Peru, Bolivia & Ecuador

Robert & Daisy Kunstaetter

Ben Box

magine Peru, Bolivia and Ecuador and you automatically
think of the Andes, the long, sinuous mountain chain that
runs the full length of all three countries and forms the
geographical and cultural spine of South America. Here, at
over 500 m, the first Incas rose from the freezing waters of
Lake Titicaca. They named their capital Cuzco, 'Navel of the
World', and built an empire that lasted until the Spanish came,
saw, conquered and converted the natives.

But old habits die hard and today indigenous customs and
beliefs are very much in evidence: in the beautiful and skilful
handicrafts; the spectacular festival costumes; the sacred
temples and pyramids; or in the burying of a llama foetus
under a new house to repel evil spirits. Often these ancient
traditions were subsumed into the 'new' religion of the
colonial masters.

It is the synthesis of ancient America and medieval Europe
that is the essence of these countries. Thousands of years of
empire-building, natural disasters, conquest, occupation and
independence have all been played out against the backdrop
of those mighty mountains, the one constant in a continent
of constant change.

COLOMBIA

To Galápagos
Islands
←

Otavalo **2**

1 ☐ QUITO

Puerto **3**
López
Baños
Riobamba Puyo

Guayaquil ECUADOR

Cuenca

Tumbes

Loja

Piura Vilcabamba

Jaén

Iquitos

Chachapoyas

Chiclayo

PERU

Trujillo Pucallpa

Huaraz **5**

BRAZIL

Pacific
Ocean

La Oroya

LIMA ☐ Huancayo

Manu
Biosphere
Reserve ◆ **6**

Puerto
Maldonado

Ayacucho *Machu* **7**
Picchu

Pisco Abancay Cuzco

Ica

Nazca
Nazca Lines

Rurrenabaque **12**

Trinidad

Galápagos Islands

Charles Darwin
Teodoro Wolf

4 *Pinta*
Marchena

Fernandina

Santiago

Santa Cruz

Isabela

San Cristóbal

Floreana *Española*

8 Juliaca **9**

Arequipa Puno *Lake*
Titicaca

BOLIVIA

Coroico

☐ LA PAZ

Cochabamba

Oruro

Santa
Cruz

Lago
Poopó

Potosí

Salar de
Uyuni **10**
Uyuni

Tupiza Tarija

CHILE

N

200 km
200 miles

ARGENTINA

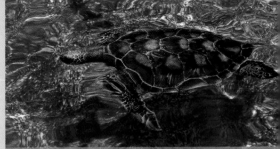
Turtle, Galápagos islands

Don't miss... See colour maps at end of book

oncepción

○ San Rafael

⑪

San José
de Chiquitos

PARAGUAY

v

Dancers, Quito, Ecuador

Itineraries for Peru, Bolivia and Ecuador

The variety that Peru, Bolivia and Ecuador can offer the visitor is enormous. The obvious attractions in Peru are Machu Picchu, the Nazca Lines and the jungle reserves of Manu and Tambopata. In Ecuador the colonial heritage of Quito and Cuenca, the wildlife extravaganza that is the Galápagos Islands, and the Oriente jungle are the major draws. Bolivia's feature attractions include the Salar de Uyuni, Madidi National Park and the Jesuit missions of Chiquitanía. Beyond these 'don't miss' destinations, all three countries share a wild natural beauty and a wealth of off-the-beaten-track experiences waiting to be appreciated. The problem is, if you're on a tight schedule, how to fit it all in. Seeing much of these countries by bus in the space of a few weeks is a forlorn hope. So you'll either need to concentrate on a smaller area or consider taking internal flights.

ITINERARY ONE: 2 weeks

The best option for a two-week visit is to limit yourself to one or two countries. As Peru is sandwiched in the middle, it is logical to combine it with a visit to either Bolivia or Ecuador. Southern Peru offers a very rewarding short circuit covering the most important and popular sites in this part of the country. Cuzco and Machu Picchu, the crown jewels of the Inca Empire, require at least four days, more if you plan to hike the Inca Trail. Beautiful Titicaca, the highest navigable lake in the world, the elegant colonial city of Arequipa, nearby Colca Canyon, and the incredible Nazca Lines could all be combined with Cuzco into a 10-day tour using air, rail and road travel.

You could then head from Lake Titicaca across the border to Copacabana and La Paz. Several interesting trips can be made from La Paz, including the ruins of the great pre-Inca city of Tiwanaku. From La Paz you can also mountain bike down the 'world's most dangerous road' to the little town of Coroico, a popular resort in the subtropical valleys of the Yungas.

An alternative to Bolivia would be to fly from Lima to the beautiful colonial city of Quito in Ecuador. One of Ecuador's great attractions is its relative compactness and much of what you want to see is only a few hours by road from the capital. Just two hours north is Otavalo, home to one of the finest craft markets in all of Latin America; while a few hours' south is the spectacular Cotopaxi National Park, the lovely Quilotoa Circuit and Baños, a popular spa town at the foot of an active volcano.

Ecuador has many excellent jungle lodges; if you don't arrange a trip to the jungle from Cuzco, it's easy to do so from Quito. You can also travel under your own steam to one of the main jungle towns and arrange a tour

TRAVEL TIP
An economical option can be to travel by land from either Ecuador or Bolivia to just inside Peru and then take a domestic flight with a Peruvian airline.

from there with a local agency. Tours can be arranged from Puyo, Tena, Misahuallí, Coca, Macas and Baños, which is on the road from the highlands to the Oriente. And then there are the Galápagos Islands, Ecuador's famed wildlife showcase. The islands are expensive to visit but well worth it. Tours range from four to 14 days; seven days is optimal, if you can afford it, to appreciate this once-in-a-lifetime experience.

Geothermal mud pools, Bolivia

Macaws, Manu National Park, Peru

ITINERARY TWO: 4 weeks

A month allows you the luxury of several further options for exploring Peru, Bolivia and Ecuador. With this amount of time you really should visit Manu National Park or the Tambopata National Reserve in Peru's southeastern jungle. These provide wonderful opportunities for watchers of birds, butterflies and animals, as well as for plant lovers. Trips to the southeastern jungle can be booked in Cuzco, which is the jumping- off point for flights or the 24-hour overland journey.

Another option in Peru is to head for Huaraz, in the Cordillera Blanca, seven hours by paved road from Lima and one of the world's top climbing and trekking destinations. A week spent exploring the Cordillera and neighbouring areas can easily be linked with the coastal archaeo-logical sites near the colonial city of Trujillo and, further north, around Chiclayo. From Chiclayo you could venture to the more remote Chachapoyas region, which contains a bewildering number of prehis-panic archaeological sites (spend at least a week here if possible).

There are several border crossings from northern Peru to the south of Ecuador. The easiest is from Piura to Loja, and an alternative adventurous route runs from Chachapoyas to Vilcabamba, once a fabled fountain of youth, today the southern terminus of Ecuador's 'gringo trail' on the fringes of Podocarpus National Park. Five hours north of Vilcabamba and Loja is Cuenca, a lovely colonial city and also

TRAVEL TIP

Fiestas are a fundamental part of life for most South Americans, taking place throughout the continent with such frequency that it would be hard to miss one, even during the briefest of stays.

Chimborazo, Ecuador

Chiquitania, Bolivia

TRAVEL TIP
The Salar de Uyuni is very impressive in the dry season under clear blue skies but the mirror effect when it is flooded is unforgettable.

a great place to buy Panama hats (yes, they're made in Ecuador!) and other crafts. There are good road links from Cuenca north to Riobamba, with access to Chimborazo (Ecuador's highest summit) and the spectacular Devil's Nose train ride. Good roads from Riobamba continue north to Quito, and northeast to Baños and the Oriente jungle.

Alternatively, you could spend more time in Bolivia. Those visiting during the dry season – April to October – would be strongly advised not to miss a trip north to Rurrenabaque, from where you can take a jungle or pampas tour and experience the amazing diversity of wildlife in Pilón Lajas Biosphere Reserve and Madidi National Park. The altiplano landscape of south-west Bolivia is dramatically different but equally remarkable. The mining city of Oruro is home to world-famous Carnival celebrations featuring the Diablada or dance of the devils. A good train service connects Oruro with Uyuni and Tupiza, starting points for tours of the Salar de Uyuni, a vast, blindingly white salt lake – one of the most bizarre and spectacular sights in the entire country. South of the Salar is Reserva Eduardo Avaroa, with deserts, volcanoes, geysers and multi-coloured lakes teeming with flamingos, all over 4000 m above sea level. The eastern lowlands of Santa Cruz form yet another markedly different region. Here the Jesuit missions of Chiquitanía and and their biannual baroque music festival are one of Bolivia's most fascinating colonial legacies.

Lake Titicaca, Peru

Isla del Sol, Bolivia

Llamas, Machu Picchu, Peru

x

Contents

Contents

Footprint features

Essentials

Planning your trip

Best time to visit Peru, Bolivia and Ecuador

Peru's high season in the highlands is from May to September. At this time the days are generally clear and sunny, though nights can be very cold at high altitude. During the wettest months in the highlands, November to April, some roads become impassable. April and May, at the tail end of the highland rainy season, is a beautiful time to see the Peruvian Andes. On the coast, high seasons are September and Christmas to February. The summer months are from December to April, but from approximately May to October much of this area is covered with *la garúa*, a blanket of cloud and mist.

The best time to visit the jungle in **Peru** and **Bolivia** is during the dry season, from April to October. During the wet season, November to April, it is oppressively hot (40°C and above) and while it only rains for a few hours at a time, it is enough to make some roads impassable. These are also the months when mosquitoes and other biting insects are at their worst, so this is not a good time to visit the jungle. As for the rest of **Bolivia**, the Altiplano does not receive much rain, so timing is not so crucial here, although hiking trails can get very muddy in the wet season. During the winter months of June and July, nights tend to be clearer but even colder than at other times. These are good months to visit the Salar de Uyuni, as the salt lake is very impressive under clear blue skies (but the mirror effect when it is flooded is also unforgettable).

Ecuador's climate is so varied and variable that any time of the year is good for a visit. In the highlands, temperatures vary more with altitude than they do with the seasons (which mainly reflect changes in rainfall). To the west of the Andes, June to September is dry and October to May is wet (but there is sometimes a short dry spell in December or January). To the east, October to February is dry and March through September is wet. There is also variation in annual rainfall from north to south, with the south being drier. In the Oriente, as in the rest of the Amazon Basin, heavy rain can fall at any time, but it is usually wettest from March to September. The Galápagos are hot from January to April, when heavy but brief showers are likely. May to December is the cooler misty season.

▶▶ See also Festivals, page 18.

What to do in Peru, Bolivia and Ecuador

Bird and wildlife watching

Peru Nearly 19% of all the bird species in the world and 45% of all neotropical birds are found in Peru. A birding trip is possible during any month as birds breed all year round. The peak in breeding activity occurs just before the rains come in Oct. The key sites, out of many, are the Manu Biosphere Reserve, Tambopata National Reserve, Abra Málaga, Iquitos, Paracas, Lomas de Lachay, the Colca Canyon, the Huascarán Biosphere Reserve and northern Peru, with its Tumbesian dry forest and Pacific slopes of the Andes. Before arranging any trip, consult **PromPerú** (www. peru.info), and www.perubirdingroutes.com (Spanish and English).

Bolivia has more than 40 well-defined ecological regions and the transition zones between them. On a trip to the Salar de Uyuni you will see Andean birdlife but also landscapes of unmatched, stark beauty. For lowland birds and animals, the main options are Rurrenabaque in the lowlands of the river Beni and the Parque Nacional Amboró,

Packing for Peru, Bolivia and Ecuador

Everybody has their own preferences, but a good principle is to take half the clothes, and twice the money, that you think you will need. Listed here are those items most often mentioned. These include an inflatable travel pillow and strong shoes (footwear over 9½ English size, or 42 European size, is difficult to find in South America). You should also take waterproof clothing and waterproof treatment for leather footwear and wax earplugs, vital for long bus trips or in noisy hotels. Also important are flip flops, which can be worn in showers to avoid athlete's foot, and a sheet sleeping bag to avoid sleeping on dirty sheets in cheap hotels. Other useful things include: a clothes line, a nailbrush, a vacuum flask, a water bottle, a universal sink plug of the flanged type that will fit any waste-pipe, string, a Swiss Army knife, an alarm clock, candles (for power cuts), a torch/flashlight, pocket mirror, a padlock for the doors of the cheapest hotels (or for tent zip if camping), a small first-aid kit, sun hat, lip salve with sun protection, contraceptives, waterless soap, dental floss (which can also be used for repairs), wipes and a small sewing kit. Always carry toilet paper, especially on long bus trips. The most security conscious may also wish to include a length of chain and padlock for securing luggage to bed or bus/train seat, and a lockable canvas cover for your rucksack. Don't forget cables and adaptors for recharging phones, laptops and other electrical equipment. Contact lens wearers note that lens solution can be difficult to find in Bolivia and Peru. Ask for it in a pharmacy, rather than an opticians. Always take out a good travel insurance policy.

---

3 hrs west of Santa Cruz, containing ecosystems of the Amazon Basin, Andean foothills and the savannahs of the Chaco plain. For table-top mountains, forests, *cerrado*, wetlands and a stunning array of wildlife, make the effort to get to Parque Nacional Noel Kempff Mercado.

Ecuador The Galápagos Islands are the top destination for reliably seeing wildlife close-up, but a number of the species from the Galápagos may also be seen in the Parque Nacional Machalilla and on other parts of the coast. An added bonus on the mainland coast is the opportunity to watch whales from Jun to Sep. A huge number of bird species in a great variety of habitats and microclimates may easily be seen. There are 5 general regions: western lowlands and lower foothills, western Andes, Inter-Andean forests and páramos, eastern Andes and Oriente jungle. The Jocotoco Foundation (www.fjocotoco.org), specializes in buying up critical bird habitat in Ecuador.

Climbing

In **Peru**, the Cordillera Blanca, with Huaraz as a base, is an ice-climber's paradise. Over 50 summits are between 5000 and 6000 m and over 20 exceed 6000 m. There is a wide range of difficulty and no peak fees are charged (although national park entrance has to be paid in the Cordillera Blanca). The Cordillera Huayhuash, southeast of Huaraz, is a bit more remote, with fewer facilities, but has some of the most spectacular ice walls in Peru. In the south of the country, the Cordilleras Vilcabamba and Vilcanota are the main destinations, but Cuzco is not developed for climbing. Climbing equipment can be hired in Huaraz but the quality can be poor.

Some of the world's best mountaineering can be found in **Bolivia**. With a dozen peaks at or above 6000 m and almost a thousand over 5000 m, most levels of skill can find something to tempt them. The season is May to Sep, with usually stable conditions Jun to

Aug. The Cordillera Real has 600 mountains over 5000 m, including 6 at 6000 m or above (Huayna Potosí is the most popular). Quimza Cruz, southeast of La Paz, is hard to get to but offers some excellent possibilities. The volcanic Cordillera Occidental contains Bolivia's highest peak, Sajama (6542 m). The Apolobamba range, northwest of La Paz, has many peaks over 5000 m.

Ecuador offers some exceptional high-altitude climbing, with 10 mountains over 5000 m – most with easy access. The 4 most frequently climbed are Cotopaxi, Chimborazo and Iliniza Norte. The other 6, Iliniza Sur, Antisana, El Altar, Sangay, Carihuairazo and Cayambe vary in degree of difficulty and/or danger. Sangay is technically easy, but extremely dangerous from the falling rocks being ejected from the volcano. Many other mountains can be climbed and climbing clubs, guiding agencies and tour operators will give advice. There are 2 seasons: Jun to Aug for the western cordillera and Dec to Feb for the eastern cordillera.

Diving and snorkelling

The Galápagos Islands are well known for their distinctive marine environments and offer more than 20 dive sites. Each island contains a unique environment and many are home to underwater life forms found nowhere else. There are excellent specialized dive-tour boats and operators but you are not allowed to dive on an ordinary Galápagos cruise. Also note that conditions in the Galápagos are difficult and for experienced divers only. Snorkelling is highly recommended, however, and you will come face to face with all manner of marine creatures. A good option for novice divers is Isla de la Plata in Machalilla National Park, on the coast of Ecuador.

Horse riding

In **Ecuador** horse rentals are available in many popular resort areas including Otavalo, Baños and Vilcabamba. Throughout the country, *haciendas* also usually offer horse riding.

Mountain biking

This is a relatively new sport in **Peru**, but dedicated cyclists are beginning to open up routes which offer some magnificent possibilities. Peru has many kilometres of trails, dirt roads and single track, but very few maps to show you where to go. There is equipment for hire and tours in the Huaraz and Cuzco areas or join an organized group to get the best equipment and guiding.

In **Bolivia**, hard-core, experienced, fit and acclimatized riders can choose from a huge range of possibilities. Either take a gamble and figure it out from a map, or find a guide and tackle the real adventure rides. Some popular rides in the La Paz region, achievable by all levels of riders, are La Cumbre to Coroico, down the so-called 'world's most dangerous road'; the Zongo Valley descent into the Yungas; Chacaltaya to La Paz, down from the (ex) world's highest ski-slope; Hasta Sorata, to the trekking paradise of Sorata. If you plan on bringing your own bike and doing some hard riding, be prepared for difficult conditions, an almost complete absence of spare parts and very few good bike mechanics. There are now a number of operators offering guided mountain biking tours, but only a few rent good quality, safe machines. Choose a reputable company, guides who speak your language and only opt for the best, US-made bikes.

Ecuador is growing in popularity as there are boundless opportunities in the Sierra, on coastal roads and in the upper Amazon Basin. Agencies which offer tours, rent equipment and can help plan routes are listed under Quito and other cities.

Parapenting/hang-gliding

Vuelo Libre (parapenting) is popular. Flying from the coastal cliffs is easy and the thermals are good. In **Peru**, the best area is the Sacred Valley of Cuzco which has excellent launch sites, thermals and reasonable landing sites. In **Ecuador** it can be done from several highland locations as well as Crucuita on the coast. The season in the Sierra is May-Oct (best Aug-Sep). Some flights in Peru have exceeded 6500 m.

Sandboarding
If you've always fancied tearing down a massive sand dune on a wooden board, then the southern coastal desert in **Peru** is the place for you. As much fun as snowboarding but without the cold or required technical expertise, sandboarding is a growing sport amongst warm-weather thrill-seekers.

Surfing
Peru is a top international surfing destination. Its main draws are the variety of waves and the year-round action. The main seasons are Sep to Feb in the north and Mar to Dec in the south, though May is often ideal south of Lima. The biggest wave is at Pico Alto (sometimes 6 m in May), south of Lima, and the largest break is 800 m at Chicama, near Trujillo.

In **Ecuador** there are a few, select surfing spots, such as Mompiche, San Mateo, Montañita and Playas, near Guayaquil. Surf is best Dec to Mar, except at Playas where the season is Jun to Sep. In the Galápagos there is good surfing at Playa Punta Carola, outside Puerto Baquerizo Moreno on San Cristóbal.

Trekking
In **Peru** there are some fabulous circuits around the peaks of the Cordillera Blanca (eg Llanganuco to Santa Cruz, and the treks out of Caraz) and Cordillera Huayhuash. The Ausangate trek near Cuzco is also good. A second type of trek is walking among, or to, ruins. The prime example is the Inca Trail to Machu Picchu, but others include those to Vilcabamba (the Incas' last home) and Choquequirao, and the treks in the Chachapoyas region. The Colca and Cotahuasi canyons also offer superb trekking. South American Explorers (www. saexplorers.org), have good information and advice on trekking and sell books.

There are many opportunities for trekking in **Bolivia**, from gentle 1-day hikes in foothills and valleys to challenging walks of several days from highlands to lowlands on Inca or golddiggers trails. The best known are: the Choro, Takesi and Yunga Cruz hikes, all of whose starting points can be reached from La Paz; the Illampu Circuit from Sorata; and the Apolobamba treks in the northwest. Various treks are outlined in the text, especially near La Paz and from Sorata.

In **Ecuador**, the varied landscape, diverse environments and friendly villages make travelling on foot a refreshing change from crowded buses. Hiking in the Sierra is mostly across high elevation *páramo*, through agricultural lands and past indigenous communities. There are outstanding views of glaciated peaks in the north and pre-Columbian ruins in the south. In the tropical rainforests of the Oriente, local guides are often required because of the difficulty in navigation and because you will be walking on land owned by local indigenous tribes. The Andean slopes are steep and often covered by virtually impenetrable cloud forests and it rains a lot. Many ancient trading routes head down the river valleys. Some of these trails are still used. Others may be overgrown and difficult to follow but offer the reward of intact ecosystems.

Volunteering in South America
In **Peru**, in Cuzco the HoPe Foundation at Hostal Marani accepts volunteers (www. hopeperu.org), as does the **Amauta Spanish School** (www.amautaspanish.com). In Huanchaco, near Trujillo, **Otra Cosa Network** (www.otracosa.info) arranges a wide range of volunteer placements in the north of the country. Projects which aim to get children away from the street and into education include **Seeds of Hope** in Huaraz (www. peruseeds.org) and **Luz de Esperanza** in Huancayo (www.peruluzdeesperanza.com).

In **Bolivia**, see www.volunteerbolivia.org.

In **Ecuador**, 'voluntourism' attracts many visitors. Several language schools operate volunteering schemes in conjunction with Spanish classes. **Fundación Arcoiris** (www.arcoiris.org.ec) works with a variety of nature conservation and sustainable community development projects in the far south of the country; **Fundación Jatun Sacha** (www.jatunsacha.org) has many different sites at which volunteers can work, all in exceptional natural areas.

Whitewater rafting

Peru has some of the finest whitewater rivers in the world. Availability is almost year-round and all levels of difficulty can be enjoyed. Cuzco is probably the rafting capital and the Río Urubamba has some very popular trips. Further afield is the Río Apurímac, which has some of the best whitewater rafting, including a trip at the source of the Amazon. In the southeastern jungle, a trip on the Río Tambopata to the Tambopata-Candamo Reserved Zone involves 4 days of whitewater followed by 2 of drifting through virgin forest; an excellent adventure which must be booked up in advance. Around Arequipa is some first-class, technical rafting in the Cotahuasi and Colca canyons and some less-demanding trips on the Río Majes. Other destinations are the Río Santa near Huaraz and the Río Cañete, south of Lima.

Ecuador is a whitewater paradise with dozens of accessible rivers, warm waters and tropical rainforest; regional rainy seasons differ so that throughout the year there is always a river to run. The majority of Ecuador's whitewater rivers share a number of characteristics. Plunging off the Andes, the upper sections are very steep creeks offering, if they're runnable at all, serious technical grade V, suitable for experts only. As the creeks join on the lower slopes they form rivers that are less steep, with more volume. Some of these rivers offer up to 100 km of continuous grade III-IV whitewater, before flattening out to rush towards the Pacific Ocean on one side of the ranges or deep into the Amazon Basin on the other. Of the rivers descending to the Pacific coast, the Blanco and its tributaries are the most frequently run. They are within easy reach of Quito, as is the Quijos on the eastern side of the Sierra. In the Oriente, the main rivers are the Aguarico and its tributary the Dué, the Napo, Pastaza and Upano.

Getting to Peru, Bolivia and Ecuador

Most international flights to the region arrive at Lima (LIM, page 42), Quito (UIO, page 422), Guayaquil (GYE, page 524), La Paz (LPB, page 304) or Santa Cruz (VVI, page 396) with the first two receiving by far the majority. There are direct flights to all three countries from **Europe**, though in many cases the choice of departure point is limited to Madrid and one or two other cities (Paris or Amsterdam, for instance). Alternatively, connections can be made in the USA (Miami, or other gateways), Buenos Aires, Rio de Janeiro or São Paulo. **Main US gateways** are Miami, Houston, Dallas, Atlanta and New York. On the west coast, Los Angeles has flights to several South America. If buying airline tickets routed through the USA, check that US taxes are included in the price. Flights from **Canada** are mostly via the USA. Likewise, flights from **Australia** and **New Zealand** are best through Los Angeles, except for the **LAN** route from Sydney and Auckland to Santiago, and **Qantas'** non-stop route Sydney–Santiago, from where connections can be made. Within **Latin America** there is plenty of choice on local carriers and some connections on US or European airlines. Enquire about 'open-jaw' flights (arriving at one airport and leaving from another). ▸▸ *For depature tax, see page 30.*

Most airlines offer discounted fares on scheduled flights through agencies who specialize in this type of fare (see Tour operators, page 31). If you buy discounted air tickets always check the reservation with the airline concerned to make sure the flight still exists. Also remember the IATA airlines' schedules change in March and October each year, so if you're going to be away a long time it's best to leave return flight coupons open. Peak times are 7 December-15 January and 10 July-10 September. If you intend travelling during those times, book as far ahead as possible. Special offers may be available February-May and September-November.

Transport in Peru, Bolivia and Ecuador

There are several daily direct flights between Lima and each of Quito, Guayaquil and La Paz with **AeroSur**, **LAN** and **TACA**, among others. When flying between Ecuador and Bolivia however, you must make a connection in Lima. **AeroSur** flies two or three times a week between La Paz and Cuzco, which can be a convenient part of a tourist itinerary. A potentially economical option (but check first as prices fluctuate), is to travel by land from either Ecuador or Bolivia to just inside Peru (eg, to Tumbes, Piura or Juliaca) and then take a domestic flight with a Peruvian airline.

Peru

Air Carriers serving the major cities are **Star Perú** ① *T01-705 9000, www.starperu.com*, **LAN** ① *T01-213 8200, www.lan.com*, **Avianca/TACA** ① *T01-511 8222, www.avianca.com*, and **Peruvian Airlines** ① *T01-716 6000, www.peruvianairlines.pe*. For destinations such as Andahuaylas, Ayacucho, Cajamarca, Jauja, Huánuco, Huaraz and Pisco, flights are offered by **LC Peru** ① *T01-204 1313, www.lcperu.pe*. Flights start at about US$100 one-way anywhere in the country from Lima, but prices vary greatly between airlines, with LAN being the most expensive for non-Peruvians. Prices often increase at holiday times (Semana Santa, May Day, Inti Raymi, 28-29 July, Christmas and New Year), and for elections. During these times and the northern hemisphere summer, seats can be hard to come by, so book early. Flight schedules and departure times often change and delays are common. In the rainy season cancellations occur. Flights into the mountains may well be put forward one hour if there are reports of bad weather. Flights to jungle regions are also unreliable. Always allow an extra day between national and international flights, especially in the rainy season. Internal flight prices are fixed in US dollars (but can be paid in soles) and have 18% tax added. Flights must be reconfirmed at least 24 hours in advance. You can do this online or in the town you will be leaving from. Be at the airport well ahead of your flight.

Bus Services along the coast to the north and south as well as inland to Huancayo, Ayacucho and Huaraz are generally good, but on long-distance journeys it is advisable to pay a bit extra and travel with a reliable company. Whatever the standard of service, accidents and hold-ups on buses do occur, especially at night; seek local advice before travelling on a night bus. All major bus companies operate modern buses with two decks on inter-departmental routes. The first deck is called *bus cama*, the second *semi-cama*. Both have seats that recline, *bus cama* further than *semi-cama*. These buses usually run late at night and are more expensive than ordinary buses which tend to run earlier in the day. Many buses have toilets and show movies. Each company has a different name for its regular and *cama* or *ejecutivo* services. **Cruz del Sur** and **Ormeño** are bus lines covering most of the country. **Cruz del Sur**, generally regarded as a class above the others, accepts Visa cards and gives 10% discount to ISIC and Under 26 cardholders (you may have to insist). There are many smaller but still excellent bus lines that run only to specific areas.

An increasing number accept internet bookings and you may find good deals on the websites. For bus lines, see page 70. For a centralized information and booking site, visit https://busportal.pe. Some bus terminals charge a usage fee of about US$0.50 which you pay at a kiosk before boarding. Many also charge for the toilet, about US$0.35 with paper and US$0.25 without. Take a blanket or warm jacket when travelling in the mountains. Where buses stop it is possible to buy food on the roadside. With the better companies you will get a receipt for your luggage, which will be locked under the bus. On local buses watch your luggage and never leave valuables on the luggage rack or floor, even when on the move. If your bus breaks down and you are transferred to another line and have to pay extra, keep your original ticket for a refund from the first company.

Combis operate between most small towns on one- to three-hour journeys. This makes it possible, in many cases, just to turn up and travel within an hour or two. Combis can be minibuses of varying age and comfort, or slightly more expensive, faster but often overfilled car colectivos, called *autos*, or *cars*. These usually charge twice the bus fare. They leave only when full. They go almost anywhere in Peru; most firms have offices. Book one day in advance and they pick you up at your hotel or in the main plaza.

Note Prices of bus tickets are raised by 60-100%, two or three days before Semana Santa, 28 July (Independence Day – Fiestas Patrias), Christmas and special local events. Tickets are sold out two or three days in advance at this time and transport is hard to come by.

Car According to the Ministry of Transport and Communications, 48% of Peru's roads are paved, including the Pan-American Highway which runs north–south through the coastal desert. The aim is for 85% to be paved by 2016. Tolls, US$1.35-2.60, are charged on most major paved roads. Some mountain roads can be impassable in the rainy season.

You must have an international driving licence to drive in Peru and be over 21 years old. If renting a car, your home driving licence will be accepted for up to six months; you must be over 25 to hire a car. Car hire rates tend to be very expensive but tourist offices and hotels should know of the cheapest companies. Always check that the vehicle you rent has a spare wheel, toolkit and functioning lights etc. The **Touring y Automóvil Club del Perú** ① *AvTrinidad Morán 698, Lince, Lima, T01-611 9999, www.touringperu.com.pe*, has offices in several provincial cities and offers help to tourists.

If bringing in your own vehicle you must provide proof of ownership; a *libreta de pasos por aduana* or *carnet de passages* is accepted and recommended, although not officially required. You cannot officially enter Peru with a vehicle registered in someone else's name. On leaving Peru there is no check on the import of a vehicle. All vehicles are required to carry Peruvian insurance (SOAT, Seguro Obligatorio para Accidentes de Tránsito) and spot checks are frequent, especially in border areas. SOAT can be purchased for as little as one month (US$10) at larger border crossings, but only during office hours (Monday-Friday 0800-1800).

Availability of fuel varies around the country and the price depends on the octane rating. Unleaded is widely available along the Pan-American Highway and in large cities but rarely in the highlands. Prices range from US$4.70-6.45 per gallon for gasoline and US$5 for diesel.

Hitchhiking Hitchhiking is difficult. Freight traffic has to stop at the police *garitas* outside each town and these are the best places to try (also toll points, but these are further from towns). Drivers usually ask for money but don't always expect to get it. In mountain and jungle areas you usually have to pay drivers of lorries, vans and even private cars; ask the driver first how much he is going to charge, and then check with locals.

Taxi Taxi prices are fixed in the mountain towns, about US$1-1.50 in urban area. Fares are not fixed in Lima although some drivers work for companies that do have standard fares. Ask locals what the price should be and always set the price beforehand; expect to pay US$3-5 in the capital. The main cities have taxis that can be hired by phone, which charge a little more, but are reliable and safe. Many taxi drivers work for commission from hotels. Choose your own hotel and find a driver who is willing to take you. Taxis at airports are more expensive; seek advice about the price in advance. In some places it is cheaper to walk out of the airport to the main road and flag down a cab. Another common form of public transport is the mototaxi, a three-wheel motorcycle with an awning covering the double-seat behind the driver. Fares are about US$1.

Train The main railways are Puno–Juliaca–Cuzco, Cuzco–Machu Picchu and Lima–Huancayo, with a continuation to Huancavelica in the Central Highlands.

Bolivia

Air All of the following offer internal air services. **Boliviana de Aviación (BoA)** ① *www. boa.bo*, flies to São Paulo and Buenos Aires; **Amaszonas** ① *T02-222 0848, www.amaszonas. com*, flies to Cuzco, Arequipa and Asunción. **TAM** ① *www.tam.bo*, the civilian branch of the Bolivian Air Force, flies to main cities as well as Uyuni and several smaller and more remote destinations. **Aerocon** ① *T03-351 1010, www.aerocon.bo*, based in Trinidad, serves mostly the northern jungle and Potosí; note that **Aerocon** has had a few accidents since 2010. **Amaszonas** flies to all main cities and between La Paz and Rurrenabaque, Trinidad and Uyuni. **Ecojet** ① *T901-105055, www.ecojet.bo*, based in Cochabamba, flies from Cochabamba to Sucre, Trinidad and Riberalta and from Sucre to Santa Cruz. Many flights radiate from La Paz, Santa Cruz or Cochabamba. Make sure you have adequate baggage insurance.

Bus Buses ply most of the main roads. Inter-urban buses are called *flotas*, urban ones *micros* or *minibuses* (vans); *trufis* are shared taxis. Larger bus companies run frequent services and offer air-conditioning, TV and other mod cons. You can usually buy tickets with reserved seats a day or two in advance. Alternatively, savings may sometimes be obtained by bargaining for fares at the last minute, although not at peak travel times like national holidays. A small charge is made for use of bus terminals; payment is before departure.

In the wet season, bus travel is subject to long delays and detours, at extra cost, and cancellations are not uncommon. On all journeys, take some food, water and toilet paper. It is best to travel by day, not just to enjoy the scenery and avoid arriving at night, but also for better road safety (also see Road safety, page 29). Bus companies are responsible for any items packed in the luggage compartment or on the roof, but only if they give you a ticket for each bag.

Car A relatively small (but growing) percentage of Bolivian roads are paved, the rest are gravel-surfaced or earth. Any road, whatever its surface, may be closed in the rainy season (December-March). Road tolls vary from US$0.50 to US$2.10 for journeys up to 100 km. On toll roads you are given a receipt at the first toll; keep it at hand as it is asked for at subsequent toll posts. The **Administradora Boliviana de Carreteras (ABC)** ① *Av Mcal Santa Cruz, Edif Centro de Comunicaciones p 8, T02-237 5000*, maintains a useful website, www. abc.gov.bo, with daily updates of road conditions, including any roadblocks due to social unrest; toll-free phone for emergencies T800-107222. Always carry spare petrol/gas and supplies and camping equipment if going off major roads. Your car must be able to cope with altitude and freezing temperatures. Take great care on the roads, especially at night. Too many truck drivers are drunk and many vehicles are driven with faulty headlights.

To bring a private vehicle into Bolivia you must have an International Driving Permit, the vehicle's registration documents and your passport. On entry you must get temporary admission from customs (free of charge) and surrender the documento departure (maximum 90 days). A carnet de passages en douane is not required, but insurance is compulsory. It is called SOAT and can be bought locally. Generally the police are helpful to foreign motorists, but stop you often and ask to see your documents, a complete first aid kit, triangle and fire extinguisher. **Automóvil Club Boliviano** ① *Av 6 de Agosto 2993 y Arce, La Paz, T02-243 1132*.

The minimum age for hiring a car is 25. Rental companies may only require your licence from home, but police ask to see an international licence. Rental of a small car costs about US$350 per week; a 4WD vehicle US$600 per week or more. *Especial*, 85 octane containing lead, US$0.54 per litre (may cost more in remote areas). Diesel costs about the same. Higher octane premium, US$0.84 per litre, is only available in La Paz, if at all. There may be fuel shortages, especially in border areas, so keep your tank full. **Note** There are restrictions on which vehicles may drive in La Paz, depending on license plate number and day of the week.

Train The western highland railway is operated by **Ferroviaria Andina (FCA)** ① *T02-241 6545, www.fca.com.bo*. There are passenger trains to Villazón from Oruro, via Atocha, Tupiza and Uyuni. There are plans to reopen to passengers the La Paz to Arica line (2014). The eastern lowland line is run by **Ferroviaria Oriental** ① *www.fo.com.bo*, with services from Santa Cruz east to the Brazilian border and south to the Argentine border at Yacuiba.

Ecuador

Air Airlines operating within Ecuador include: **Aerogal** ① *T1-800-237642 or T02-294 3100, www.aerogal.com.ec*, serving Quito, Guayaquil, Cuenca, Coca, Manta and Galápagos and international routes, code sharing with **Avianca**, to Bogotá, Cali, Medellín and Lima; **LAN** ① *T1-800-842526, www.lan.com*, with flights to Quito, Guayaquil, Cuenca, Manta and Galápagos and international routes to Miami, New York, Madrid, Cali, Medellín, Lima, Santiago and Buenos Aires; and **TAME** ① *T1-700-500800 or T02-397 7100, www.tame.com.ec*, serving Quito, Guayaquil, Cuenca, Tulcán, Latacunga, Loja, Coca, Lago Agrio, Tena, Macas, Esmeraldas, Manta, Santa Rosa (Machala) and Galápagos, as well as international flights to Bogotá, Cali, Caracas, Panamá, Habana, New York, Lima, São Paulo and Buenos Aires.

Bus Bus travel is generally more convenient and regular than in other Andean countries. Several companies use comfortable air-conditioned buses on their longer routes; some companies have their own stations, away from the main bus terminals, exclusively for these better buses. Bus company information and itineraries are found in www. ecuadorbuses.com, where tickets for some major routes can also be purchased online for US$3. **Note** Throughout Ecuador, travel by bus is safest during the daytime.

Car A very good network of paved roads runs throughout most of the country. Maintenance of major highways is franchised to private firms, who charge tolls of US$1. Roads are subject to damage during heavy rainy seasons. Always check road conditions before setting out. Unexpected potholes and other obstructions, the lack of road signs, and local drivers' tendency to use the middle of the road make driving 'an experience'. Beware of the bus drivers, who often drive very fast and rather recklessly. Driving at night is not recommended.

To bring a foreign vehicle or motorcycle into the country, its original registration document (title) in the name of the driver is required. If the driver is not the owner, a notarized letter of authorization is required. All documents must be accompanied by a Spanish translation. A 90-day permit is granted on arrival, extensions are only granted if the vehicle is in the garage for repairs. No security deposit is required and you can enter and leave at different land borders. Procedures are generally straightforward but it can be a matter of luck. Shipping a vehicle requires more paperwork and hiring a customs broker. The port of Guayaquil is prone to theft and particularly officious. Manta and Esmeraldas are smaller and more relaxed, but receive fewer ships. A valid driver's licence from your home country is generally sufficient to drive in Ecuador and rent a car, but an international licence is helpful. A valid driver's licence from your home country is generally sufficient to drive in Ecuador and rent a car, but an international licence may be helpful.

To rent a car you must be 21 and have an international credit card. Surcharges may apply to clients aged 21-25. You may pay cash, which is cheaper and may allow you to bargain, but they want a credit card for security. You may be asked to sign two blank credit card vouchers, one for the rental fee itself and the other as a security deposit, and authorization for a charge of as much as US$8000 may be requested against your credit card account if you do not purchase the local insurance. The uncashed vouchers will be returned to you when you return the vehicle. Make sure the car is parked securely at night. A small car suitable for city driving costs around US$570 per week including unlimited mileage, tax and full insurance. A 4WD or pickup truck (recommended for unpaved roads) costs about US$1240 a week. Drop-off charges are about US$112.

There are two grades of petrol, 'Extra' (82 octane, US$1.48 per US gallon) and 'Super' (92 Octane, US$1.98-2.30). Both are unleaded. Extra is available everywhere, while Super may not be available in more remote areas. Diesel fuel (US$1.03) is notoriously dirty and available everywhere.

Hitchhiking Public transport in Ecuador is so abundant that there is seldom any need to hitchhike along the major highways. On small out-of-the-way country roads however, the situation can be quite the opposite, and giving passers-by a ride is common practice and safe, especially in the back of a pick-up or truck. A small fee is usually charged, check in advance.

Taxi In cities, all taxis must use meters.

Train For information contact **Empresa de Ferrocarriles Ecuatorianos** ① *T1-800-873637*, *www.ecuadorbytrain.com*. A series of tourist rides have replaced regular passenger service along the spectacular Ecuadorean railway system, mostly restored in 2013. There are two classes of service, standard and plus; carriages are fancier in the latter and a snack is included. On some routes, an *autoferro*, a motorized railcar runs instead of the train. The following routes are on offer: Quito to Machachi, El Boliche (Cotopaxi) and Latacunga; Alausí to Sibambe via the Devil's Nose; Ambato to Urbina; Riobamba to Urbina and Colta; Ibarra to Salinas; El Tambo to Baños del Inca near Ingapirca; Durán (outside Guayaquil) to Yaguachi and Bucay; and the **Tren Crucero**, an upmarket all-inclusive tour of up to four days along the entire line from Quito to Durán. Details are given under What to do, in the corresponding cities.

Vans and shared taxis These operate between major cities and offer a faster, more comfortable and more expensive alternative to buses. Some provide pick-up and drop-off services at your hotel.

Maps and guidebooks

Peru

The **Instituto Geográfico Nacional** in Lima sells a selection of maps, see page 66. Another official site is **Ministerio de Transporte** ① *Jr Zorritos 1203, Lima centre, T01-615 7800, www.mtc.gob.pe*. Lima 2000's *Mapa Vial del Perú* (1:2,200,000) is probably the most correct road map available. Maps can also be obtained from the **South American Explorers** (see page 34).

A good tourist map of the Callejón de Huaylas and Cordillera Huayhuash, by Felipe Díaz, is available in many shops in Huaraz, including Casa de Guías. *Alpenvereinskarte Cordillera Blanca Nord 0/3a* and *Alpenvereinskarte Cordillera Blanca Süd 0/3b* at 1:100,000 are the best maps of that region, US$24, available in Huaraz and Lima, but best bought outside Peru. *Cordillera Huayhuash map*, 1:50,000 (The Alpine Mapping Guild, 2nd ed, 2004) is recommended, available in Huaraz at **Café Andino**, US$15.

Bolivia

Good maps of Bolivia are few and far between, and maps in general can be hard to find. **Instituto Geográfico Militar** (IGM, see page 320). Many IGM maps date from the 1970s and their accuracy is variable; prices also vary, US$4.50-7 a sheet. **Walter Guzmán Córdova** makes several travel and trekking maps, available from some bookshops in La Paz. The **German Alpine Club (Deutscher Alpenverein)** ① *www.alpenverein.de*, produces two maps of Sorata-Ancohuma-Illampu and Illimani, but these are not usually available in La Paz.

Ecuador

Instituto Geográfico Militar (IGM) ① *Senierges y Telmo Paz y Miño, east of Parque El Ejido, Quito, T02-397 5100, ext 2502, www.geoportaligm.gob.ec, Mon-Thu 0730-1600, Fri 0700-1430, take ID,* sell country and topographic maps in a variety of paper and digital formats for US$3-7. Maps of border and sensitive areas are 'reservado' (classified) and not available for sale without a permit. Buy your maps here, they are rarely available outside Quito.

Where to stay in Peru, Bolivia and Ecuador

There is no uniform terminology for categories of accommodation in South America, but you should be aware of the generally accepted meanings for the following. *Hotel* is the generic term, much as it is in English. *Hospedaje* means accommodation, of any kind. *Pensión* and *residencial* usually refer to more modest and economical establishments. A *posada* (inn) or *hostal* may be an elegant expensive place, while *hosterías* or *haciendas* usually offer upmarket rural lodgings. It is advisable to book in advance during school holidays and local festivals, see page 18.

Peru

Accommodation is plentiful throughout the price ranges and finding a hotel room to suit your budget should not present any problems, especially in the main tourist areas and larger towns and cities. The exception to this is during the Christmas and Easter holiday periods, Carnival, Cuzco in June and Independence celebrations at the end of July, when all hotels seem to be crowded. By law there are now four types of accommodation, each will have a plaque outside defining its status: *Hotel* (H), *Hostal* (HS), *Hostal Residencial* (HR)

Price codes

Where to stay

$$$$ over US$150	$$$ US$66-150
$$ US$30-65	$ under US$30

Price of a double room in high season, including taxes unless otherwise indicated.

Restaurants

$$$ over US$12	$$ US$7-12	$ US$6 and under

Prices for a two-course meal for one person, excluding drinks or service charge.

or *Pensión* (P). All deluxe and first-class hotels charge 18% in state sales tax (IGV) and 10% service charges. Foreigners should not have to pay the sales tax on hotel rooms; check whether it has been included. **i-Perú** ① *www.peru.info*, has a list of all accommodation registered with them. Student discounts are rare but for information on youth hostels consult **Intej** ① *www.intej.org*, or **Asociación Peruana de Albergues Turísticos Juveniles** ① *Av Casimiro Ulloa 328, Miraflores, Lima, T01-446 5488, www.limahostell.com.pe or www. hostellingperu.com.pe.* Information is also available from **Hostelling International Peru** ① *www.hostellingperu.com.pe.* **Camping** is easy in Peru, especially along the coast. There can be problems with robbery when camping near villages; ask permission to camp in a backyard or *chacra* (farmland).

Bolivia

Hotels must display prices by law. The number of stars awarded to each hotel is regulated and fairly accurate. The following terms likewise reflect the size and quality of an establishment (from largest and best, to smallest and simplest): *hotel, hostal, residencial, alojamiento* and *casa de huéspedes.* In Bolivia, a *pensión* is a simple restaurant, not a place to sleep. Youth hostels or self-styled 'backpackers' are not necessarily cheaper than hotels. A number of mid-range *residenciales* are affiliated to **Hostelling International (HI)** ① *www.hostellingbolivia.org*; some others just say they are. Another website listing hostels is www.boliviahostels.com, but they are not necessarily affiliated to HI. **Camping** is best suited to the wilderness areas of Bolivia, away from towns, villages and people. Organized campsites, car or trailer camping does not exist here. Because of the abundance of cheap hotels you should never have to camp in populated areas.

Ecuador

Outside the provincial capitals and resorts, there are few higher-class hotels, although a number of very upmarket haciendas have opened their doors to paying guests. A few are in the **Exclusive Hotels & Haciendas of Ecuador group** ① *www.ehhec.com*, but there are many other independent haciendas of good quality. Some are mentioned in the text. Larger towns and tourist centres often have more hotels than we can list. This is especially true of Quito. The hotels that are included are among the best in each category, selected to provide a variety of locations and styles. Service of 10% and tax of 12% are added to better hotel bills. Some cheaper hotels apply only the 12% tax, but check if it is included. **Camping** is possible in protected natural areas; there are very few organized campsites. It is not safe to pitch your tent at random near villages or on beaches.

Food and drink in Peru, Bolivia and Ecuador

Peru

Peru is the self-styled gastronomic capital of South America and some of the cuisine is very innovative. Along the coast the best dishes are seafood based with the most popular being *ceviche*: raw white fish marinated in lemon juice, onion and hot peppers. The staples of corn and potatoes are prevalent in highland cooking and can be found in a large and varied range of dishes. There is also an array of meat dishes with *lomo saltado* (stir-fried beef) always found on the menu and *cuy* (guinea pig) featuring as a regional delicacy. Tropical cuisine revolves around fish and the common yucca and fried bananas. Lunch is considered the main meal throughout Peru and most restaurants will serve one or two set lunches called the *menú ejecutivo* (US$2.50-4 for a three-course meal) or *menú económico* (US$2-3). A la carte meals normally cost US$5-8 but in top-class restaurants it can be up to US$80. There are many *chifas* (Chinese restaurants) all over the country which offer good reasonably priced food. Middle- and high-class restaurants may add 10% service, but not include the 18% sales tax in the bill (which foreigners do have to pay); this is not shown on the price list or menu, check in advance. Lower-class restaurants charge only tax, while cheap, local restaurants charge no taxes.

Lager-type beers are the best, especially the Cusqueña and Arequipeña brands (lager) and Trujillo Malta (porter). In Lima only Cristal and Pilsener (not related to true Pilsen) are readily available, others have to be sought out. Look out for the sweetish 'maltina' brown ale, which makes a change from the ubiquitous pilsner-type beers. The best wines are from Ica, Tacama and Ocucaje. Gran Tinto Reserva Especial and Viña Santo Tomas are reasonable and cheap. The most famous local drink is pisco which is a strong, clear brandy and forms the basis of the deliciously renowned pisco sour.

Bolivia

Bolivian cooking is usually tasty and *picante* (spicy). Recommended dishes include *sajta de pollo*, hot spicy chicken with onion, fresh potatoes and *chuño* (dehydrated potatoes), *parrillada* (mixed grill), *fricase* (juicy pork), *silpancho* (very thin fried breaded meat), and *aji de lengua*, ox-tongue with hot peppers, potatoes and *chuño* or *tunta* (another kind of dehydrated potato). *Pique macho* (roast meat, sausage, chips, onion and pepper) is especially popular. Near Lake Titicaca fish becomes an important part of the local diet and trout, though not native, is usually delicious. Bolivian soups are usually hearty and warming, including *chairo* made of meat, vegetables and *chuño*. *Salteñas* are very popular meat or chicken pasties eaten as a mid-morning snack, the challenge is to avoid spilling the gravy all over yourself. Most restaurants do not open early but many hotels include breakfast. Breakfast and lunch can also be found in markets, but eat only what is cooked in front of you. In *pensiones* and cheaper restaurants a basic lunch (*almuerzo* – usually finished by 1300) and dinner (*cena*) are normally available. The *comida del día* is the best value in any class of restaurant. Llama meat contains parasites, so make sure it has been properly cooked, and be especially careful of raw salads as many tourists experience gastrointestinal upsets. Dishes cooked in the street are not safe. Bolivia's temperate and tropical fruits are excellent and abundant. Don't miss the luscious grapes and peaches in season (February-April). Brazil nuts, called *almendras* or *castañas*, are produced in the northern jungle department of Pando and sold throughout the country.

There are several makes of local lager-type beer; Paceña and Auténtica are the best-selling brands. Singani, the national spirit, is distilled from grapes, and is cheap and strong. Good wines are produced by several vineyards near Tarija (tours are available, see page 377). The hot maize drink, *api* (with cloves, cinnamon, lemon and sugar), is good on cold mornings. Bottled water (many brands with and without gas) is readily available but make sure the seal is unbroken.

Ecuador

Ecuadorean cuisine varies extensively with region. The large cities have a wide selection of restaurants with Ecuadorean, international and fashionable fusion cuisine. In the highlands *locro de papas* (potato and cheese soup), *llapingachos* (fried potato and cheese patties), *fritada* and *hornado* (fried and roast pork, respectively), *cuy* (roast guinea pig) and *humitas* (tender ground corn steamed in corn leaves) are some of the most typical dishes. Seafood plays an important role on the coast, particularly in the very popular *ceviche* (marinaded fish or seafood, distinct from the Peruvian variety) and *encocadas* (dishes prepared in coconut milk). *Sopa de bola de verde* (plantain dumpling soup) and *patacones* (thick fried plantain chips) are also delicious coastal specialities. Most Ecuadorean food is not spicy but every table has a small bowl of *ají* (hot pepper sauce). Upmarket restaurants add 22% to the bill: 12% tax plus 10% service. All other places add the 12% tax, which is also charged on non-essential items in food shops. Tipping is not expected in the many cheaper places serving *almuerzos* and *meriendas* (set lunch and dinner).

The main beers available are Pilsener and Club. Argentine, Chilean and other imported wines can be found in major cities. The most popular local spirit is unmatured rum, called *aguardiente* (literally 'fire water'). Many excellent fruit juices include *naranjilla* and *tomate de arbol* (both tomato relatives), *maracuyá* (passion fruit), *guanábana* (soursop) and *mora* (blackberry).

Shopping in Peru, Bolivia and Ecuador

Artesenía (handicrafts) enjoy regional distinctiveness, especially in items such as textiles. Each region, village even, has its own characteristic pattern or style of cloth, so the choice is enormous. Throughout the Andes, weaving has spiritual significance as well as a practical side. Reproductions of pre-Columbian designs can be found in pottery and jewellery and many people throughout the continent make delightful items in gold and silver. Musical instruments from Bolivia, Panama hats from Ecuador and all manner of ceramics are just some of the things you can bring home with you. Craft shops abound in Lima, Cuzco, La Paz, Quito and Cuenca, but many items are sold more economically where they are made, outside the big cities. Bargaining is expected when you are shopping for handicrafts and souvenirs, but remember that most items are made by hand, and people are trying to make a living, not playing a game. You want a fair price, not the lowest one.

Peruvian crafts

Good items to buy are textiles, especially in Lima, Cuzco and Lake Titicaca. Equally common are llama- and alpaca-wool products which include ponchos, rugs, hats, gloves, sweaters and coats. The mate *burilado* (engraved gourd) is one of the most genuine images of folk art in Peru. Interesting items are bags for coca leaves, belts and knitted hats with earflaps, which can be found around Lake Titicaca. For gold and silver jewellery, Lima is the best place.

Bolivian crafts

Llama- and alpaca-wool knitted and woven items are at least as good as those from Peru and usually cheaper. Among the many items you can buy are *mantas* (ponchos), bags, *chullos* (bonnets), gold and silverware and musical instruments such as the *charango* (a mandolin traditionally with armadillo-shell sound-box, now usually of wood) and the *quena* (Inca flute), and other assorted wooden items.

Ecuadorean crafts

The huge markets at Otavalo and Saquisilí are the among best places to head for to find wall-hangings, sweaters, blankets and shawls. Authentic Panama hats are made on the coast and around Cuenca, and are sold throughout the country at a fraction of the prices in Europe. Silver jewellery, ceramics and brightly painted carvings are all very well made and there is even the opportunity to promote the conservation of the rainforest by buying some of the beautiful items made from *tagua* nut, or vegetable ivory.

Festivals in Peru, Bolivia and Ecuador

One of the major considerations of deciding when to travel, apart from the weather, is the festival calendar. Fiestas are a fundamental part of life for most South Americans, taking place throughout the continent with such frequency that it would be hard to miss one, even during the briefest of stays. This is fortunate, because arriving in any town or village during these inevitably frenetic celebrations is one of the great travelling experiences. Bolivia is especially well endowed with festivals throughout the year, some lasting a week or more.

During the main festivals and public holidays most businesses such as banks, airline offices and tourist agencies close while supermarkets and street markets may be open. This depends a lot on where you are so try to enquire locally. Sometimes holidays that fall during mid-week will be moved to the following Friday or Monday to make a long weekend, or some places will take *a día de puente* (bridging day) taking the Friday or Monday as a holiday before or after an official holiday on a Thursday or Tuesday.

Invariably, fiestas involve drinking – lots of it. There's also non-stop dancing, which can sometimes verge on an organized brawl, and throwing of water (or worse). If you chose to partake to the point of collapse due to inebriation or exhaustion, then be prepared to awake with a hangover the size of the Amazon rainforest and no recollection of what you did with your backpack.

Not all festivals end up as massive unruly parties, however. Some are solemn and elaborate holy processions, often incorporating Spanish colonial themes into predominantly ancient pagan rituals. Below is a brief list of the most important festivals in each country. Note that dates may vary from year to year.

Peru

Two of the major festival dates are **Carnaval**, which is held over the weekend before Ash Wed, and **Semana Santa** (Holy Week), which ends on Easter Sun. Carnival is celebrated in most of the Andes and Semana Santa throughout Peru.

1 May Fiesta de la Cruz is another important festival in much of the central and southern highlands and on the coast. **Jun** In Cuzco, the entire month is one huge fiesta, culminating in **Inti Raymi**, on **24 Jun**, one of Peru's prime tourist attractions. **1 Aug** National Day of the Alpaca, with events in major alpaca-rearing centres across the country. **1 Nov** Todos los Santos (All Saints) is another national festival. **8 Dec** is Festividad de la Inmaculada Concepción.

Apart from those listed above, the main holidays are: 1 Jan, New Year; 6 Jan, Bajada de Reyes; 1 May, Labour Day; 28-29 Jul, Independence (Fiestas Patrias); 7 Oct, Battle of Angamos; 24-25 Dec, Christmas.

Bolivia

2 Feb Virgen de la Candelaria, in rural communities in Copacabana, Santa Cruz departments. **Carnaval**, especially famous in Oruro, is celebrated throughout the country in Feb or Mar. There are parades with floats and folkloric dances, parties, much drinking and water throwing even in the coldest weather and nobody is spared. Many related festivities take place around the time of Carnaval. 2 weeks beforehand is **Jueves de Compadres** followed by **Jueves de Comadres**. In the Altiplano Shrove Tuesday is celebrated as **Martes de Challa**, when house owners make offerings to Pachamama and give drinks to passers-by. **Carnaval Campesino** usually begins in small towns on Ash Wednesday, when regular Carnaval ends, and lasts for 5 days, until **Domingo de Tentación**. Palm Sunday (**Domingo de Ramos**) sees parades to the church throughout Bolivia; the devout carry woven palm fronds, then hang them outside their houses. **Semana Santa** in the eastern Chiquitania is very interesting, with ancient processions, dances, and games not found outside the region. **Corpus Christi** is also a colourful festival. **3 May** Fiesta de la Invención de la Santa Cruz, various parts. **2 Jun** Santísima Trinidad in Beni Department. **24 Jun** San Juan, bonfires throughout all Bolivia. **29 Jun** San Pedro

y San Pablo, at Tiquina, Tihuanaco and throughout Chiquitania. **25 Jul** Fiesta de Santiago (St James), Altiplano and lake region. **14-16 Aug** Virgen de Urkupiña, Cochabamba, a 3-day Catholic festivity mixed with Quechua rituals and parades with folkloric dances. **16 Aug** San Roque, patron saint of dogs; the animals are adorned with ribbons and other decorations. **1-2 Nov** All Saints and All Souls, any local cemetery. Cities may be very quiet on national holidays, but celebrations will be going on in the villages. Hotels are often full at the most popular places, for instance Copacabana on Good Friday; worth booking in advance.

Apart from those listed above, the main holidays are: 1 Jan, New Year's Day; Carnaval Week, Mon, Shrove Tuesday, Ash Wednesday; Holy Week: Thu, Fri and Sat; 1 May, Labour Day; Corpus Christi (movable May-Jun); 16 Jul, La Paz Municipal Holiday; 5-7 Aug, Independence; 24 Sep, Santa Cruz Municipal Holiday; 2 Nov, Day of the Dead; Christmas Day.

Ecuador

6 Jan Reyes Magos y Día de los Inocentes, a time for pranks, which closes the Christmas-New Year holiday season. **Carnival** Mon and Tue before Lent, celebrated everywhere in the country (except Ambato) by throwing water at passers-by: be prepared to participate. **24 May** Battle of Pichincha, Independence. **Early Jun** Corpus Christi. **10 Aug** First attempt to gain the Independence of Quito. **9 Oct** Independence of Guayaquil. **3 Nov** Independence of Cuenca. **6 Dec** Foundation of Quito.

Apart from those listed above, the main holidays are: 1 Jan, New Year's Day; Easter, Holy Thu, Good Fri, Holy Sat; 1 May, Labour Day; 2 Nov, All Souls' Day; 25 Dec, Christmas Day.

Responsible travel in Peru, Bolivia and Ecuador

Since the early 1990s there has been a phenomenal growth in tourism that promotes and supports the conservation of natural environments and is also fair and equitable to local communities. In South America, this 'ecotourism' segment provides a vast and growing range of destinations and activities, for which there is a huge demand. While the authenticity of some ecotourism operators' claims needs to be interpreted with care, there are a great many whose aims and credentials are laudable and we try to highlight these in the book.

10 ways to be a responsible traveller

There are some aspects of travel that you have to accept are going to have an impact, but try to balance the negatives with positives by following these guidelines:

Cut your emissions Plan an itinerary that minimizes carbon emissions whenever possible. This might involve travelling by train, hiring a bike or booking a walking or canoeing tour rather than one that relies on vehicle transport. See below for details of carbon offset programmes. Visit www.seat61.com for worldwide train travel.

Check the small print Choose travel operators that abide by a responsible travel policy (it will usually be posted on their website). Visit www.responsibletravel.com.

Keep it local If travelling independently, try to use public transport, stay in locally owned accommodation, eat in local restaurants, buy local produce and hire local guides.

Cut out waste Take biodegradable soap and shampoo and leave excess packaging, particularly plastics, at home. The countries you are visiting may not have the waste collection or recycling facilities to deal with it.

Get in touch Find out if there are any local schools, charities or voluntary conservation organizations that you could include in your itinerary. If appropriate, take along some useful gifts or supplies. For a list of projects that could benefit from your support, see www.stuffyourrucksack.com.

Learn the lingo Practice some local words, even if it's just to say 'hello', 'thank you' and 'goodbye'. Respect local customs and dress codes and always ask permission before photographing people – including your wildlife tour guide. Once you get home, remember to honour any promises you've made to send photographs.

Avoid the crowds Consider travelling out of season to relieve pressure on popular destinations, or visit a lesser-known alternative.

Take only photos Resist the temptation to buy souvenirs made from animals or plants. Not only is it illegal to import or export many wildlife souvenirs, but their uncontrolled collection supports poaching and can have a devastating impact on local populations, upsetting the natural balance of entire ecosystems. CITES, the Convention on International Trade in Endangered Species (www.cites.org) bans international trade in around 900 species of animals and plants, and controls trade in a further 33,000 species. Several organizations, including WWF, TRAFFIC and the Smithsonian Institution have formed the Coalition Against Wildlife Trafficking (www.cawtglobal.org).

Use water wisely Water is a precious commodity in many countries. Treating your own water avoids the need to buy bottled water which can contribute to the build-up of litter. If you don't carry water treatment equipment, support places that encourage the reuse of plastic bottles.

Don't interfere Avoid disturbing wildlife, damaging habitats or interfering with natural behaviour by feeding wild animals, getting too close or being too noisy. Leave plants and shells where you find them.

Code green for hikers and campers

- Take biodegradable soap, shampoo and toilet paper, long-lasting lithium batteries and plastic bags for packing out all rubbish.
- Use a water filter instead of buying bottled water.
- Keep to trails to avoid erosion and trampling vegetation. Don't take short cuts, especially at high altitude where plants may take years to recover.
- Try to pitch your tent on non-vegetated areas; avoid particularly sensitive habitats, such as wildflower meadows and wetlands. If possible, use an existing campsite.
- Avoid damaging historical, archaeological and palaeontological sites.
- Check with landowners if camping on private land, or contact the appropriate authorities for area restrictions and permit requirements.
- For cooking use a camp stove. If you need to build a fire, use only fallen timber. Allow the fire to burn down to a fine ash which can be raked out and disposed of. Leave no trace of your fire. Observe any fire-use restrictions in place.
- If toilets, portable latrines or composting toilets are not available, dig latrines at least 50 m from water sources and camp sites. Cover the hole with natural materials and either burn or pack out your toilet paper.
- Wash clothing and cooking items well away from water sources and scatter grey water so that it filters through soil. If you must wash in streams, rivers or lakes, use biodegradable, phosphate-free soap.
- Pack out all rubbish and unused food, plus litter left by others.

Code green for animal and ecological welfare

- Do not hire any mule or horse that is lame or has open sores from badly fitting tack.
- Avoid handling, feeding or riding on marine life or aquatic mammals. Footprint does not support the keeping of marine mammals (eg dolphins) in captivity.

- Help conserve underwater and riverine environments by taking part in local clean-ups, or by diving in areas collecting data for Project AWARE (www.projectaware.org).
- Choose dive operators that use mooring buoys or drift diving techniques, rather than anchors that can damage fragile habitats.
- Never touch coral. Practice buoyancy control skills and tuck away trailing equipment.

How should I offset my carbon emissions?
Carbon offsetting schemes allow you to offset greenhouse gas emissions by donating to various projects, from tree planting to renewable energy schemes. Although some conservation groups are concerned that carbon offsetting is being used as a smoke-screen to delay the urgent action needed to cut emissions and develop alternative energy solutions, it remains an important way of counterbalancing your carbon footprint.

How does carbon offsetting work?
Carbon offsetting schemes allow you to donate to environmental projects in order to balance out your carbon footprint. For every tonne of CO_2 you generate through a fossil fuel-burning activity such as flying, you pay for an equivalent tonne to be removed elsewhere through a 'green' initiative such as tree planting or the development of renewable energy schemes. There are numerous online carbon footprint calculators (such as www.carbonfootprint.com). Alternatively, book with a travel operator that supports a carbon offset provider like TICOS (www.ticos.co.uk) or Reduce my Footprint (www.reducemyfootprint.travel). Note that some conservation groups are concerned that carbon offsetting is being used as a smoke-screen to delay the urgent action needed to cut emissions and develop alternative energy solutions.

Essentials A-Z

Accident and emergency

Peru
Emergency medical attention (Cruz Roja) T115. Fire T116. Police T105, www.pnp.gob. pe (Policía Nacional del Perú), for police emergencies nationwide. **Tourist Police**, Jr Moore 268, Magdalena, 38th block of Av Brasil, Lima, T01-460 1060/0844, daily 24 hrs They are friendly, helpful and speak English and some German.

Bolivia
Ambulance T165 in La Paz, T161 in El Alto. **Police** T110 nationwide. Robberies should be reported to the *Policía Turística*, they will issue a report for insurance purposes but stolen goods are rarely recovered. In cities which do not have a *Policía Turística* report robberies to the **Fuerza Especial de Lucha Contra el Crimen (FELCC)**, Departamento de Robos. In La Paz, see page 305.

Ecuador
For emergencies nationwide, T911. For police, T101.

Children → *See also Health, opposite.*

Travel with children can bring you into closer contact with South American families and, generally, presents no special problems. In fact the path is often smoother for family groups as officials tend to be more amenable where children are concerned.

Food Food can be a problem if the children are picky eaters. It is easier to take food such as biscuits, drinks and bread on longer trips than to rely on meal stops. Avocados are safe and nutritious for babies as young as 6 months and most older children like them too. A small immersion heater and jug for making hot drinks is invaluable, but remember that electric current varies. Try and get a dual-voltage one (110v and 220v).

Hotels In all hotels, try to negotiate family rates. If charges are per person, always insist that 2 children will occupy 1 bed only, therefore counting as 1 tariff. If rates are per bed, the same applies. You can often get a reduced rate at cheaper hotels. Sometimes when travelling with a child you will be refused a room in a hotel that is 'unsuitable'. On river boat trips, unless you have large hammocks, it may be more comfortable and cost effective to hire a 2-berth cabin for 2 adults and a child.

Transport People contemplating over-land travel in South America with children should remember that a lot of time can be spent waiting for public transport. Even then, buses can be delayed on the journey. Travel on trains allows more scope for moving about, but trains are few and far between these days. In many cases trains are luxurious and much more expensive than buses. If hiring a car, check that it has rear seat belts.

On all long-distance buses you pay for each seat, and there are no half-fares if the children occupy a seat each. For shorter trips it is cheaper, if less comfortable, to seat small children on your knee. There may be spare seats which children can occupy after tickets have been collected. In city and local excursion buses, small children generally do not pay a fare, but are not entitled to a seat when paying customers are standing. On sightseeing tours you should always bargain for a family rate – often children can go free. All civil airlines charge half for children under 12, but some military services don't have half-fares, or have younger age limits. Note that a child travelling free on a long excursion is not always covered by the operator's travel insurance; it is advisable to pay a small premium to arrange cover.

Disabled travellers

In most of South America, facilities for the disabled are severely lacking. For those in wheelchairs, ramps and toilet access are limited to some of the more upmarket, or most recently built hotels. Pavements are often in a poor state of repair or crowded with street vendors. Most archaeological sites, even Machu Picchu, have little or no wheelchair access. Visually or hearing-impaired travellers are also poorly catered for, but there are experienced guides in some places who can provide individual attention. There are also travel companies outside South America who specialize in holidays which are tailor-made for the individual's level of disability. Some moves are being made to improve the situation and Ecuador's former vice-president (until 2013) Lenín Moreno, himself a paraplegic, made huge strides in providing assistance at all levels to people with disabilities. At street level, Quito's trolley buses are supposed to have wheelchair access, but they are often too crowded to make this practical. PromPerú has initiated a programme to provide facilities at airports, tourist sites, etc. While disabled South Americans have to rely on others to get around, foreigners will find that people are generally very helpful. The **Global Access – Disabled Travel Network** website, www.globalaccessnews.com, is useful. Another informative site, with lots of advice on how to travel with specific disabilities, plus listings and links belongs to the **Society for Accessible Travel and Hospitality**, www.sath.org. **Ecuador for All** (see page 442) is a tour operator catering to travellers with special needs.

Electricty

Peru
220 volts AC, 60 cycles throughout the country, except Arequipa (50 cycles). Most 4- and 5-star hotels have 110 volts AC. Plugs are American flat-pin or twin flat and round pin combined.

Bolivia
220 volts 50 cycles AC. Sockets usually accept both continental European (round) and US-type (flat) 2-pin plugs. Also some 110-volt sockets, when in doubt, ask.

Ecuador
AC, 110 volts, 60 cycles. Sockets are for twin flat blades, sometimes with a round earth pin.

Health → *Medical facilities are listed in the Directory sections of each chapter.*

See your GP or travel clinic at least 6 weeks before departure for general advice on travel risks and vaccinations. Try phoning a specialist travel clinic if your own doctor is unfamiliar with health in the region. Make sure you have sufficient medical travel insurance, get a dental check, know your own blood group and, if you suffer a long-term condition such as diabetes or epilepsy, obtain a **Medic Alert** bracelet (www.medicalert.org.uk).

Vaccinations and anti-malarials
Confirm that your primary courses and boosters are up to date. It is advisable to vaccinate against polio, tetanus, typhoid, hepatitis A and, for more remote areas, rabies. Yellow fever vaccination is obligatory for most areas. Cholera, diphtheria and hepatitis B vaccinations are sometimes advised. Specialist advice should be taken on the best antimalarials to take before you leave.

Health risks
The major risks posed in the region are those caused by insect disease carriers

such as mosquitoes and sandflies. The key parasitic and viral diseases are malaria, South American trypanosomiasis (Chagas' disease) and dengue fever. Be aware that you are always at risk from these diseases. **Malaria** is a danger throughout the lowland tropics and coastal regions. **Dengue fever**, which is widespread, is particularly hard to protect against as the mosquitoes can bite throughout the day as well as night (unlike those that carry malaria). ITry to wear clothes that cover arms and legs and also use effective mosquito repellent. Mosquito nets dipped in permethrin provide a good physical and chemical barrier at night. **Chagas' disease** is spread by faeces of the triatomine, or assassin bugs, whereas sandflies spread a disease of the skin called **leishmaniasis**.

Some form of **diarrhoea** or intestinal upset is almost inevitable, the standard advice is always to wash your hands before eating and to be careful with drinking water and ice; if you have any doubts about the water then boil it or filter and treat it. In a restaurant buy bottled water or ask where the water has come from. Food can also pose a problem, be wary of salads if you don't know whether they have been washed or not.

There is a constant threat of **tuberculosis** (TB) and although the BCG vaccine is available, it is still not guaranteed protection. It is best to avoid unpasteurized dairy products and try not to let people cough and splutter all over you.

One of the major problems for travellers in the region is **altitude sickness**. It is essential to get acclimatized to the thin air of the Andes before undertaking long treks or arduous activities. The altitude of the Andes means that strong protection from the sun is always needed, regardless of how cool it may feel.

Websites

www.cdc.gov Centres for Disease Control and Prevention (USA).

www.nhs.uk/nhsengland/ Healthcareabroad/pages/ Healthcareabroad.aspx Department of Health advice for travellers.
www.fitfortravel.scot.nhs.uk Fit for Travel (UK), a site from Scotland providing a quick A-Z of vaccine and travel health advice requirements for each country.
www.itg.be Institute for Tropical Medicine, Antwerp.
www.nathnac.org National Travel Health Network and Centre (NaTHNaC).
www.who.int World Health Organisation.

Books

Dawood, R, editor, *Travellers' health*, 5th ed, Oxford: Oxford University Press, 2012.
Johnson, Chris, Sarah Anderson and others, *Oxford Handbook of Expedition and Wilderness Medicine*, OUP 2008.
Wilson-Howarth, Jane. *The Essential Guide To Travel Health: don't let Bugs Bites and Bowels spoil your trip*, Cadogan 2009, and *How to Shit around the World: the art of staying clean and healthy while travelling*, Travelers' Tales, US, 2011.

Internet

Email is common and public access to the internet is widespread. In large cities an hour in a cyber café will cost between US$0.50 and US$2, with some variation between busy and quiet times. Speed varies enormously, from city to city, café to café. Away from population centres service is slower and more expensive. Remember that for many South Americans a cyber café provides their only access to a computer, so it can be a very busy place and providers can get overloaded.

Language

Without some knowledge of Spanish you will become very frustrated and feel helpless in many situations. English, or any other language, is absolutely useless off the beaten track. Not all the locals speak Spanish; you will find that some people in the more remote highland parts of Bolivia and Peru, and lowland communities in Amazonia, speak only their indigenous languages (Quichua in Ecuador, Quechua in Peru and Bolivia, also Aymara in southern Peru and Bolivia), though at least one person in each village usually speaks Spanish. Some initial study or a beginners Spanish course are strongly recommended, as is a pocket phrasebook and dictionary.

Quito has the most language schools in all price ranges. Other language study centres include Cuenca, as well as Cuzco and Arequipa in Peru, Sucre and Cochabamba in Boliva. See relevant Directories for details. The following international agencies arrange language classes, homestays, educational tours and volunteer opportunities.
AmeriSpan, T215-531 7917 (worldwide), T1-800-511 0179 (USA), www.amerispan. com, offers Spanish immersion programmes, educational tours, volunteer and internship positions throughout Latin America.
Cactus, T0845-130 4775 (UK), +44-1273-359010 (international), www.cactuslanguage.com.
Spanish Abroad, 3219 East Camelback Rd No 806, Phoenix, AZ 85339, USA, T1-888-722 7623, or T602-778 6791, www.spanishabroad.com, also run courses.

LGBT (Lesbian, Gay, Bisexual, Transgendered) travellers

Much of Latin America is still quite intolerant of homosexuality. Rural areas tend to be more conservative than cities. It is therefore wise to respect this and avoid provoking a reaction. For the gay or lesbian traveller, however, Lima and Quito have active communities and there are local and international organizations which can provide information. Cuzco also has a gay scene. Useful websites include: Ecuador: www.gayecuador.com and www.quito gay. net. Peru: http://lima.queercity.info, www.

deambiente.com/web and www.gayperu. com (last 2 in Spanish).

Local customs and laws

Appearance
There is a natural prejudice in all countries against travellers who ignore personal hygiene and have a generally dirty and unkempt appearance. Most Latin Americans, if they can afford it, devote great care to their clothes and appearance; it is appreciated if visitors do likewise. Buying clothing locally can help you to look less like a tourist. As a general rule, it is better not to wear shorts in official buildings, upmarket restaurants or cinemas.

Courtesy
Remember that politeness – even a little ceremoniousness – is much appreciated. Men should always remove any headgear and say "*con permiso*" when entering offices, and be prepared to shake hands (this is much more common in Latin America than in Europe or North America); always say "*Buenos días*" (until midday) or "*Buenas tardes*" and wait for a reply before proceeding further. Always remember that the traveller from abroad has enjoyed greater advantages in life than most Latin American minor officials and should be friendly and courteous in consequence. Never be impatient. Do not criticize situations in public; the officials may know more English than you think and they can certainly interpret gestures and facial expressions. Be judicious about talking politics with strangers. Politeness can be a liability, however, in some situations; most Latin Americans are disorderly queuers. In commercial transactions (eg buying goods in a shop), politeness should be accompanied by firmness, and always ask the price first (arguing about money in a foreign language can be difficult).

Politeness should also be extended to street traders. Saying "*No, gracias*" with a smile is better than an arrogant dismissal. Whether you give money to beggars is a personal matter, but your decision should be influenced by whether a person is begging out of need or trying to cash in on the tourist trail. In the former case, local people giving may provide an indication. On giving money to children, most agree don't do it. There are times when giving food in a restaurant may be appropriate, but find out about local practice.

Money

Withdrawing cash from an ATM with a credit or debit card is by far the easiest way of obtaining money, but always have a back-up plan. ATMs are common, but cannot always be relied on and have been known to confiscate valid cards. The affiliations of banks to the Plus and Cirrus systems change often, so ask around. Always bring some US dollar bills, traveller's cheques (TCs), or both. US dollar notes are often worn and tatty in Ecuador, but will only be accepted in Peru and Bolivia if they are in good condition. Low-value US dollar bills are very useful for shopping: shopkeepers and *casas de cambio* give better exchange rates than hotels or banks. Some banks (few in Ecuador) and the better hotels will normally change TCs for their guests (often at a poor rate); some may ask to see a record of purchase before accepting. Take plenty of local currency, in small denominations, when making trips off the beaten track. Frequently, the rates of exchange on ATM withdrawals are the best available but check if your bank or credit card company imposes handling charges. Whenever possible, change money at a bank or *casa de cambio* rather than money changers on the street. Change any local currency before you leave the country or at the border.

For purchases, credit cards of the Visa and MasterCard groups, American Express (Amex), and Diners Club can be used. Transactions using credit cards are normally at an officially recognized rate of exchange; but may be subject to a surcharge of 8-12% and/or sales tax. For ATM locations, see www.visalatam.com, www.mastercard.com and www.americanexpress.com.

Another option is to take a prepaid currency card. There are many on offer, from, for example, **Caxton, FairFX, Travelex**, banks and other organizations. It pays to check their application fees and charges carefully.

Peru → *US$1 = S/2.80; €1 = S/3.73 (Aug 2014).* **Currency** The new sol (s/) is divided into 100 céntimos. Notes in circulation are: S/200, S/100, S/50, S/20 and S/10. Coins: S/5, S/2, S/1, S/0.50, S/0.20, S/0.10 and S/0.05 (being phased out). Some prices are quoted in dollars (US$) in more expensive establishments, to avoid changes in the value of the sol. **Note** A large number of forged US dollar notes (especially US$20 and larger bills) are in circulation. There are also many forged soles coins and notes. Posters in public places explain what to look for. **Cost of travelling** The average budget is US$45-60 pp a day for living fairly comfortably, including transport. Your budget will be higher the longer you stay in Lima and Cuzco and depending on how many internal flights you take. Rooms range from US$7-11 pp for the most basic *alojamiento* to US$20-40 for mid-range places, to over US$90 for more upmarket hotels (more in Lima or Cuzco). Living costs in the provinces are 20-50% below those in Lima and Cuzco. The cost of using the internet is generally US$0.60-1 per hr, but where competition is not fierce, rates vary from US$1.50 to US$4.

Bolivia → *US$1 = Bs6.90. €1 = Bs9.22 (Aug 2014)* The currency is the boliviano (Bs), divided into 100 centavos. There are notes for 200, 100, 50, 20 and 10 bolivianos, and 5, 2 and 1 boliviano coins, as well as 50, 20 and (rare) 10 centavos. Bolivianos are often referred to as pesos; expensive items, including hotel rooms, may be quoted in dollars. ATMs are not always reliable and, in addition to plastic, **you must always carry some cash**. Most ATMs dispense both Bs and US$.

Cost of travelling Bolivia is cheaper to visit than most neighbouring countries. Budget travellers can get by on US$15-20 per person per day for 2 travelling together. A basic hotel in small towns costs as little as US$5 pp, breakfast US$1.50, and a simple set lunch (*almuerzo*) around US$2.50-3.50. For around US$35, though, you can find much better accommodation, more comfortable transport and a wider choice in food. Prices are higher in the city of La Paz; in the east, especially Santa Cruz and Tarija; and in Pando and the upper reaches of the Beni. The average cost of using the internet is US$0.50 per hr.

Ecuador

The **US dollar** (US$) is the official currency of Ecuador. Only US$ bills circulate. US coins are used alongside the equivalent size and value Ecuadorean coins. Ecuadorean coins have no value outside the country. Many establishments are reluctant to accept bills larger than US$20 because of counterfeit notes or lack of change. There is no substitute for cash-in-hand when travelling in Ecuador; US$ cash in small denominations is by far the simplest and the only universally accepted option. Other currencies are difficult to exchange outside large cities and fetch a poor rate.

Cost of living/travelling Despite dollarization, prices remain modest by international standards and Ecuador is still affordable for even the budget traveller. A very basic daily travel budget in 2014 was about US$25 pp based on 2 travelling together, but allow for higher costs in main cities and resorts. For US$60 a day you can enjoy a good deal of comfort. Internet use is about US$0.60-1 per hr, US$2 in the Galápagos. Bus travel is cheap, about US$1 per hr, flights cost almost 10 times as much for the same route.

Opening hours

Peru

Banks Outside Lima and Cuzco banks may close 1200-1500 for lunch. **Government offices** Jan-Mar Mon-Fri 0830-1130; Apr-Dec Mon-Fri 0900-1230, 1500-1700, but these hours change frequently.
Other offices 0900-1700; most close on Sat. **Shops** 0900 or 1000-1230 and 1500 or 1600-2000. In the main cities, supermarkets do not close for lunch and Lima has some that are open 24 hrs. Some are closed on Sat and most are closed on Sun.

Bolivia

Banks and offices Normally open Mon-Fri 0900-1600, Sat 0900-1300, but may close for lunch in small towns. **Shops** Mon-Fri 0830-1230, 1430-1830 and Sat 0900-1200. Opening and closing in the afternoon are later in lowland provinces.

Ecuador

Banks Mon-Fri 0830-1700. **Government offices** Variable hours Mon-Fri, most close for lunch. **Other offices** 0900-1230, 1430-1800. **Shops** 0900-1900; close at midday in smaller towns, open till 2100 on the coast.

Post

Postal services vary in efficiency and prices are quite high; pilfering is frequent. All mail, especially packages, should be registered. Some countries have local alternatives to the post office. Check before leaving home if your embassy will hold mail, and for how long, in preference to the Poste Restante/General Delivery (Lista de Correos) department of a country's post office. If there seems to be no mail at the Lista under the initial letter of your surname, ask them to look under the initial of your forename or your middle name. Remember that there is no W in Spanish; look under V, or ask. To reduce the risk of misunderstanding, use title, initial and surname only. If having items sent to you by courier (such as DHL), do not use poste restante, but an address such as a hotel: a signature is required on receipt.

Peru

The central Lima post office is on Jr Camaná 195 near the Plaza de Armas. Mon-Fri 0730-1900, Sat 0730-1600. Poste Restante is in the same building but is considered unreliable. In Miraflores the main post office is on Av Petit Thouars 5201 (same hours). There are many small branches around Lima and in the rest of the country, but they are less reliable. For express service: EMS, next to central post office in downtown Lima, T533 2020.

Bolivia

The main branches of post offices in La Paz, Santa Cruz and Cochabamba are best for sending parcels. DHL and FedEx have offices in major cities.

Safety

Seek security advice before you leave from your own consulate than from travel agencies. You can contact:
British Foreign and Commonwealth Office, Travel Advice Unit, www.fco.gov.uk/en/travel-and-living-abroad. Footprint is a partner in the Foreign and Commonwealth Office's **Know before you go** campaign, www.gov.uk/knowbeforeyougo.
US State Department's Bureau of Consular Affairs, Overseas Citizens Services, T1-888-407 4747 (from overseas: T202-501 4444), www.travel.state.gov. **Australian Department of Foreign Affairs**, T+61-2-6261 3305, www.smartraveller.gov.au/.

Peru

The following notes should not hide the fact that most Peruvians are hospitable and helpful. Nevertheless, be aware that assaults may occur in Lima and centres along the Gringo Trail. Also watch for scammers who ask you, "as a favour", to change dollars into (fake) soles and for strangers who shake your hand, leaving a chemical which will knock you out when you next put your hand to your nose. Outside the Jul-Aug peak holiday period, there is less tension, less risk of crime, and more friendliness.

Although certain illegal drugs are readily available, anyone carrying any is almost automatically assumed to be a drug trafficker. If arrested on any charge the wait for trial in prison can take a year and is very unpleasant. If you are asked by the narcotics police to go to the toilets to have your bags searched, insist on taking a witness. **Drug use or purchase is punishable by up to 15 years' imprisonment. There are a number of foreigners in Peruvian prisons on drug charges.**

Many places in the Amazon and in Cuzco offer experiences with Ayahuasca or San Pedro, often in ceremonies with a shaman. These are legal, but always choose a reputable tour operator or shaman. Single women should not take part. There are plenty of websites for starting your research. See also under Iquitos, page 285. Tricks employed to get foreigners into trouble over drugs include slipping a packet of cocaine into the money you are exchanging, being invited to a party or somewhere involving a taxi ride, or simply being asked on the street if you want to buy cocaine. In all cases, a plain clothes 'policeman' will discover the planted cocaine, in your money, at your feet in the taxi, and will ask to see your passport and money. He will then return them, minus a large part of your cash. Do not get into a taxi, do not show your money, and try not to be intimidated. Beware also thieves dressed as policemen asking for your passport and wanting to search for drugs; **searching is only permitted if prior paperwork is done.** **Insurgency** Indications are that Sendero Luminoso and MRTA remain active in scattered parts of the country and to a limited degree. In the first half of 2014 there were no reports of threats to those parts of Peru of tourist interest, but it is important to be aware of the latest situation.

For up-to-date information contact the **Tourist Police** (see Accident & emergency), your embassy or consulate, fellow travellers, or **South American Explorers** (Lima T01-444 2150, Cuzco T984-245484, or in Quito). You can also contact the **Tourist Protection Bureau** (Indecopi). As well as handling complaints, they will help if you have lost, or had stolen, documents.

Bolivia

Violent crime is less common in Bolivia than some other parts of South America. Tricks and scams abound however. Fake police, narcotics police and immigration officers – usually plain-clothed but carrying forged ID – have been known to take people to their 'office' and ask to see documents and money; they then rob them. Legitimate police do not ask people for documents in the street unless they are involved in an accident, fight, etc. If approached, walk away and seek assistance from as many bystanders as possible. Never get in a vehicle with the 'officer' nor follow them to their 'office'. Many of the robberies are very slick, involving taxis and various accomplices. Take only radio taxis, identified by their dome lights and phone numbers. Always lock the doors, sit in the back and never allow other passengers to share your cab. If someone else gets in, get out at once. Also if smeared or spat-on, walk away, don't let the good Samaritan clean you up, they will clean you out instead.

The largest cities (Santa Cruz, El Alto, La Paz and Cochabamba) call for the greatest precautions. The countryside and small towns throughout Bolivia are generally safe. Note however that civil disturbance, although less frequent in recent years, remains part of Bolivian life. It can take the form of strikes, demonstrations in major cities and roadblocks (*bloqueos*), some lasting a few hrs, others weeks. Try to be flexible in your plans if you encounter disruptions and make the most of nearby attractions if transport is not running. You can often find

transport to the site of a roadblock, walk across and get onward transport on the other side. Check with locals first to find out how tense the situation is.

Road safety This should be an important concern for all visitors to Bolivia. Precarious roads, poorly maintained vehicles and frequently reckless drivers combine to cause many serious, at times fatal, accidents. Choose your transport judiciously and don't hesitate to pay a little more to travel with a better company. Look over the vehicle before you get on; if it doesn't feel right, look for another. If a driver is drunk or reckless, demand that he stop at the nearest village and let you off. Also note that smaller buses, although less comfortable, are often safer on narrow mountain roads.

Ecuador

Public safety is an important concern throughout mainland Ecuador; Galápagos is generally safe. Armed robbery, bag snatching and slashing, and holdups along the country's highways are among the most significant hazards. 'Express kidnapping', whereby victims are taken from ATM to ATM and forced to withdraw money, is a threat in major cities, and fake taxis (sometimes yellow official-looking ones, sometimes unmarked *taxis ejecutivos*) are often involved. Radio taxis are usually safer.

Secure your belongings at all times, be wary of con tricks, avoid crowds and congested urban transport, and travel only during the daytime. It is the larger cities, especially Guayaquil, Quito, Cuenca, Manta, Machala, Esmeraldas, Santo Domingo, and Lago Agrio which call for the greatest care. Small towns and the countryside in the highlands are generally safer than on the coast or in the jungle. The entire border with Colombia calls for precautions; enquire locally before travelling there.

Although much less frequent than in the past, sporadic social unrest remains part of life in Ecuador and you should not overreact. Strikes and protests are usually announced days or weeks in advance, and their most significant impact on tourists is the restriction of overland travel. It is usually best to wait it out rather than insisting on keeping to your original itinerary.

In Ecuador, drug sale, purchase, use or growing is punishable by up to 16 years' imprisonment.

Ecuador's active volcanoes are spectacular, but have occasionally threatened nearby communities. The **National Geophysics Institute** provides daily updates at www.igepn.edu.ec.

Tax

Peru
Airport tax US$31 on international flight departures; US$9.40 on internal flights (when making a domestic connection in Lima, you don't have to pay airport tax; contact airline personnel at baggage claim to be escorted you to your departure gate). Regional airports have lower departure taxes. Both international and domestic airport taxes should be included in the price of flight tickets, not paid at the airport. 18% state tax is charged on air tickets; it is included in the price of the ticket.
VAT/IGV/IVA 18%.

Bolivia
Airport tax International departure tax of US$24 is payable in dollars or bolivianos, cash only. Airport tax for domestic flights, US$2.
VAT/IVA 13%.

Ecuador
Airport tax Departure tax is included in the ticket price: Quito, US$17 for domestic flights, US$60 for international; Guayaquil, US$5 for domestic, US$30 for international; Baltra (Galápagos), US$30.
VAT/IVA 12%, may be reclaimed on departure if you show official invoices with your name and passport number; don't bother with bills under US$50. High surtaxes apply to imported luxury items.

Telephone → *Local dialling codes are listed at the beginning of each town entry.*

Peru
International phone code: +51. Easiest to use are the independent phone offices, *locutorios*, all over Lima and other cities. They take phone cards, which can be bought in *locutorios*, or in the street nearby. There are payphones throughout the country. Some accept coins, some only phone cards and some take both.

The numbering system for digital phones is as follows: for Lima mobiles, add 9 before the number, for the departments of La Libertad 94, Arequipa 95, Piura 96, Lambayeque 97; for other departments, add 9 – if not already in the number – and the city code (for example, Cuzco numbers start 984). Note also that some towns are dominated by Claró, others by Movistar (the 2 main mobile companies). As it is expensive to call between the two you should check, if spending some time in one city and using a mobile, which is the best account to have.

Red Privada Movistar (RPM) and Red Privada Claró (RPC) are operated by the respective mobile phone companies. Mobile phone users who subscribe to these services obtain a 6-digit number in addition their 9-digit mobile phone number. Both the 6- and 9-digit numbers ring on the same physical phone. The RPM and RPC numbers can be called from anywhere in Peru without using an area code, you just dial the 6 digits, and the cost is about 20% of calling the 9-digit number. This 80% discount usually also applies when calling from *locutorios*. Many establishments including hotels, tour operators and transport companies have both RPM and RPC numbers.

Bolivia
International phone code: +591. Equal tones with long pauses: ringing. Equal tones with equal pauses: engaged. IDD prefix: 00. Calls from public *cabinas* are expensive. Cellular

numbers have no city code, but carry a
3-digit prefix starting with 7.

Ecuador

International phone code: +593. Calling within
Ecuador dial the area code (02-07) + 7 digits
for land lines, 09 +8 digits for cell phones. For
local calls from a land line leave out the area
code. Calling from abroad, leave out the 0
from the area code. Phone offices are called
cabinas. **Note** Roaming may not work with
foreign cell phones, for local use it is best to buy
an Ecuadorean chip (US$6-7), but it must be
registered using a local ID (*cédula*) number.

Time

Peru GMT -5.
Bolivia GMT-4.
Ecuador GMT -5 (Galápagos, -6).

Tipping

Peru

Restaurants: service is included in the bill,
but tips can be given directly to the waiter
for exceptional service. **Taxi drivers**: none
(bargain the price down, then pay extra
for good service). **Cloakroom attendants
and hairdressers** (very high class only):
US$0.50-1. **Porters**: US$0.50. **Car wash boys**:
US$0.30. **Car 'watch' boys**: US$0.20. If going
on a trek or tour, it is customary to tip the
guide as well as the cook and porters.

Bolivia

Up to 10% in restaurants is very generous,
Bolivians seldom leave more than a few
coins. Tipping is not customary for most
services (eg taxi driver) though it is a reward
when service has been very good. Guides
expect a tip as does someone who has
looked after a car or carried bags.

Ecuador

In restaurants 10% may be included in
the bill. In cheaper restaurants, tipping is
uncommon but welcome. It is not expected
in taxis. Airport porters, US$1-2, depending
on the number of cases.

Tour operators

Amazing Peru and Beyond, Av Petit
Thouars 5356, Lima, T1-800-704 2915,
www.amazing peru.com. Wide selection
of tours in Latin America.
Andean Trails, 33 Sandport Street, Leith,
Edinburgh, EH6 6EP, UK, T0131-467 7086,
www.andeantrails.co.uk. Small group
trekking, biking and jungle tours in the
Andes and Amazon.
Aston Garcia, Salters House, Salters Lane
Industrial Estate, Sedgefield, Co Durham,
TS21 3EE, UK, T01740-582007, www.aston
garciatours.com. Tailor-made tours in
Ecuador and Peru.
Audley Travel, New Mill, New Mill Lane,
Witney, Oxfordshire, OX29 9SX, UK,

T01993-838650, www.audleytravel.com. Tailor-made trips to South America.

Condor Travel, Armando Blondet 249, San Isidro, Lima 27, T01-615 3000, www.condortravel.com. In USA T1-877-236 7199. A full range of tours, including custom-made, and services in Bolivia, Ecuador and Peru (offices in each country), with a strong commitment to social responsibility.

Discover South America, T01273-921655 (UK), www.discoversouthamerica.co.uk. British/Peruvian-owned operator offering tailor-made and classic holidays. Specialist in off-the-beaten-track destinations in Peru.

Dragoman, Camp Green, Debenham, Suffolk, IP14 6LA, UK, T01728-862211, www.dragoman.co.uk. Overland adventures.

Enchanted Adventures, www.enchanted adventures.ca. Ready-made and custom tours focusing on socially and environmentally responsible travel.

Exodus Travels, Grange Mills, Weir Rd, London, SW12 0NE, T0845-287 3647, www.exodus.co.uk.

Explore, Nelson House, 55 Victoria Rd, Farnborough, Hampshire, GU14 7PA, UK, T0843-636 8548, www.explore.co.uk.

Galápagos Classic Cruises with Classic Cruises and **World Adventures**, 6 Keyes Rd, London, NW2 3XA, T020-8933 0613, www.galapagoscruises. co.uk. Individual and group travel including cruises, diving and land-based tours to the Galápagos, Amazon, Ecuador and Peru.

HighLives, 48 Fernthorpe Rd, London, SW16 6DR, T020-8144 2629, www.highlives.co.uk. Specialists in travel to Bolivia and South America.

Journey Latin America, 12-13 Heathfield Terrace, London, W4 4JE, UK, T020-3432 5923, www.journeylatinamerica.co.uk. The specialists.

Journeyou, Lima, tollfree UK T0-808-134-9965, USA T1-855-888-2234, www.journeyou.com. Pre-packaged tours and tailor-made itineraries to suit individual travel dates and budget.

Last Frontiers, The Mill, Quainton Rd, Waddes-don, Bucks, HP18 0LP, UK, T01296-653000, www.lastfrontiers.com. South American specialists offering tailor-made itineraries, family holidays, honeymoons and Galápagos cruises.

Latin America for Less, 203 Valona Drive Round Rock, TX 78681, USA, T1-877-269 0309 (USA toll free), T020-3202 0571 (UK), www.latinamericafor less.com. Travel packages.

Latin American Travel Association, www.lata.org. For useful country information and listings of UK tour operators specializing in Latin America. Also has the LATA Foundation, www.latafoundation.org, supporting charitable work in Latin America.

Metropolitan Touring, Av de las Palmeras N45-74 y de las Orquídeas, Quito, T02-298 8300, with offices in Lima, www.metropolitan-touring.com. Long-established company with tours in Ecuador and Peru.

Neblina Forest Tours, Puembo PO Box 17 17 12 12 Quito, Ecuador, T+539-2-239 3014, www.neblinaforest.com. Birdwatching and cultural tours with a fully South American staff.

Oasis Overland, The Marsh, Henstridge, Somerset, BA8 0TF, UK, T01963-363400, www.oasisoverland.co.uk. Small-group trips to Peru and Bolivia as well as overland tours.

Rainbow Tours, Layden House, 2nd Floor, 76-86 Turnmill St, London, EC1M 5QU, UK, T020-7666 1260, www.rainbowtours.co.uk/latinamerica. Tailor-made travel.

Reef and Rainforest Tours Ltd, Dart Marine Park, Steamer Quay, Totnes, Devon, TQ9 5AL, UK, T01803-866965, www.reefandrainforest.co.uk. Tailor-made and group wildlife tours.

Select Latin America, 3.51 Canterbury Court, 1-3 Brixton Rd, Kennington Park Business Centre, London, SW9 6DE, UK, T020-7407 1478, www.selectlatinamerica.co.uk. Tailor-made holidays and small group tours.

South America Adventure Tours, 336 Kennington Lane, Suite 25, Vauxhall, London, SE11 5HY, T0845-463 3389, www.southamericaadventuretours.com. Specialize in personalized adventure tours in Ecuador and Peru.

South America Adventure Travel, www.southamericaadventure.travel. Personalized adventure tours in Argentina, Costa Rica, Ecuador and Peru.

SouthAmerica.travel, www.southamerica. travel, UK T0800-011 2959, US and Canada T1-800-747 4540, worldwide phone T+1-206-203 8800. Experienced company offering luxury tours to South America and discount flights.

Steamond, 23 Eccleston St, London, SW1W 9LX, T020-7730 8646, www.steamondtravel. com. Organizing all types of travel to Latin America since 1973, very knowledgeable and helpful.

Steppes Latin America, 51 Castle St, Cirencester, Glos, GL7 1QD, T0843-636 8412, www.steppestravel.co.uk. Tailor-made itineraries for destinations throughout Latin America.

Tambo Tours, USA, T1-888-2-GO-PERU (246- 7378), www.tambotours.com. Long-established adventure and tour specialist with offices in Peru and the US. Customized trips to the Amazon and archaeological sites of Peru, Bolivia and Ecuador.

Tribes Travel, The Old Dairy, Wood Farm, Ipswich Rd, Otley, Suffolk, IP6 9JW, UK, T01473-890499, www.tribes.co.uk. Tailor-made tours from ethical travel specialists.

Tucan, 316 Uxbridge Rd, Acton, London W3 9QP, T020-8896 1600, Av del Sol 616, of 202, AP 0637, Cuzco T51-84-241123, www.tucantravel.com.

Vaya Adventures, 1525 Shattuck Av, Suite J, Berkeley, CA 94709, USA, T888-310 3374, www.vayaadventures.com. Customized, private itineraries throughout South America.

Tourist information

South American Explorers, 126 Indian Creek Rd, Ithaca, New York 14850, www. saexplorers.org, is a non-profit educational organization staffed by volunteers, widely recognized as the best place to go for information on South America. Highly recommended as a source for specialized information, trip reports, maps, lectures, library resources. SAE helps members plan trips and expeditions, stores gear, holds post, hosts book exchanges, provides expert travel advice, etc. Annual membership fee US$60 individual (US$90 couple) includes subscription to its quarterly journal. The SAE membership card is good for many discounts throughout Ecuador, Peru and, to a lesser extent, Bolivia. The clubhouses in Quito, Lima and Cuzco are attractive and friendly.

Peru
Tourism promotion and information is handled by **PromPerú**, Edif Mincetur, C Uno Oeste 50, p 13 y 14, urb Córpac, San Isidro, T01-616 7300, or Av República de Panamá 3647, San Isidro, T01-616 7400, www.promperu.gob.pe. See also www. peru.travel. PromPerú runs an information and assistance service, **i perú**, T01-574 8000 (24 hrs). Main office: Jorge Basadre 610, San Isidro, Lima, T01-616 7300 or 7400, iperulima@promperu.gob.pe, Mon-Fri 0830-1830. Also a 24-hr office at Jorge Chávez airport; and throughout the country.

There are tourist offices in most towns, either run by the municipality, or independently. Outside Peru, information can be obtained from Peruvian embassies/consulates. **Indecopi**, T01-224 7777 (in Lima), T0800-44040 (in the Provinces), www.indecopi.gob.pe, is the government-run consumer protection and tourist complaint bureau. They are friendly, professional and helpful.

National parks
Peru has 68 national parks and protected areas. For information see El Servicio Nacional de Areas Naturales Protegidas por el Estado (Sernanp), Calle Diecisiete 355, Urb El Palomar, San Isidro, Lima, T01-717 7500, www.sernanp.gob.pe.

Useful websites
www.caretas.com.pe The most widely read weekly magazine, *Caretas*.
www.leaplocal.org Recommends good-quality guides, helping communities benefit from socially responsible tourism.

www.minam.gob.pe Ministerio del Ambiente (Spanish).

www.peruthisweek.com Informative guide and news service in English for people living in Peru.

www.peruviantimes.com The *Andean Air Mail & Peruvian Times* internet news magazine.

www.terra.com.pe TV, entertainment and news (in Spanish).

Bolivia

The **Viceministerio de Turismo**, C Mercado, Ed Ballivián, p 18, has an informative website, www.bolivia.travel.

InfoTur offices are found in most departmental capitals (addresses given under each city), at international arrivals in El Alto airport (La Paz) and Viru Viru (Santa Cruz). In La Paz at Mariscal Santa Cruz y Colombia.

National parks

Administered by the **Servicio Nacional de Areas Protegidas (SERNAP)**, Francisco Bedregal 2904 y Victor Sanjinés, Sopocachi, T02-242 6268/6272, www.sernap.gob.bo, an administrative office with limited tourist information. Better are Sernap's regional offices, addresses given in the travelling text. Involved NGOs include: **Fundación para el Desarrollo del Sistema Nacional de Areas Protegidas**, Prolongación Cordero 127, across from US Embassy, La Paz, T02-211 3364/243 1875, www.fundesnap.org; **Fundación Amigos de la Naturaleza (FAN)**, Km 7.5 Vía a La Guadria, Santa Cruz, T03-355 6800, www.fan-bo.org; **Probioma**, Calle 7 Este 29, Equipetrol, Santa Cruz, T03-343 1332, www.probioma.org.bo. See also www.biobol.org, a portal with information on Bolivia's protected areas, and the World Conservation Society's site with information on the Gran Chaco and on northwestern Bolivia, www.wcs.org/international/latinamerica/amazon_andes. See also **Ramsar**'s site, www.ramsar.org, for protected wetlands, including the Llanos de Moxos (Ríos Blanco, Matos and Yata), at 6.9 million ha the largest protected wetland in the world.

Useful websites

www.bolivia.com (Spanish) News, tourism, entertainment and information on regions.

www.bolivia-online.net (Spanish, English and German) Travel information about La Paz, Cochabamba, Potosí, Santa Cruz and Sucre.

http://lanic.utexas.edu/la/sa/bolivia Excellent database on various topics indigenous to Bolivia, maintained by the University of Texas, USA.

www.noticiasbolivianas.com All the Bolivian daily news in one place.

www.chiquitania.com Detailed information in English about all aspects of Chiquitania.

Ecuador

Ministerio de Turismo, El Telégrafo E7-58 y Los Shyris, Quito, T1-800-887476 or T02-399-9333, www.ecuador.travel. Local offices are given in the text. The ministry has a Public Prosecutors Office, where serious complaints should be reported. Outside Ecuador, tourist information can be obtained from Ecuadorean embassies.

National parks

Ecuador has an outstanding array of protected natural areas including a system of 43 national parks and reserves administered by the **Ministerio del Ambiente,** Madrid E12-102 y Andalucía, T398 7600, ext 1420, www.ambiente.gob.ec/areas-protegidas-3/. Entry to national protected areas is free except for Parque Nacional Galápagos. Some parks can only be visited with authorized guides. For information on specific protected areas, contact park offices in the cities nearest the parks, they have more information than the ministry.

Useful websites

www.ecuador.travel A good introduction. **www.ecuador.com**; **www.quito adventure.com**; **www.paisturistico.com** and **www.explored.com.ec** General guides with information about activities and national parks.

www.ecuadorexplorer.com; www. ecuador-travel-guide.org; www. ecuaworld.com and www.thebestof ecuador.com Are all travel guides; the latter includes volunteering options. www.saexplorers.org South American Explorers, has information about volunteering. www.trekkinginecuador.com and www. thefreeair.com For hiking information. www.paginasamarillas.info.ec, www. edina.com.ec and www.guiatelefonica. com.ec Telephone directories.

Visas and documentation

Peru
Tourist cards No visa is necessary for citizens of EU countries, most Asian countries, North and South America, and the Caribbean, or for citizens of Andorra, Belarus, Finland, Iceland, Israel, Liechteinstein, Macedonia, Moldova, Norway, Russian Federation, Serbia and Montenegro, Switzerland, Ukraine, Australia, New Zealand and South Africa. A Tourist Card (TAM – Tarjeta Andina de Migración) is free on flights arriving in Peru, or at border crossings for visits up to 183 days. The form is in duplicate, the original given up on arrival and the copy on departure. A new tourist card must be obtained for each re-entry. If your tourist card is stolen or lost, get a new one from **Migraciones**, Digemin, Av España 730, Breña, Lima, T01-200 1081, www. migraciones.gob.pe, Mon-Fri 0830-1300.
Tourist visas For citizens of countries not listed above (including Turkey), visas cost US$37.75 or equivalent, for which you require a valid passport, a departure ticket from Peru (or a letter of guarantee from a travel agency), 2 colour passport photos, 1 application form and proof of economic solvency. Tourist visas are valid for 183 days. In the first instance, visit the Migraciones website (as above) for visa forms.

Keep ID, preferably a passport, on you at all times. You must present your passport when reserving travel tickets. To avoid having to show your passport, photocopy the important pages of your passport – including the immigration stamp, and have it legalized by a 'Notario público'. We have received no reports of travellers being asked for onward tickets at the borders at Tacna, Aguas Verdes, La Tina, Yunguyo or Desaguadero. Travellers are not asked to show an onward flight ticket at Lima airport, but you will not be able to board a plane in your home country without one.

As of 2008, once in Peru tourists may not extend their tourist card or visa. It's therefore important to insist on getting the full number of days to cover your visit on arrival (it's at the discretion of the border official). If you exceed your limit, you'll pay a US$1-per-day fine.

Bolivia
A passport only, valid for 6 months beyond date of visit, is needed for citizens of almost all Western European countries, Israel, Japan, Canada, South American countries, Australia and New Zealand. Nationals of all other countries require a visa. US citizens can obtain a visa in advance at a Bolivian consulate or on arrival at the airport or border post. Requirements include a fee of US$135 cash (subject to change), proof of sufficient funds (eg showing a credit card) and a yellow fever vaccination certificate. Only the fee is universally enforced. Some nationalities must gain authorization from the Bolivian Ministry of Foreign Affairs, which can take 6 weeks. Other countries that require a visa do not need authorisation (visas in this case take 1-2 working days). It is best to check current requirements before leaving home. Tourists are usually granted 90 days stay on entry at airports, less at land borders. You can apply for a free extension (*ampliación*) at immigration offices in all departmental capitals, up to a maximum stay of 90 days per calendar year (180 days for nationals of Andean nations). If you overstay, the current fine is Bs20, roughly US$3 per day. Be sure to keep the green

paper with entry stamp inside your passport, you will be asked for it when you leave.

Ecuador

All visitors to Ecuador must have a passport valid for at least 6 months and an onward or return ticket, but the latter is seldom asked for. Citizens of some Middle Eastern, Asian and African countries require a visa to visit Ecuador, other tourists do not require a visa unless they wish to stay more than 90 days. Upon entry all visitors must complete an international embarkation/disembarkation card. Keep your copy, you will be asked for it when you leave.

Note You are required by Ecuadorean law to carry your passport at all times. Whether or not a photocopy is an acceptable substitute is at the discretion of the individual police officer, having it notarized can help. Tourists are not permitted to work under any circumstances.

Length of stay Tourists are granted 90 days upon arrival and there are no extensions except for citizens of the Andean Community of Nations. Visitors are not allowed back in the country if they have already stayed 90 days during the past 12 months. If you want to spend more time studying, volunteering etc, you can get a purpose specific visa (category '12-IX', about US$200 and paperwork) at the end of your 90 days as a tourist. There is no fine at present (subject to change) for overstaying but you will have difficulties on departure and may be barred from returning to Ecuador. **Dirección Nacional de Migración** (immigration) has offices in all provincial capitals; Visas for longer stays are issued by the **Ministerio de Relaciones Exteriores** (Foreign Office), through their diplomatic representatives abroad and administered in Quito by the **Dirección General de Asuntos Migratorios** and the **Dirección Nacional de Extranjería**. Visa information is found in http://cancilleria.gob.ec.

Weights and measures

Peru Metric.
Bolivia Metric, but some old Spanish measures are used for produce in markets.
Ecuador Metric, US gallons for petrol, some English measures for hardware and weights and some Spanish measures for produce.

Contents

Footprint features

At a glance

⏱ Time required 2-6 weeks.

☁ Best time Dec-Apr on the coast;
Oct-Apr in the sierra; Apr-Oct
driest in the jungles. Jun for fiestas,
especially in Cuzco; carnival is
celebrated everywhere.

✖ When not to go 28-29 Jul is a
major holiday; transport and hotels
are booked up. Roads in sierras and
jungle can be impassable Nov-Apr.
Coast is dull and damp May-Nov.

★ Don't miss ...

Cuzco, capital of the Inca world, is now one of South America's premier tourist destinations, with its access to Machu Picchu and the Inca Trail, the Sacred Urubamba Valley and a buzzing nightlife. On the border with Bolivia is Lake Titicaca, blessed with a magical light and fascinating islands. But in Peru, the Egypt of the Americas, this is just the tip of the pyramid.

The coastal desert may sound uninhabitable, yet pre-Inca cultures thrived there. They left their monuments in sculptures etched into the surface of the desert, most famously at Nazca. Civilization builders welcomed gods from the sea and irrigated the soil to feed great cities of adobe bricks. After the Incas came the Spanish *conquistadores*, who left some of their own finest monuments. You can trek forever amid high peaks and blue lakes, cycle down remote mountainsides, look into canyons deeper than any others on earth, or surf the Pacific rollers. There are enough festivals to brighten almost every day of the year, while the spiritual explorer can be led down mystical paths by a shaman.

East of the Andes the jungles stretch towards the heart of the continent with some of the richest biodiversity on earth. And, should you tire of nature, there is always Lima: loud, brash, covered in fog for half the year, but with some of the best museums, most innovative restaurants and liveliest nightlife in the country.

Lima

Lima's colonial centre and suburbs, shrouded in fog which lasts eight months of the year, are fringed by the pueblos jóvenes which sprawl over the dusty hills overlooking the city. It has a great many historic buildings, some of the finest museums in the country and its food, drink and nightlife are second to none. Although not the most relaxing of South America's capitals, it is a good place to start before exploring the rest of the country.

Arriving in Lima ➜ *Phone code: 01. Colour map 2, C2. Population: 8.6 million (metropolitan area).*
Orientation All international flights land at **Jorge Chávez Airport**, 16 km northwest of the Plaza de Armas. Transport into town by taxi or bus is easy. If arriving in the city by bus, most of the recommended companies have their terminals just south of the centre, many on Avenida Carlos Zavala. This is not a safe area and you should take a taxi to and from there.

Downtown Lima can be explored on foot by day; at night a taxi is safest. Miraflores is 15 km south of the centre. Many of the better hotels and restaurants are here and in neighbouring San Isidro. Three types of bus provide an extensive public transport system; all vehicles stop when flagged down. Termini of public transport vehicles are posted above the windscreens, with the route written on the side. However good the public transport system or smart your taxi, one thing is unavoidable, Lima's roads are congested almost throughout the whole day. Allow plenty of time to get from A to B and be patient. ➜ *For detailed information, see Transport, page 69.*

Addresses Several blocks, with their own names, make up a long street, a *jirón* (often abbreviated to Jr). Street corner signs bear both names, of the *jirón* and of the block. In the historic centre blocks also have their colonial names.

Climate Only 12° south of the equator, one would expect a tropical climate, but Lima has two distinct seasons. The winter is May-November, when a *garúa* (mist) hangs over the city, making everything look grey. It is damp and cold, 8-15°C. The sun breaks through around November and temperatures rise to 30°C or more. Note that the temperature in the coastal suburbs is lower than the centre because of the sea's influence. Protect against the sun's rays when visiting the beaches around Lima, or elsewhere in Peru.

Tourist information **i perú** has offices at **Jorge Chávez international airport** ① *T574 8000, open 24hrs;* **Casa Basadre** ① *Av Jorge Basadre 610, San Isidro, T616 7300 or 7400, Mon-Fri 0900-1800;* and **Larcomar shopping centre** ① *Módulo 10, Plaza Principal, Miraflores, T445 9400, Mon-Fri 1100-1300, 1400-2000.* There is also a **municipal tourist kiosk** ① *Pasaje Escribanos, behind the Municipalidad, near the Plaza de Armas, T632 1542, www.munlima. gob.pe.* Ask about guided walks in the city centre. There are eight **Miraflores kiosks:** Parque Central; Parque Salazar; Parque del Amor; González Prada y Avenida Petit Thouars; Avenida R Palma y Avenida Petit Thouars; Avenida Larco y Avenida Benavides; Huaca Pucllana (closed Saturday afternoon); and Ovalo Gutiérrez. **South American Explorers** ① *Enrique Palacios 956, Miraflores, T445 3306/447 7731 (dial 011-51-1 from USA), www.saexplorers.org.* See also Essentials, page 34. For an English website see www.limaeasy.com and for an upmarket city guide see www.limainside.net.

Background

Lima, capital of Peru, is built on both sides of the Río Rímac, at the foot of Cerro San Cristóbal. It was originally named *La Ciudad de Los Reyes*, in honour of the Magi, at its founding by conquistador Francisco Pizarro in 1535. From then until the independence of the South American republics in the early 19th century, it was the chief city of Spanish South America. The name Lima, a corruption of the Quechua name *Rimac* (speaker), was not adopted until the end of the 16th century.

The Universidad de San Marcos was founded in 1551, and a printing press in 1595, both among the earliest of their kind in South America. Lima's first theatre opened in 1563, and the Inquisition was introduced in 1569 (it was not abolished until 1820). For some time the Viceroyalty of Peru embraced Colombia, Ecuador, Bolivia, Chile and Argentina. There were few cities in the Old World that could rival Lima's power, wealth and luxury, which was at its height during the 17th and early 18th centuries. The city's wealth attracted many freebooters and in 1670 a protecting wall 11 km long was built round it, then destroyed in 1869. The earthquake of 1746 destroyed all but 20 houses, killed 4000 inhabitants and ended its pre-eminence. It was only comparatively recently, with the coming of industry, that Lima began to change into what it is today.

Modern Lima is seriously affected by smog for much of the year, and is surrounded by 'Pueblos Jóvenes', or settlements of squatters who have migrated from the Sierra. Villa El Salvador, a few kilometres southeast of Lima, may be the world's biggest 'squatters' camp' with 350,000 people building up an award-winning self-governing community since 1971.

Over the years the city has changed out of recognition. Many of the hotels and larger business houses have relocated to the fashionable suburbs of Miraflores and San Isidro, thus moving the commercial heart of the city away from the Plaza de Armas.

Half of the town-dwellers of Peru now live in Lima. The metropolitan area contains 8.6 million people, nearly one-third of the country's total population, and two-thirds of its industries. Callao, Peru's major port, runs into Lima; it is a city in its own right, with over one million inhabitants. Within its boundaries is the Jorge Chávez airport. The docks handle 75% of the nation's imports and some 25% of its exports. Callao has a serious theft problem, avoid being there in the evening.

Places in Lima

The traditional heart of the city, at least in plan, is still what it was in colonial days. An increasing number of buildings in the centre are being restored and the whole area is being given a new lease of life as the architectural beauty and importance of the Cercado (as it is known) is recognized. Most of the tourist attractions are in this area. Some museums are only open 0900-1300 from January-March, and some are closed in January.

Plaza de Armas (Plaza Mayor)

One block south of the Río Rímac lies the Plaza de Armas, or Plaza Mayor, which has been declared a World Heritage Site by UNESCO. Running along two sides are arcades with shops: Portal de Escribanos and Portal de Botoneros. In the centre of the plaza is a bronze fountain dating from 1650. The **Palacio de Gobierno**, on the north side of the Plaza, stands on the site of the original palace built by Pizarro. The changing of the guard is at 1145-1200. To take a tour register two days in advance at the Oficina de Turismo (ask guard for directions); the free, 45-minute tours are in Spanish and English Monday-Friday, 0830-1300, 1400-1730. The **Cathedral** ① *T427 9647, Mon-Fri 0900-1700, Sat 1000-1300; entry to* *cathedral US$3.65, ticket also including Museo Arzobispado US$11*, was reduced to rubble in the earthquake of 1746. The reconstruction, on the lines of the original, was completed 1755. Note the splendidly carved stalls (mid-17th century), the silver-covered altars surrounded by fine woodwork, mosaic-covered walls bearing the coats of arms of Lima and Pizarro and an allegory of Pizarro's commanders, the 'Thirteen Men of Isla del Gallo'. The remains of Francisco Pizarro, found in the crypt, lie in a small chapel, the first on the right of the entrance. The **Museo de Arte Religioso** in the cathedral, has sacred paintings, portraits, altar pieces and other items, as well as a café and toilets. Next to the cathedral is the **Archbishop's Palace and museum** ① *T01-427 5790, www.palacioarzobispaldelima. com, Mon-Sat 0900-1700*, rebuilt in 1924, with a superb wooden balcony. Permanent and temporary exhibitions are open to the public.

Around the Plaza de Armas

Just behind the Municipalidad de Lima is **Pasaje Ribera el Viejo**, which has been restored and is now a pleasant place, with several good cafés with outdoor seating. Nearby is the **Casa Solariega de Aliaga** ① *Unión 224, T427 7736, Mon-Fri 0930-1300, 1430-1745, US$11,*

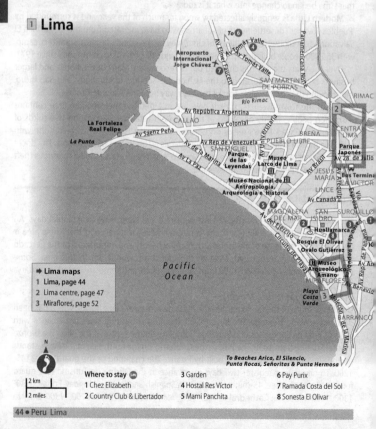

① Lima

➡ Lima maps
1 Lima, page 44
2 Lima centre, page 47
3 Miraflores, page 52

Pacific Ocean

*To Beaches Arica, El Silencio,
Punta Rocas, Señoritas & Punta Hermosa*

Where to stay		
1 Chez Elizabeth	3 Garden	6 Pay Purix
2 Country Club & Libertador	4 Hostal Res Víctor	7 Ramada Costa del Sol
	5 Mami Panchita	8 Sonesta El Olivar

knock on the door and wait to see if anyone will let you in, or contact in advance for tour operators who offer guided visits. It is still occupied by the Aliaga family and is open to the public and for functions. The house contains what is said to be the oldest ceiling in Lima and is furnished entirely in the colonial style. The **Casa de la Gastronomía Nacional Peruana** ① *Conde de Superunda 170, T426 7264, www.limacultura.pe, guided tours US$.5.25, behind the Correo Central,* has an extensive permanent collection of objects and displays on Peruvian food, historic and regional. It also has temporary exhibitions on the same theme. All signs are in Spanish.

The area from the east side of the Palacio de Gobierno (Calle Carabaya) along the second block of Ancash has been designated the tourist circuit of the Calles El Rastro y Pescadería, with the **Museo de Sitio Bodega y Quadra** ① *Ancash 213, Tue-Sun 0900-1700, free.* It stretches from the railway station to San Francisco, including the Casa de la Literatura and several historic houses. The area is to be pedestrianized.

The baroque church of **San Francisco** ① *on the 1st block of Jr Lampa, corner of Ancash, a few blocks from the Plaza de Armas, T426 7377 ext 111, www.museocatacumbas.com, daily 0930-1645, guided tours only, US$2.75, students half price, US$0.40 children,* was finished in 1674 and withstood the 1746 earthquake. The nave and aisles are lavishly decorated in Mudéjar style. The monastery is famous for the Sevillian tilework and panelled ceiling in the cloisters (1620). The Catacombs under the church and part of the monastery are well worth seeing. The late 16th-century **Casa de Jarava** or **Pilatos** ① *Jr Ancash 390*, is opposite San Francisco church. Close by, **Casa de las Trece Monedas** ① *Jr Ancash 536*, still has the original doors and window grills. **Parque de la Muralla** ① *open 0900-2000*, on the south bank of the Rímac, incorporates a section of the old city wall, fountains, stalls and street performers. There is a cycle track, toilets and places to eat both inside and near the entrance on Calle de la Soledad.

The **Palacio Torre Tagle** (1735) ① *Jr Ucayali 363, Mon-Fri during working hours*, is the city's best surviving example of secular colonial architecture. Today, it is used by the Foreign Ministry, but visitors are allowed to enter courtyards to inspect the fine, Moorish-influenced wood-carving in balconies and wrought iron work. At Ucayali 391 and also part of the Foreign Ministry is the **Centro Cultural Inca Garcilaso**, which holds cultural events. **Casa de la Rada**, or **Goyeneche** ① *Jr Ucayali 358*, opposite, is a fine mid-18th-century French-style town house which now belongs to a bank. The

SAN JUAN DE LURIGANCHO
Cerro San Cristóbal
Independencia
SANTA ANITA
Cerro El Agustino
Av N Ayllón
Av Nicolás Arriola
Vía de Evitamiento
ATE
SAN BORJA
Museo de la Nación & Gran Teatro Nacional
Av Javier Prado Este
LA MOLINA
To Puruchuco
Hipódromo de Monterrico
MONTERRICO
Av Panamericana Sur
Av Alonso de Molina
Av Aviación
Av Primavera
Museo de Oro del Perú
Av Tomás Marsano
To Chorrillos
9 Tambopacaya

El Tren Eléctrico ⎯⎯⎯
Metropolitano bus line ⎯⎯⎯

patio and first reception room are open occasionally to the public. **Museo Banco Central de Reserva** ① *Jr Ucayali at Jr Lampa, T01-613 2000 ext 2655, Tue-Fri 1000-1630, Wed 1000-1900, Sat-Sun 1000-1300, free, photography prohibited.* This is a large collection of pottery from the Vicus or Piura culture (AD 500-600) and gold objects from Lambayeque, as well as 19th- and 20th-century paintings: both sections highly recommended. **San Pedro** ① *3rd block of Jr Ucayali, Mon-Sat 0930-1145, 1700-1800,* finished by Jesuits in 1638, has marvellous altars with Moorish-style balconies, rich gilded wood-carvings in choir and vestry, and tiled throughout. Several Viceroys are buried here; the bell called *La Abuelita*, first rung in 1590, sounded the Declaration of Independence in 1821.

Between Avenida Abancay and Jr Ayacucho is **Plaza Bolívar**, where General José de San Martín proclaimed Peru's independence. The plaza is dominated by the equestrian statue of the Liberator. Behind lies the Congress building which occupies the former site of the Universidad de San Marcos. Behind the Congress is the **Mercado Municipal** (or Central) and the **Barrio Chino**, with many *chifas* and small shops selling oriental items. Block 700 of Ucayali is pedestrianized, in 'Chinese' style. The whole area is jam-packed with people. **Museo del Congreso y de la Inquisición** ① *Plaza Bolívar, C Junín 548, near the corner of Av Abancay, T311 7777, ext 5160, www.congreso.gob.pe/museo.htm, daily 0900-1700, free, students offer to show you round for a tip; good explanations in English.* The main hall, with a splendidly carved mahogany ceiling, remains untouched. The Court of Inquisition was held here from 1584; 1829-1938 it was used by the Senate. In the basement there is a recreation *in situ* of the gruesome tortures. A description in English is available at the desk.

The 16th-century **Santo Domingo church and monastery** ① *T427 6793, monastery and tombs open Mon-Sat 0900-1230, 1500-1800; Sun and holidays morning only, US$1.65,* is on the first block of Jr Camaná. The Cloister, one of the city's most attractive, dates from 1603. The second Cloister is less elaborate. Beneath the sacristy are the tombs of San Martín de Porres, one of Peru's most revered saints, and Santa Rosa de Lima (see below). In 1669, Pope Clement presented the alabaster statue of Santa Rosa in front of the altar. Behind Santo Domingo is **Alameda Chabuca Granda**, named after one of Peru's greatest singers. In the evening there are free art and music shows and you can sample foods from all over Peru. A couple of blocks beyond Santo Domingo is **Casa de Osambela** or **Oquendo** ① *Conde de Superunda 298, T427 7987 (ask Lizardo Retes Bustamante if you can visit).* It is said that José de San Martín stayed here after proclaiming independence from Spain. The house is typical of Lima secular architecture with two patios, a broad staircase leading from the lower to the upper floor, fine balconies and an observation tower. It is now the Centro Cultural Inca Garcilaso de la Vega and headquarters of various academies. A few blocks west is **Santuario de Santa Rosa** ① *Av Tacna, 1st block, T425 1279, daily 0930-1300, 1500-1800, free to the grounds,* a small but graceful church. A pilgrimage centre; here are preserved the hermitage built by Santa Rosa herself, the house in which she was born, a section of the house in which she attended to the sick, her well, and other relics.

San Agustín ① *Jr Ica 251, T427 7548, daily 0830-1130, 1630-1900, ring for entry,* is west of the Plaza de Armas: its façade (1720) is a splendid example of churrigueresque architecture. There are carved choir stalls and effigies, and a sculpture of Death, said to have frightened its maker into an early grave. The church has been restored after the last earthquake, but the sculpture of Death is in storage. **Las Nazarenas church** ① *Av Tacna, 4th block, T423 5718, daily 0700-1200, 1600-2000,* is built around an image of Christ Crucified painted by a liberated slave in 1655. This, the most venerated image in Lima, and an oil copy of El Señor de los Milagros (Lord of Miracles), encased in a gold frame, are carried on a silver litter the whole weighing nearly a ton through the streets on 18, 19, and 28 October and again on

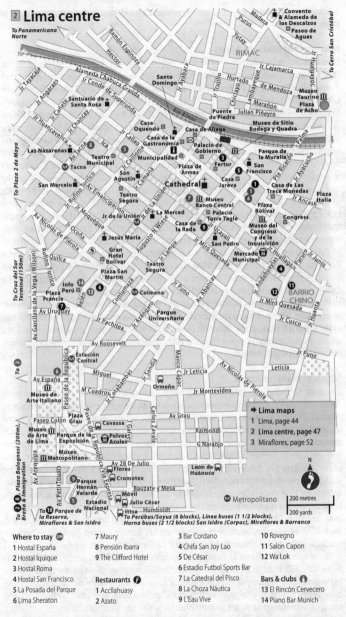

To Panamericana
Norte

Convento
& Alameda de
los Descalzos
Paseo de
Aguas

RIMAC

Ramón Espinoza

Hector

Madera

Purus

Jutay

Jr Cajamarca

To Cerro San Cristóbal

Alameda Chabuca Granda

Jr Conde de Superunda

Santo
Domingo

Hurtado
de Mendoza

Trujillo

Chiclayo

Lambayeque

Marañón

Museo
Taurino 🏛

Plaza
de Acho

Jr Tayacaja

Jr Angaraes

Jr Cañete

Santuario de
Santa Rosa

Jr Chancay

Casa
Oquendo

Casa de Aliaga

Puente
de Piedra

Julian Piñeyro

Río Rímac

Ica

Jr Callao

Casa de la
Gastronomía

Palacio de
Gobierno

Jr Huancavelica

Las Nazarenas

Av Tacna

Teatro
Municipal

Jr Callloma

Municipalidad

Plaza de
Armas

Fertur

Parque de
la Muralla

Pte Ricardo
Palma

To Plaza 2 de Mayo

M Tacna

San
Agustín

Jr Camaná

San Marcelo

Teatro
Segura

Cathedral

Casa
Jarava

San Francisco

Casa de Las
Trece Monedas

Plaza
Italia

Rufino Torrico

Av Emancipación

Jr de la Unión

La Merced

Museo
Banco Central

Jr Ancash

Av Nicolás de Piérola

Jr Moquegua

La Unión

Augusto N Wiese

Palacio
Torre Tagle

Plaza
Bolívar

Congress

Jr Ocoña

Jesús María

Casa de
la Rada

Jr Ucayali

San Pedro

Museo del
Congreso
y de la
Inquisición

Av Garcilaso de la Vega (Wilson)

Gran
Hotel
Bolívar

Jr Lampa

Jr Miró Quesada

Mercado
Municipal

M

Jr Andahuaylas

Jr Huallaga

Jr Paruro

Jr Junín

Quilca

Plaza San
Martín

Teatro
Segura

Jr Puno

Jr Abancay

BARRIO
CHINO

Jr Miró Quesada

Jr Huanta

Info
Perú

Plaza
Francia

Belén

Comunaza

M Colmena

Jr Cusco

To Cruz del Sur
Terminal (150m)

Jr Azángaro

Jr Pachitea

Parque
Universitario

Av Roosevelt

Manco Capac

Jr Leticia

Av Nicolás de Piérola

Jr Puno

Leticia

Estación
Central

Miguel

Jr Sandia

Ormeño

Av España

Paseo de la República

M Cuadros

Jr Cotabambas

Jr Montevideo

Museo de
Arte Italiano

Carlos Zavala

Paseo Colón

Plaza
Grau

Cavassa

Av Grau

Museo
de Arte
de Lima

Parque de la
Exposición

Polvos
Azules

Raimondi

G Naranjo

To 2

To 2 & 8, Plaza Bolognesi (200m),
Breña & Immigration

Museo
Metropolitano 🏛

Av 28 De Julio

Flores

Cromotex

León de
Huánuco

Parque
Hernán
Velarde

Móvil

Bauzate y Mesa

Av Petit Touars

Av Arequipa

Julio César

Estadio
Nacional

Humboldt

Ittsa

M Metropolitano

200 metres

To 2 & 8,
Breña & Immigration

To 10 Parque de
la Reserva,
Miraflores & San Isidro

To Perúbus/Soyuz (6 blocks), Línea buses (1 1/2 blocks),
Horna buses (2 1/2 blocks) San Isidro (Corpac), Miraflores & Barranco

200 yards

→ Lima maps
1 Lima, page 44
2 Lima centre, page 47
3 Miraflores, page 52

N

M Metropolitano

Where to stay 🛏
1 Hostal España
2 Hostal Iquique
3 Hostal Roma
4 Hostal San Francisco
5 La Posada del Parque
6 Lima Sheraton

7 Maury
8 Pensión Ibarra
9 The Clifford Hotel

Restaurants 🍴
1 Acllahuasy
2 Azato

3 Bar Cordano
4 Chifa San Joy Lao
5 De César
6 Estadio Futbol Sports Bar
7 La Catedral del Pisco
8 La Choza Náutica
9 L'Eau Vive

10 Rovengo
11 Salon Capon
12 Wa Lok

Bars & clubs 🍷
13 El Rincón Cervecero
14 Piano Bar Munich

1 November (All Saints' Day). *El Comercio* newspaper and local pamphlets give details of times and routes.

Northeast of Plaza de Armas

From the Plaza, passing the Palacio de Gobierno on the left, straight ahead is the **Desamparados railway station**, which now houses fascinating exhibitions on Peruvian themes. The **Puente de Piedra**, behind the Palacio de Gobierno, is a Roman-style stone bridge built in 1610, crossing the Río Rímac to the district of that name. On Jr Hualgayoc is the bullring in the **Plaza de Acho**, inaugurated on 20 January 1766, with the **Museo Taurino** ① *Hualgayoc 332, T482 3360, Mon-Sat 0800-1600, US$1, students US$0.50, photography US$2*. Apart from matador's relics, the museum contains good collections of paintings and engravings, some of the latter by Goya. There are two bullfight seasons: October to first week in December and during July. The **Convento de Los Descalzos** ① *on the Alameda de Los Descalzos in Rímac, T481 0441, daily 1000-1300, 1500-1800, except Tue, US$1, guided tour only, 45 mins in Spanish (worth it)*, was founded in 1592. It contains over 300 paintings of the Cuzco, Quito and Lima schools which line the four main cloisters and two ornate chapels. The chapel of El Carmen was constructed in 1730 and is notable for its baroque gold leaf altar. The museum shows the life of the Franciscan friars during colonial and early republican periods. The cellar, infirmary, pharmacy and a typical cell have been restored.

Cerro San Cristóbal ① *visited on a 1-hr minibus tour, departing from in front of Santo Domingo, Camaná y Conde Superunda, daily 1000-2100; departures every 15 mins, US$3*, dominates downtown Lima. It includes a look at the run-down Rímac district, passes the Convento de los Descalzos (see above), ascends the hill through one of the city's oldest shanties with its brightly painted houses and spends about 20 minutes at the summit, where there is a small museum and café. Excellent views on a clear day. The second half of the trip is a historical tour. **Urbanito buses** ① *T01-424 3650, www.urbanito.com.pe, 3 hrs, weekends and holidays*, also run from the Plaza de Armas on a tour of central Lima, which includes Cerro San Cristóbal.

South of Plaza de Armas

The Jr de La Unión, the main shopping street, runs to the Plaza de Armas. It has been converted into a pedestrian precinct which teems with life in the evening. In the two blocks south of Jr Unión, known as Calle Belén, several shops sell souvenirs and curios. **La Merced** ① *Unión y Miró Quesada, T427 8199, 0800-1245, 1600-2000 (Sun 0700-1300, 1600-2000); monastery daily 0800-1200 and 1500-1730*, is in Plazuela de la Merced. The first Mass in Lima was said here on the site of the first church to be built. The restored façade is a fine example of colonial Baroque. Inside are some magnificent altars and the tilework on some of the walls is noteworthy. A door from the right of the nave leads into the Monastery. The cloister dates from 1546. Jr de la Unión leads to **Plaza San Martín**, which has a statue of San Martín in the centre. The plaza has been restored with colourful flower beds and is now a nice place to sit and relax. On its west side is the refurbished **Gran Hotel Bolívar** ① *Jr de la Unión 958, T619 7171, www.granhotelbolivar.com.pe*, which has a huge stained-glass dome over the entrance lobby. Its **El Bolivarcito** bar calls itself 'La Catedral del Pisco Sour'.

Museo de Arte Italiano ① *Paseo de la República 250, T423 9932, Tue-Fri 0900-1900, Sat-Sun 1100-1700, US$1*, is in a wonderful neoclassical building, given by the Italian colony to Peru on the centenary of its independence. Note the remarkable mosaic murals on the outside. It consists of a large collection of Italian and other European works of art and houses the **Instituto de Arte Contemporáneo**, which has many exhibitions.

Museo de Arte de Lima ① *Paseo Colón 125, T204 0000, www.mali.pe, Tue-Sun 1000-2000, Sat 1000-1700, US$2.15 minimum, US$4.30 suggested, children, students and over-65s US$1.40, guides US$1, bilingual guides available 1030-1600, signs in English,* is in the Palacio de la Exposición, built in 1868 in Parque de la Exposición (designed by Gustave Eiffel). There are more than 7000 exhibits, giving a chronological history of Peruvian cultures and art from the Paracas civilization up to today. It includes excellent examples of 17th- and 18th-century Cuzco paintings, a beautiful display of carved furniture, heavy silver and jewelled stirrups and also pre-Columbian pottery. The Filmoteca (movie club) is on the premises and shows films just about every night; see the local paper for details, or look in the museum itself. The **Gran Parque Cultural de Lima** ① *0800-2030,* is in the grounds. Inaugurated in January 2000, this large park has an amphitheatre, Japanese garden, food court and children's activities. Relaxing strolls through this green, peaceful and safe oasis in the centre of Lima are recommended. **Museo Metropolitano** ① *Av 28 de Julio, T433 7122, www.limacultura.pe, Tue-Sun 0900-1700, US$1.40,* has audiovisual displays and temporary exhibitions about the history of Lima, also lectures and a library

In **Parque de la Reserva** is the **Circuito Mágico del Agua** ① *block 8 of Av Arequipa and going up towards the centre, Santa Beatriz, Wed-Sun and holidays 1600-2200, US$1.50,* a display of 13 fountains, the highest reaching 80 m, enhanced by impressive light and music shows four times a night, great fun and very popular.

San Borja and Surco

Museo de la Nación ① *Javier Prado Este 2465, T476 9878, www.mcultura.gob.pe/museo-de-la-nacion-exposiciones, Tue-Sun 0900-1700, closed major public holidays, US$2.50. 50% discount with ISIC card,* in the huge **Banco de la Nación** building, is the museum for the exhibition and study of the art and history of the aboriginal races of Peru. There are good explanations in Spanish and English on Peruvian history, with ceramics, textiles and displays of many ruins in Peru. It is arranged so that you can follow the development of Peruvian precolonial history through to the time of the Incas. A visit is recommended before you go to see the archaeological sites themselves. There are displays of the tomb of the Señor de Sipán, artefacts from Batán Grande near Chiclayo (Sicán culture), reconstructions of the friezes found at Huaca La Luna and Huaca El Brujo, near Trujillo, and of Sechín and other sites. A photographic record of the events of 1980-2000, **Yuyanapaq**, is also on display. Temporary exhibitions are held in the basement, where there is also a Ministerio de Cultura bookshop. The museum has a cafetería. To get there, take a taxi from downtown Lima or Miraflores US$3.20. From Avenida Garcilaso de la Vega in downtown Lima take a combi with a "Javier Prado/Aviación" window sticker. Get off at the 21st block of Javier Prado at Avenida Aviación. From Miraflores take a bus down Avenida Arequipa to Avenida Javier Prado (27th block), then take a bus with a "Todo Javier Prado" or "Aviación" window sticker.

The **Museo de Oro del Perú** ① *Alonso de Molina 1100, Monterrico, Surco (between blocks 18 and 19 of Av Primavera), Lima 33, T345 1292, www.museoroperu.com.pe, daily 1030-1800, closed 1 Jan, 1 May, 28 Jul, 25 Dec, US$11.55, children under 11 US$5.60, multilingual audioguides,* houses an enormous collection of Peruvian gold, silver and bronze objects, together with an impressive international array of arms and military uniforms from Spanish colonial times to the present day and textiles from Peru and elsewhere. Allow plenty of time to appreciate all that is on view. It is directed by the **Fundación Miguel Mujica Gallo**. 167 of its pieces can be seen in the **Sala Museo Oro del Perú**, in Larcomar (see below).

Pueblo Libre

The original museum of anthropology and archaeology is **Museo Nacional de Antropología, Arqueología e Historia** ① *Plaza Bolívar in Pueblo Libre, not to be confused with Plaza Bolívar in the centre, T463 5070, Tue-Sat 0900-1700, Sun and holidays 0900-1600, US$4, students US$1.20, guides available for groups.* On display are ceramics of the Chimú, Nazca, Mochica and Pachacámac cultures, a new display on the Paracas culture (2013), various Inca curiosities and works of art, and interesting textiles. **Museo Nacional de Historia** ① *T463 2009, Tue-Sat 0900-1700, Sun and holidays 0900-1600, US$3.65,* in a mansion occupied by San Martín (1821-1822) and Bolívar (1823-1826) is next door. It exhibits colonial and early republican paintings, manuscripts and uniforms. Take any public transport on Avenida Brasil with a window sticker saying "Todo Brasil." Get off at the 21st block called Avenida Vivanco. Walk about five blocks down Vivanco. The museum will be on your left. From Miraflores take bus SM 18 Caraballyo-Chorrillos, marked "Bolívar, Arequipa, Larcomar", get out at block 8 of Bolívar by the Hospital Santa Rosa, and walk down Avenida San Martín four blocks until you see the 'blue line'; turn left. The 'blue line' marked on the pavement, very faded, links the Museo Nacional de Antropología, Arqueología e Historia to the Museo Larco (see below), 15 minutes' walk. Taxi from downtown US$3; from Miraflores US$4.

Museo Larco de Lima ① *Av Bolívar 1515, T461 1312, www.museolarco.org, 0900-2200, 0900-1800 24 Dec-1 Jan; texts in Spanish, English and French, US$10.55 (half price for students, seniors US$8.75), disabled access, photography not permitted.* Located in an 18th-century mansion, itself built on a seventh-century pre-Columbian pyramid, this museum has a collection which gives an excellent overview on the development of Peruvian cultures through their pottery. It has the world's largest collection of Moche, Sicán and Chimú pieces. There is a Gold and Silver of Ancient Peru exhibition, a magnificent textile collection and a fascinating erotica section. Don't miss the storeroom with its vast array of pottery, unlike anything you'll see elsewhere. There is a library and computer room for your own research and a good café open during museum hours, see page 59. It is surrounded by beautiful gardens, has a new entrance and park outside. Take any bus to the 15th block of Avenida Brasil. Then take a bus down Avendia Bolívar. From Miraflores, take the SM 18 Caraballyo-Chorrillos, see above, to block 15 of Bolívar. Taxi from downtown, Miraflores or San Isidro, 15 minutes, US$4. Follow the 'blue line' marked on the pavement to the Museo Nacional de Antropología, Arqueología e Historia (see above), 15 minutes' walk.

San Isidro

To the east of Avenida La República, down Calle Pancho Fierro, is **El Olivar**, an olive grove planted by the first Spaniards which has been turned into a park. Some 32 species of birds have been recorded there. Between San Isidro and Miraflores, is **Huallamarca** ① *C Nicolás de Rivera 201 and Av Rosario, T222 4124, 0900-1700, closed Mon, US$1.75. Take bus 1 from Av Tacna, or minibus 13 or 73 to Choquechaca, then walk.* An adobe pyramid of the Maranga (Lima) culture, it dates from about AD 100-500, but has later Wari and Inca remains. There is a small site museum. There are many good hotels and restaurants in San Isidro; see Where to stay, page 55 and Restaurants, page 59.

Miraflores → *See map, page 52.*

Avenida Arequipa continues to the coast, to the most important suburb of Lima (see Where to stay, page 56; and Restaurants, page 60). Together with San Isidro and Barranco this is the social centre of Lima.

Parque Kennedy, the Parque Central de Miraflores is located between Avenida Larco and Avenida Mcal Oscar Benavides (locally known as Avenida Diagonal). This extremely well-kept park has a small open-air theatre with performances Thursday-Sunday and an arts and crafts market most evenings of the week. The house of the author **Ricardo Palma** ① *Gral Suárez 189, T445 5836, http://ricardopalma.miraflores.gob.pe, Mon-Fri 0915-1245, 1430-1700, US$2.20, includes video and guided tour*, is now a museum explaining the author's life and work. At the end of Avenida Larco and running along the Malecón de la Reserva is the renovated **Parque Salazar** and the modern shopping centre called **Centro Comercial Larcomar**. Here you will find expensive shops, hip cafés and discos and a wide range of restaurants, all with a beautiful ocean view. The 12-screen cinema is one of the best in Lima and even has a 'cine-bar' in the 12th theatre. Don't forget to check out the Cosmic Bowling Alley with its black lights and fluorescent balls. A few hundred metres to the north is the famous **Parque del Amor** where on just about any night you'll see at least one wedding party taking photos of the newly weds.

Museo Arqueológico Amano ① *Retiro 160, 11th block of Av Angamos Oeste, Miraflores, T441 2909, www.fundacionmuseoamano.org.pe, open by appointment only Mon-Fri 1500-1630, donations (photography prohibited)*. The collection is of artefacts from the Chancay, Chimú and Nazca periods, owned by the late Mr Yoshitaro Amano. It has one of the most complete exhibits of Chancay weaving, and is particularly interesting for pottery and pre-Columbian textiles, all superbly displayed and lit. Take a bus or colectivo to the corner of Avenida Arequipa y Avenida Angamos and another one to the 11th block of Avenida Angamos Oeste. Taxi from downtown US$3.20; from Parque Kennedy US$2.25.

Poli Museum ① *Almte Cochrane 466, T422 2437, tours cost US$15 per person irrespective of the size of the group, allow 2 hrs, call in advance to arrange tours*. This is one of the best private collections of colonial and pre-Columbian artefacts in Peru, including material from Sipán. At General Borgoño, eighth block s/n, turn off Avenida Arequipa at 45th block, is **Huaca Pucllana** ① *T01-445 8695, www.mirafloresperu.com/huacapuclllana/, US$4.25, students US$2, includes 45-min tour in Spanish or English, 0900-1600, closed Tue*, a pre-Inca site which is under excavation. Originally a Lima culture temple to the goddesses of sea and moon (AD 200-700), it became a Wari burial site (AD 700-900) before being abandoned. Later Ychsma occupation (AD 1000-1470) and subsequent looting followed. It has a small site museum with some objects from the site itself, a garden of traditional plants and animals and a souvenir shop (see Restaurants, page 60).

Barranco

This suburb further south was already a seaside resort by the end of the 17th century. The attractive public library, formerly the town hall, stands on the plaza. It contains the helpful **municipal tourist office** ① *T719 2046*. Nearby is the interesting *bajada*, a steep path leading down to the beach. The **Puente de los Suspiros** (Bridge of Sighs) crosses the *bajada* to the earthquake-damaged La Ermita church (only the façade has been restored) and leads towards the Malecón, with fine views of the bay. Barranco is quiet by day but comes alive at night (see Restaurants and Bars listings). The 45-minute walk from Miraflores to Barranco along the Malecón is nice in summer. There are many old mansions in the district, in a variety of styles. Several are being renovated, particularly on Calle Cajamarca and around San Francisco church. The main artistic focus is contemporary; a number of artists have their workshops here and there are several chic galleries (see also **Hotel B**, page 58). **Museo de Arte Contemporáneo de Lima (MAC Lima)** ① *Av Miguel Grau beside the municipal stadium, near Miraflores, T652 5100,* *www.mac-lima.org.pe, US$2.25, Tue-Sun 1000-1700, with guided tour*, has permanent Latin American and European collections and holds temporary exhibitions. **MATE (Asociación Mario Testino)** ① *Av Pedro de Osma 409, T251 7755, www.mate.pe, US$5.55, Tue-Sat 1100-2000, Sun 1100-1800, with audio tour (no other explanations)*, is the world-renowned fashion photographer's vision of modern art, with a shop and excellent café/restaurant. Next door, by contrast, and equally important is the **Museo de Arte Colonial Pedro de Osma** ① *Av Pedro de Osma 423, T467 0141, www.museopedrodeosma.org, Tue-Sun 1000-1800, US$6.75, students half price, guided tours in English or Spanish*, a private collection of colonial art of the Cuzco, Ayacucho and Arequipa schools.

Lima beaches

In summer (December-April) the city's beaches get very crowded at weekends and lots of activities are organized. Even though the water of the whole bay has been declared

unsuitable for swimming, Limeños see the beach more as part of their culture than as a health risk. Do not camp on the beaches as robbery is a serious threat and, for the same reason, take care on the walkways down. Don't take any belongings with you to the beach, only what is really necessary.

The *Circuito de Playas*, which begins with Playa Arica (30 km from Lima) and ends with San Bartolo (45 km from Lima), has many great beaches for all tastes. The beaches of **Miraflores**, **Barranco** and **Chorrillos** are very popular and sand and sea get dirty. It's much better to take a safe taxi 40 km south to **Punta Rocas**, **Señoritas** or **Silencio**. **Punta Hermosa** has frequent surfing and volleyball tournaments. If you really want the height of fashion head to **Asia**, Km 92-104, some 20 beaches with boutiques, hotels, restaurants and condos.

100 metres
100 yards

Where to stay
1 Albergue Turístico
   Juvenil Internacional *D3*
2 Albergue Verde *D2*
3 Alemán *A3*
4 Antigua Miraflores *B1*
5 Belmond Miraflores Park *D1*
6 Blue House *C1*
7 Casa Andina *D2*
8 Casa Andina
   Private Collection *C3*
9 Casa Andina Select *C2*
10 Casa de Baraybar *A1*
11 Casa del Mochilero *A2*
12 Casa Rodas *B3*
13 Condor's House *A1*
14 El Carmelo *B1*
15 Explorer's House *A1*
16 Flying Dog *B2 , C2*
17 Friend's House *C1*
18 Hitchhikers B&B
   Backpackers *B1*
19 Hostal El Patio *C2*
20 HosteLima *A3*
21 Inka Frog *A2*
22 José Antonio *C1*
23 JW Marriott *D1*
24 La Casa Nostra *D2*
25 La Castellana *C2*
26 Loki Backpackers *A1*
27 Pariwana *B3*

28 Pirwa *B3*
29 Pirwa B&B *A3*
30 San Antonio Abad *D3*
31 Señorial *D1*
32 Sipán *D2*
33 Sonesta Posadas del Inca
   & Café La Máquina *C2*
34 The Lighthouse *A2*

Restaurants
1 Ache & Amaz *D2*
2 Alfresco *B1*
3 AlmaZen *B2*
4 Café Café *B2*
5 Café de la Paz *B2, C2*
6 Café Tarata *C2*
7 Central *D1*
8 C'est si bon *A2*
9 Chef's Café *C2*
10 Chifa Internacional *D2*
11 El Huarike *B3*
12 El Kapallaq *B3*
13 El Parquetito *B2*
14 El Rincón Gaucho *D1*
15 Fiesta Gourmet *D2*
16 Govinda *D2*
17 Haiti *B3*
18 IK *A2*
19 La Gloria *B3*
20 La Lucha *B2*
21 La Preferida *D3*
22 Las Brujas de Cachiche *B1*
23 Las Tejas *C2*
24 La Tiendecita Blanca *B3*
25 La Trattoria *C3*
26 Lobo del Mar –
   Octavio Otani *C1*
27 Madre Natura *A3*

28 Mama Olla *C2*
29 Manifiesto *B2*
30 Panchita *B3*
31 Pizza Street *B2*
32 Punto Azul *C2*
33 Rafael *C1*
34 San Antonio *A3, D2*
35 Saqra *C2*
36 Sí Señor *B1*

Bars & clubs
37 Media Naranja *B2*
38 Murphy's *C3*
39 The Old Pub *B2*
40 Treff Pub Alemán *C2*

M Metropolitano

➡ **Lima maps**
1 Lima, page 44
2 Lima centre, page 47
3 **Miraflores, page 52**

Pachacámac

ⓘ T430 0168, http://pachacamac.cultura.pe, Tue-Sat 0900-1700, Sun 0900-1600; closed public holidays except by appointment. US$3.50, includes the museum, students US$1.75, guide US$7.

When the Spaniards arrived, Pachacámac in the Lurín valley was the largest city and ceremonial centre on the coast. A wooden statue of the creator-god, after whom the site is named, is in the site museum. Hernando Pizarro was sent here by his brother in 1533 in search of gold for Inca emperor Atahualpa's ransom. In their fruitless quest, the Spaniards destroyed images and killed the priests. The ruins encircle the top of a low hill, whose crest was crowned with a **Temple of the Sun**, now partially restored. Slightly apart is the reconstructed **House of the Mamaconas**, where the 'chosen women' spun fine cloth for the Inca and his court. An impression of the scale of the site can be gained from the top of the Temple of the Sun, or from walking or driving the 3-km circuit, which is covered by an unmade road for cars and tour buses. The site is large and it is expected that tourists will be visiting by vehicle. There are six parking areas.

◉ Lima listings

For hotel and restaurant price codes, and other relevant information, see pages 14-17.

● Where to stay

Central Lima is not as safe at night as the more upmarket areas of Miraflores, San Isidro and Barranco. If you are only staying a short time and want to see the main sites, it is convenient, but do take care. San Isidro is the poshest district while Miraflores has a good mix of places to stay, great ocean views, bookstores, restaurants and cinemas. From here you can then commute to the centre by bus (45 mins minimum) or by taxi (30 mins minimum). Barranco is a little further out. All hotels in the upper price brackets charge 18% state tax and service on top of prices. In hotels foreigners pay no tax and the amount of service charge is up to the hotel. Neither is included in the prices below, unless otherwise stated. All those listed below have received good recommendations.

Lima has several international, high-class chain hotels: JW Marriott, www.marriott.com; Lima Sheraton, www.sheraton.com.pe; Sofitel Royal Park, www.sofitel.com; Swissôtel Lima, www.lima.swissotel.com; Westin, www.starwoodhotels.com. All are recommended.

There are dozens of hostels offering dormitory accommodation and charging US$10-17 pp, usually including a simple breakfast, hot water in shared bathrooms, kitchen facilities, bar and living room. Double rooms with private bathrooms are also offered, which aren't much more expensive, starting at about US$30. Some hostels are linked to travel agents or adventure tour companies.

Lima *p43, maps p44 and p47*
Near the airport
$$$$ Ramada Costa del Sol, Av Elmer Faucett s/n, T711 2000, www.ramada.com. Within the airport perimeter. Offers day rates as well as overnights if you can't get into the city. Good service, buffet breakfast, but high-priced because of lack of competition and expensive extras.
$$ Hostal Residencial Víctor, Manuel Mattos 325, Urb San Amadeo de Garagay, Lima 31, T01-569 4662, www.hostalvictor.com. 5 mins from the airport by taxi, or phone or email in advance for free pick-up, large comfortable rooms, hot water, 10% discount for Footprint book owners, American breakfast (or packed breakfast for early departure), evening meals can be ordered locally, 2 malls with restaurants, shops, cinemas, etc, nearby, very helpful.

$$-$ Pay Purix, Av Japón (formerly Bertello Bolatti), Mz F, Lote 5, Urb Los Jazmines, 1a Etapa, Callao, T484 9118, www.paypurix. com. 3 mins from airport, can arrange pick-up (taxi US$6, US$2 from outside airport). Hostel with doubles and dorms, convenient, washing machine, English spoken, CDs, DVDs, games and use of kitchen.

Central Lima
$$$ The Clifford Hotel, Parque Hernán Velarde 27, near 1st block of Av Petit Thouars, Sta Beatriz, T433 4249, www. thecliffordhotel.com.pe. Nicely converted, republican town house in a quiet and leafy park. Rooms and suites, has a bar, café and conference room.
$$$ Maury, Jr Ucayali 201, T428 8188, hotmaury@rcp.net.pe. The most luxurious hotel in the historical centre, secure. The bar is reputed to be the home of the first-ever pisco sour (this is, of course, disputed!).
$$ La Posada del Parque, Parque Hernán Velarde 60, near 1st block of Av Petit Thouars, Santa Beatriz, between centre and San Isidro, T433 2412, www.incacountry. com. A charmingly refurbished old house with a collection of fine handicrafts, in a safe area, comfortable rooms, breakfast 0800-0930, airport transfer 24 hrs for US$18 for 1-3 passengers (US$8 pp for larger groups), no credit cards, cash only. Always check the website for special offers and gifts. The owners speak good English. Excellent value. Gay friendly. Has an agreement with the nearby Lawn Tennis Club (Arenales 200 block) for guests to eat at the good-value **Set Point** restaurant and use the gym.
$$-$ Hostal España, Jr Azángaro 105, T427 9196, www.hotelespanaperu.com. A long-standing travellers' haunt, rooms or dormitories, fine old building, motorcycle parking, laundry service, roof garden, good café, can be very busy.
$$-$ Hostal Iquique, Jr Iquique 758, Breña (discount for SAE members), T433 4724, www.hostal-iquique-lima.com. Rooms on top floor at the back are best, from singles

with shared bath to triples with private bath, well-kept if a bit noisy and draughty, use of kitchen, warm water, safe, airport pick up.
$ Hostal Roma, Jr Ica 326, T427 7576, www. hostalroma.8m.com. Over 35 years in the business, rooms sleep 1-4, private or shared bath, hot water, often full, luggage deposit and safe box, motorcycle parking, airport transfers (**Roma Tours** arranges city tours – but shop around if you want to, flight reservations). Next door is **Café Carrara**.
$ Hostal San Francisco, Jr Azángaro 127, T426 2735. Dormitories with and without bathrooms, safe, Italian/Peruvian owners, good service, café.
$ Pensión Ibarra, Av Tacna 359, 1402 y 1502, (elevator to 14th/15th floors doesn't run all hours), no sign, T427 8603/1035, pensionibarra@gmail.com. Breakfast US$4, discount for longer stay, basic, noisy, use of kitchen, balcony with views of the city, helpful owners (2 sisters), hot water, full board available (good small café almost next door). Reserve in advance; taxis can't stop outside so book airport pick-up (US$18.50) for safe arrival.

San Isidro p50, map p44
$$$$ Country Club, Los Eucaliptos 590, T611 9000, www.hotelcountry.com. Excellent, fine service, luxurious rooms, good bar and restaurant, classically stylish with a fine art collection.
$$$$ Libertador Hotels Peru, Los Eucaliptos 550, T518 6300, www.libertador. com.pe. Overlooking the golf course, full facilities for the business traveller, large comfortable rooms in this relatively small hotel, fine service, good restaurant.
$$$$ Sonesta El Olivar, Pancho Fierro 194, T712 6000, www.sonesta.com/Lima. Excellent, one of the top 5-star hotels in Lima overlooking El Olivar park, modern, good restaurant and bar, terrace, gym, swimming pool, quiet, very attentive, popular.
$$$ Garden, Rivera Navarrete 450, T200 9800, www.gardenhotel.com.pe. Good beds, small restaurant, ideal for business visitors, convenient, good value.

$$ Chez Elizabeth, Av del Parque Norte 265, San Isidro, T9980 07557, http://chezelizabeth.typepad.fr. Family house in residential area 7 mins' walk from Cruz del Sur bus station. Shared or private bathrooms, TV room, laundry, airport transfers.

$ Albergue Juvenil Malka, Los Lirios 165 (near 4th block of Av Javier Prado Este), San Isidro, T442 0162, www.youthhostelperu.com. Dormitory style, 4-8 beds per room, also private doubles (**$$**), English spoken, laundry, climbing wall, nice café, airport transfer.

San Miguel and Magdalena del Mar
South of San Isidro, on the seaward side of Pueblo Libre.

$$ Mami Panchita, Av Federico Gallessi 198 (ex-Av San Miguel), San Miguel, T263 7203, www.mamipanchita.com. Dutch/Peruvian-owned, English, Dutch and Spanish spoken, includes breakfast and welcome drink, comfortable rooms with bath, hot water, living room and bar, patio, email service, book exchange, airport transfers, 15 mins from airport, 15 mins from Miraflores, 20 mins from historical centre. Frequently recommended.

$ Tambopacaya, Jr Manco Capac 212 (block 31 of Av Brasil), Magdalena del Mar, T261 6122, www.tambopacaya.com. All rooms and dorms have private bath, hot water, use of kitchen, laundry, guided tours, airport transfers, convenient for airport and centre.

Miraflores *p50, map p52*

$$$$ Casa Andina Private Collection, Av La Paz 463, T213 4300, www.casa-andina.com. Top of the range hotel in this recommended Peruvian chain (see below), modern, well-appointed large rooms with safe, cable TV, Wi-Fi, good bathrooms. Fine food in **Alma** restaurant and good value café, **Sama**, first class service, bar, pool and gym.

$$$$ Belmond Miraflores Park, Av Malecón de la Reserva 1035, T610 4000, www.miraflorespark.com. An Orient Express hotel, excellent service and facilities, beautiful views over the ocean, top class. Rooftop, open-air, heated pool and spa

which looks out over the ocean, open to the public when you buy a spa treatment.

$$$$ Sonesta Posadas del Inca, Alcanfores 329, T241 7688, www.sonesta.com/Miraflores/. Part of renowned chain of hotels, convenient location, cable TV, a/c, restaurant.

$$$ Alemán, Arequipa 4704, T445 6999, www.hotelaleman.com.pe. No sign, comfortable, quiet, garden, excellent breakfast, smiling staff.

$$$ Antigua Miraflores, Av Grau 350 at C Francia, T201 2060, www.antigua miraflores.com. A small, elegant hotel in a quiet but central location, excellent service, tastefully furnished and decorated, gym, good restaurant. Recommended.

$$$ Casa Andina, Av 28 de Julio 1088, T241 4050, www.casa-andina.com. Also at Av Petit Thouars 5444, T447 0263, in Miraflores. These Classic hotels in this chain have similar facilities and decor. Very neat, with many useful touches, comfortable beds, fridge, safe, laundry service, buffet breakfast, other meals available. Check website for discounts and for the more upmarket **Casa Andina Select** at Schell 452, T416 7500 (**$$$$-$$$**), with disabled facilities.

$$$ Casa de Baraybar, Toribio Pacheco 216, T652 2262, www.casadebaraybar.com. 1 block from the ocean, extra long beds, a/c or fan, colourful decor, high ceilings, 24-hr room service, laundry, airport transfers free for stays of 3 nights. Bilingual staff. Recommended.

$$$ La Castellana, Grimaldo del Solar 222, T444 4662, www.castellanahotel.com. Pleasant, good value, nice garden, safe, expensive restaurant, laundry, English spoken.

$$$ José Antonio, 28 de Julio 398 y C Colón, T445 7743, www.hotelesjoseantonio.com. Good in all respects, including the restaurant, large modern rooms, jacuzzis, swimming pool, business facilities, helpful staff speak some English.

$$$ San Antonio Abad, Ramón Ribeyro 301, T447 6766, www.hotelsanantonioabad.com. Secure, quiet, helpful, tasty breakfasts, 1 free airport transfer with reservation, justifiably popular, good value.

$$$ Señorial, José González 567, T445 0139, www.senorial.com. 100 rooms, with restaurant, room service, comfortable, nice garden, parking, good services.

$$$-$$ Hostal El Patio, Diez Canseco 341, T444 2107, www.hostalelpatio.net. Very nice suites and rooms, comfortable, English and French spoken, convenient, *comedor*, gay friendly. Very popular, reservations are essential.

$$$-$$ Inka Frog, Gral Iglesias 271, T445 8979, www.inkafrog.com. Self-styled "Exclusive B&B", comfortable, nice decor, lounge with huge TV, rooftop terrace, good value.

$$ Casa Rodas, Av Petit Thouars 4712, T447 5761, and Tarapacá 250, T242 4872, www.casarodas.com. Both houses have rooms for 2, 3 or 4, good beds (**$$$** with private bath), hot water, helpful staff.

$$ El Carmelo, Bolognesi 749, T446 0575, www.hostalelcarmelo.com.pe. Great location a couple of blocks from the Parque del Amor, small restaurant downstairs serving *criolla* food and *ceviche*, good value, comfortable, breakfast extra.

$$ La Casa Nostra, Av Grimaldo del Solar 265, T241 1718. Variety of rooms (from singles to quad), all with private bath, good service, convenient, safe, money exchange, laundry, tourist information. Popular.

$$ Sipán, Paseo de la República 6171, T241 3758, www.hotelsipan.com. Very pleasant, on the edge of a residential area next to the Vía Expresa (which can be heard from front rooms). Economical meals available in restaurant, 24-hr room service, security box, secure parking. Airport transfers available.

$$-$ Albergue Turístico Juvenil Internacional, Av Casimiro Ulloa 328, San Antonio, T446 5488, www.limahostell.com.pe. Dormitory accommodation or a double private room, basic cafeteria, travel information, laundry facilities, swimming pool often empty, extra charge for breakfast, safe, situated in a nice villa; 20 mins' walk from the beach. Bus No 2 or colectivos pass Av Benavides to the centre.

$$-$ Condor's House, Martín Napanga 137, T446 7267, www.condorshouse.com. Award-winning, quiet hostel, 2 categories of dorm rooms with lockers, good bathrooms, also doubles, good meeting place, TV room with films, book exchange, *parrillada* prepared once a week, bar. Helpful staff.

$$-$ Explorer's House, Av Alfredo León 158, by 10th block of Av José Pardo, T241 5002, http://explorershouselima.com. No sign, but plenty of indications of the house number, dorm with shared bath, or double rooms with bath, hot water, laundry service, Spanish classes, English spoken, very welcoming.

$$-$ Flying Dog, Diez Canseco 117, T212 7145, www.flyingdogperu.com. Also at Lima 457 and Olaya 280, all with dorms, doubles, triples, quads. All on or near Parque Kennedy, with kitchen, lockers, but all with different features. They have others in Cuzco, Iquitos and Arequipa.

$$-$ HosteLima, Cnel Inclán 399, T242 7034, www.hostelima.com. Private double rooms and brightly painted dorms, close to Parque Kennedy, helpful staff, safe, bar/restaurant and snack shop, movie room, Play Station 3, travel information.

$$-$ The Lighthouse, Cesareo Chacaltana 162, T446 8397, www.thelighthouseperu.com. Near Plaza Morales Barros, British/Peruvian run, relaxed, small dorm or private rooms with private or shared bath. Good services, small indoor patio.

$$-$ Loki Backpackers, José Galvez 576, T651 2966, www.lokihostel.com. In a quiet area, the capital's sister to the party hostel of the same name in Cuzco, doubles or dorms, good showers, cooked breakfast extra, Fri barbecues, lockers, airport transfers.

$$-$ Pariwana, Av Larco 189, T242 4350, www.pariwana-hostel.com. Party hostel with doubles and dorms in the heart of Miraflores, individual lockers with power outlets so you can leave your gadgets charging in a safe place. Always lots going on here.

$$-$ Pirwa, González Prada 179, T444 1266 and Coronel Inclán 494 (B&B), T242 4059, www.pirwahostelsperu.com. Members of a chain of hostels in Peru (Cuzco, Arequipa, Puno, Nazca); González Prada is a bit cheaper

but both have choice of dorms and double rooms, lockers, transfers arranged, bike rental.
$ Albergue Verde, Grimaldo del Solar 459, T445 3816, www.alberguverde.com. Nice small hostal, comfortable beds, friendly owner, Arturo Palmer, airport and bus terminal pick-up.
$ Blue House, José González 475, T445 0476, www.bluehouse.com.pe. A true backpacker hostel, most rooms with bath including a double, basic but good value for the location, *terraza* with *parrilla*, films to watch.
$ Casa del Mochilero, Cesareo Chacaltana 130A, T444 9089, pilaryv@hotmail.com (casa-del-mochilero on Facebook). Ask for Pilar or Juan, dorms or double room on terrace, all with shared bath, breakfast and internet extra, hot water, lots of information.
$ Friend's House, José González 427, T446 3521, FriendsHouseLimaPeru on Facebook. Very popular, reserve in advance. Near Larcomar shopping centre, plenty of good information and help, family atmosphere. Highly recommended. They have another branch at Jr Manco Cápac 368, T446 6248, with dormitory accommodation with shared bath and hot water. Neither branch is signed, except on the bell at No 427.
$ Hitchhikers B&B Backpackers, Bolognesi 400, T242 3008, www.hhikersperu.com. Located close to the ocean, mixture of dorms (1 girl-only) and private rooms with shared or private bath (**$$**), nice patio, plenty of parking, airport transfers.

Barranco *p51*
$$$$ B, San Martín 301, T700 5106, www. hotelb.pe. Boutique hotel in an early 20th-century mansion. Beautifully redesigned as a luxury hotel in theoriginal building and a contemporary wing, eclectic design features and a large collection of mostly modern art, next to Lucía de la Puente gallery and convenient for others, blog and Facebook give cultural recommendations, highly regarded Mediterranean/Peruvian restaurant, cocktail bar, plunge pool, excellent service. In Relais y Châteaux group.

$$-$ Barranco's Backpackers Inn, Mcal Castilla 260, T247 1326, www.barranco backpackersperu.com. Ocean view, colourful rooms, all en suite, shared and private rooms, tourist information.
$$-$ Domeyer, C Domeyer 296, T247 1413, www.domeyerhostel.net. Private or shared rooms sleeping 1-3 people in a historic house. Hot water 24 hrs, laundry service, secure, gay friendly.
$$-$ Safe in Lima, Alfredo Silva 150, T252 7330, www.safeinlima.com. Quiet, Belgian-run hostal with family atmosphere, single, double and triple rooms, very helpful, airport pick-up US$28, good value, reserve in advance, lots of information for travellers.
$ The Point, Malecón Junín 300, T247 7997, www.thepointhostels.com. Rooms range from doubles to large dormitories, all with shared bath, very popular with backpackers (book in advance at weekends), laundry, gay friendly, restaurant, bar, party atmosphere most of the time, but also space for relaxing, weekly barbecues, travel centre.

🍴 Restaurants

18% state tax and 10% service will be added to your bill in middle- and upper-class restaurants. Chinese is often the cheapest at around US$5 including a drink.

Lima *p43, map p47*
Central Lima
$$$ Wa Lok, Jr Paruro 864 and 878, Barrio Chino, T427 2656. Good dim sum, cakes and fortune cookies (when you pay the bill). English spoken, very friendly. Also at Av Angamos Oeste 700, Miraflores, T447 1329.
$$ Chifa San Joy Lao, Ucayali 779. A *chifa* with a good reputation, one of several on the pedestrianized part of the Barrio Chino.
$$ L'Eau Vive, Ucayali 370, also opposite the Torre Tagle Palace, T427 5612. Mon-Sat, 1230-1500 and 1930-2130. Run by nuns, fixed-price lunch menu, Peruvian-style in interior dining room, or à la carte in either of dining rooms that open onto patio,

excellent, profits go to the poor, Ave María is sung nightly at 2100.

$$ Salon Capon, Jr Paruro 819. Good dim sum, at this recommended *chifa*. Also has a branch at Larcomar shopping centre, which is **$$**, elegant and equally recommended.

$$-$ Bar Cordano, Ancash 202 y Carabaya (in Calles El Rastro y Pescadería zone). Historic tavern serving Peruvian food and drinks, great atmosphere, favoured by politicians.

$$-$ De César, Ancash 300, T428 8740. Open 0700-2300. Old-fashioned atmosphere, apart from the 3 TVs, breakfasts, snacks, seafood, meat dishes, pastas, pizza, juices, coffees and teas. Good food.

$$-$ Rovegno, Arenales 456 (near block 3 of Arequipa), T424 8465. Italian and Peruvian dishes, home-made pasta, also serves snacks and sandwiches and has a bakery. Good value.

Acllahuasy, Jr Ancash 400. Around the corner from **Hostal España**. Daily 0700-2300. Good Peruvian dishes.

La Catedral del Pisco, Jr de la Unión 1100 esq Av Uruguay 114, T330 0079, lacatedraldelpisco@hotmail.com. Open 0800-2200. *Comida criolla*, drinks, free Peruvian coffee (excellent) or pisco sour for Footprint owners, live music at night, Wi-Fi.

Breña

$$ La Choza Náutica, Jr Breña 204 and 211 behind Plaza Bolognesi, T423 8087, www.chozanautica.com. Good *ceviche* and friendly service; has 3 other branches.

$ Azato, Av Arica 298, 3 blocks from Plaza Bolognesi, T423 0278. Excellent and cheap Peruvian dishes.

Pueblo Libre *p50*

$$$-$$ Café del Museo, at the Museo Larco, Av Bolívar 1515, T462 4757. Daily 0900-2200, seating inside and on the terrace. Specially designed interior, selection of salads, fine Peruvian dishes, pastas and seafood, a tapas bar of traditional Peruvian foods, as well as snacks, desserts and cocktails. Highly regarded.

$$-$ Antigua Taberna Quierolo, Av San Martín 1090, 1 block from Plaza Bolívar, T460 0441, http://antiguatabernaqueirolo. com. Atmospheric old bar with glass-fronted shelves of bottles, marble bar and old photos, owns bodega next door. Serves simple lunches, sandwiches and snacks, good for wine, does not serve dinner.

San Isidro *p50*

$$$ Antica Pizzería, Av Dos de Mayo 732, T222 8437. Very popular, great ambience, excellent food, Italian owner. Also in Barranco at Alfonso Ugarte 242, www.anticapizzeria.com.pe.

$$$ Chifa Titi, Av Javier Prado Este 1212, Córpac, T224 8189, www.chifatiti.com. Regarded by many as the best Chinese restaurant in Lima with over 60 years in operation.

$$$-$$ Segundo Muelle, Av Conquistadores 490, T717 9998, www.segundomuelle.com. *Ceviches* and other very good seafood dishes, including Japanese, popular.

$$ Chez Philippe, Av 2 de Mayo 748, T222 4953, www.chez-philippe.net. Pizza, pasta and crêpes, wood oven, rustic decor (same owners as **Pizza B&B** in Huaraz) and a huge choice of beers.

$$ Como Agua para Chocolate, Pancho Fierro 108, T222 0297. Dutch/Mexican-owned restaurant, specializing in Mexican food as the name suggests, also has a very amusing Dutch night once a month. SAE members get a discount.

Havanna, Miguel Dasso 165, www. havanna.pe. Branch of the Argentine coffee and *alfajores* chain, others in the city include **Larcomar**.

News Café, Av Santa Luisa 110. Mon-Fri 1000-2300, Sat 1200-2300, Sun 1200-1700. Great salads and desserts, popular and expensive. With another branch at Av Larco 657, Miraflores.

Lima's new gastronomy

Lima attracts terms such "gastronomic capital of South America", which is reflected in the fact that the Mistura festival in September 2013 attracted 500,000 visitors. There are several restaurants that are championed as the height of culinary excellence. They are often priced beyond the average traveller's budget, but a meal at one of these could be the ideal way to celebrate a special occasion. Most serve à la carte and a tasting menu. At the heart of much of today's Peruvian gastronomy are traditional ingredients, from the coast, the Andes and the jungle. The star chefs all recognize the debt they owe to the cooks of the different regions. Their skill is in combining the local heritage with the flavours and techniques that they have learnt elsewhere, without overwhelming what is truly Peruvian.

Gastón Acurio is usually credited with being the forerunner of the evolution of Peruvian cuisine. He is also recognized for his community work. With **Astrid y Gastón Casa Moreyra** (Av Paz Soldán 290, San Isidro, www.astridygaston.com),

Acurio and his wife Astrid have moved their flagship restaurant from Miraflores to this historic house in San Isidro. It has been completely remodelled and opened in 2014. Other ventures include *ceviche* at **La Mar** (Av Lar 770, Miraflores, T421 3365, www.lamarcebicheria.com), *anticuchos* at **Panchita** (Av 2 de Mayo 298, Miraflores, T242 5957, see Facebook page) and his chain of **T'anta** cafés, eg behind the Municipalidad in the city centre, at Pancho Fierro 115 in San Isidro and in Larcomar.

Central (Santa Isabel 376, Miraflores, T446 9301, www.centralrestaurante.com. pe) presents Virgilio Martínez' award-winning, sophisticated recipes fusing Peruvian ingredients and molecular cuisine.

Manifiesto (Independencia 130, Miraflores, T249 5533, www.manifiesto. pe) is billed as "Tacna meets Italy", bringing together the birthplace and family roots of chef Giacomo Bocchio.

Rafael Osterling has two restaurants in the city: **Rafael** (San Martín 300, Miraflores, T242 4149, www.rafael osterling.com), celebrated for its classic Peruvian dishes incorporating flavours

---

Miraflores *p50, map p52*

Calle San Ramón, known as 'Pizza Street' (across from Parque Kennedy), is a pedestrian walkway lined with outdoor restaurants/bars/discos open until the wee small hours. It's very popular, with good-natured touts trying to entice diners and drinkers with free offers.

$$$ El Kapallaq, Av Petit Thouars 4844, T444 4149. Mon-Fri 1200-1700 only. Prize-winning Peruvian restaurant specializing in seafood and fish, excellent *ceviches*.

$$$ El Rincón Gaucho, Av Armendáriz 580, T447 4778. Good grill, renowned for its steaks.

$$$ Huaca Pucllana, Gral Borgoño cuadra 8 s/n, alt cuadra 45 Av Arequipa, T445 4042, www.resthuacapucllana.com. Facing

the archaeological site of the same name, contemporary Peruvian fusion cooking, very good food in an unusual setting, popular with groups.

$$$ La Gloria, Atahualpa 201, T445 5705, www.lagloriarestaurant.com. Mon-Sat from 1300 and again from 2000. Popular upmarket restaurant serving Peruvian food, classic and contemporary styles.

$$$ La Preferida, Arias Araguez 698, T445 5180, http://restaurantelapreferida.com. Daily 0800-1700. Seafood restaurant and tapas bar, with delicious *ceviches*, also has a branch in Monterrico.

$$$ La Trattoria, Manuel Bonilla 106, T446 7002, www.latrattoriadimambrino. com, 1 block from Parque Kennedy. Italian from around the globe, especially the Mediterranean, and **El Mercado** (H Unanue 203, Miraflores, T221 1322), which concentrates on seafood, reflecting all the influences on Peruvian cooking.

At **IK** (Elias Aguirre 179, Miraflores, T652 1692, reservas@ivankisic.pe, see Facebook page), molecular gastronomy meets Peruvian ingredients at the late Ivan Kisic's restaurant.

Lima 27 (Santa Lucía 295 – no sign, T221 5822, www.lima27.com) is a modern restaurant behind whose black exterior you will find contemporary Peruvian cuisine. It's in the same group as **Alfresco** (Malecón Balta 790, T242 8960, www.restaurante alfresco.com), **Cala on Costa Verde** (http:// calarestaurante.com), and a new sandwich bar, **Manduca**, in Jockey Plaza.

Pedro Miguel Schiaffino's **Malabar** (Camino Real 101, San Isidro, T440 5200, http://malabar.com.pe) takes the Amazon and its produce as the starting point for its dishes, as does Schiaffino's **Amaz** (Av La Paz 1079, Miraflores, T221 9393). This eatery is in a group of four places under the Hilton Hotel. Also here is **Ache** (Av La Paz 1055, T221 9315, achecocinanikkei on Facebook) which specializes in Japanese fusion cuisine.

La Picantería (Moreno 388 y González Prada, Surquillo, T241 6676, www. picanteriasdelperu.com) serves excellent seafood, first-class *ceviche*, has a fish-of-the-day lunch menu and a good bar.

At **AlmaZen** (Federico Recavarrén 298 y Galvez, T243 0474) you will find one of the best organic slow-food restaurants in Latin America.

Beyond Lima there are many innovative restaurants in Cuzco and Arequipa and don't forget that the regional cooking that provided inspiration for Peru's growing international fame is still very much alive and well, often in much more modest surroundings than the fine dining settings of the capital. One such place that has moved to the capital is **Fiesta Gourmet** (Av Reducto 1278, T242 9009, www.restaurantfiestagourmet.com), which specializes in food from Chiclayo and the north coast: superb food in fancy surroundings.

cuisine, popular, good desserts. Has another branch, **La Bodega**, opposite entrance to Huaca Pucllana.

\$\$\$ Las Brujas de Cachiche, Av Bolognesi 472, T447 1883, www.brujasdecachiche. com.pe. Mon-Sat 1200-2400, Sun 1230-1630. An old mansion converted into bars and dining rooms, fine traditional food (menu in Spanish and English), live *criollo* music.

\$\$\$ Rosa Náutica, T445 0149, www. larosanautica.com. Daily 1230-0200. Built on old British-style pier (Espigón No 4), in Lima Bay. Delightful opulence, fine fish cuisine, experience the atmosphere by buying a beer in the bar at sunset.

\$\$\$ Saqra, Av La Paz 646, T650 8884, www.saqra.pe. Mon-Thu 1200-2400, Fri-Sat 1200-0100. Colourful and casual, indoor or outdoor seating, interesting use of ingredients from all over Peru, classic flavours with a fun, innovative twist, inspired by street food and humble dishes, vegetarian options, many organic products. Also good cocktail bar. Go with a group to sample as many dishes as possible.

\$\$\$ Sí Señor, Jr Bolognesi 706, T445 3789. Mexican food, cheerful, interesting decor, huge portions.

\$\$\$-\$\$ Chifa Internacional, Av República de Panamá 5915, T445 3997, www. chifainternacional.com. Open 1230-1530 (1600 on Sat), then from 1900, Sun 1200-2315. Great *chifa* in San Antonio district of Miraflores.

$$$-$$ Las Tejas, Diez Canseco 340, T444 4360. Daily 1100-2300. Good, typical Peruvian food, especially *ceviche*.

$$$-$$ Punto Azul, San Martín 595, Benavides 2711, with other branches in San Isidro, Surco and San Borja, http://puntoazul restaurante.com. Tue-Sun 1100-1600 (San Martín 595 also open Mon-Sat 1900-2400). Popular, well-regarded chain of seafood and *ceviche* restaurants.

$$ Café Tarata, Pasaje Tarata 260, T446 6330. Good atmosphere, family-run, good varied menu.

$$ El Huarike, Enrique Palacios 140, T241 6086. Fashionable, interesting combinations of *ceviche* and sushi, also cooked seafood dishes.

$$ El Parquetito, Lima 373 y Diez Canseco, T444 0490. Peruvian food from all regions, good menu, serves breakfast, eat inside or out.

$$ Lobo del Mar – Octavio Otani, Colón 587, T242 1871. Basic exterior hides one of the oldest *cevicherías* in Miraflores, excellent, a good selection of other seafood dishes.

$$ Mama Olla, Pasaje Tarata 248. Charming café on a pedestrian walkway, huge menu, big portions.

$ Govinda, Schell 630. Vegetarian, from Hare Krishna foundation, lunch *menú* US$3.

$ Madre Natura, Chiclayo 815, T445 2522, www.madrenaturaperu.com. Mon-Sat 0800-2100. Natural foods shop and eating place, very good.

Café Café, Martin Olaya 250, at the corner of Av Diagonal. Very popular, good atmosphere, over 100 different blends of coffee, good salads and sandwiches, very popular with 'well-to-do' Limeños. Also in Larcomar.

Café de la Paz, Lima 351, middle of Parque Kennedy. Good outdoor café right on the park, expensive, great cocktails, with another branch on Pasaje Tarata.

Café La Máquina, Alcanfores 323. Friendly small café and bar with good cocktails, interesting sandwiches and great cakes.

C'est si bon, Av Cdte Espinar 663. Excellent cakes by the slice or whole, best in Lima.

Chef's Café, Av Larco 375 and 763. Nice places for a sandwich or coffee.

Haiti, Av Diagonal 160, Parque Kennedy. Open almost round the clock daily. Great for people watching, good ice cream.

La Lucha, Av Benavides y Olaya (under Flying Dog), on Parque Kennedy, with a small branch nearby between Olaya and Benavides and another on Ovalo Gutiérrez. Excellent hot sandwiches, limited range, choice of sauces, great juices, *chicha morada* and *café pasado*. Good for a wholesome snack.

La Tiendecita Blanca, Av Larco 111 on Parque Kennedy. One of Miraflores' oldest, expensive, good people-watching, very good cakes, European-style food and delicatessen.

Pan de la Chola, Av La Mar 918, El-Pan-de-la-Chola on Facebook. Café and bakery specializing in sourdough bread, teas, juices and sweets.

San Antonio, Av 28 de Julio y Reducto (many other eating places at this junction), Av Angamos Oeste 1494, Rocca de Vergallo 201, Magdalena del Mar and Av Primavera 373, San Borja. Fashionable *pastelería* chain with hot and cold lunch dishes, good salads, inexpensive, busy.

Barranco *p51*

$$$ Canta Rana, Génova 101, T247 7274. Sun-Mon 1200-1800, Tue-Sat 1200-2300. Good *ceviche*, expensive, small portions, but the most popular local place on Sun.

$$$ La 73, Av Sol Oeste 176, casi San Martín, at the edge of Barranco. Mostly meat dishes, has a lunch menu, look for the Chinese lanterns outside, good reputation.

$$$ La Costa Verde, on Barranquito beach, T247 1244, www.restaurantecostaverde. com. Daily 1200-2400, Sun buffet. Excellent fish and wine, expensive but considered one of the best.

$$$ La Pescadería, Grau 689, T477 0966, www.lapescaderia.pe. A recommended *cevichería*.

$$$-$$ Tío Mario, Jr Zepita 214, on the steps to the Puente de Suspiros. Excellent *anticuchería*, serving delicious Peruvian kebabs, always busy, fantastic service, varied menu and good prices.

$$ Las Mesitas, Av Grau 341, T477 4199. Open 1200-0200. Traditional tea rooms-cum-restaurant, serving Creole food and traditional desserts which you won't find anywhere else, lunch *menú* served till 1400, US$3.

$$-$ Sóngoro Cosongo, Ayacucho 281, T247 4730, at the top of the steps down to Puente de Suspiros, www.songoro cosongo.com. Good-value *comida criolla*, "un poco de todo".

La Boteca, Grau 310-312. Smart-looking café-bar.

Expreso Virgen de Guadalupe, San Martín y Ayacucho. Café and vegetarian buffet in an old tram, also seating in the garden, more expensive at weekends.

Tostería Bisetti, Pedro de Osma 116, www.cafebisetti.com. Coffee, cakes and a small selection of lunchtime dishes, service a bit slow but a nice place.

⊕ Bars and clubs

Lima *p43, map p47*
Central Lima
The centre of town, specifically Jr de la Unión, has many discos. It's best to avoid the nightspots around the intersection of Av Tacna, Av Piérola and Av de la Vega. These places are rough and foreigners will receive much unwanted attention.

For latest recommendations for gay and lesbian places, check out www.gayperu.com.
El Rincón Cervecero, Jr de la Unión (Belén) 1045, www.rinconcervecero.com.pe. German-style pub, fun.

Estadio Futbol Sports Bar, Av Nicolás de Piérola 926 on the Plaza San Martín, T428 8866. Mon-Wed 1215-2300, Thu 1215-2400, Fri-Sat 1215-0300, Sun 1215-1800. Beautiful bar with a disco, international football theme, good international and Creole food.

Piano Bar Munich, Jr de la Unión 1044 (basement). Small and fun.

Miraflores *p50, map p52*
La Tasca, Av Diez Canseco 117, very near Parque Kennedy, part of the **Flying Dog** group and under one of the hostels (see Where to stay, above). Spanish-style bar with cheap beer (for Miraflores). An eclectic crowd including ex-pats, travellers and locals. Gay-friendly. Small and crowded.

Media Naranja, Schell 130, at bottom of Parque Kennedy. Brazilian bar with drinks and food.

Murphy's, Schell 619, T01-447 1082. Mon-Sat from 1600. Happy hours every day with different offers, lots of entertainment, very popular.

The Old Pub, San Ramón 295 (Pizza St), www. oldpub.com.pe. Cosy, with live music most days.

Treff Pub Alemán, Av Benavides 571-104, T444 0148, www.treff-pub-aleman.com (hidden from the main road behind a cluster of tiny houses signed "Los Duendes"). A wide range of German beers, plus cocktails, good atmosphere, darts and other games.

Barranco *p51*
Barranco is the capital of Lima nightlife. The following is a short list of some of the better bars and clubs. Pasaje Sánchez Carrión, right off the main plaza, used to be the heart of it all. Watering holes and discos line both sides of this pedestrian walkway. Av Grau, just across the street from the plaza, is also lined with bars, eg **The Lion's Head Pub**, Av Grau 268 p 2, **Déjà Vu**, No 294. Many of the bars in this area turn into discos later on.

Ayahuasca, San Martín 130. In the stunning Berninzon House from the Republican era, chilled out lounge bar with several areas for eating, drinking and dancing. Food is expensive and portions are small, but go for the atmosphere.

Barranco Beer Company, Grau 308, T247 6211, www.barrancobeer.com. Closed Mon, open from 1900 on Tue, 1200 on Wed-Sun, closes 1700 on Sun. New artisanal brewhouse.

El Dragón, N de Piérola 168, T715 5043, www.eldragon.com.pe. Popular bar and venue for music, theatre and painting.

Juanitos, Av Grau, opposite the park. Open from 1600-0400. Barranco's oldest bar, where writers and artists congregate, a perfect spot to start the evening.

La Noche, Bolognesi 307, at Pasaje Sánchez Carrión, www.lanoche.com.pe. A Lima institution and high standard, live music, Mon is jazz night, all kicks off at around 2200.

La Posada del Angel, 3 branches, Pedro de Osma 164 and 214, T247 0341, see Facebook. These are popular bars serving snacks and meals.

La Posada del Mirador, Ermita 104, near the Puente de los Suspiros (Bridge of Sighs), see Facebook. Beautiful view of the ocean, but you pay for the privilege.

Santos Café & Espirituosos, Jr Zepita 203, just above the Puente de Suspiros, T247 4609, also on Facebook. Mon-Sat 1700-0100. Favourite spot for trendy young professionals who want to drop a few hundred soles, relaxed, informal but pricey.

Sargento Pimienta, Bolognesi 757, www.sargentopimienta.com.pe. Tue-Sat from 2200. Live music, always a favourite with Limeños.

Victoria, Av Pedro de Osma 135. New upmarket pub in the beautiful Casa Cillóniz, a selection of beers, cocktails, snacks and live music.

⊕ Entertainment

Lima *p43, maps p44, p47 and p52*
Cinemas
The newspaper *El Comercio* lists cinema information in the section called *Luces*. Mon-Wed reduced price at most cinemas. Most films are in English with subtitles and cost from US$7-8.75 in Miraflores and malls, US$3-4 in the centre. The best cinema chains in the city are **Cinemark**, **Cineplanet** and **UVK Multicines**. **Filmoteca de Lima**, at **Centro Cultural PUCP** (cultural centre of the Universidad Católica), Camino Real 1075, San Isidro, T616 1616, http://cultural.pucp.edu.pe. **Cinematógrafo de Barranco**, Pérez Roca 196, Barranco, T264 4374. Small independent cinema

showing a good choice of classic and new international films.

Peñas
De Rompe y Raja, Manuel Segura 127, T636 1518, www.derompeyraja.pe. Thu, Fri, Sat. Popular for music, dancing and *criolla* food.

Del Carajo, Catalino Miranda 158, Barranco, T247 7977, www.delcarajo.com.pe. All types of traditional music.

La Candelaria, Av Bolognesi 292, Barranco, T247 1314, www.lacandelariaperu.com. Fri-Sat 2130 onwards. A good Barranco *peña*.

La Estación de Barranco, Pedro de Osma 112, T477 5030, www.laestaciondebarranco.com. Good, family atmosphere, varied shows.

Las Brisas de Titicaca, Héroes de Tarapacá 168, at 1st block of Av Brasil near Plaza Bolognesi, T715 6960, www.brisasdeltiticaca.com. A Lima institution.

Sachun, Av del Ejército 657, Miraflores, T441 0123, www.sachunperu.com. Great shows on weekdays as well.

Theatre
El Gran Teatro Nacional, at the corner of Avs Javier Prado and Aviación, San Borja. Capable of seating 1500 people, it holds concerts, opera, ballet and other dance as well as other events. Most professional plays are staged at **Teatro Segura**, Jr Huancavelica 265, T427 9491. **Teatro Municipal**, Jr Ica 377, T315 1300 ext 1767, see Facebook. Completely restored after a fire, with full programmes and with a theatre museum on Huancavelica. There are many other theatres in the city, some of which are related to cultural centres, eg **CCPUCP** (see Cinemas, above). **Instituto Cultural Peruano-Norteamericano**, Jr Cusco 446, Lima Centre, T706 7000, central office at Av Angamos Oeste 160, Miraflores, www.icpna.edu.pe. **Centro Cultural Peruano Japonés**, Av Gregorio Escobedo 803, Jesús María, T518 7450, www.apj.org.pe. All have various cultural activities. The press gives details of performances. Theatre and concert tickets booked through Teleticket, T01-613 8888, Mon-Fri 0900-1900,

www.teleticket.com.pe. For cultural events, see **Lima Cultural**, www.limacultura.pe, the city's monthly arts programme.

⊛ Festivals

Lima *p43, maps p44, p47 and p52*

18 Jan Founding of Lima. Semana Santa, or Holy Week, is a colourful spectacle with processions. **28-29 Jul** Independence, with music and fireworks in the Plaza de Armas on the evening before. **30 Aug** Santa Rosa de Lima. **Mid-Sep** Mistura, www.mistura.pe, a huge gastronomy fair in Parque Exposición, with Peruvian foods, celebrity chefs, workshops and more.
Oct The month of Our Lord of the Miracles; see Las Nazarenas church, page 46.

○ Shopping

Lima *p43, maps p44, p47 and p52*
Bookshops
Crisol, Ovalo Gutiérrez, Av Santa Cruz 816, San Isidro, T221 1010, below **Cine Planet**. Large bookshop with café, titles in English, French and Spanish. Also in Jockey Plaza Shopping Center, Av Javier Prado Este 4200, Surco, T436 0004, and other branches, www.crisol.com.pe.
Epoca, Av Cdte Espinar 864, Miraflores, T241 2951. Great selection of books, mostly in Spanish.
Ibero Librerías, Av Diagonal 500, T242 2798, Larco 199, T445 5520, in Larcomar, Miraflores, and other branches, www.iberolibros.com. Stocks Footprint Handbooks as well as a wide range of other titles.

Camping equipment
It's better to bring all camping and hiking gear from home. Camping gas (the most popular brand is **Doite**, which comes in small blue bottles) is available from any large hardware store or bigger supermarket.
Alpamayo, Av Larco 345, Miraflores at Parque Kennedy, T445 1671. Mon-Fri 1000-1330, 1430-2000, Sat 1000-1400. Sleeping mats, boots, rock shoes, climbing gear, water filters, tents, backpacks, etc, very expensive but top-quality equipment. Owner speaks fluent English and offers good information.
Altamira, Arica 880, Parque Damert, behind Wong on Ovalo Gutiérrez, Miraflores, T445 1286. Sleeping bags, climbing gear, hiking gear and tents.
Camping Center, Av Benavides 1620, Miraflores, T445 5981, www.campingperu.com. Mon-Fri 1000-2000, Sat 1000-1400. Selection of tents, backpacks, stoves, camping and climbing gear.
El Mundo de las Maletas, Preciados 308, Higuereta-Surco, T449 7850. Daily 0900-2200. For suitcase repairs.
Tatoo, CC Larcomar, locs 123-125B, T242 1938, www.tatoo.ws. For top-quality imported ranges and own brands of equipment.
Todo Camping, Av Angamos Oeste 350, Miraflores, near Av Arequipa, T2421318. Sells 100% deet, blue gas canisters, lots of accessories, tents, crampons and backpacks.

Handicrafts
Miraflores is a good place for high quality, expensive handicrafts; there are many shops on and around the top end of Av La Paz (starting at Av Ricardo Palma).
Agua y Tierra, Diez Canseco 298 y Alcanfores, Miraflores, T444 6980. Fine crafts and indigenous art.
Arte XXI, Av La Paz 678, Miraflores, T01-447 9777, www.artemania-21.com. Gallery and store for contemporary and colonial Peruvian paintings.
Artesanía Santo Domingo, Plazuela Santo Domingo, by the church of that name, in Lima centre, T428 9860. Good Peruvian crafts.
Centro Comercial El Alamo, corner of La Paz y Diez Canseco, Miraflores. *Artesanía* shops with good choice.
Dédalo, Paseo Sáenz Peña 295, Barranco, T477 0562. A labyrinthine shop selling furniture, jewellery and other items, as good as a gallery. It also has a nice coffee shop and has cinema shows. Has other branches on Parque Kennedy and at Larcomar.

Kuntur Wasi, Ocharán 182, Miraflores, opposite **Sol de Oro** hotel, look for the sign above the wall, T01-447 7173, kunturh@ speedy.com.pe. English-speaking owners are very knowledgeable about Peruvian textiles; often have exhibitions of fine folk art and crafts.

La Casa de la Mujer Artesana, Juan Pablo Ferandini 1550 (Av Brasil cuadra 15), Pueblo Libre, T423 8840, www.casadelamujer artesana.com. Mon-Fri 0900-1300, 1400-1700. A cooperative run by the Movimiento Manuela Ramos, excellent quality work mostly from *pueblos jóvenes*.

Las Pallas, Cajamarca 212, Barranco, T477 4629. Mon-Sat 0900-1900. Very high quality handicrafts, English, French and German spoken.

Luz Hecho a Mano, Berlín 399, Miraflores, T446 7098, www.luzhechoamano.com. Lovely handmade handbags, wallets and other leather goods including clothing which last for years and can be custom made.

Museo de la Nación, address above, often hosts specialist handicrafts markets presenting ore individual work from across Peru during national festivals.

There are bargains in high-quality Pima cotton. Shops selling **alpaca** items include: **Alpaca 859**, Av Larco 859, Miraflores. Good quality alpaca and baby alpaca products. **Kuna by Alpaca 111**, Av Larco 671, Miraflores, T447 1623, www.kuna.com.pe. High quality alpaca, baby alpaca and vicuña items. Also in Larcomar, loc 1-07, Museo Larco, the airport, Jockey Plaza, at hotels and in San Isidro.

Jewellery
On Cs La Esperanza and La Paz, Miraflores, dozens of shops offer gold and silverware at reasonable prices.
Ilaria, Av 2 de Mayo 308, San Isidro, T512 3530, www.ilariainternational.com. Jewellery and silverware with interesting designs. There are other branches in Lima, Cuzco, Arequipa and Trujillo.

Maps
Instituto Geográfico Nacional, Av Aramburú 1190, Surquillo, T475 9960, www.ign.gob. pe. Mon-Fri 0830-1645. It has topographical maps of the whole country, mostly at 1:100,000, political and physical maps of all departments and satellite and aerial photographs. You may be asked to show your passport when buying these maps.
Lima 2000, Av Arequipa 2625 (near the intersection with Av Javier Prado), T440 3486, www.lima2000.com.pe. Mon-Fri 0900-1300, 1400-1800. Has excellent street maps of Lima, from tourist maps, US$5.55, to comprehensive books US$18. Also has country maps (US$5.55-9.25), maps of Cuzco, Arequipa, Trujillo and Chiclayo and tourist maps of the Inca Trail, Colca, and Cordillera Blanca. **South American Explorers** (see page 42) also stocks these and IGN maps.

Markets
All are open 7 days a week until late(ish).
Av Petit Thouars, in Miraflores. At blocks 51-54 (near Parque Kennedy, parallel to Av Arequipa). An unnamed crafts market area, usually called **Mercado Inca**, with a large courtyard and lots of small flags. This is the largest crafts arcade in Miraflores. From here to C Ricardo Palma the street is lined with crafts markets.
Feria Nacional de Artesanía de los Deseos y Misterios, Av 28 de Julio 747, near junction with Av Arequipa and Museo Metropolitano. Small market specializing in charms, remedies, fortune-telling and trinkets from Peru and Bolivia.
Mercado 1, Surquillo, cross Paseo de le República from Ricardo Palma, Miraflores and go north 1 block. Food market with a huge variety of local produce. C Narciso de la Colina outside has various places to eat, including Heladería La Fiorentina, No 580, for excellent ice creams.
Parque Kennedy, the main park of Miraflores, hosts a daily crafts market from 1700-2300.
Polvos Azules, on García Naranjo, La Victoria, just off Av Grau in the centre of

town. The 'official' black market, sells just about anything; it is generally cheap and very interesting; beware pickpockets.

What to do

Lima p43, maps p44, p47 and p52

Cycling
Bike Tours of Lima, Bolívar 150, Miraflores, T445 3172, www.biketoursoflima.com. Offer a variety of day tours through the city of Lima by bike, also bicycle rentals.
BikeMavil, Av Aviación 4023, Surco, T449 8435, see Facebook page. Mon-Sat 1030-2000. Rental service, repairs, tours, selection of mountain and racing bikes.
Buenas Biclas, Domingo Elías 164, Miraflores, T241 9712, www.buenasbiclas.com. Mon-Fri 1000-2000, Sat 1000-1400. Mountain bike specialists, knowledgeable staff, good selection of bikes, repairs and accessories.
Casa Okuyama, Manco Cápac 590, La Victoria, T330 9131. Mon-Fri 0900-1300, 1415-1800, Sat 0900-1300. Repairs, parts, try here for 28-in tyres, excellent service.
Cicloturismo Peru, T99-9012 8105, www.cicloturismoperu.com. Offers good-value cycling trips around Lima and beyond, as well as bike rental. The owner, Aníbal Paredes, speaks good English, is very knowledgeable and is the owner of **Mont Blanc Gran Hotel**.
Mirabici, Parque Salazar, T673 3903. Daily 0800-1900. Bicycle hire, US$7.50 per hr (tandems available); they also run bike tours 1000-1500, in English, Spanish and Portuguese. Bikes to ride up and down Av Arequipa can be rented on Sun 0800-1300, US$3 per hr, leave passport as deposit, www.jafibike.com.
Perú Bike, T260 8225, www.perubike.com. Experienced agency leading tours, professional guiding, mountain bike school and workshop.

Diving
Peru Divers, Av Defensores del Morro 175, Chorrillos, T251 6231, www.perudivers.com. Owner Lucho Rodríguez is a certified PADI

instructor who offers certification courses, tours and a wealth of good information.

Hiking
Trekking and Backpacking Club, Jr Huáscar 1152, Jesús María, Lima 11, T423 2515, T94-3866 794, www.angelfire.com/mi2/tebac. Sr Miguel Chiri Valle, treks arranged, including in the Cordillera Blanca.

Paragliding
Aeroxtreme, Trípoli 345, dpto 503, T242 5125, www,aeroxtreme.com. One of several outfits offering parapenting in Lima, 20 years' experience.
Andean Trail Perú, T99-836 3436, www.andeantrailperu.com. For parapenting tandem flights, US$53, and courses, US$600 for 10 days. They also have a 'fun day' for US$120 to learn the basics. Trekking, kayaking and other adventure sports arranged.

Textiles/cultural tours
Puchka Perú, www.puchkaperu.com. Web-based operator specializing in textiles, folk art and markets. Fixed-date tours involve meeting artisans, workshops, visit to markets and more. In association with Maestro Máximo Laura, world-famous weaver, http://maximolauratapestries.com, whose studio in Urb Brisas de Santa Rosa III Etapa, Lima can be visited by appointment, T577 0952, karinaguilar@maximolaura.com. See also Museo Máximo Laura, page 209.

Tour operators
Do not conduct business anywhere other than in the agency's office and insist on a written contract.
The Andean Experience Co., Sáenz Peña 214, Barranco, T700 5100, www.andean-experience.com. Offers tailor-made itineraries designed to match each traveller's personal interests, style and preferences to create ideal Peru trips.
Aracari Travel Consulting, Schell 237, of 602, Miraflores, T651 2424, www.aracari.com. Regional tours throughout

Peru, also 'themed' and activity tours, has a very good reputation.

Coltur, Av Reducto 1255, Miraflores, T615 5555, www.coltur.com. Very helpful, experienced and well-organized tours throughout Peru.

Condor Travel, Armando Blondet 249, San Isidro, T615 3000, www.condortravel.com. Highly regarded operator with tailor-made programmes, special interest tours, luxury journeys, adventure travel and conventional tourism. One-stop shopping with own regional network.

Dasatariq, Av Reducto 1255, Miraflores, T447 2741, www.dasatariq.com. Also in Cuzco. Well-organized, helpful, with a good reputation.

Domiruth Travel Service S.A.C, Jr Rio de Janeiro 216-218, Miraflores, T610 6000, www.domiruth.com. Tours throughout Peru, from the mystical to adventure travel. See also **Peru 4x4 Adventures**, part of Domiruth, www.peru4x4adventures.com, for exclusive 4WD tours with German, English, Spanish, Italian and Portuguese-speaking drivers.

Ecocruceros, Av Arequipa 4964, of 202, Miraflores, T226 8530, www.islaspalomino. com. Daily departures from Plaza Grau in Callao to see the sea lions at Islas Palomino, 4 hrs with 30-40 mins wetsuit swimming with guide, snack lunch, US$48 (take ID), reserve a day in advance.

Excursiones MYG, T241 8091, www. excursionesmyg.com. Offers a variety of tours in Lima and surroundings, including historic centre, nighttime, culinary tours, Caral, and further afield.

Explorandes, C San Fernando 287, Miraflores, T200 6100, www.explorandes.com. Award-winning company. Offers a wide range of adventure and cultural tours throughout the country. Also offices in Huaraz and Cuzco (see pages 81 and 223).

Fertur Peru Travel, C Schell 485, Miraflores, T242 1900; and Jr Junín 211, Plaza de Armas, T427 2626; also in Cuzco at San Augustin 317, T084-221304; (USA/Canada T(1) 877-247 0055 toll free, UK T020-3002 3811),

www.fertur-travel.com. Mon-Fri 0900-1900, Sat 0900-1600. Siduith Ferrer de Vecchio, CEO of this agency, is highly recommended; she offers tour packages and up-to-date, correct tourist information on a national level, and also great prices on national and international flights, discounts for those with ISIC and youth cards and **South American Explorers** members. Other services include flight reconfirmations, hotel reservations and transfers to and from the airport or bus or train stations.

Il Tucano Peru, Elías Aguirre 633, Miraflores, T444 9361, 24-hr number T01-975 05375, www.iltucanoperu.com. Personalized tours for groups or individuals throughout Peru, also 4WD overland trips, first-class drivers and guides, outstanding service and reliability.

Info Perú, Jr de la Unión (Belén) 1066, of 102, T425 0414, www.infoperu.com.pe. Mon-Fri 0900-1800, Sat 0930-1400. Run by a group of women, ask for Laura Gómez, offering personalized programmes, hotel bookings, transport, free tourist information, sale of maps, books and souvenirs, English and French spoken.

InkaNatura Travel, Manuel Bañon 461, San Isidro, T440 2022, www.inkanatura.com. Also in Cuzco and Chiclayo, experienced company with special emphasis on both sustainable tourism and conservation, especially in Manu and Tambopata, also birdwatching, and on the archaeology of all of Peru.

Lima Mentor, T624 9360, www.limamentor. com. Contact through web, phone or through hotels. An agency offering cultural tours of Lima using freelance guides in specialist areas (eg gastronomy, art, archaeology, Lima at night), entertaining, finding different angles from regular tours. Half-day or full day tours.

Lima Tours, N de Piérola 589 p 18, T619 6900, www.limatours.com.pe. Very good for tours in the capital and around the country; programmes include health and wellness tours.

Peru Best Tours, Paseo de los Reyes Mz Q
Lt 9 Lima, T637 7323, USA T+1 302 319 2122,
www.perubesttours.com. Specializes in
customized cultural and activity trips in Peru.
Based in Lima with branch office in the USA.
Peru For Less, ASTA Travel Agent, Luis
García Rojas 240, Urb Humboldt, US office:
T1-877-269 0309; UK office: T+44-203-002
0571; Peru (Lima) office: T273 2486, Cuzco
T084-254800, www.peruforless.com. Will
meet or beat any published rates on the
internet from outside Peru. Good reports.
Peru Rooms, Av Dos de Mayo 1545 of 205,
San Isidro, T422 3434, www.perurooms.com.
Internet-based travel service offering 3- to
5-star packages throughout Peru, cultural,
adventure and nature tourism.
Rutas del Peru SAC, Av Enrique Palacios
1110, Miraflores, T445 7249, www.
rutasdelperu.com. Bespoke trips and
overland expeditions in trucks.
Viajes Pacífico (Gray Line), Av Paseo de la
República 6010, p 7, T610 1911, www.gray
lineperu.com. Tours throughout Peru and
within South America.
Viracocha, Av Vasco Núñez de Balboa 191,
Miraflores, T445 3986, peruviantours@
viracocha.com.pe. Very helpful, especially
with flights, adventure, cultural, mystical
and birdwatching tours.
Open-top bus tours Mirabús, T242 6699,
www.mirabusperu.com. Goes from Parque
Kennedy Tue-Sun at 1000 to Pachacámac
and back with a stop at Pántanos de Villa
wildlife sanctuary, US$30. Mirabús runs

other tours of the city and Callao (from
US$3.75 to US$28) – eg Lima half day by
day, Lima by night, Costa Verde, Callao, Gold
Museum, Miraflores. Similar services are
offered by **Turibus**, from Larcomar, T230
0909, www.turibusperu.com.
Private guides The MITINCI (Ministry
of Industry Tourism, Integration and
International Business) certifies guides
and can provide a list. Most are members
of **AGOTUR** (Asociación de Guías Oficiales
de Turismo), Av La Paz 678, Miraflores (for
correspondence only), www.agotur.com.
Book in advance. Most guides speak a
foreign language.

⊖ Transport

Lima *p43, maps p44, p47 and p52*
Air
Jorge Chávez Airport, 16 km from the
centre of Lima. Arrivals or departures flight
information T511 6055, www.lap.com.pe.

Information desks can be found in the
national and international foyers. There
is also a helpful desk in the international
Arrivals hall, which can make hotel and
transport reservations. There are many
smart shops, places to eat and drink and, in
international Arrivals, mobile phone rentals.
Global Net ATM, *casas de cambio* (money
changing kiosks) and a bank can be found
in many parts of Arrivals and Departures.
Exchange rates are marginally poorer than
outside. There are public telephones around

the airport and a **Telefónica** *locutorio*, daily 0700-2300. Internet facilities are more expensive than in the city. Most of the terminal has free Wi-Fi. There are postal services.

Transport from the airport *Remise* taxis from desks outside International Arrivals and National Arrivals: **Taxi Green**, T484 4001, www.taxigreen.com.pe; **Mitsu**, T261 7788, www.mitsoo.net; and **CMV**, T219 0266, http://cmvtaxi.pe. As a rough guide, these companies charge US$20-30 to the centre, US$22-32 to Miraflores and San Isidro, a bit more to Barranco. In the same place is the desk of **Peruvian Shuttle**, T373 5049, www. peruvian-shuttle.com, which runs private, shared and group transfers to the city; fares US$7-18 shared, depending on number of passengers, US$22-40 private. There are many taxi drivers offering their services outside Arrivals with similar or higher prices (more at night). To get to Miraflores by combi, take the "Callao-Ate" with a big red "S" ("La S"), the only direct link from the airport to Miraflores. Catch it outside of the airport, on Av Faucett, US$0. 55. From downtown Lima go to the junction of Alfonso Ugarte and Av Venezuela where many combis take the route "Todo aeropuerto – Avenida Faucett", US$0.50. At anytime other than very late at night or early in the morning luggage won't be allowed on public buses.

Note Do not take the cheapest, stopping buses to the centre along Av Faucett. They are frequently robbed. Pay more for a non-stop bus, or better still take one of the options above. Do not go to the car park exit and find a taxi without an airport permit outside the perimeter. Although much cheaper than those inside, they are not safe.

Bus
Local The bus routes are shared by buses, combis (mid-size) and colectivos (mini-vans or cars); the latter run from 0600-0100, and less frequently through the night, they are quicker and stop wherever requested. Buses and combis charge about US$0.40-0.45, colectivos a little more. On public holidays,

Sun and from 2400 to 0500 every night, a small charge is added to the fare. None is particulary safe; it is better to take a taxi (see below for recommendations).

Lima centre–Miraflores: Av Arequipa runs 52 blocks between downtown Lima and Parque Kennedy in Miraflores. There is no shortage of public transport on this avenue; they have 'Todo Arequipa' on the windscreen. When heading towards downtown from Miraflores the window sticker should say 'Wilson/Tacna'. To get to Parque Kennedy from downtown look on the windshield for 'Larco/Schell/Miraflores', 'Chorrillos/Huaylas' or 'Barranco/Ayacucho'.

Lima centre–Barranco: Lima's only urban freeway, Vía Expresa, runs from Plaza Grau in the centre of town, to the northern tip of **Barranco**. This 6-lane thoroughfare, locally known as *El Zanjón* (the Ditch), with the **Metropolitano** bus lane in the middle, is the fastest way to cross the city. Buses downtown for the Vía Expresa can be caught on Av Tacna, Av Wilson (also called Garcilaso de la Vega), Av Bolivia and Av Alfonso Ugarte.

The **Metropolitano** is a system of articulated buses running on dedicated lanes of the Vía Expresa/Paseo de la República (T01-203 9000, www.metropolitano.com. pe). The Estación Central is in front of the **Sheraton** hotel. The southern section runs to Matellini in Chorrillos (estimated journey time 32 mins). For Miraflores take stations between Angamos and 28 de Julio; for Barranco, Bulevar is 170 m from the Plaza. The northern branch runs to Naranjal in Comas, a 34-min journey. Stations Estación Central to Ramón Castilla serve the city centre. Tickets are prepaid and recharge able, from S/.5-100, each journey is S/.2 (US$0.70). Buses run from 0500-2300 daily with shorter hours on Sun and on some sections. From 0600-0900, 1635-2115 Mon-Fri express services run between certain stations. Buses are packed in rush hour.

Long distance There are many different bus companies, but the larger ones are better organized, leave on time and do not wait until the bus is full. For approximate prices, frequency and duration of trip, see destinations. Leaving or arriving in Lima by bus in the rush hour can add an extra hour to the journey. **Note** In the weeks either side of 28/29 Jul (Independence), and of the Christmas/New Year holiday, it is practically impossible to get bus tickets out of Lima, unless you book in advance. Bus prices double at these times.

Cruz del Sur, T311 5050 (telephone sales), www.cruzdelsur.com.pe. The main terminal is at Av Javier Prado 1109, La Victoria, with *Cruzero* and *Cruzero Suite* services (luxury buses) and *Imperial* service (quite comfortable buses and periodic stops for food and bathroom breaks, a cheap option with a quality company) to most parts of Peru. Another terminal is at Jr Quilca 531, Lima centre, for *Imperial* services to Arequipa, Ayacucho, Chiclayo, Cuzco, Huancayo, Huaraz, and Trujillo. There are sales offices throughout the city.

Ormeño and its affiliated bus companies depart from and arrive at Av Carlos Zavala 177, Lima centre, T427 5679; also Av Javier Prado Este 1057, Santa Catalina, T472 1710, www.grupo-ormeno.com.pe. **Ormeño** offers *Royal Class* and *Business Class* service to certain destinations. These buses are very comfortable with bathrooms, hostess, etc. They arrive and depart from the Javier Prado terminal, but the Carlos Zavala terminal is the best place to get information and buy any Ormeño ticket. **Cial**, República de Panamá 2460, T207 6900 ext 119, and Paseo de la República 646, T207 6900 ext 170, www.expresocial.com, has national coverage. **Flores**, with terminals at Av Paseo de le República 683, Av Paseo de le República 627 and Jr Montevideo 523, T332 1212, www.floreshnos.net, has departures to many parts of the country, especially the south. Some of its services are good quality.

Other companies include: **Oltursa**, Aramburú 1160, San Isidro, T708 5000, www.oltursa.pe. A reputable company offering top end services to **Nazca**, **Arequipa** and destinations in **northern Peru**, mainly at night. **Tepsa**, Javier Prado Este 1091, La Victoria, T617 9000, www.tepsa.com.pe, also at Av Gerardo Unger 6917, Terminal Plaza Norte, T533 1524 (not far from the airport, good for those short of time for a bus connection after landing in Lima). Services to the north as far as **Tumbes** and the south to **Tacna**.

Transportes Chanchamayo, Av Nicolás Arriola 535, La Victoria, T265 6850, www.transporteschanchamayo.com. To **Tarma**, **San Ramón** and **La Merced**. **Ittsa**, Paseo de la República 809, T423 5232, www.ittsabus.com. Good service to the north, **Chiclayo**, **Piura**, **Tumbes**. **Transportes León de Huánuco**, Av 28 de Julio 1520, La Victoria, T424 3893. Daily to **Huánuco**, **Tingo María**, **La Merced** and **Pucallpa**. **Línea**, Paseo de la República 941-959, Lima Centre, T424 0836, www.transporteslinea.com.pe, also has a terminal at Terminal Plaza Norte (see above under Tepsa), T533 0739. Among the best services to destinations in the **north**. **Móvil**, Av Paseo de La República 749, Lima Centre near the national stadium, T716 8000 (also Av Alfredo Mendiola 3883, Los Olivos), www.moviltours.com.pe, to **Huaraz** and **Chiclayo** by *bus cama*, and **Chachapoyas**. **Soyuz**, Av México 333, T205 2370, www.soyuz.com.pe. To **Ica** every 7 mins, well organized. As PerúBus, www.perubus.com.pe, the same company runs north to **Huacho** and **Barranca**. **Cavassa**, Raimondi 129, Lima Centre, T431 3200, also at Terminal Plaza Norte, www.turismocavassa.com.pe. To **Huaraz**. Also **Julio César**, José Gálvez 562, La Victoria, T424 8060, www.transportesjuliocesar.com.pe (also at Plaza Norte). Recommended to arrive in Huaraz and then use local transport to points beyond. Good. To **Cuzco**: **Cromotex**, Av Nicolás Arriola 898, Santa Catalina, Av Paseo de La República 659, T424 7575, www.cromotex.com.pe, also to **Arequipa**.

Bus or colectivo to Pachacámac from Lima From the Pan-American Highway (southbound) take a combi with a sticker in the window reading "Pachacámac/Lurín" (US$0.85). Let the driver know you want to get off at the ruins. A taxi will cost approximately US$5.50, but if you don't ask the driver to wait for you (an extra cost), finding another to take you back to Lima may be a bit tricky. For organized tours contact one of the tour agencies listed above.

International buses Ormeño, address above. To: **Guayaquil** (29 hrs with a change of bus at the border, US$56), **Quito** (38 hrs, US$75), **Cali** (56 hrs, US$131), **Bogotá** (70 hrs, US$141), **Caracas** (100 hrs, US$150), **Santiago** (54 hrs, US$102), **Mendoza** (78 hrs, US$159), **Buenos Aires** (90 hrs, US$148), **São Paulo** (90 hrs). A maximum of 20 kg is allowed pp. **Cruz del Sur** also has services to **Guayaquil**, 3 a week, US$85, **Buenos Aires**, US$250, and **Santiago**, US$155. El Rápido, Av Rivera Navarrete 2650, Lince, T441 6651, www.elrapidoint.com.ar. Service to Argentina and Uruguay only. Note that international buses are more expensive than travelling from one border to another on national buses.

Warning The area around the bus terminals is very unsafe; thefts and assaults are more common in this neighbourhood than elsewhere in the city. You are strongly advised either to take a bus from a company which has a terminal away from the Carlos Zavala area (eg Cruz del Sur, Oltursa, Ormeño), or to take a taxi to and from your bus. Make sure your luggage is well guarded and put on the right bus. It is also important not to assume that buses leave from the place where you bought the tickets.

Taxi
Taxis do not use meters although some have rate sheets (eg **Satelital**, T355 5555, www.3555555satelital.com). Agree the price of the journey beforehand and insist on being taken to the destination of your choice. At night, on Sunday and holidays expect a surcharge of 35-50% is made. The following are taxi fares for some of the more common routes, give or take a sol. From downtown

Lima to: Parque Kennedy (Miraflores), US$4. Museo de la Nación, US$3.75. San Isidro, US$3.75. Barranco US$4.75. From Miraflores (Parque Kennedy) to: Museo de la Nación, US$2.75. Archaeology Museum, US$3.75. Barranco, US$4.80. By law, all taxis must have the vehicle's registration number painted on the side. They are often white or yellow, but can come in any colour, size or make. Licensed and phone taxis are safest, but if hailing a taxi on the street, local advice is to look for an older driver rather than a youngster. There are several reliable phone taxi companies, which can be called for immediate service, or booked in advance; prices are 2-3 times more than ordinary taxis; eg to the airport US$15, to suburbs US$10. Some are, **Moli Taxi**, T479 0030; **Taxi Real**, T215 1414, www.taxireal.com; **Taxi Seguro**, T241 9292; **Taxi Tata**, T274 5151; **TCAM**, run by Carlos Astacio, T99-983 9305, safe, reliable. If hiring a taxi by the hour, agree on price beforehand, US$7-9. Recommended, knowledgeable drivers: **César A Canales N**, T436 6184, T99-687 3310, only speaks Spanish, reliable. **Hugo Casanova Morella**, T485 7708 (he lives in La Victoria), for city tours, travel to airport, etc. **Mario Salas Pantoja**, T99-908 1888. Very reliable and helpful, airport transfers for US$12 or hourly rate for city tours/museum visits etc. Speaks basic English. **Mónica Velásquez Carlich**, T425 5087, T99-943 0796, vc_monica@hotmail.com. For airport pick-ups, tours, speaks English, most helpful, frequently recommended. **Note** Drivers don't expect tips; give them small change from the fare.

Train
Details of the service on the Central Railway to Huancayo are given under Huancayo, page 258. The first route of the Tren Eléctrico (Metro) runs from Av Grau in the centre of Lima south to Villa El Salvador, 0600-2230. Each journey costs S/.1.50 (US$0.55); pay by swipe card S/.5 (US$1.75). To connect with the Tren Eléctrico from the Metropolitano, take a bus from Estación

Central to Grau or Gamarra. Construction work has started on the next section.

❶ Directory

Lima *p43, maps p44, p47 and p52*
Car hire Most companies have an office at the airport, where you can arrange everything and pick up and leave the car. It is recommended to test drive before signing the contract as quality varies. It can be much cheaper to rent a car in a town in the Sierra for a few days than to drive from Lima; also companies don't have a collection service. Cars can be hired from: **Paz Rent A Car**, Av Diez Canseco 319, of 15, Miraflores, T446 4395, T99-939 9853, www.perupazconsortium.com.pe. **Budget**, T204 4400, www.budgetperu. com. Prices range from US$35 to US$85 depending on type of car. Make sure that your car is in a locked garage at night.
Embassies and consulates For foreign embassies and consulates in Lima, see http://embassy.goabroad.com. **Language schools** Hispana, San Martín 377, Miraflores, T446 3045, www.hispanaidiomas. com. 20- to 60-hr travellers' programmes and other courses, also salsa, surf and gastronomy. **Instituto de Idiomas (Pontífica Universidad Católica del Perú)**, Av Camino Real 1037, San Isidro, T626 6500, http:// idiomas.pucp.edu.pe. Spanish for foreigners courses. **El Sol School of Languages**, Grimaldo del Solar 469, Miraflores, T242 7763, http://elsol.idiomasperu.com. Private tuition, also small groups. Family homestays and volunteer programmes available.
Independent teachers (enquire about rates): **AC Spanish Classes (Luis Villanueva)**, Diez Canseco 497, Miraflores, T247 7054, www. acspanishclasses.com. Flexible, reliable, helpful. **Srta Susy Arteaga**, T534 9289, T99-989 7271, susyarteaga@hotmail.com, or susyarteaga@yahoo.com. **Srta Patty Félix**, T521 2559, patty_fel24@yahoo.com.
Medical services (Also worth contacting consulate for recommendations.) **Hospitals:**

Clínica Anglo Americano, Alfredo Salazar 350, San Isidro, a few blocks from Ovalo Gutiérrez, T616 8900, www.angloamericana. com.pe. Stocks Yellow Fever and Tetanus. **Clínica Internacional**, Jr Washington 1471 y Paseo Colón (9 de Diciembre), downtown Lima, T619 6161, www.clinicainternacional. com.pe. Good, clean and professional, consultations up to US$35, no inoculations. **Instituto de Medicina Tropical**, Av Honorio Delgado 430 near the Pan American Highway in the Cayetano Heredia Hospital, San Martín de Porres, T482 3903, www.upch. edu.pe/tropicales/. Good for check-ups after jungle travel. **Clínica del Niño**, Av Brasil 600 at 1st block of Av 28 de Julio, Breña, T330 0066, www.isn.gob.pe. **Centro Anti-Rabia de Lima**, Jr Austria 1300, Breña, T425 6313. Mon-Sat 0830-1830. **Clínica Padre Luis Tezza**, Av El Polo 570, Monterrico, T610 5050, www.clinicatezza.com.pe. Clinic specializing in a wide variety of illnesses/ disorders, etc, expensive; for stomach or intestinal problems. **Clínica Ricardo Palma**, Av Javier Prado Este 1066, San Isidro, T224 2224, www.crp.com.pe. For general medical consultations, English spoken. **Clínica Good Hope**, Malecón Balta 956, Miraflores, T610 7300, www.goodhope.org.pe. Has been recommended, will make visitsto hotels; prices similar to US. **International Health Department**, at Jorge Chávez airport, T517 1845. Open 24 hrs a day for vaccinations.
Useful addresses Tourist Police, Jr Moore 268, Magdalena at the 38th block of Av Brasil, T460 1060, open daily 24 hrs. For public enquiries, Av España y Av Alfonso Ugarte, Lima, and Colón 246, Miraflores, T243 2190. They are friendly and very helpful, English spoken. It is recommended to visit when you have had property stolen. **Immigration**: Av España 730, Breña, Mon-Fri 0830-1300. Provides new entry stamps if passport is lost or stolen. **Intej**, Av San Martín 240, Barranco, T247 3230. They can extend student cards, change flight itineraries bought with student cards.

Huaraz and the Cordilleras

The spectacular Cordillera Blanca is an area of jewelled lakes and snowy mountain peaks attracting mountaineers and hikers in their thousands. Huaraz is the natural place to head for. It has the best infrastructure and the mountains, lakes and trails are within easy reach. This region, though, also has some sites of great archaeological significance, the most notable of which must be Chavín de Huantar, one of Peru's most important pre-Inca sites. Large multinational mining projects have brought new prosperity as well as social change and ecological damage to the area.

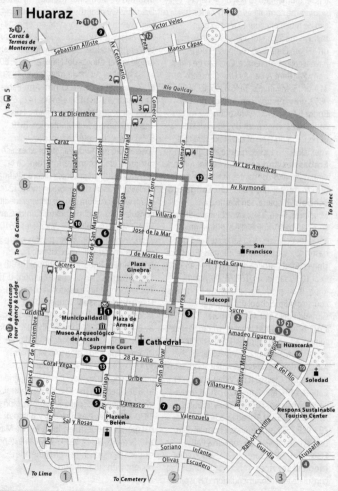

Arriving in Huaraz and the Cordilleras

North from Lima the Pan-American Highway parallels the coast. A series of roads climb up to Huaraz, in the Callejón de Huaylas, gateway to Parque Nacional Huascarán. Probably the easiest route to Huaraz is the paved road which branches east off the Pan-American Highway north of Pativilca, 203 km from Lima. The road climbs increasingly steeply to the chilly pass at 4080 m (Km 120). Shortly after, Laguna **Conococha** comes into view, where the Río Santa rises. A road branches off from Conococha to **Chiquián** (see page 93) and the **Cordilleras Huayhuash** and **Raura** to the southeast. After crossing a high plateau the main road descends gradually for 47 km until **Catac**, where another road branches east to Chavín and on to the **Callejón de Conchucos** (eastern side of the Cordillera Blanca). Huaraz is 36 km further on and the road then continues north between the towering Cordillera Negra, snowless and rising to 4600 m, and the snow-covered Cordillera Blanca. The alternative routes to the Callejón de Huaylas are via the Callán pass from Casma to Huaraz (see page 97), and from Chimbote to Caraz via the Cañón del Pato (page 96).

200 metres
200 yards

Where to stay
1 Albergue Churup *C3*
2 Alojamiento El Jacal *C3*
3 Alojamiento Soledad *C3*
4 Andino Club *D3*
5 Angeles Inn *D2*
6 Backpackers *B1*
7 Benkawasi *D1*
8 Casa Jaimes *C1*
9 Edward's Inn *B1*
10 El Patio *A1*
11 Hatun Wasi *A1*
12 Hostal Colomba *A2*
13 Hostal Quintana *C1*
14 Jo's Place *A2*
15 La Cabaña *C3*
16 La Casa de Zarela *C3*
17 Lodging Caroline *C1*
18 Lodging House Ezama *A3*
19 Olaza's B&B *D3*
20 Res NG *D2*
21 Res Sucre *C3*
22 San Sebastián *B3*

Restaurants
1 Bistro de los Andes *C2*
2 Café El Centro *C1*
3 Cafetería y Juguería *C2*
4 California Café *C1*
5 Chifa Jim Hua *D1*
6 Fuente de Salud *B1*
7 Huaraz Querido *D2*
8 Las Puyas *B1*
9 Mi Comedia *A1*
10 Panadería La Alameda *B1*
11 Panadería Montserrat *D1*
12 Papa Loca *B2*
13 Pizza Bruno *D1*

Transport
1 Sandoval/Chavín
  Express *C1*
2 Combis to Caraz *A1, A2*
3 Combis to Wilcawain *A2*
4 Julio César *B2*
5 Móvil Tours *A1*
6 Terminal de
  Transportistas
  Zona Sur *C1*
7 Trans Huandoy *A2*

➡ **Huaraz maps**
1 Huaraz, page 74
2 Huaraz centre,
  page 76

Huaraz → *Phone code: 043. Colour map 2, B2. Population: 115,000. Altitude: 3091 m.*

The main town in the Cordillera Blanca, 420 km from Lima, Huaraz is expanding rapidly as a major tourist centre, but it is also a busy commercial hub, especially on market days. It is a prime destination for hikers and a Mecca for international climbers.

Arriving in Huaraz

Tourist offices i Perú ⓘ *Pasaje Atusparia, of 1, Plaza de Armas, T428812, iperuhuaraz@ promperu.gob.pe, Mon-Sat 0800-1830, Sun 0830-1400. Also at Jr San Martín cuadra 6 s/n, open daily 0800-1100, and at Anta airport when flights arrive.* **Policía de Turismo** ⓘ *Av Luzuriaga on Plaza de Armas, around the corner from iPerú, T421351, divtueco_ huaraz@yahoo.com, Mon-Sat 0730-2100,* is the place to report crimes and resolve issues with tour operators, hotels, etc. All female officers, limited English spoken. **Indecopi** ⓘ *Av Gamarra 671, T423899, www. indecopi.gob.pe,* the government consumer protection office, is very effective but not always quick. Spanish only. Huaraz has its share of crime, especially since the arrival of mining and during the high tourist season. Women should not go to surrounding districts and sites alone. Muggings have taken place on the trails to Rataquena lookout, just above the city, and between the Monterrey thermal baths and Wilcawain ruins. See also www.andeanexplorer.com.

② Huaraz centre

N

50 metres
50 yards

Where to stay 🛏
1 Oscar's Hostal

Restaurants 🍴
1 Café Andino &
  Familia Meza Lodging
2 Chilli Heaven
3 Créperie Patrick
4 El Horno Pizzería Grill
5 Encuentro
6 Maialino
7 Pizza B&B

8 Pizzería Landauro
9 Rinconcito Minero
10 Rossanero
11 Sabor Salud
12 Trivio

Bars & clubs 🍸
13 '13 Buhos'
14 Amadeus
15 Extreme &
  Monttrek Agency
16 Taberna Tambo

➡ **Huaraz maps**
1 Huaraz, page 74
2 **Huaraz centre,**
  page 76

Places around Huaraz

Huaraz, capital of Ancash department, was almost completely destroyed in the earthquake of May 1970. The Plaza de Armas has been rebuilt. A new **Cathedral** is still being built. The setting, at the foot of the Cordillera Blanca, is spectacular. The main thoroughfare, Avenida Luzuriaga, is bursting at the seams with travel agencies, climbing equipment hire shops, restaurants, cafés and bars. A good district for those seeking peace and quiet is La Soledad, six blocks uphill from the Plaza de Armas on Avenida Sucre. Here, along Sucre as well as Jr Amadeo Figueroa, are many hotels and rooms for rent in private homes. **Museo Arqueológico de Ancash** ① *Ministerio de Cultura, Plaza de Armas, Mon-Sat 0900-1700, Sun 0900-1400*, contains stone monoliths and *huacos* from the Recuay culture, well labelled. The **Sala de Cultura SUNARP** ① *Av Centenario 530, Independencia, T421301, Mon-Fri 1700-2000, Sat 0900-1300, free*, often has interesting art and photography exhibitions by local artists.

About 8 km to the northeast is **Willkawain** ① *Tue-Fri 0830-1600, Sat-Sun 0900-1330, US$1.75, take a combi from 13 de Diciembre and Jr Cajamarca, US$0.50, 20 mins, direct to Willkawain*. The ruins (AD 700-1100, Huari Empire) consist of one large three-storey structure with intact stone roof slabs and several small structures. About 500 m past Willkawain is Ichicwillkawain with several similar but smaller structures. A well-signed trail climbs from Wilkawain to Laguna Ahuac (Aguak Cocha, 4580 m), 12 km return, a demanding acclimatization hike, no services along the way. North of Huaraz, 6 km along the road to Caraz, are the thermal baths at **Monterrey** (at 2780 m) ① *the lower pool is US$0.85; the upper pool,* which is nicer (closed Mon for cleaning), US$1.35; also individual and family tubs US$1.35 per person for 20 mins; crowded at weekends and holidays. There are restaurants and hotels. City buses along Avenida Luzuriaga go as far as Monterrey (US$0.22), until 1900; taxi US$2-3. **Note** that it is not safe to walk between Monterrey to Willkawain.

⊙ Huaraz listings

For hotel and restaurant price codes, and other relevant information, see pages 14-17.

⊙ Where to stay

Huaraz *p75, maps p74 and p76*
Hotels fill up rapidly in high season (May-Sep), especially during public holidays and special events when prices rise (beware overcharging). Touts meet buses and aggressively "suggest" places to stay. Do not be put off your choice of lodging; phone ahead to confirm.

$$$$-$$$ Andino Club, Pedro Cochachín 357, some way southeast of the centre (take a taxi after dark), T421662, www. hotelandino.com. Swiss-run hotel with very high standards, excellent restaurant, variety of rooms including panoramic views, balcony, fireplace, jacuzzi and sauna.

$$$ El Patio, Av Monterrey, 250 m downhill from the Monterrey baths, T424965, www.elpatio.com.pe. Very colonial-style with lovely gardens, comfortable rooms, singles, doubles and triples, some with balconies, also 4 lodges with fireplaces. Meals on request, bar.

$$$ Hostal Colomba, Francisco de Zela 210, just off Centenario across the river, T421501, www.huarazhotel.com. Lovely old hacienda, family-run, garden with playground and sports, safe parking, gym and well-equipped rooms sleeping 1-6, comfortable beds, restaurant.

$$$ The Lazy Dog Inn, 30 mins' drive from Huaraz (US$10 by taxi), close to the boundary of Huascarán National Park, 3.1 km past the town of Marian, close to the Quebrada Cojup, T943-789330, www. thelazydoginn.com. Eco-tourism lodge actively involved in community projects,

water recycling systems and composting toilets. Beautifully designed in warm colours, great location gives access to several mountain valleys. Organizes horse riding and hiking trips. Excellent home-cooked breakfast and dinner included. Canadian owned, English spoken. Recommended.

$$$-$$ San Sebastián, Jr Italia 1124, T426960, www.sansebastianhuaraz.com. Elegant, modern hotel, comfortable beds with duvets, parking available, helpful, good views.

$$-$ Albergue Churup, Jr Amadeo Figueroa 1257, T424200, www.churup.com. 13 rooms with private bath or 2 dorms with shared bath, hot water, fire in sitting room on 4th floor, cafeteria, use of kitchen 1800-2200, lots of information, laundry, book exchange, English spoken, Spanish classes, adventure travel tours, extremely helpful. Airport transfers and free pick-up from bus.

$$-$ Edward's Inn, Bolognesi 121, T422692, www.huaraz.com/edwards. With or without bath, nice garden, laundry, breakfast extra, insist on proper rates in low season, popular. Edward speaks English and has 30 years' experience trekking, climbing and guiding in the area. He also rents gear.

$$-$ Hatun Wasi, Jr Daniel Villayzán 268, T425055. Family-run hotel next to Jo's place. Spacious rooms, with hot water, pleasant roof terrace, ideal for breakfasts, with great views of the Cordillera.

$$-$ La Casa de Zarela, J Arguedas 1263, T421694, www.lacasadezarela.hostel.com. Hot water, use of kitchen, laundry facilities, popular with climbers and trekkers, owner Zarela who speaks English organizes groups and is very knowledgeable.

$$-$ Residencial NG, Pasaje Valenzuela 837, T421831, www.residencialng.com.

Breakfast, hot water, good value, helpful, has restaurant.

$ Alojamiento El Jacal, Jr Sucre 1044, T424612, reservaseljacal@yahoo.es. With or without shower, hot water, helpful family, garden, laundry facilities.

$ Alojamiento Soledad, Jr Amadeo Figueroa 1267, T421196, www.lodging soledad.com. Simple breakfast, private and shared bath, abundant hot water, use of kitchen, family home and atmosphere, secure, trekking information and tours. Warmly recommended.

$ Andescamp Hostel, Jr Huáscar 615, T423842, www.andescamphostel.com. See Trekking and climbing, below.

$ Angeles Inn, Av Gamarra 815, T422205, solandperu@yahoo.com. No sign, look for **Sol Andino** travel agency in same building (www.solandino.com), laundry facilities, garden, hot water, owners Max and Saul Angeles are official guides, helpful with trekking and climbing, rent equipment.

$ Backpackers, Av Raimondi 510, T421773, www.huaraz.com/backpackers. Breakfast not included. Dorms or private room with bathroom. Spacious, hot showers, good views, energetic staff, a real bargain, but heavy traffic outside.

$ Benkawasi, Parque Santa Rosa 928, 10 mins from centre, T423150, http://huarazbenkawasi.com. Doubles, also rooms for 3, 4 and dorm, hot water, breakfast US$5, laundry, games room, pick-up from bus station. Owner Benjamín Morales also has **Xtreme Bar**, **Infinite Tours** for mountain bike hire and tours of the National Park and a lodge at Playa Tortugas, near Casma (arranges downhill biking from Huaraz).

$ Casa Jaimes, Alberto Gridilla 267, T422281, 2 blocks from the main plaza, www.casa jaimes.com. Dormitory with hot showers, laundry facilities, has maps and books of the region. Noisy but otherwise good.

$ Familia Meza, Lúcar y Torre 538, behind Café Andino (enquire here), T421203. Shared bath, hot water, laundry facilities, popular with trekkers, mountaineers and bikers.

$ Hostal Quintana, Mcal Cáceres 411, T426060, www.hostal-quintana.com. English, French, Italian and Spanish spoken, mountain gear rental, 2 of the owner's sons are certified guides and can arrange itineraries, laundry facilities, café popular with trekkers.

$ Jo's Place, Jr Daniel Villayzan 276, T425505, www.huaraz.com/josplace. Safe, hot water at night, nice mountain views, garden, terrace, English owner, warm atmosphere, popular.

$ La Cabaña, Jr Sucre 1224, T423428. Shared and double rooms, hot showers, laundry, popular, safe for parking, bikes and luggage, English and French spoken, good value.

$ Lodging Caroline, Urb Avitentel Mz D-Lt 1, T422588, http://carolinelodging.com. Colourful dorms in main building or private rooms in newer annex. Gay friendly. 10-min walk from centre, free pick-up from bus station (phone ahead), hot water, tourist information, laundry, helpful. Compare tours offered here with those of established operators.

$ Lodging House Ezama, Mariano Melgar 623, Independencia, T423490, 15 mins' walk from Plaza de Armas (US$0.50 by taxi), www.huaraz.com/ezama. Light, spacious rooms, hot water, safe, helpful.

$ Oscar's Hostal, La Mar 624, T422720, cvmonical@hotmail.com. Hot water, cheap breakfast next door, good beds, cheaper in low season, helpful.

$ Residencial Sucre, Sucre 1240, T422264, filibertor@terra.com.pe. Private house, kitchen, laundry facilities, hot water, English, German and French spoken, mountaineering guide, Filiberto Rurush, can be contacted here.

🍴 Restaurants

Huaraz *p75, maps p74 and p76*

$$$ Créperie Patrick, Luzuriaga 422. Excellent crepes, fish, quiche, spaghetti and good wine.

$$$ Pizza Bruno, Luzuriaga 834. Open from 1600-2300. Best pizza, excellent crêpes and pastries, good service, French owner Bruno Reviron also has a 4WD with driver for hire.

$$$-$$ Mi Comedia, Av Centenario 351, T587954. Open 1700-2300. Wood-oven pizzas, rustic European style, very good service.

$$$-$$ Trivio, Parque del Periodista. Open for lunch and dinner. Creative food, good coffee, nice view.

$$ Bistro de los Andes, Plaza de Armas 2nd floor, T426249. Great food, owner speaks English, French and German. Plaza branch has a nice view of the plaza. Wide range of dishes including breakfasts.

$$ Chilli Heaven, Parque Ginebra, T396085. Run by a British biker, specializing in spicy food (Mexican, Indian, Thai), book exchange.

$$ El Horno Pizzería Grill, Parque del Periodista, T043-424617. Good atmosphere, fine grilled meats and nice location.

$$ Fuente de Salud, J de la Mar 562. Vegetarian, also meat and pasta dishes, serves good soups and breakfast.

$$ Huaraz Querido, Bolívar 981. Open for lunch only. Very popular place for great *ceviche* and other fish dishes.

$$ Maialino, Parque Ginebra, T940-241660. Popular for Italian and local dishes, cosy, welcoming, set meal for lunch and dinner costs US$2.50.

$$ Papa Loca, Av Raimondi 903, T978-495271, papalocarestaurant on Facebook. Tue-Sun 1700-2300. Varied menu from Peruvian to British and Irish, good quality and value. Recommended.

$$ Pizza B&B, La Mar 674, beside laundry of same name. Excellent traditional sauces for pizza and pasta, and desserts.

$$ Pizzería Landauro, Sucre, on corner of Plaza de Armas. Closed 1200-1800 and Sun. Very good for pizzas, Italian dishes, sandwiches, breakfasts, nice atmosphere.

$$ Rinconcito Minero, J de Morales 757. Breakfast, lunch, vegetarian options, coffee and snacks

$$ Sabor Salud, Luzuriaga 672, upstairs. Pizzeria with vegetarian and Italian food.

$$-$ Chifa Jim Hua, Luzuriaga y Damasco. Large, tasty portions, economical *menú*. Mon-Sat 0900-1500, 1800-2400, Sun 1800-2200.

$$-$ Encuentro, Parque del Periodista and Julian de Morales 650, www.restaurant encuentro.com. Opens 0700. Breakfast, lunch and dinners, very busy, good.

$ Las Puyas, Morales 535. Popular with gringos, good *sopa criolla* and trout, also serves breakfast.

Cafés

Café Andino, Lúcar y Torre 538, 3rd floor, T421203, www.cafeandino.com. Peruvian/American-owned café-restaurant-bar with book exchange and extensive lending library in many languages. A great place to relax and meet other travellers, nice atmosphere, warmly recommended. Owner Chris Benway also runs **La Cima Logistics**, www.lacimalogistics.com, for custom outfitting in Cordilleras Blanca and Huayhuash.

Café El Centro, 28 de Julio 592. Good breakfast for US$1.30-2, great chocolate cake and apple pie.

Cafetería y Juguería, Sucre 806. Cheap café just above the Plaza. Serves excellent yogurt and honey drinks, among other treats.

California Café, 28 de Julio 562, T428354, http://huaylas.com/californiacafe/california.htm. Excellent breakfast, great coffee and chocolate cake, book exchange. Californian owner is a good source of information on trekking in the Cordillera Huayhuash and security issues.

Panadería La Alameda, Juan de La Cruz Romero 523 near market. Excellent bread and sweets.

Panadería Montserrat, Av Luzuriaga 928. Good bakery and café, cheap, pleasant atmosphere, good for a snack.

Rossanero, Luzuriaga entre Sucre y J de Morales, 2nd floor. 'Sofa-cafe' with extensive menu, ice cream, reasonable prices.

🎵 Bars and clubs

Huaraz *p75, maps p74 and p76*
13 Buhos Bar, José de la Mar 2nd floor, above Makondo's. Afternoon, evening, and nightspot, very popular, owner makes

his own craft beer. Good music, games, nice ambience.

Amadeus, Parque Ginebra. Bar-disco.
Taberna Tambo, José de la Mar 776. Open 1000-1600, 2000-early hours. Folk music daily, disco, full on, non-stop dance mecca. Very popular with both locals and gringos.
Vagamundo, J de Morales 753. Popular bar with snacks and football tables.
Xtreme, Luzuriaga 646. Open 1900-0200. Very popular with *gringos*, soft music.

✹ Festivals

Huaraz *p75, maps p74 and p76*
Patron saints' day, El Señor de la Soledad, week starting **3 May**. Semana del Andinismo, in **Jun**, international climbing week. **San Juan** and **San Pedro** throughout the region during the last week of **Jun**. **Aug**, Inkafest mountain film festival, dates change each year.

⊙ Shopping

Huaraz *p75, maps p74 and p76*
Clothing For local sweaters, hats, gloves and wall hangings at good value, Pasaje Mcal Cáceres, off Luzuriaga, in the stalls off Luzuriaga between Morales and Sucre, Bolívar cuadra 6, and elsewhere. **Last Minute Gifts**, Lucar Y Torre 530, 2nd floor, and **Peru Magico**, Sucre ½ block from Plaza, both sell hats, clothing, souvenirs and jewelry.
Markets The central market offers various canned and dry goods, as well as fresh fruit and vegetables. Beware pickpockets in this area. There are also several supermarkets in town (see Huaraz centre map), do not leave valuables in bags you check while shopping.

⏀ What to do

Huaraz *p75, maps p74 and p76*
Try to get a recommendation from someone who has recently returned from a tour or trek, or see **South American Explorers'** recommendations in the Lima office.

All agencies run conventional tours to Llanganuco (US$12 per person, very long day) and Chavín (8-10 hrs, US$14 per person), entry tickets not included. Many hire equipment.

Horse riding
Posada de Yungar, at Yungar (about 20 km on the Carhuaz road), T421267. Swiss-run. Ask for José Flores or Gustavo Soto. US$4.50 per hr on nice horses; good 4-hr trip in the Cordillera Negra.
Sr Robinson Ayala Gride, T423813. Contact him well in advance for half-day trips (enquire at El Cortijo restaurant, on Huaraz-Caraz road, Km 6.5). He is a master paso rider.

Mountain biking
Mountain Bike Adventures, Lúcar y Torre 530, T424259, www.chakinaniperu.com. Contact Julio Olaza. US$60 pp for day trip, all included, various routes, excellent standard of equipment. Julio speaks excellent English and also runs a book exchange, sells topo maps and climbing books.

Trekking and climbing
Trekking tours cost US$50-70 pp per day, climbing US$100-140 pp per day. Many companies close in low season.
Active Peru, Gamarra 699 y Sucre, T423339, www.activeperu.com. Offers classic treks, climbing, plus standard tours to Chavín and Llanganuco, among others, good in all respects, Belgian owner speaks Dutch, German and English.
Alpa-K, Parque Ginebra 30-B, above Montañero, www.alpa-k.org. Owner Bertrand offers tours throughout Peru and has a B&B (**$**) on the premises. French, Spanish and some English spoken.
Andean Footsteps, Carretera Huaraz-Caraz Km 14, Paltay, and Jr José Olaya 103, Huaraz, T943-318820, www.andeanfootsteps.com. British/Peruvian operation (Yvonne Danson and David Maguiña), specializing in treks, climbs and tours with a commitment to using local personnel and resources. Local projects are sponsored.

Andean Kingdom, Parque Ginebra next to Casa de Guías, T425555, www.andean kingdom.com. Free information, maps, climbing wall, rock and ice climbing, including multi-day courses, treks, equipment rental, English and some Hebrew spoken, can be very busy. The company has a Refugio de Montaña, **Hatun Machay ($)**, near the excellent rock-climbing site of Hatun Machay in the Cordillera Negra, with kitchen facilities and heating, transport arranged.
Andescamp, Jr Huáscar 625, T423842, or T943-563424, www.andescamphostel.com. Popular agency and hostel, especially with budget travellers. Only qualified guides used for climbing trips. Variety of treks, mountaineering expeditions and courses, rafting, paragliding and other adventure sports. Hostel has dorms and private rooms, some with bath, and snack bar.
Cordillera Blanca Adventures, run by the Mejía Romero family, Los Nogales 108, T421934, www.cordillerablanca.org. Experienced, quality climbing/trekking trips, good guides/equipment.
Explorandes, Gamarra 835, T421960, www.explorandes.com.
Galaxia Expeditions, Parque del Periodista, T425355, www.galaxia-expeditions.com. Usual range of tours, climbing, hiking, biking, equipment hire, etc. Go to the office to buy tours direct, do not buy from unscrupulous sub-contractors.
Huascarán, Jr Pedro Campos 711, Soledad, T424504, www.huascaran-peru.com. Contact Pablo Tinoco Depaz, one of the brothers who run the company. Good 4-day Santa Cruz trip. Good food and equipment, professional service, free loan of waterproofs and pisco sour on last evening.
Kallpa, José de la Mar y Luzuriaga, p 2, T427868. Organizes treks, rents gear, arranges arrieros and mules, very helpful.
Montañero, Parque Ginebra 30-B, T426386, www.trekkingperu.com. Run by veteran mountain guide Selio Villón, German, French and English spoken.

Monttrek, Luzuriaga 646, upstairs, T421124, monttrek@terra.com.pe. Good trekking/climbing information, advice and maps, ice and rock climbing courses (at Monterrey), tours to Laguna Churup and the 'spectacular' Luna Llena tour; also hire mountain bikes, run ski instruction and trips, and river rafting. Helpful, conscientious guides. Next door in the Pizzería is a climbing wall, good maps, videos and slide shows. For new routes/maps contact Porfirio Cacha Macedo, 'Pocho', at Monttrek or at Jr Corongo 307, T423930.
Peruvian Andes Adventures, José Olaya 532, T421864, www.peruvianandes.com, www.perutrekkingclimbing.com. Run by Hisao and Eli Morales, professional, registered mountain and trekking guides. All equipment and services for treks of 3-15 days, climbing technical and non-technical peaks, or just day walks. Vegetarians catered for.
Quechua Explorer, Sucre 705 of 4, T422886, www.quechuaexplorer.com. Hiking, mountaneering, rock and ice climbing, rafting, biking, cultural and ecological tourism, experienced and friendly guides.
Quechuandes, Av Luzuriaga 522, T943-562339, www.quechuandes.com. Trekking, mountaineering, rock climbing, ice climbing, skiing, mountain biking and other adventure sports, guides speak Spanish, Quechua, English and/or French. Animal welfare taken seriously with weight limits of 40 kg per donkey.
Respons Sustainable Tourism Center, Jr Eulogio del Rio 1364, Soledad, T956-125568, www.respons.org. Sustainable tourism initiatives, community based, with trekking, homestays, tours, volunteering and other responsible travel ideas.

Guides
Aritza Monasterio, through *Casa de Guías*. Speaks English, Spanish and Euskerra.
Augusto Ortega, Jr San Martín 1004, T424888, is the only Peruvian to have climbed Everest.
Casa de Guías, Plaza Ginebra 28-g in Huaraz, T421811. Mon-Sat 0900-1300, 1600-1800. This is the climbers' and hikers'

meeting place. Has a full list of all members of the Asociación de Guías de Montaña del Perú (AGMP) throughout the country. It is useful with information, books, maps, arrangements for guides, *arrieros*, mules, etc. It operates as an agency and sells tours. Notice board, postcards and posters for sale and has a good restaurant (open 0700-1100, 1700-2300).

Christopher Benway, La Cima Logistics, cafeandino@hotmail.com. Makes custom arrangements for climbing and trekking trips.
Filiberto Rurush Paucar, Sucre 1240, T422264 (Lodging Casa Sucre), speaks English, Spanish and Quechua.
Genaro Yanac Olivera, T422825, speaks good English and some German, also a climbing guide.
Hugo Sifuentes Maguiña, Siex (Sifuentes Expeditions), Jr Huaylas 139, T426529, www.siexperu.com. Trekking, rock climbing and less adventurous tours.
Koky Castañeda, T427213, or through **Skyline Adventures**, or **Café Andino**. Speaks English and French, UIAGM Alpine certified.
Max, Misael and Saul Angeles, T456891 or 422205 (Sol Andino agency), speak some English, know Huayhuash well.
Máximo Henostrosa, T426040. Trekking guide with knowledge of the entire region.
Ted Alexander, Skyline Adventures, Pasaje Industrial 137, Cascapampa, Huaraz, T427097, www.skyline-adventures.com. US outward bound instructor, very knowledgeable.
Tjen Verheye, Jr Carlos Valenzuela 911, T422 569, is Belgian and speaks Dutch, French, German, and reasonable English, runs trekking and conventional tours and is knowledgeable about the Chavín culture.
Prices The Dirección de Turismo issues qualified guides and *arrieros* (muleteers) with a photo ID. Note down the name and card number in case you should have any complaints. Prices are currently set at: *arriero*, US$18 per day; donkey or mule, US$8 per day; trekking guides US$40-70

per day (more for foreign guides); climbing guides US$90-200 per day (more for foreign guides), depending on the difficulty of the peak; cooks US$30-40 per day; all subject to change. You are required to provide or pay for food and shelter for all *arrieros*, porters, cooks and guides. Associations of *arrieros*: **Humacchuco-Llanganuco** (for porters and cooks), T943-786497, victorcautivo@ hotmail.com. **Pashpa Arrieros**, T830540. **Musho Arrieros**, T230003/814416. **Collon Arrieros** (for llama trekking), T833417/824146.

Camping gear The following agencies are recommended for hiring gear: **Andean Kingdom, Galaxia Expeditions, Monttrek, Kallpa** and **Montañero**. Also **Skyline, Andean Sport Tours**, Luzuriaga 571, T043-421612, and **MountClimb**, Jr Mcal Cáceres 421, T426060, mountclimb@yahoo.com. Casa de Guías rents equipment and sells dried food. Check all camping and climbing equipment very carefully before taking it. Quality varies and some items may not be available, so it's best to bring your own. All prices are standard, but not cheap, throughout town. All require payment in advance, passport or air ticket as deposit and rarely give any money back if you return gear early. Many trekking agencies sell screw-on camping gas cartridges. White gas (*bencina*) is available from *ferreterías* on Raymondi below Luzuriaga and by Parque Ginebra. Along the most popular routes, campers have complained that campsites are dirty, toilet pits foul and that rubbish is not taken away by groups. Do your share to make things better.

Tour operators
Chavín Tours, José de la Mar, T421578, www.chavintours.com.pe. All local tours, long-standing agency based in Lima.
Pablo Tours, Luzuriaga 501, T421145, www.pablotours.com. For all local tours, also with many years of operation.

⊖ Transport

Huaraz *p75, maps p74 and p76*
Air LC Peru flies twice daily to/from **Lima**, 1 hr.
Bus To/from **Lima**: 7-8 hrs, US$17-30 (Móvil prices). Large selection of ordinary service and luxury coaches throughout the day. Many of the companies have their offices along Av Raymondi and on Jr Lúcar y Torre. Some recommended companies are: **Cavassa**, Jr Lúcar y Torre 446, T425767; **Rodríguez**, J de Morales 650, T429253; **Cruz del Sur**, Bolívar Mz C Lote 12, T728726; **Empresa 14**, Fitzcarrald 216, T421282, terminal at Bolívar 407; **Julio César**, Prol Cajamarca s/n, cuadra 1, T396443; **Móvil**, Av Confraternidad Internacional Oeste 451, T422555; **Oltursa**, Av Raymondi 825, T423717; **Z-Buss**, Av Raymondi, T428327.

Other long-distance buses To **Casma** via the Callán pass and Pariacoto (150 km) 7 hrs, US$12, the lower section of the road is very poor, landslides and closures are common (sit on the left for best views): **Transportes Huandoy**, Fitzcarrald 261, T427507 (terminal at Caraz 820), daily at 0800, 1000 and 1300. **Yungay Express**, Raymondi 930, T424377, 3 a day. They continue to Chimbote, 185 km. To Chimbote via Caraz and the Cañon del Pato (sit on the right for the most exciting views) **Yungay Express**, daily, US$14, 10 hrs. Other companies go to **Chimbote** via Pativilca, 7 hrs (to **Pativilca**, 160 km, 4 hrs). Most continue to **Trujillo**, all buses go at night, 8-9 hrs, US$17-30: **Línea** (Simón Bolívar 450, T726666), **Móvil** and **Empresa 14**, addresses above.

Within the Cordillera Blanca Several buses and frequent minivans run daily, 0500-2000, between Huaraz and **Caraz**,

1¼ hrs, US$2, from the parking area by the bridge on Fitzcarrald, no luggage racks, you might have to pay an extra seat for your bag. To **Chavín**, 110 km, 2 hrs (sit on left side for best views), US$6: **Sandoval/Chavín Express**, Mcal Cáceres 338, 3 a day. Also **Trans Río Mosna**, Mcal Cáceres 265, T426632, 3 a day; buses go on to Huari, 4 hrs, US$7.50.

To **Chacas**, US$7, and **San Luis**, an unforgettable ride via the 4700-m-high Punta Olímpica tunnel, US$8, at 0700 with **Virgen de Guadalupe**, Caraz 607. **Renzo**, Raymondi 821, T425371, runs to Chacas daily (0615, 1400), **Piscobamba** and **Pomabamba** (0630, best, and 1900). **Los Andes**, same office as Yungay Express, T427362, daily 0630 to **Yungay**, US$1, **Lagunas de Llanganuco**, US$7, **Yanama**, US$7, **Piscobamba**, US$8 and **Pomabamba**, US$9, 8 hrs. This route is also served by **La Perla de Alta Mayo**, daily 0630, 8 hrs to Pomabamba, US$9. To **Sihuas**, also Sandoval/Chavín Express, Tue/Fri 0800; **Perú Andino**, 1 a week, 8 hrs, US$11.

Colectivos to **Recuay**, US$0.75, and **Catac**, US$0.85, daily at 0500-2100, from Gridilla, just off Tarapacá (Terminal de Transportistas Zona Sur). To **Chiquián** for the Cordillera Huayhuash (see below). To **Huallanca** (Huánuco), the route now taken is the paved road through Conococha, Chiquián, Aquia to Huansala, then by good dirt road to Laguna Pachacoto and Huallanca to **La Unión** (paving under way). Departs Huaraz twice a day, first at 1300, with **Trans El Rápido**, Bolognesi 216, T422887, US$8. Frequent daily service from Huallanca to **Huánuco**.
Taxi Standard fare in town is about US$1, more at night; radio taxis T421482 or 422512.

Cordillera Blanca

Apart from the range of Andes running along the Chile-Argentina border, the highest mountains in South America lie along the Cordillera Blanca and are perfectly visible from many spots. From Huaraz alone, you can see more than 23 peaks of over 5000 m, of which the most notable is Huascarán (6768 m), the highest mountain in Peru. Although the snowline is receding, the Cordillera Blanca still contains the largest concentration of glaciers found in the world's tropical zone and the turquoise-coloured lakes, which form in the terminal moraines, are the jewels of the Andes. Here also is one of Peru's most important pre-Inca sites, at Chavín de Huantar.

Parque Nacional Huascarán

Established in July 1975, the park includes the entire Cordillera Blanca above 4000 m, with an area of 3400 sq km. It is a UNESCO World Biosphere Reserve and part of the World Heritage Trust. The park's objectives are to protect the flora, fauna, geology, archaeological sites and scenic beauty of the Cordillera. Take all your rubbish away with you when camping. The park charges visitors US$8 for three daytime visits; no camping, no overnight stays. For visits of up to 21-30 days (ie for trekking and climbing trips) a permit costing US$25 (70 soles) must be bought. Fees for visiting the national park are collected in the park office in Huaraz (see below) and at rangers posts at Llanganuco and Huascarán (for the Llanganuco to Santa Cruz trek), at Collón on the way up the Quebrada Ishinca. The **park office** ① *Jr Federico Sal y Rosas 555, by Plazuela Belén, T422086, pnhuascaran@sernanp.gob.pe; Mon-Fri 0830-1300, 1430-1700,* is principally administrative, with no information for visitors.

Regulations state that local guides are mandatory everywhere in the park except designated 'Recreation Zones' (areas accessible by car). Tourists must hire a licensed tour operator for all activities and those operators may only employ licensed guides, cooks, *arrieros* and porters. Fees, regulations and their implementation change frequently, always confirm details in Huaraz.

Trekking and climbing in the Cordillera Blanca

The Cordillera Blanca offers popular backpacking and trekking, with a network of trails used by the local people and some less well-defined mountaineers' routes. Most circuits can be hiked in five days. Although the trails are easily followed, they are rugged with high passes, between 4000 m and 5000 m, so backpackers should be fit and acclimatized to the altitude, and carry all equipment. Essential items are a tent, warm sleeping bag, stove, and protection against wind and rain (the weather is unreliable and you cannot rule out rain and hail storms even in the dry season). Less stamina is required if you hire mules to carry equipment. The season is from May to September, although conditions vary from year to year. The rainy season in Huaraz is December-March.

Advice to climbers The height of the Cordillera Blanca and the Callejón de Huaylas ranges and their location in the tropics create conditions different from the Alps or even the Himalayas. Fierce sun makes the mountain snow porous and glaciers move more rapidly. Deglaciation is rapidly changing the face of the Cordillera. Older maps do not provide a reliable indication of the extent of glaciers and snow fields (according to some studies 15% of the range's glaciers have disappeared since the 1970s), so local experience is important. If the rules prohibiting independent treks or climbs have not been implemented (see above), move in groups of four or more, reporting to the Casa de Guías (see page 81) or the office of the guide before departing, giving the date at which a search should begin, and leaving your embassy's telephone number, with money for the call. International recommendations are for a 300 m per day maximum altitude gain. Be wary of agencies wanting to sell you trips with very fast ascents (but ask around if this is what you want).

It is imperative that all climbers carry adequate insurance (it cannot be purchased locally). Be well prepared before setting out on a climb. Wait or cancel your trip when the weather is bad. Every year climbers are killed through failing to take weather conditions seriously. Climb only when and where you have sufficient experience. Rescue services, while better than in the past, may not be up to international standards. In the event of an emergency try calling the **Casa de Guías**, T427545 or T421811; Edson Ramírez at the national park office, T944-627946 or T943-626627; or the Police, T105. Satellite phones can be rented through the Casa de Guías and there is cell-phone coverage in some (but not all) parts of the Cordillera Blanca.

Note Before heading out on any route, always enquire locally about public safety. The Cordillera Blanca is generally safe, but muggings have taken place on the way to Laguna Churup and to the Mirador Rataquenua above Huaraz; see also above concerning Monterrey. On all treks in this area, respect the locals' property, leave no rubbish behind, do not give sweets or money to children who beg and remember your cooking utensils and tent would be very expensive for a *campesino*, so be sensitive and responsible.

Huaraz to Chavín → *For guides and prices, see Huaraz listings, page 81.*
South of Huaraz is **Olleros** (*Altitude: 3450 m*). The spectacular and relatively easy three- to four-day hike to Chavín, along a pre-Columbian trail, starts from Olleros. Some basic meals and food supplies available. At 38 km via the main road from Huaraz is **Catac** (two basic hotels and a restaurant), where a paved road branches east for Chavín.

A good place to see the impressive Puya Raimondi plants is the Pumapampa valley. A 14-km gravel road from Pachacoto goes to the park entrance (4200 m), where there is a park office. You can spend the night here. Walking up the road from this point, you will see the gigantic plants, whose flower spike, which can reach 12 m in height, takes 100 years to develop. The final flowering (usually in May) is a spectacular sight. Another good spot, and less visited, is the **Queshque Gorge**. Follow the Río Queshque from Catac (see above); it's easy to find.

From Catac to Chavín is a magnificent journey. The road passes Lago Querococha, has good views of the Yanamarey peaks and, at the top of the route, is cut through a huge rock face, entering the Cahuish tunnel at 4516 m. (The tunnel has no light and is single lane; a small stream runs inside. Cyclists must have a strong light so that trucks and buses can see them.) On the other side it descends the Tambillo valley, then the Río Mosna gorge before Chavín.

Chavín de Huantar
ⓘ *Tue-Sun 0900-1600, US$3.50, students half price, Spanish-speaking guides will take groups at an extra charge.*
Chavín de Huantar, a fortress temple, was built about 800 BC. It is the only large structure remaining of the Chavín culture which, in its heyday, is thought to have held influence in a region between Cajamarca and Chiclayo in the north to Ayacucho and Ica in the south. In December 1985, UNESCO designated Chavín a World Heritage Trust Site. The site is in good condition despite the effects of time and nature. The main attractions are the marvellous carved stone heads (*cabezas clavas*) and designs in relief of symbolic

figures and the many tunnels and culverts which form an extensive labyrinth throughout the interior of the pyramidal structure. The carvings are in excellent condition, and the best are now in the Museo Nacional Chavín. The famous Lanzón dagger-shaped stone monolith of 800 BC is found inside one of the temple tunnels. In order to protect the site some areas are closed to visitors. All the galleries open to the public have electric lights. The guard is also a guide and gives excellent explanations of the ruins. The **Museo Nacional Chavín** ① *1 km north of town and 1.6 km from the site, Tue-Sun, 0900-1700, US$3.50*, has a comprehensive collection of items, gathered from several deposits and museums, including the Tello obelisk dating from the earliest period of occupation of Chavín (c 100BC) and many impressive *cabezas clavas*.

In high season, the site is busy with tourists all day through. You will receive an information leaflet in Spanish at the entrance.

The town of Chavín → *Altitude: 3140 m.*
Just north of the ruins, Chavín, painted colonial yellow and white, has a pleasant plaza with palm and pine trees. There are a couple of good, simple hotels and restaurants; local fiesta July 13-20.

Chavín to Pomabamba → *225 km in total, gravel road, parts rough.*
From Chavín one circuit by road back to Huaraz is via Huari, San Luis, Yanama and Yungay (see page 88) but the bus service is infrequent. The road north from Chavín descends into the Mosna river canyon. The scenery is quite different from the other side of the Cordillera Blanca, very dry and hot. After 8 km it reaches **San Marcos**, the town that has been most heavily impacted by the huge **Antamina** gold mine. Hotels may be full with mine workers and public safety is a concern. After 32 km is **Huari**, perched on a hillside at 3150 m, with various simple hotels (**$ Huagancu 2**, Jr Sucre 335, T630434, clean and good value) and restaurants. **Fiesta de Nuestra Señora del Rosario** first two weeks of October, main day 7th.

There is a spectacular **two- to three-day walk** from Huari to Chacas via Laguna Purhuay. Alberto Cafferata of Caraz writes: "The Purhuay area is beautiful. It has splendid campsites, trout, exotic birds and, at its north end, a 'quenual' forest with orchids. This is a microclimate at 3500 m, where the animals, insects and flowers are more like a tropical jungle, fantastic for ecologists and photographers." A day walk to Laguna Purhuay, starting at the village of Acopalca (taxi from Huari to Acopalca US$3.50, to Puruhuay US$14) is a nice alternative for those who don't want to do the longer walk to Chacas. The lake is inside Parque Nacional Huascarán. There is a visitors' centre, food kiosk and boat rides.

In **Chacas**, 10 km south of San Luis on a paved road, is a fine church. The local fiesta (**Virgen de la Asunción**) is on 15 August, with bullfights, a famous *carrera de cintas* and fireworks. There are hostels (**$**), shops, restaurants and a small market. A spectacular paved road and 4700-m-high tunnel through Punta Olímpica, opened in 2013, connects Chacas with Carhuaz in the Callejón de Huaylas.

It is a **three-day hike** from Chacas to Marcará via the Quebradas Juytush and Honda (lots of condors to be seen). The Quebrada Honda is known as the Paraíso de las Cascadas because it contains at least seven waterfalls. From Huari the road climbs to the Huachacocha pass at 4350 m and descends to **San Luis** at 3130 m, 60 km from Huari (**$ Hostal Puñuri**, Ramón Castilla 151, T043-830408, with bath and hot water, a few basic restaurants, shops and a market).

Some 20 km north of San Luis, a road branches left to **Yanama**, 45 km from San Luis, at 3400 m. It has a good comfortable hotel (**Andes Lodge Peru**, T943-847423, www.andeslodgeperu.com, **$$**, full board available, excellent food and services, fabulous views). The village retains many traditional features and is beautifully surrounded by snow-capped peaks. A day's hike to the ruins above the town affords superb views.

A longer circuit to Huaraz can be made by continuing from San Luis 62 km to **Piscobamba**. There are a couple of basic hotels, also a few shops and small restaurants. Beyond Piscobamba by 22 km, is **Pomabamba**, worth a visit for some very hot natural springs (the furthest are the hottest). There are various hotels (**$**) near the plaza and restaurants.

From Pomabamba a dusty road runs up the wooded valley crossing the puna at Palo Seco, 23 km. The road then descends steeply into the desert-like Sihuas valley, passing through the village of Sicsibamba. The valley is crossed half an hour below the small town of **Sihuas**, a major connection point between the Callejón de Conchucos, Callejón de Huaylas, the upper Marañón and the coast. It has a few **$** hotels and places to eat. From Sihuas it is possible to travel, via Huancaspata, Tayabamba, Retamas and Chahual to Huamachuco along a road which is very poor in places and involves crossing the Río Marañón twice. Using this route, it is possible to travel from Cuzco to Quito through the Andes entirely by public transport. This journey is best undertaken in this direction though the road can take over two days (if it's not impassable) in the wet season.

Caraz → *Altitude: 2290 m. Colour map 2, B2.*

This pleasant town is a good centre for walking, parasailing and the access point for many excellent treks and climbs. Tourist facilities are expanding as a more tranquil alternative to Huaraz, and there are great views of Huandoy, Huascarán and surrounding summits in July and August. In other months, the mountains are often shrouded in cloud. Caraz has a milder climate than Huaraz and is more suited to day trips. The ruins of **Tumshukaiko** are 1.5 km from the Plaza de Armas in the suburb of Cruz Viva, to the north before the turn-off for Parón. There are seven platforms from the Huaraz culture, dating from around 2000-1800 BC, but the site is in poor shape. The **Museo Arqueológico Municipal** is on San Martín, half a block up from the plaza. The **tourist office**, at Plaza de Armas, next to the municipality, T391029 ext 143, has limited information. There are three ATMs in the centre. On 20 January is the fiesta **Virgen de Chiquinquirá**. In the last week of July is **Semana Turística**.

Treks from Caraz

A good day walk goes from Caraz by the lakes of Miramar and Pampacocha to Huaripampa, where you can get a pickup back to Caraz. A longer full-day walk with excellent views of Huandoy and Huascarán follows the foothills of the Cordillera Blanca east of the main Río Santa valley, from Caraz south through the villages of Chosica and Ticrapa. It ends at Puente Ancash on the Caraz–Yungay road, from where frequent transport goes back to Caraz.

A large stand of **Puya Raimondi** can be seen in the Cordillera Negra southwest of Caraz. Beyond Pueblo Libre is a paved road which heads west via Pamparomás and Moro to join the Panamerican highway south of Chimbote. After 45 km (1½ hours) are the Puya Raymondi plants at a place called **Winchos**, with views of 145 km of the Cordillera Blanca and to the Pacific. The plants are usually in flower May or October. Take warm clothing, food and water. You can also camp near the puyas and return the following day. The most popular way to get there is to rent a bike (US$18 per day), go up by public transport (see below), and ride back down in four or five hours. Or form a group (eg via the bulletin board at **Pony's Expeditions**, Caraz) and hire a car which will wait for you (US$60 for five). From Caraz, a minibus for Pamparomás leaves from Ramón Castilla y Jorge Chávez around 0830, two hours, US$3 (get there at about 0800 as they often leave early). From the pass (El Paso) or El Cruce it is a short walk to the plants. Return transport leaves between 1230 and 1300. If you miss the bus, you can walk back to Pueblo Libre in four hours, to Caraz in six to eight hours, but it is easy to get lost and there are not many people to ask directions along the way.

Laguna Parón ① *US$3.50*. From Caraz a narrow, rough road goes east 32 km to beautiful Laguna Parón, in a cirque surrounded by several, massive snow-capped peaks, including Huandoy, Pirámide Garcilazo and Caraz. The gorge leading to it is spectacular. It is a long day's trek for acclimatized hikers (25 km) up to the lake at 4150 m, or a four- to five-hour walk from the village of Parón, which can be reached by combi (U$2.50). Camping is possible. There is no trail around the lake and you should not attempt it as it is slippery and dangerous, particularly on the southern shore; tourists have been killed here.

Santa Cruz Valley One of the best known treks in the area is the beautiful three- to five-day route from Vaquería, over the 4750 m Punta Unión pass, to Quebrada Santa Cruz and the village of Cashapampa. It can be hiked in either direction. Starting in Cashpampa, you climb more gradually to the pass, then down to Vaquería or the Llanganuco lakes beyond. Along this 'clockwise' route the climb is gentler, giving more time to acclimatize, and the pass is easier to find, although on the other hand, if you start in Vaquería and finish in Cashapampa you ascend for one day rather than three in the other direction. You can hire an *arriero* and mule in Cashapampa. Campsites are at Llamacorral and Taullipampa before Punta Unión, and Quenoapampa (or Huaripampa) after the pass. You can end the hike at Vaquería on the Yanama–Yungay road and take a minibus or, better, an open truck from there (a beautiful run). Or end the walk a day later with a night at the Yuraccorral campsite, at the Llanganuco lakes, from where cars go back to Yungay. This trek is very popular and offered by all tour agencies in Huaraz and Caraz.

Yungay → *Colour map 2, B2.*

The main road goes on 12 km south of Caraz to Yungay which was completely buried during the 1970 earthquake by a massive mudslide; a hideous tragedy in which 20,000 people lost their lives. The earthquake and its aftermath are remembered by many older residents of the Callejón de Huaylas. The original site of Yungay, known as Yungay Viejo, desolate and haunting, has been consecrated as a *camposanto* (cemetery). The new settlement is on a hillside just north of the old town. It has a pleasant plaza and a concrete market, good on Wednesday and Sunday. October 17 is the **Virgen del Rosario** fiesta and October 28 is the anniversary of the founding of the town. The tourist office is on the corner of the Plaza de Armas.

Lagunas de Llanganuco

The Lagunas de Llanganuco are two lakes nestling 1000 m below the snowline beneath Huascarán and Huandoy. The first you come to is Laguna Chinancocha (3850 m), the second Laguna Orconcocha (3863 m). The park office is situated below the lakes at 3200 m, 19 km from Yungay. Accommodation is provided for trekkers who want to start the Llanganuco-Santa Cruz trek from here. From the park office to the lakes takes about five hours (a steep climb). For the last 1½ hours, a nature trail, Sendero María Josefa (sign on the road), takes 1½ hours to walk to the western end of Chinancocha where there is a control post, descriptive trail and boat trips on the lake. Walk along the road beside the lake to its far end for peace and quiet among the quenual trees, which provide shelter for 75% of the birdlife found in the park. .

Carhuaz → *Colour map 2, B2.*

After Yungay, the main road goes to **Mancos** (8 km south, 30 minutes) at the foot of Huascarán. There is a dormitory at **La Casita de mi Abuela**, some basic shops and restaurants. From Mancos it is 14 km to Carhuaz, a friendly, quiet mountain town with a pleasant plaza. There is very good walking in the neighbourhood (eg to thermal baths; up the Ulta valley). Market days are Wednesday and Sunday (the latter is much larger). The local fiesta of **Virgen de las Mercedes**, 14-24 September, is rated as among the best in the region.

⊛ Cordillera Blanca listings

For hotel and restaurant price codes, and other relevant information, see pages 14-17.

⊜ Where to stay

Chavín *p86*
$$-$ La Casona, Wiracocha 130, Plaza de Armas, T454116, www.lacasonachavin. com.pe. In a renovated house with attractive courtyard, single, double and triple rooms, some with balcony overlooking Plaza or courtyard, nice breakfast, laundry, parking.
$$-$ R'ikay, on 17 de Enero 172N, T454068. Set around 2 patios, modern, best in town, variety of room sizes, hot water, restaurant does Italian food in the evening. Recommended.
$ Hostal Chavín, Jr San Martín 141-151, half a block from the plaza, T454055. Pleasant courtyard, hot water, will provide breakfast for groups, best of the more basic hotels but beds are poor.
$ Inca, Wiracocha 170, T754021, www.huaraz.com/hotelinca. Rooms are cheaper without bath, good beds, hot water on request, nice garden.

Caraz *p87*
$$$-$$ Los Pinos Lodge, Parque San Martín 103 (also known as Plazuela de la Merced), T391130, www.lospinoslodge.pe. Nice comfortable rooms, patio, gardens, parking, cosy bar, tourist information. Recommended. Also have a nearby annex nearby called **Caraz Backpacker ($)**.
$$$-$$ O'Pal Inn, Km 265.5, 5 mins south of Caraz, T391015, www.opalsierraresort. com. Scenic, family bungalows, suites and

rooms, swimming pool, includes breakfast, restaurant, games room.
$$-$ La Alameda, Av Noé Bazán Peralta 262, T391177, www.hotellaalameda.com. Comfortable rooms, hot water, ample parking, pleasant gardens.
$ Caraz Dulzura, Sáenz Peña 212, about 12 blocks from the city centre, T392090, www.hostalcarazdulzura.com. Modern building in an old street, hot water, comfortable, airy rooms, restaurant and bar.
$ Chavín, San Martín 1135 just off the plaza, T391171. Get a room overlooking the street, many others have no window. Warm water, breakfast extra, guiding service, tourist info.
$ Hostal La Casona, Raymondi 319, 1 block east from the plaza, T391334. With or without bath, hot water, lovely little patio, noisy at night.
$ La Perla de los Andes, Daniel Villar 179, Plaza de Armas, next to the cathedral, T392007, http://huaraz.com/perladelos andes. Comfortable rooms, hot water, helpful, average restaurant.
$ San Marco, San Martín 1133, T391558. Comfortable rooms with private or shared bath, hot water, patio.

Yungay *p88*
$ Complejo Turístico Yungay (COMTURY), Prolongación 2 de Mayo 1012, 2.5 km south of the new town, 700 m east of main road in Aura, the only neighbourhood of old Yungay that survived, T788656. Nice bungalows, pleasant country setting, hot water, fireplace, restaurant with regional specialities, camping possible.

$ Hostal Gledel, Av Arias Graziani, north past plaza, T793048, www.huaraz.com/gledel. Owned by Sra Gamboa, who is hospitable and a good cook, shared bath, hottish water, no towels or soap, cheap meals prepared on request, nice courtyard.

$ Hostal Sol de Oro, Santo Domingo 7, T493116, www.huaraz.com/soldeoro. Most rooms with bath, hot water, comfortable, breakfast and dinner on request, good value, best in town.

Lagunas de Llanganuco *p88*

$$$$-$ Llanganuco Mountain Lodge, Lago Keushu, Llanganuco Valley, close to Huascarán park entrance (booking office in Huaraz: Gamarra 699), T943-669580, www.llanganucomountainlodge.com. 2 luxury rooms, 2 standard rooms and 10-bed dormitory. Room rate is seasonal and full board with a packed lunch, dorm beds can be with or without meals, modern, camping area, excellent food in restaurant, helpful staff, fine views and limitless possibilities for trekking (equipment rental and logistics), British-owned.

Carhuaz *p89*

$$ pp Casa de Pocha, 1.5 km out of town towards Hualcán, at foot of Nevado Hualcán, ask directions in town, T943-613058 (mob 1800-2000), www.socialwellbeing.org/lacasadepocha.htm. Including breakfast and dinner, country setting, entirely solar and wind energy powered, hot water, sauna and pool, home-produced food (vegetarian available), horses for hire, camping possible, many languages spoken. Book in advance.

$$ El Abuelo, Jr 9 de Diciembre 257, T394456, www.elabuelohostal.com. Modern, comfortable 3-star, laundry, restaurant, large garden with organic fruit and veg, parking, credit cards accepted. Knowledgeable owner is map-maker, Felipe Díaz.

$ Hostal Señor de Luren, Buin 549, 30 m from Plaza de Armas, T668806. Hot water, safe motorcycle parking, very hospitable.

$ 4 family-run *hospedajes* operate as part of

a community development project. All have private bath and hot water. The better 2 are: **Hospedaje Robri**, Jr Comercio 935, T394505. Modern. **Alojamiento Las Torresitas**, Jr Amazonas 603, T394213.

🍴 Restaurants

Chavín *p86*

$$-$ Chavín Turístico, middle of 17 de Enero. The best in town, good *menú* and à la carte, delicious apple pie, nice courtyard, popular. Also run a hostal nearby.

$$-$ La Portada, towards south end of 17 de Enero. In an old house with tables set around a pleasant garden.

$ La Ramada, towards north end of main street, 17 de Enero. Regional dishes, also trout and set lunch.

Caraz *p87*

$$ Venezia, Av Noé Bazán Peralta 231, T784813. Good home-made pasta, Italian owner.

$$-$ Entre Panes, Daniel Villar 211, half a block from the plaza. Closed Tue. Variety of excellent sandwiches, also meals. Good food, service and atmosphere.

$$-$ La Punta Grande, D Villar 595, 10 mins' walk from centre. Closes 1700. Best place for local dishes.

$$-$ La Terraza, Jr Sucre 1107, T301226. Good *menú* as well as pizza, pasta, juices, home-made ice cream, sandwiches, sweets, coffee and drinks.

$ Jeny, Daniel Villar on the plaza next to the Cathedral. Local fare at reasonable prices, ample variety.

Cafés

Café de Rat, Sucre 1266, above *Pony's Expeditions*. Breakfast, vegetarian dishes, good pizzas, drinks and snacks, darts, travel books, nice atmosphere.

El Turista, San Martín 1117. Open in morning and evening only. Small, popular for breakfast, ham omelettes and ham sandwiches are specialities.

Heladería Caraz Dulzura, D Villar on the plaza. Home-made ice cream.
Panificadora La Alameda, D Villar y San Martín. Good bread and pastries, ice cream, popular with locals. The excellent *manjar blanco* for which the town earned it's nickname 'Caraz dulzura' is sold here and at several other shops on the same street.

Yungay *p88*
$$ Alpamayo, Av Arias Graziani s/n. At north entrance to town, good for local dishes, lunchtime only.
$ Café Pilar, on the main plaza. Good for juices, cakes and snacks.

Carhuaz *p89*
$$ La Bicharra, just north of Carhuaz on main road, T943-780893 (mob). Innovative North African/Peruvian cooking, lunch only, busy at weekends, call ahead to check if they are open on weekdays.

🍷 Bars and clubs

Caraz *p87*
Airu Resto Bar, at Los Pinos Lodge, Parque San Martín. Open 1800-2200. Serves wines and piscos.

⭘ Shopping

Caraz *p87*
Camping supplies Fresh food in the market. Some dried camping food is available from **Pony's Expeditions**, who also sell camping gaz canisters and white gas.

⏣ What to do

Caraz *p87*
Agencies in Caraz arrange treks in the Cordillera Huayhuash, as well as more local destinations.
Apu-Aventura, Parque San Martín 103, 5 blocks west of plaza, T391130, www.apu aventura.pe. Range of adventure sports and equipment rental.

Pony's Expeditions, Sucre 1266, near the Plaza de Armas, T391642, www.pony expeditions.com. Mon-Sat 0800-2200. English, French, Italian and Quechua spoken. Owners Alberto and Aidé Cafferata are knowledgeable about treks and climbs. They arrange local tours, offer accommodation at **Pony's Lodge ($$)** and **Backpacker Los Ponys ($)**, trekking, transport for day excursions, and rental of a 4WD vehicle with driver (US$125 per day plus fuel). Also maps and books for sale, equipment hire and mountain bike rental (US$18 for a full day). Well organized and reliable. Highly recommended.

⊖ Transport

Chavín *p86*
Bus It is much easier to get to Chavín (even walking!) than to leave the place by bus. All buses to **Huaraz** originate in Huari or beyond. They pass through Chavín at irregular hours and may not have seats available. Buying a ticket at an agency in Chavín does not guarantee you will get a seat or even a bus. For buses from **Huaraz**, see under Huaraz. Sandoval/Chavín Express goes through around 1200, 1600 and 1700 daily, **Río Mosna** at 0430 and then 4 between 1600-2200. Bus to Huaraz takes 2 hrs. To **Lima**, 438 km, 12 hrs, US$14, with Trans El Solitario and Perú Andino daily. Locals prefer to travel to Huaraz and then take one of the better companies from there.

To other destinations in the Callejón de Conchucos, either use buses coming from Huaraz or Lima, or hop on and off combis which run between each town. To **San Marcos**, 8 km, and **Huari**, 38 km, take one of the cars or combis which leave regularly from the main plaza in Chavín, every 20 mins and 30 mins respectively. There are buses during the day from Lima and Huaraz which go on to **Huari**, with some going on to **San Luis**, a further 61 km, 3 hrs; **Piscobamba**, a further 62 km, 3 hrs; and **Pomabamba**, a further 22 km, 1 hr; such as El Solitario which passes through Chavín at 1800.

Chavín to Pomabamba p86
Huari
Bus Terminal Terrestre at Av Circunvalación Baja. To **Huaraz**, 4 hrs, US$5.50, **Sandoval/Chavín Express** 3 a day. Also runs to **San Luis** and **Lima**.

Yanama
Bus Daily between **Yungay** and Yanama over the 4767-m Portachuelo de Llanganuco (3 hrs, US$7.50), continuing to Pomabamba.

Pomabamba
To **Piscobamba**, combis depart hourly, 1 hr, US$1.50. There are no combis from Piscobamba to San Luis. To **Lima**, 18 hrs, US$15, via San Luis (4 hrs, US$5), Huari (6 hrs, US$7.50) and Chavín (9 hrs, US$9) with El Solitario Sun, Mon and Thu at 0800; via **Yungay** and **Huaraz** with La Perla del Alto Mayo, Wed, Thu, Sat, Sun, 16 hrs.

Sihuas
Bus To **Pomabamba**, combi from Av 28 de Julio near the market at 1100, 4 hrs, US$7 (returns 0200). To **Huaraz**, via Huallanca, with Cielo Azul, daily at 0830, 10 hrs, US$11. To **Tayabamba**, for the Marañón route north to Huamachuco and Cajamarca: Andía passes through from Lima on Sat and Sun at 0100, La Perla del Alta Mayo passes through Tue, Thu 0000-0200; also Garrincha Wed, Sun around 0800; all 8 hrs, US$11, the beginning of a long wild ride. To **Huacrachuco**, Andía, passes through Wed, Sat 0100. To **Chimbote**, Corvival on Wed, Thu and Sun morning, 9 hrs, US$9; La Perla del Alta Mayo Tue, Thu, Sun. To **Lima** (19 hrs, US$20) via Chimbote, Andía Tue, Sun 0200, Wed, Sat 1600; and 3 other companies once or twice a week each.

Caraz p87
Bus From Caraz to **Lima**, 470 km, 9 companies, daily, US$11-30 (El Huaralino, T996-896607, Huaraz Buss, T943-469736, Zbuss, T391050, Cooperativa Ancash, T391126, all on Jr Cordova; Rochaz, Pasaje

Olaya, T794375, Cavassa, Carretera Central, T392042, Yungay Express, Av Luzuriaga, T391492, Móviltours, east end of town, www.moviltours.com.pe, Rodríguez, Daniel Villar, T635631), 10-11 hrs. All go via Huaraz and Pativilca. To **Chimbote**, Yungay Express, via Huallanca, Casma and Cañon del Pato, 3 daily, US$9, 7 hrs. Sit on right for best views. To **Trujillo**, via Casma with Móviltours. To **Huaraz**, combis leave 0400-2000, 1¼ hrs, US$2, no luggage racks, you might have to pay an extra seat for your bag. They leave from a terminal on the way out of town, where the south end of C Sucre meets the highway. To **Yungay**, 12 km, 15 mins, US$0.70. To **Huallanca** and **Yuramarca** (for the Cañon del Pato), combis and cars leave from Córdova y La Mar, 0700-1600, US$2.50.

Treks from Caraz p88
Laguna Parón
To the village of **Parón**, *colectivos* from Ramón Castilla y Jorge Chávez, close to the market, 1 hr, US$1.50. Taxi from Caraz to the lake, US$40-45 for 4 passengers. Pony's Expeditions who make daily departures to Laguna Parón at 0800, US$60 for 4, including 1-hr visit to the lake and 1-hr walk. Also, you can hire a bike (US$18 per day), take a car up and ride back down.

Santa Cruz Valley
To **Cashapampa** (Quebrada Santa Cruz) colectivo/minbus from Ramón Castilla y Jorge Chávez, Caraz, leave when full from 0600 to 1530, 1½ hrs, US$2. Yanama to Yungay combis can be caught at Vaquería between 0800-1400, US$4, 2 hrs.

Yungay p88
Buses and colectivos run all day to **Caraz**, 12 km, US$0.50, and **Huaraz**, 54 km, 1½ hrs, US$1. To lakes **Llanganuco**, combis leave when full, especially 0700-0900, from Av 28 de Julio 1 block from the plaza, 1 hr, US$2.50. To **Yanama**, via the Portachuelo de Llanganuco Pass, 4767m, 58 km, 3½ hrs,

US$5; stopping at María Huayta (for the Llanganuco–Santa Cruz trek), after 2 hrs, US$3. To **Pomabamba**, via Piscobamba, Trans Los Andes, daily at 0700-0730, the only company with a ticket office in Yungay; **Transvir** and **La Perla de Alta Mayo** buses coming from Huaraz, 0730, stop if they have room, 6-7 hrs, US$6. After passing the Llanganuco lakes and crossing the Portachuelo the buses descend to Puente Llacma, where it is possible to pick up buses and combis heading south to San Luis, Chacas and Huari.

Carhuaz *p89*

All transport leaves from the main plaza. To **Huaraz**, colectivos and buses leave 0500-2000, US$1, 40 mins. To **Caraz**, 0500-2000, US$1, 1 hr. Buses from Huaraz to **Chacas** in the Cordillera Blanca, 87 km, 4 hrs, US$5.75, pass through Carhuaz about 40 mins after leaving Huaraz. The road works its way up the Ulta valley to the pass at Punta Olímpica from where there are excellent views. The dirt road is not in good condition due to landslides (can be closed in the wet season). **Renzo** daily buses pass through en route to **San Luis** (see page 86), a further 10 km, 1½ hrs.

Cordillera Huayhuash

The Cordillera Huayhuash, lying south of the Cordillera Blanca, has azure trout-filled lakes interwoven with deep *quebradas* and high pastures around the hem of the range and is perhaps the most spectacular cordillera for its massive ice faces that seem to rise sheer out of the Puna's contrasting green. You may see tropical parakeets in the bottom of the gorges and condors circling the peaks. The complete circuit is very tough; allow 10-12 days. Fees are charged by every community along the way, adding up to about US$80 for the entire circuit. Take soles in small denominations and insist on getting a receipt every time. The trail head is at **Cuartel Huain**, between Matacancha and the **Punta Cacanan** pass (the continental divide at 4700 m). There are up to eight high passes over 4600 m, depending on the route. A half-circuit is also possible, but there are many other options. Both ranges are approached from Chiquián in the north, **Oyón**, with links to Cerro de Pasco to the southeast, **Churín** in the south or Cajatambo to the southwest. The area offers fantastic scenery and insights into rural life.

Chiquián is a town of narrow streets and overhanging eaves. **Semana Turística**: first week of July. Buy all your food and supplies in Huaraz as there are only basic supplies in Chiquián and almost nothing in the hamlets along the route. **Mule hire** It may take a day to bring the mules to your starting point from Llamac or Pocpa where they are kept. (Very basic supplies only can be bought in either village.) Ask for mules (US$6 per day) or horses (US$7 per day) at the hotels or restaurants in Chiquián. A guide for the Huayhuash is Sr Delao Callupe, ask for him in Chiquián.

Cajatambo is the southern approach to the Cordillera Huayhuash, a small market town with a beautiful 18th-century church and a lovely plaza. There are various hotels (**$**) and some good restaurants around the plaza. Note that the road out of Cajatambo is not for the fainthearted. For the first three to four hours it is no more than a bus-width, clinging to the cliff edge.

For hotel and restaurant price codes, and other relevant information, see pages 14-17.

⊜ Where to stay

Cordillera Huayhuash *p93*
$ Hostal San Miguel, Jr Comercio 233, Chiquián, T447001. Nice courtyard and garden, clean, many rooms, popular.
$ Hotel Huayhuash, 28 de Julio 400, Chiquián, T447049. Private bathroom, hot water, restaurant, laundry, parking, modern, great views, information and tours.
$ Los Nogales de Chiquián, Jr Comercio 1301, T447121, http://hotelnogaleschiquian. blogspot.com. Traditional design, with private or shared bath, hot water, cafeteria, parking. Recommended.

❼ Restaurants

Cordillera Huayhuash *p93*
$ El Refugio de Bolognesi and **Yerupajá**, on Tarapacá, both offer basic set meals.
$ Panificadora Santa Rosa, Comercio 900, on the plaza, Chiquián, for good bread and sweets, has coin-operated phones and fax.

⊖ Transport

Cordillera Huayhuash *p93*
Coming from Huaraz, the road is now paved beyond Chiquián to Huansala, on the road to Huallanca (Huánuco). 2 bus companies run from **Huaraz to Chiquián**, 120 km, 3½ hrs: El Rápido, at Bolognesi 216, T422887, at 1345, and Chiquián Tours, on Tarapacá behind the market. From Chiquián to Huaraz: buses leave the plaza at 0500 daily, US$1.75, except El Rápido, Jr Figueredo 216, T447049, at 0500 and 1330, US$3.65. Also colectivo Chiquián-Huaraz 1500, 3 hrs, US$2.45 pp. There is also a connection from **Chiquián to Huallanca** (Huánuco) with buses from Lima in the early morning and combis during the day, which leave when full, 3 hrs, US$2.50. From Huallanca there are regular combis on to La Unión, 1 hr, US$0.75, and from there transport to Huánuco. From Cajatambo buses depart for **Lima** at 0600, US$9, daily with Empresa Andina (office on plaza next to Hostal Cajatambo), **Tour Bello**, 1 block off the Plaza, and Turismo Cajatambo, Jr Grau 120 (in Lima, Av Carlos Zavala 124 corner of Miguel Aljovin 449, T426 7238).

North coast

The north of Peru has been described as the Egypt of South America, as it is home to many ruined pre-Inca treasures. Many tourists pass through without stopping on their way to or from Ecuador, missing out on one of the most fascinating parts of the country. Along a seemingly endless stretch of desert coast lie many of the country's most important pre-Inca sites: Chan-Chán, the Moche pyramids, Túcume, Sipán, Batán Grande and El Brujo. The main city is Trujillo, while Chiclayo is more down to earth, with one of the country's largest witchdoctors' market. The coast is also famous for its deep-sea fishing, surfing, and the unique reed fishing boats at Huanchaco and Pimentel. Inland lies colonial Cajamarca, scene of Atahualpa's last stand. Further east, where the Andes meet the jungle, countless unexplored ancient ruins await the more adventurous traveller.

North of Lima

The Pan-American Highway is four-lane (several tolls, about US$2.65) to Km 101, by **Huacho**, which is by-passed, 19 km east of **Puerto Huacho** (several hotels in Huacho, and good restaurants, eg **Cevichería El Clásico**, Calle Inca s/n, open 1000-1800; **La Estrella**, Avenida 28 de Julio 561). The beaches south of the town are clean and deserted.

Caral and Paramonga → *Phone code: 01.*
A few kilometres before Barranca (by-passed by the Highway) a turning to the right (east) at Km 184 leads to **Caral** ① *0900-1700; entry US$4, all visitors must be accompanied by an official guide, US$7 per group, in the car park is the ticket office, toilets, handicrafts stalls; for details, Proyecto Especial Caral, Av Las Lomas de la Molina 327, Urb Las Lomas, Lima 12, T205 2500, www.caralperu.gob.pe, UNESCO World Heritage Site.* This ancient city, 26 km from the coast, dates from about 2600 BC. Many of the accepted theories of Peruvian archaeology have been overturned by Caral's age and monumental construction. It appears to be easily the oldest city in South America. The dry, desert site lies on the southern fringes of the Supe valley, along whose flanks there are more ruins, 19 out of 32 of which have been explored. Caral covers 66 ha and contains eight significant pyramidal structures. To date seven have been excavated by archaeologists from the University of San Marcos, Lima. They are undertaking careful restoration on the existing foundations to re-establish the pyramidal tiers. It is possible to walk around the pyramids. A viewpoint provides a panorama across the whole site. The site is well organized, criss-crossed by marked paths which must be adhered to. Allow at least two hours for your visit. You can stay or camp at the **Casa del Arqueólogo**.

Some 4 km beyond the turn-off to Huaraz at Pativilca, beside the Panamericana, are the well preserved ruins of the **Chimú temple of Paramonga** ① *US$1.80; caretaker may act as guide.* Set on high ground with a view of the ocean, the fortress-like mound is reinforced by eight quadrangular walls rising in tiers to the top of the hill. Between Pativilca and Chimbote the mountains come down to the sea. The road passes by a few very small protected harbours in tiny rock-encircled bays, such as **Huarmey**, with a fine beach and **($)** **Jaime Crazy** ① *Manuel Scorza 371 y 373, Sector B-8, Huarmey, T043-400104, www.jaimecrazyperu.com*, a hostel offering trips to beaches, archaeological sites, farming communities, volunteering and all sorts of activities.

Casma and Sechín → *Phone code: 043. Colour map 2, B2. Population: 22,600.*
Casma has a pleasant Plaza de Armas, several parks and two markets including a good food market. It is a base from where to explore **Sechín** ① *daily 0800-1800, photography best around midday, US$1.80 (children and students half price); ticket also valid for the Max Uhle Museum by the ruins and Pañamarca*, an archaeological site in the Nepeña Valley, north of Casma. Frequent colectivos leave from in front of the market in Casma, US$0.50 per person, or motorcycle taxi US$1, one of the most important ruins 5 km away on the Peruvian coast. It consists of a large square temple completely faced with about 500 carved stone monoliths narrating, it is thought, a gruesome battle in graphic detail. The style is unique in Peru for its naturalistic vigour. The complex as a whole is associated with the pre-Chavín Sechín culture, dating from about 1600 BC. Three sides of the large stone temple have been excavated and restored, but you cannot see the earlier adobe buildings inside the stone walls because they were covered up and used as a base for a second storey, which has been completely destroyed.

Chimbote → *Phone code: 043. Colour map 2, B2. Population: 296,600.*
The port of Chimbote serves the national fishing industry and the smell of the fishmeal plants is overpowering. As well as being unpleasant it is also unsafe. Take extensive

precautions, always use taxis from the bus station to your hotel and don't venture far.
Note The main street, Avenida Víctor Raul Haya de la Torre, is also known by its old name, José Pardo. At weekends boat trips go around the bay to visit the cliffs and islands to see the birdlife and rock formations.

Chimbote to Callejón de Huaylas

Just north of Chimbote, a road branches northeast off the Pan-American Highway and goes up the Santa valley following the route of the old Santa Corporation Railway which used to run as far as **Huallanca** (Ancash – not to be confused with the town southeast of Huaraz), 140 km up the valley. At Chuquicara, three hours from Chimbote (paved – very rough thereafter), is Restaurante Rosales, a good place to stop for a meal (you can sleep here, too, but it's very basic). At Huallanca there are also places to stay and eat. Fuel is available. At the top of the valley by the hydroelectric centre, the road goes through the very narrow and spectacular **Cañon del Pato**. You pass under tremendous walls of bare rock and through almost 40 tunnels, but the flow of the river has been greatly reduced by the hydroelectric scheme. After this point the road is paved to the Callejón de Huaylas and south to Caraz and Huaraz.

An alternative road for cyclists (and vehicles with a permit) is the 50-km private road known as the 'Brasileños', used by the Brazilian company Odebrecht which has built a water channel for the Chavimochic irrigation scheme from the Río Santa to the coast. The turn-off is 35 km north of the Santa turning, 15 km south of the bridge in Chao, on the Pan-American Highway at Km 482. It is a good all-weather road via Tanguche. Permits are obtainable from the Chavimochic HQ at San José de Virú, US$7.50, or from the guard at the gate on Sunday.

◉ North of Lima listings

For hotel and restaurant price codes, and other relevant information, see pages 14-17.

⦿ Where to stay

Casma and Sechín *p95*
$$ El Dorado Inn, Av Garcilazo de la Vega Mz J, Lt 37, T411795. 1 block from the Panamericana. With fan, pool, restaurant and tourist information.
$$ Hostal El Farol, Túpac Amaru 450, T411064, www.elfarolinn.com. Very nice, rooms and suites, hot water, swimming pool, pleasant garden, good restaurant, parking, information.
$ Gregori, Luis Ormeño 530, T711073. Rooms with or without bath, café downstairs.
$ Las Dunas, Luis Ormeño 505, T711057. An upgraded and enlarged family home, welcoming.

Chimbote *p95*
Plenty of hotels, so try to negotiate a lower rate.
$$ Cantón, Bolognesi 498, T344388. Modern, higher quality than others, has a good but pricey chifa restaurant.
$$ Ivansino Inn, Av José Pardo 738, T321811, www.ivansinoinn.com. Includes breakfast, comfortable, modern.
$ Hostal El Ensueño, Sáenz Peña 268, 2 blocks from Plaza Central, T328662. Cheaper rooms without bath, very good, safe, welcoming.
$ Hostal Karol Inn, Manuel Ruiz 277, T321216. Hot water, good, family-run, laundry, cafetería.
$ Residencial El Parque, E Palacios 309, on plaza, T345572. Converted old home, hot water, nice, secure.

🍴 Restaurants

Casma and Sechín *p95*
Cheap restaurants on Huarmey. The local
ice cream, *Caribe*, is available at Ormeño 545.
$ Tío Sam, Huarmey 138. Specializes
in fresh fish, wins awards for its *ceviche*.
Recommended.
$ Venecia, Huarmey 204.
Local dishes, popular.

⏰ What to do

Casma and Sechín *p95*
Sechín Tours, in Hostal Monte Carlo, Casma,
T411421. Organizes tours in the local area.
The guide, Renato, only speaks Spanish but
has knowledge of local ruins and can be
contacted at renatotours@yahoo.com.

⊖ Transport

North of Lima *p94*
Bus AméricaMóvil (Av Luna Pizarro 251,
La Victoria, T01-423 6338; in Huacho T01-
232 7631) and Zeta (Av Abancay 900,
T01-426 8087; in Huacho T01-239 6176)
run every 20-30 mins Lima–Huacho,
from 0600 to 2000, 2½ hrs, US$6 (more
expensive at weekends).

Caral and Paramonga *p95*
Bus To **Barranca** stops opposite the service
station (*el grifo*) at the end of town. From
Lima to Barranca, 3½ hrs, US$7.50. As bus
companies have their offices in Barranca,
buses will stop there rather than at Pativilca
or Paramonga. Bus from Barranca to **Casma**
155 km, several daily, 2½ hrs, US$6. From
Barranca to **Huaraz**, take a minibus from
C Lima to the gas station in Pativilca where
you can catch a bus, colectivo or truck on
the good, paved road to Huaraz.

To **Caral**, Empresa Valle Sagrado Caral
leave from terminal at Berenice Dávila,
cuadra 2, Barranca, US$2.75 shared, or US$35
private service with 1½ hrs at the site. Taxi
to the ruins US$10 one way. The ruins are

25 km along a road which runs up the Supe
valley from Km 184 of the Panamericana
(signed). Between Kms 18 and 19 of this
road a track leads across the valley to the
ruins, though the river may be impassable
Dec-Mar, 30 mins. Tours from Lima usually
allow 1½ hrs at Caral, with a 3-hr journey
each way, stopping for morning coffee and
for lunch in Huacho on the return.

Buses run only to Paramonga port (3 km
off the Highway, 4 km from the Paramonga
ruins, about 15 mins from Barranca).
Taxi From Paramonga to the ruins
and return after waiting, US$9, otherwise
take a Barranca–Paramonga port bus, then
a 3 km walk.

Casma and Sechín *p95*
Bus Half hourly from **Lima** to **Chimbote**
which can drop you off in Casma, 370 km,
6 hrs, US$18. If going to **Lima** many of the
buses from Trujillo and Chimbote stop
briefly opposite the petrol station, block 1 of
Ormeño or, if they have small offices, along
blocks 1-5 of Av Ormeño. To **Chimbote**,
55 km, it is easiest to take a Los Casmeños
colectivo, which depart when full from
in front of the petrol station, block 1 of
Ormeño, or from Plaza Poncianos, 45 mins,
US$.50. To **Trujillo** it is best to go first to
Chimbote bus station and then take an
América Express bus. To **Huaraz** (150 km),
via Pariacoto, buses come from Chimbote,
6-7 hrs, US$12. **Transportes Huandoy**,
Ormeño 166, T712336, departs at 0700,
1100 and 1400, while **Yungay Express**,
Ormeño 158, departs at 0600, 0800 and
1400. This difficult but beautiful trip is worth
taking in daylight. From Casma the first
50 km are paved, a good dirt road follows
for 20 km to **Pariacoto** (basic lodging).
From here to the **Callán pass** (4224 m) the
road is rough (landslides in rainy season),
but once the Cordillera Negra has been
crossed, the gravel road is better with lovely
views of the Cordillera Blanca (150 km to
Huaraz). Most Huaraz buses go via Pativilca,
which is further but the road is much better,

6 hrs, **Móvil Tours** and **Trans Chinchaysuyo**, all run at night.

Chimbote p95
Warning Under no circumstances should you walk to the centre: minibus costs US$0.50, taxi US$1.50. There are no hotels near the terminal; some companies have ticket offices in the centre.

Bus The station is 4 km south on Av Meiggs. From **Lima**, to Chimbote, 420 km, 5½ hrs, US$15-20. Frequent service with many companies. To **Trujillo**, 130 km, 2 hrs, US$6, **América Express** buses every 20 mins till 2100. To **Huaraz** most companies, with the best buses, go the 'long way round', ie down the Pan-americana to Pativilca, then up the paved highway, 7 hrs, US$14. The main companies start in Trujillo and continue to **Caraz**. To Huaraz via Pariacoto, 7 hrs, US$14, **Trans Huandoy** (Etseturh), T354024, at 0600, 1000 and 1300, 7 hrs, and Yungay Express at 0500, 0700 and 1300. To **Caraz** via Cañón del Pato, 7-8 hrs, US$12, Yungay Express at 0830 (for a description of this route see above). Sit on the left-hand-side for the best views. If arriving from Caraz via the Cañón del Pato there is usually time to make a connection to Casma or Trujillo/Huanchaco and avoid overnighting in Chimbote. If travelling to Caraz, take **Línea** 0600 or earlier from Trujillo to make the 0830 bus up the Cañón del Pato. If overnighting is unavoidable, Casma is near enough to stay in but you will need to buy your Caraz ticket the day before; the bus station is on the Casma side of Chimbote.

Trujillo and around → *Phone code: 044. Colour map 2, B2. Population: 1,539,774.*

The capital of La Libertad Department, 548 km from Lima, disputes the title of second city of Peru with Arequipa. The compact colonial centre, though, has a small-town feel. The greenness surrounding the city is a delight against the backdrop of brown Andean foothills and peaks. Founded by Diego de Almagro in 1534 as an express assignment ordered by Francisco Pizarro, it was named after the latter's native town in Spain. Nearby are some of Peru's most important Moche and Chimú archaeological sites and a stretch of the country's best surfing beaches.

Arriving in Trujillo
Orientation The **airport** is west of the city; the entry to town is along Avenida Mansiche. There is no central bus terminal. **Bus stations** are spread out on four sides of the city beyond the inner ring road, Avenida España. There are few hotels around them, but plenty of taxis. Insist on being taken to your hotel of choice. A new Terminal Terrestre is being built.» *See also Transport, page 109.*

Trujillo is best explored on foot. The major sites outside the city, Chan Chán, the Moche pyramids and Huanchaco beach are easily reached by public transport, but take care when walking around. A number of recommended guides run tours to these and other places. **Note** The city is generally safe, but take care beyond the inner ring road, Avenida España, as well as obvious places around bus stops and terminals, and at ATMs and internet cafés.

Tourist offices i perú ① *Diego de Almagro 420, Plaza de Armas, T294561, iperutrujillo@ promperu.gob.pe, Mon-Sat 0900-1800, Sun 1000-1400.* Also useful: **Municipalidad de Trujillo, Sub-Gerencia de Turismo** ① *Av España 742, T044-244212, anexo 119, sgturismo@ munitrujillo.gob.pe.* The **Tourist Police** ① *Independencia 572, in the Ministerio de Cultura building, policia_turismo_tru@hotmail.com, Mon-Sat 0800-2000,* provide useful information and can help with reports of theft, some speak English. **Indecopi** ① *Santo Toribio de Mogrovejo 518, Urb San Andrés II etapa, T295733, sobregon@indecopi.gob.pe*, for tourist complaints. **Gobierno Regional de la Libertad** ① *Dirección de Turismo, Av España 1800, T296221*, for information on regional tourism. Useful websites include www.xanga.com/TrujilloPeru and www.laindustria.com.

Places in Trujillo

The focal point is the pleasant and spacious **Plaza de Armas**. The prominent sculpture represents agriculture, commerce, education, art, slavery, action and liberation, crowned by a young man holding a torch depicting liberty. Fronting it is the **Cathedral** ① *0700-1230, 1700-2000*, dating from 1666, with its **museum of religious paintings and sculptures** ① *Mon-Fri 0900-1300, 1600-1900, Sat 0900-1300, US$1.45*, next door. Also on the Plaza are the **Hotel Libertador**, the colonial-style Sociedad de Beneficencia Pública de Trujillo and the Municipalidad. The **Universidad de La Libertad**, second only to that of San Marcos at Lima, was founded in 1824. Two beautiful colonial mansions on the plaza have been taken over. The Banco Central de Reserva is in the Colonial-style **Casa Urquiaga (or Calonge)** ① *Pizarro 446, Mon-Fri 0930-1500, Sat-Sun 1000-1330, free 30-min guided tour, take passport*, which contains valuable pre-Columbian ceramics. The other is **Casa Bracamonte (or Lizarzaburu)** ① *Independencia 441*, which houses the Seguro Social de Salud del Perú and has occasional exhibitions. Opposite the Cathedral on Independencia, is the **Casa Garci Olguín** (Caja Nuestra Gente), recently restored but boasting the oldest façade in the city and Moorish-style murals. The buildings that surround the Plaza, and many others in the vicinity, are painted in bright pastel colours. Near the Plaza de Armas is the spacious 18th-century **Palacio Iturregui**, now occupied by the **Club Central** ① *Jr Pizarro 688, restricted entry to patio, US$1.85 to see the ceramics, 0830-1000*. An exclusive and social centre of Trujillo, it houses a private collection of ceramics. **Casa Ganoza Chopitea** ① *Independencia 630 (see Casona Deza under Restaurants, page 106)*, is considered architecturally the most representative of the viceroyalty in the city. It combines baroque and rococo styles and is also known for the pair of lions that adorn its portico.

Other mansions, still in private hands, include **Casa del Mayorazgo de Facalá** ① *Pizarro 314, another entrance on Bolognesi, Mon-Fri 0915-1230*, now Scotiabank. **Casa de la Emancipación** ① *Jr Pizarro 610 (Banco Continental), Mon-Sat, 0900-1300, 1600-2000*, is a museum in the building where independence from Spain was planned and was the first seat of government and congress in Peru. The **Casa del Mariscal de Orbegoso** ① *Orbegoso 553, open 0930-2000*, is the **Museo de la República** owned by the BCP bank. It also holds temporary exhibitions. **Museo Haya de la Torre (Casa del Pueblo)** ① *Orbegoso 664, Mon-Sat 0900-1300, 1600-2000, free*, is a small, well-presented museum about the life of the founder of the APRA party and one of the leading 20th-century socialists in the Americas, in the house in which he was born. It holds a cinema club once a week.

One of the best of the many churches is the 17th-century **La Merced** ① *at Pizarro 550, 0800-1200, 1600-2000, free*, with picturesque moulded figures below the dome. **El Carmen** ① *at Colón y Bolívar, open for Mass Sun 0700-0730*, church and monastery, has been described as the 'most valuable jewel of colonial art in Trujillo' but it is rarely open. Likewise **La Compañía** ① *near Plaza de Armas*, now an auditorium for cultural events.

Museo de Arqueología ① *Junín 682 y Ayacucho, Casa Risco, T249322, Mon-Fri 0830-1430, US$1.85*, houses a large and interesting collection of thematic exhibits. The **Museo del Juguete** ① *Independencia 705 y Junín, Mon-Sat 1000-1800, Sun 1000-1300, US$1.85, children US$0.70, café open 0900-2300*, is a toy museum containing examples from prehistoric times to 1950, collected by painter Gerardo Chávez. Downstairs is the Espacio Cultural Angelmira with a café bar; in a restored *casona*, worth a visit. Gerardo Chávez has opened the **Museo de Arte Moderno** ① *Av Industrial, 3.5 km from centre, T215668, 0930-1700, Sun 0930-1400, US$3.50, students half price,* which has some fine exhibits, a peaceful garden and friendly staff. The basement of the **Cassinelli garage** ① *Av N de Piérola 607,*

Trujillo

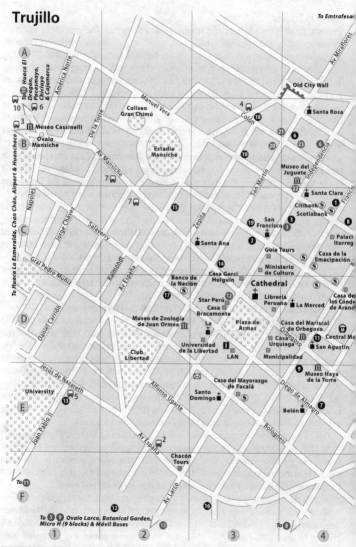

T231801, behind a petrol station, 1000-1300, 1430-1800, US$2.45, contains a private collection of Mochica and Chimú pottery which is recommended. **Museo de Zoología de Juan Ormea**① *Jr San Martín 368, Mon-Fri 0700-1850, US$0.70*, has interesting displays of Peruvian animals. There is also a **botanical garden**① *Mon-Sat 0800-1700, free*, about half a block beyond the Ovalo Larco, southwest of the city centre.

200 metres
200 yards

Where to stay
1 Casa de Clara *F6*
2 Chan Chán Inn *A5*
3 Colonial *C4*
4 Continental *D4*
5 El Gran Marqués *F2*
6 El Mochilero *B4*
7 Gran Bolívar *B5*
8 Hostal El Centurión *F4*
9 Hostal Malibú *F2*
10 Hostería El Sol *A1*
11 Kallpa *F1*
12 Libertador *D3*
13 Res Vanini *F2*
14 Turismo *D5*

Restaurants
1 Asturias, Café Oviedo, Demarco & Romano *C4*
2 Café Amaretto *C3*
3 Casona Deza *C4*
4 Cevichería Puerto Mori *B4*
5 Chelsea *B5*
6 Dulcería Doña Carmen *B4*
7 El Chileno *E4*
8 El Kluv *C4*
9 El Mochica *E4*
10 El Sol *B3*
11 Juguería San Agustín *D4*
12 Le Nature *F2*
13 Pizzería Pizzanino *E1*
14 Rincón de Vallejo *C3*
15 Rincón de Vallejo 2 *C2*
16 Romano-Rincón Criollo *F3*
17 Sabor Supremo *D2*
18 Sal y Pimienta *B3*
19 Trujillo Señorial *C3*

Bars & clubs
20 Canana *B3*
21 El Estribo *B4*
22 Juguete *C4*
23 Stradivarius *B4*

Transport
1 Buses to Huaca del Sol y de la Luna *D6*
2 Combi A to Chan Chán & Huanchaco *E2, E5*
3 Combis A & B; & Micros B, H & H-Corazón: to Chan Chán & Huanchaco *B1*
4 Combi B & Micro B: to Chan Chán & Huanchaco *A4, B3*
5 Micro H to Chan Chán & Huanchaco *E1*
6 El Dorado *B1*
7 Ittsa *B2, C2*
8 Oltursa & Flores *A5*
9 Ormeño *A5*
10 Turismo Díaz, Horna & Tarapoto Tours *B1*

Huacas del Sol and de la Luna

ⓘ *0900-1600 (last entry, but site open till sunset), US$4 (students US$2, children US$0.40), booklet in English or Spanish US$2.85. All tickets are sold at the Museo Huacas de Moche – see below. You have to go with a guide on a 1-hr tour in English, French or Spanish. Groups can be up to 25 people and quite rushed. See Proyecto Huaca de la Luna, Jr San Martín 380, Trujillo, T221269, www.huacas.com. The visitors' centre (T834901) has a café showing videos and a souvenir shop and good toilets. In an outside patio craftsmen reproduce ceramics in designs from northern Peru.*

A few kilometres south of Trujillo are the huge and fascinating Moche pyramids, the Huaca del Sol and the Huaca de la Luna. Until the Spaniards destroyed a third of it in a vain search for treasure, Huaca del Sol was the largest man-made structure in the western hemisphere, at 45 m high. It consisted of seven levels, with 11 or 12 phases of construction over the first six centuries AD. Today, about two thirds of the pyramid have been lost and it is closed to the public. Huaca de la Luna, 500 m away, received scant attention until extensive polychrome moulded decorations were uncovered since 1990. The colours on these remarkable geometric patterns and deities have faded little and it is now possible to view impressive friezes of the upper four levels on the northern exterior wall of the *huaca*. The highest mural is a 'serpent' which runs the length of the wall, beneath it there are repeated motifs of 'felines' holding decapitated heads of warriors, then repeated motifs of 'fishermen' holding fish against a bright blue background and, next, huge 'spider/crab' motifs. The bottom two levels show dancers or officials grimly holding hands and, below them, victorious warriors following naked prisoners past scenes of combat and two complex scenes, similar to those at Huaca Cao Viejo at El Brujo (see below). Combined with intricate, brightly painted two-dimensional motifs in the sacrificial area atop the huaca, and with new discoveries in almost every excavation, Huaca de la Luna is now a truly significant site well worth visiting.

The **Templo Nuevo**, or Plataforma III, represents the period 600 to 900 AD and has friezes in the upper level showing the so-called Rebellion of the Artefacts, in which weapons take on human characteristics and attack their owners. Also new was the **Museo Huacas de Moche** ⓘ *5 mins' walk from Huaca de la Luna, www.huacasdemoche.pe, daily 0900-1600, US$1, students US$0.75, children US$0.40*, the site museum. Three halls display objects found in the huacas, including beautiful ceramics, arranged thematically around the Moche themselves, the cermonial complex, daily life, the deities of power and of the mountains and priests who worshipped them. Food is available on Sunday at the nearby town of Moche.

Chan Chán

ⓘ *5 km from Trujillo. 0900-1600, arrive well before that. Site may be covered up if rain is expected. Tickets cost US$3.80 (US$2 with ISIC card, children US$0.35), include entrance fees for Chan Chán, Huaca El Dragón and Huaca La Esmeralda (for 2 days). Official guides, US$10, wait by the souvenir shops, toilets here too. See note about safety, page 110.*

These vast, unusually decorated crumbling ruins of the imperial city of the Chimú domains are the largest adobe city in the world. The ruins consist of 10 great compounds built by Chimú kings. The 11- to 12-m-high perimeter walls surrounded sacred enclosures with usually only one narrow entrance. Inside, rows of storerooms contained the agricultural wealth of the kingdom, which stretched 1000 km along the coast from near Guayaquil to the Carabayllo Valley, north of Lima.

Most of the compounds contain a huge walk-in well which tapped the ground water, raised to a high level by irrigation further up the valley. Each compound also included a platform mound which was the burial place of the king, with his women and his treasure, presumably maintained as a memorial. The Incas almost certainly copied this system and transported it to Cuzco where the last Incas continued building huge enclosures. The Chimú surrendered to the Incas around 1471 after 11 years of siege and cutting off the irrigation canals.

The dilapidated city walls enclose an area of 28 sq km containing the remains of palaces, temples, workshops, streets, houses, gardens and a canal. What is left of the adobe walls bears either well-restored, or modern fibreglass fabrications of moulded decorations showing small figures of fish, birds, fishing nets and various geometric motifs. Painted designs have been found on pottery unearthed from the debris of a city ravaged by floods, earthquakes, and *huaqueros* (grave looters). The **Ciudadela de Nik-An** (formerly called Tschudi) is the part that visitors see.

The **site museum** ① *US$1, 0830-1630*, on the main road, 100 m before the turn-off, has objects found in the area, displays and signs in Spanish and English.

The partly restored temple, **Huaca El Dragón** ① *0930-1630 (in theory), on the west side of the Pan-American Highway in the district of La Esperanza; combis from Huayna Cápac y Los Incas, or Av España y Manuel Vera marked 'Arco Iris/La Esperanza', taxi costs US$2, dating from Huari to Chimú times (AD 1000-1470)*, is also known as **Huaca Arco Iris** (rainbow), after the shape of friezes which decorate it. The poorly preserved **Huaca La Esmeralda** is at Mansiche, between Trujillo and Chan Chán, behind the church and near the Mall Aventura shopping centre. Buses to Chan Chán and Huanchaco pass the church at Mansiche.

El Brujo
① *Daily 0900-1600, US$4 (US$2 with ISIC card, children US$0.35). Shops and toilets at the entrance. See www.fundacionwiese.com.*

A complex collectively known as El Brujo, 60 km north of Trujillo, is considered one of the most important archaeological sites on the north coast. Covering 2 sq km, it was a ceremonial centre for up to 10 cultures, including the Moche. Huaca Cortada (or El Brujo) has a wall decorated with high relief stylized figures. Huaca Prieta is, in effect, a giant rubbish tip dating back 5000 years, which once housed the very first settlers. It was first investigated by the US archaeologist Junius Bird in the late 1940s leading him to establish the chronology of prehistoric Peru that prevails today, cementing the place of this unremarkable *huaca* in Peruvian history. Huaca Cao Viejo has extensive friezes, polychrome reliefs up to 90 m long, 4 m high and on five different levels. The mummy of a tattooed, pregnant woman, La Señora de Cao, dating from AD 450, has also been found. Her mausoleum, with grave goods, can be visited in an excellent, purpose-built museum. In front of Cao Viejo are the remains of one of the oldest Spanish churches in the region. It was common practice for the Spaniards to build their churches near these ancient sites in order to counteract their religious importance. Excavations will continue for many years. Trujillo travel agencies run tours and there is a trail system for exploring the site.

Huanchaco and around
An alternative to Trujillo is this fishing and surfing village, full of hotels, guest houses and restaurants. It is famous for its narrow pointed fishing rafts, known as *caballitos* (little horses) *de totora*, made of totora reeds and depicted on Mochica, Chimú and other cultures' pottery. Unlike those used on Lake Titicaca, they are flat, not hollow, and ride the breakers rather like surfboards (fishermen offer trips on their *caballitos* for US$1.75, be prepared to get wet; groups should contact Luis Gordillo, El Mambo, T461092). You can see

fishermen returning in their reed rafts at about 0800 and 1400 when they stack the boats upright to dry in the fierce sun. Overlooking Huanchaco is a huge church (1535-1540) from the belfry of which are extensive views. There is a post office at Grau y Manco Capac, open Monday-Saturday 1300-1800.

Puerto Chicama (**Malabrigo**), is claimed by surfers as the best surf beach in Peru, with the longest left-hand point-break in the world. The best waves are March-October (high point May-June) and the sand is clean. It is 70 km north of Trujillo, turn off Panamericana at Paiján. There is a 1-km-long fishing pier, huge, abandoned warehouses and the remains of the railway to Casa Grande cooperative from the town's sugar-exporting days. There are a few *hospedajes* and simple places to eat in town (shop early by the market for fresh seafood) and a string of small places line the clifftop south of town, Distrito El Hombre. The best places to eat are here (eg **Chicama**, Arica 625); avoid the shacks that line the beach.

⊙ Trujillo and around listings

For hotel and restaurant price codes, and other relevant information, see pages 14-17.

◉ Where to stay

Trujillo *p98, map p100*

$$$$ El Gran Marqués, Díaz de Cienfuegos 145-147, Urb La Merced, T481710, www.elgran marques.com. Price includes breakfast, modern, minibar, pool, sauna, jacuzzi, restaurant.

$$$$ Libertador, Independencia 485, Plaza de Armas, T232741, www.libertador. com.pe. Modern hotel in historic building, lovely place to stay. Comfortable rooms, excellent service, swimming pool in a flower-filled patio, sauna, cafetería and restaurant, breakfast extra, excellent buffet lunch on Sun.

$$$ Gran Bolívar, Bolívar 957, T222090, www.granbolivarhotel.net. In converted 18th-century house, restaurant and room service, café, bar, laundry, gym, parking.

$$$-$$ Kallpa, Díaz de las Heras s/n, Urb Vista Hermosa, T281266, www.kallpa hotel.pe. A smart new boutique hotel, welcoming, English spoken, well below usual boutique hotel prices.

$$ Colonial, Independencia 618, T258261, www.hostalcolonial.com.pe. Attractive but small rooms, hot showers, basic breakfast, good restaurant, especially for set lunch.

$$ Continental, Gamarra 663, T241607, www.perunorte.com/hcontinental. Modern but old-fashioned hotel opposite the market, with hot water, good breakfast, helpful, safe.

$$ Hostal El Centurión, Paraguay 304, Urb El Recreo, T201526, www.hostalelcenturion. com. About 20 mins' walk from the Plaza, modern, good rooms, well kept, safe but no a/c, simple restaurant, good service.

$$ Hostal Malibú, Av Larco 1471, Urb La Merced, T284811, www.hostalmalibu.com. Variety of rooms, restaurant, room service, minibar, laundry, massage, currency exchange. Also sister hotel of same name at Av Larco 1000, Huanchaco.

$ Casa de Clara, Cahuide 495, T243347, http://trujilloperu.xanga.com. Backpackers' hostal, hot water, good food, helpful, information, lodging packages with meals and tours, laundry service, use of kitchen with permission and charge for gas, meeting place and lots going on, many languages spoken (see Clara Bravo and Michael White, What to do, below). Restaurants nearby.

$ Chan Chán Inn, Av Ejército 307, T298583, chanchaninn@hotmail.com. Close to several bus terminals so noisy, with or without breakfast, popular with backpackers, café, laundry, money exchange, information.

$ El Mochilero, Independencia 887, T297842, Elmochilerotrujilloperuoficial on Facebook. A variety of dorms and rooms, only one with bath, electric showers, breakfast US$1.75, fridge for guests' use. Tours arranged, information.

$ Hostería El Sol, Brillantes 224, Urb Santa Inés, T231933, hosteriaelsol@gmail.com, near bus terminals on Av Nicolás de Piérola. With hot shower, restaurant, all meals available.

$ Residencia Vanini, Av Larco 237, outside Av España, T200878, enriqueva@hotmail.com. Youth hostel in a converted private house, a good option but not in the centre, some rooms with bath, others with shared shower.

$ Turismo, Gamarra 747, T244181. Central, good services, restaurant, parking, travel agency.

El Brujo p103

$ Hospedaje Jubalu, Libertad 105, Magdalena de Cao, T995-670600. With hot water. No internet in town and limited shopping.

Huanchaco p103

$$$-$$ Bracamonte, Los Olivos 160, T461162, www.hotelbracamonte.com.pe. Comfortable, modern, contemporary decor, good, pool, secure, good restaurant offers lunch *menú* and some vegetarian dishes, English spoken, laundry service, games room. Highly recommended.

$$$-$$ Hostal Huankarute, La Rivera 312, T461705, www.hostalhuankarute.com. On the sea-front, with small pool, bar, sun terrace, bicycle rental; some rooms larger, more luxurious and more pricey, all with ocean view. Recommended.

$$$-$$ Las Palmeras, Av Larco 1150, sector Los Tumbos, T461199, www.laspalmerasde huanchaco.com. One of the best, rooms with terrace, hot water, dining room, pool and gardens. Rooms on top floor with sea view cost more than ground floor rooms with pool view.

$$ El Malecón, Av La Rivera 322, T461275, www.hostalelmalecon.com. Overlooking the sea, some rooms with terrace, hot water, café, helpful staff.

$$ Hostal Huanchaco, Larco 185 on Plaza, T461272, www.huanchacohostal.com. With hot water, pool, good but pricey cafetería, video, pool table.

$$ Hostal Los Esteros, Av Larco 618, T461300, www.losesteroshuanchaco.com. Rooms with sea view for 1-4 people, hot water, laundry, restaurant, safe parking, bicycle hire, can arrange surfing and *caballitos de totora* trips.

$$ Residencial Sol y Mar, La Rivera 400, T461120, ctsolymar1@hotmail.com. Breakfast extra, with pool, restaurant and garden.

$$-$ Hostal Cocos Beach, Av Larco 1500, Los Tumbos, T461023, www.hostelcoco sbeach.com. Opposite the beach, rooms with beds and bunks, hot water, restaurant, surfing lessons, car rental, tours arranged.

$$-$ Huanchaco Inn, Los Pinos 528, T461158. Rooms with and without bath, hot water, use of kitchen, laundry service, small pool.

$ Cherry's, Los Pinos 448, T462066. Owner Juan Carlos speaks English, rooms with private or shared bath, hot water, kitchen, shop, bar, roof terrace, laundry, even a small swimming pool.

$ Hospedaje My Friend, Los Pinos 533, T461080. Dorm rooms with shared bath upstairs, with hot water, TV room, information. Tours arranged, but service is erratic. Popular place with surfers, good for meeting others and for a meal in the restaurant on ground floor (open 0800-1800).

$ La Casa Suiza, Los Pinos 308, T461285, www.lacasasuiza.com. This Huanchaco institution has a variety of rooms with/ without bath, breakfast US$3, BBQ on the roof, book exchange.

$ Las Brisas, Raymondi 146, T461186, http://facebook.com/lasbrisashuanchaco. Hot water, café, comfortable.

$ McCallum Lodging, Los Ficus 460, T462350, http://mccallumlodginghouse. wordpress.com/the-hostel/. Private rooms and dorms, hot water, hammocks, home-cooked meals available and recipes shared, laundry, baggage and surfboard storage, family atmosphere, highly considered by locals and tourists.

$ Ñaylamp, Av Víctor Larco 123, northern end of seafront in El Boquerón, T461022, www.hostalnaylamp.com. Rooms set around a courtyard with patios and garden, others have sea view, dorms, hammocks, good beds, hot water, camping, tents available to hire, laundry, safe, Italian food, good breakfasts.

Puerto Chicama
At Distrito El Hombre (several close out of season):

$$$ Chicama Beach, T576130, www.chicamabeach.com. 3-star, hot water, swimming pool for kids and adults, restaurant, bar, laundry, parking, open all year.

$$$ Chicama Surf Resort, T576206, www.chicamasurf.com. Exclusive, with surfing classes, boats to the waves, spa, restaurant, infinity pool, open all year.

$ El Hombre is the backpacker place, OK, very friendly.

$ Hostal Los Delfines, T943-296662. Owner Tito Venegas, guests can use well-equipped kitchen, rooms with balcony, hot water, spacious.

$ Sueños de Chicama, is the furthest from town and the cheapest.

In town there are several cheaper places; Hostal El Naipe, Tacna 395, is arguably the best.

🍴 Restaurants

Trujillo *p98, map p100*
A speciality is *shambar*, a thick minestrone made with pork, served on Mon. All along Pizarro are restaurants to suit all tastes and budgets. On the west side of the central market at Grau y Ayacucho are several small, cheap restaurants. On sale everywhere is *turrón*, a nougat-type sweet.

$$$ Romano-Rincón Criollo, Estados Unidos 162, Urb El Recreo, 10-min walk from centre, T244207. Northern Peruvian cuisine, *menú* for US$5.60, smart.

$$$-$$ El Mochica, Bolívar 462. Good typical food with live music on special occasions.

$$ Casona Deza, Independencia 630, T434866, CasonaDezaCafe on Facebook. Open 0800-2200, from 0900 on Sun. An atmospheric pizzeria in a restored colonial house with period furniture and a patio surrounded by frescoes.

$$ Chelsea, Estete 675, T257032. Open 1145-1645, 1700-0100, on Sun. Restaurant/bar. Buffet Criollo US$8.70, special shows on Fri (live music, fee US$3.50) and Sat (Marinera dance show, US$5.25). Recommended.

$$ Demarco, Pizarro 725. Popular at midday for lunchtime menus and for its cakes and desserts, good service.

$$ Le Nature, Marcelo Corne 338, in a residential district off Av Larco, T209674. Mon-Thu 1000-2200, Fri, Sun 1000-1600, Sat 1900-2200. Probably the best vegetarian food in town.

$$ Pizzería Pizzanino, Av Juan Pablo II 183, Urb San Andrés, opposite University. Good for pizzas, pastas, meats, desserts, evening only.

$$ Romano, Pizarro 747. International food, good *menú*, breakfasts, coffee, excellent milkshakes, cakes.

$$-$ Cevichería Puerto Mori, Estete 482, T346752. Very popular, they serve only good seafood. At the same location are 2 more fish restaurants, but not of the same quality.

$ Asturias, Pizarro 741. Nice café with a reasonable *menú*, good pastas, cakes and sandwiches.

$ Café Oviedo, Pizarro 737. With soups, vegetarian options, good salads and cakes, helpful.

$ El Sol, Zepita 203, T345105. Mon-Sat 0800-2200, Sun 0800-1600. Vegetarian, lunch *menú* and à la carte.

$ Juguería San Agustín, Bolívar 526. Good juices, good *menú*, sandwiches, ice creams, popular, excellent value. Also at Av Larco Herrera y Husares de Junín.

$ Rincón de Vallejo, Orbegoso 303. Good *menú*, typical dishes, very crowded at peak times. Second branch at Av España 736.

$ Sabor Supremo, Diego de Almagro 210, T220437. Menú US$1.75, also à la carte, vegetarian food, vegan on special request.
$ Sal y Pimienta, Colón 201. Very popular for lunch, US$1 and US$1.85, close to buses for Huanchaco and Chan Chán.
$ Trujillo Señorial, Gamarra 353, T204873. Mon-Sat 1300-1530. Restaurant and hotel school, good *menú* US$2.60-3, food nicely presented, good value.

Cafés

Café Amaretto, Gamarra 368. Smart, good selection of real coffees, "brilliant" cakes, sweets, snacks and drinks.
Casona Deza, Independencia 630. Comfortable café/bar selling home-made pasta and pizza and good coffee in an old mansion.
Dulcería Doña Carmen, San Martín 814. Serves local specialities such as *alfajores*, *budin*, *king kong*, etc.
El Chileno, Ayacucho 408. Café and ice cream parlour, popular.
El Kluv, Junín 527 (next to Metro Market). Italian owned, fresh, tasty pizzas at noon and in the late afternoon.
Fitopán, Bolívar 406. Good selection of breads, also serves lunches.

Huanchaco *p103*

There are about 30 restaurants on the beachfront, recommended on Av Larco are
$$ Estrella Marina, No 740, **Los Herrajes**, No 1020, **Lucho del Mar**, No 750. Many close in the low season and at night.
$$$ Big Ben, Av Larco 1182, near A Sánchez, T461869. Open 1130-1730. Seafood and international, very good.
$$$ Club Colonial, La Rivera 514, on the beachfront, T461015. Open 1100-2300. A smart restaurant and bar, French-speaking Belgian owner.
$$$ El Mochica, Av Larco 700, T461963. Same owners and quality as this restaurant in Trujillo, due to reopen after rebuilding in 2014.
$$$ Huanchaco Beach, Av Larco 602, T461484. One of the best for quality in town, popular with tours.

$$$-$$ El Kero, Av La Ribera 612, T461184. Open 0800-midnight. Very popular meeting place and good restaurant.
$$$-$$ El Sombrero, Av Larco 800. Smart new restaurant serving good *ceviche* and seafood, most tables have great sea view.
$$ Casa Tere, Plaza de Armas, T461197. For best pizzas in town, also pastas, burgers and breakfasts.
$$ La Barca, Raimondi 117, T461855. Very good seafood, well-run, popular.
$$ Sabes?, Av Larco 920, T461555. Opens at 2000. Pub with food, internet café, popular, British-owned.
$$-$ Menuland, Los Pinos 250, T773579. Managed by a German/Peruvian couple, English, German, Italian spoken. Peruvian and international dishes, breakfast, lunch *menú* for US$1.75. Also has 2 double rooms (**$**), book exchange.
$ La Charapita, Húascar 162. Modest but popular restaurant serving large portions.

Cafés

Argolini, Av Rivera 400. Convenient for people staying in the Los Pinos/Los Ficus area for fresh bread, cakes, ice cream, coffee and juices.
Chocolate, Av Rivera 772. Open 0730-1900. Dutch/Peruvian management, serves breakfast, also some vegetarian food, coffee and cakes. Also offers B&B.

Bars and clubs

Trujillo *p98, map p100*
Bar/Café Juguete, Junín y Independencia. Open to midnight. An old style café serving good coffee. Has a good pasta restaurant attached.
Bar/Café Stradivarius, Colón 327. Open in the evenings only. An attractive café with sofas,
Canana, San Martín 788, T232503. Bars and restaurant, disco, live music at weekends (US$1.50-3), video screens (also has travel agency). Recommended, but take care on leaving.

El Estribo, San Martín 809, T204053.
A club playing a wide genre of sounds
and attracting a mixed crowd.

✹ Festivals

Trujillo *p98, map p100*
The 2 most important festivals are the
National Marinera Contest (end of **Jan**) and
the **Festival Internacional de La Primavera**
(last week of **Sep**), with cultural events,
parades, beauty pageants and Trujillo's
famous **Caballos de Paso**.

Huanchaco *p103*
In the 1st week of **May** is the **Festival del
Mar**, a celebration of the disembarkation
of Taycanamo, the leader of the Chimú
period. A procession is made in Totora
boats. **29 Jun, San Pedro**, patron saint of
fishermen: his statue is taken out to sea on
a huge totora-reed boat. There are also surf
competitions. Carnival and New Year are
also popular celebrations.

○ Shopping

Trujillo *p98, map p100*
Bookshops **Librería Peruana**, Pizarro 505,
just off the Plaza. Best selection in town, also
postcards, ask for Sra Inés Guerra de Guijón.
SBS, Jr Bolívar 714 and in Mall Aventura,
Av Mansiche block 20, also in Plaza Real
Mall, Prol Av César Vallejo (behind UPAO
University), California (take taxi or green
California micro A).
Handicrafts **120 Artesanía por Descubrir**,
Las Magnolias 403, California, www.tienda
120.blogspot.com. Art gallery designs and
handmade crafts, near Real Plaza. **APIAT**,
craft market, Av España y Zela. The largest
craft market in the city, good for ceramics,
totora boats, woodwork and leather,
competitive prices. **Artesanía del Norte**,
at Dulcería La Libertad, Jr Pizarro 758, and
at the Huacas del Sol y de la Luna, www.
artesaniadelnorte.com. Sells items mostly
to the owner, Mary Cortijo's, design using

traditional techniques. **Trama Perú**, Pizarro
754, T243948, www.tramaperu.com. Daily
1000-2200. High-quality, handmade art
objects, authorized Moche art replicas.
Markets **Mercado Central**, on Gamarra,
Ayacucho and Pasaje San Agustín. **Mercado
Unión**, between Av Santa and Av Perú.
A little safer than others, also has repairs
on shoes, clothes and bags.

Huanchaco *p103*
El Quibishi, entrance to Huanchaco at
south end of beach. Main *artesanía* market;
also has a food section.

○ What to do

Trujillo *p98, map p100*
Tour operators
Prices vary and competition is fierce so shop
around for the best deal. Few agencies run
tours on Sun and often only at fixed times
on other days. Their groups are usually large.
To Chan Chán, El Dragón and Huanchaco,
4-4½ hrs for US$8-9 pp. To Huacas del Sol
and de la Luna, 2½-3 hrs for US$8-9 pp.
To El Brujo, US$27-34 pp, 4-5 hrs. City tours
cost US$3.50 pp, 2-2½ hrs. Prices do not
include entrance fees.
Chacón Tours, Av España 106-112,
T255212. Sat afternoon and Sun morning.
Recommended for flights etc, not local tours.
Guía Tours, Independencia 580, T234856.
Also Western Union agent.

Guides
Many hotels work on a commission basis
with taxi drivers and travel agencies. If you
decide on a guide, make your own direct
approach and always agree what is included
in the price. The Tourist Police (see Directory)
has a list of guides; average cost US$7 per
hr. Beware of cowboy outfits herding up
tourists around the plazas and bus terminals
for rapid, poorly translated tours. Also
beware scammers offering surfing or salsa
lessons and party invitations. **Clara Bravo**,
Cahuide 495, T243347, http://trujilloperu.

xanga.com. An experienced tourist guide who speaks Spanish, English, German and understands Italian; archaeological tour US$20 for 6 hrs, city tour US$7 pp, US$53 per car to El Brujo, with extension to Sipán, Brüning Museum and Túcume possible (tours in Lambayeque involve public transport, not included in cost). Clara works with English chartered accountant **Michael White** (same address, microbewhite@ yahoo.com, also speaks German, French and Italian), who provides transport. He is very knowledgeable about tourist sites. They run tours any day of the week; 24-hr attention, accommodate small groups. **Luis Ocas Saldaña**, Jr José Martí 2019, T949-339593, guianorteperu@hotmail.com. Very knowledgeable, helpful, covers all of northern Peru. **Gustavo Prada Marga**, at Chan Chán, an experienced guide. **Alfredo Ríos Mercedes**, riosmercedes@hotmail.com, T949-657978. Speaks English. **Jannet Rojas Sánchez**, Alto Mochica Mz Q 19, Trujillo, T949-344844. Speaks English, enthusiastic, works also for **Guía Tours**. **José Soto Ríos**, Atahualpa 514, dpto 3, T949-251489. He speaks English and French.

Huanchaco *p103*
Surfing
There are plenty of surf schools. Equipment rental US$8.75/day, one lesson US$14-15.50. See also **Casa Amelia**, Av Larco 1150, T461351, http://casaamelia.net.
Indigan, Deán Saavedra 582 (next to soccer field), T462591. Jhon and Giancarlos Urcía for lessons, surf trips and rentals. Also offer lodging at their home.
Muchik, Av Larco 650, T462535, www.escueladetablamuchik.com. Instructors Chico and Omar Huamanchumo are former surf champions, also repairs. Arrange trips to other surf sites.
Olas Norte, Los Ficus 450, see Facebook. Individual and group lessons, prices include full equipment.
Onechako, Av La Ribera Norte, escuelasurfonechako@hotmail.com.

Owner Tito Lescano. *Caballito de totora* riding lessons. Surf trips to other surf beaches in the north. Restaurant/bar.
Yenth Ccora, Av Larco 500, T949-403871, http://yenthccora.blogspot.co.uk. Surfing equipment manufacture, repair, rental and surfing school.

⊖ Transport

Trujillo *p98, map p100*
Air To **Lima**, 1 hr, daily flights with **LAN, Star Perú** and **Avianca/TACA**. Taxi to airport, US$6-8 depending on length of journey. The military **Grupo Aéreo 42** (J Alfonso Ugarte 642, Centro Cívico, T995-566264), has passenger flights on 2 routes in the north: Trujillo, Chiclayo, Chachapoyas, Tarapoto, Chiclayo, Trujillo (twice a week) and Trujillo, Chiclayo, Cajamarca, Mendoza, Juanjui, Tarapoto, Yurimaguas, Iquitos (out Wed, return Thu, plus Iquitos, Yurimaguas, Tarapoto, Chiclayo, Trujillo on Sun).
Bus Micros (small buses with 25 or more seats) and combis (up to 15 passengers), on all routes, cost US$0.50-0.60; colectivos (cars carrying 6 passengers), US$0.50, tend to run on main avenues starting from Av España. None is allowed inside an area bounded by Av Los Incas in the east to Ovalo Mansiche in the west and the north and south perimeters of Av España.

A large new bus terminal for southbound buses has been built between Ovalos Grau and La Marina. Over time all bus companies will relocate here, but at the time of writing many maintain their own terminals.
Note On Fri-Sun nights year round the better bus services must be pre-booked 2-3 days in advance. To and from **Lima**, 561 km, 9-10 hrs in the better class buses, average fare US$22-32, 10 hrs or more in the cheaper buses, US$11-16. There are many bus companies doing this route, among those recommended are: **Cruz del Sur**, Amazonas 437 near Av Ejército, T261801, the only one with a morning service to Trujillo at 0800; **Turismo Díaz**,

Nicolás de Piérola 1079 on Panamericana Norte, T201237; **Línea**, Av América Sur 2857, T297000, 3 levels of service, also to **Chimbote** hourly, **Huaraz**, 9 hrs, **Cajamarca** 5 a day, **Chiclayo**, hourly (from Carrión by Av Mansiche, T235847, on the hour), and **Piura**, 2300. Also **Flores** (Av Ejército 346, T208250), **Ittsa** (Av Juan Pablo 1110, T284644, for southern destinations, Av Mansiche 145, T222541, for northern destinations – good service), **Móvil**, Av América Sur 3959, T286538. **Oltursa**, Av Ejército 342, T263055, 3 *bus cama* services to Lima.

Small **Pakatnamú** buses leave when full, 0400-2100, from Av N de Piérola 1092, T206594, to **Pacasmayo**, 102 km, 1¼ hrs, US$5.50. To **Chiclayo**, 4 hrs from Trujillo, from US$5.50, several companies. Among the best are **Emtrafesa**, Av Túpac Amaru 185, T471521, on the half-hour every hour; also to **Jaén**, 9 hrs; **Piura**, 6 hrs, US$15 (Ittsa's 1330, or Línea's 1415 buses are good choices); Ittsa also goes to **Talara**, 2200, 9 hrs, US$16.

Direct buses to **Huaraz**, 319 km, via Chimbote and Casma (169 km), with **Línea** and **Móvil**, 8 hrs, US$17-30. There are several buses and colectivos to **Chimbote**, with **América Express** from Av La Marina 315, 135 km, 2 hrs, US$6, departures every 30 mins from 0530 (ticket sales from 0500); then change at Chimbote (see above – leave Trujillo before 0600 to make a connection from 0800). Ask Clara Bravo and Michael White (see Guides, above) about transport to Caraz avoiding Chimbote (a worthwhile trip via the Brasileños road and Cañón del Pato).

To **Cajamarca**, 300 km, 7-8 hrs, US$10-27: with **Línea**, and **Emtrafesa**, see above, at 2145. To **Huamachuco**, 170 km, 5-6 hrs, see page 136.

Taxi Taxis in town charge US$1 within Av España and US$1.20 within Av América; always use official taxis, which are mainly yellow, or cooperative taxis, which have the company logo on the side. Beware of overcharging, check fares with locals. Taxi from in front of Hotel Libertador, US$12 per hr, about the same as a tour

with an independent guide or travel agent for 1-2 people.

Huacas del Sol and de la Luna *p102*
Combis every 15 mins from Ovalo Grau and, less safe, Galvez y Los Incas. They leave you a long walk from the site. On the return go to Ovalo Grau for onward connections. US$0.40. Taxis about US$5; few at site for return, unless you ask driver to wiat.

Chan Chán *p102*
Take any transport between Trujillo and Huanchaco (see below) and ask to get out at the turn-off to Chan Chán, US$0.50. A taxi is US$5 from Trujillo to the ruins, US$1 from museum to ruins, US$3 to Huanchaco. **Note** There are police at the entrance to the site, but it is a 25-min walk to the ticket office. Take care if not taking a car on this track. On no account walk the 4 km from Chan Chán or on to Buenos Aires beach, as there is serious danger of robbery and of being attacked by dogs.

El Brujo *p103*
The complex can be reached by taking one of the regular buses from Trujillo to Chocope, US$1.25, every 10 mins, 1 hr, and then a colectivo to Magdalena de Cao, US$0.75 (leave when full), 15 mins, then a mototaxi taking up to 3 people to the site, US$7.50 including 1½ hr wait.

Huanchaco *p103*
2 combi routes run between Trujillo and Huanchaco, A and B, **Caballitos de Totora** company (white and black). 4 micros run between Trujillo and Huanchaco: A, B (also known as Mercado Mayorista), H (UPAO) and H-Corazón (with red heart, Mercado Hermelinda), **Transportes Huanchaco**, red, yellow and white. They run 0500-2030, every 5-10 mins. Fare is US$0.75 for the journey (25 mins by combi, 45-60 mins by microbus). The easiest place to pick up any of these combis or micros is Ovalo Mansiche, 3 blocks northwest of Av España

in front of the Cassinelli museum. In Trujillo, combi A takes a route on the south side of Av España, before heading up Av Los Incas. Combi B takes the northerly side of Av España. Micro A from Huanchaco goes to the 28 de Julio/Costa Rica junction where it turns west along Prolongación César Vallejo, passing the UPAO university and Plaza Real shopping centre, continuing to the Av El Golf (the terminus for return to Huanchaco on almost the same route). From Huanchaco to the city centre on other routes, ask the cobrador to let you off near C Pizarro on Av España. For the **Línea, Móvil Tours** and southern bus terminals, take micro H. It also goes to Ovalo Grau where you can catch buses to the Huacas del Sol and de la Luna. For **Cruz del Sur, Ormeño, Flores**, etc, take combi or micro B from Huanchaco. For **Oltursa** take micro H, Taxis US$4-5.

Puerto Chicama
Combis from Trujillo (Santa Cruz terminal, Av Santa Cruz, 1 block from Av America Sur), US$2, 1½ hrs. Also **Dorado** buses, Av N de Piérola 1062, T291778, US$2 (via Chocope, US$0.75, and Paiján, US$0.60 to Chicama). Buses stop just off Plaza Central, opposite Comisaria.

❶ Directory

Trujillo *p98, map p100*
Medical services Hospital Belén, Bolívar 350, T245281. **Clínica Peruano Americana**, Av Mansiche 810, T231261, English spoken, good. **Useful addresses** Immigration: Av Larco 1220, Urb Los Pinos, T282217. Mon-Fri 0815-1230, 1500-1630.

Huanchaco *p103*
Medical services Centro de Salud, Jr Atahualpa 128, T461547.

Chiclayo and around

Lambayeque department, sandwiched between the Pacific and the Andes, is a major agricultural zone, especially for rice and sugar cane. It boasts a distinctive cuisine and musical tradition, and an unparalleled ethnographic and archaeological heritage. Chiclayo's witchcraft market is famous and excavations at nearby adobe pyramid cities are uncovering fabulous treasures.

Chiclayo → *Phone code: 074. Colour map 2, B1. Population: 750,000.*
Since its inception in the 16th century, Chiclayo has grown to become a major commercial hub, but it is best known for the spectacular cache of prehispanic archaeological treasures that lie at its doorstep. **Tourist offices: i perú** ① *Sáenz Peña 838, T205703, iperuchiclayo@ promperu.gob.pe, 0900-1900, Sun 0900-1300; also at the airport (daily).* For complaints and tourist protection, **Indecopi** ① *Los Tumbos 245, Santa Victoria, T206223, aleyva@indecopi. gob.pe, Mon-Fri 0800-1300, 1630-1930.* The **tourist police** ① *Av Sáenz Peña 830, T236700, ext 311, 24 hrs a day,* are very helpful and may store luggage and take you to the sites themselves. There are tourist kiosks on the Plaza and on Balta.

In the city itself, on the Plaza de Armas, is the 19th-century neoclassical **Cathedral**, designed by the English architect Andrew Townsend. The private **Club de la Unión** is on the Plaza at the corner of Calle San José. The new Palacio Municipal contains a Centro Documental de la Memoria Histórica de Chiclayo. Continue five blocks north on Balta, the busiest commercial street, to the **Mercado Modelo**, one of northern Peru's liveliest and largest daily markets. Don't miss the handicrafts stalls (see **Monsefú**) and the well-organized section (off Calle Arica on the south side) of ritual paraphernalia used by traditional curers and diviners (*curanderos*): herbal medicines, folk charms, curing potions, and exotic objects including dried llama foetuses to cure all manner of real and imagined illnesses. At **Paseo de Artesanías**, 18 de Abril near Balta south of the Plaza, stalls sell handicrafts in a quiet, custom-built open-air arcade. Another relaxing spot here is the **Paseo de las Musas**, with its gardens and imitation Greek statues.

Monsefú and the coast

The traditional town of **Monsefú**, southwest, is known for its music and handicrafts; there's a good market, four blocks from the plaza. Handicraft stalls open when potential

Chiclayo

Where to stay
1 Casa de la Luna *B1*
2 Costa del Sol *C3*
3 Embajador *A3*
4 Garza *C3*
5 Gran Hotel Chiclayo *B1*
6 Hosp Concordia *C3*
7 Hosp San Eduardo *C3*
8 Inti *B2*
9 Muchik Hostel *B3*
10 Pirámide Real *C3*
11 Santa Rosa *B2*
12 Sicán *C2*
13 Sol Radiante *C2*
14 Sunec *C2*

Restaurants
1 Balta 512 *C3*
2 Boulevar *B2*
3 Café 900 *C3*
4 Café Astoria *C2*
5 D'Onofrio *C3*
6 El Huaralino *C1*
7 Fiesta *B1*
8 Hebrón *C3*
9 Kaprichos *A3*
10 La Panadería *B2*
11 La Parra *C3*
12 La Plazuela *B1*
13 Las Américas *B3*
14 Roma *C3*
15 Tradiciones *C2*

Transport
1 Brüning Express to Lambayeque *B1*
2 Cial *C1*
3 Civa *C3*
4 Colectivos to Lambayeque *A2*
5 Colectivos to Puerto Etén *A3*
6 Cruz del Sur *C3*
7 Emtrafesa *C3*
8 Línea *C2*
9 Móvil *C2*
10 Oltursa *B1*
11 Tepsa *C2*
12 Transportes Chiclayo *B1*

customers arrive (see Festivals, page 118). Beyond Monsefú are three ports serving the Chiclayo area. **Pimentel**, 8 km from Chiclayo, is a beach resort which gets very crowded on Sundays and during the summer (US$4 to rent a chair and sunshade). Most of the seafront has been bought up by developers, but the main plaza is an oasis of green. There are several seafood restaurants (**El Muelle de Pimentel**, Rivera del Mar cuadra 1, T453142, is recommended). You can walk along the restored pier for US$0.25. Sea-going reed boats (*caballitos de totora*) are used by fishermen and may be seen from the pier returning mid-morning or late morning or late afternoon on the beach. The surfing between Pimentel and the Bayovar Peninsula is excellent, reached from Chiclayo (14.5 km) by road branching off from the Pan-American Highway. Nearby **Santa Rosa** has little to recommend it other than to see the realities of the fisherfolks' life and it is not safe to walk there from Pimentel. The most southerly is **Puerto Eten**, a quaint port with some nice wooden buildings on the plaza, 24 km by road from Chiclayo. Its old railway station has been declared a national heritage. In the adjacent roadstead, Villa de Eten, panama hats are the local industry, but it is not as picturesque. The ruined Spanish town of **Zaña**, 51 km south of Chiclayo, was destroyed by floods in 1726, and sacked by English pirates on more than one occasion. There are ruins of five colonial churches and the convents of San Agustín, La Merced and San Francisco.

Lambayeque

About 12 km northwest from Chiclayo is Lambayeque, a good base from which to explore the Chiclayo area. Its narrow streets are lined by colonial and republican houses, many retaining their distinctive wooden balconies and wrought-iron grill-work over the windows, but many in very bad shape. On Calle 2 de Mayo see especially **Casa de la Logia o Montjoy**, whose 64-m-long balcony is said to be the longest in the colonial Americas. It has been restored and can be visited (free). At 8 de Octubre 345 is **Casona Descalzi** ① *T283433, 1100-1700 daily*, which is well preserved as a good restaurant. It has 120 carved iguana heads on the ceiling. **Casona Iturregui Aguilarte**, at No 410, is, by contrast, seriously neglected. Also of interest is the 16th-century **Complejo Religioso Monumental de San Francisco de Asís** and the baroque church of the same name which stands on Plaza de Armas 27 de Diciembre.

The reason most people visit is to see the town's two museums. The older of the two is the **Brüning Archaeological Museum** ① *0900-1700, US$2.75, a guided tour costs an extra US$2.75*, in a modern building, specializing in Mochica, Lambayeque/Sicán and Chimú cultures. Three blocks east is the more recent **Museo de las Tumbas Reales de Sipán** ① *Av Juan Pablo Vizcardo y Guzmán 895, T283977, www.museotumbasrealessipan.pe, 0900-1700, closed Mon, US$3.55, moto taxi from plaza US$0.60*, shaped like a pyramid. The magnificent treasure from the tomb of 'The Old Lord of Sipán' (see below), and a replica of the Lord of Sipán's tomb are displayed here. A ramp from the main entrance takes visitors to the third floor, from where you descend, mirroring the sequence of the archaeologists' discoveries. There are handicrafts outside and in the museum shop and a **tourist office** ① *Tue-Sun 1030-1400, 1500-1730*.

On the plaza in **Mórrope**, on the Pan-American Highway 20 km north of Lambayeque, is one of the earliest churches in northern Peru, **San Pedro de Mórrope** (1545), an adobe and *algarrobo* structure beautifully renovated and painted. It contains the tomb of the cacique Santiago Cazusol. Next to it is the more modern parish church.

Sipán

ⓘ *Daily 0900-1700, entrance for tombs and museum is US$2.85; guide at site US$8 (may not speak English). To visit the site takes about 3-4 hrs. There are comedores outside the site.*

At this imposing complex a short distance east of Chiclayo (turn-off well signed in the centre of Pomalca), excavations since 1987 in one of three crumbling pyramids have brought to light a cache of funerary objects considered to rank among the finest examples of pre-Columbian art. Peruvian archaeologist Walter Alva, former leader of the dig, continues to probe the immense mound that has revealed no less than 12 royal tombs filled with 1800-year-old offerings worked in precious metals, stone, pottery and textiles of the Moche culture (circa AD 1-750). In the most extravagant Moche tomb discovered, El Señor de Sipán, a priest was found clad in gold (ear ornaments, breast plate, etc), with turquoise and other valuables.

In another tomb were found the remnants of what is thought to have been a priest, sacrificed llama and a dog, together with copper decorations. In 1989 another richly appointed, unlooted tomb contained even older metal and ceramic artefacts associated with what was probably a high-ranking shaman or spiritual leader, called 'The Old Lord of Sipán'. Three tombs are on display, containing replicas of the original finds. **Museo de Sitio Huaca Rajada** ⓘ *daily 0900-1700, US$2.85*, concentrates on the finds at the site, especially Tomb 14 (the 'Sacerdote-Guerrero', or Priest-Warrior), the decorative techniques of the Moche and the roles that archaeologists and local communities play in protecting these precious discoveries. You can wander around the previously excavated areas of the Huaca Rajada to get an idea of the construction of the burial mound and adjacent pyramids. For a good view, climb the large pyramid across from the excavated Huaca Rajada.

A 4000-year-old temple, **Ventarrón**, was uncovered about 20 km from Sipán in 2007 by Walter Alva; his son, Ignacio, is now in charge of the dig. It predates Sipán by some 2000 years and shows three phases of development. Its murals, which appear to depict a deer trapped in a net, are claimed to be the oldest in the Americas and there is evidence of cultural exchange with as far away as the Amazon. A project to build a site museum and improved access will take until 2015, until then entry, with guide, is US$2.

East from Pomalca is Chongoyape, just before which is the turning to the **Chaparrí** private ecological reserve, 34,000 ha, set up and run by the Comunidad Muchik Santa Catalina de Chongoyape, 75 km from Chiclayo. Visitors can go for the day or stay at the **Chaparrí EcoLodge** ⓘ *US$10.50 for entry to the reserve, www.chaparri.org, for day visits T978-896377, see Where to stay, below*. All staff and guides are locals; for every 10 people you have to have a local guide (this provides work and helps to prevent rubbish). There are no dogs or goats in the area so the forest is recuperating; it contains many bird and mammal species of the dry forest, including white-winged guan and spectacled bear. There is a Spectacled Bear Rescue Centre where bears rescued from captivity live in semi-wild enclosures. The Tinajones reservoir is good for birdwatching.

Túcume

ⓘ *T835026, www.museodesitiotucume.com, open 0800-1700, US$4.50, students US$1, children US$0.30, guide US$7.*

About 35 km north of Chiclayo, not far from the Panamericana and Túcume Nuevo, lie the ruins of this vast city built over 1000 years ago. A short climb to the two *miradores* on **Cerro La Raya** (or **El Purgatorio**) offers the visitor an unparalleled panoramic vista of 26 major pyramids, platform mounds, walled citadels and residential compounds flanking a ceremonial centre and ancient cemeteries. One of the pyramids, Huaca Larga, where excavations are still being undertaken, is the longest adobe structure in the world, measuring 700 m long, 280 m wide and over 30 m high. There is no evidence of occupation of Túcume previous to the Sicán, or Lambayeque people who developed the site AD 1000-1375 until the Chimú conquered the region, establishing a short reign until the arrival of the Incas around 1470. The Incas built on top of the existing structure of **Huaca Larga** using stone from Cerro La Raya. Among the other pyramids which make up this huge complex are: **Huaca El Mirador** (90 m by 65 m, 30 m high), **Huaca Las Estacas, Huaca Pintada** and **Huaca de las Balsas**, which is thought to have housed people of elevated status such as priests. A walkway leads around the covered pyramid and you can see many mud reliefs including fishermen on rafts.

Not much of the site is open to view, only the miradores mentioned above and the walk through the site there, as lots of study is going on. There is a pleasant dry forest walk to Huaca I, with shade, bird- and lizard-watching. A new site museum is due to open in late 2014.

The town of **Túcume Viejo** is a 20-minute walk beyond the site. Look for the side road heading towards a new park, opposite which is the ruin of a huge colonial church made of adobe and some brick. The surrounding countryside is pleasant for walks through mango trees and fields of maize. **Fiesta de la Purísima Concepción**, the festival of the town's patron saint, is eight days prior to Carnival in February, and also in September.

Ferreñafe and Sicán

The colonial town of **Ferreñafe**, 20 km northeast of Chiclayo, is worth a visit, especially for the **Museo Nacional Sicán** ① *T286469, Museo-Nacional-Sican on Facebook, Tue-Sun 0900-1700, US$4, students half price, good explanations in Spanish, café and gift shop*. This excellent new museum on the outskirts of town houses objects of the Sicán (Lambayeque) culture from near Batán Grande. **Tourist office**: the **Mincetur** ① *on the Plaza de Armas, T282843, citesipan@mincetur.gob.pe*, is helpful.

The entrance to **El Santuario Histórico Bosque de Pómac** ① *visitors' centre, dalemandelama@gmail.com, 0900-1700, free, a guide (Spanish only) can be hired with transport, US$3.45, horses for hire US$6*, which includes the ruins of **Sicán**, lies 20 km beyond Ferreñafe along the road to Batán Grande (from the Panamericana another entrance is near Túcume). Visiting is not easy because of the arid conditions and distances involved: it is 10 km to the nearest *huaca* (pyramid). At the visitors' centre food and drinks are available and camping is permitted. The guide covers a two-hour tour of the area which includes at least two *huacas*, some of the most ancient carob trees and a mirador (viewpoint), which affords a beautiful view across the emerald green tops of the forest with the enormous pyramids dramatically breaking through. Sicán has revealed several sumptuous tombs dating to AD 900-1100. The ruins comprise some 12 large adobe pyramids, arranged around a huge plaza, measuring 500 m by 250 m, with 40 archaeological sites in total. The city, of the Sicán (or Lambayeque culture), was probably moved to Túcume (see above), 6 km west, following 30 years of severe drought and then a devastating El Niño related flood in AD 1050-1100. These events appear to have provoked a rebellion in which many of the remaining temples on top of the pyramids were burnt and destroyed. The forest itself has good birdwatching possibilities.

North of Chiclayo

On the old Pan-American Highway 885 km from Lima, **Olmos** is a tranquil place (several hotels and **Festival de Limón** last week in June). A paved road runs east from Olmos over the Porculla Pass, branching north to Jaén and east to Bagua Grande (see page 149).

Olmos is the best base for observing the critically endangered white-winged guan, a bird thought extinct for 100 years until its rediscovery in 1977. On the outskirts is the white-winged guan captive breeding centre, **Zoocriadero Bárbara d'Achille** ① *Km 103, Olmos*, which also has an aviary of rescued birds, and the **Asociación Cracidae Perú** ① *(director Fernando Angulo Pratolongo), Torres Paz 708, Chiclayo, T074-238748*. Captive breeding started in 1979 and the first reintroduction into the wild was made in 2001 at **Chaparrí Ecolodge** (see page 114). One place where the guans can be seen in the wild is Quebrada Limón (or Frejolillo), where guides from the local community check on the guans' whereabouts in order to take visitors to see them in the early morning. Ask at the breeding centre for how to get there.

The old Pan-American Highway continues from Olmos to Cruz de Caña and Piura. At Lambayeque the new Pan-American Highway branches off the old road for 190 km straight across the **Sechura Desert**, a large area of shifting sands separating the oases of Chiclayo and Piura. **Note** Solo cyclists should not cross the desert as muggings have occurred. Take the safer, inland route. In the desert, there is no water, fuel or accommodation. Do not attempt this alone.

◉ Chiclayo and around listings

For hotel and restaurant price codes, and other relevant information, see pages 14-17.

◉ Where to stay

Chiclayo *p111, map p112*
$$$ Costa del Sol, Balta 399, T227272, www.costadelsolperu.com. Non-smoking rooms, smart, small pool, sauna, jacuzzi, Wi-Fi, ATM. Páprika restaurant, good value Sun buffets, vegetarian options.
$$$ Gran Hotel Chiclayo (Casa Andina Select), Villareal 115, T511-2139739, www.casa-andina.com. Large, modern hotel for corporate and leisure guests, pool, safe car park, changes dollars, jacuzzi, entertainments, restaurant. Now operated by Casa Andina.
$$$ Inti, Luis Gonzales 622, T235931, www.intihotel.com.pe. More expensive rooms with jacuzzi, family rooms available, welcome cocktail, airport transfer included, parking, safe and fridge in room, restaurant, helpful staff.
$$$ Sunec, Izaga 472, T205110, www.sunechotel.com.pe. Modern hotel in a central location, parking and small pool, opened in 2013.

$$ Embajador, 7 de Enero 1388, 1½ blocks from Mercado Modelo, T204729, http://hotelembajadorchiclayo.com. Modern, bright, good facilities, 20 mins' walk from centre, small comfortable rooms, small restaurant, excellent service, free pick-up from bus office, tours arranged.
$ Hospedaje Concordia, 7 de Enero Sur 235, Urb San Eduardo, T209423. Rooms on 2nd floor bigger than 3rd, modern, pleasant, no meals, laundry service, view of Parque San Eduardo.
$ Hospedaje San Eduardo, 7 de Enero Sur 267, Urb San Eduardo, T208668. No meals, colourful decor, modern bathrooms, fan, Wi-Fi, public phone, quiet, hot water.
$ Muchik Hostel, Vicente de la Vega 1127. Singles, doubles and dorm, with fan, pleasant common area, safe.
$ Pirámide Real, MM Izaga 726, T224036. Compact and spotless, good value, no meals, safe in room, fan, very central.
$ Santa Rosa, L González 927, T224411. Rooms with windows are bright and spacious, best at rear. Hot water, fan, laundry, good value.
$ Sicán, MM Izaga 356, T208741, hsican@hotmail.com. With breakfast, hot water, fan, comfortable, restaurant and bar, laundry, parking, welcoming and trustworthy.

$ Sol Radiante, Izaga 392, T237858. Hot water, comfortable, pleasant, family-run, laundry, tourist information. Pay in advance.

Lambayeque p113

$$$ Hostería San Roque, 2 de Mayo 437, T282860, www.hosteriasanroque.com. In a fine, extensive colonial house, beautifully refurbished, helpful staff, bar, swimming pool, lunch on request. Single, double, triple, quad rooms and dorm for groups of 6, **$**.
$ Hostal Libertad, Bolívar 570, T283561, www.hostallibertad.com. 1½ blocks from plaza, big rooms, fridge, secure.
$ Hostal Real Sipán, Huamachuco 664, opposite Brüning Museum. Modern, an option if arriving late at night.

Mórrope

$$-$ La Casa del Papelillo, San Pedro 357, T955-624734, http://lacasadelpapelillo.blogspot.com/. 3 rooms in a remodelled 19th-century home, one with private bath, includes breakfast, communal areas, cultural events, discounts for community volunteer work. Owner Cecilia is knowledgeable and helpful.

Sipán: Chaparrí p114

$$$$ EcoLodge Chaparrí, T984-676249 or in Chiclayo T452299, www.chaparrilodge.com. A delightful oasis in the dry forest, 6 beautifully decorated cabins (more being built) and 5 double rooms with shared bath, built of stone and mud, nice and cool, solar power. Price is for 3 meals and a local guide for one day, first-class food. Sechuran foxes in the gardens; hummingbirds bathe at the pool about 0600 every day. Recommended.

Túcume p114

$$ pp Los Horcones, T951-831705, www.loshorconesdetucume.com. Rustic luxury in the shadow of the pyramids, with adobe and algarrobo rooms set in lovely garden with lots of birdlife. Good food, pizza oven, breakfast included. Note that if rice is being grown nearby in Jan-May there can be a serious mosquito problem.

North of Chiclayo: Olmos p115

$$$ Los Faiques, Humedades Alto, Salas, T979-299932, www.losfaiques-salas.com. Very pretty place in a quiet forest setting, buffet breakfast, excellent restaurant.
$ El Remanso, San Francisco 100, T427158, elremansolmos@yahoo.com. Like an hacienda with courtyards, small pool, whitewashed rooms, colourful bedding, flowers and bottled water in room, hot water (supposedly). Price is full board, good restaurant. Charming owner. Several other places to stay.

🍴 Restaurants

Chiclayo p111, map p112
For delicious, cheap *ceviche*, go to the **Nativo** stall in the Mercado Central, a local favourite.
$$$ El Huaralino, La Libertad 155, Santa Victoria. Wide variety, international and creole, but mixed reports of late.
$$$ Fiesta, Av Salaverry 1820 in 3 de Octubre suburb, T201970, www.restaurant fiesta gourmet.com. Gourmet local dishes, excellent food and service, beautifully presented, daily and seasonal specials, fabulous juices, popular business lunch place.
$$$ Sabores Peruanos, Los Incas 136. Tue-Sun 1200-1700. Great Peruvian seafood and meat dishes.
$$ Balta 512, Balta 512, T223598. First-class local food, usually good breakfast, popular with locals.
$$ Boulevar, Colón entre Izaga y Aguirre. Good, friendly, *menú* and à la carte.
$$ Hebrón, Balta 605. For more upmarket than average chicken, but also local food and *parrilla*, good salads. Also does an excellent breakfast and a good buffet at weekends.
$$ Kaprichos, Pedro Ruíz 1059, T232721. Chinese, delicious, huge portions.
$$ Las Américas, Aguirre 824. Open 0700-0200. Good service.
$$ Roma, Izaga 706. Open all day. Wide choice, breakfasts, snacks and meals.
$$ Tradiciones, 7 de Enero Sur 105, T221192. Daily 0900-1700. Good variety

of local dishes, including *ceviche*, and drinks, nice atmosphere and garden, good service.
$ Café Astoria, Bolognesi 627. Open 0800-1200, 1530-2100. Breakfast, good-value *menú*.
$ La Parra, Izaga 746. Chinese and creole, *parrillada*, very good, large portions, cheerful.
$ La Plazuela, San José 299, Plaza Elías Aguirre. Good food, seats outside.
Café 900, MM Izaga 900, www.cafe900.com. Nice atmosphere in a remodeled old house, good food, popular with locals, sometimes has live music.
D'Onofrio, Balta y Torres Paz. Good ice cream.
La Panadería, Lapoint 847. Good choice of breads, including *integral*, snacks and soft drinks.

Lambayeque *p1203*

A Lambayeque speciality is the 'King Kong', a giant *alfajor* biscuit filled with manjar blanco and other sweets. San Roque brand (www.sanroque.com.pe), sold throught Peru, is especially good.
$$ Casona Descalzi, address above. Open for lunch only. Good menu, including traditional northern dishes.
$$ El Cántaro, 2 de Mayo 180, http://restaurant elcantaro.com. Lunch only. For traditional local dishes, à la carte and a good *menú*.
$$ El Pacífico, Huamachuco 970, T283135. Open for lunch only. Renowned for its enormous plates of *arroz con pato* and *causa norteña*.
$$ El Rincón del Pato, A Leguía 270. Lunch only. Offers 40 different duck dishes.
$$-$ Sabor Norteño, Bolívar 440. One of the few restaurants open in the early evening.
$ Café Cultural La Cucarda, 2 de Mayo 263, T284155. Open evening only. Small alternative café, decorated with rescued antiques, delicious pastries, pies and cakes. Recommended.

⊕ Festivals

Chiclayo *p111, map p112*
6 Jan Reyes Magos in Mórrope, Illimo and other towns, a recreation of a medieval pageant in which pre-Columbian deities become the Wise Men. On **4 Feb** Túcume devil dances (see below). **14 Mar** El Señor Nazareno Cautivo, in Lambayeque and Monsefú, whose main celebration of this festival is **14 Sep**. Holy Week, traditional Easter celebrations and processions in many villages. **2-7 Jun** Divine Child of the Miracle, Villa de Eten. **27-31 Jul** Fexticum in Monsefú, traditional foods, drink, handicrafts, music and dance. **5 Aug** Pilgrimage from the mountain shrine of **Chalpón** to **Motupe**, 90 km north of Chiclayo; the cross is brought down from a cave and carried in procession through the village. At **Christmas** and **New Year**, processions and children dancers (*pastorcitos* and *seranitas*) can be seen in many villages, eg **Ferreñafe, Mochumi, Mórrope**.

⊙ What to do

Chiclayo *p111, map p112*
Lambayeque's museums, Sipán and Túcume (see Around Chiclayo) can easily be visited by public transport. Local operators run 3-hr tours to Sipán; Túcume and Lambayeque (5 hrs); Sicán is a full-day tour including Ferreñafe and Pómac; also to Zaña and coastal towns.
InkaNatura, Manuel María Izaga 730, of 203, T979-995024, www.inkanatura.net. Mon-Fri 0915-1315, 1515-1915, Sat 0915-1315. Run historical and nature tours throughout northern Peru. Good service.

Horse riding
Rancho Santana, in Pacora, T979-712145, www.cabalgatasperu.com. Relaxing tours on horseback, half-day (US$15.50), 1-day (US$22.50) or 3-day tours, including to Santuario Bosque de Pómac, Sicán ruins and Túcume, Swiss-run (Andrea Martin), good horses. Also **$** a bungalow, a double

room and camping (tents for hire) at the ranch with safe parking for campervans. Frequently recommended.

⊖ Transport

Chiclayo *p111, map p112*
Air José Abelardo Quiñones González airport 1 km from town, T233192; taxi from centre US$4. Arrive 2 hrs before flight; be prepared for manual search of hand luggage; no restaurant or bar in departure lounge.

Daily flights to/from **Lima** and **Piura** with LAN (MM Izaga 770) and StarPerú (MM Izaga 459, T225204), direct or via **Trujillo**. The military **Grupo Aéreo 42** (Av Balta 901, T979-975537) has passenger flights to Chiclayo originating in Trujillo or Iquitos; see page 109 for routes and schedules.
Bus No terminal terrestre; most buses stop outside their offices on Bolognesi. To **Lima**, 770 km, US$25-36: Civa, Av Bolognesi 714, T223434; Cruz del Sur, Bolognesi 888, T225508; Ormeño, Haya de la Torre 242, 2 blocks south of Bolognesi, T234206; Ittsa, Av Bolognesi 155, T233612; Línea, Bolognesi 638, T222221, *especial* and *bus cama* service; Móvil, Av Bolognesi 195, T271940 (goes as far as Tarapoto); Oltursa, ticket office at Balta e Izaga, T237789, terminal at Vicente de la Vega 101, T225611; Tepsa, Bolognesi 504-36 y Colón, T236981; Transportes Chiclayo, Av L Ortiz 010, T223632. Most companies leave from 1900 onwards. To **Trujillo**, 209 km, with Emtrafesa, Av Balta 110, T600660, every 15 mins, 4 hrs, US$5.50, and Línea, as above. To **Piura**, 4 hrs, US$5.50, Transportes Chiclayo leave 15 mins throughout the day; also Línea and Emtrafesa and buses from the Cial/Flores terminal, Bolognesi 751, T239579. To **Sullana**, US$8.50. To **Tumbes**, US$9, 9-10 hrs; with Cial, Cruz del Sur or El Dorado. Some companies on the route northwards arrive full from Lima. Many buses go on to the **Ecuadorean border** at **Aguas Verdes**. Go to the *Salida* on Elías Aguirre, mototaxi drivers know where it is, be there by 1900. All buses stop here after

leaving their terminals to try and fill empty seats, so discounts may be possible. To **Cajamarca**, 260 km, US$9-20, eg Línea, 4 a day; others from Tepsa terminal, Bolognesi y Colón, eg Días, T224448. To **Chachapoyas**, US$13.50-25: Civa 1730 daily, 10-11 hrs; Transervis Kuelap, in Tepsa station, 1830 daily, Móvil, at 2000. To **Jaén**, US$7.75-9.60, many companies, but Móvil US$11.55-15.50. To **Tarapoto**, 18 hrs, US$25-29, with Móvil, also Tarapoto Tours, Bolognesi 751, T636231. Civarun to **Guayaquil** at 1825, *semi-cama* US$34.75, *cama* US$42.50, also Super Semería, US$25, 12 hrs, via Piura, Máncora, Tumbes; they also go to Cuenca.
Taxi Mototaxis are a cheap way to get around; US$1 anywhere in city.

Monsefú and the coast *p112*
Combis to **Monsefú** cost US$0.75 from Balta y Pedro Ruiz, or Terminal Epsel, Av Castañeda Iparraguirre s/n. The **ports** may be visited on a half-day trip. Combis leave from Av L Ortiz and San José, Chiclayo, to Pimentel, US$1.10. Taxi Chiclayo–Pimentel US$6, 20 mins. Colectivos to Eten leave from 7 de Enero y Arica.

Lambayeque *p113*
Colectivos from **Chiclayo** US$0.75, 25 mins, from Pedro Ruíz at the junction with Av Ugarte. Also Brüning Express combis from Vicente de la Vega entre Angamos y Av L Ortiz, every 15 mins, US$0.50. Trans Lambayeque colectivo from Plaza Elias Aguirre, US$0.90, Some major bus lines have offices in Lambayeque and can drop you off there.

Sipán *p114*
Combis to Sipán leave from Plaza Elías Aguirre and from terminal Epsel, US$1, 1 hr.

Chaparrí
Take a public bus from Leoncio Prado y Sáenz Peña, Chiclayo, to **Chongoyape** (1¼ hrs, US$1.50), then a mototaxi to **Chaparrí**, US$10.

Túcume p114

Combis from **Chiclayo**, Av Leguía, 15 m from Angamos, US$1, 45 mins; mototaxi from highway/new town to ruins US$0.75. Combi Túcume-**Lambayeque**, US$0.75, 25 mins.

Ferreñafe and Sicán p115

Colectivos from Terminal Epsel, Chiclayo, to the centre of Ferreñafe leave every few mins, or from 8 de Octubre y Sáenz Peña, 40 mins, U$1, take a mototaxi to the

museum, 5 mins, US$1.75. Alternatively, combis for Batán Grande depart from Av N de Piérola, Chiclayo, and pass the museum every 15-20 mins, 40 mins, US$1.

Ⓘ Directory

Chiclayo p111, map p112
Medical services Ambulance: Max Salud, 7 de Enero 185, T234032.

Piura and around → Phone code: 073. Colour map 2, A1. Population: 377,500.

A proud and historic city, Piura was founded in 1532, three years before Lima, by the *conquistadores* left behind by Pizarro. The city has two well-kept parks, Cortés and Pizarro (with a statue of the conquistador, also called Plaza de las Tres Culturas), and public gardens. Old buildings are kept in repair and new buildings blend with the Spanish style of the old city. Three bridges cross the Río Piura to Castilla, the oldest from Calle Huancavelica, for pedestrians (Puente San Miguel), another from Calle Sánchez Cerro, and the newest from Avenida Panamericana Norte, at west end of town. The winter climate, May-September, is very pleasant although nights can be cold and the wind piercing; December-March is very hot.

Tourist offices Information at **i Peru** Ⓘ *Ayacucho 377, T320249, iperupiura@promperu. gob.pe, Mon-Sat 0830-1900, Sun 0830-1400. Also at the airport.* **Dirección Regional de Turismo** Ⓘ *Av Fortunato Chirichigno, Urb San Eduardo, T308229, at the north end of town, helpful when there are problems, open 0900-1300, 1600-1800.* **Indecopi** Ⓘ *Av Los Cocos 268, Urb Club Grau, T308549, dnavarro@indecopi.gob.pe.*

Places in Piura

Standing on the **Plaza de Armas** is the **cathedral**, with gold covered altar and paintings by Ignacio Merino. A few blocks away is **San Francisco**, where the city's independence from Spain was declared on 4 January 1821, nearly eight months before Lima. The birthplace of Admiral Miguel Grau, hero of the War of the Pacific with Chile, is **Casa Museo Grau** Ⓘ *Jr Tacna 662, opposite the Centro Cívico, 0800-1300, 1600-1900, free.* It is a museum and contains a model of the *Huáscar*, the largest Peruvian warship in the War of the Pacific, which was built in Britain. It also contains interesting old photographs. Local craftwork is sold at the **Mercado Modelo**. The small **Museo Municipal Vicús** Ⓘ *Sullana, near Huánuco, Mon-Sat 0800-2200, Sun 0800-1200*, includes 60 gold artefacts from the local Vicús culture. It also has an art section.

Catacaos 12 km to the southwest of Piura, is famous for its *chicha*, *picanterías* (local restaurants, some with music), tooled leather, gold and silver filigree jewellery, wooden articles, straw hats (expensive) and splendid celebrations in Holy Week. About 2 km south of Catacaos is the **Narihualá** archaeological site.

The port for the area, 50 km from Piura, **Paita** is flanked on three sides by a towering, sandy bluff. It is a major fishing port with a long history. Several colonial buildings survive. Bolívar's mistress, Manuela Sáenz, lived the last 24 years of her life in Paita, after being exiled from Quito. She supported herself until her death in 1856 by weaving, embroidering and making candy, after refusing the fortune left her by her husband. On a bluff looming over Paita is a small colonial fortress built to repel pirates, who attacked it frequently. Nearby beaches include **Colán**, to the north, with various hotels, restaurants and a long sandy beach (beware the stingrays); and less developed **Yasila**, a fishing village to the south.

Piura

Where to stay	Restaurants	
1 California	1 Alex Chopp's	8 Ganímedes
2 El Almirante	2 Brosti Chopp	9 Italia
3 El Sol	3 Carburmer &	10 La Pera Madura
4 Esmeralda	Picantería Los Santitos	11 Romano
5 Hosp Aruba	4 Chalán de la Avenida	
6 Hostal Los Jardines	5 Chalán del Norte	
7 Hostal Moon Night	6 D'Pauli	
8 LP Los Portales	7 El Otro Romano &	
9 San Miguel	Piura Tours	

N

100 metres
100 yards

⊕ Piura and around listings

For hotel and restaurant price codes, and other relevant information, see pages 14-17.

⊜ Where to stay

Piura and around *p120, map p121*
To be sure of a room in Piura, book the hotel of your choice in advance.
$$$$ LP Los Portales, Libertad 875, Plaza de Armas, T321161, www.losportales hoteles.com.pe. Includes welcome cocktail, attractively refurbished, the city's social centre, elegant, hot water, pleasant terrace, nice pool.
$$$ Esmeralda, Loreto 235, T331205, www.hotelesmeralda.com.pe. Variety of room sizes, hot water, frigobar, comfortable, good, restaurant.
$$ El Almirante, Ica 860, T335239. With fan, modern, laundry, meals, parking, owner is knowledgeable about the Ayabaca area.
$$ El Sol, Sánchez Cerro 411, T324461. Hot water, frigobar, small pool, snack bar, parking, payment in advance, some rooms can be noisy.
$$ San Miguel, Lima 1007, Plaza Pizarro, T305122, www.sanmigueldepiura.com. Modern, comfortable, café.
$$-$ Hostal Los Jardines, Av Los Cocos 136, T326590, www.hotellosjardines.com. Hot water, laundry, parking, good value.
$ California, Jr Junín 835, upstairs, T328789. Shared or private bath, own water-tank, some hot water, mosquito netting on windows, roof terrace, brightly decorated. The best of the hostels in this area.
$ Hospedaje Aruba, Junín 851, T303067. Small rooms, no windows, but comfortable, shared bath, fan on request.
$ Hostal Moon Night, Junín 899, T336174. Comfortable, modern, spacious, with or without bath, cold water.

⊘ Restaurants

Piura and around *p120, map p121*
$$$ Carburmer, Libertad 1014, T332380. Very good lunches and dinners, also serves pizza.
$$$ Picantería Los Santitos, in the same precinct is Carburmer. Lunch only, wide range of traditional dishes in a renovated colonial house.
$$ Alex Chopp's, Huancavelica 538, T322568. A la carte dishes, seafood, fish, chicken and meats, beer, popular at lunchtime.
$$ Brosti Chopp, Arequipa 780, T303753. Similar, but with lunch *menú* for US$1.45.
$$ Romano, Ayacucho 580. Mon-Sat 0700-2300. Popular with locals, extensive menu, excellent set meal for US$1.55. Recommended. Also has **$$ El Otro Romano**, Ayacucho 579, Tue-Sun 0900-1700, offering the same fare.
$ Ganímedes, Lima 440, T329176. A good vegetarian restaurant, very popular set lunch, à la carte is slow but well worth it.
$ Italia, Grau 172. For breakfasts, snacks, desserts and juices.

Cafés
Chalán del Norte several branches for sandwiches, sweets, and very good ice cream, Tacna 520 on Plaza de Armas, Grau 173 and 450 (**Chalán de la Avenida**).
D'Pauli, Lima 541. Sweets, cakes and ice cream.
La Pera Madura, Arequipa 168, next to Cine Municipal. Daily 1700-2300. For local specialities, plus tamales and other snacks.

⊘ What to do

Piura and around *p120, map p121*
Piura Tours, C Ayacucho 585, T326778, piuratours@speedy.com.pe. The manager Mario speaks good English.

⊖ Transport

Piura and around *p120, map p121*
Air Capitán Guillermo Concha airport is in Castilla, 10 mins from the centre by taxi (US$1.85). It has gift shops and 2 car rental agencies (see below). Daily flights with **LAN** (Av Grau 140) to **Lima** via **Chiclayo**. Flights with **Saereo** Mon, Wed, Fri, 1325, to **Machala** (Santa Rosa) US$87, **Guayaquil** US$120 and **Quito** US$185, one way.
Bus Most companies are on Av Sánchez Cerro, blocks 11, 12 and 13. To **Lima**, 1038 km, 14-15½ hrs, US$30-45. Most buses stop at the major cities on route; **Ittsa**, Sánchez Cerro 1142, T308645; **Línea**, Sánchez Cerro 1215, T327 821; **Tepsa**, Loreto 1195, T306345. To **Chiclayo** and **Lambayeque**, 190 km, 4 hrs, from US$5.50, **Trans Chiclayo**, Sánchez Cerro 1121, T308455; several others. Also several daily buses to **Trujillo**, 7 hrs, 487 km, US$15, to travel by day change in Chiclayo. To **Tumbes**, 282 km, 4½ hrs, US$8.50, several buses daily, eg **Cruz del Sur** (Av Circunvalación 160, T337094, also to Lima), **Cial** (Bolognesi 817, T304250) and **Emtrafesa** (Los Naranjos 255, T337093, also to Chiclayo and Trujillo); also colectivos, US$12. To **Paita**, **Trans Dora**, Sánchez Cerro 1391, every 20 mins, 1 hr, US$1.50; also from Paita terminal on Av Gullman, just off Sánchez Cerro. To **Máncora**, US$5.50, 3 hrs, with **Eppo**, T304543, www.eppo.com.pe.
    To Ecuador To **Machala** and **Guayaquil**, the fastest route if you are heading directly to Quito, **CIFA**, Los Naranjos y Sánchez Cerro (cuadra 11-12) opposite Emtrafesa, T305925, 5 a day, Machala US$7, 6 hrs, Guayaquil US$13-17, 9 hrs. **Ecuatoriana Pullman**, on Av Loreto, 0830, 2030 to **Guayaquil** via Sullana, Tumbes and Machala, US$17-20, 10 hrs. Otherwise, go to Tumbes and travel on from there for the Aguas Verdes crossing. To **Loja**, the best option if you want to visit the southern or central highlands of Ecuador, **Transportes Loja**, Sánchez Cerro 1480, T305446, at 0930, 1300, 1900, US$12, 8-9 hrs, to **Macará** US$5. Or **Unión Cariamanga**, Sánchez Cerro (cuadra 18) y Av Vice, Urb Santa Ana, T969-900135, at 1330 and 2000. Alternatively take a bus to **Sullana**, 38 km, 30 mins (US$0.50), **Eppo**, **Sullana Express** and **Turismo del Norte**, all on 1100 block of Sánchez Cerro; also colectivos (US$1). To **La Tina** on the Ecuadorean frontier, is a further 128 km, 1¾ hrs, US$3.50. It's best to take an early bus to Sullana (start at 0430, leave when full), then a colectivo (see under Sullana).

Catacaos *p120*
Combis From **Piura** to Catacaos leave when full from bus terminal at block 12 of Av Sánchez Cerro, US$0.50, 20 mins.

⊕ Directory

Piura and around *p120, map p121*
Car hire Ramos, T348668, www.ramos rentacars.com. At airport, and others.
Consulates Ecuadorean consulate, Av Chirichigño 505 y F Elguero, Urb El Chipe, T308027. Mon-Fri 0800-1400. **Immigration** Av Integración Urbana y Av Sullana, T335536.

North to Ecuador

Sullana, built on a bluff over the fertile Chira valley, is a busy, modern place 38 km north of Piura. Here the Pan-American Highway forks. To the east it crosses the Peru-Ecuador border at La Tina and continues via Macará to Loja and Cuenca. The excellent paved road is very scenic. The more frequently used route to the border is the coastal road which goes from Sullana northwest towards the Talara oilfields, and then follows the coastline to Máncora and Tumbes.

Border at La Tina–Macará The border crossing is problem-free and both sides are open 24 hours. A new international bridge was opened in 2013 and there are plans to build a border complex. In the meantime immigration, customs and other services are housed in temporary quarters nearby; officials are generally helpful. There are no money changers right at the bridge, only at the park in Macará where vehicles leave for the border. On the Peruvian side, there is one *hospedaje* and several eating places on the road down to the bridge. On the Ecuadorean side, Macará is a small city with all services, 2.5 km past the bridge.

Máncora and Punta Sal

Máncora, a resort stretching along the Panamerican Highway, is popular with young Limeños, Chileans and Argentines and as a stop-off for travellers, especially surfers, on the Peru-Ecuador route. Development here has been rapid and haphazard. The area is crowded and noisy during the December-February high season, beaches can get dirty, drugs and scams (many involving mototaxis) abound and public safety is an important concern. Enquire locally about which sections are currently safe. More tranquil beaches such as Las Pocitas and Vichayito are being developed to the south. Surfing on this coast is best November-March and boards and suits can be hired from several places on Avenida Piura, US$10 per day. **Tourist office**: i Perú ① *Av Piura 250, Thu-Sun 1000-1700*. See www.vivamancora.com.

At 22 km north of Máncora, Km 1187, is the turn-off for **Punta Sal**, marked by a large white arch (El Arco) over the track leading into Punta Sal (2 km). Punta Sal boasts a 3-km-long white sandy beach and a more upmarket clientèle than Máncora, with accommodation (and prices) to match. There is no town centre nor services such as banks, ATMs or restaurants independent of hotels; it is very quiet in the low season. There is one bank and various ATMs in Máncora. Taking a taxi from Máncora to Punta Sal is safest, 20 minutes, US$14; mototaxi 40 minutes, US$10. **Zorritos**, 27 km south of Tumbes, is an important fishing centre with a good beach. At **Caleta La Cruz** is the only part of the Peruvian coast where the sea is warm all year, 16 km southwest of Tumbes. It was here that Pizarro landed in 1532. Regular colectivos, US$0.30 each way.

Tumbes and around → *Phone code: 072. Colour map 2, A1. Population: 94,750.*

The most northerly of Peruvian towns (265 km north of Piura), Tumbes is a garrison town. Most tourists stop only briefly to get transport connections to the beaches to the south, or to Ecuador to the north. The most striking thing is the bright and cheery modern public buildings. The **Malecón Benavides**, a long promenade beside the Tumbes river, has rainbow-coloured archways and a monstrous statue called El Beso (the Kiss). The Plaza de Armas sports a large structure of many colours and even the **cathedral** ① *entry during morning and evening Mass*, (1903, restored in 1985) has green and pink stripes. Calles Bolívar and San Martín (Paseo de la Concordia) make for a pleasant wander and there is a small artesans' market at the top end of San Martín (approaching Plaza Bolognesi). On Calle Grau, there are the tumble-down colonial houses, many of which are no longer in use. **Tourist office** is in the **Centro Cívico** ① *Bolognesi 194, 2nd level, on the plaza, T524940, dirceturtumbes@gmail.com, Mon-Fri 0730-1300, 1400-1630*. **Pronaturaleza** ① *Bq 0B-14, 4 Etapa, Urb Casas Fonavi, T993-583445, comunicaciones@ pronaturaleza.org*, has specialized information about national parks in the area, of which there are three important ones: The **Santuario Nacional los Manglares de Tumbes** protects 3000 ha of Peru's remaining 4750 ha of mangrove forest.

The **Parque Nacional Cerros de Amotape** protects 90,700 ha of varied habitat, but principally the best preserved area of dry forest on the west coast of South America. The **Zona Reservada de Tumbes** (75,000 ha) lies northeast of Tumbes between the Ecuadorean border and Cerros de Amotape. It protects dry equatorial forest and tropical rainforest. The Río Tumbes crocodile, which is a UN Red-data species, is found at the river's mouth, where there is a small breeding programme, and in its upper reaches.

Border with Ecuador The best way to cross this border is on one of the international buses that run between Peru (Piura, Máncora or Tumbes) and Ecuador (Huaquillas, Machala, Guayaquil or Cuenca). If travelling from further south in Peru, do not take a bus all the way to the border; change to an Ecuador-bound bus in Piura, Máncora or Tumbes. Formalities are only carried out at the new bridge, far outside the border towns of **Aguas Verdes** (Peru) and **Huaquillas** (Ecuador). There are two border complexes called **CEBAF (Centro Binacional de Atención Fronteriza)**, open 24 hours on either side of the bridge. Both complexes have Peruvian and Ecuadorean immigration officers so you get your exit and entry stamps in the same place. If crossing with your own vehicle however, you may have to stop at both border complexes for customs.

If you do not take one of the international buses then the crossing is hot, harrowing and transport between the two sides via the new bridge and border complex is inconvenient and expensive (see Transport, below). Travellers often fall vicitim to thefts, muggings, shakedowns by minor officials and countless scams on both sides. Never leave your baggage unattended and do your own arithmetic when changing money. Those seeking a more relaxed crossing to or from Ecuador should consider La Tina–Macará or Namballe–La Balsa.

◉ North to Ecuador listings

For hotel and restaurant price codes, and other relevant information, see pages 14-17.

◉ Where to stay

North to Ecuador: Sullana *p123*
Take care by the market. Do not arrive at night.
$$ Hostal La Siesta, Av Panamericana 400, T502264, www.lasiestasullana.com. At entrance to town, hot water, fan, pool, restaurant, laundry.
$ Hospedaje San Miguel, C J Farfán 204, T502789. Private/shared bath, good showers, basic, helpful, rooms sprayed against mosquitoes, café.
$ Hostal Lion's Palace, Grau 1030, T502587. With fan, patio, pleasant, quiet, no breakfast.

Máncora and Punta Sal *p124*
Máncora town
There are at least 50 hotels in and around Máncora, heavily booked in high sesaon. The

main strip of the Panamericana is known as Av Piura from the bridge for the first couple of blocks, then Av Grau to the end of town. The better hotels are at the southern end of town, with a small concentration of mid-range hotels just over the bridge. Hotels to the left look onto the beach directly in front of the best surf and often have beach entrances as well as road entrances. As the most popular with tourists, they are all noisy at night from nearby discos, which go on until around 0200 week nights and 0600 at weekends. Prices can increase by 100% or more in high season (Dec-Mar). Many hotels have even higher rates for Christmas, New Year, Easter and Independence Day holidays when the resort is full to bursting. When checking into any hotel, expect to pay up front and make sure you get a receipt as you will most likely be asked to pay again the next time the receptionist sees you. Take every precaution with your valuables, theft is common. Mosquitoes are bad at certain times of the year, so take plenty of bug spray.

$$$ Don Giovanni, Pje 8 de Noviembre s/n, T258525, www.dongiovannimancora.com. 3-storey Indonesian-style beachfront hotel, includes breakfast, restaurant and ice cream parlour, kitesurfing classes available.

$$ Del Wawa, beachfront, T258427, www.delwawa.com. This relaxed and spacious Spanish-owned hotel is popular with serious surfers and kitesurfers. Hotel service poor, rooms noisy, food average, but great location and nice restaurants round the corner.

$$ Kon Tiki, Los Incas 200, T258138, www.kontikimancora.net. On hill with lighhouse, great views, cabins with thatched roofs, hammocks, kitchen facilities, bar. Transport to/from bus station provided. Advance booking required.

$$ Las Olas, beachfront, T258099, www.lasolasmancora.com. Smart, cabin-style rooms, top floor rooms have best view of ocean, hammocks and gardens, includes breakfast.

$$ Punta Ballenas Inn, Km 1164, south of Cabo Blanco bridge at the south entrance to town, T630844, www.puntaballenas.com. Lovely setting on beach, garden with small pool, expensive restaurant.

$$-$ Kokopelli Beachpackers, Av Piura 209, T258091, www.hostelkokopelli.com. Popular hostel 3 mins' walk from beach, with pool, bar, good food, good meeting place, lots of facilities. Rooms for 2, 4 or 8, mixed or female only, all with bath, hot water.

$$-$ Laguna Surf Camp, T01-99 401 5628, www.vivamancora.com/lagunacamp. 50 m from the sea, thatched roofs, cabins sleeping up to 6 people (US$11 pp), also cabins around small communal area with hammocks, pool and restaurant. Good surf lessons, helpful staff.

$$-$ Loki del Mar, Av Piura 262, T258484, www.lokihostel.com. In the **Loki** group of hostels, seafront, bright white and modern muti-storey building, doubles with private bath or dorms with 4-6 beds and lockable closets, bar, restaurant, pool, lots of activities.

Be ready for loud music and parties. Advance booking required.

$ Casa del Turista, Av Piura 224, T258126. Family-run, TV, roof terraces giving sea views, good value and location.

Quebrada Cabo Blanco
Crossing the bridge into Máncora, a dirt track leads downhill to the right, to the Quebrada Cabo Blanco, signed to **La Posada Youth Hostel**. The many hotels at the end of the track require better lighting for guests returning at night (robberies have occurred), but the hotels are relatively quiet and relaxing.

$$ Kimbas Bungalows, T258373, www.kimbasbungalowsmancora.com. Relaxed spot with charming thatched bungalows, Balinese influences, nice garden with hammocks, pool, some rooms have hot water, good value. Recommended.

$$ La Posada, T258328, hlaposada@hotmail.com. IYHF affiliated hostel, dorms (US$20 pp), camping (US$12 pp) and rooms with private bath, fan, garden with hammocks, pool, cooking facilities, parking,

Las Pocitas and Vichayito
South of Máncora, a stretch of beautiful beach with rocks on the shore, behind which little pools (or *pocitas*) form at low tide. Vichayito, a separate beach around a headland from Las Pocitas, is better reached from Los Organos than Máncora. There are over 40 hotels in this area.

$$$$ Arennas, Antigua Panamericana Norte Km 1213, T258240, www.lasarenasdemancora.com. Smart, luxury pool or beachfront suites, all modern facilities, with central bar and restaurant serving imaginative dishes, beautiful pool, palm-lined beach frontage, very romantic.

$$$ Las Pocitas, Antigua Panamericana Norte Km 1215, T258432, www.laspocitasmancora.com. Great location, rooms with ocean views, lovely palm-lined beach, terrace, pool, restaurant and bar.

$$$ Máncora Beach Bungalows, Antigua Panamericana Norte Km 1215, Lima T01-201 2060, www.mancora-beach.com. Comfortable rooms with ceiling fan, terrace and hammocks, good restaurant, good value for this price range.

$$$ Puerto Palos, along the old Pan-American Highway 2 km south of Máncora (10 mins by mototaxi, US$2), T258199, www.puertopalos.com. Variety of rooms, fan, suites have a/c. Excellent, nice pool overlooking ocean, hammocks, sunbeds, umbrellas, good restaurant.

$$ Marcilia Beach Bungalows, Antigua Panamericana Norte Km 1212, T09-9468 5209, www.marciliadevichayito.com. Nice rustic bamboo cabins with ocean views, includes breakfast, family-run.

Punta Sal

There is a huge new resort of the Colombian **Royal Decameron** group here, www.decameron.com.

$$$$ Punta Sal, Panamericana Norte Km 1192, Punta Sal Chica, T596700/540088, www.puntasal.com.pe. A beautiful complex of bungalows along a fine sandy beach, with pool, bar decorated with photos of big game fishing, fine restaurant. Most deals are all-inclusive, but massages and whale-watching trips are extra. Good food and service.

$$$-$ Waltako Beach Town, Panamericana 1199, Canoas de Punta Sal, T998-141976, www.waltakoperu.com. Thatched cabins for 2, 4 or 6 people, with kitchenette, porch and hammock. Camping on the beach if you bring your own tent. Restaurant and bar, bicycles, quad bikes and horses for hire. Volunteers welcomed for conservation and reforestation work.

$$ Hospedaje El Bucanero, at the entrance to Playa Punta Sal, set back from the beach, T540118, www.elbucaneropuntasal.com. The most happening place in Punta Sal, popular with travellers, rates rise in high season, a variety of rooms, pool, restaurant, bar and gardens.

$$ Huá, on the beach at the entrance to Playa Punta Sal, T540023, www.hua-puntasal.com. A rustic old wooden building, pleasant terrace overlooking ocean, hammocks, quiet, restful, good food, friendly service.

$$-$ Las Terrazas, opposite Sunset Punta Sal, T507701. One of the more basic and cheaper hotels in Punta Sal in operation since 1989, restaurant has sea view, some rooms better than others, those with own bath and sea view twice the price. Helpful owners.

$ Hospedaje Orillas del Mar, San Martín 496, Cancas. The best of the basic *hostales* lining the beach and Panamericana; a short walk from Punta Sal Chica beaches.

Zorritos

$ Hostal Grillo Tres Puntas, Panamericano Norte Km 1235, T794830, www.casagrillo.net. On the beach, rustic bamboo cabins, quiet and peaceful. Great food prepared by Spanish chef-owner, León, who breeds Peruvian hairless dogs. Lukewarm showers, Wi-Fi in dining area, camping possible on the beach.

Tumbes and around *p124*

Av Tumbes is still sometimes referred to by its old name of Teniente Vásquez. At holiday times it can be very difficult to find a room.

$$$ Costa del Sol, San Martín 275, Plazuela Bolognesi, T523991, www.costadelsolperu.com. The only high class hotel in town, hot water, minibars, a/c, good restaurant, garden, pool, excellent service. Parking for an extra fee. Rooms which look onto the Plaza Bolognesi are noisy.

$$ Lourdes, Mayor Bodero 118, 3 blocks from main plaza, T522966. Welcoming place. Narrow corridor leading to cell-like rooms which are plushly decorated with a mixture of antique and modern furniture. Good bathrooms, fans in each room.

$$-$ Asturias, Av Mcal Castilla 307, T522569. Comfortable, hot water, a/c or fan, restaurant, bar and laundry. Accepts credit cards.

$ Hostal Tumbes, Filipinas s/n, off Grau, T522203, or T972 852954. Small, dark, basic but cleanish rooms with fans and bath. Good cheap option.

🍴 Restaurants

Máncora and Punta Sal *p124*
Máncora
Máncora is packed with restaurants. Plenty of sushi, pizza and grills; most are pricey, the cheaper places are north along Av Piura. At a small open-air commercial centre called **The Birdhouse** are: **Green Eggs and Ham**, open 0730-1300 for great breakfasts at US$3.35, 8 options including waffles, pancakes or eggs and bacon, plus optional extra portions, juice or coffee included. **Papa Mo´s** milk bar, directly underneath Green Eggs and Ham, with comfy seats which are practically on the beach and a selection of drinks.

Along the main strip of the Panamericana:
$$$ Pizzería Mamíferos, Av Piura 346. Tue-Sun 1800-2300. Wood-oven pizzas and lasagna.
$$$-$$ Josil, near **The Birdhouse**. Closed Sun. Very good Sushi bar.
$$$-$$ Tao , Av Piura. Closed Wed. Good Asian food and curries.
$$ Angela's Place/Cafetería de Angela, Av Piura 396, www.vivamancora.com/deangela. Daily 0800-2300. A great option for a healthy breakfast or lunch and heaven for vegetarians and wholefood lovers, home-made bread, yogurts, fresh fruit etc.
$$ Don César, hard to find, ask around or take a mototaxi. Closed Sun. Good fresh sea food, very popular with locals.
$ Café La Bajadita, Av Piura, has an impressive selection of delicious home-made desserts and cakes.

Tumbes and around *p124*
Cheap restaurants on the Plaza de Armas, Paseo de la Concordia and near the markets.
$$-$ Budabar, Grau 309, on Plaza de Armas, T525493. One of a kind chill-out lounge offering traditional food and comfy seating with outdoor tables and cheap beer, popular in the evenings.
$$-$ Chifa Wakay, Huáscar 413. Open evenings only. A large, well-ventilated smart restaurant offering the usual Chifa favourites.

$$-$ Classic, Tumbes 185. Look for it almost under the bridge over the river, heading south. Popular for local food.
$$-$ Los Gustitos, Bolívar 148. Excellent menús and à la carte. Popular, good atmosphere at lunchtime.
$ Sí Señor, Bolívar 119 on the plaza. Good for snacks, cheap lunch menus.
Cherry, San Martín 116. Open 0800-1400, 1700-2300. Tiny café offering an amazing selection of cakes and desserts, also fresh juices, shakes, sandwiches, hot and cold drinks and traditional *cremoladas* (fruit juice with crushed ice).

🎯 What to do

Máncora and Punta Sal *p124*
Many agencies on Av Piura offer day trips to Manglares de Tumbes and Isla del Amor for snorkelling, as well as private transport in cars and vans.
Iguanas Trips, Av Piura 306, T632762, www.iguanastrips.com. Run by Ursula Behr, offers a variety of adventure tourism trips, horseriding and camping in the nearby national parks and reserve zones.
Samana Chakra, in the eponymous hotel, T258604, www.samanachakra.com. Yoga classes, US$5 per hr.
Surf Point Máncora, on the beach next to Hostal del Wawa. Surf classes US$17.50 per hr, kitesurfing (season Mar-Sep) US$50 per hr. Various board rentals.

🚌 Transport

North to Ecuador: Sullana *p123*
Bus Several bus companies including Ormeño share a Terminal Terrestre outside the centre. To **Tumbes**, 244 km, 4-5 hrs, US$8, several buses daily. To **Chiclayo** and **Trujillo** see under Piura. To **Lima**, 1076 km, 14-16 hrs, several buses daily, most coming from Tumbes, luxury overnight via Trujillo with **Ittsa** (T503705), also with **Ormeño** and **Tepsa** (José de Lama 236, T502120). To **Máncora**, Eppo, frequent, 2½ hrs, US$4.50.

Border with Ecuador: La Tina–Macará
p124

Bus Buses leave frequently from Ecuadorean side for Loja, so even if you are not taking the through bus (see under Piura), you can still go from Sullana to Loja in a day. From the border to Sullana, cars may leave before they are full, but won't charge extra.

Shared taxis Station wagons leave from Sullana to the international bridge from Terminal Terrestre La Capullana, off Av Buenos Aires, several blocks beyond the canal. They leave when full, US$8 per person, 1¾ hrs. It's best to take a taxi or mototaxi to and from the terminal. From the border to Macará is 2.5 km; pick-ups charge US$0.50 pp, or US$1.50 for whole vehicle.

Máncora and Punta Sal *p124*

Bus To **Sullana** with Eppo, every 30 mins, 0400-1830, US$4.50, 3½ hrs; to **Piura**, US$5.50, 4 hrs;. also colectivos, 2 hrs, US$9; to **Tumbes** (and points in between), minibuses leave when full, US$5.50, 1½ hrs. Several companies to **Lima**, US$28-70, 18 hrs; to **Chiclayo**, Tran Chiclayo, US$17.50, 6 hrs; **Trujillo** US$25, 9 hrs. To **Ecuador: Machala** (US$14, 5 hrs) and **Guayaquil** (US$17.50, 8 hrs), CIFA and Super Semería, at 0800, 1100 and 1300; Guayaquil direct at 2300 and 2330; **Cuenca**, Super Semería at 2300 and 2400, US$20.

Tumbes and around *p124*

Air Daily flights to and from **Lima** (LAN, Bolognesi 250).

Bus Daily to and from **Lima**, 1320 km, 18-20 hrs, depending on stopovers, US$34-45 regular fare), US$60 (Cruz del Sur VIP, Tumbes Norte 319, T896163). **Civa**, Av Tumbes 518, T525120. Several buses daily. Cheaper buses usually leave 1600-2100, more expensive ones 1200-1400. Except for luxury service, most buses to Lima stop at major cities en route. Tickets to anywhere between Tumbes and Lima sell quickly, so if arriving from Ecuador you may have to stay overnight. Piura is a good place for connections in the daytime. To **Sullana**, 244 km, 3-4 hrs, US$8, several buses daily. To **Piura**, 4-5 hrs, 282 km, US$8.50 with **Trans Chiclayo** (Tumbes 466, T525260), **Cruz del Sur, El Dorado** (Piura 459, T523480) 6 a day; **Comité Tumbes/ Piura** (Tumbes N 308, T525 977), US$12 pp, fast cars, leave when full, 3½ hrs. To **Chiclayo**, 552 km, 7-8 hrs, US$9, several each day with **Cruz del Sur, El Dorado**, and others. To **Trujillo**, 769 km, 10-11 hrs, from US$15, **Ormeño** (Av Tumbes s/n, T522228), **Cruz del Sur, El Dorado, Emtrafesa**, Tumbes Norte 596, T522894. Transport to the border with Ecuador, see below.

To Ecuador CIFA, Av Tumbes 958, to **Machala**, US$4, and **Guayaquil**, 5 a day, luxury bus at 1000, US$8.50, 5 hrs to Guayaquil.

Border with Ecuador *p125*
Between Tumbes and the border
If you cannot cross on an international bus (the preferred option), then take a taxi from Tumbes to the new bridge, 17 km, US$12; bridge to **Huaquillas**, US$2.50-5. **Entering Peru** From the new bridge to: **Tumbes,** city or airport, US$17; **Punta Sal**, US$50; **Máncora**, US$60.

● Directory

Máncora and Punta Sal *p124*
Medical services Clínica Medical Center, Av Panamericana s/n, T258601.

Tumbes and around *p124*
Consulates Ecuadorean Consulate, Bolívar 129, p 3, Plaza de Armas, T525949, consultum@ speedy.com.pe. Mon-Fri 0800-1400. **Medical services** 24 Hour Emergency Clinic, Av Mariscal Castilla 305, T525341. Consultancy hours Mon to Fri 0800-1400.

Northern Highlands

Leaving the Pacific coast behind, you climb in a relatively short time up to the Sierra. It was here, at Cajamarca, that the defeat of the Incas by the Spaniards began, bringing about cataclysmic change to this part of the world. But, unlike this well-documented event, the history of the Incas' contemporaries and predecessors has to be teased out of the stones of their temples and fortresses, which are shrouded in cloud in the 'Eyebrow of the Jungle'.

Trujillo to Cajamarca

To the northeast of Trujillo is Cajamarca, an attractive colonial town surrounded by lovely countryside and the commercial centre of the northern mountain area. It can be reached by the old road (now paved) via Huamachuco and Cajabamba, or via Ciudad de Dios. The former road takes two hours from Huamachuco to Cajabamba and three hours from Cajabamba via San Marcos to Cajamarca (as opposed to nine hours via Ciudad de Dios, see below). It is also more interesting, passing over the bare *puna* before dropping to the Huamachuco valley.

Huamachuco → *Colour map 2, B2. Altitude: 3180 m. www.munihuamachuco.gob.pe.*
This colonial town formerly on the royal Inca Road, 181 km from Trujillo, has the largest main plaza in Peru, with fine topiary, and a controversial modern **cathedral**. There is a colourful **Sunday market**, with dancing in the plaza, and the Founding of Huamachuco festival, second week in August, with spectacular fireworks and the amazing, aggressive male dancers, called *turcos*. **Museo Municipal Wamachuko** ① *Sucre 195, Mon-Sat 0900-1300, 1500-1900, Sun 0900-1200, free,* displays artefacts found at nearby **Cerro Amaru** (a hill-top system of wells and water worship) and **Marca Huamachuco** ① *daily 0900-1700, allow 2 hrs, 4 hrs to explore fully.* Access is via a poor vehicle road or a mule track (preferable for walking), off the road to Sanagorán, there is an archway at the turn-off, 5 km from Huamachuco, mototaxi to turn-off US$2; combis to Sanagorán in the morning. These hilltop pre-Inca fortifications rank in the top 10 archaeological sites in Peru. They are 3 km long, dating back to at least 300 BC though many structures were added later. Its most impressive features are: El Castillo, a remarkable circular structure with walls up to 8 m high located at the highest point of the site, and El Convento complex, five circular structures of varying sizes towards the northern end of the hill. The largest one has been partially reconstructed. The extensive Huari ruins of **Wiracochapampa** are 3 km north of town, 45 minutes' walk, but much of the site is overgrown.

   Cajabamba is a small market town and a useful stop-over point between Cajamarca and Huamachuco. A new thermal bath complex, **La Grama**, is 30 minutes by combi (US$1) from Cajabamba, with a pool, very hot individual baths and an adjoining small *hostal*.

Pacasmayo → *Colour map 2, B1. Population: 12,300.*
Pacasmayo, 102 km north of Trujillo, is the port for the next oasis north. It has a nice beach front with an old Customs House and a very long pier. Resort El Faro is 1 km away, with surfing at the point and kite- and windsurfing closer to town. There are maritime festivals at New Year and Semana Santa. Away from the front it is a busy commercial centre.

   Some 20 km further north on the Panamericana is the main road connection from the coast to Cajamarca at a junction called **Ciudad de Dios**. The paved 175 km road branches off the Pan-American Highway soon after it crosses the Río Jequetepeque. The river valley has terraced rice fields and mimosas may often be seen in bloom, brightening the otherwise dusty landscape.

Cajamarca → *Phone code: 076. Colour map 2, B2. Population: 201,000. Altitude: 2750 m.*

At Cajamarca Pizarro ambushed and captured Atahualpa, the Inca emperor. This was the first showdown between the Spanish and the Incas and, despite their huge numerical inferiority, the Spanish emerged victorious, executing Atahualpa in the process. The nearby **Yanacocha gold mine** ⓘ *www.yanacocha.com.pe*, has brought new wealth to the town (and major ecological concerns and social problems) and Cajamarca is the hub of tourism development for the whole of the northwest via the *Circuito Turístico Nororiental* (Chiclayo-Cajamarca-Chachapoyas). **Tourist offices: Dirección Regional de Turismo** and **Ministerio de Cultura** ⓘ *in the Conjunto Monumental de Belén, Belén 631, T362601, cajamarca@mcultura.gob.pe, Mon-Fri 0900-1300, 1500-1730*. **Sub-Gerencia de Turismo of the Cajamarca Municipality** ⓘ *Av Alameda de los Incas, Complejo Qhapac Ñan, T363626, www.municaj.gob.pe,* opposite UNC university on the road to Baños del Inca. The **University tourist school** ⓘ *Del Batán 289, T361546, Mon-Fri 0830-1300, 1500-2200,* offers free advice and leaflets. **Indecopi** ⓘ *Apurímac 601, T363315, mcastillo@indecopi.gob.pe.*

Cajamarca

Where to stay		
1 Cajamarca	10 La Casona del Inca	6 El Pez Loco
2 Costa del Sol	11 Los Balcones de	7 El Zarco
3 El Cabildo	La Recoleta	8 Heladería Holanda
4 El Cumbe Inn		9 Om-Gri
5 El Ingenio	**Restaurants**	10 Pascana
6 El Portal del Marqués	1 Bella's Café Lounge	11 Pizzería El Marengo
7 Hosp Los Jazmines	2 Casa Club	12 Pizzería Vaca Loca
8 Hostal Becerra	3 Cascanuez	13 Querubino
9 Hostal Perú	4 De Buena Laya	14 Salas
	5 Don Paco	15 Sanguchón.com

N

100 metres
100 yards

Complejo Belén ① *Tue-Sat 0900-1300, 1500-1800, Sun 0900-1300, US$1.55, valid for more than 1 day, a ticket is also valid for the Cuarto de Rescate, a guide for all the sites costs US$2.85 (US$5.75-8.50 for guides in other languages).* The complex comprises the tourist office and Institute of Culture, a beautifully ornate church, considered the city's finest. See the inside of the dome, where eight giant cherubs support an intricate flowering centrepiece. In the same courtyard is the **Museo Médico Belén**, which has a collection of medical instruments. Across the street is a maternity hospital from the colonial era, now the **Archaeological and Ethnological Museum**, Junín y Belén. It has a range of ceramics from all regions and civilizations of Peru. The **Cuarto de Rescate** ① *entrance at Amalia Puga 750, Tue-Sat 0900-1800, Sun 0900-1300,* is not the actual ransom chamber but in fact the room where Atahualpa was held prisoner. A red line on the wall is said to indicate where Atahualpa reached up and drew a mark, agreeing to have his subjects fill the room to the line with treasure. A new roof protects the building from the weather and pollution.

You can also visit the plaza where Atahualpa was ambushed and the stone altar set high on **Santa Apolonia hill** ① *US$0.60, take bus marked Santa Apolonia/Fonavi, or micro A,* where he is said to have reviewed his subjects. There is a road to the top, or you can walk up from Calle 2 de Mayo, using the steep stairway. The view is worth the effort, especially at sunrise (but go in a group).

The **Plaza de Armas**, where Atahualpa was executed, has a 350-year-old fountain, topiary and gardens. The **Cathedral** ① *0800-1000, 1600-1800,* opened in 1776, is still missing its belfry, but the façade has beautiful baroque carving in stone. On the opposite side of the plaza is the 17th-century **San Francisco Church** ① *Mon-Fri 0900-1200, 1600-1800,* older than the Cathedral and with more interior stone carving and elaborate altars. The attached **Museo de Arte Colonial** ① *Mon-Sat 1430-1800, US$1, entrance is behind the church on Amalia Puga y Belén,* is filled with colonial paintings and icons. The guided tour of the museum includes entry to the church's spooky catacombs.

The city has many old colonial houses with garden patios, and 104 elaborately carved doorways: see the **Bishop's Palace**, across the street from the Cathedral; the **palace of the Condes de Uceda**, at Jr Apurímac 719 (now occupied by BCP bank); and the **Casa Silva Santiesteban** (Junín y 2 de Mayo).

Museo Arqueológico Horacio H Urteaga ① *Del Batán 289, Mon-Fri 0700-1445, free, donations accepted,* of the Universidad Nacional de Cajamarca, has objects of the pre-Inca Cajamarca and other cultures. The university maintains an experimental arboretum and agricultural station, the **Museo Silvo-agropecuario** ① *Km 2.5 on the road to Baños del Inca,* with a lovely mural at the entrance.

Excursions About 6 km away are the sulphurous thermal springs of **Los Baños del Inca** ① *0500-2000, T348385, www.ctbinca.com.pe, US$0.70, combis marked Baños del Inca cost US$0.20, 15 mins, taxis US$2.30.* The water temperature is at least 72° C. Atahualpa tried the effect of these waters on a festering war wound and his bath is still there. The complex is renewed regularly, with gardens and various levels of accommodation (see Where to stay, below). The main baths are divided into five categories, with prices ranging from US$1.75-2.10, all with private tubs and no pool. Sauna US$3.50, massage US$7 (take your own towel; soaps are sold outside). Only spend 20 minutes maximum in the water; obey instructions; many of the facilities allow bathers in shifts, divided by time and/or sex.

Other excursions include **Llacanora**, a typical Andean village in beautiful scenery (13 km southeast; nice walk downhill from Baños del Inca, two hours). **Ventanillas de Otusco** ① *8 km, 0800-1800, US$1.10, combi US$0.20,* part of an old pre-Inca cemetery, has a gallery of secondary burial niches. There are good day walks in this area; local sketch maps available.

A road goes to **Ventanillas de Combayo** ① *occasional combis on weekdays; more transport on Sun when a market is held nearby, 1 hr, some 20 km past the burial niches of Otusco*. These are more numerous and spectacular, being located in an isolated, mountainous area, and distributed over the face of a steep 200-m-high hillside.

Cumbe Mayo, a *pampa* on a mountain range, is 20 km southwest of Cajamarca. It is famous for its extraordinary, well-engineered pre-Inca channels, running for 9 km across the mountain tops. It is said to be the oldest man-made construction in South America. The sheer scale of the scene is impressive and the huge rock formations of Los Frailones ('big monks') and others with fanciful names are strange indeed. On the way to Cumbe Mayo is the Layzón ceremonial centre. There is no bus service; guided tours run from 0900-1300 (recommended in order to see all the pre-Inca sites); taxi US$15. To walk up takes three to four hours (take a guide, or a tour, best weather May-September). The trail starts from the hill of Santa Apolonia (Silla del Inca), and goes to Cumbe Mayo straight through the village and up the hill; at the top of the mountain, leave the trail and take the road to the right to the canal. The walk is not difficult and you do not need hiking boots. Take a good torch. The locals use the trail to bring their goods to market.

The **Porcón** rural cooperative, with its evangelical faith expressed on billboards, is a popular excursion, 30 km northwest of Cajamarca. It is tightly organized, with carpentry, bakery, cheese and yoghurt-making, zoo and vicuñas. A good guide helps to explain everything. If not taking a tour, contact **Cooperativa Agraria Atahualpa Jerusalén** ① *Chanchamayo 1355, Fonavi 1, T825631*.

Some 93 km west of Cajamarca is the mining town of Chilete, 21 km north of which on the road to San Pablo is **Kuntur Wasi**. The site was devoted to a feline cult and consists of a pyramid and stone monoliths. Extensive excavations are under way and significant new discoveries are being made (excellent site museum). There are two basic *hostales* in Chilete; very limited facilities.

⊕ Trujillo to Catamarca listings

For hotel and restaurant price codes, and other relevant information, see pages 14-17.

⊕ Where to stay

Huamachuco *p130*
$$ Real, Bolívar 250, T441402, www.hotel realhuamachuco.com. Modern, sauna, majority of fittings are wood, pleasant with good service.
$$ Santa María, Grau 224, T348334. An enormous new, sparsely furnished edifice offering the best-quality rooms in town, with restaurant.
$$-$ Hostal Santa Fe, San Martín 297, T441019, www.actiweb.es/luisnv83/. Good value, hot water, parking, restaurant.

$ Hostal Huamachuco, Castilla 354, on the plaza, T440599. With private or shared hot showers, small rooms but large common areas, good value, has parking.

Cajabamba
$ Hostal Flores, Leoncio Prado 137, on the Plaza de Armas, T551086. With electric shower, cheaper without bath, clean but rooms are gloomy, nice patio; no breakfast.

Pacasmayo *p130*
$$ La Estación, Malecón Grau 69, T521515, www.hotellaestacion.com.pe. Restaurant on ground floor, all meals extra, some rooms with terrace overlook sea, others face street, fan, good beds.

$$ Libertad, Leoncio Pardo 1-D, T521937, www.hotellibertad.com. 2 km from beach by petrol station, safe, restaurant/bar, parking, efficient and nice.

$$ Pakatnamú, Malecón Grau 103, T522368, www.activeb.es/hotelpakatnamu. Historic building on seafront with verandahs and balconies, rooms and suite have seaview.

$ Duke Kahanamoku, Ayacucho 44, T521889, www.eldukepacasmayo.com. Surfing place, with classes and board rental, breakfast extra, hot water.

Cajamarca p131, map p131

$$$$ Costa del Sol, Cruz de Piedra 707, T362472, www.costadelsolperu.com. On the Plaza de Armas, part of a Peruvian chain, with airport transfer, welcome drink; restaurant, café and bars, pool, spa, casino, business centre.

$$$ El Ingenio, Av Vía de Evitamiento 1611-1709, T368733, www.elingenio.com. Colonial style buildings 1½ blocks from new El Quinde shopping mall. With solar-powered hot water, spacious, very relaxed.

$$ Cajamarca, Dos de Mayo 311, T362532, hotelcajamarca@gmail.com. 3-star in beautiful colonial mansion, sizeable rooms, hot water, food excellent in Los Faroles restaurant.

$$ El Cabildo, Junín 1062, T367025. Includes breakfast, in historic monument with patio and modern fountain, full of character, elegant local decorations, comfortable, breakfast served.

$$ El Cumbe Inn, Pasaje Atahualpa 345, T366858, www.elcumbeinn.com. Includes breakfast and tax, comfortable, variety of rooms, hot water, evening meals on request, small gym, will arrange taxis, very helpful.

$$ El Portal del Marqués, Del Comercio 644, T368464, www.portaldelmarques.com. Attractive converted colonial house, laundry, safe, parking, leased restaurant **El Mesón del Marqués** has good lunch *menú*. Casino with slot machines.

$$ La Casona del Inca, 2 de Mayo 458-460, Plaza de Armas, T367524,

www.casonadelincaperu.com. Upstairs, old building, traditional style, some rooms overlooking plaza, some with interior windows, good beds, breakfast in café on top floor, tours, laundry.

$$ Los Balcones de la Recoleta, Amalia Puga 1050, T363302, hslosbalcones@speedy. com.pe. Beautifully restored 19th-century house, central courtyard full of flowers, some rooms with period furniture, internet.

$ Hospedaje Los Jazmines, Amazonas 775, T361812. In a converted colonial house with courtyard and café, 14 rooms with hot water, all profits go to disabled children, guests can visit the project's school and help.

$ Hostal Becerra, Del Batán 195, T367867. With hot water, modern, pleasant, will store luggage until late buses depart.

$ Hostal Perú, Amalia Puga 605, on Plaza, T365568. With hot water, functional rooms in old building around central patio used by **El Zarco** restaurant, wooden floors, credit cards taken.

Los Baños del Inca

$$$$-$$$ Laguna Seca, Av Manco Cápac 1098, T584300, www.lagunaseca.com.pe. In pleasant surroundings with thermal streams, private hot thermal baths in rooms, swimming pool with thermal water, restaurant, bar, health spa with a variety of treatments, disco, horses for hire.

$$$ Hostal Fundo Campero San Antonio, 2 km off the Baños road (turn off at Km 5), T368237. An old *hacienda*, wonderfully restored, with open fireplaces and gardens, 15 mins walk along the river to Baños del Inca, riding on *caballos de paso*, own dairy produce, fruit and vegetables, catch your own trout for supper; try the *licor de sauco*.

$$-$ Los Baños del Inca, see above, T348385. Various accommodation: bungalows for 2 to 4 with thermal water, fridge; **Albergue Juvenil**, not IYFH, hostel rooms with bunk beds or double rooms, private bath, caters to groups, basic. Camping possible. Restaurant offers full board.

🍴 Restaurants

Huamachuco *p130*

$$-$ Bull Grill, R Castilla 364. Smart new place specializing in meat dishes, with a cool bar at the back.

$ Café Somos, Bolognesi 665. Good coffee, large turkey/ham sandwiches and excellent cakes.

$ Doña Emilia, Balta 384, on Plaza de Armas. Good for breakfast and snacks.

$ El Viejo Molino, R Castilla 160. Specializes in local cuisine, such as *cuy*.

Cajabamba

$ Cafetería La Otuscana, Grau 929. Daily 0730-2200. Good bakery, sweets and sandwiches.

$ Don Lucho, Jr Leoncio Prado 227. Good local trout and other à la carte dishes.

Cajamarca *p131, map p131*

$$$ Pascana, Av Atahualpa 947. Well-known and recommended as the best in town, near the new Qhapac Ñan Municipality. Their **Taberna del Diablo** is the top disco in town.

$$$ Querubino, Amalia Puga 589, T340900. Mediterranean-style decoration, a bit of everything on the menu, including pastas, daily specials, breakfasts, cocktails, coffees, expensive wines otherwise reasonable, popular.

$$ Casa Club, Amalia Puga 458-A, T340198. Open 0800-2300. *Menú*, including vegetarian, and extensive selection à la carte, family atmosphere, slow but attentive service.

$$ Don Paco, Amalia Puga 390, T362655. Opposite San Francisco. Typical, including *novo andino*, and international dishes, tasty food, desserts, drinks.

$$ El Pez Loco, San Martín 333. Recommended for fish dishes.

$$ Om-Gri, San Martín 360, near the Plaza de Armas. Opens 1300 (1830 Sun). Good Italian dishes, small, informal, French spoken.

$$ Pizzería El Marengo, Junín 1201. Good pizzas and warm atmosphere, T368045 for delivery.

$$ Salas, Amalia Puga 637, on the main plaza, T362867. Open 0700-2200. A Cajamarca tradition, fast service, excellent local food (try their *cuy frito*), best *tamales* in town.

$$-$ De Buena Laya, 2 de Mayo 343. With a rustic interior, popular with hostales, offers *novo cajamarquino* cuisine; lunchtime *menú* US$3.50.

$$-$ El Zarco, Jr Del Batán 170, T363421. Sun-Fri 0700-2300. Very popular, also has short *chifa* menu, good vegetarian dishes, excellent fish, popular for breakfast.

$ Pizzería Vaca Loca, San Martín 330. Popular, best pizzas in town.

Cafés

Bella's Café Lounge, Junín 1184, T345794. For breakfasts, sandwiches, great desserts and coffee from Chanchamayo, Wi-Fi, a place to linger, check emails and relax, owner Raul speaks English. Popular with visitors to the city.

Cascanuez, Amalia Puga 554. Great cakes, extensive menu including *humitas*, breakfasts, ice creams and coffees, highly regarded.

Heladería Holanda, Amalia Puga 657 on the Plaza de Armas, T340113. Dutch-owned, easily the best ice creams in Cajamarca, 50 flavours (but not all on at the same time), try *poro poro*, *lúcuma* or *sauco*, also serves coffee. Four branches, including at Baños del Inca. Ask if it is possible to visit their factory. They assist deaf people and single mothers.

Sanguchón.com, Junín 1137. Best burgers in town, sandwiches, also popular bar.

⊛ Festivals

Cajamarca *p131, map p131*

The **pre-Lent Carnival** is very spectacular and regarded as one of the best in the country; it is also one of the most raucous. In Porcón, 16 km to the northwest, **Palm Sunday** processions are worth seeing.

24 Jun San Juan in Cajamarca, Chota, Llacanora, San Juan and Cutervo. An agricultural fair is held in **Jul** at Baños del Inca; on the first Sun in **Oct** is the Festival Folklórico in Cajamarca.

Shopping

Cajamarca p131, map p131
Handicrafts Specialities including gilded mirrors and cotton and wool saddlebags (*alforjas*). Items can be made to order. The market on Amazonas is good for *artesanía*. There are stalls near the Belén complex (Belén and/or 2 de Mayo) and along the steps up to Santa Apolonia hill. At Jr El Comercio 1045, next to the Police office, is a **Feria Artesenal**, as well as **El Molino** at 2 de Mayo. All offer a good range of local crafts.

What to do

Cajamarca p131, map p131
Agencies around the Plaza de Armas offer trips to local sites and further (eg Kuntur Wasi, Kuélap), trekking on Inca trails, riding *caballos de paso* and handicraft tours. Cumbe Mayo, US$6.50-8.50, 4-5 hrs at 0930. Porcón, US$6.50-8.50, 4-5 hrs at 0930. Otusco, US$4.50-7, 3-3½ hrs at 1530. City tour, US$7, 3 hrs at 0930 or 1530. Kuntur Wasi is a full day. There are also 2 day/3 night tours to Kuélap and Cutervo National Park.
Cumbemayo Tours, Amalia Puga 635 on the plaza, T362938. Guides in English and French, standard tours.
Mega Tours, Amalia Puga 691 on the plaza, T341876, www.megatours.org. Conventional tours, full day and further afield, ecotourism and adventures.

Transport

Huamachuco p130
Bus To/from **Trujillo**, 170 km, 5-6 hrs, US$9-15: the best service is **Fuentes** (J Balta 1090, Huamachuco, T41090 and Av R Palma 767, Trujillo, T204581); **Tunesa**

(Suárez 721, T441157). To **Cajabamba**, **Trans Los Andes**, Pje Hospital 109, 3 combis a day, 2 hrs, US$7.50.

Cajabamba
Bus To/from **Cajamarca**, 127 km, US$7.50, 3 hrs, several companies. Combis, 3 hrs, US$8.

Cajamarca p131, map p131
Air To/from **Lima**: LC Peru (Comercio 1024, T361098), daily except Sat, LAN (Cruz de Piedra 657) and Star Perú (Junín 1300, T367243). The military **Grupo Aéreo 42** (Amalia Pugla 605, T970-029134) has passenger flights to Cajamarca originating in Trujillo or Iquitos; see page 109 for routes and schedules. Airport 5 km from town; taxi US$8.
Bus Buses in town charge US$0.35. To **Lima**, 870 km, 12-14 hrs, US$27-53, including several luxury services, many buses daily. To **Trujillo**, 295 km, 7 hrs, US$10-27, regular buses daily 0900-2230 most continue to Lima. To **Chiclayo**, 265 km, 6 hrs, US$9-20, several buses daily; you have to change buses to go on to Piura and Tumbes. To **Celendín**, 107 km, 3½ hrs, US$6, usually 2 a day with CABA, Royal Palace's and Rojas. To **Chachapoyas**, 336 km, 11-12 hrs, US$18, **Virgen del Carmen**, Atahualpa 333A, T983-915869, at 0500, to **Leymebamba**, US$11.55, 9-10 hrs. The route follows a paved road through beautiful countryside. Among the bus companies are: **CABA**, Atahualpa 299, T366665 (Celendín); **Civa**, Ayacucho 753, T361460 (Lima); **Cruz del Sur**, Atahualpa 606, T361737 (Lima). **Emtrafesa**, Atahualpa 315, T369663 (to Trujillo). **Línea**, Atahualpa 318, T363956 (Lima, Trujillo, Chiclayo). **Móvil**, Atahualpa 405, T340873 (Lima). **Rojas**, Atahualpa 309, T340548 (to Cajabamba; Celendín); **Royal Palace's**, Reina Forje 130, T343063 (Lima, Trujillo, Celendín); **Tepsa**, Sucre y Reina Forje, T363306 (Lima); **Turismo Días**, Av Evitamiento s/n, T344322 (to Lima, Chimbote, Trujillo, Chiclayo).
Taxi US$2 within city limits. Mototaxis US$0.75. Radio taxi: El Sol, T368897, 24 hrs. Taxi Super Seguro, T507090.

Chachapoyas region

Cajamarca is a convenient starting point for the trip east to the department of Amazonas, which contains the archaeological riches of the Chachapoyans, also known as Sachupoyans. Here lie the great pre-Inca cities of Vilaya (not yet developed for tourism) and the immense fortress of Kuélap, among many others. It is also an area of great natural beauty with waterfalls, notably Gocta, cliffs and caves. The road is paved but prone to landslides in the rainy season. It follows a winding course through the mountains, crossing the wide and deep canyon of the Río Marañón at Balsas. The road climbs steeply with superb views of the mountains and the valleys below. The fauna and flora are spectacular as the journey alternates between high mountains and low forest.

Celendín → *Phone code: 076. Colour map 2, B2.*
East from Cajamarca, this is the first town of note, with a pleasant plaza and cathedral, predominantly blue. Festival 16 July to 3 August (**Virgen del Carmen**). There is also a fascinating local market on Sunday which is held in three distinct areas. At 0630 the **hat market** is held by the Alameda, between Ayacucho and 2 de Mayo at Jorge Chávez. You can see hats at every stage of production, but it is over within an hour or so. Then at 0930 the **potato market** takes place at 2 de Mayo y Sucre and, at the other end of town, the **livestock market** on Túpac Amaru. The most popular local excursion is to the hot springs and mud baths at **Llanguat**, 20 km, US$2.75 by limited public transport. Multired ATM beside **Banco de la Nación** on 2 de Mayo may not accept all foreign cards; take cash.

Leymebamba and around → *Phone code: 041. Colour map 2, B2. Altitude: 2250 m.*
There are plenty of ruins – many of them covered in vegetation – and good walking possibilities around this pleasant town at the source of the Utcubamba River. The main attraction in the area is its spectacular museum, see below.

La Congona, a Chachapoyan site, is well worth the effort, with stupendous views. It consists of three hills: on the vegetation-covered conical hill in the middle, the ruins are clustered in a small area, impossible to see until you are right there. The other hills have been levelled. La Congona is the best preserved of three sites in this area, with 30 round stone houses (some with evidence of three storeys) and a watch tower. The two other sites, **El Molinete** and **Cataneo**, are nearby. All three sites can be visited in a day but a guide is advisable. It is a brisk three hours' walk from Leymebamba, first along the rough road to Fila San Cristóbal, then a large trail. The road starts at the bottom of Jr 16 de Julio.

At **Laguna de los Cóndores**, in 1996, a spectacular site consisting of six burial *chullpas*, containing 219 mummies and vast quantities of ceramics, textiles, woodwork, *quipus* and everyday utensils from the late Inca period, was discovered near a beautiful lake in a lush cloudforest setting. The trip to Laguna de los Cóndores takes 10-12 hours on foot and horseback from Leymebamba. An all-inclusive tour for the three-day muddy trek can be arranged at Leymebamba hotels (ask for Sinecio or Javier Farge) or with Chachapoyas operators, US$70 per person. The artefacts were moved to the excellent **Museo Leymebamba** ① *outside San Miguel, on the road to Celendín, T041-816803, www. museoleymebamba.org, Tue-Sun about 0930-1630, entry US$5.75. Taxi from Leymebamba US$2.75, mototaxi US$2.* From Leymebamba, walk to the village of 2 de Mayo, ask for the trail to San Miguel, then take the footpath uphill, the road is much longer. It is beautifully laid-out and very informative. Across the road is **Kentitambo** (T971-118273, **$$$$-$$$** in two comfortable cabins, restaurant, lovely grounds with hummingbirds), **Kentikafe**, offering snacks, and **Mishqui**, offering meals on request.

The road to Chachapoyas follows the Utcubamba River north. In the mountains rising from the river, are a number of archaeological sites. Before **Yerbabuena** (important Sunday market, basic *hospedaje*), a road heads east to **Montevideo** (basic *hospedaje*) and beyond to the small village of San Pedro de Utac, where you can hike up to the impressive but overgrown ruins of Cerro Olán.

The burial *chullpas* of **Revash**, of the Revash culture (AD 1250), are reached from either **San Bartolo** (30-45 minutes' walk) or a trail starting past **Puente Santo Tomás** (1½ to two hours' walk). Both access points are along roads going west from Yerbabuena.The town of **Jalca Grande** (or La Jalca), at 2800 m, is reached along a road going east at **Ubilón**, north of Yerbabuena. Jalca Grande has the remains of a Chachapoyan roundhouse, a stone church tower, a small **museum** ① *US$1.80*, with ceramics and textiles, and one very basic *hospedaje*.

Tingo → *Phone code: 041. Colour map 2, B2. Altitude: 1800 m.*

Situated at the junction of the Tingo and Utcubamba rivers, 40 km north of Leymebamba and 37 km south of Chachapoyas, Tingo is the access for Kuélap. A road climbs steeply from Tingo to **Choctámal**, where it divides. The left branch climbs east to Lónguita, María, Quizango and Kuélap.

Kuélap → *Altitude: 3000 m.*

① *0800-1700, US$4.30, guides available for US$7 per group (Rigoberto Vargas Silva has been recommended). The ticket office at the car park has a small but informative Sala de Interpretacion.* Kuélap is a spectacular pre-Inca walled city which was re-discovered in 1843. It was built continuously from AD 500 up to Inca times and is said to contain three times more stone than the Great Pyramid at Giza in Egypt. The site lies along the summit of a mountain crest, more than 1 km in length. The massive stone walls, 585 m long by 110 m wide at their widest, are as formidable as those of any pre-Columbian city. Some reconstruction has taken place, mostly of small houses and walls, but the majority of the main walls on all levels are original, as is the inverted, cone-shaped main temple. The structures have been left in their cloud forest setting, the trees covered in bromeliads and moss, the flowers visited by hummingbirds.

Chachapoyas → *Phone code: 041. Colour map 2, B2. Population: 30,000. Altitude: 2350 m.*

The capital of the Department of Amazonas, founded in 1538 retains its colonial character. The city's importance as a crossroads between the coast and jungle began to decline in the late 1940s, however archaeological and ecological tourism have grown gradually since the 1990s and have brought increasing economic benefits to the region. The cathedral, with a lovely modern interior, stands on the spacious Plaza de Armas. **Ministerio de Cultura Museum** ① *Ayacucho 904, T477045, amazonas@mcultura.gob.pe, Mon-Fri 0800-1300, 1500-1700, free*, contains a small collection of artefacts and mummies, with explanations in Spanish. The **Museo Santa Ana** ① *Jr Santa Ana 1054, T790988, Sun-Fri 0900-1300, 1500-1800, US$2*, has colonial religious art and pre-Hispanic ceramics and textiles. Jr Amazonas, pedestrianized from the Plaza de Armas uphill to Plaza Burgos, makes a pleasant stroll. **Tourist offices**: i Perú ① *on the Plaza de Armas, T477292, iperuchachapoyas@promperu. gob.pe, Mon-Sat 0900-1800, Sun 0900-1300.* **Huancas** ① *autos leave from Jr Ortiz Arrieta 370, 0600-1800, 20 mins, US$1.15 or 2-hr walk*, is a small village to the north of Chacha where rustic pottery is produced. Walk uphill from town to the **Mirador** ① *1 km from the plaza, US$0.70, viewing tower, crafts on sale*, for magnificent views into the deep canyon of the Río Sonche, with tumbling waterfalls. At **Huanca Urco**, 5 km from Huancas, past the large prison complex, are ruins, remains of an Inca road and another *mirador* with fine views including Gocta Waterfall in the distance.

Levanto, due south of Chachapoyas, was built by the Spaniards in 1538, directly on top of the previous Chachapoyan structures, as their first capital of the area. Nowadays Levanto is an unspoilt colonial village overlooking the massive canyon of the Utcubamba River. Kuélap can, on a clear day, be seen on the other side of the rift. A 30-minute walk from Levanto towards Chachapoyas are the overgrown ruins of **Yalape**, which seems to have been a massive residential complex, extending over many hectares. Local people can guide you to the ruins.

Chachapoyas

Where to stay 🛏
1 Aventura Backpackers Lodge *A1*
2 Belén *A1*
3 Casa Vieja *A1*
4 Casona Monsante *B2*
5 Chachapoyas Backpackers *B2*
6 El Dorado *A1*
7 Las Orquídeas *A1*
8 Posada del Arriero *B1*
9 Puma Urco *B2*
10 Quiocta *B2*
11 Revash *B2*
12 Rumi Huasi *A2*
13 Vilaya *B2*
14 Vista Hermosa *A1*

Restaurants 🍴
1 Batán del Tayta *B2*
2 Dulcería Santa Elena *B2*
3 El Edén *A2*
4 El Tejado *A1*
5 Fusiones *A1*
6 Heladería San Antonio *B2*
7 La Tushpa *B1*
8 Matalaché *B3*
9 Panadería Café San José *B2*
10 Paraíso de las Pizzas *A1*
11 Romana *B1*

Transport 🚍
1 Cars to Huancas & Mendoza *A1*
2 Cars to Lamud & Luya *A1*
3 Combis to Bagua Grande & Moyobamba *A1*
5 Combis to Pedro Ruiz *A1*
6 Trans Rollers to Kuelap & Pizuquia *A2*
7 Cars to Pedro Ruiz & Bagua Grande *A2*
8 Civa *A2*
9 Virgen del Carmen to Celendín & Cajamarca *A2*
10 Karlita to Leymebamba *A2*
12 Móvil Tours *B3*
13 El Expreso & Transervis Kuelap *B3*
14 GH Bus *A3*

East of Chachapoyas

In the district of Soloco, south of the Chachapoyas-Mendoza road is **Parjugsha**, Peru's largest cave complex, about 300 m deep and with some 20 km of galeries (10 km have been explored and connected). Spelunking experience is essential.

The road east from Chachapoyas continues on to **Mendoza** (2½ hours), centre of the coffee producing region of Rodríguez de Mendoza. It is the starting point of an ethnologically interesting area in the Guayabamba Valley, where there is an unusually high incidence of fair-skinned people. Close by are the caves at Omia, Tocuya thermal baths, Mirador Wimba and Santa Natalia waterfall. For information ask for Michel Ricardo Feijoó Aguilor in the municipal office, mifeijoo@gmail.com; he can help tourists arrange a guide, accommodation, etc. A recommended guide is Alfonso Saldana Pelaez, fotoguiaalsape@gmail.com.

Northwest of Chachapoyas

On a turn-off on the Chachapoyas-Pedro Ruiz road, at Km 37, is the village of **Luya**. Here the road divides, one branch goes north to **Lamud**, a convenient base for several interesting sites, such as San Antonio and Pueblo de los Muertos, and the **Quiocta cave** ① *entry US$2, tours from Chachapoyas, or arranged at the Lamud Oficina de Turismo; it's 30 mins by car from Lamud, then a 10-min walk.* The cave is 560 m long, 23 m deep, has four chambers with stalactites and stalagmites and a stream running through it. There are petroglyphs at the mouth, a man-made wall, human skulls set in depressions and other, partly buried human remains

The second road goes south and west to Cruzpata, the access for **Karajía** ① *US$2, take binoculars*, where remarkable, 2.5-m-high sarcophagi set into an impressive cliff face overlook the valley. The viewpoint is 2½ hours' walk from Luya or 30 minutes from Cruzpata (*autos from Luya to Cruzpata, 0600-1700, US$3, one hour*). **Chipuric** is another site 1½ hours' walk from Luya. In a lush canyon, 1½ hours' walk from the road to Luya is **Wanglic**, a funeral site with large circular structures built under a ledge. Nearby is a beautiful waterfall, a worthwhile excursion. Ask for directions in Luya. Best to take a local guide (US$7 a day). The road to Luya and Lamud is unpaved, see Chachapoyas Transport for how to get there.

⊙ Chachapoyas region listings

For hotel and restaurant price codes, and other relevant information, see pages 14-17.

● Where to stay

Celendín *p137*

$$-$ Hostal Celendín, Unión 305, Plaza de Armas, T555041, hcgustavosd1@hotmail.com. Some rooms with plaza view, central patio and wooden stairs, hot water, pleasant, has 2 restaurants: Rinconcito Shilico, 2 de Mayo 816, and Pollos a la brasa Gusys.

$ Hostal Imperial, Jr Dos de Mayo 568, 2 blocks from the plaza, T555492. Large rooms, good mattresses, hot water, Wi-Fi, parking, decent choice.

$ Loyer's, José Gálvez 410, T555210. Patio with wooden balcony all round, nice, singles, doubles and family rooms.

$ Maxmar, Dos de Mayo 349, T555330. Cheaper without bath, hot shower extra, basic, parking, good value, owners Francisco and Luis are very helpful.

$ Mi Posada, Pardo 388, next to Atahualpa bus, T631908. Includes breakfast, small cheerful rooms, family atmosphere.

$ Orange B&B, Jr Unión 333, T770590, www.celendinperu.com. One bedroom in family of the owners of the original *hostal*, which is being built in a new location on the edge of town. See the website for developments. In the meanwhile you can

ask for advice on the area by emailing Susan van der Wielen in advance. Tours offered. This is also the HQ for **Proyecto Yannick**, a charity for children and the families of children with Down's Syndrome, www. proyectoyannick.org. See the website or contact Orange if you would like to help.
$ Raymi Wasi, Jr José Gálvez 420, T976-551133. With electric shower, cheaper without, large rooms, has patio, quiet, parking, good value, restaurant and karaoke.

Leymebamba *p137*
$$ La Casona, Jr Amazonas 223, T630301, www.casonadeleymebamba.com. Nicely refurbished old house with balcony, attractive common area, restaurant upstairs with good view over roof tops, simple rooms with solar hot water, arrange tours and horses.
$ Laguna de los Cóndores, Jr Amazonas 320, ½ a block from the plaza, T797908. Nice courtyard, breakfast available, electric shower, also runs the shelter at Laguna de los Cóndores and offers tours of 1-8 days.
$ La Petaca, Jr Amazonas 426, on the plaza, T999-020599. Good rooms with hot water, breakfast available, café, helpful.

Tingo *p138*
$$ Estancia Chillo, 5 km south of Tingo towards Leymebamba, T630510/979-340444. On a 9-ha farm, dinner and breakfast included, with bath, hot water, transport, horse riding. Friendly family, a lovely country retreat. The walk from Chillo to Kuélap is shorter than from Tingo.
$ Albergue León, along the south bank of the Río Tingo, just upriver from the highway, T941 715685, hildegardlen@yahoo.es. Basic, private or shared bath, electric shower, guiding, arrange horses, run by Lucho León who is knowledgeable.
$ Albergue Tingo, on the main highway, just north of the Río Tingo, T941-732251. Adequate rooms with electric shower, restaurant.

Choctámal
$$ Choctámal Marvelous Spatuletail Lodge, 3 km from village towards Kuélap at Km 20, T041-941-963327, www.marvelous spatuletail.com. Book in advance. Heated rooms, hot showers, hot tub, telescope for star-gazing. Meals US$8-10. Offers horse riding and a chance to see the endangered Marvellous spatuletail hummingbird.

María
2½ hrs from Kuélap on the vehicle road to Choctámal has 10 *hospedajes*, some with bath and hot water; meals available. All these places are in the **$** range.

Kuélap *p138*
Walking up from Tingo, the last house to the right of the track (**El Bebedero**) offers very basic rooms with bed, breakfast and dinner, helpful. It may be fully booked by archaeologists, but **Gabriel Portocarrero**, the caretaker, runs a hostel just below the ruins, basic, friendly. **Sra Juanita**, T989-783432, the home of archaeologist Arturo Ruiz Estrada, basic rooms with shared bath, cold water, includes breakfast, good.

Chachapoyas *p138, map p139*
$$$ Casa Andina Classic, Km 39 Carretera Pedro Ruiz (13 km from Chacha), T969-335840, www.casa-andina.com. Colonial-style hacienda some way outside Chachapoyas, some rooms in modern annex, with safe, pool, gardens, restaurant, Wi-Fi in public areas.
$$$ Casa Vieja, Chincha Alta 569, T477353, www.casaviejaperu.com. Converted old house with lovely courtyard, very nicely decorated, all rooms different, comfy beds, family atmosphere, good service, living room and *comedor* with open fire, includes breakfast, good café, Wi-Fi and library. Repeatedly recommended.
$$ Casona Monsante, Amazonas 746, T477702, www.lacasonamonsante.com. Converted colonial house with patio, orchid garden, comfortable rooms decorated with antiques.

$$ Las Orquídeas, Ayacucho 1231, T478271, www.hostallasorquideas.com. Converted home, nicely decorated rooms, hot water, large garden.

$$ Posada del Arriero, Grau 636, T478945, www.posadadelarriero.net. Old house nicely refurbished in modern style, rooms are a bit plain, courtyard, helpful staff.

$$ Puma Urco, Amazonas 833, T477871, www.hotelpumaurco.com. Comfortable rooms, includes breakfast, TV, frigobar, Wi-Fi, **Café Café** next door, hotel and café receive good reports, run tours with **Turismo Explorer**.

$$ Vilaya, Ayacucho 734, T477664. Ample carpeted rooms, parking.

$$-$ Quiocta, Amazonas 721, T477698. Brightly painted rooms, hot water, family-run.

$$-$ Revash, Grau 517, Plaza de Armas, T477391, revash9@hotmail.com. Traditional house with patio, stylish decor, steaming hot showers, breakfast available, helpful owners, good local information, popular. Operate tours and sell local crafts.

$ Aventura Backpackers Lodge, Jr Amazonas 1416, www.chachapoyas hostal.com. Dorms with bunk beds, use of kitchen, good value.

$ Belén, Jr Ortiz Arrieta 540, Plaza de Armas, T477830, www.hostalbelen.com. With hot water, nicely furnished, pleasant sitting room overlooking the Plaza, good value.

$ Chachapoyas Backpackers, Jr Dos de Mayo 639, T478879, www.chachapoyas backpackers.com. Simple 2- and 3-bed dorms with shared bath, electric shower, a good budget option, same owners as **Turismo Explorer** tour operator. Lovely family-run place. Recommended.

$ El Dorado, Ayacucho 1062, T477047, ivvanovt@hotmail.com. With bathroom, electric shower, helpful staff, a good economical option.

$ Rumi Huasi, Ortiz Arrieta 365, T791100. With and without bath, electric shower, small rooms, simple and good.

$ Vista Hermosa, Puno 285, T477526. Nice ample rooms, some have balconies, electric shower, good value.

Levanto

$ Levanto Marvelous Spatuletail Lodge, behind the church, T478838, www. marvelousspatuletail.net. 2 circular buildings with tall thatched roofs, 4 bedrooms with 2 external bathrooms, can accommodate 12 people, hot shower, lounge with fireplace and kitchen, meals US$8-10, must book ahead.

Northwest of Chachapoyas *p140*
$ Hostal Kuélap, Garcilaso de la Vega 452, on the plaza, Lamud. With or without bath or hot water, basic.

🍴 Restaurants

Celendín *p137*
$$-$ La Reserve, José Gálvez 313. Good quality and value, extensive menu, from Italian to *chifa*.

$ Carbón y Leña, 2 de Mayo 410. For chicken, *parrillas* and pizzas.

$ Juguería Carolin, Bolognesi 384. Daily 0700-2200. One of the few places open early, for juices, breakfasts and caldos.

Chachapoyas *p138, map p139*
$$$ Batán del Tayta, La Merced 604. Closed Sun. Excellent innovative local cuisine, generous portions. Recommended.

$$ El Tejado, Santo Domingo 424. Daily for lunch only, but hours vary. Excellent upscale *comida criolla*. Large portions, attentive service, nice atmosphere and setting. Good-value *menú ejecutivo* on weekdays.

$$ La Tushpa, Jr Ortiz Arrieta 753. Mon-Sat 1300-2300. Good grilled meat and *platos criollos*, wine list, very clean kitchen, attentive service.

$$ Paraíso de las Pizzas, Chincha Alta 355. Open to 2200. Good pizzas and pastas, family-run.

$$-$ Romana, Amazonas 1091. Daily 0700-2300. Choice of set meals and à la carte, good service.

$ El Edén, Grau by the market. Sun-Thu 0700-2100, Fri 0700-1800. Simple vegetarian, a variety of dishes à la carte and economical set meals.

$ Matalaché, Ayacucho 616. Daily 0730-1530, 1800-2230. Famous for their huge *milanesa* (breaded beef); also serves *menú*.

Dulcería Santa Elena, Amazonas 800. Open 0900-2230. Old-fashioned home-made desserts.

Fusiones, Chincha Alta 445. Mon-Sat 0730-1130, 1600-2100. Breakfast, fair-trade coffee, juices, snacks, Wi-Fi, book exchange, volunteer opportunities.

Heladería San Antonio, 2 de Mayo 521 and Amazonas 856. Good home-made ice cream, try the *lúcuma* and *guanábana* flavours.

Panadería Café San José, Ayacucho 816. Mon-Sat 0630-2200. Bakery and café, good breakfasts, sweets and snacks.

What to do

Chachapoyas *p138, map p139*
The cost of full-day trips depends on season (higher Jul-Sep), distance to a site, number of passengers and whether meals are included. Several operators have daily departures to Kuélap, US$15-19, Gocta, US$13.50-15, Quiocta and Karajía, US$19-27, and Museo de Leymebamba and Revash, US$31-39. All-inclusive trekking tours to Gran Vilaya cost about US$46-50 pp per day.

Amazon Exepdition, Jr Ortiz Arrieta 508, Plaza de Armas, T798718, http://amazonexpedition.com.pe. Day tours and multi-day treks.

Andes Tours, at Hostal Revash. Daily trips to Kuélap and Gocta, other tours to ruins, caves and trekking. Also less-visited destinations, combining travel by car, on horseback and walking.

Cloudforest Expeditions, Jr Puno 368, T477610, www.kuelapnordperu.com. English and German spoken.

Nuevos Caminos, at Café Fusiones, T479170, www.nuevoscaminostravel.com. Alternative community tourism throughout northern Peru, volunteer opportunities.

Turismo Explorer, Jr Grau 509, T478162. Daily tours to Kuélap, Gocta and other

destinations, trekking tours including Laguna de los Cóndores and other archaeological sites, transport service.

Vilaya Tours, T+51(0)41 477506, www.vilayatours.com. All-inclusive treks to off-the-beaten-path destinations throughout northern Peru. Run by Robert Dover, a very experienced and knowledgeable British guide, book ahead.

Guides Martín Chumbe, T941-994650, martin.chumbe@yahoo.es, or through **Restaurante Las Rocas**, Jr Ayacucho, at the Plaza. Specializes in longer trips.

Transport

Celendín *p137*
Bus To **Cajamarca**, 107 km, 3½ hrs: with Royal Palace's, Jr Unión y José Gálvez, by Plaza de Armas, at 1400 daily; also **CABA** 2 a day, and **Rojas** 3 a day. Cars to Cajamarca leave when full from Ovalo Agusto Gil, Cáceres y Amazonas, 2½ hrs, US$9 pp. From the same place they go to **Chachapoyas**, 6 hrs, US$18 pp. **Virgen del Carmen**, Cáceres 112 by Ovalo A Gil, T792918, to Chachapoyas, daily at 0900, US$11.55, 6 hrs to **Leymebamba**, US$7.75.

Leymebamba and around *p137*
To **Chachapoyas**, 2½ hrs (fills quickly, book ahead), cars US$7.75; *combis* US$4, eg **Transportes Karlita**, Jr Amazonas corner 16 de Julio on the plaza, 0400 and 0500, **Mi Cautivo**, Jr San Agustín ½ block from the plaza, Mon-Sat 0500 and 0700, Sun 1100 and 1700, **Hidalgo Tours**, Jr Bolívar 608, 0500. **Virgen del Carmen**, Jr 16 de Julio at Plaza, buses from Cajamarca pass Leymebamba at about 1400 en route to Chacha; from Chacha they pass at 0800 for Celendín US$7.75, and Cajamarca US$11.55, 8 hrs.

Kuélap *p138*
There are 4 options: **1)** Take a tour from Chachapoyas (3 hrs each way in vehicle, including lunch stop on return, 3 hrs at the site). **2)** Hire a vehicle with driver in

Chachapoyas, US$45 per vehicle, or US$54 with wait. **3)** Take Trans Rollers combi from Chachapoyas to the end of the road, near the ruins. It returns right away, so you will have to spend the night at Kuélap, María (2-2½ hrs walk), Choctámal (4-5 hrs walk) or Tingo (see option 4). From Tingo you may get transport back to Chachapoyas later in the day. **4)** Take a combi from Chachapoyas to Tingo, spend the night, then take the 5 hrs' strenuous walk uphill from Tingo; take waterproofs, food and drink, and start early as it gets very hot. Only the fit should try to ascend and descend in one day on foot. In the rainy season it is advisable to wear boots; at other times it is hot and dry (take all your water with you as there is nothing on the way up).

Chachapoyas p138, map p139
Air The military **Grupo Aéreo 42** (Grau 505, T947-490770) has passenger flights to Chachapoyas originating in **Trujillo** or **Iquitos**; see page 109 for routes and schedules.
Bus To **Chiclayo** (9 hrs, US$15-25), **Trujillo** (12 hrs, US$23-29) and **Lima** (20-22 hrs, US$44-52), best is **Móvil**, Libertad 464, T478545; to Lima daily at 1300; to Trujillo and Chiclayo at 1930. **Civa**, Salamanca y Ortiz Arrieta, T478048 (to Chiclayo also at 1815). **Transervis Kuelap**, Jr Union 330, T478128, to Chiclayo Tue and Sat at 1900, other days at 2000. **GH Bus**, station at C Evitamiento (take a taxi), tickets can be bought on Jr Grau entre Trujillo y Amazonas, T479200, to Lima at 1030, to Chiclayo at 2000, to Trujillo 1930. **El Expreso**, Jr Unión 330, to Chiclayo 1930 daily. To **Celendín** (8-9 hrs) and **Cajamarca** (11-12 hrs): **Virgen del Carmen**, Salamanca 956, 0500 daily, US$11.55 to Celendín, US$18 to Cajamarca, 11 hrs. To **Pedro Ruiz** (1 hr), for connections to Chiclayo, Jaén, or Tarapoto, cars leave from Grau 310 y Salamanca, 0600-1800 (1800-2200 they depart from Grau in front of the market), US$3.85; combis every 2 hrs 0600-1800, from Ortiz Arrieta 370, US$2, also **Diplomáticos** vans, as they fill 0500-

1900, from Libertad cuadra 10. To **Bagua Grande** for connections to Jaén, cars from Grau between Libertad and Salamanca 0600-1800 and Grau by the market 1800-0600, US$8.50, 2 hrs, also combis/vans with **Evangelio Poder de Dios**, Jr Libertad 1048, US$6. This company also goes to **Moyobamba** (connections to Tarapoto), 0700, US$9.75, 5 hrs.
Regional To **Kuélap** US$6, 3 hrs (will only go to Kuélap if they have enough passengers); **María** US$6, 2½ hrs; **Lónguita** US$4.60, 2 hrs; **Choctámal** US$3.85, 1½ hrs; **Tingo** US$3.10, 1 hr: with Roller's, Grau y Salamanca, combi or car, at 0400 (return from Kuélap around 0700); with **Sr José Cruz**, Grau 331, combi or car at 0530 (returns from María at 0800); with **Trans Shubet**, Pasaje Reyes off Grau, cars to Lónguita around 1400-1500. To **Tingo**, also with **Brisas del Utcubamba**, Grau 332, cars bound for Magdalena, 0500-1800 or transport going to Yerbabuena or Leymebamba. Vehicles going to Chachapoyas pass Tingo from 0500. To **Leymebamba**, 83 km, 3 hrs, US$4, reserve ahead: **Transportes Karlita**, Salamanca cuadra 9, 1300, 1600; **Mi Cautivo**, Pasaje David Reina y Grau, vans at 1200 and 1600; **Hidalgo Tours**, Jr Grau corner Pasaje David Reina, at 1300. For **Revash**, Comité Santo Tomás, to **Santo Tomás**, at 1000, 1300, 1500 (return at 0300, 0400, 0500), US$4.30, 3 hrs; get off at **Cruce de Revash** (near Puente Santo Tomás), US$4.30, 2½ hrs; or with the same company to **San Bartolo** at 1400 (return 0600), US$4.30, 3 hrs. To **Jalca Grande**, from Jr Hermosura y Salamanca, 2 combis depart Mon-Fri from 1330 onwards, US$4.30, 3 hrs (return 0300-0400). To **Levanto**, cars from Av Cuarto Centenario y Sociego southeast end of town, daily 1200-1300, US$2.90. To **Mendoza** (86 km), Guayabamba, Ortiz Arrieta 372, US$7.75, 2½ hrs, combis from same address US$6. To **Luya** and **Lamud**, from Libertad y Chincha Alta, cars 0400-1800, US$2.85, 1 hr to Lamud, same price to Luya.

Chachapoyas to the Amazon

From Chachapoyas the road heads north through the beautiful Utcubamba canyon for one hour to a crossroads, **Pedro Ruíz** (two hotels and other lodgings; basic restaurants), where you can return to the coast, head to Jaén for Ecuador, or continue east to Tarapoto and Yurimaguas, making the spectacular descent on a paved road from high Andes to jungle. In the rainy season, the road may be subject to landslides. On route to Tarapoto are **Rioja** (198 km, with several hotels), Nueva Cajamarca (reported unsafe) and Moyobamba.

Gocta

South of Pedro Ruíz is the spectacular **Gocta Waterfall** (771 m, the upper waterfall is 231 m, the lower waterfall is 540 m), one of the highest in the world. From Pedro Ruiz, take the Chachapoyas road for 18 km to Cocahuayco where there are two roads up to Gocta, along either bank of the Cocahuayco River. The first turn-off leads up to the village of **San Pablo de Valera** (1934 m, 6 km from main road, 20 minutes by car) from which it is a one- to 1½-hour walk to a mirador, and then 30-60 minutes to the base of the upper waterfall, 6.3 km in all. The second turn-off, 100 m further on the main road, leads up to the village of **Cocachimba** (1796 m, 5.3 km, 20 minutes), from which it is a 1½- to 2½-hour, 5.5-km walk to the base of the lower waterfall, of which there is an impressive view. Both routes go through about 2 km of lovely forest; the San Pablo trail is somewhat flatter. A trail connecting both banks starts on the San Pablo side at the mirador. It is a much smaller trail than the others, quite steep and not signposted past the mirador. There is a suspension foot-bridge over the main river. It joins the Cocachimba trail about three quarters of the way to the base of the lower falls. If you start the hike at San Pablo and finish at Cocachimba you can arrange transport to return to San Pablo at the end of the day. Or you can take transport to San Pablo to begin the hike if lodged in Cocachimba. The ride is about 30 minutes. To see both sides in one day you need to start very early, but this is a great way to get the full experience. Each community offer similar services: entry fee is US$4, guides (compulsory) cost US$11, horses can be hired for US$11 (they can only go part of the way), rubber boots and rain ponchos are available for hire, US$1.20 (it is always wet by the falls). The best time to visit is May-September, the dry season. In the wet season the falls are more spectacular, but it is cold, rainy and the trails may be slippery. Both towns have a **community tourist information office** ① *San Pablo, T041-631163, daily 0800-1730; and Cocachimba, T041-630569, daily 0800-1730*. Several more waterfalls in this area are now becoming accessible, including **Yumbilla**, 895 m (124 m higher than Gocta), although in eight tiers. For more information about expeditions to Yumbilla, other falls and related projects, see the Florida-based NGO, **Amazon Waterfalls Association**, www.amazonwaterfalls.org.

Moyobamba → *Phone code: 042. Colour map 2, B2. Population: 14,000. Altitude: 900 m.*

Moyobamba, capital of San Martín department, is a pleasant town, in the attractive Río Mayo valley. The area is renowned for its orchids and there is a Festival de la Orquídea over three days around 1 November. Among several places to see orchids is **Orquideario Waqanki** ① *www.waqanki.com, 0700-1800, US$0.55*, where the plants have been placed in trees. Just beyond are **Baños Termales San Mateo** ① *5 km southeast, 0600-2200, US$0.55*, which are worth a visit. **Puerto Tahuishco** is the town's harbour, a pleasant walk north of the centre, where boat trips can be taken. **Morro de Calzada** ① *Rioja combi to the Calzada turn-off, US$0.55, mototaxi to the start of the trail US$2.50*, is an isolated outcrop in white sand forest, good for birdwatching. A path through forest leads to the top and a lookout (1½ hours), but enquire about public safety beforehand. The main road that goes to Pomacochas and Pedro Ruiz climbs through the **Bosque de Protección Alto Mayo**, with the Long-whiskered Owlet reserve and the Abra Patricia pass (Rioja T558467).

Tourist offices: Oficina Municipal de Información ① *Jr Pedro Canga 262, at Plaza, T562191 ext 541, Mon-Fri 0800-1300, 1430-1715, no English spoken*. **Dircetur** ① *Jr San Martín 301, T562043, Mon-Fri 0800-1300, 1430-1730*, has leaflets and map, English spoken. Also see www.moyobamba.net.

Tarapoto → Phone code: 042. Colour map 2, B2. Altitude: 350 m. Population: 120,000

Tarapoto, the largest commercial centre in the region, is a very friendly place. Information from: **Oficina Municipal de Información** ① *Jr Ramírez Hurtado, at plaza, T526188, Mon-Sat 0800-1300, 1500-2000, Sun 0900-1300*, and **Dircetur** ① *Jr Angel Delgado Morey, cuadra 1, T522567*. **Lamas** 22 km from Tarapoto, off the road to Moyobamba, has a native community, descendants of the Chancas people, who live in the Wayku neighbourhood below the centre. There is a small **Museo Los Chankas** ① *Jr San Martín 1157, daily 0830-1300, 1430-1800, US$1.15*, with ethnological and historical exhibits. In upper part of town is a *mirador*, opposite is **$ Hosp Girasoles** (T042-543439, stegmaiert@yahoo.de, breakfast available, nice views, pizzeria and friendly knowledgeable owners). Cars from Tarapoto: Avenida Alfonso Ugarte, cuadra 11, US$1.45, 30 minutes.

Tarapoto stands at the foot of the forested hills of the **Area de Conservación Regional Cordillera Escalera** (149,870 ha), good for birdwatching and walking. By the conservation area and within easy reach of town are the 9-ha **El Amo del Bosque Sector** ① *Urawasha 5 km walk (9 km by car) from town, T524675 (after 1900)*, knowledgeable owner Sr José Macedo, offers guided tours; and 20-ha **Wayrasacha** ① *6-km walk (10 km by car) from the city, T522261, www.wayrasacha.com.pe*, run by Peruvian-Swiss couple, César Ramírez and Stephanie Gallusser, who offer day trips, overnight stays in a basic shelter and volunteer opportunities, English and French spoken. Within the conservation area, about 15 km from Tarapoto on the spectacular road to Yurimaguas are the 50-m falls of **Ahuashiyacu** ① *US$1.15, tours available or transport from La Banda de Shilcayo*. This is a popular place with locals. There are many other waterfalls in the area. Past Ahuashiyacu, the road climbs to a tunnel (stop at the police control for birdwatching, mototaxi US$6), after which you descend through beautiful forest perched on rocky cliffs to Pongo de Caynarachi (several basic *comedores*), where the flats start.

⊙ Chachapoyas to the Amazon listings

For hotel and restaurant price codes, and other relevant information, see pages 14-17.

⊙ Where to stay

Gocta p145
San Pablo
$ Hospedaje Las Gardenias, T941-718660, Basic rooms with shared bath, cold water, economical meals available.

Gocta, just outside town on the way to the falls, T984-007033. A comfortable hotel with camping facilities, under construction in 2014.

Cocachimba
$$$ Gocta Andes Lodge, Cocachimba, T041-630552 (Tarapoto T042-522225), www.goctalodge.com. Beautifully located lodge overlooking the waterfall, ample rooms with balconies, lovely terrace with

pool, restaurant. Packages available with other hotels in the group.

$ Hospedaje Gallito de la Roca, T630048. Small simple rooms with shared bath, cold water, economical meals available.

$ Hospedaje Las Orquídeas, T631265. Simple rooms in a family home, shared bath, cold water, restaurant.

Moyobamba p145

$$$ Puerto Mirador, Jr Sucre, 1 km from centre, T562050, www.hotelpuertomirador. com. Buffet breakfast, lovely grounds, views overlooking river valley, pool, good restaurant, credit cards accepted.

$$ Orquídea del Mayo, Jr San Martín 432, T561049, orquideadelmayohostal@hotmail. com. Modern comfortable rooms with bath, hot water.

$$ Río Mayo, Jr Pedro Canga 415, T564193. Central, modern comfortable rooms, frigobar, small indoor pool, parking.

$$-$ El Portón, Jr San Martín 449, T866121, casahospedajeelporton@hotmail.com. Pleasant modern rooms with fan, hot water, nice grounds with hammocks, kitchen facilities.

$ Atlanta, Alonso de Alvarado 865, T562063, atlantainn@hotmail.com. Hot water, parking, fan, good value but front rooms noisy.

$ Cobos, Jr Pedro Canga 404, T562153. Private bath, cold water, simple but good.

$ La Cueva de Juan, Jr Alonso de Alvarado 870, T562488, lacueva870@hotmail.com. Small courtyard, private bath, hot water, central but reasonably quiet, good value.

Tarapoto p146

Several **$** *alojamientos* on Alegría Arias de Morey, cuadra 2, and cheap basic hotels by the bus terminals.

$$$ Puerto Palmeras, Carr Belaúnde Terry Km 614, T524100. Large, modern complex, popular with families, lots of activities and entertainment. Nice rooms, helpful staff, good restaurant, pleasant grounds with pool, mountain bikes, horses and small zoo, airport transfers. Private reserve outside town.

$$$ Puma Rinri Lodge, Carretera Shapaja-Chasuta Km 16, T526694, www.pumarinri. com. Lodge/resort hotel on the shores of the Río Huallaga, 30 km east of Tarapoto. Offers a variety of all-inclusive packages.

$$ Huingos Lodge, Prolongación Alerta cuadra 6, Sector Takiwasi, T524171, www.huingoslodge.com. Nice cabins in lovely grounds by the Río Shilcayo, fan, electric shower, frigobar, kitchen facilities, hammocks, HI afiliated, mototaxi from bus stations US$1.55-2.

$$ La Patarashca, Jr San Pablo de la Cruz 362, T528810, www.lapatarashca.com. Very nice hotel with large rooms, cheaper without a/c, rustic, restaurant, electric shower, large garden with hammocks, tours arranged.

$$ Luna Azul, Jr Manco Capac 276, T525787, www.lunaazulhotel.com. Modern, central, includes breakfast and airport transfers, with bath, hot water, a/c or fan, frigobar.

$$-$ El Mirador, Jr San Pablo de la Cruz 517, 5 blocks uphill from the plaza T522177, www.elmiradortarapoto.blogspot.com. With bath, electric shower, fan, Wi-Fi, laundry facilities, breakfast available, hammocks on rooftop terrace with nice views, tours arranged. Family-run and very welcoming.

$$-$ La Posada Inn, San Martín 146, T522234, laposada_inn@yahoo.es. Convenient but ageing town centre hotel, a/c or fan, electric shower, fridge, nice atmosphere. **El Merendero** restaurant on ground floor.

$ San Antonio, Jr Jiménez Pimentel 126, T525563. Rooms with private bath, hot water and fan, good value.

🍴 Restaurants

Moyobamba p145

$$-$ Kikeku, Jr Pedro Canga 450, next to casino. Open 24 hrs. Good *chifa*, also *comida criolla*, large portions, noisy.

$$-$ La Olla de Barro, Pedro Canga 398. Daily 0800-2200. Tourist place serving regional food and other Peruvian dishes.

$ El Avispa Juane, Jr Callao 583.
Mon-Sat 0730-1600, Sun 0800-1500.
Regional specialities, menu Mon-Sat
and snacks, popular.
$ La Buena Salud, 25 de Mayo 227, by
market. Sun-Fri 0800-1500. Vegetarian
set meals, breakfast and fruit juices.
Helados La Muyuna, Jr Pedro Canga 529.
Good natural jungle fruit ice cream.

Tarapoto *p146*

Several restaurants and bars around Jr San
Pablo de la Cruz corner Lamas – a lively area
at night.
$$$-$$ Chalet Venezia, Jr Alegría Arias de
Morey 298, www.restaurantcafechalet
venezia.com. Tue-Sun 1200-2300. Upmarket
Italian-Amazonian fusion cuisine, wine list,
elegant decor, interior or terrace seating.
$$$-$$ Real Grill, Jr Moyobamba on
the plaza. Daily 0830-2400. Regional and
international food. One of the best in town.
$$-$ Chifa Cantón, Jr Ramón Castilla 140.
Mon-Fri 1200-1600, Sat-Sun 1200-2400.
Chinese, very popular and clean.
$ El Manguaré, Jr Moyobamba corner Manco
Cápac. Mon-Sat 1200-1530. Choice of set
meals and à la carte, good food and service.
Café Plaza, Jr Maynas corner Martínez,
at the plaza. Open 0730-2300. Breakfast,
coffee, snacks, juices, Wi-Fi, popular.
Helados La Muyuna, Jr Ramón Castilla 271.
Open 0800-2400 except closed Fri from
1700 until Sat at 1830. Good natural ice
cream and drinks made with jungle fruits,
fruit salads,

⊜ Transport

Chachapoyas to the Amazon *p145*
Pedro Ruíz Many buses on the **Chiclayo–
Tarapoto** and Chiclayo–**Chachapoyas**
routes pass through town. Bus fare
to Chiclayo US$11.50-19; to Tarapoto
US$11.50-15.50. Cars or combis are more
convenient for Chacha or Bagua. To
Chachapoyas, cars US$4, combis US$2, 1 hr.
To **Bagua Grande**, cars US$4.75, combis

US$4, 1hr. To **Jaén**, Trans Fernández bus
from Tarapoto passes Pedro Ruiz about
1400-1500 or take a car to Bagua Grande
and transfer there. To **Moyobamba**, cars
US$10.70, 4 hrs. To **Nueva Cajamarca**, cars
US$9.75, combis US$7.75, 3-3½ hrs, then a
further 20 mins to **Rioja**, car US$1.15, combi
US$0.75. From Rioja to **Moyobamba**, 21 km,
20 mins, car US$1.15, combi, US$0.75.

Gocta *p145*

The easiest way to get to Gocta is with a tour
from Chachapoyas; in high season there are
also tours from Pedro Ruiz. Cocahuayco, near
the turn-offs for San Pablo and Cocachimba
is 16 km from Pedro Ruiz and about 35 km
from Chachapoyas. A taxi from Pedro Ruiz
to San Pablo or Cocachimba costs US$2
pp (there are seldom other passengers to
share) or US$10 for the vehicle. Sr Fabier,
T962-922798, offers transport service to San
Pablo, call ahead to find out when he will be
in Pedro Ruiz. A moto-taxi from Pedro Ruiz
costs US$6, beware of overcharging and
dress warmly, it is windy and cold. Cars and
mototaxis wait at 5 Esquinas, along the road
to Chachapoyas, 4 blocks from the highway.
A taxi from Chachapoyas costs US$30, or
US$38 with 5-6 hrs wait. Arrange return
transport ahead or at the tourist offices in
San Pablo or Cocachimba. It is difficult to
get transport from Cocahuayco to either
Chachapoyas or Pedro Ruiz, passing vans
are generally full.

Moyobamba *p145*

Long distance The bus terminal is
12 blocks from the centre on Av Grau
(mototaxi US$0.55). No service originating
in Moyobamba, all buses are on route to/
from Tarapoto. Several companies heading
west to **Pedro Ruiz** (US$9, 4 hrs), **Jaén**
(US$9, 7 hrs), **Chiclayo** (US$15-US$23,
12 hrs). To book on long-haul buses, you
may have to pay the fare to the final
destination even if you get off sooner.
Regional Empresa San Martín, Benavides
276, and ETRISA, Benavides 244: cars to

Tarapoto, US$7.75, vans US$4, 2 hrs; to **Rioja** US$1.15, 20 mins, vans US$0.75; to **Nueva Cajamarca**, US$2, vans US$1.55, 40 mins. Combis cost about 50% less on all routes. To **Chachapoyas**, Evangelio Poder de Dios, Grau 640, at 1500, US$9.75, 5 hrs.

Tarapoto p146

Air US$3 per taxi airport to town, mototaxi US$1.15. To **Lima**, with LAN (Ramírez Hurtado 183, on the plaza, T529318), **Avianca/TACA** and **Star Perú** (San Pablo de la Cruz 100, T528765) daily. **Star Perú** to **Iquitos** daily (Mon, Wed, Fri via Pucallpa), LAN to Iquitos Mon, Thu. The military **Grupo Aéreo 42** (J Martínez de Compañón 688, T972-990630) has passenger flights to Tarapoto originating in **Trujillo** or **Iquitos**; see page 109 for routes and schedules.

Buses From Av Salaverry, blocks 8-9, in Morales; mototaxi from centre, US$1.15, 20 mins. To **Moyobamba**, 116 km, US$3.85, 2 hrs; to **Pedro Ruiz**, US$11.50-15.50 (companies going to Jaén or Chiclayo), 6 hrs; **Chiclayo**, 690 km, 15-16 hrs, US$25-29; and **Lima**, US$46-52, *cama* US$64, 30 hrs. To **Jaén**, US$13.50-15.50, 9-10 hrs, **Fernández** 4 a day. For **Chachapoyas**, go to Moyobamba and take a van from there. To **Piura** US$23, 16 hrs, with **Sol Peruano**, at 1200. To **Tingo María**, US$27, and **Pucallpa**, US$35, Mon, Wed, Fri 0500, Tue, Thu, Sat 0830, **Transamazónica** and **Transmar** alternate days; there have been armed hold-ups on this route.

Regional To **Moyobamba**, cars with **Empresa San Martín**, Av Alfonso Ugarte 1456, T526327 and **ETRISA**, Av Alfonso Ugarte 1096, T521944, both will pick you up from your hotel, US$7.70, 2 hrs; combis with **Turismo Selva**, Av Alfonso Ugarte, cuadra 11, US$4, 2½ hrs. To **Yurimaguas**, **Gilmer Tours**, Av Alfonso Ugarte 1480, frequent minibuses, US$5.75, 2½ hrs; cars with **Empresa San Martín**, see above, US$7.75, 2 hrs; **Turismo Selva** vans US$4, 8 daily.

Chachapoyas to Ecuador and the coast

The road from Pedro Ruíz (see page 145) goes west to Bagua Grande and then follows the Río Chamaya. It climbs to the Abra de Porculla (2150 m) before descending to join the old Pan-American Highway at Olmos (see page 115). From Olmos you can go southwest to Chiclayo, or northwest to Piura. **Bagua Grande** is the first town of note heading west. It has several hotels (eg **$$-$ Río Hotel**, Jr Capac Malku 115, www.riohotelbaguagrande. blogspot.com, good) but is hot, dusty and unsafe. Pedro Ruiz or Jaén are more pleasant places to spend the night.

To Ecuador

Some 50 km west of Bagua Grande, a road branches northwest at Chamaya to **Jaén** (*Phone code: 076; Colour map 2, B2; Population: about 100,000*), a convenient stopover en route to the jungle or Ecuador. It is a modern city surrounded by rice fields. A **Museo Hermógenes Mejía Solf** ① *2 km south of centre, T976-719590, Mon-Fri 0800-1400, mototaxi US$0.60*, displays pre-Columbian artefacts from a variety of cultures and newly-discovered temples close to Jaén, at Monte Grande and San Isidro, are revealing more finds, dating back possibly to 3500 BC. Festival, **Nuestro Señor de Huamantanga**, 14 September.

A road runs north to **San Ignacio** (109 km, first 55 km are paved), near the border with Ecuador. San Ignacio (fiesta 30 July) is a pleasant town with steep streets in the centre of a coffee growing area. The nearby hills offer excursions to waterfalls, lakes, petroglyphs and ancient ruins. West of San Ignacio is the **Santuario Tabaconas-Namballe** ① *Sernanp, Huancabamba s/n, Sector Santiago, downhill from the centre in San Ignacio, T968-218439*, a 32,125-ha reserve, at 1700-3800 m protecting the spectacled bear, mountain tapir and several ecosystems including the southernmost Andean *páramo*. From San Ignacio the unpaved road, being widened, runs 45 km through green hills to **Namballe**. The border is 15 minutes from town at **La Balsa**, with a simple lodging and a simple *comedor*, a few small shops and money changers, but no lodgings. To leave Perú head directly to immigration (0830-1300, 1500-2000, otherwise find the officer at his house), when entering see immigration first, then the PNP and return to immigration. From the frontier transport goes to Zumba and then to Vilcabamba and Loja. ►► *See Transport, page 151.*

◉ Chachapoyas to Ecuador and the coast listings

For hotel and restaurant price codes, and other relevant information, see pages 14-17.

⬤ Where to stay

To Ecuador *p149*
Jaén
$$ Casa del Sol, Mcal Castilla 140, near Plaza de Armas, T434478, hotelcasadelsol@ hotmail.com. Modern confortable rooms with frigobar, parking, suites with jacuzzi.
$$ El Bosque, Mesones Muro 632, T431184, hoteleraelbosque@speedy.com.pe. On main road by bus terminals. Quiet rooms at the back, gardens, frigobar, solar hot water, pool, good restaurant.
$$ Hostal Valle Verde, Mcal Castilla 203, Plaza de Armas, T432201. Modern, large comfortable rooms and beds, a/c or fan, hot water, frigobar, parking.
$$ Prim's, Diego Palomino 1341, T431039, www.primshotel.com. Includes breakfast, good service, comfortable, hot water, a/c or fan, frigobar, Wi-Fi, friendly, small pool.
$ Cancún, Diego Palomino 1413, T433511. Good rooms with hot water, fan, good value.
$ Danubio, V Pinillos 429, T433110. Older place, nicely refurbished, many different rooms and prices, some cheaper rooms have cold water only, fan, good.

North of Jaén
$ Gran Hotel San Ignacio, Jr José Olaya 680 at the bottom of the hill, T076-356544, granhotel-sanignacio@hotmail.com. Restaurant for breakfast and good lunch *menú*, modern comfortable rooms, upmarket for San Ignacio.

$ Hostal Maldonado, near the plaza, Namballe, T076-830011 (community phone). Private bath (cheaper without), cold water, basic.
$ La Posada, Jr Porvenir 218, San Ignacio, T076-356180. Simple rooms which are cheaper without bath or hot water, restaurant.
$ Sol de la Frontera, 1 km north of Namballe, 4 km from La Balsa, T976 116781, T01-247 8881 in Lima, www.hotelsoldela frontera.com. British-run by Isabel Wood. Comfortable rooms in bungalows, bathtubs, gas water heaters, continental breakfast, set in 2.5 ha of countryside. A good option if you have your own vehicle or bring some food. Meals only available for groups with advance booking. Camping and campervans.

❼ Restaurants

To Ecuador *p149*
Jaén
$$-$ La Cabaña, Bolívar 1332 at Plaza de Armas. Daily 0700-0000. Daily specials at noon, à la carte in the evening, popular.
$$-$ Lactobac, Bolívar 1378 at Plaza de Armas. Daily 0730-0000. Variety of à la carte dishes, snacks, desserts, good *pollo a la brasa*. Very popular.
$ Ebenezer, Mcal Ureta 1360. Sun-Thu 0700-2130, Fri 0700-1600. Simple vegetarian restaurant serves economical midday *menú* and à la carte.
$ Gatizza, Diego Palomino 1503. Mon-Sat 0830-1800. Tasty and varied *menú*.
Cenfrocafé, San Martín 1528. Mon-Sat 0730-1330, 1600-2300. Serve a variety of coffees, sandwiches, *humitas* and desserts, Wi-Fi.

Cenfrocafé, www.cenfrocafe.com.pe, is a Jaén-based coffee farmers organization.

⊖ Transport

Chachapoyas to Ecuador and the coast p149
Many buses pass through **Bagua Grande** en route from Chiclayo to Tarapoto or Chachapoyas and vice versa. Cars to **Jaén** from Mcal Castilla y Angamos at the west end of town, US$4, combis US$2.50, 1 hr. From R Palma 308 at the east end of town, cars leave to **Pedro Ruiz**, US$4.60, combis US$4, 1 hr; to **Chachapoyas**, US$9.75, combis US$5.75, 2½ hrs.

To Ecuador p149
Jaén
Bus Terminals are strung along Mesones Muro, blocks 4-7, south of centre; many ticket offices, always enquire where the bus actually leaves from. Some companies also have offices in the centre: eg Civa, Mcal Ureta 1300 y V Pinillos (terminal at Bolívar 935). To **Chiclayo**: US$7.75-15.50, 6 hrs, many companies, **Móvil** more expensive than others. Cars to Chiclayo from terminal at Mesones Muro cuadra 4, US$27, 5 hrs. To **Lima**: Móvil at 1500, 16 hrs, *bus cama* US$46, *semi-cama* US$38.50. Civa, 1700, US$35-42. Service to Lima also goes through

Trujillo. To **Piura** via Olmos: **Sol Peruano**, at 2200, US$15.50, 8 hrs. To **Tarapoto**, 490 km, US$13.50-15.50, 9-10 hrs; **Fernández**, 4 a day. To **Moyobamba**, US$11.50-13.50, 7 hrs, same service as Tarapoto, likewise to **Pedro Ruiz**: US$6-7.75, 3½ hrs. To **Bagua Grande**, cars from Mesones Muro cuadra 6, 0400-2000, US$4, 1hr; combis from cuadra 9, US$2.50. To **Chamaya**: cars from Mesones Muro cuadra 4, 0500-2000, US$1, 15 mins. To **San Ignacio** (for Ecuador), cars from Av Pacamuros, cuadra 19, 0400-1800, US$7.75, 2 hrs; combis from cuadra 17, US$4.60, 3 hrs.

North of Jaén
Bus From San Ignacio to **Chiclayo**, with Civa, Av San Ignacio 386, daily at 1830, US$11.55, 10-11 hrs; with **Trans Chiclayo**, Av San Ignacio 406, 1945 daily. To **Jaén**, from *óvalo* at south end of Av Mariano Melgar: prices above.

To **Namballe** and **La Balsa** (border with Ecuador), cars leave from Sector Alto Loyola at north end of town, way above the centre, US$6 to Namballe, US$6.55 to La Balsa, 1½ hrs. Taxi or moto-taxi Namballe-La Balsa, US$1.15. In Ecuador, *rancheras* (open-sided buses) run from La Balsa to Zumba at 1200, 1700 and 1915, US$1.75, 1¾ hrs; Zumba to La Balsa 0800, 1430 and 1700. There are Ecuadorean military controls before and after Zumba; keep your passport to hand.

South coast

The Pan-American Highway runs all the way south from Lima to the Chilean border. This part of Peru's desert coast has its own distinctive attractions. The most famous, and perhaps the strangest, are the mysterious Nazca Lines, whose origin and function continue to puzzle scientists the world over. But Nazca is not the sole archaeological resource here: remains of other pre-Columbian civilizations include outposts of the Inca empire itself. Pisco and Ica are the main centres before Nazca. The former, which is near the famous Paracas marine reserve, is named after the latter's main product, the pisco grape brandy and a number of places are well known for their bodegas.

South from Lima

Beyond the beaches which are popular with Limeños the road passes near several towns: eg Chincha with its Afro-Peruvian culture. The Paracas peninsula, near Pisco, is one of the world's great marine bird reserves and was home to one of Peru's most important ancient civilizations. Further south, the Ica valley, with its wonderful climate, is home to that equally wonderful grape brandy, pisco. Most beaches have very strong currents and can be dangerous for swimming; if unsure, ask locals.

Cañete Valley

A paved road runs inland from Cañete, mostly beside the Río Cañete, to **Lunahuaná** (40 km). It is 8 km beyond the Inca ruins of **Incawasi**, which dominated the valley. In the week it's very quiet, but on Sunday the town is full of life with pisco tastings from the valley's *bodegas*, food and handicrafts for sale in the Plaza and lots of outdoor activities. Several places offer rafting and kayaking: from November-April rafting is at levels IV-V. May-October is low water, levels I-II only. A festival of adventure sports is held every February. **Fiesta de la Vendimia**, grape harvest, first weekend in March. At the end of September/beginning October is the **Fiesta del Níspero** (medlar festival). There are several hotels, ranging from **$$** to **$**, and *restaurantes campestres* in the area. **Tourist office** in the Municipalidad (T284 1006), opposite the church, open daily.

Beyond Lunahuaná the road ascending the Cañete Valley leaves the narrow flood-plain and runs 41 km, paved, through a series of gorges to the San Jerónimo bridge. A side road heads to Huangáscar and the village of Viñac, where **Mountain Lodges of Peru** has its **Viñak-Reichraming Lodge** (**$$$** pp full board, T01-421 6952, www.refugiosdelperu.com, see page 247), a wonderful place to relax or go horse riding or walking (superb views, excellent food). The main road carries on to market town of **Yauyos** (basic accommodation, 5 km off the road). After the attractive village of **Huancaya** (several *hospedajes*, T01-810 6086/7, municipal phone, and ask for details) the valley is transformed into one of the most beautiful upper valleys in all Peru, on a par with Colca. Above Huancaya the high Andean terrain lies within the **Reserva Paisajística Nor Yauyos-Cochas** (Sernanp contact Juan Carlos Pilco, pilco_traveler@hotmail.com; regional office RPNYC, Avenida Francisco Solano 107, San Carlos, Huancayo T064-213064) and the river descends through a series of absolutely clear, turquoise pools and lakes, interrupted by cascades and white water rapids. The valley has perhaps the best pre-Columbian terracing anywhere in Peru. Further upstream **Llapay** is a good base because it is in the middle of the valley (**$** Hostal Llapay, basic but very friendly, will open at any hour, restaurant). Beyond Llapay, the Cañete valley narrows to an exceptionally tight canyon, with a road squeezed between nothing but rock and rushing water for the steep climb to the 4600-m pass. Beyond, the road drops to Huancayo (see page 253).

Pisco and around → *Phone code: 056. Colour map 2, C3. Population: 82,250.*

The largest port between Callao and Matarani is a short distance to the west of the Pan-American Highway and 237 km south of Lima. In August 2007, an earthquake of 7.9 on the Richter scale struck the coast of Peru south of Lima killing 519 people, with 1366 injured and 58,500 homes destroyed. Hardest hit was the province of Ica; in the city of Pisco almost half of all buildings were destroyed. Also affected was **Chincha Alta**, 35 km north of Pisco, where the negro/criollo culture thrives. The famous festival, **Verano Negro**, is at the end of February while, in November, the **Festival de las Danzas Negras** is held in El Carmen, 10 km south. In October 2011, another earthquake, this time of 6.9 on the Richter scale, occurred off the coast of Ica, leaving one dead, 1705 homeless and 515 damaged or destroyed houses.

A 317-km paved road goes to Ayacucho in the sierra, with a branch to Huancavelica. At Castrovirreyna it reaches 4600 m. The scenery on this journey is superb. **Tambo Colorado**, one of the best-preserved Inca ruins in coastal Peru, is 38 km from the San Clemente junction, up the Pisco valley. It includes buildings where the Inca and his retinue would have stayed. Many of the walls retain their original colours. On the other side of the road is the public plaza and the garrison and messengers' quarters. The caretaker will act as a guide, he has a small collection of items found on the site. See https://www.facebook.com/TamboColorado for details of a French research project here.

Paracas National Reserve

① *US$1.75 pp; agency tours cost US$9 in a bus with 20 people, 1100-1500.*

Down the coast 15 km from Pisco Puerto is the bay of **Paracas**, sheltered by the Paracas peninsula. The name means 'sandstorm' (these can last for three days, especially in August; the wind gets up every afternoon, peaking at around 1500). Paracas can be reached by the coast road from San Andrés, passing the fishing port and a large proportion of Peru's fishmeal industry. Alternatively, go down the Pan-American Highway to 14.5 km past the Pisco turning and take the road to Paracas across the desert. In town is the **Museo Histórico de Paracas** ① *Av Los Libertadores Mz JI Lote 10, T955-929514, www.museohistoricoparacas. com*, with exhibits from the pre-Columbian cultures of the region.

The peninsula, a large area of coast to the south and the Ballestas Islands is a national reserve (Peru's most visited in 2013), and one of the best marine reserves, with the highest concentration of marine birds in the world. It's advisable to see the peninsula as part of a tour: it is not safe to walk alone and it is easy to get lost. The **Julio C Tello** site museum was being rebuilt in 2014 after the 2007 earthquake. Tours follow a route through the reserve, including to a *mirador* of **La Catedral** rock formation, which collapsed in 2007. Longer tours venture into the deserts to the south. About 14 km from the museum is the pre-Columbian Candelabra (**Candelabro** in Spanish) traced in the hillside, at least 50 m long, best seen from the sea (sit on left side of boat). The tiny fishing village of **Lagunilla** is 5 km from the museum across the neck of the peninsula. Eating places there are poor value (watch out for prices in dollars), but almost all tours stop for lunch here.

Ballestas Islands

Trips to the **Islas Ballestas** leave from the jetties in Paracas town. The islands are spectacular, eroded into numerous arches and caves (*ballesta* means bow, as in archery), which provide shelter for thousands of seabirds, some of which are very rare, and hundreds of sea lions. The book *Las Aves del Departamento de Lima* by Maria Koepcke is useful (see also www.avesdelima.com/playas.htm). You will see, close up, thousands of inquisitive sea lions, guano birds, pelicans, penguins and, if you're lucky, dolphins swimming in the bay. Most boats are speedboats with life jackets, some are very crowded; wear warm clothing and protect against the sun. The boats pass Puerto San Martín and the Candelabra en route to the islands.

Ica and Huacachina → *Phone code: 056. Colour map 2, C3. Population: 161,410.*

Ica, 70 km southeast of Pisco, is Peru's chief wine centre and is famous for its *tejas*, a local sweet of *manjarblanco*. It suffered less damage than Pisco, but one side of the Plaza de Armas collapsed in the earthquake. The **Museo Regional** ① *Av Ayabaca, block 8, T234383, Mon-Wed 0800-1900, Thu-Sun 0900-1800, US$4, students US$2.15, tip guides US$4-5, take bus 17 from the Plaza de Armas (US$0.50)*, has mummies, ceramics, textiles and trepanned skulls from the Paracas, Nazca and Inca cultures. It has a good, well-displayed collection of Inca *quipus* and clothes made of feathers. Behind the building is a scale model of the Nazca lines with an observation tower; a useful orientation before visiting the lines. The kiosk outside sells copies of motifs from the ceramics and textiles. **Dircetur** ① *Av Grau 148, T238710, ica@mincetur.gob.pe*. Some tourist information is available at travel agencies.

Wine *bodegas* that you can visit are: **La Caravedo**, Panamericana Sur 298, T01-9833 4729, with organic production and sophisticated presentation; **El Carmen**, on the right-hand side when arriving from Lima (has an ancient grape press made from a huge tree trunk); **El Catador** ① *Fondo Tres Esquinas 102, T962629, elcatadorcristel@yahoo.es, 1000-1800, US$1.50, 10 km outside Ica, in the district of Subtanjalla, combi from the 2nd block of Moquegua, every 20 mins, US$0.75, taxi takes 10 mins, good tours in Spanish*. The shop sells home-made wines, pisco and crafts associated with winemaking. In the evening it is a restaurant-bar with dancing and music, best visited during harvest, late February to early April. Near El Catador is **Bodega Alvarez**, whose owner, Umberto Alvarez, is very hospitable. The town of Ocucaje is a popular excursion from Ica for tours of the **Ocucaje winery** ① *Ctra Panamericana Sur, Km 335.5, T01-251 4570, www.ocucaje.com*, which makes wines and *pisco*.

About 5 km from Ica, round a palm-fringed lake and amid amazing sand dunes, is the oasis and summer resort of **Huacachina** ① *take a taxi from Ica for US$1.75, or colectivo from Bolívar black 2 in Ica, return from behind Hotel Mossone, US$0.75*, a popular hang-out for people seeking a change from the archaeology and chill of the Andes. Plenty of cheap hostels and bars have opened, playing pop and grunge as opposed to pan-pipe music. Paddleboats can be rented and sandboarding on the dunes has become a major pastime. For the inexperienced, note that sandboarding can be dangerous. Dune buggies also do white-knuckle, rollercoaster tours for US$20 (plus a municipal small fee), most start between 1600 and 1700 for sunsets, some at 1000, 2½ hours.

◉ South from Lima listings

For hotel and restaurant price codes, and other relevant information, see pages 14-17.

● Where to stay

Pisco and around *p152*
$$ Posada Hispana Hostal, Bolognesi 222, T536363, www.posadahispana.com. Some rooms with loft and bath, also rooms with shared bath, hot water, can accommodate groups, comfortable, breakfast extra, has **Café de la Posada**, information service, English, French, Italian and Catalan spoken.
$$-$ El Candelabro, Callao y Pedemonte, T532620, www.hoteleselcandelabro.com. Modern, pleasant, all rooms with bath, fridge, restaurant.
$$-$ Hostal San Isidro, San Clemente 103, T536471, http://sanisidrohostal.com. With or without bath, hot water, safe, welcoming, nice pool and cafeteria, pizzeria, free laundry facilities, games room, English spoken, parking. Breakfast not included, free coffee

in mornings, use of kitchen. Arranges dune buggy tours and other excursions.
$$-$ San Jorge Residencial, Jr Barrio Nuevo 133, T532885, www.hotelsanjorge residencial.com. Smart and modern. Hot water, secure parking, breakfast is served in the restaurant, also lunch and dinner, swanky and spacious, café/bar in garden.
$ Hostal Los Inkas Inn, Prol Barrio Nuevo Mz M, Lte 14, Urb San Isidro, T536634. Affordable, rooms and dorms have private bath, fan, safes, rooftop games area, small pool.
$ Hostal Tambo Colorado, Av Bolognesi 159, T531379, www.hostaltambocolorado. com. Welcoming, helpful owners are knowledgeable about the area, hot water, small café/bar, use of kitchen.

Paracas *p153*
$$$$ Hotel Paracas Luxury Collection Resort, Av Paracas 173, T581333, www. libertador.com.pe. The reincarnation of the

famous **Hotel Paracas**, as a resort with spa, pools, excellent rooms in cottages around the grounds, access to beach, choice of restaurants, bar.

$$$$ La Hacienda Bahía Paracas, Lote 25, Urb Santo Domingo, T01-213 1000, www.hoteleslahacienda.com. Next to Doubletree but not connected, rooms and suites, some with access straight to pool, spa, choice of restaurants, bar.

$$$$-$$$ Doubletree Guest Suites Paracas, Lote 30-34, Urb Santo Domingo on the outskirts, T01-617 1000, www.doubletree.com. Low rise, clean lines and a comfortable size, built around a lovely pool, on beach, water sports, spa, all mod cons and popular with families.

$$$ El Mirador, at the turn-off to El Chaco, T545086, www.elmiradorhotel.com. Hot water, good service, boat trips arranged, meals available, large pool, tranquil gardens, relaxing.

$$$ Gran Palma, Av Principal Mz D lote 03, half block from plaza, T01-665 5932, www.hotelgranpalma.com. Central, convenient for boats, best rooms have sea view, buffet breakfast on the terrace.

$$ Brisas de la Bahía, Av Principal, T531132, www.brisasdelabahia.com. Good, family-run hostal, convenient position for waterfront and bus stops, ask for a back room, good breakfast.

$$ Los Frayles, Av Paracas Mz D lote 5, T545141, www.hostallosfrayles.com. Variety of simple, well-kept rooms, ocean view, breakfast extra, roof terrace, tourist information, transfers to/from bus arranged.

$$ Mar Azul, Alan García Mz B lote 20, T534542, www.hostalmarazul.com. Family-run overlooking the sea although most rooms face away from ocean, comfortable, hot water, breezy roof terrace with sea view for breakfast (included), helpful owner Yudy Patiño. Also **Ballestas Expeditions** for local tours.

$$ Santa María, Av Paracas s/n, T545045, www.hostalsantamariaparacas.com. Smart rooms, hot water, no view. **El Chorito** restaurant, mainly fish and seafood. Also has

Santa María 2, round the corner in lovely converted house (same contact numbers), not all rooms have view but has rooftop terrace. **Santa María 3**, under construction on the approach road, will have more facilities and pool.

$ Backpackers House, Av Los Libertadores, beside museum, T635623, www.paracasbackpackershouse.com.pe. Rooms with and without bath, private and dorms, at high season prices rise to **$$-$**. Good value, comfortable, tourist information.

$ Hostal El Amigo, El Chaco, T545042, hostalelamigo@hotmail.com. Simple, hot water, no food, no internet but very helpful staff.

Ica and Huacachina p153
Ica

Hotels are fully booked during the harvest festival and prices rise. Many hotels are in out of town residential neighbourhoods, insist taxis go to the hotel of your choice.

$$$$-$$$ Las Dunas, Av La Angostura 400, T256224, www.lasdunashotel.com. Lima office: Av Vasco Núñez de Balboa 259, Lima, T213 5000. Variety of rooms and suites. Prices are reduced on weekdays. Packages available. Complete resort with restaurant, swimming pool, many sporting activities and full-day programmes.

$$$ Villa Jazmín, Los Girasoles Mz C-1, Lote 7, Res La Angostura, T258179, www.villajazmin.net. Modern hotel in a residential area near the sand dunes, 8 mins from the city centre, solar heated water, restaurant, buffet breakfast, pool, tours arranged, airport and bus transfers, helpful staff, tranquil and very good.

$$ Princess, Santa Magdalena D-103, Urb Santa María, T215421, www.hotelprincess.com.pe. Taxi ride from the main plaza, small rooms, hot water, frigobar, pool, tourist information, helpful, peaceful, very good.

$ Arameli, Tacna 239, T239107. 1 block from the Plaza de Armas, is a nice place to stay, good value, café on 3rd floor.

Huacachina

$$$ Mossone, east end of the lake, T213630, www.dmhoteles.pe. Faded elegance, hacienda-style with a view of the lagoon, full board available, good buffet breakfast, large rooms, bilingual staff, lovely courtyard, bicycles and sandboards, large, clean swimming pool.

$$ Hostal Huacachinero, Av Perotti, opposite Hostal Salvatierra, T217435, http://elhuacachinero.com. Spacious rooms, sparsely furnished but comfortable beds, nice atmosphere, pool, outside bar and restaurant, parking, offers tours and buggy rides.

$$ Hostería Suiza, Malecón 264, T238762, hostesuiza@terra.com.pe. Overlooking lake, lovely grounds, quiet, safe parking.

$ Carola del Sur (also known as Casa de Arena II), Av Perotti s/n, T237398. Basic rooms, popular, small pool, restaurant/bar, hammocks, access to Casa de Arena's bigger pool, noisy at night, pressure to buy tours.

$ Casa de Arena, Av Perotti s/n, T215274. Basic rooms and dorms, thin walls, bar, small pool, laundry facilities, board hire, popular with backpackers but grubby, check your bill and change carefully, don't leave valuables unattended, disco next door.

$ Hostal Rocha, T222256, kikerocha@ hotmail.com. Hot water, with or without bath, family-run, kitchen and laundry facilities, board hire, small pool, popular with backpackers, but a bit run-down.

$ Hostal Salvatierra, T232352, http:// salvaturgroup.galeon.com. An old building, with or without bath, not on waterfront, charming, pool, relaxing courtyard, rents sandboards, good value.

See also **Desert Adventures**, under What to do, below.

🍴 Restaurants

Pisco and around *p152*
$$-$ As de Oro, San Martín 472, T532010. Closed Mon. Good food, not cheap but always full at lunchtime, swimming pool.

$ Café Pirata, Callao 104, T534343. Open 0630-1500, 1800-2200, closed Sun. Desserts, pizzas, sandwiches, coffee and lunch menu.
$ Chifa Lisen, Av San Martín 325, T535527. Open 1230-1530, 1800-2200. Chinese food and delivery.

Paracas *p153*
Several eating places on the Malecón by Playa El Chaco, all with similar menus and prices (in our **$$** range) and open for breakfast, eg **Bahía**; **Brisa Marina**, varied menu, mainly seafood; **Johnny y Jennifer**. All have vegetarian options. Better value *menús* are available at lunchtime on the main road, eg **Lobo Fino**. Higher quality food within walking distance of the centre is at the **Hotel Paracas'** restaurant and **Trattoria**, **$$$**, both open to the public.

Ica and Huacachina *p153*
$$-$ Anita, Libertad 133, Plaza de Armas. Local dishes, breakfast, à la carte a bit expensive for what's offered, but set menus at US$4.50 are good value.
$ Carne y pescao, Av Juan José Elías 417, T228157. Seafood and, at night, grilled chicken and *parrilladas*.
$ Plaza 125, C Lima 125, T211816. On the plaza, regional and international food as well as breakfast, good-value set lunches.
D'lizia, Lima 155, Plaza de Armas, T237733, www.delizia.com.pe. Also in the Patio de comidas at Plaza Vea mall and in Urb Moderna. Modern and bright, for breakfasts, lunches, sandwiches, snacks, ice cream, cakes and sweets, juices and drinks.
Tejas Helena, Cajamarca 137. The best *tejas* and locally made chocolates are sold here.

Huacachina
$ La Casa de Bamboo, Av Perotti s/n, next to Hostería Suiza, T776649. Café-bar, English breakfast, marmite, Thai curry, falafel, vegetarian and vegan options, book exchange, games.
$ Moroni, T238471. Open 0800 till late. Only restaurant right on the lake shore, serving a variety of Peruvian and international foods.

⚘ Festivals

Ica and Huacachina *p153*
Festival Internacional de la Vendimia wine harvest in early **Mar**. The image of El Señor de Luren, in a fine church in Parque Luren, draws pilgrims from all Peru in **Oct** (3rd Mon), when there are all-night processions; celebrations start the week before.

⏱ What to do

Paracas *p153*
There are agencies all over town offering trips to the Islas Ballestas, the Paracas reserve, Ica, Nazca and Tambo Colorado. A 2-hr boat tour to the islands costs US$13-15 pp, including park entrance fee and tax, departure 0800. Usually, agencies will pool clients together in 1 boat, 40 people per boat. Do not book tours on the street. An agency that does not pool clients is **Huacachina**, based in Ica, with an office in Paracas, T056-215582, www.huacachinatours.com.
Zarcillo Connections, Independencia A-20, Paracas, T536636, www.zarcilloconnections.com. With long experience for trips to the Paracas National Reserve, Tambo Colorado, trekking and tours to Ica, Chincha and the Nazca Lines and surrounding sites. Agent for **Cruz del Sur** buses. Also has its own hotel, **Zarcillo Paradise**, in Paracas.

Ica and Huacachina *p153*
In Ica, agencies offer city tours, Nazca Lines, Paracas, Islas Ballestas, buggies and sandboarding: **AV Dolphin Travel**, C Municipalidad 132, of 4, T256234, www.av-dolphintravelperu.com; **Desert Travel**, Lima 171, inside Tejas Don Juan on Plaza, T227215, desert_travel@hotmail.com.
Desert Adventures, Huacachina, T228458, www.desertadventure.net. Frequently recommended for sandboarding and camping trips into the desert by 4WD and buggies, French, English and Spanish spoken. Also to beaches, Islas Ballestas and Nazca Lines flights. Has an associated hostel,

Desert Nights, which has a good reputation, English spoken, food available.
Ica Desert Trip, Bolívar 178, T237373, www.icadeserttrip.com. Roberto Penny Cabrera (speaks Spanish and English) offers 1-, 2- and 3-day trips off-road into the desert, archaeology, geology, etc. 4 people maximum, contact by email in advance. Take toilet paper, something warm for the evening, a long-sleeved loose cotton shirt for daytime and long trousers. Recommended, but "not for the faint-hearted".

⊖ Transport

Cañete Valley *p152*
Soyuz bus Lima-**Cañete** every 7 mins, US$5; combi Cañete-**Lunahuaná**, US$2.75. Cars run from the Yauyos area to **Huancayo**, US$7.50. Ask locally where and when they leave. Public transport between villages is scarce and usually goes in the morning. When you get to a village you may have to wait till the early evening for places to open up.

Pisco and around *p152*
Air Capitán RE Olivera airport is being redeveloped from a military base into an alternative airport for Lima. By 2017 it expected to be a major international hub. LCPerú's Lima–Pisco–Cuzco flights offer views of the Nazca Lines. They also have Nazca overflights from Pisco in large-windowed Twin Otter Vistaliners (www.lcperu.pe), as does **Aerodiana** (Av Casimiro Ulloa 227, San Antonio, Lima, T447 6824, www.aerodiana.com.pe).
Bus Buses drop passengers at San Clemente on Panamericana Sur (**El Cruce**); many bus companies and tour agencies have their offices here. It's a 10-km taxi ride from the centre, US$8, US$10 to Paracas. Colectivos leave from outside Banco Continental (plaza) for El Cruce when full, US$2. To **Lima**, 242 km, 4 hrs, US$7.50. The best company is **Soyuz**, every 7 mins. **Ormeño** has an office in Pisco plaza and will take you to El Cruce to meet their 1600 bus.

Flores is the only company that goes into Pisco town, from Lima and Ica, but buses are poor and services erratic. To **Ica**, US$1.25 by bus, 45 mins, 70 km, with **Ormeño**, also colectivos. To **Nazca**, 210 km, take a bus to Ica and then change to a colectivo. To **Ayacucho**, 317 km, 8-10 hrs, US$12-20, several buses daily, leave from El Cruce, book in advance and take warm clothing as it gets cold at night. To **Huancavelica**, 269 km, 12-14 hrs, US$12, with **Oropesa**, coming from Ica. To Arequipa, US$17, 10-12 hrs, 2 daily. To **Tambo Colorado** from near the plaza in Pisco, 0800, US$2.50, 3 hrs; also colectivos, US$2 pp. Alight 20 mins after the stop at Humay; the road passes right through the site. Return by bus to Pisco in the afternoon. For transport back to Pisco wait at the caretaker's house. Taxi from Pisco US$30. Tours from Pisco agencies US$15 with guide, minimum 2 people.

Paracas *p153*
Cruz del Sur has 2 direct buses a day to its Paracas terminal, regular bus from US$9, luxury services US$30-35 from **Lima**, US$15 to **Nazca**. Agencies in Paracas sell direct transfers between Paracas and Huacachina, Pelican Perú, 1100 daily, US$7, comfortable and secure.
Taxi From **Pisco** to Paracas about US$3; combis when full, US$1.75, 25 mins.

Ica and Huacachina *p153*
Bus All bus offices are on Lambayeque blocks 1 and 2 and Salaverry block 3. To **Pisco**, 70 km, as above; to Paracas junction US$1.15. To **Lima**, 302 km, 4 hrs, US$21-34, on upmarket buses, several daily including **Soyuz** (Av Manzanilla 130, every 7 mins 0600-2200) and **Ormeño** (at Lamba yeque 180). To **Nazca**, 140 km, 2 hrs, several buses (US$3.50) and colectivos (US$5) daily, including **Ormeño**, **Flores**, 4 daily, and **Cueva** (José Elias y Huánuco), hourly on the hour 0600-2200. To **Arequipa** the route goes via Nazca (see Nazca).

Nazca and around

Set in a green valley amid a perimeter of mountains, Nazca's altitude puts it just above any fog which may drift in from the sea. The sun blazes the year round by day and the nights are crisp. Nearby are the mysterious, world-famous Nazca Lines. Overlooking the town is Cerro Blanco (2078 m), the highest sand dune in the world, popular for sandboarding and parapenting.

Nazca Town → *Phone code: 056. Colour map 2, C3. Population: over 50,000. Altitude: 598 m.*
In the town of Nazca (140 km south of Ica via Pan-American Highway, 444 km from Lima) there are two important museums. **Museo Antonini** ① *Av de la Cultura 600, eastern end of Jr Lima, T523444, cahuachi@terra.com.pe or CISRAP@numerica.it, 0900-1900, ring the bell, US$6, including guide. 10-min walk from the plaza, or short taxi ride.* This museum houses the discoveries of Professor Orefici and his team from the huge pre-Inca city at Cahuachi (see below), which, Orefici believes, holds the key to the Nazca Lines. Many tombs survived the huaqueros and there are displays of mummies, ceramics, textiles, amazing *antaras* (panpipes) and photos of the excavations. In the garden is a prehispanic aqueduct. Recommended. The **Maria Reiche Planetarium** ① *Hotel Nazca Lines, T522293, shows usually at 1900 and 2115 in English, 2000 in Spanish; US$7 (students half price),* offer introductory lectures every night about the Nazca Lines, based on Reiche's theories, which cover archaeology and astronomy. The show lasts about 45 minutes, after which visitors are able to look at the moon, planets and stars through telescopes. There is a small

market at Lima y Grau, the Mercado Central at Arica y Tacna and a supermarket, Raulito, at Grau 245. The **Virgen de la Guadalupe** festival takes place 29 August-10 September. **Tourist police** ① *Av Los Incas cuadra 1, T522105.*

Nazca Lines

Cut into the stony desert about 22 km north of Nazca, above the Ingenio valley on the Pampa de San José, along the Pan-American Highway, are the famous Nazca Lines. Large numbers of lines, not only parallels and geometrical figures, but also designs such as a dog, an enormous monkey, birds (one with a wing span of over 100 m), a spider and a tree. The lines, best seen from the air, are thought to have been etched on the Pampa Colorada sands by three different groups – the Paracas people 900-200 BC, the Nazcas 200 BC-AD 600 and the Huari settlers from Ayacucho at about AD 630.

The Nazcas had a highly developed civilization which reached its peak about AD 600. Their polychrome ceramics, wood carvings and adornments of gold are on display in many of Lima's museums. The Paracas was an early phase of the Nazca culture, renowned for the superb technical quality and stylistic variety in its weaving and pottery. The Huari empire, in conjunction with the Tiahuanaco culture, dominated much of Peru from AD 600-1000.

Origins of the lines The German expert, Dr Maria Reiche, who studied the lines for over 40 years, mostly from a step ladder, died in 1998, aged 95. She maintained that they represent some sort of vast astronomical pre-Inca calendar. In 1976 Maria Reiche paid for a platform, the mirador, from which three of the huge designs can be seen – the Hands,

Nazca

Where to stay	
1 Alegría	10 Posada Guadalupe
2 Casa Andina Classic	11 Sol de Nasca
3 Hostal Alegría	
4 Maison Suisse	**Restaurants**
5 Majoro	1 Chifa Guang Zhou
6 Nasca	2 Coffee Break
7 Nazca Lines	3 El Huarango &
8 Paredones Inn	Travel Service
9 Posada de Don Hono	4 Fuente de Soda Jumbory
	5 Kañada

6 La Choza	
7 La Taberna	
8 Los Angeles	
9 Mamashana &	
Vía La Encantada	
10 Panadería	
11 Rico Pollo	

200 metres
200 yards

N

the Lizard and the Tree. Her book, *Mystery on the Desert*, is on sale for US$10 (proceeds to conservation work) in Nazca. In January 1994 Maria Reiche opened a small **museum** ⓘ *US$1. At the Km 421 marker, 5 km from town, take micro from in front of Ormeño terminal, US$0.75, frequent.* Viktoria Nikitzhi, a colleague of Maria Reiche, gives one-hour lectures about the Nazca Lines at **Dr Maria Reiche Center** ⓘ *US$5, Av de los Espinales 300, 1 block from Ormeño bus stop, T969 9419, viktorianikitzki@hotmail.com.* She also organizes tours in June and December (phone in advance to confirm times; also ask about volunteer work). See the Planetarium, above. Another good book is *Pathways to the Gods: the mystery of the Nazca Lines*, by Tony Morrison (Michael Russell, 1978).

Other theories abound: claims that the lines are the tracks of running contests (Georg A von Breunig, 1980, and English astronomer Alan Sawyer); that they represent weaving patterns and yarns (Henri Stirlin) and that the plain is a map demonstrating the Tiahuanaco Empire (Zsoltan Zelko). Johan Reinhard proposes that the Lines conform to fertility practices throughout the Andes, in common with the current use of straight lines in Chile and Bolivia.

Another theory is that the ancient Nazcas flew in hot-air balloons, based on the idea that the lines are best seen from the air (Jim Woodman, 1977 and, in part, the BBC series *Ancient Voices*). A related idea is that the lines were not designed to be seen physically from above, but from the mind's eye of the flying shaman. Both theories are supported by pottery and textile evidence which shows balloonists and a flying creature emitting discharge from its nose and mouth. There are also local legends of flying men. Thhe depiction in the desert of creatures such as a monkey or killer whale also indicates the qualities needed by the shaman in his spirit journeys.

After six years' work at La Muña and Los Molinos, Palpa (43 km north of Nazca), and using photogrammetry, Peruvian archaeologist Johny Isla and Markus Reindel of the Swiss-Liechtenstein Foundation deduced that the lines on both the Palpa and Nazca plains are offerings dedicated to the worship of water and fertility, two elements which also dominate on ceramics and on the engraved stones of the Paracas culture. Isla and Reindel believe that the Palpa lines predate those at Nazca and that the lines and drawings themselves are scaled up versions of the Paracas drawings. This research proposes that the Nazca culture succumbed not to drought, but to heavy rainfall, probably during an El Niño event.

Other excursions

The Nazca area is dotted with over 100 cemeteries and the dry, humidity-free climate has perfectly preserved invaluable tapestries, cloth and mummies. At **Chauchilla** ⓘ *30 km south of Nazca, last 12 km a sandy track, US$3,* grave robbing *huaqueros* ransacked the tombs and left bones, skulls, mummies and pottery shards littering the desert. A tour takes about two hours. Gold mining is one of the main local industries and a tour usually includes a visit to a small family processing shop where the techniques used are still very old-fashioned.

To the **Paredones ruins and aqueduct** ⓘ *US$3.55 entry also includes 4 other archealogical sites: El Telar Geoglyphs, Acueductos de Cantayoc, Las Agujas Geoglyphs and Acueductos de Ocongalla.* The ruins, also called Cacsamarca, are Inca on a pre-Inca base; they are not well preserved. The underground aqueducts, built 300 BC-AD 700, are still in working order and worth seeing. Cantayoc Aqueducts, Las Agujas and El Telar Geoglyphs are a 30 minutes to one-hour walk through Buena Fe (or organize a taxi from your hotel), to see markings in the valley floor and ancient aqueducts which descend in spirals into the ground. The markings consist of a triangle pointing to a hill and a *telar* (loom) with a spiral depicting the threads. Climb the mountain to see better examples.

Cahuachi ① *US$3.50 entry, US$17 pp on a tour, US$12-15 in private taxi, minimum 2 people; see also the Museo Antonini, above,* one hour to the west of the Nazca Lines along a rough dirt track, comprises some 30 pyramids. Only 5% of the site has been excavated so far, some of which has been reconstructed. It could be larger than Chan Chán, making it the largest adobe city in the world. Some 4 km beyond Cahuachi is a site called **El Estaquería**, thought to have been a series of astronomical sighting posts, but more recent research suggests the wooden pillars were used to dry dead bodies and therefore it may have been a place of mummification.

Reserva Nacional De San Fernando is a gathering place for birds, continental and oceanic mammals. It was established in 2011 as a national reserve to protect migratory and local wild life such as the Humboldt penguin, sea lions, the Andean fox, condor, guanaco, dolphins and whales. San Fernando is located in the highest part of the Peruvian coastal desert, in the same place as Cerro Blanco, the highest dune in the world. Here is where the Nazca Plate lifts the continental plate, generating moist accumulation in the ground with resulting seasonal winter flora and a continental wildlife corridor between the high coastal mountains and the sea. Full-day and two-day/one-night tours are offered by some agencies in town.

Road from Nazca towards Cuzco

Two hours out of Nazca on the newly paved road to Abancay and Cuzco is the **Reserva Nacional Pampas Galeras** at 4100 m, which has a vicuña reserve. There is an interesting Museo del Sitio, also a military base and park guard here. Entry is free. At Km 155 is **Puquio**, then it's another 185 km to **Chalhuanca**. Fuel is available in both towns. There are wonderful views on this stretch, with lots of small villages, valleys and alpacas.

South of Nazca

Ten kilometres north of the fishing village of **Chala** (*Phone code: 054*, 173 km from Nazca, many restaurants) are the large pre-Columbian ruins of **Puerto Inca** on the coast. This was the port for Cuzco. The site is in excellent condition: the drying and store houses can be seen as holes in the ground (be careful where you walk). On the right side of the bay is a cemetery, on the hill a temple of reincarnation, and the Inca road from the coast to Cuzco is clearly visible. The road was 240 km long, with a staging post every 7 km so that, with a change of runner at every post, messages could be sent in 24 hours. The site is best appreciated when the sun is shining.

◉ Nazca and around listings

For hotel and restaurant price codes, and other relevant information, see pages 14-17.

◉ Where to stay

Nazca *p158, map p159*
If arriving by bus beware of touts who tell you that the hotel of your choice is closed, or full. If you phone or email the hotel they will pick you up at the bus station free of charge day or night.

$$$ Casa Andina Classic, Jr Bolognesi 367, T01-213 9739, www.casa-andina.com. This recommended chain of hotels' Nazca property, offering standardized services in distinctive style. Bright, modern decor, central patio with palm trees, pool, restaurant.
$$$ Maison Suisse, opposite airport, T522 434, www.nazcagroup.com. Comfortable, safe car park, expensive restaurant, pool, suites with jacuzzi, good giftshop, shows video of Nazca Lines. Also has camping

facilities. Its packages include flights over Nazca Lines.

$$$ Majoro, Panamericana Sur Km 452, T522490, www.hotelmajoro.com.
A charming old hacienda about 5 km from town past the airstrip so quite remote, beautiful gardens, pool, slow and expensive restaurant, quiet and welcoming, good arrangements for flights and tours.

$$$ Nazca Lines, Jr Bolognesi 147, T522293.
With a/c, rather dated rooms with private patio, hot water, peaceful, restaurant, safe car park, pool (US$9-10.50 pp includes sandwich and drink), they can arrange package tours which include 2-3 nights at the hotel plus a flight over the lines and a desert trip.

$$$-$$ Oro Viejo, Callao 483, T521112, www.hoteloroviejo.net. Has a suite with jacuzzi and comfortable standard rooms, nice garden, swimming pool, restaurant and bar. Recommended.

$$ Alegría, Jr Lima 166, T522497, www.hotelalegria.net. Small breakfast, bus terminal transfers. Rooms with hot water, cafeteria, pool, garden, English, Hebrew, Italian and German spoken, laundry facilities, book exchange, restaurant, ATM, parking, OK but can be noisy from disco and traffic. Also has a tour agency and guests are encouraged to buy tours (see What to do), flights and bus tickets arranged.

$$ La Encantada, Callao 592, T522930, www.hotellaencantada.com.pe. Pleasant modern hotel with restaurant, laundry and parking.

$$ Paredones Inn, Jr Lima 600, T522181. 1 block from the Plaza de Armas, modern, colourful rooms, great views from roof terrace, laundry service, bar, suites with minibar, microwave, jacuzzi, helpful staff.

$$ Posada de Don Hono, Av María Reiche 112, T506822, laposadadedonhono1@ hotmail.com. Small rooms and nice bungalows, good café, parking.

$ Hostal Alegría, Av Los Incas 117, opposite Ormeño bus terminal, T522497. Basic, hot water, hammocks, nice garden, camping, restaurant.

$ Nasca, C Lima 438, T522085, marionasca13@ hotmail.com. Hot water, with or without bath, laundry facilities, new annexe at the back, nice garden, safe motorcycle parking.

$ Posada Guadalupe, San Martín 225, T522249. Family-run, lovely courtyard and garden, hot water, with or without bath, good breakfast, relaxing. (Touts selling tours are nothing to do with hotel.)

$ Sol de Nasca, Callao 586, T522730. Rooms with and without hot showers, restaurant, pleasant, don't leave valuables in luggage store.

South of Nazca p161

$$$-$$ Puerto Inka, 2 km along a side road from Km 610 Panamericana Sur (reservations T054-778458), www.puertoinka.com.pe. Bungalows on the beautiful beach, hammocks outside, indoor games room, disco, breakfast extra, great place to relax, kayaks, boat hire, diving equipment rental, pleasant camping US$5, low season discounts, used by tour groups, busy in summer.

❶ Restaurants

Nazca p158, map p159

$$$-$$ Vía La Encantada, Bolognesi 282 (website as hotel above). Modern, stylish with great food, fish, meat or vegetarian, good value lunches.

$$-$ Mamashana, Bolognesi 270. Rustic style with a lively atmosphere, for breakfast, grills, pastas and pizzas.

$$-$ La Choza, Bolognesi 290. Nice decor with woven chairs and thatched roof, all types of food, live music at night. Single women may be put off by the crowds of young men hanging around the doors handing out flyers.

$$-$ La Taberna, Jr Lima 321, T521411. Excellent food, live music, popular with gringos, it's worth a look just for the graffiti on the walls.

$ Chifa Guang Zhou, Bolognesi 297, T522036. Very good.

$ El Huarango, Arica 602. National and international cuisine. Relaxed family atmosphere and deliciously breezy terrace.
$ Kañada, Lima 160, nazcanada@yahoo.com. Cheap, good *menú*, excellent pisco sours, nice wines, popular, display of local artists' work, email service, English spoken, helpful.
$ Los Angeles, Bolognesi 266. Good, cheap, try *sopa criolla*, and chocolate cake.
$ Rico Pollo, Lima 190. Good local restaurant with great chicken dishes.
Coffee Break, Bolognesi 219. Open 0700-2300 except Sat. For real coffee and good pizzas.
Fuente de Soda Jumbory, near the cinema. Good *almuerzo*.
Panadería, Bolognesi 387.

⏲ What to do

Nazca *p158, map p159*
All guides must be approved by the Ministry of Tourism and should have an official identity card. Touts (*jaladores*) operate at popular hotels and the bus terminals using false ID cards and fake hotel and tour brochures. They are rip-off merchants who overcharge and mislead those who arrive by bus. Only conduct business with agencies at their office, or phone or email the company you want to deal with in advance. Some hotels are not above pressurising guests to purchase tours at inflated prices. Taxi drivers usually act as guides, but most speak only Spanish. Do not take just any taxi on the plaza for a tour, always ask your hotel for a reputable driver.
Air Nasca Travel, Jr Lima 185, T521027, guide Susi recommended. Very helpful and competitive prices. Can do all types of tours around Nazca, Ica, Paracas and Pisco.
Algería Tours, Lima 186, T523431, http://alegriatoursperu.com. Offers inclusive tours, guides with radio contact and maps can be provided for hikes to nearby sites. Guides speak English, German, French and Italian. They also offer adventure tours, such as mountain biking from 4000 m in the Andes down to the plain, sandboarding, and more.

Félix Quispe Sarmiento, 'El Nativo de Nazca'. He has his own museum, Hantun Nazca, at Panamericana Sur 447 and works with the Ministerio de Cultura, tours off the beaten track, can arrange flights, knowledgeable, ask for him at Kañada restaurant.
Fernández family, who run the Hotel Nasca, also run local tours. Ask for the hotel owners and speak to them direct.
Huarango Travel Service, Arica 602, T522141, huarangotravel@yahoo.es. Tours around Ica, Paracas, Huacachina, Nazca and Palpa.
Mystery Peru, Simón Bolívar 221, T01-435 0051, T956-691155, www.mysteryperu.com. Owned by Enrique Levano Alarcón, based in Nazca with many local tours, also packages throughout Peru.
Nazca Perú 4x4, Bolognesi 367 (in Casa Andina), T522928, or T975-017029. Tubular 4WD tours to San Fernando National Reserve and other off-the-beaten-track locations.

Tours of the Nazca Lines
On land Taxi-guides to the mirador, 0800-1200, cost US$5-8 pp, or you can hitch, but there is not always much traffic. Travellers suggest the view from the hill 500 m back to Nazca is better. Go early as the site gets very hot. Or take a taxi and arrive at 0745 before the buses.
By air Small planes take 3-5 passengers to see the Nazca Lines. Flights last 30-35 mins and are controlled by air traffic personnel at the airport to avoid congestion. The price for a flight is around US$130 pp. You also have to pay US$10 airport tax. It is best to organize a flight with the airlines themselves at the airport. They will weigh you and select a group of passengers based on weight, so you may have to wait a while for your turn. Flights are bumpy with many tight turns – many people get airsick so it's wise not to eat or drink just before a flight. Best times to fly are 0800-1000 and 1500-1630 when there is less turbulence and better light (assuming there is no fog). Make sure you clarify everything before

getting on the plane and ask for a receipt. Also let them know in advance if you have any special requests. Taxi to airport, US$5, bus, US$0.25 (most tours include transport). **Note** Be aware that fatal crashes by planes flying over the lines do occur. Some foreign governments advise tourists not to take these flights and some companies will not provide insurance for passengers until safety and maintenance standards are improved. **Aero Diana**, see above under Pisco, Air, and **Aero Paracas**, T01-641 7000, www. aeroparacas.com, offer daily flights over the Lines.

Alas Peruanas, T522444, http://alas peruanas.com. Flights can also be booked at Hotel Alegría. Experienced pilots. They also offer 1-hr flights over the Palpa and Llipata areas, where you can see more designs and other rare patterns (US$130 pp, minimum 3) and Nazca and Palpa combined (US$250). See the website for promotional offers. All **Alas Peruanas** flights include the BBC film of Nazca.

⊕ Transport

Nazca *p158, map p159*
Bus It is worth paying the extra for a good bus – reports of robbery on the cheaper services. Over-booking is common.

To **Lima**, 446 km, 7 hrs, several buses and colectivos daily, US$23-26. **Ormeño**, T522058, *Royal Class* at 0530 and 1330 from Hotel Nazca Lines, normal service from Av Los Incas, 6 a day; **Civa**, Av Guardia Civil,

T523019, normal service at 2300; **Cruz del Sur**, Lima y San Martín, T523713, via Ica and Paracas, luxury service, US$39-55. **Ormeño** to **Ica**, 2 hrs, US$3.50, 4 a day. For **Pisco** (210 km), 3 hrs, buses stop 5 km outside town (see under Pisco, Transport), so change in Ica for direct transport into Pisco. To **Arequipa**, 565 km, 9 hrs, US$19-22.50, or US$28-52 *bus cama* services: **Ormeño**, from Av Los Incas, Royal Class at 2130, 8 hrs, also **Cruz del Sur** and **Oltursa**, Av los Incas 103, T522265, reliable, comfortable and secure on this route. Delays are possible out of Nazca because of drifting sand across the road or because of mudslides in the rainy season. Travel in daylight if possible. Book your ticket on previous day.

Buses to Cuzco, 659 km, via **Chalhuanca** and **Abancay** (13 hrs). The highway from Nazca to Cuzco is paved and is safe for bus travellers, drivers of private vehicles and motorcyclists. To **Cuzco** with **Ormeño**, US$50, and **Cruz del Sur**, 2015, 2100, US$50-70.

South of Nazca: Puerto Inca *p161*
Taxi from **Chala** US$8, or take a colectivo to Nazca as far as the turn-off for Puerto Inca, Km 610, if it has space, about US$6, beware overcharging.

⊕ Directory

Nazca *p158, map p159*
Useful addresses Police: at Av Los Incas, T522105, or T105 for emergencies.

Arequipa and the far south

The colonial city of Arequipa, with its guardian volcano, El Misti, is the ideal place to start exploring southern Peru. It is the gateway to two of the world's deepest canyons, Colca and Cotahuasi, whose villages and terraces hold onto a traditional way of life and whose skies are home to the magnificent condor. From Arequipa there are routes to Lake Titicaca and to the border with Chile.

Arequipa → *Phone code: 054. Colour map 3, B1. Population: 1 million. Altitude: 2380 m.*

The city of Arequipa, 1011 km from Lima, stands in a beautiful valley at the foot of El Misti volcano, a snow-capped, perfect cone, 5822 m high, guarded on either side by the mountains Chachani (6057 m), and Pichu-Pichu (5669 m). The city has fine Spanish buildings and many old and interesting churches built of sillar, a pearly white volcanic material almost exclusively used in the construction of Arequipa. The city was re-founded on 15 August 1540 by an emissary of Pizarro, but it had previously been occupied by Aymara Indians and the Incas. It is the main commercial centre for the south and is a busy place. Its people resent the general tendency to believe that everything is run from Lima. It has been declared a World Cultural Heritage site by UNESCO.

Arriving in Arequipa
Orientation The **airport** is 7 km west. It takes about half an hour to town. The main **bus terminal** is south of the centre, 15 minutes from the centre by colectivo, 10 minutes by taxi. ▶ *See also Transport, page 175.*

The main places of interest and the hotels are within walking distance of the Plaza de Armas. If you are going to the suburbs, take a bus or taxi. A cheap tour of the city can be made in a *Vallecito* bus, 1½ hours for US$0.50. It is a circular tour which goes down Calle Jerusalén and Calle San Juan de Dios. Alternatively an **open-top bus** ① *T203434, www.bustour.com.pe, US$17 for 4 hrs*, tours the city and nearby attractions from Portal San Agustín, Plaza de Armas at 0900 and 1400 daily.

Climate The climate is delightful, with a mean temperature before sundown of 23°C, and after sundown of 14°C. The sun shines on 360 days of the year. Annual rainfall is less than 150 mm.

Security There have been recent reports of taxi drivers in collusion with criminals to rob both tourists and locals. Ask hotels, restaurants, etc, to book a safe taxi for you. Theft can be a problem in the market area and the park at Selva Alegre. Be very cautious walking anywhere at night. The police are conspicuous, friendly, courteous and efficient, but their resources are limited.

Tourist office i perú ① *central office is in the Plaza de Armas, Portal de la Municipalidad 110, T223265, iperuarequipa@promperu.gob.pe, Mon-Sat 0830-1930, Sun 0830-1600*, also in the airport Arrivals hall, T444564, only open when flights are arriving. **Municipal tourist office** ① *in the Municipalidad, on the south side of the Plaza de Armas, No 112 next to iPerú, T211021*. The local guides' association, **Adegopa** ① *Claustros de la Compañía, tienda 11, Morán 118, http://adegopa.org or adegopa.blogspot.co.uk*, offers a variety of tours and activities. **Indecopi** ① *Hipólito Unanue 100-A, Urb Victoria, T212054, mlcornejo@indecopi. gob.pe*. The **Tourist Police** ① *Jerusalén 315, T201258, open 24 hrs*, are very helpful with complaints or giving directions.

Places in Arequipa

The elegant **Plaza de Armas** is faced on three sides by arcaded buildings with many restaurants, and on the fourth by the massive **Cathedral**, founded in 1612 and largely rebuilt in the 19th century. It is remarkable for having its façade along the whole length of the church (entrance on Santa Catalina and San Francisco). Inside is the fine Belgian organ and elaborately carved wooden pulpit. The Cathedral has a **museum** ① *www. museocatedralarequipa.org.pe, Mon-Sat 1000-1700*, which outlines the history of the building, its religious objects and art and the belltower. Behind the Cathedral there is an alley with handicraft shops and places to eat.

Santa Catalina Convent ① *Santa Catalina 301, T608282, www.santacatalina.org. pe, 0900-1700 (high season from 0800, last admission 1600), evening visits till 2000 on Tue and Thu, US$12.50*. This is by far the most remarkable sight, opened in 1970 after four centuries of mystery. The convent has been beautifully refurbished, with period furniture, pictures of the Arequipa and Cuzco schools and fully equipped kitchens. It is a complete miniature walled colonial town of over 2 ha in the middle of the city at Santa Catalina 301, where about 450 nuns lived in total seclusion, except for their women servants. The few remaining nuns have retreated to one section of the convent, allowing visitors to see a maze of cobbled streets and plazas bright with geraniums and other flowers, cloisters and buttressed houses. These have been painted in traditional white, orange, deep red and blue. On Tuesday and Thursday evenings the convent is lit with torches, candles and blazing fireplaces, very beautiful. There is a good café, which sells cakes, sandwiches, baked potatoes and a special blend of tea. There are tours of 1½ hours, no set price, many of the guides speak English or German (a tip of US$6 is expected).

Museo Santuarios de Altura ① *La Merced 110, T215013, www.ucsm.edu.pe/santury, Mon-Sat 0900-1800, Sun 0900-1500, US$5.25 includes a 20-min video of the discovery in English followed by a guided tour in English, French, German, Italian or Spanish (tip the guide), discount with student card, tour lasts 1 hr*. It contains the frozen Inca mummies found on Mount Ampato; the mummy known as 'Juanita' is fascinating as it is so well preserved. From January to April, Juanita is often jetting round the world, and is replaced by other child sacrifices unearthed in the mountains.

Arequipa is said to have the best preserved colonial architecture in Peru, apart from Cuzco. As well as the many fine churches, there are several fine seignorial houses with large carved tympanums over the entrances. Built as single-storey structures, they have mostly withstood earthquakes. They have small patios with no galleries, flat roofs and small windows, disguised by superimposed lintels or heavy grilles. Good examples are the 18th-century **Casa Tristán del Pozo**, or **Gibbs-Ricketts house** ① *San Francisco 108, Mon-Sat 0915-1245, 1600-1800*, with its fine portal and puma-head waterspouts (now a bank). **Casa del Moral** ① *Moral 318 y Bolívar, Mon-Sat 0900-1700, Sun 0900-1300, US$1.80, US$1 for students*, also known as Williams house. It is now a bank and has a museum. **Casa Goyeneche** ① *La Merced 201 y Palacio Viejo*, also a bank office, ask the guards to let you view the courtyard and fine period rooms. The oldest district is **San Lázaro**, a collection of tiny climbing streets and houses quite close to the **Hotel Libertador**, where you can find the ancient **Capilla de San Lázaro**.

Among the many fine churches is **La Compañía** ① *General Morán y Alvarez Thomas*, the main façade (1698) and side portal (1654) are striking examples of the florid Andean *mestizo* style. To the left of the sanctuary is the **Capilla Real** (Royal Chapel) ① *Mon-Fri 0900-1230, 1500-1930, Sat 1130-1230, 1500-1800, Sun 0900-1230, 1700-1800, with Mass every day at 1200, free but donations box by the main altar*. Its San Ignacio chapel has a beautiful polychrome cupola. Also well worth seeing is the church of **San Francisco** ① *Zela 103,*

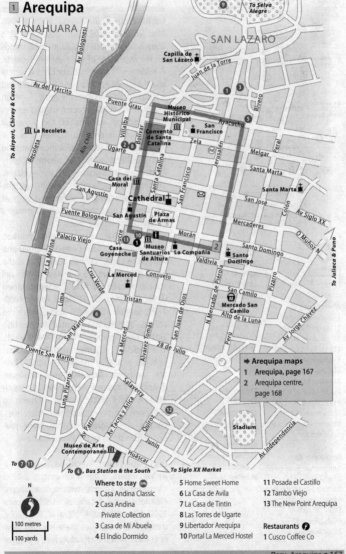

1 Arequipa

→ Arequipa maps
1 Arequipa, page 167
2 Arequipa centre, page 168

Where to stay 🛏
1 Casa Andina Classic
2 Casa Andina
   Private Collection
3 Casa de Mi Abuela
4 El Indio Dormido
5 Home Sweet Home
6 La Casa de Avila
7 La Casa de Tintin
8 Las Torres de Ugarte
9 Libertador Arequipa
10 Portal La Merced Hostel
11 Posada el Castillo
12 Tambo Viejo
13 The New Point Arequipa

Restaurants 🍴
1 Cusco Coffee Co

2 Arequipa centre

➡ **Arequipa maps**
1 Arequipa, page 167
2 Arequipa centre, page 168

50 metres

50 yards

Where to stay 🛏
1 Casablanca Hostal *B1*
2 Casa de Melgar *A2*
3 Hostal Regis *A1*
4 Hostal Santa Catalina *A1*
5 Hostal Solar *A2*
6 La Casa de Margott *A2*
7 La Fiorentina *A2*
8 La Posada del Cacique *A2*
9 La Posada del Virrey *A2*
10 Los Andes B&B *B1*
11 Sonesta Posadas del Inca *B1*

Restaurants 🍴
1 Antojitos de Arequipa *B2*
2 Ary Quepay *A2*
3 Bóveda San Agustín *B1*
4 Bruno Pizzería *A1*
5 Café Capriccio *B2*
6 Café Manolo *B2*
7 Café Valenzuela *B2*
8 Chicha *B1*
9 Crepísimo *A1*
10 El Asador *A1*
11 El Turko *B2*
12 Fez *B1*
13 La Alemana *B1*
14 La Canasta *B2*
15 Lakshmivan *A1*
16 La Trattoria del Monasterio *A1*
17 Mandala *A2*
18 Paladar 1900 *B1*
19 Qochamama *A1*
20 Ras El Hanout y los 40 Sabores *A1*
21 Sonccollay *B1*
22 Suri *B2*
23 Wayrana *B1*
24 Zig Zag *A1*

Bars & clubs 🍸
25 Casona Forum & Déjà Vu *A1*
26 Farren's *B1*

US$1.65, opposite which is the interesting **Museo Histórico Municipal** ① *Plaza San Francisco 407, Mon-Fri 0900-1700, US$0.70*, with much war memorabilia and some impressive photos of the city in the aftermath of several notable earthquakes. **La Recoleta** ① *Jr Recoleta 117, T270966, Mon-Sat 0900-1200, 1500-1700, US$1.50*, a Franciscan monastery built in 1647, stands on the other side of the river, on Recoleta. A seldom-visited gem it contains a variety of exhibits. As well as several cloisters and a religious art museum, the pre-Columbian art museum contains ceramics and textiles produced by cultures of the Arequipa area. Most impressive however is the museum of Amazon exploration featuring many artifacts as well as photos of early Franciscan missionaries in the Amazon. The library, containing many antique books, is available for supervised visits at 45 minutes past the hour for 15 minutes when the museum is open.

The central **San Camilo market**, between Perú, San Camilo, Piérola and Alto de la Luna, is worth visiting, as is the **Siglo XX market**, to the east of the rail station. **Museo de Arte Contemporáneo** ① *Tacna y Arica 201, T221068, Tue-Fri 1000-1700, Sat-Sun 1000-1400, US$1*, in the old railway station, is dedicated to painting and photography from 1900 onwards. The building is surrounded by gardens and has a Sunday market. Universidad de San Agustín's **Archaeological Museum** ① *Alvarez Thomas y Palacio Viejo, T288881, Mon-Fri 0815-1700*, has an interesting collection of ceramics and mummies, tracing the region's history from pre-Columbian times to the Republican era.

Excursions near Arequipa

At **Yanahuara**, 2 km northwest, is a 1750 *mestizo*-style church, with a magnificent churrigueresque façade, all in sillar (opens 1500). On the same plaza is a *mirador*, through whose arches there is a fine view of El Misti with the city at its feet, a popular spot in the late afternoon. The **Museo Pre Inca de Chiribaya** ① *Miguel Grau 402, www. museochiribaya.org, Mon-Sat 0830-1900, Sun 0900-1500*, has a good collection of vessels and well-preserved textiles from a culture that had a high importance in the area before the arrival of the Incas. To get to Yanahuara, cross the Puente Grau, turn right up Avenida Bolognesi.

Some 3 km past **Tingo**, beside the Río Sabandía on the Huasacanche road, is **La Mansión del Fundador** ① *0900-1700, US$4.50*. Originally owned by the founder of Arequipa, Don Garcí Manuel de Carbajal, it has been restored as a museum with original furnishings and paintings; also has cafetería and bar.

About 8 km southeast of Arequipa is the **Molino de Sabandía** ① *US$3.75, ring bell for admission; round trip by taxi US$6*. This is the first stone mill in the area, built in 1621. It has been fully restored and the guardian diverts water to run the grinding stones when visitors arrive. Adjoining Sabandía is **Yumina** ① *tourist fee of US$6 payable, which may be asked for on the bus to Chivay*, with many Inca terraces which are still in use.

Climbing El Misti and Chachani At 5822 m, El Misti volcano offers a relatively straightforward opportunity to scale a high peak. There are three routes for climbing the volcano; all take two days. The northeast route starts from the Aguada Blanca reservoir, reached by 4WD, from where a four-hour hike takes you to the Monte Blanco camp at 4800 m. Then it's a five- to six-hour ascent to the top. Two hours takes you back down to the trail. The southwest route involves taking a 4WD vehicle to the trailhead at Pastores (3400 m), followed by a hike of five or six hours to a camp at 4700 m. A five-hour climb takes you to the summit, before a three-hour descent to the trail. A southern route (Grau) also starts at 3400 m, with a camp at 4610 m, followed by a five-hour hike to the summit and a two-hour descent. Be prepared for early starts and take plenty of water, food and protection against the weather. Favoured months are May to September.

Climbing Chachani (6057 m), northwest of El Misti, is also popular. This peak retains its icy covering longer than El Misti, though this is fast disappearing. Remember that both summits are at a very high altitude and that this, combined with climbing on scree, makes it hard going for the untrained. Always contact an experienced guiding agency or professional guide in Arequipa as you should never climb alone (see What to do, page 174).

⊕ Arequipa listings

For hotel and restaurant price codes, and other relevant information, see pages 14-17.

⊖ Where to stay

Arequipa *p165, maps p167 and p168*
When arriving by bus, do not believe taxi drivers who say the hotel of your choice is closed or full. This applies to many of the popular hotels, drivers will try to take you to another hotel which pays them a high commission. Phone in advance, or ring the door bell and check for yourself.
$$$$ Casa Andina Private Collection, Ugarte 403, T226907, www.casa-andina.

com. Luxury hotel in a restored 18th-century mansion, former Casa de la Moneda.
5 large suites in colonial building, 36 rooms in modern extension off 2nd courtyard. Gourmet restaurant, room service, business centre, roof terrace with views.
$$$$ Libertador Arequipa, Plaza Simón Bolívar, Selva Alegre, T215110, www. libertador.com.pe. Safe, large comfortable rooms, good service, swimming pool (cold), gardens, good meals, pub-style bar, cocktail lounge, squash court.
$$$$ Sonesta Posadas del Inca, Portal de Flores 116, T215530, www.sonesta.com/ arequipa. On Plaza de Armas, all the services

associated with this chain, comfortable modern rooms, Inkafé restaurant and bar overlooking plaza, good food, tiny outdoor pool, business centre with internet.

$$$ Casa Andina Classic, C Jerusalén 603, T202070, www.casa-andina.com. Part of the attractive **Casa Andina** chain, with breakfast, comfortable and colourful, central, modern, good restaurant, safe, parking.

$$$-$$ La Casa de Margott, Jerusalén 304, T229517, www.lacasademargott.com. Family-run, bright with a massive palm tree in patio, spacious, convenient, small bar/café, security box.

$$ Casablanca Hostal, Puente Bolognesi 104, a few metres from the Plaza de Armas, T221327, www.casablancahostal.com. Super stylish *hostal*, lovely minimalist rooms in a colonial building. Ambient lighting, rooms with exposed stone walls, hot water, most with balcony.

$$ Casa de Mi Abuela, Jerusalén 606, T241206, www.lacasademiabuela.com. Safe, hot water, laundry, swimming pool, rooms at the back are quieter and overlook the garden, English spoken, parking, restaurant and piano bar, breakfast or evening snacks on patio or in beautiful garden.

$$ Hostal Solar, Ayacucho 108, T241793, www.hostalsolar.com. Colonial building, hot water, good breakfast served in nice patio, sun lounge on roof, very secure, multilingual staff.

$$ La Casa de Avila, San Martín 116, Vallecito, T213177, www.casadeavila.com. Rooms with hot water on 2 floors around spacious, sunny garden, computers for guests' use, can arrange airport/bus station pick-up, recommended Spanish courses held in the garden and other activities.

$$ La Casa de Tintin, Urbanización San Isidro F1, Vallecito, T284700, www.hoteltintin.com. 15 mins' walk, 5 mins by taxi from the Plaza de Armas, Belgian/Peruvian-owned, hot water, garden, terrace, sauna, massage, laundry service, restaurant, café and bar, mountain bike rental, very pleasant and comfortable.

$$ Posada el Castillo, Pasaje Campos 105, Vallecito, T201828, www.posadaelcastillo.com. Dutch/Peruvian-owned, in an old house decorated with utensils found in the renovation, 20 mins by taxi from city centre. Variety of rooms and suites, some with balcony and view of El Misti, wonderful breakfast in new annexe, pool, lovely gardens, a good choice.

$$-$ Portal La Merced Hostel, La Merced 131, T330481, PortalLaMercedHostel on Facebook. Quiet, central, private rooms and dorms, beds only so-so, good breakfast, good service, laundry, travel agency.

$ Casa de Melgar, Melgar 108, T222459, www.lacasademelgar.com. 18th-century building, excellent rooms with bath, hot water (solar), safe, courtyard, good breakfast buffet. Good taxi driver (Angel).

$ El Indio Dormido, Av Andrés Avelino Cáceres B-9, T427401, http://members.tripod.com/h_indio_dormido/. Close to bus terminal, free transport to centre, rooms with bath, kitchen, cafeteria, parking, laundry, TV room, very helpful, family-run.

$ Home Sweet Home, Rivero 509A, T405982, www.homesweethome-peru.com. Run by María and daughter Cathy, who runs a travel agency and speaks Spanish, English, Italian, French, very helpful, warm and inviting atmosphere, substantial fresh breakfast included. Private or shared bath, hot water all day, simple rooms.

$ Hostal Regis, Ugarte 202, T226111, hostalregis@hotmail.com. Colonial house, French-style interior, hot water all day, use of fridge and laundry facilities, sun terrace with good views, street-facing rooms with sound-proofed windows, safe deposit, video rental and guide books and English language magazines for reference, tours arranged, but poor breakfast.

$ Hostal Santa Catalina, Santa Catalina 500, T243705, www.hostalsantacatalinaperu.com. On busy corner, rooms arranged around a courtyard, roof terrace with great views, helpful staff. Simple rooms with fridge, private or shared bath, hot water, laundry, security box. Can arrange trips and accommodation in other cities.

$ La Fiorentina, Puente Grau 110, T202571. With or without bath, hot water, comfortable, family atmosphere, tours arranged, laundry facilities, café bar and TV room.

$ La Posada del Cacique, Puente Grau 219 and at Jerusalén 404, T202170, posadadelcacique@ yahoo.es. At Puente Grau is an old house with tall ceilings, teeny patio, sun terrace, hot water, English spoken, family atmosphere, private or shared bath, also dorm accommodation, breakfast available, laundry service, will pick up from terminal. Jerusalén branch is good value and helpful, with roof terrace, bar, café/restaurant.

$ La Posada del Virrey, Puente Grau 103, T224050. Spacious rooms with and without bath, dorms, hot water, kitchen and laundry facilities, helpful, café bar, small patio.

$ Las Torres de Ugarte, Ugarte 401, T283532, www.hotelista.com. Round the corner from Santa Catalina convent, hot water, laundry service, reflexology, roof terrace, parking, safe, luggage store. Some rooms are bungalow style in colonial part at the back.

$ Los Andes Bed & Breakfast, La Merced 123, T330015, www.losandesarequipa.com. Good value, kitchen use, hot water, large rooms with waxed wood floors and minimalist decor, TV rooms, pleasant roof terrace.

$ Lula's B&B, in Cayma, T272517, 959 992995, www.bbaqpe.com. Same owners as Ari Quipay language school, Lula (Peruvian) and her husband (Swiss) speak Spanish, English, German and French, with airport/bus terminal pick-up, modern, charming, quiet, meals available.

$ The New Point Arequipa, Palacio Viejo 325, T286920, www.thepointhostels.com. Very central, small, medium and large dorms, great place to meet other travellers, information on nightlife, lots of services (laundry, DVDs etc), games room and travel centre.

$ Tambo Viejo, Av Malecón Socabaya 107, IV Centenario, T288195, www.tamboviejo.com. 5 blocks south of the plaza near the rail

station. 15 rooms ranging from double with bath to dormitory, quiet, English and Dutch spoken, walled garden, hot water, choice of 8 fresh breakfasts (extra), vegetarian restaurant, laundry service, safe deposit, coffee shop, bar, book exchange (2 for 1), money changed, tourist information for guests, bike rental, luggage store extra, tours and volcano climbs arranged. For a small fee, you can use the facilities if passing through. Free pick-up from bus terminal 0700-2300 (call when arriving), US$10 for airport pick-up.

🍴 Restaurants

Arequipa *p165, maps p167 and p168*

$$$ Chicha, Santa Catalina 210, int 105, T287360. The menu of mostly local and fusion dishes is created by Gastón Acurio, fine dining in a historic building opposite Santa Catalina.

$$$ Paladar 1900, San Francisco 227. In the same group as **El Turko**, stylish, contemporary design, Peruvian cuisine with a modern twist.

$$$ Wayrana, Santa Catalina 200, T285641. Traditional Arequipa dishes with a modern twist, specializing in sea food, *cuy*, and alpaca. Beautiful colonial building with stylish interior design.

$$$ Zig Zag, Zela 210, T206020. In a colonial house, European (including Swiss) and local dishes, meats include ostrich and alpaca, delicious. Book in advance.

$$$-$$ El Cebillano, C Misti 110, Yanahuara, T484866. Excellent *cevichería* in Yanahuara suburb, with good seafood, attentive service and long queues at weekends.

$$$-$$ La Trattoria del Monasterio, Santa Catalina 309, T204062, www.latrattoria delmonasterio.com. A fusion of Italian and Arequipeño styles and ingredients, in a cloister in the Convento.

$$ Ary Quepay, Jerusalén 502. Open 1000-2400. Excellent local meat and vegetarian dishes, very touristy but fun.

$$ Café-Restaurante Bóveda San Agustín, Portal San Agustín 127-129, T243596. Opens at 0700. Attractive, downstairs bar type atmosphere, upstairs balcony overlooking the Plaza de Armas, good value breakfasts and lunches, evening specials.

$$ Crepísimo at Santa Catalina 208, T206620. Great coffee and a huge variety of sweet and savoury crepes, magazines and board games.

$$ Sonccollay, Portal de San Agustin 149, www.sonccollay.com. Open 0800-2200. Serving 'Inca and Pre-Inca' dishes, stone-cooked alpaca steaks and meats are a speciality (you can view the kitchen), entertaining owner, copious *chicha* and generous pisco sours. It has a seafood branch, **Qochamama**, Ugarte 300 p 2, T231407, which is more of a bar in the evening.

$$-$ El Asador, Zela 201, T223414. Good value for alpaca steaks, *parrillada*, pleasant atmosphere, good music.

$ Bruno Pizzería, Jerusalén y Santa Marta. Pizzas and pastas with good lunch and dinner menus.

$ El Turko, San Francisco 223-25. Open 0700-2200. Bright café/bar selling kebabs, coffee, breakfasts recommended, good sandwiches. Has a branch at the airport.

$ Fez, San Francisco 229 and **Istanbul**, San Francisco 231-A. More up-market restaurants run by same company as **El Turko**. Delicious falafel and Middle Eastern fast food, including vegetarian. Good coffee, pleasant courtyard.

$ Lakshmivan, Jerusalén 408, T228768. Vegetarian wholefood restaurant, set breakfast, lunch and dinner options for under US$2.50, pleasant courtyard, good value and healthy, but slow service.

$ Mandala, Jerusalén 207, T229974. Good-value vegetarian, breakfast, 3 set menus for lunch, buffet, dinner, friendly staff.

$ Ras El Hanout y los 40 Sabores, Santa Catalina 300 B-1, T212424, www.rasel hanout40.com. Moroccan 'resto-lounge', breakfast, tagines, keftas, salads, juices and world music.

Cafés

Antojitos de Arequipa, Morán 125-A. An Arequipeñan institution, sells traditional sweets.

Café Capriccio, Mercaderes 121. Not that cheap, but excellent coffee, cakes, etc. Very popular with local business people. Also has **Capriccio Gourmet** on Santa Catalina, which is also good.

Café Manolo, Mercaderes 107 and 113. Great cakes and coffee, also cheap lunches.

Café Valenzuela, Morán 114. Fantastic coffee (also sells beans and ground coffee), locals' favourite.

La Canasta, Jerusalén 115. Excellent baguettes twice daily, also serves breakfast and delicious apple and brazil nut pastries, courtyard seating.

Cusco Coffee Co, La Merced 135, T281152. Good variety of coffees, cakes, average sandwiches, comfy sofas, Wi-Fi.

La Alemana, San Francisco 137. Wide choice of sausages, plus very good *empanadas* and sandwiches. Good value and popular.

Suri, Portal de Flores 128, T237202. The best chicken pie in Arequipa and more, great for a cheap quick snack while you look out on the Plaza.

Typical Arequipeño food is available at the San Camilo market. *Picanterías*, also called *restaurantes típicos*, are also places to find highly spiced dishes. The local chocolate is excellent: **La Ibérica**, in Patio del Ekeko, Mercaderes 141 (see Shopping), also at Morán 160, is top quality, but expensive. There are mini *chocolaterías* everywhere.

🔊 Bars and clubs

Arequipa *p165, maps p167 and p168*

Casona Forum, San Francisco 317. Opens 1800 every day. Huge complex which hosts the **Retro Bar, Zero** pool bar, **Forum Rock Café, Terrasse** lounge and **Chill Out Sofa Bar**. With live music, underground club with huge imitation waterfall and top floor classy restaurant with great views of the city.

Déjà Vu, San Francisco 319-B. Open 2000-2400. Café/restaurant and bar, good food, DJ evenings, shows movies, has rooftop bar and often live music, weekend drinks specials, popular.

Farren's, Pasaje Catedral. Good meeting place, pool table, great music.

⊛ Festivals

Arequipa *p165, maps p167 and p168*
A full list of the department's many festivals is available locally from **iPerú**.
10 Jan Sor Ana de Los Angeles y Monteagudo, festival for the patron saint of Santa Catalina monastery. **Mar-Apr** Semana Santa celebrations involve huge processions every night, culminating in the burning of an effigy of Judas on Easter Sunday in the main plazas of Cayma and Yanahuara, and the reading of his will, containing criticisms of the city authorities. **27 Apr** The celebration of the apostle Santiago. May is known as the **Mes de Las Cruces**, with ceremonies on hilltops throughout the city. **3 Aug** A procession through the city bearing the images of Santo Domingo and San Francisco. **6-31 Aug** Fiesta Artesanal del Fundo El Fierro is a sale and exhibition of *artesanía* from all parts of Peru, taking place near Plaza San Francisco. **6-17 Aug** Celebration of the city's anniversary (the 15th, many events including a mass ascent of El Misti). **2 Nov** Day of the Dead celebrations in cemeteries.

⊙ Shopping

Arequipa *p165, maps p167 and p168*
Alpaca goods, textiles and clothing
Alpaca 21, Jerusalén 115, of 125, T213425. Recommended.
Kuna by Alpaca 111, in the Patio del Ekeko (see below), Casona Santa Catalina, Santa Catalina 210, Local 1-2, T282485, in the Hotel Libertador, T223303, www.kuna. com.pe. High-quality alpaca and wool products. See also www.incalpaca.com.
Las Clausulas de La Compañía, Morán 140. Handicrafts shopping centre in a colonial setting, containing many alpaca knitwear outlets including a factory outlet in the second patio.

Michell y Cia, Juan de la Torre 101, T202525, www.michell.com.pe. Factory outlet, excellent place for alpaca yarn in huge variety of colours, also a clearance room for baby and adult alpaca yarn is sold. They also sell other types of wool. Alpaca garments also for sale. 1920s machinery on display. Michell has opened an outlet, **Sol Alpaca**, Santa Catalina 210 (inside La Casona Santa Catalina), T221454, with branches in Lima and Cuzco, for their latest lines in alpaca and pima cotton clothing.
Millma's Baby Alpaca, Pasaje Catedral 117, T205134, millmas@hotmail.com. 100% baby alpaca goods, run by Peruvian family, high quality, beautiful designs, good prices.

Bookshops
Librería El Lector, San Francisco 213. Wide selection, including of Peruvian authors, book exchange in various languages (2 for 1), stocks *Footprint*.
Librerías San Francisco has branches at Portal de Flores 138, San Francisco 102-106 and 133-135. Books on Arequipa and Peru, some in English.
SBS Book Service, San Francisco 125, T205317. Has a good selection of travel books etc.

Markets
The covered market opposite the Teatro Municipal in C Mercaderes is recommended for knitted goods, bags, etc.
Note that in both Arequipa and Cuzco it is becoming common to find painted and unpainted souvenir condor feathers in the markets. Condors are being killed for this trade. It is illegal in Peru to sell or purchase condor feathers and the crime carries a sentence of 4 years in prison.
Fundo del Fierro, the large handicraft market behind the old prison on Plaza San Francisco, is also worth a visit.

Shopping centres
Patio del Ekeko, Mercaderes 141. A commercial centre with upmarket

handicrafts, **Kuna by Alpaca** 111 (see above), **Ilaria** for fine jewellery, **La Ibérica** chocolate shop (also at Morán 160), café, internet, cinema and **Museo de Arte Textil** upstairs (Mon-Sat 1000-2030, Sun 1000-1530).

⏱ What to do

Arequipa *p165, maps p167 and p168*
Climbing, cycling, rafting and trekking
International recommendations are for a 300 m per day maximum altitude gain. Be wary of agencies wanting to sell you trips with very fast ascents.
Julver Castro, who has an agency called **Mountrekk**, T601833, julver_mountrekk@ hotmail.com. A climbing guide recommended as experienced and "full of energy".
Colca Trek, Jerusalén 401 B, T206217, www.colcatrek.com.pe. Knowledgeable and English-speaking Vlado Soto is one of the best guides for the Cotahuasi Canyon and is recommended for climbing, trekking and mountain biking in the Colca Canyon. He also rents equipment and has topographical maps.
Cusipata, Jerusalén 402-A, T203966, www. cusipata.com (shared office with **Andina Travel**). Recommended as the best local rafting operator, very popular half-day trips, run 6-day trips on the Río Colca. May-Dec, Río Chili 1-day kayak courses, also trekking and mountain bike tours.
Naturaleza Activa, Santa Catalina 211, T204182, naturactiva@yahoo.com. Experienced guides, knowledgeable, climbing and trekking.
Sacred Road Tours, Jerusalén 400, T212332, www.sacredroad.com. Arranges hiking and rock climbing in Colca Canyon and elsewhere, experienced guides led by Arcadio Mamani, equipment available.
Selern Services, Urb Puerta Verde F13, José LB y Rivero, Arequipa, T348685, see Facebook. Trekking, adventure tourism, mountain climbing.
Volcanyon Travel, C Villalba 414, T205078, mario-ortiz@terra.com.pe. Trekking and

some mountain bike tours in the Colca Canyon, also volcano climbing.
Carlos Zárate Aventuras, Santa Catalina 204, of 3, T202461. Run by Carlos Zárate of the Mountaineering Club of Peru. Good family-run business that always works with qualified mountain guides. A specialist in mountaineering and exploring, with a great deal of information and advice and some equipment rental. Carlos also runs trips to one of the supposed sources of the Amazon, Nevado Mismi, as well as trekking in the Cotahuasi canyon and climbing tougher peaks such as Coropuna.

Tour operators
Many agencies on Jerusalén, Santa Catalina and around Plaza de Armas sell air, train and bus tickets and offer tours of Colca, Cotahuasi, Toro Muerto and city. Prices vary greatly so shop around; check carefully what is included in the cheapest tours and that there are enough people for the tour to run. Travel agents frequently work together to fill buses and there are lots of touts. Many tourists prefer to contract tours through their hotel. If a travel agency puts you in touch with a guide, make sure he/ she is official. The following have been recommended as helpful and reliable.
Al Travel Tours, Santa Catalina 203, of 7, ask for Miguel Fernández T959-391436/971-858704 (mob), www.aitraveltours.com. Peruvian/Dutch tour operator offering cultural and adventure tours for groups or individuals, volunteer work and Spanish courses, large book exchange.
Andina Travel Service, Jerusalén 309-402A, T225082, www.andinatravelaqp.com. Good tours of Colca Canyon, guide Gelmond Ynca Aparicio is very enthusiastic.
Colca Explorer, Mariscal Benavides 201 Selva Alegre, T202587, www.colca-explorer. com. Agency associated with **Amazonas Explorer** in Cuzco, with many options in Colca and southern Peru: from classic local tours to horse riding, mountain biking, fishing in remote lakes, climbing,

treks and visiting alpaca farms on
the altiplano.

Colca Journeys, C Rodríguez Ballón
533, Miraflores, T973-901010, www.
colcajourneys.com. Specializes in and
operates tours to the Colca Valley and
Cotahuasi Valley.

Giardino Tours, at Casa de Mi Abuela
(see above), T221345, www.giardinotours.
com. Professional company offering tours
and transport, has own properties in
Arequipa and Colca (eg delightful **La Casa
de Mamayacchi** in Coporaque), community
tourism options, good information.

Land Adventure, Residencial La Peña
A-20, Sachaca (outside city), T959-941570,
www.landadventures.net. 'Sustainable' tour
operator with good guides for communities
in Colca, trekking, climbing, downhill biking.

Pablo Tour, Jerusalén 400-AB-1, T203737,
www.pablotour.com. Family-run agency,
owns several hostals in Cabanaconde and
knows area well, 3-day mixed tours in
the Colca Canyon with mountain biking,
trekking and rafting, free tourist information,
maps for sale, bus and hotel reservation
service. Son Edwin Junco Cabrera can
sometimes be found in the office, he
speaks fluent French and English.

Vita Tours, Jerusalén 302, T284211,
www.vitatours.com.pe. Tours in the
Arequipa area, including to the coast,
and in the Colca Canyon where they
have a hotel, **La Casa de Lucila**.

⊖ Transport

Arequipa *p165, maps p167 and p168*
Air
Rodríguez Ballón airport is 7 km from town,
T443464. Two desks offer hotel reservations
and free transport to town; also car rentals.
To and from **Lima**, 1 hr 10 mins, several daily
with **LAN**, **Peruvian Airlines** (also to **Tacna**)
and **Star Perú**. LAN and Star Perú also serve
Juliaca, 30 mins, LAN continuing to **Cuzco**,
1 hr 10 mins from Arequipa. Local buses and
combis go to about 500 m from the airport,

look for ones marked 'Río Seco', 'Cono-
Norte' or 'Zamacola'. Best to use a radio
taxi company listed below.

Bus
A new urban rapid transit system, **Arequipa
Bus** is being introduced, with dedicated bus
lanes and less polluting vehicles.

There are 2 terminals at Av Andrés A
Cáceres s/n, Parque Industrial, south of the
centre, 15 mins by colectivo US$0.50, or
taxi US$2.50. The older **Terminal Terrestre**
has a tourist office, shops and places to
eat. The newer **Terrapuerto**, across the car
park, has a tourist office (which makes hotel
reservations) and its own *hostal* (**$** without
breakfast), T421375. Terminal tax US$0.50.
Buses may not depart from the terminal
where you bought your ticket. All the bus
companies have offices in Terminal Terrestre
and several also have offices in Terrapuerto.

Note Theft is a serious problem in the
bus station area. Take a taxi to and from the
bus station and do not wander around with
your belongings. No one is allowed to enter
the terminal 2100-0500, so new arrivals
cannot be met by hoteliers between those
hours; best not to arrive at night.

To **Lima**, 1011 km, 16-18 hrs, services from
US$22 to US$56. **Cruz del Sur** (T427375),
Enlaces (T430333), **Tepsa** (T054-608079),
Ormeño (T424187) are recommended.
The road is paved but drifting sand and
breakdowns may prolong the trip.

To **Nazca**, 566 km, 9 hrs, US$19-22.50
(US$30-52 on luxury services), several buses
daily, mostly at night; most buses continue
to Ica (US$30-42) and Lima. Also US$12 to
Chala, 8 hrs. To **Moquegua**, 213 km, 3 hrs,
US$7.50-12, several buses and colectivos
daily. To **Tacna**, 320 km, 6-7 hrs, from US$18,
17 buses daily with **Flores**.

To **Cuzco**, all buses go via Juliaca or
Puno, US$14-47, 10 hrs. Most companies
go overnight, eg **Enlaces**, **Cial**, **Ziva** and
Ormeño, but a few in daytime. There is a
quick paved road to **Juliaca**, US$11-27,
4-5 hrs (Cruz del Sur; also **Trans Julsa**,

T430843, hourly buses, reliable), and **Puno**, 5 hrs, US$11-27 **Cruz del Sur**. Most buses and colectivos continue to Puno.

Taxi

US$8 airport to city (can be shared). From US$1 around town. **Alo 45**, T454545; **Taxitel**, T452020; **Taxi 21**, T212121; **Turismo Arequipa**, T458888.

🅓 Directory

Arequipa *p165, maps p167 and p168*

Language courses Centro de Intercambio Cultural Arequipa (CEICA), Urb Universitaria G-9, T250722, www. ceica-peru.com. Individual classes US$145 for 20 hrs' tuition, US$109 for groups of 3 or more, rooms with families (US$90 per week for a single room with breakfast, US$107 half board, US$119 full board), also dance lessons, history and cultural classes, excursions. **Escuela de Español Ari Quipay (EDEAQ)**, T272517, T959 992995 (mob), www.edeaq.com. Peruvian/Swiss-run, experienced, multilingual staff, recognized by Peruvian Ministry of Education, in a colonial house near the Plaza de Armas, one-to-one and group classes, home stay available (see **Lula's B&B** under Where to stay). **Instituto Cultural Peruano Alemán**, Ugarte 207, T228130, www.icpa.org.pe. Good language classes. **Llama Education**, Casabella, lote A6, Cerro Colorado, T274069, www.arequipaspanish.com/index. html. Professional, with personal attention, owner María Huaman is very helpful. Individual and small group tuition, home

stays and cultural exchanges. **Spanish School Arequipa**, Av San Martín 116, T213177, www.spanishschoolarequipa. com. Standard Spanish lessons or courses tailored for travellers or volunteers, accommodation with families or on site at Casa de Avila, see above. **Silvana Cornejo**, 7 de Junio 118, Cerrito Los Alvarez, Cerro Colorado, T254985, silvanacor@yahoo. com. Negotiable rates for group, she speaks German fluently. Her sister Roxanna also is a teacher. **Cecilia Pinto Oppe**, Puente Grau 108 (in Hostal La Reyna), T959-961638, www.cepesmaidiomasceci.com. Good-value lessons, held in a café which helps orphaned children. **Carlos Rojas Núñez**, Filtro 405, T285061, carlrojas@mixmail. com. Private or group lessons to students of all levels, encourages conversation, knowledgeable on culture and politics.

Medical services Hospitals: Regional Honorio Delgado, Av A Carrión s/n, T238465/231818 (inoculations). **Central del Sur**, Filtro y Peral s/n, T214430 in emergency. Clinics: **Clinic Arequipa SA**, Puente Grau y Av Bolognesi, T599000, www.clinicarequipa.com.pe, fast and efficient with English-speaking doctors and all hospital facilities. **Paz Holandesa**, Villa Continental, C 4, No 101, Paucarpata, T432281, www.pazholandesa.com. Dutch foundation dedicated to helping the impoverished, which also has a travel clinic for tourists. Dutch and English spoken, 24-hr service. Highly recommended (see their website if you are interested in volunteering). **Emergencies**: Ambulance T289800; also **San Miguel**, T283330 (24 hrs).

Colca Canyon → *You must buy a tourist ticket for US$26.50 (valid 10 days), at a checkpoint on the road to Chivay when entering the canyon.*

The Colca Canyon is deep: twice as deep as the Grand Canyon. The Río Colca descends from 3500 m above sea level at Chivay to 2200 m at Cabanaconde. In the background looms the grey, smoking mass of Sabancaya, one of the most active volcanoes in the Americas, and its more docile neighbour, Ampato (6288 m). Unspoiled Andean villages lie on both sides of the canyon, inhabited by the Cabana and Collagua peoples, and some of the extensive pre-Columbian terraced fields are still in use. High on anyone's list for visiting the canyon is an early-morning trip to the Cruz del Cóndor, to see these majestic birds at close quarters. From January to April is the rainy season, but this makes the area green, with lots of flowers. This is not the best time to see condors. May to December is the dry, cold season when there is more chance of seeing the birds. Conditions vary annually, though.

From Arequipa there are two routes to **Chivay**, the first village on the edge of the Canyon: the old route, via Cayma, and the new paved route, through Yura, following the railway, longer but quicker. The two routes join at Cañahuas where you can change buses to/from Juliaca or Chivay without going to Arequipa. The road from Cañahuas to Puno via Patahuasi, Imata and Juliaca has been improved with a daily tourist transport service (see Transport, below). It can be cold in the morning, reaching 4825 m in the Pata Pampa pass, but the views are worth it. Cyclists should use the Yura road; better condition and less of a climb at the start. The old dirt route runs north from Arequipa, over the altiplano. About an hour out of Arequipa is the **Aguada Blanca National Vicuña Reserve**. If you're lucky, you can see herds of these rare animals near the road. This route affords fine views of the volcanoes Misti, Chachani, Ampato and Sabancaya. Chivay is the chief linking point between the two sides of the canyon; there is a road bridge over the river here (others at Yanque and Lari). The road continues northeast to **Tuti** (small handicrafts shop), and **Sibayo** (*pensión* and grocery store). A long circuit back to Arequipa heads south from Sibayo, passing through **Puente Callalli**, **Chullo** and **Sumbay**. This is a little-travelled road, but the views, with vicuña, llamas, alpacas and Andean duck are superb. Crossing the river at Chivay going west to follow the canyon on the far side, you pass the villages of **Coporaque**, **Ichupampa** (a footbridge crosses the river between the two villages and foot and road bridges connect the road between Coporaque and Ichupampa with Yanque), **Lari**, **Madrigal** (footbridge to Maca) and **Tapay** (connected to Cabanaconde by a footbridge).

Chivay to Cabanaconde

Chivay (3600 m) is the gateway to the canyon. The **Maria Reiche Planetarium and Observatory** ① *in the grounds of the Casa Andina hotel, 6 blocks west of the Plaza between Huayna Capac and Garcilazo (www.casa-andina.com), US$6, discounts for students*, makes the most of the Colca's clear Southern Hemisphere skies with a powerful telescope and two 55-minute presentations per day at 1830 (Spanish) and 1930 (English). There is a very helpful **tourist office** in the Municipalidad on the west side of the plaza (closed at weekends). The tourist police, also on the plaza, can give advice about locally trained guides. **Traveller's Medical Center** (**TMC**) ① *Ramón Castilla 232, T531037*. There is a Globalnet ATM close to the plaza.

The hot springs of **La Calera** ① *US$5.25 to bathe, half price just to go in, regular colectivos (US$0.25), taxi (US$1.50) or a 1-hr walk from town*, are 4 km away and are highly recommended after a hard day's trekking.

From Chivay, the main road goes west along the Colca Canyon. The first village encountered is **Yanque** (8 km, excellent views), with an interesting church containing superbly renovated altar pieces and paintings, a museum on the opposite side of the plaza, and a bridge to the villages on the other side of the canyon. A large thermal swimming pool is 20 minutes walk from the plaza, beside the renovated colonial bridge on the Yanque-Ichupampa road, US$0.75. The road continues paved to **Achoma** (Hospedaje Cruz del Cóndor on the plaza and a campsite) and **Maca**, which barely survived an earthquake in November 1991. Then comes the tiny village of **Pinchollo**, with **Hospedaje Refugio del Geyser** (Calle Melgar s/n, behind municipality, T959-007441/958-032090, basic with good local information). From here it is a 30-minute walk on a dirt track to the geyser

Hatun Infiernillo. The Mirador, or **Cruz del Cóndor** ① *where you may be asked to show your tourist ticket*, is at the deepest point of the canyon. The view is wonderful and condors can be seen rising on the morning thermals (0900, arrive by 0800 to get a good spot) and sometimes in the late afternoon (1600-1800). Camping here is officially forbidden, but if you ask the tourist police in Chivay they may help. **Milagros'** 0630 bus from Chivay stop here very briefly at around 0800 (ask the driver to stop), or try hitching with a tour bus at around 0600. Buses from Cabanaconde stop at about 0700 (**Andalucía**) or 0830 (**Reyna**), which leave Cabanaconde's plaza 30 minutes earlier.

From the Mirador it is a 20-minute ride in tourist transport, 40 minutes by local bus on a paved road to **Cabanaconde** (3287 m). You can also walk, three hours by the road, or two hours by a short cut following the canyon. It is the last village in the Colca Canyon, friendly, typical, but basic (it does have 24-hour electricity). The views are superb and condors can be seen from the hill just west of the village, a 15-minute walk from the plaza, which also gives views of the agrcultural terraces, arguably the most attractive in the valley, to the south of the village. Cabanaconde is an excellent base for visiting the region, with interesting trekking, climbing, biking and horse riding. Many are keen to encourage respectful tourism in the area and several locally owned tourism businesses have opened in the village.

There's a friendly tourist information office, T280212, willing to give plenty of advice, if not maps. It's a good place to find trekking guides and muleteers (US$30 a day mule and guide).

Two hours below Cabanaconde is **Sangalle**, an 'oasis' of palm trees and swimming areas and three campsites with basic bungalows and toilets (three to 4½ hours back up, ask for the best route in both directions, horses can be hired to carry your bag up, US$5.85), a beautiful spot, recommended. A popular hike involves walking east on the Chivay road to the Mirador de Tapay (before Cruz del Cóndor), then descending to the river on a steep track (four hours, take care). Cross the bridge to the north bank. At the village of San Juan de Chuccho you can stay and eat at a basic family hostel, of which there are several. **Hostal Roy** and **Casa de Rebelino ($)** are both good. US$2 will buy you a good meal. From here pass **Tapay** (also possible to camp here) and the small villages of Malata and Cosnirhua, all the time heading west along the north side of the Río Colca (take a guide or ask local directions). After about three hours walking, cross another bridge to the south bank of the Río Colca, follow signs to Sangalle, spend the night and return to Cabanconde on the third day. This route is offered by many Arequipa and local agencies.

⊙ Colca Canyon listings

For hotel and restaurant price codes, and other relevant information, see pages 14-17.

⊖ Where to stay

Chivay to Cabanconde *p177*
Chivay
$$$ Casa Andina, Huayna Cápac s/n, T531020, www.casa-andina.com. Attractive cabins with hot showers and a cosy bar/dining area, a member of the recommended hotel chain, heating, parking.

$$$ Estancio Pozo del Cielo, C Húascar B-3, Sacsayhuaman-Chivay over the Puente Inca from Chivay amid pre-Inca terraces, T531041 (Alvarez Thomas 309, Arequipa, T205838), www.pozodelcielo.com.pe. Very comfortable, warm rooms, good views, good service and restaurant.

$$ Colca Inn, Salaverry 307, T531088, www.hotelcolcainn.com. Good mid-range option, modern, hot water, decent restaurant, basic breakfast.

$$ Cóndor Wasi, Av Polonia s/n, on the road to La Calera hot springs, 1 km from

Chivay, T799032, T959-444956, condorwasi@hotmail.com. Rustic rooms with bath, hot water, very tranquil.

$$ Posada del Colca, Salaverry 325, T959-784940, laposadadelcolca@hotmail.com, also on Facebook. Central, good rooms, hot water.

$ Hospedaje Restaurant Los Portales, Arequipa 603, T531164, www.losportales dechivay.com. Good value, though beds have rather 'floppy' mattresses. Restaurant downstairs.

$ La Casa de Lucila, M Grau 131, T531109, http://vitatours.com.pe. Comfortable, hot water, coffee, guides available.

$ La Pascana, Puente Inca y C Siglo XX 106, T531001, hrlapascana@hotmail.com. Northwest corner of the Plaza. Excellent value with spacious en suite rooms, hot water, most rooms overlook a pleasant garden. Parking and a good restaurant.

$ Rumi Wasi, Sucre 714, 6 blocks from plaza (3 mins' walk), T531146. Good rooms, hot water, helpful, mountain bike rental (in poor condition).

Yanque

$$$$ Colca Lodge, across the river from Yanque, T531191, office at Mariscal Benavides 201, Selva Alegre, Arequipa, T202587, www.colca-lodge.com. Very relaxing, with beautiful hot springs beside the river, spend at least a day to make the most of the activities on offer. Day passes available. Rooms heated with geothermal energy, solar heated water.

$$$$ Las Casitas del Colca, Av Fundo La Curiña s/n, Yanque, T959-672688, www.lascasitasdelcolca.com. Under new management of the GHL group, with luxury cottages made of local materials with underfloor heating and plunge pools. Has a gourmet restaurant, bar, vegetable garden and farm, offers cookery and painting courses, the spa offers a variety of treatments, swimming pool.

$$$ Collahua, Av Collahua cuadra 7, Yanque, or in Arequipa at Mercaderes 212, Galerías Gamesa, T226098, www.hotelcollahua.com. Modern bungalows just outside Yanque, with heating, solar-powered 24-hr hot water and plush rooms, pool, restaurant.

$$$ Eco Inn, Lima 513, Yanque, T 837112, www.ecoinnhotels.com. Perched high on a bluff with incredible views over the valley and newly-restored Ullo Ullo ruins. Large, comfortable rooms in cabins, restaurant open from 0530 for buffet breakfast, Wi-Fi in lobby and restaurant.

$$ Tradición Colca, on main road. In Arequipa C Argentina 108, Urb Fecia JL Bustamante y Rivero, T424926, www.tradicion colca.com. Adobe construction, rooms with private bathroom, gas stove. Spa treatment room in the garden, massages, sauna, jacuzzi (1800-2045). Restaurant, bar, games room, observatory and planetarium (30 min session at 1900, free for guests), horse riding from 2 hrs to 2 days, guided hiking tour to Ullu Ullu, also has a travel agency in Arequipa.

$ Casa Bella Flor Sumaq Wayta Wasi, Cuzco 303, T253586, www.casabellaflor.com. Charming small lodge run by Sra Hilde Checca, flower-filled garden, tasteful rooms, good meals (also open to non-residents), Hilde's uncle, Gregorio, guides visitors to pre-Columbian sites.

$ Rijchariy Colca Lodge, on the track leading down to the footbridge over the river, T764610. Great views, garden, comfortable rooms, restaurant.

Cabanaconde

$$ Kuntur Wassi, C Cruz Blanca s/n, on the hill above the plaza, T233120, www.arequipacolca.com. Excellent, 3-star, fine traditional meals on request. Creative design with rooms spaced between rock gardens and waterfalls. Viewing 'tower' and conference centre above. Owners Walter and María very welcoming and knowledgeable about treks.

$$ Posada del Conde, C San Pedro, T441030. Smart hotel and a lodge. Cheaper in low season, with hot shower, comfortable beds, good food. Local guides and horses for hire.

$ Hostal Valle del Fuego, 1 and 2 blocks from the plaza on C Grau y Bolívar, T959-611241, www.hvalledelfuego.com. Rooms with comfortable beds, all with hot water, laundry facilities, restaurant. The Junco family have plenty of information, with a small family 'empire', including the Arequipa agency **Pablo Tour**, the **Oasis Paradise** in Sangalle (discounts for clients of Valle del Fuego) and a bar, the **Casa de Pablo Club** at the end of the street. They usually meet the incoming buses. Popular.

$ Majestic Colca, Miguel Grau s/n near C San Pedro, T958-060433. Modern, hot water, rooftop terrace and restaurant.

$ Pachamama Home, San Pedro 209, T767277, T959-316322, www.pachamamahome.com. Backpacker hostel, with and without bath, family atmosphere, hot water, lots of information, good bar/pizzería **Pachamama** next door, try the Colca Sour, made from a local cactus. You can help with teaching and activities for village children.

$ Virgen del Carmen, Av Arequipa s/n, T832159, 5 blocks up from the plaza. Hot showers, may even offer you a welcoming glass of *chicha*.

🍴 Restaurants

Chivay *p177*
Several restaurants serve buffet lunches for tour groups, US$5 pp, also open to the general public. Of the few that open in the evening, most have folklore shows and are packed with tour groups. When walking in the valley meals and drinks can be taken in any of the larger lodges. For local cheeses and dairy products, visit **Productos del Colca**, Av 22 de Agosto in the central market.

$$ El Balcón de Don Zacarías, Av 22 de Agosto 102 on plaza, T531108. Breakfast, the best lunch buffet in town, à la carte menu, novo andean and international cuisine.

$$-$ Lobos Pizzería, José Gálvez 101, T531081. Has good pizzas and pastas, fast service and good bar, popular. Has mountain biking information and **Isuiza Turismo y Aventura** agency, T959-860870.

$$-$ McElroys's Irish Pub, on the plaza. Bar run by a Peruvian and an Irishman, warm, good selection of drinks (sometimes including expensive Guinness), sandwiches, pizza, pasta and music. Mountain bikes for hire. Accepts Visa.

$$-$ Yaraví, Plaza de Armas 604, T489109. Arequipeña food, vegetarian options and the most impressive coffee machine in town.

$ Innkas Café-Bar, main plaza No 706, T531209. Coffee, sandwiches, *menú*, pizzas, pool table, nice atmosphere.

$ Ruadhri Irish Pub, Av Salaverry 202. Nothing Irish about it, but still a popular hang-out offering pizzas, pastas and sandwiches, has happy hour and a pool table.

Cabanaconde *p178*
$$-$ Casa de Pablo Club, C Grau. Excellent fresh juices and pisco sour, cable TV (football!), small book exchange and some equipment hire.

$ Las Brisas del Colca, main plaza, T631593. Pleasant, serves breakfast, tourist menu, à la carte dishes, juices and sandwiches.

$ Don Piero, signposted just off main plaza. Excellent choice and good information.

$ Pizzería Bar Bon Appetit, Jorge Chávez s/n, main plaza, T630171. Pizzas, pastas, breakfast, and vegetarian.

$ Rancho del Colca, on plaza. Mainly vegetarian.

🎉 Festivals

Colca Canyon *p176*
Many in the Colca region: **2-3 Feb** Virgen de la Candelaria, Chivay, Cabanaconde, Maca, Tapay. **Feb**: Carnaval, Chivay. **3 May** Cruz de la Piedra, Tuti. **13 Jun** San Antonio, Yanque, Maca. **14 Jun** San Juan, Sibayo, Ichupampa. **21 Jun** Anniversary of Chivay. **29 Jun** San Pedro y San Pablo, Sibayo. **14-17 Jul** La Virgen del Carmen, Cabanaconde. **25 Jul** Santiago Apóstol, Coporaque. **26 Jul-2 Aug** Virgen Santa Ana, Maca.

15 Aug Virgen de la Asunta, Chivay.
8 Dec Immaculada Concepción, Yanque,
Chivay. **25 Dec** Sagrada Familia, Yanque.
Many of these festivals last several days and
involve traditional dances and customs.

⏻ What to do

Colca Canyon *p176*
Tours
It is not always possible to join a tour in
Chivay; it is best to organize it in Arequipa
and travel with a group. From Arequipa a '1-
day' tour to the Mirador at Cruz del Cóndor
costs US$25-30: depart Arequipa at 0400,
arrive at the Cruz del Cóndor at 0800-0900,
expensive lunch stop at Chivay and back
to Arequipa by 2100. For many, especially
for those with altitude problems, this is too
much to fit into one day (the only advantage
is that you don't have to sleep at high
altitude). 2-day tours are about US$30-40 pp
with an overnight stop in Chivay or Yanque;
more expensive tours range from US$45
to US$90. Most agencies will have a base
price for the tour and then different prices
depending on which hotel you pick. Allow
at least 2-3 days to appreciate the Colca
Canyon fully, more if planning on trekking.

Trekking
There are many hiking possibilities in the
area, with *hostales* or camping for longer
treks. Make sure to take enough water, or
purification, as it gets very hot and there
is not a lot of water available. Moreover,
sun protection is a must. Some treks are
impossible if it rains heavily in the wet
season, but this is very rare. Ask locals
for directions as there are hundreds of
confusing paths going into the canyon.
In Cabanaconde trekking and adventure
sports can be organized quite easily at short
notice. Buy food for longer hikes in Arequipa.
Topographical maps are available at the
Instituto Geográfico Nacional in Lima, and

at Colca Trek or Pablo Tour in Arequipa. See
above for some of the the main treks.

Chivay *p177*
Ampato Adventure Sports, Plaza de
Armas (close to **Lobos Pizzería**), Chivay,
T531073, www.ampatocolca.com. Offer
information and rent good mountain
bikes, but rarely open.
Colca-Turismo, Av Salaverry 321, Chivay,
T503368, guide Zacarías Ocsa Osca,
zacariasocsa@hotmail.com, seems to
offer a professional service.

Cabanaconde *p178*
Chiqui Travel & Expeditions, San Pedro
s/n, T958-063602. Small, but professional
and reliable, organizes trekking, biking
and horse riding.
Guías Locales Aproset, T958-099332.
Association of local guides, can organize
arrieros and mules for independent treks.

⛟ Transport

Colca Canyon *p176*
Bus La Reyna (T430612), Trans Milagros,
T531115, and Andalucía, T694060, have
almost hourly departures daily from
Arequipa to **Chivay**, US$4.50, 6 hrs, some
continuing to **Cabanaconde**, US$6, a further
75 km, 2 hrs. Buses return to Arequipa
from bus station in Chivay, 3 blocks from
the main plaza, next to the stadium. None
offers a secure service; it may be better
to take tourist transport, even if staying a
few days, then join another group for the
return. Combis and colectivos leave from the
terminal to any village in the area. Ask the
drivers. **Chivay-Cabanaconde** Bus at 0500.
Buses run infrequently in each direction,
fewer on Sun. Buses leave Cabanaconde for
Arequipa from 0730 to 1500 from the Plaza
de Armas. To **Cuzco** from Chivay take a bus
to Cañahuas and change there for a bus to
Juliaca, then carry on to Cuzco.

Cotahuasi Canyon

Toro Muerto

① *US$2; entrance 2 km from the road, site 2 km from the entrance.*

West of Arequipa, a dirt road branches off the Pan-American to Corire, Aplao (small museum containing Wari cultural objects from the surrounding area) and the Río Majes valley. The **world's largest field of petroglyphs**, covering 5 sq km, at Toro Muerto is near Corire, where there are several hotels and restaurants near the plaza and excellent shrimp restaurants by the river. For Toro Muerto, turn off on the right heading back out of Corire; one-hour walk; ask directions. The higher you go, the more interesting the petroglyphs, though some have been ruined by graffiti. The designs range from simple llamas to elaborate human figures and animals and are thought to be Wari (AD 700-1100) in origin. The sheer scale of the site, some 6000 sculpted rocks, is awe-inspiring and the view is wonderful (UNESCO World Heritage Site). Take plenty of water, sunglasses and sun cream. At least an hour is needed to visit the site.

Cotahuasi Canyon

Beyond Aplao the road heads north through **Chuquibamba**, where the paving ends (festivals 20 January; 2-3 February; 15 May), traversing the western slopes of Nevado Coropuna (6425 m), before winding down into **Cotahuasi** (*Phone code: 054; Population: 3200; Altitude: 2680 m*). The peaceful colonial town nestles in a sheltered hanging valley beneath Cerro Huinao. Its streets are narrow, the houses whitewashed. There is a small museum with **tourist information** ① *Centenario 208, Mon-Fri 0800-1300, 1400-1700, helpful*, Local festival is 4 May.

Several kilometres away a canyon has been cut by the Río Cotahuasi, which flows into the Pacific as the Río Ocuña. At its deepest, at Ninochaca (just below the village of Quechualla), the canyon is 3354 m deep, 163 m deeper than the Colca Canyon and the deepest in the world. From this point the only way down the canyon is by kayak and it is through kayakers' reports since 1994 that the area has come to the notice of tourists (it was declared a Zona de Reserva Turística in 1988). There is little agriculture apart from some citrus groves, but in Inca times the road linking Puerto Inca and Cuzco ran along much of the canyon's course. Note that the area is not on the tourist route and information is hard to come by.

Following the Río Cotahuasi to the northeast up the valley, you come to **Tomepampa** (10 km), a neat hamlet at 2700 m, with painted houses and a chapel. The hot springs (33° to 38°C) of **Luicho** ① *18 km from Cotahuasi, 24 hrs, US0.50-1.75*, are a short walk from the road, across a bridge. Beyond is **Alca** (20 km, at 2750 m, one *hostal*), above which are the small ruins of Kallak, Tiknay and a "stone library" of rock formations. All these places are connected by buses and combis from Cotahuasi. Buses leave Alca for Arequipa around 1400, combis hourly from 0600-1800. **Puica** ① *connected to Alca by combi (2 hrs, US$1.50*, is the last village of any significance in the valley, hanging on a hillside at nearly 3700 m. Nearby attractions include: Churca and a vast prairie of Puya Raimondi cacti; the Ocoruro geysers; and the ruins of Maucallacta. Horses can be hired for US$5 a day, and locals can act as guides.

One of the main treks in the region follows the Inca trade road from Cotahuasi to Quechualla. From the football pitch the path goes through Piro, the gateway to the canyon, and Sipia (three hours, two suspension bridges to cross), near which are the powerful, 150-m-high Cataratas de Sipia (take care near the falls if it is windy). Combis from Cotahuasi to Velinga go to within an hour's walk of the Cataratas; they leave 0630 and

1200, passing the Sipia drop off one hour later; return four hours later. It's best to visit at midday. A road is being built from this point to the falls, and may be complete by the time you read this. The next three-hour stretch to Chaupo is not for vertigo sufferers as the road (track) is barely etched into the canyon wall, 400 m above the river in places. At Chaupo ask permission to camp; water is available. Next is Velinga (currently the end of the road), from where you can reach the dilapidated but extensive ruin of Huña, and the charming village of **Quechualla** at 1980 m. The deepest part of the canyon is below Quechualla. Ask Sr Carmelo Velásquez Gálvez for permission to sleep in the schoolhouse.

Several tour operators in Arequipa run four-day trips to Cotahuasi, taking in the Sipia falls and the Puya Raimondi cacti. They can also organize adventure activities. **Cotahuasi Trek** (www.cotahuasitrek.com) is a specialist adventure company based in Cotahuasi, owned by Marcio Ruiz, locally renowned guide.

⊕ Cotahuasi Canyon listings

For hotel and restaurant price codes, and other relevant information, see pages 14-17.

⬤ Where to stay

Cotahuasi *p182*
$$ Valle Hermoso, Tacna 108-110, T581057, www.hotelvallehermoso.com. Nice and cosy, includes breakfast, beautiful views of the canyon, comfortable rooms, large garden, restaurant uses home-grown fruit and veg.
$ Casa Primavera, in Tomepampa, T212982. Family-run hostel, some rooms with private bath, kitchen facilities, courtyard and common areas, meals on request.
$ Cotahuasi, Arequipa 515, T581029/959-397163, hotel_cotahuasi@hotmail.com. New, with TV, hot water, clean.
$ Hostal Alcalá II, Arequipa 116, T581090. Very good, hot showers, excellent beds, doubles and triples. Run by same family as
$ Hostal Alcalá, main plaza, Alca, T452258. One of the best hostales in the valley, 2 rooms with shower, others shared, hot water, restaurant, good food. Prices vary according to season and demand.
$ Hostal Fany Luz, Independencia 117, T581002. Basic but amenable, shared hot showers, double room with cold water only.

⊘ Restaurants

Cotahuasi *p182*
3 small restaurants/bars on Jr Arequipa offer basic fare, best is BuenSabor, opposite Hostal Alcalá II. There are many well-stocked *tiendas*, particularly with fruit, vegetables and local wine.
$ El Pionero, Jr Centenario. Clean, good *menú*.
$ R y M, on main square, prepares typical soups.

⊖ Transport

Toro Muerto *p182*
Empresa Del Carpio buses to **Corire** leave from **Arequipa** main terminal hourly from 0500, 3-4 hrs, US$5. Ask to be let out at the beginning of the track to Toro Muerto, or from the plaza in Corire take a taxi, US$10 including 2-hr wait.

Cotahuasi *p182*
There is a modern bus station 10 mins' walk from the Plaza. Buses daily from **Arequipa** bus terminal, 10-11 hrs, US$11: Cromotex at 1700 and 1800; Reyna at 1630; all return from Cotahuasi at the same times. They stop for refreshments in Chuquibamba, about halfway. Both companies continue to **Tomepampa** and **Alca**.

Cotahuasi *p182*
Useful services PNP, on plaza; advisable to register with them on arrival and before leaving. **Maps:** some survey maps in Municipalidad and PNP; they may let you make photocopies (shop on the corner of the plaza and Arequipa). Sr Chávez has photocopies of the sheets covering Cotahuasi and surroundings. The *Lima 2000* 1:225,000 map of the Colca and Cotahuasi canyons has information about the small villages throughout the canyon as well as about interesting places to visit.

South to Chile

Moquegua → *Phone code: 053. Colour map 3, B1. Population: 110,000. Altitude: 1412 m.*
This town 213 km from Arequipa in the narrow valley of the Moquegua River enjoys a sub-tropical climate. The old centre, a few blocks above the Pan-American Highway, has winding, cobbled streets and 19th-century buildings. The Plaza de Armas, with its mix of ruined and well-maintained churches, colonial and republican façades and fine trees, is one of the most interesting small-town plazas in the country. **Museo Contisuyo** ① *on the Plaza de Armas, within the ruins of Iglesia Matriz, T461844, www.museocontisuyo.com, daily 0800-1300, 1430-1730, Tue 0800-1200, 1600-2000, US$0.50*, covers the cultures which thrived in the Moquegua and Ilo valleys, including the Huari, Tiahuanaco, Chiribaya and Estuquiña, who were conquered by the Incas. Artefacts are well displayed and explained in Spanish and English. **Día de Santa Catalina**, 25 November, is the anniversary of the founding of the colonial city. **Dircetur regional tourist office** ① *Ayacucho 1060, T462236, moquegua@mincetur.gob.pe, Mon-Fri 0800-1630*.

A highly recommended excursion is to **Cerro Baúl** (2590 m) ① *30 mins by colectivo, US$2*, a tabletop mountain with marvellous views and many legends, which can be combined with the pleasant town of Torata, 24 km northeast.

The Carretera Binacional, from the port of Ilo to La Paz, has a breathtaking stretch from Moquegua to Desaguadero at the southeastern end of Lake Titicaca. It skirts Cerro Baúl and climbs through zones of ancient terraces to its highest point at 4755 m. On the altiplano there are herds of llamas and alpacas, lakes with waterfowl, strange mountain formations and snow-covered peaks. At Mazo Cruz there is a PNP checkpoint where all documents and bags are checked. Approaching Desaguadero the Cordillera Real of Bolivia comes into view. The road is fully paved and should be taken in daylight.

Tacna → *Phone code: 052. Colour map 3, B2. Population: 174,366. Altitude: 550 m.*
Only 36 km from the Chilean border and 56 km from the international port of Arica, Tacna has free-trade status. It is an important commercial centre and Chileans come for cheap medical and dental treatment. Around the city the desert is gradually being irrigated. The local economy includes olive groves, vineyards and fishing. Tacna was in Chilean hands from 1880 to 1929, when its people voted by plebiscite to return to Peru. Above the city (8 km away, just off the Panamericana Norte), on the heights, is the **Campo de la Alianza**, scene of a battle between Peru and Chile in 1880. The cathedral, designed by Eiffel, faces the Plaza de Armas, which contains huge bronze statues of Admiral Grau and Colonel Bolognesi. They stand at either end of the Arca de los Héroes, the triumphal arch which is the symbol of the city. The bronze fountain in the Plaza is said to be a duplicate of the one in the Place de la Concorde (Paris) and was also designed by Eiffel. The **Parque de la Locomotora** ① *daily 0700-1700, US$0.30; knock at the gate under the clock tower on Jr 2 de*

Mayo for entry, near the city centre, has a British-built locomotive, which was used in the War of the Pacific. There is a very good railway museum at the station.

Tourist offices **i perú** ① *San Martín 491 (Plaza de Armas), T425514, Mon-Sat 0830-1930, Sun 0830-1400*. Also at the airport in the Arrivals hall which is usually manned when flights are scheduled to arrive, and **Terminal Terrestre Internacional** ① *Mon-Sat 0830-1500*. There is another office at the **border** ① *Thu-Sat 0830-1730*. A city map and regional information is available from **Dircetur** ① *Blondell 50, p 3, T422784, Mon-Fri 0730-1530*. See also www. turismotacna.com. **Tourist police** ① *Pasaje Calderón de la Barca 353, inside the main police station, T414141 ext 245*.

Border with Chile

There is a checkpoint before the border, which is open 0800-2300 (24 hours Friday and Saturday). You need to obtain a Peruvian exit stamp and a Chilean entrance stamp; formalities are straightforward (see below). If you need a Chilean visa, you have to get it in Tacna (address below). Peruvian time is one hour earlier than Chilean time March-October; two hours earlier September/October to February/March (varies annually). No fruit or vegetables are allowed into Chile or Tacna.

Tacna

Where to stay 🛏
1 Copacabana
2 Dorado
3 El Mesón
4 Gran Hotel Tacna
5 Hostal Anturio
6 Hostal Bon Ami
7 La Posada del Cacique
8 Roble 18 Residencial

Restaurants 🍴
1 Café Zeit
2 Cusqueñita
3 Da Vinci
4 Fu-Lin
5 Il Pomodoro
6 Koyuki
7 Un Limón
8 Verdi

400 metres
400 yards

Crossing by private vehicle For those leaving Peru by car buy *relaciones de pasajeros* (official forms, US$0.45) from the kiosk at the border or from a bookshop; you will need four copies. Next, return your tourist card, visit the PNP office, return the vehicle permit and finally depart through the checkpoints.

Exchange Money-changers can be found at counters in the international bus terminal; rates are much the same as in town.

⊚ South to Chile listings

For hotel and restaurant price codes, and other relevant information, see pages 14-17.

⊜ Where to stay

Moquegua *p184*
Most hotels do not serve breakfast.
$ Alameda, Junín 322, T463971.
Includes breakfast, large comfortable rooms, welcoming.
$ Hostal Adrianella, Miguel Grau 239, T463469. Hot water, safe, helpful, tourist information, close to market and buses, bit faded.
$ Hostal Carrera, Jr Lima 320-A (no sign), T462113. With or without bath, solar-powered hot water (best in afternoon), laundry facilities on roof, good value.
$ Hostal Plaza, Ayacucho 675, T461612. Modern and comfortable, good value.

Tacna *p184, map p185*
$$$ Gran Hotel Tacna, Av Bolognesi 300, T424193, www.granhoteltacna.com. Includes breakfast, internet, pool open to non-guests with purchases in restaurant or bar, disco, gardens, safe car park, English spoken.
$$ Copacabana, Arias Aragüez 370, T421721, www.copahotel.com. With breakfast, good rooms, restaurant, pizzería.
$$ Dorado, Arias Aragüez 145, T415741, www.doradohoteltacna.com. Modern and comfortable, good service, restaurant.
$$ El Mesón, H Unanue 175, T425841, www.mesonhotel.com. Central, modern, comfortable, safe.
$ Hostal Anturio, 28 de Julio 194 y Zela, T244258. Cafeteria downstairs, breakfast extra, good value.

$ Hostal Bon Ami, 2 de Mayo 445, T244847. With or without bath, hot water best in afternoon, simple, secure.
$ La Posada del Cacique, Arias Aragüez 300-4, T247424, laposada_hostal@hotmail. com. Antique style in an amazing building built around a huge spiral staircase.
$ Roble 18 Residencial, H Unanue 245, T241414, roble18@gmail.com. One block from Plaza de Armas. Hot water, English, Italian, German spoken.

⊘ Restaurants

Moquegua *p184*
$ Moraly, Lima y Libertad. Mon-Sat 1000-2200, Sun 1000-1600. The best place for meals. Breakfast, good lunches, *menú* US$1.75.

Tacna *p184, map p185*
$$ DaVinci, San Martín 596 y Arias Araguez, T744648. Mon-Sat 1100-2300, bar Tue-Sat 2000-0200. Pizza and other dishes, nice atmosphere.
$$ Il Pomodoro, Bolívar 524 y Apurimac. Closed Sun evening and Mon 1200. Upscale Italian serving set lunch on weekdays, pricey à la carte in the evening, attentive service.
$ Cusqueñita, Zela 747. Open 1100-1600. Excellent 4-course lunch, large portions, good value, variety of choices. Recommended.
$ Fu-Lin, Arias Araguez 396 y 2 de Mayo. Mon-Sat 0930-1600. Vegetarian Chinese.
$ Koyuki, Bolívar 718. Closed Sun evening. Generous set lunch daily, seafood and à la carte in the evening. Several other popular lunch places on the same block.

$ Un Limón, Av San Martín 843, T425182. *Ceviches* and variety of seafood dishes.
Café Zeit, Deústua 150, CafeZeit on Facebook. German-owned coffee shop, cultural events and live music as well as quality coffee and cakes.
Verdi, Pasaje Vigil 57. Café serving excellent *empanadas* and sweets, also set lunch.

⊖ Transport

Moquegua *p184*
Bus All bus companies are on Av Ejército, 2 blocks north of the market at Jr Grau, except Ormeño, Av La Paz casi Balta. From **Lima**, US$30-42, 15 hrs, many companies with executive and regular services. To **Tacna**, 159 km, 2 hrs, US$6, hourly buses with **Flores**, Av del Ejército y Andrés Aurelio Cáceres. To **Arequipa**, 3½ hrs, US$7.50-12, several buses daily. Colectivos for these 2 destinations leave when full from Av del Ejercito y Andrés Aurelio Cáceres, almost double the bus fare – negotiate. To **Desaguadero** and **Puno**, San Martín-Nobleza, 4 a day, 6 hrs, US$12. **Mily Tours**, Av del Ejército 32-B, T464000, colectivos to Desaguadero, 4 hrs, US$20.

Tacna *p184, map p185*
Air The airport (T314503) is at Km 5 on the Panamericana Sur, on the way to the border. To go from the airport directly to Arica, call the bus terminal (T427007) and ask a colectivo to pick you up on its way to the border, US$7.50. Taxi from airport to Tacna centre US$5-6. To **Lima**, 1½ hrs; daily flights with **LAN** (Av San Martín 259, T428346) and **Peruvian Airlines** (Av San Martín 670 p 2, T412699, also to **Arequipa**).
Bus Two bus stations on Hipólito Unánue, T427007, 1 km from the plaza (colectivo US$0.35, taxi US$1 minimum). One terminal is for international services (ie Arica), the other for domestic, both are well organized, local tax US$0.50, baggage store, easy to make connections to the border, Arequipa or Lima. To **Moquegua** and **Arequipa**, 6 hrs (prices

above) frequent buses with **Flores** (Av Saucini behind the Terminal Nacional, T426691). Also **Trans Moquegua Turismo** and **Cruz del Sur**. To **Nazca**, 793 km, 12 hrs, several buses daily, en route for Lima (fares US$3 less than to Lima). Several companies daily to **Lima**, 1239 km, 21-26 hrs, US$26-62 *bus-cama*, eg **Oltursa** or Civa. **Cruz del Sur** (T425729), charges US$43. Buses to **Desaguadero**, **Puno** and **Cuzco** leave from Terminal Collasuyo (T312538), Av Internacional in Barrio Altos de la Alianza neighbourhood; taxi to centre US$1. **San Martín-Nobleza** in early morning and at night to **Desaguadero**, US$22, and **Puno**, US$18, 8-10 hrs.

At **Tomasiri**, 35 km north of Tacna, passengers' luggage is checked. Do not carry anything on the bus for anyone else. Passports may be checked at Camiara, a police checkpoint some 60 km from Tacna. **Sernanp** also has a post where any fruit will be confiscated in an attempt to keep fruit fly out of Peru.

To **La Paz**, Bolivia, the quickest and cheapest route is via Moquegua and Desaguadero; it also involves one less border crossing than via Arica and Tambo Colorado.

Border with Chile: Tacna *p185*
Road 56 km, 1-2 hrs, depending on waiting time at the border. Buses to Arica charge US$2.50 and colectivo taxis US$7.50 pp. All leave from the international terminal in Tacna throughout the day. Colectivos which carry 5 passengers only leave when full. As you approach the terminal you will be grabbed by a driver or his agent and told that the car is "just about to leave". This is hard to verify as you may not see the colectivo until you have filled in the paperwork. Once you have chosen a driver/agent, you will be rushed to his company's office where your passport will be taken from you and the details filled out on a Chilean entry form. You can change your remaining soles at the bus terminal. It is 30 mins to the Peruvian border post at Santa Rosa, where all exit formalities are carried out. The driver will hustle you

through all the procedures. A short distance beyond is the Chilean post at Chacalluta, where again the driver will show you what to do. All formalities take about 30 mins. It's a further 15 mins to Arica's bus terminal. A Chilean driver is more likely to take you to any address in Arica.

Train Station is at Av Albaracín y 2 de Mayo. In 2014 no trains were running on the cross-border line to **Arica**.

ⓘ Directory

Tacna *p184, map p185*
Consulates Bolivia, Av Bolognesi 175, Urb Pescaserolli, T245121, Mon-Fri 0830-1630. **Chile**, Presbítero Andía block 1, T423063. Open Mon-Fri 0800-1300.
Useful addresses Immigration, Av Circunvalación s/n, Urb El Triángulo, T243231.

Lake Titicaca

Straddling Peru's southern border with Bolivia are the sapphire-blue waters of mystical Lake Titicaca, a huge inland sea which is the highest navigable lake in the world. Its shores and islands are home to the Aymara and Quechua, who are among Peru's oldest peoples. Here you can wander through traditional villages where Spanish is a second language and where ancient myths and beliefs still hold true. Newly paved roads climb from the coastal deserts and oases to the high plateau in which sits Lake Titicaca (Arequipa–Yura–Santa Lucía–Juliaca–Puno; Moquegua–Desaguadero–Puno). The steep ascents lead to wide open views of pampas with agricultural communities, desolate mountains, small lakes and salt flats. It is a rapid change of altitude, so be prepared for some discomfort and breathlessness.

Puno and around → *Phone code: 051. Colour map 3, B2. Population: 100,170. Altitude: 3855 m. See map, page 190.*

On the northwest shore of Lake Titicaca, Puno is capital of its department and Peru's folklore centre with a vast array of handicrafts, festivals and costumes and a rich tradition of music and dance. Puno gets bitterly cold at night: from June to August the temperature at night can fall to -25°C, but generally not below -5°C.

Arriving in Puno

Tourist offices i perú ⓘ *Jr Lima y Deústua, near Plaza de Armas, T365088, iperupuno@ promperu. gob.pe, daily 0830-1930.* Helpful English-speaking staff, good information and maps. Municipal website: www.munipuno.gob.pe. **Dircetur** ⓘ *Ayacucho 684, T364976, puno@mincetur.gob.pe,* with a desk at the Terminal Terrestre. **Indecopi** ⓘ *Jr Deústua 644, T363667, jpilco@indecopi. gob.pe,* is the consumer protection bureau. **Tourist police** ⓘ *Jr Deústua 558, T354764, daily 0600-2200.* Report any scams, such as unscrupulous price changes, and beware touts (see page 194).

Places around Puno

The **Cathedral** ⓘ *Mon-Fri 0800-1200, 1500-1800, Sat-Sun until 1900,* completed in 1657, has an impressive baroque exterior, but an austere interior. Across the street from the Cathedral is the **Balcony of the Conde de Lemos** ⓘ *Deústua y Conde de Lemos, art gallery open Mon-Fri 0800-1600* where Peru's Viceroy stayed when he first arrived in the city. The **Museo Municipal Dreyer** ⓘ *Conde de Lemos 289, Mon-Sat 1030-2200, Sun 1600-2200, US$5 includes 45-min guided tour,* has been combined with the private collection of

Sr Carlos Dreyer. A short walk up Independencia leads to the **Arco Deústua**, a monument honouring those killed in the battles of Junín and Ayacucho. Nearby, is a mirador giving fine views over the town, the port and the lake beyond. The walk from Jr Cornejo following the Stations of the Cross up a nearby hill, with fine views of Lake Titicaca, has been recommended, but be careful and don't go alone (the same applies to any of the hills around Puno, eg Huajsapata).

Avenida Titicaca leads to the port from where boats go to the islands. From its intersection with Avenida Costanera towards the pier, one side of the road is lined with the kiosks of the **Artesanos Unificados de Puno**, selling crafts. Closer to the port are food kiosks. On the opposite side of the road is a shallow lake where you can hire **pedal boats** ① *US$0.70 pp for 20 mins*. At the pier are the ticket counters for transport to the islands. The **Malecón Bahía de los Incas**, a lovely promenade along the waterfront, extends to the north and south; it is a pleasant place for a stroll and for birdwatching. The **Yavari** ① *0815-1715, free but donations of US$6 welcome to help with maintenance costs*, the oldest ship on Lake Titicaca, is berthed near the entrance to the **Sonesta Posada del Inca** hotel and is you have to go through the hotel to get to it. Alternatively, a boat from the port costs US$2 return, with wait. The ship was built in England in 1862 and was shipped in kit form to Arica, then by rail to Tacna and by mule to Lake Titicaca. The journey took six years. The *Yavari* was launched on Christmas Day 1870. Project addresses: England: 12 Back Lane, Great Bedwyn, Wiltshire SN8 3NX, yavarilarken@gmail.com. In Puno: T051-369329, yavariguldentops@hotmail.com. Visit www.yavari.org. Another old ship is the **MN Coya** ① *moored in Barrio Guaje, beyond the Hotel Sonesta Posada del Inka, T368156, has a restaurant on board*, built in Scotland and launched on the lake in 1892. Berthed next to Coya is Hull (UK)-built *MS Ollanta*, which sailed the lake from 1926 to the 1970s.

Around Puno

Anybody interested in religious architecture should visit the villages along the western shore of Lake Titicaca. An Inca sundial can be seen near the village of **Chucuito** (19 km), which has an interesting church, La Asunción, and houses with carved stone doorways.

Juli, 80 km, has some fine examples of religious architecture. **San Pedro** on the plaza, is the only functioning **church** ① *open 0630-1130, 1400-1600, except Tue when only for Mass at 0700 and Sun for Mass at 0730, 1100 and 1800, free, but donations appreciated*. It contains a series of paintings of saints, with the Via Crucis scenes in the same frame, and gilt side altars above which some of the arches have baroque designs. **San Juan Letrán** ① *daily 0800-1600, US$1.50*, has two sets of 17th-century paintings of the lives of St John the Baptist and of St Teresa, contained in sumptuous gilded frames. San Juan is a museum. It also has intricate *mestizo* carving in pink stone. **La Asunción** ① *daily 0800-1630, US$1.20*, is also a museum. The nave is empty, but its walls are lined with colonial paintings with no labels. The original painting on the walls of the transept can be seen. Its fine bell tower was damaged by earthquake or lightning. Outside is an archway and atrium which date from the early 17th century. Needlework, other weavings, handicrafts and antiques are offered for sale in town. Colectivo Puno–Juli US$1.50; return from Juli outside market at Ilave 349.

A further 20 km along the lake is **Pomata** (bus from Juli US$0.75, US$2 from Puno), whose red sandstone church of **Santiago Apóstol** ① *daily 0700-1200, 1330-1600, US$1, but if guardian is not there, leave money on table*, has a striking exterior and beautiful interior, with superb carving and paintings. At **Zepita**, near Desaguadero, the 18th-century Dominican church is also worth a visit.

Near Puno are the *chullpas* (pre-Columbian funeral towers) of **Sillustani** ① *32 km from Puno on a good road, US$2, take an organized tour; about 3-4 hrs, leave 1430, US$15-18, tours usually stop at a Colla house on the way, to see local products*, in a beautiful setting on a peninsula in Lake Umayo. John Hemming writes: "Most of the towers date from the period of Inca occupation in the 15th century, but they are burial towers of the Aymara-speaking Colla tribe. The engineering involved in their construction is more complex than anything the Incas built – it is defeating archaeologists' attempts to rebuild the tallest 'lizard' *chullpa*." There is a museum and handicraft sellers wait at the exit. Photography is best in the afternoon light, though this is when the wind is strongest. The scenery is barren, but impressive. There is a small community at the foot of the promontory.

Puno

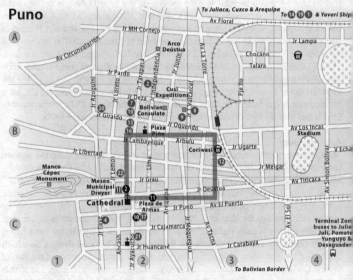

Where to stay 🛏

1 Casa Andina Private
  Collection Puno *A4*
2 Casa Andina Tikarani *B2*
3 Casona Colón Inn
  Puno centre
4 Conde de Lemos *C2*
5 El Buho *Puno centre*
6 Hacienda Puno *Puno centre*
7 Hosp Res Margarita *B2*
8 Hostal Imperial &
  Los Uros *B3*
9 Hostal Italia *B2*

10 Hostal Los Pinos *B2*
11 Hostal Pukara
  Puno centre
12 Inka's Rest *B3*
13 Intiqa *B2*
14 Libertador Lago
  Titicaca *A4*
15 Plaza Mayor *Puno centre*
16 Posada Don Giorgio *B2*
17 Puno Plaza *C2*
18 Sillustani *Puno centre*
19 Sonesta Posadas del Inca *A4*
20 Tambo Real *B2*

21 The Point *C1*
22 Tierra Viva Plaza *B2*

Restaurants 🍴

1 Cafetería Mercedes
  Puno centre
2 Casa del Corregidor *C2*
3 Casa Grilll La Estancia
  Puno centre
4 Chifa Nan Hua *B2*
5 Don Piero &
  Positive Bar *Puno centre*
6 Govinda *Puno centre*

200 metres
200 yards

Llachón → *Population: 1300.*

At the eastern end of the Península de Capachica, which encloses the northern side of the Bahía de Puno, the pretty farming villages of Llachón, Santa María and Ccotos have become a focus of community-based tourism. On Capachica there are currently six organizations, each with a dozen or more families and links to different tour operators in Puno, Cuzco or abroad. The scenery is very pretty, with sandy beaches, pre-Inca terracing, trees and flowers. The view of the sunset from the Auki Carus hill is reckoned to be better even than from Taquile. Visitors share in local activities and 70% of all produce served is from the residents' farms. Throughout the peninsula the dress of the local women is very colourful, with four-cornered hats called *monteros*, matching vests and colourful *polleras*. The peninsula is good for hiking, mountain biking and sailing; boats can be hired. Off the east coast of the peninsula is the island of Ticonata, whose community tourism association offers accommodation in round houses and various activities (www.ticonatatours.com). It's a short boat ride from Ccotos, or from Amantaní. Motor boats from Puno take 3½ hours.

Puno centre

IncAbar *Puno centre*
Internacional *Puno Centre*
La Hostería *Puno Centre*
0 La Plaza *C2*
1 Mojsa *C2*
2 Pizzería/Trattoria El Buho *Puno centre*
3 Ricos Pan *Puno centre*
4 Tradiciones del Lago *Puno centre*
5 Tulipans *Puno centre*
6 Ukukus *Puno centre*
7 Vida Natural *C3*

Bars & clubs 🌢
18 Pub Ekeko's *Puno Centre*

⊙ Puno and around listings

For hotel and restaurant price codes, and other relevant information, see pages 14-17.

⊜ Where to stay

Puno *p188, map p190*
A number of luxury hotels are opening in and around the city. Prices vary according to season. Many touts try to persuade tourists to go to a hotel not of their own choosing. Be firm.

$$$$ Casa Andina Private Collection Puno, Av Sesquicentenario 1970, T363992. This recommended chain's lakeshore luxury property. The group also has **$$ Casa Andina Tikarani**, Independencia 185, T367803, heating, non-smoking rooms, safe, central, business centre. Visit www.casa-andina.com.

$$$$ Libertador Lago Titicaca, on Isla Esteves linked by a causeway 5 km northeast of Puno (taxi US$3), T367780, www.libertador.com.pe. Modern hotel with every facility, built on a Tiahuanaco-period site, spacious, good views, phone, bar, good restaurant, disco, good service, parking.

$$$$ Sonesta Posadas del Inca, Av Sesquicentenario 610, Huaje, 5 km from Puno on the lakeshore, T364111, www.sonesta.com/laketiticaca/. 62 rooms with heating, facilities for the disabled, local textile decorations, good views,

Inkafé restaurant has an Andean menu, folklore shows.

$$$ Hacienda Puno, Jr Deústua 297, T356109, www.lahaciendapuno.com. Refurbished colonial house, with buffet breakfast, rooms and suites with good bathrooms, restaurant with local specialities, comfortable.

$$$ Intiqa, Jr Tarapacá 272, T366900, www.intiqahotel.com. Built around a sunny courtyard with good restaurant. Stylish, rooms have heaters, professional staff. Associated with **La Casa de Wiracocha**, at No 260, for select Peruvian handicrafts.

$$$ Plaza Mayor, Deústua 342, T366089, www.plazamayorhostal.com. Comfortable, well-appointed, good big beds, buffet breakfast, hot water, laundry, restaurant.

$$$ Puno Plaza, Jr Puno 425, T351424, http://tierravivahoteles.com. Tastefully decorated modern hotel overlooking the Plaza de Armas, includes buffet breakfast, very comfortable rooms, all with bathtub or jacuzzi, heater, safety box, good restaurant.

$$$-$$ Tierra Viva Plaza, Jr Grau 270, 1 block from plaza, T367520, www.tierra vivahoteles.com. Heating, non-smoking rooms, safe, central, business centre, parking.

$$ Casona Colón Inn, Tacna 290, T351432, www.coloninn.com. Colonial style, good rooms with hot shower, good service, safe, restaurant **Sol Naciente** and pizzería **Europa**, the Belgian manager Christian Nonis is well known, especially for his work on behalf of the people on Taquile island.

$$ Conde de Lemos, Jr Puno 681, T369898, www.condelemosinn.com. Convenient, comfy, plush modern hotel, heating, washing machine, elevator, wheel chair friendly, restaurant.

$$ El Buho, Lambayeque 142, T366122, www.hotelbuho.com. Hot water, nice rooms with heaters, restaurant, safe, discount for Footprint book owners, travel agency for trips and flights.

$$ Hostal Imperial, Teodoro Valcarcel 145, T352386, www.hostalimperial.com. Basic but big rooms, good hot showers, safe, helpful, stores luggage, comfortable.

$$ Hostal Italia, Teodoro Valcarcel 122, T367706, www.hotelitaliaperu.com. 2 blocks from the station. With breakfast, cheaper in low season, good, safe, hot water, good food, small rooms, staff helpful.

$$ Hostal Pukara, Jr Libertad 328, T368448, pukara@terra.com.pe. Excellent, English spoken, helpful service, central, quiet, free coca to drink in evening, American breakfast included, dining room on top floor, lots of stairs.

$$ Posada Don Giorgio, Tarapacá 238, T363648, www.posadadongiorgio.com. Comfortable, hot water, large rooms, nicely decorated, traditional architecture.

$$ Sillustani, Tarapacá 305 y Lambayeque, T351881, www.sillustani.com. Hot water, safety deposit, heaters, well-established, popular, reservations advised.

$$ Tambo Real, Jr Santiago Giraldo 362, T366060, www.tamborealtitikaka.com. Good value, bright rooms, good bathrooms, family-owned, helpful, tea and coffee in the lobby all day.

$$ pp MN Yavari, Muelle del Hotel Sonesta Posadas del Inca, T369329 (in Lima T01-255 7268), reservasyavari@gmail.com. B&B is available on board, 3 twin bunk rooms with shared bath. Dinner served on request downstairs in the Victorian saloon.

$ Hospedaje Residencial Margarita, Jr Tarapacá 130, T352820, www.hostal margaritapuno.com. Large building, family atmosphere, cold rooms, heaters on request, hot water, tours can be arranged.

$ Hostal Los Pinos, Tarapacá 182, T367398, hostalpinos@hotmail.com. Family-run, helpful, small breakfast, cold rooms, heater on request, hot showers, safe, laundry facilities, tours organized.

$ Inka's Rest, Pasaje San Carlos 158, T368720, http://inkasresthostel.com. Several sitting areas hot water, heating, double or twin rooms with private or shared bath and a dorm, cooking and laundry facilities, a place to meet other travellers, reserve ahead.

$ Los Uros, Teodoro Valcarcel 135, T352141, www.losuros.com. Private or shared bath, hot water, breakfast available, quiet at back, small charge to leave luggage, laundry, heating costs extra.

$ The Point, Av Ayacucho 515-517, T351427, www.thepointhostels.com. Quieter than some of the other Point hostels, 1 block from main plaza, with dorms for 1-4 people, each with bath, hot water, bar, restaurant, travel centre, hammocks.

Around Puno: Chucuito *p189*
$$$$ Titilaka Lodge, Comunidad de Huencalla s/n, on a private peninsula near Chucuito, T01-700 5111 (Lima), www.titilaka.com. Luxury boutique hotel offering all-inclusive packages in an exclusive environment on the edge of the lake. Plenty of activities available.
$$ Las Cabañas, Jr Tarapacá 538, T369494, T951-751196, www.chucuito.com. Rooms and cottages, lakeside, breakfast included, other meals available, events and conferences held here, will collect you from Puno if you phone in advance.
$ Sra Nely Durán Saraza, Chucuíto Occopampa, T951-586240 (mob). 2 nice rooms, one with lake view, shared bath, hot water, breakfast and dinner available, very welcoming and interesting.

Llachón *p191*
Families offer accommodation on a rotational basis and, as the community presidents change each year, the standard of facilities changes from year-to-year and family-to-family. All hosts can arrange boat transport to Amantaní. Among those who offer lodging (**$** per bed, meals extra) are: Tomás Cahui Coila, **Centro Turístico Santa María Llachón**, T951-923595, www.exploretiticaca.com; **Primo Flores**, Santa María, T951-821392/951-680040/951-410901, primopuno@hotmail.com; **Valentín Quispe**, T951-821392 (mob), llachon@yahoo.com. But do recognize that there are other families who accept guests.

❶ Restaurants

Puno *p188, map p190*
$$ IncAbar, Lima 348, T368031. Open for breakfast, lunch and dinner, interesting dishes in creative sauces, fish, pastas, curries, café and couch bar, nice decor.
$$ Internacional, Moquegua 201, T352502. Very popular, excellent trout, good pizzas, service variable.
$$ La Hostería, Lima 501, T365406. Good set meal and à la carte dishes including local fare like alpaca and *cuy*, pizza, also breakfast, music in the evening.
$$ La Plaza, Puno 425, Plaza de Armas. Good food, international dishes and *comida nueva andina*, good service.
$$ Mojsa, Lima 635 p 2, Plaza de Armas. Good international and *novo andino* dishes, also has an arts and crafts shop.
$$ Tradiciones del Lago, Lima 418, T368140, www.tradicionesdelago.com. Buffet, à la carte and a big selection of Peruvian food.
$$ Tulipans, Lima 394, T351796. Sandwiches, juices and a lunchtime menu are its staples. One of the few places in Puno with outdoor seating in a pleasant colonial courtyard, a good option for lunch.
$$-$ Don Piero, Lima 360. Huge meals, live music, try their '*pollo coca-cola*' (chicken in a sweet and sour sauce), slow service, popular, tax extra.
$$-$ Pizzería/Trattoria El Buho, Lima 349 and at Jr Libertad 386, T356223. Open 1800 onwards. Excellent pizza, lively atmosphere, pizzas US$2.35-3.
$ Casa Grilll La Estancia, Libertad 137, T51-365469. Salad bar, huge steaks, grilled meat and peruvian food. Very popular with locals for huge lunches and a few beers.
$ Chifa Nan Hua, Arequipa 378. Tasty Chinese, big portions.
$ Govinda, Deústua 312. Closes at 2000. Cheap vegetarian lunch menus.
$ Ukukus, Libertad 216 and Pje Grau 172, T367373/369504. Good combination of Andean and *novo andino* cuisine as well as pizzas and some Chinese *chifa* style.

$ Vida Natural, Tacna 141. Breakfast, salads, fruits, also vegetarian meals midday and evening.

Cafés
Cafetería Mercedes, Jr Arequipa 144. Good menú US$1.50, bread, cakes, snacks, juices.
Casa del Corregidor, Deústua 576, aptdo 2, T365603. In restored 17th-century building, sandwiches, good snacks, coffee, good music, great atmosphere, nice surroundings with patio. Also has a Fair Trade store offering products directly from the producers.
Ricos Pan, Jr Lima 424. Mon-Sat 0600-2300. Café and bakery, great cakes, excellent coffees, juices and pastries, breakfasts and other dishes. Branches at Arequipa cuadra 3 and Moquegua 330.

Bars and clubs

Puno *p188, map p190*
Dómino, Libertad 443. Happy hour 2000-2130 Mon-Thu. "Megadisco", good.
Positive, Jr Lima 382. Drinks, large-screen TV, modern music, occasional heavy metal groups.
Pub Ekeko's, Lima 355. Happy hour 2000-2200. Live music every night.

Festivals

Puno *p188, map p190*
Feb At the **Fiesta de la Virgen de la Candelaria**, 1st 2 weeks in **Feb**, bands and dancers from all the local towns compete in a *Diablada*, or Devil Dance. The festivities are better at night on the streets than the official functions in the stadium. Check the dates in advance as Candelaria may be moved if pre-Lentern carnival coincides with it. A candlelight procession through darkened streets takes place on **Good Friday**. **3 May** Festividad de las Cruces, celebrated with Masses, a procession and the Alasita festival of miniatures.
29 Jun Colourful festival of **San Pedro**, with a procession at Zepita (see page 189). **4-5 Nov** Pageant dedicated to the founding of Puno and the emergence of Manco Cápac and Mama Ocllo from the waters of Lake Titicaca.

Shopping

Puno *p188, map p190*
Markets Puno is the best place in Peru to buy alpaca wool articles, bargaining is appropriate. Along the avenue leading to the port is the large **Mercado Artesanal Asociación de Artesanos Unificados**, daily 0900-1800. Closer to the centre are **Mercado Coriwasi**, Ugarte 150, daily 0800-2100 and **Central Integral de Artesanos del Perú (CIAP)**, Jr Deústua 576, Mon-Sat 1000-1800. The **Mercado Central**, in the blocks bound by Arbulú, Arequipa, Oquendo and Tacna has all kinds of food, including good cheeses as well as a few crafts. Beware pickpockets in the market. You will be hassled on the street and outside restaurants to buy woollen goods, so take care.

What to do

Puno *p188, map p190*
Watch out for unofficial tour sellers, *jalagringos*, who offer hotels and tours at varying rates, depending on how wealthy you look. They are everywhere: train station, bus offices, airport and hotels. Ask to see their guide's ID card. Only use agencies with named premises, compare prices and only hand over money at the office, never on the street or in a hotel.

Agencies organize trips to the Uros floating islands (see page 196) and the islands of Taquile and Amantaní, as well as to Sillustani, and other places. The standard tour is 2 days, 1 night, visiting the Uros, staying in either Taquile or Amantaní and then visiting the other island the next day (from US$26.50 pp). Choose an agency that allows you to pay direct for your lodging so you know that the family is benefiting. Make sure that you settle all details before embarking on the tour. We have received good reports on the following:

All Ways Travel, Casa del Corregidor, Deústua 576, p 2, T353979, and at Tacna 281, p 2, T355552, www.titicacaperu.com. Very helpful, kind and reliable, speak German, French, English and Italian. They offer a unique cultural tour to the islands of Anapia and Yuspique in Lake Wiñaymarka, beyond the straits of Tiquina, "The Treasure of Wiñaymarka", departures Thu and Sun.

CEDESOS, Centro para el Desarrollo Sostenible (Centre for Sustainable Development), Jr Moquegua 348 Int p 3, T367915, www.cedesos.org. A non-profit NGO which offers interesting tours of Capachica peninsula with overnight stops in family homes, going to the less visited islands where there are few tourists.

Cusi Expeditions, Jr T Varcarcel 164, T369072, reservascusi@terra.com.pe. They own most of the boats which operate the standard tours of the Islands. You will very likely end up on a Cusi tour so it's best to buy from them directly to get the best price and the most accurate information.

Edgar Adventures, Jr Lima 328, T353444, www.edgaradventures.com. English, German and French spoken, very helpful and knowledgeable. Constantly exploring new areas, lots of off-the-beaten-track tours, eg kayaking tour of Llachón. Community-minded, promote responsible tourism. Consistently recommended.

Kontiki Tours, Jr Melgar 188, T353473, www.kontikiperu.com. Receptive tour agency specializing in special interest excursions.

Nayra Travel, Jr Lima 419, of 105, T337934, www.nayratravel.com. Small agency run by Lilian Cotrado and her helpful staff, traditional local tours and a variety of options in Llachón. Can organize off-the-beaten track excursions for a minimum of 2 people. Recommended.

Peru Up to Date, Arequipa 340, T950-857371, www.peruuptodate.com. New, offers tours in the Puno and Titicaca area.

Pirámide Tours, Jr Rosendo Huirse 130, T366107, www.titikakalake.com. Out of the ordinary and classic tours, flexible, personalized service, modern fast launches, very helpful, works only via internet, overseas clients.

Titikaka Explorers, Jr Puno 633 of 207, T368903, www.titikaka-explorer.com. Good service, helpful.

⊖ Transport

Puno *p188, map p190*

Bus All long-distance buses, except some Cuzco services and buses to La Paz (see below), leave from the Terminal Terrestre, which is at 1 de Mayo 703 y Victoria, by the lake, T364733. It has a tourist office, snack bars and toilets. Platform tax US$0.50. Small buses and colectivos for Juliaca, Ilave and towns on the lake shore between Puno and Desaguadero, including Yunguyo, leave from the Terminal Zonal, Av Bolívar between Jrs Carabaya and Palma. To **Juliaca**, 44 km, 1 hr, bus US$1, minbus US$2. Daily buses to **Arequipa**, 5 hrs via Juliaca, 297 km, most buses take this route, US$15 (**Destinos**, **Julsa**, **Señor de Milagros**, or **Sur Oriente**, most have a morning and evening bus – better quality buses go at night); **Cruz del Sur**, T368524, US$19-25. To **Moquegua**, US$7.50-9, and **Tacna**, US$18. To **Lima**, 1011 km, 21 hrs, all buses go through **Arequipa**, sometimes with a change of bus. See Arequipa, page 175. For services to La Paz or Copacabana (Bolivia), see page 202.

To **Cuzco**, 388 km, 5-7 hrs. There are 3 levels of service: regular via Juliaca, US$12, 7 hrs; direct, without stopping in Juliaca, with **Tour Perú**, Jr Tacna, T365517, www.tourperu.com.pe, at 0800, US$15 and 2130 (*bus cama* US$18), 6 hrs; tourist service with 5 stops (Pukará, Sicuani for lunch, La Raya, Raqchi and Andahuaylillas), leave at 0730, US$60, includes lunch, 10 hrs, with **Inka Express**, Jr Tacna 346 and at the Terminal Terrestre, T365654, www.inkaexpress.com.pe (leaves from the Terminal and may pick up from hotel on request), **First Class**, Tacna 280-300, T364640, or **Turismo Mer**, Jr Tacna 336, T367223, www.turismomer.com. In high season, reserve 2 days ahead. **Note** It is advisable to travel by day, for safety as well as for the views. If you wish to travel by bus and cannot go direct, it is no problem to take separate buses to Juliaca, then to Sicuani, then to Cuzco.

To **Puerto Maldonado**, several daily along Route 4 of the Interoceanic Highway, a dramatic road via Juliaca, the San Gabán gorge and **Mazuko**, where the branches of the new road from Cuzco, Puerto Maldonado and Juliaca converge, **Transporte Santa Cruz**, US$27, 10-12 hrs. Other services start from Juliaca or from Arequipa via Juliaca.

Boats on Lake Titicaca Boats to the islands leave from the terminal in the harbour (see map); *trici-taxi* from centre, US$1.

Taxi 3-wheel 'Trici-Taxis', cost about US$0.25 per km and are the best way to get around.

Trains The railway runs from Puno to Juliaca (44 km), where it divides, to Cuzco (381 km) and Arequipa (279 km; no passenger service). To **Cuzco**, *Andean Explorer*, US$156, Cuzco to Puno US$268, Mon, Wed, Fri (Apr-Oct) and Sat at 0800, arriving in Cuzco at about 1800; try to sit on the right hand side for the views. The train stops at La Raya. The ticket office is open 0700-1700 Mon-Fri, 0700-1200 Sat, Sun and holidays; in high season buy several days in advance, passport required. The station is well guarded by police and sealed off to those without tickets.

Llachón p191

Boats Only 1 weekly public boat from Llachón to **Puno**, Fri 0900, returning to Llachón Sat 1000, US$1.50, 3½ hrs. The daily 0800 boat to Amantaní may drop you off at Colata (at the tip of the peninsula), a 1-hr walk from Llachón, confirm details in advance. Returning to Puno, you can try to flag down the boat from Amantaní which passes Colata between 0830 and 0930. In Santa María (Llachón), boats can be hired for trips to **Amantaní** (40 mins) and **Taquile** (50 mins), US$30 return, minimum 10 passengers. **Combis** run daily from Bellavista market (known as El Contrabando) in Puno to **Capachica**, from 0700 to1600, 1½ hrs, US$1.35, where you get another combi or bus to **Llachón**, leave when full, 30 mins, US$1.

⊙ Directory

Puno *p188, map p190*
Consulates Bolivia, Jr Arequipa 136, T351251, consular visas take about 48 hrs, Mon-Fri 0800-1400. **Useful addresses** Immigration: Ayacucho 280, T357103, Mon-Fri 0800-1300, 1500-1700.

The islands

The Uros
ⓘ *US$2 entry.*

The people of Uros or the 'floating islands' in Puno Bay fish, hunt birds and live off the lake plants, most important of which are the reeds they use for their boats, houses and the very foundations of their islands. Visitors to the floating islands encounter more women than men. These women wait every day for the tour boats to sell their handicrafts. The few men one does see might be building or repairing boats or fixing their nets. The rest are out on the lake, hunting and fishing. The Uros cannot live from tourism alone and it is better to buy handicrafts or pay for services than just to tip. They glean extra income from tourists offering overnight accommodation in reed houses, selling meals and providing Uro guides for two-hour tours. Organized tour parties are usually given a boat building demonstration and the chance to take a short trip in a reed boat. Some islanders will also greet boat loads of tourists with a song and will pose for photos. The islanders, who are very friendly, appreciate gifts of pens, paper, etc for their two schools. This form of tourism on the Uros Islands is now well-established and, whether it has done irreparable harm or will ultimately prove beneficial, it takes place in superb surroundings. Take drinking water as there is none on the islands.

Taquile
ⓘ US$3 to land. Contact Munay Taquile, the island's community-based travel agency, Titicaca 508, Puno, T351448, www.taquile.net
Isla Taquile, 45 km from Puno, on which there are numerous pre-Inca and Inca ruins, and Inca terracing, is only about 1 km wide, but 6-7 km long. Ask for the (unmarked) **museum of traditional costumes**, which is on the plaza. There is a co-operative shop on the plaza that sells exceptional woollen goods, which are not cheap, but of very fine quality. Each week different families sell their products. Shops on the plaza sell postcards, water and dry goods. The principal festivals are from 2-7 June, and the **Fiesta de Santiago** from 25 July to 2 August, with many dances in between. Native guides in Taquile, some speaking English and/or German, charge US$5 for two-hour tours. If you are staying over, you are advised to take some food, particularly fruit, bread and vegetables, water, plenty of small-value notes, candles and a torch, toilet paper and a sleeping bag. Take precautions against sunburn and take warm clothes for the cold nights. It is worth spending a night on Taquile to observe the daily flurry of activity around the boatloads of tourists: demonstrations of traditional dress and weaving techniques, the preparation of trout to feed the hordes. When the boats leave, the island breathes a gentle sigh and people slowly return to their more traditional activities.

Amantaní
ⓘ US$3 to land.
Another island worth visiting, is Amantaní, very beautiful and peaceful. There are six villages and ruins on both of the island's peaks, **Pacha Tata** and **Pacha Mama**, from which there are excellent views. There are also temples and on the shore there is a throne carved out of stone, the **Inkatiana**. On both hills, a fiesta is celebrated on 15-20 January, **Pago a la Tierra or San Sebastián**. The festivities are very colourful, musical and hard-drinking. There is also a festival on 9 April, **Aniversario del Consejo** (of the local council), and a **Feria de Artesanías**, 8-16 August. The residents make beautiful textiles and sell them quite cheaply at the Artesanía Cooperativa. They also make basketwork and stoneware. The people are Quechua speakers, but understand Spanish. Islanders arrange dances for tour groups (independent travellers can join in), visitors dress up in local clothes and join the dances. Small shops sell water and snacks.

Anapia and Yuspique
In the Peruvian part of the Lago Menor are the islands of **Anapia**, a friendly, Aymara-speaking community, and **Yuspique**, on which are ruins and vicuñas. The community has organized committees for tourism, motor boats, sailing boats and accommodation with families (**All Ways Travel**, see page 195, arranges tours). To visit Anapia independently, take a colectivo from Yunguyo to Tinicachi and alight at Punta Hermosa, just after Unacachi. Boats to Anapia leave Punta Hermosa on Sunday and Thursday at 1300 (they leave Anapia for Yunguyo market on the same days at 0630); bus from Puno on Sunday, Tuesday, Thursday, US$6. It's two hours each way by boat. On the island ask for José Flores, who is very knowledgeable about Anapia's history, flora and fauna. He sometimes acts as a guide.

The islands listings

For hotel and restaurant price codes, and other relevant information, see pages 14-17.

Where to stay

The Uros *p196*
Oscar Coyla, T051-951-824378 is the representative for the Uros community. Accommodation costs US$5 pp, simple meals are extra or US$10 pp full board including tour. **René Coyla Coila**, T051-951-743533 is an official tour guide who can advise on lodging and **Armando Suaña**, T051-951-341374 is another native guide offering accommodation in Kantati.

Taquile *p197*
The Community Tourism Agency **Munay Taquile** (see above) can arrange accommodation in a **Casa Rural**, **Albergue Rural**, or **Hotel Rural**. Someone will approach you when you get off the boat if you don't have anything booked in advance. Lodging rates US$15-25 pp full board. Most Taquileños have a room in which they can accommodate visitors (*Casa Rural*). Since some families have become the favourites of tour groups they have been able to build bigger and better facilities (eg with showers and loos) (*Albergue* or *Hotel Rural*) and those which are in need of the income are often shunned as their facilities may be more basic. Instead of staying in the busy part around the main square, the Huayllano community is hosting visitors. This is on the south side of the island. Contact **Alipio Huatta Cruz**, T051-951-668551 or T951-615239 or you can arrange a visit with **All Ways Travel**, see page 195.

Amantaní *p197*
The **Presidente del Comité Turístico de Amantaní** is Senón Tipo Huatta, T051-951-832 308. Rate is up to US$25 pp full board. If you are willing to walk to a more distant communities, you might get a better price and you are helping to share the income. Some families that one can contact are:
$$ Kantuta Lodge, T051-630238, T951-636172, www.kantutalodge.com, run by Richard Cari and family, full board; **Hospedaje Jorge Cari**, basic, but nice family, great view of lake from room, or **Ambrosio Mamani**; or **Familia Victoriano Calsin Quispe**, Casilla 312, Isla Amantaní, T051-360220/363320.

Restaurants

Taquile *p197*
There are many small restaurants around the plaza and on the track to the Puerto Principal (eg Gerardo Huatta's **La Flor de Cantuta**, on the steps; **El Inca** on the main plaza). Meals are generally fish, rice and chips, omelette and *fiambre*, a local stew. Meat is rarely available and drinks often run out. Breakfast consists of pancakes and bread.

Amantaní *p197*
There is 1 restaurant, **Samariy**. The artificially low price of tours allows families little scope for providing anything other than basic meals, so take your own supplies if you so wish.

Transport

The Uros *p196*
Boat Asociación de Transporte los Uros, at the port, T368024, aeuttal@hotmail.com, 0800-1600. Motorboat US$5, 0600-1600 or whenever there are 10 people. Agencies charge US$12-15.

Taquile *p197*
Boats Centro de Operadores de Transporte Taquile, at the port, T205477, 0600-1100, 1400-1800. In high season, boats go at 0730 and 0800, stopping at the **Uros** on the way, returning at 1400 and 1430, in low season only one boat travels, US$7.50 one way. Organized tours cost US$18-25.

Amantaní *p197*
Boats Transportes Unificados Amantaní,
at the port, T369714, 0800-1100. 2 daily
boats at 0815, one direct, the 2nd one stops
at Uros, they return at 0800 the next day, one
directo **Puno**, the 2nd one stops at **Taquile**.
US$7.50 one way direct, US$18 return with
stops at **Uros** and Taquile. Amantaní-Taquile
costs US$3. If you stop in Taquile on the way
back, you can continue to Puno at 1200 with
the Amantaní boat or take a Taquile boat at
1400 (also 1430 in high season). Purchasing
one-way tickets gives you more flexibility if
you wish to stay longer on the islands.

To Cuzco

Juliaca → *Phone code: 051. Colour map 3, B2. Population: 134,700. Altitude: 3825 m.*
Freezing cold at night, hygienically challenged and less than safe, Juliaca, 289 km northeast
of Arequipa, is not particularly attractive. As the commercial focus of an area bounded by
Puno, Arequipa and the jungle, it has grown very fast into a noisy chaotic place with a
large impermanent population, lots of contraband and more *tricitaxis* than cars. Monday,
market day, is the most disorganized of all. A Sunday woollens market, **La Dominical**, is
held near the exit to Cuzco. The handicrafts gallery, **Las Calceteras**, is on Plaza Bolognesi.
Túpac Amaru market, on Moquegua seven blocks east of railway line, is a cheap market.
Tourist office, Dircetur ⓘ *Jr Noriega 191, p 3, T321839, Mon-Fri 0730-1530.*

The unspoiled little colonial town of **Lampa**, 31 km northwest of Juliaca is known as
the 'Pink City'. It has a splendid church, La Inmaculada, containing a copy of Michelangelo's
'Pietà' cast in aluminium (guided tours of the church, crypt and mausoleum, US$3.50),
many Cuzqueña school paintings and a carved wooden pulpit. To see a plaster copy of
the 'Pietà' in the Municipalidad, a donation is requested. **Kampac Museo** ⓘ *Jr Ayacucho y
Alfonso Ugarte, T951-820085, owner Profesor Jesús Vargas can be found at the shop opposite,
no charge for admission and tour but contributions appreciated,* small private museum
featuring an eclectic collection of sculptures and ceramics from a number of Peruvian
cultures. Lampa has a small Sunday market and celebrates a fiesta of **Santiago Apóstol** on
6-15 December. There is a fine colonial bridge just south of the town.

At Pucará, 63 km west of Juliaca on the road to Cuzco, Route 4, a fully paved branch
of the Interoceanic Highway, heads north across the vast alpaca-grazed altiplano to
Macusani (4400 m, always cold, basic hotels). The dramatic road then descends past the
mining supply towns of Olachea and San Gabán, to Puente Iñambari, Mazuko and Puerto
Maldonado. This off-the-beaten-path route through the Cordillera Carabaya connects
Lake Titicaca and the southern jungle (see Transport below). Along the way are rock
formations, petroglyphs and the glaciated summits of Allin Cápac surrounded by lakes
and valleys ideal for trekking.

Puno to Cuzco
The road Puno–Juliaca–Cuzco is fully paved and in good condition. Bus services are an
acceptable alternative to the train, at an average altitude of 3500 m. There is much to see
on the way, but neither the daytime buses nor the trains make frequent stops. You would
have to be using your own transport, or taking buses from town to town to sample what
the places en route have to offer, eg pottery bulls at Pucará (rooms available at the station);
knitted alpaca ponchos and pullovers and miniature llamas at Santa Rosa (rooms available).
There are also hotels in **Ayaviri**, whose speciality is a mild, creamy cheese (US$4 per kg).

The road and railway crosses the altiplano, climbing to **La Raya**, the highest pass on
the line; 210 km from Puno, at 4321 m (local market; toilets US$0.20). Up on the heights

breathing may be a little difficult, but the descent along the Río Vilcanota is rapid. To the right of **Aguas Calientes**, the next station, 10 km from La Raya, are steaming pools of hot water in the middle of the green grass; a startling sight (US$0.15). The temperature of the springs is 40°C, and they show beautiful deposits of red ferro-oxide. Communal bathing pools and a block of changing rooms have been opened. At **Maranganí**, the river is wider and the fields greener, with groves of eucalyptus trees.

At 38 km beyond La Raya pass is **Sicuani** (*Phone code: 084; Altitude: 3690 m*), an important agricultural centre. Excellent items of llama and alpaca wool and skins are sold on the railway station and at the Sunday morning market. Around Plaza Libertad are several hat shops. The bus terminal is in the newer part of town, which is separated from the older part and the Plaza by a pedestrian walkway and bridge. Several hotels (**$**) lie on the west side of the pedestrian bridge. (For more information about places between Sicuani and Cuzco, see page 231.)

● To Cuzco listings

For hotel and restaurant price codes, and other relevant information, see pages 14-17.

● Where to stay

Juliaca *p199*
The town has water problems in dry season.
$$$ Hotel Don Carlos, Jr 9 de Diciembre 114, Plaza Bolognesi, T323600, www.hotelesdon carlos.com. Comfortable, modern facilities, hot water, heater, good service, breakfast, restaurant and room service. Also has **Suites Don Carlos**, Jr M Prado 335, T321571.
$$ Royal Inn, San Román 158, T321561, www.royalinnhoteles.com. Rooms and suites with heaters, includes breakfast, good restaurant (**$$-$**).
$$ Sakura, San Román 133, T322072, hotelsakura@hotmail.com. Quiet, hot water, basic rooms in older section with shared bath.
$$-$ Hostal Luquini, Jr Brasesco 409, Plaza Bolognesi, T321510. Comfortable, patio, helpful staff, reliable hot water in morning only, motorcycle parking.

Lampa
$ Hospedaje Estrella, Jr Municipal 540. Simple rooms, with or without private bath, hot water, very friendly, breakfast included, a good alternative to staying in Juliaca.

● Restaurants

Juliaca *p199*
$ Dory's, Jr San Martín 347. Sun-Thu 0800-2000, Fri 0800-1400. Simple vegetarian.
$ El Asador, Unión 119. Open 1800-2400. Chicken, grill and pizza, good food and service, pleasant atmosphere.
Ricos Pan, Jr San Román y Jorge Chávez. Good bakery with café, popular.

● Transport

Juliaca *p199*
Air Manco Cápac airport is small but well organized. To/from **Lima**, 2¼ hrs, 3 a day with LAN (T322228 or airport T324448) via **Arequipa** (30 mins), **Cuzco** and direct, StarPerú (T326570) once a day via Arequipa, and **Avianca/TACA**, Beware overcharging for ground transportation. If you have little luggage, regular taxis and combis stop just outside the airport parking area. Taxi from Plaza Bolognesi, US$2.75; taxi from airport US$3.50, or less from outside airport gates. Airport transfers from **Puno** US$5.50 pp with Camtur, Jr Tacna 336, of 104, T951 967652 and Rossy Tours, Jr Tacna 308, T366709. Many Puno hotels offer an airport transfer. Taxi between Puno and the airport, about US$30. If taking regular public transport to Juliaca and a taxi to the airport from there,

allow extra time as the minibuses might drive around looking for passengers before leaving Puno.

Bus To **Puno**, minibuses from Jr Brasesco near Plaza Bolognesi, leave when full throughout the day, US$2, 1 hr. To **Capachica** for Llachón, from Cerro Colorado market, leave when full 0500-1700, US$2, 1½ hrs. To **Lampa**, cars (US$1) and combis (US$0.75) leave when full from Av Circunvalación, block 6 west, 30 mins.

Long distance The terminal terrestre is at the east end of San Martín (cuadra 9, past the Circunvalación). Most bus companies have their offices nearby on San Martín. To **Lima**, US$38 normal, US$70 'Imperial', 20 hrs; with **Ormeño** 1630, 2000. To **Cuzco**, US$8-17, 5-6 hrs; **Power** (T321952) hourly, several others. To **Arequipa**, US$15, 4-5 hrs,

Julsa (T331952) hourly, several others. To **Puerto Maldonado** via **Mazuko**, where the branches of the Interoceanic Highway from Cuzco, Puerto Maldonado and Juliaca converge, US$27, 12 hrs; several companies leave from M Nuñez cuadra 11, "El Triángulo" by the exit to Cuzco, 1300-1500. To **Macusani**, Alianza (Av Ferrocarril y Cahuide) 1300, 1700, 1815, US$3.50, 3 hrs; **Jean** (M Núñez y Pje San José), 0845, 1330, 1800; also minibuses from Pje San José, leave when full, US$4.25. See below for how to get to the Bolivian border and page 202 for transport.

Puno to Cuzco: Sicuani *p200*
Bus To Pucará, Ayaviri and Azángaro, from Las Mercedes terminal. To **Cuzco**, 137 km, US$1.50.

Border with Bolivia → *Peruvian time is 1 hr behind Bolivian time.*

There are three different routes across the border:

Puno-La Paz via Yunguyo and Copacabana Peruvian immigration is five minutes' drive from **Yunguyo** and 500 m from the Bolivian post; open 0700-2000 (Peruvian time), Bolivian immigration is open 0730-1930 (Bolivian time). Be aware of corruption here and look out for official or unofficial people trying to charge you a fee, on either side of the border (say that you know it is illegal and ask why only gringos are approached to pay the 'embarkation tax').

Bolivian consulate is at Jr Grau 339, T856032, near the main plaza in Yunguyo, open Monday-Friday 0830-1500. US citizens need a visa for Bolivia, it can be obtained in advance or right at the border (see Bolivia chapter for details). There are a couple of *casas de cambio* on the Peruvian side of the border offering slightly lower rates than in Yunguyo, but better rates than the shops on the Bolivian side. US dollars cash and soles can also be exchanged at *cambios* in Copacabana. In Yunguyo best rates for US dollars cash and Bolivianos at **Farmacia Loza**, Jr Bolognesi 567, Plaza 2 de Mayo. Also *cambios* on Plaza de Armas, and street changers who deal in dollars, bolivianos and euros.

Puno-Desaguadero Desaguadero is a bleak unsavoury place, with poor restaurants and dubious accommodation. Friday is the main market day, when the town is packed. There is a smaller market on Tuesday and at other times Desaguadero is deserted. There is no need to stop here as all roads to it are paved and if you leave La Paz, Moquegua or Puno early enough you should be at your destination before nightfall. Minibuses Puno-Desaguadero hourly 0600-1900, 2½ hours, US$2. Taxi US$33. **Peruvian border office** is open 0700-2000, Bolivian 0830-2030 (both local time). It is easy to change money on the Peruvian side. This particular border crossing allows you to stop at Tiahuanaco en route.

Along the east side of Lake Titicaca This is the most remote route, via **Huancané**, **Moho** (several basic *hostales*), **Cambria** (access to Isla Suasi), **Conima** and **Tilali**. Some walking may be involved between Tilali and **Puerto Acosta** (Bolivia, 13 km). Make sure you get an exit stamp in Puno, post-dated by a couple of days. From Juliaca there are minibuses to Huancané, Moho and Tilali, the last village in Peru with very basic lodgings (see Transport, below). The road is all paved. From Tilali it is 3-km walk to the international frontier. Puerto Acosta in Bolivia is a further 10 km. You must get a preliminary entry stamp at the police station on the plaza, then the definitive entry stamp at Migración in La Paz.

◉ Border with Bolivia listings

For hotel and restaurant price codes, and other relevant information, see pages 14-17.

◉ Where to stay

Border with Bolivia: Yunguyo *p201*
$ Hostal Isabel, San Francisco 110, near Plaza de Armas, T951-794228. With or without bath, nice rooms and courtyard, electric shower, parking, friendly. A few other cheap places to stay.

North shore of Lake Titicaca
$$$$ Hotel Isla Suasi, T01-213 9739, a Casa Andina Private Collection hotel, www.casa-andina.com. This is the only house on this tiny, tranquil, private island. There are beautiful gardens, best Jan-Mar. The non-native eucalyptus trees are being replaced by native varieties. You can take a canoe around the island to see birds and the island has vicuñas, a small herd of alpacas and vizcachas. The sunsets from the highest point are beautiful. Facilities are spacious, comfortable and solar-powered, rooms with bath, hot water, hot water bottles. Price includes full board, national drinks, entrance to island, all transport (suite boat from Puno 2¼ hrs direct), services and taxes. Massage room and sauna, internet extra.

◉ Transport

Border with Bolivia: Yunguyo *p201*
Bus The road is paved from Puno to Yunguyo and the lakeside scenery is interesting. From Puno to **Copacabana**,

US$8, 3 hrs, and **La Paz**, US$18, the best direct services are with **Tour Peru**, Jr Tacna, www.tourperu.com.pe, direct service to Copacabana leave Puno daily at 0730, and to La Paz at 0700. **Panamericano**, Jr Tacna 245, T369010, and **Litoral** (at Terminal Terrestre, cheaper, but thefts reported on night buses).

To **Yunguyo**, from the Terminal Regional in Puno, minibuses hourly 0600-1900, 2½ hrs, US$2.70 (return from Jr Cusco esq Arica, 1 block from Plaza 2 de Mayo). From Yunguyo to the border (Kasani), from Jr Titicaca y San Francisco, 1 block from Plaza de Armas, shared taxis US$0.30 pp, taxi US$2.50, 5 mins. From Kasani to Copacabana, minibuses US$0.50, taxi US$3, 8 km, 15 mins. **Note** Don't take a taxi Yunguyo-Puno without checking its reliability first, driver may pick up an accomplice to rob passengers.
To La Paz by hydrofoil or catamaran There are luxury services combining bus and boat travel from Puno to La Paz by **Crillon Tours** hydrofoil, www.titicaca.com, with connections to tours, from La Paz, to Cuzco and Machu Picchu. Similar services, by catamaran, are run by **Transturin**, www.transturin.com (Jr Puno 633, of 3, Puno).

East side of Lake Titicaca *p202*
From Juliaca, minibuses for **Moho** via **Huancané** depart when full throughout the day from Jr Moquegua y Av El Maestro, north of Mercado Tupac Amaru, US$2.20, 1½ hrs. Minibuses for **Tilali** depart when full from Jr Lambayeque y Av Circunvalación

Este, also near the market, US$3.60, 3 hrs. On market days trucks may go to Puerto Acosta and La Paz. Try hitching to catch bus from **Puerto Acosta** to **La Paz** (daily) about 1400 (note Bolivian time is 1 hr ahead of Peru), more frequent service on Sun, 5 hrs, US$6. If you miss the bus, ask the truck to drop you off 25 km further in Escoma, from where there are frequent minivans to La Paz. Buses leave La Paz for Puerto Acosta at 0600 daily. Transport from Puerto Acosta to border only operates on market days, mostly cargo trucks.

Cuzco

The ancient Inca capital is said to have been founded around AD 1100, and since then has developed into a major commercial and tourism centre of 428,000 inhabitants, most of whom are Quechua. Today, colonial churches, monasteries and convents and extensive pre-Columbian ruins are interspersed with countless hotels, bars and restaurants that cater to the over one million tourists who visit every year. Almost every central street has remains of Inca walls, arches and doorways; the perfect Inca stonework now serves as the foundations for more modern dwellings. This stonework is tapered upwards (battered); every wall has a perfect line of inclination towards the centre, from bottom to top. The curved stonework of the Temple of the Sun, for example, is probably unequalled in the world.

Arriving in Cuzco → *Phone code: 084. Colour map 4, C3. Altitude: 3310 m.*

Orientation The **airport** is to the southeast of the city and the road into the centre goes close to Wanchac station, at which **trains** from Puno arrive. The **bus terminal** is near the Pachacútec statue in Ttio district. Transport to your hotel is not a problem from any of these places by taxi or in transport arranged by hotel representatives.

The centre of Cuzco is quite small and possible to explore on foot. Taxis in Cuzco are cheap and recommended when arriving by air, train or bus and especially when returning to your hotel at night. On arrival in Cuzco, respect the altitude: two or three hours rest after arriving makes a great difference; avoid meat and smoking, eat lots of carbohydrates and drink plenty of clear, non-alcoholic liquid; remember to walk slowly. To see Cuzco and the surrounding area properly (including Pisac, Ollantaytambo, Chinchero and Machu Picchu) you need five days to a week, allowing for slowing down because of the altitude. → *See Transport, page 226.*

Tourist information **Official tourist information** ① *Portal Mantas 117-A, next to La Merced church, T222032, Mon-Sat 0800-2000, Sun 0800-1300.* **i perú** ① *at the airport, T237364, daily 0800-1600; also at Av El Sol 103, of 102, Galerías Turísticas, T252974; iperucusco@promperu. gob.pe, daily 0830-1930.* **Dircetur** ① *Plaza Túpac Amaru Mz 1 Lte 2, Wanchac, T223761, Mon-Fri 0800-1300,* gives out good map. Other information sources include **South American Explorers** ① *Atocsaycuchi 670, T245484, www.saexplorers.org, Mon-Fri 0930-1700, Sat 0930-1300.* It's worth making the climb up the steps to the large new clubhouse which has a garden. Sells good city map, members get many local discounts, has comprehensive recycling centre. As with SAE's other clubhouses, this is the place to go for specialized information, member-written trip reports and maps. Also has rooms for rent. For full details on South American Explorers, see page 34. Many churches close to visitors on Sunday. See also www.aboutcusco.com and www.cuscoonline.com.

Inca society

Cuzco was the capital of the Inca empire – one of the greatest planned societies the world has known – from its rise during the 11th century to its death in the early 16th century. (See John Hemming's *Conquest of the Incas* and B C Brundage's *Lords of Cuzco* and *Empire of the Inca*.) It was solidly based on other Peruvian civilizations which had attained great skill in textiles, building, ceramics and working in metal. Immemorially, the political structure of the Andean *indígena* had been the *ayllu*, the village community; it had its divine ancestor, worshipped household gods, was closely knit by ties of blood to the family and by economic necessity to the land, which was held in common. Submission to the *ayllu* was absolute, because it was only by such discipline that food could be obtained in an unsympathetic environment. All the domestic animals, the llama and alpaca and the dog, had long been tamed, and the great staple crops, maize and potatoes, established. What the Incas did – and it was a magnificent feat – was to conquer enormous territories and impose upon the variety of *ayllus*, through an unchallengeable central government, a willing spiritual and economic submission to the State. The common religion, already developed by the classical Tiwanaku culture, was worship of the Sun, whose vice-regent on earth was the absolute Sapa Inca. Around him, in the capital, was a religious and secular elite which never froze into a caste because it was open to talent. The elite was often recruited from chieftains defeated by the Incas; an effective way of reconciling local opposition. The mass of the people were subjected to rigorous planning. They were allotted land to work, for their group and for the State; set various tasks (the making of textiles, pottery, weapons, ropes, etc) from primary materials supplied by the functionaries, or used in enlarging the area of cultivation by building terraces on the hill-sides. Their political organization was simple but effective. The family, and not the individual, was the unit. Families were grouped in units of 10, 100, 500, 1000, 10,000 and 40,000, each group with a leader responsible to the next largest group. The Sapa Inca crowned the political edifice; his four immediate counsellors were those to whom he allotted responsibility for the northern, southern, eastern and western regions (suyos) of the empire.

Equilibrium between production and consumption, in the absence of a free price mechanism and good transport facilities, must depend heavily upon statistical information. This the Incas raised to a high degree of efficiency by means of their *quipus*: a decimal system of recording numbers by knots in cords. Seasonal variations were guarded against by creating a system of state barns in which provender could be stored during years of plenty, to be used in years of scarcity. Statistical efficiency alone required that no one should be permitted to leave his home or his work. The loss of personal liberty was the price paid by the masses for economic security. In order to obtain information and to transmit orders quickly, the Incas built fine paved pathways along which couriers sped on foot. The whole system of rigorous control was completed by the greatest of all their monarchs, Pachacuti, who also imposed a common language, Quechua, as a further cementing force.

Visitors' tickets A combined entry ticket, called *Boleto Turístico de Cusco* (BTC), is available to most of the sites of main historical and cultural interest in and around the city, and costs as follows: 130 soles (US$46/35) for all the sites and valid for 10 days; or 70 soles (US$25/19) for either the museums in the city, or Sacsayhuaman, Qenqo, Puka Pukara and Tambo Machay, or Pisac, Ollantaytambo, Chinchero and Moray; the 70 soles ticket is valid for one day. The BTC can be bought at the offices of **Cositic** ⓘ *Av El Sol 103, of 102, Galerías Turísticas, T261465, Mon-Sat 0800-1800, Sun 0800-1300, or Yuracpunku 79-A (east of centre, go along Recoleta), www.cosituc.gob.pe or www.boletoturisticocusco.net*, or at any of the sites included in the ticket. For students with an ISIC card the BTC costs 70 soles (US$25), which is only available at the Cosituc office upon presentation of the ISIC card. Take your ISIC card when visiting the sites, as some may ask to see it. Photography is not allowed in the churches, nor in museums.

Entrance tickets for the Santo Domingo/Qoricancha, the Inka Museum (El Palacio del Almirante) and La Merced are sold separately, while the Cathedral (including El Triunfo and La Sagrada Familia), La Compañía, San Blas and the Museo de Arte Religioso del Arzobispado are included on a religious buildings ticket which costs 50 soles (US$17.50) and is valid for 10 days. Each of these sites may be visited individually. Machu Picchu ruins and Inca trail entrance tickets are sold electronically at www.machupicchu.gob.pe, at the **Dirección Regional de Cultura Cusco** ⓘ *Av de la Cultura 238, Condominio Huáscar, T236061, www.drc-cusco.gob. pe, Mon-Fri 0715-1600, and other outlets listed on the www.machupicchu.gob.pe website.*

Security Police patrol the streets and stations, but still be vigilant. On no account walk back to your hotel after dark from a bar or club, strangle muggings and rape do occur. Pay for a taxi called by the club's doorman and make sure the taxi is licensed. Other areas in which to take care include San Pedro market (otherwise recommended), the San Cristóbal area, and at out-of-the-way ruins. Also take special care during Inti Raymi. **Tourist Police** ⓘ *Plaza Túpac Amaru, Wanchac, T512351 or T235123, polturcusco_74@hotmail.com*. If you need a *denuncia* (report for insurance purposes), which is available from the Banco de la Nación, they will type it out. Always go to the police when robbed, even though it will cost you some time. **Indecopi** ⓘ *Av Manco Inca 209, Wanchac, T252987, mmarroquin@indecopi.gob.pe; toll free T0800-44040 (24-hr hotline, not available from payphones,* is the consumer protection bureau.

Places in Cuzco

The heart of the city in Inca days was *Huacaypata* (the place of tears) and *Cusipata* (the place of happiness), divided by a channel of the Saphi River. Today, Cusipata is Plaza Regocijo and Huacaypata is the Plaza de Armas, around which are colonial arcades and four churches. To the northeast is the early 17th-century baroque **Cathedral** ⓘ *US$9, daily 1000-1800*. It is built on the site of the Palace of Inca Wiracocha (*Kiswarcancha*). The high altar is solid silver and the original altar *retablo* behind it is a masterpiece of Andean wood carving. The earliest surviving painting of the city can be seen, depicting Cuzco during the 1650 earthquake. In the far right hand end of the church is an interesting local painting of the Last Supper replete with *cuy, chicha,* etc. In the sacristy are paintings of all the bishops of Cuzco. The choir stalls, by a 17th-century Spanish priest, are a magnificent example of colonial baroque art. The elaborate pulpit and the sacristy are also notable. Much venerated is the crucifix of El Señor de los Temblores, the object of many pilgrimages and viewed all over Peru as a guardian against earthquakes. The tourist entrance to the Cathedral is through the church of **La Sagrada Familia** (1733), which stands to its left as you face it. Its gilt main altar has been renovated. **El Triunfo** (1536), on the right of the

Cathedral, is the first Christian church in Cuzco, built on the site of the Inca Roundhouse (the *Suntur Huasi*). It has a statue of the Virgin of the Descent, reputed to have helped the Spaniards repel Manco Inca when he besieged the city in 1536.

On the southeast side of the plaza is the beautiful **La Compañía de Jesús** ⓘ *US$3.55, or by religious buildings ticket, daily 0900-1750*, built on the site of the Palace of the Serpents (*Amarucancha*, residence of Inca Huayna Capac) in the late 17th century. Its twin-towered exterior is extremely graceful, and the interior rich in fine murals, paintings and carved altars. Nearby is the **Santa Catalina church** ⓘ *Arequipa at Santa Catalina Angosta, daily 0900-1200, 1300-1700, except Fri 0900-1200, 1300-1600, joint ticket with Santo Domingo US$5.25*, convent

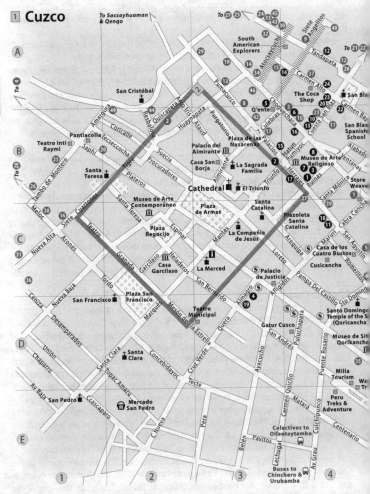

1 **Cuzco**

and museum, built upon the foundations of the *Acllahuasi* (House of the Chosen Women). There are guided tours by English-speaking students; tip expected. **Museo Machupicchu** (Casa Concha) ⓘ *Santa Catalina Ancha 320, T255535, Mon-Sat 0900-1700, US$7*, is a new museum which features objects found by Hiram Bingham during his initial excavations of Machu Picchu in 1912, returned by Yale University to the Peruvian government in 2010

If you continue down Arequipa from Santa Catalina you come to Calle Maruri. Between this street at Santo Domingo is **Cusicancha** ⓘ *US$1.75, Mon-Fri 0730-1600, sometimes open at weekends*, an open space showing the layout of the buildings as they would have been in Inca times.

➡ **Cuzco maps**
1 Cuzco, page 206
2 Around Plaza de Armas, page 208

Where to stay 🛏
1 Albergue Casa Campesina C4
2 Albergue Municipal B2
3 Andenes al Cielo B4
4 Cahuide A1
5 Casa Andina Koricancha C4
6 Casa Andina Private Collection Cusco C5
7 Casa Andina San Blas B5
8 Casa Cartagena A3
9 Casa de la Gringa A4
10 Casa Elena B4
11 Casa San Blas & Tika Bistro B4
12 Casona Les Pleiades A4
13 El Arqueólogo & Divina Comedia Restaurant A3
14 El Balcón Colonial A3
15 El Grial A3
16 El Mercado C1
17 El Monasterio B3
18 Estrellita C5
19 Flying Dog Hostel A3
20 Hitchhikers B&B Backpackers Hostel B2
21 Hosp El Artesano de San Blas A4
22 Hosp Inka A4
23 Hostal Amaru B4
24 Hostal Casa de Campo A3
25 Hostal El Balcón B1
26 Hostal Killipata B1
27 Hostal Kuntur Wasi A3
28 Hostal Loki B1
29 Hostal María Esther A3
30 Hostal Pakcha Real A4
31 Hostal Qorichaska C1
32 Hostal Tikawasi A3
33 La Encantada A3
34 Los Apus Hotel & Mirador A3
35 Maison de la Jeunesse D4
36 Mamá Simona Hostel C1
37 Marani A4
38 Niños/Hotel Meloc C1
39 Novotel C4
40 Palacio del Inka Luxury Collection C4
42 Palacio Nazarenas B3
43 Pensión Alemana A3
44 Piccola Locanda & L'Osteria Restaurant B2
45 Quinua Villa Boutique A3
46 Rumi Punku A3
47 Sonesta Hotel Cusco E6
48 The Blue House A4
49 The Walk on Inn B2

Restaurants 🍴
1 Aldea Yanapay B4
2 A Mi Manera B3
3 Baco B4
4 Café El Ayllu D3
5 Café Punchay A3
6 Chocolate B4
7 Cositas Café y Arte B4
8 El Encuentro B4
9 El Paisa E5
10 Granja Heidi B4
11 Inkanato C4
12 Inka Panaka A4
13 Jack's Café B4
14 Juanito's Sandwich Café A4
15 Justina B3
16 Kuska...fé B4
17 La Bodega 138 B4
18 Le Soleil C4
19 Los Toldos D3
20 Macondo A4
21 Manu Café E6
22 Pachapapa B4
23 Panadería El Buen Pastor A4
24 Venezia A4

Bars & clubs 🍷
25 Bar 7 A3
26 Km 0 (Arte y Tapas) A4
27 Museo del Pisco B4

100 metres
100 yards

N

La Merced ① *on Plazoleta Espinar, Calle Márquez, church Mon-Fri 0800-1700, Sat 0900-1600; monastery and museum 1430-1700, except Sun, US$1.* The church was first built 1534 and rebuilt in the late 17th century. Attached is a very fine monastery with an exquisite cloister. Inside the church are buried Gonzalo Pizarro, half-brother of Francisco, and the two Almagros, father and son. The church is most famous for its jewelled monstrance, which is on view in the monastery's museum during visiting hours.

Much **Inca stonework** can be seen in the streets and most particularly in the Callejón Loreto, running southeast past La Compañía de Jesús from the main plaza. The walls of the Acllahuasi (House of the Chosen Women) are on one side, and of the **Amarucancha** on the other. There are also Inca remains in Calle San Agustín, to the east of the plaza. The stone of 12 angles is in Calle Hatun Rumiyoc halfway along its second block, on the right-hand side going away from the Plaza. The **Palacio Arzobispal** stands on Hatun Rumiyoc y Herrajes, two blocks northeast of Plaza de Armas. It was built on the site of the palace occupied in 1400. It contains the **Museo de Arte Religioso** ① *0800-1800, included on the religious buildings ticket, or US$5.35,* a collection of colonial paintings and furniture. The collection includes the paintings by the indigenous master, Diego Quispe Tito, of a 17th-century Corpus Christi procession that used to hang in the church of Santa Ana.

The **Palacio del Almirante**, just north of the Plaza de Armas, is impressive. It houses the **Museo Inka** ① *Cuesta del Almirante 103, T237380, Mon-Fri 0800-1900, Sat 0900-1600,*

② Around Plaza de Armas

US$4, which is run by the Universidad San Antonio de Abad, the museum exhibits the development of culture in the region from pre-Inca, through Inca times to the present day: textiles, ceramics, metalwork, jewellery, architecture, technology. See the collection of miniature turquoise figures and other offerings to the gods. Weaving demonstrations are given in the courtyard. On the northwest side of the Plaza de las Nazarenas, No 231, is **Museo de Arte Precolombino** ⓘ *www.map.org.pe, 0900-2200, US$7, US$3.50 with student card; under same auspices as the Larco Museum in Lima, MAP Café (see Restaurants, page 216)*, housed in the **Casa Cabrera**. This beautiful museum is set around a spacious courtyard and contains many superb examples of pottery, metalwork (largely in gold and silver), wood carvings and shells from the Moche, Chimú, Paracas, Nazca and Inca cultures. There are some vividly rendered animistic designs, giving an insight into the way Peru's ancient people's viewed their world and the creatures that inhabited it. Every exhibit carries explanations in English and Spanish. Highly recommended. The **Convento de las Nazarenas**, also on Plaza de las Nazarenas, is now a hotel. You can see the Inca-colonial doorway with a mermaid motif, but ask permission to view the lovely 18th-century frescos inside. In the San Blas district, now firmly on the tourist map, the small church of **San Blas** ⓘ *Plazoleta San Blas, Carmen Bajo, 0800-1800, on the religious buildings ticket, or US$5.35* has a beautiful carved *mestizo* cedar pulpit, which is well worth seeing. **Museo Máximo Laura** ⓘ *Carmen Alto 133, T227383, http://museomaximolaura.com, daily 1000-2000,*

50 metres
50 yards

displays 24 prize-winning exhibits by this celebrated textile artist (see page 67), with workshop, gallery and shop. See also Shopping, page 220.

Santo Domingo, southeast of the main Plaza, was built in the 17th century on the walls of the **Qoricancha, Temple of the Sun** ① *Mon-Sat 0830-1730, Sun 1400-1700 (closed holidays), US$2, or joint ticket with Santa Catalina US$5.25, English-speaking guides, tip of US$2-3 expected*, and from its stones. Excavation has revealed more of the five chambers of the Temple of the Sun, which shows the best Inca stonework to be seen in Cuzco. The Temple of the Sun was awarded to Juan Pizarro, the younger brother of Francisco, who willed it to the Dominicans after he had been fatally wounded in the Sacsayhuaman siege. The baroque cloister has been gutted to reveal four of the original chambers of the great Inca temple – two on the west have been partly reconstructed in a good imitation of Inca masonry. The finest stonework is in the celebrated curved wall beneath the west end of Santo Domingo. This was rebuilt after the 1950 earthquake, at which time a niche that once contained a shrine was found at the inner top of the wall. Below the curved wall was a garden of gold and silver replicas of animals, maize and other plants. Excavations have revealed Inca baths below here, and more Inca retaining walls. The other superb stretch of late Inca stonework is in Calle Ahuacpinta outside the temple, to the east or left as you enter.

Museo de Sitio Qorikancha (formerly Museo Arqueológico) ① *Av El Sol, Mon-Sat 0900-1200, 1300-1700, Sun 0800-1400, entrance by BTC*, is under the garden below Santo Domingo. It contains a limited collection of pre-Columbian items, Spanish paintings of imitation Inca royalty dating from the 18th century, and photos of the excavation of Qoricancha. The palace called **Casa de los Cuatro Bustos**, whose colonial doorway is at San Agustín 400, is now the **Hotel Libertador**. The general public can enter the hotel from Plazoleta Santo Domingo, opposite the Temple of the Sun/Qoricancha.

Museo de Historia Regional ① *in the Casa Garcilaso, C Garcilaso y Heladeros, 0730-1700, entrance by BTC*, tries to show the evolution of the Cuzqueño school of painting. It also contains Inca agricultural implements, colonial furniture and paintings. **San Francisco** ① *on Plaza San Francisco, 3 blocks southwest of the Plaza de Armas, 0600-0800, 1800-2000*, is an austere church reflecting many indigenous influences. Its monastery is being rebuilt and may be closed. **San Pedro** ① *in front of the San Pedro market, Mon-Sat 1000-1200, 1400-1700*, was built in 1688. Its two towers were made from stones brought from an Inca ruin.

Museo de Plantas Sagradas, Mágicas y Medicinales ① *Santa Teresa 351, T222214, www.museoplantascusco.org, Mon-Sat 0800-2100, Sun 0800-1800, US$5.50*, has nine exhibition rooms detailing the history and uses of plants such as coca, Ayahuasca and San Pedro.

Above Cuzco, on the road up to Sacsayhuamán, is **San Cristóbal**, built to his patron saint by Cristóbal Paullu Inca. The church's atrium has been restored and there is a sidewalk access to the Sacsayhuamán Archaeological Park. North of San Cristóbal, you can see the 11 doorway-sized niches of the great Inca wall of the **Palacio de Colcampata**, which was the residence of Manco Inca before he rebelled against the Spanish and fled to Vilcabamba.

Sacsayhuaman

① *Daily 0700-1730; free student guides, give them a tip.*

There are some magnificent Inca walls in this ruined ceremonial centre, on a hill in the northern outskirts. The Incaic stones are hugely impressive. The massive rocks weighing up to 130 tons are fitted together with absolute perfection. Three walls run parallel for over 360 m and there are 21 bastions. Sacsayhuaman was thought for centuries to be a fortress, but the layout and architecture suggest a great sanctuary and temple to the Sun, which rises exactly opposite the place previously believed to be the Inca's throne – which was probably an altar, carved out of the solid rock. Broad steps lead to the altar from either side. The hieratic, rather than the military, hypothesis was supported by the discovery in 1982 of the graves of priests, who would have been unlikely to be buried in a fortress. The precise functions of the site, however, will probably continue to be a matter of dispute as very few clues remain, owing to its steady destruction. The site is about a 30-minute walk up Pumacurco from Plaza de las Nazarenas. A new Gran Museo del Tawantinsuyo was under construction here in 2014.

Along the road from Sacsayhuaman to Pisac, past a radio station, is the temple and amphitheatre of **Qenqo** with some of the finest examples of Inca stone carving *in situ*, especially inside the large hollowed-out stone that houses an altar. On the same road are **Puka Pukara** (Red Fort, but more likely to have been a *tambo*, or post-house), wonderful views; and the spring shrine of **Tambo Machay**, which is in excellent condition. Water still flows by a hidden channel out of the masonry wall, straight into a little rock pool traditionally known as the Inca's bath. Take a guide to the sites and visit in the morning for the best photographs. Carry your multi-site ticket, there are roving ticket inspectors. You can visit the sites on foot, a pleasant walk of at least half a day through the countryside; take water, sun protection, and watch out for dogs. Alternatively, take the Pisac bus or the Señor del Huerto combi up to Tambo Machay (US$0.70) and walk back.

◉ Cuzco listings

For hotel and restaurant price codes, and other relevant information, see pages 14-17.

● Where to stay

Cuzco *p203, maps p206 and p208*
Book more expensive hotels several months in advance, particularly for the week or so around **Inti Raymi**, when prices are greatly increased. Prices given are for the high season in Jun-Aug. When there are fewer tourists hotels may drop their prices by as much as half. Always check for discounts. Be wary of unlicensed hotel agents for medium-priced hotels who are often misleading about details; their local nickname is *jalagringos* (gringo pullers), or *piratas*. Taxis and tourist minibuses meet new arrivals and (should) take you to the hotel of your choice, but be insistent. Since it is cold here and many hotels have no heating, ask for an *estufa*, a heater which some places will provide for an extra charge. Many places will store your luggage when you go trekking, but always check valuables

and possessions before and after depositing them with hotel/hostel staff.

International chain hotels in Cuzco include **JW Marriott** (www.marriott.com), **Novotel** (www.novotel.com) and **Sonesta** (www.sonesta.com).

Around the Plaza de Armas
$$$$ Andean Wings, Siete Cuartones 225, T243166, www.andeanwingshotel.com. In a restored 17th-century house, in the same group as **Casa de la Gringa** and **Another Planet**, 5-star, intimate, suites, some with jacuzzi, are individually designed (one is accessible for the disabled), spa, restaurant and bar.
$$$$ The Fallen Angel Guest House, Plaza Nazarenas 221, T258184, www.fallenangel incusco.com. A 4-room luxury hotel above the restaurant of the same name. Each suite is decorated in its own lavish style (with living room, dining room, bathroom, feather duvets, heating), very comfortable and a far cry from the usual adaptation of colonial buildings elsewhere in the city. With all amenities, excellent service.

$$$$ La Casona Inkaterra, Plazoleta Las Nazarenas 113, T223010, www.inkaterra.com. A private, colonial-style boutique hotel in a converted 16th-century mansion, built on the site of Manco Cápac's palace. 11 exclusive suites, all facilities, concierge service with activities and excursions, highly-regarded and the height of luxury.

$$$ Casa Andina Classic – Cusco Plaza, Portal Espinar 142, T231733, www.casa-andina.com. 40-room hotel near plaza, ATM and safe deposit box. Equally recommendable are **Casa Andina Koricancha**, San Agustín 371, T252633, **Casa Andina Catedral**, Santa Catalina Angosta 149, T233661, and the **Casa Andina San Blas**, Chihuampata 278, San Blas, T263964, all of which are in the same vein.

$$$ Loreto Boutique Hotel, Pasaje Loreto 115, T226352, www.loretoboutiquehotel.com. Great location; 12 spacious rooms with original Inca walls, upgraded to "boutique" status. Laundry service, will help organize travel services including guides and taxis, free airport pick-up.

$$$ Marqueses, Garcilaso 256, T264249, www.hotelmarqueses.com. Spanish colonial style, with 16th/17th-century style religious paintings and 2 lovely courtyards. Rooms have heavy curtains and some are a little dark; luxury rooms have bath and shower. Buffet breakfast.

$$$ Sonesta Posadas del Inca, Portal Espinar 108, T712 6060, www.sonesta.com. Includes buffet breakfast, warmly decorated rooms with heating, safe, some rooms on 3rd floor have view of Plaza, very helpful, English spoken, restaurant with Andean food, excellent service.

$$$ Tierra Viva Cusco Plaza, Suecia 345, T245858, www.tierravivahoteles.com. Boutique hotel in the former residence of Gonzalo Pizarro. Rooms and suites have comfortable beds, heating, minibar, safe, with excellent breakfast. Exemplary service, airport transfers.

$$-$ EcoPackers Hostel, Santa Teresa 375, T231800, www.ecopackersperu.com.

Ecologically friendly, well-regarded hostal in a colonial *casona*, double rooms with en suite or dorms for 4-18 people, communal kitchen, games room, bar, large-screen TV room, Wi-Fi, garage for bicycles or motorcycles.

$ Hostal Resbalosa, Resbalosa 494, T224839, www.hostalresbalosa.com. Private or shared bath, hot water in the mornings and evenings, ask for a room with a view, dorm beds, laundry facilities, full breakfast extra.

$ Hostal Royal Frankenstein, San Juan de Dios 260, 2 blocks from the Plaza de Armas, T236999, www.hostal-frankenstein.net. Eccentric place but a frequent favourite, with private or shared bath, hot water, safe, kitchen, small charge for computer, heater and laundry, German-owned, German and English spoken.

$ Pariwana, Mesón de la Estrella 136, T233751, www.pariwana-hostel.com. Variety of rooms in a converted colonial mansion with courtyard, from doubles with bath to dorms sleeping 10, also girls only dorm, restaurant, bar/lounge, English spoken, lots of activities.

$ Pirwa Hostels, T244315, www.pirwahostelscusco.com. This chain of hostels offers a range of rooms from private doubles with bath to dorms, in colonial buildings, lockers, 24-hr reception: **Pirwa Suecia**, Suecia 300, the B&B branch; **Pirwa Posada del Corregidor**, Portal de Panes 151 (Plaza de Armas); **Pirwa Backpackers San Blas**, Carmen Alto 283, and **Pirwa Backpackers Colonial**, Plaza San Francisco 360.

$ The Point, Mesón de la Estrella 172, T252266, www.thepointhostels.com. Dormitory accommodation, also has doubles and singles, hot showers, good party atmosphere.

Beyond the Plaza, including San Blas
$$$$ Casa Andina Private Collection Cusco, Plazoleta de Limacpampa Chico 473, T232610, www.casa-andina.com. The most upmarket and comfortable in this group, in a 16th-century mansion with 4 courtyards, enriched oxygen available in the rooms, plus

a gourmet restaurant serving local cuisine and a bar with an extensive pisco collection.

$$$$ Casa Cartagena, Pumacurco 336, T261171, www.casacartagena.com. In a converted monastery and national heritage building, super-deluxe facilities with Italian design and colonial features, 4 levels of suite, **La Chola** restaurant, extensive complimentary Qoya spa, enriched oxygen system, and all services to be expected in a Luxury Properties group hotel.

$$$$ El Mercado, C Siete Cuartones 306, T582640, www.elmercadotunqui.com. On the site of a former market close to the Plaza de Armas, owned by **Mountain Lodges of Peru**, superior rooms and suites, restaurant, bar, helpful staff.

$$$$ El Monasterio (Belmond), C Palacios 136, Plazoleta Nazarenas, T604000, www. monasteriohotel.com. 5-star, beautifully restored Seminary of San Antonio Abad (a Peruvian National Historical Landmark), including the Baroque chapel, spacious comfortable rooms with all facilities (some rooms offer an oxygen-enriched atmosphere to help clients acclimatize), very helpful staff (buffet breakfast open to non-residents, will fill you up for the rest of the day), good restaurants, lunch and dinner à la carte, business centre with internet for guests.

$$$$ Palacio del Inka Luxury Collection, Plazoleta Santo Domingo 259, T231961, www. libertador.com.pe. 5-star, good, especially the service, warm and bright, **Inti Raymi** restaurant, excellent, live music in the evening.

$$$$ Palacio Nazarenas (Belmond), Plazoleta Nazarenas 144, T582222, www.palacionazarenas.com. Housed in a beautifully restored building, outdoor swimming pool, spa, history booklet and cooking classes. Opened in 2013.

$$$$-$$$ Casa San Blas, Tocuyeros 566, just off Cuesta San Blas, T237900, www. casasanblas.com. An international-standard boutique hotel with bright, airy rooms decorated with traditional textiles. Breakfast, served in the **Tika Bistro** downstairs. Pleasant balcony with good views, attentive service.

$$$ El Arqueólogo, Pumacurco 408, T232522, www.hotelarqueologo.com. Includes breakfast, hot water, heating extra, helpful, French and English spoken, will store luggage, garden, cafeteria and kitchen. Same group as **Vida Tours**, Ladrillo 425, T227750, www.vidatours.com. Traditional and adventure tourism.

$$$ Los Apus Hotel & Mirador, Atocsaycuchi 515 y Choquechaca, San Blas, T264243, www.losapushotel.com. Includes breakfast and airport transfer, full of character, very clean and smart, central heating, disabled facilities.

$$$ Rumi Punku, Choquechaca 339, T221102, www.rumipunku.com. An Inca doorway leading to a sunny courtyard, comfortable rooms, helpful staff, safe, sauna, jacuzzi, gym.

$$$-$$ Andenes al Cielo, Choquechaca 176, T222237, www.andenesalcielo.com. At the foot of the San Blas district, 15 rooms in renovated historic home, most expensive rooms have fireplaces, all with either balconies or patios, heating. Buffet breakfast, free airport pick up, gym.

$$$-$$ Cahuide, Saphi 845, T222771, www.hotelcahuide-cusco.com. Hot water, good rooms and suites, quiet, good laundry service, helpful, good value breakfasts.

$$$-$$ Hostal Casa de Campo, Tandapata 298 (at the end of the street), T244404, www. hotelcasadecampo.com. Some of the top rooms have a *lot* of steps up to them, hot water, includes bus/airport/rail transfer with reservations, 10% discount for Footprint book owners, safe deposit box, sun terrace, quiet, relaxing, all rooms have great views, Dutch and English spoken, take a taxi after dark.

$$$-$$ Hostal El Balcón, Tambo de Montero 222, T236738, www.balconcusco. com. Warm atmosphere, very welcoming, quiet, laundry, sauna, bar, meals on request, English spoken, wonderful views, beautiful garden.

$$$-$$ Hostal Tikawasi, Tandapata 491, T231609, www.tikawasi.com. Includes heating, family-run, lovely garden overlooking the city. Stylish, modern rooms with good views, comfortable beds.

$$$-$$ La Encantada, Tandapata 354, T242206, www.encantadaperu.com. Good beds, rooftop spa, fabulous views of the city. Swiss-Peruvian owned.

$$$-$$ Piccola Locanda, Resbalosa 520, T252551, www.piccolalocanda.com. Steep walk up from the Plaza de Armas, colourful Peruvian/Italian-run B&B. Rooftop terrace with 360° views, excellent restaurant L'Osteria, a TV room, pleasant courtyard. Private or shared bath. Associated with **Perú Etico** tour company and 2 children's projects.

$$$-$$ Quinua Villa Boutique, Pasaje Santa Rosa A-8, T242646, www.quinua. com.pe. A beautifully built living museum, 5 different apartments, each with a different theme and kitchen.

$$$-$ Hostal Amaru, Cuesta San Blas 541, T225933, www.amaruhostal.com. Private or shared bath. Price includes airport/train/bus pick-up. Oxygen, kitchen for use in the evenings, laundry, book exchange. Rooms around a pretty colonial courtyard, some with no windows, good beds, pleasant, relaxing, some Inca walls. Also has **$$ Hostal Amaru II**, Chihuampata 642, San Blas, T223521, www.amaruhostal2.com, and **$$-$ Hostería de Anita**, Alabado 525-5, T225933, www.amaruhostal.com/hosteria_ de_anita, with rooms or dorm beds, safe, quiet, good breakfast.

$$ Casa Elena, Choquechaca 162, T241202, www.casaelenacusco.com. French/Peruvian hostel, very comfortable, helpful staff, good choice.

$$ Casona Les Pleiades, Tandapata 116, T506430, www.casona-pleiades.com. Small guesthouse in renovated colonial house, cosy and warm, generous hosts, hot water, video lounge and book exchange, café, free airport pickup with reservation, lots of info, being expanded in 2014.

$$ El Grial, Carmen Alto 112, T223012, www.hotelelgrial.com. Family-run, 2 star hostel, in a 17th-century building, coffee shop, laundry service.

$$ Hostal Kuntur Wasi, Tandapata 352-A, San Blas, T227570, www.hospedajekuntur wasi.com. Great views, cheaper without bath, use of kitchen and laundry (both extra), owner speaks a bit of English and is very helpful and welcoming, a pleasant place to stay.

$$ Hostal María Esther, Pumacurco 516, T224382, http://hostalmariaesther.free.fr/. Very comfortable, helpful, garden.

$$ Marani, Carmen Alto 194, San Blas, T249462, www.hostalmarani.com. Full of character, set around a courtyard, breakfast available, Dutch-owned hostel associated with **Hope Foundation** (www.stichtinghope. org), which builds schools, helps teachers and hospitals, good value.

$$ Niños/Hotel Meloc, Meloc 442, T231424, www.ninoshotel.com. Modern decor in colonial building. Hot water, excellent breakfast extra, restaurant, laundry service, luggage store, English spoken, run as part of the Dutch foundation **Niños Unidos Peruanos** and all profits are invested in projects to help street children. Also has **Niños 2/Hotel Fierro**, on C Fierro 476, T254611, with all the same features.

$$ Pensión Alemana, Tandapata 260, San Blas, T226861, www.cuzco.com.pe. Colonial-style modern building. Swiss owned, welcoming, comfortable, discount in low season.

$$-$ Flying Dog Hostel, Choquechaca 469, T253997, www.flyingdogperu.com. Shared and private rooms and family suites, bar, living room with TV and DVD, buffet breakfast.

$$-$ Hitchhikers B&B Backpackers Hostel, Saphi 440, T260079, www.hhikersperu.com. Located close to the plaza, mixture of dorms and 1- to 3-bed private rooms with private or shared bath, laundry service.

$$-$ Hostal Loki, Cuesta Santa Ana 601, T243705, www.lokihostel.com/en/cusco. Huge hostel in a restored viceroy's residence on the steep Cuesta Santa Ana, dorms and rooms set around a beautiful courtyard, comfortable beds, hot water, free internet. A great meeting place.

$$-$ Mamá Simona Hostel, Ceniza 364, San Pedro, near the market, T260408, www.mamasimona.com. Traditional old house with rooms around a courtyard, doubles (with heating) and dorms, duvets, shared bathrooms, hot water, towel rental, full breakfast available, laundry service, helpful.

$$-$ Hostal Qorichaska, Nueva Alta 458, some distance from centre, T228974, www.qorichaskaperu.com. Rooms are clean and sunny, the older ones have traditional balconies. Also has dorms, mixed and men or women only. Laundry service. A good choice.

$ Albergue Casa Campesina, Av Tullumayo 274, T233466. Shared bath, lovely place, funds support the Casa Campesina organization (www.cbc.org.pe), which is linked to local *campesina* communities (see also Store of the Weavers under Shopping, below).

$ The Blue House, Kiskapata 291 (parallel and above Tandapata), T242407, www.thebluehouse.info. Cosy family hostal, good value. Reductions for longer stays, meals (except breakfast) US$3, hot shower, DVDs, great views.

$ Casa de La Gringa, Tandapata y Pasñapacana 148, T241168, www.casadelagringa.com. Each room individually decorated, lots of art and colour, 24-hr hot water, DVD, CD player in the common areas, heaters in the main lounges. See also Another Planet (Tour operators), below.

$ El Balcón Colonial, Choquechaca 350, T238129, balconcolonial@hotmail.com. Family house, fairly basic rooms, hot showers, good home cooking, use of family kitchen, laundry facilities extra, comfortable, safe, generous hosts.

$ Estrellita, Av Tullumayo 445, parte Alta, T234134. Most rooms with shared bath, 2 with private bath, basic but excellent value, safe parking available for bikes.

$ Hospedaje El Artesano de San Blas, Suytucato 790, San Blas, T263968, manosandinas@yahoo.com. Many bright and airy rooms overlooking courtyard, quiet, taxis leave you at Plaza San Blas, then it's a steep walk uphill for 5-10 mins.

$ Hospedaje Inka, Suytuccato 848, T231995, http://hospedajeinka.weebly.com. Taxis leave you at Plaza San Blas, walk steeply uphill for 5-10 mins, or phone the hostal. Private or shared bath. Wonderful views, spacious rooms, very helpful owner, Américo.

$ Hostal Killipata, Killichapata 238, just off Tambo de Montero, T236668, www.hospedajekillipatacusco.com. Family-run lodging with variety of room sizes, private or shared bath, good showers, hot water and fully equipped kitchen. Breakfast is extra.

$ Hostal Pakcha Real, Tandapata 300, San Blas, T237484, www.hostalpakchareal.com. Family-run, hot water, relaxed, with or without bath. Breakfast, cooking and laundry facilities extra. Airport/train/bus pick-up, but call ahead if arriving late.

$ The Walk on Inn, Suecia 504, T235065, www.walkoninn.com.pe. 2 blocks from the Plaza, private or shared bathrooms, breakfast extra, laundry service, free airport/bus station pick-up.

Youth hostels

$ Albergue Municipal, Quiscapata 240, San Cristóbal, T252506, albergue@municusco.gob.pe. Dormitories and double rooms, great views, bar, cafeteria, laundry, discount for members, luggage store.

$ El Procurador del Cusco, Coricalle 440, Prolongación Procuradores, T243559, http://hostelprocuradordelcusco.blogspot.com. Price includes use of the basic kitchen (no fridge) and laundry area, with or without bath, basic rooms, but upstairs is better, helpful, good value.

$ Maison de la Jeunesse (affiliated to HI, www.hihostels.com), Av El Sol, Cuadra 5, Pasaje Grace, Edif San Jorge (down a small side street opposite Qoricancha) T235617, hostellingcusco@hotmail.com. Double rooms with bath or a bed in a dorm with shared bath; HI discount. TV and video room, lockers, cooking facilities and hot water.

❼ Restaurants

Cuzco *p203, maps p206 and p208*
Around the Plaza de Armas
There are many good cheap restaurants on Procuradores, Plateros and Tecseccocha.
$$$ **Chicha**, Plaza Regocijo 261, p 2 (above El Truco), T240520. Daily 1200-2400. Specializes in regional dishes created by restaurateur Gastón Acurio (see under Lima, Restaurants), Peruvian cuisine of the highest standards in a renovated colonial house, at one time the royal mint, tastefully decorated, open-to-view kitchen, bar with a variety of pisco sours, good service.
$$$ **Cicciolina**, Triunfo 393, 2nd floor, T239510. Sophisticated cooking focusing largely on Italian/Mediterranean cuisine, impressive wine list. Good atmosphere, great for a special occasion.
$$$ **El Truco**, Plaza Regocijo 261. Open 0900-0100. Excellent local and international dishes, buffet lunch 1200-1500, nightly folk music at 2045, next door is **Taberna del Truco**.
$$$ **Fallen Angel**, Plazoleta Nazarenas 320, T258184. Sun from 1500. International and *Novo Andino* gourmet cuisine, great steaks, genuinely innovative interior design, worth checking out their events.
$$$ **Fusiones**, Av El Sol 106, T233341. Open 1100-2300. In the La Merced commercial centre, 2nd floor. *Novo Andino* and international cuisine in a chic contemporary setting, fine wines.
$$$ **Incanto**, Santa Catalina Angosta 135, T254753. Daily 1100-2400. Under same ownership as **Inka Grill** and with the same standards, restaurant has Inca stone work and serves Italian dishes (pastas, grilled meats, pizzas), and desserts, accompanied by an extensive wine list. Also Peruvian delicatessen.
$$$ **Inka Grill**, Portal de Panes 115, Plaza de Armas, T262992. Specializing in *Novo Andino* cuisine, also home-made pastas, wide vegetarian selection, live music, excellent coffee and home-made pastries 'to go'.
$$$ **Kusikuy**, Suecia 339, T292870. Mon-Sat 0800-2300. Local, national and international

dishes, good service, set lunch unbeatable value at only US$2.
$$$ **La China**, Santa Teresa 364, 2nd floor, T506462. Reportedly one of the best *chifas* in Cuzco.
$$$ **La Retama**, Portal de Panes 123, 2nd floor, T226372. Good food (also *Novo Andino*) and service, live music and dance, art exhibitions.
$$$ **Limo**, Portal de Carnes 236, T240668. On 2nd floor of a colonial mansion overlooking the Plaza de Armas, Peruvian cuisine of the highest standard, with strong emphasis on fish and seafood, fine pisco bar, good service and atmosphere.
$$$ **MAP Café**, in Museo de Arte Precolombino, Plaza de las Nazarenas 231. Café by day (1000-1830), from 1830 to 2200 serves superb international and Peruvian-Andean cuisine, innovative children's menu, minimalist design and top-class service.
$$$ **Pachacútec Grill and Bar**, Portal de Panes 105, Plaza de Armas. International cuisine, seafood and Italian specialities, folk music nightly.
$$$ **Tunupa**, Portal Confiturias 233, p 2, Plaza de Armas. Large restaurant, small balcony overlooking Plaza, international, Peruvian and *Novo Andino* cuisine, good buffet US$15, nicely decorated, cocktail lounge, live music and dance at 2030.
$$$ **Tupananchis**, Portal Mantas 180, T245159. Tasty *Novo Andino* and fusion cuisine in a sophisticated atmosphere.
$$ **Greens Organic**, Santa Catalina Angosta 135, upstairs, T243379. Exclusively organic, but not wholly vegetarian, ingredients in fusion cuisine and a fresh daily buffet, very good.
$$ **Pucará**, Plateros 309. Mon-Sat 1230-2200. Peruvian and international food (no language skills required as a sample plate of their daily menu is placed in the window at lunchtime), nice atmosphere.
$$ **Sara**, Santa Catalina Ancha 370, T261691. Vegetarian-friendly organic café bistro, stylish and modern setting, menu includes both traditional Peruvian dishes as well as pasta and other international dishes.

$ El Encuentro, Santa Catalina Ancha 384, Choquechaca 136 and Tigre 130. One of the best value eateries in Cuzco, 3 courses of good healthy vegan food and a drink for US$2, very busy at lunchtime.

$ El Fogón, Plateros 365. Huge local *menú del día*, good solid food at reasonable prices. Very popular.

$ Víctor Victoria, Tecseccocha 466, T252854. Israeli and local dishes, first-class breakfasts, good value.

Cafés

Amaru, Plateros 325, p 2. Limitless coffee and tea, great bread and juices, even on 'non-buffet' breakfasts, colonial balcony. Also has bar.

Café El Ayllu, Almagro 133, T232357, and Marqués 263, T255078. Classical/folk music, good atmosphere, superb range of milk products, wonderful apple pastries, good selection for breakfast, great juices, quick service. A Cuzco institution.

Café Halliy, Plateros 363. Popular meeting place, especially for breakfast, good for comments on guides, has good snacks and 'copa Halliy' (fruit, muesli, yoghurt, honey and chocolate cake), also good vegetarian *menú* and set lunch.

Café Perla, Santa Catalina Ancha 304, on the plazoleta, T774130. Extensive menu of light meals, sandwiches, desserts and coffee, including beans for sale roasted on the premises. Popular.

Dolce Vita, Santa Catalina Ancha 366. Open 1000-2100. Delicious Italian ice cream.

Dos por Tres, Marquez 271. Popular for over 20 years, great coffee and cakes.

La Bondiet, Plaza Espinar y Plateros 363. Clean, simple café with a huge selection of sweet and savoury pastries, *empanadas*, good sandwiches, juices and coffee. A local favourite.

La Tertulia, Procuradores 44, p 2. Open until 2300. Breakfast served 0630-1300, includes muesli, bread, yoghurt, eggs, juice and coffee, all you can eat for US$3, superb value, vegetarian buffet daily 1800-2200, set dinner and salad bar for US$3.50, also

fondue and gourmet meals, book exchange, newspapers, classical music.

Yahuu! Juice Bar, Portal Confituría 249 and Marqués 200. Fresh inexpensive juices and smoothies as well as sandwiches (at Portal Confituría).

Yaku Mama, Procuradores 397. Good for breakfast, unlimited fruit and coffee.

Beyond the Plaza, including San Blas

$$$ A Mi Manera, Triunfo 393, T222219. Imaginative *Novo Andino* cuisine with open kitchen. Great hospitality and atmosphere.

$$$ Baco, Ruinas 465, T242808. Wine bar and bistro-style restaurant, same owner as Cicciolina. Specializes in BBQ and grilled meats, also veggie dishes, pizzas and good wines. Unpretentious and comfy, groups welcome.

$$$ Pachapapa, Plazoleta San Blas 120, opposite church of San Blas, T241318. A beautiful patio restaurant in a colonial house, good Cusqueña and other dishes, at night diners can sit in their own, private colonial dining room, attentive staff.

$$$-$$ Divina Comedia, Pumacurco 406, T437640. Daily 1230-1500, 1830-2300. An elegant restaurant just 1 block from the Monasterio hotel, diners are enter tained by classical piano and singing. Friendly atmosphere with comfortable seating, perfect for a special night out, reasonable prices.

$$ El Paisa, Av El Sol 819, T501717. Open 0900-1700. Typical northern Peruvian dishes including *ceviche* and goat.

$$ Granja Heidi, Cuesta San Blas 525, T238383. Delicious yoghurt, granola, ricotta cheese and honey and other great breakfast options. Also vegetarian dishes, a very good midday *menú* and steak at night. Highly recommended.

$$ Inkanato, San Agustín 280, T222926. Good food, staff dressed in Inca outfits and dishes made only with ingredients known in Inca times, calls itself a "living museum".

$$ Inka Panaka, Tandapata 140, T235034. Artistic flair, gallery of local artists' work. *Novo Andino* cuisine, and tasty innovative treats. Several vegetarian options, also breakfast.

$$ Jack's Café, Choquechaca y San Blas, T806960. Excellent varied menu, generous portions, relaxed atmosphere, can get very busy at lunchtime, expect a queue in high season.

$$ Justina, Palacios 110. Mon-Sat from 1800. Good value, good quality pizzería, with wine bar. It's at the back of a patio.

$$ La Bodega 138, Herrajes 138, T260272. Excellent pizza, good salads and pasta. Warm and welcoming.

$$ Le Soleil, C San Agustin 275, in La Lune hotel, T240543, www.restaurantele soleilcusco.com. Closed Wed. Excellent restaurant using local products to make classic French cuisine.

$$ Los Toldos, Almagro 171 and San Andrés 219. Grilled chicken, fries and salad bar, also *trattoria* with home-made pasta and pizza, delivery T229829.

$$ Macondo, Cuesta San Blas 571, T229415. Interesting restaurant with an imaginative menu, good food, well-furnished, gay friendly.

$$ The Muse, C Triunfo 338, 2nd floor, T242030. Restaurant lounge serving an international menu, lots of veggie options, live music every night, balcony seating, Wi-Fi. British owner Claire is a great source of information.

$$-$ Aldea Yanapay, Ruinas 415, p 2. Good café serving breakfast, lunch and dinner. Run by a charity which supports children's homes (www.aldeayanapay.org).

$ Café Punchay, Choquechaca 229, T261504. German-owned vegetarian restaurant, with a variety of pasta and potato dishes, good range of wines and spirits, large screen for international sports and you can bring a DVD for your own private movie showing.

$ Kushka...fé, Choquechaca 131-A and Espaderos 142, T258073. Great food and value in a nice setting, English spoken.

$ Venezia, Carmen Alto 154, San Blas. Only 4 tables, "exquisite gourmet" food at ridiculously low prices, opened in 2013.

Cafés

Chocolate, Choquechaca 162. Good for coffee and cakes, but don't miss the gourmet chocolates.

Cositas Café y Arte, Pasaje Inca Roca 108 and 110, T236410. Inventive local cuisine in a small, art-filled café. Profits support local social projects such as arts and crafts which are on sale in the café.

Juanito's Sandwich Café, Qanchipata 596. Great grilled veggie and meaty burgers and sandwiches, coffee, tea and hot chocolate. Juanito himself is a great character and the café stays open late.

Manu Café, Av Pardo 1046. Good coffee and good food too.

Panadería El Buen Pastor, Cuesta San Blas 579. Very good bread, *empanadas* and pastries, proceeds go to a charity for orphans and street children.

🌙 Bars and clubs

Cuzco *p203, maps p206 and p208*
Bars
Bar 7, Tandapata 690, San Blas, T506472. Good food and drinks in a trendy bar which specializes in local ingredients.

Cross Keys Pub, Triunfo 350 (upstairs), T229227, www.cross-keys-pub-cusco-peru. com. Open 1100-0130. Run by Barry Walker of **Manu Expeditions**, a Mancunian and ornithologist, cosy, darts, cable sports, pool, bar meals, plus daily half price specials Sun-Wed, great pisco sours, very popular, great atmosphere, free Wi-Fi.

Indigo, Tecseccocha 2, p 2, T260271. Shows 3 films a day. Also has a lounge and cocktail bar and serves Asian and local food. A log fire keeps out the night-time cold.

Km 0 (Arte y Tapas), Tandapata 100, San Blas. Mediterranean themed bar tucked in behind San Blas, good snacks and tapas, with live music every night (around 2200).

Los Perros Bar, Tecseccocha 436. Open 1100-0100. Great place to chill out on comfy couches, excellent music, welcoming, good coffee, tasty meals available (including

vegetarian), book exchange, English and other magazines, board games. Has a take-away only branch at Suecia 368, open 2400 to 0600 for good quality, post-club food.
Museo del Pisco, Santa Catalina Ancha 398, T262709, museo-del-pisco on Facebook. A bar where you can sample many kinds of pisco; tapas-style food served.
Norton Rat's Tavern, Santa Catalina Angosta 116. Open 0700-0230. On the corner of the Plaza de Armas, fine balcony, also serves meals, cable TV, popular, English spoken, pool, darts, motorcycle theme. Also runs Hostal Gocta Cusco.
Paddy's Pub, Triunfo 124 on the corner of the plaza. Open 1300-0100. Irish theme pub, deservedly popular, good grub.
Rosie O'Grady's, Santa Catalina Ancha 360, T247935. Open 1100 till late (food served till 2400). Good music, tasty food, good value.

Clubs
El Garabato Video Music Club, Espaderos 132, p 3. Daily 1600-0300. Dance area, lounge for chilling, bar, live shows 2300-0030 (all sorts of styles) and large screen showing music videos.
Extreme, C Suecia. Movies in the late afternoon and early evening, but after midnight this place really gets going with an eclectic range of music, from 60s and 70s rock and pop to techno and trance.
Kamikaze, Plaza Regocijo 274, T233865. *Peña* at 2200, good old traditional rock music, candle-lit cavern atmosphere, entry US$2.50.
Mama Africa, Portal de Panes 109. Cool music and clubber's spot, good food with varied menu, happy hour till 2300, good value.
Mythology, Portal de Carnes 298, p 2. Mostly an early 80s and 90s combination of cheese, punk and classic, popular. Food in served in the jungle-themed Lek Café. They also show movies in the afternoons.
Ukuku's, Plateros 316. US$1.35 entry, very popular, good atmosphere, good mix of music including live shows nightly. Also has a restaurant at Carmen Alto 133, good value and fabulous views.

⊙ Entertainment

Cuzco *p203, maps p206 and p208*
Folklore Regular nightly folklore show at Centro Qosqo de Arte Nativo, Av El Sol 604, T227901. Show from 1900 to 2030, entrance on BTC ticket. **Teatro Inti Raymi**, Saphi 605, nightly at 1845, US$4.50, well worth it. **Teatro Municipal**, C Mesón de la Estrella 149 (T227321 for information 0900-1300 and 1500-1900). Refurbished in 2013. Plays, dancing and shows, mostly Thu-Sun. They also run classes in music and dancing from Jan to Mar which are great value.

⊛ Festivals

Cuzco *p203, maps p206 and p208*
Carnival in Cuzco is a messy affair with flour, water, cacti, bad fruit and animal manure being thrown about in the streets.
Easter Monday: procession of El Señor de los Temblores (Lord of the Earthquakes), starting at 1600 outside the Cathedral. A large crucifix is paraded through the streets, returning to the Plaza de Armas around 2000 to bless the tens of thousands of people who have assembled there.
2-3 May Vigil of the Cross takes place at all mountaintops with crosses on them, a boisterous affair. **Jun** Q'Olloriti, the Snow Star Festival, is held at a 4700 m glacier north of Ocongate (Ausangate) 150 km southeast of Cuzco. Several agencies offer tours. (The date is moveable.) On **Corpus Christi** day, the Thu after Trinity Sunday, all the statues of the Virgin and of saints from Cuzco's churches are paraded through the streets to the Cathedral. The Plaza de Armas is surrounded by tables with women selling *cuy* (guinea pig) and a mixed grill called *chiriuchu* (*cuy*, chicken, tortillas, fish eggs, water-weeds, maize, cheese and sausage) and lots of Cusqueña beer. **24 Jun** The pageant of **Inti Raymi**, the Inca festival of the winter solstice, is enacted in Quechua at 1000 at the Qoricancha, moving on to Sacsayhuaman at 1300. Tickets for the

stands can be bought a week in advance from the Emufec office, Santa Catalina Ancha 325, US$80, less if bought Mar-May. Travel agents can arrange the whole day for you, with meeting points, transport, reserved seats and packed lunch. Those who try to persuade you to buy a ticket for the right to film or take photos are being dishonest. On the night before Inti Raymi, the Plaza de Armas is crowded with processions and food stalls. Try to arrive in Cuzco 15 days before Inti Raymi. **28 Jul** Peruvian Independence Day. Prices shoot up during these celebrations. **Aug** On the last Sun is the **Huarachicoy** festival at Sacsayhuaman, a spectacular re-enactment of the Inca manhood rite, performed in dazzling costumes by boys of a local school. **8 Sep** **Day of the Virgin** is a colourful procession of masked dancers from the church of Almudena, at the southwest edge of Cuzco, near Belén, to the Plaza de San Francisco. There is also a splendid fair at Almudena, and a free bull fight on the following day. **1 Nov** All Saints' Day, celebrated everywhere with bread dolls and traditional cooking. **8 Dec** Cuzco day, when churches and museums close at 1200. **24 Dec** Santuranticuy, 'the buying of saints', with a big crafts market in the plaza, very noisy until early hours of the 25th. This is one of the best festivals with people from the mountains coming to celebrate Christmas in Cuzco.

O Shopping

Cuzco p203, maps p206 and p208
Arts and crafts
In the Plaza San Blas and the surrounding area, authentic Cuzco crafts still survive. A market is held on Sat. Many leading artisans welcome visitors. Among fine objects made are Biblical figures from plaster, wheatflour and potatoes, reproductions of pre-Columbian ceramics and colonial sculptures, pious paintings, earthenware figurines, festive dolls and wood carvings.

Cuzco is the weaving centre of Peru and excellent textiles can be found at good value. Be very careful of buying gold and silver objects and jewellery in and around Cuzco. Do not buy condor feathers, painted or unpainted, as it is illegal to sell or purchase them. Condors are being killed for this trade. The prison sentence is 4 years.
Agua y Tierra, Plazoleta Nazarenas 167, and Cuesta San Blas 595, T226951. Excellent quality crafts from rainforest communities.
Apacheta, San Juan de Dios 250, T238210, www.apachetaperu.com. Replicas of Pre-Inca and Inca textiles, ceramics, alpaca goods, contemporary art gallery, books on Andean culture.
Inkantations, Choquechaca 200. Radical baskets made from natural materials in all sorts of weird and wonderful shapes. Also ceramics and Andean weavings. Interesting and original.
Mercado Artesanal, Av El Sol, block 4, is good for cheap crafts.
Pedazo de Arte, Plateros 334B. A tasteful collection of Andean handicrafts, many designed by Japanese owner Miki Suzuki.
La Pérez, Urb Mateo Pumacahua 598, Huanchac, T232186. A big co-operative with a good selection; they will arrange a free pick-up from your hotel.
Seminario, Portal de Carnes 244, Plaza de Armas, sells the ceramics of Seminario-Behar (see under Urubamba, page 234), plus cotton, basketry, jewellery, etc.

Bookshops
Centro de Estudios Regionales Andinos Bartolomé de las Casas, Av Tullumayo 465, T233472, www.cbc.org.pe. Mon-Sat 1100-1400, 1600-1900. Good books on Peruvian history, archaeology, etc.
Jerusalem, Heladeros 143, T235408. English books, guidebooks, postcards, book exchange (3 for 1).

Camping equipment
For renting equipment, there are several places around the Plaza area. Check the

equipment carefully as it is common for parts to be missing. A deposit of US$100 is asked, plus credit card, passport or plane ticket. White gas (*bencina*), US$1.50 per litre, can be bought at hardware stores, but check the purity. Stove spirit (*alcoól para quemar*) is available at pharmacies; blue gas canisters, costing US$5, can be found at hardware stores and camping shops. You can also rent equipment through travel agencies.

Edson Zuñiga Huillca, Mercado Rosaspata, Jr Abel Landeo P-1, 3 mins from Plaza de Armas, T802831. For repair of camping equipment and footwear, also equipment rental, open 24 hrs a day, 7 days a week, English and Italian spoken.

Tatoo, Plazoleta Espinar, T254211, www. tatoo.ws. High-quality hiking, climbing and camping gear, not cheap, but Western brand names and their own lines.

Fabrics and alpaca clothing

Alpaca Golden, Portal de Panes 151, T251724, alpaca.golden@terra.com.pe. Also at Plazoleta Nazarenas 175. Designer, producer and retailer of fine alpaca clothing.

The Center for Traditional Textiles of Cuzco, Av El Sol 603, T228117, www.textiles cusco.org. A non-profit organization that seeks to promote, refine and rediscover the weaving traditions of the Cuzco area. Tours of workshops, weaving classes, you can watch weavers at work. Also run 3-day weaving courses. Over 50% of the price goes direct to the weaver. Recommended.

Hilo, Carmen Alto 260, T254536. Fashionable items designed individually and handmade on-site. Run by Eibhlin Cassidy, she can adjust and tailor designs.

Josefina Olivera, Portal Comercio 173, Plaza de Armas. Daily 1100-2100. Sells old textiles and weavings, expensive but worth it to save pieces being cut up to make other item.

Kuna by Alpaca 111, Plaza Regocijo 202, T243233, www.kuna.com.pe. High-quality alpaca clothing with outlets also in hotels **El Monasterio**, **Libertador** and **Machu Picchu Sanctuary Lodge**.

Store of Weavers (Asociación Central de Artesanos y Artesanas del Sur Andino Inkakunaq Ruwaynin), Av Tullumayo 274, T233466. Store run by 6 local weaving communities, some of whose residents you can see working on site. All profits go to the weavers themselves.

Food and natural products

Choco Museo, Garcilaso 210, 2nd floor, also in Ollantaytambo, T244765, www.chocomuseo. com. Offers chocolate making classes and runs trips to their cocoa plantation.

The Coca Shop, Carmen Alto 115, San Blas, T260774. Tiny shop selling an interesting selection of sweets and chocolates made using coca leaf flour. There is also plenty of information about the nutritional values of coca leaves.

La Cholita, Av El Sol and at airport. Special chocolates made with local ingredients.

Jewellery

Calas, Siete Angelitos 619-B, San Blas. Handmade silver jewellery in interesting designs and alpaca goods from the community of Pitumarca.

Ilaria, Portal Carrizos 258, T246253. Branches in hotels **Monasterio**, **Libertador** and at the airport. For recommended jewellery and silver.

Inka Treasure, Triunfo 375, T227470. With branches at Av Pardo 1080, Plazoleta Nazarenas 159 and Portal de Panes 163. Also at the airport and the airport in Juliaca. Fine jewellery including goldwork, mostly with pre-Columbian designs, and silver with the owner's designs. Tours of workshops at Av Circunvalación, near Cristo Blanco. The stores also incorporte the work of famed jeweller Carlos Chakiras.

Mullu, Triunfo 120, T229831. Mon-Sat 1000-2100. Contemporary silver jewellery with semi-precious stones and cotton clothing with interesting designs.

Spondylus, Cuesta San Blas 505, T226929. A good selection of interesting gold and silver jewellery and fashion tops with Inca and pre-Inca designs.

Markets

Wanchac, Av Garcilaso (southeast of centre) and **San Pedro Market**, opposite Estación San Pedro, sell a variety of goods. **El Molino**, beyond the Terminal Terrestre, sells everything under the sun at knockdown prices, but quality not guaranteed and nothing touristy, fascinating, crowded, don't take valuables and go there by colectivo or taxi. **Confraternidad**, beside the Wanchaq train station, is similar to El Molino and closer to town.

Music

Taki Museo de Música de los Andes, Hatunrumiyoc 487-5. Shop and workshop selling and displaying musical instruments, owner is an ethno-musicologist. Recommended for anyone interested in Andean music.

◑ What to do

Cuzco *p203, maps p206 and p208*
For a list of recommended Tour operators for Manu, see page 297. There are many travel agencies in Cuzco. The sheer number and variety of tours on offer is bewildering and prices for the same tour can vary dramatically. Always remember that you get what you pay for and that, in a crowded market, organization can sometimes be a weak point. In general you should only deal directly with the agencies themselves. You can do this when in town, or you can raise whatever questions you may have in advance (or even in Cuzco), and get replies in writing, by email. Other sources of advice are visitors returning from trips, who can give the latest information, and the trip reports for members of the South America Explorers. Students will normally receive a discount on production of an ISIC card. Do not deal with guides who claim to be employed by agencies listed below without verifying their credentials. City tours cost about US$10-15 for 4 hrs; check what sites are included and that the guide is experienced.

Only a restricted number of agencies are licensed to operate **Inca Trail** trips. Sernanp, Av José Gabriel Cosio 308, Urb Magisterial, 1 etapa, T229297, www.sernanp.gob.pe, verifies operating permits (see Visitors' tickets, above, for Dirección de Cultura office). Unlicensed agencies will sell Inca Trail trips, but pass clients on to the operating agency. This can cause confusion and booking problems at busy times. Current advice is to book your preferred dates as early as possible, between 2 months and a year in advance, depending on the season when you want to go, then confirm nearer the time. There have been many instances of disappointed trekkers whose bookings did not materialize. Don't wait to the last minute and check your operator's cancellation fees.
Note See page 245, under Inca Trails, for regulations governing the trail. Note also that many companies offer treks as alternatives to the Inca Trail and its variations to Machu Picchu. Unlike the Inca Trail, these treks are unregulated. Ensure that the trekking company does not employ the sort of practices (such as mistreating porters, not clearing up rubbish) which are now outlawed on the trails to Machu Picchu.

The Cuzco soccer stadium was renovated in 2014 and, If you are a fan, it is worth going to see a game.

Inca Trail and general tours

Amazon Trails Peru, Tandapata 660, T437374, or T984-714148, www.amazon trailsperu.com. Trekking tours around the area, including the Inca Trail, Salkantay and Choquequirao. Also well-equipped and well-guided trips to Manu.
Alpaca Expeditions, Heladeros 157, T254278. Offers responsible treks focusing on the Inca Trail.
Andean Treks, Av Pardo 705, T225701, www.andeantreks.com. Manager Tom Hendrickson uses high-quality equipment and satellite phones. This company organizes itineraries, from 2 to 15 days with a wide variety of activities in this area and further afield.

Andina Travel, Plazoleta Santa Catalina 219, T251892, www.andinatravel.com. Specializes in trekking and biking, notably the Lares Valley and Inca Trail, working with local communities.

Big Foot, Triunfo 392 (oficina 213), T233836, www.bigfootcusco.com. Tailor-made hiking trips, especially in the remote corners of the Vilcabamba and Vilcanota mountains; also the Inca Trail.

Ch'aska, Garcilaso 265 p 2, of 6, T240424, https://chaskatours.com. Dutch-Peruvian company offering cultural, adventure, nature and esoteric tours. They specialize in the Inca Trail, but also llama treks to Lares, treks to Choquequirao.

Culturas Peru, Tandapata 354A, T243629, www.culturasperu.com. Swiss-Peruvian company offering adventure, cultural, ecological and spiritual tours. Also specialize in alternative Inca trails.

Destinos Turísticos, Portal de Panes 123, oficina 101-102, Plaza de Armas, T228168, www.destinosturisticosperu.com. The owner speaks Spanish, English, Dutch and Portuguese and specializes in package tours from economic to 5-star budgets. Advice on booking jungle trips and renting mountain bikes. Very helpful.

EcoAmerica Peru, T999-705538, www.eco americaperu.com. Associated with **America Tours** (La Paz, Bolivia). Owned by 3 experienced consultants in responsible travel, conservation and cultural heritage.

Specializes in culture, history, nature, trekking, biking and birding tours. Knowledgeable guides, excellent customer service for independent travellers, groups or families. Also sell tours and flights to Bolivia.

Enigma Adventure, Jr Clorinda Matto de Turner 100, Urb Magisterial 1a Etapa, T222155, www.enigmaperu.com. Run by Spaniard Silvia Rico Coll. Well-organized, innovative trekking expeditions including a luxury service, Inca Trail and a variety of challenging alternatives. Also cultural tours to weaving communities, Ayahuasca therapy, climbing and biking.

Explorandes, Paseo Zarzuela Q-2, Huancaro, T238380, www.explorandes.com. Experienced high-end adventure company. Arrange a wide variety of mountain treks; trips available in Peru and Ecuador, book through website also arranges tours across Peru for lovers of orchids, ceramics or textiles. Award-winning environmental practices.

Fertur, C San Agustín 317, T221304, www.fertur-travel.com. Mon-Fri 0900-1900, Sat 0900-1200. Cuzco branch of the Lima tour operator, see page 68.

Gatur Cusco, Puluchapata 140 (a small street off Av El Sol 3rd block), T223496, www.gaturcusco.com. Esoteric, ecotourism, and general tours. Owner Dr José (Pepe) Altamirano is knowledgeable in Andean folk traditions. Excellent conventional tours, bilingual guides and transportation. Guides

speak English, French, Spanish and German. They can also book internal flights.

Habitats Peru, Condominio La Alborada B-507, T246271, www.habitatsperu.com. Bird watching and mountain biking trips offered by Doris and Carlos. They also run a volunteer project near Quillabamba.

Hiking Peru, Portal de Panes 109, of 6, T247942, T984-651414, www.hikingperu.com. 8-day treks to Espíritu Pampa; 7 days/6 nights around Ausangate; 4-day/3-night Lares Valley Trek.

Inca Explorers, C Peru W-18, T241070, www.incaexplorers.com. Specialist trekking agency for small group expeditions in socially and environmentally responsible manner. Also 2-week hike in the Cordillera Vilcanota (passing Nevado Ausangate), and Choquequirao to Espíritu Pampa.

InkaNatura Travel, Ricardo Palma J1, T255255, www.inkanatura.com. Offers tours with special emphasis on sustainable tourism and conservation. Knowledgeable guides.

Llama Path, San Juan de Dios 250, T240822, www.llamapath.com. A wide variety of local tours, specializing in Inca Trail and alternative treks, involved in environmental campaigns and porter welfare. Many good reports.

Machete Tours, Triunfo 392, T224829, T440 351 (Lima office), www.machetetours.com. Peruvian and Danish owners. Tours cover all Peru and also Bolivia and Chile. All guides speak good English. Adventure tours arranged using local accommodation or family camping areas. Tours are eco-friendly and benefit the local community.

Peru Treks, Av Pardo 540, T222722, www.perutreks.com. Trekking agency set up by Englishman Mike Weston and his wife Koqui González. They pride themselves on good treatment of porters and support staff and have been consistently recommended for professionalism and customer care, a portion of profits go to community projects. The company specializes in trekking and cultural tours in the Cuzco region. Treks offered include Salkantay, the Lares Valley and Vilcabamba Vieja.

Q'ente, Choquechaca 229, p 2, T222535, www.qente.com. Their Inca Trail service is recommended. Also private treks to Salkantay, Ausangate, Choquequirao, Vilcabamba and Q'eros. Horse riding to local ruins costs US$35 for 4-5 hrs. Very good, especially with children.

Sky Travel, Santa Catalina Ancha 366, interior 3-C (down alleyway near Rosie O'Grady's pub), T261818, www.skyperu.com. English spoken. General tours around city and Sacred Valley. Inca Trail with good-sized double tents and a dinner tent (the group is asked what it would like on the menu 2 days before departure). Other trips include Vilcabamba and Ausangate (trekking).

Southamerica Planet, Garcilaso 210, of 201 (2nd floor, T251145, www.southamericaplanet.com. Peruvian/Belgian-owned agency offering the Inca Trail, other treks around Cuzco and packages within Peru, as well as Bolivia and Patagonia.

Tambo Tours, 4405 Spring Cypress Rd, Suite 210, Spring, TX 77388, USA, T1-888-2-GO-PERU (246-7378), T001-281 528 9448, www.2GOPERU.com. Long established adventure and tour specialist with offices in Peru and the US. Customized trips to the Amazon and archaeological sites of Peru, Bolivia and Ecuador.

Tanager Tours, T01-669 0825, T984-742711, T984-761790 (mob), www.tanagertours.com. Specializes in birdwatching tours throughout Peru but all will also arrange other tours. Owners live in Cuzco but currently no office. Most of their tours are arranged via the internet and they contact clients at their accommodation.

T'ika Trek, no storefront, UK T07768-948366, www.tikatrek.com. Run by Fiona Cameron, a long-term resident of Peru and keen hiker and biker. With over 10 years in the Cuzco tourism business Fiona provides high-quality personalized tours all over Peru as well as to the Galápagos Islands (Ecuador). Focus is on small groups and families.

Trekperu, Av República de Chile B-15, Parque Industrial, Wanchac, T261501, www.trekperu.com. Experienced trek operator as well as other adventure sports and mountain biking. Offers 'culturally sensitive' tours. Cusco Biking Adventure includes support vehicle and good camping gear (but providing your own sleeping bag).

United Mice, Av Pachacútec 454 A-5, T221139, www.unitedmice.com. Inca Trail and alternative trail via Salkantay and Santa Teresa, well-established and reputable. Good guides who speak languages other than Spanish. Discount with student card, good food and equipment. City and Sacred Valley tours and treks to Choquequirao.

Wayki Trek, Av Pardo 506, T224092, www.waykitrek.net. Budget travel agency with a hostel attached, recommended for their Inca Trail service. Owner Leo knows the area very well. Treks to several almost unknown Inca sites and interesting variations on the 'classic' Inca Trail with visits to porters' communities. Also treks to Ausangate, Salkantay and Choquequirao.

Rafting, mountain biking and trekking

When looking for an operator please consider more than just the price of your tour. Competition between companies in Cuzco is intense and price wars can lead to compromises in safety. Consider the quality of safety equipment (lifejackets, etc) and the number and experience of rescue kayakers and support staff. On a large and potentially dangerous rivers like the Apurímac and Urubamba (where fatalities have occurred), this can make all the difference.

Amazonas Explorers, Av Collasuyo 910, Miravalle, PO Box 722, www.amazonas-explorer.com. Experts in rafting, inflatable canoeing, mountain biking, horse riding and hiking. English owner Paul Cripps has great experience. Most bookings from overseas (in UK, T01874-658125, Jan-Mar; T01437-891743, Apr-Dec), but they may be able to arrange a trip for travellers in Cuzco with advance notice. Rafting and inflatable canoeing includes Río Urubamba, Río Apurímac, Río Tambopata (including

Lake Titicaca). Also 5-day/4-night Inca Trail, alternatives to the Inca Trail and Choquequirao to Machu Picchu, an excellent variation of the Ausangate Circuit and a trek to Espíritu Pampa. Multi-activity and family trips are a speciality. Mountain biking trips all use state-of-the-art equipment, expert guides and support vehicles where appropriate. All options are at the higher end of the market and are highly recommended. Amazonas Explorer are members of www.onepercentfortheplanet. org, donating 1% of their turnover to a tree-planting project in the Lares watershed.

Apumayo, Jr Ricardo Palma N-5, Santa Mónica, Wanchaq, T246018, www.apumayo. com. Mon-Sat 0900-1300, 1600-2000. Urubamba rafting (from 0800-1530 every day); 3- to 4-day Apurímac trips. Also mountain biking to Maras and Moray in Sacred Valley, or from Cuzco to the jungle town of Quillabamba. This company also offers tours for disabled people, including rafting.

Apus Perú, Cuichipunco 366, T232691, www.apus-peru.com. Conducts most business by internet, specializes in alternatives to the Inca Trail, strong commitment to sustainability, well-organized. Associated with **Threads of Peru** NGO which helps weavers.

Eric Adventures, Urb Santa María A1-6, San Sebastián, T272862, www.ericadventures. com. Specialize in many adventure activities. They clearly explain what equipment is included in their prices and what you will need to bring. They also rent motorcross bikes for US$70-90 per day, mountain bikes and cars and 4WDs. Prices are more expensive if you book by email. A popular company.

Medina Brothers, contact Christian or Alain Medina on T225163 or T984-653485/ T984-691670. Family-run rafting company with good equipment and plenty of experience. They usually focus on day rafting trips in the Sacred Valley, but services are tailored to the needs of the client.

Pachatusan Trek, Villa Union Huancaro G-4, B 502, T231817, www.pachatusantrek.com.

Offers a wide variety to treks, as alternatives to the Inca Trail, professional and caring staff, "simply fantastic".

River Explorers, Pasaje Los Zafiros B-15, T260926 or T958-320673, www.river explorers.com. An adventure company offering mountain biking, trekking and rafting trips (on the Apurímac, Urubamba and Tambopata). Experienced and qualified guides with environmental awareness.

Terra Explorer Peru, T237352, www. terraexplorerperu.com. Offers a wide range of trips from high-end rafting in the Sacred Valley and expeditions to the Colca and Cotahuasi canyons, trekking the Inca Trail and others, mountain biking, kayaking (including on Lake Titicaca) and jungle trips. All guides are bilingual.

Cultural tours

Milla Tourism, Av Pardo 800, T231710, www.millaturismo.com. Mon-Fri 0800-1300, 1500-1900, Sat 0800-1300. Mystical tours to Cuzco's Inca ceremonial sites such as Pumamarca and The Temple of the Moon. Guide speaks only basic English. They also arrange cultural and environmental lectures and courses.

Shamans and drug experiences

San Pedro and Ayahuasca have been used since before Inca times, mostly as a sacred healing experience. If you choose to experience these incredible healing/ teaching plants, only do so under the guidance of a reputable agency or shaman and always have a friend with you who is not partaking. If the medicine is not prepared correctly, it can be highly toxic and, in rare cases, severely dangerous. Never buy from someone who is not recommended, never buy off the streets and never try to prepare the plants yourself.

Another Planet, Tandapata y Pasñapacana 148, San Blas, T241168, or T974-792316, www.anotherplanetperu.org. Run by Lesley Myburgh, who operates mystical and adventure tours in and around Cuzco, and is

an expert in San Pedro cactus preparation. She arranges San Pedro sessions for healing in the garden of her house outside Cuzco. Tours meet at **La Casa de la Gringa**, see Where to stay, above.

Etnikas Travel & Shamanic Healing, Herrajes 148, T244516, www.etnikas.com. A shamanic centre now offering travel for mind, body and spirit and the sale of natural products from the Andes and the jungle. Expensive but serious in their work.

Sumac Coca Travel, San Agustín 245, T260311. Mystical tourism, offering Ayahuasca and San Pedro ceremonies, and also more conventional cultural tourism. Professional and caring.

Private guides

As most of the sights do not have any information or signs in English, a good guide can really improve your visit. Either arrange this before you set out or contract one at the sight you are visiting. A tip is expected at the end of the tour. Tours of the city or Sacred Valley cost US$50 for half-day, US$65 full day; a guide to Machu Picchu charges US$80 per day. A list of official guides is held by **Agotur Cuzco**, C Heladeros 157, Of 34-F, p 3, T233457. **South American Explorers** has a list and contact details for recommended local guides. See also www.leaplocal.org.

⊖ Transport

Cuzco p203, maps p206 and p208
Air

The airport is at Quispiquilla, near the bus terminal, 1.6 km from centre, airport information T222611/601. **Note** The airport can get very busy. Check in 2 hrs before your flight. Flights may be delayed or cancelled during the wet season, or may leave early if the weather is bad. To **Lima**, 55 mins, over 30 daily flights with **Avianca/TACA**, **Star Perú**, **LAN**, **Peruvian Airlines** and **LC Perú** (on its Lima, Pisco, Cuzco route). To **Arequipa**, 30 mins daily with **LAN**. To **Juliaca** (for Puno), 1 hr daily with **LAN**. To **Puerto Maldonado**,

30 mins, with **LAN** and **Star Perú**. To **La Paz**, **Amaszonas** (www.amaszonas.com) 1 hr daily except Sat. Taxi to and from the airport costs US$3.50 (US$7.25 from the official taxi desk). Colectivos cost US$0.30 from Plaza San Francisco or outside the airport car park. Many representatives of hotels and travel agencies operate at the airport, with transport to the hotel with which they are associated. Take your time to choose your hotel, at the price you can afford. Also in baggage retrieval are mobile phone rentals, ATMs, LAC Dollar money exchange, an Oxyshot oxygen sales stand and an **i perú** office. There are phone booths, restaurant, cafeteria and a Tourist Protection Bureau desk.

Bus

Long distance Terminal on Av Vallejo Santoni, block 2 (Prolongación Pachacútec), colectivo from centre US$0.50, taxi US$2. Platform tax US$0.35. Buses to **Lima** (20-24 hrs) go via **Abancay**, 195 km, 5 hrs (longer in the rainy season), and **Nazca**, on the Panamerican Highway. This route is paved but floods in the wet season often damage large sections of the highway. If prone to travel sickness, be prepared on the road to Abancay, there are many, many curves, but the scenery is magnificent. At Abancay, the road forks, the other branch going to **Andahuaylas**, a further 138 km, 10-11 hrs from Cuzco, and **Ayacucho**, another 261 km, 20 hrs from Cuzco. On both routes at night, take a blanket or sleeping bag to ward off the cold. All buses leave daily from the Terminal Terrestre. **Molina**, who also have an office on Av Pachacútec, just past the railway station, have buses on both routes. They run 3 services a day to Lima via Abancay and Nazca, and one, at 1900, to Abancay and Andahuaylas. **Cruz del Sur**'s service to Lima via Abancay leaves at 0730 and 1400, while their more comfortable services depart at 1500 and 1630. **San Jerónimo** and **Los Chankas** have buses to Abancay, Andahuaylas and Ayacucho at 1830. **Turismo Ampay** and **Turismo Abancay** go 3 times

a day to Abancay, and **Expreso Huamanga** once. **Bredde** has 5 buses a day to Abancay. Fares: Abancay US$18, Andahuaylas US$22, Nazca US$28, Lima also US$38-49; also US$50-70 (*Cruz del Sur Cruzero* and *VIP* classes). In Cuzco you may be told that there are no buses in the day from Abancay to Andahuaylas; this is not so as **Señor de Huanca** does so. If you leave Cuzco before 0800, with luck you'll make the connection at 1300 – worth it for the scenery. **Ormeño** has a service from Cuzco to Lima via Arequipa which takes longer (22 hrs), but is a more comfortable journey.

To Lake Titicaca and Bolivia To **Juliaca**, 344 km, 5-6 hrs, US$8-17. The road is fully paved, but after heavy rain buses may not run. To **Puno**, via Juliaca, US$8-17; direct, US$15 (*bus cama* US$18), 6 hrs. Tourist service with 5 stops, First Class and Inka Express (Av La Paz C-32, Urb El Ovalo, Wanchac, T247887, www.inkaexpress.com), calling at Andahuayllas church, Raqchi, La Raya, Sicuani and Pucará, US$60, lunch included. **Note** It is safest to travel by day on the Juliaca-Puno-Cuzco route.

To **Arequipa**, 521 km, US$14-47; Cruz del Sur use the direct paved route via Juliaca and have a *Cruzero* services at 2000 and 2030, 10 hrs, US$25-47. Other buses join the new Juliaca–Arequipa road at Imata, 10-12 hrs (eg **Carhuamayo**, 3 a day).

To **Puerto Maldonado**, Móvil (Terminal Terrestre, T238223), Transportes Iguazú, Machupicchu, Palomino and Mendivil, all from Terminal Terrestre, several daily, see page 299.

To the **Sacred Valley**: To **Pisac**, 32 km, 1 hr, US$1.50, from C Puputi on the outskirts of the city, near the Clorindo Matto de Turner school and Av de la Cultura. Colectivos, minibuses and buses leave whenever they are full, between 0600 and 1600. Buses returning from Pisac are often full. The last one back leaves around 2000. Taxis charge about US$20 for the round trip. To Pisac, **Calca** (18 km beyond Pisac) and **Urubamba** a further 22 km, buses leave from Av Tullumayo 800 block, Wanchac, US$1.50. Combis and colectivos leave from 300 block of Av Grau, 1 block before crossing the bridge, for **Chinchero**, 23 km, 45 mins, US$1.50; and for **Urubamba** a further 25 km, 45 mins, US$1.50 (or US$2.25 Cuzco–Urubamba direct, US$2.25 for a seat in a colectivo taxi). To **Ollantaytambo** from Av Grau, 0745, 1945, US$4, or catch a bus to Urubamba. Also Cruz del Sur, at Terminal Terrestre, 3 a day, 2 hrs, US$7. Direct taxi-colectivo service to Ollantaytambo from C Pavitos, leaves when full, US$5. Tours can be arranged to Chinchero, Urubamba and Ollantaytambo with a Cuzco travel agency. To Chinchero, US$9 pp; a taxi costs US$35 round-trip. Usually only day tours are organized for visits to the valley, US$25-30. Using public transport and staying overnight in Urubamba, Ollantaytambo or Pisac allows more time to see the ruins and markets.

Taxi

In Cuzco they are recommended when arriving by air, train or bus. They have fixed prices but you have to stay alert to overpricing: in the centre US$1.50 in town (50% more after 2100 or 2200). In town it is advisable to take municipality-authorized taxis that have a sticker with a number on the window and a chequerboard pattern on the side. Safer still are licensed taxis, which have a sign with the company's name on the roof, not just a sticker in the window. These taxis are summoned by phone (*llama taxi*) and are more expensive (Aló Cusco T222222, Ocarina T247080). Trips to **Sacsayhuaman**, US$10; ruins of **Tambo Machay** US$15-20 (3-4 people); day trip US$50-85.

Train

To Juliaca and Puno, **Perú Rail** trains leave from the Av El Sol station, Estación Wanchac, T238722. When arriving in Cuzco, a tourist bus meets the train to take visitors to hotels whose touts offer rooms. Machu Picchu trains leave from Estación San Pedro, opposite the San Pedro market.

The train to **Puno**, the *Andean Explorer* leaves at 0800, Mon, Wed, Fri (Apr-Oct) and Sat, arriving at Puno around 1800, sit on the left for views. The train makes a stop to view the scenery at La Raya. Always check whether the train is running, especially in the rainy season, when services may be cancelled. Cuzco to Puno costs US$268, Puno to Cuzco US$156. The ticket office at Wanchac station is open Mon-Fri 0700-1700, Sat, Sun and holidays 0700-1200. The **Perú Rail** office at Portal de Carnes 214 is open Mon-Fri 1000-2200, Sat, Sun and holidays 1400-2300 (take your passport or a copy when buying tickets). Buy tickets on www.perurail.com, or through a travel agent. Meals are served on the train. To **Ollantaytambo** and **Machu Picchu**, see page 244.

Directory

Cuzco *p203, maps p206 and p208*
Banks Most banks are on Av El Sol and all have ATMs. There are also ATMs around the Plaza de Armas, in San Blas and on Av Cultura. Many travel agencies and **casas de cambio** change dollars. **LAC Dollar**, Av El Sol 150, T257762, Mon-Sat 0900-2000, has a delivery service to central hotels. Street changers hang around Av El Sol blocks 2-3. **Consulates** For foreign consulates in Cuzco, see http://embassy.goabroad.com. Bolivia, Av Osvaldo Baca 101, p 1, Urb Magisterio, T231845, Mon-Fri 0900-1200, 1500-1700. **Language schools** Academia Latinoamericana de Español, Plaza Limacpampa 565, T243364, www.latinoschools.com. The same company also has schools in Ecuador (Quito) and in Bolivia (Sucre). They can arrange courses that include any combination of these locations using identical teaching methods and materials. Professionally run with experienced staff. Many activities per week, including dance lessons and excursions to sites of historical and cultural interest. Good homestays. Private classes US$170 for 20 hrs, groups also available. **Acupari**, the German-Peruvian Cultural Association, San Agustín

307, T242970, www.acupari.com. Spanish classes are run here. **Amauta Spanish School**, Suecia 480, T262345, www.amautaspanish. com. Spanish classes, one-to-one or in small groups, also Quechua classes and workshops in Peruvian cuisine, dance and music, group tuition (2-6 people) US$140 for 20 hrs. They have pleasant accommodation on the same street, as well as a free internet café for students, and can arrange excursions and help find voluntary work. They also have a school in Urubamba and can arrange courses in Tambopata, Lima and Argentina. **Amigos Spanish School**, Zaguán del Cielo B-23, T242292, www.spanishcusco.com. Certified, experienced teachers, friendly atmosphere. All profits support a foundation for disadvantaged children. Private lessons or US$150 for 20 hrs of classes in a small group. Comfortable homestays and extra-curricular activities available, including a 'real city tour' through Cuzco's poor areas or cooking classes. **Excel**, Cruz Verde 336, T235298, www. excel-spanishlanguageprograms-peru.org. Very professional, US$7 per hr for private one-to-one lessons. US$229 for 20 hrs with 2 people, or US$277 with homestay, one-on-one for 20 hrs. **Fairplay Spanish School**, Pasaje Zavaleta C-5, Wanchac, T984-789252, www.fairplay-peru.org. This relatively new NGO teaches Peruvians who wouldn't normally have the opportunity (Peruvian single mothers, for example) to become Spanish teachers themselves over several months of training. The agency then acts as an agent, allowing these same teachers to find work with visiting students. Classes with these teachers cost US$4.50 or US$6 per hr, of which 33% is reinvested in the NGO, the rest going direct to the teachers. Can also arrange volunteer work and homestay programmes. **San Blas Spanish School**, Carmen Bajo 224, T247898, www.spanishschoolperu.com. Groups, with 4 clients maximum, US$110 for 20 hrs tuition (US$210 one-to-one). **Massage and therapies** Casa de la Serenidad, Santa María P-8, San Sebastián, T984-671867, www.shamanspirit.net. A shamanic therapy centre run by a Swiss-American healer and Reiki Master who uses medicinal 'power' plants. It also has bed and breakfast and has received very good reports. **Medical services** Clinics: Hospital Regional, Av de la Cultura, T227661, emergencies T223691. **Clínica Pardo**, Av de la Cultura 710, T240387. 24 hrs daily, trained bilingual personnel, complete medical assistance coverage with international insurance companies, highly regarded. **Clínica Paredes**, Calle Lechugal 405, T225265, www. sos-mg.com. 24 hrs daily, excellent service, emergency doctors speak good English. **Motorcycle hire** Perú Mototours, Saphi 578, T232742, www.perumototours.com. Helpful, good prices and machines. **Useful addresses** Migraciones, Av El Sol s/n, block 6 close to post office, T222741, Mon-Fri 0800-1300. **ISIC-Intej office**, Portal de Panes 123, of 107 (CC Los Ruiseñores), T256367, cusco@ intej.org. Issues international student cards.

Southeast from Cuzco

There are many interesting villages and ruins on this road. The ruins of **Tipón** ① *US$3.60*, between the villages of Saylla and Oropesa, are extensive and include baths, terraces, irrigation systems, possibly an agricultural laboratory and a temple complex, accessible from a path leading from just above the last terrace (5-km climb from village; take a combi from Cuzco to Oropesa, then a taxi). **Oropesa**, whose church contains a fine ornately carved pulpit, is the national 'Capital of Bread'. Try the delicious sweet circular loaves known as *chutas*.

At **Huambutío**, north of the village of Huacarpay, the road divides; northwest to Pisac and north to **Paucartambo**, on the eastern slope of Andes. This remote town, 80 km east of Cuzco, has become a popular tourist destination. In the Centro Cultural is the Museo de los Pueblos, with exhibits on the history, culture, textiles and society of the region, including the **Fiesta de la Virgen del Carmen** (Mamacha Carmen). This is a major attraction, with masked dancers enacting rituals and folk tales: 15-17 July. (There is basic accommodation in town.) From Paucartambo, in the dry season, you can go 44 km to **Tres Cruces**, along the Pilcopata road, turning left after 25 km. Tres Cruces gives a wonderful view of the sunrise in June and July: peculiar climactic conditions make it appear that three suns are rising. Tour agencies in Cuzco can arrange transport and lodging.

Further on from Huacarpay are the Huari (pre-Inca) ruins of **Piquillacta** ① *daily 0700-1730, US$3.60*. Buses to Urcos from Avenida Huáscar in Cuzco will drop you at the entrance on the north side of the complex, though this is not the official entry. The Piquillacta Archaeological Park also contains the Laguna de Huacarpay (known as Muyna in ancient times) and the ruins that surround it: Kañarakay, Urpicancha and the huge gateway of Rumicolca. A guide will help to find the more interesting structures. It's good to hike or cycle and birdwatch around the lake.

Andahuaylillas is a village 32 km southeast from Cuzco, with a fine early 17th-century church (the 'Andean Sistine Chapel'), with frescoes, a splendid doorway and a gilded main altar. Taxi colectivos go there from block 17 of Av La Cultura (opposite university), as does the *Oropesa* bus (from Avenida Huáscar in Cuzco) via Tipón, Piquillacta and Rumicolca. The next village, **Huaro**, also has a church whose interior is entirely covered with colourful frescoes.

Beyond Andahuaylillas is **Urcos**, whose lake is a popular picnic spot (follow the clear path). There are three very basic hostales. A spectacular road from Urcos crosses the Eastern Cordillera to Puerto Maldonado in the jungle (see page 291). Some 47 km after passing the snow line Hualla-Hualla pass, at 4820 m, the super-hot thermal baths of **Marcapata** ① *173 km from Urcos, US$0.20,* provide a relaxing break.

Some 82 km from Urcos, at the base of **Nevado Ausangate** (6384 m), is the town of **Ocongate**, which has two hotels on the Plaza de Armas and the **Parador de Ausangate** (T221601, www.paradordelausangate.com), which can arrange hiking, horse riding, fishing and biking. Beyond Ocongate is **Tinqui**, the starting point for hikes around Ausangate and in the Cordillera Vilcanota. On the flanks of the Nevado Ausangate is Q'Olloriti, where a church has been built close to a glacier and has become a place of pilgrimage (see Cuzco, Festivals, page 219).

Hiking around Ausangate ① *Entry US$7.50 at Tinqui.* The hike around the mountain of Ausangate takes five days: spectacular, but quite hard, with a pass over 5000 m and camping above 4000 m, so you need to be acclimatized. Temperatures in high season (April-October) can drop well below zero at night. It is recommended to take a guide and/

or *arriero*. *Arrieros* and mules can be hired in Tinqui for US$12 per day for an *arriero*, US$10 for a mule, but more for a saddle horse. *Arrieros* also expect food. Make sure you sign a contract with full details. Buy all food supplies in Cuzco. Maps are available at the **IGN** in Lima or **South American Explorers**, who also have latest information.

From Urcos to Sicuani (see page 200), the road passes **Cusipata** (with an Inca gate and wall), **Checacupe** (with a lovely church) and **Tinta**, 23 km from Sicuani (church with brilliant gilded interior and an interesting choir vault). There are frequent buses and trucks to Cuzco, or take the train from Cuzco. Continuing to Sicuani, **Raqchi** is the scene of the region's great folklore festival starting on 24 June, **Wiracocha**, when dancers come from all over Peru. Raqchi is also the site of the **Viracocha Temple** ① *US$3, take a bus or truck from Cuzco towards Sicuani, US$2.50*. John Hemming wrote: "What remains is the central wall, which is adobe above and Inca masonry below. This was probably the largest roofed building ever built by the Incas. On either side of the high wall, great sloping roofs were supported by rows of unusual round pillars, also of masonry topped by adobe. Nearby is a complex of barracks-like buildings and round storehouses. This was the most holy shrine to the creator god Viracocha, being the site of a miracle in which he set fire to the land – hence the lava flow nearby. There are also small Inca baths in the corner of a field beyond the temple and a straight row of ruined houses by a square. The landscape is extraordinary, blighted by huge piles of black volcanic rocks." You can do a homestay here with pottery classes and a walk to the extinct volcano.

⊙ Southeast from Cuzco listings

For hotel and restaurant price codes, and other relevant information, see pages 14-17.

⊙ Where to stay

Ausangate *p230*
$ Ausangate, Tinqui. Very basic, but warm, friendly atmosphere.
$ Hostal Tinqui Guide, on the right-hand side as you enter Tinqui. Meals available. Sr Crispin, the owner, is knowledgeable and can arrange guides, mules, etc. He and his brothers can be contacted in Cuzco on T227768. All have been recommended as reliable sources of trekking and climbing information, for arranging trips. Also recommended is Teofilo Viagara, who lives 30 mins above the village; ask around to contact him by radio.

⊙ Transport

Southeast from Cuzco: Paucartambo *p230*
Bus A minibus leaves daily for Paucartambo from Av Huáscar in **Cuzco**, US$8, 3-4 hrs; alternate days Paucartambo-Cuzco. Trucks and a private bus leave from the Coliseo, behind Hospital del Seguro in Cuzco, 5 hrs, US$3. Agencies in Cuzco arrange round trips on 15-17 Jul.

Ausangate *p230*
Bus From Cuzco, to **Tinqui** from Av Tomasatito Condemayta, corner of the Coliseo Cerrado in Cuzco, daily at 1600, 3-4 hrs, US$7. **Huayna Ausangate** is a recommended company, ticket office near the Coliseo Cerrado.

Sacred Valley of the Incas

The name conjures up images of ancient rulers and their god-like status, with the landscape itself as their temple. And so it was, but the Incas also built their own tribute to this dramatic land in monuments such as Machu Picchu, Ollantaytambo, Pisac and countless others. For the tourist, the famous sights are now within easy reach of Cuzco, but the demand for adventure, to see lost cities in a less 21st-century context, means that there is ample scope for exploring. But if archaeology is not your thing, there are markets to enjoy, birds to watch, trails for mountain-biking and a whole range of hotels to relax in. The best time to visit is April to May or October to November. The high season is June-September, but the rainy season, from December to March, is cheaper and pleasant enough.

Pisac → *Phone code: 084. Colour map 4, C3.*

Pisac, 30 km north of Cuzco, has a traditional Sunday morning **market**, at which local people sell their produce in exchange for essential goods. It is also a major draw for tourists who arrive after 0800 until 1700. Pisac has other, somewhat less crowded but more commercial markets every second day. Each Sunday at 1100 there is a Quechua Mass. On the plaza are the church and a small interesting **Museo Folklórico**. The **Museo Comunitario Pisac** ① *Av Amazonas y Retamayoc K'asa, museopisac@gmail.com, daily 1000-1700, free but donations welcome*, has a display of village life, created by the people of Pisac. There are many souvenir shops on Bolognesi. Local fiesta: 15 July.

The Sacred Valley

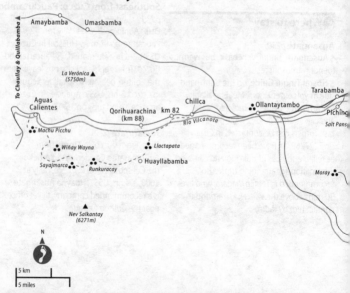

High above the town on the mountainside is a superb **Inca fortress** ⓘ *0700-1730, guides charge about US$5, you must show your BTC multi-site ticket to enter.* The walk up to the ruins begins from the plaza (but see below), past the Centro de Salud and a control post. The path goes through working terraces, giving the ruins a context. The first group of buildings is Pisaqa, with a fine curving wall. Climb then to the central part of the ruins, the Intihuatana group of temples and rock outcrops in the most magnificent Inca masonry. Here are the Reloj Solar ('Hitching Post of the Sun') – now closed because thieves stole a piece from it, palaces of the moon and stars, solstice markers, baths and water channels. From Intihuatana, a path leads around the hillside through a tunnel to Q'Allaqasa, the military area. Across the valley at this point, a large area of Inca tombs in holes in the hillside can be seen. The end of the site is Kanchiracay, where the agricultural workers were housed. Road transport approaches from this end. The descent takes 30 minutes. At dusk you will hear, if not see, the *pisaca* (partridges), after which the place is named. Even if going by car, do not rush as there is a lot to see and a lot of walking to do. Road transport approaches from the Kanchiracay end. The drive up from town takes about 20 minutes. Walking up, although tiring, is recommended for the views and location. It's at least one hour uphill all the way. The descent takes 30 minutes on foot. Combis charge US$0.75 per person and taxis US$7 one way up to the ruins from near the bridge. Then you can walk back down (if you want the taxi to take you back down, usually from a lower level, it will be another US$7).

Pisac to Urubamba

Calca, 2900 m, is 18 km beyond Pisac. There are basic hotels and eating places and buses stop on the other side of the divided plaza. **Fiesta de la Vírgen Asunta** 15-16 August. The

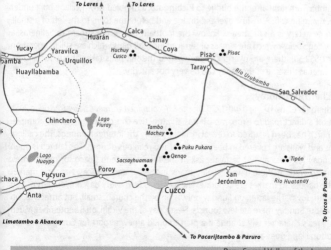

ruins of a small Inca town, **Huchuy Cuzco** ① *US$7.15 for trek and entry*, are dramatically located on a flat esplanade almost 600 m above Calca, from where a road has been built to the ruins. Alternatively, a steep trail goes to the site from behind the village of Lamay, across the river. A magnificent one- or two-day trek leads to Huchuy Cuzco from Tambo Machay, the route once taken by the Inca from his capital to his country estate.

The **Valle de Lares** is beautiful for walking and cycling, with its magnificent mountains, lakes and small villages. You start near an old hacienda in Huarán (2830 m), cross two passes over 4000 m and end at the hot springs near Lares. From this village, transport runs back to Calca. Alternatively, you can add an extra day and continue to Ollantaytambo. You can also start in Lares and end in Yanhuara. Several agencies in Cuzco offer trekking and biking tours to the region. Miguel Angel Delgado in Cuzco, T973-275881, mikyyuta@ yahoo.com, has been recommended as a trekking guide for this area.

About 3 km east of Urubamba, **Yucay** has two grassy plazas divided by the restored colonial church of Santiago Apóstol, with its oil paintings and fine altars. On the opposite side from Plaza Manco II is the adobe palace built for Sayri Túpac (Manco's son) when he emerged from Vilcabamba in 1558. In Yucay monks sell milk, ham and eggs from their farm on the hillside.

Urubamba → *Phone code: 084. Altitude: 2863 m.*
Like many places along the valley, Urubamba is in a fine setting with snow-capped peaks in view. Calle Berriózabal, on the west edge of town, is lined with pisonay trees. The large market square is one block west of the main plaza. The main road skirts the town and the bridge for the road to Chinchero is just to the east of town. Visit **Seminario-Bejar Ceramic Studio** ① *Berriózabal 111, T201002, www.ceramicaseminario.com*. Pablo Seminario and his workshop have investigated and use pre-Columbian techniques and designs, highly recommended. For local festivals, May and June are the harvest months, with many processions following ancient schedules. Urubamba's main festival, **El Señor de Torrechayoc**, occupies the first week of June.

About 6 km west of Urubamba is **Tarabamba**, where a bridge crosses the Río Urubamba. Turn right after the bridge to **Pichingoto**, a tumbled-down village built under an overhanging cliff. Also, just over the bridge and before the town to the left of a small, walled cemetery is a salt stream. Follow the footpath beside the stream to Salineras, a small village below which are a mass of terraced Inca salt pans which are still in operation (entry US$2.50); there are over 5000. The walk to the salt pans takes about 30 minutes. Take water as this side of the valley can be very hot and dry.

Chinchero and Moray
Chinchero (3762 m) ① *site 0700-1730, on the BTC combined entrance ticket (see page 205)*, is just off a direct road to Urubamba. It has an attractive church built on an Inca temple. The church has been restored to reveal in all their glory the interior paintings. The ceiling, beams and walls are covered in beautiful floral and religious designs. The church is open on Sunday for Mass and at festivals; ask in the tourist office in Cuzco for other times. Recent excavations there have revealed many Inca walls and terraces. The food market and the handicraft market are separate. The former is held every day, on your left as you come into town. The latter, on Sunday only, is up by the church, small, but attractive. On any day but Sunday there are few tourists. Fiesta, day of the Virgin, on 8 September. Much of the area's character will change if a plan to build a new airport for Cuzco on nearby agricultural land goes ahead.

At Moray, there are three 'colosseums', used by the Incas, according to some theories, as a sort of open-air crop nursery, known locally as the laboratory of the Incas. The great depressions contain no ruined buildings, but are lined with fine terracing. Each level is said to have its own microclimate. It is a very atmospheric place which, many claim, has mystical power, and the scenery is absolutely stunning (entry US$3.50, or by BTC). The most interesting way to get to Moray is from Urubamba via the Pichingoto bridge over the Río Urubamba. The path passes by the spectacular **salt pans**, still in production after thousands of years, taking 1½ to two hours to the top. The village of Maras is about 45 minutes further on, then it's 9 km by road or 5 km through the fields to Moray. Tour companies in Cuzco offer cycle trips to Moray. There are no hotels at all in the area, so take care not to be stranded. (See Transport, for further details on how to get there.)

Ollantaytambo → *Colour map 4, B2. Phone code: 084. Altitude: 2800 m.*
① *Inca ruins open 0700-1730. If possible arrive very early, 0700, before the tourists. Admission is by BTC visitor's ticket, which can be bought at the site. Guides at the entrance.*

The Inca town, or *Llacta*, on which the present-day town is based is clearly seen in the fine example of Inca *canchas* (blocks), which are almost entirely intact and still occupied behind the main plaza. Entering Ollantaytambo from Pisac, the road is built along the long wall of 100 niches. Note the inclination of the wall: it leans towards the road. Since it was the Inca's practice to build with the walls leaning towards the interiors of the buildings, it has been deduced that the road, much narrower then, was built inside a succession of buildings. The road out of the plaza leads across a bridge, down to the colonial church with its enclosed *recinto*. Beyond is Plaza Araccama (and car park) with the entrance to the archaeological site.

The so-called **Baño de la Ñusta** (bath of the princess) is of grey granite, and is in a small area between the town and the temple fortress. Some 200 m behind the Baño de la Ñusta along the face of the mountain are some small ruins known as Inca Misanca, believed to have been a small temple or observatory. A series of steps, seats and niches have been carved out of the cliff. There is a complete irrigation system, including a canal at shoulder level, some 6 inches deep, cut out of the sheer rock face. The flights of terraces leading up above the town are superb, and so are the curving terraces following the contours of the rocks overlooking the Urubamba. These terraces were successfully defended by Manco Incas warriors against Hernando Pizarro in 1536. Manco Inca built the wall above the site and another wall closing the Yucay valley against attack from Cuzco. These are visible on either side of the valley.

The temple itself was started by Pachacútec, using Colla Indians from Lake Titicaca – hence the similarities of the monoliths facing the central platform with the Tiahuanaco remains. The massive, highly finished granite blocks at the top are worth the climb to see. The Colla are said to have deserted halfway through the work, which explains the many unfinished blocks lying about the site.

On the west side of the main ruins, a two-dimensional 'pyramid' has been identified in the layout of the fields and walls of the valley. A fine 750 m wall aligns with the rays of the winter solstice on 21 June. It can be appreciated from a high point about 3.5 km from Ollantaytambo.

For hotel and restaurant price codes, and other relevant information, see pages 14-17.

◎ Where to stay

Pisac *p232*

$$$ Royal Inka Pisac, Carretera Ruinas Km 1.5, T203064, www.royalinkahotel. pe. Converted hacienda with olympic-size swimming pool (US$3.50 per day), sauna and jacuzzi for guests only, very pleasant, provides guides. This chain also has **Royal Inkas I** and **II** in Cuzco.

$$ Hostal Varayoc, Mcal Castilla 380, T223638, luzpaz3@hotmail.com. Renovated hotel around a colonial courtyard with working bread oven. Decor is smart and bathrooms are modern.

$$ Melissa Wasi, 15 mins' walk from Pisac Plaza, close to the river, T797589. A family-run bed and breakfast with rooms and small bungalows. Very homely, English spoken.

$$ Paz y Luz, T203204, www.pazyluzperu. com. 10-15 mins' walk from Pisac Plaza, close to the river. American-owned, pleasant garden, nicely designed rooms, breakfast included. Diane Dunn offers healing from many traditions (including Andean), sacred tours, workshops and gatherings.

$$ Pisac Inn, at the corner of Pardo on the Plaza, Casilla Postal 1179, Cuzco, T203062, www.pisacinn.com. Bright and charming local decor, pleasant atmosphere, private and shared bathrooms, hot water, sauna and massage. Good breakfast, the **Cuchara de Palo** restaurant serves meals using local ingredients, plus pizza and pasta, café.

$ Res Beho, Intihuatana 642, T203001. Ask for room in main building, good breakfast, owner's son will act as guide to ruins at weekend.

Pisac to Urubamba *p234*
Yucay
$$$$ Sonesta Posadas del Inca Sacred Valley, Plaza Manco II de Yucay 123,

T201107, www.sonesta.com. Converted 300-year-old monastery, it is like a little village with plazas, chapel, 69 comfortable, heated rooms, price includes buffet breakfast. Lots of activities can be arranged, canoeing, horse riding, mountain biking, etc. **Inkafe** restaurant is open to all, serving Peruvian, fusion and traditional cuisine with a US$15 buffet. Recommended.

$$$ La Casona de Yucay, Plaza Manco II 104, T201116, www.hotelcasonayucay.com. This colonial house was where Simón Bolívar stayed during his liberation campaign in 1824. With heating, 2 patios and gardens, **Don Manuel** restaurant and bar.

$$$ The Green House, Km 60.2 Huaran, T984-770130, www.thegreenhouseperu. com. A charming, Wi-Fi-free retreat, only 4 rooms, breakfast included, comfortable lounge, restaurant, small kitchen for guests, beautiful garden, restricted internet. No children under 10. Information on walks and day trips in the area. Activities include hiking, biking, horse riding and rafting. Intimate, beautiful and relaxing.

Urubamba *p234*

$$$$ Casa Andina Private Collection Sacred Valley, paradero 5, Yanahuara, between Urubamba and Ollantaytambo, T984-765501, www.casa-andina.com. In its own 3-ha estate, with all the facilities associated with this chain, plus **Valle Sagrado Andean Cottage** for family and long-stay accommodation, 'Sacred Spa', gym, planetarium, good restaurant, adventure options.

$$$$ Río Sagrado (Belmond), Km 76 Carretera Cuzco–Ollantaytambo, T201631, www.rio sagrado.com. 4 km from Urubamba, set in beautiful gardens overlooking the river with fine views. Rooms and villas, **Mayu Wilka** spa, restaurant and bar, offers various packages.

$$$$ Sol y Luna, Fundo Huincho, west of town, T201620, www.hotelsolyluna.com.

Award-winning bungalows and suites set off the main road in lovely gardens, pool, excellent gourmet restaurant, wine tastings, spa, handicrafts shop. Also has **Wayra** lounge bar and dining room, open to non-guests, for freshly cooked, informal lunches. Arranges adventure and cultural activities and traditional tours. Profits go to **Sol y Luna** educational association.

$$$$ Tambo del Inka, Av Ferrocarril s/n, T581777, www.luxurycollection.com/vallesagrado. A resort and spa on the edge of town, in gardens by the river. Completely remodelled with a variety of rooms and suites, fitness centre, swimming pools, **Hawa** restaurant, bar, business facilities and lots of activities arranged.

$$$ Casa Colibrí, Km 2.5 on road to Ollantaytamba, T205003, www.casacolibriecolodge.com. Delightful, spacious rooms and casitas made of local stone, wood and adobe, set in beautiful gardens to attract bees, butterflies and hummingbirds. Very restful, hammocks, meditation room, excellent homegrown food, swings and table tennis, popular with couples, families and yoga groups.

$$ Las Chullpas, Querocancha s/n, 3 km from town, T201568, www.chullpas.pe. Very peaceful, excellent breakfast, vegetarian meals, English and German spoken, Spanish classes, natural medicine, treks, riding, mountain biking, camping US$3 with hot shower. Mototaxi from town US$2.50, taxi (ask for Querocancha) US$4.

$$ Posada Las Tres Marías, Zavala 307, T201006, www.posadatresmarias.com. A little way from the centre, quiet. Comfortable, hot water, no TV, lovely garden and shady terrace, can provide early breakfast.

$ Hospedaje Buganvilla, Jr Convención 280, T205102, T984-618900. Sizable rooms with hot water, breakfast on request, quiet, bright, good value, very pleasant.

$ Hospedaje Los Jardines, Jr Convención 459, T201331, www.hospedajelosjardines.blogspot.co.uk. Attractive guesthouse with comfortable rooms, hot water, non-smoking,

delicious breakfast US$3.25 extra (vegans catered for), safe, lovely garden, laundry. **Sacred Valley Mountain Bike Tours** also based here.

Chinchero p234

$$ La Casa de Barro, Miraflores 157, T306031 www.lacasadebarro.com. Modern hotel, with hot water, heating, bar, restaurant serving 'fusion' food using organic local produce, tours arranged.

Ollantaytambo p235

$$$$ Pakaritampu, C Ferrocarril s/n, T204020, www.pakaritampu.com.Modern, well-appointed rooms, TV room, restaurant and bar, laundry, safe and room service. Adventure sports can be arranged. Lunch and dinner are extra. Excellent quality and service, but room 8 looks onto the railway station car park.

$$$ El Albergue Ollantaytambo, within the railway station gates, T204014, www.elalbergue.com. Owned by North American artist Wendy Weeks. Also has **Café Mayu** on the station and a good restaurant. Characterful rooms, rustic elegance, some larger than others, some with safe, lovely gardens, great showers and a eucalyptus steam sauna. Books for sale and exchange, also handicrafts. Private transport can be arranged to nearby attractions, also mountain-biking, rafting and taxi transfers to the airport.

$$$ Hostal Sauce, C Ventiderio 248, T204044, www.hostalsauce.com.pe. Smart, simple decor and views of the ruins from 3 of the 6 rooms as well as from the dining room, food from own farm.

$$ Apu Lodge, Calle Lari, T797162, www.apulodge.com. On the edge of town, great views of the ruins and surrounding mountains. Run by Scot Louise Norton and husband Arturo, good service, quiet, nice garden, good buffet breakfast, can help organize tours and treks. They work with **Leap Local** (www.leaplocal.org) guides project.

$$ Hostal Iskay II, Patacalle s/n, T204004, www.hostaliskay.com. In the Inca town. Great location but car access is difficult. Only 6 rooms, hot water, free tea and coffee, use of kitchen. Good reports.

$$ Hostal K'uychipunku, K'uychipunku 6, T204175. Close to Plaza Araccama, hot water, modern, some rooms with view, courtyard.

$$ Hotel Sol Ollantay, C Ventiderio s/n by the bridge between the 2 plazas, T204130, www.hotelsolperu.com. Tastefullly renovated with good views from most rooms, hot water.

$$ KB Tambo, between the main plaza and the ruins, T204091, http://kbperu.com. Spacious, comfortable rooms, suites, garden view or standard, comfy mattresses, heaters on request, hot water, flower-filled garden, good restaurant (**$$**), breakfast extra. Reserve in advance. Also offers adventure tours.

$$ Las Orquídeas, near the start of the road to the station, T204032. Hot water, fairly small but nice rooms, flower-filled patio, discounts for 2 or more nights.

$$ Tika Wasi, C Convencion s/n, T204166, www.tikawasihotel.com. Great location close to the archaeological site, good service and comfortable rooms.

$ Hostal Chaska Wasi, Plaza de Armas, T204045. Private rooms and dorms, hammocks, hot showers, free hot drinks, laundry. Owner Katy is very friendly.

$ Hostal Plaza Ollantaytambo, beside the police station on the main plaza, T436741, hostalplazaollantaytambo@gmail.com. Basic rooms but with private bath, hot water and Wi-Fi. Opened in 2013.

$ Hostal Tambo, C Horno, north of the plaza, T773262 or T984-489094, paula1_79@ hotmail.com. Cheaper for groups, breakfast extra. Once past the door you emerge into a garden full of fruit trees and flowers. Small, rooms for up to 3 people, basic, shared bath downstairs in the courtyard, hot water.

Camping
Restaurant Huatucay, at the edge of the Inca town, between Patacalle and the road to Patacancha, has camping for US$3.60 pp. There are toilets, a minimarket and the restaurant serves typical food.

🍴 Restaurants

Pisac *p232*
$$-$ Miski Mijuna Wasi, on the Plaza de Armas, T203266. Serves tasty local food, typical and Novo Andino, also international dishes. Has a *pastelería* also.

$$-$ Mullu, Plaza de Armas 352 and Mcal Castilla 375, T208182. Tue-Sun 0900-1900. Café/restaurant related to the **Mullu** store in Cuzco, also has a gallery promoting local artists.

$ Doña Clorinda, on the plaza opposite the church. Tasty food, including vegetarian.

$ Valle Sagrado, Av Amazonas 116 (the main street where buses go towards Urubamba). Good quality, generous portions and a lunchtime buffet that includes vegetarian options. Go early before the tour groups arrive.

Bakery, Mcal Castilla 372. Good wholemeal bread, excellent cheese *empanadas*.

Blue Llama Café, corner of the plaza opposite Pisac Inn, T203135, www.bluellama cafe.com. Cute, colourful café with a huge range of teas, good coffee, breakfasts and daily menus.

Ulrike's Café, C Pardo 613, T203195. Has possibly the best apple crumble with ice cream, excellent coffee, smoothies and a wide range of international dishes. Good value 3-course daily *menú*. A good place to chill out.

Urubamba *p234*
$$$ Tunupa, on road from Urubamba to Ollantaytambo, on riverbank. Buffet lunch 1200-1500, US$15, dinner 1800-2030. Same owners as Tunupa in Cuzco, colonial-style hacienda, excellent food and surroundings, pre-Columbian and colonial art exhibitions.

$$$-$$ El Huacatay, Arica 620, T201790, http://elhuacatay.com. Mon-Sat. A small restaurant with a reputation for fine, creative fusion cuisine (local, Mediterranean, Asian).

$$ Coffee Tree, Plaza de Armas, www.
perucoffeetree.com. Daily 0700-2200,
closed Feb. Has a proper coffee machine.
Breakfast, lunch and dinner available.
$$ El Fogón, Parque Pintacha, T201534.
Peruvian food.
$$ El Maizal, on the main road, before the
bridge, T201454. Country-style restaurant,
buffet service with a variety of *Novo Andino*
and international choices, beautiful gardens,
open daytime only.
$$ Tres Keros, Av Señor de Torrechayoc,
T201701. Novo Andino cuisine, try the
lamb chops.
$ La Chepita, Av 1 de Mayo, M6, in a small
plaza. The place to go on Sun for regional
food in the biggest portions you have ever
seen. Get 1 plate between 2.
$ Pizza Wasi, Av Mcal Castilla 857, T434751
for delivery. Good pizzas and pastas. Mulled
wine served in a small restaurant with nice
decor, good value. Has another branch on
Plaza Araccama in Ollantaytambo.

Ollantaytambo *p235*

There are restaurants all over town offering
menú turístico, pizzas, pastas, juices and
hot drinks.
$$ Heart´s Café, Av Ventiderio s/n,
T204013, www.heartscafe.org. Open
0700-2100. Mainly wholefood restaurant
serving international and Peruvian dishes,
including vegetarian, box lunch and
takeaway available, good coffee. All profits
to education and self-help projects in the
Sacred Valley. Deservedly popular.
$$ Il Cappuccino and **Kusicoyllor**, Plaza
Araccama. Good coffee and continental
and American breakfasts. Also serves *menú
turístico*, lunch and dinner, desserts, juices
and light meals.
$$ Mayupata, Jr Convención s/n, across
bridge on the way to the ruins, on the left,
T204083. Opens 0600 for breakfast, and
serves lunch and dinner. International
choices and a selection of Peruvian dishes,
desserts, sandwiches and coffee. Bar has
fireplace; river view, relaxing atmosphere.

$$ Papa's, C Horno at the plaza, T436700.
Restaurant and lounge open 1000-2200.
Serving Tex-Mex, local dishes, pizzas, soups,
salads, and desserts.
$$ Tawachaki, close to the Ollantaytambo
ruin. Good alpaca steak and great views of
the ruins.
$$-$ Alcázar Café, C del Medio, 50 m
from Plaza, T204034. Vegetarian, but also
offers meat and fish, and pasta. Arranges
excursions to Andean communities.
$ La Ñusta, Plaza de Armas corner of Chaupi
Calle, ask here about their *hospedaje*. Popular,
good food, snacks, soups, salads and juices.
Calicanto, on the righthand side just before
the bridge leading to Plaza Araccama. For
coffees and light meals, etc, overlooking
the river that divides the town.

⊛ Festivals

Ollantaytambo *p235*

On the Sun following Inti Raymi, there is a
colourful festival, the **Ollanta-Raymi**. **6 Jan**
The Bajada de Reyes Magos (the Magi), with
dancing, a bull fight, local food and a fair.
End-May/early-Jun 50 days after Easter,
Fiesta del Señor de Choquekillca, patron
saint of Ollantaytambo, with several days
of dancing, weddings, processions, Masses,
feasting and drinking. **29 Oct** The town's
anniversary, with lots of dancing in traditional
costume and many local delicacies for sale.

⚙ What to do

Urubamba *p234*

Horse riding Perol Chico, 5 km from
Urubamba at Km 77, T084-974-798 890/974-
780020, www.perolchico.com. Dutch/Peruvian
owned and operated, 1- to 14-day trips, good
horses, riding is Peruvian Paso style.
Trekking Haku Trek, contact Javier
Saldívar, T984-613001, www.hakutrek.com.
Cooperative tourism project in the
Chicón valley (the mountain valley above
Urubamba), run by residents of the
community, 1- and 2-day hiking trips based

at a simple eco-lodge; profits are used to fund reforestation of the area.

⊖ Transport

Urubamba *p234*
Bus Terminal, west of town on the main road, about 3 km from centre. From Urubamba to **Calca**, **Pisac** (US$2, 1 hr) and **Cuzco**, about 2 hrs, US$2.25; also buses to Cuzco via Chinchero, same fare. Combis run to **Ollantaytambo**, 45 mins, US$0.75.

Chinchero and Moray *p234*
Road There is a paved road from the main road between Chinchero and Urubamba to the village of Maras and from there an unmade road in good condition leads to Moray, 9 km. Ask in Maras for the best route to walk, other than on the main road. Any bus between Urubamba and Cuzco via Chinchero passes the clearly marked turning to Maras. From the junction taxi colectivos charge US$2.50 pp to Maras, or you can walk (30 mins). There is public transport from Chinchero to Maras; it stops running between 1700 and 1800. Taxi to Moray, 1-hr wait then take you to the salt pans, from where you can walk back to the Urubamba-Ollantaytambo road, US$25.

Ollantaytambo *p235*
Bus Colectivos leave all day for Urubamba and Cuzco from 1 block east of the main plaza. Direct bus Ollantaytambo to **Cuzco** at 0715 and 1945, US$4; also Cruz del Sur, 3 a day, US$7. Direct taxi colectivo service from C Pavitos, Cuzco, leaves when full US$3.60 to Ollantaytambo. Minibuses and taxis leave the small Terminal de Transportes just up from Ollantaytambo station (10-15 mins' walk from the plaza) at train times for Urubamba and Cuzco, US$6 shared to either place, but they may try to charge much more as a private service only. Say you'll go to the colectivo terminal and they may reduce the price. Transfers and tours with **Aló K'antuyoc**, at the hostel of that name on Av Ferrocarril, T204147. See also under trains to and from Machu Picchu, page 244. There are colectivos and mototaxis at the Plaza for the station when trains are due. You won't be allowed in the station unless you have previously bought a ticket (and it is best to buy tickets in Cuzco).

Machu Picchu → *Colour map 4, B2.*

There is a tremendous feeling of awe on first witnessing Machu Picchu. The ancient citadel (42 km from Ollantaytambo by rail) straddles the saddle of a high mountain (2380 m) with steep terraced slopes falling away to the fast-flowing Urubamba river snaking its hairpin course far below in the valley floor. Towering overhead is Huayna Picchu, and green jungle peaks provide the backdrop for the whole majestic scene. Machu Picchu is a complete Inca city. For centuries it was buried in jungle, until Hiram Bingham stumbled upon it in 1911. It was then explored by an archaeological expedition sent by Yale University. The ruins – staircases, terraces, temples, palaces, towers, fountains and the famous Intihuatana (the so-called 'Hitching Post of the Sun') – require at least a day. Take time to appreciate not only the masonry, but also the selection of large rocks for foundations, the use of water in the channels below the Temple of the Sun and the surrounding mountains.

Arriving at Machu Picchu
Entrance to Machu Picchu The site is open from 0600 to 1730. Only 2500 visitors are allowed entry each day. Entrance fee to Machu Picchu only is 128 soles (US$45.50), 65 soles for Peruvians, 63 soles with ISIC card (US$23 and US$22.40 approximately). To climb Huayna Picchu you have to buy a ticket for site entry and the climb and specify whether you are going to go 0700-0800 or 1000-1100 (only 400 people are allowed up at one time), 152 soles

(US$54). There is also a combined Machu Picchu and Museum ticket, 150 soles (US$53.30). There is a fourth Machu Picchu and Montaña ticket for 142 soles (US$50.50). Because of the limit on numbers it is wise to reserve your ticket online in advance at www.machupicchu. gob.pe. You can pay online with Visa or at a number of outlets given on the website. These include branches of Banco de la Nación, **Centro Cultural de Machu Picchu** ① *Av Pachacútec cuadra 1, Aguas Calientes, 0500-2200 (also i perú here, of 4, T211104, iperumachupicchu@ promperu.gob.pe, daily 0900-1300, 1400-2000)*, **Dirección Regional de Cultura** in Cuzco (see page 205), **AATC** ① *C Nueva Baja 424, Cuzco*, offices of **PerúRail** and **Inca Rail** in Cuzco, **Hotel Monasterio**. Other websites offer tickets for sale, at an inflated price. Do not buy (fake) tickets on the street in Cuzco. You can deposit your luggage at the entrance for a small fee, but small bags may be taken into the ruins. Guides are available at the site, they are often very knowledgeable and worthwhile. The official price for a guide is US$80 for a full tour for one to 10 people. Site wardens are also informative, in Spanish only. A guarded gate by the river in Aguas Calientes opens only at 0530, so it is not possible to walk up to the ruins to be there before the first buses. After 1100 the ruins fill rapidly with visitors who have arrived by train. It is best to arrive before then. The **Sanctuary Lodge** is located next to the entrance, with a self-service restaurant. Take your own food and drink if you don't want to pay hotel prices, and take plenty of drinking water. Note that food is not officially allowed into the site and drink can only be carried in canteens/water bottles. There are toilets at the entrance. Sandflies are a problem, especially in the dry season, so take insect repellent and wear long clothes. Also take protection against the sun and rain showers.

New regulations were announced in early 2014 but had not yet come into effect at the close of this edition. They would require that all visitors be accompanied by a guide, that they follow one of the three established routes without turning back and that they limit stops at certain places to there to five minutes; all in the interest of mitigating crowding and maintaining an orderly flow of tourists through the site. Be aware also that entry may be limited to morning-, or afternoon-only tickets.

Around the site

Huayna Picchu, the mountain overlooking the site (on which there are also ruins), has steps to the top for a superlative view of the whole site, but it is not for those who are afraid of heights and you shouldn't leave the path. The climb takes up to 90 minutes but the steps are dangerous after bad weather. Visitors are given access to the main path at 0700 and 1000 daily, latest return time 1500 (maximum 200 people per departure). Check with the Ministerio de Cultura in Aguas Calientes or Cuzco for current departure times and to sign up for a place. Another trail to Huayna Picchu, down near the Urubamba, is via the Temple of the Moon, in two caves, one above the other, with superb Inca niches inside. For the trail to the Temple of the Moon: from the path to Huayna Picchu, take the marked trail to the left. It is in good shape, although it descends further than you think it should and there are very steep steps on the way. After the Temple you may proceed to Huayna Picchu, but this path is overgrown, slippery in the wet and has a crooked ladder on an exposed part about 10 minutes before reaching the top (not for the faint-hearted). It is safer to return to the main trail to Huayna Picchu, although this adds about 30 minutes to the climb. The round trip takes about four hours. Before doing any trekking around Machu Picchu, check with an official which paths may be used, or which are one-way.

The famous Inca bridge is about 45 minutes along a well-marked trail south of the Royal Sector. The bridge (on which you cannot walk) is spectacularly sited, carved into a vertiginous cliff-face. East of the Royal Sector is the path leading up to **Intipunku** on the

Inca Trail (60 minutes, fine views). Climbing Machu Picchu mountain is another excellent option which gives a completely different view of the site and surrounding valleys. The route is steep and takes up to three hours.

Aguas Calientes

Those with more time should spend the night at Aguas Calientes (also known as Machu Picchu Pueblo) and visit the ruins early in the morning, when fewer people are around. Most hotels and restaurants are near the railway station, on the plaza, or on Avenida Pachacútec, which leads from the plaza to the **thermal baths** ① *0500-2030, US$3.15, 10 mins' walk from the town,* (a communal pool, smelling of sulphur, best early in the morning) good bar for cocktails in the pool. You can rent towels and bathing costumes (US$3) at several places on the road to the baths; basic toilets and changing facilities and showers for washing *before* entering the baths; take soap and shampoo, and keep an eye on valuables. The **Museo Manuel Chávez Ballón** ① *Carretera Hiram Bingham, Wed-Sun 0900-1600, see above for tickets,* displays objects found at Machu Picchu.

⊕ Machu Picchu listings

For hotel and restaurant price codes, and other relevant information, see pages 14-17.

⊖ Where to stay

Machu Picchu *p240*

$$$$ Machu Picchu Sanctuary Lodge, reservations as for the **Hotel Monasterio** in Cuzco, which is under the same management (Belmond), T084-984-816956, www.sanctuary lodge.net. Comfortable, good service, helpful staff, food well-cooked and presented. Electricity and water 24 hrs a day, prices are all-inclusive, restaurant for residents only in the evening, but the buffet lunch is open to all. Usually fully booked well in advance, try Sun night as other tourists find Pisac market a greater attraction.

Aguas Calientes *p242*

$$$$ Casa del Sol, Av Imperio de los Incas 608, on the railroad, T211118, www.hoteles casadelsol.com. 5-storey hotel with lift/ elevator, different room categories with river or mountain views, nice restaurant, beautiful spa. Shower service and changing room available after check out.

$$$$ Inkaterra Machu Picchu Pueblo, Km 104, 5 mins' walk along the railway from town, T211122. Reservations: C Andalucía 174, Miraflores, Lima, T01-610 0400; in Cuzco at Plaza las Nazarenas 113 p2, T234010, www.inkaterra.com. Beautiful colonial-style bungalows in village compound surrounded by cloud forest, lovely gardens with a lot of steps between the public areas and rooms, pool, excellent restaurant, offer tours to Machu Picchu, several guided walks on and off the property, buffet breakfasts included in price. Good baggage service to coordinate with train arrivals and departures. Also has the **Café Inkaterra** by the railway line.

$$$$ Sumaq Machu Picchu, Av Hermanos Ayar Mz 1, Lote 3, T211059, www.sumaq hotelperu.com. Award-winning 5-star hotel on the edge of town, between railway and road to Machu Picchu. Suites and luxury rooms with heating, restaurant and bar, spa.

$$$ Gringo Bill's (Hostal Q'oñi Unu), Colla Raymi 104, T211046, www.gringobills.com (in Cuzco Av El Sol 520, T223663). With hot water, laundry, money exchange, pretty rooms, good beds, balconies, lot of coming and going, good restaurant, breakfast from 0500, packed lunch available. Views of the plaza are now obscured by the monstrous new municipal building.

$$$ La Cabaña, Av Pachacútec Mz 20, Lote 3, T211048, www.lacabanamachu picchu.com. With hot water, café, laundry service, helpful, popular with groups.

$$$ Presidente, Av Imperio de los Incas, at the old station, T211034, www.hostal presidente.com. Adjoining **Hostal Machu Picchu**, see below, more upmarket but little difference, rooms without river view cheaper.

$$$-$$ Hostal Wiracocha Inn, C Wiracocha, T211088, www.wiracochainn.com. Hot water, small garden, helpful, popular with groups, also has higher-priced suites.

$$$-$$ Rupa Wasi, Huanacaure 105, T211101, www.rupawasi.net. Charming 'eco-lodge' up a small alley off Collasuyo, laid back, comfortable, great views from the balconies, purified water available, organic garden, good breakfasts, half-board available, excellent restaurant, **The Tree House**, and cookery classes.

$$ Hospedaje Quilla, Av Pachacútec 23 between Wiracocha and Tupac Inka Yupanki, T211009. Hot water, rents bathing gear for the hot springs.

$$ Hostal Imperio de los Inkas, Av Pachacútec 602, at the old station, T211105, totemsito@gmail.com. Functional, quiet, family-owned *hostal*, group rates, good value.

$$ Hostal Machu Picchu, Av Imperio de los Incas 135, at the old station, T211065, sierrandina@gmail.com. Functional, quiet, Wilber, the owner's son, has travel information, hot water, nice balcony over the Urubamba, grocery store.

$$ Hostal Místico, Av Pachacútec Mz 19 lote 12, T211051, http://elmisticohostal.com. Good breakfast, free Wi-Fi but pay for use of computer, quiet, new-wave-ish, comfortable, near thermal baths.

$$-$ Las Bromelias, Colla Raymi, T211145, just off Plaza before Gringo Bill's. Cheaper without bath, small, hot water.

$ Hostal Pirwa, C Túpac Inka Yupanki 103, T214315, www.pirwahostelscusco.com. In the same group as in Cuzco, Lima and elsewhere.

$ Terrazas del Inca, C Wiracocha M-18-4, T211114, www.terrazasdelinca.com. Safety deposit box, kitchen use, helpful staff.

Camping The only official campsite is in a field by the river, just below Puente Ruinas station, toilets, cold showers, US$6 per tent. Do not leave your tent and belongings unattended.

⑦ Restaurants

Aguas Calientes *p242*

The old station and Av Pachútec are lined with eating places, many of them *pizzerías*. Tax is often added as an extra to the bill.

$$$ Café Inkaterra, on the railway, just below the **Machu Picchu Pueblo Hotel**. US$15 for a great lunch buffet with scenic views of the river.

$$ Indio Feliz, C Lloque Yupanqui, T211090. Great French cuisine, excellent value and service, set 3-course meal for US$20, good pisco sours in the new bar, great atmosphere.

$$ Inka Wasi, Av Pachacútec. Very good choice, has an open fire, full Peruvian and international menu available.

$$ Inka's Pizza Pub, on the plaza. Good pizzas, also changes money.

$$ Pueblo Viejo, Av Pachacútec (near plaza). Good food in a spacious but warm environment. Price includes use of the salad bar.

$$ Toto's House, Av Imperio de los Incas, on the railway line. Same owners as **Pueblo Viejo**. Good value and quality *menú*, buffet from 1130-1500.

$ Discovery, Plaza de Armas, T211355. The best coffee and internet connection in Aguas Calientes. Several computers and Wi-Fi.

$ Govinda, Av Pachacútec y Túpac Inka Yupanki. Vegetarian restaurant with a cheap set lunch.

La Boulangerie de Paris, Jr Sinchi Roca, www.laboulangeriedeparis.net. Coffee, sandwiches, quiche and great French bread.

⑪ Bars and clubs

Aguas Calientes *p242*

Wasicha Pub, C Lloque Yupanqui. Good music and atmosphere, the place to party after the Trail.

✈ Transport

Machu Picchu *p240*

Bus Buses leave **Aguas Calientes** for Machu Picchu as they fill from 0530 until 1500, 25 mins. US$19 return, US$10 single, children US$10, valid 48 hrs. The bus stop in Aguas Calientes is 50 m from the railway station, with the ticket office opposite. Tickets can also be bought in advance at **Consettur** in Cuzco, Av Infancia 433, Wanchaq, T222125, www.consettur.com, which saves queuing when you arrive in Aguas Calientes. Buses return from the ruins to Aguas 0700-1730. The walk up from Aguas Calientes follows a poor path and crosses the motor road (take care). The road is also in poor condition and landslides can cause disruptions.

Train 2 companies operate: **PerúRail** (Av Pachacútec, Wanchac Station, T581414, www.perurail.com) to Machu Picchu from Poroy, near Cuzco, from Urubamba and from Ollantaytambo. **Inca Rail**, joint operation with Andean Railways (Portal de Panes 105, Plaza de Armas, Cuzco, T233030, or Lima T613 5288, www.incarail.com) from Ollantaytambo to Machu Picchu. They go to Aguas Calientes (the official name of this station is 'Machu Picchu'). The station for the tourist trains at Aguas Calientes is on the outskirts of town, 200 m from the **Pueblo Hotel** and 50 m from where buses leave for Machu Picchu ruins. There is a paved road between Aguas Calientes and the start of the road up to the ruins. **Note** Services may be disrupted in the rainy season, especially Jan-Feb.

There are 4 classes of **PerúRail** tourist train: **Vistadome** (recommended, US$87 one-way from Poroy, US$60-84 from Ollantaytambo); **Expedition** (US$77 Poroy-Machu Picchu one-way, US$56-65 from Ollantaytambo); **Auto Vagón** (from the Hotel Tambo del Inka in Urubamba, US$80); and the luxurious **Belmond Hiram Bingham** service with meals, drinks and entertainment (US$356 one way from Poroy). Services from Poroy and Urubamba run once a day; those from Ollantaytambo 5 times a day each.

Seats can be reserved even if you're not returning the same day. These trains have toilets, video, snacks and drinks for sale. You must have your original passport to travel on the trains to Machu Picchu. Tickets for all trains may be bought at Wanchac station and Portal de Carnes 214, Plaza de Armas, in Cuzco, at travel agencies, or via PerúRail's website, www.perurail.com.

Inca Rail has 4 trains a day Ollantayambo-Machu Picchu, 0640, 0720, 1115 and 1636, returning 0830, 1430, 1612 and 1900), US$47-67 one way tourist class, US$135 one way executive class. Carriages have a/c and heating, snacks and drinks served.

Tourists may not travel on the local train to Machu Picchu, but there are ways to avoid the train. Take a bus from Cuzco towards Quillabamba at 0800, 0900 or 1900, US$9. It is best not to travel overnight; confirm all bus and train times locally, especially in the rainy season. Get out at **Santa María** (about 7 hrs) where minibuses wait to go to **Santa Teresa**, 2 hrs, US$7. From Santa Teresa you have to cross the bridge over the Río Urubamba and walk 6 km to the Central Hidroeléctrica, a nice, flat road, or take a combi, US$4. From the Hidroeléctrica train station it's 40 mins on the local train to **Aguas Calientes** (US$20 for tourists, about 3 a day in high season) or you can walk along the railway in 2-3 hrs (at Km 114.5 is **$** pp **Hospedaje Mandor**, about 2 km from bridge to Machu Picchu). To return, walk or take the local train from Aguas Calientes to Santa Teresa to catch a bus to Santa María, then take a bus back to Cuzco. If using this route, don't forget you can pre-book your ticket for Machu Picchu online or in Cuzco, if you don't want to buy it in Aguas Calientes.

Another option is to take a **Machu Picchu By Car** tour, which agencies in Cuzco run over 1 or 2 nights. Passengers are taken to the Hidroeléctrica station via **Ollantaytambo** and **Abra Málaga**, with an overnight stay in Aguas Calientes, or Santa Teresa. The tour includes transport, lodging, Machu Picchu entry, some meals and guide, US$115-160 pp.

Inca trails

The most impressive way to reach Machu Picchu is via the centuries-old Inca Trail that winds its way from the Sacred Valley near Ollantaytambo, taking three to five days. The spectacular hike runs from Km 88, Qorihuayrachina (2299 m), a point immediately after the first tunnel 22 km beyond Ollantaytambo station. A sturdy suspension bridge has now been built over the Río Urubamba. Guided tours generally start at Km 82, Piscacucho, reached by road. Rules for hiking the trail are detailed below. What makes this hike so special is the stunning combination of Inca ruins, unforgettable views, magnificent mountains, exotic vegetation and extraordinary ecological variety.

Arriving at the Inca Trail
Equipment The Inca Trail is rugged and steep, but the magnificent views compensate for any weariness which may be felt. It is cold at night, however, and weather conditions change rapidly, so it is important to take not only strong footwear, rain gear and warm clothing but also food, water, water purification for when you fill bottles from streams, insect repellent, a supply of plastic bags, coverings, a good sleeping bag, a torch/flashlight and a stove for preparing hot food and drink to ward off the cold at night. A stove using white gas (*bencina,* available from hardware stores in Cuzco) is preferable. A tent is essential, but if you're hiring one in Cuzco, check carefully for leaks. Walkers who have not taken adequate equipment have died of exposure.

All the necessary equipment can be rented; see page 220 under Camping equipment and What to do. Good maps of the Trail and area can be bought from **South American Explorers** in Lima or Cuzco. If you have any doubts about carrying your own pack, reasonably priced porters/guides are available. Carry a day-pack for your water, snacks, etc, in case you walk faster than the porters and you have to wait for them to catch you up.

The above applies only to those who trek with a licensed guide (see below). Most people sign on with an agency, which should provide all gear. Independent trekking is not permitted.

Tours Travel Agencies in Cuzco arrange transport to the start, equipment, food, etc, for an all-in price for all treks that lead to the Machu Picchu Historical Sanctuary. Prices start at about US$540-620 per person for a four-day/three-night trek on the Classic Inca Trail and rise according to the level of service given. If the price is significantly lower, you should be concerned as the company will be cutting corners and may not be paying the environment the respect the regulations were designed to instil. All are subject to strict rules and must be licensed. Tour operators taking clients on any of the Inca Trails leading to the Machu Picchu Historical Sanctuary have to pass an annual test. Groups of up to seven independent travellers who do not wish to use a tour operator are allowed to hike the trails if they contract an independent, licensed guide to accompany them, as long as they do not contact any other persons such as porters or cooks. There is a maximum of 500 persons per day, including guides and porters, allowed on the Classic Inca Trail. Operators pay US$15 for each porter and other trail staff; porters are not permitted to carry more than 20 kg. Littering is banned, as is carrying plastic water bottles (canteens only may be carried). Pets and pack animals are prohibited. Groups have to use approved campsites only.

Trail tickets On all hiking trails (Km 82 or Km 88 to Machu Picchu, Salkantay to Machu Picchu, and Km 82 or Km 88 to Machu Picchu via Km 104) adults must pay US$95, students and children under 15 US$47. On the Camino Real de los Inkas from Km 104 to Wiñay-Wayna and Machu Picchu the fee is US$55 per adult, US$31 for students and children and Salkantay to Huayllabamba and Km 88, US$95. All tickets must be bought at the Dirección de Cultura office in Cuzco; tickets are only sold on presentation of a letter from a licensed tour operator on behalf of the visitor, including full passport details. Tickets are non-refundable and cannot be changed so make sure you provide accurate passport details to your tour operator. None is sold at the entrance to any of the routes. See page 222 on the need to reserve your place on the Trail in advance. You can save a bit of money by arranging your own transport back to Ollantaytambo in advance, either for the last day of your tour, or by staying an extra night in Aguas Calientes and taking the early morning train, then take a bus back to Cuzco. Make sure your return train ticket to Cuzco has your name on it (spelt absolutely correctly) for the tourist train, otherwise you have to pay for any changes.

Advice Four days would make a comfortable trip (though much depends on the weather). Allow a further day to see Machu Picchu when you have recovered from the hike. You cannot take backpacks into Machu Picchu; leave them at ticket office. The first two days of the Trail involve the stiffest climbing, so do not attempt it if you're feeling unwell. Leave all your valuables in Cuzco and keep everything inside your tent, even your shoes. Security has, however, improved in recent years. Always take sufficient cash to tip porters and guides at the end (S/.50-100 each, but at your discretion). Avoid the July-August high season and check conditions in the rainy season from November to April (note that this can vary). In the wet it is cloudy and the paths are very slippery and difficult. **The Trail is closed each February for cleaning and repair.**

The Trail
The trek to the sacred site begins either at Km 82, **Piscacucho**, or at Km 88, **Qorihuayrachina**, at 2600 m. In order to reach Km 82 hikers are transported by their tour operator in a minibus on the road that goes to Quillabamba. From Piri onward the road follows the riverbank and ends at Km 82, where there is a bridge. The Inca Trail equipment, food, fuel and field personnel reach Km 82 (depending on the tour operator's logistics) for the Sernanp staff to weigh each bundle before the group arrives. When several groups are leaving on the same day, it is more convenient to arrive early. Km 88 can only be reached by train, subject to schedule and baggage limitations. The train goes slower than a bus, but you start your walk nearer to Llaqtapata and Huayllabamba. (See below for details of variations in starting points for the Inca Trail.)

The walk to **Huayllabamba**, following the Cusichaca River, needs about three hours and isn't too arduous. Beyond Huayllabamba, a popular camping spot for tour groups, there is a camping place about an hour ahead, at **Llulluchayoc** (3200 m). A punishing 1½-hour climb further is **Llulluchapampa**, an ideal meadow for camping. If you have the energy to reach this point, it will make the second day easier because the next stage, the ascent to the first pass, **Warmiwañuska** (Dead Woman's Pass) at 4200 m, is tough; 2½ hours.

Afterwards take the steep path downhill to the Pacaymayo ravine. Beware of slipping on the Inca steps after rain. Tour groups usually camp by a stream at the bottom (1½ hours from the first pass). It is no longer permitted to camp at **Runkuracay**, on the way up to the second pass (a much easier climb, 3900 m). Magnificent views near the summit in clear weather. A good overnight place is about 30 minutes past the Inca ruins at **Sayacmarca** (3500 m), about an hour on after the top of the second pass.

A gentle two-hour climb on a fine stone highway leads through an Inca tunnel to the third pass. Near the top there's a spectacular view of the entire Vilcabamba range. You descend to Inca ruins at **Phuyupatamarca** (3650 m), well worth a long visit, even camping overnight.

From there steps go downhill to the magnificent ruins of **Wiñay-Wayna** (2700 m, entry US$5.75), with impressive views of the cleared terraces of Intipata. Access is possible, but the trail is not easily visible. There is a campsite which gets crowded and dirty. After Wiñay-Wayna there is no water and no camping till the official site below Puente Ruinas. The path from this point goes more or less level through jungle until the steep staircase up to the **Intipunku** (two hours), where there's a fine view of Machu Picchu, especially at dawn, with the sun alternately in and out, clouds sometimes obscuring the ruins, sometimes leaving them clear.

Get to Machu Picchu as early as possible, preferably before 0830 for best views but in any case before the tourist trains in high season.

Alternative Inca trails

The **Camino Real de los Inkas** starts at Km 104, where a footbridge gives access to the ruins of Chachabamba and the trail which ascends, passing above the ruins of Choquesuysuy to connect with the main trail at Wiñay-Wayna. This first part is a steady, continuous ascent of three hours (take water) and the trail is narrow and exposed in parts. Many people recommend this short Inca Trail. Good hiking trails from Aguas Calientes (see page 242) have been opened along the left bank of the Urubamba, for day hikes crossing the bridge of the hydroelectric plant to Choquesuysuy. A three-night trek goes from Km 82 to Km 88, then along the Río Urubamba to Pacaymayo Bajo and Km 104, from where you take the Camino Real de los Inkas.

Two treks involve routes from **Salkantay**: one, known as the **High Inca Trail** joins the classic Trail at Huayllabamba, then proceeds as before on the main Trail through Wiñay Wayna to Machu Picchu. To get to Salkantay, you have to start the trek in Mollepata, northwest of Cuzco in the Apurímac valley. **Ampay** buses run from Arcopata on the Chinchero road, or you can take private transport to Mollepata (three hours from Cuzco). Salkantay to Machu Picchu this way takes three nights. The second Salkantay route, known as the **Santa Teresa Trek**, takes four days and crosses the 4500-m Huamantla Pass to reach the Santa Teresa valley, which you follow to its confluence with the Urubamba. The goal is the town of Santa Teresa from where you can go to La Hidroeléctrica station for the local train to Aguas Calientes (see page 244). On this trek, **Machu Picchu Lodge to Lodge** ① *Mountain Lodges of Peru, T084-243636 (in Lima T01-421 6952, in North America T1-510-525 8846, in Europe T43-664-434 3340), www.mountainlodgesofperu.com*, a series of lodges have been set up. Fully guided tours take seven days, going from lodge to lodge, which are at Soraypampa (**Salkantay Lodge and Adventure Resort**), Huayraccmachay (**Wayra Lodge**), Collpapampa (**Colpa Lodge**) and Lucmabamba (**Lucma Lodge**). Contact **Mountain Lodges of Peru** for rates, departure dates and all other details, also for their new five- or seven-day, Lodge-to-Lodge route from Lamay to Ollantaytambo (http://laresadventure.com).

Inca Jungle Trail This is offered by several tour operators in Cuzco: on the first day you cycle downhill from Abra Málaga to Santa María (see Train, page 244), 2000 m, three to four hours of riding on the main Quillabamba–Cuzco highway with speeding vehicles inattentive to cyclists on the road. It's best to pay for good bikes and back-up on this section. Some agencies also offer white-water rafting in the afternoon. The second day is a hard 11-km trek from Santa María to Santa Teresa. It involves crossing three adventurous bridges and bathing in the hot springs at Santa Teresa (US$1.65 entry). The third day is a six-hour trek from Santa Teresa to Aguas Calientes. Some agencies offer ziplining as an alternative. The final day is a guided tour of Machu Picchu.

Vitcos and Vilcabamba

The Incas' last stronghold is reached from **Chaullay**, a village on the road between Ollantaytambo and Quillabamba. The road passes through Peña, a beautiful place with snowy peaks on either side of the valley, then the climb to the pass begins in earnest – on the right is a huge glacier. Soon on the left, Verónica begins to appear in all its huge and snowy majesty. After endless zig-zags and breathtaking views, you reach the Abra Málaga pass (road is paved to here). The descent to the valley shows hillsides covered in lichen and Spanish moss. At Chaullay, the road crosses the river on the historic Choquechaca bridge.

From Chaullay you can drive, or take a daily bus or truck (four to seven hours) to the village of **Huancacalle**, the best base for exploring the nearby Inca ruins of **Vitcos**, with the palace of the last four Inca rulers from 1536 to 1572, and **Yurac Rumi** (or **Chuquipalta**), the impressive sacred white rock of the Incas. There are a few restaurants, shops and basic places to stay at Huancacalle. There are two hostals: $ **El Ultimo Refugio de Manco Inca**, T846010, clean hostal run by the Quispicusi family that also run the INC office, excellent information; and $ **Sixpac Manco**, managed by the Cobos family. Alternatively villagers will let you stay on their floor, or you can camp near the river below the cemetery. Allow time for hiking to, and visiting Vitcos. It takes one hour to walk from Huancacalle to Vitcos, 45 minutes Vitcos to Chuquipalta, 45 minutes Chuquipalta to Huancacalle. Horses can be hired.

The road from Chaullay continues to **Vilcabamba La Nueva**. You can also hike from Huancacalle; a three-hour walk through beautiful countryside with Inca ruins dotted around. There is a missionary building run by Italians, with electricity and running water, where you may be able to spend the night.

Vilcabamba Vieja

Travellers with ample time can hike from Huancacalle to **Espíritu Pampa**, the site of the **Vilcabamba Vieja** ruins (entry US$11), a vast pre-Inca ruin with a neo-Inca overlay set in deep jungle at 1000 m. The site is reached on foot or horseback from Pampaconas. From Chaullay, take a truck to Yupanca, Lucma or Pucyura: there rent horses or mules and travel through breathtaking countryside to Espíritu Pampa. From Huancacalle a trip will take three or four days on foot, with a further day to get to Chihuanquiri and transport back to Quillabamba. The Ministerio de Cultura charge for this trek is US$38, students US$19. It is advisable to take local guides and mules. Ask around in Huancacalle for guides. The **Sixpac Manco** hostal has various guides and other people in the village will offer their services. Distances are considerable and the going is difficult. *Sixpac Manco*, by Vincent R Lee (available in Cuzco), has accurate maps of all archaeological sites in this area, and describes two expeditions into the region by the author and his party, following in the footsteps of Gene Savoy, who first identified the site in the 1960s. His book, *Antisuyo*, is also recommended reading. The best time of year is May to November, possibly December. Outside this period it is very dangerous as the trails are very narrow and can be thick with mud and very slippery. Insect repellent is essential, also painkillers and other basic medicines. Make enquiries about safety in Cuzco before setting out on treks in this area.

For hotel and restaurant price codes, and other relevant information, see pages 14-17.

⊖ Transport

Huancacalle *p248*
Bus 4 companies leave Cuzco's bus terminal for **Quillabamba**, taking 6-8 hrs

for the 233 km, depending on season, US$9 (**Ampay** is best company). Then take a combi from Quillabamba, 0900 and 1200, US$3.30 to Huancacalle, 3-4 hrs. On Fri they go all the way to Vilcabamba. You can also take a taxi.

West from Cuzco

Beyond Anta on the Abancay road, 2 km before Limatambo at the ruins of **Tarahuasi** (US$6), a few hundred metres from the road, is a very well-preserved **Inca temple platform**, with 28 tall niches, and a long stretch of fine polygonal masonry. The ruins are impressive, enhanced by the orange lichen which give the walls a honey colour.

Along the Abancay road 100 km from Cuzco, is the exciting descent into the Apurímac canyon, near the former Inca suspension bridge that inspired Thornton Wilder's *The Bridge of San Luis Rey*.

Choquequirao
ⓘ *Entry US$13.50, students US$6.75.*

Choquequirao is another 'lost city of the Incas', built on a ridge spur almost 1600 m above the Apurímac. It is reckoned to be a larger site than Machu Picchu, but with fewer buildings. The main features of Choquequirao are the **Lower Plaza**, considered by most experts to be the focal point of the city. The **Upper Plaza**, reached by a huge set of steps or terraces, has what are possibly ritual baths. A beautiful set of slightly curved agricultural terraces run for over 300 m east-northeast of the Lower Plaza.

The **Usnu** is on a levelled hilltop, ringed with stones and giving awesome 360° views. The **Ridge Group**, still shrouded in vegetation, is a large collection of unrestored buildings some 50-100 m below the Usnu. The **Outlier Building**, isolated and surrounded on three sides by sheer drops of over 1.5 km into the Apurímac Canyon, possesses some of the finest stonework within Choquequirao. **Capuliyoc**, nearly 500 m below the Lower Plaza, is a great set of agricultural terraces, visible on the approach from the far side of the valley. One section of terraces is decorated with llamas in white stone.

There are three ways in to Choquequirao. None is a gentle stroll. The shortest way is from **Cachora**, a village on the south side of the Apurímac, reached by a side road from the Cuzco-Abancay highway, shortly after Saywite. It is four hours by bus from Cuzco to the turn-off, then a two-hour descent from the road to Cachora (from 3695 m to 2875 m). Guides (Celestino Peña is the official guide) and mules are available in Cachora. From the village you need a day to descend to the Río Apurímac then seven hours to climb up to Choquequirao. Allow one or two days at the site then return the way you came. This route is well signed and in good condition, with excellent campsites and showers en route. Horses can be hired to carry your bags. The second and third routes take a minimum of eight days and require thorough preparation. You can start either at Huancacalle, or at Santa Teresa, between Machu Picchu and Chaullay. Both routes involve an incredible number of strenuous ascents and descents. You should be acclimatized for altitudes ranging from 2400 m to between 4600 and 5000 m and be prepared for extremes of temperature. In each case you end the trail at Cachora. It is possible to start either of these long hikes at Cachora, continuing even from Choquequirao to Espíritu Pampa. Note, the government approved the construction of an aerial cableway to Choquequirao in 2013, due for completion in late 2015.

Saywite → *3 km from the main road at Km 49 from Abancay, 153 km from Cuzco, US$4, students US$2. Altitude: 3500 m.*

Beyond the town of Curahuasi, 126 km from Cuzco, is the large carved rock of Saywite. It is a UNESCO World Heritage Site. The principal monolith is said to represent the three regions of jungle, sierra and coast, with the associated animals and Inca sites of each. It is fenced in, but ask the guardian for a closer look. It was defaced, allegedly, when a cast was taken of it, breaking off many of the animals' heads. Six further archaeological areas fall away from the stone and its neighbouring group of buildings. The site is more easily reached from Abancay than Cuzco.

◉ West from Cuzco listings

For hotel and restaurant price codes, and other relevant information, see pages 14-17.

◉ Where to stay

Choquequirao *p249*
$$ pp Casa de Salcantay, Prolongación Salcantay s/n, Cachora, T984 281171, www.salcantay.com. Price includes breakfast, dinner available if booked in advance. Dutch-run hostel with links to community projects, comfortable, small, Dutch, English, German spoken, can help with arranging independent treks, or organize treks with tour operator.

$$ pp Los Tres Balcones, Jr Abancay s/n, Cachora, www.choquequirau.com. Hostel designed as start and end-point for the trek to Choquequirao. Breakfast included, comfortable, hot showers, restaurant and pizza oven, camping. Shares information with internet café. They run a 5-day trek to

Choquequirao, US$500-650 (depending on numbers), with camping gear (but not sleeping bag), all meals and lunch at the hostel afterwards, entrance to the ruins, horses to carry luggage, transport from Cuzco and bilingual tour guide.

$ La Casona de Ocampo, San Martín 122, Cachora, T237514. Rooms with hot shower all day, free camping, owner Carlos Robles is knowledgeable.

◉ Transport

Choquequirao *p249*
From Cuzco take the first Abancay bus of the morning with **Bredde** at 0600, buy your ticket the night before to get a seat. Buses run from Abancay (Jr Prado Alto entre Huancavelica y Núñez) to **Cachora** at 0500 and 1400, return 0630 and 1100, 2 hrs, US$2.50. Cars run from the Curahuasi terminal on Av Arenas, Abancay, US$10 for whole vehicle.

Central Highlands

The Central Andes have many remote mountain areas with small typical villages, while larger cities of the region include Ayacucho and Huancayo. The vegetation is low, but most valleys are cultivated. Secondary roads are often in poor condition, sometimes impassable in the rainy season; the countryside is beautiful with spectacular views and the people are friendly. Three paved roads, from Lima, Pisco and Nazca, connect the Central Highlands to the coast. Huancayo lies in a valley which produces many crafts; the festivals are very popular and not to be missed.

Lima to Huancayo

The Central Highway more or less parallels the course of the railway between Lima and Huancayo (335 km). With the paving of roads from Pisco to Ayacucho and Nazca to Abancay, there are now more options for getting to the Sierra and the views on whichever ascent you choose are beyond compare. You can also reach the Central Highlands from Cuzco (via Abancay and Andahuaylas) and from Huaraz (via La Unión and Huánuco), so Lima is not the sole point of access overland.

Chosica and Marcahuasi
Chosica (860 m) is the real starting place for the mountains, 40 km from Lima. It's warm and friendly and a great place to escape the big city. Beyond the town looms a precipitous range of hills almost overhanging the streets. There are some basic *hostales* and, outside town, weekend resorts (see www.chosica.com). Up the Santa Eulalia valley 40 km beyond Chosica, is **Marcahuasi**, a table mountain (US$4) about 3 km by 1 km at 4000 m, near the village of **San Pedro de Casta**. There are three lakes, a 40-m-high 'monumento a la humanidad', and other mysterious lines, gigantic figures, sculptures, astrological signs and megaliths, which the late Daniel Ruzo describes in his book, *La Culture Masma*, Extrait de l'Ethnographie, Paris, 1956. A more widely accepted theory is that the formations are the result of wind erosion. The trail starts south of the village of San Pedro, and climbs southeast. It's three hours' walk to the *meseta*; guides are advisable in misty weather. Donkeys for carrying bags cost US$8 to hire, horses US$10. Tourist information is available at the municipality on the plaza. At shops in San Pedro you can buy everything for the trip, including bottled water. Tours can be arranged with travel agencies in Lima.

Chosica to Huancayo
For a while, beyond Chosica, each successive valley looks greener and lusher, with a greater variety of trees and flowers. Between Río Blanco and **Chicla** (Km 127, 3733 m), Inca contour-terraces can be seen quite clearly. After climbing up from **Casapalca** (Km 139, 4154 m), there are glorious views of the highest peaks, and mines, from the foot of a deep gorge. The road ascends to the Ticlio Pass, before the descent to **Morococha** and **La Oroya**. A large metal flag of Peru can be seen at the top of Mount Meiggs, not by any means the highest in the area, but through it runs Galera Tunnel, 1175 m long, in which the Central Railway reaches its greatest altitude, 4782 m. The railway itself is a magnificent feat of engineering, with 58 bridges, 69 tunnels and six zigzags, passing beautiful landscapes. It is definitely worth the ride on the new tourist service (see Transport, below). **La Oroya** (3755 m) is the main smelting centre for the region's mining industry. It stands at the fork of the Yauli and Mantaro rivers. Any traveller, but asthmatics in particular, beware, the

pollution from the heavy industry causes severe irritation. (For places to the east and north of La Oroya, see page 269.)

Jauja The old town of Jauja (*Phone code: 064; Population: 16,000; Altitude: 3400 m, www. jaujaperu.info*), 80 km southeast of La Oroya, was Pizarro's provisional capital until the founding of Lima. It has a colourful Wednesday and Sunday market. The **Museo Arqueológico Julio Espejo Núñez** ① *Jr Cusco 537, T361163, Mon and Wed 1500-1900, Sun 0900-1200, 1400-1700, donations welcome, knock on door of La Casa del Caminante opposite where the creator and curator lives*, is a quaint but endearing mix of relics from various Peruvian cultures, including two mummies, one still wrapped in the original shroud. The **Cristo Pobre** church is supposedly modelled after Notre Dame and is something of a curiosity. Department of Junín **tourist office** ① *Jr Grau 528, T362897, junin@mincetur.gob.pe*. On a hill above Jauja there is a fine line of Inca storehouses, and on hills nearby the ruins of Huajlaasmarca, with hundreds of circular stone buildings from the Huanca culture (John Hemming). There are also ruins near the **Paca lake**, 3.5 km away. The western shore is lined with restaurants; many offer weekend boat trips, US$1 (combi from Avenida Pizarro US$0.50).

On the road to Huancayo 18 km to the south, is **Concepción** (*Altitude: 3251 m*), with a market on Sunday. From Concepción a branch road (6 km) leads to the **Convent of Santa Rosa de Ocopa** ① *0900-1200 and 1500-1800, closed Tue, 45-min tours start on the hour, US$1.25, colectivos from the market in Concepción, 15 mins, US$0.50*, a Franciscan monastery set in beautiful surroundings. It was established in 1725 for training missionaries for the jungle. It contains a fine library with over 25,000 volumes, a biological museum and a large collection of paintings.

⚉ Lima to Huancayo listings

For hotel and restaurant price codes, and other relevant information, see pages 14-17.

◉ Where to stay

Chosica and Marcahuasi: San Pedro de Casta *p251*
Locals in town will put you up, **$**; ask at tourist information at the municipality. Take all necessary camping equipment for Marcahuasi trek.
$ Marcahuasi, just off the plaza. Private or shared bath, the best hotel in San Pedro; it also has a restaurant.

Chosica to Huancayo: La Oroya *p251*
$ Hostal Chavín, Tarma 281; and **$ Hostal Inti**, Arequipa 117, T391098. Both basic.

Jauja *p252*
$ Hostal Manco Cápac, Jr Manco Cápac 575, T361620, T99-974 9119. Central, good

rooms, private or shared rooms, garden, good breakfast and coffee.
$ Hostal María Nieves, Jr Gálvez 491, 1 block from the Plaza de Armas, T362543. Safe, helpful, large breakfast, hot water all day, parking. Good.

◉ Restaurants

Chosica to Huancayo: La Oroya *p251*
$$ El Tambo, 2 km outside town on the road to Lima. Good trout and frogs, sells local cheese and *manjar*, recommended as the best in and around town, buses on the Lima route stop here.

Jauja *p252*
$ Centro Naturista, Huarancayo 138 (no sign). Fruit salad, yoghurt, granola, etc, basic place.
$ D'Chechis, Jr Bolívar 1166, T368530. Lunch only, excellent.

$ Ganso de Oro, R Palma 249, T362166. Good restaurant in hotel of same name (which is not recommendable), varied prices, unpretentious.

$ La Rotonda, Tarapacá 415, T368412. Good lunch *menú* and pizzas in the evening.

⊖ Transport

Chosica *p251*

Bus Colectivos for Chosica leave from Av Grau, **Lima**, when full, between 0600 and 2100, US$1. Most buses on the Lima-La Oroya route are full; colectivo taxi to La Oroya US$7.50, 3 hrs, very scenic, passing the 2nd highest railway in the world.

San Pedro de Casta/Marcahuasi

Bus To San Pedro de Casta minibuses leave **Chosica** from Parque Echenique, opposite market, 0900 and 1500, 4 hrs, US$3.50; return 0700 and 1400.

Chosica to Huancayo: La Oroya *p251*

Bus To **Lima**, 4½ hrs, US$8. To **Jauja**, 80 km, 1½ hrs, US$2. To **Tarma**, 1½ hrs, US$2.50.

To **Cerro de Pasco**, 131 km, 3 hrs, US$3. To **Huánuco**, 236 km, 6 hr, US$7.50. Buses leave from Zeballos, adjacent to the train station. Colectivos also run on all routes.

Jauja *p252*

Air LC Peru has 2 daily flights from **Lima** to Francisco Carle airport, just outside Jauja, 45 mins, price includes transfer to Huancayo (marketed 'Lima–Huancayo').

Bus To **Lima**: US$15; with Cruz del Sur, Pizarro 220, direct, 6 hrs, US$22-29 *bus cama*. Most companies have their offices on the Plaza de Armas, but their buses leave from Av Pizarro. To **Huancayo**, 44 km, takes 1 hr and costs US$2.25. Combis to Huancayo from 25 de Abril y Ricardo Palma, 1¼ hrs, US$2.50. To **Cerro de Pasco**, Turismo Central from 25 de Abril 144, 5 hrs, US$6. Turismo Central also goes to **Huánuco**, 8 hrs, US$15. To **Tarma**, US$3, hourly with Trans Los Canarios and Angelitos/San Juan from Jr Tarma; the latter continues to **Chanchamayo**, US$8. Colectivos to Tarma leave from Junín y Tarma when full.

Huancayo and around → *Phone code: 064. Colour map 2, C3. Population: over 500,000. Altitude: 3271 m.*

The city is in the Mantaro Valley. It is the capital of Junín Department and the main commercial centre for inland Peru. All the villages in the valley produce their own original crafts and celebrate festivals all year round. At the important festivals in Huancayo, people flock in from far and wide with an incredible range of food, crafts, dancing and music. The Sunday market gives a little taste of this every week (it gets going after 0900), but it is better to go to the villages for local handicrafts. Jirón Huancavelica, 3 km long and four stalls wide, still sells clothes, fruit, vegetables, hardware, handicrafts and traditional medicines and goods for witchcraft. There is also an impressive daily market behind the railway station and a large handicrafts market between Ancash and Real, block 7, offering a wide selection.

Tourist offices The regional office is in Jauja; see above. Small **tourist information booth** ① *Plaza Huamanmarca, Real 481, T238480/233251.* **Indecopi** ① *Moquegua 730, El Tambo, T245180, abarrientos@indecopi.gob.pe,* is the consumer protection office.

The **museum** ① *at the Salesian school, north of the river on Pasaje Santa Rosa, Mon-Fri 0900-1800, Sun 1000-1200, US$1.75,* is a fascinating cabinet of curiosities with everything ranging from two-headed beasts to a collection of all the coins of the United States of America. The **Parque de Identidad Wanka** ① *on Jr San Jorge in the Barrio San Carlos northeast of the city, entry free, but contributions are appreciated,* is a mixture of surrealistic construction interwoven with native plants and trees and the cultural history of the Mantaro Valley.

Mantaro Valley

The whole Mantaro Valley is rich in culture. On the outskirts of town is **Torre-Torre**, impressive, eroded sandstone towers on the hillside. Take a bus to Cerrito de la Libertad and walk up. The ruins of **Warivilca** (15 km) ⓘ *1000-1200, 1500-1700 (museum mornings only), US$0.15, take a micro for Chilca from C Real*, are near **Huari**, with the remains of a pre-Inca temple of the Huanca tribe. Museum in the plaza, with deformed skulls, and modelled and painted pottery of successive Huanca and Inca occupations of the shrine.

Huancayo

Where to stay 🛏
1 Casa Alojamiento de
  Aldo y Soledad Bonilla *C2*
2 El Marquez *A2*
3 Hosp Familiar Tachi *B2*
4 Hosp Piccolo *B2*
5 Kiya *B2*
6 La Casa de La Abuela *A3*
7 Los Balcones *A2*
8 Peru Andino *A3*
9 Presidente *C2*
10 Retama Inn *C2*
11 Turismo *B2*

Restaurants 🍴
1 A La Leña *B2*
2 Café El Parque *B2*
3 Chifa El Centro *B2*
4 Chifa Xu *B2*
5 Detrás de la Catedral *B2*
6 Donatelo's *B2*
7 El Inka *A2*
8 El Olímpico *B2*
9 El Paraíso *C2*
10 ImaginArte *A2*
11 La Cabaña *B3*
12 La Pérgola *A2*
13 Panadería Koky *B2*
14 Pizzería Antojitos *B2*

East of the Mantaro River The villages of **Cochas Chico** and **Cochas Grande**, 11 km away, are where the famous *mate burilado*, or gourd carving, is done. You can buy them cheaply direct from the manufacturers, but ask around. Beautiful views of the Valle de Mantaro and Huancayo. *Micros* leave from the corner of Amazonas and Giráldez, US$0.25.

Hualahoyo (11 km) has a little chapel with 21 colonial canvasses. **San Agustín de Cajas** (8 km) makes fine hats, and **San Pedro** (10 km) makes wooden chairs; **Hualhuas** (12 km) fine alpaca weavings which you can watch being made. The weavers take special orders; small items can be finished in a day. Negotiate a price.

The town of **San Jerónimo** is renowned for the making of silver filigree jewellery; Wednesday market. Fiesta on the third Saturday in August. There are ruins two to three hours' walk above San Jerónimo, but seek advice before hiking to them.

Between Huancayo and Huancavelica, **Izcuchaca** is the site of a colonial bridge over the Río Mantaro. On the edge of town is a fascinating pottery workshop whose machinery is driven by a water turbine (plus a small shop). A nice hike is to the chapel on a hill overlooking the valley; about one to 1½ hours each way.

◉ Huancayo and around listings

For hotel and restaurant price codes, and other relevant information, see pages 14-17.

◯ Where to stay

Huancayo *p253, map p254*
Prices may be raised in Holy Week.
Note The Plaza de Armas is called Plaza Constitución.
$$$ Presidente, C Real 1138, T231275, http://huancayo.hotelpresidente.com.pe. Helpful, classy, safe, serves breakfast, restaurant, convention centre.
$$$ Turismo, Ancash 729, T235611, http://turistases.hotelpresidente.com.pe/. Restored colonial building, same owner as Presidente, with more atmosphere, elegant, rooms quite small, Wi-Fi extra, quiet. Restaurant (**$$-$**) serves good meals, fine service.
$$$-$$ El Marquez, Puno 294, T219202, www.elmarquezhuancayo.com. Good value, efficient, popular with local business travellers, safe parking.
$$ Kiya, Giráldez 107, T214955, www.hotel kiya.com. Comfortable although ageing, hot water, helpful staff. Spectacular view of Plaza.
$ Casa Alojamiento de Aldo y Soledad Bonilla, Huánuco 332, ½ block from Mcal Cáceres bus station, T232103. Cheaper without full board, colonial house, owners

speak English, laundry, secure, relaxing, nice courtyard, tours arranged, best to book ahead.
$ Hospedaje Familiar Tachi, Huamanmarca 125, T219980, saenz_nildy@hotmail.com. Central but not the safest area, small, comfortable, hot water, private or shared showers, family-run, nice atmosphere and views from terrace.
$ Hospedaje Piccolo, Puno 239. With hot water, good beds, well-kept.
$ La Casa de la Abuela, Prolongación Cusco 794 y Gálvez, T234383, www.incasdelperu. org/casa-de-la-abuela. Doubles with or without private bath and dorms, 15 mins out of town. Hot shower, light breakfast, laundry facilities, meals available, sociable staff, owner speaks English, good meeting place, free pickup from bus station if requested in advance. Discount for Footprint readers.
$ Los Balcones, Jr Puno 282, T214881. Comfortable rooms, hot water, helpful staff, elevator (reasonable wheelchair access). View of the back of the Cathedral.
$ Peru Andino, Pasaje San Antonio 113-115, 1 block Parque Túpac Amaru, in 1st block of Francisco Solano (left side of Defensoría del Pueblo), 10-15 mins' walk from the centre (if taking a taxi, stress that it's *Pasaje* San Antonio), T223956. Hot showers, several

rooms with bath, laundry and kitchen facilities, breakfast and other meals on request, safe area, cosy atmosphere, run by Sra Juana and Luis, who speak some English, organize trekking and mountain bike tours, bike hire, Spanish classes. Can pick up guests at Lima airport with transfer to bus station.
$ Retama Inn, Ancash 1079, T219193, http://hotelretamainnhuancayo.blogspot.co.uk/. All amenities, comfortable beds, hot water, TV, café/bar, helpful, breakfast extra.

Mantaro Valley *p254*
In Izcuchaca, ask in stores off the plaza. Many locals are enthusiastic about renting a room to a gringo traveller for a night. You may well make a friend for life.

Restaurants

Huancayo *p253, map p254*
Breakfast is served in Mercado Modelo from 0700. Better class, more expensive restaurants, serving typical dishes for about US$5, plus 18% tax, drinks can be expensive. Lots of cheap restaurants along Av Giráldez.
$$ Detrás de la Catedral, Jr Ancash 335 (behind Cathedral as name suggests), T212969. Pleasant atmosphere, excellent dishes. Charcoal grill in the corner keeps the place warm on cold nights. Considered by many to be the best in town.
$$ El Olímpico, Giráldez 199. Long-established, one of the more upscale establishments offering Andean and Creole dishes; the real reason to go is the owner's model car collection displayed in glass cabinets.
$$ La Cabaña, Av Giráldez 652. Pizzas, ice cream, *calentitos*, and other dishes, excellent atmosphere, live folk music Thu-Sun.
$$ Pizzería Antojitos, Puno 599. Attractive, atmospheric pizzería with live music some nights.
$$-$ Chifa Xu, Giráldez 208. Good food at reasonable prices, always-bustling atmosphere.

$ A La Leña, Paseo la Breña 144 and on Ancash. Good rotisserie chicken and salads, popular.
$ Chifa El Centro, Giráldez 238, T217575. Another branch at Av Leandra Torres 240. Chinese food, good service and atmosphere.
$ Donatelo's, Puno 287. Excellent pizza and chicken place, with nice atmosphere, popular.
$ La Pérgola, Puno 444. Pleasant atmosphere, overlooking the plaza, 4-course *menú*.

Cafés

Café El Parque, Giráldez y Ancash, on the main plaza. Popular place for juices, coffee and cakes.
El Inka, Puno 530. Popular *fuente de soda*, with coffee, Peruvian food, desserts, milkshakes.
El Paraíso, Arequipa 428, and another opposite at No 429. Both vegetarian places, OK.
ImaginArte, Jr Ancash 260. Open from 1800. Principally an art gallery, often displaying work based on ethnic Peruvian culture. Good coffee and cakes.
Panadería Koky, Ancash y Puno, serves Hotel Marquez. Open 0700-2300, lunch 1230-1530. Good for breakfasts, lunches, sandwiches, capuccino and pastries, fancy atmosphere, free Wi-Fi.

Bars and clubs

Huancayo *p253, map p254*
Peñas All the *peñas* have folklore shows with dancing, open normally Fri, Sat and Sun from 1300 to 2200. Entrance fee is about US$3 pp. Eg **Ollantaytambo**, Puno, block 2, and **Taki Wasi**, Huancavelica y 13 de Noviembre.

Festivals

Huancayo *p253, map p254*
There are so many festivals in the Mantaro Valley that it is impossible to list them all. Nearly every day of the year there is some sort of celebration in one of the villages.

Jan 1-6, New Year celebrations; 20, San Sebastián y San Fabián (recommended in Jauja). **Feb** There are carnival celebrations for the whole month, with highlights on 2, Virgen de la Candelaria, and 17-19 Concurso de Carnaval. **Mar-Apr** Semana Santa, with impressive Good Friday processions. **May** Fiesta de las Cruces throughout the whole month. **Jun** 15 Virgen de las Mercedes; 24, San Juan Bautista; 29, Fiesta Patronal. **Jul** 16, Virgen del Carmen; 24-25, Santiago. **Aug** 4, San Juan de Dios; 16, San Roque; 30, Santa Rosa de Lima. **Sep** 8, Virgen de Cocharcas; 15, Virgen de la Natividad; 23-24, Virgen de las Mercedes; 29, San Miguel Arcángel. **Oct** 4, San Francisco de Asís; 18, San Lucas; 28-30 culmination of month-long celebrations for El Señor de los Milagros. **Nov** 1, Día de Todos los Santos. **Dec** 3-13, Virgen de Guadalupe; 8, Inmaculada Concepción; 25, Navidad (Christmas).

O Shopping

Huancayo p253, map p254
Thieves in the market hand out rolled up paper and pick your pocket while you unravel them.
Crafts All crafts are made outside Huancayo in the many villages of the Mantaro Valley, or in Huancavelica. The villages are worth a visit to learn how the items are made.
Casa de Artesano, on the corner of Real and Paseo La Breña, at Plaza Constitución. Has a wide selection of good-quality crafts.

O What to do

Huancayo p253, map p254
Tour operators
American Travel & Service, Plaza Constitución 122, of 2 (next to the Cathedral), T211181, T964-830220. Wide range of classical and more adventurous tours in the Mantaro Valley and in the Central Jungle. Transport and equipment

rental possible. Most group-based day tours start at US$8-10 pp.
Incas del Perú, Av Giráldez 652, T223303, www.incasdelperu.org. Associated with the La Cabaña restaurant and La Casa de la Abuela. Run jungle, biking and riding trips throughout the region, as well as language and volunteer programs. Very popular with travellers in the region.
Peruvian Tours, Plaza Constitución 122, p 2, of 1, T213069. Next to the Cathedral and American Travel & Service. Classic tours of the Mantaro valley, plus day trips up to the Huaytapallana Nevados above Huancayo, plus long, 16-hr excursions to Cerro de Pasco and Tarma.

Guides
Marco Jurado Ames, T201260 or T964-227050 (mob), andinismo_peru@yahoo.es. Rock climbing and mountaineering, organizes long-distance treks on the 'hidden paths of Peru'. Many of these include Huancayo, such as a trek to Machu Picchu from the Amazon lowlands via Choquequirao and Inca Trail to Pariaccacca in the central Andes. Can start in Huancayo or Lima.

O Transport

Huancayo p253, map p254
Bus The new bus terminal for buses to many destinations is 3 km north of the centre in the Parque Industrial. Some companies retain their own terminal in the centre, eg **Cruz del Sur**, Av Ferrocarril N 151, T223367. There are regular buses to **Lima**, 6-7 hrs on a good paved road, US$11-28 (Oltursa fares). For other fares and daytime buses take a bus from/to Yerbateros terminal in Lima (San Luis district, taxi there US$4.50), US$12. Travelling by day is recommended for the fantastic views and for safety; most major companies go by night (take warm clothing). Recommended companies:, **Turismo Central** and **Transportes Rogger**, Lima 561, T233488.

To **Ayacucho**, 319 km, 9-10 hrs, US$15-17 with **Molina**, C Angaráes 334, T224501, 3 a day, recommended; 1 a day with **Turismo Central** US$13. The road is paved for the first 70 km, then in poor condition and is very difficult in the wet. Take warm clothing. (**Note** If driving to Ayacucho and beyond, roads are "amazingly rough". Don't go alone. Count kilometres diligently to keep a record of where you are: road signs are poor.) After Izcuchaca, on the railway to Huancavelica, there is a good road to the Quichuas hydroelectric scheme, but after that it is narrow with hair-raising bends and spectacular bridges. The scenery is staggering.

To **Huancavelica**, 147 km, 5 hrs, US$4. Many buses daily, including **Transportes Yuri**, Ancash 1220, 3 a day. The road has been paved and is a delightful ride, much more comfortable than the train (if you can find a driver who will not scare you to death). A private car from Huancayo costs US$18-23 pp depending on your negotiating skills.

To **Cerro de Pasco**, 255 km, 5 hrs, US$7.50. Several departures. Alternatively, take a bus to La Oroya, about every 20 mins, from Av Real about 10 blocks north of the main plaza. From La Oroya there are regular buses and colectivos to Cerro. The road to La Oroya and on to Cerro is in good condition. To **Huánuco**, 7 hrs, **Turismo Central** at 2115, US$9, good service.

To **Chanchamayo** Angelitos/San Juan, Ferrocarril 161 and Plaza Amazonas, every 1½ hrs, and **Tans Los Canarios** hourly service via Jauja to Tarma, 3 hrs, US$6, some of which continue on to La Merced, 5 hrs, US$7.50.

To **Yauyos**, cars at 0500 from Plaza de los Sombreros, El Tambo, US$7.50. It is a poor road with beautiful mountain landscapes before dropping to the valley of Cañete; cars go very fast.

To **Jauja**, 44 km, 1 hr. Colectivos and combis leave every few mins from Huamanmarca y Amazonas, and Plaza Amazonas, US$2.50. Ones via San Jerónimo

and Concepción have 'Izquierda' on the front. Taxi to Jauja US$15, 45 mins. Most buses to the Mantaro Valley leave from several places around the market area. Buses to **Hualhuas** and **Cajas** leave from block 3 of Pachitea. Buses to **Cochas** leave from Amazonas y Giráldez.

Train There are 2 unconnected railway stations. The Central station serves **Lima**, via La Oroya: there is irregular service, about once a month, operated by **Ferrocarril Centro Andino**, Av José Gálvez Barrenechea 566, p 5, San Isidro, Lima, T01-226 6363, see www.ferrocarrilcentral.com.pe for next departure date. There are *turístico* and *clásico* fares, US$125 and US$70 return, respectively. The train leaves Lima at 0700, 11 hrs, returning at 0700, 3 or 4 days later. Coaches have reclining seats, heating, restaurant, tourist information, toilets, and nurse with first aid and oxygen. Tickets are sold online and by Lima agencies.

From the small station in Chilca suburb (15 mins by taxi, US$2), trains run to **Huancavelica**, on a narrow gauge (3 ft), Mon-Sat 0630, 1230, Sun 1400. There are 38 tunnels and the line reaches 3676 m. This "classic" Andean train journey on the *Tren Macho* takes 7 hrs and has fine views, passing through typical mountain villages where vendors sell food and crafts. In some places, the train has to reverse and change tracks.

⊙ Directory

Huancayo *p253, map p254*
Language classes Incas del Perú (see What to do, above) organizes Spanish courses for beginners for US$100 per week, including accommodation at **Hostal La Casa de La Abuela**, see above, and all meals, also home-stays and weaving, playing traditional music, Peruvian cooking and lots of other things. **Katia Cerna** is a recommended teacher, T225332, katiacerna@hotmail.com. She can arrange home stays; her sister works in adventure tourism.

Huancavelica is a friendly and attractive town, surrounded by huge, rocky mountains. It was founded in the 16th century by the Spanish to exploit rich deposits of mercury and silver. It is predominantly an indigenous town, and people still wear traditional costume. There are beautiful mountain walks in the neighbourhood. The Cathedral, located on the Plaza de Armas, has an altar considered to be one of the finest examples of colonial art in Peru. Also very impressive are the five other churches in town. The church of San Francisco, for example, has no less than 11 altars. Sadly, though, most of the churches are closed to visitors. **Tourist office**: Dircetur ① *Jr Victoria Garma 444, T452938.* Very helpful.

Bisecting the town is the Río Huancavelica. South of the river is the main commercial centre. North of the river, on the hillside, are the **thermal baths** ① *0600-1500, US$0.15 for private rooms, water not very hot, US$0.10 for the hot public pool, also hot showers, take a lock for the doors.* The handicraft sellers congregate in front of the Municipalidad on M Muñoz and the Biblioteca on the Plaza de Armas (V Toledo). Most handicrafts are transported directly to Lima, but you can still visit craftsmen in neighbouring villages. The Potaqchiz hill, just outside the town, gives a fine view, about one hour walk up from San Cristóbal. **Ministerio de Cultura** ① *Plazoleta San Juan de Dios, T453420,* is a good source of information on festivals, archaeological sites, history, etc. Gives courses on music and dancing, and lectures some evenings. There is also an interesting but small **Museo Regional** ① *Arica y Raimondi, Mon-Sat 1000-1300, 1500-1900.*

Huancavelica to Ayacucho

The direct route from Huancavelica to Ayacucho (247 km) goes via **Santa Inés** (4650 m), 78 km. Out of Huancavelica the road climbs steeply with switchbacks between herds of llamas and alpacas grazing on rocky perches. Around Pucapampa (Km 43) is one of the highest habitable *altiplanos* (4500 m), where the rare and highly prized ash-grey alpaca can be seen. Snow-covered mountains are passed as the road climbs to 4853 m at the Abra Chonta pass, 23 km before Santa Inés. By taking the turn-off to Huachocolpa at Abra Chonta and continuing for 3 km you'll reach one of the highest drivable passes in the world, at 5059 m. Nearby are two lakes (Laguna Choclacocha) which can be visited in 2½ hours. Some 52 km beyond Santa Inés at the Abra de Apacheta (4750 m), 98 km from Ayacucho, the rocks are all the colours of the rainbow, and running through this fabulous scenery is a violet river. See Transport, below, for road services and lodging options on this route.

There is another route to Ayacucho from Huancayo, little used by buses, but which involves not so much climbing for cyclists. Cross the pass into the Mantaro valley on the road to **Quichuas**. Then to **Anco** and **Mayocc** (lodging). From here the road crosses a bridge after 10 km and in another 20 km reaches **Huanta** in the picturesque valley of the same name. It celebrates the **Fiesta de las Cruces** during the first week of May. Its Sunday market is large and interesting. Then it's a paved road 48 km to Ayacucho. On the road from Huanta, 24 km from Ayacucho, is the site of perhaps the oldest known human settlement in South America, 20,000 years old, evidence of which was found in the cave of **Pikimachay**. The remains are now in Lima's museums.

For hotel and restaurant price codes, and other relevant information, see pages 14-17.

Where to stay

Huancavelica *p259*

$$$ Presidente, Plaza de Armas, T452760, http://huancavelica.hotelpresidente.com. pe/. Lovely colonial building, higher-priced suites available, heating, parking, safe, laundry, restaurant and café.

$ Ascención, Jr Manco Capac 481 (Plaza de Armas), T453103. A hidden treasure, no sign, use wooden door next to the Comisaría and follow the sign that says "Hotel". Very comfortable, wooden floors, with or without bath, hot water.

$ Camacho, Jr Carabaya 481, T453298. Shared showers, hot water morning only, secure, old-fashioned, good value.

$ La Portada, Virrey Toledo 252, T453603. Large rooms with private bath or small, basic rooms with shared bath with extra charge for TV. Lots of blankets, unlimited coca tea, helpful staff, good value, secure metal doors. Women may be put off by the public urinal in the shared shower area, but there is a better bathroom by the cafeteria.

$ San José, Jr Huancayo 299, T452958. Solar hot water in daytime, cheaper without bath or TV, secure, nice beds, helpful but basic.

Huancavelica to Ayacucho *p259*

$ Alojamiento Andino, in Santa Inés, and a very friendly restaurant, El Favorito, where you can sleep. Several others.

$ Hostal Recreo Sol y Sombra, in Quichuas. Charming, small courtyard, helpful, basic.

Restaurants

Huancavelica *p259*

$$-$ Mochica Sachún, Av Virrey Toledo 303. Great *menú* US$1.50, full meals available, sandwiches, friendly.

$$-$ Roma II, Manco Capac 580, T452608. Open 1800-2300. Pizzas, smells delicious, friendly staff, delivery available.

$ Chifa El Mesón, Manchego Muñoz 153, T453570. Very popular, standard *chifa* fare. Delivery available.

$ Joy, Virrey Toledo 230. Creole and regional dishes, sandwiches, long-established, award-winning, bright. Also **Joy Campestre**, Av de los Incas 870. Serves typical Peruvian regional dishes in leisurely country environment.

Festivals

Huancavelica *p259*

The whole area is rich in culture. Fiesta de los Reyes Magos y los Pastores, **4-8 Jan**. Fiesta del Niño Perdido is held on **2nd Sun in Jan**. Pukllaylay Carnavales, celebration of the first fruits from the ground (harvest), **20 Jan-mid Mar**. Semana Santa, Holy Week. Toro Pukllay festival **last week of May, 1st week of Jun**. Fiesta de Santiago is held in **May and Aug** in all communities. Los Laijas or Galas (scissors dance), **22-28 Dec**.

Transport

Huancavelica *p259*

Bus All bus companies have their offices on, and leave from the east end of town, around Parque M Castilla, on Muñoz, Iquitos, Tumbes and O'Donovan. To **Huancayo**, 147 km, 5 hrs, US$4, paved road, Transportes Yuri and Transportes Ticllas (O'Donovan 500). To **Lima** via Huancayo, 445 km, 13 hrs minimum, US$14. Most buses to Huancayo go on to Lima, there are several a day. The other route is to **Pisco**, 269 km, 12 hrs, US$12 and **Ica**, US$13, 1730 daily, with Oropesa, O'Donovon 599. Buy your ticket 1 day in advance. The road is poor until it joins the Ayacucho-Pisco road, where it improves. Most of the journey is done at night. Be prepared for sub-zero temperatures in the early morning as the bus passes snowfields, then for temperatures of 25-30°C as the bus descends to the coast.

Train See under Huancayo; trains leave for Huancayo Mon-Sat 0630, 1230, Sun 0630.

Huancavelica to Ayacucho *p259*

There is no direct transport from Huancavelica to Ayacucho, other than 0430 on Sat with **San Juan Bautista** (Plazoleta Túpac Amaru 107, T803062), US$8. Otherwise you have to go to **Rumichaca** just beyond Santa Inés on the paved Pisco–Ayacucho road, also with **San Juan Bautista**, 0430, 4 hrs, then wait for a passing bus to Ayacucho at 1500, US$3, or try to catch a truck. Rumichaca has only a couple of foodstalls and some filthy toilets. This route is one of the highest continuous roads in the world. The journey is a cold one but spectacular as the road rarely drops below 4000 m for 150 km. The best alternative is to take a colectivo Huancavelica–**Lircay**, a small village with **$** unnamed *hostal* at Sucre y La Unión, with bath and hot water, much better than Hostal El Paraíso, opposite, also with bath, cheaper without (**Transportes 5 de Mayo**, Av Sebastián Barranca y Cercado, US$7.55, 2½ hrs, leave when full). The same company runs from Lircay Terminal Terrestre hourly from 0430 to Julcamarca (colonial church, **Hostal Villa Julcamarca**, near plaza, no tap water, really basic), 2½ hrs, US$6, then take a minibus from Julcamarca plaza to Ayacucho, US$4, 2 hrs; beautiful scenery all the way. Another option is to take the train to Izcuchaca, stay the night and take the colectivo (see above).

Ayacucho → *Phone code: 066. Colour map 2, C3. Population: 170,000. Altitude: 2748 m.*

A week can easily be spent enjoying Ayacucho and its hinterland. The climate is lovely, with warm, sunny days and pleasant balmy evenings, and the people are very hospitable. Semana Santa celebrations are famous throughout South America. Ayacucho was founded on 25 April 1540. On the Pampa de Quinua, on 9 December 1824, the decisive Battle of Ayacucho was fought, bringing Spanish rule in Peru to an end. In the middle of the festivities, the Liberator Simón Bolívar decreed that the city be named Ayacucho, 'Place of the Dead', instead of its original name, Huamanga.

The city is built round the Plaza Mayor, the main plaza, with the Cathedral, Municipalidad, Universidad Nacional de San Cristóbal de Huamanga (UNSCH) and various colonial mansions facing on to it. It is famous for its Semana Santa celebrations, its splendid market and its 33 churches. **Tourist offices**: i Perú ① *Portal Municipal 45, on the Plaza, T318305, iperuayacucho@promperu.gob.pe, daily 0830-1930, Sun 0830-1430.* Very helpful. Also has an office at the airport. **Dirección Regional de Industria y Turismo** (Dircetur) ① *Asamblea 481, T312548. Mon-Fri 0800-1700*, friendly and helpful. **Tourist Police** ① *Arequipa cuadra 1, T312055.*

Places in Ayacucho

The **Cathedral** ① *daily 1700-1900, Sun 0900-1700*, built in 1612, has superb gold leaf altars. It is beautifully lit at night. On the north side of the Plaza Mayor, at Portal de la Unión 37, are the **Casona de los Marqueses de Mozobamba del Pozo**, also called Velarde-Alvarez. Recently restored as the **Centro Cultural de la UNSCH**, frequent artistic and cultural exhibitions are held here; see the monthly Agenda Cultural. The **Casona Chacón** ① *Portal de la Unión 28, in the BCP building*, displays temporary exhibitions. North of the Plaza is **Santo Domingo** (1548) ① *9 de Diciembre, block 2, Mass daily 0700-0800*. Its fine façade has triple Roman arches and Byzantine towers.

Jr 28 de Julio is pedestrianized for two blocks. A stroll down here leads to the prominent **Arco del Triunfo** (1910), which commemorates victory over the Spaniards. Through the

Ayacucho

To Museo Anfasep & Terrapuerto Plaza Wari (bus station)

To 🚌 1

To Pisco & Lima

Mercado Artesanal Shosaku Nagase

Quinua

Libertad

Garcilaso de la Vega

Manco Capac

Pje Cáceres

Los Andes

Miller

To Combis for Huari, Quinua & Huanta

Cruz del Sur

9 de Diciembre

Asamblea

Dirceur

Av Mariscal Cáceres

Colectivos to Julcamarca

Bellido

Santo Domingo

Casona de los Marqueses de Mozobamba del Pozo

Tres Máscaras

Sol

Cuzco

Callao

Prefectura

Plaza Mayor

Municipalidad

Cathedral

iPerú

Arequipa

Lima

Casas de Cambio

La Compañía de Jesús

Centro Turístico Cultural San Cristóbal

Casa Jaúregui

La Merced

San Martín

Río Alameda

To 🚌 7, Airport & Cuzco

Liberated

Grau

28 de Julio

Nazareno

Carlos F Vivanco

Arco del Triunfo

Av Ramón Castilla

Londres

Huancasolar

Santa Clara

Mercado de Abastos Carlos F Vivanco

San Francisco de Asís

2 de Mayo

S J de Dios

Mercado 12 de Abril

Raymondi

C Chorro

Museo Andrés A Cáceres (Casona Vivanco)

N

100 metres
100 yards

Santa Teresa

San Cristóbal

To Barrio Santa Ana

To 🚌 1

Where to stay 🛏
1 El Marqués de Valdelirios
2 Florida
3 Grau
4 Hosp El Centro
5 Hostal 3 Máscaras
6 La Crillonesa
7 Marcos
8 San Francisco de Paula
9 Santa Rosa
10 ViaVia Café Ayacucho

Restaurants 🍴
1 Cabo Blanco
2 Chifa Wa Lin
3 La Casona
4 La Italiana
5 Lalo's Pan
6 La Miel
7 Las Flores
8 Mía Pizza
9 Miskycha
10 Nino
11 Portal 1
12 Wallpa Sua

arch is the church of **San Francisco de Asís** (1552) ① *28 de Julio, block 3, daily for morning Mass and 1730-1830*. It has an elaborate gilt main altar and several others. Across 28 de Julio from San Fancisco is the **Mercado de Abastos Carlos F Vivanco**, the packed central market. As well as all the household items and local produce, look for the cheese sellers, the breads and the section dedicated to fruit juices.

Santa Clara de Asís ① *Jr Grau, block 3, open for Mass*, is renowned for its beautifully delicate coffered ceiling. It is open for the sale of sweets and cakes made by the nuns (go to the door at Nazareno 184, it's usually open). On the 5th block of 28 de Julio is the late 16th-century **Casona Vivanco**, which houses the **Museo Andrés A Cáceres** ① *Jr 28 de Julio 508, T066-812360, Mon-Sat 0900-1300, 1400-1800. US$1.25*. The museum has baroque painting, colonial furniture, republican and contemporary art, and exhibits on Mariscal Cáceres' battles in the War of the Pacific. Further south still, on a pretty plazuela, is **Santa Teresa** (1683) ① *28 de Julio, block 6, daily Mass, usually 1600*, with its monastery. The nuns here sell sweets and crystallized fruits and a *mermelada de ají*, made to recipe given to them by God; apparently it is not picante. **San Cristóbal** ① *Jr 28 de Julio, block 6, rarely open*, was the first church to be founded in the city (1540), and is one of the oldest in South America. With its single tower, it is tiny compared with Santa Teresa, which is opposite.

The 16th-century church of **La Merced** ① *2 de Mayo, open for Mass*, is the second oldest in the city. The high choir is a good example of the simplicity of the churches of the early period of the Viceroyalty. **Casa Jáuregui**, opposite, is also called **Ruiz de Ochoa** after its original owner. Its outstanding feature is its doorway, which has a blue balcony supported by two fierce beasts with erect penises.

Museo de Anfasep (Asociación Nacional de Familiares de Secuestrados Detenidos y Desaparecidos del Perú) ① *Prol Libertad 1226, 15 mins' walk from Mercado Artesanal Shosaku Nagase, or mototaxi, entry free but give a donation*, provides an insight into the recent history of this region during the violence surrounding the Sendero Luminoso campaign and the government's attempts to counter it.

For a fascinating insight into Inca and pre-Inca art and culture, a visit to **Barrio Santa Ana** is a must. The district is full of *artesanía* shops, galleries and workshops (eg **Wari Art Gallery** ① *Jr Mcal Cáceres 302, T312529, acwari@hotmail.com*, for textiles, and **Julio Gálvez** ① *Plazoleta Santa Ana 12, T314278*, for remarkable sculptures in alabaster – *piedra de huamanga*). Galleries are closed on Sunday.

Excursions

The Inca ruins of **Vilcashuamán** are 120 km the south, beyond Cangallo. Vilcashuamán was an important provincial capital, the crossroads where the road from Cuzco to the Pacific met the empire's north-south highway. Tours can be arranged with travel agencies in Ayacucho, US$13 per person, only with eight passengers, full day tour (0500-1800), including **Intihuatana** (Inca baths about one hour uphill from the village of Vischongo, one hour from Vilcashuamán, also Puya Raimondi plants at Titankayuq national sanctuary, one hour walk from Vischongo); alternatively stay overnight (three hotels, **$**, basic but clean). Market day is Wednesday. Buses and colectivos run from Avenida Cuzco 350, daily 0400-1500, four hours, US$7.50.

A good road going north from Ayacucho leads to **Huari** ① *22 km from Ayacucho, 0800-1700, US$1*, dating from the 'Middle Horizon' (AD 600-1000), when the Huari culture spread across most of Peru. This was the first urban walled centre in the Andes. The huge irregular stone walls are up to 3-4 m high and rectangular houses and streets can be made out. The most important activity here was artistic: ceramics, gold, silver, metal and alloys such as bronze, which was used for weapons and for decorative objects. The ruins now lie in an extensive *tuna* cactus forest (don't pick the fruit). There is a museum at the site.

Quinua village, 37 km northeast of Ayacucho, has a charming cobbled main plaza and many of the buildings have been restored. There is a small market on Sunday. Nearby, on the Pampa de Quinua, a 44-m-high obelisk commemorates the battle of Ayacucho. A reenactment of the battle is held on 9 December, with college students playing the roles of Royalist and South American soldiers. The village's handicrafts are recommended, especially ceramics. Most of the houses have miniature ceramic churches on the roof. San Pedro Ceramics, at the foot of the hill leading to the monument, and Mamerto Sánchez, Jr Sucre, should be visited, but there are many others. **Fiesta de la Virgen de Cocharcas**, around 8 September. Trips can be arranged to Huari, La Quinua village and the battlefield; US$12 per person, minimum four people. Combis leave from Paradero a Huari Quinua, corner of Jirón Ciro Alegría and Jirón Salvador Cavero, when full from 0700; 40 minutes to Huari, US$1, then on to Quinua, 25 minutes, US$0.75 (US$1.50 from Ayacucho – ask the driver to go all the way to the Obelisco for an extra US$0.75).

◉ Ayacucho listings

For hotel and restaurant price codes, and other relevant information, see pages 14-17.

◉ Where to stay

Ayacucho *p261, map p262*

$$ San Francisco de Paula, Jr Callao 290, T312353, www.hotelsanfranciscodepaula. com. A bit like a museum with a nice patio, popular choice. Comfortable rooms and some suites with hot water. Will book El Encanto de Oro in Andahuaylas.

$$ Santa Rosa, Jr Lima 166, T314614, www.hotelsantarosa.com.pe. Lovely colonial courtyard in building with historical associations, roof terrace, warm rooms, hot water, attentive staff, car park, good restaurant with good value *menú*.

$$ ViaVia Café Ayacucho, Portal Constitución 4, Plaza de Armas, T312834, www.viaviacafe.com. Single, double and triple rooms with private bath, solar hot water 24 hrs, TV room, Spanish, Dutch and English spoken. The attached ViaVia restaurant and travellers' café overlooks the Plaza, offering international and Peruvian food, a lunch *menú*, lounge and live music on Sat, cultural events and tourist information.

$ El Marqués de Valdelirios, Alameda Valdelirios 720, T317040. Lovely colonial-style mansion, beautifully furnished, pick-up from the airport, hot water, bar, reserve at least 24 hrs in advance.

$ Florida, Jr Cuzco 310, T312565. Small, pleasant, quiet, patio with flowers, hot water from electric showers.

$ Grau, Jr San Juan de Dios 192, T312695, hotelgrau192@hotmail.com. Rooms on 3rd floor by the markets, with or without bath, hot water, laundry facilities, good value, safe but noisy, breakfast extra.

$ Hospedaje El Centro, Av Cáceres 1048, T313556. Rooms without bath and TV are cheaper than with, large rooms, hot water, good value, on a busy avenue.

$ Hostal 3 Máscaras, Jr 3 Máscaras 194, T312921, www.hoteltresmascaras.galeon. com. New rooms with bath better, but with less character, than the old ones without, nice colonial building with patio, hot water, breakfast extra, car park.

$ La Crillonesa, El Nazareno 165, T312350, www.hotelcrillonesa.com. Good value, hot water, laundry facilities, great views from roof terrace, loads of information, very helpful, Carlos will act as a local tour guide and knows everyone.

$ Marcos, 9 de Diciembre 143, T316867. Comfortable, modern, in a cul-de-sac half a block from the Plaza, quiet, hot water, price includes breakfast in the cafetería.

🍴 Restaurants

Ayacucho *p261, map p262*
Those wishing to try *cuy* should do so in Ayacucho as it's a lot cheaper than Cuzco. For a cheap, healthy breakfast, try *maca*, a drink of maca tuber, apple and quinoa, sold outside the market opposite Santa Clara, 0600-0800.
$$ Las Flores, Jr José Olaya 106, Plaza Conchopata, east of city. Daily 0900-1900. Specializes in *cuy*. Taxi US$1 from centre.
$$ Miskycha, Jr Callao 274. In a colonial mansion with regional decoration, good typical food and pleasant, helpful staff.
$$-$ La Casona, Jr Bellido 463. Open 1200-2200. Dining under the arches and in dining room, regional specialities, try their *puca picante*, *mondongo* and *cuy*, and a wide menu.
$$-$ Los Manglares de Tumbes, Av 26 de Enero 415, T315900. The best-established *cevichería* of several on this avenue, also does home delivery.
$$-$ Nino, Jr 9 de Diciembre 205, on small plaza opposite Santo Domingo church, T814537. Daily. Pleasant decor, terrace and garden (look for the owls in the trees); chicken, *parrillas*, pastas, pizzas, including take-away.
$ Cabo Blanco, Av Maravillas 198, T818740, close to Shosaku Nagase market (see Shopping). Open 0800-1800. *Ceviches*, seafood and fish dishes, small place with personal service. Also serves, beers, wines and cocktails.
$ Chifa Wa Lin, Asamblea 257. Very popular Chinese, said to be the best in town.
$ La Italiana, Jr Bellido 486, T317574. Open 1700-2300. Pizzería with a huge wood-burning oven for all to see.
$ Mía Pizza-Pizzería Karaoke, Av Mcal Cáceres 1045, T313273. Open 1800-0200. Pizzas *a la leña*, pastas and karaoke (also has a bar to get you in the mood for singing).
$ Wallpa Sua, Jr Garcilazo de la Vega 240. A good chicken place, also with *parrillas*.

There are other chicken places in town, eg Tutos, Jr Bellido 366, T312154 for delivery.

Cafés
Centro Turístico Cultural San Cristóbal, 28 de Julio 178, some expensive cafés (eg Lalo's, No 115, open 0900-2100, café, pizza delivery and bar) as well as other restaurants; all have tables in the pleasant courtyard.
La Miel, Portal Constitución 11-12, on the Plaza, T317183, 2 locations. Good coffee, hot drinks, juices, shakes, cakes and snacks, also ice creams.
Lalo's Pan, Mcal Cáceres 1243. For breakfasts, burgers and pies.
Portal 1, Portal Constitución 1. A good café on the corner of the plaza serving snacks, light meals and ice cream.

✹ Festivals

Ayacucho *p261, map p262*
The area is well known for its festivals throughout the year. Almost every day there is a celebration in one of the surrounding villages. Check with the tourist office. **Carnival in Feb** is reported as a wild affair. **Semana Santa** begins on the Fri before Holy Week. There follows one of the world's finest Holy Week celebrations, with candle-lit nightly processions, floral 'paintings' on the streets, daily fairs (the biggest on Easter Saturday), horse races and contests among peoples from all central Peru. All accommodation is fully booked for months in advance. Many people offer beds in their homes during the week. Look out for notices on the doors and in windows of transport companies.
25 Apr Anniversary of the founding of Huamanga province. **1-2 Nov** Todos Los Santos and Día de los Muertos.

🛍 Shopping

Ayacucho *p261, map p262*
Handicrafts Ayacucho is a good place to buy local crafts including filigree silver, which often uses *mudéjar* patterns. Also look out for

little painted altars which show the manger scene, carvings in local alabaster, harps, or the pre-Inca tradition of carving dried gourds. The most famous goods are carpets and *retablos*. In both weaving and *retablos*, scenes of recent political strife have been added to more traditional motifs. For carpets, go to Barrio Santa Ana, see under Places above. **Familia Pizarro**, Jr UNSCH 278, Barrio Belén, T313294. Works in textiles and *piedra huamanga* (local alabaster) and Carnival masks, good quality and all pieces individually made. They also have rooms for visitors to stay and take classes. **Mercado 12 de Abril**, Chorro y San Juan de Dios. For fruit and vegetables. **Shosaku Nagase**, on Jr Quinua y Av Maravillas, opposite Plazoleta de María Parado de Bellido. A large handicraft market.

☼ What to do

Ayacucho *p261, map p262*
A&R Tours, Jr 9 de Diciembre 130, T311300, www.viajesartours.com. Open daily 0800-2000, offers tours in and around the city. **Morochucos Rep's**, Jr 9 de Diciembre 136, T317844, www.morochucos.com. Dynamic company with tours locally and to other parts of Peru, flight and bus tickets. **Urpillay Tours**, Portal Constitución 4, T315074, urpillaytours@ terra.com. All local tours and flight tickets. **Wari Tours**, Lima 138, T311415. Local tours. **Willy Tours**, Jr 9 de Diciembre 107, T314075. Personal guides, also handles flight and bus tickets.

☎ Transport

Ayacucho *p261, map p262*
Air From/to **Lima**, 55 mins, with LC Peru (Jr 9 de Diciembre 160, T316 012) daily. StarPerú, Portal Constitución 17, T316660. Taxi airport-city centre US$3.
Bus Bus terminal **Terrapuerto Plaza Wari** at final Av Javier Pérez de Cuéllar s/n, T311710, northwest of centre, 10 mins. All bus companies are installed here, but some may retain sales counters in the centre (eg **Cruz del Sur**, Av Mcal Cáceres 1264, T312813). To **Lima**, 8 hrs on a good paved road, via Ica; several companies US$14-22 (**Molina** has the most services), plus **Cruz del Sur** US$26 *regular*, US$37 *suite* and *VIP* services, Tepsa US$37 presidencial; and Civa, US$26-41. For **Pisco**, 332 km, take a Ica/Lima bus and get out at San Clemente, 5 hrs, 10 mins from Pisco, and take a bus or combi (same fare to San Clemente as for Ica).

To **Huancayo**, 319 km, 9-10 hrs, US$15-18, 3 daily with **Molina**, also **Turismo Central**, Manco Cápac 499, T317873, US$13 at 2030. The road is paved but poor as far as Huanta, thereafter it is rough, especially in the wet season, except for the last 70 km (paved). The views are stunning.

For **Huancavelica**, take a Libertadores 0730, or **Molina** 0800 bus as far as **Rumichaca**, US$3, where combis wait at 1030 for Huancavelica, 4 hrs. Otherwise take a Huancayo bus as far as **Izcuchaca**, then take another bus, a longer route.

Ayacucho to Cuzco

Beyond Ayacucho are two highland towns, Andahuaylas and Abancay, which are possible stopping, or bus-changing places on the road to Cuzco. The road towards Cuzco climbs out of Ayacucho and crosses a wide stretch of high, treeless páramo before descending through Ocros to the Río Pampas (six hours from Ayacucho). It then climbs up to **Chincheros**, 158 km from Ayacucho, and Uripa (good Sunday market).

Andahuaylas

Andahuaylas is about 80 km further on, in a fertile valley. It offers few exotic crafts, but beautiful scenery, great hospitality and a good market on Sunday. On the north side is the Municipalidad, with a small **Museo Arqueológico**, which has a good collection of pre-Columbian objects, including mummies. A good nearby excursion is to the **Laguna de Pacucha** ⓘ *colectivo from Av Los Chankas y Av Andahuaylas, at the back of the market, US$1, 40 mins*. On the shore is the town of Pacucha with a family-run hostal (**$** on road from plaza to lake) and various places to eat. A road follows the north shore of the lake and a turn-off climbs to **Sóndor** ⓘ *US$0.65*, an Inca archaeological site at 3300 m. Various buildings and small plazas lead up to a conical hill with concentric stone terracing and, at the summit, a large rock or *intihuatana*. Each 18-19 June **Sóndor Raymi** is celebrated. Taxi from Andahuaylas, US$10; walk from Pachuca 8-10 km, or take a colectivo to Argama (also behind Andahuaylas market), which passes the entrance. With any form of public transport you will have to walk back to Pacucha, unless very lucky. **Tourist office: Dircetur** ⓘ *Av Túpac Amaru 374, T421627*.

Abancay → *Phone code: 084; Altitude: 2378 m*

Nestled between mountains in the upper reaches of a glacial valley, the friendly town of Abancay is first glimpsed when you are many kilometres away. The town is growing in importance now that the paved Lima–Nazca–Cuzco road passes through. **Tourist office** ⓘ *Lima 206, 0800-1430*, or **Dircetur**, *Av Arenas 121, p 1, T321664, apurimac@mincetur.gob.pe*. **Santuario Nacional de Ampay** ⓘ *US$1.50*, north of town, has lagoons called Angasccocha (3200 m) and Uspaccocha (3820 m), a glacier on Ampay mountain at 5235 m and flora and fauna typical of these altitudes. By public transport, take a colectivo to Tamburco and ask the driver where to get off. To get to the glacier you need two days' trekking, with overnight camping. See page 249 for sites of interest between Abancay and Cuzco.

⊚ Ayacucho to Cuzco listings

For hotel and restaurant price codes, and other relevant information, see pages 14-17.

⊜ Where to stay

Andahuaylas *p266*
$ El Encanto de Apurímac, Jr Ramos 401 (near Los Chankas and other buses), T723527. With hot water, very helpful.
$ El Encanto de Oro, Av Pedro Casafranca 424, T723066, www.encantodeoro.4t.com. Modern, comfy, hot water, laundry service, restaurant, organizes trips on request. Reserve in advance.
$ Las Américas, Jr Ramos 410, T721646. Near buses, bit gloomy in public areas, rooms are fine if basic, cheaper without bath, hot water, helpful.
$ Sol de Oro, Jr Juan A Trelles 164, T721152. Good value, good condition, hot water, laundry service, garage, tourist information, restaurant alongside, near buses.

Abancay *p267*
$$-$ Turistas, Av Díaz Barcenas 500, T321017, www.turismoapurimac.com. The original building is in colonial style, rooms a bit gloomy, breakfast not included. Newer rooms on top floor (best) and in new block are more expensive, including breakfast. Good restaurant (**$$**), wood panelled bar, parking.
$ Apurímac Tours, Jr Cuzco 421, T321446. Modern building, rooms with bath have tiny bathrooms, hot water, good value, helpful.
$ Hostal Arenas, Av Arenas 192, T322107. Well-appointed rooms, good beds, hot showers, helpful service, restaurant.
$ Imperial, Díaz Barcenas 517, T321538. Great beds, hot water, spotless, very helpful, parking, good value, cheaper without bath or breakfast.

🍴 Restaurants

Andahuaylas *p266*

$ El Dragón, Jr Juan A Trellas 279.
A recommended *chifa* serving huge
portions, excellent value (same owner
as Hotel El Encanto de Apurímac).
$ Il Gatto, Jr G Cáceres 334. A warm pizzería,
with wooden furniture, pizzas cooked in a
wood-burning oven.
$ Nuevo Horizonte, Jr Constitución 426.
Vegetarian and health food restaurant,
open for breakfast.

Abancay *p267*

$ Focarela Pizzería, Díaz Bárcenas 521, T083-
322036. Simple but pleasant decor, pizza
from a wood-burning oven, fresh, generous
toppings, popular (ask for *vino de la casa*).
$ Pizzería Napolitana, Díaz Barcenas 208.
Wood-fired clay oven, wide choice of toppings.

🎯 What to do

Abancay *p267*

Apurímak Tours, at Hotel Turistas, see
Where to stay. Run local tours and 1- and
2-day trips to Santuario Nacional de Ampay:
1-day, 7 hrs, US$40 per person for 1-2 people
(cheaper for more people). Also a 3-day
trip to Choquequirao including transport,
guide, horses, tents and food, just bring your
sleeping-bag, US$60 pp.
Carlos Valer, guide in Abancay – ask for
him at **Hotel Turistas**, very knowledgeable
and kind.

🚌 Transport

Ayacucho to Cuzco *p266*

Ayacucho to Andahuaylas, 261 km, takes
10-11 hrs (more in the rainy season), the
road is being paved. It's in good condition
when dry, but landslides occur in the wet.
The scenery is stunning. Daytime buses stop
for lunch at Chumbes (4½ hrs), which has a
few restaurants, a shop selling fruit, bread
and refrescos, and some grim toilets. **Los
Chankas**, Pasaje Cáceres 150, T312391, at
0630 (without toilet) and 1900 (with toilet),
US$15. **Celtur**, Pasaje Cáceres 174, T313194,
1830, US$15. Los Chankas' 1900 and Celtur
are direct to **Cuzco**, but you still have to
change buses in Andahuaylas. There are no
other direct buses to Abancay or Cuzco.

Andahuaylas to Ayacucho Los
Chankas, Av José María Arguedas y
Jr Trelles, T722441, 0600 and 1800 or 1840,
one coming from Cuzco. To **Abancay**, **Señor
de Huanca**, Av Martinelli 170, T721218,
3 a day, 5 hrs, US$6; Los Chankas at 0630,
US$7.50. To **Cuzco**, San Jerónimo, Av José
María Arguedas 425, T801767, via Abancay,
1800 or 1830, also 1900 Sun, US$22,
and Los Chankas. To **Lima**, buses go via
Ayacucho or Pampachiri and Puquio:
US$20. On all night buses, take a blanket.

In **Abancay**, 138 km from Andahuaylas,
5 hrs, the new Terminal Terrestre is on
Av Pachacútec, on the west side of
town. Taxi to centre US$1, otherwise it's
a steep walk up to the centre. Several
companies have offices on or near the El
Olivo roundabout at Av Díaz Bárcenas y
Gamarra, others on Av Arenas. Buses go to
Cuzco, **Andahuaylas**, and **Nazca** (464 km,
via Chalhuanca and Puquio), continuing
to **Lima**. To **Cuzco**, 195 km, takes 4½ hrs,
US$14-18. To Lima, Oltursa, US$66, Tepsa
US$71. The scenery en route is dramatic,
especially as it descends into the Apurímac
valley and climbs out again.

Bus companies, all leave from Terminal
Terrestre; office addresses are given: **Bredde**,
Gamarra 423, T321643, 5 a day to Cuzco.
Los Chankas, Díaz Bárcenas 1011, El Olivo,
T321485. **Molina**, Gamarra 422, T322646. 3 a
day to Cuzco, to Andahuaylas at 2330. **San
Jerónimo**, to Cuzco at 2130 and Andahuaylas
at 2130. **Señor de Huanca**, Av Arenas 198,
T322377, 3 a day to Andahuaylas. Several
others to Lima and Cuzco.

East and north of La Oroya

A paved road heads north from La Oroya towards Cerro de Pasco and Huánuco. Just 25 km north of La Oroya a branch turns east towards Tarma, then descends to the little-visited jungles of the Selva Central. This is a really beautiful run. North of La Oroya the road crosses the great heights of the Junín pampa and the mining zone of Cerro de Pasco, before losing altitude on its way to the Huallaga Valley. On this route you can connect by road to the Cordillera Blanca via La Unión.

Tarma and around → *Phone code: 064. Colour map 2, C3. Population: 55,000. Altitude: 3050 m.*

Founded in 1534, Tarma, 60 km from La Oroya, is a growing city but still has a lot of charm. The **Semana Santa celebrations** are spectacular, with a very colourful Easter Sunday morning procession in the main plaza. Accommodation is hard to find at this time, but you can apply to the Municipalidad for rooms with local families. The town is also notable for its locally made fine flower-carpets. Good, friendly market around Calle Amazonas and Ucayali. The surrounding countryside is beautiful. **Tourist office** ① *2 de Mayo 775 on the Plaza, T321010, ext 107, turismo@munitarma.gob.pe, Mon-Fri 0800-1300, 1500-1800, very helpful; see www.tarma.info.* Around 8 km from Tarma, the small town of **Acobamba** has *tapices* made in San Pedro de Cajas which depict the Crucifixion. There are festivities during May. About 2 km up beyond the town is the **Santuario de Muruhuay**, with a venerated picture painted on the rock behind the altar.

Beyond Tarma the road is steep and crooked but there are few places where cars cannot pass one another. In the 80 km between Tarma and La Merced the road, passing by great overhanging cliffs, drops 2450 m and the vegetation changes dramatically from temperate to tropical. The towns of San Ramón and La Merced are in the province of **Chanchamayo**. **San Ramón** (*population 25,000*) is 11 km before La Merced and has several hotels ($$$-$) and restaurants. There are regular combis and colectivos between the two towns. **La Merced** (*population 20,000*) lies in the fertile Chanchamayo valley. Asháninka Indians can usually be found around the central plaza selling bows, arrows, necklaces and trinkets. There is a festival in the last week of September. There are several hotels ($$-$) and restaurants. For information, visit **Dircetur** ① *Pardo 110, San Ramón, T064-331265.*

About 25 km from La Merced along the road to Oxapampa, a road turns northeast to **Villa Rica**, centre of an important coffee growing area (hotels and restaurants). A very poor dirt road continues north to Puerto Bermúdez and beyond to join the Tingo María-Pucallpa road at Von Humboldt, 86 km from Pucallpa. **Puerto Bermúdez** is a great base for exploring further into the San Matías/San Carlos national reserve in the Selva Central Peruana, with trips upriver to the Asháninka communities. Tours are arranged by **Albergue Humboldt** (see Where to stay, below). To go further downriver to Pucallpa, there is road transport via Ciudad Constitución, about US$20 over two stages.

North of La Oroya

A paved road runs 130 km north from La Oroya to Cerro de Pasco. It runs up the Mantaro valley through canyons to the wet and mournful Junín pampa at over 4250 m, one of the world's largest high-altitude plains. An obelisk marks the battlefield where the Peruvians under Bolívar defeated the Spaniards in 1824. Blue peaks line the pampa in a distant wall. This windswept sheet of yellow grass is bitterly cold and the only signs of life are the youthful herders with their sheep and llamas. The road follows the east shores of the Lago Junín. The town of **Junín** lies some distance south of the lake and has the somewhat desolate feel of a high *puna* town, bisected by the railway (two hotels, $, **Leo** is very dirty).

The **Junín National Reserve** ① *US$5, ticket from Sernanp in Junín, Jr San Martín 138, T064-344146*, protects one of the best birdwatching sites in the central Andes where the giant coot and even flamingos may be spotted. It is easiest to visit from the village of Huayre, 5 km south of Carhuamayo, from which it is a 20-minute walk down to the lake. Fishermen are usually around to take visitors out on the lake. Carhuamayo is the best place to stay: **Gianmarco**, Maravillas 454, and **Patricia**, Tarapacá 862, are the best of several basic *hostales*. There are numerous restaurants along the main road.

Cerro de Pasco → *Phone code: 063. Population: 70,000. Altitude: 4330 m.*

This long-established mining centre, 130 km from La Oroya, is not attractive, but is nevertheless very friendly. Copper, zinc, lead, gold and silver are mined here, and coal comes from the deep canyon of Goyllarisquisga, the 'place where a star fell', the highest coal mine in the world, 42 km north of Cerro de Pasco. The town is sited between Lago Patarcocha and the huge abyss of the mine above which its buildings and streets cling precariously. Nights are bitterly cold.

Southwest of Cerro de Pasco by 40 km is **Huayllay**, near which is the **Santuario Huayllay (Bosque de Piedras)** ① *US$1, camping is permitted within the Sanctuary; Sernanp in Junín administers the site and there is a Comité del Santuario Nacional de Huayllay*. These unique weathered limestone formations are in the shape of a tortoise, elephant, alpaca, etc. At the Sanctuary (4100-4600 m), 11 tourist circuits through the spectacular rock formations have been laid out. The village of Huallay is 6 km southwest the sanctuary; it has a municipal hostel and other hotels. A festival of sports and music is held here 6-8 September. The Central Highway from Cerro de Pasco continues northeast another 528 km to Pucallpa, the limit of navigation for large Amazon river boats. The western part of this road (Cerro de Pasco-Huánuco) has been rebuilt into an all-weather highway. The sharp descent along the nascent **Río Huallaga** is a tonic to travellers suffering from *soroche*. The road drops 2436 m in the 100 km from Cerro de Pasco to Huánuco, and most of it is in the first 32 km. From the bleak high ranges the road plunges below the tree line offering great views. The only town of any size before Huánuco is **Ambo**.

Huánuco → *Phone code: 062. Colour map 2, B2/3. Population: 118,814. Altitude: 1894 m.*

This is an attractive Andean town on the Upper Huallaga with an interesting market. **Tourist office** ① *Gen Prado 716, on the Plaza de Armas, T512980.* A website giving local information is www.webhuanuco.com. About 5 km away on the road west to La Unión is **Kótosh** (*Altitude: 1912 m*) ① *US$0.75, including a guide around a marked circuit which also passes through a small botanical garden of desert plants, taxi US$5 from the centre, with 30 mins' wait.* At this archaeological site, the Temple of Crossed Hands, the earliest evidence of a complex society and of pottery in Peru, dates from 2000 BC. From Huánuco, a spectacular but very poor dirt road leads to **La Unión**, capital of Dos de Mayo district. It's a fast developing town with a couple of hotels ($) and restaurants, but electricity can be a problem and it gets very cold at night. On the pampa above La Unión is the large archaeological site of **Huánucopampa** or **Huánuco Viejo** ① *US$1.50, allow 2 hrs*, a 2½-hour walk from the town, an important Inca administrative centre with residential quarters (taxi US$6.50-9.50 with wait). It has impressive stonework and a fine section of Inca road running north and south. The route to the Callejón de Huaylas goes through **Huallanca**, an attractive town, with mining projects nearby. See Transport, below.

For hotel and restaurant price codes, and other relevant information, see pages 14-17.

⊙ Where to stay

Tarma and around *p269*

$$$ Hacienda Santa María, 2 km out of town at Vista Alegre 1249, Sacsamarca, T321232, www.haciendasantamaria.com. A beautiful (non-working) 17th-century hacienda, beautiful gardens and antique furniture. Includes breakfast. Excellent guides for local day trips.

$$$ Los Portales, Av Castilla 512, T321411, www.losportaleshoteles.com.pe. On the edge of town, hot water, heating, 1950s building with old furnishings, includes breakfast, good restaurant.

$$$-$$ Hacienda La Florida, 6 km from Tarma, T341041, www.haciendalaflorida. com. 18th-century working hacienda owned by German-Peruvian couple Inge and Pepe, who also arrange excursions. Variety of rooms sleeping 1-4, adjoining family rooms, dorm for groups and an independent house; all with hot water, meals available, lots of home-grown organic produce. Also camping for US$5.

$$ Normandie, beside the Santuario de Muruhuay, Acobamba, T064-341028, Lima T01-365 9795, www.hotelnormandie.com. pe. Rooms with hot water, bar, restaurant, tours offered.

$ El Caporal, Lima 616, T323636, hostalel caporal@yahoo.es. Includes breakfast, good location, comfortable, hot water.

$ Hospedaje Residencial El Dorado, Huánuco 488, T321914, www.hospedajeel doradotarma.com. Hot water, rooms set round a patio, 1st floor better, safe, welcoming, secure parking.

$ Hostal Aruba, Jr Moquegua 452 near the market, T322057. Hot water, nice rooms with tile floors, good value.

$ Hostal Central, Huánuco 614, T322625. Cheaper without bath, hot water, laundry,

bit rundown but popular, has observatory (opens Fri 2000, US$1 for non-guests).

$ La Colmena, Jauja 618, T321157. Well-maintained old building, convenient for Huancayo buses.

Puerto Bermúdez

$ Albergue Cultural Humboldt, by the river port (La Rampa), T063-963-722363, http://alberguehumboldt.free.fr. The owner, Basque writer Jesús, has created a real haven for backpackers, with maps, library and book exchange. Rooms sleep 1-3, or there are hammocks and tents. Meals available, Spanish and Peruvian food. Jesús arranges tours, from day trips to camping and trekking in primary forest. Recommended.

Cerro de Pasco *p270*

$ Hostal Arenales, Jr Arenales 162, near the bus station, T723088. Modern, TV, hot water in the morning.

$ Señorial, Jr San Martín 1, in the district of San Juan, 5 mins north of Cerro by taxi, T422802, hotelsenorial@hotmail.com. The most comfortable in town, hot water, fine view across the mine pit.

$ Welcome, Av La Plata 125, opposite the entrance to the bus station, T721883. Some rooms without window, hot water 24 hrs.

Huánuco *p270*

$$$ Grand Hotel Huánuco (Inka Comfort), Jr D Beraún 775, T514222, www.grandhotel huanuco.com. With restaurant, pool, sauna, gym and parking.

$ El Roble, Constitución 629, T512515. Without bath, cheap and good value.

$ Hostal Miraflores, Valdizán 560, T512848, www.granhostalmiraflores.com. Hot water, private bathroom, quiet, safe, laundry service.

$ Imperial, Huánuco 581, T518737. With hot showers, quiet and helpful. Recommended.

$ Las Vegas, 28 de Julio 940, on Plaza de Armas, T512315. Small rooms, hot water, restaurant next door. Good.

Huallanca

$ Hostal Yesica, L Prado 507. Hot water, shared bathroom, the best of the basic ones.
$ Hotel Milán, 28 de Julio 107. Modern, hot water, best in town, good restaurant.

🍴 Restaurants

Tarma and around *p269*
$ Chavín, Jr Lima 270 at Plaza de Armas. Daily 0730-2230. Very good quality and variety in set meals (weekdays only), also à la carte.
$ Chifa Roberto Siu, Jr Lima 569 upstairs. A good option for Chinese food, popular with locals.
$ Comedor Vegetariano, Arequipa 695. Open 0700-2100, but closed Fri after lunch and Sat. Vegetarian, small and cheap, sells great bread.
$ Señorial/Pollería El Braserito, Huánuco 138. Señorial is open daily 0800-1530, El Braserito, daily 1800-2300. Good *menú*, extensive choice of à la carte dishes.

Cerro de Pasco *p270*
$ Los Angeles, Jr Libertad, near the market. Excellent *menú* for US$1.50. Recommended.
$ San Fernando, bakery in the plaza. Opens at 0700. Great hot chocolate, bread and pastries.

Huánuco *p270*
$ Chifa Men Ji, 28 de Julio, block 8. Good prices, nice Chinese food.
$ Govinda, Prado 608. Reckoned to be the best vegetarian restaurant.
$ La Olla de Barro, Gral Prado 852, close to main plaza. Serves typical food, good value.
$ Pizzería Don Sancho, Prado 645. Best pizzas in town.

🎉 Festivals

Huánuco *p270*
20-25 Feb Carnaval Huanqueño.
3 May La Cruz de Mayo. **16 Jul** Fiesta de la Virgen del Carmen. **12-18 Aug** Tourist

Week in Huánuco. **28-29 Oct** Fiesta del Señor de Burgos, the patron of Huánuco.
25 Dec Fiesta de los Negritos.

🚌 Transport

Tarma and around *p269*
Bus To **Lima**, 231 km (paved), 6 hrs, US$15. Transportes Junín, Amazonas 667, 7 a day, with *bus cama* night bus (in Lima: Av Nicolás Arriola 198, T01-224 9220). Trans La Merced, Vienrich 420, 3 a day. Trans Los Canarios, Jr Amazonas 694 (2 daily) start in Tarma. Transportes Chanchamayo, Callao 1002, T321882, 2 a day, en route from Chanchamayo. To **Jauja**, US$2, and **Huancayo**, US$3, Transportes Angelitos/San Juan, from the stadium, 0800-1800, every 1½ hrs; Trans Los Canarios about 1 per hr, 0500-1800; Trans Junín at 1200 and 2400. Colectivos depart when full from Callao y Jauja, 2 hrs, US$4, and 3 hrs, US$6, respectively. To **Cerro de Pasco**, Empresa Junín, Amazonas 450, 4 a day, 3 hrs, US$2.50. Also colectivos when full, 2 hrs, US$4. Buses to **La Oroya** leave from opposite the petrol station on Av Castilla block 5, 1 hr, US$1.50, while colectivos leave from the petrol station itself, 45 mins, US$2. To **Chanchamayo**, Transportes Angelitos/San Juan, 13 daily, 0600-2100, to La Merced US$1.75; Trans Junín, 4 a day, to San Ramón US$1.75, 1½ hrs, La Merced US$2.75, 2 hrs. Combis, US$1.75, and colectivos, US$4, from the stadium to La Merced.

Colectivos and Canary Tours combis to **Acobamba** and up to **Muruhuay**, 15 mins, US$0.30 and 0.45 respectively.

Note The local names for colectivos are '*carros*' and '*stations*'.

San Ramón
Air Flights leave from San Ramón. There is a small airstrip where **Aero Montaña**, T064-331074, rfmamsa@hotmail.com, has air taxis that can be chartered (*viaje especial*) to the jungle towns, with a maximum of 3 people, but you have to pay for the pilot's return

to base. Flights cost US$250 per hr. **Puerto Bermúdez** takes 33 mins. You can also just go to the air base, across the river, on the east side of town.

La Merced

Bus Many buses go here from **Lima**: Expreso Satipo, Junín, La Merced and Chanchamayo each have several buses during the day, US$8 *regular*, US$11 *cama* upper level, US$12.50 *cama* lower level, 7-8 hrs. To **Tarma** Transportes Angelitos/ San Juan, hourly, 2½ hrs, US$1.75, or colectivos, just over 1 hr, US$4. To **Puerto Bermúdez**, Empresa Transdife and Villa Rica have 4WD pick-ups between 0400 and 0600 and may pick up passengers at their hotels. You must purchase tickets in advance, the vehicles get very full. US$14 in front, US$8 in the back (worth spending the extra money), 8-10 hrs or more.

Cerro de Pasco *p270*

Bus There is a large bus station. To **Lima** several companies including Carhuamayo and Transportes Apóstol San Pedro, hourly 0800-1200, plus 4 departures 2030-2130, 8 hrs, US$8. If there are no convenient daytime buses, you could change buses in La Oroya. To **Carhuamayo**, **Junín** and **La Oroya**: buses leave when full, about every 20-30 mins, to Carhuamayo 1 hr, US$1; to Junín 1½ hrs, US$1; to La Oroya, 2½ hrs, US$2. Colectivos also depart with a similar frequency, 1½ hrs, US$2.50, to La Oroya. To **Tarma**, Empresa Junín, 0600, 1500, 3 hrs, $2.50. Colectivos also depart hourly, 1½ hrs, US$4. To **Huancayo**, various companies leave throughout the day, 5 hrs, US$4. To **Huánuco**, buses and cars leave when full, about half hourly, 2½ hrs and 1½ hrs, US$2 and US$4 respectively.

Huayllay

Minibuses to Huallay from Cerro de Pasco's terminal leave throughout the day, about 1 hr, US$1. They return until 1800-1900.

Huánuco *p270*

Air Airport T513066. From **Lima**, StarPerú and **LCPeru** (2 de Mayo 1355, T518113), daily, 55 mins.

Bus To **Lima**, US$18-25, 8 hrs. León de Huánuco, Malecón Alomía Robles 821, 3 a day. Also Bahía Continental, Valdizán 718, recommended, Transportes El Rey, 28 de Julio 1215 (28 de Julio 1192, La Victoria, Lima). The majority of buses of all companies leave 2030-2200, most also offer a bus at 0900-1000. A colectivo to Lima, costing US$23, leaves at 0400, arriving at 1400; book the night before at Gen Prado 607, 1 block from the plaza. Recommended. To **Cerro de Pasco**, 3 hrs, US$2, colectivos under 2 hrs, US$4. All leave when full from the Ovalo Carhuayna on the north side of the city, 3 km from the centre. To **Huancayo**, 7 hrs, US$6: Turismo Central, Tarapacá 530, at 2100. Colectivos run to **Tingo María**, from block 1 of Prado close to Puente Calicanto, 2½ hrs, US$5. Also Etnasa, 3-4 hrs, US2. For **Pucallpa**, take a colectivo to Tingo María, then a bus from there. This route has many checkpoints and robberies can occur. Travel by day and check on the current situation regarding safety. To **La Unión**, Turismo Unión, daily 0730, 7 hrs, US$5; also Turismo Marañón daily 0700. This is a rough road operated also by El Niño colectivos, Aguilar 530, leave when full, US$7.15.

La Unión

Bus To **Huánuco**: Turismo Unión, Jr Comercio 1224 daily at 0600, US$8, 7 hrs. Also Turismo Marañón, Jr Comercio 1309, daily at 0700 (no afternoon/evening departures). *El Niño* colectivos, Jr Comercio 12, T062-515952, 5 hrs. To **Huallanca (Huánuco)**, combis leave from the market, about hourly, when full and follow the attractive Vizcarra valley, 1 hr, US$2. *El Rápido* runs to **Huaraz** 0400, 4½ hrs, US$8, or change in Huallanca. Combis leave when full about half hourly, from the corner of Comercio y 28 de Julio in Huallanca for La Unión. They also go to Laguna Pacahacoto from where another combi can be taken to Huaraz.

Amazon Basin

Cooled by winds sweeping down from the Andes but warmed by its jungle blanket, this region contains important tropical flora and fauna. In the north of the region, Iquitos, on the Amazon itself, is the centre of jungle exploration. It is a very varied landscape, with grasslands and tablelands of scrub-like vegetation, inaccessible swamps, and forests up to 2000 m above sea level. The principal means of communication in the jungle is by its many rivers, the most important being the Amazon, which rises high up in the Andes as the Marañón, then joins the Ucayali to become the longest river in the world. The northern tourist area is based on the River Amazon itself with, at its centre, a sizeable city, Iquitos. Although it has lost its rubber-boom dynamism, Iquitos is still at the heart of life on the river. There are jungle lodges upstream and down, each with its own speciality and level of comfort, but none more than half a day away by fast boat. To get right into the wilds, head for Peru's largest national reserve, Pacaya-Samiria, accessed by boat from Iquitos or the little town of Lagunas.

North from Huánuco to Pucallpa

Huánuco to Tingo María

The journey to Tingo María from Huánuco, 135 km, is very dusty but gives a good view of the jungle. Some 25 km beyond Huánuco the road begins a sharp climb to the heights of Carpish (3023 m). A descent of 58 km brings it to the Huallaga River again; it then continues along the river to Tingo María. The road is paved from Huánuco to Tingo María, including a tunnel through the Carpish hills. Landslides along this section are frequent and construction work causes delays. Although this route is reported to be relatively free from terrorism, robberies do occur and it is advisable to travel only by day.

Situated on the middle Huallaga, in the Ceja de Montaña, on the edge (literally 'eyebrow') of the mountains, **Tingo María** *(Phone code: 062; Population: 20,560; Altitude: 655 m; Annual rainfall: 2642 mm)* is isolated for days in the rainy season. The altitude prevents the climate from being oppressive. The Cordillera Azul, the front range of the Andes, covered with jungle-like vegetation to its top, separates it from the jungle lowlands to the east. The mountain which can be seen from all over the town is called La Bella Durmiente (the Sleeping Beauty). The meeting here of highlands and jungle makes the landscape extremely striking. Bananas, sugar cane, cocoa, rubber, tea and coffee are grown. The main crop of the area, though, is coca, grown on the *chacras* (smallholdings) in the countryside, and sold legitimately and otherwise in Tingo María. A small university outside the town, beyond the **Hotel Madera Verde**, has a little **museum/zoo** ① *free but a small tip would help to keep things in order*; it also maintains botanical gardens in the town. About 6.5 km from Tingo, on a rough road, is a fascinating cave, the **Cueva de las Lechuzas** ① *US$1 for the cave, take a torch, and do not wear open shoes, getting there: take a motorcycle-taxi from town, US$1.75; cross the Río Monzón by new bridge.* There are many oilbirds in the cave and many small parakeets near the entrance. **Tourist office** ① *Av Ericson 158, T562310, perucatapress@gmail.com.* Note that Tingo María is a main narco-trafficking centre and although the town is generally safe, it is not safe to leave it at night. Always keep to the main routes.

Tingo María to Pucallpa

From Tingo María to the end of the road at Pucallpa is 255 km, with a climb over the watershed – the Cordillera Azul – between the Huallaga and Ucayali rivers. The road is in poor shape for most of the journey, but some paving is in progress. Travel by day: it is safer the views are tremendous as you go from the high jungle to the Amazon Basin. Sit on the righthand side of the bus. When the road was being surveyed it was thought that the lowest pass over the Cordillera Azul was over 3650 m high, but an old document stating that a Father Abad had found a pass through these mountains in 1757 was rediscovered, and the road now goes through the pass of Father Abad, a gigantic gap 4 km long and 2000 m deep. At the top of the pass is a Peruvian Customs house; the jungle land to the east is a free zone. Coming down from the pass the road bed is along the floor of a magnificent canyon, the Boquerón Abad. It is a beautiful trip through luxuriant jungle, ferns and sheer walls of bare rock, punctuated by occasional waterfalls plunging into the roaring torrent below. East of the foot of the pass the all-weather road goes over the flat pampa, with few bends, to the village of **Aguaytía** (narcotics police outpost, gasoline, accommodation and restaurants). From Aguaytía the road continues for 160 km to Pucallpa – five hours by bus. There is a service station three hours before Pucallpa.

Pucallpa → *Phone code: 061. Colour map 2, B3. Population: 400, 000.*

Pucallpa is a rapidly expanding jungle town on the Río Ucayali, navigable by vessels of 3000 tons from Iquitos, 533 nautical miles away. Different 'ports' are used depending on the level of the river, they are all just mud banks without any facilities (see Transport, below).The economy of the area includes sawmills, plywood factories, oil refinery, fishing and boat building. Large discoveries of oil and gas are being explored. Local festivals are **Carnival** in February, **San Juan** on 24 June, and the Ucayali regional fair in October. The town is hot and dusty between June and November and muddy from December to May. **Note** There is narcotics activity in the area. The city itself is safe enough to visit, but don't travel at night. **Museo Regional** ① *Carretera Federico Basadre Km 4.2, park entry US$1.10, Mon-Fri 0800-1630, Sat and Sun 0900-1730,* has some good examples of Shipibo ceramics, as well as some delightful pickled snakes and other reptiles. **Tourist office Dircetur** ① *Jr 2 de Mayo 111, T578400, ucayali@mincetur.gob.pe, Mon-Fri 0730-1300, 1330-1515.* Information also at **Gobierno Regional de Ucayali (GOREU)** ① *Raimondi block 220, T575018, www.regionucayali.gob.pe.*

Around Pucallpa The main attraction is **Lago Yarinacocha** ① *to the northeast of Pucallpa, 20 mins by colectivo or bus along Jr Ucayali, US$0.50, or 15 mins by taxi,* an oxbow lake linked to the Río Ucayali by a canal at the northern tip of its west arm. River dolphins can be seen here. Puerto Callao, also known as Yarinacocha or Yarina, is the main town, at the southern tip, reached by road from Pucallpa. There are a number of restaurants and bars here and it is popular at weekends. From Yarina, a road continues along the western arm to **San José**, **San Francisco** and **Santa Clara** (bus US$0.75). The area is populated by the Shipibo people, who make ceramic and textile crafts. The area between the eastern arm of the lake and the Río Ucayali has been designated as a reserve. Here, towards the northwestern shore of the east arm is the beautifully located **Jardín Botánico Chullachaqui** ① *free,* which can be reached by boat from Puerto Callao to Pueblo Nueva Luz de Fátima, 45 minutes, then one hour's walk to the garden (ask at Moroti-Shobo on the Plaza de Armas in Puerto Callao).

For hotel and restaurant price codes, and other relevant information, see pages 14-17.

◉ Where to stay

Tingo María *p274*

$$$-$$ Madera Verde, Av Universitaria s/n, out of town on the road to Huánuco, near the University, T561800. Wooden chalets, cabins and rooms in beautiful surroundings, breakfast included, restaurant, 2 swimming pools, butterfly farm, free entry to wildlife rescue centre.

$$ Albergue Ecológico Villa Jennifer, Km 3.4 Carretera a Castillo Grande, 10 mins from Tingo María, T962-603509, www.villa jennifer.net. Danish-Peruvian owned, includes breakfast, 2- to 4-night packages, US$50-90, and tours to local sites, pool, mini-zoo, birdwatching, restaurant, laundry service, phone ahead to arrange bus station pick-up. Rooms are surrounded by local flora, with lots of birdlife.

$$ Nueva York, Av Alameda Perú 553, T562406, joferjus@hotmail.com. Central and noisy, cheaper without bath and TV, laundry, good value, restaurant.

$ Hostal Marco Antonio, Jr Monzón 364, T562201. Quiet, restaurant of the same name next door.

Pucallpa *p275*

$$$ Sol del Oriente, Av San Martín 552, T575154, www.soldelorientehoteles.com. Price includes breakfast and airport transfer, a/c, pool, mini-zoo, good restaurant, bilingual guides.

$$$-$$ Grand Hotel Mercedes, Raimondi 610, T575120, www.granhotelmercedes. com. Pucallpa's first hotel, still family-run, with some refurbished rooms, modern facilities with old-fashioned ambiance, includes breakfast, hot water, a/c, fridge, pool, restaurant.

$$-$ Antonio's, Jr Progreso 545, T573721, antonios_hs@hotmail.com. A variety of

rooms and prices, cheaper in older rooms or with fan, breakfast extra, cable TV, garden, pool, jacuzzi, parking, airport pick-up.

$$-$ Arequipa, Jr Progreso 573, T571348, www.hostal-arequipa.com. Good, a/c or fan, breakfast, comfortable, safe, restaurant, pool.

$ Barbtur, Raimondi 670, T572532. Cheaper without bath, central, good beds, cold water, friendly but noisy.

$ Komby, Ucayali 360, T571562. Cold water, fan, ample rooms, pool, very noisy street but back rooms are quiet, good value.

$ La Suite de Petita's Inn, Jr Fitzcarraldo 171, T572831. Includes simple breakfast, cold water, fan, fridge, parking.

Around Pucallpa: Yarinacocha *p275*

$$$ Jana Shobo Amazonian Lodge, Lake Yarinacocha, T596943, www.otaku.ch/ cyberboogie/JanaShoboweb/index_EN.htm. Small lodge is set in 10 ha of forest on the lakeshore. Bunk beds or camping. Price includes meals and airport transfer, packages and tours available. Living room, reading room and kitchen.

$$$ pp Pandisho Amazon Ecolodge, north of the village of 11 de Agosto, towards the northern tip of the eastern shore of the west arm, T061-799214, www.amazon-ecolodge. com (in Pucallpa, Pasaje Bolívar 261, T961-994227). Full board, good resort with cabins by the lakeshore, includes packages of varying length and rainforest expeditions. Also has lodges in Pacaya-Samiria, near Pucallpa at Honoria and near Iquitos.

$ Los Delfines, opposite Electroucayali in Puerto Callao. With bath, fan, fridge, some with TV.

◉ Restaurants

Tingo María *p274*

$ El Antojito 2, Jr Chiclayo 458. Local food.

$ Girasol, Av Raimondi 253, T562065. Chicken, burgers, cakes and fruit juices.

Pucallpa *p275*

$$-$ C'est si bon, Jr Independencia 560 y Pasaje Zegarra, Plaza de Armas. Daily 0800-2400. Chicken, snacks, drinks, sweets, ice cream.

$$-$ Chifa Xin Xin, Jr Tarapacá 515 and Av Raimondi 603. Daily 1200-1600 and 1830-2300. Authentic Chinese cooking, set meals and à la carte.

$$-$ El Viajero, Jr Libertad 374. Sun-Fri 0800-1630. Choice of good set meals, also à la carte, very popular.

$$-$ La Favorita, Jr Adolfo Morey e Inmaculada. Daily 0800-1600. Regional and home cooking, good set meals Mon-Sat and *parrilladas* on Sun, popular.

$ Tropitop Heladería, Jr Sucre y Tarapacá 401 (Plaza de Armas). Good, cheap, typical breakfasts.

◯ Shopping

Pucallpa *p275*

Many Shibipo women carry and sell their products around Pucallpa and Yarinacocha. **Agustín Rivas**, at Jr Tarapacá 861, above a small restaurant whose entrance is at No 863 (ask for it). For local wood carvings visit the workshop of this sculptor, whose work is made from huge tree roots.

Artesanías La Anaconda, Pasaje Cohen by Plaza de Armas, good selection of indigenous crafts.

⊖ Transport

Tingo María *p274*

Bus To **Huánuco**, 119 km, 3-4 hrs, US$2 with **Etnasa** (not recommended – theft and drug-trafficking); take a micro, US$2, or colectivo, US$5, 2 hrs, several daily. Direct buses continue to Lima, 10 hrs, with **Trans Rey**, US$22 *bus cama*, **León de Huánuco** and **Bahía Continental** (recommended, T01-424 1539), US$15. To **Pucallpa**, 5 hrs, US$15. **Ucayali Express** colectivos leave from Raimondi y Callao and **Selva Express**, Av Tito Jaime 218, T562380. Buses take 7-8 hrs, US$8.50, eg **Etposa**.

Pucallpa *p275*

Air To **Lima** and **Iquitos**, daily 1 hr, flights with **LAN** (Jr Tarapacá 805 y San Martín, T579840) and **Star Perú** (7 de Junio 865, T590585). Airport taxis charge US$6 to town, outside taxis charge US$3.

Bus There are regular bus services to **Lima**, several companies, 18-20 hrs (longer in the rainy season, Nov-Mar), US$11-12.50 *regular*. **Transmar**, Av Raimondi 770, T579778 (in Lima Av Nicolás de Pierrola 197, T01-265 0190), US$17.50 *regular*, US$28 *bus cama* with a/c, US$25 *bus cama* without a/c. To **Tingo María**, bus US$8.50, 7-8 hrs, bound for Lima, also **Etposa**, 7 de Junio 843, at 1700. Or 5 hrs, US$15 by combi, leave from early morning, **Turismo Ucayali**, 7 de Junio 799, T593002, and **Selva Express**, Jr 7 de Junio 841, T579098. Take blankets as the crossing of the Cordillera at night is bitterly cold.

Ferry Boats to all destinations dock around Puerto Inmaculada, 2 blocks downriver from the Malecón Grau, at the bottom of Jr Inmaculada, unless the water level is very high, in which case they dock at Puerto Manantay, 4 km south of town. To **Iquitos** down the Ucayali and Amazon rivers, 3-4 days, longer if the water level is low and larger boats must travel only by day, hammock US$40, berth US$140 double. **Henry** is a large company with departures Mon, Wed, Fri and Sat from Puerto Henry at the bottom of Jr Manco Capac, by Jr Arica; their newer boats, *Henry 6* and *7*, have some cabins with private bath. Another good boat is *Pedro Martín 2* sailing from Puerto Inmaculada.

You must ask around for the large boats to Iquitos. A mototaxi to any of the ports costs US$0.75 from the Plaza de Armas, taxis charge US$3. Departure times are marked on chalk boards on the deck. Schedules seem to change almost hourly. Do not pay for your trip before you board the vessel, and only pay the captain. Some boat captains may allow you to live on board a couple of days before sailing. Bottled drinking water can be bought in Pucallpa, but not cheaply. See General hints for river travel, page 287.

Pucallpa *p275*
Cultural centres Art school: Usko Ayar Amazonian School of Painting, in the house of artist Pablo Amaringo (died 2009), a former *vegetalista* (healer), Jr LM Sánchez Cerro 465-467, see Facebook page. The school provides art classes for local people, and is dependent upon selling their art. The internationally renowned school welcomes overseas visitors for short or long stays to study painting and learn Spanish and/ or teach English with Peruvian students.
Police Policia Nacional, Jr Independencia 3rd block, T575211.

Yurimaguas and Pacaya-Samiria

Yurimaguas

The Río Huallaga winds northwards for 930 km. The Upper Huallaga is a torrent, dropping 15.8 m per kilometre between its source and Tingo María. The Lower Huallaga moves through an enervation of flatness, with its main port, Yurimaguas, below the last rapids and only 150 m above the Atlantic Ocean, yet distant from that ocean by over a month's voyage. Between the Upper and Lower lies the Middle Huallaga: the third of the river which is downstream from Tingo María and upstream from Yurimaguas.

Downriver of Tingo María, beyond Bellavista, the orientation is towards **Yurimaguas** (*Phone code: 065; Population: 25,700*), which is connected by road with the Pacific coast, via Tarapoto (120 km) and Moyobamba (see page 145). It's a very relaxed jungle town and, as the roadhead on the lower Río Huallaga, is an ideal starting point for river travel in the Peruvian Amazon. A colourful Mercado Central is open from 0500-1200, full of fruit and animals, many, sadly, for the pot. Excursions in the area include the gorge of Shanusi and the lakes of Mushuyacu and Sanango. **Concejo Regional tourist office** ① *Mariscal Castilla 118, of 2, Mon-Fri 0745-1545, www.yurimaguas.net.*

Pacaya-Samiria

All river traffic to Iquitos stops at **Lagunas**, 12 hours from Yurimaguas, one of the entry points to the Pacaya-Samiria Reserve. The **reserve office** ① *Iquitos, SERNANP, Jorge Chávez 930/942, T223555, www.pacayasamiria.org, Mon-Fri 0700-1300, 1500-1700,* has general information and an updated list of tour operators authorized to enter the reserve. Entry costs US$2 for a day visit, US$23 for three days, US$46 for seven days, payable at the ranger stations. Pacaya-Samiria Reserve, at 2,080,000 ha, is the country's second largest protected area. It is bounded by the rivers Marañón and Ucuyali, narrowing to their confluence near the town of Nauta. The reserve's waterways and wetlands provide habitat for several cats including puma and jaguar, manatee, tapir, river dolphins, giant otters, black cayman, boas, 269 species of fish and 449 bird species. Many of the animals found here are in danger of extinction. There are 208 population centres in the area of the reserve, 92 within the park, the others in the buffer zone. Five native groups plus *colonos* live in the region.

The reserve can only be visited with an authorized guide arranged through a tour operator or a local community tourism association. Native guides generally speak only Spanish and native tongues. A list of authorized community associations is found in the reserve's web page and iPerú in Iquitos has a list of authorized operators. Most of the reserve is off-limits to tourists, but eight areas have been set up for visitors, these have shelters or camping areas, conditions are generally simple and may require sleeping in hammocks. Trips are mostly on the river and often include fishing. Four circuits are most commonly offered. All are rich in wildlife. **1)** The basin of the Yanayacu and Pucate rivers is the most frequently visited; Laguna El Dorado is an important attraction in this area. It is accessed from **Nauta** on the Marañón, two hours by paved road from Iquitos and three hours by *peque peque* or 1½ hours by *deslizador* from there to the reserve. Note that Nauta has pirate guides; best arrange a tour with an operator. **2)** The middle and lower Samiria, accessed from Leoncio Prado (with a couple of *hospedajes*), 24 hours by *lancha* from Iquitos along the Marañón. Several lakes are found in this area. **3)** The lower Pacaya, mostly flooded forest, accessed from Bretaña, on the Canal de Puinahua, a shortcut on the Ucayali, 24 hours by *lancha* from Iquitos. This area is less frequently visited than others. **4)** The Tibilo-Pastococha area in the western side of the park, also in the Samiria basin, accessed from Lagunas on the Río Huallaga, 10-12 hours by *lancha* or three hours by *deslizador* from Yurimaguas and 48 hours by *lancha* from Iquitos. Another way of visiting the reserve is on a cruise, sailing along the main rivers on the periphery of the park. These tours are offered by some Iquitos operators.

⦿ Yurimaguas and Pacaya-Samiria listings

For hotel and restaurant price codes, and other relevant information, see pages 14-17.

⦿ Where to stay

Yurimaguas *p278*

$$$-$$ Río Huallaga, Arica 111, T768329, www.riohuallagahotel.com. Nice modern hotel overlooking the river, safety box, pool, bar, rooftop restaurant with lovely views.

$$-$ Luis Antonio, Av Jaúregui 407, T352061, hostal_luis_antonio@hotmail.com. Cold water, small pool, a/c at extra cost, breakfast, very helpful.

$$-$ Posada Cumpanama, Progreso 403, T352905, http://posadacumpanama. blogspot.com. Rooms cheaper with shared bath, breakfast extra, tastefully decorated, pool, very pleasant.

$ Hostal Akemi, Jr Angamos 414, T352237, www.hostalakemi.com. Decent rooms with hot water, cheaper without a/c, some with frigobar, restaurant, pool, helpful owner, good value.

$ Hostal El Caballito, Av Jaúregui 403, T352864. Cold water, small bathroom, fan, pleasant, good value.

$ Hostal El Naranjo, Arica 318, T352650, www.hostalelnaranjo.com.pe. A/c or fan, hot water, frigobar, small pool, with restaurant.

Pacaya-Samiria *p278*

$$$$ Pacaya Samiria Amazon Lodge, T065-225769 (Iquitos), www.pacayasamiria. com.pe. Beautifully designed lodge on a hill overlooking the Marañón, just inside the reserve but close to road and town. All buildings in indigenous style, with balconies and en suite bathrooms, restaurant, bar. Community visits and specialist birdwatching trips included in the price, but boat trips (also included) can be long. Camping trips can be arranged deeper inside the reserve.

Lagunas

Basic places in town include: all **$ Eco**, Jr Padre Lucero, near cemetery, T503703; **Hostal Miraflores**, Miraflores 1 block from plaza; **Samiria**, Jr José Cárdenas, near the market.

Nauta

Basic places in town include: all **$ La Granja Azul**, near entrance to town; **Nauta Inn**, Manuel Pacaya by Laguna Sapi Sapi, T411025.

⦿ What to do

Yurimaguas *p278*

Samiria Expeditions, Río Huallaga Hotel, www.peruselva.com. Tours to lakes, day and multi-day trips to Pacaya-Samiria, work with Hauyruro Tours in Lagunas.

Pacaya-Samiria *p278*

Community associations in many of the villages around the reserve run tours. **Consorcio Rumbo al Dorado**, www. yacutayta.org, groups 3 communities in the Yanayacu-Pucate region. In the community of San Martín de Tipishca in the Samiria Basin are **Asiendes** (Asociación Indígena en Defensa de la Ecología Samiria), T965-861748, asiendesperu@hotmail.com and **Casa Lupuna**. 5 associations operate in Lagunas; a tour operator is **Huayruro Tours**, T065-401203, www.peruselva.com. In Bretaña the **Gallán family** offer tours. Community tours cost US$46-70 pp per day, agency tours arranged in Iquitos start at US$80. Make sure you know exactly what is included: park fees, lodging, food, transport, guide. Also what the trip involves: most of the day in a canoe, walking, hunting, fishing, type of accommodation.

⊖ Transport

Yurimaguas *p278*
Air The military **Grupo Aéreo 42** (Bolívar 128, T981-664986) has passenger flights to Yurimaguas originating in Trujillo or Iquitos; see page 109 for routes and schedules.
Bus The road to Tarapoto is paved. **Paredes Estrella**, Mariscal Cáceres 220, 0830 daily to **Lima** (32-34 hrs, US$38.50) via **Tarapoto** (US$4), **Moyobamba** (US$7.75, 5-6 hrs), **Pedro Ruiz** (US$17.50), **Chiclayo** (US$27) and **Trujillo** (US$33). Also Ejetur, 0500 to Lima. Faster than the bus to Tarapoto are: **Gilmer Tours**, C Victor Sifuentes 580, frequent minibuses, US$5.75, 2½ hrs; cars (eg **San Martín**) US$7.75; and combis (Turismo Selva, Mcal Cáceres 3rd block) US$4.
Ferry There are 6 docks in all. To **Iquitos** from Embarcadero La Boca, 3 days/2 nights, **Eduardo/Gilmer** company is best, Elena Pardo 114, T352552 (see under Iquitos, Tansport). To **Lagunas** for Pacaya Samiria Reserve, from Embarcadero Abel Guerra at 0900, US$11.55, 10 hrs.

❸ Directory

Yurimaguas *p278*
Banks Several banks with ATMs. Casa de cambio Progreso, Progreso 117, changes US$ cash.

Iquitos and around → *Phone code: 065. Colour map 2, A4. Population: 600,000.*

Iquitos stands on the west bank of the Amazon and is a chief town of Peru's jungle region. Some 800 km downstream from Pucallpa and 3646 km from the mouth of the Amazon, the city is completely isolated except by air and river. Its first wealth came from the rubber boom (late 19th century to second decade of 20th century). The main economic activities are logging, commerce and petroleum and it is the main starting point for tourists wishing to explore Peru's northern jungle. It is hot, dirty and noisy from the tens-of-thousands of mototaxis and motorcycles that fill the streets.

The incongruous **Iron House/Casa de Fierro** stands on the Plaza de Armas, designed by Eiffel for the Paris exhibition of 1889. It is said that the house was transported from Paris by a local rubber baron and is constructed entirely of iron trusses and sheets, bolted together and painted silver. It now houses a pharmacy. Of special interest are the older buildings, faced with *azulejos* (glazed tiles). They date from the rubber boom of 1890 to 1912, when the rubber barons imported the tiles from Portugal and Italy and ironwork from England to embellish their homes. The **Casa de Barro** on the Plaza (house of the controversial rubber baron Fitzcarrald), is now a bank. **Museo Amazónico** ① *Malecón Tarapacá 386, T234221, Mon-Sat 0800-1300, 1430-1730, Sun 0800-1230, free, some guides speak English, tip expected*, in the Prefectura, has displays of native art and sculptures by Lima artist Letterstein. **Museo de Culturas Indígenas Amazónicas** ① *Malecón Tarapacá 332, T235809, 0800-*

1930, US$5.25, the private museum of Dr Richard Bodmer, who owns the **Casa Morey** hotel (see below), celebrating cultures from the entire Amazon region. Ask here about historic Amazonian boats (www.amazoneco.com). The waterfront by Malecón Maldonado, known as 'Boulevard', is a pleasant place for a stroll and gets busy on Friday and Saturday evenings.

Belén, the picturesque, lively waterfront district, is worth visiting, but is not safe at night. Most of its huts are built on rafts to cope with the river's 10 m change of level during floods (January-July); now they're built on stilts. On Pasaje Paquito are bars serving local sugar

Iquitos

Where to stay 🛏
1 Casa Morey
2 El Dorado Isabel
3 El Dorado Plaza
4 El Sitio
5 Flying Dog Hostel
6 Green Track Hostel
7 Hostal El Colibrí
8 La Casa Fitzcarraldo
9 La Casona
10 Las Amazonas Inn
11 Marañón
12 Royal Inn
13 Samiria Jungle
14 Sol del Oriente
15 Victoria Regia

Restaurants 🍴
1 Amazon Bistro
2 Antica Pizzería
3 Ari's Burger
4 Chez Maggy Pizzería
5 El Carbón
6 El Sitio
7 Fitzcarraldo
8 Helados La Muyuna
9 Huasaí
10 La Gran Maloca
11 María's Café
12 Panadería Tívoli
13 Yellow Rose of Texas

Bars & clubs 🍸
14 Arandú
15 Camiri
16 La Parranda
17 Noa Noa

cane rum. The main plaza has a bandstand made by Eiffel. In the high season canoes can be hired on the waterfront for a tour of Belén, US$3 per hour. The market at the end of the Malecón is well worth visiting, though you should get there before 0900 to see it in full swing.

Tourist offices: i perú ① *Jr Napo 161, of 4, T236144, iperuiquitos@promperu.gob.pe, Mon-Sat 0900-1800, Sun 0900-1300*, also at the airport, at flight times. Both offices are helpful. If arriving by air, go first to this desk. They will give you a list of hotels, a map, tell you about the touts outside the airport etc. Both www.iquitosnews.com and www.iquitostimes.com have articles, maps and information. See also www.jungle-love.org. **Indecopi** ① *Putumayo 464, T243490, jreategui@indecopi.gob.pe, Mon-Fri 0830-1630*.

Excursions

There are pleasant beaches at **Tipishca** on the Río Nanay, reached in 20 minutes by boat from Puerto de Santa Clara near the airport, it gets quite busy at weekends, and, quieter, **Santa Rita**, reached from Puerto de Pampa Chica, on a turn-off, off the road to the airport. Beaches appear when the river is low, July-September. **Pilpintuhuasi Butterfly Farm** ① *near the village of Padre Cocha, T232665, www.amazonanimalorphanage.org, US$7.75, students US$4, includes guided tour, Tue-Sun 0900-1600, guided tours at 0930, 1100, 1330 and 1500*, as well as butterflies, has a small well-kept zoo, Austrian/Peruvian-run. Colectivo from Bellavista to Padre Cocha takes 20 minutes, walk from there. If the river is high, boats can reach Pilpintuhuasi directly (no need to walk), a speedboat charges US$25 return including waiting time (pay at the end).

Along the road to Nauta, which is 100 km from Iquitos, are several attractiosn and balnearios. At Km 4.5 on the road to Nauta is **Centro de Rescate Amazónico** ① *http://gonzalomatosuria.blogspot.com/p/fundacion-iquitos-centro-de-rescate_20.html, daily 0900-1500, free, must show ID*, where orphaned manatees are nursed until they can be released. A good place to see this endangered species. The beautiful **Lake Quistococha** in lush jungle is at Km 6.5, with a fish hatchery at the lakeside. There's a two-hour walk through the surrounding jungle on a clearly marked trail, bars and restaurants on the lakeside and a small beach. Boats are for hire on the lake and swimming is safe but take insect repellent against sandflies.

Allpahuayo-Mishana Reserve ① *SERNANP, Jorge Chávez 930/942, T223555, Mon-Fri 0700-1300, 1500-1700, reserve fees: US$8.50, students US$6.25*. On the Río Nanay, some 25 km south of Iquitos by the Nauta road or two hours by boat from Bellavista, this reserve protects the largest concentration of white sand jungle (*varillales*) in Peru. Part of the Napo ecoregion, biodiversity here is among the highest in the Amazon Basin. It has several endangered species including two primates, several endemic species; the area is rich in birds (475 species have been recorded). Within the reserve are **Zoocriadero BIOAM**, Km 25, a good birdwatching circuit in land belonging to the Instituto Nacional de Innovación Agraria (INIA); **Jardín de Plantas Medicinales y Frutales** ① *at Km 26.8, 0800-1600, guiding 0800-1000*; and at Km 28, **El Irapay** interpretation centre ① *Mon-Sat 0830-1430*, with a trail to Mishana village by the river.

Border with Brazil

Details on exit and entry formalities seem to change frequently, so when leaving Peru, check in Iquitos first at Immigration or with the Capitanía at the port. Boats stop in Santa Rosa for Peruvian exit formalities. Santa Rosa has five simple hotels, **Diana** and **Las Hamacas** are reported better than the others, price around US$15 for a double.

For hotel and restaurant price codes, and other relevant information, see pages 14-17.

⚙ Where to stay

Iquitos *p280, map p281*
Around Peruvian Independence Day (27 and 28 Jul) and Easter, Iquitos can get crowded and prices rise at this time.
$$$$ El Dorado Plaza, Napo 258 on main plaza, T222555, www.grupo-dorado.com. Good accommodation and restaurant, bar, business-type hotel, pool, prices include service, small breakfast, welcome drink and transfer to/from airport. Also owns **$$$ El Dorado Isabel**, Napo 362, T232574.
$$$$ Samiria Jungle, Ricardo Palma 159, T223232, www.samiriajunglehotel.com. Modern upmarket hotel, includes airport transfers, large suites and rooms, frigobar, bathtub, restaurant, bar, pool, meeting rooms.
$$$ Casa Morey, Raymondi y Loreto, Plaza Ramón Castilla, T231913, www.casamorey. com. Boutique hotel in a beautifully restored historic rubber-boom period mansion. Great attention to detail, includes airport transfers, ample comfortable rooms, pool, good library.
$$$ Sol del Oriente, Av Quiñónez Km 2.5 on the way to the airport, T260317, www. soldelorientehoteles.com. Airport transfers, pool, internet in hall, nice gardens, deco a bit kitsch.
$$$ Victoria Regia, Ricardo Palma 252, T231983, www.victoriaregiahotel.com. Free map of city, safe deposit boxes in rooms, good restaurant, indoor pool.
$$$-$$ La Casa Fitzcarraldo, Av La Marina 2153, T601138, http://casafitzcarraldo.com/. Prices vary according to room. Includes breakfast and airport transfer, with Wi-Fi, satellite TV, minibar, 1st-class restaurant, treehouse, pool in lovely gardens, captive animals. The house was the home of Walter Saxer, the executive-producer of Werner Herzog's famous film, lots of movie and celebrity memorabilia.

$$$-$$ Marañón, Fitzcarrald y Nauta 289, T242673, http://hotelmaranon.com. Multi-storey hotel, spotless comfortable rooms, a/c, convenient location, small pool.
$$ Royal Inn & Casino, Aguirre 793, T224244, www.royalinncasinohotel.com. Modern, comfortable, frigobar and, bidet, airport transfer, good.
$$-$ Flying Dog Hostel, Malecón Tarapacá 592, T223755, www.flyingdogperu.com. Nice old house, pleasant 4 bed dorms and private rooms with bath and a/c or fan, clean kitchen, lockers, arrange tours.
$$-$ Hostal Colibrí, Raymondi 200, T241737, hostalelcolibri@hotmail.com. 1 block from Plaza and 50 m from the river so can be noisy, nicely refurbished house, a/c or fan, hot water, secure, good value, breakfast extra, helpful staff.
$$-$ La Casona, Fitzcarald 147, T234 394, www.hotellacasonaiquitos.com.pe. In building dating from 1901, now modernized, hot water, fan or a/c, kitchen facilities, small patio, pool, popular with travellers. Opposite, at Fitzcarald 152, is Hostal La Casona Río Grande, with smaller rooms, fan. Transport to either from the airport with advance reservation.
$ Green Track Hostel, Ricardo Palma 540, T997 829118, www.greentrack-travel.com. Nice hostel, dorms with a/c or fan, 1 private room with bath, free pick up with advanced booking, English spoken, helpful owners, tours arranged to Tapiche Ohara's Reserve.
$ El Sitio, Ricardo Palma 541, T234932. Fan, private bath, cold water, good value.
$ Las Amazonas Inn, Ricardo Palma 460, T225367, las_amazonas_inn_iquitos@ yahoo.es. Simple rooms with electric shower, a/c, kitchen facilities, breakfast available, pleasant owner.

⚙ Restaurants

Iquitos *p280, map p281*
Local specialities Try palm heart salad (*chonta*), or *a la Loretana* dish on menus;

also try *inchicapi* (chicken, corn and peanut soup), *cecina* (fried dried pork), *tacacho* (fried green banana and pork, mashed into balls and eaten for breakfast or tea), *juanes* (chicken, rice, olive and egg, seasoned and wrapped in bijao leaves and sold in restaurants) and the *camu-camu*, an acquired taste, said to have one of the highest vitamin C concentrations in the world. For a good local breakfast, go to the Mercado Central, C Sargento Lores, where there are several kioskos outside, popular and cheap. Avoid eating endangered species such as paiche, caiman or turtle, which are sometimes on menus. Try the local drink *chuchuhuasi*, made from the bark of a tree, which is supposed to have aphrodisiac properties (for sale at Arica 1046), and *jugo de cocona*, and the alcoholic *cola de mono* and *siete raices* (aguardiente mixed with the bark of 7 trees and wild honey), sold at **Musmuqui**, Raymondi 382, Mon-Sat from 1900.

$$$ Al Frío y al Fuego, on the water, go to Embarcadero Turístico and their boat will pick you up, T224862. Mon 1830-2300, Tue-Sat 1130-1600 and 1830-2300, Sun 1130-1600. Good upscale floating restaurant with regional dishes, seafood specialities.
$$$ Fitzcarraldo, Malecón Maldonado 103 y Napo. Smart, pizza, also good pastas and salads.
$$$ La Gran Maloca, Sargento Lores 170, opposite Banco Continental. Closes 2000 on Sun, other days 2300. A/c, high class regional food.
$$ Ari's Burger, Plaza de Armas, Próspero 127. Medium-priced fast food, breakfasts, popular with tourists but hygiene questionable.
$$ Yellow Rose of Texas, Putumayo 180. Open 24 hrs so you can wait here if arriving late at night. Varied food including local dishes, Texan atmosphere, good breakfasts, lots of information, also has a bar, Sky TV and Texan saddle seats.
$$-$ Antica Pizzería, Napo 159. Sun-Thu 0700-2400, Fri-Sat 0700-0100. Very nice

pizza and Italian dishes, pleasant ambiance especially on the upper level, also serves breakfast, try the *desayuno Loretano*.
$$-$ Arapaíma Gigas, Carr a Zungarococha Km 1. Open for lunch. Just outside the city, a restaurant with its own fish farm in a lake. They catch whatever you request and cook it immediately; *ceviche* de paiche on Sun.
$$-$ Chez Maggy Pizzería, Raymondi 177. Daily 1800-0100. Wood oven pizza and home-made pasta.
$ El Carbón, La Condamine 115. Open 1900-2300 only. Grilled meats, salads, regional side-dishes such as tacacho and patacones.
$ El Sitio, Sargento Lores 404. Mon-Sat 1930-2230. A simple place for *anticuchos* for all tastes including vegetarian, popular.
$ Huasaí, Fitzcarrald 131. Open 0715-1615, closed Mon. Varied and innovative menu, popular, good food and value, go early.

Cafés

Amazon Bistro, Malecón Tarapacá 268. Upscale French bistro/bar on the waterfront, drinks, snacks, breakfasts and meal of the day. Trendy and popular.
Helados La Muyuna, Jr Próspero 621. Good natural jungle fruit ice cream. Second location on Napo near Malecón.
María's Café, Nauta 292. Opens 0800, closed Mon and 1230-1600. Breakfasts, sandwiches, burgers, coffee and cakes, with desserts of the day.
Panadería Tívoli, Ricardo Palma, block 3, a variety of good bread and sweets.

Bars and clubs

Iquitos *p280, map p281*
Arandú, Malecón Maldonado. Good views of the river.
Camiri, Pevas at the shore. Floating bar, pleasant atmosphere.
La Parranda, Pevas, cuadra 1. Drinks, live music, dancing, Latin music, 80s rock.
Noa Noa, Pevas y Fitzcarrald. Popular disco with cumbia and Latin music.

Iquitos *p280, map p281*
5 Jan Founding of Iquitos. **Feb-Mar**
Carnival. **3rd week in Jun** Tourist week.
24 Jun San Juan. **28-30 Aug** Santa Rosa
de Lima. **8 Dec** Immaculate Conception,
celebrated in Punchana, near the docks.

🛍 Shopping

Iquitos *p280, map p281*
Hammocks in Iquitos cost about US$12.
Amazon arts and crafts can be found at:
Mercado Artesanal Anaconda, by the
waterfront at Napo. **Asociación de Artesanos
El Manguaré**, kiosks on Jr Nauta, block 1.
Comisesa, Arica 471, sells rubber boots, torches
(flashlights), rain ponchos and other gear.
Mad Mick's Trading Post, Putumayo 163,
top floor, next to the Iron House, hires out
rubber boots for those going to the jungle.
Mercado Artesanal de Productores, 4 km
from the centre in the San Juan district, on the
road to the airport, take a colectivo. Cheapest
in town with more choice than elsewhere.

🎯 What to do

Iquitos *p280, map p281*
Jungle tours from Iquitos Agencies
arrange 1-day or longer trips to places of
interest with guides speaking some English.
Package tours booked in your home country,
over the internet or in Lima are much more
expensive than those booked locally. Take
your time before making a decision and
don't be bullied by the hustlers at the airport
(they get paid a hefty commission). You
must make sure your tour operator or guide
has a proper licence (check with i perú).
Do not go with a company which does not
have legal authorization; there are many
unscrupulous people about. Find out all the
details of the trip and food arrangements
before paying (a minimum of US$50 per
day). Speed boats for river trips can be hired
by the hour or day at the Embarcadero

Turístico, at the intersection of Av de la
Marina and Samánez Ocampo in Punchana.
Prices vary greatly, usually US$15-20 per hr,
US$80 for speedboat, and are negotiable.
In fact, all prices are negotiable, except
Muyuna, **Heliconia Lodge** and **Explorama**,
who do not take commissions.

There are several agencies that arrange
river cruises in well-appointed boats. Most
go to the Pacaya-Samiria region, very few
towards Brazil. In addition to the vessels of
Aqua and **Delfín** (see below), other options
include *La Amatista* of the **Dorado** hotel
group, the *Aquamarina*, *Arapaima* and
Queen Violeta group and *Estrella Amazónica*.
Contact a company like **Rainforest Cruises**,
www.rainforestcruises.com, for options.

General information and advice
Take a long-sleeved shirt, waterproof coat
and shoes or light boots on jungle trips
and binoculars and a good torch, as well
as espirales to ward off the mosquitoes
at night – they can be bought from
pharmacies in Iquitos. Premier is the most
effective local insect repellent. The dry
season is from Jul-Sep (Sep is the best
month to see flowers and butterflies).

This is an important place for Ayahuasca
tourism. There are legitimate shamans
as well as charlatans. **Karma Café**, Napo
138, is the centre of the scene in town.
See also the work of Alan Shoemaker,
who holds an International Amazonian
Shamanism Conference every year, **Soga
del Alma**, Rómulo Espinar 170, Iquitos 65,
alanshoemaker@hotmail.com. Before taking
Ayahuasca in a ceremony with a shaman,
read the note on page 28.
Amazon Yarapa River Lodge, Av La Marina
124, www.yarapa.com. On the Río Yarapa,
in a pristine location, award-winning in its
use of ecofriendly resources and work with
local villages, flexible and responsible, its
field laboratory is associated with Cornell
University. Arranges trips to Pacaya-Samiria.
Aqua Expeditions, Iquitos 1167, T601053,
www.aquaexpeditions.com. Luxury river

cruises of 3, 4, or 7 nights on the *M/V Aria* (from US$2835 pp) and the *M/V Aqua* (from US$2685 pp), both designed by architect Jordi Puig to look like floating town houses rather than boats, with massive picture windows in each a/c suite. Amazing food with local delicacies on the gourmet tasting menu, good shore excursions with knowledgeable local guides.

Blue Morpho Tours, Av Guardia Civil 515, T263454, www.bluemorphotours.com. A rustic camp on Carretera Nauta, Km 52.5. Centre for shamanic studies and workshops, 9-day shamanic trips, all inclusive except for bar and snacks.

Chullachaqui Eco Lodge, Raymondi 138, Iquitos, T965-705919, http://amazoniantrips.com/chullachaqui-eco-lodge/. 2 hrs by speed boat up the Amazon on the Río Tapira. Thatched timber cabins, basic accommodation, private bath, communal dining room, hammock room, insect screens, tours with naturalist guides to see river dolphins and other wildlife.

Cumaceba Amazonia Tours, Putumayo 184 in the Iron House, T232229, www.cumaceba.com. Overnight visits to Cumaceba Lodge, 35 km from Iquitos, and tours of 1-4 nights to the Botanical Lodge on the Amazon, 80 km from Iquitos, birdwatching tours, Ayahuasca ceremonies.

Dawn on the Amazon, Malecón Maldonado 185 y Nauta, T223730, www.dawnonthe amazon.com. Offer a variety of day tours around Iquitos on the luxurious 20 passenger *Dawn on the Amazon.III* (US$199 pp). Also offer custom-made cruises for several days. Their wooden vessels are decorated with carvings of jungle themes. Also has a bar/restaurant in town.

Delfín, Av Abelardo Quiñones Km 5, San Juan Bautista, T262721, www.delfinamazon cruises.com. Luxury cruises on the *Delfín I* and *Delfín II* (the cheaper of the 2), 3- and 4-night expeditions to Pacaya-Samiria, with daily activities including kayaking, bird and wildlife watching, fresh organic food, from US$2400 pp.

Explorama Tours, by the riverside docks on Av La Marina 340, T252530, www.explorama.com, are highly recommended, with over 40 years in existence, certainly the biggest and most established. Their sites are: **Ceiba Tops**, 40 km (1½ hrs) from Iquitos, is a comfortable resort, 75 a/c rooms with electricity, hot showers, pool with hydromassage and beautiful gardens. The food is good and, as in all Explorama's properties, is served communally. There are attractive walks and other excursions, a recommended jungle experience for those who want their creature comforts, US$340 pp for 1 night/2 days. **Explorama Lodge** at Yanamono, 80 km from Iquitos, 2½ hrs from Iquitos, has palm-thatched accommodation with separate bathroom and shower facilities connected by covered walkways, cold water, no electricity, good food and service. US$455 for 3 days/2 nights. **Explornapo Lodge** at Llachapa on the Sucusai creek (a tributary of the Napo), is in the same style as Explorama Lodge, but is further away from Iquitos, 160 km (4 hrs), and is set in 105,000 ha of primary rainforest, so is better for seeing wildlife, US$1,120 for 5 days/4 nights (all 2014 basic prices). Nearby is the impressive canopy walkway 35 m above the forest floor and 500 m long, 'a magnificent experience and not to be missed'. It is associated with the Amazon Center for Tropical Studies (ACTS), a scientific station, only 10 mins from the canopy walkway. **Explor Tambos**, 2 hrs from Explornapo, offer more primitive accommodation, 8 shelters for 16 campers, bathing in the river, offers the best chance to see fauna. Close to Explornapo is the ReNuPeRu medicinal plant garden, run by a curandero.

Gerson Pizango, T965-013225. Local, English-speaking and award-winning guide who will take you to his village 2½ hrs by boat, from where you can trek and camp or stay and experience village life. Expert at spotting wildlife, knowledgeable about medicinal plants, interesting and varied expedities benefitting the community. In the village, accommodation is in a hut by the riverside where there are pink and grey dolphins, private room with mosquito net. US$50-70 pp per day depending on length of trip and size of party, includes food, water, camping gear, boots, raincoats, torches, binoculars, fishing rods, machetes.

Heliconia Lodge, Ricardo Palma 259, T231959 (Lima T01-421 9195), www. heliconialodge.com.pe. On the Río Amazonas, 80 km from Iquitos. Surrounded by rainforest, islands and lagoons full of wildlife, this is a beautiful place for resting, birdwatching, looking for pink dolphins, jungle hikes. Organized packages from 1 to 4 nights, all-inclusive. Good guides, food and flexible excursions according to guest's request. The lodge has a traditional, rustic yet comfortable design, swimming pool, hot water and electricity at certain times of day and 1700 to 2200.

Muyuna Amazon Lodge, Putumayo 163, ground floor, T242858, www.muyuna.com. 140 km from Iquitos, also on the Yanayacu, before San Juan village. 1- to 5-night packages available. Everything is included in the price. Good guides, accommodation, food and service; very well organized and professional, flexible, radio contact, will collect passengers from airport if requested in advance. Amenities are constantly updated with new ecological considerations. It is easy to see animals here and you can even find rareties such as the piuri (wattled curaçao, *Crax globulosa*). They offer birdwatching trips. Because of the isolated location they guarantee that visitors will see animals. Also visits to the Butterfly Farm and manatee rescue centre and city tours. Highly recommended.

Paseos Amazónicos Ambassador, Pevas 246, T231618, www.paseosamazonicos.com, operates the **Amazonas Sinchicuy Lodge**. The lodge is 1½ hrs from Iquitos on the Sinchicuy river, 25 mins by boat from the Amazon river. The lodge consists of several wooden buildings with thatched roofs on stilts, cabins with bathroom, no electricity

but paraffin lamps are provided, good food, and plenty activities, including visits to local villages. Recommended. They also have **Tambo Yanayacu** and **Tambo Amazónico** lodges, organize visits to Pacaya-Samiria and local tours.

Tapiche Ohara's Reserve, contact through **Green Track Hostel**, www.greentrack-jungle. com. On the Río Tapiche, a tributary of the Ucayali, 11 hrs up river from Iquitos. Fully screened wood cabins with thatched roofs, custom designed trips according to the visitor's interests, 4 nights/5 days US$840 pp.

⊖ Transport

Iquitos *p280, map p281*
Air Francisco Secada Vigneta airport, T260147. Taxi to the airport costs US$6; *mototaxi* (motorcycle with 2 seats), US$3.10. A bus from the airport, US$0.75, goes from the main road; most go through the centre of town. To **Lima**, daily; **LAN** (direct or via Tarapoto), **Peruvian Airlines** and **Star Perú** (direct or via Tarapoto, also daily to Pucallpa). The military **Grupo Aéreo 42** has passenger flights to Iquitos originating in Trujillo; see page 109 for routes and schedules.

Ferry General hints for river travel: large passenger and cargo vessels are called *lanchas*, smaller faster craft are called *rápidos* or *deslizadores* (speedboats). *Yates* are small to medium wooden colectivos, usually slow, and *chalupas* are small motor launches used to ferry passengers from the lanchas to shore. For information about boats, go to the corresponding ports of departure for each destination, except for speed boats to the Brazil/Colombian border which have their offices clustered on Raymondi block 3. When river levels are very high departures may be from alternative places.

Lanchas leave from Puerto Henry and Masusa, 2 km north of the centre, a dangerous area at night. The first night's meal is not included. Always deal directly with boat owners or managers, avoid touts and middle-men. All fares are negotiable.

You can buy either a ticket to sling your hammock on deck, or for a berth in a cabin sleeping 2 to 4 people.

A hammock is essential. A double, of material (not string), provides one person with a blanket. Board the boat many hours in advance to guarantee hammock space. If going on the top deck, try to be first down the front; take rope for hanging your hammock, plus string and sarongs for privacy. On all boats, hang your hammock away from lightbulbs (they aren't switched off at night and attract all sorts of strange insects) and away from the engines, which usually emit noxious fumes. Guard your belongings from the moment you board. It's safer to club together and pay for a cabin in which to lock your belongings, even if you sleep outside in a hammock. There is very little privacy; women travellers can expect a lot of attention. There are adequate washing and toilet facilities, but the food is rice, chicken and beans (and whatever can be picked up en route) cooked in river water. Stock up on drinking water, fruit and tinned food. Vegetarians must take their own supplies. There is usually a bar on board. Take plenty of prophylactic enteritis tablets; many contract dysentery on the trip. Also take insect repellent and a mosquito net. If arriving in Iquitos on a regular, slow boat, take extreme care when disembarking. Things get very chaotic at this time and theft and pickpocketing is rife. Some of the newer boats have CCTV to deter theft.

To **Pucallpa**, 4-5 days up river along the Amazon and Ucayali (can be longer if the water level is low), larger boats must travel only by day, hammock US$40, berth US$140 double. **Henry** (T263948) is a large company with 4 departures per week from Puerto Henry; *Henry 5, 6* and *7* have some cabins with bath. Another good boat is *Pedro Martín 2* from Puerto Masusa. To **Yurimaguas**, 3-4 days up river along the Amazon, Marañón and Huallaga, hammock space US$40, berth US$119-134 double. The **Eduardo/ Gilmer** company, T960404, with 8 boats is

recommended, they sail from Puerto Masusa several per week, but not Sun; *Eduardo I* and *Gilmer IV* have berths with bath for US$192.

The most convenient way to travel to the border with Brazil and Colombia is on a *rápido* to **Santa Rosa**, 8-10 hrs downriver, US$75, Tue-Sun, from the Embarcadero Turístico at 0600; be at the port 0445 for customs check, board 0500-0530. Motorized canoes cross from Santa Rosa to **Tabatinga** (Brazil) US$1.75 pp and **Leticia** (Colombia), US$1.65 pp. From Santa Rosa to Iquitos, Tue-Sun at 0400, board 0300, 10-12 hrs upstream, get immigration entry stamp the day before. *Rápidos* carry life jackets and have bathrooms, a simple breakfast and lunch are included in the price. Luggage limit is 15 kg. Purchase tickets in advance from company offices, open Mon-Sat. In Iquitos: **Golfinho**, Raymondi 378, T225118, www.transportegolfinho.com; **Transtur**, Raymondi 384, T221356. In Tabatinga: **Golfinho**, Marechal Mallet 306, T3412 3186; **Transtur**, Marechal Mallet 290, T8113 5239. Tickets are also on sale in Leticia, but the price is higher. *Lanchas* to Santa Rosa, which may continue Islandia, leave from the Puerto Pesquero or Masusa (enquire at T250440), Mon-Sat at 1800 (depart Santa Rosa at 1200), 2-3 days downriver, US$31 in hammock, US$50 in cabin.

To **Pantoja** (for Ecuador), 5-7 days up river on the Napo, a route requiring plenty of time, stamina and patience. There are irregular departures once or twice a month; ask in Iquitos about sailings, eg **Radio Moderna** (Iquitos T250440), or T830055 – a private phone in Pantoja village. Fare is about US$38, US$3 per day extra for berth if you can get one. The vessels are usually cargo boats which carry live animals, some of which are slaughtered en route. Crowding and poor sanitation are problems on some of the boats. Take a hammock, cup, bowl, cutlery, extra food and snacks, drinking water or purification, insect repellent, toilet paper, soap, towel, cash dollars and soles in small notes. To shorten the voyage, or visit towns along the way, you can go to **Indiana**, daily departures from **Muelle de Productores** in Iquitos, US$5, 45 mins, then take a mototaxi to **Mazán** on the Río Napo. From Mazán, there are *rápidos* to **Santa Clotilde** on Mon, Tue, Thu, Fri and Sat at 0600 (Santa Clotilde to Mazán Tue, Wed, Fri, Sat and Sun), US$31 includes a snack, 4-5 hrs, information from **Familia Ruiz**, Iquitos T251410. You can board boats in Mazan or Santa Clotilde. There is no public transport from Pantoja to **Nuevo Rocafuerte** (Ecuador), you must hire a private boat, US$60 per boat. For details of boats beyond Nuevo Rocafuerte, see Ecuador chapter, Coca, Transport, River.

Excursions: To **Nauta**, Trans del Sur buses from Libertad y Próspero, 0530-1900, US$3.10, 2 hrs; vans from Av Aguirre cuadra 14 by Centro Comercial Sachachorro, leave when full, US$4, 1½ hrs.

To **Lake Quistococha**, combis leave every hour until 1500 from Moore y Bermúdez, Iquitos, US$1; the last one back leaves at 1700. City bus from Tacna y Mcal Cáceres, US$0.40.

❶ Directory

Iquitos *p280, map p281*
Consulates Brazil, Sargento Lores 363, T235153, www.abe.mre.gov.br. Mon-Fri 0800-1400, visas issued in 2 days. Colombia, Calvo de Araujo 431, T231461, Mon-Fri 0800-1100. **Note** There is no Ecuadorean consulate. If you need a visa, you must get it in Lima or in your home country. **Medical services** Clínica Ana Stahl, Av la Marina 285, T252535. **Useful addresses** Immigration: Mcal Cáceres 18th block, T235371, Mon-Fri 0800-1615. Tourist police: Sargento Lores 834, T242081.

Southeastern jungle

The southern *selva* is in Madre de Dios department, which contains the Manu National Park (2.04 million ha), the Tambopata National Reserve (254,358 ha) and the Bahuaja-Sonene National Park (1.1 million ha). The forest of this lowland region (*Altitude: 260 m*) is technically called Sub-tropical Moist Forest, which means that it receives less rainfall than tropical forest and is dominated by the floodplains of its meandering rivers. The most striking features are the former river channels that have become isolated as ox-bow lakes. These are home to black caiman and giant otter. Other rare species living in the forest are jaguar, puma, ocelot and tapir. There are also howler monkeys, macaws, guans, currasows and the giant harpy eagle. As well as containing some of the most important flora and fauna on Earth, the region also harbours gold-diggers, loggers, hunters, drug smugglers and oil-men, whose activities have endangered the unique rainforest. Moreover, the construction of the *Interoceánica*, a road linking the Atlantic and Pacific oceans via Puerto Maldonado and Brazil, will certainly bring more uncontrolled colonization in the area, as seen so many times in the Brazilian Amazon.

Arriving in Manu
Access to Manu The multiple use zone of Manu Biosphere Reserve is accessible to anyone and several lodges exist in the area (see Lodges in Manu, below). The reserved zone is accessible by permit only. Entry is strictly controlled and visitors must visit the area under the auspices of an authorized operator with an authorized guide. Permits are limited and reservations should be made well in advance. In the reserved zone the only accommodation is in the comfortable **Manu Lodge** or in the comfortable but rustic **Casa Machiguenga** in the Cocha Salvador area. Several companies have tented safari camp infrastructures, some with shower and dining facilities, but all visitors sleep in tents. The

entrance fee to the Reserved Zone is 150 soles per person (about US$55) and is included in package tour prices.

Useful addresses **In Lima** Asociación Peruana para la Conservación de la Naturaleza (APECO) ① *Parque José Acosta 187, p 2, Magdalena del Mar, T01-264 0094, comunicapeco@ apeco.org.pe*. **Pronaturaleza** ① *Doña Juana 137, Urb Los Rosales, Santiago de Surco, T01-271 2662, and in Puerto Maldonado, Jr Cajamarca cuadra 1 s/n, T082-571585, comunicaciones@ pronaturaleza.org*. **In Cuzco** **Perú Verde** ① *Ricardo Palma J-1, Santa Mónica, Cuzco, T084-226392, www.peruverde.org*. This is a local NGO that can help with information and has free video shows about Manu National Park and Tambopata National Reserve. Friendly and helpful and with information on research in the jungle area of Madre de Dios. The **Amazon Conservation Association (ACCA)** ① *Av Oswaldo Baca 402, Urb Magisterio, Cuzco, T084-222329, www.amazon conservation.org, Jr Cusco 499, T082-573237, Puerto Maldonado* is another NGO whose mission is to protect biodiversity by studying ecosystems and developing conservation tools to protect land while suporting local communities. Further information can be obtained from the **Manu National Park Office** ① *Av Micaela Bastidas 310, Cuzco, T084-240898, open 0800-1400*. They issue the permit for the Reserved Zone.

Climate The climate is warm and humid, with a rainy season from Novemer to March and a dry season from April to October. Cold fronts from the South Atlantic, called *friajes*, are characteristic of the dry season, when temperatures drop to 15-16° C during the day, and 13° C at night. Always bring a sweater at this time. The best time to visit is during the dry season when there are fewer mosquitoes and the rivers are low, exposing the beaches. This is also a good time to see nesting and to view animals at close range, as they stay close to the rivers and are easily seen. Note that this is also the hottest time. A pair of binoculars is essential and insect repellent is a must.

Manu Biosphere Reserve
No other reserve can compare with Manu for the diversity of life forms; it holds over 1000 species of birds and covers an altitudinal range from 200 m to 4100 m above sealevel. Giant otters, jaguars, ocelots and 13 species of primates abound in this pristine tropical wilderness, and uncontacted indigenous tribes are present in the more remote areas, as are indigenous groups with limited access.

The reserve is one of the largest conservation units on Earth, encompassing the complete drainage of the Manu River. It is divided into the **Manu National Park** (1,692,137 ha), where only government sponsored biologists and anthropologists may visit with permits from the Ministry of Agriculture in Lima; the **Reserved Zone** (257,000 ha) within the Manu National Park, set aside for applied scientific research and ecotourism; and the **Cultural Zone** (92,000 ha), which contains acculturated native groups and colonists, where the locals still employ their traditional way of life. Among the ethnic groups in the Cultural Zone are the Harakmbut, Machiguenga and Yine in the Amarakaeri Reserved Zone, on the east bank of the Alto Madre de Dios. They have set up their own ecotourism activities. Associated with Manu are other areas protected by conservation groups, or local people (for example the Blanquillo reserved zone) and some cloud forest parcels along the road. The **Nahua-Kugapakori Reserved Zone**, set aside for these two nomadic native groups, is the area between the headwaters of the Río Manu and headwaters of the Río Urubamba, to the north of the alto Madre de Dios.

Cuzco to Puerto Maldonado via Mazuko

This route is Cuzco–Urcos–Quincemil–Mazuko–Puerto Maldonado. Bus details are given under Transport, below. The road from Cuzco to Puerto Maldonado has been upgraded as part of the Interoceánica highway and the road's susceptibility to bad weather has declined. **Quincemil**, 240 km from Urcos on the road to Mazuko, is a centre for alluvial gold-mining with many banks. Hunt Oil is building a huge oil and gas facility here; its exploration lot controversially overlaps the Amarakaeri Communal Reserve. Accommodation is available in $ **Hotel Toni**, friendly, clean, cold shower, good meals. The changing scenery is magnificent. Puente Iñambari is the junction of three sections of the Interoceanic Highway, from Cuzco, Puerto Maldonado and Juliaca. However, this is only a small settlement and transport stops 5 km further north at Mazuko. In the evenings, Mazuko is a hive of activity as temperatures drop and the buses arrive. There is regular traffic to Puerto Maldonado, including colectivos, three hours, US$11. $ **Hostal Valle Sagrado** is the best of many places to stay. The highway beyond Mazuko cuts across lowland rainforest, large areas of which have been cleared by migrants engaged in small-scale gold mining. Their encampments of plastic shelters, shops and prostibars now line the highway for several kilometres. A worthwhile stop on the route is the **Parador Turístico Familia Méndez**, Km 419, 45 minutes from Puerto Maldonado, www.paradormendez.com, which prepares local dishes from home-grown ingredients and has a trail network on the surrounding forest.

Cuzco to Puerto Maldonado via Pilcopata and Itahuania

The arduous 255 km trip over the Andes from Cuzco to Pilcopata takes about eight to 12 hours by bus or truck (10 hours to two days in the wet season). On this route, too, the scenery is magnificent. From Cuzco you climb up to the pass before Paucartambo (very cold at night), before dropping down to this mountain village at the border between the departments of Cuzco and Madre de Dios. The road then ascends to the second pass (also cold at night), after which it goes down to the cloud forest and then the rainforest, reaching **Pilcopata** at 650 m (eight hours).

Pilcopata to Itahuania After Pilcopata, the route is hair-raising and breathtaking, passing through **Atalaya**, the first village on the Alto Madre de Dios River and tourist port for hiring boats to Boca Manu (basic accommodation). The route continues to Salvación, where a park office and park entrance are situated. There are basic hostals and restaurants. Basic restaurants can be found in Pilcopata and Atalaya.

The road, which bypasses the previous port of **Shintuya**, continues to **Itahuania**, the starting point for river transport. Rain often disrupts wheeled transport, though. The road is scheduled to continue to Nuevo Edén, 11 km away, and Diamante, so the location of the port will be determined by progress on the road. Eventually, the road will go to Boca Colorado. **Note** It is not possible to arrange trips to the Reserved Zone of the National Park from Itahuania, owing to park regulations. All arrangements, including permits, must be made in Cuzco.

Itahuania to Puerto Maldonado Cargo boats leave for the gold mining centre of Boca Colorado on the Río Madre de Dios, via Boca Manu, but only when the boat is fully laden (see Transport below). Very basic accommodation can be found here, but it is not recommended for lone women travellers. From Colorado you can take a colectivo taxi to Puerto Carlos, cross the river, then take another colectivo to Puerto Maldonado; 4½ hours in all.

Boca Manu is the connecting point between the rivers Alto Madre de Dios, Manu and Madre de Dios. It has a few houses, an air strip and some food supplies. It is also the entrance to the Manu Reserve and to go further you must be part of an organized group. The park ranger station is located in Limonal. You need to show your permit here. Camping is allowed if you have a permit. There are no regular flights from Cuzco to Boca Manu. These are arranged the day before, if there are enough passengers. Check at Cuzco airport; or with the tour operators in Cuzco.

To the Reserved Zone Upstream on the Río Manu you pass the **Manu Lodge** (see Where to stay, below), on the Cocha Juárez, three or four hours by boat. You can continue to Cocha Otorongo, 2½ hours and Cocha Salvador, 30 minutes, the biggest lake with plenty of wildlife. From here it is two to three hours to Pakitza, the entrance to the National Park Zone. This is only for biologists with a special permit.

Between Boca Manu and Colorado is **Blanquillo**, a private reserve (10,000 ha). Bring a good tent with you and all food if you want to camp and do it yourself, or alternatively accommodation is available at the **Tambo Blanquillo** (full board or accommodation only). Wildlife is abundant, especially macaws and parrots at the macaw lick near **Manu Wildlife Centre**. There are occasional boats to Blanquillo from Shintuya; six to eight hours.

Puerto Maldonado → *Phone code: 082. Colour map 2, C5. Pop: 45,000. Altitude: 250 m.*

Puerto Maldonado is an important starting point for visiting the south eastern jungles of the Tambopata Reserve or departing for Bolivia or Brazil. It overlooks the confluence of the rivers Tambopata and Madre de Dios and, because of the gold mining and timber industries, the immediate surrounding jungle is now cultivated. A bridge, as part of the Interoceánica highway, has been built across the Río Madre de Dios. Even before its completion business activity in the town was growing fast. There are tourist offices at the airport and at **Dircetur** ① *Urb Fonavi, take a moto-taxi to the Posta Médica which is next door*.

The beautiful and tranquil **Lago Sandoval** is a one-hour boat ride along the Río Madre de Dios, and then a 5-km walk into the jungle (parts of the first 3 km are a raised wooden walkway; boots are advisable). Entry to the lake costs US$9.50. You must go with a guide; this can be arranged by the boat driver. Boats can be hired at the Madre de Dios port for about US$25 a day, minimum two people (plus petrol) to go to Lago Sandoval (don't pay the full cost in advance).

Jungle tours from Puerto Maldonado

Trips can be made to **Lago Valencia**, 60 km away near the Bolivian border, four hours there, eight hours back. It is an ox-bow lake with lots of wildlife. Many excellent beaches and islands are located within an hour's boat ride. Mosquitoes are voracious. If camping, take food and water.

It is quite easy to arrange a boat and guide from Puerto Maldonado (see Tour operators below) to the **Tambopata National Reserve** (**TNR**) ① *Sernanp, Av 28 de Julio 482, Puerto Maldonado, T573278*, between the rivers Madre de Dios, Tambopata and Heath. Some superb ox-bow lakes can be visited and the birdwatching is wonderful.

The **Bahuaja-Sonene National Park**, declared in 1996, stretches from the Heath River across the Tambopata, incorporating the Río Heath National Sanctuary. It is closed to visitors.

Río Las Piedras

Lying to the northeast of, and running roughly parallel to the Río Manu, this drainage runs some 700 km from rainforest headwaters in the Alto Purús region. The lower, more easily accessible section of the river, closer to Puerto Maldonado and outside state protection, runs through rich tropical forests, very similar to those in the Manu and Tambopata areas. Close to 600 species of birds, at least eight primate species and some of the Amazon's larger mammals, giant otter, jaguar, puma, tapir and giant anteater, are all present. Hunting pressure has resulted in wildlife being shier than in Manu or Tambopata, but this remains an excellent wildlife destination. See www.arbioperu.org and www.relevantfilms.co.uk/propied/las-piedras/.

To Iberia and Iñapari

Daily public transport runs to **Iberia** and **Iñapari** on the border with Brazil. This section of the Interoceánica road takes a lot of traffic and can be dangerous for motorcyclists as a result. No primary forest remains along the road, only secondary growth and small *chacras* (farms). There are picturesque *caseríos* (settlements) that serve as processing centres for the brazil nut. Some 70% of the inhabitants in the Madre de Dios are involved in the collection of this prized nut.

Iberia, Km 168, has three hotels, the best is **$ Hostal Aquino**, basic, cold shower. It's a small frontier town, much quieter and more laid back than Iñapari on the border. The old Fundo María Cristina rubber plantation, now a research centre, can be visited to see the whole rubber production process. Allow one hour; five minutes south of town, US$0.50 by mototaxi.

Iñapari, at the end of the road, Km 235, has a growing problem with Haitian refugees trying to enter Brazil by the back door. Hundreds are stuck in transit. The town has a basic hotel and a restaurant, but **Assis Brasil** across the border is much more attractive and has three hotels, two restaurants and shops. A suspension bridge now links the two countries.

There is a road from Assis Brasil into Brazil and connections to Cobija in Bolivia from Brasiléia. There are no exchange facilities en route and poor exchange rates for Brazilian currency at Iñapari. Crossing between Peru and Bolivia on this route is not easy.

Crossing to Brazil

Public transport stops near immigration in **Iñapari**. Exit stamps can be obtained at immigration, open 0930-1300, 1500-1930 daily (Brazilian side 0830-1200, 1400-1830). In Assis Brasil, there is no Policía Federal office. You have to travel on to Brasiléia to obtain your Brazil entry stamp at Policía Federal in the Rodoviária (bus station). You must have a yellow fever certificate to enter Brazil.

◉ Southeastern jungle listings

For hotel and restaurant price codes, and other relevant information, see pages 14-17.

◉ Where to stay

Manu Biosphere Reserve *p290*
Lodges in Manu
Most jungle lodges are booked as package deals for 3 days, 2 nights, or longer, with meals, transport and guides, see websites below for offers.

Amazon Yanayacu Lodge, Cahuide 824, Punchana, T065-250822, www.amazon yanayaculodge.com. About 1 hr by boat above Diamante village on the southern bank of the Madre de Dios, close to a small parrot *collpa* (mineral lick). Using local river transport to arrive at the lodge rates are very reasonable, prices depend on length of stay. The lodge also offers several different itineraries in Manu.

Amazonia Lodge, on the Río Alto Madre de Dios just across the river from Atalaya, T084-816131, www.amazonialodge.com; in Cuzco at Matará 334, p 3, T084-231370. An old tea hacienda run by the Yabar Calderón family, famous for its bird diversity and fine hospitality, a great place to relax, meals included, birding or natural history tours available, contact Santiago in advance and he'll arrange a pick-up.

Casa Machiguenga, near Cocha Salvador, upriver from Manu Lodge. Contact **Manu Expeditions** or **Apeco** NGO, T084-225595. Machiguenga-style cabins run by local communities with NGO help.

Cock of the Rock Lodge, on the road from Paucartambo to Atalaya at 1600 m, www.tropicalnaturetravel.com. Next to a Cock of the Rock *lek*, 10 private cabins with en-suite bath.

Erika Lodge, on the Alto Madre de Dios, 25 mins from Atalaya, offers basic accommodation and is cheaper than the other, more luxurious lodges. Contact **Manu Ecological Adventures** (see below).

Manu Cloud Forest Lodge, at Unión, at 1800 m on the road from Paucartambo to Atalaya, owned by **Manu Nature Tours**, 6 rooms with 16-20 beds.

Manu Learning Centre, Fundo Mascoitania, a 600-ha reserve within the cultural zone, T84-262433, www.crees-expeditions.com. 45 mins from Atalaya by boat, a conservation and volunteer programme run by the crees foundation, now welcoming tourists here and at their new, luxury lodge, **Romero Rainforest Lodge**, a day away by boat.

Manu Lodge, on the Manu river, 3 hrs upriver from Boca Manu towards Cocha Salvador, run by **Manu Nature Tours** and only bookable as part of a full package deal with transport.

Manu Wildlife Center, 2 hrs down the Río Madre de Dios from Boca Manu, near the Blanquillo macaw lick. Book through **Manu Expeditions**, which runs it in conjunction with the conservation group **Peru Verde**, www.manuwildlifecenter.com. 22 double cabins, with private bathroom and hot water. Also canopy towers for birdwatching and a tapir lick.

Pantiacolla Lodge, 30 mins downriver from Shintuya. Owned by the Moscoso family. Book through **Pantiacolla Tours** (see page 299).

Cuzco to Puerto Maldonado via Pilcopata and Itahuania *p291*

Turismo Indigena Wanamei, Av El Sol 814 p 2, of 212, Cuzco, T234608, T984-754708, or Av 26 de Diciembre 276, Puerto Maldonado, T082-572 539, www.ecoturismowanamei.com. An initiative by the people of the Amarakaeri Communal Reserve, located between Manu and Tambopata. They offer 4- to 9-day trips starting and ending in Cuzco. Accommodation includes lodges, communities and camping. The trips aim not only to offer excellent wildlife viewing opportunities but also an insight in to the daily life of indigenous peoples. It's advised that you speak Spanish.

$ Hospedaje Manu, Boca Colorado, on street beside football field. Cell-like rooms, open windows and ceilings but comfy mattresses and mosquito netting.

$ Sra Rubella in Pilcopata. Very basic but friendly.

$ Yine Lodge, next to Boca Manu airport. A cooperative project run between **Pantiacolla Tours** and the Yine community of Diamante, who operate their own tours into their community and surroundings. Also **$ Hostal** in Boca Manu run by the community. Basic accommodation.

Puerto Maldonado *p292*

New hotels catering for business travellers are springing up.

$$$ Don Carlos, Av León Velarde 1271, T571029, www.hotelesdoncarlos.com. Nice view over the Río Tambopata, a/c, restaurant, airport transfers, good.

$$$ Wasaí Lodge & Expeditions, Plaza Grau 1, T572290, www.wasai.com. In a beautiful location overlooking the Madre de Dios River, with forest surrounding cabin-style rooms, shower, small pool with waterfall, good restaurant (local fish a speciality). They can organize local tours and also have a lodge on the Río Tambopata (see page 297).

$$$-$$ Cabañaquinta, Cuzco 535, T571045, www.hotelcabanaquinta.com. A/c or fan, frigobar, laundry, free drinking water, good restaurant, lovely garden, very comfortable, airport transfer. Request a room away from the Interoceanic Highway.

$$ Anaconda Lodge, 600 m from airport, T982-611039 (mob), www.anaconda junglelodge.com. With private or shared bath, Swiss/Thai-owned bungalows, hot showers, swimming pool, Thai restaurant or Peruvian food and pizza if you prefer, tours arranged, has space for camping, very pleasant, family atmosphere.

$$ Paititi Hostal, G Prada 290 y Av León Velarde, T574667, see Facebook page. All mod-cons, executive and standard rooms. Reserve in advance.

$$ Perú Amazónico, Jr Ica 269, T571799, peruamazonico@hotmail.com. Modern, comfortable and good.

$ Amarumayo, Libertad 433, 10 mins from the centre, T573860. Comfortable, with pool and garden, good restaurant.

$ Hospedaje El Bambú, Jr Puno 837, T793880. Basic and small but well-kept rooms with fan, family atmosphere, breakfast and juices not included in price but served in dining room. A good budget option.

$ Hospedaje Español, González Prada 670, T572381. Comfortable, set back from the road, in a quiet part of town.

$ Hospedaje La Bahía, 2 de Mayo 710, T572127. Cheaper without bath or TV, large rooms, a good choice.

$ Tambopata Hostel, Av 26 de Diciembre 234, www.tambopatahostel.com. The only real backpacker hostel in town, dorm beds, hammocks or camping. Nice atmosphere, they also organize local tours.

Jungle tours from Puerto Maldonado: Tambopata *p292*

Some of the lodges along the Tambopata river offer guiding and research placements to biology and environmental science graduates. For more details send an SAE to **TReeS**: UK – J Forrest, PO Box 33153, London, NW3 4DR, www.tambopata.org.uk.

Lodges on the Río Madre de Dios

Most jungle lodges are booked as package deals for 3 days, 2 nights, or longer, with meals, transport and guides, see websites below for offers.

$$ Casa de Hospedaje Mejía, to book T571428, visit **Ceiba Tours**, L Velarde 420, T573567, turismomejia@hotmail.com. Attractive but basic rustic lodge close to Lago Sandoval, full board can be arranged, canoes are available.

Eco Amazonia Lodge, on the Madre de Dios, 1 hr down-river from Puerto Maldonado (office Jr Lambayeque 774, T573491). In Lima: Enrique Palacios 292, Miraflores, T01-242 2708, in Cuzco Garcilazo 210, of 206, T084-236159, www.ecoamazonia.com.pe. Basic bungalows and dormitories, good for birdwatching, has its own Monkey Island with animals taken from the forest.

El Corto Maltés, Billinghurst 229, Puerto Maldonado, T573831, www.cortomaltes-amazonia.com. On the Madre de Dios, halfway to Sandoval which is the focus of most visits. Hot water, huge dining room, well run.

Estancia Bello Horizonte, 20 km northeast of Puerto Maldonado, Loreto 252, Puerto Maldonado, T572748, www.estanciabellohorizonte.com. In a nice stretch of forest overlooking the old course of the Madre de Dios, now a huge aguajal populated with macaws. A small lodge with bungalows for 30 people, with private bath, hot water, pool, butterfly house. Transport, all meals and guide (several languages offered) included, US$220 for 3 days/2 nights. The lodge belongs to APRONIA, an organization that trains and provides employment for orphaned children. Suitable for those wanting to avoid a river trip.

Inkaterra Reserva Amazónica Lodge, 45 mins by boat down the Madre de Dios. To book: **Inkaterra**, Andalucía 174, Miraflores L18, Lima, T01-610 0400; Plaza Nazarenas 167 p 2, Cuzco T084-245314, and Cuzco 436, Puerto Maldonado, www.inkaterra.com. Tastefully redecorated hotel in the jungle with suites and bungalows, solar power, good food in huge dining room supported by a big tree. Jungle tours in its own 10,000 ha plus their new canopy walk; also tours to Lago Sandoval.

Sandoval Lake Lodge, 1 km beyond Mejía on Lago Sandoval, book through InkaNatura, address under Manu, Tour operators. Usual access is by canoe after a 3-km walk or rickshaw ride, huge bar and dining area, electricity, hot water.

Lodges on the Tambopata

Lodges on the Tambopata are reached by vehicle to Bahuaja port, 15 km up river from Puerto Maldonado by the community of Infierno, then by boat. Under a new scheme, a central booking office is being set up to offer the services of over 15 small lodges and *casas de hospedaje* along the Tambopata river under the names: **Tambopata Ecotourism Corridor** and **Tambopata Homestays** (www.tambopataecotours.com). Further details on the website of location, style of accommodation, facilities, cost, etc. See lodge websites for prices of packages offered.

Explorers Inn, book through **Peruvian Safaris**, Alcanfores 459, Miraflores, Lima, T01-447 8888, www.peruviansafaris.com. Just before the La Torre control post, adjoining the TNR, in the part where most research work has been done, 58 km from Puerto Maldonado. 2½ hrs up the Río Tambopata (1½ hrs return), one of the best places in Peru for seeing jungle birds (580 plus species have been recorded), butterflies (1230 plus species), also giant river otters, but you probably need more

than a 2-day tour to benefit fully from the location. Offers tours through the adjoining community of La Torre. The guides are biologists and naturalists undertaking research in the reserve. They provide interesting wildlife treks, including to the macaw lick (*collpa*).

Posada Amazonas Lodge, on the Tambopata river, 1½ hrs by vehicle and boat upriver from Puerto Maldonado. Book through **Rainforest Expeditions**, San Francisco de Paula Ugariza 813, Of 201, San Antonio-Miraflores, Lima, T01-241 4880, reservations at T01-997 903650, www.perunature.com. A collaboration between the tour agency and the local native community of Infierno. Attractive rooms with cold showers, visits to Lake Tres Chimbadas, with good birdwatching including the Tambopata Collpa. Offers trips to a nearby indigenous primary health care project where a native healer gives guided tours of the medicinal plant garden. Service and guiding is very good. The **Tambopata Research Centre**, the company's more intimate, but comfortable lodge, about 6 hrs further upriver. Rooms are smaller than Posada Amazonas, shared showers, cold water. The lodge is next to the famous Tambopata macaw clay lick. 2 hrs from Posada Amazonas, Rainforest Expeditions also has the **Refugio Amazonas**, close to Lago Condenados. It is the usual stopover for those visiting the collpa. 3 bungalows accommodate 70 people in en suite rooms, large, kerosene lit, open bedrooms with mosquito nets, well designed and run, atmospheric. There are many packages at the different lodges and lots of add-ons.

Tambopata Eco Lodge, on the Río Tambopata, to make reservations Nueva Baja 432, Cuzco, T084-245695, operations office Jr Gonzales Prada 269, Puerto Maldonado, T571726, www.tambopatalodge.com. Rooms with solar-heated water, good guides, excellent food. Trips go to Lake Condenado, some to Lake Sachavacayoc, and to the Collpa de Chuncho, guiding mainly in English and Spanish, naturalists programme provided.

Wasaí Lodge and Expeditions, Río Tambopata, 120 km (3 hrs by speedboat) upriver from Puerto Maldonado, contact Las Higueras 257, Residencial Monterrico, La Molina, Lima 12, T01-436 8792, or Plaza Grau 1, Puerto Maldonado, T082-572290, www.wasai.com. Kayaking, zipline, fishing, photography tours, mystic tours, wildlife observation, volunteering, etc. Also tours to the Chuncho Clay Lick and Sandoval Lake. Guides in English and Spanish.

Río Las Piedras
Amazon Rainforest Conservation Centre, contact Pepe Moscoso, Jr Los Cedros B-17, Los Castaños, Puerto Maldonado, T082-573655, www.laspiedrasamazontour. com. Roughly 8 hrs up Río Las Piedras, overlooking a beautiful oxbow lake, Lago Soledad, which has a family of giant otters. Comfortable bungalows, with bath and hot water. Activities include a viewing platform 35 m up an ironwood tree, a hide overlooking a macaw lick, and walks on the extensive trail network. Most trips break the river journey half way at **Tipishca Lodge**, overlooking an oxbow lake with a family of otters (same website as above).
Las Piedras Biodiversity Station, T082-573922. A small lodge in a 4000-ha concession of 'primary' rainforest 90 km up the Río Las Piedras. Visitors camp en route to the lodge. 20 beds in 10 rooms, central dining-room, shared bath, no electricity, library, guiding in English/ Spanish. Minimum package is for 4 days/ 3 nights. Birdwatching trips cost more.

🍽 Restaurants

Puerto Maldonado p292
$$-$ Burgos's, León Velarde 129. Serves traditional dishes and has a good set lunch menu.
$$-$ Carne Brava, on the Plaza de Armas. One of the smart new joints for a steak and chips.

$$-$ El Hornito/Chez Maggy, on the plaza. Cosy, good pizzas, busy at weekends.
$$-$ Kuskalla, Av 26 de Diciembre 195. Peruvian/Brazilian fusion food with views of the Madre de Dios and Tambopata rivers.
$ D'Kaoba, Madre de Dios 439. Serves the most delicious *pollos a la brasa* in town.
$ La Casa Nostra, Velarde 515. Sells huge fruit juices for US$0.50, as well as *tamales*, *papas rellenas* and enormous fancy cakes, great coffee.
$ Namaste, Av León Velarde 469. Moroccan and Indian food, sandwiches, breakfasts and set lunches, in chilled out surroundings.
Gustitos del Cura, Loreto 258, Plaza de Armas. Open 0800-2300, closed Wed. Ice cream and juice parlour run by the APRONIA project for homeless teenagers, offering unusual flavours.

🍸 Bars and clubs

Puerto Maldonado p292
El Asadero, Arequipa 246, east side of Plaza. Popular *menú* at lunchtime, great sandwiches later in the day, cool bar in the evening.
El Witite, Av León Velarde 153. Fri and Sat. A popular, good disco, latin music.
Le Boulevard, behind El Hornito. Live music, popular.
T-Saica, Loreto 335. An atmospheric bar with live music at weekends.
Vikingo, León Velarde 158. A popular bar and open-air disco.

⏰ What to do

Manu Biosphere Reserve p290
Warning Beware of pirate operators on the streets of Cuzco who offer trips to the Reserved Zone of Manu and end up halfway through the trip changing the route "due to emergencies", which, in reality means they have no permits to operate in the area. Some unscrupulous tour guides will offer trips to see the uncontacted tribes of Manu. On no account make any attempt to view these very vulnerable people. The following

companies organize trips into the Multiple Use and Reserved Zones. Contact them for more details.

Amazon Trails Peru, C Tandapata 660, San Blas, Cuzco, T084-437374, or T984-714148, www.amazontrailsperu.com. Offers tours to Manu National Park and Blanquillo clay lick; runs 2 lodges in Manu. Operated by ornithologist Abraham Huamán, who has many years' experience guiding in Manu, and his German wife Ulla Maennig. Well-organized tours with knowledgeable guides, good boatmen and cooks, small groups, guaranteed departure dates. Also trekking in Cuzco area. Run the **Amazon Hostel** next door to office in Cuzco (T236770).

Bonanza Tours, Suecia 343, T084-507871, www.bonanzatoursperu.com. 3- to 8-day tours to Manu with local guides, plenty of jungle walks, rafting, kayaking and camp-based excursions with good food. Tours are high quality and good value.

Expediciones Vilca, Plateros 359, Cuzco, T084-244751, www.manuvilcaperu.com. Offers tours at economical prices.

Greenland Peru, in Cuzco: Celasco Astete C-12, T246572, www.greenlandperu.com. Fredy Domínguez is an Amazonian and offers good-value trips to Manu with comfortable accommodation and transport and excellent food cooked by his mother. Experienced, knowledgeable and enthusiastic, he speaks English.

InkaNatura, in Cuzco: Ricardo Palma J1, T084-255255, in Lima: Manuel Bañón 461, San Isidro, T01-440 2022, www.inkanatura.com. Tours to Manu Wildlife Centre and Sandoval Lake Lodge (see above) with emphasis on sustainable tourism and conservation. Knowledgeable guides. They also run treks in Cuzco area.

Manu Adventures, Plateros 356, Cuzco, T084-261640, www.manuadventures.com. This company operates one of the most physically active Manu programmes, with options for a mountain biking descent through the cloudforest and 3 hrs of whitewater rafting on the way to **Erika Lodge** on the upper Río Madre de Dios. Also jungle specialists.

Manu Expeditions and Birding Tours, Jr Los Geranios 2-G, Urb Mariscal Gamarra, 1a Etapa, Cuzco, T084-225990, www.manuexpeditions.com. Owned by ornithologist Barry Walker, 3 trips available to the reserve and Manu Wildlife Center.

Manu Learning Centre, Fundo Mascoitania, a 600-ha private reserve near Salvación, operated by CREES, San Miguel 250, Cuzco, T084-262433 (in UK 5-6 Kendrick Mews, London, SW7 3HG, T020-7581 2932), www.crees-manu.org. A multi-use centre in the Cultural Zone for ectourism, research, volunteers and school groups for rainforest conservation and community development. They run expeditions, tours and field courses.

Manu Nature Tours, Av Pardo 1046, Cuzco, T084-252721, www.manuperu.com. Owned by Boris Gómez Luna, run lodge- based trips, owners of **Manu Lodge** and part owners of **Manu Cloudforest Lodge**; Manu is the only lodge in the Reserved Zone, open all year, situated on an oxbow lake, providing access to the forest, guides available; activities include river-rafting and canopy-climbing. Highly recommended for experiencing the jungle in comfort.

Oropéndola, Av Circunvalación s/n, Urb Guadalupe Mz A Lte 3, Cuzco, T084-241428, www.oropendolaperu.org. Guide Walter Mancilla Huamán is an expert on flora and fauna. 5-, 7- and 9-day tours from US$800 pp plus park entrance. Good reports of attention to detail and to the needs of clients.

Pantiacolla Tours SRL, Garcilaso 265, interior, p 2, of 12, Cuzco, T084-238323, www.pantiacolla.com. Run by Marianne van Vlaardingen and Gustavo Moscoso. They have tours to the **Pantiacolla Lodge** (see Where to stay, page 294) and also 8-day camping trips. Pantiacolla has started a community-based ecotourism project, called the **Yine Project**, with the people of Diamante in the Multiple Use Zone.

Puerto Maldonado *p292*
Guides

All guides should have a carnet issued by the Ministry of Tourism (DIRCETUR), which also verifies them as suitable guides for trips to other places and confirms their identity. Check that the carnet has not expired. Reputable guides are **Hernán Llave Cortez**, **Romel Nacimiento** and the **Mejía** brothers, all of whom can be contacted on arrival at the airport, if available. Also recommended: **Carlos Borja Gama**, a local guide offering specialist birdwatching and photography trips as well as traditional jungle tours, speaks several languages. Contact him through Wasaí or see www.carlosexpeditions.com. **Víctor Yohamona**, T082-982-686279 (mob), victorguideperu@hotmail.com. Speaks English, French and German. Boat hire can be arranged through the Capitanía del Puerto (Río Madre de Dios), T573003. **Perú Tours**, Loreto 176, T082-573 244. Organize local trips. See also **Ceiba Tours**, under **Casa de hospedaje Mejía**, above.

⊙ Transport

Cuzco to Puerto Maldonado: via Urcos and Mazuko *p291*
Bus The *Interoceánica* is paved all the way. There are many daily buses, US$19-30 (*económico* or *semi-cama*), 10-11 hrs, from the Terminal Terrestre in **Cuzco** with **Transportes Iguazú** (one of the cheapest, less reliable, no toilet), **Mendivil**, **Machupicchu**, **Palomino** and **Móvil Tours** (one of the better companies, at Tambopata 529, Puerto Maldonado, T082-795785). All are on Av Tambopata, blocks 3 and 5 in Puerto Maldonado. There are also daily buses from **Mazuko** to Puerto Maldonado with **Transportes Bolpebra** and **Transportes Señor de la Cumbre**, 4 hrs, US$6.

Juliaca to Puerto Maldonado: via Mazuko
Road The 4th stage of the Interoceanic Highway is now open and several buses run daily from Arequipa and Puno, stopping in Juliaca, crossing the altiplano and joining the Cuzco-Puerto Maldonado section of the Highway at Puente Iñambari, 5 km from the gold-mining town of Mazuko. **Trans Continental Sur**, **Aguilas** and **Santa Cruz** buses leave Juliaca 1300-1500, 12 hrs, US$27. **Trans Wayra** from Puno (US$27) and Arequipa; **Trans Mendivil** from Cuzco (US$30), Puno and Arequipa.

Cuzco to Puerto Maldonado: via Pilcopata and Itahuania *p291*
Road From the Coliseo Cerrado in Cuzco 3 buses run to **Pilcopata** Mon, Wed, Fri, returning same night, US$10. They are fully booked even in low season. The best are **Gallito de las Rocas**; also **Unancha** from C Huáscar near the main plaza. Trucks to Pilcopata run on same days, returning Tue, Thu, Sat, 10 hrs, in wet season, less in the dry. Only basic supplies are available after leaving Cuzco, so take all camping and food essentials, including insect repellent. Transport can be disrupted in the wet

season because the road is in poor condition, although improvements are being made. *Camioneta* service runs between Pilcopata and **Salvación** to connect with the buses, Mon, Wed, Fri. The same *camionetas* run **Itahuania-Shintuya-Salvacion** regularly, when sufficient passengers, probably once a day, and 2 trucks a day. On Sun, there is no traffic. To **Boca Manu** you can hire a boat in Atalaya, several hundred dollars for a *peke peke*, more for a motor boat. It's cheaper to wait or hope for a boat going empty up to Boca Manu to pick up passengers, when the fare will be US$15 per passenger. Itahuania-Boca Manu in a shared boat is US$7.50. A private, chartered boat would be over US$100. From Itahuania, cargo boats leave for the gold mining centre of **Boca Colorado** on the Río Madre de Dios, via Boca Manu, but only when the boat is fully laden; about 6-8 a week, 9 hrs, US$20. From Boca Colorado colectivos leave from near football field for Puerto Carlos, 1 hr, US$5, ferry across river 10 mins, US$1.65; colectivo Puerto Carlos-Puerto Maldonado, 3 hrs, US$10, rough road, lots of stops (in Puerto Maldonado **Turismo Boca Colorado**, Tacna 342, T082-573435, leave when full). Tour companies usually use own vehicles for the overland trip from Cuzco to Manu.

Puerto Maldonado *p292*
Air To **Lima**, daily with **LAN** and **Star Perú** via Cuzco. Moto-taxi from town to airport US$2.25, taxi US$3.50, 8 km.

Road and ferry A standard journey by moto-taxi in town costs US$0.60, a ride on a motorbike US$0.30. For **Boca Manu** and **Itahuania** take a colectivo to **Boca Colorado** (see above) and then take a cargo boat (no fixed schedule). From Itahuania there is transport to Pilcopata and Cuzco. To **Iberia** and **Iñapari** for Brazil, daily combis from Jr Ica y Jr Piura, recommended companies are **Turismo Imperial** and Turismo **Real Dorado**. To Iberia 2½ hrs, US$6.50; to Iñapari 3½ hrs, US$8.50. **Móvil** (see above) also have daily service to **Rio Branco** (Brazil), 1200, US$35. To **Juliaca**, several companies offer daily services via San Gabán, at 1900 and 1700 respectively, 18 hrs, US$17. For all routes, ask around the bus offices for colectivo minibuses.

Directory

Puerto Maldonado *p292*
Consulates Bolivian Consulate, on the north side of the plaza. **Motorcycle hire** Scooters and mopeds can de hired from **San Francisco** and others, on the corner of Puno and G Prado for US$1.75 per hr, off-road motorbikes cost US$3.50 per hr. Passport and driver's licence must be shown. **Useful addresses** Peruvian immigration, 28 de Julio 465, get your exit stamp here.

Contents

Bolivia

At a glance

⊚ **Time required** 2-4 weeks, but don't try to do too much; distances are long and land transport is slow.

🌣 **Best time** Altiplano: all year is good, Jun and Jul are clearest and coldest at night, and busiest. Feb-Apr are good for festivals, but this is wet season. Alasitas in La Paz in late Jan should not be missed. For climbing May-Sep.

✕ **When not to go** Nov-Mar is the rainy season, heaviest in lowlands but check road conditions everywhere at this time of year.

BRAZIL

Assis
Brasil
Brasiléia
Cobija
Puerto
Rico
Riberalta
Guayaramerín
El Chorro

PERU

Puerto
Pardo
Puerto Heath

Parque
Nacional
Madidi
5
Reyes
Rurrenabaque
Yucumo
Guanay
Sorata
Caranavi
Coroico
Chulumani
2
Sta Ana
de Yacuma
San Joaquín
Magdalena
Pilón Lajas
Biosphere
Reserve
San Borja
San Ignacio
de Moxos
San Javier
Casarebe
Trinidad
Caimanes
Perseverancia
Parque Nacional
Noel Kempff Mercado
San
Pablo
Baia
Grande
San Ignacio
de Velasco
San Matías
Santa Ana

Lake
Titicaca
Carabuco
Copacabana
1
LA PAZ
Villa
Tunari
Puerto
Villarroel
San Javier
San
Ramón
Concepción
San
Miguel
6
San Rafael

Parque
Nacional
Sajama
Cochabamba
Parque
Nacional
Totora
Torotoro
Buena
Vista
Montero
Santa Cruz
de la Sierra
San José
de Chiquitos
Roboré

Oruro
Tambo
Quemado
Sacabaya
Sabaya
Parque
Nacional
Amboró
Aiquile
Samaipata
Parque
Nacional
Kaa-Iya
Quijarro/
Puerto
Suárez

Huanuni
Challapata
Lago
Poopó
La Higuera
Abapó

Sucre
Tarabuco
Potosí
Monteagudo
Camiri
Boyuibe

Salar de
Uyuni
Llica
Colchane
Cerdas
Camargo
Villamontes
Hito Villazón

Chiguana
Uyuni
4
San
Vicente
Tupiza
Tarija
Yacuiba
Ibibobo
Pocitos
Bermejo
Fortín Infante
Rivarola

PARAGUAY

Reserva Fauna Andina
Eduardo Avaroa
Laguna
Colorada
Hito
Cajones
Laguna
Verde
Villazón

CHILE

ARGENTINA

N

100 km
100 miles

On Bolivia's Altiplano you are so far up it will make your head spin. Every day in La Paz, one of the highest seats of government in the world transforms itself from a melee of indigenous markets and modern business into a canyon of glittering stars as the lights come on at nightfall.

Bolivia has some of the most bio-diverse conservation areas in South America: Amboró, Kaa-lya (the continent's largest), Madidi and Noel Kempff Mercado, all with an incredible range of habitats and variety of flora and fauna. If you fancy a trek, there are adventurous trails within a day of the capital, while anyone nostalgic for the revolutionary days of the 1960s can follow the Che Guevara Trail. For an exhilarating bike ride, head for Coroico, where in less than an hour you can go from mountain heights to the lush Yungas valleys, through waterfalls and round hairpin bends – but do go with an expert.

In Bolivia you learn to expect the unexpected. On the largest salt flat on earth, a vast blinding-white expanse, you lose track of what is land and what is sky. At Carnaval in Oruro, dancers wear masks of the scariest monsters you could ever dream of. To visit the mines at Potosí, once the silver lode for the Spanish Empire, you should buy coca leaves and other gifts for the miners. In the surreal Reserva Nacional de Fauna Andina Eduardo Avaroa, volcanoes overlook lakes of blue, white, green and red, where flamingos feed, and Dalí-esque rock structures dot the Altiplano. In the Bolivian Amazon you can swim with pink river dolphins or fish for piranhas.

Before you go home, you can fill your bags with everything from the beautiful autumnal colours of the textiles, to packs of dried llama foetuses. The latter are said to protect homes from evil spirits but are unlikely to ingratiate you with most customs and agriculture officers.

La Paz and around

The minute you arrive in La Paz, the highest seat of government in the world, you realize this is no ordinary place. El Alto airport is at a staggering 4061 m above sea level. The sight of the city, lying hundreds of metres below, at the bottom of a steep canyon and ringed by snow-peaked mountains, takes your breath away – literally – for at this altitude breathing can be a problem.

The Spaniards chose this odd place for a city on 20 October 1548, to avoid the chill winds of the plateau, and because they had found gold in the Río Choqueyapu, which runs through the canyon. The centre of the city, Plaza Murillo, is at 3636 m, about 400 m below the level of the Altiplano and the sprawling city of El Alto, perched dramatically on the rim of the canyon.

Arriving in La Paz → *Phone code: 02. Population: La Paz: 912,512, El Alto: 1,079,698.*

Orientation La Paz has the highest commercial **airport** in the world, high above the city at El Alto. A taxi from the airport to the centre takes about 30 minutes. There are three main **bus terminals**; the bus station at Plaza Antofagasta, the cemetery district for Sorata, Copacabana and Tiwanaku, and Minasa bus station in Villa Fátima for the Yungas, including Coroico, and northern jungle. A system of cable cars (*teleféricos*) is under construction. The red line, between El Alto and Vita, west of the main bus station, is scheduled to open in 2014. There are three types of city bus: *puma katari* (a fleet of new buses operating since March 2014), *micros* (small, old buses) and faster, more plentiful minibuses. *Trufis* are fixed-route collective taxis, with a sign with their route on the windscreen. Taxis come in three types: regular honest taxis, fake taxis and radio taxis, the safest, which have a dome light and number.

The city's main street runs from **Plaza San Francisco** as Avenida Mariscal Santa Cruz, then changes to Avenida 16 de Julio (more commonly known as El Prado) and ends at **Plaza del Estudiante**. The business quarter, government offices, central university (UMSA) and many of the main hotels and restaurants are in this area. Banks and exchange houses are clustered on Calle Camacho, between Loayza and Colón, not far from **Plaza Murillo**, the traditional heart of the city. From the Plaza del Estudiante, Avenida Villazón splits into Avenida Arce, which runs southeast towards the wealthier residential districts of **Zona Sur**, in the valley, 15 minutes away; and Avenida 6 de Agosto which runs through **Sopocachi**, an area full of restaurants, bars and clubs. Zona Sur has shopping centres, supermarkets with imported items and some of the best restaurants and bars in La Paz (see page 318). It begins after the bridge at La Florida beside the attractive Plaza Humboldt. The main road, Avenida Ballivián, begins at Calle 8 and continues up the hill to San Miguel on Calle 21 (about a 20-minute walk).

Sprawled around the rim of the canyon is **El Alto**, Bolivia's second-largest city (after Santa Cruz, La Paz is third). Its population of more than one million is mostly indigenous migrants from the countryside and its political influence has grown rapidly. El Alto is connected to La Paz by motorway (toll US$0.25) and by a road to Obrajes and the Zona Sur. Minibuses from Plaza Eguino leave regularly for Plaza 16 de Julio, El Alto, more leave from Plaza Pérez Velasco for La Ceja, the edge of El Alto. Intercity buses to and from La Paz always stop at El Alto in an area called *terminal*, off Avenida 6 de Marzo, where transport companies have small offices. If not staying in La Paz, you can change buses here and save a couple of hours. There is accommodation nearby, but the area is not safe, especially at night.
➤➤ *See Transport, page 323, for full details.*

Best time to visit La Paz Because of the altitude, nights are cold the year round. In the day, the sun is strong, but the moment you go into the shade or enter a building, the temperature falls. From December-March, the summer, it rains most afternoons, making it feel colder than it actually is. Temperatures are even lower in winter, June-August, when the sky is always clear. The two most important festivals, when the city gets particularly busy, are **Alasitas** (last week of January and first week of February) and **Festividad del Señor del Gran Poder** (end May/early June). ▶▶ *See Festivals, page 319.*

Tourist offices The **Gobierno Municipal de La Paz** has information centres at: **Plaza del Estudiante** ① *at the lower end of El Prado between 16 de Julio and México, T237 1044, Mon-Fri 0830-1200, 1430-1900, Sat-Sun 0900-1300, very helpful, English and French spoken*; **El Prado InfoTur** ① *Mariscal Santa Cruz y Colombia, Mon-Fri 0830-1900, Sat-Sun 0930-1300*; **Bus terminal** ① *T228 5858, Mon-Fri 0600-2200, Sat 0800-1600, Sun 1400-2200, holidays 0800-1200, 1600-2000*; **Plaza Pérez Velasco** ① *opposite San Francisco, under the pedestrian walkway, Mon-Fri 0830-1200, 1430-1700*; and **Tomás Katari** ① *Av Bautista y José María Aliaga, by the cemetery, Mon-Fri 0900-1700*. They also have information booths at the Museo Costumbrista on Calle Jaén, Valle de la Luna and Muela del Diablo. Tourist office for **El Alto: Dirección de Promoción Turística** ① *C 5 y Av 6 de Marzo, Edif Vela, p 5, also at arrivals in airport, T282 9281, Mon-Fri 0800-1200, 1400-1800.*

Health Travellers arriving in La Paz, especially when flying directly from sea level, may experience mild altitude sickness. If your symptoms are severe, consult a physician. See Health in Essentials.

Safety The worst areas for crime are around Plaza Murillo and the Cemetery neighbourhood where local buses serve Copacabana and Tiwanaku. **Tourist police** ① *T222 5016*, now patrol these bus stops during the daytime, but caution is still advised. Other areas, particularly upscale Sopocachi, are generally safer. **Warning for ATM users**: scams to get card numbers and PINs have flourished, especially in La Paz. The tourist police post warnings in hotels. ▶▶ *See also Safety, page 29.*

Places in La Paz

There are few colonial buildings left in La Paz; probably the best examples are in **Calle Jaén** (see below). Late 19th- and early 20th-century architecture, often displaying European influence, can be found in the streets around Plaza Murillo, but much of La Paz is modern. The **Plaza del Estudiante** (Plaza Franz Tamayo), or a bit above it, marks a contrast between old and new styles, between the commercial and the more elegant. The **Prado** itself is lined with high-rise blocks dating from the 1960s and 1970s.

Around Plaza Murillo

Plaza Murillo, three blocks north of the Prado, is the traditional centre. Facing its formal gardens are the **Cathedral**, the **Palacio Presidencial** in Italian renaissance style, known as the **Palacio Quemado** (burnt palace) twice gutted by fire in its stormy 130-year history, and, on the east side, the **Congreso Nacional**. In front of the Palacio Quemado is a statue of former President Gualberto Villarroel who was dragged into the plaza by a mob and hanged in 1946. Across from the Cathedral on Calle Socabaya is the **Palacio de los Condes de Arana** (built 1775), with beautiful exterior and patio. It houses the **Museo Nacional**

1 La Paz

To ①②⑲, Bus Station, El Alto, Airport,
Titicaca, Tiwanaku & Oruro

Where to stay 🛏
1 Adventure Brew B&B *A2*
2 Adventure Brew Hostel *A2*
3 Arthy's Guesthouse *A2*
4 Bacoo *A3*
5 Casa Fusión *E5*
6 El Rey Palace *D4*
7 Estrella Andina *B2*
8 Europa & Café El Consulado *C4*
9 Hostal Copacabana *B2*
10 Hostal República *B4*
11 La Joya *B1*
12 La Loge & La Comedie Restaurant *E5*
13 Mitru La Paz *E5*
14 Onkel Inn 1886 *C3*
15 Radisson Plaza *D5*
16 Rosario *B2*
17 Stannum *E5*
18 Tambo de Oro *A3*
19 Wild Rover Backpackers Hostel *B4*

Restaurants 🍴
1 Alexander Coffee *C4, E5*
2 Arco Iris *E4*
3 Armonía *E5*
4 Beatrice *E4*
5 Café Soho *A3*
6 Fridolín *E5*
7 Ken-Chan *D4*
8 Kuchen Stube *E5*
9 La Terraza *C4, E5*
10 Maphrao On *E6*
11 Mongo's *E5*
12 Olive Tree *E6*
13 Reineke Fuchs *E5*
14 Rendezvous *E5*
15 Sancho Panza *E5*
16 Vienna *D4*

Bars & clubs 🍸
17 Equinoccio *E4*
18 Marka Tambo & Etno Café *A3*
19 Tetekos *C4*
20 Thelonius Jazz Bar *E4*

N

100 metres
100 yards

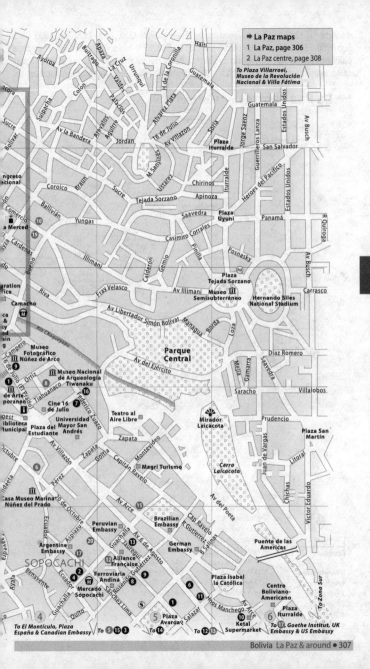

de Arte ① *T240 8542, www.mna.org.bo, Tue-Fri 0900-1230, 1500-1900, Sat 1000-1700, Sun 0900-1330, closed for renovations in 2014, US$1.50*. It has a fine collection of colonial paintings including many works by Melchor Pérez Holguín, considered one of the masters of Andean colonial art, and which also exhibits the works of contemporary local artists.

② La Paz centre

➡ La Paz maps
1 La Paz, page 306
2 La Paz centre, page 308

N

| 100 metres |
| 100 yards |

Where to stay 🛌
1 Arcabucero *C1*
2 El Solario *B1*
3 Fuentes *C1*
4 Gloria *B2*
5 Hosp Milenio *A3*

6 Hostal Naira *C2*
7 La Casona *B2*
8 La Posada de la
  Abuela Obdulia *C1*
9 Loki *A1, C3*
10 Milton *D1*
11 Muzungu *B1*
12 Posada El Carretero *A3*
13 Presidente &
   La Kantuta Restaurant *B2*
14 Sagárnaga *C1*
15 Torino *B3*

Restaurants 🍴
1 100% Natural *C1*
2 Alexander Coffee *B3*
3 A Lo Cubano *C1*
4 Angelo Colonial *C1*
5 Banais *B2*
6 Café del Mundo *C1*
7 Café Illampu *C1*
8 Colonial Pot *C1*
9 La Cueva *C2*
10 Pepe's *C1*
11 Pizzería Italia *C1*

12 Sol y Luna *C2*
13 Star of India *C2*
14 Steakhouse *C1*

Bars & clubs 🍸
15 Hard Rock Café *B1*
16 Oliver's English Tavern *C2*
17 Peña Parnaso *C2*

Calle Comercio, running east-west across the Plaza, has most of the stores and shops. West of Plaza Murillo, at Ingavi 916, in the palace of the Marqueses de Villaverde is the **Museo Nacional de Etnografía y Folklore** ① *T240 8640, www.musef.org.bo, Mon-Fri 0900-1230, 1500-1900, Sat 0900-1630, Sun 0900-1430, US$3, filming costs US$6.* Various sections show the cultural richness of Bolivia by region through textiles and other items. It has a *videoteca*.

Northwest of Plaza Murillo is **Calle Jaén**, a picturesque colonial street with a restaurant/peña, a café, craft shops, good views and four museums (known as **Museos Municipales** ① *Tue-Fri 0930-1230, 1500-1900, Sat 1000-1700, Sun 0900-1330, US$1.50 each*) housed in colonial buildings. **Museo Costumbrista Juan de Vargas** ① *on Plaza Riosinio, at the top of Jaén, T228 0758, US$0.60*, has miniature displays depicting incidents in the history of La Paz and well-known Paceños, as well as miniature replicas of reed rafts used by the Norwegian Thor Heyerdahl, and the Spaniard Kitin Muñoz, to prove their theories of ancient migrations. **Museo del Litoral Boliviano** ① *T228 0758*, has artefacts of the War of the Pacific, and interesting selection of old maps. **Museo de Metales Preciosos** ① *T228 0329*, is well set out with Inca gold artefacts in basement vaults, also ceramics and archaeological exhibits, and **Museo Casa Murillo** ① *T228 0553*, the erstwhile home of Pedro Domingo Murillo, one of the martyrs of the La Paz independence movement of 16 July 1809, has a good collection of paintings, furniture and national costumes. **Museo Tambo Quirquincho** ① *C Evaristo Valle, south of Jaén, Plaza Alonso de Mendoza, T239 0969, Tue-Fri, 0930-1230, 1500-1900, Sat-Sun, 0900-1300, US$1.20*, displays modern painting and sculpture, carnival masks, silver, early 20th-century photography and city plans, and is recommended.

Plaza San Francisco up to the cemetery district

At the upper end of Avenida Mcal Santa Cruz is the **Plaza San Francisco** with the **church and monastery of San Francisco** ① *open for Mass at 0700, 0900, 1100 and 1900, Mon-Sat, and also at 0800, 1000 and 1200 on Sun.* Dating from 1549, this is one of the finest examples of colonial religious architecture in South America and well worth seeing. The **Centro Cultural Museo San Francisco** ① *Plaza San Francisco 503, T231 8472, Mon-Sat 0900-1800, US$2.80, allow 1½-2 hrs, free guides available but tip appreciated, some speak English and French*, offers access to various areas of the church and convent including the choir, crypt (open 1400-1730), roof, various chapels and gardens. Fine art includes religious paintings from the 17th, 18th and 19th centuries, plus visiting exhibits and a hall devoted to the works of Tito Yupanqui, the indigenous sculptor of the Virgen de Copacabana. There is a pricey but good café at entrance. Behind the San Francisco church a network of narrow cobbled streets rise steeply up the canyon walls. Much of this area is a street market. Handicraft shops, travel agencies, hotels and restaurants line the lower part of **Calle Sagárnaga** (here you find the highest concentration of tourists and pick-pockets). The **Mercado de Brujas**, 'witchcraft market', on Calles Melchor Jiménez and Linares, which cross Santa Cruz above San Francisco, sells charms, herbs and more gruesome items like llama foetuses. The excellent **Museo de la Coca** ① *Linares 914, T231 1998, Mon-Sat 1000-1900, Sun 1000-1600, US$2, www.cocamuseum.com, shop with coca products for sale*, is devoted to the coca plant, its history, cultural significance, medical values and political implications, with explanations in five languages. Nearby is the recommended **Museo de Arte Texil Andino Boliviano** ① *Linares 906, daily 1000-1900, Sun 1000-1700, US$1.20*, a small collection of old traditional weavings (not to be confused with the larger **Museo de Textiles Andinos Bolivianos** in Miraflores).

Further up, from Illampu to Rodríguez and in neighbouring streets, is the produce-based **Rodríguez market** ① *daily, but best on Sun morning*. Turning right on Max Paredes,

Tiny treats

One of the most intriguing items for sale in Andean markets is *Ekeko*, the god of good fortune and plenty and one of the most endearing of the Aymara folk legends. He is a cheery, avuncular little chap, with a happy face, a pot belly and short legs. His image, usually in plaster of Paris, is laden with various household items, as well as sweets, confetti and streamers, food, and with a cigarette dangling cheekily from his lower lip. Believers say that these statues only bring luck if they are received as gifts. The *Ekeko* occupies a central role in the festival of Alacitas, the Feast of Plenty, which takes place in La Paz at the end of January. Everything under the sun can be bought in miniature: houses, trucks, buses, suitcases, university diplomas; you name it, you'll find it here. The idea is to have your mini-purchase blessed by a *Yatiri*, an Aymara priest, and the real thing will be yours within the year.

heading north, is **Avenida Buenos Aires**, where small workshops turn out the costumes and masks for the Gran Poder festival, and with great views of Illimani, especially at sunset. Continuing west along Max Paredes towards the **cemetery district**, the streets are crammed with stalls selling every imaginable item. Transport converges on the cemetery district (for more information see page 323). See also Safety, page 305.

The Prado, Sopocachi, Miraflores and Zona Sur

Museo de Arte Contemporáneo Plaza ① *Av 16 de Julio 1698, T233 5905, daily 0900-2100, US$2.20*. In a 19th-century house which has been declared a national monument, there is a selection of contemporary art from national and international artists. Just off the Prado (down the flight of stairs near the Maria Auxiliadora church) is **Museo Nacional de Arqueología** or **Tiahuanaco** (Tiwanaku) ① *Tiwanacu 93 entre Bravo y F Zuazo, T231 1621, www.bolivian.com/arqueologia, closed for renovation in 2014*. It contains good collections of the arts and crafts of ancient Tiwanaku and items from the eastern jungles. It also has an exhibition of gold statuettes and objects found in Lake Titicaca. On Avenida Libertador Simón Bolívar, from where there are views of Mount Illimani, is the modern **Mercado Camacho** produce market. In Sopocachi district, by Plaza España, is **El Montículo**, a park with great views of the city and Illimani. In the residential district of Miraflores, east of the centre, on Plaza Tejada Sorzano, outside the Hernán Siles national football stadium is the **Museo Semisubterráneo**, a sunken garden full of replicas of statues and artefacts from Tiwanaku, but difficult to get to because of the traffic. At the north end of Avenida Busch are Plaza Villarroel and **Museo del la Revolución Nacional** ① *Tue-Fri 0930-1200, 1500-1800, Sat-Sun 1000-1200, US$0.15*, a memorial of the 1952 revolution and a mausoleum with tombs of former presidents.

Around La Paz

South of La Paz

To the south of the city are dry hills of many colours, topped by the **Muela del Diablo**, a striking outcrop. Here is the **Valle de la Luna**, or 'Valley of the Moon' (US$3), with impressive eroded hills; the climate in this valley is always much warmer than in the city. For transport details see page 323. About 3 km from the bridge at Calacoto the road forks, get out of the minibus at the turning and walk a few minutes east to the Valle entrance, or get out at the football field which is by the entrance. Take good shoes and water, but do not go alone, armed robbery has occurred. Just past the Valle de la Luna is **Mallasa** where there are several small roadside restaurants and cafés and the **Hotel Oberland** (see page 316). To the southeast of La Paz and best accessed from the La Paz–Oruro road are the **Yungas de Inquisivi** and **Quime**, see page 343.

Tiwanaku

ⓘ *The site is open 0900-1700, US$12, including entry to museums. Allow 4 hrs to see the ruins and village. See also Transport, page 323.*

This remarkable archaeological site, 72 km west of La Paz, near the southern end of Lake Titicaca, takes its name from one of the most important pre-Columbian civilizations in South America. It is the most popular excursion from La Paz, with facilities being improved as a result. Many archaeologists believe that Tiwanaku existed as early as 1600 BC, while the complex visible today probably dates from the eight to the 10th centuries AD. The site may have been a ceremonial complex at the centre of an empire which covered almost half Bolivia, southern Peru, northern Chile and northwest Argentina. It was also a hub of trans-Andean trade. The demise of the Tiwanaku civilization, according to studies by Alan Kolata of the University of Illinois, could have been precipitated by the flooding of the area's extensive system of raised fields (*Sukakollu*), which were capable of sustaining a population of 20,000. The Pumapunku section, 1 km south of the main complex may have been a port, as the waters of the lake used to be much higher than they are today. The raised field system is once again being used in parts of the Titicaca area.

One of the main structures is the **Kalasasaya**, meaning 'standing stones', referring to the statues found in that part: two of them, the Ponce monolith (centre of inner patio) and the Fraile monolith (southwest corner), have been re-erected. In the northwest corner is the Puerta del Sol, originally at Pumapunku. Its carvings, interrupted by being out of context, are thought to be either a depiction of the creator god, or a calendar. The motifs are exactly the same as those around the Ponce monolith. The **Templo Semisubterráneo** is a sunken temple whose walls are lined with faces, all different, according to some theories depicting states of health, the temple being a house of healing; another theory is that the faces display all the ethnicities of the world. The **Akapana**, originally a pyramid (said to have been the second largest in the world, covering over 28,000 sq m), still has some ruins on it. Plastering of the Akapana's walls was halted in 2009 when UNESCO, among others, declared it inappropriate. At **Pumapunku**, some of whose blocks weigh between 100 and 150 tonnes, a natural disaster may have put a sudden end to the construction before it was finished. There is a small **Museo Lítico** at the ticket office, with several large stone pieces and, at the site, the **Museo Regional Arqueológico**, containing a well-illustrated explanation of the raised field system of agriculture. Many other artefacts are in the **Museo Nacional de Arqueología** in La Paz.

Written guide material is difficult to come by; hiring a guide costs US$20 for two hours, some speak English but don't be bullied into taking one if you prefer to go on your own. Locals sell copies of Tiwanaku figures; cheaper here than in La Paz.

Nearby **Tiwanaku village**, with several basic hotels and eateries, still has remnants from the time of independence and the 16th-century church used pre-Columbian masonry. In fact, Tiwanaku for a long while was the 'quarry' for the altiplano. For the **Willkakuti**, winter solstice festival on 21 June, there is an all-night vigil and colourful dances. There is also a colourful local festival on the Sunday after Carnaval.

By road to Chile

The main route to Chile is via Tambo Quemado (see page 343), but an alternative route, on which there are no trucks, is to go by good road direct from La Paz via Viacha to **Santiago de Machaco** (130 km, petrol); then 120 km on a very bad road to the border at **Charaña** (basic **Alojamiento Aranda**; immigration behind railway station). From Visviri, on the Chilean side of the frontier (no services), a regular road runs to Putre. A motorized railway car also runs from Viacha to Charaña on Monday and Thursday at 0800 (four hours, US$4.30), returning Tuesday and Friday at 1200. There is no train service on the Chilean side.

Trekking and climbing near La Paz

Three so-called 'Inca Trails' link the Altiplano with the Yungas, taking you from the high Andes to the sub-tropics, with dramatic changes in weather, temperature and vegetation. Each has excellent sections of stonework and they vary in difficulty from relatively straightforward to quite hard-going. In the rainy season going can be particularly tough. ▸▸ *For details of how to reach the starting point of each trail, see Transport sections on page 325.*

Takesi Trail Start at **Ventilla** (see below), walk up the valley for about three hours passing the village of Choquekhota until the track crosses the river and to the right of the road, there is a falling-down brick wall with a map painted on it. The Takesi and Alto Takesi trails start here, following the path to the right of the wall. The road continues to Mina San Francisco. In the first hour's climb from the wall is excellent stone paving which is Inca or pre-Inca, depending on who you believe, either side of the pass at 4630 m. There are camping possibilities at Estancia Takesi and in the village of Kakapi you can sleep at the simple **Kakapi Tourist Lodge**, 10 beds with good mattresses, solar shower and toilet. It is run by the local community and sponsored by Fundación Pueblo. It is also possible to camp. You also have to pass the unpleasant mining settlement of Chojlla, between which and Yanakachi is a gate where it is necessary to register and often pay a small 'fee'. Yanakachi has a number of good places to stay, several good hikes and an orphanage you can help at. The Fundación Pueblo office on the plaza has information. Buy a minibus ticket on arrival in Yanakachi or walk 45 minutes down to the La Paz–Chulumani road for transport. The trek can be done in one long day, especially if you organize a jeep to the start of the trail, but is more relaxing in two or three. If you take it slowly, though, you'll have to carry camping kit. Hire mules in Choquekhota for US$10 per day plus up to US$10 for the muleteer. A two- to three-day alternative is from Mina San Francisco to El Castillo and the village of Chaco on the La Paz–Chulumani road. This trek is called La Reconquistada and has the distinction of including a 200-m disused mining tunnel.

Choro Trail (La Cumbre to Coroico) Immediately before the road drops down from La Cumbre to start the descent to Las Yungas, there is a good dirt road leading up to the *apacheta* (narrow pass) where the trail starts properly. Cloud and bad weather are normal at La Cumbre (4660 m): you have to sign in at the Guardaparque post on the way to the pass. The trail passes Samaña Pampa (small shop, sign in again, camping US$0.60), Chucura (pay US$1.50 fee, another shop, camping), Challapampa (camping possible, US$1.20, small shop), the Choro bridge and the Río Jacun-Manini (fill up with water at both river crossings). At Sandillani is a lodge (**$$-$**). There is good paving down to Villa Esmeralda, after which is Chairo (lodging and camping), then to Yolosa. It takes three days to trek from La Cumbre to Chairo, from where you can take a truck to Puente Yolosita, the turn-off for Cocoico on the new road. From Puente Yolosita trucks run uphill to Coroico when they fill, US$0.80, 15 minutes. The Choro Trail has a reputation for unfriendliness and occasional robbery, take care.

Huayna Potosí Huayna Potosí (6088 m) is normally climbed in two days, with one night in a basic shelter at 5300 m or camped on a glacier at 5600 m. Acclimatization and experience on ice are essential, and the mountain is dangerous out of season. There are four shelters: a community-run shelter 10 minutes up from the pass, one by the lake, very cold; **Refugio Huayna Potosí** at 4780 m, with toilets and shower, run by the tour operator of the same name, and a basic shelter at 5300 m owned by the same operator. Average cost is US$120 per person for two-day tour for three people (US$200 for one) including all equipment except sleeping bag. The starting point for the normal route is at Zongo. A three-day trek in the area is also offered. See Climbing, hiking and trekking, page 320, for tour operators.

◉ La Paz and around listings

For hotel and restaurant price codes, and other relevant information, see pages 14-17.

● Where to stay

El Alto *p304*
$$ Alexander Palace, Av Jorge Carrasco 61 y C 3, Ceja, Zona 12 de Octubre, T282 3376, www.bit.ly/alexanderpalacehotel. Modern, with breakfast, **$** pp in dorm, parking, disco.
$ Orquídea, C Dos 22 y Av 6 de Marzo, Villa Bolívar A, near bus terminals, T282 6487. Comfortable heated rooms, cheaper with shared bath, electric showers, good value. Better than others in the area.

Around Plaza Murillo *p305, maps p306 and p308*
$$$ Gloria, Potosí 909, T240 7070, www.hotelgloria.com.bo. Modern, central, includes buffet breakfast, 2 restaurants (1 is vegetarian), good food and service, runs **Gloria Tours** (www.gloria tours.com.bo) and also owns **Gloria Urmiri** resort, 2 hrs from La Paz. Recommended.
$$$ Presidente, Potosí 920 y Sanjines, T240 6666, www.hotelpresidente-bo.com. The 'highest 5-star in the world'. Excellent service, comfortable, heating, good food, gym and sauna, pool, all open to non-

residents, bar. See also **Urban Rush**, under What to do, below.
$$-$ Hostal República, Comercio 1455, T220 2742, www.hostalrepublica.com. Old house of former president, more expensive in apartment, with and without bath, hot water, good café, quiet garden, book ahead and ask for room on upper floor.
$ Adventure Brew Bed & Breakfast, Av Montes 533, T246 1614, www.the adventurebrewbedandbreakfast.com. Mostly private rooms with bath, cheaper in dorms for 8, includes pancake breakfast, use of kitchen, free beer from microbrewery every night, rooftop bar with great views and spa, nightly BBQs, good value, popular meeting place.
$ Adventure Brew Hostel, Av Montes 504, T291 5896, www.theadventurebrewhostel. com. More economical than B&B above, 8 to 12-bed dorms, with shared hot showers, includes pancake breakfast and a free beer every night, rooftop terrace with great views of the city and Illimani, basement bar, travel agency and bank, lively young crowd, convenient to the bus station, associated with **Gravity Bolivia** (see What to do).
$ Arthy's Guesthouse, Montes 693, T228 1439, http://arthyshouse.tripod.com. Shared bath, warm water, safe, helpful, popular with bikers, English spoken, 2400 curfew.

$ Bacoo, Calle Alto de la Alianza 693, T228 0679, www.bacoohostel.com. Some rooms with private bath, cheaper in dorm, jacuzzi, restaurant and bar, garden, ping-pong and pool, arrange tours.

$ Hosp Milenio, Yanacocha 860, T228 1263, hospedajemilenio@hotmail.com. Economical, shared bath, electric shower, basic, family house, homely and welcoming, popular, helpful owner, quiet, kitchen, breakfast extra, security boxes, great value.

$ Loki, Loayza 420, T211 9024 and Av América 120, esq Plaza Alonso de Mendoza, T245 7300, www.lokihostel.com. Members of a chain of popular party hostels. The Loayza location has a more subdued atmosphere with double rooms, more dorms at América, TV room, computer room, bar (meals available), tour operator.

$ Posada El Carretero, Catacora 1056, entre Yanacocha y Junín, T228 5271, elcarretero posada@gmail.com. Very economical single and double rooms (cheaper with shared bath), also dorms, hot showers, helpful staff, good atmosphere and value.

$ Tambo de Oro, Armentia 367, T228 1565. Near bus station, cheaper with shared bath, hot showers, good value if a bit run down, safe for luggage.

$ Torino, Socabaya 457, T240 6003, www.hoteltorino.com.bo. Ask for better rooms in new section, older ones are run-down, cheaper without bath. Old backpackers' haunt, free book exchange, cultural centre, travel agency, good service. Restaurant next door for breakfast and good-value lunch (Mon-Fri 1200-1500).

$ Wild Rover Backpackers Hostel, Comercio 1476, T211 6903, www.wildrover hostel.com. Party hostel in renovated colonial-style house with courtyard and high-ceilings, dorms with 6-10 beds and doubles with shared bath, bar, TV room, book exchange, meals available, helpful staff speak English.

Plaza San Francisco up to the cemetery district *p309, maps p306 and p308*

$$$ La Casona, Av Mcal Santa Cruz 938, T290 0505, www.lacasonahotelboutique. com. Boutique hotel in beautifully restored former San Francisco convent dating to 1860, nice rooms (those in front get street noise), suites have jacuzzi, includes buffet breakfast and some museum entry fees, heating, safe box, terrace and cupola with nice views, very good restaurant, new in 2012.

$$$ Rosario, Illampu 704, T245 1658, www. hotelrosario.com. Sauna, laundry, internet café (free for guests, great view), good restaurant with buffet breakfast, stores luggage, no smoking, very helpful staff. Highly recommended. **Turisbus** travel agency downstairs (see Tour operators, page 323), Cultural Interpretation Centre explains items for sale in nearby 'witches' market'.

$$ Estrella Andina, Illampu 716, T245 6421, juapame_2000@hotmail.com. Cheaper in low season, all rooms have a safe and are decorated individually, English spoken, family-run, comfortable, tidy, helpful, roof terrace, heaters, money exchange, very nice. Also owns **$ Cruz de los Andes**, Aroma 216, T245 1401, same style but shares premises with a car garage.

$$ Fuentes, Linares 888, T231 3966. Cheaper without bath, hot water, variety of rooms and prices, nice colonial style, comfortable, sauna, good value, family-run.

$$ Hostal Naira, Sagárnaga 161, T235 5645, www.hostalnaira.com. Hot water, comfortable but pricey, rooms around courtyard, some are dark, price includes good buffet breakfast in **Café Banais**, safety deposit boxes.

$$ La Posada de la Abuela Obdulia, C Linares 947, T233 2285, http://hostal abuelaposada.com. Very pleasant inn.

$$ Milton, Illampu 1126-1130, T236 8003, www.hotelmiltonbolivia.com. Hot water, psychedelic 1970s style wallpaper in many rooms, restaurant, laundry, excellent views from roof, popular.

$ Arcabucero, C Viluyo 307 y Linares, T231 3473, arcabucero-bolivia@hotmail.com. Price rises in high season, pleasant new rooms in converted colonial house, excellent value but check the beds, breakfast extra.

$ El Solario, Murillo 776, T236 7963. Central, shared bath medical services, taxi and travel agency, good value, gets crowded.

$ La Joya, Max Paredes 541, T245 3841, www.hotelajoya.com. Cheaper without bath, modern and comfy, lift, area unsafe at night but provides transfers.

$ Muzungu Hostel, Illampu 441, T2451640, muzunguhostel@hotmail.com. Rooms with 1-4 beds, with and without bath and cheaper rate for dorms, several common areas, good restaurant (closed Sun) and bar, breakfast and 1 drink per day included.

$ Onkel Inn 1886, Colombia 257, T249 0456, onkelinn@gmail.com. Hostel in a remodelled 19th-century house, rooms with and without bath, doubles, triples and bunks. Jacuzzi, laundry facilities, café and bar, HI affiliated. Also in Copacabana.

$ Sagárnaga, Sagárnaga 326, T235 0252, www.hotel-sagarnaga.com. Cheaper in plain rooms without TV, solar hot water, 2 ATMs, English spoken, *peña*, popular with tour groups, helpful owner.

The Prado, Sopocachi, Miraflores and Zona Sur *p310, map p306*

$$$$ Casa Grande, Av Ballivián 1000 y C 17, T279 5511, and C 16 8009, T277 4000, both in Calacoto, www.casa-grande. com.bo. Beautiful, top-quality apartments on Ballivian and hotel suites under a greenhouse dome on C16, buffet breakfast, pool and spa, airport transfers at night only, restaurants, very good service.

$$$$ Europa, Tiahuanacu 64, T231 5656, www.hoteleuropa.com.bo. Next to the Museo Nacional de Arqueología. Excellent facilities and plenty of frills, health club, several restaurants, parking. Recommended.

$$$$ Stannum, Av Arce 2631, Torre Multicine, p 12 , T214 8393, www.stannum hotels.com. Boutique hotel on the 12th floor of an office building with lovely views of Illimani and the city, above mall and cinema complex. Comfortable rooms with minimalist decor, includes breakfast, bathtub, heating, a/c, fridge, restaurant, bar, gym, spa, airport transfers, no smoking anywhere on the premisies, new in 2013.

$$$$-$$$ Radisson Plaza, Av Arce 2177, T244 1111, www.radisson.com/lapazbo. 5-star hotel with all facilities, includes breakfast, gym, pool and sauna, excellent buffet in restaurant (see Restaurants, below).

$$$ El Rey Palace, Av 20 de Octubre 1947, T241 8541, www.hotelreypalace.com. Large suites with heating, excellent restaurant, stylish.

$$$ Mitru La Paz, 6 de Agosto 2628, Edif Torre Girasoles, T243 2242, www. hotelmitrulapaz.com. Modern hotel on the 1st 3 floors of the highest building in La Paz (37 storeys). Includes breakfast and complimentary hot drinks, bright ample rooms most with bathtubs, heating, safe boxes, fridge, convenient location for Sopocachi dining, good value for its price category, new in 2013.

$$$-$$ La Loge, Pasaje Medinacelli 2234, Sopocachi, T242 3561, www.lacomedie-lapaz.com/es/loge. Above, and owned by, **La Comedie** restaurant, elegant apart-hotel rooms, a good option with all services.

$$ Sopocachi, T214 0933, www.casafusion. com.bo. Lovely hotel with modern comfortable rooms, includes buffet breakfast, heating, good value, new in 2013.

South of La Paz *p310*

$$ Allkamari, near Valle de las Animas, 30 mins from town on the road to Palca, T279 1742, www.casalunaspa.com. Reservations required, cabins for up to 8 in a lovely valley between the Palca and La Animas canyons, a place to relax and star-gaze, **$** pp in dorm, solar heating, jacuzzi included, meals on request, horse and bike rentals, massage, shamanic rituals, taxi from Calacoto US$7, bus No 42 from the cemetery to within 1 km.

$$ Oberland, Mallasa, El Agrario 3118, near main road, 12 km from La Paz centre, T274 5040, www.h-oberland.com. A Swiss-owned, chalet-style restaurant (excellent, not cheap) and hotel (also good) with older resort facilities, lovely gardens, spa, sauna, covered pool (open to public – US$2 – very hot water), volleyball, tennis. Permit camping with vehicle, US$4 pp. Recommended.

$$-$ Colibrí Camping, C 4, Jupapina, near Mallasa, 30 mins from La Paz, T7629 5658, www.colibricamping.com. Cabins, teepee, tents and sleeping bags for hire or set up your own tent for US$7 pp, nice views, details about transport in their website.

🍴 Restaurants

Around Plaza Murillo *p305, maps p306 and p308*

$$ La Kantuta, in Hotel Presidente, Potosí 920, T240 6666. Excellent food, good service. La Bella Vista on the top floor is fancier.

Cafés
Alexander Coffee, Potosí 1091. Part of a chain, sandwiches, salads, coffee, pastries.
Café Soho, Jaén 747. Mon-Sun 0930-2300. Cosy café with small courtyard, inside and outside seating, local artwork.

Plaza San Francisco up to the cemetery district *p309, maps p306 and p308*

$$$-$$ Steakhouse, Tarija 243B, T231 0750, www.4cornerslapaz.com. Daily 1500-2300. Good cuts of meat, large variety of sauces and a great salad bar in a modern environment.
$$ La Cueva, Tarija 210B, T231 4523, www.4cornerslapaz.com. Daily 1130-late. Small cosy Mexican restaurant, quick service, wide selection of tequilas.
$$ Pizzería Italia, Illampu 840, T246 3152, and 809, 2nd floor, T245 0714. Thin-crust pizza, and pasta.
$$-$ A Lo Cubano, Sagárnaga 357, entre Linares y Illampu, T245 1797. Mon-Sat 1200-

2200. *Almuerzo* for US$3.65, but it runs out fast, also other choices of good Cuban food, good value.
$$-$ Angelo Colonial, Linares 922, T215 9633. Open early for breakfast. Vegetarian options, good music, internet, can get busy with slow service. Has a *hostal* at Av Santa Cruz 1058.
$$-$ Colonial Pot, Linares 906 y Sagárnaga. Bolivian dishes and a variety of main courses including vegetarian, set meal US$4.35 and à-la-carte, pastries, snacks, hot and cold drinks, quiet, homely, music, exceptional value.
$$-$ Sol y Luna, Murillo 999 y Cochabamba, T211 5323, www.solyluna-lapaz.com. Mon-Fri 0900-0100, Sat-Sun 1700-0100. Dutch run, breakfast, *almuerzo* and international menu, coffees and teas, full wine and cocktail list, live music Mon and Thu, movies, Wi-Fi, guide books for sale, book exchange, salsa lessons.
$$-$ Star of India, Cochabamba 170, T211 4409. British-run Indian curry house, will deliver, including to hotels.
$$-$ Tambo Colonial, in Hotel Rosario (see above). Excellent local and international cuisine, good salad bar, buffet breakfast, peña at weekend.
$ 100% Natural, Sagárnaga 345. Range of healthy, tasty fast foods ranging from salads to burgers and llama meat, good breakfasts.

Cafés
Banais, Sagárnaga 161, same entrance as Hostal Naira. Coffee, sandwiches and juices, buffet breakfast, set lunch, laid-back music and computer room.
Café del Mundo, Sagárnaga 324, www.cafe-delmundo.com. Swedish-owned, breakfasts, pancakes, waffles, sandwiches, coffees, teas and chocolate.
Café Illampu, Linares 940, upstairs. Mon-Sat 0800-2000, Sun 0930-1700. La Paz branch of the Swiss-run Sorata café known for its sandwiches, bread and cakes. Also salads, llama sausages, and European specialities like *roesti* and *spaetzle*. Recommended.
Pepe's, Pasaje Jiménez 894, off Linares. All-day breakfasts, sandwiches, omelettes,

tables outside, cards and dominoes, magazines and guidebooks.

The Prado, Sopocachi, Miraflores and Zona Sur *p310, map p306*

$$$ Chalet la Suisse, Av Muñoz Reyes 1710, Cota Cota, T279 3160, www. chaletlasuisse.com. Open 1900-2400, booking is essential on Fri. Serves excellent fondue, steaks.

$$$ Gustu, C 10 No 300, Calacoto, T211 7491, www.restaurantgustu.com. Upmarket restaurant with remarkable food and cookery school. Part of the Nordic cuisine pioneers, aimed at stimulating Bolivian gastronomy and giving opportunities to vulnerable people through the MeltingPot Foundation, www.meltingpot-bolivia.org.

$$$-$$ La Comedie, Pasaje Medinacelli 2234, Sopocachi, T242 3561. Mon-Fri 1200-1500, 1900-2300, Sat-Sun from 1900. 'Art café restaurant', contemporary, French menu, good salads, wine list and cocktails. See also La Loge under Where to stay.

$$ Beatrice, Guachalla y Ecuador, opposite Sopocachi market. Open 1200-2200, closed Tue. Excellent home-made pasta, good value and very popular with locals.

$$ El Consulado, Bravo 299 (by Hotel Europa), T211 7706. Open 0900-2000. Serves lunch and coffee and drinks in the evening. In gorgeous setting with outdoor seating and covered terrace, includes high-end handicraft store, book exchange, Wi-Fi, photo gallery, organic coffee and food, pricey but worth it.

$$ Maphrao On, Hnos Manchego 2586, near Plaza Isabela la Católica, T243 4682. Open 1200-1400, 1900-2400. Thai and Southeast Asian food, warm atmosphere, good music.

$$ Reineke Fuchs, Pje Jáuregui 2241, Sopocachi, T244 2979, and Av Montenegro y C 18, San Miguel, T277 2103, www.reineke fuchs.com. Mon-Fri 1200-1430 and from 1900, Sat from 1900 only. German-style bar/ restaurant, many imported German beers, also set lunch from US$5.

$$ Suma Uru, Av Arce 2177 in Radisson Plaza Hotel, T244 1111. *Almuerzo* Mon-Fri for US$8 and excellent buffet, in 5-star setting on Sun 1200-1500, US$11.60. Friendly to backpackers.

$$-$ Ken-Chan, Bat Colorado 98 y F Suazo, p 2 of Japanese Cultural Center, T244 2292. Open 1800-2300. Japanese restaurant with wide variety of dishes, popular.

$$-$ Mongo's, Hnos Manchego 2444, near Plaza Isabela la Católica, T244 0714. Open 1830-0300, live music Tue, club after midnight. Excellent Mexican fare and steaks, open fires, bar (cocktails can be pricey), popular with gringos and locals.

$$-$ Rendezvous, Sargento Carranza 461, end of Sánchez Lima, Sopocachi, T291 2459. Mon-Sat 1900-2200. Mediterranean cuisine, excellent variety and quality, best to book as usually full. Also has a very nice small hotel above the restaurant.

$$-$ Sancho Panza, Av Ecuador 738 y Gutiérrez, T242 6490, Sopocachi. Tue-Sat 1200-1500, 1900-2300, Sun 1200-1500. Mediterranean and Spanish tapas, also good-value set lunches.

$$-$ Vienna, Federico Zuazo 1905, T244 1660, www.restaurantvienna.com. Mon-Fri 1200-1400, 1830-2200, Sun 1200-1430. Excellent German, Austrian and local food, great atmosphere and service, live piano music, popular.

$ Armonía, Av Ecuador 2286, above bookstore. Mon-Sat 1230-1400. Nice varied vegetarian buffet with organic produce from proprietors' farm. Recommended.

$ Como en Casa, Av del Ejercito 1115, on the road through the Parque Urbano towards Miraflores. Open 1100-1500. Good value set meals, meat and vegetable options, good service and atmosphere.

$ Olive Tree, Campos 334, Edificio Iturri, T243 1552. Mon-Fri 1100-2200, Sat 1100-1500. Good salads, soups and sandwiches, attentive service.

Cafés

Alexander Coffee (Café Alex), Av 16 de Julio 1832, also at 20 de Octubre 2463 Plaza Avaroa, Av Montenegro 1336, Calacoto, and the airport. Open 0730-2400. Excellent coffee, smoothies, muffins, cakes and good salads and sandwiches, Wi-Fi.

Arco Iris, F Guachalla 554 y Sánchez Lima, Sopocachi. Also in Achumani, C 16 by the market. Bakery and handicraft outlet of Fundación Arco Iris (www.arcoirisbolivia.org), which works with street children, good variety of breads, pastries, meats and cheeses.

Fridolín, Av 6 de Agosto 2415; and Prolongación Montenegro, San Miguel. Daily 0800-2200. *Empanadas*, *tamales*, savoury and sweet (Austrian) pastries, coffee, breakfast, Wi-Fi.

Kuchen Stube, Rosendo Gutiérrez 461, Sopocachi. Mon-Fri 0800-2000, Sat-Sun 0800-1900. Excellent cakes, coffee and German specialities, also *almuerzo* Mon-Fri.

La Terraza, 16 de Julio 1615, 0630-0030; 20 de Octubre 2171 y Gutiérrez; and Av Montenegro 1576 y C 8, Calacoto, both 0730-2400. Excellent sandwiches and coffee, pancakes, breakfasts, Wi-Fi.

into nightclub around 2400, popular with locals and tourists, especially on Sun.

Oliver's English Tavern, Murillo y Cochabamba. Fake English pub serving breakfast from 0600, curries, sandwiches, fish and chips, pasta, sports channels, music, dress up parties and more. Pub crawl tours (see What to do, below) start here.

The Prado, Sopocachi, Miraflores and Zona Sur *p310, map p306*

Equinoccio, Sánchez Lima 2191, Sopocachi. Thu-Sat, cover charge US$2.10, or more for popular bands. Top venue for live rock music and bar.

Glam, Sánchez Lima 2237, next to Ferroviaria Andina. Thu-Sat from 2100. Good place to go dancing, live salsa on Fri.

Hallwrights, Sánchez Lima 2235, next to Glam. Mon-Sat 1700-2400. The only wine bar in La Paz.

Tetekos, C México 1553. Loud music, cheap drinks, popular with locals and backpackers.

Thelonius Jazz Bar, 20 de Octubre 2172, Sopocachi, T242 4405. Wed-Sat shows start at 2200. Renowned for jazz, cover charge US$3-5.

🍷 Bars and clubs

The epicentre for nightlife in La Paz is currently Plaza Avaroa in Sopocachi. Clubs are clustered around here and crowds gather Fri and Sat nights.

Around Plaza Murillo *p305, maps p306 and p308*

Etno Café, Jaén 722, T228 0343. Mon-Sat 1930-0300. Small café/bar with cultural programmes including readings, concerts, movies, popular, serves artisanal and fair trade drinks (alcoholic or not).

San Francisco up to the cemetery district *p309, maps p306 and p308*

Hard Rock Café, Santa Cruz 399 e Illampu, T211 9318, www.hardrockcafebolivia. lobopages.com. Serves Hard Rock fair, turns

🎭 Entertainment

For current information on cinemas and shows, check *La Prensa* or *La Razón* on Fri, or visit www.laprensa.com.bo or www.la-razon.com. Also look for *Bolivian Express* (in English) and *Mañana*, both free monthly magazines with listings of concerts, exhibits, festivals, etc.

Around Plaza Murillo *p305, maps p306 and p308*

Bocaisapo, Indaburo 654 y Jaén. Thu-Fri 1900-0300. Live music in a bar; no cover charge, popular.

Marka Tambo, Jaén 710, T228 0041. Thu-Sat 2100-0200, also Mon-Sat 1230-1500 for lunch. US$6 for evening show, food and drinks extra, live shows with traditional dancing and music (*peña*), touristy but recommended.

Plaza San Francisco up to the cemetery district *p309, maps p306 and p308*

Peña Parnaso, Sagárnaga 189, T231 6827. Daily starting at 2030, meals available, purely for tourists but a good way to see local costumes and dancing.

Cinemas Films mainly in English with Spanish subtitles cost around US$3.50-4. See www.cinecenter.com.bo, http://megacenter.irpavi.com and www.multicine.com.bo; the latter has the most comfortable halls. **Cinemateca Boliviana**, Oscar Soria (prolong Federico Zuazo) y Rosendo Gutiérrez, T244 4090, www.cinematecaboliviana.org. Municipal theatre with emphasis on independent productions.

Theatre Teatro Municipal Alberto Saavedra Pérez has a regular schedule of plays, opera, ballet and classical concerts, at Sanjinés e Indaburo, T240 6183. The National Symphony Orchestra is very good and gives inexpensive concerts. Next door is the **Teatro Municipal de Cámara**, which shows dance, drama, music and poetry. **Casa Municipal de la Cultura 'Franz Tamayo'**, almost opposite Plaza San Francisco, hosts a variety of exhibitions, paintings, sculpture, photography, etc, mostly free. Free monthly guide to cultural events at information desk at entrance. The **Palacio Chico**, Ayacucho y Potosí, in old Correo, operated by the Secretaría Nacional de Cultura, also has free exhibitions (good for modern art), concerts and ballet, Mon-Fri 0900-1230, 1500-1900.

✦ Festivals

La Paz *p304, maps p306 and p308*
Starting **24 Jan** Alasitas, in Parque Central up from Av del Ejército, also in Plaza Sucre/San Pedro, recommended. Carnaval in **Feb** or **Mar. End May/early Jun** Festividad del Señor del Gran Poder, the most important festival of the year, with a huge procession of costumed and masked dancers on the 3rd Sat after Trinity. **Jul** Fiestas de Julio, a month of concerts and performances

at the Teatro Municipal, with a variety of music, including the University Folkloric Festival. **8 Dec**, festival around Plaza España, colourful and noisy. On **New Year's Eve** there are fireworks displays; view from higher up. See page 18 for national holidays and festivals outside La Paz.

✦ Shopping

La Paz *p304, maps p306 and p308*
Camping equipment Kerosene for pressure stoves is available from a pump in Plaza Alexander, Pando e Inca. **Ayni Sport Bolivia**, Jiménez 806, open Mon-Sun 1030-2100. Rents and sometimes sells camping equipment and mountain gear (trekking shoes, fleeces, climbing equipment etc). **Caza y Pesca**, Edif Handal Center, No 9, Av Mcal Santa Cruz y Socabaya, T240 9209. English spoken. **The Spitting Llama**, Linares 947 (inside Hostal La Posada de la Abuela), T7039 8720, www.thespittingllama.com. Sell camping gear including GPS units, used books, guidebooks, issue ISIC cards, English spoken, helpful; branches in Cochabamba and Copacabana. **Tatoo Bolivia**, Illampu 828, T245 1265, www.tatoo.ws. Tatoo clothing plus outdoor equipment including backpacks, shoes, etc. English and Dutch spoken. For camping stove fuel enquire at **Emita Tours** on Sagárnaga.

Handicrafts Above Plaza San Francisco (see page 309), up Sagárnaga, by the side of San Francisco church (behind which are many handicraft stalls in the Mercado Artesanal), are booths and small stores with interesting local items of all sorts. The lower end of Sagárnaga is best for antiques. **Galería Dorian**, Sagárnaga 177, is an entire gallery of handicraft shops; includes **Tejidos Wari**, unit 12, for high-quality alpaca goods, will make to measure, English spoken. On Linares, between Sagárnaga and Santa Cruz, high-quality alpaca goods are priced in US$. Also in this area are many places making fleece jackets, gloves and hats, but shop around for value and service. **Alpaca**

Style, C 22 No 14, T271 1233, Achumani. Upmarket shop selling alpaca and leather clothing. **Arte y Diseño**, Illampu 833. Makes typical clothing to your own specifications in 24 hrs. **Artesanía Sorata**, Linares 900, T245 4728, and Sagárnaga 363. Specializes in dolls, sweaters and weavings. **Ayni**, Illampu 704, www.aynibolivia.com. Fair trade shop in Hotel Rosario, featuring Aymara work. **Comart Tukuypaj**, Linares 958, T231 2686, and C 21, Galería Centro de Moda, Local 4B, San Miguel, www.comart-tukuypaj. com. High-quality textiles from an artisan community association. **Incapallay**, Linares 958, p 2, www.incapallay.org. A weavers' cooperative from Tarabuco and Jalq'a communities, near Sucre. **Jiwitaki Art Shop**, Jaén 705, T7725 4042. Run by local artists selling sketches, paintings, sculptures, literature, etc. Open Mon-Fri 1100-1300, 1500-1800. **LAM** shops on Sagárnaga. Good quality alpaca goods. **Millma**, Sagárnaga 225, T231 1338, and Claudio Aliaga 1202, Bloque L-1, San Miguel, closed Sat afternoon and Sun. High-quality alpaca knitwear and woven items and, in the San Miguel shop, a permanent exhibition of ceremonial 19th and 20th century Aymara and Quechua textiles (free). **Mother Earth**, Linares 870, T239 1911. 0930-1930 daily. High-quality alpaca sweaters with natural dyes. **Toshy** on Sagárnaga. Top-quality knitwear.

Jewellery Good jewellery stores with native and modern designs include **King's**, Loayza 261, between Camacho and Mercado also at Torre Ketal, C 15, Calacoto and **Mi Joyita**, Av Mariscal Santa Cruz 1351, El Prado.

Maps IGM: head office at Estado Mayor, Av Saavedra 2303, Miraflores, T214 9484, Mon-Thu 0900-1200, 1500-1800, Fri 0900-1200, take passport to buy maps. Also office in Edif Murillo, Final Rodríguez y Juan XXIII, T237 0116, Mon-Fri 0830-1230, 1430-1830, some stock or will get maps from HQ in 24 hrs. **Librería IMAS**, Av Mcal Santa Cruz entre Loayza y Colón, Edif Colón, T235 8234. Ask to see the map collection. Maps are also sold in the Post Office on the stalls opposite the Poste Restante counter.

Markets In addition to those mentioned in the Plaza San Francisco section (page 309), the 5-km sq **Feria 16 de Julio, El Alto** market is on Thu and Sun (the latter is bigger). Take any minibus that says La Ceja and get off at overpass after toll booth (follow crowd of people or tell driver you're going to La Feria), or take 16 de Julio minibus from Plaza Eguino. Arrive around 0900; most good items are sold by 1200. Goods are cheap, especially on Thu. Absolutely everything imaginable is sold here. Be watchful for pickpockets, just take a bin liner to carry your purchases. **Mercado Sopocachi**, Guachalla y Ecuador, a well-stocked covered market selling foodstuffs, kitchen supplies, etc.

Musical instruments Many shops on Pasaje Linares, the stairs off C Linares, also on Sagárnaga/Linares, for example **Walata 855**.

☼ What to do

La Paz *p304, maps p306 and p308*
City tours
The **Teleférico** promises a spectacular overview of La Paz (see Transport). **Sightseeing**, T279 1440, city tours on a double-decker bus, 2 circuits, downtown and Zona Sur with Valle de la Luna (1 morning and 1 afternoon departure to each), departs from Plaza Isabel la Católica and can hop on at Plaza San Francisco, tour recorded in 7 languages, US$9 for both circuits, Mon-Fri at 0830 and 1430, Sat-Sun at 0900 and 1430. Free walking tours of La Paz are given by Red C&P, www.redcapwalkingtours.com, 1100 and 1400 every day from Plaza San Pedro, 2½ hrs; they also offer pub crawl and local food tours. See also **La Paz On Foot** tour operator, below.

Climbing, hiking and trekking
Guides must be hired through a tour company. There is a mountain rescue group, **Socorro Andino Boliviano**, Calle 40 Villa Aérea, T246 5879.

Andean Summits, Muñoz Cornejo 1009 y Sotomayor, Sopocachi, T242 2106, www.andeansummits.com. For mountaineering and other trips off the beaten track, contact in advance.

Bolivian Mountains, Rigoberto Paredes 1401 y Colombia, p 3, San Pedro, T249 2775, www.bolivianmountains.com (in UK T01273-746545). High-quality mountaineering with experienced guides and good equipment, not cheap.

Climb On. Brand new outfit (ask at **Gravity** or **Kanoo** – see below) offering all-inclusive tours, ½ day or longer, routes for beginners and experts.

Climbing South America, Murillo 1014 y Rodríguez, Ed Provenzal PB, of 1, T215 2232, www.climbingsouthamerica.com. Climbing and trekking in Bolivia, Argentian and Chile, equipment rental, Australian run.

Refugio Huayna Potosí, Sagárnaga 308 e Illampu, T245 6717, www.huayna-potosi.com. Climbing and trekking tours, run 2 mountain shelters on Huayna Potosí and climbing school.

Football

Popular and played on Wed and Sun at the **Siles Stadium** in Miraflores (Micro A), which is shared by both La Paz's main teams, Bolívar and The Strongest. There are reserved seats.

Golf

Mallasilla is the world's highest golf course, at 3318 m. Non-members can play here on weekdays, US$85.

Tour operators

America Tours, Av 16 de Julio 1490 (El Prado), Edificio Avenida pb, No 9, T237 4204, www.america-ecotours.com. Cultural and ecotourism trips to many parts of the country, rafting, trekking and horse riding, English spoken. Highly professional and recommended.

Andean Base Camp, Illampu 863, T246 3782. Overland tours throughout Bolivia, Swiss staff, good reports.

Andean Secrets, General Gonzales 1314 y Almirante Grau, San Pedro (Mon-Fri 1500-1900, Sat 0900-1730, Sun 1000-1400), T7729 4590, quimsacruz_bolivia@hotmail.com, www.andean-secrets.com. Female mountain guide Denys Sanjines specializes in the Cordillera Quimsa Cruz.

Barracuda Biking Company, Illampu 750, inside **Hostal Gloria**, of 4, T245 9950, info@barracudabiking.com. Bike trips to Coroico at a lower price than the upmarket companies.

Bolivian Journeys, Sagárnaga 363, p 2, T235 7848, www.bolivianjourneys.org. Camping, mountain bike tours, equipment rental, maps, English and French spoken, helpful.

Crillon Tours, Camacho 1223, T233 7533, www.titicaca.com. A company with over 50 years' experience. Joint scheduled tours with Lima arranged. Fixed departures and luxury camper service to Salar de Uyuni (www.uyuni.travel), trips throughout Bolivia, including the Yungas, Sajama and Lauca, community and adventure tourism and much more. ATM for cash. Recommended. Full details of their Lake Titicaca services on page 334. See www.alwa.travel for their deluxe overlanding scheme.

Deep Rainforest, Galería Dorian, Sagárnaga 189, of 9A, T215 0385, www.deep-rainforest.com. Off the beaten track trekking, climbing, canoe trips from Guanay to Rurrenabaque, rainforest and pampas trips.

Enjoy Bolivia, Plaza Isabel La Católica, Edif Presidente Bush, of 2, T243 5162, www.njboltravel.com. Wide selection of tours and transport service. Airport and bus terminal transfers, van service to Oruro (US$13 pp shared, US$90 private).

Fremen Tours, Av 20 de Octubre 2396, Edif María Haydee, p 10, T242 1258, www.andes-amazonia.com. Customized tours and special interest travel throughout Bolivia, including **Tayka** hotels around Salar de Uyuni and Reina de Enín riverboat.

Gloria Tours, Potosí 909, T240 7070, www.gloriatours.com.bo. Good service. See **Hotel Gloria**, page 313.

Gravity Bolivia, Av 16 de Julio 1490 (El Prado), Edif Avenida, ground floor, of 10, T231 3849, www.gravitybolivia.com. A wide variety of mountain biking tours throughout Bolivia, including the world-famous downhill ride to Coroico. They offer a zipline at the end of the ride, or independently (www.ziplinebolivia.com). Also bike rides more challenging than Coroico, including single-track and high-speed dirt roads, with coaching and safety equipment. Also have cycle spares, very knowledgeable service. Book on website in advance or by phone until 2200, T7721 9634. Recommended.

Kanoo Tours, Illampu 832 entre Sagárnaga y Santa Cruz, T246 0003, www.kanootours.com. Also at **Adventure Brew Hostel**. Sells **Gravity Bolivia** tours (see above), plus Salar de Uyuni, Rurrenabaque jungle trips and Perú.

La Paz On Foot, Prol Posnanski 400, Miraflores, T224 8350/7154 3918, www.lapazonfoot.com; new shop and information centre at Indaburo 710 esq C Jaeno. Walking city tours, walking and sailing trips on Titicaca, tours to Salar de Uyuni, multi-day treks in the Yungas and Apolobamba and regional tours focused on Andean food and biodiversity which also include Peru, northern Chile and Argentina. Recommended.

Lipiko Tours, Av Mariscal Santa Cruz 918 y Sagárnaga, Galeria La República, T214 5129, www.travel-bolivia.co.uk. Tailor-made tours for all budgets, 4WD tours, trekking, climbing and adventure sport, trips to

Amazon and national parks. Also runs trips to Peru.

Magri Turismo, Capitán Ravelo 2101, T244 2727, www.magriturismo.com. Recommended for tours throughout Bolivia, flight tickets. Own **La Estancia** hotel on the Isla del Sol.

Moto Andina, Urb La Colina N°6 Calle 25, Calacoto, T7129 9329, www.moto-andina.com (in French). Motorcycle tours of varying difficulty in Bolivia, contact Maurice Manco.

Mundo Quechua, Av Circunvalación 43, Achumani, Zona Sur, T279 6145, www.mundoquechua.com. Daily tours to the Cordillera Real, private transport in and around La Paz, custom made climbing, trekking and 4WD tours throughout Bolivia. Also extensions to Peru and Argentina. English and French spoken, good service.

Peru Bolivian Tours, Calle Capitán Ravelo 2097, esquina Montevideo, Edif Paola Daniela, 1st piso, oficina 1-A, T244 5732, www.perubolivian.com. More than 20 years' experience, arranges special programmes throughout Bolivia and Peru.

Topas Travel, Carlos Bravo 299 (behind Hotel Plaza), T211 1082, www.topas.bo. Joint venture of Akhamani Trek (Bolivia), Topas (Denmark) and the Danish embassy, offering trekking, overland truck trips, jungle trips and climbing, English spoken, restaurant and *pensión*.

Transturin, Av Arce 2678, Sopocachi, T242 2222, www.transturin.com. Full travel services with tours in La Paz and throughout

Bolivia. Details of their Lake Titicaca services on page 335.

Tupiza Tours, Villalobos 625 y Av Saavedra, Edif Girasoles, ground floor, Miraflores, T224 5254, www.tupizatours.com. La Paz office of the Tupiza agency. Specialize in the Salar and southwest Bolivia, but also offer tours around La Paz and throughout the country.

Turisbus, Av Illampu 704, T245 1341, www.turisbus.com. Lake Titicaca and Isla del Sol, Salar de Uyuni, Rurrenbaque, trekking and Bolivian tours. Also tours and tickets to Puno and Cuzco.

Turismo Balsa, Av 6 de Agosto 3 y Pinilla, T244 0620, www.turismobalsa.com. City and tours throughout Bolivia. Owns **Hotel Las Balsas**, in beautiful lakeside setting at Puerto Pérez on Lake Titicaca, T02-289 5147, 72 km from La Paz, with excellent restaurant.

Urban Rush, T240 6666, www.urbanrush bolivia.com. Go to **Hotel Presidente** 1300-1700 for abseiling or rap jumping from one of the tallest buildings in La Paz, gaining popularity quickly.

⊖ Transport

La Paz *p304, maps p306 and p308*
Air
La Paz has the highest commercial **airport** in the world, at El Alto (4061 m); T281 0240. **Cotranstur** minibuses, T231 2032, white with 'Cotranstur' and 'Aeropuerto' written on the side and back, go from Plaza Isabel La Católica, stopping all along the Prado and Av Mcal Santa Cruz to the airport, 0615-2300, US$0.55 (allow about 1 hr), best to buy an extra seat for your luggage, departures every 4 mins. Shared transport from Plaza Isabel La Católica, US$3.50 pp, carrying 4 passengers, also private transfers from **Enjoy Bolivia**, see Tour operators, page 321. Radio-taxi is US$9 to centre, US$14 to Zona Sur. Prices are displayed at the airport terminal exit. There is an **Info Tur** office in arrivals with a *casa de cambio* next to it (dollars, euros cash and TCs, poor rates; open 0530-1300, 1700-0300,

closed Sun evening – when closed try the counter where departure taxes are paid). Several ATMs in the departures hall. The international and domestic departures hall is the main concourse, with all check-in desks. There are separate domestic and international arrivals. Bar/restaurant and café upstairs in departures. For details of air services, see under destinations.

Bus
City buses There are 3 types of city bus: the modern puma katari, introduced in Mar 2014, with 3 lines along different routes, mostly from El Alto through the centre to the Zona Sur, US$0.25-0.30 depending on route, additional lines will be added; *micros* (small, old buses), which charge US$0.20 a journey; and minibuses (small vans), US$0.20-0.35 depending on the journey. *Trufis* are fixed-route collective taxis, with a sign with their route on the windscreen, US$0.45 pp in the centre, US$0.55 outside.

Long distance For information, T228 5858. Buses to: **Oruro**, **Potosí**, **Sucre**, **Cochabamba**, **Santa Cruz**, **Tarija**, **Uyuni**, **Tupiza**, and **Villazón**, leave from the main terminal at Plaza Antofagasta (micros 2, M, CH or 130), see under each destination for details. Taxi to central hotels, US$1.40. The terminal (open 0400-2300) has a tourist booth by the main entrance, ATMs, internet, a post office, **Entel**, restaurant, luggage store and travel agencies. Touts find passengers the most convenient bus and are paid commission by the bus company. To **Oruro** van service with **Enjoy Bolivia**, see Tour operators, page 321, US$13 pp shared, US$90 private.

To **Copacabana**, several bus companies (tourist service) pick-up travellers at their hotels (in the centre) and also stop at the main terminal, tickets from booths at the terminal (cheaper) or agencies in town. They all leave about 0800 (**Titicaca Bolivia** also at 1400), 3½ hrs, US$3.60-4.50 one way, return from Copacabana about 1330. When there are not enough passengers for each company, they pool them. **Diana Tours**, T235 0252, **Titicaca Bolivia**, T246 2655, Turisbus, T245 1341 (more expensive), many others. You can also book this service all the way to Puno, US$7.

Public buses to **Copacabana**, **Tiwanaku**, **Desaguadero** (border with Peru) and **Sorata**, leave from the Cemetery district. To get there, take any bus or minibus marked 'Cementerio' going up C Santa Cruz (US$0.15-0.22). On Plaza Reyes Ortiz are **Manco Capac**, and **2 de Febrero** for **Copacabana** and **Tiquina**. From the Plaza go up Av Kollasuyo and at the 2nd street on the right (Manuel Bustillos) is the terminal for minibuses to **Achacachi**, **Huatajata** and **Huarina**, as well as **Trans Unificada** and **Flor del Illampu** minibuses for **Sorata**. Several micros (20, J, 10) and minibuses (223, 252, 270, 7) go up Kollasuyo. Taxi US$2 from downtown, US$4.30 from Zona Sur. Buses to **Coroico, the Yungas and northern jungle** leave from Terminal Minasa in Villa Fátima (25 mins by micros B, V, X, K, 131, 135, or 136, or *trufis* 2 or 9, which pass Pérez Velasco coming down from Plaza Mendoza, and get off at Minasa terminal, Puente Minasa). See Safety, page 305.

International buses From main bus terminal: to **Buenos Aires**, US$102, 2 a week with Ormeño, T228 1141, 54 hrs via Santa Cruz and Yacuiba; via Villazón with Río Paraguay, 3 a week, US$75, or **Trans Americano**, US$85. Alternatively, go to Villazón and change buses in Argentina. To **Arica** via the frontier at Tambo Quemado and Chungará, **Pullmanbus** at 0630 (good), **Cuevas** at 0700, **Zuleta** at 0600, **Nuevo Continente** at 1230 except Sat, **Litoral**, T228 1920, Sun-Thu 1230, US$26. Connecting service for Iquique or Santiago. To **Puno** and **Cuzco**, luxury and indirect services, see under Lake Titicaca, page 336. Direct to Cuzco, 12 hrs with **Litoral**, US$23 via Desaguadero and Puno (5 hrs, US$8). To **Lima**, Ormeño daily at 1430, US$90, 27 hrs; **Nuevo Continente** at 0830, US$88, 26 hrs, via Desaguadero, change to **Cial** in Puno.

Cable car

Teleférico A system of 3 lines of cable cars joining neighbourhoods along the edge of the altiplano, including El Alto, with the centre of the city and the Zona Sur, are under construction in 2014. The red line from La Ceja, El Alto, to the old train station, 3 blocks above Plaza Eguino, in an area known as Vita in the northwest of the city, was due to start operating in mid-2014.

Car hire

Imbex, C11, No 7896, Calacoto, T212 1012, www.imbex.com. Wide range of well-maintained vehicles; Suzuki jeeps from US$60 per day, including 200 km free for 4-person 4WD. Also office in Santa Cruz, T311001. Recommended. **Kolla Motors**, Rosendo Gutierrez 502 y Ecuador, Sopocachi, T241 9141, www.kollamotors.com. 6-seater 4WD Toyota jeeps, insurance and gasoline extra. **Petita Rent-a-car**, Valentín Abecia 2031, Sopocachi Alto, T242 0329, www.rentacarpetita.com. Swiss owners Ernesto Hug and Aldo Rezzonico. Recommended for personalized service and well-maintained 4WD jeeps, minimum rental 1 week. Their vehicles can also be taken outside Bolivia. Also offer adventure tours (German, French, English spoken). Ernesto has a highly recommended garage for VW and other makes, Av Jaimes Freyre 2326, T241 5264.

Taxi

Taxis are often, but not always, white. Taxi drivers are not tipped. There are 3 types: standard taxis which may take several passengers at once (US$0.45-1.75 for short trips within city limits), fake taxis which have been involved in robberies, and radio taxis which take only one group of passengers at a time. Since it is impossible to distinguish between the first two, it is best to pay a bit more for a radio taxi, especially at night. These have a dome light, a unique number (note this when getting in) and radio communication (eg **Gold**, T241 1414, in the centre, T272 2722 in Zona Sur, **Servisur**, T271

9999). They charge US$1.40-2.20 in centre, more to suburbs and at night.

Train

Ferroviaria Andina (FCA), Sánchez Lima 2199 y Fernando Guachalla, Sopocachi, T241 6545, www.fca.com.bo, Mon-Fri 0800-1600. Sells tickets for the **Oruro-Uyunui-Tupiza-Villazón** line; see schedule and fares under Oruro Transport (page 348). Tickets for *ejecutivo* class sold up to 2 weeks in advance, for *salón* 1 week. Must show passport to buy tickets. Also operate a **tourist train** from **El Alto** station, C 8, Villa Santiago I, by Cuartel Ingavi, the 2nd Sun of each month at 0800, to **Guaqui** via Tiwanaku; returning from Guaqui at 1500; US$4.35 *ejecutivo*, US$2.90 *popular*, confirm all details in advance.

South of La Paz *p310*

For Valle de la Luna, Minibuses 231, 273 and 902 can be caught on C México, the Prado or Av 6 de Agosto. Alternatively take Micro 11 ('Aranjuez' large, not small bus) or ones that say 'Mallasa' or 'Mallasilla' along the Prado or Av 6 de Agosto, US$0.65, and ask driver where to get off. Most of the travel agents organize tours to the Valle de la Luna. There are brief, 5-min stops for photos in a US$15 tour of La Paz and surroundings; taxis cost US$6, US$10 with a short wait.

Tiwanaku *p311*

To get to Tiwanaku, tours booked through agencies cost US$12 (not including entry fee or lunch). Otherwise take any **Micro** marked 'Cementerio' in La Paz, get out at Plaza Félix Reyes Ortiz, on Mariano Bautista (north side of cemetery), go north up Aliaga, 1 block east of Asín to find Tiwanaku micros, US$2, 1½ hrs, every 30 mins, 0600 to 1500. Tickets can be bought in advance. **Taxi** costs US$30-55 return (shop around), with 2 hrs at site. Some **buses** go on from Tiwanaku to Desaguadero; virtually all Desaguadero buses stop at the access road to Tiwanaku, 20-min walk from the site. Return buses (last back 1700) leave from south side of the Plaza in village. Minibuses (vans) to **Desaguadero**, from José María Asín y P Eyzaguirre (Cemetery district) US$2, 2 hrs, most movement on Tue and Fri when there is a market at the border. **Note** When returning from Tiwanaku (ruins or village) to La Paz, do not take an empty minibus. We have received reports of travellers being taken to El Alto and robbed at gun point. Wait for a public bus with paying passengers in it.

Takesi Trail *p312*

Take a **Líneas Ingavi** bus from C Gral Luis Lara esq Venacio Burgoa near Plaza Líbano, San Pedro, going to **Pariguaya** (2 hrs past Chuñavi), daily at 0800, US$3, 2 hrs. On Sun, also minibuses from C Gral Luis Lara y Boquerón, hourly 0700-1500. To **Mina San Francisco**: hire a **jeep** from La Paz; US$85, takes about 2 hrs. **Veloz del Norte** (T02-221 8279) leaves from Ocabaya 495 in Villa Fátima, T221 8279, 0900 daily, and 1400 Thu-Sun, US$3, 3½ hrs, continuing to Chojlla. From Chojlla to La Paz daily at 0500, 1300 also on Thu-Sun, passing **Yanakachi** 15 mins later.

Choro Trail *p312*

To the *apacheta* pass beyond **La Cumbre**, take a **taxi** from central La Paz for US$20, 45 mins, stopping to register at the Guardaparque hut. Buses from Villa Fátima to Coroico and Chulumani pass La Cumbre. Tell driver where you are going, US$2.80. The trail is signed.

Huayna Potosí *p313*

The mountain can be reached by transport arranged through tourist agencies (US$100) or the refugio, **taxi** US$45. **Minibus** Trans Zongo, Av Chacaltaya e Ingavi, Ballivián, El Alto, daily 0600, 2½ hrs, US$1.80 to Zongo, check on return time. Also minibuses from the Ballivián area that leave when full (few on Sun). If camping in the Zongo Pass area, stay at the site near the white house above the cross.

La Paz *p304, maps p306 and p308*
Embassies and consulates For all foreign embassies and consulates in La Paz, see http://embassy.goabroad.com.
Language schools Instituto Exclusivo, Av 20 de Octubre 2315, Edif Mechita, T242 1072, www.instituto-exclusivo. com. Spanish lessons for individual and groups, accredited by Ministry of Education. Instituto de La Lengua Española, María Teresa Tejada, C Aviador esq final 14, No 180, Achumani, T279 6074, T7155 6735. One-to-one lessons US$7 per hr. Recommended. Speak Easy Institute, Av Arce 2047, between Goitía and Montevideo, T244 1779, speakeasyinstitute@yahoo.com. US$6 for one-to-one private lessons, cheaper for groups and couples, Spanish and English taught. Private Spanish lessons from: Isabel Daza, Murillo 1046, p 3, T231 1471, T7062 8016. US$4 per hr. Enrique Eduardo Patzy, Méndez Arcos 1060, Sopocachi, T241 5501 or T776-22210, epatzy@hotmail. com. US$6 an hr one-to-one tuition, speaks English and Japanese. Recommended.
Medical services For hospitals, doctors and dentists, contact your consulate or the tourist office for recommendations.
Health and hygiene: Ministerio de Desarollo Humano, Secretaría Nacional de Salud, Av Arce, near Radisson Plaza, yellow fever shot and certificate, rabies and cholera shots, malaria pills, bring own syringe. Centro Piloto de Salva, Av Montes y Basces, T245 0026, 10 mins walk from Plaza San Francisco, for malaria pills, helpful. Laboratorios Illimani, Edif Alborada p 3, of 304, Loayza y Juan de la Riva, T231 7290, open 0900-1230, 1430-1700, fast, efficient, hygienic. Tampons may be bought at most *farmacias* and supermarkets. Daily papers list pharmacies on duty (de turno). For contact lenses, Optalis, Comercio 1089. **Useful addresses** Immigration: to renew a visa go to Migración Bolivia, Camacho 1468, T211 0960. Mon-Fri 0830-1230, 1430-1830, go early. Allow 48 hrs for visa extensions. Tourist Police: C Hugo Estrada 1354, Plaza Tejada Sorzano frente al estadio, Miraflores, next to Love City Chinese restaurant, T800-140081, 0900-1800, or in office hours T222 5016. Open 0830-1800, for police report for insurance claims after theft.

Lake Titicaca

Lake Titicaca is two lakes joined by the Straits of Tiquina: the larger, northern lake (Lago Mayor, or Chucuito) contains the Islas del Sol and de la Luna; the smaller lake (Lago Menor, or Huiñamarca) has several small islands. The waters are a beautiful blue, reflecting the hills and the distant cordillera in the shallows of Huiñamarca, mirroring the sky in the rarified air and changing colour when it is cloudy or raining. A boat trip on the lake is a must.

Arriving at Lake Titicaca
Getting there A paved road runs from La Paz to the southeastern shore of the lake. One branch continues north along the eastern shore, another branch goes to the Straits of Tiquina (114 km El Alto–San Pablo) and Copacabana. A third road goes to Guaqui and Desaguadero on the southwestern shore. ▸▸ *See also Transport, page 335.*

La Paz to Copacabana
Huatajata Along the northeast shore of the lake is Huatajata, with Yacht Club Boliviano and **Crillon Tours' International Hydroharbour** and **Inca Utama Hotel** (see below). Reed

boats are still built and occasionally sail here for the tourist trade. There are several small but interesting exhibits of reed boats that were used on long ocean voyages. Beyond here is **Chúa**, where there is fishing, sailing and **Transturin's** catamaran dock (see below).

Islands of Lake Huiñamarca

On **Suriqui** (one hour from Huatajata) in Lake Huiñamarca, a southeasterly extension of Lake Titicaca, you can see reed *artesanías*. The late Thor Heyerdahl's *Ra II*, which sailed from Morocco to Barbados in 1970, his *Tigris* reed boat, and the balloon gondola for the Nazca (Peru) flight experiment (see the Nazca Lines in the Peru chapter), were also constructed by the craftsmen of Suriqui. Reed boats are still made on Suriqui, probably the last place where the art survives. On **Kalahuta** there are *chullpas* (burial towers), old buildings and the uninhabited town of Kewaya. On **Pariti** there is Inca terracing and the **Museo Señor de los Patos**, with weavings and Tiwanku-era ceramics.

From Chúa the main road reaches the east side of the Straits at **San Pablo** (clean restaurant in blue building, toilets at both sides of the crossing). On the west side is San Pedro, the main Bolivian naval base, from where a paved road goes to Copacabana and the border. Vehicles are transported across on barges, US$5. Passengers cross separately, US$0.20 (not included in bus fares) and passports may be checked. Expect delays during rough weather, when it can get very cold.

Copacabana → *Phone code: 02. Colour map 3, B2. Population: 5515. Altitude: 3850 m.*
A popular little resort town on Lake Titicaca, 158 km from La Paz by paved road, Copacabana is set on a lovely bay and surrounded by scenic hills. **Municipal tourist office**

Copacabana

Where to stay	7 La Cúpula	Restaurants
1 Chasqui del Sol	8 Las Olas	1 Aransaya
2 Ecolodge	9 Leyenda	2 Café Bistrot Copacabana
3 Emperador	10 Pacha	3 La Orilla
4 Gloria Copacabana	11 Rosario del Lago	4 Puerta del Sol
5 Kantutas	12 Sonia	5 Snack 6 de Agosto
6 Kotha Kahuaña	13 Utama	6 Sujna Wasi

① 16 de Julio y 6 de Agosto, Wed-Sun 0800-1200, 1400-1800. There are two unreliable ATMs in town, best bring some cash.

Red de Turismo Comunitario *① 6 de Agosto y 16 de Julio, T7729 9088, Mon-Sat 0800-1230, 1300-1900,* can arrange tours to nearby communities. At major holidays (Holy Week, 3 May, and 6 August), the town fills with visitors.

Copacabana has a heavily restored, Moorish-style **basilica** *① open 0700-2000; minimum 5 people at a time to visit museum, Tue-Sat 1000-1100, 1500-1600, Sun 1000-1100, US$1.50, no photos allowed.* It contains a famous 16th-century miracle-working Virgen Morena (Dark Lady), also known as the Virgen de Candelaria, one of the patron saints of Bolivia. The basilica is clean, white, with coloured tiles decorating the exterior arches, cupolas and chapels. It is notable for its spacious atrium with four small chapels; the main chapel has one of the finest gilt altars in Bolivia. There are 17th- and 18th-century paintings and statues in the sanctuary. Vehicles decorated with flowers and confetti are blessed in front of the church.

On the headland which overlooks the town and port, **Cerro Calvario**, are the Stations of the Cross (a steep 45-minute climb – leave plenty of time if going to see the sunset). On the hill behind the town is the **Horca del Inca**, two pillars of rock with another laid across them; probably a sun clock, now covered in graffiti. There is a path marked by arrows, boys will offer to guide you: fix price in advance if you want their help.

There are many great hikes in the hills surrounding Copacabana. North of town is the **Yampupata Peninsula**. It is a beautiful 17 km (six hours) walk to the village of Yampupata at the tip of the peninsula, either via Sicuani on the west shore or Sampaya on the east shore, both picturesque little towns. There are also minibuses from Copacabana to Yampupata, where you can hire a motorboat or rowboat to Isla del Sol or Isla de la Luna; boats may also be available from Sampaya to Isla de la Luna.

Isla del Sol

The site of the main Inca creation myth (there are other versions) is a place of exceptional natural beauty and spiritual interest. Legend has it that Viracocha, the creator god, had his children, Manco Kapac and Mama Ocllo, spring from the waters of the lake to found Cuzco and the Inca dynasty. A sacred rock at the island's northwest end is worshipped as their birthplace. Near the rock are the impressive ruins of **Chincana**, the labyrinth, a 25-minute walk from the village of Challapampa, with a basic **museum** *① US$1.45 includes landing fee and entry to Chincana.* Near the centre of the island is the community of Challa with an **ethnographic museum** *① US$2.15, includes trail fees.* Towards the south end of the island is the **Fuente del Inca**, a spring reached by Inca steps leading up from the lake and continuing up to the village of Yumani. Near the southeast tip of the island, 2 km from the spring, are the ruins of **Pilcocaina** *① US$0.70 include landing fees,* a two storey building with false domes and nice views over the water. You must pay the fees even if you don't visit the museums or ruins. Keep all entry tickets, you may be asked for them at other locations. Several restored pre-Columbian roads cross the island from north to south.

The three communities are along the east shore of the island. All have electricity (Yumani also has internet), accommodation and simple places to eat. The island is heavily touristed and gets crowded in high season. Touts and beggars can be persistent, especially in Yumani. Tour operators in Copacabana offer half- and full-day 'tours' (many are just transport, see page 336) but an overnight stay at least is recommended to appreciate fully the island and to enjoy the spectacular walk from north to south (or vice-versa) at a comfortable pace. In a day trip, you will barely have time for a quick look at Chincana and you will see Pilcocaina from the boat. Note that it is a steep climb from the pier to the town of Yumani. Local guides are available in Challapampa and Yumani.

Southeast of Isla del Sol is the smaller **Isla de la Luna**, which may also be visited. The community of Coati is located on the west shore, an Inca temple and nunnery on the east shore.

Border with Peru

West side of Lake Titicaca The road goes from La Paz 91 km west to the former port of **Guaqui** (at the military checkpoint here, and other spots on the road, passports may be inspected). The road crosses the border at **Desaguadero** 22 km further west and runs along the shore of the lake to Puno. Bolivian immigration is just before the bridge, open 0830-2030 (Peru is one hour earlier than Bolivia). Get exit stamp, walk 200 m across the bridge then get entrance stamp on the other side. Get Peruvian visas in La Paz. There are a few hotels and restaurants on both sides of the border; very basic in Bolivia, slightly better in Peru. Money changers on Peruvian side give reasonable rates. Market days are Friday and Tuesday: otherwise the town is dead.

Via Copacabana From Copacabana a paved road leads 8 km south to the frontier at Kasani, then to Yunguyo, Peru. Do not photograph the border area. For La Paz tourist agency services on this route see International buses, page 324, and What to do, page 334. The border is open 0730-1930 Bolivian time (one hour later than Peruvian time). International tourist buses stop at both sides of the border; if using local transport walk 300 m between the two posts. Do not be fooled into paying any unnecessary charges to police or immigration. Going to Peru, money can be changed at the Peruvian side of the border. Coming into Bolivia, the best rates are at Copacabana.

East side of Lake Titicaca

From Huarina, a road heads northwest to Achacachi (market Sunday; fiesta 14 September). Here, one road goes north across a tremendous marsh to **Warisata**, then crosses the altiplano to Sorata (see below). At Achacachi, another road runs roughly parallel to the shore of Lake Titicaca, through **Ancoraimes** (Sunday market, the church hosts a community project making dolls and alpaca sweaters, also has dorms), **Carabuco** (with colonial church), **Escoma**, which has an Aymara market every Sunday morning, to **Puerto Acosta**, 10 km from the Peruvian border. It is a pleasant, friendly town with a large plaza and several simple places to stay and eat. The area around Puerto Acosta is good walking country. From La Paz to Puerto Acosta the road is paved as far as Escoma, then good until Puerto Acosta (best in the dry season, approximately May to October). North of Puerto Acosta towards Peru the road deteriorates and should not be attempted except in the dry season. There is a smugglers' market at the border on Wednesday and Saturday, the only days when transport is plentiful. You should get an exit stamp in La Paz before heading to this border (only preliminary entrance stamps are given here). There is a Peruvian customs post 2 km from the border and 2 km before Tilali, but Peruvian immigration is in Puno.

Sorata → *Phone code: 02. Colour map 3, B2. Population: 2523. Altitude: 2700 m.*

Sorata, 163 km from La Paz along a paved road, is a beautiful colonial town nestled at the foot of Mount Illampu; all around it are views over steep lush valleys. The climate is milder and more humid compared to the altiplano. Nearby are some challenging long-distance treks as well as great day-hikes. The town has a charming plaza, with views of the snow-capped summit of Illampu on a clear day. The main fiesta is 14 September. There is no ATM in Sorata, take cash.

A popular excursion is to **San Pedro cave** ⓘ *0800-1700, US$3, toilets at entrance*, beyond the village of San Pedro. The cave has an underground lake (no swimming allowed) and is lit. It is reached either by road, a 12 km walk (three hours each way), or by a path high above the Río San Cristóbal (about four hours, impassable during the rainy season and not easy at any time). Get clear directions before setting out and take sun protection, food, water, etc. Taxis and pick-ups from the plaza, 0600-2200, US$11 with a 30-minute wait. The **Mirador del Iminiapi** (Laripata) offers excellent views of town and the Larecaja tropical valleys. It is a nice day-walk or take a taxi, US$11 return.

Trekking and climbing from Sorata
Sorata is the starting point for climbing **Illampu** and **Ancohuma**. All routes out of the town are difficult, owing to the number of paths in the area and the very steep ascent.

Sorata

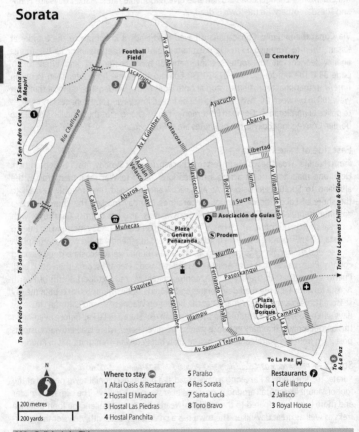

Where to stay 🛏
1 Altai Oasis & Restaurant
2 Hostal El Mirador
3 Hostal Las Piedras
4 Hostal Panchita
5 Paraíso
6 Res Sorata
7 Santa Lucía
8 Toro Bravo

Restaurants 🍴
1 Café Illampu
2 Jalisco
3 Royal House

Experience and full equipment are necessary. You can hire trekking guides and mules (see What to do, page 335). The three- to four-day trek to **Lagunas Chillata and Glaciar** is the most common and gets busy during high season. Laguna Chillata can also be reached by road or on a long day-hike with light gear, but mind the difficult navigation and take warm clothing. Laguna Chillata has been heavily impacted by tourism (remove all trash, do not throw it in the pits around the lake) and groups frequently camp there. The **Illampu Circuit**, a six- to seven-day high-altitude trek (three passes over 4000 m, one over 5000 m) around Illampu, is excellent. It can get very cold and it is a hard walk, though very beautiful with nice campsites on the way. Some food can be bought in Cocoyo on the third day. You must be acclimatized before setting out. Another option is the Trans-Cordillera Trek, 10-12 days from Sorata to Huayna Potosí, or longer all the way to Illimani at the opposite (south) end of the Cordillera Real. Some communities charge visitors fees along the way.

Cordillera Apolobamba

The Area Protegida Apolobamba forms part of the Cordillera Apolobamba, the north extension of the Cordillera Real. The range itself has many 5000 m-plus peaks, while the conservation area of some 560,000 ha protects herds of vicuña, huge flocks of flamingos and many condors. The area adjoins the Parque Nacional Madidi (see page 388). This is great trekking country and the four- to six-day **Charazani to Pelechuco** (or vice versa) mountain trek is one of the best in the country (see Footprint's *Bolivia Handbook* for details). It passes traditional villages and the peaks of the southern Cordillera Apolobamba.

Charazani is the biggest village in the region (3200 m), with hot springs (US$0.75). Its three-day fiesta is around 16 July. There are some cheap *alojamientos*, restaurants and shops. **Pelechuco** (3600 m) is a smaller village, also with cheap *alojamientos*, cafés and shops. The road to Pelechuco goes through the Area Protegida, passing the community of Ulla Ulla, 5 km outside of which are the reserve's HQ at La Cabaña. Visitors are welcome to see the orphaned vicuñas. There are economical community hostels at the villages of Lagunillas and Agua Blanca. Basic food is available in the communities. For information, contact SERNAP, www.sernap.gob.bo.

◉ Lake Titicaca listings

For hotel and restaurant price codes, and other relevant information, see pages 14-17.

◉ Where to stay

La Paz to Copacabana *p326*
Huatajata
$$ Hotel Titicaca, between Huatajata and Huarina, Km 80 from La Paz, T289 5180 (in La Paz T290 7000). Beautiful views, sauna, pool, good restaurant. It's very quiet during the week.

$ Máximo Catari's Inti Karka Hotel, on the lakeshore, T7197 8959, erikcatari@hotmail. com. Rooms are cheaper with shared bath. Also restaurant, open daily, average prices.

Copacabana *p327, map p327*
$$$ Rosario del Lago, Rigoberto Paredes y Av Costanera, T862 2141, reservations La Paz T244 1756, www.hotelrosario.com/ lago. Comfortable rooms with lake views, beautifully furnished, good restaurant, small museum, **Turisbus** office (see Transport below), parking. Efficient and attentive service.
$$ Chasqui del Sol, Av Costanera 55, T862 2343, www.chasquidelsol.com. Lakeside hotel, café/breakfast room has great views, trips organized, video room, parking.
$$ Ecolodge, 2 km south along the lakeshore, T862 2500 (or T245 1626, **Hostal Copacabana**, La Paz). Small comfortable cabins in a quiet out-of-the way location,

nice grounds. Only breakfast available, solar hot water, helpful owner.

$$ Gloria Copacabana, 16 de Julio y Manuel Mejía, T862 2094, La Paz T240 7070, www.hotelgloria.com.bo. Full board available, bar, café and restaurant with international and vegetarian food, gardens, parking. Same group as Gloria in La Paz.

$$ Las Olas, lake-end of Pje Michel Pérez past La Cúpula, T7250 8668, www.hostallasolas.com. Tastefully decorated suites, each in its own style. All have kitchenettes, heaters, lovely grounds and views, outdoor solar-heated jacuzzi, a special treat. Warmly recommended.

$$ Utama, Michel Pérez, T862 2013, www.utamahotel.com. Comfortable rooms, hot water, good showers, restaurant, book exchange.

$$-$ La Cúpula, Pje Michel Pérez 1-3, 5 mins' walk from centre, T6708 8464, www.hotelcupula.com. Variety of rooms and prices from suite with jacuzzi to comfortable rooms with shared bath, reliable hot water, sitting room with TV and video, fully equipped kitchen, library, book exchange, attentive service, excellent restaurant (**$$** with vegetarian options, great breakfast). Popular, advance booking advised. Highly recommended.

$ Emperador, C Murillo 235, T862 2083. Very economical, even cheaper without

bath, electric showers, newer rooms at the back, popular, helpful, tours arranged.

$ Kantutas, Av Jaúregui esquina Bolívar, on Plaza Sucre, T862 2093. Good rooms, a decent option in the middle price range, convenient location for transport.

$ Kotha Kahuaña, Av Busch 15, T862 2022. Very economical, cheaper without bath, simple kitchen facilities, quiet, hospitable, basic but good value.

$ Leyenda, Av Costanera y Germán Busch, T7067 4097, hostel.leyenda@gmail.com. Lakeshore hotel with eclectic decor, rooms elaborately decorated with local motifs, electric shower.

$ Sonia, Murillo 253, T7196 8441. Rooms are cheaper without bath, good beds, big windows, roof terrace, laundry facilities, breakfast in bed on request, very helpful, good value. Recommended.

Isla del Sol *p328*
Yumani

Most of the *posadas* on the island are here. Quality varies; ignore the touts and shop around for yourself. Please conserve water, it is hauled up the steep hill by donkeys.

$$ Palla Khasa, 600 m north of town on the main trail to Challapampa, T7321 1585, pallakhasa@gmail.com. Includes good breakfast, nice cabins, large rooms, good beds, restaurant with fine views,

nice location and grounds, family-run, solar electricity, changes US$ and other currencies. Book in advance.
$ Imperio del Sol, on the way up to town, 500 m below the Casa Cultural, about the middle of the steps, T7196 1863, www.hotel imperiodelsol.com. Nice hotel, comfortable rooms, small garden. Recommended.
$ Inti Kala, at the top of the hill, T7194 4013, javierintikala@hotmail.com. Cheaper without bath, electric shower, fantastic views, could use a coat of paint, serves good meals.
$ Templo del Sol, at the top of the hill, T7400 5417. Comfortable rooms, cheaper without bath, electric shower, great views, comfy beds, could use a coat of paint, good restaurant.

Challa
Located mid-island on the east shore, about 200 m below the main north-south trail. Most hostels are on the beach, the town is uphill.
$ Inca Beach, on the beach, T7353 0309. Simple rooms with bath, electric shower, kitchen and laundry facilities, meals available, nice common area, camping possible, good value.
$ Qhumpuri, on hillside above beach, T7472 6525. Simple 2-room units with nice views, private toilet, shared electric shower, tasty meals available.

Challapampa
$ Cultural, 1 block from beach, T7190 0272. Clean rooms, cheaper without bath, nice terrace, does not include breakfast.
$ Manco Kapac, by the dock, T7128 8443. Basic clean rooms, shared bath, electric shower, camping possible, does not include breakfast.
$ Wipala, 1 km north on trail to Chincana, T7257 0092. Simple rooms, electric shower, lovely quiet location, does not include breakfast.

Tour group accommodation
La Posada del Inca, a restored colonial hacienda, owned by **Crillon Tours**, only available as part of a tour with Crillon, see page 321. **Magri Turismo** also owns a hotel on the island, **La Estancia**, www.ecolodge-laketiticaca.com. See La Paz, Tour operators on page 322. See also **Transturin's** overnight options on page 335.

Sorata *p329, map p330*
$$ Altai Oasis, T213 3895, www.altaioasis.com. At the bottom of the valley in a beautiful setting, 15-min steep downhill walk from town, or taxi US$2. Cabins, rooms with bath (cheaper with shared bath), dorms and camping (US$5 pp). Very good restaurant (**$$**), bar, lovely grounds, pool, peaceful, very welcoming, family-run by the Resnikowskis, English and German spoken. Warmly recommended.
$ Hostal El Mirador, Muñecas 400, T7350 5453. Cheaper with shared bath, hot water, kitchen, laundry facilities, terrace.
$ Hostal Las Piedras, just off Ascarrunz, T7191 6341, laspiedras2002@yahoo.de. Rooms with and without bath, good mattresses, electric shower, very nice, good breakfast with home-made products available, very helpful, English and German spoken. Recommended.
$ Hostal Panchita, on plaza, T213 4242. Simple rooms, shared bath, electric shower, sunny courtyard, washing facilities, does not include breakfast, good value.
$ Paraíso, Villavicencio 117. With electric shower, basic rooms, terrace, breakfast available.
$ Res Sorata, on plaza, T213 6672. Cheaper without bath, electric shower, restaurant, large but scruffy grounds, poor beds, a bit run down overall but still adequate.
$ Santa Lucía, Ascarrunz, T213 6686. Rooms are cheaper with shared bath, electric shower, carpeted rooms, patio, does not include breakfast, not always open.
$ Toro Bravo, below petrol station at entrance to town, T7725 5255. With electric shower, ample grounds and rooms (upstairs rooms are better), small pool, restaurant, a bit faded but good value.

🍴 Restaurants

La Paz to Copacabana *p326*
Huatajata
$$-$ Inti Raymi, next to Inca Utama hotel.
With fresh fish and boat trips. There are
other restaurants of varying standard, most
lively at weekends and in the high season.

Copacabana *p327, map p327*
Excellent restaurants at hotels **Rosario
del Lago** and **La Cúpula**. Many touristy
places on Av 6 de Agosto toward the
lakeshore, all similar.
$$ Café Bistrot Copacabana, Cabo Zapana
y 6 de Agosto, upstairs. Daily 0730-2100.
Varied menu, international dishes, vegetarian
options, French and English spoken.
$$-$ La Orilla, Av 6 de Agosto, close to
lake. Daily 1000-2200 (usually). Warm,
atmospheric, tasty food with local and
international choices.
$ Aransaya, Av 6 de Agosto 121. Good
restaurant and café.
$ Puerta del Sol, Av 6 de Agosto. Good trout.
$ Snack 6 de Agosto, Av 6 de Agosto,
2 branches. Good trout, big portions, some
vegetarian dishes, serves breakfast.
$ Sujna Wasi, Jaúregui 127. Daily 0730-
2300. Serves breakfast, vegetarian lunch,
wide range of books on Bolivia, slow service.

Sorata *p329, map p330*
There are several **$$-$** Italian places on the
plaza, all quite similar.
$$-$ Café Illampu, 15 min walk on the way
to San Pedro cave. Closed Tue and Dec-Mar.
Excellent sandwiches, bread and cakes,
camping possible. Offers tours with
own 4WD vehicle, Swiss-run, English
and German spoken.
$$-$ Jalisco, on plaza. Mexican and Italian
dishes, sidewalk seating.
$ Royal House, off Muñecas by the market.
Decent set lunch, friendly.

⚜ Festivals

Copacabana *p327, map p327*
Note At these times hotel prices quadruple.
1-3 Feb Virgen de la Candelaria, massive
procession, dancing, fireworks, bullfights.
Easter, with candlelight procession on Good
Friday. **23 Jun** San Juan, also on Isla del Sol.
4-6 Aug La Virgen de Copacabana.

Sorata *p329, map p330*
14 Sep Fiesta Patronal del Señor de la
Columna, is the main festival.

⏰ What to do

Lake Titicaca *p326*
Crillon Tours, La Paz, see page 321. Run
a hydrofoil service on Lake Titicaca with
excellent bilingual guides. Tours stop at
their Andean Roots cultural complex at
Inca Utama. Very experienced company.
The **Inca Utama Hotel and Spa ($$$)** has
a health spa based on natural remedies
and Kallawaya medicine; the rooms
are comfortable, with heating, electric
blankets, good service, bar, restaurant, Wi-Fi,
reservations through **Crillon Tours** in La
Paz. Crillon is Bolivia's oldest travel agency
and is consistently recommended. Also at
Inca Utama is an observatory (*alajpacha*)
with 2 telescopes and retractable roof for
viewing the night sky, an Altiplano Museum,
a floating restaurant and bar on the lake
(**La Choza Náutica**), a 252-sq-m floating
island and examples of different Altiplano
cultures. Health, astronomical, mystic and
ecological programmes are offered. The
hydrofoil trips include visits to Andean
Roots complex, Copacabana, Islas del Sol
and de la Luna, Straits of Tiquina and the
Cocotoni community. See Isla del Sol, Where
to stay, for **La Posada del Inca**. Crillon has a
sustainable tourism project with Urus-Iruitos
people from the Río Desaguadero area on
floating islands by the Isla Quewaya. Trips
can be arranged to/from Puno and Juli (bus
and hydrofoil excursion to Isla del Sol) and

from Copacabana via Isla del Sol to Cuzco and Machu Picchu. Other combinations of hydrofoil and land-based excursions can be arranged (also highland, Eastern lowland, jungle and adventure tours). See www.titicaca.com and www.uyuni.travel for details. All facilities and modes of transport connected by radio.

Transturin (see also La Paz, Tour operators, page 322) run catamarans on Lake Titicaca, either for sightseeing or on the La Paz-Puno route. The catamarans are more leisurely than the hydrofoils of **Crillon** so there is more room and time for on-board meals and entertainment, with bar, video and sun deck. From their dock at Chúa, catamarans run 2-day/1-night cruises starting either in La Paz or Copacabana. Puno may also be the starting point for trips. Overnight cruises involve staying in a cabin on the catamaran, moored at the Isla del Sol, with lots of activities. On the island, Transturin has the Inti Wata cultural complex which has restored Inca terraces, an Aymara house, the underground Ekeko museum and cultural demonstrations and activities. There is also a 30-passenger totora reed boat for trips to the Pilcocaina Inca palace. All island-based activities are community-led and for catamaran clients only. Transturin runs through services to Puno without many of the formalities at the border. Transturin offers last-minute programmes with 40% discount rates in Puno, Cuzco and La Paz, if booked 6 days prior to departure only. You can book by phone or by email, but ask first, as availability depends on date.

Turisbus (www.turisbus.com, see La Paz, Tour operators page 323 and **Hoteles Rosario**, La Paz, and **Rosario del Lago**, Copacabana) offer guided tours in the fast launches *Titicaca Explorer I* (28 passengers) and *II* (8 passengers) to the Isla del Sol, returning to Copacabana via the Bahía de Sicuani for trips on traditional reed boats. Also La Paz-Puno, with boat excursion to Isla del Sol, boxed lunch and road transport, or with additional overnight at **Hotel Rosario del Lago**.

Copacabana *p327, map p327*
Town is filled with tour agencies, all offering excursions to floating islands on imitation reed vessels, and tours to Isla del Sol (see Transport, below). Kayak and pedal-boat rentals on the beach, US$3 per hr.

Sorata *p329, map p330*
Trekking guides
It may be cheaper to go to Sorata and arrange trekking there than to book a trek with an agency in La Paz. Buy necessary foods and supplies in La Paz, Sorata shops have basic items.
Asociación de Guías, Sucre 302 y Guachalla, leave message at Res Sorata (T213 6672); hires guides, porters and mules. Prices vary: guides approximately US$30 per day, mules US$15 per day. Porters take maximum 2 mules, remember you have to feed your guide/porter.
Eduardo Chura, T7157 8671, guiasorata@yahoo.com, is an independent local trekking guide.

⊖ Transport

La Paz to Copacabana *p326*
Huatajata
Bus La Paz–Huatajata, US$1, frequent minibuses from Bustillos y Kollasuyo, Cementerio district, daily 0400-1800, continuing to Tiquina.

Islands of Lago Huiñamarca *p327*
Boat Máximo Catari (see **Huatajata**, Where to stay, above) and Paulino Esteban (east end of town, T7196 7383) arrange trips to the islands in Lago Huiñamarca for US$15 per hr.

Copacabana *p327, map p327*
If arriving in Bolivia at Copacabana and going to La Paz, be sure to arrive there before dark. See also Safety on page 305.
Bus To/from **La Paz**, US$2.15 plus US$0.30 for Tiquina crossing, 4 hrs, throughout the day with **Manco Capac**, **2 de Febrero**. Both

have offices on Copacabana's main plaza (but leave from Plaza Sucre) and in La Paz at Plaza Reyes Ortiz, opposite entrance to cemetery. Buy ticket in advance at weekends and on holidays. **Diana Tours** and others daily at 1330, from Plaza Sucre, 16 de Julio y 6 de Agosto, US\$3.50-4.50, take you to Sagárnaga e Illampu in the tourist district, but will not drop you off at your hotel. (See also Border with Peru via Copacabana, below.)

Isla del Sol *p328*

Boat Boat companies have ticket booths at the beach, by the bottom of Av 6 de Agosto; there are also agencies selling boat and bus tickets along Av 6 de Agosto. All departures are at 0830, unless otherwise noted, and boats arrive back at Copacabana around 1730. The crossing from Copacabana to Yumani takes about 1½ hrs, to Challpampa 2 hrs. Return tickets are only valid on the same day, get a one way fare if you plan to stay overnight. **Andes Amazonía** run full-day trips Copacabana-Challapampa-Yumani-Copacabana, US\$5. If you wish to walk, you can be dropped off at Challapampa around 1030-1100 and picked up at Yumani at 1530 (boats leave punctually, so you will have to walk quickly to see the ruins in the north and then hike south to Yumani and down to the pier). They also have a 1330 departure to Yumani, returning 1600, with a 10-min stop at Pilcocaina on the way back. Unión Marinos, run Copacabana–Challapampa–Copacabana, US\$4.30; they depart Challapampa at 1330. Titicaca Tours run Copacabana–Coati (Isla de la Luna)–Yumani–Copacabana, US\$4.30; they stop for 1 hr at Coati and depart Yumani at 1530. One way fares from Copacabana to Yumani US\$2.85, to Challapampa US\$3.60. Boats also run from Challa to Copacabana Wed, Sat, Sun at 0700, returning 1330, US\$1.50 one way.

From **Yampupata**: to Yumani by motorboat, US\$13 per boat (US\$3 pp by rowboat); to Isla de la Luna, US\$26 per boat.

Border with Peru *p329*
Via Guaqui and Desaguadero
Bus Road paved all the way to Peru. Buses from La Paz to Guaqui and Desaguadero depart from J M Asín y P Eyzaguirre, Cementerio, from 0500, US\$1.50, shared taxi US\$3, 2 hrs. From Desaguadero to **La Paz** buses depart 4 blocks from bridge, last vehicle 2000.

Via Copacabana
Bus Several agencies go from La Paz to **Puno**, with a change of bus and stop for lunch at Copacabana, or with an open ticket for continuing to Puno later. They charge US\$8 and depart La Paz 0800, pick-up from hotel. From Copacabana they continue to the Peruvian border at Kasani and on to Puno, stopping for immigration formalities and changing money (better rates in Puno). Both **Crillon Tours** (page 321) and **Transturin** (page 322) have direct services to Puno without a change of bus at the border. From Copacabana to Puno, **Trans Titicaca** (www.titicacabolivia.com) at 0900, 1330, 1830 and other agencies at 1330, offices on 6 de Agosto, US\$4-5, 3 hrs. Also **Turisbus** (www.turisbus.com) to Puno from Hotel Rosario del Lago at 1330, US\$9. To go to **Cuzco**, you will have to change in Puno where the tour company arranges connections, which may involve a long wait, check details (US\$14-22 La Paz–Cuzco). In high season, book at least a day in advance. It is always cheaper, if less convenient, to buy only the next segment of your journey directly from local bus companies and cross the border on your own. *Colectivo* Copacabana (Plaza Sucre)–**Kasani** US\$0.60 pp, 15 mins, Kasani–**Yunguyo**, where Peruvian buses start, US\$0.30 pp.

East side of Lake Titicaca *p329*
Bus La Paz (Reyes Cardona 772, Cancha Tejar, Cementerio district, T238 2239)–**Puerto Acosta**, 5 hrs, US\$4, Tue-Sun 0500. Transport past Puerto Acosta only operates on market days, Wed and Sat, and is mostly cargo trucks.

Bus Puerto Acosta–La Paz at about 1500. There are frequent minivans to La Paz from **Escoma**, 25 km from Puerto Acosta; trucks from the border may take you this far.

Sorata *p329, map p330*

Bus Minibuses throughout the day from **La Paz** with Trans Unificada (C Manuel Bustillos 683 y Av Kollasuyo in the Cementerio district, T238 1693); also Perla del Illampu (Manuel Bustillos 615, T238 0548), US$2.50, 3½ hrs. Booking recommended on Fri. In Sorata they leave from C Samuel Tejerina, near the exit to La Paz. To or from **Copacabana** and **Peru**, change buses at Huarina but they are often full so start early and be prepared for a long wait.

Jeeps run from La Paz (C Choroique y Tarapacá, T245 0296, often full), via Sorata to **Santa Rosa** (US$15, 13 hrs), on the road to **Mapiri** and **Guanay**, a rough route with interesting vegetation and stunning scenery. Onward transport can be found in Santa Rosa. From Guanay private boats may be arranged to **Rurrenabaque**, and vehicles run to Caranavi and thence to Coroico. Sorata–Coroico by this route is excellent for offroad motorcycling. If travelling by public transport it is easier to go La Paz–Coroico–Caranavi–Guanay–Santa Rosa–Sorata–La Paz, than vice versa.

Cordillera Apolobamba *p331*
Charazani
Bus From Calle Reyes Cardona 732, off Av Kollasuyo, Cemetery district, La Paz, daily with Trans Altiplano, 0600-0630, 7 hrs, US$3.50, very crowded. Return to La Paz at 1800; also has 0900 on Sat and 1200 Mon and Fri.

Pelechuco
Bus From **La Paz** Trans Provincias del Norte leaves daily 0600-0700 from Ex Tranca de Río Seco in El Alto, passing through Qutapampa, Ulla Ulla and Agua Blanca to Pelechuco, 10-12 hrs, US$5, sometimes on sale 24 hrs before departure at the booking office in Calle Reyes Cardona. Return to La Paz between 0300 and 0400 most days.

The Yungas

Only a few hours from La Paz are the subtropical valleys known as the Yungas. These steep, forested slopes, squeezed in between the Cordillera and the Amazon Lowlands, provide a welcome escape from the chill of the capital. The warm climate of the Yungas is also ideal for growing citrus fruit, bananas, coffee and especially coca.

La Paz to the Yungas
The roads from La Paz to Nor- and Sud-Yungas go via **La Cumbre**, a pass at 4725 m about one hour northeast of the city. The road out of La Paz circles cloudwards over La Cumbre; all around are towering snowcapped peaks. The first village after the pass is **Unduavi**, where there is a check point, a petrol station, and roadside stalls. Beyond Unduavi an unpaved road branches right 75 km to Chulumani and the Sud-Yungas. Beyond Sud-Yungas, to the southeast, are the Yungas de Inquisivi, see Quime, page 343. The paved road contnues to Cotapata, where it again divides: right is the old unpaved road to Yolosa, the junction 8 km from Coroico (this is the popular cycling route). To the left, the new paved road goes via Chuspipata and Puente Yolosita, where an unpaved road climbs steeply to Coroico. Between Yolosita and Yolosa (see below) is Senda Verde (www.sendaverde.com), an animal refuge, eco-lodge and restaurant with opportunities for volunteering. In addition, from Puente Villa on the Unduav–Chulumani road, an unpaved road runs to Coripata and Coroico. For the La Cumbre–Coroico hike (Choro), see page 312.

All roads to Coroico drop some 3500 m to the green subtropical forest in 70 km. The best views are in May to June, when there is less chance of fog and rain. The old road, the so-called "World's Most Dangerous Road", is steep, twisting, clinging to the side of sheer cliffs, and it is slippery in the wet. It is a breathtaking descent (best not to look over the edge if you don't like heights) and its reputation for danger is more than matched by the beauty of the scenery. Many tourists go on a mountain-bike tour: it is your responsibility to choose top quality bikes (with hydraulic disc brakes) and a reputable company which offers bilingual guides, helmet, gloves, vehicle support throughout the day (see La Paz, Tour operators, page 321). Many bike companies take riders back to La Paz the same day, but Coroico is worth more of your time. In Yolosa, at the end of the bike ride, is a three-segment zipline (total 1555 m) operated by **Gravity Bolivia**; see page 322 and www. ziplinebolivia.com. The road is especially dangerous when it is raining (mid-December to mid-February), be sure the bike is in top shape and be extra cautious.

Coroico → *Phone code: 02. Colour map 3, B2. Population 2903. Altitude: 1750 m*

The little town of Coroico, capital of the Nor-Yungas region, is perched on a hill amid beautiful scenery. The hillside is covered with orange and banana groves and coffee plantations. Coroico is a first-class place to relax with several good walks. A colourful four-day festival is held 19-22 October. On 2 November, All Souls' Day, the cemetery is festooned with black ribbons. A good walk is up to the waterfalls, starting from **El Calvario**. Follow the stations of the cross by the cemetery, off Calle Julio Zuazo Cuenca, which leads steeply uphill from the plaza. Facing the chapel at El Calvario, with your back to the town, look for the path on your left. This leads to the falls which are the town's water supply (Toma de Agua) and, beyond, to two more falls. **Cerro Uchumachi**, the mountain behind El Calvario, can be climbed following the same stations of the cross, but then look for the faded red and white antenna behind the chapel. From there it's about two hours' steep walk to the top (take water). A third walk goes to the pools in the **Río Vagante**, 7 km off the road to Coripata; it takes about three hours. **Tourist information** ⓘ *at the Prefectura, Monse y Julio Zuazo Cuenca, corner of the main plaza.* In the interests of personal safety, women in particular should not hike alone in this area.

Caranavi → *Phone code: 02. Colour map 3, B2. Population 21,883. Altitude: 600 m.*

From the junction at Puente Yolosita the paved road follows the river 11 km to Santa Bárbara, then becomes gravel for 65 km to Caranavi, an uninspiring town 156 km from La Paz. From here the road continues towards the settled area of the Alto Beni, at times following a picturesque gorge. Market days are Friday and Saturday. There is a range of hotels and *alojamientos* and buses from La Paz (Villa Fátima) to Rurrenabaque pass through. Beyond Caranavi, 70 km, is **Guanay** at the junction of the Tipuani and Mapiri rivers (basic lodging).

Chulumani and Sud-Yungas → *Phone code: 02. Colour map 3, B2/3. Population 3650. Altitude: 1750 m.*

The road from Unduavi to Chulumani goes through **Puente Villa**, where a branch runs north to Coroico through Coripata. The capital of Sud Yungas is **Chulumani** is a small town with beautiful views, 124 km from La Paz. There are many birds in the area and good hiking. The 24 August fiesta lasts 10 days and there is a lively market every weekend. **Tourist office** ⓘ *in the main plaza, open irregular hours, mostly weekends.* There is no ATM in Chulumani, take cash. **Irupana** (*altitude 1900 m*), 31 km east of Chulmani (minibus or shared taxi US$2), is a friendly little place with a lovely location, delightful climate, more good walking and birdwatching, and a couple of very nice places to stay. The 500-ha **Apa Apa Reserve** ① *5 km from Chulumani on the road to Irupana (see Where to stay, below)*, is the one of the last areas of original Yungas forest with lots of birds, other wildlife, hiking trails and pleasant accommodation.

◉ The Yungas listings

For hotel and restaurant price codes, and other relevant information, see pages 14-17.

◉ Where to stay

Coroico *p338*

Hotel rooms are hard to find at holiday weekends and prices are higher.
$$$-$$ El Viejo Molino, T279 7329, www. hotelviejomolino.com. 2 km on road to Caranavi. Upmarket hotel and spa with pool, gym, jacuzzi, games room, restaurant, etc.
$$ Gloria, C Kennedy 1, T289 5554, www.hotelgloria.com.bo. Traditional resort hotel, full board, pool, restaurant with set lunches and à la carte, internet, free transport from plaza.
$$-$ Bella Vista, C Héroes del Chaco 7 (2 blocks from main plaza), T213 6059, www.coroicobellavista.blogspot.com. Beautiful rooms and views, includes breakfast, cheaper without bath, 2 racquetball courts, terrace, bike hire, restaurant, pool.
$$-$ Esmeralda, on the edge of town, 10 mins uphill from plaza (see website for transport), T213 6027, www.hotelesmeralda. com. Most rooms include breakfast, cheaper in dorms, hot showers, satellite TV and DVD, book exchange, good buffet restaurant, sauna, garden, pool, can arrange local tours and transport to/from La Paz and Coroico bus stop.
$$-$ Hostal Kory, at top of steps leading down from the plaza, T7156 4050, info@ hostalkory.com. Rooms with shared bath are cheaper, electric showers, restaurant, huge pool, terrace, good value, helpful.
$ Don Quijote, 500 m out of town, on road to Coripata, T213 6007, www.donquijote. lobopages.com. Economical, electric shower, pool, quiet, nice views.

$ El Cafetal, Miranda, 10-min walk from town, T7193 3979. Rooms with and without bath, very nice, restaurant with excellent French/Indian/vegetarian cuisine, French-run.
$ Los Silbos, Iturralde 4043, T7350 0081. Cheap simple rooms with shared bath, electric showers, good value.
$ Matsu, 1 km from town (call for free pick-up, taxi US$2), T7069 2219. Economical, has restaurant, pool, views, quiet, helpful.
$ Residencial de la Torre, Julio Zuazo Cuenca, ½ block from plaza. Welcoming place with courtyard, cheap sparse rooms, no alcoholic drinks allowed.
$ Sol y Luna, 15-20 mins beyond **Hotel Esmeralda**, La Paz contact: Maison de la Bolivie, 6 de Agosto 2464, Ed Jardines, T244 0588, www.solyluna-bolivia.com. Excellent accommodation in fully equipped cabins, apartments and rooms with and without bath, splendid views, restaurant (vegetarian specialities), camping US$3 pp (not suitable for cars), garden, pool, shiatsu massage (US$15-20), good value, Sigrid (owner) speaks English, French, German, Spanish.

Chulumani and Sud-Yungas *p338*

Chulumani suffers from water shortages, check if your hotel has a reserve tank.
$ Apa Apa, 5 km from town on road to Irupana, then walk 20 mins uphill from turn-off, or taxi from Chulumani US$3.50, T7254 7770, La Paz T213 9640, apapayungas@ hotmail.com. A lovely old hacienda with simple rooms, private bath, hot water, delicious meals available, home-made ice cream, pool, large campsite with bathrooms and grills, tours to Apa Apa Reserve, family-run by Ramiro and Tildy Portugal, English spoken.

$ Country House, 400 m out of town on road to cemetery, T7528 2212, La Paz T274 5584. With electric shower, lovely tranquil setting, pool and gardens, library, breakfast and other home-cooked meals available, family-run. Enthusiastic owner Xavier Sarabia is hospitable and offers hiking advice and tours, English spoken.
$ Hostal Familiar Dion, Alianza, ½ block below plaza, T289 6034. Cheaper without bath, electric shower, very well maintained, restaurant, attentive.
$ Huayrani, Junín y Cornejo, uphill from centre near bus stops, T213 6351. Electric shower, nice views, pool, parking.

Irupana
$ Bougainville Hotel, near the centre of town, T213 6155. Modern rooms, electric shower, pizzería, pool, family-run, good value.
$ Nirvana Inn, uphill at the edge of town past the football field, T213 6154. Comfortable cabins on beautiful grounds with great views, pool, parking, flower and orchid gardens lovingly tended by the owners. Includes breakfast, other meals on request.

🍴 Restaurants

Coroico *p338*
$$ Bamboos, Iturralde y Ortiz. Good Mexican food and pleasant atmosphere, live music some nights with cover charge. Happy hour 1800-1900.
$$-$ Back-stube, Pasaje Adalid Linares, 10 m from the main square. Mon 0830-1200, Wed-Fri 0830-1430, 1830-2200, Sat-Sun 0830-2200. National and international food, vegetarian options, à la carte only, breakfasts, pastries, top quality, terrace with panoramic views, nice atmosphere.
$$-$ Carla's Garden Pub, Pasaje Adalid Linares, 50 m from the main plaza. Open lunch until late. Sandwiches, snacks, pasta and international food, BBQ for groups of 5 or more. Lots of music, live music at weekends. Garden, hammocks, games, nice atmosphere.

$ Pizzería Italia, 2 with same name on the plaza. Daily 1000-2300. Pizza, pasta, snacks.

Chulumani and Sud-Yungas *p338*
$ La Cabaña Yungeña, C Sucre 2 blocks below plaza. Tue-Sun. simple set lunch and dinner.
Couple of other places around plaza, all closed Mon. Basic eateries up the hill by bus stops.

⚙ What to do

Coroico *p338*
Cycling
CXC, Pacheco 79, T7157 3015, www. cxccoroico.lobopages.com. Good bikes, US$20 for 6 hrs including packed lunch, a bit disorganized but good fun and helpful, English and German spoken.

Horse riding
El Relincho, Don Reynaldo, T7191 3675, 100 m past **Hotel Esmeralda** (enquire here), US$25 for 4 hrs with lunch.

⊖ Transport

Coroico *p338*
Bus From La Paz all companies are Minasa terminal, Puente Minasa, in Villa Fátima: buses and minibuses leave throughout the day US$4.25, 2½ hrs on the paved road. **Turbus Totaí**, T221 6592, and several others. Services return to La Paz from the small terminal down the hill in Coroico, across from the fooball field. All are heavily booked at weekends and on holidays.
Pick-ups from the small mirador at Pacheco y Sagárnaga go to **Puente Yolosita**, 15 mins, US$0.70. Here you can try to catch a bus to **Rurrenabaque**, but there's more chance of getting a seat in **Caranavi**, where La Paz-Rurre buses pass through in the evening, often full. Caranavi-Rurre 12 hrs, US$6-7, **Flota Yungueña**, at 1800-1900, **Turbus Totaí** 2100-2200, and others. See also **Deep Rainforest**, La Paz (page 321). For Guanay to **Sorata** via **Mapiri** and **Santa Rosa**, see page 337.

Chulumani and Sud-Yungas *p338*
Bus From **La Paz**, several companies from Villa Fátima, leave when full, US$3.60, 4 hrs: eg **San Cristóbal**, C San Borja 408 y 15 de Abril, T221 0607. In Chulumani most buses leave from the top of the hill by the petrol station; minibuses and taxis to local villages from plaza.

ⓘ Directory

Coroico *p338*
Language classes Siria León Domínguez, T7195 5431. US$5 per hr, also rents rooms and makes silver jewellery, excellent English. **Medical services** Hospital is the best in the Yungas.

Southwest Bolivia

The mining town of Oruro, with one of South America's greatest folkloric traditions, shimmering salt flats, coloured lakes and surrealistic rock formations combine to make this one of the most fascinating regions of Bolivia. Add some of the country's most celebrated festivals and the last hide-out of Butch Cassidy and the Sundance Kid and you have the elements for some great and varied adventures. The journey across the altiplano from Uyuni to San Pedro de Atacama is a popular route to Chile and there are other routes south to Argentina.

Oruro and around → *Phone code: 02. Colour map 3, B3. Population: 240,996. Altitude: 3725 m.*

The mining town of Oruro is the gateway to the altiplano of southwest Bolivia. It's a somewhat drab, dirty, functional place, which explodes into life once a year with its famous carnival, symbolized by La Diablada. To the west is the national park encompassing Bolivia's highest peak: Sajama. The **tourist office** ⓘ *Bolívar y Montes 6072, Plaza 10 de Febrero, T525 0144, Mon-Fri 0800-1200, 1430-1830,* is helpful and informative. The Prefectura and the Policía de Turismo jointly run information booths in front of the **Terminal de Buses** ⓘ *T528 7774, Mon-Fri 0800-1200, 1430-1830, Sat 0830-1200*; and opposite the **railway station** ⓘ *T525 7881, same hours.*

Although Oruro became famous as a mining town, there are no longer any working mines of importance. It is, however, a railway terminus and the commercial centre for the mining communities of the altiplano, as well as hosting the country's best-known carnival (see La Diablada, page 344). The Plaza 10 de Febrero and surroundings are well maintained and several buildings in the centre hint at the city's former importance. The **Museo Simón Patiño** ⓘ *Soria Galvarro 5755, Mon-Fri 0830-1130, 1430-1800, Sat 0900-1500, US$1,* was built as a mansion by the tin baron Simón Patiño, it is now run by the Universidad Técnica de Oruro and contains European furniture and temporary exhibitions. There is a view from the Cerro Corazón de Jesús, near the church of the Virgen del Socavón, five blocks west of Plaza 10 de Febrero at the end of Calle Mier.

The **Museo Sacro, Folklórico, Arqueológico y Minero** ⓘ *inside the Church of the Virgen del Socavón, entry via the church daily 0900-1145, 1500-1730, US$1.50, guided tours every 45 mins,* contain religious art, clothing and jewellery and, after passing through old mining tunnels and displays of mining techniques, a representation of El Tío (the god of the underworld). **Museo Antropológico** ⓘ *south of centre on Av España y Urquidi, T526 0020, Mon-Fri 0900-1200, 1400-1800, Sat-Sun 1000-1200, 1500-1800, US$0.75, guide mandatory, getting there: take micro A heading south or any trufi going south.* It has a unique collection of stone llama heads as well as impressive carnival masks.

The **Museo Mineralógico y Geológico** ① part of the University, T526 1250, Mon-Fri 0800-1200, 1430-1700, US$0.70, getting there: take micro A south to the Ciudad Universitaria, has mineral specimens and fossils. **Casa Arte Taller Cardozo Velásquez** ① Junín 738 y Arica, east of the centre, T527 5245, Mon-Sat 1000-1200, 1500-1800, US$1. Contemporary Bolivian painting and sculpture is displayed in the Cardozo Velásquez home, a family of artists.

There are thermal baths outside town at **Obrajes** ① 23 km from Oruro, minibuses leave from Caro y Av 6 de Agosto, US$1, 45 mins; baths open 0700-1800, US$1.50, Oruro office: Murgía 1815 y Camacho, T525 0646.

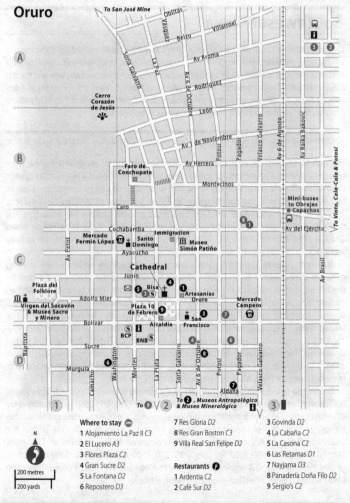

Oruro

Where to stay 🛏
1 Alojamiento La Paz II C3
2 El Lucero A3
3 Flores Plaza C2
4 Gran Sucre D2
5 La Fontana D2
6 Repostero D3
7 Res Gloria D2
8 Res Gran Boston C3
9 Villa Real San Felipe D2

Restaurants 🍴
1 Ardentia C2
2 Café Sur D2
3 Govinda D2
4 La Cabaña C2
5 La Casona C2
6 Las Retamas D1
7 Nayjama D3
8 Panadería Doña Filo D2
9 Sergio's C2

Quime → *Population: 3000.*

North of Oruro, one hour by bus (two to three hours south of La Paz) is the junction at Conani, where there are several places to eat and stay. From here a road, mostly paved, runs over the altiplano to the Tres Cruces pass (over 5000 m) before dropping 2000 m on a spectacular road to Quime, a town in the Yungas de Inquisivi, at the southern edge of the Cordillera Quimsa Cruz. It can also be reached along scenic secondary roads from Chulumani in Sud-Yungas and Cochabamba. It's an increasingly popular escape from La Paz, to relax or hike in the cordillera. Excursions include to Aymara mining communities and waterfalls and mountain biking trips, including a downhill from Tres Cruces. The main festival is from 23 July (Santiago). There are basic services, but no ATMs.

Parque Nacional Sajama

A one-day drive to the west of Oruro is the **Parque Nacional Sajama** ① *park headquarters in Sajama village, T02-513 5526 (in La Paz SERNAP T02-242 6303), www.biobol.org, US$4.25 payable to community of Sajama*, established in 1939 and covering 100,230 ha. The park contains the world's highest forest, consisting mainly of the rare queñual tree (Polylepis tarapacana) which grows up to an altitude of 5500 m. The scenery is wonderful with views of several volcanoes, including Sajama – Bolivia's highest peak at 6542 m – Parinacota and Pomerape (jointly called Payachatas). The road is paved and leads across the border into the Parque Nacional Lauca in Chile. You can trek in the park, with or without porters and mules, but once you move away from the Río Sajama or its major tributaries, lack of water is a problem. There is basic accommodation in Sajama village (see below) as well as a more comfortable and expensive option at **Tomarapi** on the north side of the mountain; see page 346.

Sajama village → *Population: 500. Altitude: 4200 m.*

In Sajama village, visitors are billeted in basic family-run *alojamientos* on a rotating basis (about US$4.50 per person). All are basic to very basic, especially the sanitary facilities; no showers or electricity, solar power for lighting only. Alojamientos may provide limited food, so take your own supplies. It can be very windy and cold at night; a good sleeping bag, gloves and hat are essential. Crampons, ice axe and rope are needed for climbing the volcanoes and can be hired in the village. Maps are hard to find. Local guides charge US$50-70 per day. Pack animals can be hired, US$8 per day including guide. Good bathing at the Manasaya thermal complex, 6 km northwest of village, entry US$4.25; jeeps can be rented to visit, US$8-16. Many villagers sell alpaca woolen items.

By road to Chile

The shortest and most widely used route from La Paz to Chile is the road to **Arica** via the border at **Tambo Quemado** (Bolivia) and **Chungará** (Chile). From La Paz take the highway south towards Oruro. Immediately before Patacamaya, turn right at green road sign to Puerto Japonés on the Río Desaguadero, then on to Tambo Quemado. Take extra petrol (none available after Chilean border until Arica), food and water. The journey is worthwhile for the breathtaking views.

Bolivian **customs and immigration** are at Tambo Quemado, where there are a couple of very basic places to stay and eat. Border control is open daily 0800-2000. Shops change bolivianos, pesos chilenos and dollars. From Tambo Quemado there is a stretch of about 7 km of 'no-man's land' before you reach the Chilean frontier at Chungará. Here the border crossing, which is set against the most spectacular scenic backdrop of Lago Chungará

La Diablada

Starting on the Saturday before Ash Wednesday, Los Carnavales de Oruro include the famous **Diablada** ceremony in homage to the miraculous Virgen del Socavón, patroness of miners, and in gratitude to Pachamama, the Earth Mother. The Diablada was traditionally performed by indigenous miners, but several other guilds have taken up the custom. The carnival is especially notable for its fantastically elaborate and imaginative costumes.

The **Sábado de Peregrinación** starts its 5 km route through the town at 0700, finishing at the Sanctuary of the Virgen del Socavón, and continues into the early hours of Sunday. There the dancers invoke blessings and ask for pardon.

At dawn on Sunday, **El Alba** is a competition of all participating musicians at Plaza del Folklore near the Santuario, an amazing battle of the bands. The **Gran Corso** or **La Entrada** starts at 0800 on the Sunday, a more informal parade (many leave their masks off) along the same route.

Monday is **El Día del Diablo y del Moreno** in which the Diablos and Morenos, with their bands, bid farewell to the Virgin. Arches decorated with colourful woven cloths and silverware are set up on the road leading to the Santuario, where a Mass is held. In the morning, at Avenida Cívica, the Diablada companies participate in a play of the Seven Deadly Sins. This is followed by a play about the meeting of the Inca Atahualpa with Pizarro, performed by the Fraternidad Hijos del Sol. At night, each company has a private party.

On Tuesday, **Martes de Chall'a**, families get together, with ch'alla rituals to invoke ancestors, unite with Pachamama and bless personal possessions. Throughout Carnaval everyone throws water and sprays foam at everyone else (plastic tunics are sold for US$0.20 by street vendors).

The Friday before Carnaval, traditional miners' ceremonies are held at mines,

and Volcán Parinacota, is thorough but efficient; open 0800-2000. Expect a long wait at weekends and any day behind lines of lorries. Drivers must fill in 'Relaciones de Pasajeros', US$0.25 from kiosk at border, giving details of driver, vehicle and passengers. Do not take any livestock, plants, fruit, vegetables, coca or dairy products into Chile.

An alternative crossing from Oruro: several bus companies travel southwest to Iquique, via the border posts of **Pisiga** (Bolivia) and **Colchane** (Chile). The road is paved from Oruro to Toledo (32 km) and from Opoquari to Pisiga via Huachachalla (about 100 km). The rest of the 170 km road in Bolivia is unpaved; on the Chilean side it's paved all the way to Iquique, 250 km. There is also service from Oruro to Arica via Patacamaya and Tambo Quemado.

South of Oruro

Machacamarca, about 30 minutes south of Oruro, has a good **railway museum** ① *Wed and Fri 0900-1200, 1500-1700*. Further south, the road runs between the flat plain of Lago Poopó and the Cordillera Azanaque, a very scenic ride. There are thermal baths at **Pazña**, 91 km from Oruro. About 65 km south is the **Santuario de Aves Lago Poopó** (a Ramsar site), an excellent bird reserve on the lake of the same name. The lake dries up completely in winter. The closest place to Oruro to see flamingos and other birds is **Lago Uru Uru** (the northern section of the Poopó lake system), go to Villa Challacollo on the road to Pisiga (minibuses 102, 10, 5 or blue micros) and walk from there. Birds start arriving with the first rains in October or November. Further along, at Km 10 is Chusakeri, where chullpas can be seen on the hillside.

including the sacrifice of a llama. Visitors may only attend with advance permission.

Preparations for Carnaval begin four months before the actual event, on the first Sunday of November, and rehearsals are held every Sunday until one week before Carnaval, when a plain clothes rehearsal takes place, preceded by a Mass for participants. In honour of its syncretism of ancestral Andean traditions and Catholic faith, the Oruro Carnaval has been included on UNESCO's Heritage of Humanity list.

Seating Stands are erected along the entire route and must be purchased from the entrepreneurs who put them up. Tickets are for Saturday and Sunday, there is no discount if you stay only one day. A prime location is around Plaza 10 de Febrero where the companies perform in front of the authorities, seats run US$35-55, some are sold at the more expensive hotels. Along Avenida 6 de Agosto seats cost US$20-25, good by the TV cameras, where performers try their best.

Where to stay During Carnaval, accommodation costs two to three times more than normal and must be booked well in advance. Hotels charge for Friday, Saturday and Sunday nights. You can stay for only one night, but you'll be charged for three. Locals also offer places to stay in their homes, expect to pay at least US$10 per person per night.

Transport The maximum fare is posted at the terminal, but when demand is at its peak, bus prices from La Paz can triple. Buses get booked up quickly, starting Friday and they do not sell tickets in advance. There's usually no transport back to La Paz on Tuesday, so travel on Monday or Wednesday. Many agencies organize day trips from La Paz on Saturday, departing 0430, most will pick you up from your hotel. They return late, making for a tiring day. Trips cost US$45-60, and include breakfast, a snack and sometimes a seat for the parade.

Access to the lake is a little closer from **Huari**, 15 minutes south of Challapata. Huari (124 km south of Oruro, paved) is a pleasant little town with a large brewery; there is a small museum and Mirador Tatacuchunita, a lookout on nearby Cerro Sullka. Sunsets over the lake are superb. There are a couple of basic *alojamientos*, eg **25 de Mayo**, two blocks from the plaza towards Challapata, shared bath, cold water in morning only. It is about an 8 km walk from Huari to the lake, depending on the water level. Near the lake is the Uru-Muratos community of **Llapallapani** with circular adobe homes, those with straw roofs are known as *chillas* and those with conical adobe roofs are *putukus*. Cabins in putuku style form part of a community tourism programme. Boats can be hired when the water level is high, at other times Poopó is an unattainable mirage. There is good walking in the Cordillera Azanaque behind Huari; take food, water, warm clothing and all gear. **Challapata** (fiesta 15-17 July) has several places to stay, eg **Res Virgen del Carmen**, by main plaza, and a gas station.

Atlantis in the Andes Jim Allen's theory of Atlantis (www.atlantisbolivia.org) is well known around Oruro. **Pampa Aullagas**, the alleged Atlantis site, is 196 km from Oruro, southwest of Lago Poopó. Access is from the town of **Quillacas** along a road that branches west from the road to Uyuni just south of Huari, or from the west through Toledo and Andamarca. A visit here can be combined with visits to the Salar de Coipasa.

Southwest of Lago Poopó, off the Oruro-Pisiga-Iquique road (turn off at **Sabaya**), is the **Salar de Coipasa**, 225 km from Oruro. It is smaller and less visited than the Salar de Uyuni, and has a turquoise lake in the middle of the salt pan surrounded by mountains with gorgeous views and large cacti. Coipasa is northwest of the Salar de Uyuni and travel from one to the other is possible with a private vehicle along the impressive **Ruta Intersalar**. Along the way are tombs, terracing and ancient irrigation canals at the archaeological site of **Alcaya** ① *US$1.25*, gradually being developed by the local community (near **Salinas de Garci Mendoza**, locally known as Salinas). At the edge of the Salar de Uyuni is **Coquesa** (lodging available), which has a mirador and tombs with mummies (US$1.25 entry to each site). Nearby are the towering volcanic cones of Cora Cora and Tunupa. Access to the north end of the Salar de Uyuni is at **Jirira**, east of Coquesa, with a salt hotel (see Where to stay) and airstream camper vans run by **Crillon Tours** (www.uyuni.travel).

Note: Getting stranded out on the altiplano or, worse yet on the salar itself, is dangerous because of extreme temperatures and total lack of drinking water. It is best to visit this area with a tour operator that can take you, for example, from Oruro through the salares to Uyuni. Travellers with their own vehicles should only attempt this route following extensive local inquiry or after taking on a guide to avoid becoming lost or bogged. The edges of the salares are soft and only established entry points or ramps (*terraplenes*) should be used to cross onto or off the salt.

⊙ Oruro and around listings

For hotel and restaurant price codes, and other relevant information, see pages 14-17.

⊜ Where to stay

Oruro *p341, map p342*
$$ Flores Plaza, Adolfo Mier 735 at Plaza 10 de Febrero, T525 2561, www.floresplaza hotel.com. Comfortable carpeted rooms, central location.
$$ Gran Sucre, Sucre 510 esq 6 de Octubre, T527 6800, hotelsucreoruro@entelnet.bo. Refurbished old building (faded elegance), rooms and newer suites, heaters on request, internet in lobby, helpful staff.
$$ Samay Wasi, Av Brasil 232 opposite the bus terminal, T527 6737, www.hotelessamay wasi.com. Carpeted rooms, discount for IYHF members, has a 2nd branch in Uyuni.
$$ Villa Real San Felipe, San Felipe 678 y La Plata, south of the centre, T525 4993, www.hotelvillarealsanfelipe.com. Quaint hotel, nicely furnished but small rooms, heating, buffet breakfast, sauna and whirlpool, restaurant, tour operator.
$ El Lucero, 21 de Enero 106 y Brasil, opposite the terminal, T528 5884. Multi-storey hotel, reliable hot water, front rooms noisy, good value.

$ La Fontana, off Bakovic, opposite the bus terminal, T527 9412. Simple rooms, does not include breakfast, restaurant, good service, helpful owner.
$ Repostero, Sucre 370 y Pagador, T525 8001. Hot water, parking, restaurant serves set lunch. Renovated carpeted rooms are more expensive but better value than their old rooms.
$ Res Gran Boston, Pagador 1159 y Cochabamba, T527 4708. Refurbished house, rooms around a covered patio, cheaper with shared bath, good value.

Quime *p343*
$ Hostal Rancho Colobrí, 4 blocks from main plaza (ask directions), http://rancho colibri.wordpress.com. 8 rooms with shared bath, breakfast extra but has a fully-equipped kitchen. Owner Marko Lewis has masses of information on the area (website is also helpful).
2 other basic, slightly cheaper *alojamientos* in town: Santiago and Quime.

Parque Nacional Sajama *p343*
$$ Tomarapi Ecolodge, north of Sajama in Tomarapi community, near Caripe, T02-241 4753, represented by **Millenarian Tourism &**

Travel, Av Sánchez Lima 2193, La Paz, T02-241 4753, www.boliviamilenaria.com. Including full board (good food) and guiding service with climbing shelter at 4900 m, helpful staff, simple but comfortable, with hot water, heating.

South of Oruro *p344*
$ Alojamiento Paraíso, Sabaya. Take sleeping bag, shared bath, cold water, meals on request or take own food, sells petrol.
$ Doña Wadi, Salinas de Garci Mendoza, C Germán Busch, near main plaza, T513 8015. Shared bath, hot water, basic but clean, meals available.
$ Posada Doña Lupe, Jirira. Partly made of salt , hot water, cheaper without bath, use of kitchen but bring your own food, no meals available, caters to tour groups, pleasant, comfortable.
$ Zuk'arani, on a hillside overlooking Salinas de Garci Mendoza and the Salar, T2513 7086, zukarani@hotmail.com. 2 cabins for 4, with bath, hot water, cheaper in rooms with shared bath, hot water, meals on request.

🍴 Restaurants

Oruro *p341, map p342*
$$ La Cabaña, Junín 609. Sun and Mon 1200-1530 only, Comfortable, smart, good international food, bar.
$$ Nayjama, Aldana 1880. Good regional specialities, very popular for lunch, huge portions.
$$-$ Las Retamas, Murguía 930 esq Washington. Mon-Sat 0930-2330, Sun 0930-1430. Excellent quality and value for set lunches (**$**), Bolivian and international dishes à la carte, very good pastries at **Kuchen Haus**, pleasant atmosphere, attentive service, a bit out of the way but well worth the trip. Recommended.
$ Ardentia, Sorria Galvarro y Junín, open 1900-2200. Home cooking, tasty pasta and meat dishes.
$ La Casona, Pres Montes 5970, opposite Post Office. *Salteñas* in the morning, closed midday. Good *pizzería* at night.

$ Govinda, 6 de Octubre 6071. Mon-Sat 0900-2130. Excellent vegetarian.
$ Sergio's, La Plata y Mier, at Plaza 10 de Febrero. Very good pizza, hamburgers, snacks; also pastries in the afternoon, good service.

Cafés
Café Sur, Arce 163, near train station. Tue-Sat. Live entertainment, seminars, films, good place to meet local students.
Panadería Doña Filo, 6 de Octubre esq Sucre. Closed Sun. Excellent savoury snacks and sweets, takeaway only.

🍸 Bars and clubs

Oruro *p341, map p342*
Bravo, Montesinos y Pagador. Open 2100-0300. Varied music.
Imagine, 6 de Octubre y Junín. Open 2200-0400. Latin and other music.

🛍 Shopping

Oruro *p341, map p342*
Camping equipment Camping Oruro, Pagador 1660, T528 1829, camping_oruro@hotmail.com.
Crafts On Av La Paz the blocks between León and Belzu are largely given over to workshops producing masks and costumes for Carnaval. **Artesanías Oruro**, A Mier 599, esq S Galvarro. Lovely selection of regional handicrafts produced by 6 rural community cooperatives; nice sweaters, carpets, wall-hangings.
Markets Mercado Campero, V Galvarro esq Bolívar. Sells everything, also *brujería* section for magical concoctions. **Mercado Fermín López**, C Ayacucho y Montes. Food and hardware. C Bolívar is the main shopping street. **Global**, Junín y La Plata. Well stocked supermarket. **Irupana**, S Galvarra y A Mier. Natural food and snacks.

⚙ What to do

Oruro *p341, map p342*
Asociación de Guías Mineros, contact
Gustavo Peña, T523 2446. Arranges visits
to San José mine.
Freddy Barrón, T527 6776, lufba@hotmail.
com. Custom-made tours and transport,
speaks German and some English.

⊖ Transport

Oruro *p341, map p342*
Bus Bus terminal 10 blocks north of centre
at Bakovic and Aroma, T525 3535, US$0.25
terminal use fee, luggage store, ATMs.
Micro 2 to centre, or any saying 'Plaza 10 de
Febrero'. To **Challapata** and **Huari**: several
companies go about every hour, US$1,
1¾ hrs, and Huari, US$1.25, 2 hrs, last bus
back leaves Huari about 1630. You can also
take a bus to Challapata and a shared taxi
from there to Huari, US$0.30. Daily services
to: **La Paz** at least every hour 0400-2200,
US$2-3.40, 4 hrs; also tourist van service
with **Enjoy Bolivia**, see La Paz Tour operators,
page 321. Note that in 2014, work was in
progress to widen the La Paz to Oruro
highway to 4 lanes, causing travel delays.
Cochabamba, US$3.35-4, 4 hrs, frequent.
Potosí, US$2.70-4, 5 hrs, several daily. **Sucre**,
all buses around 2000, US$7, 9 hrs. **Tarija**,
2 departures at 2030, US$9.30-14.50, 14 hrs.
Uyuni, several companies, all depart 1900-
2100, US$4.35 regular, US$7.25 semi-cama,
7-8 hrs. **Todo Turismo**, offers a tourist bus
departing from La Paz at 2100, arrange
ahead for pick-up in Oruro at midnight,
US$27. To **Tupiza**, via Potosí, **Boquerón** at
1230, **Illimani** at 1630 and 2000, US$9.75-
12.40, 11-12 hrs, continuing to Villazón,
US$10-13, 13-14 hrs. **Santa Cruz**, Bolívar
at 2000, US$8.70, *bus cama* at 2130, US$14,
11 hrs. To **Pisiga** (Chilean border), **Trans
Pisiga**, Av Dehene y España, T526 2241,
at 2000 and 2030, or with Iquique bound
buses, US$3.75, 4-5 hrs. **International
buses** (US$2 to cross border): to **Iquique**

via Pisiga, US$13-14, 8 hrs, buses leave
around 1200 coming from Cochabamba.
Arica via Patacamaya and Tambo Quemado,
several companies daily around 1100-1300
and 2300, US$22 normal, US$26-29 semi-
cama, US$33 cama, 8 hrs, some continue to
Iquique, 12 hrs.
Train The station is at Av Velasco Galvarro
y Aldana, T527 4605, ticket office Mon-Fri
0800-1200, 1430-1800, Sun 0830-1120,
1530-1800. Tickets for *ejecutivo* class are sold
up to 2 weeks in advance, 1 week for *salón*.
Tickets can also be purchased in La Paz, see
page 325. **Ferroviaria Andina** (FCA, www.
fca.com.bo), runs services from Oruro to
Uyuni, **Tupiza** and **Villazón**. Expreso del Sur
runs Tue and Fri at 1530, arriving in Uyuni
at 2220, and **Wara Wara** on Sun and Wed at
1900, arriving in Uyuni at 0220.
  Fares Expreso del Sur to **Uyuni**, *Ejecutivo*
US$17, *Salón* US$8.60; **Tupiza**, 12½ hrs:
US$34, US$15.30 respectively; **Villazón**:
15½ hrs, US$40, US$18 respectively. **Wara
Wara del Sur to Uyuni**: *Ejecutivo* US$14.60,
Salón US$6.70; **Tupiza**, 13½-14 hrs: US$26,
US$11.40 respectively; **Villazón**, 17 hrs:
US$31.40, US$14.30 respectively.

Quime *p343*
To get to Quime, take any bus from La Paz to
Oruro or Cochabamba and get out at Conani,
2-3 hrs (likewise get out at Conani coming
from Oruro or Cochabamba). Change to a
bus, minibus or taxi (wait till full) to Quime,
1½ hrs, US$3.55. Direct buses from La Paz
to Quime, 5 hrs, are **Inquisivi** from the bus
terminal (T282 4734) and **Apóstol Santiago**
from El Alto (T259 7544), US$3.55.

Parque Nacional Sajama *p343*
To get to the park, take a La Paz-Oruro bus
and change at Patacamaya. Minivans
from Patacamaya to Sajama Sun-Fri 1200,
3 hrs, US$2.50. Sajama to **Patacamaya**
Mon-Fri 0600, some days via **Tambo
Quemado**, confirm details and weekend
schedule locally. From Tambo Quemado
to Sajama about 1530 daily, 1 hr, US$0.65.

Or take a La Paz-Arica bus, ask for Sajama, try to pay half the fare, but you may be charged full fare.

South of Oruro *p344*
To **Coipasa** ask if **Trans Pisiga**, address above, is running a fortnightly service. If not, you can take one of the buses for Iquique and get off at the turn-off, but it's difficult to hire a private vehicle for onward transportation in this sparsely populated area. Salinas de Garci Mendoza from **Oruro**,

Trans **Cabrera**, C Tejerina y Caro, daily except Sat (Mon, Wed Fri, Sun 1900, Tue, Thu 0830, Sun also at 0730). Return to Oruro same days, US$3.40, 7 hrs.

ⓘ Directory

Oruro *p341, map p342*
Useful addresses Immigration, S Galvarro 5744 entre Ayacucho y Cochabamba, across from Museo Simón Patiño, T527 0239, Mon-Fri 0830-1230, 1430-1830.

Uyuni → *Phone code: 02. Colour map 3, C3. Population: 18,000. Altitude: 3670 m.*

Uyuni lies near the eastern edge of the Salar de Uyuni and is one of the jumping-off points for trips to the salt flats, volcanoes and lakes of southwest Bolivia. With the arrival of regular flights to Uyuni and the paving of the Uyuni-Potosí road, tourism in the area is changing fast, with new hotels and new packages being offered. Still a commercial and communication centre, Uyuni was, for much of the 20th century, important as a major railway junction. Two monuments dominate Avenida Ferroviaria: one of a railway worker, erected after the 1952 Revolution, and the other commemorating those who died in the Chaco War. Most services are near the station. **Museo Arqueológico y Antropológico de los Andes Meridionales** ① *Arce y Potosí, Mon-Fri 0830-1200, 1400-1800, Sat-Sun 0900-1300, US$0.35*, is small museum with local artefacts. The market is at Potosí y Bolívar. Fiesta 11 July. There is a Railway Cemetery of sorts outside town with engines from 1907 to the 1950s, now rusting hulks. **Pulacayo**, 25 km from Uyuni on the road to Potosí, is a town at the site of a 19th-century silver mine. The train cemetery here is more interesting and contains the first locomotive in Bolivia and the train robbed by Butch Cassidy and the Sundance Kid.

Tourist office Dirección de Turismo Uyuni ① *at the clock tower, T693 2060, Mon-Sat 0800-1200, 1430-1830, Sun 0900-1200*. **Subprefectura de Potosí** ① *Colón y Sucre, Mon-Fri 0800-1200, 1430-1830, Sat 0800-1200*, departmental information office, the place to file complaints in writing. There is only one ATM in Uyuni which does not always work, take cash.

Salar de Uyuni

Crossing the Salar de Uyuni, the largest and highest salt lake in the world, is one of the great Bolivian trips. Driving across it is a fantastic experience, especially during June and July when the bright blue skies contrast with the blinding white salt crust. Farther south, and included on most tours of the region, is the **Reserva Eduardo Avaroa** (REA, see below) with the towering volcanoes, multi-coloured lakes with abundant birdlife, weird rock formations, thermal activity and endless puna that make up some of most fabulous landscapes in South America. For information on the north shore of the salar, see South of Oruro, page 344.

Trips to the Salar de Uyuni originating in Uyuni enter via the *terraplén* (ramp) at **Colchani** (Museo de la Llama y de la Sal; see also Where to stay, below) and include stops to see traditional salt mining techniques and the Ojos del Agua, where salt water bubbles to the surface of the slat flat, perhaps a call at a salt hotel (see Where to stay, below) and a visit to the **Isla Incahuasi** ① *entry US$5*. This is a coral island, raised up from the ocean bed, covered in tall cactii. There is a walking trail with superb views, a café, basic lodging and toilets. If on an extended tour (see below), you may leave the Salar by another *terraplén*, eg Puerto Chuvica in the southwest. Some tours also include **Gruta de la Galaxia**, an interesting cave at the edge of the Salar.

The Salar de Uyuni contains what may be the world's largest lithium deposits and the Bolivian government has announced plans to build large-scale extraction facilities. A pilot plant was recently operating (away from usual tourist routes) and concern has been expressed about the impact of more extensive lithium mining.

San Cristóbal

The original village of San Cristóbal, southwest of Uyuni, was relocated in 2002 to make way for a huge open-pit mine, said to be one of the largest silver deposits in South America. The original church (1650) had been declared a national monument and was therefore rebuilt in its entirety. Ask at the Fundación San Cristóbal Office for the church to be opened as the interior artwork, restored by Italian techniques, is worth seeing. The fiesta is 27-28 July.

Reserva Nacional de Fauna Andina Eduardo Avaroa

① *SERNAP office at Colón y Avaroa, Uyuni, T693 2225, www.biobol.org, Mon-Fri 0830-1230, 1430-1800; entry to reserve US$22 (Bs150, not included in tour prices; pay in bolivianos). Park ranger/entry points are near Laguna Colorada, Lagunas Verde and Blanca, close to the Chilean border, and at Sol de Mañana, near Quetena Chico.*

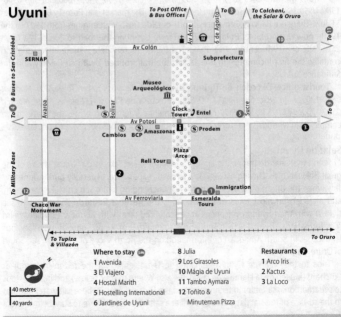

Uyuni

To Post Office & Bus Offices
To ③
To Colchani, the Salar & Oruro
To ⑪

Av Colón

SERNAP

Subprefectura

To ① & Buses to San Cristóbal

Avaroa

Bolivar

Fie Ⓢ

Museo Arqueológico

Clock Tower ▪ Entel

Av Potosí

Cambios BCP Amazonas ⓘ Ⓢ Prodem

Sucre

To ⑨ ⑥

Plaza Arce ❶

Reli Tour ❷

Immigration

❽ ❶

Av Ferroviaria

Esmeralda Tours

To Military Base

Chaco War Monument

To Tupiza & Villazón

To Oruro

40 metres
40 yards

Where to stay		
1 Avenida	8 Julia	Restaurants
3 El Viajero	9 Los Girasoles	1 Arco Iris
4 Hostal Marith	10 Mágia de Uyuni	2 Kactus
5 Hostelling International	11 Tambo Aymara	3 La Loco
6 Jardines de Uyuni	12 Toñito &	
	Minuteman Pizza	

In the far southwest of Bolivia, in the Lípez region, is the 714,745-ha Reserva Nacional Eduardo Avaroa (REA). There are two access routes from Uyuni (one via the Salar) and one from Tupiza. This is one of Bolivia's prime attractions and tour vehicles criss-cross the puna every day, many on the route from Uyuni to San Pedro de Atacama (Chile). Roads are still unmarked rugged tracks, however, and may be impassable in the wet season. **Laguna Colorada** at 4278 m, 346 km southwest of Uyuni, is just one of the highlights of the reserve, its shores and shallows encrusted with borax and salt, an arctic white counterpoint to the flaming red, algae-coloured waters in which the rare James flamingos, along with the more common Chilean and Andean flamingos, breed and live. **Laguna Verde** (lifeless because it is laden with arsenic) and its neighbour **Laguna Blanca**, near the Chilean border, are at the foot of Volcán Licancábur, 5868 m. Between Lagunas Colorada and Verde there are thermal pools at Laguna Blanca (blissful water, a challenge to get out into the bitter wind – no facilities) and at Polques, on the shores of Río Amargo/Laguna Salada by the Salar de Chalviri. A *centro comunal* at Polques has dining room, changing room and toilets. All these places are on the 'classic' tour route, across the Salar de Uyuni to **San Juan**, which has a museum of local *chullpas*, and is where most tour companies stop: plenty of lodgings. Other tours stop at **Culpina K**. Then you go to the Salar de Chiguana, Mirador del Volcán de Ollagüe, Cinco Lagunas, a chain of small, flamingo-specked lagoons, the much-photographed Arbol de Piedra in the Siloli desert, then Laguna Colorada (spend the second night here: **Hospedaje Laguna Colorada**, the newer and better **$ Don Humberto** in Huayllajara, and **Campamento Ende**). From Colorada you go over the Cuesta del Pabellón, 4850 m, to the Sol de Mañana geysers (not to be confused with the Sol de Mañana entry point), the Desierto de Dalí, a pure sandy desert as much Daliesque for the spacing of the rocks, with snow-covered peaks behind, as for the shape of the rocks themselves, and Laguna Verde (4400 m).

Jurisdiction of the reserve belongs to the villages of **Quetena Chico** and Quetena Grande, to the east of Laguna Colorada. The villagers run lodging in the reserve: Quetena Chico runs *hospedajes* at Laguna Colorada. Quetena Grande runs La Cabaña at Hito Cajónes (see below). In Quetena Chico is the reserve's visitors information centre, **Centro Ecológico Ch'aska** ① *daily 0730-1800*, informative displays about the region's geology, vulcanology, fauna, flora and human history; a worthwhile stop. The village has two cheap *hospedajes* (**Piedra Preciosa** and **Hostal Quetena**, hot water extra), and places to eat.

Sadly, lakes in the reserve are gradually drying-up, most noticeably Laguna Verde. This has been attributed to global climate change but the real reason may be massive underground water consumption by Bolivian, Chilean and Argentine mines.

From Tupiza Tour operators in Tupiza run trips to the REA and Salar de Uyuni and go to places not included on tours from Uyuni. These include the beautiful **Lagunas Celeste** and **Negra** below Cerro Uturunco, which is near Quetena Chico; the **Valle de las Rocas**, 4260 m, between the villages of **Alota** and **Villa Mar** (a vast extension of rocks eroded into fantastic configurations, with polylepis trees in sheltered corners); and isolated communities in the puna. The high altitude scenery is out of this world. With the exception of Quetena Chico, *alojamientos* in the villages on the tour routes cannot be booked. You turn up and search for a room. All provide kitchen space for the tour's cook or independent traveller to prepare meals, take your own stove, though. See also **Tayka** in Salar de Uyuni, Where to stay, below. There is public transport from Uyuni into the region, but rarely more than one bus a week, with several hours rough travelling. If travelling independently, note that there are countless tracks and no signposts.

Crossing into Chile

There is a REA ranger station near Lagunas Blanca and Verde: if going from Bolivia, have your park entry receipt at hand, if crossing from Chile pay the entry fee here. Alongside is a *refugio*, La Cabaña; US$5 pp in comfortable but very cold dorms, solar-powered lighting, hot water seldom works, cooking facilities but take your own food (in high season book in advance – tour agencies can do this by radio). There is good climbing and hiking in the area with outstanding views. You must register at the ranger station before heading out and they may insist that you take a guide (eg to climb Licancábur, US$30 for guide plus US$40 for transport). Mind the altitude, intense solar radiation and lack of drinking water.

From the ranger station it's 5 km to the border at Hito Cajones (on the Chilean side called Hito Cajón), 4500 m. Bolivian immigration open 0800-2100, charges US$2 in any currency. If you plan to cross to Chile here, you should first go to the immigration office in Uyuni (see Directory, page 356). There are no services or facilities at the border. A further 6 km along a good dirt road into Chile is the intersection with the fully paved road from San Pedro de Atacama to Paso de Jama, the border between Chile and Argentina. From here it's 40 km (2000 m downhill) to San Pedro. Chilean customs and immigration are just outside San Pedro and can take 45 minutes at busy times. ▸▸ *See Transport, page 355.*

⊙ Uyuni listings

For hotel and restaurant price codes, and other relevant information, see pages 14-17.

● Where to stay

Uyuni *p349, map p350*
Many hotels fill early, reservations are advised in high season, but new hotels are opening (eg Samay Wasi, Av Potosí 965, www.hotelessamaywasi.com). Be conservative with water use, this is a very dry area, water is scarce and supplied at limited hours (better hotels have reserve tanks).

$$$ Jardines de Uyuni, Potosí 113, T693 2989, www.hotelesrusticosjardines.com. Tastefully decorated, comfortable, heating, open fire in the lounge, small pool, parking.

$$$ Mágia de Uyuni, Av Colón 432, T693 2541, www.hostalmagiauyuni.com. Nice ample rooms and suites upstairs with heating, cheaper in older colder rooms downstairs (ask for a heater), parking.

$$ Los Girasoles, Santa Cruz 155, T693 3323, www.girasoleshotel.hostel.com. Buffet breakfast, bright and warm (especially 2nd floor), comfortable, nice decor, heaters, cheaper in old section, internet extra.

$$ Tambo Aymara, Camacho s/n y Colón, T693 2227, www.tamboaymara. com. Lovely colonial-style modern hotel, large comfortable rooms, heating, Belgian/Bolivian owned, operate their own tours.

$$-$ Toñito, Av Ferroviaria 48, T693 3186, www.bolivianexpeditions.com. Spacious rooms with good beds, solar-powered showers and heating in new wing, cheaper in old section with electric showers, parking, book exchange, tours.

$ Avenida, Av Ferroviaria 11, near train station, T693 2078. Simple but well maintained, cheaper with shared bath, hot water (shared showers 0700-2100), long patio with laundry facilities, family-run, helpful, good value, popular and often full.

$ El Viajero, Cabrera 334 y 6 de Agosto, near bus terminals, T02-693 3549. Basic rooms, cheaper with shared bath, electric shower, parking.

$ Hostal Marith, Av Potosí 61, T693 2174. Basic, cheaper with shared bath and in dorm, electric showers from 0830, patio with laundry facilities, tours (have salt hotel at Atulcha near the salar).

$ Hostelling International, Potosí y Sucre, T693 2228 (listed on www.hihostels.com).

Cheaper with shared bath, hot water, modern and popular but poor beds, discount for IYHF members.

$ Julia, Ferroviaria 314 y Arce, T693 2134, www.juliahoteluyuni.com. Spacious rooms, cheaper with shared bath, electric showers, internet extra.

Salar de Uyuni and Reserva Eduardo Avaroa *p349 and p350*

These *hoteles de sal* are generally visited on tours, seldom independently.

$$$$-$$$ Luna Salada, 5 km north of Colchani near the edge of the salar, T7242 9716, La Paz T02-278 5438, www.lunasalada hotel.com.bo. Lovely salt hotel, comfortable rooms, hot water, ample common areas with lovely views of the Salar, salt floors, skylights make it warm and cosy, reserve ahead.

$$$$-$$$ Palacio de Sal, on the edge of the salar, near the ramp outside Colchani, www.palaciodesal.com.bo. Book through Hidalgo Tours, Potosí, T02-622 9512. Spacious, luxury salt hotel, decorated with large salt sculptures, heating, sauna, lookout on 2nd storey with views of the salar.

$$$ Mallku Cueva, outside Villa Mar, along the route from Tupiza to the reserve, T617 9014, www.hotelesrusticosjardines.com. Nicely decorated upmarket hotel with all services, including Wi-Fi.

$$$ Tayka, Uyuni office: Sucre 7715 entre Uruguay y México, T693 2987, La Paz T7205 3438, www.taykahoteles.com. A chain of 4 upmarket hotels in Salar de Uyuni-REA area, operating in conjunction with local communities. The hotels have comfortable rooms with bath, hot water, heating, restaurant, price includes breakfast, discounts in low season. The Hotel de Sal (salt hotel) is in Tahua, on the north shore of the Salar; the Hotel de Piedra (stone hotel) is in San Pedro de Quemes, on the south shore of the Salar; the Hotel del Desierto (desert hotel) is in Ojo de Perdiz in the Siloli Desert, north of Laguna Colorada; the Hotel del Volcán (volcano

hotel) is in San Pablo de Lípez, between Uturunco Volcano and Tupiza.

$ Alojamiento del Museo de Sal, on the road to the Salar from Colchani, by the *tranca*, T7272 0834. Simple cheap salt hotel, shared bath, kitchen facilities, dining area used by groups, has a small museum with salt sculptures, reserve ahead, good value.

San Cristóbal *p350*

$$ Hotel San Cristóbal, in centre, T7264 2117. Purpose-built and owned by the community. The bar is inside a huge oil drum, all metal furnishings. The rest is comfortable if simple, hot water, good breakfast, evening meal extra.

There are also a couple of inexpensive *alojamientos* in town.

❼ Restaurants

Uyuni *p349, map p350*
Plaza Arce has various tourist restaurants serving mostly mediocre pizza.

$$-$ Kactus, Bolívar y Ferroviaria. Daily 0830-2200. Set lunches and international food à la carte, also sells pastries and whole-wheat bread, slow service.

$$-$ La Loco, Av Potosí y Camacho, T693 3105. Mon-Sat 1600-0200 (food until about 2130), closed Jan-Feb. International food with a Bolivian and French touch, music and drinks till late, open fire, popular, reserve in Jul-Aug. Also run a small exclusive guest-house: La Petite Porte (**$$$** www.hotel-lapetiteporte-uyuni.com).

$ Arco Iris, Plaza Arce. Daily 1600-2230. Good Italian food, pizza, and atmosphere, occasional live music.

$ Extreme Fun Pub, Potosí 9. Restaurant/pub, pleasant atmosphere, good service, videos, friendly owner is very knowledgeable about Bolivia.

$ Minuteman, pizza restaurant attached to Toñito Hotel (see above), good pizzas and soups, also breakfast.

⚙ What to do

Uyuni *p349, map p350*
There are over 70 agencies in Uyuni offering salar tours and quality varies greatly. You generally get what you pay for but your experience will depend more on your particular driver, cook and companions than the agency that sells you the tour. Travel is in 4WD Landcruisers, cramped for those on the back seat, but the staggering scenery makes up for any discomfort. Always check the itinerary, the vehicle, the menu (especially vegetarians), what is included in the price and what is not. Trips are usually 3-4 days: Salar de Uyuni, Reserva Eduardo Avaroa, and back to Uyuni or on to San Pedro de Atacama (Chile); or Tupiza to Uyuni, San Pedro de Atacama or back to Tupiza. Prices range from US$50-350 pp plus park fee of Bs 150 (US$22) The cheapest tours are not recommended and usually involve crowding, insufficient staff and food, poor vehicles (fatal accidents have taken place) and accommodation. The best value is at the mid- to high-end, where you can assemble your own tour for a tank of 4-5 passengers, with driver, cook, good equipment and services. Three factors often lead to misunderstandings between what is offered and what is actually delivered by the tour operator: 1) agencies pool clients when there are not enough passengers to fill a vehicle. 2) Agencies all over Bolivia sell Salar tours, but booking from far away may not give full information on the local operator. 3) Many drivers work for multiple agencies and will cut tours short. If the tour seriously fails to match the contract and the operator refuses any redress, complaints can be taken to the Subprefectura de Potosí in Uyuni (see above) but don't expect a quick refund or apology. Try to speak to travellers who have just returned from a tour before booking your own, and ignore touts on the street and at the rail or bus stations.

Tour operators
Andes Travel Office (ATO), in Hotel Tambo Aymara (see above), T693 2227, tamboaymara@gmail.com. Upmarket private tours, Belgian/Bolivian-owned, English and French spoken, reliable.
Atacama Mística, Av Ferroviaria s/n, T693 3607, www.atacamamistica.cl. Chilean-Bolivian company, daily tours with transfer to San Pedro de Atacama, also transfers between San Pedro and Uyuni, good service.
Creative Tours, Sucre 362, T693 3543, www.creativetours.com.bo. Long-established company, partners in the Tayka chain of hotels, see below. Premium tours in the region and throughout the country, with offices in Uyuni, Cochabamba and Trinidad, and representatives in the main cities.
Esmeralda, Av Ferroviaria y Arce, T693 2130, esmeraldaivan@hotmail.com. Economical end of market.
Hidalgo Tours, Av Potosí 113 at Hotel Jardines de Uyuni, www.salardeuyuni.net. Well established Salar/REA operator, runs Palacio de Sal and Mallku Cueva hotels, also in Potosí.
Oasis Odyssey, Av Ferroviaria, T693 3175, www.oasistours-bo.com. Also have office in Sucre.
Reli Tours, Av Arce 42, T693 3209.

San Cristóbal *p350*
Llama Mama, T7240 0309. 60 km of exclusive bicycle trails descending 2-3 or 4 hrs, depending on skill, 3 grades, US$20 pp, all inclusive, taken up by car, with guide and communication.

⊖ Transport

Uyuni *p349, map p350*
Air To/from La Paz , Amaszonas, Potosí y Arce, T693 3333, 1 or 2 daily, US$143, also TAM 3 times a week.
Bus Most offices are on Av Arce and Cabrera. To La Paz, US$12-17, 11 hrs, daily at 2000 (La Paz-Uyuni at 1900) with Panasur, www.uyunipanasur.com, Cruz del Norte, and

Trans Omar, www.transomar.com; or transfer in Oruro. Tourist buses with **Todo Turismo**, T693 3337, daily at 2000, US$33 (La Paz office, Plaza Antofagasta 504, Edif Paola, p1, opposite the bus terminal, T02-211 9418, daily to Uyuni at 2100), note this service does not run if the road is poor during the rainy season. **Oruro**, several companies 2000-2130, US$6, 7 hrs; Todo Turismo (see above), US$20. To **Potosí** several companies around1000 and 1900, US$5.50, 6 hrs, spectacular scenery. To **Sucre**, 6 de Octubre and **Emperador** at 1000, US$10, 9 hrs; or transfer in Potosí. To **Tupiza** US$7.50, 8 hrs, via **Atocha**, several companies daily at 0600 and 2030 (from Tupiza at 1000 and 1800), continuing to **Villazón** on the Argentine border, US$10, 11 hrs. For **Tarija** change in Potosí or Tupiza. Regional services to villages in **Nor- and Sud-López** operate about 3 times a week, confirm details locally. To **Pulacayo** take any bus for Potosí.

Road and train A road and railway line run south from Oruro, through Río Mulato, to Uyuni (323 km, each about 7 hrs). The road is sandy and, after rain, very bad, especially south of Río Mulato. The train journey is more comfortable. **Expreso del Sur** leaves for **Oruro** on Wed and Sat at 2350, arriving 0710 the next day. **Wara Wara del Sur** leaves on Tue and Fri at 0115, arriving 0910 (prices for both under Oruro, page 348). To **Atocha**, **Tupiza** and **Villazón** Expreso del Sur leaves Uyuni on Tue and Fri at 2220, arriving, respectively, at 0045, 0400 and 0705. **Wara Wara** leaves on Mon and Thu at 0220, arriving 0500, 0835 and 1205. The ticket office (T693 2320) opens Mon-Fri 0900-1200, 1430-1800, Sat-Sun 1000-1100, and 1 hr before the trains leave. It closes once tickets are sold – get there early or buy through a tour agent (more expensive).

Advance preparations are required to drive across the salar and REA. Fuel is not easily available in the López region, so you must take jerrycans. A permit from the Dirección General de Substancias Controladas in La Paz is required to fill jerrycans; you will be authorized to fill only two 60 l cans. Fuel for vehicles with foreign plates may be considerably more expensive than for those with local plates.

Travelling to Chile Chile is 1 hr ahead of Bolivia from mid-Oct to Mar. Chile does not allow coca, dairy produce, tea bags, fruit or vegetables to be brought in.

The easiest way is to go to San Pedro de Atacama as part of your tour to the Salar and REA (see above). **Colque Tours** runs 2 minibuses daily from near the ranger station at Hito Cajones to San Pedro de Atacama, departing 1000 and 1700, US$6.50, 1 hr including stop at immigration. At other times onward transport to San Pedro must be arranged by your agency, this can cost up to US$60 if it is not included in your tour. The ranger station may be able to assist in an emergency. **Hostal Marith** (see Uyuni, Where to stay) and Atacama Mística tour operator run transport service from Uyuni to San Pedro de Atacama, US$30, confirm details in advance.

From Uyuni to **Avaroa** and on to **Calama**, Centenario, Cabrera y Arce, Sun, Mon, Wed, Thu at 0330, transfer at the border to **Intertrans** (daily from Calama to Ollagüe) or Atacama, Thu, Mon 2000. To Avaroa, US$6, 4½ hrs; to Calama US$15, 4 hrs; allow 2 hrs at the border.

If driving your own vehicle, from **Colchani** it is about 60 km across to the southern shore of the **Salar**. Follow the tracks made by other vehicles in the dry season. The salt is soft and wet for about 2 km around the edges so only use established ramps. It is 20 km from the southern shore to Colcha K military checkpoint. From there, a poor gravel road leads 28 km to San Juan then the road enters the Salar de Chiguana, a mix of salt and mud which is often wet and soft with deep tracks which are easy to follow; 35 km away is Chiguana, another military post, then 45 km to the end of this Salar, a few kilometres before border at Ollagüe. This latter part is the most dangerous; very slippery with little traffic. Or take the route that tours use to Laguna Colorada and continue to Hito Cajones. **Atacama Mística** of Uyuni will let you follow one of their groups if you arrange in advance. There is no fuel between Uyuni and Calama (Chile) if going via Ollagüe, but expensive fuel is sold in San Pedro de Atacama. Keep to the road at all times; the road is impassable after rain.

① Directory

Uyuni *p349, map p350*
Useful addresses Immigration: Av Ferroviaria entre Arce y Sucre, T693 2062, Mon-Fri 0830-1230, 1430-1830, Sat-Sun 0900-1100, for visa extensions, also register here before travel to Chile.

Tupiza → *Phone code: 02. Colour map 3, C3. Population: 25,709. Altitude: 2975m.*

Set in a landscape of colourful, eroded mountains and stands of huge cactii (usually flowering December-February), Tupiza, 200 km south of Uyuni, is a pleasant town with a lower altitude and warmer climate, making it a good alternative for visits to the Reserva Eduardo Avaroa and the Salar. Several Tupiza operators offer Salar, REA and local tours. Beautiful sunsets over the fertile Tupiza valley can be seen from the foot of a statue of Christ on a hill behind the plaza.

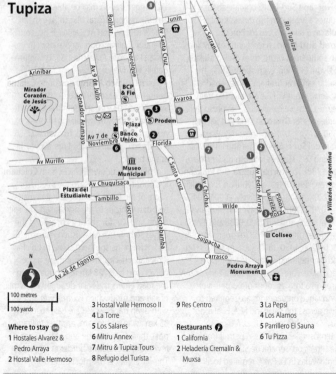

Tupiza

100 metres
100 yards

Where to stay 🛏
1 Hostales Alvarez & Pedro Arraya
2 Hostal Valle Hermoso
3 Hostal Valle Hermoso II
4 La Torre
5 Los Salares
6 Mitru Annex
7 Mitru & Tupiza Tours
8 Refugio del Turista
9 Res Centro

Restaurants 🍴
1 California
2 Heladería Cremalín & Muxsa
3 La Pepsi
4 Los Alamos
5 Parrillero El Sauna
6 Tu Pizza

There is good hiking around Tupiza but be prepared for sudden changes of climate including hailstorms, and note that dry gullies are prone to flash flooding. A worthwhile excursion is to **Quebrada Palala** with the nearby 'Stone Forest'; here is the hamlet of Torre Huayco, part of a community tourism project, Circuitos Bioculturales. **Oploca**, a small town 17 km northwest of Tupiza with a lovely colonial church, is also part of the project, as is Chuquiago, 30 km south of Tupiza, along the rail line. Each has a small *eco-albergue* (\$ pp, with breakfast, simple comfortable rooms, kitchen) and guides. A circuit can be done in one to three days by bicycle, horse, trekking, jeep, or a combination of these (US\$35-50 per day, ask tour operators in Tupiza). The routes are very scenic and the villages are tranquil. You can arrange to spend a couple of days relaxing there.

Tupiza is the base for **Butch Cassidy and the Sundance Kid tours**. The statue in the main plaza is to **Victor Carlos Aramayo** (1802-1882), of the 19th century mining dynasty. Butch and Sundance's last holdup was of an Aramayo company payroll at Huaca Huañusca on 4 November 1908. They are believed (by some, see *Digging Up Butch and Sundance*, by Anne Meadows, Bison Books, 2003) to have died soon afterwards at the hands of a police patrol in **San Vicente**, a tiny mining camp at 4500 m, but no grave in the San Vicente cemetery has yet to be positively identified as theirs. There is a small museum with local artifacts but no lodging or other services. Visits can be arranged by Tupiza agencies.

There are two ATMs in Tupiza, beside Tu Pizza restaurant and at Banco FIE. Don't rely on them, though; take cash.

South to Argentine border

Villazón The Argentine border is at Villazón *(Phone code: 02; Population: 37,133; Altitude: 3443 m)*, 81 km south of Tupiza. There is a museum about the Chicha culture at the plaza. Of traditional villages in the surroundings, those to the west, like Berque, are known for their pottery. Many *casas de cambio* on Av República de Argentina, leading to the border, change US\$, pesos and euros, all at poor rates. There are banks and an ATM in town. The border area must not be photographed.

Border with Argentina The Bolivian immigration office is on Avenida República de Argentina just before bridge, open daily 0600-2000, taxi from Villazón bus terminal US\$0.50 pp. Queuing begins at 0500 and there may be long delays. Argentine immigration (open 0700-2400 Argentine time, see below) is on the other side of the bridge, 10 blocks from La Quiaca bus terminal, taxi US\$1. Change all your bolivianos in Villazón as there is nowhere to do so in La Quiaca or beyond. Entering Bolivia, boys offer to wheel your bags uphill to the bus stations, US\$1, but they will ask for more. The Argentine consulate is at Plaza 6 de Agosto 121, T597 2011, Monday-Friday 0800-1300. **Note** Argentine time is one hour later than Bolivia, two hours when Buenos Aires adopts daylight saving.

⊙ Tupiza listings

For hotel and restaurant price codes, and other relevant information, see pages 14-17.

⊜ Where to stay

Tupiza *p356, map p356*
\$\$-\$ Mitru, Av Chichas 187, T694 3001, www.hotelmitru.com. Pleasant ample grounds with pool, nice atmosphere, a variety of rooms and prices, the more expensive rooms have king-size beds, a/c and hair driers, cheaper in older section with private bath and even cheaper with shared bath. All include good buffet breakfast with bread made on the premises, reliable solar hot water, parking, luggage store,

book exchange, Wi-Fi. Very helpful and knowledgeable, popular, reserve ahead in high season. Warmly recommended.

$ Hostal Alvarez, Av P Arraya 492, T694 5327. Near the bus and train stations, Small 10-room hostel, brighter rooms on 2nd storey, cheaper with shared bath, extra charge for a/c and breakfast, new in 2013.

$ Hostal Pedro Arraya, Av P Arraya 494, T694 2734, www.hostalpedroarraya.com. Convenient to bus and train stations, small rooms, cheaper with shared bath, hot water, breakfast available, laundry facilities, terrace, family-run.

$ Hostal Valle Hermoso, Av Pedro Arraya 478, T694 2592, www.vallehermosotours. com. Breakfast available, cheaper with shared bath, cheaper in dorm. TV/breakfast room, book exchange, motorbike parking. Second location, **Valle Hermoso II**, Av Pedro Arraya 585, T694 3441, near the bus station, 3 simple rooms with bath, several dorms with bunk beds, same prices as No 1, 10% discount for IYHF members in both locations.

$ La Torre, Av Chichas 220, T694 2633, www. latorretours-tupiza.com. Lovely refurbished house, newer rooms at back, comfortable, cheaper with shared bath and no TV, great service, good value. Recommended.

$ Los Salares, C Ecuador s/n, Zona Chajrahuasi, behind petrol station, T694 5813, www.lossalares.hostel.com. 9 rooms, 1 without bath (cheaper), continental breakfast and kitchen, parking, a bit out of town.

$ Mitru Annex, Avaroa 20, T694 3002, www.tupizatours.com. Nicely refurbished older hotel, buffet breakfast, cheaper with shared bath, good hot showers, Wi-Fi, use of pool and games room at **Hotel Mitru**.

$ Refugio del Turista, Av Santa Cruz 240, T694 3155, www.tupizatours.com. Refurbished home with garden, shared bath, reliable hot water, well-equipped kitchen, laundry facilities, parking and electric outlet for camper-vans, popular budget option, good value.

$ Res Centro, Av Santa Cruz 287, T694 2705. Nice patio, couple of rooms with private bath, most shared, basic but clean, hot water, parking, helpful owner, good value.

Villazón *p357*

$ Hostal Plaza, Plaza 6 de Agosto 138, T597 3535. Adequate rooms, cheaper without bath, electric shower, includes simple breakfast, good restaurant, **La Perla**, underneath hotel, also internet below.

$ Olimpo, Av República Argentina y Chorolque 116, T597 2219. Among the better hotels in town, cheaper with shared bath, includes simple breakfast.

$ Tierra Andina, 25 de Mayo 52, T594 5133. Another good option, with and without bath and most economical in 4-bed dorms, includes a very basic breakfast.

🍴 Restaurants

Tupiza *p356, map p356*

Several touristy pizza places on C Florida are mediocre to terrible, also watch your belongings here. The best options are just outside town (all **$$-$**), they serve grilled meat and good regional specialities like *picante de cabrito* (spicy goat) but open only Sat or Sun midday – go early. These include: La Campiña, in Tambillo Alto, 45 mins' walk north along the river; and La Estancia, 2 km north in Villa Remedios. There are food stalls upstairs in the market but mind the cleanliness.

$$-$ Café Muxsa, Cochabamba 133 y Florida, on Plaza, Tue-Sun 1700-2200. A variety of good-quality sandwiches, tacos and salads, nicely served, good coffee, pastries, Wi-Fi, popular.

$ California, Cochabamba 413, 2nd floor. Set lunches, hamburgers and snacks in the evening when service is slow.

$ Los Alamos, Av Chichas 157. Open 0800-2400. Local and international dishes, good atmosphere, average food, good juices, large portions, popular with tourists.

$ Parrillero El Sauna, Av Santa Cruz entre Avaroa y Junín. Tue-Sun from 1700. Very good *parrilladas* with Argentine meat, salad buffet.

$ Tu Pizza, Sucre y 7 de Noviembre, on Plaza. Mon-Sat 1830-2300. Cute name, variety of pizzas, very slow service.
Heladería Cremalín, Cochabamba y Florida, on Plaza, ice cream, juices and fruit shakes.
La Pepsi, Avaroa s/n, Mon-Sat 0830-1830. *Salteñas* in the morning, also very good sweet and savoury pastries, sandwiches, juices, cappuccino.

⏺ What to do

Tupiza *p356, map p356*
1-day jeep tours US$35 pp for group of 5; horse riding 3-, 5- and 7-hr tours, the latter includes lunch, US$10 per hr, multi-day tours US$70 per day; 2-day San Vicente plus colonial town of Portugalete US$80 pp (plus lodging); Salar de Uyuni and REA, 4 days with Spanish speaking guide, US$200 pp for a group of 5, plus Bs150 (US$22) park fee. Add US$23 pp for English speaking guide.
La Torre Tours, in Hotel La Torre (see above), Salar/REA tours and local trips on jeep, bicycle, walking or horse riding.
Tupiza Tours, in Hotel Mitru (see above), www.tupizatours.com. Highly experienced and well organized for Salar/REA and local tours. Also offer 1-day 'triathlon' of horse riding, biking and jeep, US$50 pp for group of 5, a good way to see the area if you only have 1 day; Butch Cassidy tours; paseos bioculturales, and extensions to the Uyuni tour. Have offices in La Paz and Tarija, and offer tours in all regions of Bolivia. Highly recommended.
Valle Hermoso Tours, in Hostal Valle Hermoso 1 (see above), www.vallehermoso tours.com. Offers similar tours on horse or jeep, as do several other agencies and most Tupiza hotels.

⏺ Transport

Tupiza *p356, map p356*
Bus There is small, well-organized, bus terminal at the south end of Av Pedro Arraya. To **Villazón** several buses daily,

USUS2.75, 2 hrs; also **ATL** minibuses from opposite terminal, leave when full, US$4. To **Potosí**, several companies around 1000 and 2100, US$5, 8 hrs. To **Sucre**, Expreso Villazón at 1500, **Trans Illimani** at 2030 (more comfortable but known to speed), US$11, 12 hrs; or transfer in Potosí. To **Tarija**, several around 1930-2030, US$9, 6 hrs (change here for **Santa Cruz**). To **Uyuni**, several companies around 1000 and 1800, US$8, 8 hrs. To **Oruro**, Trans Illimani at 1300, 1800, US$15, 12 hrs; continuing to **Cochabamba**, US$19, 17 hrs. To **La Paz** several at 1200 and 1730-2030, US$19, 16-17 hrs. Agent for the Argentine company **Balut** at terminal sells tickets to Jujuy, Salta, Buenos Aires or Córdoba (local bus to the border at Villazón, then change to Balut), but beware overcharging or buy tickets directly from local companies once in Argentina.
Train Train station ticket office open Mon-Sat 0800-1100, 1530-1730, and early morning half an hour before trains arrive. To **Atocha**, **Uyuni** and **Oruro**: Expreso del Sur Wed and Sat at 1815; **Wara Wara** Mon and Thu at 1825. Fares are given under Oruro, page 348.

Villazón *p357*
Bus Bus terminal is near plaza, 5 blocks from the border. Lots of company offices. Taxi to border, US$0.50 or hire porter, US$1, and walk. From **La Paz**, several companies, 18 hrs, US$16-28 (even though buses are called 'direct', you may have to change in Potosí), depart La Paz 1630, depart **Villazón** 0830-1000 and 1830-1900. To **Potosí** several between 0800-0900 and 1830-1900, US$9, 10 hrs. To **Tupiza**, several daily, US$2.75. To **Tarija**, US$5.50, 7 hrs. Tickets for buses in **Argentina** are sold in Villazón but beware of scams and overcharging. Buy only from company offices, never from sellers in the street. Safer still, cross to La Quiaca and buy onward tickets there.
Road The road north from Villazón through Tupiza, Potosí and Sucre, to Cochabamba or Santa Cruz is paved. About 30% of the scenic

road to Tarija is paved. A second road from
Tupiza to Tarija is mostly paved.

Train Station about 1 km north of border
on main road, T597 2565. To Tupiza, Atocha,
Uyuni and Oruro: Expreso del Sur Wed and
Sat at 1530; Wara Wara Mon and Thu at 1530.
Fares are given under Oruro, page 348.

❶ Directory

Tupiza p356, map p356
Useful addresses Public Hospital,
on Suipacha opposite the bus terminal.
IGM office, Bolívar y Avaroa, on Plaza, p 2.

Central and Southern Highlands

*This region boasts two World Cultural Heritage sites, the mining city of Potosí, the source of
great wealth for colonial Spain and of indescribable hardship for many Bolivians, and Sucre,
the white city and Bolivia's official capital. In the south, Tarija is known for its fruit and wines
and its traditions which set it apart from the rest of the country.*

Potosí → *Phone code: 02. Colour map 3, C3. Population: 175,562. Altitude: 3977 m.*

Potosí is the highest city of its size in the world. It was founded by the Spaniards on 10 April
1545, after they had discovered indigenous mine workings at Cerro Rico (4824 m), which
dominates the city. Immense amounts of silver were once extracted. In Spain 'es un Potosí'
(it's a Potosí) is still used for anything superlatively rich.

By the early 17th century Potosí was the largest city in the Americas, but over the next
two centuries, as its lodes began to deteriorate and silver was found elsewhere, Potosí
became little more than a ghost town. It was the demand for tin – a metal the Spaniards
ignored – that saved the city from absolute poverty in the early 20th century, until the
price slumped because of over-supply. Mining continues in Cerro Rico (mainly tin, zinc,
lead, antimony and wolfram) to this day.

Arriving in Potosí

Orientation The bus terminal (Nueva Terminal) is on Avenida de las Banderas at the north
end of the city. The airport, 5 km out of town on the Sucre road, has no scheduled flights.
▶▶ *See also Transport, page 366.*

Tourist office InfoTur Potosí ⓘ *C Ayacucho, behind the façade of Compañía de Jesús church,
T623 1021, Mon-Fri 0830-1230, 1430-1800, Sat 0900-1200.* Also a kiosk on Plaza 6 de Agosto,
staffed sporadically by tourist police; and information office at bus terminal, Monday-Friday
0800-1200, 1430-1800. Beware scams involving fake plainclothes policemen. The official
police wear green uniforms and work in pairs. ▶▶ *See also Safety, page 29.*

Places in Potosí

Large parts of Potosí are colonial, with twisting streets and an occasional great mansion
with its coat of arms over the doorway. The city is a UNESCO World Heritage site. Some of
the best buildings are grouped round the Plaza 10 de Noviembre. The old Cabildo and the
Royal Treasury – Las Cajas Reales – are both here, converted to other uses. The massive
Cathedral faces Plaza 10 de Noviembre.

The **Casa Nacional de Moneda**, or Mint, ⓘ *on C Ayacucho, T622 2777, www.bolivian.
com/cnm, Tue-Sat 0900-1230, 1430-1830, Sun 0900-1230, entry US$3, plus US$3 to take*

photos, US$6 for video, entry by regular, 2-hr guided tour only (in English or French if there are 10 or more people, at 0900, 1030, 1430 and 1630), is nearby. Founded in 1572, rebuilt 1759-1773, it is one of the chief monuments of civil building in Hispanic America. Thirty of its 160 rooms are a museum with sections on mineralogy, silverware and an art gallery in a splendid salon on the first floor. One section is dedicated to the works of the acclaimed

Potosí

To **2**, Train Station, Ex Terminal & Nueva Terminal

To **6**, Airport & Sucre

To Oruro & La Paz

To San Martín Church (200m)

Where to stay
1 Carlos V *C3*

2 Cima Argentum *A1*
3 Coloso Potosí *B3*
4 El Turista *D2*
5 Hostal Colonial *C3*
6 Hostal Eucaliptus *C3*
7 Hostal Gran Libertador *D3*
8 Hostal Patrimonio *C3*
9 Hostal San Marcos *D3*
10 Hostal Tukos *C3*

11 Koala Den *B3*
12 La Casona *D3*
13 Res Sumaj *B1*

Restaurants
1 4060 Café *C3*
2 Café La Plata *C3*
3 Café Manzana Mágica *B2*
4 Chaplin *C2*

5 Confitería Cherry's *C3*
6 Doña Eugenia *A3*
7 El Fogón *C2*
8 Kaypichu *C3*
9 La Taberna *B2*
10 Potocchi *C3*
11 Santa Clara *C2, C3*
12 Torre de Pizza *C2*

100 metres
100 yards

17th- to 18th-century religious painter Melchor Pérez de Holguín. Elsewhere are coin dies and huge wooden presses which made the silver strips from which coins were cut. The smelting houses have carved altar pieces from Potosí's ruined churches. You can't fail to notice the huge, grinning mask of Bacchus over an archway between two principal courtyards. Erected in 1865, its smile is said to be ironic and aimed at the departing Spanish. Wear warm clothes; it's cold inside.

Potosí has many outstanding colonial churches. **Convento y Museo de Santa Teresa** ① *Santa Teresa y Ayacucho, T622 3847, http://museosantateresa.blogspot.co.uk, only by guided tour in Spanish or English, Mon-Sat 0900-1230, 1500-1800; Sun 0900-1200, 1500-1800, museum is closed Tue and Sun morning; US$3, US$1.50 to take photos, US$25 for video*, has an impressive amount of giltwork inside and an interesting collection of colonial and religious art. Among Potosí's baroque churches, typical of 18th-century Andean or 'mestizo' architecture, are the Jesuit **Compañía church and bell-gable** ① *Ayacucho entre Bustillos y Oruro*, whose beautiful façade hides the modern tourist office building, and whose tower has a **mirador** ① *0800-1200, 1400-1800, 30 mins later Sat-Sun, US$1.40*. **San Francisco** ① *Tarija y Nogales, T622 2539, Mon-Fri 0900-1100, 1430-1700, Sat 0900-1100, US$2.15*, with a fine organ, worthwhile for the views from the tower and roof, museum of ecclesiastical art, underground tunnel system. **San Lorenzo** (1728-1744) ① *Héroes del Chaco y Bustillos, Mass 0700-1000*, with a rich portal and fine views from the tower. **San Martín** ① *on Hoyos, T622 3682, Mon-Fri 1000-1200, 1500-1830, Sat 1500-1800, free*, with an uninviting exterior, is beautiful inside, but is normally closed for fear of theft. Ask the German Redemptorist Fathers to show you around; their office is just to the left of the church. **La Merced** ① *Hoyos y Millares, US$1.40 for museo sacro and mirador, US$0.70 for mirador only (with café)*, views of Cerro Rico and the city are great. **San Agustín** ① *Bolívar y Quijarro, open only for Mass*, has crypts and catacombs (much of the city was interconnected by tunnels in colonial times).

Teatro Omiste (1753) *on Plaza 6 de Agosto*, has a fine façade. The **Museo Universitario** ① *C Bolívar 54 y Sucre, T622 7310, Mon-Fri 0800-1200, 1400-1800, US$0.70*, displays archaeology, fossils, costumes, musical instruments and some good modern Bolivian painting. Guided tour to the *mirador* (tower) offers great views, US$0.70. **Museo del Ingenio de San Marcos** ① *La Paz 1565 y Betanzos, T622 6717, 1000-1500, US$1.40; textiles museum and shop Mon-Sat 1430-2200; restaurant 1200-1500, 1900-2200*. This is a well-preserved example of the city's industrial past, with machinery used in grinding down the silver ore. It also has cultural activities and an exhibition of Calcha textiles. **Museo Etno-indumentario** ① *Av Serrudo 152, T622 3258, Mon-Fri 0900-1200, 1500-1800, Sat 0900-1200, US$1.40, includes tour*. This fascinating museum displays in detail the dress, customs and histories of Potosí department's 16 provinces.

In Potosí, 2000 colonial buildings have been catalogued. Among the better preserved examples is the house of the Marqués de Otavi, now the BNB bank, on Junín between Matos and Bolívar. Next to Hostal Gran Libertador, Millares between Nogales and Chuquisaca, is a doorway with two rampant lions in low relief on the lintel. The Casa de las Tres Portadas (house of the three arches) is now Hostal Tukos, on Bolívar near La Paz.

Mine tours

For many, the main reason for being in Potosí is to visit the mines of Cerro Rico. The state mines were closed in the 1980s and are now worked as cooperatives by small groups of miners in medieval conditions. An estimated 14,000 miners work in 49 cooperatives, some 800 are children. *The Devil's Miner* is a recommended documentary film about child labour in the mines, shown regularly by Potosí agencies and Sucre cafés.

A tour to the mines and ore-processing plant involves meeting miners and seeing them at work first-hand. Mine entrances are above 4000 m and temperatures inside can reach 40ºC, with noxious dust and gasses. You should be acclimatized, fit and have no heart or breathing problems, such as asthma. The length and difficulty of tours varies, up to five hours; you can ask for a shorter, less gruelling, visit if you wish. Not all tours visit the processing plant.

Guided tours are conducted by former miners; by law all guides have to work with a tour agency and carry an ID card issued by the Prefectura. Essential equipment is provided: helmet, lamp and usually protective clothing but large size boots may not be available. Wear old clothes and take torch and a handkerchief or mask to filter the dusty air. The smaller the tour group, the better. Some are as large as 20 people, which is excessive. Tours cost about US$20 per person for two people, US$10 for four, and include transport. Many agencies say they give part of their proceeds to miners but such claims are difficult to verify. You can also contribute directly, for example by taking medicines to the health centre (*Posta Sanitaria*) on Cerro Rico. Saturday and Sunday are the quietest days (Sunday is the miners' day off). **Note** Tourists are not allowed to buy dynamite to give to miners.

Museo Histórico Minero Diego Huallpa ① *by Mina Pailaviri on Cerro Rico, city buses P, Q, 70 and others, T623 1143, Mon-Sat 0900-1200, 1430-1800, Sun 0900-1500, US$10*, has exhibits of minerals and mining techniques, two-hour visits include mine tunnels with mannequins instead of real miners.

Tarapaya

A good place to freshen up after visiting the mines (or to spend a day relaxing) is Tarapaya, 21 km on the road to Oruro, where there are **thermal baths** ① *public pools US$0.60, private baths US$1.20 per hr, family baths US$2.80*, and cabins for rent. On the other side of the river from Tarapaya is a 60-m diameter crater lake, whose temperature is 30-34ºC; take sun protection. Below the crater lake are boiling ponds, not fit for swimming. **Balneario Miraflores** (25 km) ① *pools US$0.35, private baths US$2.80*, has hotter water than Tarapaya, but is not as clean. Minibuses run to both *balnearios* from outside Chuquimia market on Avenida Universitaria, 0600-1800, US$0.55; taxi US$8.50. Last vehicle back to Potosí from Miraflores at 1800.

⊙ Potosí listings

For hotel and restaurant price codes, and other relevant information, see pages 14-17.

⊖ Where to stay

Potosí *p360, map p361*
Unless otherwise stated hotels have no heating.
$$$ Coloso Potosí, Bolívar 965, T622 2627, www.potosihotel.com. Comfortable modern rooms with frigo-bar, heating, bath tubs and nice views. Small indoor pool, sauna, parking.
$$$-$$ Hostal Patrimonio, Matos 62, T622 2659, www.hostalpatrimonio.com. Bright, warm, modern hotel. Heating, frigo-bar and safe in each room, sauna and jacuzzi (suites each have their own).

$$ Cima Argentum, Av Villazón 239, T622 9538, www.hca-potosi.com. Modern comfortable rooms and suites, warm and bright, heating, frigo-bar and safe in each room.
$$ El Turista, Lanza 19, T622 2492. Older place but well maintained, heating, nice common areas, helpful staff, great view from top rooms.
$$ Hostal Colonial, Hoyos 8, T622 4809, www.hostalcolonialpotosi.com. Older place but well located, carpeted, heating, bathtubs, frigo-bar.
$$ Hostal Gran Libertador, Millares 58, T622 7877. Colonial-style hotel, good buffet breakfast, cafeteria, comfortable rooms, central heating, quiet, helpful, parking.

$$-$ Hostal Tukos (Las Tres Portadas), Bolívar 1092, T623 1025. Old colonial house with spacious rooms, skylights, warm and nice.
$ Carlos V, Linares 42, T623 1010, frontdesk@hostalcarlosv.com. Cheaper rooms without bath, hot water, kitchen facilities.
$ Hostal Eucalyptus, Linares 88, T622 3738, www.koalabolivia.com. Pleasant bright rooms, cheaper with shared bath, heating, good breakfast, 350 m from the main plaza.
$ Hostal San Marcos, La Paz y Periodista, T623 001, hostalsanmarcos@hotmail.com. Colonial house, nice comfortable rooms, heating, cooking facilities.
$ Koala Den, Junín 56, T622 6467, papamilla@hotmail.com. Private rooms with bath and breakfast (cheaper in dorm), heating, TV and video, use of kitchen, popular and often full.
$ La Casona, Chuquisaca 460, T623 0523, www.hotelpotosi.com. Cheaper with shared bath and in dorm, courtyard, kitchen facilities.
$ Res Sumaj, Gumiel 12, T622 2336, hoteljer@entelnet.bo. Basic, small dark rooms with shared bath, helpful, 10% IYHF discount.

🍴 Restaurants

Potosí p360, map p361
$$ 4060 Café, Hoyos y Sucre. Open 1600-late, food until 2300. Restaurant/bar serving good meals, varied menu, large portions, nice atmosphere, heating. Recommended.
$$ El Fogón, Frías 58 y Oruro. Daily 1200-2300. Restaurant/grill, good food and atmosphere.
$$-$ Kaypichu, Millares 16. Tue-Sun 0700-1300, 1700-2300. Breakfast, vegetarian options, *peña* in high season.
$$-$ La Taberna, Junín 12, open all day. Bolivian and international food, set lunch and à la carte in the evening, good service.
$$-$ Potocchi, Millares 24, T622 2759. Open 0800-2230. International and local dishes, can accommodate special diets with advance notice, *peña* in high season.
$ Doña Eugenia, Santa Cruz y Ortega. Open 0900-1300. Typical food such as the

warming kalapurca soup with corn and meat (be careful it is hot) and *chicharrón de cerdo*, fried pork rinds.
$ Torre de Pizza, Matos 14. Open 0700-2200. Pizza, pasta, vegetarian options, also breakfast, family-run, attentive service.

Cafés
Café La Plata, Tarija y Linares at Plaza 10 de Noviembre. Mon-Sat 1000-2200. Upmarket place for coffee, sweets and drinks. Nice atmosphere, English and French spoken.
Café Manzana Mágica, Oruro 239. Meat-free meals only, a popular, small café.
Chaplin, Matos y Quijarro. Mon-Fri 0830-1200. Breakfasts and excellent *tucumanas* (fried empanadas).
Confitería Cherry's, Padilla 8. Open 0800-2230. Small economical place, good cakes, breakfast.
Santa Clara, Quijarro 32 y Matos, also Sucre 33 y Bolívar and other locations. Mon-Sat 0700-2300. Popular with locals for afternoon snacks.

⊛ Festivals

Potosí p360, map p361
Fiesta de Manquiri: on 3 consecutive Sat at the end of **May**/beginning of **Jun** llama sacrifices are made at the cooperative mines in honour of *Pachamama*. **Carnaval Minero**, 2 weeks before Carnaval in Oruro, includes Tata Ckascho, when miners dance down Cerro Rico and El Tío (the *Dios Minero*) is paraded. **San Bartolomé**, or **Chutillos**, is held from the middle of **Aug**, with the main event being processions of dancers on the weekend closest to the **24-26**; Sat features Potosino, and Sun national, groups. Costumes can be hired in *artesanía* market on C Sucre. Hotel and transport prices go up by 30% for the whole of that weekend.
10 Nov, Fiesta Aniversario de Potosí. Potosí is sometimes called the 'Ciudad de las Costumbres', especially at Corpus Cristi, Todos Santos and Carnaval, when special sweets are prepared, families go visiting friends, etc.

O Shopping

Potosí *p360, map p361*
Mercado Artesanal, at Sucre y Omiste. Mon-Sat 0830-1230, 1430-1830. Sells handwoven cloth and regional handicrafts. Several craft shops on C Sucre between Omiste and Bustillos. **Mercado Central**, Bustillos y Bolívar, sells mainly meat and some produce. There are several other markets around town.

O What to do

Potosí *p360, map p361*
All agencies offer mine tours (see page 362), trips to the Salar de Uyuni and REA (see page 354) and trekking at Kari-Kari lakes. **Claudia Tours**, Ayacucho 7, T622 5000, turismoclaudiabolivia@gmail.com. City tours, mines and trekking; also in Uyuni, Av Ferroviaria opposite Hotel Avenida. **Hidalgo Tours**, La Paz 1133, T622 9512, www.salardeuyuni.net; also Av Potosí 113, Uyuni. Specialized services in Potosí and to Salar de Uyuni. Guide Efraín Huanca has been recommended for mine tours. Pioneering tour operator for the Uyuni salt flats and the lagoons, having the first salt hotel in the world, the **Palacio de Sal Hotel**. **Koala Tours**, Ayacucho 5, T622 2092, www.koalabolivia.com. Owner Eduardo Garnica speaks English and French. Their mine tours are popular and have been recommended. **Silver Tours**, Quijarro 12, T622 3600, www.silvertours.8m.com. Economical mine tours. **Sin Fronteras**, Ayacucho 17 y Bustillos, T622 4058, frontpoi@entelnet.bo. Owner Juan Carlos Gonzales speaks English and French and is very helpful. Also hires camping gear. **Turismo Potosí**, Lanza 12 y Chuquisaca, T622 8212. Guide and owner Santos Mamani has been recommended.

O Transport

Potosí *p360, map p361*
Air The airport is about 7 km from Potosí on the road to Sucre. Aerocon, Plaza del Estudiante, Edif 4º Centenario, T6960 7526, Mon-Sat from La Paz at 0615, to La Paz at 0800, 1 hr, US$139 one way.
Bus Large modern bus terminal (Nueva Terminal, use fee US$0.30) with ATMs, luggage store, information office, Tourist Police and food court. **Note** it is far from the centre: taxi US$2; city buses F, I, 150, US$0.20, but there are no city buses or taxis late at night; not safe to go out on the street, try to arrive by day or wait inside until morning. Daily services: **La Paz** several companies 1900-2230, US$7, 10 hrs by paved road; *bus cama* US$16 (departures from La Paz 1830-2030). To travel by day, go to **Oruro**, San Miguel and others, all day, US$4.50, 5 hrs. **Cochabamba** several companies 1830-2030, US$7.50, 10 hrs; San José at 0500 and 1530. **Sucre** frequent service 0630-1800, US$2.50, 3 hrs; also shared taxis from behind the old bus terminal, Cielito Lindo, T624 3381, 2½ hrs, US$6 pp, drop-off at your hotel. For **Santa Cruz** change in Sucre or Cochabamba. **Tupiza** several companies around 0730 and 2000, US$5, 8 hrs; continuing to **Villazón**, US$9, 10 hrs. **Tarija** several companies 1800-1830, US$8.50, 11 hrs, spectacular journey. To go by day take a bus to **Camargo**, 6 hrs, US$6, then change. Buses to **Uyuni** leave from either side of the railway line at Av Toledo y Av Universitaria, 1000-1200 and 1800-2000, US$5, 5-6 hrs on a new road, superb scenery; book in advance.
Train Station is at Av Sevilla y Villazón, T622 3101, www.fca.com.bo. A 25-passenger railcar to **Sucre** Tue, Thu, Sat 0800, 6 hrs, US$3.60; confirm details in advance.

O Directory

Potosí *p360, map p361*
Useful addresses Migración: Calama 188 entre Av Arce y Av Cívica, T622 5989. Mon-Fri 0830-1230, 1430-1830. **Police station**: on Plaza 10 de Noviembre.

Founded in 1538 as La Plata, it became capital of the Audiencia of Charcas in 1559. Its name was later changed to Chuquisaca before the present name was adopted in 1825 in honour of the second president of the new republic. Sucre is sometimes referred to as La Ciudad Blanca, owing to the tradition that all buildings in the centre are painted in their original colonial white. This works to beautiful effect and in 1991 UNESCO declared the city a World Heritage Site. There are two universities, the older dating from 1624. From 1825 to 1899 Sucre was the only capital of Bolivia; it remains the constitutional capital as it is home to Bolivia's judicial branch although La Paz is the administrative one. *La capitalidad* remains an emotionally charged issue among *sucrenses*, who strive to see Sucre regain its status as the only capital.

Arriving in Sucre

Orientation Airport is 5 km northwest of town. The bus terminal is on north outskirts of town, 3 km from centre. ▸▸ *See also Transport, page 373.*

Tourist office Dirección de Turismo de la Alcaldía ① *Argentina 65, p 2, Casa de la Cultura, T643 5240, www.sucreturistico.gob.bo, Mon-Fri 0800-1200, 1400-1800*, some English spoken; also have information kiosks at the airport, bus terminal, **Plazuela Libertad** ① *Destacamento 111 y Arenales* and **La Recoleta** ① *Polanco e Iturrichia*. **Tourist office** ① *Estudiantes 25, T644 7644, open Mon-Fri 0900-1200, 1500-1830*, staffed by university students (open only during term). **Safety** Caution is advised after 2200 and in market areas.

Places in Sucre centre

Plaza 25 de Mayo is large, spacious, full of trees and surrounded by elegant buildings. Among these are the **Casa de la Libertad** ① *T645 4200, Tue-Sat 0900-1230, 1430-1800, US$2.15 with tour; US$5.80 video*. Formerly the Assembly Hall of the Jesuit University, where the country's Declaration of Independence was signed, this house contains a famous portrait of Simón Bolívar by the Peruvian artist Gil de Castro, admired for its likeness. Also on the Plaza are the beautiful 17th century **Cathedral** and **Museo Eclesiástico** ① *Ortiz 61, T645 2257, Mon-Fri 1000-1200, 1500-1700, US$1.45*. Worth seeing are the famous jewel-encrusted Virgin of Guadalupe, 1601, and works by Viti, the first great painter of the New World, who studied under Raphael.

  San Felipe Neri ① *entrance through school, Ortiz 165 y Azurduy, T645 4333, Mon-Sat 1400-1800, US$1.45 (extra charge for photos)*. Visits include the neoclassical church with its courtyard, the crypt and the roof (note the penitents' benches), which offers fine views over the city. The monastery is used as a school. Diagonally opposite is the church of **La Merced** ① *T645 1338*, which is notable for its gilded central and side altars. **San Miguel** ① *Arenales 10, T645 1026, Mass Mon-Sat 0800 and 1915, Sun 1100, no shorts, short skirts or short sleeves allowed*, completed in 1628, has been restored and is very beautiful with Moorish-style carved and painted ceilings, *alfarjes* (early 17th century), pure-white walls and gold and silver altar. In the Sacristy some early sculpture can be seen. Santa Mónica, Arenales y Junín, is perhaps one of the finest gems of Spanish architecture in the Americas, but has been converted into the theatre and hall for Colegio Sagrado Corazón. **San Francisco** (1581) ① *Ravelo y Arce, Mass daily 0700 and 1900, Sun also 1030 and 1700*, has altars coated in gold leaf and 17th century ceilings; one of its bells summoned the people of Sucre to struggle for independence. **San Lázaro** (1538) ① *Calvo y Padilla, Mass daily 0700, Sun also*

1900. This is regarded as the first cathedral of La Plata (Sucre). On the nave walls are six paintings attributed to Zurbarán; it has fine silverwork and alabaster in the Baptistery. San Miguel, San Francisco and San Lázaro are only open during Mass. **Monasterio de Santa Clara** ① *Calvo 212, Mass daily 0730, museum open Mon-Fri 1400-1800, Sat 1400-1730, US$2,*

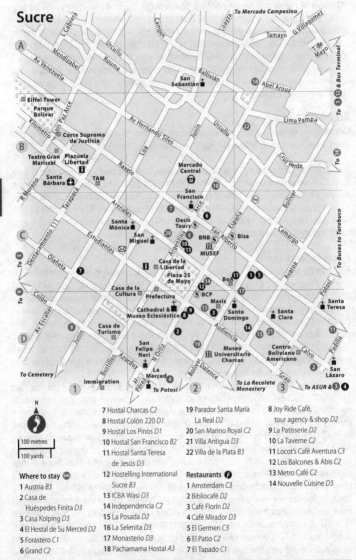

Sucre

Where to stay
1 Austria *B3*
2 Casa de Huéspedes Finita *D3*
3 Casa Kolping *D3*
4 El Hostal de Su Merced *D2*
5 Forastero *C1*
6 Grand *C2*
7 Hostal Charcas *C2*
8 Hostal Colón 220 *D1*
9 Hostal Los Pinos *D1*
10 Hostal San Francisco *B2*
11 Hostal Santa Teresa de Jesús *D3*
12 Hostelling International Sucre *B3*
13 ICBA Wasi *D3*
14 Independencia *C2*
15 La Posada *D2*
16 La Selenita *D2*
17 Monasterio *D3*
18 Pachamama Hostal *A3*
19 Parador Santa María La Real *D2*
20 San Marino Royal *C2*
21 Villa Antigua *D3*
22 Villa de la Plata *B3*

Restaurants
1 Amsterdam *C3*
2 Bibliocafé *D2*
3 Café Florín *D2*
4 Café Mirador *D3*
5 El Germen *C3*
6 El Patio *C2*
7 El Tapado *C1*
8 Joy Ride Café, tour agency & shop *D2*
9 La Patisserie *D2*
10 La Taverne *C2*
11 Locot's Café Aventura *C3*
12 Los Balcones & Abis *C2*
13 Metro Café *C2*
14 Nouvelle Cuisine *D3*

good guided tours in Spanish, Displays paintings by Bitti, sculptures, books, vestments, some silver and musical instruments (including a 1664 organ). Small items made by the nuns on sale.

The excellent **Museo de Arte Indígena ASUR** (Museo Téxtil Etnográfico) ① *Pasaje Iturricha 314, opposite Casa Kolping in La Recoleta, T645 6651, www.asur.org.bo, Mon-Fri 0830-1200, 1430-1800, Sat from 0930, US$2.25, English and French-speaking guides*, displays regional textiles and traditional techniques, shop sells crafts. Near the main plaza is the **Museo Nacional de Etnografía y Folklore (MUSEF)** ① *España 74 y San Alberto, T645 5293, Tue-Fri 0930-1230, 1430-1830, Sat 0930-1230, free*, with an impressive exhibit of masks. The **Museo Universitario Charcas** ① *Bolívar 698, T645 3285, Mon-Fri 0800-1200, 1400-1800, Sat 0800-1200, US$0.50, photos extra*, has anthropological, archaeological and folkloric exhibits, and colonial collections and presidential and modern-art galleries.

Four blocks northwest of Plaza 25 de Mayo is the **Corte Suprema de Justicia** ① *Luis Paz Arce 352, Mon-Fri 1000-1200, 1500-1800, free*, the seat of Bolivia's national judiciary and what remains of the city's official status as capital of Bolivia. To enter you must be smartly dressed and leave your passport with the guard; guides can be found in the public relations office. The nearby **Parque Bolívar** contains a monument and a miniature of the Eiffel Tower and Arc de Triomphe in honour of one of Bolivia's richest 20th-century tin barons, Francisco Argandoña, who created much of Sucre's splendour. At the downhill-end of the park is Fuente del Bicentenario, where a **sound and light show** ① *Thu-Sun 1900-2100*, is displayed. The **obelisk** opposite the Teatro Gran Mariscal, in Plazuela Libertad, was erected with money raised by fining bakers who cheated on the size and weight of their bread. Also on this plaza is the Hospital Santa Bárbara (1574).

Around Sucre

Southeast of the city, at the top of Dalence is **La Recoleta**, a lookout with arches, offering good views over the city. Here, within the Franciscan convent of La Recoleta is the **Museo de la Recoleta** ① *Plaza Pedro de Anzúrez, T645 1987, Mon-Sat 0900-1130, 1500-1800, US$1.45 for entrance to all collections, guided tours only*. It is notable for the beauty of its cloisters and gardens; the carved wooden choir stalls above the nave of the church are especially fine (see the martyrs transfixed by lances). In the grounds is the Cedro Milenario, a 1400-year-old cedar. Behind Recoleta monastery a road flanked by Stations of the Cross ascends an attractive hill, **Cerro Churuquella**, with large eucalyptus trees on its flank, to a statue of Christ at the top.

About 5 km south on the Potosí road is the **Castillo de la Glorieta** ① *Mon-Sat 0830-1200, 1300-1700, US$4.30, take Micro 4 marked Liceo Militar*. The former mansion of the Argandoña family, built in a mixture of contrasting European styles with painted ceilings, is in the military compound. Ask to see the paintings of the visit of the pope, in a locked room. Some 3 km north of Sucre is **Cal Orcko**, considered the world's largest paleontological site, where tracks from eight types of dinosaur have been identified (inside the Fancesa cement works, not open to the public). Nearby is **Parque Cretácico** ① *T645 7392, Mon-Thu 0900-1700, Fri-Sat 1000-2000, Sun 1000-1700, US$4.35, children US$0.75, crowded at weekends*, with fibreglass dinosaurs, recorded growls, a 30-minute guided tour and binoculars through which (for an extra US$0.30) you can look at the prints on Cal Orcko, 300 m away. The **Sauro Tours** bus leaves daily 0930, 1200, 1430 from corner of cathedral, US$1.75 return, or take Micro 4 from Calle Junín.

Tarabuco → *Colour map 3, C3. Altitude: 3295 m.*

Tarabuco, 64 km southeast of Sucre, is best known for its colourful indigenous market on Sunday, with local people in traditional dress. It starts around 0930-1000 and is very popular with tourists. Textiles are sold in a purpose-built market on Calle Murillo. Next to the market is a small museum, **Incapallay** ⓘ *Murillo 25, T646 1936, www.incapallay. org, Sun 0930-1400*, run by a weavers' association. The *Pujllay* independence celebration on the third Sunday in March is very vibrant. No one sleeps during this fiesta but basic accommodation and meals are available. The market is not held at Carnaval (when all Tarabuco is dancing in Sucre), Pujllay, Easter Sunday or All Saints' Day.

◉ Sucre listings

For hotel and restaurant price codes, and other relevant information, see pages 14-17.

◉ Where to stay

Sucre *p367, map p368*
\$\$\$ Parador Santa María La Real, Bolívar 625, T643 9630, www.parador.com.bo. Tastefully restored and upgraded colonial house, bathtub, safety box, frigobar, heating.
\$\$\$ Refugio Andino Bramadero, 30 km from the city towards Ravelo, details from Raul y Mabel Cagigao, Avaroa 472, T645 5592, bramader@yahoo.com, or **Restaurant Salamandra** (Avaroa 510, good food). Cabins or rooms, well-furnished, full board, drinks and transport included, excellent value, owner Raul can advise on hikes and astronomy, book in advance. Recommended.
\$\$\$ Sky Hacienda, in Mosoj Llacta, by Yotala, 19 km south of Sucre along the road to Potosí, T643 0045, www.skyhacienda.com. Upmarket hotel in a rural setting, nice views from the rooms with heating, jacuzzi, restaurant, nice patio and garden, pool, horse riding, bicycles, minimum stay 2 nights, no children under 12. Transfers to airport and bus station are extra.
\$\$\$ Villa Antigua, Calvo 237, T644 3437, www.villaantiguahotel.com. Tastefully restored colonial house with garden, internet room, gym, large rooftop terrace has great views, some suites with kitchenette, airport transfers.
\$\$\$-\$\$ Monasterio, Calvo 140, T644 0181, www.hotelmonasteriosucre.com. Beautiful

16th-century house with colonial and neoclassic architecture. Elegant common areas, heated rooms and suites, restaurant serves international dishes, quiet terrace, airport transfers.
\$\$ Casa Kolping, Pasaje Iturricha 265, La Recoleta, T642 3812. Pleasant, lovely location with nice views, good **Munay Pata** restaurant (**\$\$-\$**),internet lounge, wheelchair access, parking.
\$\$ El Hostal de Su Merced, Azurduy 16, T644 2706, www.desumerced.com. Beautifully restored colonial building, lots of character, owner and staff speak French and English, good breakfast buffet, sun terrace, restaurant. Recommended.
\$\$ Hostal Santa Teresa de Jesús, San Alberto 431, T645 4189, santateresadejesushostal@hotmail.com. Refurbished colonial house, restaurant, comfortable, garage. Recommended.
\$\$ Independencia, Calvo 31, T644 2256, www.independenciahotel.com. Historic colonial house, opulent salon, spiral stairs, lovely garden, comfortable, some rooms with bathtub, café, attentive service.
\$\$ La Posada, Audiencia 92, T646 0101, www.hotellaposada.com.bo. Smart, colonial-style, good restaurant. Recommended.
\$\$ La Selenita, J Mostajo 145, T643 4239, laselenitasucre@yahoo.fr. Pleasant guesthouse with 4 cabins for 2-3 persons, 2 types of breakfast with home-made bread and jam available, nice gardens, quiet, panoramic views of the colonial city, French/Belgian-run, new in 2012.

$$ San Marino Royal, Arenales 13, T645 1646, www.sanmarinoroyalhotel.com.bo. Nicely converted colonial house, frigobar, cafetería, **$$$** for suite with jacuzzi.

$$-$ Hostelling International Sucre, G Loayza 119 y Ostria Gutiérrez, T644 0471, www.hostellingbolivia.org. Functional hostel 1½ blocks from bus terminal, cheaper without bath and in dorms, breakfast available, garden, internet extra, parking, discount for HI members.

$$-$ ICBA Wasi, Avaroa 326, T645 2091, www.icba-sucre.edu.bo. Part of Insituto Cultural Boliviano-Alemán, imaginatively designed, spotless rooms with solar hot water, some with kitchenette. Recommended.

$ Austria, Av Ostria Gutiérrez 506, by bus station, T645 4202, www.hostalaustria.com. bo. Hot showers, good beds and carpeted rooms, cafetería, parking, cheaper with shared bath and no breakfast, parking extra.

$ Casa de Huéspedes Finita, Padilla 233 (no sign), T645 3220, delfi_eguez@hotmail. com. Some rooms with bath, good breakfast, hot water, heaters, tasty lunch available on request, garden, terrace, also apartments with fully equipped kitchens for longer stays. Good value and recommended.

$ Forastero, Destacamento 111 No 394, T7181-3654, pichicamichel@hotmail.com. 2 adjacent houses, one with comfortable rooms with and without bath, the second with economical dorms with 3 to 7 beds, bath and individual safety boxes, good hot showers, kitchen facilities, common areas, restaurant (quinoa specialities) in nice garden, tours, discounts for groups and long stays, helpful, enthusiastic owner, English spoken. Recommended.

$ Grand, Arce 61, T645 2461. Older hotel but well maintained, comfortable (ask for room 18), ground floor at the back is noisy, some rooms dark, electric showers, good value lunch in **Arcos** restaurant, Wi-Fi in patio, motorcycle parking.

$ Hostal Charcas, Ravelo 62, T645 3972, hostalcharcas@yahoo.com. Cheaper without bath or TV, good value, huge breakfast extra, hot showers, at times runs bus to Tarabuco on Sun.

$ Hostal Colón 220, Colón 220, T645 5823, colon220@bolivia.com. Very nice guesthouse, cheaper with shared bath, laundry, helpful owner speaks English and German and has tourist information, coffee room.

$ Hostal los Pinos, Colón 502, T645 5639. Comfortable, hot showers, garden, quiet, peaceful, parking.

$ Hostal San Francisco, Av Arce 191 y Camargo, T645 2117. Colonial building, electric showers, breakfast available, quiet, patio, good value.

$ Pachamama Hostal, Arce 450, T645 3673, hostal_pachamama@hotmail.com. Simple rooms with bath, electric shower, pleasant patio, parking, good value.

$ Villa de la Plata, Arce 369, T645 6849, villadelaplata888@gmail.com. Good value apartments with kitchenette, discounts for long stays, popular.

❷ Restaurants

Sucre *p367, map p368*
Sausages and chocolates are among the locally produced specialities.

$$ El Huerto, Ladislao Cabrera 86, San Matías, T645 1538. Daily 1130-1600 and Thu-Sun 1830-2100. International food with salad bar, good *almuerzo*, in a beautiful garden. Take a taxi there at night.

$$ El Tapado, Olañeta 165 y Loa, T643 8778. Open daily, all day. Extensive breakfast and dinner menu, llama dishes, sandwiches, a choice of drinks including micro brews, parties in the patio on Fri and Sat night.

$$ La Taverne of the **Alliance Française**, Arce 35. Mon-Sat 1200-1500, 1800-2230, Sun 1900-2200. Lovely terrace seating, weekly lunch specials, international food, also regular cultural events.

$$-$ El Germen, San Alberto 231. Mon-Sat 0800-2200. Mostly vegetarian, set lunches, excellent breakfast, German pastries, book exchange, German magazines. Recommended.

$$-$ Los Balcones, Plaza 25 de Mayo 33, upstairs. Open 1200-2400. Good food, popular with locals, set lunch with salad bar, views over plaza.
$$-$ Nouvelle Cuisine, Avaroa 537. Daily 1100-2300. Excellent *churrasquería* (grill), good value.

Cafés
Abis, Plaza 25 de Mayo 32. Belgian-owned café and *heladería*, with coffees, breakfasts, sandwiches, light meals, ice cream.
Amsterdam, Bolívar 426. Mon-Fri from 1200, Sun from 1530. Drinks, snacks and meals, book exchange, Wi-Fi, live music Wed-Thu. Dutch-run, works with a programme for migrant children from the countryside.
Bibliocafé, N Ortiz 38, near plaza. Pasta and light meals. *Almuerzo* 1200-1500, 1800-0200, Sun 1900-2400. Music and drinks, Wi-Fi.
Café Florín, Bolívar 567. Daily 0730-0200, weekends to 0300. Breakfast, sandwiches, snacks and international meals (**$$**), large portions, micro-brews. Sunny patio, Wi-Fi, tour bookings, cosy atmosphere, Dutch-run
Café Mirador, Pasaje Iturricha 297, La Recoleta. Open 0930-2000. Very good garden café, fine views, good juices, snacks and music, popular.
El Patio, San Alberto 18. Small place for delicious *salteñas/empanadas*.
Joy Ride Café, N Ortiz 16, www.joyridebol.com. Daily 0730-2300. Great international food and drink, music, Wi-Fi, very popular, upstairs lounge shows films, also cultural events.
La Patisserie, Audiencia 17. 0830-1230, 1530-2030. French-owned, popular for crêpes, salads and puddings.
Locot's Café Aventura, Bolívar 465, T691 5958. Mon-Sat 0800-2400, Sun 1100-2300. Bar serving international and Mexican food, live music and theatre, Wi-Fi, also offer many types of adventure sports: mountain biking, hiking, riding, paragliding.
Metro Café, Calvo 2 on Plaza 25 de Mayo. A variety of coffees, sandwiches, breakfasts, pastries, desserts, juices; delicious and good service.

🍸 Bars and clubs

Sucre *p367, map p368*
Mitos, Pje Tarabuco y Junín. Thu-Sat 2200-0300. Disco, popular with travellers.
Stigma, Bolívar y Camargo. Varied music, young crowd.
Tabaco's, Eduardo Berdecio, east of centre. Varied music, popular with university students.

⊛ Festivals

Sucre *p367, map p368*
24-26 May Independence celebrations, most services, museums and restaurants closed on 25. **8 Sep** Virgen de Guadalupe, 2-day fiesta. **21 Sep** Día del Estudiante, music around main plaza. **Oct/Nov** Festival Internacional de la Cultura, 2nd week, shared with Potosí.

⊙ Shopping

Sucre *p367, map p368*
Handicrafts ASUR, opposite Casa Kolping in La Recoleta. Weavings from around Tarabuco and from the Jalq'a. Weavings are more expensive, but of higher quality than elsewhere. **Artesanías Calcha**, Arce 103, opposite San Francisco church. Recommended, knowledgeable proprietor. Several others nearby. **Bolsa Boliviana**, Calvo 64, non-profit with many nice items, especially bags. **Casa de Turismo**, Bustillos 131, several craft shops and tour operators under one roof. **Centro Cultural Masis**, Bolívar 561, T645 3403, www.losmasis.com. Teaches local youth traditional music and culture and has items for sale; visitors welcome at events and exhibitions. **Incapallay**, Audiencia 97 y Bolívar, T646 1936, www.incapallay.org. Fair trade shop selling textiles by Tarabuco and Jalq'a weavers; also in Tarabuco and La Paz. Artisans sell their wares at the **La Recoleta** lookout. **Chocolates Para Tí**, Arenales 7, Audiencia 68, at the airport and bus terminal. One of the best chocolate shops in

Sucre. **Taboada, Arce y Arenales**, at airport and bus terminal, www.taboada.com.bo. Also very good.

Markets The central market is colourful with some stalls selling *artesanía*, but beware of theft and crafty vendors.

What to do

Sucre *p367, map p368*

Bolivia Specialist, N Ortiz 30, T643 7389, www.boliviaspecialist.com. Dutchman Dirk Dekker's agency for local hikes, horse riding and 4WD trips, all sorts of tours throughout Bolivia and Peru, bus and plane tickets, loads of information and connections.

Candelaria Tours, JJ Pérez 303-305 y Colón, T646 0289, www.candelariatours. com. Hikes around Sucre, tours to weaving communities, English spoken.

Cóndor Trekkers, Loa 457, T7289 1740, www.condortrekkers.org. Not-for-profit trekking company using local guides supported by volunteers, city walks and treks around Sucre, proceeds go to social projects, first aid carried.

Joy Ride Tourism, N Ortiz 2, at corner of Plaza, T645 7603, www.joyridebol.com. Mountain- and motor-biking, hiking, climbing, horse riding, paragliding, tours to Potosí and Salar de Uyuni.

L y D, final Panamá 127 y Comarapa, Barrio Petrolero, T642 0752, turismo_lyd@hotmail. com. Lucho and Dely Loredo and son Carlos (who speaks English) offer custom-made tours using private or public transport, to regional communities and attractions, and further afield.

Oasis Tours, Arce 95, of 2, T643 2438, www.oasistours-bo.com. City walking tour, indigenous communities, Chataquila, Inca Trail. Also sell bus tickets and have their own office in Uyuni for Salar trips. Very helpful owner.

Seatur, Plaza 25 de Mayo 24, T646 2425. Local tours, hiking trips, English, German, French spoken.

Transport

Sucre *p367, map p368*

Air **Juana Azurduy de Padilla** airport is 5 km northwest of town (T645 4445). BoA (Calvo 94, T691 2325) 3 per week to Cochabamba. TAM (Arenales 217, T646 0944) daily to **La Paz**, **Santa Cruz** and **Cochabamba**, 5 weekly to **Tarija** and 2 weekly to **Yacuiba**. Aerocon (at airport, T645 0007) flies to **Trinidad**. Ecojet (T901-105055), daily to **Santa Cruz**. Airport tax US$1.60. Micros 1, D and F go from entrance to Av Hernando Siles, a couple of blocks from main plaza, US$0.20, 25 mins. Taxi US$3.50.

Bus Bus terminal is on north outskirts of town, 3 km from centre on Ostria Gutiérrez, T644 1292; taxi US$1.15; Micro A or 3. Daily to/from **La Paz** several companies at 1700-2000, 12 hrs, regular US$7-10, *semi-cama* US$12-13, *cama* US$18-20. To **Cochabamba**: several companies daily at 1830-1930, 9 hrs via Aiquile; at 2100 via Oruro, 12 hrs, US$6-7.50. To **Potosí**: frequent departures between 0630 and 1800, US$2.15-2.50, 3 hrs. Shared taxis with pick up service: **Cielito Lindo**, at Casa de Turismo, Bustillos 131, T643 2309, **Cielito Express**, T643 1000 and **Expreso Dinos**, T643 7444, both outside the bus terminal, 2½ hrs, US$6 pp. To **Oruro**: 2000-2200, 4 companies via Potosí, 8 hrs, US$7-8.70. To **Tarija**: 4 companies, at 1500-1600, 14 hrs, US$9-14 via Potosí. To **Uyuni**: direct at 0830, **6 de Octubre**, 9 hrs, **Emperador** 0700, 1230, with change and 2-hr wait in Potosí, US$7.25-10. Or catch a bus to Potosí and change; try to book the connecting bus in advance. To **Villazón** via Potosí and Tupiza: at 1330, 1730, 6 de Octubre, 12 hrs, US$11.60; to **Tupiza**, 9 hrs, US$9.50. To **Santa Cruz**: many companies 1600-1730, 15 hrs, US$10-12; *semi-cama* US$15.

To Tarabuco Minivans leave when full from C Túpac Yupanqui (Parada de Tarabuco), daily starting 0630, US$1, 1¼ hrs on a good paved road. To get to the Parada take a micro "C" or "7" from the Mercado

Central. Also buses to Tarabuco from Av de las Américas y Jaime Mendoza, same fare and times. Tourist bus from the Cathedral on Sun at 0830, US$5 round-trip, reserve at Oasis Tours (address above); also **Real Audiencia**, depart San Alberto 181 y España, T644 3119, at 0830, return 1330; you must use the same bus you went on. Shared taxi with **Cielito Lindo** (see transport to Potosí above), Sun at 0900, US$5 return.

Car hire Imbex, Serrano 165, T646 1222, www.imbex.com. Recommended.

Road 164 km from **Potosí** (fully paved), 366 km to **Cochabamba** (mostly paved except for some segments in the Puente Arce–Aiquile–Epizana segment, which were being paved in 2014).

Taxi US$0.60 per person within city limits.

Train Station at El Tejar, 1 km south on Potosí road, take Micro 4, T644 0751, www.fca.com.bo. A 25-passenger railcar to **Potosí**, Mon, Wed, Fri at 0800, US$3.60, 6 hrs;. tickets go on sale at 0600, confirm details in advance.

① Directory

Sucre *p367, map p368*

Language classes The Instituto Cultural Boliviano-Alemán (ICBA, Goethe Institute), Avaroa 326, T645 2091, www.icba-sucre. edu.bo, runs Spanish, German, Portuguese and Quechua courses. **Alianza Francesa**, Aniceto Arce 35, T645 3599, www.sucre. alianzafrancesa.org.bo, also offers Spanish and French classes. **Centro Boliviano Americano**, Calvo 301, T644 1608, www. cbasucre.org, is also recommended for language courses. These centres run cultural events, have libraries and branches in La Paz. **Academia Latinoamericana de Español**, Dalence 109, T646 0537, www. latinoschool.com. Professional, good extracurricular activities, US$90 for 20 hrs per week (US$120 for private teacher – higher prices if you book by phone or email). **Bolivian Spanish School**, C Kilómetro 7 250, T644 3841, www.bolivianspanishschool. com. Near Parque Bolívar, pleasant school, good value, excellent teachers. **Continental Spanish School**, Olañeta 224, T643 8093, www.schoolcontinental. com. Good teachers and fun activities. **Fox Academy**, San Alberto 30, T644 0688, www.foxacademysucre.com. Spanish and Quechua classes, US$5 per hr, non-profit, proceeds go to teaching English to children, volunteering arranged. **Casa Andina de Lenguas**, Loayza 119, T644 0471, www. spanish-viva-online.net. At HI Hostelling Sucre, www.hostellingbolivia.org, US$6 per hr. **Sucre Spanish School**, Calvo 350, T643 6727, www.sucrespanishschool.com, US$6 per hr, salsa and cooking classes, friendly and flexible. **Medical services** Hospital Santa Bárbara, Ayacucho y R Moreno, Plazuela Libertad, T646 0133, public hospital. Hospital Cristo de las Américas, Av Japón s/n, T644 3269, private hospital. **Useful addresses** Immigration: Bustillos 284 entre La Paz y Azurduy, T645 3647, Mon-Fri 0830-1230, 1430-1830.

Tarija → *Phone code: 04. Colour map 3, C4. Population: 234,422. Altitude: 1840 m.*

Tarija has a delightful climate and streets and plazas planted with flowering trees. Still known for its fruit, wines and strong cultural heritage which sets it apart from the rest of the country, it has also experienced an economic boom and rapid growth since 2005 due to natural gas development in the department. The best time to visit is from January to April, when the fruit is in season. Founded 4 July 1574 in the rich valley of the Río Guadalquivir, the city declared itself independent of Spain in 1807, and for a short time existed as an independent republic before joining Bolivia. In Plaza Luis de Fuentes there is a statue to the city's founder, Capitán Luis de Fuentes Vargas. The **Dirección de Turismo** ① *Ingavi y Gral Trigo, T667 2633, Mon-Fri 0800-1200, 1500-1900*, is helpful, city and departmental map.

Dirección Municipal de Turismo ① *C 15 de Abril y Mcal Sucre, T663 3581, Mon-Fri 0800-1200, 1430-1830, helpful, city map, some English spoken; also have a booth at the Terminal de Buses, T666 7701, 0700-1100, 1430-2200.* In the wine producing area of **Valle de la Concepción, Información Turística** ① *Plaza Principal, T667 2854, Mon-Sat 0800-1600,* offer maps and pamphlets. Note that blocks west of C Colón have a small O before number (oeste), and all blocks east have an E (este); blocks are numbered from Colón outwards. All streets north of Avenida Las Américas are preceded by N (norte).

Places in Tarija The oldest and most interesting church in the city is the **Basílica de San Francisco** ① *corner of La Madrid y Daniel Campos, 0700-1000, 1800-2000, Sun 0630-1200, 1800-2000.* It is beautifully painted inside, with praying angels depicted on the ceiling and the four evangelists at the four corners below the dome. The library is divided into old and new sections, the old containing some 15,000 volumes, the new a further 5000. To see the library, go to the door at Ingavi O-0137. Behind the church is the **Museo Fray Francisco Miguel de Mari** ① *Colón y La Madrid, T664 4909, www.franciscanosdetarija.com/ pag/ced/museo.htm, 1000-1100, 1600-1700, US$2.85,* with colonial and contemporary art collections, colonial books, the oldest of which is a 1501 *Iliad,* 19th-century photograph albums and other items. **Casa Dorada** ① *Trigo e Ingavi (entrance on Ingavi), http:// casadelaculturatarija.com, guided tours Mon-Fri at 0900, 1000, 1100, 1500, 1600, and 1700, US$0.70.* Begun in 1886 and also known as the Maison d'Or, it is now part of Casa de la Cultura. It belonged to importer/exporter Moisés Narvajas and his wife Esperanza Morales and has been beautifully restored inside and out. Tarija's **Museo de Arqueología y Paleontología** ① *Trigo y Lema, Mon-Fri 0800-1200, 1500-1800, Sat 0900-1200, 1500-1800, US$0.45,* contains a palaeontological collection (fossils, remains of several Andean elephants of the Pleistocene), as well as smaller mineralogical, ethnographic and anthropological collections. The outskirts of the city can be a good place to look for **fossils,** but report any finds to the university.

About 15 km north of the centre is the charming village of **San Lorenzo.** Just off the plaza is the **Museo Méndez** ① *0900-1230, 1500-1830, minimum US$0.30 entry,* the house of the independence hero Eustaquio Méndez, 'El Moto'. The small museum exhibits his weapons, his bed, his 'testimonio'. At lunchtime on Sunday, many courtyards serve cheap meals. Minibuses from Domingo Paz y J M Saracho, every five minutes, US$0.30. The road to San Lorenzo passes **Tomatitas** (5 km) a popular picnic and river bathing area, from where good day trips include the waterfalls at **Coimata** and the valley at **Rincón de la Victoria.** There is a spectacular one- to two-day Camino del Inca from Tajzara in **Reserva de Sama** to Pinos Sud, from where public transport can take you back to the city. For information contact **SERNAP** ① *Av Jaime Paz 1171, T665 0605,* or the NGO **Prometa** ① *Alejando del Carpio 659, T664 1880, www.prometa.org.bo.*

Tarija is proud of its **wine and singani** (brandy) production. Not all wineries receive visitors. To visit a *bodega,* contact its shop in town beforehand to make arrangements or, better yet, take a tour (see What to do, page 377) which provides transport and allows you to visit several different bodegas on the same day. **Campos de Solana** ① *15 de Abril E-0259 entre Suipacha y Méndez, T664 5498.* Increasingly recognized for their selection of fine wines (the Malbec is highly regarded), as well as the popular Casa Real brand of singani. The Campos de Solana bodega is in El Portillo, 6 km on road to Bermejo and the Casa Real bodega is in Santa Ana, about 15 km off the road to Bermejo. **Casa Vieja** ① *15 de Abril 540, T667 2349,* a traditional *bodega artesanal,* small-scale winery, located in Valle de la Concepción, 25 km from Tarija. Interesting and recommended. **El Potro** ① *C José*

María Villena, San Gerónimo near the airport, T7298 8832, daily 1000-1900. Guided tours and wine-tasting. **La Concepción** ① *Colón y La Madrid, T665 1514.* Wines (try their Cabernet Sauvignon) and Rujero singani, bodega in Valle de Concepción. Wine shops (*vinotecas*) include: **Las Duelas Calamuchita** ① *opposite the sports field in village of Calamuchita, T666 8943, daily 0900-1700.* Small winery, *vinos artesanales*, wine-tasting and regional preserves. **La Vinoteca** ① *Ingavi O-0731 y Gral Trigo, Mon-Sat 0900-1900.* For wine, cheese and ham.

To Argentina → *Bolivia is 1-2 hrs behind Argentina, depending on the time of year.*
The road to Villazón (see page 357) is the shortest route to Argentina; 189 km, but a tiring trip along a winding, scenic mountain road. The alternative route via Bermejo is the most easily reached from Tarija; 210 km all paved, the views are also spectacular (sit on right). **Bermejo** (*Population: 13,000, Altitude: 415 m*) is well supplied with places to sleep and eat, there are many *casas de cambio*. Be prepared for up to four hours at customs and immigration here; it's very hot. An international bridge crosses the river from Bermejo to Aguas Blancas, Argentina. A third option, from Tarija to the Yacuiba/Pocitos border (see page 406), is 290 km away.

⊙ Tarija listings

For hotel and restaurant price codes, and other relevant information, see pages 14-17.

⬤ Where to stay

Tarija *p374*
Some hotels may offer low-season discounts, May-Aug.
$$$$-$$$ Los Parrales Resort, Urb Carmen de Aranjuez Km 3.5, T664 8444 , www.los parraleshotel.com. Large luxury hotel offering fine views over the city and surrounding hills. Includes buffet breakfast, pool, spa, gym, Wi-Fi in communal areas. Non-guests can pay to use the pool and other facilities.
$$$ Terravina, Bolívar E 525 y Santa Cruz, T666 8673, terravinatarija@gmail.com. Modern boutique hotel with a wine theme, rooms with fridge and heating and fully furnished 1-2 bedroom apartments, 2 rooms on the ground floor are equipped for handicapped guests, includes buffet breakfast.
$$ Hostal Carmen, Ingavi O-0784, T664 3372, www.hostalcarmentarija.com. Older place but well maintained, excellent buffet breakfast, hot water, heating, airport transfers available. Often full, advance booking advised, very helpful, good value. Recommended.

$$ La Pasarela, 10 km north of Tarija near the village of Coimata, T666 1333, www. lapasarelahotel.com. Belgian-owned hotel with good restaurant/bar, country views, tranquil, family atmosphere, living room, jacuzzi, swimming pool, mountain bikes, laundry and camping.
$$ Mitru Tarija, Avaroa 450, entre Isaac Attie y Delgadillo, T664 3930, www. hotelmitru.com. Modern hotel, comfortable rooms with a/c, heating, garden with hammocks, new in 2014.
$ Alojamiento Familiar, Rana S 0231 y Navajas, T664 0832. Shared bath, hot shower, cheap, helpful, close to bus terminal, traffic noise.
$ Miraflores, Sucre 920, T664 3355. Hot water, cheaper rooms with shared bath are simple, popular place but indifferent service.
$ Res Rosario, Ingavi O-0777, T664 2942. Simple rooms, cheaper with shared bath, hot water, good budget option, family atmosphere, helpful.

❼ Restaurants

Tarija *p374*
Many restaurants (and much else in town) close between 1400 and 1600.

$$$ Carnes y Tintos, Av España 1788 y Juan José Echalar, half a block from Av Las Américas, T666 0815. Grill, very good for prime local and Argentine meat and an extensive list of local wines.

$$ Don Pepe Rodizio, D Campos N-0138, near Av Las Américas. Stylish restaurant serving tasty daily set lunch, all-you-can-eat *rodizio* on weekends for US$10.

$$ El Fogón del Gringo, La Madrid O-1053, Plaza Uriondo. Mon-Sat 1900-2300, on Fri-Sun also 1200-1430. Upmarket *parillada* includes excellent salad bar.

$$ La Taberna Gattopardo, on main plaza. Daily 0800-2100. Pizza, *parrillada* with Argentine beef, local wines, deserts, snacks, excellent salads, popular meeting place, Wi-Fi.

$ Miiga Comida Coreana, Cochabamba 813 y Ballivian. Open every night except Tue. Sushi with salmon and a small but tasty range of Korean dishes

$ El Molino, Ingavi O-550 entre Saracho y Campero. Midday only. Tasty and healthy vegetarian set lunch.

$ El Patio, Sucre N-0458. Mon-Sat. Good set lunch with small salad bar, pleasant seating in patio, also great *tucumanas al horno*.

DeliGelato, Colón N-0421, Plaza Sucre. Daily until 2130. Good ice cream.

Nougat Café-Bar, Gral Trigo corner 15 de Abril. Daily 0800-2400. Nicely decorated. European-style café. Breakfast, à la carte dishes, snacks and sweets, Wi-Fi.

Pastelería Jenny, 15 de Abril 0215. Good coffee and cakes.

⊕ Festivals

Tarija *p374*
Tarija is known for its fiestas. **Carnaval Chapaco** in **Feb/Mar** is lively and colourful; **Compadres** and **Comadres**, celebrated on the Thu preceding carnival, are an important part of the tradition. **Fiesta de la Vendimia**, held Feb/Mar in Valle de la Concepción, 25 km from Tarija, is a week-long vintage and art festival. During **Easter** week, Mar/Apr, communities such as San Lorenzo and Padcaya welcome visitors with colourful arches and flowers to **La Pascua Florida** processions. **Abril en Tarija**: cultural events are held throughout Apr. **15 Aug-14 Sep** La Virgen de Chaguaya, 45 km pilgrimage from the city to the Santuario Chaguaya, south of El Valle. For less devoted souls, Línea P *trufi* from Plaza Sucre, Tarija, to Padcaya, US$1; bus to Chaguaya and Padcaya from terminal daily, 0700, returns 1700, US$1.35. **San Roque**,**16 Aug-1st week Sep**, is Tarija's main festival. A procession on the 1st Sun takes the richly dressed saint's statue around the various churches. *Chunchos*, colourfully attired male devotees of the saint, dance in processions and women throw flowers from the balconies. No alcohol is consumed. On **2nd Sun in Oct** the flower festival commemorates the **Virgen del Rosario** (celebrations in the surrounding towns are recommended, eg San Lorenzo and Padcaya).

⊙ What to do

Tarija *p374*
Bolivian Wine Tours, Méndez entre Avaroa y Av Las Américas, T7022 5715. Speciality tours to vineyards and wine cellars (*bodegas*) focusing not only on the production of high-altitude wines but also on local culture.

Educación y Futuro, at the Ecosol shop, Virgino Lema y Suipacha, Plazuela Sucre, T666 4973, www.educacionyfuturo.com. An NGO offering homestays with rural families, cheese making and guided trekking.

Sur Bike, Ballivián 601 e Ingavi, T7619 4200. Cycling trips in the countryside outside Tarija US$27-41, for a day trip including snack. Bike rentals US$16.50 per day.

Tupiza Tours, at hotel Mitru, T7022 5715, www.tupizatours.com. Tarija contact of the Tupiza agency.

VTB, at Hostal Carmen (see Where to stay above), T663 3281, www.vtbtourtarija. com. All tours include a free city tour; 4-6 hr trips including bodegas, US$23 pp;

comprehensive 10 hr "Tarija and surroundings in 1 Day", US$35; can also try your hand at excavation with palaeontology specialist! Good vehicles, recommended. **Viva Tours**, Bolivar 251, Edif Ex-Hansa, of 6, T663 8325, auriventur@hotmail.com. Vineyard tours US$30 with lunch.

⊖ Transport

Tarija *p374*
Air BoA (General Trigo 327, T611 1389) flies Mon-Sat to **Cochabamba**, Sun to **La Paz**. TAM (La Madrid O-0470 entre Trigo y Campero, T662 2734), to either **La Paz**, **Sucre**, **Santa Cruz** or **Yacuiba**, depending on day of week. Aerocon (Ballivián 525, T665 8634) flies to **Santa Cruz**. Shared taxi from airport to centre, US$0.75 pp, or *micro* A from Mercado Central which drops you 1 block away. Some hotels have free transport to town, you may have to call them. Airport information T664 3135.
Bus The bus station is southeast of centre on Av Las Américas (30-min walk from centre), T666 6701. Note that the **Copa Moya** bus company has a poor safety record. To **La Paz** several buses at 0700-

0800 and 1700 (935 km) 17 hrs, US$14, via Potosí and **Oruro** (US$12.50); check which company operates the best buses. To **Potosí**, several additional departures 1630-1800, 10 hrs, US$10. To **Sucre** at 1630 and 1800, US$12.50. To **Tupiza**, Diamante, 1930, and **Juárez**, 2030, US$9.50, 6 hrs. To **Santa Cruz** via Villamontes, several companies at 1830, US$14, 17 hrs. To get to Villamontes in daylight, take a **La Guadalupana** or **La Entreriana** bus from Parada del Chaco (east end of Av Las Américas) to **Entre Ríos**, US$3, 3½ hrs, some continue to Villamontes (spectacular route), mostly in daylight.
To Argentina: to **Villazón**, several companies daily, 1930-2030, 8 hrs, US$5.50. To **Bermejo**, shared taxis leave when full from opposite the bus station, US$5.50, 3 hrs; bus US$3, 4 hrs. Buses to **Yacuiba** US$7, 9 hrs, most depart in the evening.

⊕ Directory

Tarija *p374*
Useful addresses Immigration, Ingavi O-0789, T664 3450, Mon-Fri 0830-1230, 1430-1830. Visa renewals in 48 hrs.

Cochabamba and around → *Phone code: 04. Colour map 3, B3. Population: 650,038. Altitude: 2570 m.*

Set in a bowl of rolling hills at a comfortable altitude, Cochabamba enjoys a wonderfully warm, dry and sunny climate. Its parks and plazas are a riot of colour, from the striking purple of the bougainvillaea to the subtler tones of jasmine, magnolia and jacaranda. Bolivia's fourth largest city was founded in 1574 and in colonial times it was the 'breadbasket' of Bolivia, providing food for the great mining community of Potosí. Today it is an important commercial centre. Many visitors particularly enjoy La Cancha market, one of the largest in Bolivia, as well as Cochabamba's very good dining and nightlife.

Fertile foothills surrounding the city still provide much of the country's grain, fruit and coca. Markets, colonial towns and archaeological sites are all close by too. Conquering the challenging Cerro Tunari is a must for all adventurers. Further afield, the dinosaur tracks and great scenery at Torotoro National Park are worth the trip. The paved lowland route to Santa Cruz de la Sierra has much more transport than the rough old road over the mountains via Comarapa and Samaipata. Both offer access to Carrasco and Amboró national parks. There is an animal refuge by Villa Tunari, along the lowland road.

Arriving in Cochabamba

Orientation The city is served by paved roads from La Paz and Santa Cruz. Neither airport, nor bus station are far from the centre. Buses and taxis serve both. The city is divided into four quadrants based on the intersection of Avenida Las Heroínas running west to east, and Avenida Ayacucho running north to south. In all longitudinal streets north of Heroínas the letter N (Norte) precedes the four numbers. South of Heroínas the numbers are preceded by S (Sur). In all transversal streets west of Ayacucho the letter O (Oeste) precedes the numbers and all streets running east are preceded by E (Este). The first two numbers refer to the block, 01 being closest to Ayacucho or Heroínas; the last two refer to the building's number. ▶ *See also Transport, page 386.*

Tourist information **Dirección de Turismo de la Alcaldía** ① *Plaza Colón 448, T425 8030-8035, Mon-Fri 0800-1200, 1430-1830*, is the best option. Other offices at the bus station and Jorge Wilstermann airport (0700-1100, 1500-2200). The **departmental tourist office** ① *Colombia E-0340, entre 25 de Mayo y España, T450 5392, Mon-Fri 0800-1200, 1430-1830*. **Tourist police** ① *Plaza 14 de Septiembre, north side, T450 3880*. The unofficial web resource for the city is www.bolivia-online.net.

Safety Both Cochabamba city and department have public safety issues. Do not venture into any of the hills around town on foot (including San Pedro with the Cristo de la Concordia, San Sebastián and La Coronilla), take only radio taxis (marked with stickers on the back doors) at night, and mind your belongings in markets, on public transport, and other crowded places where you should wear your bag in front. In the main towns in the coca growing region of Chapare tourists are reasonably safe. ▶ *See also Safety, page 29.*

Places in Cochabamba

At the heart of the old city is the arcaded **Plaza 14 de Septiembre** with the **Cathedral** ① *Mon-Fri 0800-1200, 1700-1900, Sat-Sun 0800-1200*, dating from 1571, but much added-to. Of the colonial churches nearby, the **Convent and Museum of Santa Teresa** ① *Baptista y Ecuador, T422 1252, Mon-Fri 0830-1200, 1430-1800, Sat 1430-1700, US$3, camera US$ 3.50 extra, guides included*, original construction 1760-1790, has a beautiful interior.

Museo Arqueológico ① *Aguirre y Jordán, T425 0010, www.museo.umss.edu.bo, Mon-Fri 0800-1800, Sat 0830-1200, US$3, free student guide in Spanish (English Mon-Fri 1300-1600)*. Part of the Universidad de San Simón, one of the most complete museums in Bolivia, displaying artefacts including Amerindian hieroglyphic scripts, mummies, and pre-Inca textiles, through to the colonial era. **Casona Santiváñez** ① *Santiváñez O-0156, Mon-Fri 0800-1200, 1430-1800, free*, has a nice colonial patio, and exhibition of paintings and historic photographs.

From Plaza Colón, at the north end of the old town, the wide **Avenida Ballivián** (known as **El Prado**) runs northwest to the wealthy modern residential areas; along it you can find restaurants and bars. Also in the north is the Patiño family's **Palacio Portales** ① *Av Potosí 1450, T448 6414, guided tours in Spanish Tue-Fri 1530, 1630, 1730, in English 1600, 1700, 1800, Sat in Spanish at 0930, 1000, 1100, English 1100, 1130, Sun Spanish 1100, English 1030, 1130, US$1.50. The gardens are open Tue-Fri 1500-1830, Sat-Sun 0930-1130*. Built in French renaissance style, furnished from Europe and set in 10 ha of gardens inspired by Versailles, the Patiño mansion was finished in 1927 but never occupied. It is now the **Centro Cultural Simón I Patiño** ① *http://portal.fundacionpatino.org*, with an excellent art gallery in the basement. Take a taxi (five minutes from the centre) or micro G from Avenida San Martín.

Cochabamba

Where to stay 🛏
1 Aranjuez *A3*
2 Gina's *A2*
3 Gran Hotel
   Cochabamba *A3*
4 Hostal Florida *C2*
5 Hostal Maya *B1*
6 Hostal Ñawpa House *B2*
7 Monserrat *A2*
8 Regina *A2*
9 Res Familiar *C2*
10 Res Familiar Annex *B2*

Restaurants 🍴
1 Brazilian Coffee *A2*
2 Café París *B2*
3 Casablanca *A2*
4 Churrasquería Tunari *A3*
5 Doña Alcira *A3*
6 Ganesha *A2*
7 La Cantonata *A2*
8 La Estancia *A3*
9 Los Castores *A2*
10 Paprika *A3*
11 Sole Mío *A3*

Bars & clubs 🍸
12 Cocafé *A2*
13 La Muela del Diablo *A3*
14 Na Cunna *A3*

Next to Palacio Portales is the very nice **Museo de Historia Natural Alcide d'Orbigny** ① *Av Potosí 1458 y Av América, T448 6969, Mon-Fri 0900-1230, 1500-1830, free*, named after the famous 19th-century French naturalist. It houses natural history collections of international importance.

To the south of the old town lie the bus and train stations and one of the best markets in Bolivia. The huge and fascinating **La Cancha market** ① *between Esteban Arze, Punata, República and Pulacayo*, is open all week but best on Wednesday and Saturday when it is packed with campesinos and trading spills over into surrounding streets. It has a vast array of foodstuffs and local goods. Souvenirs can be found at San Antonio on Avenida Esteban Arze y Punata, well worth a visit, but watch your valuables.

Around Cochabamba

Parque Nacional Tunari, 300,000 ha, is just outside the city (see www.biobol.org). Despite this proximity, it remains a beautiful unspoilt natural area and a good place for acclimatization to altitude. There are llamas and alpacas above 4000 m and even the occasional condor. The highest point in the park, Cerro Tunari (5035 m), offers magnificent views, even as far as Illimani. It can be climbed in a day trip; going with a local operator is recommended. **Note** Armed attacks of visitors have taken place along the marked trail from the park entrance in the north of the city. Safer alternatives, although not signposted, are along the south flank of the mountain, either reached from above Hacienda Pairumani (see below) or from **Berghotel Carolina**, which arranges tours with pack animals (see page 383).

Quillacollo, 13 km west of the city, has a produce Sunday market and a famous festival (see page 385). Take any micro or trufi marked "Quillacollo" along Av Heroínas. Some 8 km beyond town is the turn-off to the beautiful **Hacienda Pairumani** ① *T426 0083 to check if it is open, Mon-Fri 1500-1600, Sat 0900-1130*, centre of the Patiño agricultural foundation, also known as **Villa Albina**, built in 1925-1932, furnished from Europe and inhabited by Patiño's wife, Albina. Pairumani can be reached from Avenida Aroma in Cochabamba or by Trufi 211 from Plaza Bolívar in **Quillacollo**.

Some 27 km west of Cochabamba are **Inka-Rakay** ruins, with fine views of the Cochabamba valley and the mountains around the ruins. A day trip to the ruins can end at the plaza in nearby Sipe Sipe or one of its local restaurants with a bowl of *guarapo* (wine-based drink) and a plate of *charque* (sun-dried beef), served with potatoes, eggs and corn; best at weekends. Or take trufi "Sipe Sipe" from Plaza Bolivar in Quillacollo and get off at the church on the main square, then ask for the way up to the ruins.

Tarata, 33 km southeast of Cochabamba, is a colonial town with a traditional arcaded plaza on which stand the church (daily 0800-1300) and the Casa Consistorial. In the plaza, the **clock tower** ① *Mon-Fri 0800-1200, 1330-1700, Sat-Sun 0800-1200*, houses a German timepiece with chimes. Inside the **Franciscan Convent** ① *Mon-Sat 0930-1130, 1430-1800, US$0.30, guided visits from Casa de Cultura y Turismo, main square, T457 8727*, overlooking the town, are the remains of the martyr, San Severino, patron saint of the town, more commonly known as the 'Saint of Rain'; festival, on the last Sunday of November, attracts thousands of people. Large procession on 3 May, day of La Santa Cruz, with fireworks and brass band. Market days Thursday and Sunday (bus US$0.65, one hour, last returns 1900). For fine alpaca products, visit **Doña Prima Fernández Prado** ① *Arce E-0115, opposite the convent*, who sells sweaters, bags and textiles from two rooms off a beautiful colonial patio. The local sausages are nationally famous. Beyond Tarata are Cliza, Mizque and Aiquile, along a scenic rail line. A *ferrobus*, a bus running on train tracks, has irregular service on this route; enquire if it is running (T455 6208).

Parque Nacional Torotoro

① *Entry US$15, payable at the Oficina de Turismo, Calle Cochabamba, Main Plaza, T7227 0968, T04-413 5736, www.biobol.org*. In the department of Potosí, but best reached from Cochabamba (136 km), is **Torotoro**, a small village, set amid beautiful rocky landscape in the centre of the Parque Nacional Torotoro, covering an area of 21,693 ha. It can also be reached along a dusty road from Sucre. Attractions include caves, a canyon, waterfalls, ruins, rock paintings, and thousands of incredible fossilized dinosaur tracks, some of which can be seen by the Río Torotoro just outside the village. Near the community of **Wayra K'asa**, about 8 km northwest of Torotoro, **Umajalanta cave**, the largest in Bolivia, has many stalactites, stalagmites and a lake with endemic blind fish; 7 km have been explored and are open to caving (head torch and helmet are required and for hire at the entrance). In the Cañón de Torotoro, 4 km from the village, are the fantastic **El Vergel** waterfalls and the walk along the river bed is great fun if you like rock-hopping and skipping over pools. The views over the canyon from the observation lookout are amazing and you can also see a number of endemic birds; on the way to the lookout are dinosaur prints. Fossils can be seen at Siete Vueltas, 5 km from the village. Itas, in the community of Ovejerías, 21 km from Torotoro, offers lovely views of the surrounding ridges and canyons, interesting rock formations (some resemble gothic cathedrals), rock paintings and, with a little luck, condors. By the community of Molle Cancha is a turtle cemetery.

Tours or day trips can be organized by the **Asociación de Guías** ① *Main Plaza across from the Oficina de Turismo*. Every visitor gets a map and a personal guide; Mario Jaldín, T7141 2381, is excellent. Going with a local guide is compulsory. Four-wheel-drive tours are also offered by **El Mundo Verde Travel** (www.elmundoverdetravel.com), which can also provide transport from Sucre, and other Cochabamba agencies.

Cochabamba to Santa Cruz

The lowland road from Cochabamba through Villa Tunari to Santa Cruz is fully paved but prone to landslides after heavy rain. **Villa Tunari** is a relaxing place and holds an annual Fish Fair the first weekend of August, with music, dancing and food. **Parque Ecoturístico Machía**, just outside town, is managed by **Inti Wara Yassi** ① *T04-413 6572, www.intiwarayassi.org, entrance US$0.90, US$2 for camera, US$3.60 for video, donations welcome, open daily 0900-1600*. This 36-ha park includes a well-signposted 3-km interpretive trail, which explains the park's ecology and other good trails through semi-tropical forest. There are panoramic lookouts, waterfalls and a wide variety of wildlife. The park is run by an animal rescue organization, which attempts to rehabilitate captive animals and return them to the wild. They also operate two other parks, one about half way between Santa Cruz and Trinidad and another near Rurrenabaque. For volunteer opportunities, contact them in advance.

Parque Nacional Carrasco South of Villa Tunari, this park covers 622,600 ha between 300 and 4500 m. It has 11 ecological life zones, superb birdwatching and many rivers, waterfalls, canyons and pools. Access is from Villa Tunari, Totora and Monte Punku – Sehuencas. From the park entrance closest to Villa Tunari, a cable car takes you across the river for a 2½-hour walking circuit to the Cavernas de Repechón (Oil-bird caves). Guides may be hired from the **Kawsay Wasi community** ① *T7939 0894, www.tusoco.com*. Julián (T7480 9714) has been recommended. See www.biobol.org.

The highland road to Santa Cruz The 500 km highland road from Cochabamba to Santa Cruz is very scenic. Some sections are unpaved and the newer lowland route is preferred by most transport. Between Monte Punku (Km 119) and Epizana is the turn-off to Pocona and Inkallajta. To reach the ruins follow the road for 13 km as far as the village of Collpa, then take the left fork for a further 10 km. The Inca ruins of **Inkallajta** (1463-1472, rebuilt 1525), on a flat spur of land at the mouth of a steep valley, are extensive and the main building of the fortress is said to have been the largest roofed Inca building. There are several good camping sites near the river and some basic facilities and services. The mountain road continues to **Epizana**, junction for the road to Sucre (being paved in 2014) via the beautiful colonial village of **Totora** and the more modern town of **Aiquile**. Past Epizana the road from Cochabamba goes on to **Pojo**, Comarapa and Samaipata (see page 403).

◉ Cochabamba and around listings

For hotel and restaurant price codes, and other relevant information, see pages 14-17.

◎ Where to stay

Cochabamba *p378, map p380*
However attractive their prices, places to stay south of Av Aroma and near the bus station are unsafe at all times.
$$$ Aranjuez, Av Buenos Aires E-0563, T428 0076, www.aranjuezhotel.com. The most beautiful of the luxury hotels with a nice garden and lots of style, 4-star, small, good restaurant, jazz in the bar Fri-Sat night, small pool open to public (US$1). Recommended.
$$$ Gran Hotel Cochabamba, Plaza de la Recoleta E-0415, T448 9520, www. granhotelcochabamba.com. One of the best hotels in Cochabamba, pool, tennis courts, business centre, airport transfers, parking.
$$ Ginas, México 346 entre España y 25 de Mayo, T422 2925, www.ginashostal.web.bo. Has a variery of rooms for 1-5 persons, includes breakfast, safe box in rooms, convenient location in the heart of the city, monthly rates available.
$$ Monserrat, España 0342, T452 1011, http://hotelmonserrat.com. In the bohemian zone with bars and restaurants, sauna, cafetería, buffet breakfast.
$$ Regina, Reza 0359, T425 4629, www. hotelreginabolivia.com/regina. Spacious, efficient, with breakfast, restaurant.
$ Hostal Florida, 25 de Mayo S-0583, T425 7911. Cheaper with shared bath, hot water, noisy, popular, safe deposit box, breakfast.

$ Hostal Maya, Colombia 710 y Suipacha, T425 9701. Includes breakfast, private bath, hot water, central.
$ Hostal Ñawpa House, España 250, T452 7723. Simple rooms with electric shower, large courtyard, laundry facilities, book exchange.
$ Res Familiar, Sucre E-0554, T422 7988. Very pleasant, secure, cheaper without bath, good showers, sunny courtyard. Its annex at 25 de Mayo N-0234 (entre Colombia y Ecuador), T422 7986, is also pleasant, with a big courtyard, shared bath, hot water, comfortable.

Around Cochabamba *p381*
$$$-$$ Berghotel Carolina, Pairumani, at the foot of the Cerro Tunari, T7213 0003, www.berghotelcarolina.com. Arranges private transport (25 mins) from Plaza Bolívar in Quillacollo. Mountain lodge with 5 comfortable rooms with private bath and 2 with shared bath, restaurant, bar, living room with fireplace, sauna and large terrace. Organizes guided 2-day walking tours with tent to the Laguna Cajón (4100 m), Cerro Tunari and other peaks in Parque Tunari. Walking trails start right from the lodge.
$$ El Poncho Eco Center, Marquina, Quillacollo, T439 2283, T7648 6666, www.elponcho.org. Ecological cabins, restaurant and pool.

Parque Nacional Torotoro *p382*
An upmarket community run hotel is under construction in Wayra K'asa, by the cave, due to open in late 2014. The following are in the village of Torotoro:

$$ Hostal Asteria, in the centre of the village, T6707 3401, La Paz office T02-211 6552. Colonial-style hotel, restaurant serving all meals, living room with books and DVDs, beautiful patio, parking.

$$ Villa Etelvina, 15-min walk from plaza, T7073 7807, www.villaetelvina.com. Bungalow for 4 with private bath, cheaper in rooms with shared bath, includes breakfast, beautiful garden, parking.

$ El Molino, 1.5 km from the village, T7647 5999, Cochabamba office T04-402 6172, www.elmolinotorotoro.com. Beautiful Spanish-style country house surrounded by mountains and a river, comfortable rooms with private bath, nice common areas, fireplace, bar, pool table, indoor patio.

$ Hostal Las Hermanas, on main road from Cochabamba, 1 block before plaza on the left, T7221 1257. Basic rooms, cheaper with shared bath, Doña Lily serves delicious food and is very attentive.

Cochabamba to Santa Cruz:
Villa Tunari *p382*

$$ Victoria Resort, on the road to Santa Cruz, 4 km before Villa Tunari on the right, T413 6538, www.victoria-resort.com. Modern, cabaña style, 500 m from the main road in the middle of the forest, quiet, large pool, breakfast buffet.

$ El Puente Jungle Lodge, Av de la Integración, 4 km from town, T458 0085, www.hotelelpuente.com.bo (or book in advance through **Salar Amazon Tours**, see below). Cabins from 2 persons to family-size surrounded by tropical vegetation, with breakfast and bath, pool, zipline, stream and natural pools.

$ Hostal Mirador, on road to Santa Cruz, before first bridge, T7795 5766, boborgne36@yahoo.fr. With bath, small pool and tower with views of river San Mateo.

The highland road to Santa Cruz:
Totora *p382*

$ Casa de Huespedes Villa Eva, on main road, T7437 1530. Well furnished

country house with large living room, fully equipped kitchen, and comfortable rooms with private bath.

Restaurants

Cochabamba *p378, map p380*
The restaurant and nightlife district is on España, Ecuador, Mayor Rocha and Av Ballivian (El Prado), and north of the Río Rocha on the Pasaje Boulevard de la Recoleta and Av Pando. Those on very tight budgets can find an edible lunch at the **Mercado 25 de Mayo** at 25 de Mayo entre Sucre y Jordán.

$$ Churrasquería Tunari, Pasaje Boulevard de la Recoleta, T448 8153. The most delicious meat you can find in Cochabamba.

$$ La Cantonata, España y Mayor Rocha, T425 9222. Good Italian restaurant. Recommended.

$$ La Estancia, Pasaje Blvd de la Recoleta 786, T424 9262. Best steak in town, salads and international food in this traditional restaurant.

$$ Sole Mio, Av América 826 y Pando, T428 3379. A smart Neapolitan pizza restaurant, delicious, also good for desserts. Attentive service.

$$-$ Ganesha, Mayor Rocha E-0375. Closed Sun. Good filling vegetarian food, buffet lunch and breakfast, mostly soy-protein based dishes.

$$-$ Paprika, Chuquisaca 688 y Antezana, www.paprika.com.bo. Opens in the evening. Nice atmosphere, international food, good cocktails and desserts.

Cafés
Brazilian Coffee, Av Ballivián 537 just off Plaza Colón. Open 24 hrs. Upmarket, tables on pavement.

Café París, Bolívar, corner of Plaza 14 de Septiembre. Serves good coffee and crêpes.

Casablanca, 25 de Mayo entre Venezuela y Ecuador. Attractive, buzzing, good food and a wide selection of coffee, popular for wine and cocktails in the evening.

Doña Alcira, Plazuela La Recoleta. Serves traditional *empanaditas* and *helados de canela* (cinnamon ice cream).
Los Castores, Ballivián y Oruro. Popular, good for *salteñas*.

Parque Nacional Torotoro *p382*
Several small restaurants in town including **Pensión La Huella**, and **El Comedor**, at the food market 2 blocks above the main plaza, good local food, cheap but clean.

Cochabamba to Santa Cruz: Villa Tunari *p382*
There are several eating places on both sides of the main road to Santa Cruz. The more expensive ones are on the riverside. The more popular food stalls 1 block from the bus terminal serve different fish dishes and have also a cheap daily menu. Upstairs at the market (breakfast and lunch) is a very cheap option.

🍷 Bars and clubs

Cochabamba *p378, map p380*
Cocafé, Antezana y Ecuador. Caring, family atmosphere, good place for foreigners to meet. Street musicians always pass by to show off their skills.
La Muela del Diablo, Potosí 1392 y Portales, next to Palacio Portales. Bolivian rock music, theatre groups, German beer.
Na Cunna, Av Salamanca 577, T452 1982. Opens in the evenings, Fri live music. Irish pub and restaurant. They also serve Guinness.

🎭 Entertainment

Cochabamba *p378, map p380*
Theatre mARTadero, Av 27 de Agosto entre Ollantay y Ladislao Cabrera, T458 8778, www.martadero.org. Cultural and artistic centre for local and international artists, exhibitions, and events, in a refurbished slaughterhouse. Daily 1500-1800. Micros/ trufis P, Q, and 212 to Plaza de los Arrieros.

Teatro Achá, España 280 y Plaza 14 de Septiembre, T425 8054. The city's oldest cultural centre, with monthly presentations.
Teatro Hecho a Mano, Venezuela 0655 entre Lanza y Antezana, T452 9790. Theatre school. For cinema, see www.cinecenter.com.bo.

🎉 Festivals

Cochabamba *p378, map p380*
Carnaval is celebrated 15 days before **Lent**. Rival groups (*comparsas*) compete in music, dancing, and fancy dress, culminating in El Corso on the last Sat of the Carnaval. **Mascaritas** balls also take place in the carnival season, when the young women wear long hooded satin masks. **14 Sep Día de Cochabamba**.

Around Cochabamba *p381*
Fiesta de la Virgen de Urkupiña (www. urcupina.com), in Quillacollo, **14-15 Aug**. Plenty of transport from Cochabamba, hotels all full. Be there before 0900 to be sure of a seat, as you are not allowed to stand in the street. The 1st day is the most colourful with all the groups in costumes and masks, parading and dancing in the streets till late at night. Many groups have left by the 2nd day and dancing stops earlier. The 3rd day is dedicated to the pilgrimage.

🛍 Shopping

Cochabamba *p378, map p380*
Camping gear, maps, etc The Spitting Llama, España N-301 y Ecuador, T489 4540, www.thespittingllama.com. IGM, 16 de Julio S-237, T425 5503, Mon-Thu 0800-1200, 1430-1800, Fri 0800-1200, sells topographic maps of Cochabamba department.
Handicrafts Artesanos Andinos, Pasaje Catedral, T450 8367. An artisans' association selling textiles. Fotrama, Bolívar 0349, entre San Martín y 25 de Mayo, www.fotrama.com. High-quality alpaca clothing.

⚙ What to do

Cochabamba p378, map p380
Adventure sports
Cochabamba is growing in popularity for parapenting, with several outfits offering tamdem jumps and courses more cheaply than other places, starting at US$30-35 and US$200-250 respectively.

AndesXtremo, La Paz 138 entre Ayacucho y Junín, T452 3392, www.andesxtremo. com. Adventure sports company offering parapenting, climbing, rafting and trekking, good value, professional staff. Recommended.

Bolivia Cultura, Ecuador 342 entre 25 de Mayo y España, T452 7272, www.bolivia cultura.com. Tours to Torotoro. They run year-round tours for 3 and 4 days to all the major sites and can arrange longer trips.

D'Orbigny Travel, Pasaje de la Promotora 344 entre España y Heroínas, T451 1367. Run by an enthusiastic Bolivian couple, excursions in Cochabamba department and throughout Bolivia. Recommended.

El Mundo Verde Travel, no storefornt, T653 44272, www.elmundoverdetravel.com. Great for local information, regional experts offer tours to Torotoro, Pico Tunari and Chapare and throughout Bolivia; day trips and adventure tours. Dutch/Bolivian-run. English, Dutch and Spanish spoken. Recommended.

Fremen Tours, Tumusla 245 entre Ecuador y Colombia, T425 9392, www.frementours. com. Offers tours throughout the country, including their own facilities at Villa Tunari and on the *Reina de Enín* riverboat.

Salar Amazon Tours, Condominio Los Faros 4 en Pasaje la Sevillana (Zona Templo Mormón), T458 0085, www.salaramazon. com. Offer salar and jungle tours and Reina de Enín cruises, also run **Hotel El Puente** in Villa Tunari.

⊕ Transport

Cochabamba p378, map p380
Air Jorge Wilstermann airport, T412 0400. Airport bus is Micro B from Heroínas

y Ayacucho, US$0.40; taxis from airport to centre US$4. Arrive 2 hrs ahead for international flights. Cochabamba is an air transport hub with several daily flights to/from **La Paz** (35 mins) and **Santa Cruz** (40 mins) with **Amaszonas**, Av Libertador Bolívar 1509, Edif El Solar, PB, T479 4200, **Boliviana de Aviacion**, Jordán 202 y Nataniel Aguirre, T901-105010 and **TAM** Militar, Buenos Aires entre Av Santa Cruz y América, T441 1545). **Aerocon**, Ancieto Padilla 755, T448 9210, **Ecojet**, Plazuela Constitucion 0879 entre 16 de Julio y Chuquisaca, T901-105055, and **TAM** have flights to **Trinidad**, with connections to other northern cities.

Bus *Micros* and *colectivos*, US$0.25; *trufis*, US$0.30. Anything marked 'San Antonio' goes to the market. *Trufis* C and 10 go from bus terminal to the city centre. **Long distance** The main bus terminal is on Av Aroma y Ayacucho, 600-700 m south of Plaza 14 de Septiembre (T155). To **Santa Cruz**, almost hourly 0600-2130, 12 hrs, US$7.50; Trans Copacabana *semi-cama*, 2130, US$10; Bolívar *bus-cama*, US$15; all via the paved lowland road through Villa Tunari. See page 382. To **Mairana, Samaipata** and **Santa Cruz**, along the old mountain road via Epizana and Comarapa, a beautiful ride, **Trans Carrasco**, 6 de Agosto y República, T456-9348, daily at 0730 to Santa Cruz (14 hrs), 1200 to Mairana (11 hrs), US$6. El Mundo Verde Travel offers 4WD tours from Cochabamba to **Samaipata**. To/from **La Paz** almost hourly 0530-2300, 7 hrs, US$6 (Trans Copacabana *semi-cama*, 2230, US$8.50, Bolívar *bus-cama*, 2230, 2300, US$12.50). To **Oruro**, 0600-1730 (Sun last bus at 2100), 4 hrs, US$3.35-4. To **Potosí**, departures at 2000 (US$7), 2100 (*semi-cama*, US$11) with Bolívar and Trans Copacabana, 10 hrs. Daily to **Sucre**, 8 hrs, several companies (Bolívar and Trans Copacabana at 1930, 2000 US$7, 2030 *semi-cama*, US$8.50). To **Sucre** by day; go to Aiquile by bus (several from Av 6 de Agosto entre Av República y Av Barrientos, none before

1200) or **ferrobus** (see page 381), then a bus at 0200-0300 passing en route to Sucre, or Fri and Sun, 2000. **Regional** Local buses leave from Av Barrientos y Av 6 de Agosto, near La Coronilla for **Tarata**, **Punata** and **Cliza**. From Av 6 de Agosto y Av República to **Totora**. Av Oquendo y 9 de Abril (be careful in this area), to **Villa Tunari**, US$4.50, 4-5 hrs, several daily; **Puerto Villarroel**, US$7.75, 6 hrs (from 0800 when full, daily).
Taxi About US$0.75 from anywhere to the Plaza, more expensive to cross the river; double after dark.

Parque Nacional Torotoro *p382*
Bus Buses and minivans from the end of Av República y Vallegrande, daily at 1800; return to Cochabamba Mon-Sat at 0600; Sun at 1300 and 1500; US$3, 4-5 hrs in the dry season, 7-8 hrs in the wet season, on a cobbled road. There is no bus service from Sucre, it takes 14 hrs in a private vehicle along a road opened in 2013.

The highland road to Santa Cruz: Inkallajta *p382*
Take a trufi from 0500 onwards from 6 de Agosto y Manuripi (Av República) in Cochabamba (ask for the "Parada Pocona"). For 3 people the trufi will drop you off at the entrance to the Inca ruins (US$3 pp). Arrange with the driver to pick you up at a specific time to return to Cochabamba. If alone, ask to get off after arriving in Collpa at a big green sign, where the road to the ruins turns off to the right. Walk along the cobbled road for approximately 10 km to the ruins. Trufis return from Pocona to

Cochabamba when full till 1600. Taxis from Pocona charge around US$14 one way to the ruins.

ⓘ Directory

Cochabamba *p378, map p380*
Language classes Beyond Bolivia, www.beyondsouthamerica.com. Dutch organization which offers language classes Spanish/Portuguese, homestays and recommended volunteer programmes and interships. **Bolivia Sostenible**, Julio Arauco Prado 230, Zona Las Cuadras, T423 3786, www.boliviasostenible.org. Offers home stays and paid placements for volunteers. **Centro de Idiomas Kori Simi**, Lanza 727, entre La Paz y Chuquisaca, T425 7248, www.korisimi.com. Spanish and Quechua school run by staff from Switzerland, Germany and Bolivia, also offers activity programme, homestays and volunteer placements. **Runawasi**, Maurice Lefebvre 0470, Villa Juan XXIII, Av Blanco Galindo Km 4.5, T424 8923, www.runawasi.org. Spanish, Quechua and Aymara, also has accommodation. **Volunteer Bolivia**, Ecuador E-0342, T452 6028, www.volunteerbolivia.org. Bolivian/US-run organization which offers language classes, homestays and a recommended volunteer programme. There are many qualified language teachers in the city.
Medical facilities For hospitals, doctors and dentists, contact your consulate or the tourist office for advice. **Useful addresses** Immigration Office: Av Ballivián 720 y La Paz, T452 4625, Mon-Fri 0830-1230, 1430-1830.

Northern Lowlands

Bolivia's Northern Lowlands account for about 70% of national territory. Flat savannahs and dense tropical jungle stretch northwards from the great cordilleras, sparsely populated and, until recently, rarely visited by tourists. Improved roads and frequent flights, particularly to Rurrenabaque and Trinidad, are opening up the area and wildlife and rainforest expeditions are becoming increasingly popular. Most people head to Rurrenabaque. If seeking hard travel off the beaten track, try Cobija, Riberalta or Guayaramerín, all near the border with Brazil. Beni department has 53% of the country's birds and 50% of its mammals, but destruction of forest and habitat by loggers and colonists is proceeding at an alarming rate.

Madidi and Rurrenabaque

Caranavi to San Borja

From Caranavi, a road runs north to Sapecho, where a bridge crosses the Río Beni. Beyond Sapecho (7 km from the bridge), the road passes through Palos Blancos (several cheap lodgings). The road between Sapecho and Yucumo, three hours from Sapecho *tránsito*, is a good all-weather gravel surface. There are basic *hospedajes* and restaurants in **Yucumo** where a road branches northwest, fording rivers several times on its way to Rurrenabaque. Taking the eastern branch from Yucumo it is 50 km (one to two hours) to **San Borja**, a small, relatively wealthy cattle-raising centre with simple hotels and restaurants clustered near the plaza. From San Borja the road goes east to Trinidad via **San Ignacio de Moxos** (see page 394). The road passes through part of the Pilón Lajas Reserve (see below).

Parque Nacional Madidi

ⓘ *Headquarters in San Buenaventura, about 4 blocks upriver from the plaza, T03-892 2540. US$18 entry is collected near the dock in San Buenaventura. Insect repellent and sun protection are essential. See www.biobol.org.*

Parque Nacional Madidi is quite possibly the most bio-diverse of all protected areas on the planet. It is the variety of habitats, from the freezing Andean peaks of the Cordillera Apolobamba in the southwest (reaching nearly 6000 m), through cloud, elfin and dry forest to steaming tropical jungle and pampas (neo-tropical savannah) in the north and east, that account for the array of flora and fauna within the park's boundaries. In an area roughly the size of Wales or El Salvador (1,895,740 ha) are an estimated 900 bird species, 10 species of primate, five species of cat (with healthy populations of jaguar and puma), giant anteaters and many reptiles. Madidi is at the centre of a bi-national system of parks that spans the Bolivia–Peru border. The Heath river on the park's northwestern border forms the two countries' frontier and links with the Tambopata National Reserve in Peru. To the southwest the Area Protegida Apolobamba protects extensive mountain ecosystems. It is easiest to visit the lowland areas of Madidi through Rurrenabaque.

Pilón Lajas Biosphere Reserve and Indigenous Territory

ⓘ *HQ at Campero y Germón Busch, Rurrenabaque, T892 2246, crtmpilonlajas@yahoo.com, entrance fee US$25.*

Beyond the Beni River in the southeast runs the Pilón Lajas Biosphere Reserve and Indigenous Territory (400,000 ha), home to the Tsimane and Mosetene peoples. Together with Madidi, it constitutes approximately 60,000 sq km, one of the largest systems of protected land in the neotropics. Unfortunately, much of this land is under pressure from logging interests, especially along the western border of the reserve. Set up under the auspices of UNESCO, Pilón Lajas has one of the continent's most intact Amazonian rainforest ecosystems, as well as an incredible array of tropical forest animal life. NGOs have been working with the people of La Unión, Playa Ancha, Nuevos Horizontes and El Cebú to develop sustainable forestry, fish farming, cattle ranching and *artesanía*.

Rurrenabaque → *Phone code: 03. Population: 15,197. Altitude: 200 m.*

The charming, picturesque jungle town of Rurre (as the locals call it), on the Río Beni, is the main jumping off point for tours in the Bolivian Amazon and pampas, from 2-4 day trips through to full expeditions. Across the river is the smaller town of San Buenaventura (canoe US$0.15). Despite its growth as a trading, transport and ecotourism centre, Rurre is a pleasant town to walk around, although the climate is usually humid. Market day is Sunday. **Dirección Regional de Turismo** ⓘ *Avaroa y Vaca Díez, Mon-Fri 0800-1200, 1400-1800, Sat 0900-1100*, has general information and a bulletin board for posting comments on tours; read this before booking a tour and write your own feedback. Bicycles rented at US$2 per hour. There are two ATMs, both on Comercio near the intersection with Aniceto.

Forty minutes upstream from Rurre is **San Miguel del Bala**, in a beautiful setting, 3 km from the entrance to Madidi. This community lodge gives a good taste of the jungle, offers day trips, well-laid-out trails and has en suite cabins where you can stay, bar and a pool fed by a waterfall. It is owned and operated by the indigenous Tacana community. Community tourism is also being developed at **Santa Rosa de Yacuma**, 100 km northeast of Rurre, for information contact **FAN** (page 35).

ⓔ Madidi and Rurrenabaque listings

For hotel and restaurant price codes, and other relevant information, see pages 14-17.

ⓔ Where to stay

Madidi *p388*
Chalalán Ecolodge is 5 hrs upriver from Rurrenabaque, at San José de Uchupiamonas, in Madidi National Park. La Paz office: Sagárnaga 189, Edif Shopping Doryan, of 22, T02-231 1451; in Rurrenabaque, C Comercio entre Campero y Vaca Díez, T892 2419, www.chalalan. com. This is Bolivia's top ecotourism project, founded by the local Quechua-Tacana community, Conservation International and the Interamerican Development Bank, and now has a well-deserved international reputation. Accommodation is in thatched cabins, and activities include fantastic wildlife-spotting and birdwatching, guided and self-guided trails, river and lake

activities, and relaxing in pristine jungle surroundings. 3-day/2-night packages cost US$350 pp (US$320 with shared bath), plus transport to Rurre and national park fees.
San Miguel del Bala, 40-min boat trip upriver from Rurre (office at C Comercio entre Vaca Díez y Santa Cruz), T892 2394, www.sanmigueldelbala.com. 7 cabins in a delightful setting, good bathrooms, nice public areas, good restaurant, attentive staff, 3 days/2 nights cost US$240 pp. Advance booking required. Highly recommended.

Pilón Lajas *p388*
Mapajo, Mapajo Ecoturismo Indígena, Santa Cruz entre Avaroa y Comercio, Rurrenabaque, T892 2317, http://mapajo-ecoturismo-indigena.blogspot.co.uk. A community-run ecolodge 3 hrs by boat from Rurrenebaque has 6 *cabañas* without electricity (take a torch), shared cold showers and a dining room serving traditional meals.

3 days/2 nights cost US$250 pp. You can visit the local community, walk in the forest, go birdwatching, etc. Take insect repellent, wear long trousers and strong footwear. Recommended.

Rurrenabaque *p389*
In high season hotels fill up very quickly.
$$ El Ambaibo, Santa Cruz entre Bolívar y Busch, T892 2107. Includes breakfast and airport transfer, large pool (US$3 for non-guests), parking, a step up from the average in Rurre.
$$ Safari, Comercio on the outskirts downriver (can be a hot walk), T892 2410. A peaceful spot with beautiful garden and comfortable rooms, pool, terrace and a good restaurant. Recommended.
$ Asaí, Vaca Díez y Busch, T892 2439. Electric showers, cheap, quiet, laundry area, courtyard and hammocks, breakfast extra.
$ Beni, Comercio y Arce, along the river, T892 2408. Best rooms have a/c and TV, hot showers, cheaper with fan and without bath, kitchen facilities. Spacious, good service.
$ El Curichal, Comercio 1490, T892 2647, elcurichal@hotmail.com. Nice courtyard, hammocks, laundry and small kitchen facilities, helpful staff, will change cash and TCs. Popular economy option.
$ Hostal Pahuichi, Comercio y Vaca Díez, T892 2558. Some big rooms with electric shower, fan, rooftop views, cheap and good.
$ Mirador del Lobo, upstream end of Comercio, contact through El Lobo in La Paz, T02-245 1640. Cheap rooms in large breezy building overlooking the river, some rooms with electric shower.
$ Oriental, on plaza, T892 2401. Hot showers, fan, small breakfast included, quiet, hammocks in peaceful garden, family-run. A good option.
$ Res Jislene, C Comercio entre La Paz y Beni, T892 2526. Erlan Caldera and family are very hospitable, hot water, fan, hammock area, cheap basic rooms, good breakfast if booked in advance, information, helpful.

$ Santa Ana, Avaroa entre Vaca Díez y Campero, T892 2399. Cheap basic rooms, laundry, pleasant hammock area in garden.

❼ Restaurants

Rurrenabaque *p389*
$$ Camila's, Avaroa y Campero. Daily 0800-0130. International food, *parrillada* on Sun, pool tables, fast service.
$$ Casa del Campo, Vaca Díez y Avaroa. Daily 0700-2100. Good sandwices, juices, fresh organic food, great salad selection, breakfast, delicious desserts, garden, friendly staff but very slow service.
$$ Juliano's, Santa Cruz entre Bolívar y Avaroa. Daily 1200-1430, 1800-late. French and Italian food, good presentation and service. Recommended.
$$-$ Luna Café, Comercio entre Santa Cruz y Vaca Diez. Open 0800-2200. International meals, pizza, snacks and drinks.
$$-$ Pizzería Italia & Monkey's Bar, Avaroa entre Santa Cruz y Vaca Díez. Open 0900-0100. Big pizzas, imaginative pastas, lively crowd, big-screen TV, pool tables.
$ La Cabaña, Santa Cruz, by the river. Mon-Sat 0800-2200, Sun 0800-1600. Wide selection of international and Bolivian food.

Cafés
French Bakery, Vaca Díez entre Avaroa y Bolívar. Mon-Sat 0600-1200. Run by Thierry. Delicious croissants and *pain au chocolat*, get there early.
Moskkito Bar, Vaca Díez y Avaroa. Cool bar for tall jungle tales. Burgers, pizzas, rock music and pool tables.
Pachamama, south end of Avaroa. Open 1200-2230. English/Israeli café/bar, snacks, films (US$3), board games and a book exchange.
Ron, an American expat, drives round town in a kit car offering banana bread, cinnamon rolls, granola bars and his views on the sad state of the world. Catch him while they're hot, at the corner of Santa Cruz and Avaroa.

❶ What to do

Rurrenabaque p389

There are 2 types of tours, jungle or pampas. Both cost about US$80 pp plus US$13.50 park fee for a typical 3-day tour. Prices and quality both vary but booking in Rurre is usually cheaper than in La Paz. Jungle tours normally involve travelling by boat on the Río Beni. Lodging is either in purpose-built camps on higher-end tours, or tents at the budget end. Tours are long enough for most people to get a sense of life in the jungle. In the rainy season the jungle is very hot and humid with many more biting insects and far fewer animals to be seen. In the more open terrain of the Pampas you will see a lot more wildlife. Pampas tours involve 4-hr jeep ride to the Río Yacuma at either end, and a series of boat trips. You may have to wade through knee-deep water; wear appropriate shoes. You might see howler, squirrel and capuchin monkeys, caiman, capybara, pink dolphins, possibly anacondas and a huge variety of birds. You will not see jaguars. One-day trips are not recommended as they spend most of the time travelling, unless going to San Miguel del Bala.

Rurrenabaque has thrived on its steadily increasing number of visitors but also suffered the consequences of haphazard growth in tourism. Not all of the many tour operators here are reputable nor do all tourists in Rurre behave responsibly. Many agencies offer ecologically unsound practices such as fishing, feeding monkeys, catching caiman or handling anaconda. Before signing up for a tour, check the bulletin board at the Dirección Municipal de Turismo and try to talk to other travellers who have just come back. Post your own comments after you return. Go with an established company as competition has been forcing down prices and, consequently, the quality of tours. Some operators pool customers, so you may not go with the company you booked with. There are many more agencies in town than those listed below. Shop around and choose carefully.

Tour operators

Aguilar Tours, Av Avaroa, T892 2478, www.aguilar.lobopages.com. Jungle and pampas tours.

Bala Tours, Av Santa Cruz y Comercio, T3892 2527, www.balatours.com. Arranges Pampas and jungle tours, with their own lodge in each (with bath and solar power). English-speaking guides. Combined trips to Pampas and jungle arranged. Recommended.

Donato Tours, Avaroa entre Pando y Arce, T892 2571, http://donatotours.com. Regular tours plus the opportunity to stay in a community in Pilón Lajas for 1 to 20 days.

Lipiko Tours, Av Santa Cruz s/n, between Bolívar and Avaroa, T892 2221, www.travel-bolivia.co.uk.

Madidi Travel, Comercio y Vaca Díez, T892 2153, in La Paz, Linares 968, T02-231 8313, www.madidi-travel.com. Specializes in tours to the private Serere Sanctuary in the Madidi Mosaic (details on website), minimum 3 days/2 nights, good guiding.

Mashaquipe Tours, Avaroa y Arce, http://mashaquipe.com.bo. Jungle and pampas tours run by an organization of indigenous families with a lodge in Madidi National Park.

❸ Transport

Caranavi to San Borja p388

Bus See page 340 for buses in Caranavi. **Yucumo** is on the La Paz–Caranavi–Rurrenabaque and San Borja bus routes. Rurrenabaque–La Paz bus passes through about 1800. If travelling to Rurrenabaque by bus take extra food in case there is a delay (anything from road blocks to flat tyres to high river levels). **Flota Yungueña** daily except Thu at 1300 from San Borja to **La Paz**, 19 hrs via Caranavi. Also San Borja to **Rurrenabaque**, **Santa Rosa**, **Riberalta**, **Guayaramerín** about 3 times a week. Minibuses and *camionetas* normally run daily between San Borja and **Trinidad**

throughout the year, US$15, about 7 hrs including 20 mins crossing of Río Mamoré on ferry barge (up to 14 hrs in wet season). Gasoline available at Yolosa, Caranavi, Yucumo, San Borja and San Ignacio.

Rurrenabaque *p389*
Air Several daily flights to/from **La Paz** with **Amaszonas**, Comercio entre Santa Cruz y Vaca Diez, T892 2472, US$95; and 3 a week with **TAM**, Santa Cruz y Avaroa, T892 2398, US$68. Amaszonas also flies to **Trinidad** and **Santa Cruz**. Book flights as early as possible and buy onward ticket on arrival. Check flight times in advance; they change frequently. Delays and cancellations are common. Airport taxes US$2. Airlines provide transport to/from town, US$1.
Bus To/from **La Paz** via Caranavi with Flota Yungueña, Totaí and Vaca Díez; 18-20 hrs, US$8.50, daily at 1030 and Sat-Mon also at 1900. Some continue to **Riberalta** (US$17, 13 hrs from Rurre), **Guayaramerín** (US$18, 15 hrs) or **Cobija** (US$32, 30 hrs). Rurrenabaque-**Riberalta** may take 6 days or more in the wet season. Take lots of food, torch and be prepared to work. To **Trinidad**, with Trans Guaya (buses) or Trans Rurrenabaque (minibuses) daily, Flota Yungueña Mon, Wed, via **Yucumo** and **San Borja**, US$18, check that the road is open.

⊙ Directory

Rurrenabaque *p389*
Immigration Arce entre Bolívar y Busch, T892 2241, Mon-Fri 0830-1230, 1430-1830, same-day extensions.

Riberalta to Brazil

Riberalta → *Phone code: 03. Colour map 3, A3. Population: 97,982. Altitude: 175 m.*
This town, at the confluence of the Madre de Dios and Beni rivers, is off the beaten track and a centre for brazil nut production. It's very laid back, but take care if your bus drops you in the middle of the night and everything is closed. There are places to eat on the plaza and near the airport. Change cash in shops and on street.

Guayaramerín and border with Brazil → *Phone code: 03. Colour map 3, A3. Population: 39,010.*
Guayaramerín is a cheerful, prosperous little town on the bank of the Río Mamoré, opposite the Brazilian town of Guajará-Mirim. There are several restaurants and cafés around the plaza. It has an important *Zona Libre*. Passage between the two towns is unrestricted; boat trip US$1.65 (more at night).

Bolivian immigration Avenida Costanera near port; open 0800-1100, 1400-1800. Passports must be stamped here when leaving, or entering Bolivia. On entering Bolivia, passports must also be stamped at the Bolivian consulate in Guajará-Mirim. The Brazilian consulate is on 24 de Septiembre, Guayaramerín, T855 3766, open 0900-1300, 1400-1700; visas for entering Brazil are given here. To enter Brazil you must have a yellow fever certificate, or be inoculated at the health ministry (free). Exchange cash at the dock on the Bolivian side where rates are written up on blackboards (no traveller's cheques), although there is an ATM at the Banco do Brasil in Guajará-Mirim; no facilities for cash.

Cobija → *Phone code: 03. Colour map 3, A2. Population: 55,692.*
The capital of the lowland Department of Pando lies on the Río Acre which forms the frontier with Brazil. A new, single-tower suspension bridge crosses the river to Brasiléia. As a duty-free zone, shops in centre have a huge selection of imported consumer goods at bargain prices. Brazilians and Peruvians flock here to stock up. As this is a border area,

watch out for scams and cons. **Bolivian immigration** ⓘ *Av Internacional 567, T842 2081, open daily 0900-1800.* **Brazilian consulate** ⓘ *Av René Barrientos s/n, T842 2110, Mon-Fri 0830-1230.* There are *casas de cambio* on Avenida Internacional and Avenida Cornejo. Most shops will accept dollars or reais, and exchange money.

⦿ Riberalta to Brazil listings

For hotel and restaurant price codes, and other relevant information, see pages 14-17.

⬡ Where to stay

Riberalta *p392*
Ask for a fan and check the water supply.
\$\$ Colonial, Plácido Méndez 1, T852 3018. Charming colonial casona, large, well-furnished rooms, no singles, nice gardens and courtyard, comfortable, good beds, helpful owners.
\$ Alojamiento Comercial Lazo, NG Salvatierra. With a/c, cheaper with fan, comfortable, laundry facilities, good value.
\$ Res Los Reyes, near airport, T852 2628. With fan, cheap, safe, pleasant, but noisy disco nearby on Sat and Sun.

Guayaramerín *p392*
\$\$ San Carlos, 6 de Agosto, 4 blocks from port, T855 3555. With a/c, hot showers, changes dollars cash, TCs and reais, swimming pool, reasonable restaurant.
\$ Santa Ana 25 de Mayo, close to airport, T855 3900. With bath, fan, cheap and recommended.

Cobija *p392*
\$\$ Diana, Av 9 de Febrero 123, T842 3653, www.dianahotel.boliviafull.com. A/c, TV, safe, buffet breakfast, pool.
\$\$ Nanijos, Av 9 de Febrero 147, T842 2230. Includes breakfast, a/c, TV, *comedor* does good lunch, helpful.
\$\$ Triller, Av Internacional 640, T842 2024. With a/c (cheaper with fan) and bath, restaurant.

⬥ What to do

Riberalta *p392*
Riberalta Tours, Av Sucre 634, T852 3475, www.riberaltatours.com. Multi-day river and jungle tours, airline tickets, very helpful.

⬤ Transport

Riberalta *p392*
Air Flights to **Trinidad** and **Cobija** with Aerocon (at airport, T852 4679). TAM (Av Suárez Chuquisaca, T852 3924) to **Trinidad, Santa Cruz, Cochabamba** and **La Paz**. Expect cancellations in the wet season.
Bus Roads to all destinations are appalling, even worse in the wet season. Several companies (including Yungueña) to **La Paz**, via **Rurrenabaque** and **Caranavi** daily, 35 hrs to 3 days or more, US\$27. To **Trinidad** via Rurrenabaque and San Borja, 25-35 hrs. To **Guayaramerín** 7 daily, US\$5, 2 hrs. To **Cobija** several companies, none with daily service, 10-11 hrs.
River Cargo boats carry passengers along the **Río Madre de Dios**, but they are infrequent. There are no boats to Rurrenabaque.

Guayaramerín *p392*
Air Daily flights to **Trinidad**, with onward connections, with **Aerocon** (25 de Mayo y Beni, T855 5025). TAM has same services as for Riberalta.
Bus Buses leave from General Federico Román. Same long-haul services as Riberalta, above. To **Riberalta** 2 hrs, US\$5, daily 0700-1730.
River Check the notice of vessels leaving port on the Port Captain's board, prominently displayed near the immigration

post on the riverbank. Boats sailing up the Mamoré to **Trinidad** are not always willing to take passengers.

Cobija *p392*
Air Daily flights to **Riberalta** and **Trinidad**, with onward connections, with **Aerocon**, Leoncio Justiniano 43, T842 4575. TAM (Av 9 de Febrero 49, T842 2267), to **La Paz** or **Trinidad** on alternating days.
Bus Flota Yungueña and Flota Cobija to **La Paz** via Riberalta and Rurrenabaque, 2-3 days or more, US$30-40. To **Riberalta** with several bus companies, depart from 2 de Febrero, most on Wed, Fri, Sun at 0600; good all-weather surface; 2 river crossings on pontoon rafts, takes 10-11 hrs.

Taxi US$0.60 in centre, but more expensive beyond, charging according to time and distance, expensive over the international bridge to Brasiléia. Besides taxis there are motorbike taxis (US$0.60). **Brasiléia** can also be reached by **canoe**, US$0.35. The bridge can be crossed on foot as well, although one should be dressed neatly in any case when approaching Brazilian customs. Entry/exit stamps (free) are necessary and yellow fever vaccination certificate also, when crossing into Brazil. From Brasiléia **Real Norte**, has buses to **Rio Branco**, US$7.60, and **Assis Brasil**, US$4, and Taxis Brasileiros run to Rio Branco, US$10.

Cochabamba to Trinidad

Villa Tunari to the Lowlands
Another route into Beni Department is via the lowland road between Cochabamba and Santa Cruz. At Ivirgazama, east of Villa Tunari, the road passes the turn-off to **Puerto Villarroel**, 27 km further north, from where cargo boats ply irregularly to Trinidad in about four to 10 days. You can get information from the Capitanía del Puerto notice board, or ask at docks. There are only a few basic places to sleep in Villarroel and very few stores.

Trinidad → *Phone code: 03. Colour map 3, B3. Population: 101,293. Altitude: 327 m.*
The hot and humid capital of the lowland Beni Department is a dusty city in the dry season, with many streets unpaved. Primarily a service centre for the surrounding ranches and communities, most travellers find themselves in the area for boats up and down the Río Mamoré. There are two ports, Almacén and Varador, check at which one your boat will be docked. Puerto Varador is 13 km from town on the Río Mamoré on the road between Trinidad and San Borja; cross the river over the main bridge by the market, walk down to the service station by the police checkpoint and take a truck, US$1.70. Almacén is 8 km from the city. The main mode of transport in Trinidad is the motorbike (even for taxis, US$0.40 in city); rental on plaza from US$2 per hour, US$8 per half day. Transport can be arranged from the airport. **Tourist office** ① *in the Prefectura building at Joaquín de Sierra y La Paz, ground floor, T462 4831, www.trinidad. gob.bo; also at Centro de Informacion Turistica, 6 de Agosto, next to Hotel Campanario.*

About 5 km from town is the Laguna Suárez, with plenty of wildlife; swimming is safe where the locals swim, near the café with the jetty (elsewhere there are stingrays and alligators). Motorbike taxi from Trinidad, US$1.30.

San Ignacio de Moxos → *Electricity is supplied in town from 1200-2400.*
San Ignacio de Moxos, 90 km west of Trinidad, is known as the folklore capital of the Beni Department. It's a quiet town with a mainly indigenous population; 60% are *Macheteros*, who speak their own language. San Ignacio still maintains the traditions of the Jesuit missions with big fiestas, especially during Holy Week and the **Fiesta del Santo Patrono de Moxos**, the largest festival in the Beni, at the end of July.

For hotel and restaurant price codes, and other relevant information, see pages 14-17.

⊙ Where to stay

Trinidad *p394*

$$$$ Flotel Reina de Enín, river cruise, see What to do, below.

$$ Campanario, 6 de Agosto 80, T462 4733. Rooms with a/c and frigobar, meeting room, restaurant, bar, pool.

$$ Jacaranda Suites, La Paz entre Pedro de la Rocha y 18 de Noviembre, T462 2446. Good services, restaurant, pool, meeting rooms, internet.

$ Copacabana, Tomás Villavicencio, 3 blocks from plaza, T462 2811. Good value, some beds uncomfortable, cheaper with shared bath, helpful staff.

$ Monteverde, 6 de Agosto 76, T462 2750. With a/c (cheaper with fan), frigobar, owner speaks English. Recommended.

$ Res 18 de Noviembre, Av 6 de Agosto 135, T462 1272. With and without bath, welcoming, laundry facilities.

San Ignacio de Moxos *p394*

There are some cheap *alojamientos* on and around the main plaza.

⊘ Restaurants

Trinidad *p394*

$$ Club Social 18 de Noviembre, N Suárez y Vaca Díez on plaza. Good-value lunch, lively, popular with locals.

$$ El Tábano, Villavicencio entre Mamore y Nestor Suarez. Good fish and local fare, relaxed atmosphere.

$$ La Estancia, Barrio Pompeya, on Ibare entre Muibe y Velarde. Excellent steaks.

$$ Pescadería El Moro, Bolívar 707 y 25 de Diciembre. Excellent fish. Also several good fish restaurants in Barrio Pompeya, south of plaza across river.

$ La Casona, Plaza Ballivián. Good pizzas and set lunch, closed Tue.

Heladería Oriental, on plaza. Good coffee, ice cream, cakes, popular with locals.

⊙ What to do

Trinidad *p394*

Most agents offer excursions to local *estancias* and jungle tours. Most *estancias* can also be reached independently in 1 hr by hiring a motorbike.

Flotel Reina de Enín, Av Comunidad Europea 624, T 7391 2965, www.amazon cruiser.com.bo. Cruises on the Mamoré River within in the Ibaré-Mamoré Reserve. Comfortable berths with bath, US$445 pp for 3 day/2 night cruise includes all activities: dolphin watching, horse riding, visiting local communities, jungle walks, swimming and piranha fishing.

La Ruta del Bufeo, T462 7739, www.laruta delbufeo.blogspot.com. Specializes in river tours for seeing dolphins.

Moxos, 6 de Agosto 114, T462 1141. Multi-day river and jungle tours with camping. Recommended.

Paraíso Travel, 6 de Agosto 138, T462 0692. Offers excursions to Laguna Suárez, Rio Mamoré, camping and birdwatching tours.

⊙ Transport

Villa Tunari to the Lowlands: Puerto Villarroel *p394*

From Cochabamba you can get a bus to **Puerto Villarroel** (see Cochabamba Transport, Bus), **Puerto San Francisco**, or **Todos Santos** on the Río Chapare.

Trinidad *p394*

Air Daily flights with **Aerocon** (6 de Agosto y 18 de Noviembre, T462 4442) and TAM (Bolívar 42, T462 2363) to **La Paz**, **Santa Cruz**, **Cochabamba**, **Cobija**, **Riberalta** and **Guayaramerín** (Aerocon also to Sucre).

Amaszonas (18 de Noviembre 267, T462 2426) Mon, Wed, Fri to **Rurrenabaque**. Airport, T462 0678. Mototaxi to airport US$1.20.
Bus Bus station is on Rómulo Mendoza, between Beni and Pinto, 9 blocks east of main plaza. Motorbike taxis will take people with backpacks from bus station to centre for US$0.45. To **Santa Cruz** (10 hrs on a paved road, US$8-18) and **Cochabamba** (US$12-17, 20 hrs), with Copacabana, **Mopar** and **Bolívar** mostly overnight (*bus cama* available). To **Rurrenabaque**, US$18, 12-20 hrs. Enquire locally what services are running to San Borja and **La Paz**. Similarly to **Riberalta** and **Guayaramerín**.

River Cargo boats down the Río Mamoré to **Guayaramerín** take passengers, 3-4 days, assuming no breakdowns, best organized from Puerto Varador (speak to the Port Captain). **Argos** is recommended as friendly, US$22 pp, take water, fresh fruit, toilet paper and ear-plugs; only for the hardy traveller.

San Ignacio de Moxos p394
Bus The Trinidad to San Borja bus stops at the **Donchanta** restaurant for lunch, otherwise difficult to find transport to San Borja. Minibus to Trinidad daily at 0730 from plaza, also *camionetas*, check road conditions and times beforehand.

Santa Cruz and Eastern Lowlands

In contrast to the highlands of the Andes and the gorges of the Yungas, eastern Bolivia is made up of vast plains stretching to the Chaco of Paraguay and the Pantanal wetlands of Brazil. Agriculture is well developed and other natural resources are fully exploited, bringing a measure of prosperity to the region. There are a number of national parks with great biodiversity, such as Amboró and Noel Kempff Mercado. Historical interest lies in the pre-Inca ceremonial site at Samaipata, the beautiful Jesuit Missions of Chiquitos and, of much more recent date, the trails and villages where Che Guevara made his final attempt to bring revolution to Bolivia.

Santa Cruz → *Phone code: 03. Colour map 3, B4. Population: 1,566,000. Altitude: 416 m.*

A little over 50 years ago, what is now Bolivia's largest city was a remote backwater, but rail and road links ended its isolation. The exploitation of oil and gas in the Departments of Santa Cruz and Tarija, and a burgeoning agribusiness sector, helped fuel rapid development. Since the election of Evo Morales in 2006 however, *Cruceños* have been concerned about the impact of his economic policies, perceived as favouring the highlands. There is considerable local opposition to the national government and Santa Cruz has spearheaded the eastern lowland departments' drive for greater autonomy from La Paz. The city is modern and busy, far removed from most travellers' perceptions of Bolivia. The centre still retains a bit of its former air, however, and the main plaza – 24 de Septiembre – is well cared for and a popular meeting place. During the extended lunchtime hiatus locals (who call themselves *cambas*) take refuge in their homes from the heat or rain, and the gridlock traffic eases. December to March is the hottest and rainiest time of the year.

Arriving in Santa Cruz
Orientation The international **airport** is at **Viru-Viru**, 13 km from the centre, reached by taxi or micro. Regional flights operate from **El Trompillo** airport, south of the centre on the Segundo Anillo. Long distance and regional **buses** leave from the combined bus/train terminal, **Terminal Bimodal**, Avenida Montes on the Tercer Anillo. The city has eight ring

roads, Anillos 1, 2, 3, 4 and so on, the first three of which contain most sites of interest to visitors. The neighbourhood of Equipetrol, where many upscale hotels, restaurants and bars are situated, is northwest of the centre in the Tercer (3rd) Anillo.

Santa Cruz

To **6 9**, Av San Martin & Barrio Equipetrol

To **3 4 10**, Av Monseñor Rivero & Viru-Viru Airport

Tourist information There is a **departmental tourist office** ① *Junín 22 on main plaza, T334 6776, Mon-Fri 0800-1200, 1500-1800; also a desk at Viru-Viru airport, 0700-2000.* **InfoTur** ① *Sucre y Potosí, inside the Museo de Arte, T339 9581, Mon-Fri 0800-1200, 1500-1900.* **APAC** ① *Av Busch 552 (2nd Anillo), T333 2287, www.festivalesapac.com,* has information about cultural events in the department of Santa Cruz. See also www.destinosantacruz.com.

Health and safety Dengue fever outbreaks are common during the wet season (Jan-Mar), take mosquito precautions. Take great care in crowds and market areas and take only radio taxis at night. ▸▸ *See also Safety, page 29.*

Places in Santa Cruz

The Plaza 24 de Septiembre is the city's main square with the huge **Cathedral** (also a basilica) ① *museum, T332 4683, Mon-Fri 1500-1800, US$1.50.* You can climb to a mirador in the cathedral **bell tower** ① *daily 0800-1200, 1500-1900, US$0.50,* with nice views of the city. **Manzana Uno**, the block behind the Cathedral, has been set aside for rotating art and cultural exhibits. **El Casco Viejo**, the heart of the city, with its arcaded streets and buildings with low, red-tiled roofs and overhanging eaves, retains a slight colonial feel, despite the profusion of modern, air-conditioned shops and restaurants. The **Museo de Historia** ① *Junín 141, T336 5533, Mon-Fri 0800-1200, 1500-1830, free* has several displays including archaeological pieces from the Chané and Guaraní cultures and explorers' routes. **Museo de Arte Contemporáneo** ① *Sucre y Potosí, T334 0926, Mon-Fri 0900-1200, 1500-2000, Sat-Sun 1500-1900, free,* houses contemporary Bolivian and international art in a nicely restored old house.

Some 12 km on the road to Cotoca are the **Botanical Gardens** ① *micro or trufi from C Suárez Arana, 15 mins, open daily 0800-1700, entry US$0.50,* a bit run-down but with many walking trails, birds and several forest habitats. **Parque Ecológico Yvaga Guazu** ① *Km 12.5 Doble Vía a La Guardia, taxi US$5, T352 7971, www.parqueyvagaguazu.org, daily 0800-1600, US$9 for 2-hr guided tour in Spanish (more for English-speaking guide),* 14 ha of tropical gardens with native and exotic species, plants for sale, restaurant serves Sunday buffet lunch. **Biocentro Güembé** ① *Km 7 Camino a Porongo, taxi US$7, T370 0700, www.biocentroguembe.com, daily 0830-1800, US$13 includes guided tour in Spanish or English,* is a resort with accommodation ($$$ range), restaurant, butterfly farm, walk-in aviary, swimming pools and other family recreation.

⊙ Santa Cruz listings

For hotel and restaurant price codes, and other relevant information, see pages 14-17.

⊖ Where to stay

Santa Cruz *p396, map p397*
$$$$ Los Tajibos, Av San Martín 455, Barrio Equipetrol, T342 1000, www.lostajiboshotel.com. Set in 6 ha of lush gardens, one of several hotels in this price bracket in the city and the most traditional, all facilities including business centre, art gallery, restaurants and spa. Weekend discounts.
$$$ Cortez, Cristóbal de Mendoza 280 (Segundo Anillo), T333 1234, www.hotelcortez.com. Traditional tropical hotel with restaurant, pool, gardens, meeting rooms, parking, good for dining and nightlife.
$$$ Royal Lodge, Av San Martín 200, Equipetrol, T343 8000. With restaurant and bar, pool, airport transfers. Excellent option for its location and price range.
$$$ Senses, Sucre y 24 de Septiembre, just off main plaza, T339 6666, www.senses

corp.com. Self-styled boutique hotel in the heart of the city, minimalist decor, includes all services.

$$$ Villa Magna, Barrón 70, T339 9700, www.villamagna-aparthotel.com. Fully furnished apartments with small pool, Wi-Fi, parking, attentive owner and staff, English and German spoken, from daily to monthly rates.

$$-$ Hostal Río Magdalena, Arenales 653 (no sign), T339 3011, www.hostalrio magdalena.com. Comfortable rooms, downstairs ones are dark, with a/c or fan, small yard and pool, popular.

$$ Bibosi, Junín 218, T334 8548, htlbibosi@ hotmail.com. Includes breakfast, private bath, electric shower, a/c, cheaper with fan, Wi-Fi in lobby, good value.

$$ Copacabana, Junín 217, T336 2770, hotelcopacabanascz@hotmail.com. Very good, popular with European tour groups, rooms cheaper without a/c, restaurant.

$$ Jodanga, C El Fuerte 1380, Zona Parque Urbano, Barrio Los Chóferes, T339 6542, www.jodanga.com. Good backpacker option 10 mins' walk from Terminal Bimodal, cheaper with fan and without bath, cheaper still in dorm, kitchen, bar, swimming pool, billiards, DVDs, nice communal areas, laundry, helpful owner and multilingual staff.

$ Milán, René Moreno 70, T339 7500, www.hotelmilan.web.bo. Some rooms with a/c, hot water, central location.

$ Res Bolívar, Sucre 131, T334 2500, www.residencialbolivar.com. Includes good breakfast, cheaper with shared bath and in dorm, lovely courtyard with hammocks, rooms can get hot, alcohol prohibited, popular.

$ Sarah, C Sara 85, T332 2425, hotel.sarah@ hotmail.com. Simple rooms which cost less without a/c, screened windows, small patio, good value.

❶ Restaurants

Santa Cruz *p396, map p397*
Santa Cruz has the best meat in Bolivia, try a local *churrasquería* (grill). Av San Martín in

Barrio Equipetrol, and Av Monseñor Rivero are the areas for upmarket restaurants and nightlife. Both are away from the centre, take a taxi at night. Some restaurants close Mon.

$$$-$$ La Creperie, Arenales 135. Mon-Sat 1900-2400. Serves good crêpes, fondues and salads.

$$$-$$ Los Hierros, Av Monseñor Rivero 300 y Castelnau. Daily 1200-1500, 1900-2400. Popular upmarket grill with salad bar.

$$$-$$ Michelangelo, Chuquisaca 502. Mon-Fri 1200-1430, 1900-2330, Sat evenings only. Excellent Italian cuisine, a/c.

$$ Ken, Uruguay 730 (1er Anillo), T333 3728. 1130-1430, 1800-2300, closed Wed. Sushi and authentic Japanese food, popular.

$$ La Casona, Arenales 222, T337 8495. Open 1130-1500, 1900-2400. German-run restaurant, very good food.

$$ Pizzería Marguerita, Junín y Libertad, northwest corner of the plaza. Open 0830-2400. A/c, good service, coffee, bar. Popular with expats, Finnish owner speaks English and German.

$$ Rincón Brasilero, Libertad 358. Daily 1130-1430,1930-2330. Brazilian-style buffet for lunch, pay by weight, very good quality and variety, popular; pizza and à la carte at night. Recommended.

$$ Tapekuá, Ballivián y La Paz, T334 5905. French and international food, good service, live entertainment some evenings.

$$-$ El Chile, Av Las Américas 60. Daily 1200-1500, 1700-2400. Mexican and Bolivian food, good set lunch with salad bar, à la carte at night.

$$-$ Los Lomitos, Uruguay 758 (1er Anillo), T332 8696. Daily 0800-2400. Traditional *churrasquería* with unpretentious local atmosphere, excellent Argentine-style beef.

$$-$ Vegetarian Center, Aroma 64, entre Bolívar y Sucre. Mon-Sat 1200-1500. Set lunch or pay-by-weight buffet.

$ Pizzería El Horno, 3er Anillo, frente a Hospital Oncológico, Equipetrol, T342 8042; also Av Roque Aguilera 600, Las Palmas; and Lagunillas 134, Braniff. Daily 1100-2300. True Italian pizza, very popular.

$ Su Salud, Quijarro 115. Mon-Thu 0800-2100, Fri and Sun 0800-1700. Tasty vegetarian food, filling lunches, sells vegetarian products.

Cafés

There are lots of very pleasant a/c cafés where you can get coffee, ice cream, drinks, and snacks.

Alexander Coffee, Junín y Libertad near main plaza, and Av Monseñor Rivero 400 y Santa Fe. For good coffee and people watching.

Café 24, downstairs at René Moreno y Sucre, on the main plaza. Daily 0830-0200. Breakfast, juices, international meals, wine rack, nice atmosphere, Wi-Fi.

Café Lorca, upstairs at René Moreno y Sucre, on the main plaza. Mon-Thu 0900-0100, Fri-Sat 0900-0300, Sun 1800-2400. Meals and drinks, Spanish wines, small balcony with views over plaza, live music Tue-Sat from 2100, part of a cultural project, see www.lorcasantacruz.org.

Freddo, Monseñor Rivero 245. Good expensive ice cream imported from Argentina.

Fridolín, 21 de Mayo 168, Pari 254, Av Cañoto y Florida, and Monseñor Rivero y Cañada Strongest. All good places for coffee and pastries.

Horno Caliente, Chuquisaca 604 y Moldes, also 24 de Septiembre 653. Salteñas 0730-1230, traditional local snacks and sweets 1530-1930. Popular and very good.

🕭 Bars and clubs

Santa Cruz *p396, map p397*

Bar Irlandés Irish Pub, 3er Anillo Interno 1216 (between Av Cristo Redentor and Zoológico). Irish-themed pub, food available, Irish owner, live music Wed, Fri and Sat evenings. Also **Café Irlandés**, Plaza 24 de Septiembre, overlooking main plaza. Popular.

Kokopelli, Noel Kempff Mercado 1202 (3er Anillo Interno), bar with Mexican food and live music.

⊕ Festivals

Santa Cruz *p396, map p397*

Cruceños are famous as fun-lovers and their music, the *carnavalitos*, can be heard all over South America. Of the various festivals, the brightest is **Carnaval**, renowned for riotous behaviour, celebrated for the **15 days before Lent** Music in the streets, dancing, fancy dress and the coronation of a queen. Water and paint throwing is common – no one is exempt. **24 Sep** is the local holiday of Santa Cruz city and department.

The **Festival de Música Renacentista y Barroca Americana "Misiones de Chiquitos"** is held in **late Apr through early May** every even year in Santa Cruz and the Jesuit mission towns of the Chiquitania. It is organized by **Asociación Pro Arte y Cultura** (APAC), Av Busch 552, Santa Cruz, T333 2287, www.festivalesapac.com, and celebrates the wealth of sacred music written by Europeans and indigenous composers in the 17th and 18th centuries. APAC sells books, CDs, and videos and also offers – in both Santa Cruz and the mission towns – a schedule of musical programmes. The festival is very popular: book hotels at least 2-3 weeks in advance. Every odd year the city of Santa Cruz APAC holds a **Festival Internacional de Teatro**, and every Aug and Dec a **Festival de la Temporada** in Santa Cruz and major towns of Chiquitania, featuring *musica misional* with local performers.

Cultural centres with events and programmes: Centro Cultural Santa Cruz, René Moreno 369, T335 6941, www.culturabcb.org.bo. Centro Simón I Patiño, Independencia y Suárez de Figueroa 89, T 337 2425, www.fundacionpatino.org. Exhibitions, galleries, and bookstore on Bolivian cultures. See also **Centro Boliviano Americano**, Cochabamba 66, T334 2299, www.cba.com.bo; Centro Cultural Franco Alemán, 24 de Septiembre on main plaza, T335 0142, www.ccfrancoaleman.org; Centro de Formación de la Cooperación Española, Arenales 583, T335 1311, www.aecid-cf.bo.

For cinema, **Cine Center**, Av El Trompillo (2do Anillo) entre Monseñor Santiesteban y René Moreno, www.cinecenter.com.bo.

O Shopping

Santa Cruz *p396, map p397*
Handicrafts Bolivian Souvenirs, Shopping Bolívar, loc 10 and 11, on main plaza, T333 7805; also at Viru-Viru airport. Expensive knitwear and crafts from all over Bolivia. **Paseo Artesanal La Recova**, off Libertad, ½ block from Plaza. Many different kiosks selling crafts. **Vicuñita Handicrafts**, Ingavi e Independencia, T333 4711. Wide variety of crafts from the lowlands and the altiplano, very good.
Jewellery Carrasco, Velasco 23, T336 2841, and other branches. For gemstones. RC Joyas, Bolívar 262, T333 2725. Jewellery and Bolivian gems.
Markets Los Pozos, between Quijarro, Campero, Suárez Arana and 6 de Agosto; is a sprawling street market for all kinds of produce. **Siete Calles**, Isabel la Católica y Vallegrande, mainly clothing. **Mercado Nuevo**, at Sucre y Cochabamba.

O What to do

Santa Cruz *p396, map p397*
Bird Bolivia, T358 2674, www.birdbolivia. com. Specializes in organized birding tours, English spoken.
Forest Tour, Galería Casco Viejo, upstairs, No 115, T337 2042, www.forestbolivia.com. Environmentally sensitive tours to Refugio los Volcanes, birdwatching, national parks, Chiquitania and Salar de Uyuni. English spoken.
Magri Turismo, Velarde 49 y Irala, T334 4559, www.magriturismo.com. Long-established agency for airline tickets and tours.
Misional Tours, Los Motojobobos 2515, T360 1985, www.misionaltours.com. Covers all of Bolivia, specializing in Chiquitania, Amboró, and Santa Cruz. Tours in various languages.

Ruta Verde, 21 de Mayo 318, T339 6470, www.rutaverdebolivia.com. Offers national parks, Jesuit missions, Amazonian boat trips, Salar de Uyuni, and tailor-made tours, Dutch/Bolivian-owned, English and German also spoken, knowledgeable and helpful.

O Transport

Santa Cruz *p396, map p397*
Air Viru-Viru, open 24 hrs, airline counters from 0600; *casa de cambio* changing cash US$ and euros at poor rates, 0630-2100; various ATMs; luggage lockers 0600-2200, US$5.50 for 24 hrs; ENTEL for phones and internet, plus a few eateries. Taxi US$10, micro from Ex-Terminal (see below), or El Trompillo, US$1, 45 min. From airport take micro to Ex-Terminal then taxi to centre. Domestic flights with **Boliviana de Aviación (BoA)** and **TAM (Bolivia)**, to **La Paz**, **Cochabamba**, **Sucre**, **Tarija** and **Cobija**. International flights to **Asunción**, **Buenos Aires**, **Salta**, **Lima**, **Madrid**, **Miami**, **Washington**, **Santiago** and **São Paulo**.
El Trompillo is the regional airport operating daily 0500-1900, T352 6600, located south of the centre on the Segundo Anillo. It has a phone office and kiosk selling drinks, but no other services. Taxi US$1.50, many micros. **TAM** has flights throughout the country, different destinations on different days. **Aerocon** flies via **Trinidad** to various towns in the northern jungle.
Bus Most long-distance buses leave from the combined bus/train terminal, **Terminal Bimodal**, Av Montes on the Tercer Anillo, T348 8382; police check passports and search luggage here; taxi to centre, US$1.50. Terminal fee, US$0.50, left luggage US$0.50, there are ATMs and *cambios*. Regional buses and vans leave either from behind the Terminal Bimodal (use pedestrian tunnel under the rail tracks) or from near the Ex-Terminal (the old bus station, Av Irala y Av Cañoto, 1er Anillo, which is no longer functioning). To **Cochabamba**, via the lowland route, many depart 0600-0930

and 1630-2130, US$8-16, 8-10 hrs, also **Trans Carrasco** vans leave when full across the street from the Terminal Bimodal, US$15; via the old highland route, **Trans Carrasco**, depart from the main plaza in El Torno, 30 km west of Santa Cruz, daily at 1200 (from Mairana daily at 0800 and 1500), US$6, 14 hrs. Direct to **Sucre** via Aiquile, around 1600, US$7.50-15, 12-13hrs. To **Oruro**, US$11-20, 14-15 hrs, and **La Paz** between 1630-1900, US$11-25, 15-16 hrs; change in Cochabamba for daytime travel. To **Camiri** (US$4, 4-5 hrs), **Yacuiba** (border with Argentina), US$7-16, 8 hrs and **Tarija**, US$13-26, 17-24 hrs. To **Trinidad**, several daily after 2000, 9 hrs, US$7-15. To **San José de Chiquitos**, US$7-10, 5 hrs, **Roboré**, US$7-10, 7 hrs, and **Quijarro** (border with Brazil), at 1030 and between 1700-2000, US$12-22, 8-10 hrs. Also vans to San José, leave when full, US$10, 4½ hrs. To **San Ignacio de Velasco**, US$10, 10 hrs; **Jenecherú** *bus-cama* US$18; also **Expreso San Ignacio** vans leave when full, US$20, 8 hrs.

International Terminal fee US$1.50. To **Asunción**, US$52-64, 20-24 hrs via Villamontes and the Chaco, at 1930, with **Yacyretá**, T362 5557, Mon, Tue, Thu, Sat; **Stel Turismo**, T349 7762, daily; **Pycazú**, daily, and **Palma Loma**. Other companies are less reliable. See page 406 for the route to Paraguay across the Chaco. To **Buenos Aires** daily departures around 1900, US$70-90, 36 hrs, several companies. To **São Paulo** via Puerto Suárez, with **La Preferida**, T364 7160, Mon, Wed, Fri, US$140, 2 days. **Taxi** About US$1-1.50 inside 1er Anillo (more at night), US$2 inside 3er Anillo, fix fare in advance. Use radio-taxis at night (eg **Matico**, T335 6666).

Train Ferroviaria Oriental, at Terminal Bimodal, T338 7300, www.fo.com.bo, runs east to **San José de Chiquitos**, **Roboré** and **Quijarro** on the Brazilian border. The **Ferrobus** (a rail-car with the fastest most luxurious service) leaves Santa Cruz Tue, Thu, Sun 1800, arriving Quijarro 0700 next day, US$33.60; **Expreso Oriental** (an express train), Mon, Wed, Fri 1450, arriving 0729, US$14.30; There is also little-used weekly train service south to **Yacuiba** on the Argentine frontier; buses are much faster.

ⓘ Directory

Santa Cruz *p396, map p397*
Car hire Avis, Av Cristo Redentor Km. 3.5, T343 3939, www.avis.com.bo. **Barron's**, Av Alemana 50 y Tajibos, T342 0160. Outstanding service and completely trustworthy. **IMBEX**, C El Carmen 123, entre Av Suárez Arana y Av Charcas, T311 1000, www.imbex.com. **Localiza**, Cristo Redentor entre 2do y 3er Anillo, T341 4343; also at airport, T341 4343; www.localiza.com. **Medical services** Santa Cruz is an important medical centre with many hospitals and private clinics. **Clínica Foianini**, Av Irala 468, www.clinicafoianini. com, is among the better regarded and more expensive; **San Juan de Dios**, Cuellar y España, is the public hospital. **Useful addresses** Immigration, Av El Trompillo (2do Anillo) near El Deber newspaper, T351 9574, Mon-Fri 0830-1200, 1430-1800; busy office, give yourself extra time. **Fundación Amigos de la Naturaleza (FAN)**, Km 7.5 Vía a La Guadria, T355 6800, www.fan- bo.org. **SERNAP**, Calle 9 Oeste 138, frente a la Plaza Italia, Barrio Equipetrol, T339 4310, Mon-Fri 0800-1200, 1400-1800.

Southwest of Santa Cruz

The highlights of this area known as Los Valles Cruceños, are southwest of Santa Cruz: the Inca site of El Fuerte by the pleasant resort town of Samaipata, nearby Parque Nacional Amboró and the Che Guevara Trail, on which you can follow in the final, fatal footsteps of the revolutionary.

Samaipata → *Phone code: 03. Colour map 3, B4. Population 3000. Altitude: 1650 m.*

From Santa Cruz the old mountain road to Cochabamba runs along the Piray gorge and up into the highlands. Some 100 km from Santa Cruz is Samaipata, a great place to relax midweek, with good lodging, restaurants, hikes and riding, and a growing ex-pat community. A two-hour walk takes you to the top of Cerro de La Patria, just east of town, with nice views of the surrounding valleys. Local *artesanías* include ceramics, paintings and sculpture. At weekends the town bursts into life as crowds of Cruceños come to escape the city heat and to party. See www.samaipata.info and www.guidetosamaipata.com.

The **Museo de Arqueología** houses the tourist information office and a collection of ceramics with anthropomorphic designs, dating from 200 BC to AD 300, and provides information on the nearby pre-Inca ceremonial site commonly called **El Fuerte** ① *daily 0900-1630, museum Mon-Fri 0830-1200, 1400-1800, Sat-Sun 0830-1600, US$8 for El Fuerte and Museum, US$0.85 for museum only, ticket valid 4 days, Spanish- and English-speaking guides available at El Fuerte, US$12.* This sacred structure (altitude 1990 m) consists of a complex system of channels, basins, high-relief sculptures, etc, carved out of one vast slab of rock. Some suggest that Amazonian people created it around 1500 BC, but it could be

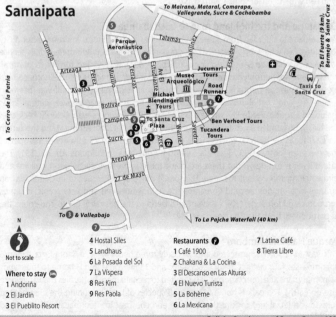

Samaipata

To Mairana, Mataral, Comarapa, Vallegrande, Sucre & Cochabamba

To El Fuerte (9 km), Bermejo & Santa Cruz

To Cerro de la Patria

Parque Aeronáutico

Museo Arqueológico

Jucumari Tours

Road Runners

Michael Blendinger Tours

Plaza

To Santa Cruz

Ben Verhoef Tours

Tucandera Tours

Taxis to Santa Cruz

To 3 & Valleabajo

To La Pajcha Waterfall (40 km)

N

Not to scale

Where to stay
1 Andoriña
2 El Jardín
3 El Pueblito Resort
4 Hostal Siles
5 Landhaus
6 La Posada del Sol
7 La Víspera
8 Res Kim
9 Res Paola

Restaurants
1 Café 1900
2 Chakana & La Cocina
3 El Descanso en Las Alturas
4 El Nuevo Turista
5 La Bohème
6 La Mexicana
7 Latina Café
8 Tierra Libre

later. There is evidence of subsequent occupations and that it was the nethermost outpost of the Incas' Kollasuyo (their eastern empire). Behind the rock are poorly excavated remains of a city. It is not permitted to walk on the rock, so visit the museum first to see the excellent model. El Fuerte is 9 km from Samaipata; 3 km along the highway to Santa Cruz, then 6 km up a rough, signposted road (taxi US$6 one way, US$13 return with two hours' wait); two to three hours' walk one way. Pleasant bathing is possible in a river on the way to El Fuerte.

In addition to tours to El Fuerte and the Ruta del Che (see below), many other worthwhile excursions can be made in the Samaipata area. Impressive forests of giant ferns can be visited around **Cerro La Mina** and elsewhere in the Amboró buffer zone. Also **Cuevas**, 20 km east of town, with waterfalls and pools, often visited together with El Fuerte. Further east are forest and sandstone mountains at **Bella Vista/Codo de los Andes**. There is a wonderful hike up to the **Mirador de Cóndores**, with many condors and nearby the the 25-m-high **La Pajcha** waterfall, 40 km south of Samaipata. **Postrervalle** is a quaint hamlet with many interesting walks and mountain bike trails. There is good birdwatching throughout the region, especially around Mataral (see below), and tour operators in Samaipata can arrange all of the above trips.

The little village of **Bermejo**, 40 km east of Samaipata on the road to Santa Cruz, provides access to the strikingly beautiful **Serranía Volcanes** region, abutting on Parque Nacional Amboró. Here is the excellent **Refugio Los Volcanes** ① *T03-337 2042, www.refugiovolcanes.net*, a small lodge with a 15-km trail system, with good birdwatching, orchids and bromeliads. Ginger's Paradise, some 2 km from Bermejo (www. gingersparadise.com), offers an organic, communal alternative, popular with backpackers (you can work to offset some room costs).

Comarapa and the highland road to Cochabamba

Past Samaipata the road from Santa Cruz continues west 17 km to **Mairana**, a hot dusty roadside town where long-distance buses make their meal stops and there is daily service to Cochabamba (see Santa Cruz transport, page 401). It is 51 km further to **Mataral**, where there are petroglyphs and the road to Vallegrande branches south. Another 57 km west is **Comarapa** (altitude 1800 m), a tranquil agricultural centre half-way between Santa Cruz and Cochabamba. The town provides access to several lovely natural areas including **Laguna Verde** (12 km, taxi US$11.50 with two hours wait, or walk back over the hills), surrounded by cloud forest bordering Parque Nacional Amboró; and the **Jardín de Cactáceas de Bolivia**, where the huge *carpari* cactus and 25 other endemic species may be seen (entry US$0.75, take a *trufi* from Comarapa to Pulquina Abajo, US$1). The Jardín itself is run-down but there are many more impressive cactii, good walking and birdwatching throughout the area. The tourist office at El Parquecito in Comarapa can arrange local guides. Beyond Comarapa the road is unpaved and very scenic. It climbs through cloud forest past the village of **La Siberia** to the pass at El Churo and enters the department of Cochabamba (see page 382).

Parque Nacional Amboró

This vast (442,500 ha) protected area lies only three hours west of Santa Cruz. Amboró encompasses four distinct major ecosystems and 11 life zones and is home to thousands of animal, plant and insect species (it is reputed to contain more butterflies than anywhere else on earth). The park is home to over 850 species of birds, including the blue-horned curassow, quetzal and cock-of-the-rock, red and chestnut-fronted macaws, hoatzin and cuvier toucans, and most mammals native to Amazonia, such as capybaras, peccaries, tapirs, several species of monkey, and jungle cats like the jaguar, ocelot and margay, and the spectacled bear. There are also numerous waterfalls and cool, green swimming pools, moss-ridden caves and large tracts of virgin rainforest. The park itself is largely inaccessible, but there is good trekking in the surrounding 195,100-ha buffer zone which is where most tours operate. The best time of year to visit the park is during April to October. There are two places to base yourself: Samaipata (see above) to access the southern highland areas of the park, and Buena Vista (see below) for northern lowland sections. You cannot enter the park without a guide, either from a tour operator, or from a community-based project. The park is administered by **SERNAP**, for their Santa Cruz office see page 402. There are also park offices in Samaipata and Buena Vista. Note that there are many biting insects so take repellent, long-sleeved shirts, long trousers and good boots. See www.biobol.org.

Buena Vista → Phone code: 04. Colour map 3, B4.

This sleeply little town is 100 km northwest of Santa Cruz by paved road (see www. buenavistabolivia.com). No ATM in town, but US$ cash can be changed. There is an interpretation office one block from the plaza, T932 2055. Three kilometres from town is **Eco-Albergue Candelaria** ① *T7781 3238 or contact in advance through Hacienda El Cafetal (page 407)*, a community tourism project offering cabins in a pleasant setting, activities and tours. From Buena Vista there are five tourist sites for entering the national park: **Villa Amboró** ① *T03-343 1332, www.probioma.org.bo*, good for hiking; the community can arrange horse riding. Get there either by 4WD, or take a taxi-trufi to Las Cruces (35 km from Buena Vista) and then hike to the refuge (about two hours). **Macuñucu**, about 2 km from Villa Amboró, is an entrance favoured by tour operators. **La Chonta** ① *T6773 5333, www. lachontaamboro.wordpress.com*, a community-based ecotourism lodge, offers tours to the forest and to farming communities with local guides. Take a taxi-trufi via Haytú to the Río Surutú and from there walk or horse ride 2½ hours. Further along the road to Cochabamba is **Mataracú**, used by the operators, with natural pools, waterfalls and dinosaur fossils. It has the private **Mataracú Tent Camp** ① *T03-342 2372*, and other camping options. At **Cajones de Ichilo** ① *T0763 02581, 0600-0900, 1800-2200*, a community lodge 70 km west from Buena Vista in Cochabamba department in mountainous scenery with a large river, there are trails which offer a good chance of seeing mammals and, with luck, the horned currasow, one of the most endangered species of bird in Bolivia.

Vallegrande and La Higuera

Some 115 km south of the Santa Cruz-Cochabamba road is La Higuera, where Che Guevara was killed. On 8 October each year, visitors, most from outside Bolivia, gather there to celebrate his memory. La Higuera is reached through the town of Vallegrande where, at **Hospital Nuestro Señor de Malta** ① *no fee, but voluntary donation to the health station*, you can see the old laundry building where Che's body was shown to the international press on 9 October 1967. Near Vallegrande's air strip you can see the results of excavations carried out in 1997 which finally unearthed his physical remains (now in Cuba), ask an airport attendant to see the site. Vallegrande has a small **archaeological museum** ① *US$1.50*, above which is the **Che Guevara Room** ① *free*.

The schoolhouse in La Higuera (60 km south of Vallegrande) where Che was executed is now a museum. Another **museum** ① *T03-942 2003*, owned by René Villegas, is open when he is in town. Guides, including Pedro Calzadillo, headmaster of the school, will show visitors to the ravine of El Churo (or Yuro), where Che was captured on 8 October 1967.

Tours organized by agencies in Santa Cruz and Samaipata follow some of the last movements of Che and his band.

To Paraguay and Argentina
South of Santa Cruz a good paved road passes through Abapó, Camiri (**Hotel Premier**, Avenida Busch 60, T952 2204, is a decent place to stay), Boyuibe, Villamontes – access for the Trans-Chaco route to Paraguay – and Yacuiba, on the border with Argentina.

Villamontes → *Phone code: 04. Colour map 3, C4.*
Villamontes, 500 km south of Santa Cruz, is renowned for fishing. It holds a Fiesta del Pescado in August. It is a hot, friendly, spread-out city on the north shore of the Río Pilcomayo, at the base of the Cordillera de Aguaragüe. The river cuts through this range (Parque Nacional Aguaragüe) forming **El Angosto**, a beautiful gorge. The road to Tarija, 280 km west, is cut in the cliffs along this gorge. At Plaza 6 de Agosto is the **Museo Héroes del Chaco** ① *Tue-Sun 0800-1200, 1400-1800, US$0.30*, with photographs, maps, artefacts, and battle models of the 1932-1935 Chaco War. There is no ATM, but banks, **Prodem** and various *cambios* are on Avenida Méndez Arcos.

From Villamontes, the road to Paraguay runs east to **Ibibobo** (70 km). The first 30 km is paved, thereafter it's gravel and further paving is in progress. Motorists and bus travellers should carry extra water and some food, as climatic conditions are harsh and there is little traffic in case of a breakdown. Bolivian exit stamps are given at Ibibobo. If travelling by bus, passports are collected by driver and returned on arrival at Mcal Estigarribia (Paraguay), with Bolivian exit stamp. Paraguayan immigration and thorough drugs searches take place in Mcal Estigarribia. See Santa Cruz Transport (page 401) for international bus services. From Ibibobo to the Bolivian frontier post at Picada Sucre is 75 km, then it's 15 km to the actual border and another 8 km to the Paraguayan frontier post at **Fortín Infante Rivarola**. There are customs posts, but no police, immigration nor any other services at the border.

Yacuiba → *Colour map 3, C4. Population: 11,000.*
Yacuiba is a prosperous city (reported less-than-safe due to drug running) at the crossing to Pocitos in Argentina. Hotels include **Valentín**, San Martín 1153, www.valentinhotelbolivia.com, and **París**, Comercio 1175 y Campero, T04-682 2182 (both **$$**). The train service from Santa Cruz is slow and poor, road travel is a better option, or **Aerocon** flights to Santa Cruz (Santa Cruz 1336, T468 3841). In Yacuiba, there are ATMs on Campero. Argentine consul at Comercio y Sucre. Passengers leaving Bolivia must disembark at Yacuiba, take a taxi to Pocitos on the border (US$0.40, beware unscrupulous drivers) and walk across to Argentina.

◉ Southwest of Santa Cruz listings

For hotel and restaurant price codes, and other relevant information, see pages 14-17.

◉ Where to stay

Samaipata *p403, map p403*
Rooms may be hard to find at weekends in high season.

$$$$-$$$ El Pueblito Resort, camino a Valle Abajo, 20 mins' walk uphill from town, T944 6383, www.elpueblitoresort.com. Fully-equipped cabins and rooms, pool, restaurant and bar set around a mock colonial plaza, with shops and meditation chapel.
$$ Landhaus, C Murillo uphill from centre, T944 6033, www.samaipata-landhaus.com.

Cabins and rooms in nice ample grounds, small pool, hammocks, parking, sauna (extra), craft shop, good breakfast available. Older rooms are cheaper and good value.

$$ La Posada del Sol, C Arteaga, 3 blocks north of plaza, T7211 0628, www.laposadadelsol.net. Most rooms with bath, electric shower, nice grounds, restaurant, views, US/Bolivian-run.

$$ La Víspera, 1.2 km south of town, T944 6082, www.lavispera.org. Dutch-owned organic farm with accommodation in 4 cosy cabins with kitchen, camping US$4-7 pp, breakfast and lunch available in **Café-Jardín** (0800-1500 daily), book exchange, maps for sale. A peaceful slow-paced place; owners Margarita and Pieter are very knowledgeable and can arrange excursions and horse riding. They also sell medicinal and seasoning herbs. Highly recommended.

$ Andoriña, C Campero, 2½ blocks from plaza, T944 6333, www.andorinasamaipata.com. Tastefully decorated hostel, cheaper without bath, good breakfast, kitchen, bar, good views, volunteer opportunites. Dutch/Bolivian-run, enthusiastic owners Andrés and Doriña are very knowledgeable, English spoken.

$ El Jardín, C Arenales, 2 blocks from market, T7311 4461. With electric shower, cheaper in dorm, ample grounds, camping US$3 pp, kitchen facilities, Belgian/Bolivian-run.

$ Hostal Siles, C Campero, T944-6408. Simple rooms, cheaper with shared bath electric shower, kitchen and laundry facilities, good value.

$ Paola, C Terrazas, diagonal to the plaza, T944 6093. Simple rooms, cheaper without bath, electric shower, restaurant serves set meals, internet (extra), kitchen and laundry facilities.

$ Res Kim, C Terrazas, near plaza, T944 6161. Cheaper with shared bath, family-run, spotless, good value.

Comarapa p404

$ El Paraiso, Av Comarapa 396 (main road to Cochabamba), T946 2045. Pleasant economical hotel, electric shower, nice garden, parking, decent restaurant, popular.

Buena Vista p405

$$$-$$ Hacienda El Cafetal, 5.5 km south of town (taxi from plaza US$3), T935 2067. Comfortable suites for up to 5 people, double rooms, restaurant, bar, birdwatching platform, on a working coffee plantation (tours available), with shade forest.

$$ Buenavista, 700 m out of town, T03-932 2104, www.buenavistahotel.com.bo. Pretty place with rooms, suites and cabins with kitchen, viewing platform, pool, sauna, very good restaurant, horse riding.

$ La Casona, Av 6 de Agosto at the corner of the plaza, T03-932 2083. Small simple rooms with fan, shared bath, electric shower, courtyard in hammocks, plants and birds, good value.

$ Quimori, 1 km east of Buena Vista, T03-932 2081. Includes breakfast, other meals with advance notice, pool, nice grounds, tours in dry season, family-run.

$ Res Nadia, T03-932 2049. Cheaper without bath, simple, small, family-run.

Vallegrande and La Higuera p405

$ Hostal Juanita, M M Caballero 123, Vallegrande, T942 2231. Cheaper without bath, electric shower, good value, Doña Juanita is kind.

$ La Casa del Telegrafista, La Higuera, T6773 3362, casadeltelegrafista@gmail.com. Small, welcoming French-owned posada, rooms with shared bath, lovely garden, great views, meals on request, camping (US$2), horseback and mountain bike tours, US$15, also bikes for hire.

$ Res Vallegrande, on the plaza, Vallegrande. Basic accommodation.

Villamontes p406

$$ El Rancho, Av Méndez Arcos opposite the train station, 15 blocks from the centre, T672 2059, rancho@entelnet.bo. Lovely rooms, frigobar, nice grounds and pool, parking, excellent restaurant.

$ Gran Hotel Avenida, Av Méndez Arcos 3 blocks east of Plaza 15 de Abril, T672 2106. Helpful owner, parking.

$ Res Raldes, Cap Manchego 171, 1½ blocks from Plaza 15 de Abril, T672 2088, fernandoarel@gmail.com. Well maintained, family-run, electric shower, cheaper with shared bath and fan, nice courtyard, small pool, parking.

⑦ Restaurants

Samaipata *p403, map p403*
$$ El Descanso en Las Alturas, C Arteaga, uphill from plaza, opens mostly on weekends. Wide choice including good steaks and pizzas.
$$ La Mexicana, C Rubén Terrazas near the plaza. Tue-Sun 1100-1500 and 1800-2300. Nice restaurant/bar with very good Mexican food. Also serves breakfast Sat-Sun.
$$ Latina Café, Bolívar, 3 blocks from plaza. Fri-Tue 1800-2200, Sat-Sun also 1200-1430. Nice upmarket restaurant/bar with very good Bolivian and international food including vegetarian. French/Bolivian-run and recommended.
$$-$ Chakana, Terrazas on plaza. Daily 0800-2300. Bar/restaurant/café serving *almuerzos*, good snacks, salads, cakes and ice cream, outside seating, book exchange, Dutch-owned.
$$-$ Tierra Libre, Sucre ½ block from plaza. Open 1200-2200, Sun 1200-1500, closed Wed. Nice terrace with outdoor seating, good meat and vegetarian, pleasant atmosphere.
$ Café 1900, Sucre on plaza. Daily 0800-2300. Good set lunch, sandwiches and crêpes.
$ El Nuevo Turista, opposite the gas station on the highway. Good local dishes.
$ La Boheme, Sucre y Terrazas, diagonal to plaza. Daily 1200-2400. Trendy Australian-run bar for drinks and snacks.
$ La Cocina, Sucre by the plaza. Tue-Sat 1900-2200. Middle Eastern and Mexican fast food with home-made breads.

Buena Vista *p405*
$$-$ La Plaza, on the plaza. Elegant restaurant/bar with a terrace, wide range of international dishes, good service.

$ El Patujú, on the plaza. The only café in town, serving excellent local coffee, teas, hot chocolate and a range of snacks. Also sells local produce and crafts.

⚙ What to do

Samaipata *p403, map p403*
Cycling
Club de Ajedrez, Bolivar near the museum, rents bikes.

Massage
Samaipata Spa, at the end of C Bolivar, T7263 6796, www.samaipataspa.com. Daily 0900-1200, 1500-2000. Offers massage, yoga and alternative therapies.

Wine tasting
Two bodegas located outside Samaipata are Uvairenda (www.uvairenda.com) and Vargas (www.vitivinicolavargas.com).

Tour operators
Samaipata has many tour operators, more than we can list. Except as noted, all are on C Bolívar near the museum. Most day trips cost about US$20-25 pp in a group of 4.
Ben Verhoef Tours, Campero 217, T944 6365, www.benverhoeftours.com. Dutch-owned, English, German and Spanish also spoken. Offer tours along La Ruta del Che and throughout the area.
Jucumari Tours, T944 6129, erwin-am@ hotmail.com. Run by Edwin Acuña, who has a 4WD vehicle.
Michael Blendinger, T944 6227, www. discoveringbolivia.com. German guide raised in Argentina who speaks English, runs fully equipped 4WD tours, short and long treks, horse rides, specialist in nature and archaeology.
Road Runners, T944 6193. Olaf and Frank speak English, German and Dutch, enthusiastic, lots of information and advice.
Tucandera Tours, T7316 7735, tucandera. tours@hotmail.com. Saul Arias and Elva Villegas are biologists, excellent for nature

tours and birdwatching, English spoken, competitive prices. Recommended.

Buena Vista *p405*
Amboró Travel & Adventure on the plaza, T7160 0691, amborotravel@hotmail.com. Prices include transport to and from the park, guide and meals. Recommended.
Puertas del Amboró, corner of the plaza, T03-932 2059. They also offer full packages.

⊖ Transport

Samaipata *p403, map p403*
Bus From **Santa Cruz** to Samaipata, only Sucre-bound buses leave from the Terminal Bimodal. Taxis Expreso Samaipata in Santa Cruz at Av Omar Chávez 1147 y Soliz de Holguín, T333 5067 (Samaipata T944 6129), leave when full Mon-Sat 0530-2030 (for Sun book in advance), US$4.50 per person shared; or US$20 in private vehicle, 2½ hrs. Returning to Santa Cruz, they pick you up from your hotel in Samaipata. Buses leaving Santa Cruz for **Sucre** and other towns pass through Samaipata between 1800 and 2100; tickets can be booked with 1 day's notice through **Hotel El Nuevo Turista**, at main road opposite petrol station. To get to **Samaipata** from **Sucre**, buses leave at night and arrive 0500-0600 (set your alarm in case the driver forgets to stop for you), stopping in Mataral or Mairana for breakfast, about half an hour before Samaipata.

Comarapa *p404*
To/from **Santa Cruz** with Turismo Caballero (T350 9626) and Trans Comarapa (T7817 5576), both on Plazuela Oruro, Av Grigotá (3er Anillo), 3 daily each, US$4.50, 6 hrs. To **Cochabmaba**, 2 buses a day pass through from Mairana.

Buena Vista *p405*
Sindicato 10 de Febrero in Santa Cruz at Izozog 668 y Av Irala, 1er Anillo behind ex-terminal, T334 8435, 0730-1830, US$3 pp (private vehicle US$15), 2½ hrs. Also another shared taxi company nearby, and 'Linea 102' buses from regional section of Terminal Bimodal. From Buena Vista, the access to the park is by gravel road, 4WD jeep or similar recommended as rivers have to been crossed. All operators and community eco-lodge coordinators offer transport.

Vallegrande and La Higuera *p405*
Bus Flota Vallegrande has 2 daily buses morning and afternoon from Santa Cruz to **Vallegrande** via **Samaipata** (at 1130 and 1630), 5 hrs, US$5. Best to book in advance. From Vallegrande market, a daily bus departs 0815 to **Pucará** (45 km), from where there is transport (12 km) to **La Higuera**. Taxi Vallegrande-La Higuera US$25-30.

Villamontes *p406*
Bus To **Yacuiba**, Coop El Chaco, Av Méndez Arcos y Ismael Montes, hourly 0630-1830, US$1.35, 1½ hrs. Cars from Av Montenegro y Cap Manchego, hourly or when full, 0630-1830, US$2, 1½ hrs. Long distance buses from terminal on Av Méndez Arcos, 13 blocks east of Plaza 15 de Abril (taxi US$0.40 pp). To **Tarija** via Entre Ríos, mostly unpaved (sit on the right for best views), US$5-6, 10-11 hrs, several companies 1730-1930; for day travel, **Copacabana** may depart at 1030, 2-3 per week from the terminal; Guadalupana, Wed and Sat at 0930, from Coop El Chaco office. To **Santa Cruz**, several companies daily, US$4.50-8.50, some bus cama, 7-8 hrs.

To **Asunción**, buses from Santa Cruz pass through 0200-0300, reserve a day earlier, US$35, about 15 hrs. 5 companies, offices all on Av Montenegro, either side of Av Méndez Arcos. Best are **Stel**, T672 3662, or Vicky Vides T7735 0934; Yaciretá, T672 2812, or Betty Borda, T7740 4111.

Yacuiba *p406*
Bus To **Santa Cruz**, about 20 companies, mostly at night, 14 hrs, US$8-15. To **Tarija**, daily morning and evening.

Eastern Bolivia

The vast and rapidly developing plains to the east of the Eastern Cordillera are Bolivia's richest area in natural resources. For the visitor, the beautiful churches and rich traditions of the former Jesuit missions of Chiquitos are well worth a visit. Here too are some of the country's largest and wildest protected natural areas. This combination of natural beauty, living indigenous culture and Jesuit heritage make the region one of Bolivia's hidden gems.

Jesuit Missions of Chiquitos

Nine Jesuit missions survive east of Santa Cruz, six of which – San Javier, Concepción, San Rafael, Santa Ana, San Miguel and San José de Chiquitos – have churches which are UNESCO World Heritage Sites. Many of these were built by the Swiss Jesuit, Padre Martin Schmidt and his pupils. Besides organizing *reducciones* and constructing churches, Padre Schmidt wrote music (some is still played today on traditional instruments) and he published a Spanish-Chiquitano dictionary based on his knowledge of all the dialects of the region. He worked in this part of the then-Viceroyalty of Peru until the expulsion of the Jesuits in 1767 by order of Charles III of Spain. One of the best ways to appreciate this region is at the bi-annual **Festival de Música Renacentista y Barroca Americana**, held every even year (see page 400), but the living legacy of the missions can be appreciated year-round. Church services are exceptionally well attended, with Chuiquitano musicians and choirs sometimes performing at Sunday Mass. The centres of the towns have been beautifully refurbished and are a pleasure to stroll around.

Access to the mission area is by bus or train from **Santa Cruz**: a paved highway runs north to San Ramón (180 km) and on north, to San Javier (40 km further), turning east here to Concepción (60 km), then to San Ignacio de Velasco (160 km, of which the first 30 are paved). A newly paved road runs south from San Ignacio either through San Miguel, or Santa Ana to meet at San Rafael for the continuation south to San José de Chiquitos. Access is also possible by the paved Santa Cruz–Puerto Suárez highway, which goes via San José de Chiquitos. By rail, leave the Santa Cruz–Quijarro train at San José and from there travel north by bus. The most comfortable way to visit is by jeep, in about five days. The route is straightforward and fuel is available. For information see www.chiquitania.com for extensive historical and practical information.

San Javier (or San Xavier) The first Jesuit mission in Chiquitos (1691), its church built by Padre Schmidt between 1749 and 1752. Some of the original wooden structure has survived more or less intact and restoration was undertaken between 1987 and 1992 by the Swiss Hans Roth, himself a former Jesuit. Subtle designs and floral patterns cover the ceiling, walls and carved columns. One of the bas-relief paintings on the high altar depicts Martin Schmidt playing the piano for his indigenous choir. It is a fine 30 minute walk (best in the afternoon light) to **Mirador El Bibosi** and the small **Parque Piedra de Los Apóstoles**. There is also good walking or all-terrain cycling in the surrounding countryside (no maps, ask around), thermal swimming holes at **Aguas Calientes**, and horse riding from several hotels. Patron saint's fiesta, 3 December, but 29 June, Feast of Saints Peter and Paul, is best for viewing traditional costumes, dances and music. Tourist guides' association has an office in the **Alcaldía** ① *T7761 7902, or 7763 3203 for a guide*. Information also from the **Casa de Cultura** ① *on the plaza, T963 5149*.

Concepción The lovely town is dominated by its magnificent **cathedral** ① *0700-2000, tours 1000, 1500, donation invited*, completed by Padre Schmidt and Juan Messner in

1756 and totally restored by Hans Roth (1975-1986). The interior of this beautiful church has an altar of laminated silver. In front of the church is a bell-cum-clock tower housing the original bells and behind it are well-restored cloisters. On the plaza, forming part of the Jesuit complex, is the **Museo Misional** ① *Mon-Sat 0800-1200, 1430-1830, Sun 1000-1230, US$3.50*, which has an *artesanía* shop. The ticket also gives entry to the **Hans Roth Museum**, dedicated to the restoration process. Visit also the **Museo Antropológico de la Chiquitania** ① *16 de Septiembre y Tte Capoblanco, 0800-1200, 1400-1800, free*, which explains the life of the indigenous peoples of the region. It has a café and guesthouse. Fiesta de la Inmaculada Concepción: 8 December. An orchid festival is held in the second week of October. The **Municipal tourist office** ① *Lucas Caballero y Cabo Rodríguez, one block from plaza, T964 3057*, can arrange trips to nearby recreational areas, ranches and communities. An **Asociación de Guías Locales** ① *south side of plaza, contact Ysabel Supepi, T7604 7085; or Hilario Orellana, T7534 3734*, also offers tours to local communities many of which are developing grass-roots tourism projects: eg **Santa Rita**, **San Andrés** and **El Carmen**. With a week's advance notice, they can also organize private concerts with 30 to 40 musicians. Various restaurants in town. Many places sell wood carvings, traditional fabrics and clothing.

San Ignacio de Velasco This is the main commercial and transport hub of the region, with road links to Brazil. A lack of funds for restoration led to the demolition of San Ignacio's replacement Jesuit church in 1948, the original having burnt down in 1808. A modern replica contains the elaborate high altar, pulpit and paintings and statues of saints. Tourist information office at **Casa de la Cultura** ① *La Paz y Comercio, on the plaza, T962 2056 ext 122, culturayturismo.siv@gmail.com, Mon-Fri 0800-1200, 1430-1830*, can help organize guides and visits to local music schools. The **Centro Artesanal** ① *Santa Cruz entre Bolívar y Oruro, Mon-Sat 0800-1930, Sun 0800-1200*, sells lovely textile and wood crafts. There is community tourism in the villages of **San Juancito**, 18 km from San Ignacio, where organic coffee is grown, and **San Rafael de Sutuquiña**, 5 km; both have artisans. **Laguna Guapomó** reservoir on the edge of San Ignacio is good for swimming and fishing. Patron saint's day, preceded by a cattle fair, 31 July. There is only one ATM in town, best take some cash.

Santa Ana, San Rafael and San Miguel de Velasco These three small towns are less visited than some others along the missions circuit. Allow at least two days if travelling independently from San Ignacio: you can take a bus to Santa Ana in the afternoon, stay overnight, then continue to San Rafael the next afternoon and return to San Ignacio via San Miguel on Tuesday, Thursday or Sunday (see Transport, page 417). A day trip by taxi from San Ignacio costs about US$65 or an all-inclusive tour can be arranged by **Parador Santa Ana** (see Where to stay, page 415). Local guides are available, US$10.

The church in Santa Ana (town founded 1755, church constructed 1773-80, after the expulsion of the Jesuits), is a lovely wooden building. It is the most authentic of all the Jesuit *templos* and Santa Ana is a particularly authentic little village. The tourist office on the plaza can provide guides. Simple economical accommodation at **Comunidad Valenciana**, T980 2098. **Fiesta de Santa Ana:** 26 July.

San Rafael's church was completed by Padre Schmidt in 1748. It is one of the most beautifully restored, with mica-covered interior walls and frescoes in beige paint over the exterior. Patron saint's day, with traditional dancing, 24 October. **$ Hotel Paradita**, T962 4008, and others; restaurants near the plaza; tourist information office T962 4022.

The frescoes on the façade of the church (1752-1759) at San Miguel depict St Peter and St Paul; designs in brown and yellow cover all the interior and the exterior side walls. The mission runs three schools and a workshop; the sisters are very welcoming and will gladly show tourists around. There is a **Museo Etnofolclórico**, off the Plaza at Calle Betania; next door is the Municipalidad/Casa de la Cultura, with a tourist information office, T962 4222. San Miguel has many worksops and rivals San Ignacio for the quality of its Jesuit-inspired art. Patron saint's day: 29 September.

San José de Chiquitos → *Phone code: 03. Colour map 3, B5.*

One complete side of the plaza is occupied by the superbly restored frontage of the Jesuit mission complex of four buildings and a bell tower, begun in the mid-1740s. Best light for photography is in the afternoon. The stone buildings, in Baroque style, are connected by a wall. They are the workshops (1754); the church (1747) with its undulating façade; the four-storey bell-tower (1748) and the mortuary (*la bóveda* – 1750), with one central window but no entrance in its severe frontage. The complex and **Museo** ① *Mon-Fri 0800-1200, 1430-1800, Sat-Sun 0900-1200, 1500-1800, entry US$3*, are well worth visiting. Behind are the *colegio* and workshops, which house the **Escuela Municipal de Música**, visits to rehearsals and performances can be arranged by the tourist office. **InfoTur** ① *in the Municipio, C Velasco, ½ block from plaza, T972 2084, Mon-Fri 0800-1200, 1430-1830*, has information and arranges various tours; there is internet upstairs. On Mondays, Mennonites bring their produce to San José and buy provisions. The colonies are 50 km west and the Mennonites, who speak English, German, plattdeutsch and Spanish, are happy to talk about their way of life. **Fiesta de San José** is 1 May, preceded by a week of folkloric and other events. There is only one ATM in town, best take some cash.

About 2 km south from San José is the 17,000 ha **Parque Nacional Histórico Santa Cruz la Vieja** ① *www.biobol.org*. It has a monument to the original site of Santa Cruz (founded 1561) and a *mirador* with great views. The park's heavily forested hills contain much animal and bird life. There are various trails for hiking; guides can be organized by the tourist office in San José. It gets very hot so start early, allow over one hour to get there on foot (or hire a vehicle) and take plenty of water and insect repellent. There is also good walking with lovely views at **Cerro Turubó** and the **Serranía de San José**, both outside San José.

East of San José de Chiquitos

Paving of the highway from Santa Cruz east to Brazil in 2011 opened up this once isolated region of friendly villages surrounded by natural wonders. The **Serranía de Chiquitos** is a flat-topped mountain range running east-west, north of the highway and railroad. It is filled with rich vegetation, caves, petroglyphs, waterfalls, birds and butterflies. These hills are part of the 262,000-ha **Reserva Valle de Tucavaca** (www.biobol.org) which protects unique Chiquitano dry forest and offers great hiking opportunities. Various community tourism projects are underway in the area and local guides are available in the towns.

The village of **Chochís**, 80 km east of San José de Chiquitos, is known for its sanctuary of the Virgen Asunta built by Hans Roth in 1988 (one of his few major works not connected with restoring Jesuit missions). The large sanctuary is built at the foot of an impressive red sandstone outcrop called **La Torre**, 2 km from town. Along the rail line from Chochís toward La Torre is a signed trail leading to the **Velo de Novia** waterfall, a pleasant one- to two-hour walk. A much more challenging hike climbs 800 m to the flat top of **Cerro de Chochís**, where you can camp or return to town in a long day; guide required.

Sixty kilometers east of Chochís is **Roboré**, the regional centre and transport hub. The **Oficina Municipal de Turismo** ① *Rubén Terrazas, one block from plaza, T974 2276*, has information about local excursions including **Los Helechos** and **Totaisales**, two lovely bathing spots in the forest. Roboré is an old garrison town dating back to the Chaco War and retains a strong military presence. The local fiesta is 25 October.

Seven kilometres east of Roboré, a paved road branches northeast and in 14 km reaches the particularly friendly village of **Santiago de Chiquitos**. Founded in 1754, Santiago was one of the last missions built in Chiquitania. There are good accommodations and more good walking to a fine *mirador*, natural stone arches and caves with petroglyphs; guides available in town. A poor road continues 150 km past Santiago to **Santo Corazón**, a still-isolated Jesuit mission town (the last one built, 1760) inside **Area Natural de Manejo Integrado San Matías** ① www.biobol.org.

Aguas Calientes is 32 km east of Roboré along the rail line and highway to Brazil. The hot little village is unimpressive but nearby is a river of crystal-clear thermal water, teeming with little fish and bird life. There are several spots with facilities for bathing and camping, which is preferable to the basic accommodations in town. There are many tiny biting sandflies, so your tent should have good netting. Soaking in the thermal water amid the sights and sounds of the surrounding forest at dawn or on a moonlit night is amazing.

Parque Nacional Noel Kempff Mercado
① *Park office in San Ignacio de Velasco, C Oruro y Cochabamba, T962 2747, Mon-Fri 0830-1200, 1430-1800; additional information from SERNAP and FAN, both in Santa Cruz (page 402), also www.biobol.org.*
In the far northeast corner of Santa Cruz Department, Parque Nacional Noel Kempff Mercado (named after a Bolivian conservation pioneer who was killed while flying over the park), is one of the world's most diverse natural habitats. This World Heritage Site covers 1,523,446 ha and encompasses seven ecosystems, within which are 139 species of mammal (including black jaguars), 620 species of bird (including nine types of macaw), 74 species of reptile and 110 species of orchid. Highlights include the **Huanchaca** or **Caparú Plateau**, which with its 200-500 m sheer cliffs and tumbling waterfalls is a candidate for Sir Arthur Conan Doyle's *Lost World* (Colonel Percy Fawcett, who discovered the plateau in 1910, was a friend of Conan Doyle).

This outstanding natural area received about 40 visitors in 2012-2013. Organizing a trip requires time, money and flexibility; there is no infrastructure, visitors must be self-sufficient and take all equipment including a tent. The authorities sometimes restrict access, enquire in advance. Operators in Santa Cruz (see page 401) may be able to arrange all-inclusive tours. Otherwise, the best base is San Ignacio, which has some provisions but more specialized items should be brought from Santa Cruz.

The southwestern section of the park is reached from the village of **Florida**, where there is a ranger station and a community tourism project offering basic accommodation and guides (guide compulsory, US$25 per day, www.parquenoelkempffmercado.blogspot.com). It is 65 km from Florida to the trailhead (pickup US$60 one way), which provides access to the 80-m high **El Encanto** waterfall and the climb to the plateau; allow five to six days for the return excursion. To reach Florida from San Ignacio, either hire a 4WD (US$100 per day), or there is one bus a week in the dry season (June to November, see Transport, page 418).

In the northeastern section of the park are the great **Arco Iris** and **Federico Ahlfeld** waterfalls, both on the Río Paucerna and accessible mid-December to May when water levels are sufficiently high. Access is either from the Bolivian village of **Piso Firme** or the Brazilian town of **Pimenteiras do Oeste**; in all cases you must be accompanied by a Bolivian boatman/guide, available in Piso Firme and organized by the park office in San Ignacio. It is six to seven hours by motorized canoe from Piso Firme to a shelter near the Ahlfeld waterfall, and a full day's walk from there to Arco Iris. There is, in principle, one bus a week to Piso Firme from Santa Cruz and another from San Ignacio in the dry season (see Transport, page 418).

To Brazil
There are four routes from Santa Cruz: by air to Puerto Suárez, by rail or road to Quijarro (fully paved except for 40 km between Santa Cruz and San José de Chiquitos), by road to San Matías (a busy border town reported unsafe due to drug smuggling), and via San Ignacio de Velasco to either Vila Bela or Pontes e Lacerda (both in Brazil). Puerto Suárez is near Quijarro and this route leads to Corumbá on the Brazilian side, from where there is access to the southern Pantanal. The San Matías and Vila Bela/Pontes roads both link to Cáceres, Cuiabá and the northern Pantanal in Brazil. There are immigration posts of both countries on all routes except Vila Bela/Pontes. If travelling this way get your Bolivian exit stamp in San Ignacio (immigration office near **Jenecherú** bus station) and Brazilian entry stamp in Cáceres or Vilhena. There may be strict customs and drugs checks entering Brazil, no fresh food may be taken from Bolivia.

Quijarro and Puerto Suárez → *Phone code: 03. Colour map 3, C6.*
The eastern terminus of the Bolivian road and railway is **Quijarro**. It is quite safe by day, but caution is recommended at night. The water supply is often unreliable. Prices are much lower than in neighbouring Brazil and there are some decent places to stay. **Rossy Tours** (C Costa Rica, four blocks toward river from train station, T978 2022), offers 4WD tours to **Parque Nacional Otuquis** in the Bolivian Pantanal, and various boat trips. ATMs and banks are at the border.

On the shores of Laguna Cáceres, 8 km west of Quijarro, is **Puerto Suárez**, with a shady main plaza. There is a nice view of the lake from the park at the north end of Avenida Bolívar.

Border with Brazil
The neighbourhood by the border is known as Arroyo Concepción. You need not have your passport stamped if you visit Corumbá for the day. Otherwise get your exit stamp at Bolivian immigration (see below), entry stamp at Brazilian border complex. Yellow Fever vaccination is compulsory to enter Bolivia and Brazil, have your certificate at hand when you go for your entry stamp, otherwise you may be sent to get revaccinated. Bolivian immigration is at the border at Arroyo Concepción (0800-1200, 1400-1730 daily), or at Puerto Suárez airport, where Bolivian exit/entry stamps are also issued. There is one ATM at Arroyo Concepción, at the Hotel Pantanal. Money changers right at the border offer the worst rates, better to ask around in the small shops past the bridge. There are Brazilian consulates in Puerto Suárez and Santa Cruz. See Transport, below, for taxis from the border.

⊕ Eastern Bolivia listings

For hotel and restaurant price codes, and other relevant information, see pages 14-17.

⊖ Where to stay

Jesuit Missions of Chiquitos *p410*
San Javier
$ Alojamiento San Xavier, C Santa Cruz, T963 5038. Cheaper without bath, electric shower, garden, nice sitting area. Recommended.

$ Residencial Chiquitano, Av Santa Cruz (Av José de Arce), ½ block from plaza, T963 5072. Simple rooms, fan, large patio, good value.

Concepción
$$ Gran Hotel Concepción, on plaza, T964 3031. Excellent service, buffet breakfast, pool, gardens, bar, very comfortable. Highly recommended.

$$ Hotel Chiquitos, end of Av Killian, T964 3153, hotel_chiquitos@hotmail.com. Colonial style construction, ample rooms, frigobar, pool, gardens and sports fields, orchid nursery, parking. Tours available. Recommended.

$ Colonial, Ñuflo de Chávez 7, ½ block from plaza, T964 3050. Economical place, hammocks on ample veranda, parking, breakfast available.

$ Las Misiones, C Luis Caballero, 1 block from church, T964 3021. Small rooms, nice garden, small pool, also has an apartment, good value.

$ Oasis Chiquitano, C Germán Bush, 1½ blocks from plaza. Buffet breakfast, pool, nice patio with flowers.

$ Residencial Westfalia, Saucedo 205, 2 blocks from plaza, T964 3040. Cheaper without bath, German-owned, nice patio, good value.

San Ignacio de Velasco

$$$ La Misión, Libertad on plaza, T962 2333, www.hotel-lamision.com. Upmarket hotel, restaurant, meeting rooms, pool, parking, downstairs rooms have bath tubs.

$$ Apart Hotel San Ignacio, 24 de Septiembre y Cochabamba, T962 2157, www.aparthotel-sanignacio.com. Comfortable rooms, nice grounds, pool, hammocks, parking. Despite the name, no apartments or kitchenettes.

$$ Parador Santa Ana, Libertad entre Sucre y Cochabamba, T962 2075, www. paradorsantaana.blogspot.com. Beautiful house with small patio, tastefully decorated, 5 comfortable rooms, good breakfast, knowledgeable owner arranges tours, credit cards accepted. Recommended.

$$ San Ignacio, Libertad on plaza, T962 2283. In a beautifully restored former episcopal mansion, non-profit (run by diocese, funds support poor youth in the community), breakfast.

$ Res Bethania, Velasco y Cochabamba, T962 2367. Simple rooms with shared bath, electric shower, small patio, economical and good value.

San José de Chiquitos *p412*

$$$ Villa Chiquitana, C 9 de Abril, 6 blocks from plaza, T7315 5803, www. villachiquitana.com. Charming hotel built in traditional style, restaurant open to public, frigobar, pool (US$3 for non-guests), garden, parking, craft shop, tour agency. French run.

$ Turubó, Bolívar on the plaza, T972 2037, hotelturubo@hotmail.com. With a/c or fan, electric shower, variety of different rooms, ask to see one before checking-in, good location.

East of San José de Chiquitos *p412*
Chochís

$ Ecoalbergue de Chochís, 1 km west of town along the rail line, T7263 9467; Santa Cruz contact: Probioma, T343 1332, www.probioma.org.bo. Simple community-run lodging in 2 cabins, shared bath, cold water, small kitchen, screened hammock area, camping US$3.50 pp, meals on advance request.

$ El Peregrino, on the plaza, T7313 1881. Simple rooms in a family home, some with fan and fridge, shared bath, electric shower, ample yard, camping possible.

Roboré

$$ Anahí, Obispo Santiesteban 1½ blocks from plaza, T974 2362. Comfortable rooms with electric shower, nice patio, parking, kitchen and washing facilities, owner runs tours.

$$ Choboreca, C La Paz, T974 2566. Nice hotel, rooms with a/c.

Several other places to stay in town.

Santiago de Chiquitos

$$ Beula, on the plaza, T337 7274, pachecomary@hotmail.com. Comfortable hotel in traditional style, good breakfast, frigobar. Unexpectedly upmarket for such a remote location.

$ El Convento, on plaza next to the church, T7890 2943. Former convent with simple rooms, one has private bath, lovely garden, hot and no fan but clean and good value.

$ Panorama, 1 km north of plaza, T313 6286, katmil@bolivia.com. Simple rooms with shared bath and a family farm, friendly owners Katherine and Milton Whittaker sell excellent home-made dairy products and jams, they are knowledgeable about the area and offer volunteer opportunities.

There are also various *alojamientos familiares* around town, all simple to basic.

Aguas Calientes
$$ Cabañas Canaan, across the road from Los Hervores baths, T7467 7316. Simple wooden cabins, cold water, fan, restaurant, rather overpriced but better than the basic places in town.
$ Camping Miraflores, 1 km from town on the road to Los Hervores baths, T7262 0168, www.aguascalientesmiraflores. com.bo. Lovely ample grounds with clean bathrooms, electric showers, barbeques, small pier by the river.

Quijarro *p414*
$$$-$$ Bibosi, Luis Salazar s/n, 4½ blocks east of train station, T978 2044. Variety of rooms and prices, some with a/c, fridge, cheaper with fan and shared bath, breakfast, pool, patio, restaurant, upscale for Quijarro.
$$ Tamengo, Costa Rica 57, Barrio Copacabana, 6 blocks toward river from train station, T978 3356, www.hosteltrail.com/ hostels/tamengo resort. Located by the river, all rooms with a/c (cheaper with shared bath and in dorm), restaurant and bar, pool, sports fields, book exchange. Day-use of facilities by visitors US$8.50. Arranges tours and volunteer opportunities.
$ Gran Hotel Colonial, Av Luis de la Vega, 2 blocks east of train station, T978 2037. With a/c (cheaper with fan and private bath; even cheaper with shared bath). Restaurant serves good set lunch.
Willy Solís Cruz, Roboré 13, T7365 5587, wiland_54@hotmail.com. For years Willy has helped store luggage and offered local information and assistance. His home is open to visitors who would like to rest, take a shower,

do laundry, cook or check the internet while they wait for transport; a contribution in return is welcome. He speaks English, very helpful.

Puerto Suárez *p414*
$ Beby, Av Bolívar 111, T976 2270. Private bath, a/c, cheaper with shared bath and fan.
$ Casa Real, Vanguardia 39, T976 3335, www.hotelenpuertosuarez.com. A/c, frigobar, Wi-Fi, parking, tours.

❼ Restaurants

Jesuit Missions of Chiquitos *p410*
San Javier
$$ Ganadero, in Asociación de Ganaderos on plaza. Excellent steaks. Other eateries around the plaza.

Concepción
$ El Buen Gusto, north side of plaza. Set meals and regional specialities.

San Ignacio de Velasco
$ Club Social, Comercio on the plaza. Daily 1130-1500. Decent set lunch.
Panadería Juanita, Comercio y Sucre. Good bakery.
Mi Nonna, C Velasco y Cochabamba. 1700-2400, closed Tue. Café serving cappuccino, sandwiches, salads and pasta.

San José de Chiquitos *p412*
$$ Sabor y Arte, Bolívar y Mons Santisteban, by the plaza. Tue-Sun 1800-2300. International dishes, for innovation try their coca-leaf ravioli, nice ambience, French-Bolivian run.
$$-$ Rancho Brasilero, by main road, 5 blocks from plaza. Daily 0900-1530. Good Brazilian-style buffet, all you can eat grill on weekends.

East of San José de Chiquitos *p412*
Roboré
$ Casino Militar, on the plaza, daily for lunch and dinner. Set meals and à la carte. Several other restaurants around the plaza.

Santiago de Chiquitos

$ Churupa, ½ block from plaza. Set meals (go early or reserve your meal in adavance) and à la carte. Best in town.

⊛ Festivals

The region celebrates the **Festival de Música Renacentista y Barroca Americana** every even year. Many towns have their own orchestras, which play Jesuit-era music on a regular basis. **Semana Santa** (Holy Week) celebrations are elaborate and interesting throughout the region.

⊖ Transport

Jesuit Missions of Chiquitos *p410*
San Javier
Trans Guarayos, T346 3993, from Santa Cruz Terminal Bimodal regional departures area, 7 a day, 4 hrs, US$4.50, some continue to **Concepción**. Several others including **Jenecherú**, T348 8618, daily at 2000, US$6, *bus-cama* US$10, continuing to Concepción and **San Ignacio**. Various taxi-*trufi* companies also operate from regional departures area, US$5, 3½ hrs.

Concepción
Bus To/from **Santa Cruz**, Trans Guarayos, US$5, 5 hrs, and **Jenecherú**, as above, US$6; various others. To **San Ignacio de Velasco**, buses pass though from Santa Cruz (many at night); also **Flota 31 del Este** (poor buses) from C Germán Busch in Concepción, daily at 1700, 5-6 hrs, US$4.25. Concepción to **San Javier**, 1 hr, US$1.50.

San Ignacio de Velasco
Bus From **Santa Cruz**, many companies from Terminal Bimodal depart 1900-2000, including **Jenecherú** (most luxurious buses, see above), US$10, bus cama US$17-30, 11 hrs; returning 1800-1900. For daytime service **31 del Este** (slow and basic) at 1100. Also *trufis* from regional departures area 0900 daily (with minimum 7 passengers),

US$17, 8 hrs. To **San José de Chiquitos**, see San José Transport, below. To **San Rafael** (US$3, 2½ hrs) via **Santa Ana** (US$1.50,1 hr) **Expreso Baruc**, 24 de Septiembre y Kennedy, daily at 1400; returning 0600. To **San Miguel**, *trufis* leave when full from Mercado de Comida, US$1.75, 40 mins. To **San Matías** (for Cáceres, Brazil) several daily passing through from Santa Cruz starting 0400, US$12, 8 hrs. To **Pontes e Lacerda** (Brazil), **Rápido Monte Cristo**, from Club Social on the plaza, Wed and Sat 0900, US$22, 8-9 hrs; returning Tue and Fri, 0630. All roads to Brazil are poor. The best option to Pontes e Lacerda is via Vila Bela (Brazil), used by **Amanda Tours** (T7608 8476 in Bolivia, T65-9926 8522 in Brazil), from El Corralito restaurant by the market, Tue, Thu, Sun 0830, US$28; returning Mon, Wed, Fri 0600.

San José de Chiquitos *p412*
Bus To **Santa Cruz** many companies pass through starting 1700 daily, US$6. Also *trufis*, leave when full, US$10, 4 hrs. To **Puerto Suárez**, buses pass through1600-2300, US$10, 4 hrs. To **San Ignacio de Velasco** via San Rafael and San Miguel, **Flota Universal** (poor road, terrible buses), Mon, Wed, Fri, Sat at 0700, US$7, 5 hrs, returning 1400; also **31 de Julio**, Tue, Thu, Sun from San Ignacio at 0645, returning 1500.
Train Westbound, the **Ferrobus** passes through San José Tue, Thu, Sat at 0150, arriving Santa Cruz 0700; **Expreso Oriental**, Mon, Wed, Fri 0109, arriving 0740. Eastbound, the **Ferrobus** passes through San José Tue, Thu, Sun 2308, arriving Quijarro 0700 next day; **Expreso Oriental** Mon, Wed, Fri 2100, arriving 0729 next day. See Santa Cruz Transport (page 402) and www.fo.com.bo for fares and additional information.

East of San José de Chiquitos *p412*
Bus To **Chochís** from San Jose de Chiquitos, with **Perla del Oriente**, daily 0800 and 1500, US$3.50, 2 hrs; continuing to **Roboré**, US$1, 1 hr more; Roboré to San José via Chochís 0815 and 1430. Roboré

bus terminal is by the highway, a long walk from town, but some buses go by the plaza before leaving; enquire locally. From **Santiago de Chiquitos** to Roboré, Mon-Sat at 0700, US$1.50, 45 mins; returning 1000; taxi Roboré–Santiago about US$15. Buses to/from Quijarro stop at **Aguas Calientes**; taxi Roboré–Aguas Calientes about US$22 return. From Roboré to **Santa Cruz**, several companies, US$7-20, 7-9 hrs; also *trufis* 0900, 1400, 1800, US$14.50, 5 hrs. From Roboré to **Quijarro** with Perla del Oriente, 4 daily, US$4.50, 4 hrs; also *trufis* leave when full, US$8, 3 hrs.

Train All trains stop in Roboré (see www. fo.com.bo), but not in Chochís or Aguas Calientes. Enquire in advance if they might stop to let you off at these stations.

Parque Nacional Noel Kempff Mercado *p413*
Road/us All overland journeys are long and arduous, take supplies. The following are subject to frequent change and cancellation, always enquire locally. **San Ignacio–Florida**, Trans Velasco, Av Kennedy y 24 de Septiembre, T7602 3269, dry season only (Jun-Nov), Sat 0900, US$10, at least 10 hrs; same company runs **San Ignacio–Piso Firme**, dry season only, Fri 1000, US$18, 24 hrs or more, returning Sun 1400. **Santa Cruz–Piso Firme** (via Santa Rosa de la Roca, not San Ignacio), Trans Bolivia, C Melchor Pinto entre 2do y 3er Anillo, T336 3866, Thu morning, US$24, 24 hrs or more; returning Sun. For **Pimenteiras do Oeste** (Brazil) see San Ignacio Transport (above) to Pontes e Lacerda and make connections there via Vilhena.

Quijarro and Puerto Suárez *p414*
Air Puerto Suárez airport is 6 km north of town, T976 2347; airport tax US$2. Flights to **Santa Cruz** with TAM, 3 times a week, US$85. Don't buy tickets for flights originating in Puerto Suárez in Corumbá, these cost more.

Bus Buses from Quijarro pick up passengers in Puerto Suárez on route to **Santa Cruz**, many companies, most after 1800 (**Trans Bioceánico** at 1030), US$12-22, 8-10 hrs.

Taxi Quijarro to the border (**Arroyo Concepción**) US$0.70 pp; to **Puerto Suárez** US$1 pp, more at night. If arriving from Brazil, you will be approached by Bolivian taxi drivers who offer to hold your luggage while you clear immigration. These are the most expensive cabs (US$5 to Quijarro, US$15 to Puerto Suárez) and best avoided. Instead, keep your gear with you while your passport is stamped, then walk 200 m past the bridge to an area where other taxis wait (US$0.70 pp to Quijarro). Colectivos to Puerto Suárez leave Quijarro when full from Av Bolívar corner Av Luis de la Vega, US$1.

Train With paving of the highway from Santa Cruz train service is in less demand, but it remains a comfortable and convenient option. Ticket office in Quijarro station Mon-Sat 0730-1200, 1430-1800, Sun 0730-1100. Purchase tickets directly at the train station (passport required; do not buy train tickets for Bolivia in Brazil). The **Ferrobus** leaves Quijarro Mon, Wed, Fri 1800, arriving Santa Cruz 0700 next day; **Expreso Oriental**, Tue, Thu, Sun 1450, arriving 0740 next day. See Santa Cruz Transport (page 402) and www.fo.com.bo for fares and additional information.

Contents

Footprint features

Ecuador

At a glance

◉ **Time required** 2-5 weeks.

☽ **Best time** Jun-Aug, Christmas and New Year are good for fiestas.

✖ **When not to go** Jun-Sep and Dec-Jan are the busiest times. All year is good from a climatic point of view. In the highlands, the wettest months are Oct-Nov and Feb-May; Jan-May are hottest and rainiest on Pacific coast. In the jungle, wet months are Mar-Sep.

COLOMBIA

Pacific
Ocean

To The Galápagos Islands 6

San Lorenzo
Limones
La Tola
Mataje
Rioverde
Atacames
Tonchigüe
Esmeraldas
Punta Galeras
Muisne
Viche
Maldonado
Tulcán
Lita
La Libertad
San Gabriel
Bolívar
Apuela
Ibarra
La Bonita
El Conejo
Cojimíes
PV Maldonado
Otavalo
Cotacachi
Cayambe
Lumbaquí
Lago Agrio
Cuyabeno Reserve
Pedernales
Santo Domingo
de los Tsáchilas
Mindo
Calderón
QUITO
Sangolquí
Reventador
Shushufindi
Tarapoa
Cuyabeno
Jama
San Isidro
Machachi
Cotopaxi NP
Baeza
Coca
Napo
Aguarico
Pañacocha
Nuevo
Rocafuerte
Canoa
Bahía de
Caráquez
San Vicente
Chugchilán
Lasso
Vol
Cotopaxi
Loreto
Archidona
Yasuní NP
Tiputini
Crucita
Chone
Zumbahua
Latacunga
Tena
Shiripuno
Nashino
Manta
Quevedo
Pujilí
Misahuallí
Portoviejo
Ambato
Baños
Puyo
Villano
Curaray
Cononaco
Sucre
Jipijapa
Balzar
Riobamba
El Altar
(5319m)
Sarayacu
Conambo
Curaray
Puerto López
Guaranda
Guamote
Vol Sangay
(5230m)
Montañita
Manglaralto
Valdivia
Babahoyo
Guamote
Palmira
Macas
Montalvo
Conambo
Pintuyaco
Durán
Bucay
Alausí
Huigra
Sucúa
Guayaquil
Chanduy
El Morro
Puná
Cañar
Paute
Méndez
San José de
Morona
Posorja
I Puná
Azogues
Gualaceo
Santiago
Golfo de
Guayaquil
Cuenca
Plan de
Milagro
I Sta Clara
Girón
Sígsig
Gualaquiza
Machala
Oña
El Pangui
Huaquillas
Arenillas
Santa Rosa
Piñas
Saraguro
Puyango
Zaruma
Loja
Yantzaza
Alamor
Catacocha
Podocarpus NP
Vilcabamba
Zamora
Zapotillo
Macará
Cariamanga
Amaluza
Valladolid
Zumba
La Balsa

PERU

★ **Don't miss ...**
1 Quito, page 422.
2 Otavalo, page 458.
3 Cuenca, page 503.
4 Vilcabamba, page 520.
5 Northern Oriente, page 559.
6 Galápagos Islands, page 576.

50 km
50 miles

N

Tucked in between Peru and Colombia, this country is small enough for you to have breakfast with scarlet macaws in the jungle, lunch in the lee of a snow-capped peak and, at tea time, be eyeballed by an iguana whose patch of Pacific beach you have just borrowed.

A multitude of national parks and conservation areas emphasize the incredible variety of Ecuador. They include mangroves; an avenue of volcanoes (many of them active) striding across the Equator; and forests growing on the dry Pacific coast, in the clouds and under the Amazonian rains – not forgetting all the animals and birds that flourish in these habitats. In fact, as Ecuador is one of the richest places in the world for birds, with some of the planet's most beautiful species, the country is a prime birdwatching destination.

The capital, Quito, and the southern highland city of Cuenca, are two of the gringo centres of South America, bursting at the seams with language schools, tour operators and restaurants. The smaller towns and villages of Ecuador offer the most authentic experience. Indulge your senses at one of their many markets, with dizzying arrays of textiles, ceramics, carvings and other crafts, not to mention the cornucopia of fresh produce.

The exotic wildlife of the Galápagos Islands will also keep you enthralled, whether it's watching an albatross take off on its flight path, swimming with marine iguanas, sea lions and penguins, or admiring the sexual paraphernalia of the magnificent frigatebird. If the Galápagos are beyond your budget, then Isla de la Plata in Parque Nacional Machalilla is a more accessible alternative for seeing marine life.

Quito

Few cities have a setting to match that of Quito, the second highest capital in Latin America after La Paz. The city is set in a hollow at the foot of the volcano Pichincha (4794 m). The city's charm lies in its colonial centre – the Centro Histórico as it's known – a UNESCO World Heritage Site, where cobbled streets are steep and narrow, dipping to deep ravines. From the top of Cerro Panecillo, 183 m above the city level, there is a fine view of the city below and the encircling cones of volcanoes and other mountains.

North of the colonial centre is modern Quito with broad avenues lined with contemporary office buildings, fine private residences, parks, embassies and villas. Here you'll find Quito's main tourist area in the district known as La Mariscal, bordered by Avenidas Amazonas, Patria, 12 de Octubre and Orellana.

Arriving in Quito → *Phone code: 02. Colour map 1, A4. Population: 1,670,000. Altitude: 2850 m.*

Orientation **Mariscal Sucre airport** is about 30 km northeast of the city. Long-distance bus services leave from terminals at the extreme edges of the city, **Quitumbe** in the south and **Carcelén** in the north. Some bus services also run to their own offices in modern Quito. There are four parallel public transit lines running north to south on exclusive lanes: the *Trole*, *Ecovía*, *Metrobus* and *Universidades*, as well as city buses.

Both colonial Quito and La Mariscal in modern Quito can be explored on foot, but getting between the two requires some form of public transport, using taxis is the best option. Quito is a long city stretching from north to south, with Pichincha rising to the west. Its main arteries run the length of the city and traffic congestion along them is a serious problem. Avenida Occidental or Mariscal Sucre is a somewhat more expedite road to the west of the city. The Corredor Periférico Oriental or Simón Bolívar is a bypass to the east of the city running 44 km between Santa Rosa in the south and Calderón in the north. Roads through the eastern suburbs in the Valle de los Chillos and Tumbaco can be taken to avoid the city proper. **Note** There are vehicular restrictions on weekdays 0700-0930 and 1600-1930, based on the last digit of the license plate, seniors are exempt. Colonial Quito is closed to vehicles Sunday 0900-1600 and main avenues across the city close Sunday 0800-1400 for the *ciclopaseo* (page 441).

Most places of historical interest are in colonial Quito, while the majority of the hotels, restaurants, tour operators and facilities for visitors are in the modern city to the north. The street numbering system is based on N (Norte), E (Este), S (Sur), Oe (Oeste), plus a number for each street and a number for each building, however, an older system of street numbers is also still in use. Note that, because of Quito's altitude and notorious air pollution, some visitors may feel some discomfort: slow your pace for the first 48 hours.
▸▸ *See also Transport, page 444.*

Tourist information **Empresa Metropolitana Quito Turismo/Quito Visitor's Bureau** ① *T299 3300, www.quito.com.ec,* has information offices with English-speaking personnel, brochures and maps, and an excellent website. They also run walking tours of the colonial city, see Paseos Culturales, page 440. **Airport** ① *in Arrivals area, T281 8363, open 24 hrs.* **Bus station** ① *Terminal Quitumbe, T382 4815, daily 0900-1730.* **Train station** ① *T261 7661, Mon-Fri 0800-1630.* **Colonial Quito** ① *Plaza de la Independencia, El Quinde craft shop at Palacio Municipal, Venezuela y Espejo, T257 2445, Mon-Fri 0900-1800, Sat 0900-2000, Sun 0900-1700.* **La Mariscal** ① *República del Cacao, Reina Victoria 258 y Pinto, near Plaza Foch,*

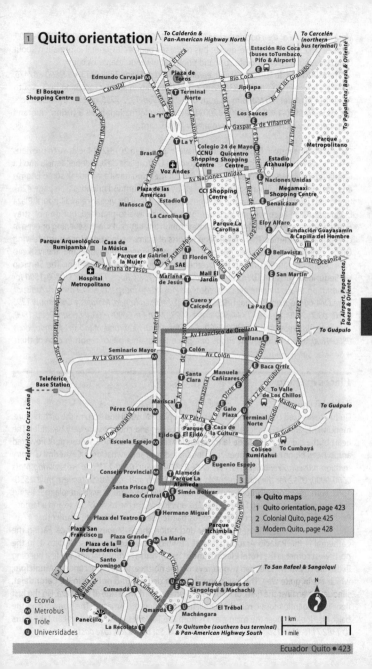

1 Quito orientation

To Calderón &
Pan-American Highway North

To Carcelén
(northern
bus terminal)

Estación Río Coca
(buses toTumbaco,
Pifo & Airport)

Av El Inca

Río Coca

Edmundo Carvajal Ⓜ

Plaza de
Toros

Jipijapa

Av de los Granados

Carvajal

Av 10 de Agosto

Av La Prensa

El Bosque
Shopping Centre ◼

Terminal
Norte

Av de los Shyris

Los Sauces

Av Gaspar de Villarroel

Av Eloy Alfaro

To Papallacta, Baeza & Oriente

La 'Y' Ⓜ

Av Amazonas

La Y Ⓣ

Av de Diciembre

Brasil Ⓜ

Colegio 24 de Mayo
CCNU
Shopping
Centre

Quicentro
Shopping
Centre

Estadio
Atahualpa

Av América

Voz Andes ✚

Av Naciones Unidas

Naciones Unidas Ⓔ

Parque
Metropolitano

Plaza de las
Américas

CCI Shopping
Centre

Megamaxi
Shopping Centre ◼

Mañosca Ⓜ

Estadio Ⓣ

Benalcázar Ⓔ

Av Rep del Salvador

La Carolina Ⓣ

Parque La
Carolina

Eloy Alfaro Ⓔ

Fundación Guayasamín
& Capilla del Hombre ▥

Parque Arqueológico
Rumipamba ◼

Casa de
la Música

San
Gabriel Ⓜ

Av Atahualpa

Av Eloy Alfaro

Bellavista Ⓔ

Vía Interocéanica

Parque de
la Mujer

Av Mariana de Jesús

El Florón Ⓔ

SAE ◼

Av República

San Martín Ⓔ

Hospital
Metropolitano ◼

Mariana
de Jesús Ⓣ

Mall El
Jardín

Av Occidental (Mariscal Sucre)

Cuero y
Caicedo Ⓣ

La Paz Ⓔ

Teleférico
Base Station ◼

Av América

Av Francisco de Orellana

Av de Agosto

Orellana Ⓔ

González Suárez

To Guápulo

Teleférico to Cruz Loma

Seminario Mayor Ⓜ

Av La Gasca

Colón Ⓣ

Av Colón

Baca Ortiz Ⓣ

Av Coruña

Santa
Clara Ⓣ

Manuela
Cañizares Ⓣ

Ecovía

To Airport, Papallacta, Baeza & Oriente

Mariscal Ⓜ

Av 6 de Diciembre

Av 12 de Octubre

To Valle
de Los Chillos

Pérez Guerrero Ⓣ

Av Amazonas

Galo
Plaza Ⓤ

Madrid

To Guápulo

Av Universitaria

Av Patria

Ejido Ⓣ Ⓔ

Casa de
la Cultura Ⓣ Ⓔ

Terminal
Norte

Escuela Espejo Ⓣ

Parque
El Ejido

L de Guevara

To Cumbayá

Consejo Provincial Ⓜ

Alameda
Parque La
Alameda

Eugenio Espejo Ⓤ

Coliseo
Rumiñahui Ⓤ

3

Santa Prisca Ⓜ

Banco Central Ⓣ Ⓤ

Simón Bolívar Ⓤ

➡ Quito maps

1 Quito orientation, page 423
2 Colonial Quito, page 425
3 Modern Quito, page 428

Plaza del Teatro Ⓣ

Hermano Miguel Ⓣ

Plaza San
Francisco

Plaza Grande

La Marín Ⓤ

Av Velasco Ibarra

Parque
Itchimbía

Plaza de la
Independencia

Av Pichincha

Santo
Domingo

Av Cumandá

To San Rafael & Sangolquí

N

Av Bahía de Caráquez

Cumandá Ⓤ

El Playón (buses to
Sangolquí & Machachi)

Panecillo

Qmandá Ⓤ

El Trébol

Machángara

La Recoleta Ⓣ

To Quitumbe (southern bus terminal)
& Pan-American Highway South

1 km

1 mile

Ⓔ Ecovía
Ⓜ Metrobus
Ⓣ Trole
Ⓤ Universidades

kiosk in the patio of the chocolate shop/café, T255 1566, Mon-Fri 0900-1800, Sat 0900-1400; also sell tickets for the double-decker bus tours, see page 440. General information about Quito is found at www.in-quito.com and photos at www.quitoenfotos.com.

The **Ministerio de Turismo** ① *El Telégrafo E7-58 y Los Shyris, T399 9333 or T1-800-887476, www.ecuador.travel, Mon-Fri 0830-1730*, offers information at their reception desk. **South American Explorers** ① *Mariana de Jesús Oe3-32 y Ulloa, T222 7235, quitoclub@saexplorers. org, Mon-Fri 0930-1700, Sat 0900-1200.* They offer information, have a hiking club and members may store gear. Local discounts with SAE card.

Safety Public safety in Quito appears to have improved in 2013-2014 relative to previous years, however, it is still not a safe city. In colonial Quito, Plaza de la Independencia and La Ronda are patrolled by officers from the **Policía Metropolitana** who speak some English and are very helpful. El Panecillo is patrolled by neighbourhood brigades (see page 426). In modern Quito, La Carolina and La Mariscal districts call for vigilance at all hours. Plaza El Quinde (Calle Foch y Reina Victoria) in La Mariscal is also patrolled, but do not stray outside its perimeter at night. Do not walk through any city parks in the evening or even in daylight at quiet times. There have been reports of scams on long-distance buses leaving Quito, especially to Baños; do not give your hand luggage to anyone and always keep your things on your lap, not in the overhead storage rack nor on the floor. The **Servicio de Seguridad Turística** ① *HQ at Reina Victoria N21-208 y Roca, T254 3983, 0800-1800 for information, 24 hrs for emergencies; offices at: Plaza de la Independencia, Pasaje Arzobispal, Chile Oe4-66 y García Moreno, T295 5785, 0800-2400; La Ronda, Morales y Guayaquil, T295 6010, 0800-2400; airport, T394 5000, ext 3023, Mon-Fri 0600-2400, Sat-Sun 0600-1800; Terminal Quitumbe, Tue-Fri 0800-2400, Sat-Mon 0730-1800; and Mitad del Mundo, daily 0800-1800*, offers information and is one place to obtain a police report in case of theft.
➤➤ *See also Safety, page 29.*

Places in Quito

Colonial Quito
Quito's revitalized colonial district is a pleasant place to stroll and admire the architecture, monuments and art. At night, the illuminated plazas and churches are very beautiful. The heart of the old city is **Plaza de la Independencia** or **Plaza Grande**, whose pink-flowered arupo trees bloom in September. It is dominated by a somewhat grim **Cathedral** ① *entry through museum, Venezuela N3-117, T257 0371, Tue-Sat, 0900-1745, no visits during Mass 0600-0900, US$2 for the museum, night visits to church and cupolas on request*, built 1550-1562, with grey stone porticos and green tile cupolas. On its outer walls are plaques listing the names of the founding fathers of Quito, and inside are the tomb of Sucre and a famous Descent from the Cross by the indigenous painter Caspicara. There are many other 17th- and 18th-century paintings; the interior decoration shows Moorish influence. Facing the Cathedral is the **Palacio Arzobispal**, part of which now houses shops. Next to it, in the northwest corner, is the **Hotel Plaza Grande** (1930), with a baroque façade, the first building in the old city with more than two storeys. On the northeast side is the concrete **Municipio**, which fits in quite well. The low colonial Palacio de Gobierno or **Palacio de Carondelet**, silhouetted against the flank of Pichincha, is on the northwest side of the Plaza. On the first floor is a gigantic mosaic mural of Orellana navigating the Amazon. The ironwork on the balconies looking over the main plaza is from the Tuilleries in Paris. Visitors can take **tours** ① *T382 7118, Mon 1500-1900, Tue-Sun 0900-1900, Sat until 2200, take passport or copy.*

2 Colonial Quito

➡ **Quito maps**
1 Quito orientation, page 423
2 Colonial Quito, page 425
3 Modern Quito, page 428

200 metres
200 yards

Julio Matovelle
Guatemala
Rubén Darío
Carchi
Galápagos
Babahoyo
Mideros
Alianza
Quinga
Simón Bolívar
Av 24 de Mayo
Loja

Santa Prisca
Santa Prisca
Briceño
Caldas
Vargas
Oriente
Esmeraldas
Manabi
Olmedo
Mejía
Chile
Espejo
Junín
Sucre
Morales (La Ronda)
Morales
Ambato
Loja
Agoyán
Villavicencio

Astronomical
Observatory
Parque La
Alameda
Banco
Central
Simón
Bolívar
Banco
Central
To 4 + 12
San Blas
Antepara
Hermano
Miguel
Mercado
Central
To Baeza
La Marín
Santa
Catalina
Plaza
Lucinda
Toledo
Milagros
Sucre
Cumandá
(Northbound)
Cumandá
(Southbound)
Plaza
de La
Recoleta
La Recoleta
La Recoleta
To train
station &
Quitumbe
bus terminal

Parque
García Moreno
La Basílica
San Juan
Santa
Bárbara
Plaza del
Teatro Teatro Sucre
El Carmen
Bajo
Casa de
Benalcázar
Museo de Arte
Colonial
Palacio
Arzobisp
Plaza
Grande
San
Agustín
La Merced
La Concepción
Plaza
La Merced
Palacio de
Gobierno
Plaza de la
Independencia
Municipio
Centro Cultural
Metropolitano
Cathedral
La Compañía
El Sagrario
Casa de
Sucre
San Francisco
Church & Museum
Cantuña Chapel
Plaza
San
Francisco
Casa del
Alabado
San
Roque
Santa
Clara
El Carmen
Alto
Museo de
la Ciudad
El Robo
Plaza
Santo
Domingo
Santo Domingo
Church & Museum
Santo Domingo
(Southbound)
Plaza Victoria
San Sebastián
San Diego,
Convent
& Museum
Plaza
San Diego
Cementerio
San Diego
PANECILLO
**Virgen
de Quito**

To Yaku, Museo del Agua

To Yaku, Museo del Agua

Where to stay 🛏
1 Casa Gangotena *C2*
2 Catedral Internacional *B2*
3 Community Hostel *B3*
4 Guayunga *A3*
5 Huasi Continental *C3*
6 La Casona de La Ronda *C3*
7 Patio Andaluz *B2*

8 Plaza Grande *B2*
9 Quito Cultural *B3*
10 Relicario del Carmen *B2*
11 San Francisco
   de Quito *C2*
12 Secret Garden *A3*

Restaurants 🍴
1 Caffeto *B3*
2 El Ventana *A1, D2*
3 Govinda *B2*
4 Heladería San Agustín *B2*
5 Los Geranios *C3*
6 San Ignacio & Casa María
  Augusta Urrutia Museum *C2*

7 Tianguez *C1*
8 Vista Hermosa *B2*

🇪 Ecovía
Ⓜ Metrobus
🇹 Trole
🇺 Universidades

From Plaza de la Independencia two main streets, Venezuela and García Moreno, lead straight towards the Panecillo. Parallel with Venezuela is Calle Guayaquil, the main shopping street. These streets all run south from the main plaza to meet Calle Morales, better known as **La Ronda**, one of the oldest streets in the city. This narrow cobbled pedestrian way and its colonial homes with wrought iron balconies have been refurbished and house a hotel, restaurants, bars, cultural centres and shops. It is a quaint corner of the city growing in popularity for a night out or an afternoon stroll. On García Moreno N3-94 is the beautiful **El Sagrario** ① *Mon-Fri, 0800-1800, Sat-Sun 1000-1400, no entry during Mass, free*, church with a gilded door. The **Centro Cultural Metropolitano** is at the corner of Espejo, housing the municipal library, a museum for the visually impaired, temporary art exhibits and the **Museo Alberto Mena Caamaño** ① *entry on C Espejo, T395 2300, ext 155, www.centrocultural-quito.com, Tue-Sun 0900-1730, US$1.50*. This wax museum depicts scenes of Ecuadorean colonial history. The scene of the execution of the revolutionaries of 1809 in the original cell is particularly vivid. The fine Jesuit church of **La Compañía** ① *García Moreno N3-117 y Sucre, T258 1895, Mon-Thu 0930-1830, Fri 0930-1730, Sat and holidays 0930-1600, Sun 1230-1600, US$4, students US$2*, has the most ornate and richly sculptured façade and interior. Many of its most valuable treasures are in vaults at the Banco Central. Diagonally opposite is the **Casa Museo María Augusta Urrutia** ① *García Moreno N2-60 y Sucre, T258 0103, Tue-Fri 1000-1800, Sat-Sun 0930-1730, US$2*, the home of a Quiteña who devoted her life to charity, showing the lifestyle of 20th-century aristocracy.

Housed in the fine restored, 16th century Hospital San Juan de Dios, is the **Museo de la Ciudad** ① *García Moreno 572 y Rocafuerte, T228 3879, www.museociudadquito.gob.ec, Tue-Sun 0930-1730, US$3, free entry on the last Sat of each month, foreign language guide service US$6 per group (request ahead)*. A very good museum which takes you through Quito's history from prehispanic times to the 19th century, with imaginative displays; café by the entrance overlooking La Ronda. Almost opposite on García Moreno are the convent and museum of **El Carmen Alto** ① *T228 1513, Wed-Sun 0930-1600, US$3, request ahead for guiding in English*. In 2013, this beautifully refurbished cloister opened its doors to the public for the first time since 1652.

On **Cerro Panecillo** ① *Mon-Thu 0900-1700, Fri-Sun 0900-2100, US$1 per vehicle or US$0.25 per person if walking, for the neighbourhood brigade; entry to the interior of the monument US$2*, there is a statue of the Virgen de Quito and a good view from the observation platform. Although the neighbourhood patrols the area, it is safer to take a taxi (US$6 return from the colonial city, US$10 from La Mariscal, with a short wait). In the museum of the monastery of **San Diego** ① *Calicuchima 117 y Farfán, entrance to the right of the church, T317 3185, Tue-Sat 1000-1300, 1400-1700, Sun 1000-1400, US$2*, (by the cemetery of the same name, just west of Panecillo). Guided tours (Spanish only) take you around four colonial patios where sculpture and painting are shown. Of special interest are the gilded pulpit by Juan Bautista Menacho and the Last Supper painting in the refectory, in which a *cuy* and *humitas* have taken the place of the paschal lamb.

Plaza de San Francisco (or Bolívar) is west of Plaza de la Independencia; here are the great church and monastery of the patron saint of Quito, **San Francisco** ① *daily 0800-1200, 1500-1800*. The church was constructed by the Spanish in 1553 and is rich in art treasures. A modest statue of the founder, Fray Jodoco Ricke, the Flemish Franciscan who sowed the first wheat in Ecuador, stands nearby. See the fine wood-carvings in the choir, a high altar of gold and an exquisite carved ceiling. There are some paintings in the aisles by Miguel de Santiago, the colonial *mestizo* painter. The **Museo Franciscano Fray Pedro Gocial** ① *in the church cloisters to the right of the main entrance, T295 2911, Mon-Sat 0900-1730, Sun 0900-*

1300, US$2, has a collection of religious art. Also adjoining San Francisco is the **Cantuña Chapel** ① *Cuenca y Bolívar, T295 2911, 0800-1200, 1500-1800, free*, with sculptures. Not far to the south along Calle Cuenca is the excellent archaeological museum **Museo Casa del Alabado** ① *Cuenca 335 y Rocafuerte, T228 0940, Tue-Sat 0930-1730, Sun 1000-1600, US$4, guides extra, excellent art shop*. An impressive display of pre-Columbian art from all regions of Ecuador, amongst the best in the city. North of San Francisco is the church of **La Merced** ① *Chile y Cuenca, 0630-1200, 1300-1800, free*, with many splendidly elaborate styles. Nearby is the **Museo de Arte Colonial** ① *Cuenca N6-15 y Mejía, T228 2297, Tue-Sat 0900-1630, US$2*, housed in a 17th-century mansion, it features a collection of colonial sculpture and painting.

At **Plaza de Santo Domingo** (or Sucre), southeast of Plaza de la Independencia, is the church and monastery of **Santo Domingo** ① *daily 0630-1230, 1700-1830*, with its rich wood-carvings and a remarkable Chapel of the Rosary to the right of the main altar. In the monastery is the **Museo Dominicano Fray Pedro Bedón** ① *T228 0518, Mon-Sat 0915-1400, 1500-1630, US$2*, another fine collection of religious art. In the centre of the plaza is a statue of Sucre, facing the slopes of Pichincha where he won his battle against the Royalists. Just south of Santo Domingo, in the old bus station, is **Parque Qmanadá** ① *Tue-Sun 0900-1300, 1500-1800, busy on weekends*, with swimming pool, sport fields, gym and activities. **Museo Monacal Santa Catalina** ① *Espejo 779 y Flores, T228 4000, Mon-Fri 0900-1700, Sat 0900-1200, US$2.50*, said to have been built on the ruins of the Inca House of the Virgins, depicts the history of cloistered life. Many of the heroes of Ecuador's struggle for independence are buried in the monastery of **San Agustín** ① *Chile y Guayaquil, Mon-Sat 0715-1200, 1430-1715, Sun 0715-1315*, which has beautiful cloisters on three sides where the first act of independence from Spain was signed on 10 August 1809. Here is the **Museo Miguel de Santiago** ① *Chile 924 y Guayaquil, T295 1001, www.migueldesantiago.com, Mon-Fri 0900-1230, 1400-1700, Sat 0900-1230, US$2*, with religious art.

The **Basílica** ① *on Parque García Moreno, Carchi 122 y Venezuela, northeast of Plaza de la Independencia, T228 9428, 0900-1700 daily, US$2*, is very large, has many gargoyles (some in the shape of Ecuadorean fauna), stained glass windows and fine, bas relief bronze doors (begun in 1926; some final details remain unfinished due to lack of funding). Climb above the coffee shop to the top of the clock tower for stunning views. The **Centro de Arte Contemporáneo** ① *Luis Dávila y Venezuela, San Juan, T398 8800, Tue-Sun 0900-1700, free*, in the beautifully restored Antiguo Hospital Militar, built in the early 1900s, has rotating art exhibits. To the west of the city, the **Yaku Museo del Agua** ① *El Placer Oe11-271, T251 1100, www.yakumuseoagua.gob.ec, Tue-Sun 0900-1700, US$3, take a taxi*, has great views. Its main themes are water and nature, society and heritage, also a self-guided *eco-ruta*; great for children. Another must for children, south of the colonial city, is the **Museo Interactivo de Ciencia** ① *Tababela Oe1-60 Y Latorre, Chimbacalle, T251 1100*. East of the colonial city is **Parque Itchimbía** ① *T228 2017, park open daily 0600-1800, exhibits 0900-1630*, a natural look-out over the city with walking and cycle trails and a cultural centre housed in a 19th-century 'crystal palace' which came from Europe, once housed the Santa Clara market.

Modern Quito

Parque La Alameda has the oldest **astronomical observatory** ① *T257 0765, ext 101, http://oaq.epn.edu.ec, museum Tue-Sat 1000-1700, US$2, observations on clear nights, call ahead for schedule*, in South America dating to 1873 (native people had observatories long before the arrival of the Europeans). There is also a splendid monument to Simón Bolívar, lakes, and in the northwest corner a spiral lookout tower with a good view. On Fridays and Saturdays from 1900 to 2100, there are very nice sound and light shows.

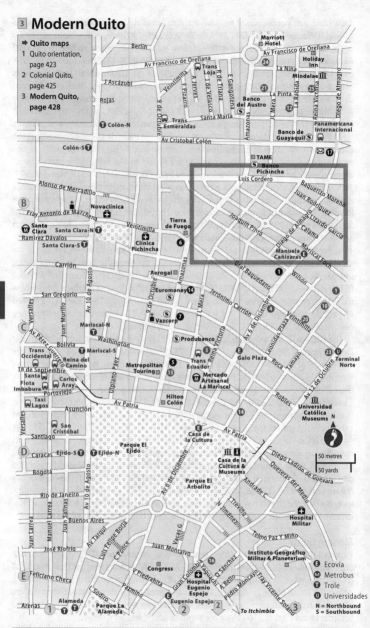

3 Modern Quito

Quito maps
1 Quito orientation, page 423
2 Colonial Quito, page 425
3 **Modern Quito, page 428**

Berlin

Av Francisco de Orellana

Marriott Hotel

Av Francisco de Orellana

Holiday Inn

La Niña

Mindalae

J Ascázubi

Rojas

9 de Octubre

Trans Loja

Veintimilla

A Jerves

F Pizarro

R de Triana

E Gangotena

La Pinta

La Rábida

Mera

Reina Victoria

Diego de Almagro

Trans Esmeraldas

Santa María

Banco del Austro

Amazonas

Panamericana Internacional

Colón-N

Av Cristóbal Colón

Banco de Guayaquil

Colón-S

TAME

Banco Pichincha

Alonso de Mercadillo

Luis Cordero

Baquerizo Moreno

Fray Antonio de Marchena

Novaclínica

Juan Rodríguez

Santa Clara

Santa Clara-N

Veintimilla

Tierra de Fuego

Joaquín Pinto

Lizardo García

Ramírez Dávalos

Santa Clara-S

Clínica Pichincha

Catama

Diego de Almagro

Mariscal Foch

Carrión

Manuela Cañízares

Wilson

San Gregorio

Aerogal

Gral Baquedano

Av 10 de Agosto

Euromoney

Jerónimo Carrión

Av Pérez Guerrero

Juan Murillo

Mera

Vazcorp

Av 6 de Diciembre

Versalles

Mariscal-N

Leonidas Plaza

Veintimilla

Washington

Produbanco

Tamayo

Bolivia

Mariscal-S

Reina Victoria

Galo Plaza

Roca

Trans Occidental

Reina del Camino

Ulpiano Páez

Metropolitan Touring

Trans Ecuador

18 de Septiembre

Santa Flota Imbabura

Carlos Aray

Mercado Artesanal La Mariscal

Robles

Av 12 de Octubre

Terminal Norte

Taxi Lagos

Portoviejo

Hilton Colón

Asunción

San Cristóbal

Av Patria

Santiago

Casa de la Cultura

Av Patria

Universidad Católica Museums

Caracas

Ejido-S

Ejido-N

Casa de la Cultura & Museums

Diego Ladrón de Guevara

Bogotá

Parque El Ejido

Queseras del Medio

50 metres

50 yards

Río de Janeiro

Av 10 de Agosto

Av 6 de Diciembre

Parque El Arbolito

Andrade C

Manuel Larrea

Juan Larrea

Juan Salinas

Buenos Aires

J Treviño

J Nimenezin

José Riofrío

Av Tarqui

Luis Felipe Borja

C Ponce

Vaca G

Hospital Militar

Feliciano Checa

Juan Montalvo

Telmo Paz Y Miño

Congress

Gran Colombia

Yaguachi

Q Sánchez

Instituto Geográfico Militar & Planetarium

Ecovía

V Piedrahita

A Bello

Metrobus

Alameda

S Odrio

Hospital Eugenio Espejo

Pazmín

Pedro Moncayo

Fray Vicente Solano

Trole

Universidades

Arenas

Parque La Alameda

Eugenio Espejo

To Itchimbía

N = Northbound
S = Southbound

A short distance north of Parque La Alameda, opposite Parque El Ejido and bound by 6 de Diciembre, Patria, 12 de Octubre and Parque El Arbolito, is the **Casa de la Cultura**, a large cultural and museum complex. If you have time to visit only one museum in Quito, it should be the **Museo Nacional** ① *entrance on Patria, T222 3258, Tue-Fri 0900-1700, Sat-Sun 1000-1600, free, guided tours in English by appointment*, housed in the north side of the Casa de la Cultura. The **Sala de Arqueología** is particularly impressive with beautiful pre-Columbian ceramics, the **Sala de Oro** has a nice collection of prehispanic gold objects, and the **Sala de Arte Colonial** with religious art from the Quito School. On the east side of the complex are the museums administered by the **Casa de la Cultura** ① *enter from Patria and go left around the building, T290 2272, ext 420, Tue-Sat 0900-1300, 1400-1645, US$2*: **Museo de Arte Moderno**, paintings and sculpture since 1830 also rotating exhibits and **Museo de Instrumentos Musicales**, an impressive collection of musical instruments, said to be the second in importance in the world. Also on the east side are an art gallery for temporary exhibits and the **Agora**, a large open space used for concerts. On the west side are halls for temporary art exhibits, in the original old building, and the entrance to the **Teatro Nacional**, with free evening performances. On the south side are the **Teatro Demetrio Aguilera Malta** and other areas devoted to dance and theatre. Near the Casa de la Cultura, in the Catholic

La Mariscal detail

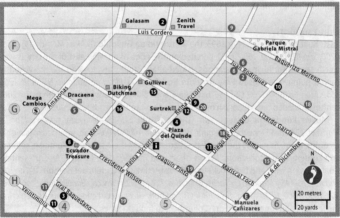

Where to stay			
1 Anahi *C3*	13 Hothello *C2*	3 Chez Alain *H4*	15 Sushi/Siam *G5*
2 Backpackers Inn *G6*	14 La Cartuja *D3*	4 Coffee Bar *G5*	16 The Magic Bean *G5*
3 Café Cultura *C2*	15 La Casa Sol *H6*	5 Coffee Tree *C2*	17 Yu Su *B3*
4 Casa Helbling *C3*	16 L'Auberge Inn *E2*	6 El Hornero *B2*	
5 Casa Joaquín *G4*	17 Nü House *G5*	7 Ethnic Coffee *C2*	
6 Cayman *F6*	18 Posada del Maple *G6*	8 Kallari *G4*	**Bars & clubs**
7 City Art Hotel Silberstein *G4*	19 Queen's Hostel *H5*	9 La Boca del Lobo *G5*	18 Bungalow Six *G5*
8 El Arupo *F6*	20 Sierra Madre *C3*	10 La Petite Mariscal *G6*	19 Cherusker *H5*
9 El Cafecito *F6*	21 Travellers Inn *A3*	11 Las Menestras de	20 El Aguijón *G5*
10 Fuente de Piedra I *C3*		la Almagro *H4, H5*	21 Finn McCool's *H5*
11 Fuente de Piedra II *H4*	**Restaurants**	12 Mama Clorinda *G5*	22 No Bar *F5*
12 Hostal de la Rábida *A3*	1 Baalbek *C3*	13 Paléo *F5*	23 Seseribó *C3*
	2 Chandani Tandoori *F5*	14 Sakti *C2*	24 Turtle's Head *A3*
			25 Varadero *A3*

University's **cultural centre** ① *12 de Octubre y Roca, T299 1700, ext 1710, Mon-Fri 0900-1900, Sat1000-1700*, are the **Museo Jijón y Caamaño**, with a private collection of archaeological objects, historical documents and art, very well displayed (closed for relocation in 2014); the **Museo Weilbauer**, with archaeological and photo collections; and temporary exhibits.

A focal point in La Mariscal, north of Parque El Ejido, is **Plaza del Quinde**, also called **Plaza Foch** (Reina Victoria y Foch), a popular meeting place surrounded by cafés and restaurants. At the corner of Reina Victoria and La Niña, known as **Plaza Yuyu**, is the excellent **Museo Mindalae** ① *T223 0609, daily 0900-1800, US$3, 1st Sun of each month free*, which exhibits Ecuadorean crafts and places them in their historical and cultural context, as well as temporary exhibits, a good fair-trade, non-profit shop and restaurant. (For another handicrafts museum and shop, see **Folklore**, page 439.)

North of La Mariscal is the large **Parque La Carolina**, a favourite recreational spot at weekends. Around it is the banking district, several shopping malls, hotels and restaurants. In the park is the **Jardín Botánico** ① *T333 2516, www.jardinbotanicoquito.com, Mon-Fri 1000-1700, Sat-Sun 0900-1700, US$3.50*, which has a good cross section of Andean flora. Also the **Vivarium** ① *T227 1820, daily 0930-1300, 1330-1730, US$3*, dedicated to protect endangered snakes, reptiles and amphibians, and the **Museo de Ciencias Naturales** ① *T244 9824, Mon-Fri 0800-1300,1345-1645, US$2*. Beyond La Carolina, on the grounds of Quito's former airport, is **Parque Bicentenario**, with sports fields and a great cycling track, right on the old tarmac.

Quito suburbs

East Built by Indian slaves in 1693, the **Santuario de Guápulo** ① *Mass Mon-Fri 1900, Sat 0700, Sun 0700-1200, 1600-1700*, perched on the edge of a ravine east of the city, is well worth seeing for its many paintings, gilded altars, stone carvings and the marvellously carved pulpit. The **Museo Fray Antonio Rodríguez** ① *Plaza de Guápulo N27-138, T256 5652, Mon-Fri 0900-1700, US$1.50*, has religious art and furniture, from the 16th to the 20th centuries. Guided tours (Spanish only) include a visit to the beautiful Santuario.

Museo Fundación Guayasamín ① *Bosmediano E15-68, Bellavista, northeast of La Mariscal, T244 6455, www.guayasamin.org, Tue-Sun 1000-1700, US$6, take a taxi*, is highly recommended. As well as the eponymous artist's works there are pre-Columbian, colonial and contemporary collections. Works of art and jewellery are for sale. Also presenting Guayasamín's work and five blocks from the museum is **La Capilla del Hombre** ① *Lorenzo Chávez E18-143 y Mariano Calvache, Bellavista, T244 8492, www.capilladelhombre.com, Tue-Sun 1000-1700, US$6 (US$1 discount if visiting both sites)*, a collection of murals depicting the fate of Latin America from pre-Columbian to modern times.

In the eastern suburb of San Rafael is **La Casa de Kingman Museo** ① *Portoviejo 111 y Dávila, 1 block from San Rafael park, Valle de los Chillos, T286 1065, undergoing restoration in 2014*. This is a collection of the renowned artist's work, in his home, alongside other colonial, republican and 20th-century art. Take a taxi or a *Vingala* bus from Isabel La Católica y Mena Caamaño, behind Universidad Católica.

West For spectacular views ride the **Teleférico** ① *Av Occidental above La Gasca, T222 1320, daily 0800-2000, US$8.50, children and seniors US$6.50, take a Trans Alfa bus bound for Comuna Obrero Independiente from the Seminario Mayor, América y Colón, or a taxi from the same place (US$1.50)*. The cable car is part of a complex with an amusement park, shops and food courts. It climbs to 4050 m on the flanks of Pichincha, where there are walking trails, including one to the summit of Rucu Pichincha, and horse riding just past the fence.

Parque Arqueológico y Ecológico Rumipamba ① *east side of Av Occidental just north of Mariana de Jesús, Wed-Sun 0830-1600, free, some English speaking guides*, is a 32-ha park on the slopes of Pichincha, where vestiges of human occupation of several pre-Inca periods, dating from 1500 BC to AD 1500, have been found. There are walking trails in some pockets of native vegetation. Northwest of Rumipamba, in the neighbourhood of San Vicente de la Florida is **Museo de Sitio La Florida** ① *C Antonio Costas y Villacrés, T380 3043, Wed-Sun 0800-1600, free, some English speaking guides, at north end of Marín-San Vicente bus line*. At this necropolis of the Quitus people, 10- to 17-m-deep burial chambers, dating to AD 220-640, have been excavated. The elaborate dress and jewellery found in the tombs suggests most were prominent citizens.

Mitad del Mundo and around

The location of the equatorial line here (23 km north of central Quito) was determined by Charles-Marie de la Condamine and his French expedition in 1736, and agrees to within 150 m with modern GPS measurements. The monument forms the focal point of a leisure park built as a typical colonial town, with restaurants, gift shops, post office, travel agency, and has a very interesting **ethnographic museum** ① *T239 4806, 0900-1700 daily (very crowded on Sun), entry to complex US$3, children US$1.50, includes entrance to the pavilions; entry to the ethnographic museum US$3 (includes guided tour in Spanish or English)*, depicting indigenous cultures. There is also an interesting **model of old Quito**, about 10 m sq, with artificial day and night and an **insectarium**. The **Museo Inti-Ñan** ① *200 m north of the monument, T239 5122, www.museointinan.com.ec, 0930-1700 daily, US$4*, is eclectic, very interesting, has lots of fun activities and gives Equator certificates for visitors. Research about the equator and its importance to prehistoric cultures is carried out near Cayambe, by an organization called **Quitsa-to** ① *www.quitsato.org, daily 0800-1700, US$2*.

ⓦ Quito listings

For hotel and restaurant price codes, and other relevant information, see pages 14-17.

ⓦ Where to stay

For websites with extensive lists of hotels see Where to stay, page 14. For lodgings near the airport, see Quito suburbs below. Near the Quitumbe bus terminal are a few simple establisments catering to short stay customers and there is one simple hostal (**$ Madrid**) opposite the Carcelén bus terminal, along busy Avenida Eloy Alfaro. Large international chain hotels are represented in the city and meet their international standards. For more information see: www.sheraton.com, www.radisson.com, www.swissotel.com, www.hilton.com, www.hojo.com (**Howard Johnson**), www.hiexpress.com (**Holiday Inn**), www.danncarltonquito.com, www.marriott.com, www.mercure.com, www.bestwestern.com, www.hotelquito.com (**Compass**).

Colonial Quito *p424, map p425*
$$$$ Casa Gangotena, Bolívar y Cuenca, T400 8000, www.casagangotena.com. Superb location by Plaza San Francisco, luxury accommodation in beautifully refurbished classic family home with rooms and suites, fine restaurant.
$$$$ Patio Andaluz, García Moreno N6-52 y Olmedo, T228 0830, www.hotelpatio andaluz.com. Beautifully reconstructed 16th-century mansion with large arches, balconies and patios, exclusive restaurant with Ecuadorean and Spanish cuisine, library, gift shop.
$$$$ Plaza Grande, García Moreno N5-16, Plaza de la Independencia, T251 0777,

www.plazagrandequito.com. Exclusive top-of-the-line hotel with an exceptional location, 15 suites including a presidential suite for US$2000, jacuzzi in all rooms, climate control, 3 restaurants including La Belle Epoque, gourmet French cuisine and a wine cellar, mini-spa, 110/220V outlets.

$$$ Catedral Internacional, Mejía Oe6-36 y Cuenca, T295 5438. Nicely restored colonial house with 15 carpeted rooms, heaters, small patio, popular restaurant, spa.

$$$ La Casona de La Ronda, Morales Oe1-160 y Guayaquil, T228 7538, www.lacasona delaronda.com. Tastefully refurbished colonial house in the heart of La Ronda, comfortable rooms and suite, restaurant.

$$$ Relicario del Carmen, Venezuela 1041 y Olmedo, T228 9120, www.hotelrelicariodel carmen.com. Beautifully refurbished colonial house, good restaurant, cafeteria, good rooms and service, no smoking.

$$ Quito Cultural, Flores N4-160 y Chile, T228 8084, www.hostalquitocultural.com. Nicely refurbished colonial house, bright, rooftop terrace with nice views, patio with plants, a bit pricey.

$$ San Francisco de Quito, Sucre Oe3-17 y Guayaquil, T295 1241. Converted colonial building, breakfast served in attractive patio or underground cloisters, restaurant, suites are particularly good value, well run by owners, rooms to the street can be noisy.

$$-$ Community Hostel, Cevallos N6-78 y Olmedo, T228 5108, communityhostel@ gmail.com. Popular hostel with 2 double rooms and dorms for 4-6 (cheaper) comfy beds, shared bath (may have to wait for toilet in the morning), good showers, very clean and efficient, nice sitting area, breakfast available, kitchen facilities, helpful staff.

$ Huasi Continental, Flores N3-08 y Sucre, T295 7327. Colonial house, restaurant, private or shared bath, parking, good value.

In between the colonial and modern cities

$$$$ Mansión del Angel, Los Ríos N13-134 y Pasaje Gándara, T254 0293,

www.mansiondelangel.com.ec. Luxurious hotel decorated with antiques in a beautifully renovated mansion, 15 ample rooms and a palacial suite, dinner available, nice gardens, lovely atmosphere.

$$-$ L'Auberge Inn, Colombia N15-200 y Yaguachi, T255 2912, www.auberge-inn-hostal.com. Nice spacious rooms, duvets, private or shared bath, excellent hot water, restaurant, spa, cooking facilities, parking, lovely garden, terrace and communal area, tour operator, helpful, good atmosphere. Highly recommended.

$$-$ Secret Garden, Antepara E4-60 y Los Ríos, T295 6704, www.secretgarden quito.com. Restored house, some rooms small and dark, lovely roof-top terrace restaurant, private or shared bath, cheaper in dorm, popular meeting and party place, can be noisy. Ecuadorean/Australian-owned, also run a rustic lodge between Pasochoa and Cotopaxi, www.secretgardencotopaxi.com.

$ Chicago, Los Ríos N17-30 y Briceño, T228 1695. Popular family-run hostel, small rooms, cheaper in dorm, laundry and cooking facilities, a good economy option.

$ Guayunga, Antepara E4-27 y León, T228 3127, www.guayunga.com. Nice hostel with a few double rooms with and without bath and dorms for 3-9 (cheaper), interior patio, nice rooftop terrace with great views, parking.

Modern Quito *p427, map p428*

$$$$ Le Parc, República de El Salvador N34-349 e Irlanda, T227 6800, www.leparc. com.ec. Modern hotel with 30 executive suites, full luxury facilities and service, restaurant, spa, gym.

$$$$ Nü House, Foch E6-12 y Reina Victoria, T255 7845, www.nuhousehotels. com. Modern luxury hotel with minimalist decor, restaurant, some suites with jacuzzi, all furnishings and works of art are for sale.

$$$ Anahi, Tamayo N23-95 y Wilson, T250 8403, www.anahihotelquito.com. Very nice tastefully decorated suites, each one is different, ample bathrooms, buffet breakfast, safety box, fridge, terrace with nice views, good value.

$$$ Café Cultura, Robles E6-62, T250 4078, www.cafecultura.com. A well-established hotel with ample suites, social areas including wood-panelled library with fireplace, restaurant, attentive service. Planning to relocate.

$$$ Casa Joaquín, Pinto E4-376 y JL Mera, T222 4791, www.hotelcasajoaquin.com. Nicely refurbished hotel in the heart of La Mariscal, covered patio makes it warm, good service, a bit pricey, Belgian-run, new in 2013.

$$$ Cayman, Rodríguez E7-29 y Reina Victoria, T256 7616, www.hotelcaymanquito.com. Pleasant hotel, lovely dining room, cafeteria, rooms a bit small, sitting room with fireplace, parking, garden, very good.

$$$ City Art Hotel Silberstein, Wilson E5-29 y JL Mera, T603 2213, www.cityart silberstein.com. 10 comfortable rooms and suites in an attractively refurbished building, includes buffet breakfast.

$$$ Hostal de la Rábida, La Rábida 227 y Santa María, T222 2169, www.hostalrabida.com. Lovely converted home, bright comfortable rooms, good restaurant, parking, British/Italian-run. Recommended.

$$$ Finlandia, Finlandia N32-129 y Suecia, T224 4288, www.hotelfinlandia.com.ec. Pleasant small hostel in residential area, buffet breakfast, restaurant, spacious rooms, sitting room with fireplace, small garden, parking, airport pick-up extra, helpful staff.

$$$ Fuente de Piedra I & II, Wilson E9-80 y Tamayo, T255 9775 and JL Mera N23-21 y Baquedano, T290 1332, www.ecuahotel.com. Nicely decorated modern hotels, comfortable, some rooms are small, nice sitting areas, pleasant.

$$$ La Cartuja, Plaza 170 y 18 de Septiembre, T252 3577, www.hotelacartuja.com. In the former British Embassy, beautifully decorated, spacious comfortable rooms, cafeteria, parking, lovely garden, very helpful and hospitable. Highly recommended.

$$$ La Casa Sol, Calama 127 y 6 de Diciembre, T223 0798, www.lacasasol.com.

Nice small hotel with courtyard, 24-hr cafeteria, very helpful, English and French spoken, also run **Casa Sol** in Otavalo. Recommended.

$$$ Sierra Madre, Veintimilla E9-33 y Tamayo, T250 5687, www.hotelsierramadre.com. Fully renovated villa, comfortable, restaurant, nice sun roof, parking, English spoken.

$$$ Villa Nancy, Muros N27-94 y 12 de Octubre, T256 2483, www.hotelvillanancy.com. Quaint hotel in quiet residential area, buffet breakfast, parking, homely and comfortable, helpful multilingual staff. Recommended.

$$ El Arupo, Rodríguez E7-22 y Reina Victoria, T255 7543, www.hostalelarupo.com. Good hotel, cooking facilities, English and French spoken. Recommended.

$$ Hothello, Amazonas N20-20 y 18 de Septiembre, T256 5835. Small bright hotel, tastefully decorated rooms, heating, helpful multilingual staff.

$$ Queen's Hostel/Hostal de la Reina, Reina Victoria N23-70 y Wilson, T255 1844. Nice small hotel, popular among travellers and Ecuadoreans, cafeteria, cooking facilities, sitting room with fireplace.

$$-$ Casa Helbling, Veintimilla E8-152 y 6 de Diciembre, T222 6013, www.casahelbling.de. Very good, popular hostel, spotless, breakfast available, private or shared bath, laundry and cooking facilities, English, French and German spoken, pleasant atmosphere, good information, tours arranged, luggage storage, parking. Highly recommended.

$$-$ Casona de Mario, Andalucía 213 y Galicia (La Floresta), T254 4036, www.casona demario.com. Popular hostel, private or shared bath, hot water, laundry facilities, well-equipped kitchen, parking, sitting room, nice garden, book exchange, long-stay discounts, Argentine owner. Repeatedly recommended.

$$-$ Posada del Maple, Rodríguez E8-49 y 6 de Diciembre, T254 4507, www.posadadelmaple.com. Popular hostel, private or shared bath, also dorms, cooking facilities, warm atmosphere, free tea and coffee.

$$-$ Travellers Inn, La Pinta E4-435 y Amazonas, T255 6985, www.travellers ecuador.com. In a nicely converted home, includes good breakfast, private or shared bath, parking, nice common area, bike rentals. Recommended.

$ Backpackers Inn, Rodríguez E7-48 y Reina Victoria, T250 9669, www.backpackersinn. net. Popular hostel, breakfast available, private or shared bath, also dorms, laundry and cooking facilities, adequate dorms.

$ El Cafecito, Cordero E6-43 y Reina Victoria, T223 4862, www.cafecito.net. Popular with backpackers, good café including vegetarian, cheaper in dorm (US$8), 1 room with bath, relaxed atmosphere but can get noisy at night, Canadian-owned.

Quito suburbs p430

$$$$ Hacienda Rumiloma, Obispo Díaz de La Madrid, T254 8206, www.hacienda rumiloma.com. Luxurious hotel in a 40-ha hacienda on the slopes of Pichincha. Sumptuous suites with lots of attention to detail, lounges with antiques, good pricey restaurant, bar with fireplace, nice views, personalized attention from owners, ideal for someone looking for a luxurious escape not far from the city.

$$$ Hostería San Jorge, Km 4 via antigua Quito-Nono, to the west of Av Mariscal Sucre, T339 0403, www.eco-lodgesanjorge. com. Converted 18th-century hacienda on a 80-ha private reserve on the slopes of Pichincha, full board available, good pricey restaurant, heating, pool, sauna and jacuzzi, horse riding and birdwatching. Operates several nature reserves.

Quito airport

A hotel by the airport was under construction in 2014. Towns near the airport with accommodation include: Tababela, off highway E-35, 10 mins from the airport towards Quito (airport taxi US$10). Nearby, by the junction of E-35 and the Vía Interoceánica, is **Pifo**, also about 10 mins from the airport (taxi US$10). From Pifo you can go northwest to Quito, southwest to Sangolquí and points south or east to Papallacta and Oriente. **Puembo**, past Pifo on the Vía Interoceánica, is 20 mins from the airport (taxi US$15-20) and closer to Quito. **Checa**, north of the airport on the E-35, is about 15 mins away (taxi US$12-15). Further north on the E-35 is **El Quinche**, about 20 mins from the airport (taxi US$15-20). The latter 2 are convenient if going to Otavalo and points north, without going to Quito.

$$$ Garden Hotel San José, Manuel Burbano s/n, Barrio San José, Puembo, T239 0276, T1-800-180180, www.hosteriasanjose. com. 18th-century hacienda with 4 ha of grounds, modern rooms, restaurant, pool, spa, airport transfers US$10 pp.

$$$ Hostal Su Merced, Julio Tobar Donoso, Puembo, T239 0251, www.sumerced.com. Nicely refurbished 18th-century hacienda house, well-appointed rooms with bathtubs, includes traditional breakfast, restaurant, sauna, gardens, airport transfers US$15 per vehicle.

$$ Hostal El Parque, 29 de Abril y 24 de Septiembre, opposite the main park in Tababela, T259 9008, patriciogarzon70@ hotmail.com. Private or shared bath, gardens, meals available, airport transfers US$5 per vehicle.

$$ Hostal MarShyl, E-35 y Cuenca, El Quinche, T238 8327, www.marshyl.com. Functional rooms in 4-storey hotel, package rate including breakfast and airport transfers.

$$ Hostería San Carlos, Justo Cuello y Maldonado, Tababela, T359 9057, www. hosteriasancarlostababela.com. Hacienda style inn with ample grounds, restaurant, pool, jacuzzi, rooms with bath and dorms (US$18 pp), airport transfers US$5 per person.

$ Nevada, E-35 Km 26, outside Pifo, near the turn-off for Sangolquí, T238 0074. Simple economical rooms, noisy.

❶ Restaurants

Eating out in Quito is excellent, varied, upmarket and increasingly cosmopolitan.

There are many elegant restaurants offering Ecuadorean and international food, as well as small simple places serving set meals for US$2-50, the latter close by early evening and on Sun.

Colonial Quito p424, map p425

$$$ El Ventanal, Carchi y Nicaragua, west of the Basílica, in Parque San Juan, take a taxi to the parking area and a staff member will accompany you along a footpath to the restaurant, T257 2232, www.elventanal.ec, Tue-Sat 1100-1500, 1800-2200, Sun 1200-1600. International nouvelle cuisine with a varied menu including a number of seafood dishes, fantastic views over the city. 2nd branch with traditional Ecuadorean menu at Loja Oe4-09 y Venezuela, T228 5103.

$$$ Theatrum, Plaza del Teatro, 2nd floor of Teatro Sucre, T228 9669, www.theatrum.com.ec. Mon-Fri 1230-1600, 1930-2330, Sat-Sun 1900-2300. Excellent creative gourmet cuisine in the city's most important theatre, wide selection of fruit desserts which come with an explanatory card.

$$$-$$ Los Geranios, Morales Oe1-134, T295 6035. Mon-Fri 0900-2400, Sat 0900-0200, Sun 0900-1200. Upscale *comida típica*, in a nicely restored La Ronda house.

$$ Hasta la Vuelta Señor, Pasaje Arzobispal, 3rd floor. Mon-Sat 1100-2300, Sun 1100-2100. A *fonda quiteña* perched on an indoor balcony with *comida típica* and snacks, try *empanadas* (pasties) or a *seco de chivo* (goat stew).

$$ Tianguez, Plaza de San Francisco under the portico of the church. Mon-Tue 0930-1830, Wed-Sun 0930-2400. International and local dishes, good coffee, snacks, sandwiches, popular, also craft shop (closes 1830), run by **Fundación Sinchi Sacha**.

$$ Vista Hermosa, Mejía 453 y García Moreno. Mon-Sat 1400-2400, Sun 1200-2100. Good meals, drinks, pizza, live music on weekends, lovely terrace-top views of the colonial centre.

$$-$ San Ignacio, García Moreno N2-60, at Museo María Agusta Urrutia, Mon-Thu 0800-1930, Fri-Sat 0800-2100, Sun 0800-1530. Good popular set lunch (US$4-4.50) with a choice of dishes and buffet salad bar; à la carte in the evening.

$ Govinda, Esmeraldas Oe3-115 y Venezuela. Mon-Sat 0800-1600. Vegetarian dishes, good value economical set meals and à la carte, also breakfast.

Cafés

Caffeto, Chile 930 y Flores. Mon-Sat 0800-1930. Variety of coffees, snacks, sandwiches, sweets.

Heladería San Agustín, Guayaquil N5-59 y Chile. Mon-Fri 1000-1630, Sat-Sun 1030-1530. Coffee, traditional home-made cakes, ices and lunch, a Quito tradition since 1858.

Modern Quito p427, map p428

There are many restaurants serving good economical set lunches along both Pinto and Foch, between Amazonas and Cordero.

$$$ Carmine, Catalina Aldaz N34-208 y Portugal, T333 2829, www.carmineristorante.com. Mon-Sat 1200-1530, 1900-2230, Sun 1200-1800. Creative international and Italian cuisine.

$$$ Chez Jérôme, Whymper N30-96 y Coruña, T223 4067. Mon-Fri 1230-1530, 1930-2330, Sat 1930-2330. Excellent French cuisine, traditional and modern dishes with a touch of local ingredients, good ambience and service.

$$$ La Boca del Lobo, Calama 284 y Reina Victoria, T223 4083. Sun-Wed 1700-2330, Thu-Sat 1700-0100. Stylish bar-restaurant with eclectic food, drink, decor, and atmosphere, good food and cocktails, popular, good meeting place.

$$$ La Choza, 12 de Octubre N24-551 y Cordero, T223 0839. Mon-Fri 1200-1600, 1800-2200, Sat-Sun 1200-1700. Traditional Ecuadorean cuisine, good music and decor.

$$$ La Gloria, Valladolid N24-519 y Salazar, La Floresta, T252 7855. Daily 1200-1530, 1900-2200. Very innovative Peruvian and international cuisine, excellent food and service, same ownership as **Theatrum**.

$$$ La Petite Mariscal, Almagro N24-304 y Rodríguez, T09-8772 8010.

Upmarket European cuisine with an Ecuadorean touch.

$$$ Sake, Paul Rivet N30-166 y Whymper, T252 4818. Mon-Sat 1230-1530, 1830-2300, Sun 12305-1600, 1830-2200. Sushi bar and other Japanese dishes, very trendy, great food and decor.

$$$ San Telmo, Portugal 440 y Casanova, T225 6946. Mon-Sat 1200-2300, Sun until 2200. Good Argentine grill, seafood, pasta, pleasant atmosphere, great service.

$$$ Zazu, Mariano Aguilera 331 y La Pradera, T254 3559, www.zazuquito.com. Mon-Fri 1230-1500, 1900-2230, Sat 1900-2230. Very elegant and exclusive dinning. International and Peruvian specialities, extensive wine list, attentive service, reservations required.

$$$-$$ La Briciola, Toledo 1255 y Salazar, T254 7138, www.labriciola.com.ec. Daily 1200-2400. Extensive Italian menu, excellent food, homely atmosphere, very good personal service.

$$ Chez Alain, Baquedano E5-26 y JL Mera. Mon-Fri 1200-1530. Choice of good 4-course set lunches, pleasant relaxed atmosphere. Recommended.

$$ Il Risotto, Eloy Alfaro N34-447 y Portugal. Sun-Fri 1200-1500, 1800-2300. Very popular and very good Italian cooking, live music Thu and Fri. A Quito tradition.

$$ Mama Clorinda, Reina Victoria N24-150 y Calama. Daily 1100-2300. Ecuadorean cuisine à la carte and set meals, filling, good value.

$$ Paléo, Cordero E5-36 y JL Mera. Mon-Sat 1200-1500 1830-2200. Authentic Swiss specialities such as rösti and raclette. Also good economical set lunch, pleasant ambiance. Recommended.

$$ Pekín, Whymper N26-42 y Orellana. Mon-Sat 1200-1500, 1900-2230, Sun 1200-2030. Excellent Chinese food, very nice atmosphere.

$$ Sushi/Siam, Calama E5-104 y JL Mera. Mon-Sat 1200-2300, Sun 1200-1600. Sushi bar, small portions, pleasant atmosphere with nice balcony, good-value happy hour 1700-1900.

$$ The Magic Bean, Foch E5-08 y JL Mera and Portugal y Los Shyris. Daily 0700-2200. Fine coffees and natural food, more than 20 varieties of pancakes, good salads, large portions, outdoor seating (also popular lodging, **$**).

$$-$ Baalbek, 6 de Diciembre N23-123 y Wilson. Daily 1200-1800. Authentic Lebanese cuisine, great food and atmosphere, friendly service.

$$-$ El Hornero, Veintimilla y Amazonas, República de El Salvador N36-149 y Naciones Unidas and on González Suárez. Daily 1200-2300. Very good wood oven pizzas, try one with choclo (fresh corn). Recommended.

$$-$ Las Palmeras, Japón N36-87 y Naciones Unidas, opposite Parque la Carolina. Daily 0800-1700. Very good *comida Esmeraldeña*, try their hearty viche soup, outdoor tables, popular, good value. Recommended.

$ Chandani Tandoori, JL Mera 1312 y Cordero. Mon-Sat 1100-2200. Good authentic Indian cuisine, economical set meals, popular, good value. Recommended.

$ Las Menestras de la Almagro, Almagro y Foch and Veintimilla y JL Mera. Mon-Sat 1200-2400, Sun 1230-2100. Breakfast, economical set lunches and a choice of *menestras* (grilled meat or chicken with stewed beans or lentils) and other local fare; large portions.

$ Sakti, Carrión E4-144 y Amazonas. Mon-Fri 0830-1800. Good quality and value vegetarian food, breakfast, set lunches and à la carte, fruit juices, great desserts (also a few rooms, **$$-$**).

$ Yu Su, Almagro y Colón, edif Torres de Almagro. Mon-Fri 1230-1600, 1800-2000, Sat 1230-1600. Very good sushi bar, pleasant, Korean-run, takeaway service.

Cafés

Coffee Bar, Reina Victoria y Foch, open 24 hrs. Popular café serving a variety of snacks, pasta, burguers, coffee, Wi-Fi. Very similar are **Coffee Tree**, Amazonas y Washington, and **Coffee O**, next to Museo Mindalae, La Niña y Reina Victoria.

Ethnic Coffee, Amazonas y Roca, Edif Hotel Mercure Alameda. Mon-Fri 0930-2100. Nice café with gourmet coffee as well as a wide range of desserts, meals and drinks.

Kallari, Wilson y JL Mera, www.kallari.com. Mon-Fri 0800-1830, Sat 0900-1830. Fair-trade café, breakfast, snacks, salad and sandwich set lunches, organic coffee and chocolate, crafts, run by an association of farmers and artisans from the Province of Napo working on rainforest and cultural conservation.

⑪ Bars and clubs

Note that a law forbids the sale and consumption of alcohol on Sun. In Colonial Quito, nightlife is concentrated along La Ronda.

Modern Quito *p427, map p428*
Bungalow Six, Almagro N24-139 y Calama. Tue-Sat 1900-0200, Sun 1200-1900. US-style sports bar and club. Popular place to hang out and watch a game or a film, dancing later on, varied music, cover US$5 (Thu free), ladies' night on Wed, happy hour 2000-2200.
Cherusker, Pinto y Diego de Almagro esquina. Mon-Fri 1500-2330, Fri-Sat 1500-0130. Various micro-brews and German food.
El Aguijón, Calama E7-35 y Reina Victoria. Tue-Sat 2100-0300. Bohemian bar/club, varied music, nice atmosphere, after 2200 entry US$6 with 1 free drink. Also concerts, theatre, art.
El Pobre Diablo, Isabel La Católica y Galicia E12-06, La Floresta. Mon-Sat 1230-0200. Relaxed atmosphere, friendly, jazz, sandwiches, snacks and nice meals, live music Wed, Thu and Sat, a popular place to hang out and chill.
Finn McCool's, Almagro N24-64 y Pinto. Daily 1100-0200. Irish-run pub, Irish and international food, darts, pool, table football, sports on TV, Wi-Fi, popular meeting place.
Flash Back, González Suárez N27-205 y Muros. Club, mostly English music, rock and 1980s music, older crowd, cover US$12.
La Juliana, 12 de Octubre N24-722 y Coruña. Thu-Sat 2130-0300. Popular club, live 1990s Latin music, cover US$12.
No Bar, Calama E5-01 y JL Mera. Mon-Sat 1900-0300. Good mix of Latin and Euro

dance music, busy at weekends. Free drinks for women until 2200, Thu-Sat after 2200 entry US$5 with 1 free drink.
Ramón Antiguo, Mena Caamaño E12-86 e Isabel la Católica. 2100-0200. Live music Fri-Sat, cover US$5-10 depending on band. Great for salsa and other hip tropical music, popular with locals.
Seseribó, Veintimilla 325 y 12 de Octubre, T256 3598. Thu-Sat 2100-0100. Caribbean music and salsa, a must for *salseros*, very popular, especially Thu and Fri, cover US$8. Recommended.
Turtle's Head, La Niña 626 y JL Mera, T256 5544. Mon-Tue 1700-0300, Wed-Sat 1230-0300. Microbrews, fish and chips, curry, pool table, darts, fun atmosphere.
Varadero, Reina Victoria N26-99 y La Pinta. Mon-Thu 1200-2400, Fri-Sat 1800-0300. Bar-restaurant, live Cuban music Wed-Sat, meals, snacks, good cocktails, older crowd.

❷ Entertainment

Quito *p422, maps p423, p425 and p428*
There are always many cultural events taking place in Quito, usually free of charge. **Culturas** monthly agenda is available at the tourist office and museums. Films are listed daily in *El Comercio*, www.elcomercio.com.

Cinema
Casa de la Cultura, Patria y 6 de Diciembre, T290 2272. Shows foreign films, often has documentaries, film festivals.
Ocho y Medio, Valladolid N24-353 y Guipuzcoa, La Floresta, T290 4720. Cinema and café, good for art films, programme available at **Libri Mundi** and elsewhere. There are several multiplexes, eg **Cinemark**, www.cinemark.com.ec and **Multicines**, www.multicines.com.ec

Dance schools
One-to-one or group lessons are offered for US$4-6 per hr.
Ritmo Tropical, Amazonas N24-155 y Calama, T255 7094, www.ritmotropicalsalsa.com, salsa, capoeira, merengue, tango and more.

Salsa y Merengue School, Foch E4-256 y Amazonas, T222 0427, also cumbia.

Music
Classical The **Orquesta Sinfónica Nacional**, T250 2815, performs at Teatro Sucre, Casa de la Música, Teatro Escuela Politécnica Nacional, in the colonial churches and regionally. **Casa de la Música**, Valderrama s/n y Mariana de Jesús, T226 7093, www.casadelamusica.ec, concerts by the Orquesta Sinfónica Nacional, Orquesta Filarmónica del Ecuador, Orquesta de Instrumentos Andinos and invited performers. Excellent acoustics.
Folk Folk shows at Palacio Arzobispal (entrance on C Venezuela, minimum donation US$1): Fri and Sat at 1930, Sun at 1200. Folk music is popular in *peñas* which come alive after 2230. **Noches de Quito**, Washington E5-29 y JL Mera, T223 4855. Thu-Sat 2000-0300, show starts 2130. Varied music, entry US$6. **Ñucanchi**, Av Universitaria Oe5-188 y Armero, T254 0967. Thu-Sat 2000-0300, show starts at 2130. Ecuadorean and other music, including Latin dance later in the night, entry US$8-10.
Ecuadorean folk ballet Ballet Andino Humanizarte, at Casa 707, Morales 707, La Ronda, T257 3486. Thu 2100, Fri-Sat 2130, US$5; plays and comedies are also often in their repertoire, restaurant on the premises.
Jacchigua, at Teatro Demetrio Aguilera Malta, Casa de la Cultura, 6 de Diciembre y Patria, T295 2025, www.jacchiguaesecuador.com. Wed at 1930. Entertaining, colourful and touristy, reserve ahead, US$30.
Saruymanda, at Palacio Arzobispal, Venezuela y Chile, Fri at 1930, minimum donation US$1, see above.

Theatre
Agora, open-air theatre of Casa de la Cultura, 12 de Octubre y Patria. Stages plays, concerts.
Teatro Bolívar, Espejo 847 y Guayaquil, T258 2486, www.teatrobolivar.org. Despite restoration work there are tours, presentations and festivals.

Teatro Sucre, Plaza del Teatro, Manabí N8-131 y Guayaquil, T295 1661. Beautifully restored 19th-century building, the city's main theatre.

⊛ Festivals

Quito *p422, maps p423, p425 and p428*
New Year, Años Viejos: life-size puppets satirize politicians and others. At midnight on 31 Dec a will is read, the legacy of the outgoing year, and the puppets are burnt; good at Parque Bicentenario, where a competition is held, very entertaining and good humoured. On New Year's day everything is shut. **6 Jan** (may be moved to the weekend), colourful **Inocentes** procession from Plaza de Santo Domingo at 1700. **Palm Sunday**, colourful procession from the Basílica, 0800-1000. The solemn **Good Friday** processions are most impressive. **24 May** is Independence, commemorating the Battle of Pichincha in 1822 with early morning cannon-fire and parades, everything closes. **Aug:** Agosto Arte y Cultura, organized by the municipality, cultural events, dance and music in different places throughout the city. The city's main festival, Día de Quito, celebrated **1-6 Dec**, commemorates the foundation of the city with elaborate parades, bullfights, performances and music in the streets, very lively. Hotels charge extra, everything except a few restaurants shuts on 6 Dec. Foremost among **Christmas** celebrations is the **Misa del Gallo**, Midnight Mass. Nativity scenes can be admired in many public places. Over Christmas, Quito is crowded, hotels are full and the streets are packed with vendors and shoppers.

○ Shopping

Quito *p422, maps p423, p425 and p428*
Shops open generally 0900-1900 on weekdays, some close at midday and most shut Sat afternoon and Sun. Shopping centres are open at weekends. In modern

Quito much of the shopping is done in malls. For purchasing maps see page 14.

Camping

Camping gas is available in many of the shops listed below, white gas is not.

Aventura Sport, Quicentro Shopping, 2nd level. Tents, good selection of glacier sunglasses, upmarket.

Camping Sports, Colón E6-39 y Reina Victoria. Sales only, well stocked.

Equipos Cotopaxi, 6 de Diciembre N20-36 y Patria. Ecuadorean and imported gear for sale.

Explora, Plaza Foch and several other locations in the city. Clothing and equipment for adventure sports. Also have public bulletin boards for travellers.

The Explorer, Reina Victoria N24-43 y Pinto, Plaza Foch. Sales and rentals, very helpful, will buy US or European equipment, also run tours.

Los Alpes, Reina Victoria N23-45 y Baquedano. Sales and good rental prices.

Mono Dedo, Rafael León Larrea N24-36 y Coruña, La Floresta, www.monodedo.com. Climbing equipment, part of a rock climbing club, lessons.

Tatoo, JL Mera N23-54 y Wilson and CC La Esquina in Cumbayá, www.ec.tatoo.ws. Quality backpacks and outdoor clothing.

Chocolate

Ecuador has exported its fine cacao to the most prestigious chocolatiers around the world for over 100 years. Today, quality chocolate is on offer in specialized shops and food stores.

Galería Ecuador, Reina Victoria N24-263 y García. Shop and café featuring Ecuadorean gourmet organic coffee and chocolate as well as some crafts.

República del Cacao, Reina Victoria y Pinto, Plaza Foch; Morales Oe1-166, La Ronda and at the airport. Chocolate boutique and café.

Handicrafts

Note that there are controls on export of arts and crafts. Unless they are obviously new handicrafts, you may have to get a permit from the **Instituto Nacional de Patrimonio Cultural** (Colón Oe1-93 y 10 de Agosto, T254 3527, offices also in other cities), before you can mail or take things home. Permits cost US$5 and take time.

A wide selection can be found at the following craft markets: **Mercado Artesanal La Mariscal**, Jorge Washington, between Reina Victoria and JL Mera, daily 1000-1800, interesting and worthwhile; **El Indio**, Roca E4-35 y Amazonas, daily 0900-1900; and **Centro de Artesanías CEFA**, 12 de Octubre1738 y Madrid, Mon-Sat 0930-1830.

On weekends, crafts are sold in stalls at **Parque El Ejido** and along the Av Patria side of this park, artists sell their paintings. There are crafts and art shops along La Ronda and souvenir shops on García Moreno in front of the Palacio Presidencial

Recommended shops with an ample selection are:

Camari, Marchena 260 y Versalles. Fair Trade shop run by an artisan organization.

The Ethnic Collection, Amazonas y Roca, Edif Hotel Mercure Alameda, www.ethniccollection.com. Wide variety of clothing, leather, bags, jewellery and ceramic items. Also café next door.

Folklore, Colón E10-53 y Caamaño, also at **Hotel Hilton Colón** and **Hotel Patio Andaluz**. The store of the late Olga Fisch, who for decades encouraged craftspeople to excel. Attractive selection of top quality, pricey handicrafts and rugs. Small museum upstairs.

Galería Latina, JL Mera 823 y Veintimilla. Fine selection of alpaca and other handicrafts from Ecuador, Peru and Bolivia, visiting artists sometimes demonstrate their work.

Hilana, 6 de Diciembre N23-10 y Veintimilla, www.hilana.com.ec. Beautiful unique 100% wool blankets, ponchos and clothing with Ecuadorean motifs, excellent quality, purchase by metre possible, reasonable prices.

Kallari (see page 437) crafts from the Oriente sold at this café.

La Bodega, JL Mera 614 y Carrión. Recommended for antiques and handicrafts.

Marcel Creations, Roca 766, entre
Amazonas y 9 de Octubre. Panama hats.
Mindalae (page 430), nice crafts at museum.
Productos Andinos, Urbina 111 y Cordero.
Artisan's co-op, good selection, unusual items.
Saucisa, Amazonas N22-18 y Veintimilla,
and a couple other locations in La Mariscal.
Very good place to buy Andean music
and instruments.

Jewellery
Argentum, JL Mera 614. Excellent selection,
reasonably priced.
Ari Gallery, Bolívar Oe6-23, Plaza de San
Francisco. Fine silver with ancestral motifs.
Taller Guayasamín, at the museum, see
page 430. Jewellery with native designs.

⏱ What to do

Quito p422, maps p423, p425 and p428
Birdwatching and nature
The following are specialized operators:
Andean Birding, www.andeanbirding.com;
BirdEcuador, www.birdecuador.com;
Neblina Forest, www.neblinaforest.com;
Pluma Verde, www.plumaverdetours.com.

City tours
Paseos Culturales. Walking tours of
the colonial city led by English- or
French-speaking officers of the Policía
Metropolitana start at the Plaza de la
Independencia tourist information office,
Venezuela y Espejo, T257 2445. Departures
with minimum 2 passengers at 0900, 1000,
1100, 1130 and 1400. There are 2 choices:
Vida Cotidiana, includes visits to museums,
Tue-Sun, 2½ hrs, US$15, children and seniors
US$7.70, includes museum entrance fees;
and **Fachadas**, a daily historic buildings
walking tour, 2 hrs, US$4. Arrange ahead
for evening tours, US$5.
Quito Tour Bus, T245 8010, www.quito
tourbus.com. Tours on double-decker bus,
stops at 12 places of interest, it starts and
ends at Naciones Unidas, south side. You can
alight at a site and continue later on another

bus. Hourly, 0900-1600, 3-hr ride, US$12,
children and seniors US$6, ticket valid all
day. Night tour US$10.

Climbing, trekking and walking
The following Quito operators specialize in
this area, many also offer conventional tours
and sell Galápagos and jungle tours. Note
that independent guides are refused entry
to national parks.
Andes Explorer, T247 2306, www.andes-
explorer.com. Good-value budget mountain
and jungle trips.
Campo Base, T259 9737, campobase_ec@
yahoo.com. Climbing, trekking, horse riding
and cycling tours, run by Diego Jácome, very
experienced climbing guide. Also operate a
mountain lodge 15 km south of Sangolquí,
good for acclimatization at 3050 m.
Campus Trekking, T234 0601, www.
campustrekking.com.ec. Good-value
trekking, climbing and cultural tours,
8- to 15-day biking trips, taylor made
itineraries. Also run **Hostería Pantaví**
near Ibarra, 8 languages spoken.
Climbing Tours, Amazonas N21-221 y
Roca, T254 4358, www.climbingtour.com.
Climbing, trekking and other adventure
sports. Tours to regional attractions, also
sell Galápagos and jungle tours. Well-
established operator.
Compañía de Guías, Valladolid N24-70 y
Madrid, T290 1551, www.companiadeguias.
com. Climbing and trekking specialists.
Speak English, German, French and Italian.
Cotopaxi Cara Sur, contact Eduardo Agama,
T09-9800 2681, www.cotopaxicarasur.com.
Offers climbing and trekking tours, runs
Albergue Cara Sur on Cotopaxi.
Latitud 0°, Mallorca N24-500 y Coruña,
La Floresta, T254 7921, www.latitud0.com.
Climbing specialists, French spoken.
Original Ecuador, T323 7512, www.original
ecuador.com. Runs 4- and 7-day highland
tours which involve walking several hours
daily, also custom made itineraries.
Sierra Nevada, Pinto E4-152 y Cordero,
T255 3658, www.sierranevada.ec.

Adventure expeditions: climbing, trekking, rafting and jungle, experienced multilingual guides. Also run a good hotel: www.hotelsierranevada.com.
TribuTrek, T09-9282 5404, www.tributrek. com. Hiking and trekking, cultural and budget tours.

Cycling and mountain biking

Quito has many bike paths and bike lanes on city streets, but mind the traffic and aggressive drivers. The city organizes a **ciclopaseo,** a cycle day, every Sun 0800-1400. Key avenues are closed to vehicular traffic and thousands of cyclists cross the city in 29 km from north to south. This and other cycle events are run by **Fundación Ciclópolis**, Equinoccio N17-171 y Queseras del Medio, T322 6502, www.ciclopolis.ec; they also hire bikes, US$5.60 per *ciclopaseo* (must book Mon-Fri), US$11.20 per day on other days. Rentals also from **La Casa del Ciclista**, Eloy Alfaro 1138 y República, near the ciclopaseo route, T254 0339, US$3 per hr, US$12 per day. If staying a long time in the city, sign up with BiciQ, to use their bikes stationed throughout town. **Biciacción**, www.biciaccion.org, has information about routes in the city and organizes trips outside Quito.
Mountain bike tours Many operators offer bike tours, the following are specialists:
Aries, T09-9981 6603, www.aries bikecompany.com. 1- to 3-day tours, all equipment provided.
Biking Dutchman, Foch E4-283 y Amazonas, T256 8323, after hours T09-9420 5349, www.biking-dutchman.com. 1- and several-day tours, great fun, good food, very well organized, English, German and Dutch spoken, pioneers in mountain biking in Ecuador.

Horse riding

Horse riding tours are offered on Pichincha above the gate of the *teleférico* (see page 430).
Green Horse Ranch, see page 454.
Ride Andes, T09-9973 8221, www.rideandes.

com. Private and set date tours in the highlands including stays in haciendas, also in other South American countries.

Motorbiking
Freedom Bike Rental, JL Mera N22-37 y Veintimilla, T250 4339, www.freedom bikerental.com. Motorcycle rentals US$75-200 per day, scooter US$25, good equipment including mountain bikes, route planning, also tours.

Paragliding
Escuela Pichincha de Vuelo Libre, Carlos Endara Oe3-60 y Amazonas, T225 6592 (office hours), T09-9993 1206, parapent@ uio.satnet.net. Offers complete courses for US$450 and tandem flights for US$65-US$105 (Pichincha).

Tour operators
Most operators also sell Galápagos cruises and jungle tours.
Advantage Travel, Gaspar de Villarroel 1100 y 6 de Diciembre, T336 0887, www.advantagecuador.com. Tours on the **Manatee** floating hotel on Río Napo and to Machalilla.
Andando Tours – Angermeyer Cruises, Moreno Bellido E6-167 y Amazonas, T323 8631, www.andandotours.com. Operate the *Mary Anne* sailing vessel and *Anahi* catamaran, as well as land-based highland tours, see www.humboltexpeditions.com.
Andean Travel Company, Amazonas N24-03 y Wilson, p 3, T222 8385, www.andeantc.com. Dutch/Ecuadorean-owned operator, wide range of tours including trekking and cruises on the *Galapagos Voyager*, *Galapagos Odyssey* and *Galapagos Grand Odyssey* vessels.
Creter Tours, Pinto E5-29 y JL Mera, T254 5491, www.cretertours.com.ec. Operate the *Treasure of Galapagos* catamaran and sell island-hopping tours.
Dracaena, Pinto E4-375 y Amazonas, T290 6644, www.amazondracaena.com. Runs good budget jungle tours to Cuyabeno and climbing and trekking trips, popular.

EcoAndes, Baquedano E5-27 y JL Mera, T222 0892, www.ecoandestravel.com. Classic and adventure tours, volunteer opportunities Also operate hotels in Quito.
Ecoventura, La Niña E8-52 y Almagro, T323 7393, www.ecoventura.com. Operate first-class Galápagos cruises and sell mainland tours.
Ecuador for All, T237 7430, www.ecuador forall.com. Specialized tours to all regions of Ecuador for the mobility and hearing impaired traveller.
Ecuador Galapagos Travels (EGT), Veintimilla E10-78 y 12 de Octubre, Edif El Girón, Torre E, of 104, T254 7286, www. galapagos-cruises.ec, www.ecuadortravels.ec. Wide range of traditional and adventure tours throughout Ecuador; tailor-made itineraries.
Ecuador Journeys, Manabi S1-146, Cumbaya, T603 5548, www.ecuadorian journey.com. Adventure tours to off-the-beaten-path destinations, day tours, treks to volcanos, jungle trips, run **Emerald Forest Lodge** in Pañacocha, tours to expat hotspots.
Ecuador Treasure, Wilson E4266 y JL Mera, T09-9546 5822/09-8938 6999, www.ecuador treasure.com. Climbing, horse riding, cycling and trekking tours. Run **Chuquirahua Lodge**, near Reserva Los Ilinizas.
Enchanted Expeditions, de las Alondras N45-102 y de los Lirios, T334 0525, www. enchantedexpeditions.com. Operate the *Cachalote* and *Beluga* Galápagos vessels, sell jungle trips to Cuyabeno and highland tours. Very experienced.

Equateur Voyages Passion, in L'Auberge Inn, Gran Colombia N15-200 y Yaguachi, T322 7605, www.magical-ecuador.com. Full range of adventure tours, run in highlands, coast and jungle. Also custom-made itineraries.
Galacruises Expeditions, 9 de Octubre N22-118 y Veintimilla, pb, T252 3324, www.islasgalapagos.travel. Galápagos cruises on the *Sea Man II* catamaran and other vessels. Also island hopping and land tours on Isabela, where they operate Casa Isabela on the Beach.
Galasam, Amazonas N24-214 y Cordero, T290 3909, www.galasam.net. Has a fleet of boats in different categories for Galápagos cruises. City tours, full range of highland tours and jungle trips to **Siona Lodge** in Cuyabeno.
Galextur, Portugal E10-271 y 6 de Diciembre, T226 9626, www.galextur.com. Run land-based Galápagos tours with daily sailings. Operate **Hotel Silberstein** in Puerto Ayora and **City Art Hotel Silberstein** in Quito. Good service.
Geo Reisen, Shyris N36-46 y Suecia, T243 6081. Specializing in cultural, adventure and nature tours adapted for individuals, groups or families.
Gulliver, JL Mera N24-156 y Calama, T290 5036, www.gulliver.com.ec. Wide range of economical adventure and traditional tours. Operate **Hostería Papagayo** south of Quito.
Happy Gringo, Catalina Aldaz N34-155 y Portugal, Edif Catalina Plaza, of 207, T512

3486, www.happygringo.com. Tailor-made tours throughout Ecuador, Quito city tours, Otavalo, sell Galápagos, jungle and other destinations,good service. Recommended. .

Klein Tours, Eloy Alfaro N34-151 y Catalina Aldaz, also Shyris N34-280 y Holanda, T226 7000, www.kleintours.com. Operate the *Galapagos Legend* and *Coral I* and *II* cruise ships. Also run community-based tours in Imbabura and highland tours with tailor-made itineraries, English, French and German spoken.

Latin Trails, T286 7832, www.latintrails.com, www.galapagoscatamarans.com, www.galapagosodyssey.com. Run cruises in various Galápagos vessels and offer a variety of land trips in several countries.

Metropolitan Touring, Av Las Palmeras N45-74 y Las Orquídeas, Amazonas N20-39 y 18 de Septiembre, Amazonas N40-80 y Naciones Unidas and at shopping centres, T1800-115115, T298 8200, www.metropolitan-touring.com. A large organization operating in Ecuador, Peru, Chile and Argentina. Run several luxury Galápagos vessels, the **Finch Bay Hotel** in Puerto Ayora, Casa Gangotena in Quito and Mashpi Lodge west of Quito. Also adventure, cultural and gastronomy tours.

Positiv Turismo, Jorge Juan N33-38 y Atahualpa, T600 9401, www.positivturismo. com. Cultural trips, Cuyabeno, trekking and special interest tours, Swiss-run.

Pure! Ecuador, Muros N27-94 y González Suárez, T512 3358, www.pure-ecuador. com. A Dutch/local operator offering tours throughout Ecuador and the Galápagos, trips to **Cotococha Amazon Lodge**, and tailor-made tours.

Quasar Náutica, T244 6996, T1-800 247 2925 (USA), www.quasarnautica.com. Offer 7- to 10-day naturalist and diving Galápagos cruises on 8- to 16-berth yachts.

Rolf Wittmer Turismo/Tip Top Travel, Foch E7-81 y Almagro, T252 6938, www. rwittmer.com. Run first class yachts: *Tip Top II*, *III* and *IV*. Also tailor-made tours throughout Ecuador.

Safari Tours, Reina Victoria N25-33 y Colón, Edif Banco de Guayaquil, p11, T255 2505, www.safari.com.ec. Daily 0930-1830. Adventure travel, personalized itineraries, mountain climbing, cycling, rafting, trekking and cultural tours. Also book Galápagos tours. Recommended.

Surtrek, Reina Victoria N24-151 y Calama, T250 0660, www.surtrek.com. Wide range of tours in all regions, helicopter and ballon flights, birdwatching, rafting, horse riding, mountain biking and jungle tours, also sell domestic flights and run **Las Cascadas Lodge**. .

Tierra de Fuego, Amazonas N23-23 y Veintimilla, T250 1418, www.ecuador tierradefuego.com. Provide transport and tours throughout the country, domestic flight tickets, Galápagos bookings and operate the *Guantanamera* yacht.

Tropic Journeys in Nature, Pasaje Sánchez Melo Oe1-37 y Av Galo Plaza, T240 8741, www.destinationecuador.com. Environmental and cultural jungle tours to the **Huaorani Ecolodge**, see page 564; also day trips, Quito city, coast, highlands, lodge-to-lodge mountain treks, Amazon lodges and Galápagos land-based and multisport tours. Community-based tourism working with and donating a percentage of all profits to **Conservation in Action**. Winner of awards for responsible tourism.

Yacu Amu Experiences, Checoslovaquia E10-137 y 6 de Diciembre, T246 1511, www.yacuamu.com. Tailor-made adventure, nature and cultural trips for active couples, families and small groups.

Zenith Travel, JL Mera N24-234 y Cordero, T252 9993, www.zenithecuador.com. Good-value Galápagos cruises as well as various land tours in Ecuador and Peru. All gay Galápagos cruises available. Multilingual service, knowledgeable helpful staff, good value.

Train rides

The lovely refurbished train station, **Estación Eloy Alfaro (Chimbacalle)**, with a railway museum and working concert hall, is 2 km south of the colonial city **at** Maldonado y Sincholagua, T1-800-873637, T265 6142, www.trenecuador.com, Mon-Fri 0800-1630. *Tren Crucero*, a luxury tourist train, runs about twice per month (but not every month) in either direction between Quito and Durán, outside Guayaquil, part of the route is run with a historic steam locomotive. The complete route takes 4 days and costs US$1270 one way, you can also take it for segments from 1 to 3 days. The tour includes visits to places of interest and accommodation in luxury inns. See www.trenecuador.com/crucero for details. Tourist trains run Thu-Sun and holidays from Quito to **Machachi** (at 0815, US$15-20), **El Boliche** (0815, US$20-25) and **Latacunga** (motorized rail car at 0800, transport only US$12 return, you cannot purchase tickets to board at Latacunga.). If you go only to Machachi, you will have a long wait for the returning train, so it is a better option to go to El Boliche. At the station in the latter is **Restaurante Nuna**, and nearby, **Área Nacional de Recreación El Boliche**, a protected area abutting on Parque Nacional Cotopaxi. There are lovely views of Cotopaxi and Los Ilinizas. Purchase tickets in advance by phone, or at the station or **El Quinde craft shop**, Palacio Municipal, Venezuela y Espejo. You need each passenger's passport number and age to purchase tickets. Tours start with a visit to the railway museum.

Whitewater rafting

Río Blanco/Toachi tours cost US$87. **Ríos Ecuador** (see Tena operators), T260 5828, www.riosecuador.com. Very professional, rafting and kayaking trips of 1-6 days, also kayak courses. Highly recommended. **Sierra Nevada** (see page 440), excellent trips from 1 to 3 days, minimum 5 passengers, chief guide Edison Ramírez (fluent English/French) is certified by **French Association des Rivieres des Eaux Rapides**.

Mitad del Mundo *p431*
Calimatours, 30 m east of monument, Mitad del Mundo, T239 4796, www.mitaddelmundo tour.com. Tours to Pululahua and other sites in the vicinity.

⊘ Transport

Quito *p422, maps p423, p425 and p428*
Air
Details of internal air service are given under the respective destinations. Quito's new **Mariscal Sucre Airport** opened in 2013, T395 4200, www.quitoairport.aero (has information about current arrival and departures, airport services and airlines). It is in Tababela, off Highway E-35, about 30 km northeast of the city, at 2134 m above sea level. The tourist information office (arrivals level, T281 8363, open 24 hrs), will assist with hotel bookings. Set taxi rates to different zones of the city are posted by arrivals (US$24.50 to La Mariscal, US$26 to colonial Quito, US$33 to Quitumbe bus station, US$26.50 to Carcelén station); taxi rates from the city to the airport are about 12% cheaper. Aero Servicios express bus, T604 3500, T1-800-237673, runs 24 hrs per day, between the new airport and the old airport in northern Quito (Parque Bicentenario), US$8, US$4 seniors and children. From Tababela, departures are hourly from 2400 to 0600 and every 30 mins during the day, taking a taxi from the old airport to your hotel is recommended; from Quito, departures are hourly from 1800 to 0300 and every 30 mins the rest of the day. HATS, T323 0113 or T09-8336 1610, shuttle bus to/from hotels in La Mariscal, US$16 pp, minimum 4 passengers. Regional buses with limited stops, run every 15 mins, 0600-2145, between the airport and Terminal Quitumbe in the south and Terminal Río Coca in the north, US$2. Van services are good value for groups (US$35-40, minimum 3 passengers, US$5 per additional person), but require advanced arrangements: **Trans-Rabbit**,

T290 2690, www.transrabbit.com.ec, or **Achupallas Tour**, T255 1614.

Note There is only one access road from the city to the airport and traffic is congested. It may take as much as 2 hrs to reach the airport, allow enough time. Additional access roads were under construction in 2014, one from Calderón in the north of Quito is due to be completed by the end of the year. If going to the airport from other cities, take a bus that bypasses Quito along highway E-35 (available from Baños, Ambato and Ibarra), get off at the airport roundabout and take the regional bus 4.5 km from there. If coming from the east (Papallacta, Baeza or Oriente), go as far as Pifo and transfer to the regional bus there.

Bus
Local Quito has 4 parallel mass transit lines running from north to south on exclusive lanes, covering almost the length of the city. There are several transfer stations where you can switch from one line to another without cost. Feeder bus lines (*alimentadores*) go from the terminals to outer suburbs. Within the city the fare is US$0.25; the combined fare to some suburbs is US$0.40. Public transit is not designed for carrying heavy luggage and is often crowded. **Trole** (T266 5016, Mon-Fri 0500-2345, weekends and holidays 0600-2145, plus hourly overnight service with limited stops) is a system of trolley buses which runs along Av 10 de Agosto in the north of the city, C Guayaquil (southbound) and C Flores (northbound) in colonial Quito, and mainly along Av Maldonado and Av Teniente Ortiz in the south. The northern terminus is north of 'La Y', the junction of 10 de Agosto, Av América and Av de la Prensa; south of the colonial city are important transfer stations at El Recreo, known as Terminal Sur, and Morán Valverde; the southern terminus is at the Quitumbe bus station. Trolleys do not necessarily run the full length of the line, the destination is marked in front of the vehicle. Trolleys have a special entrance for wheelchairs. **Ecovía** (T243 0726, Mon-Sat 0500-2200, Sun and holidays 0600-2200), articulated buses, runs along Av 6 de Diciembre from Estación Río Coca, at C Río Coca east of 6 de Diciembre, in the north, to La Marín transfer station and on to Cumandá, east of colonial Quito. **Metrobus** (T346 5149, Mon-Fri 0530-2230, weekends and holidays 0600-2100) also runs articulated buses along Av de la Prensa and Av América from Terminal La Ofelia in the north to La Marín in the south. **Universidades** articulated buses run from 12 de Octubre y Veintimilla to Quitumbe bus terminal. There are also 2 types of **city buses**: *Selectivo* are red, and *Bus Tipo* are royal blue, both cost US$0.25. Along Av Universitaria and at the El Tejar and San Roque tunnels on Av Mariscal Sucre (Occidental) are interchanges where you can change buses without paying a second fare. Many bus lines go through La Marín and El Playón Ecovía/Metrobus stations. Extra caution is advised here: pickpockets abound and it is best avoided at night. For Quito Tour Bus, see page 440.

Short distance Outer suburbs are served by green *Interparroquial* buses. Those running east to the valleys of Cumbayá, Tumbaco and the airport leave from the Estación Río Coca (see Ecovía above). Buses southeast to Valle de los Chillos leave from El Playón Ecovía/Metrobus station and from Isabel la Católica y Mena Caamaño, behind Universidad Católica. Buses going north (ie Calderón, Mitad del Mundo) leave from La Ofelia Metrobus station. Regional destinations to the north (ie Cayambe) and northwest (ie Mindo) leave from a regional station adjacent to La Ofelia Metrobus station. Buses west to Nono from the Plaza de Cotocollao, to Lloa from C Angamarca in Mena 2 neighbourhood. Buses south to Machachi from El Playón, La Villaflora and Quitumbe. Buses to Baeza and El Chaco leave from Don Bosco E1-136 y Av Pichincha in La Marín.

Long distance Quito has 2 main bus terminals: **Terminal Quitumbe** in the southwest of the city, T398 8200, serves destinations south, the coast via Santo Domingo, Oriente and Tulcán (in the north). It is served by the Trole (line 4: El Ejido-Quitumbe, best taken at El Ejido) and the Universidades articulated buses, however it is advisable to take a taxi, about US$6, 30-45 mins to the colonial city, US$8-10, 45 mins-1 hr to La Mariscal. Arrivals and tourist information are on the ground floor. Ticket counters (destinations grouped and colour coded by region), and departures in the upper level. Left luggage (US$0.90 per day) and food stalls are at the adjoining shopping area. The terminal is large, allow extra time to reach your bus. Terminal use fee US$0.20. Watch your belongings at all times. On holiday weekends it is advisable to reserve the day before. The smaller **Terminal Carcelén**, Av Eloy Alfaro, where it meets the Panamericana Norte, T396 1600, serves destinations to the north (including Otavalo) and the coast via the Calacalí–La Independencia road. It is served by feeder bus lines from the northern terminals of the Trole, Ecovía and Metrobus, a taxi costs about US$5, 30-45 mins to La Mariscal, US$7, 45 mins-1 hr to colonial Quito. Ticket counters are organized by destination. See under destinations for fares and schedules; these are also listed in www.ecuadorbuses.com, where for US$3 you can also purchase tickets online for buses departing Quito. A convenient way to travel between Quitumbe and Carcelén is to take a bus bound for Tulcán, **Trans Vencedores** or **Unión del Carchi** (Booth 12), every 30 mins during the day, hourly at night, US$1, 1 hr; from Carcelén to Quitumbe, wait for a through bus arriving from the north; taxi between terminals, US$15.

Several companies run better quality coaches on the longer routes and some have terminals in modern Quito (departures at night), these include: **Flota Imbabura**, Larrea 1211 y Portoviejo, T223 6940, for **Cuenca** and **Guayaquil**; Transportes Ecuador, JL Mera N21-44 y Washington, T250 3842, hourly to **Guayaquil**; Transportes Esmeraldas, Santa María 870 y Amazonas, T250 9517, for **Esmeraldas**, **Atacames**, **Coca**, **Lago Agrio**, **Manta** and **Huaquillas**. Reina del Camino, Larrea y 18 de Septiembre, T321 6633, for **Bahía**, **Puerto López** and **Manta**; Carlos Aray Larrea y Portoviejo, T256 4406, for **Manta** and **Puerto López**; Transportes Occidentales, 18 de Septiembre y Versalles, for **Esmeraldas**, **Atacames**, **Salinas** and **Lago Agrio**; Transportes Loja, Orellana y Jerves, T222 4306, for **Loja** and **Lago Agrio**; San Cristóbal, Larrea y Asunción, T290 0457, for **Tulcán** and **Guayaquil**; in the same office is **Transportes Chimborazo**, for Riobamba. **Transportes Baños**, for **Baños** and Oriente destinations, has a ticket counter at Santa María y JL Mera, but buses leave from Quitumbe. **Panamericana Internacional**, Colón E7-31 y Reina Victoria, T255 7133, ext 126 for national routes, ext 125 for international, for **Huaquillas**, **Machala**, **Cuenca**, **Loja**, **Manta**, **Guayaquil** and **Esmeraldas**. Also run international service to **Lima**, daily, changing buses in Aguas Verdes and Túmbes, US$85, 38 hrs. **Ormeño Internacional**, from Perú, Shyris N35-52 y Portugal, of 3B, T245 6632, Tue and Thu to **Lima**, US$90, Sat to **Bogotá**, US$90, Tue to **Caracas**, US$130. **Rutas de América**, Selva Alegre Oe1-72 y 10 de Agosto, T250 3611, www.rutasenbus.com, to **Lima**, 1 weekly, US$65; to **Caracas**, 2 weekly, US$135, 2½ days, does not go into Colombian cities, but will let passengers off by the roadside (eg Popayán, Palmira for Cali or Ibagué for Bogotá, all US$55). The route to **Peru** via Loja and Macará takes much longer than the Huaquillas route, but is more relaxed. Don't buy Peruvian (or any other country's) bus tickets here, they're much cheaper outside Ecuador.

Shared taxis and vans offer door-to-door service and avoid the hassle of reaching Quito's bus terminals. Reserve at least

2 days ahead. Taxis Lagos to **Otavalo** and **Ibarra**, see page 463. **Servicio Express**, T03-242 6828 (Ambato) or T09-9924 2795, to **Ambato** (US$12) or **Latacunga** (US$10), 9 daily (fewer on Sun). **Montecarlo Trans Vip**, T03-294 3054 (Riobamba) or T09-8411 4114, to **Riobamba**, US$15. **Autovip**, T600 2582, to **Puyo**, US$30; to **Baños**, US$20. **Río Arriba/Atenas** Washington y Páez, T252 1336, to **Cuenca**, daily at 2300, US$25, 6 hrs. **Sudamericana Taxis**, to **Santo Domingo**, see page 551. **Esmetur Express** T06-271 5498 (Esmeraldas) or T09-9226 0857, to **Esmeraldas**, US$25.

Taxi

Taxis are a cheap (from US$1) and efficient way to get around the city. Authorized taxis display a unit number on the windshield, the driver's photograph and have a working meter. They are safer and cheaper than unauthorized taxis. Expect to pay US$1-2 more at night when meter may not be used. At night it is safer to use a radio taxi, these have black markings in front, ie: **Taxi Americano**, T222 2333; **Taxi Amigo**, T222 2222; **City Taxi**, T263 3333. Make sure they give you the taxi number so that you get the correct vehicle, some radio taxis are unmarked. Taxis from the near suburbs have a red markings and those from the outer suburbs green. Note the registration and the licence plate numbers if you feel you have been seriously overcharged or mistreated. You may then complain to the transit police or tourist office. To hire a taxi by the hour costs from US$8 in the city, more out of town. For trips outside Quito, agree the fare beforehand: US$70-85 a day. Outside luxury hotels cooperative taxi drivers have a list of agreed excursion prices and most drivers are knowledgeable.

Train

There is no regular passenger service. For tourist rides, see Train rides, page 443.

Mitad del Mundo and around *p431*
Bus From Quito take a 'Mitad del Mundo' feeder bus from La Ofelia station on the Metrobus (transfer ticket US$0.15), or from the corner of Bolivia y Av América (US$0.40). Some buses continue to the turn-off for Pululahua or Calacalí beyond. An excursion by **taxi** to Mitad del Mundo (with 1 hr wait) is US$25, or US$30 to include Pululahua. Just a ride from La Mariscal costs about US$15.

ⓘ Directory

Quito *p422, maps p423, p425 and p428*
Banks The highest concentration of banks and ATMs is in modern Quito. Many are along Av Amazonas, both in La Mariscal and La Carolina, and along Naciones Unidas between Amazonas and Los Shyris. In colonial Quito there are banks near the main plazas. To change TCs, **Banco del Pacífico**, Naciones Unidas E7-95 y Shyris and Amazonas y Veintimilla and *casas de cambio*: All open Mon-Fri 0900-1730, Sat 0900-1245. **Euromoney**, Amazonas N21-229 y Roca, T252 6907. Change 10 currencies, 2% commission for Amex US$ TCs; **Mega Cambios**, Amazonas N24-01 y Wilson, T255 5849. 3% commission for US$ TCs, change cash euros, sterling, Canadian dollars; **Vazcorp**, Amazonas N21-169 y Roca, T252 9212. Change 11 currencies, 1.8% comission for US$ TCs, good rates, recommended. **Car hire** All the main international car rental companies are at the airport. For rental procedures see Driving in Ecuador, page 12. A local company is: **Simon Car Rental**, Los Shyris 2930 e Isla Floreana, T243 1019, www.simoncarrental. com, good rates and service. **Achupallas Tours**, T255 1614, and **Trans-Rabbit**, T290 2690, www.transrabbit.com.ec, rent vans for 8-14 passengers, with driver, for trips in Quito and out of town. **Embassies and consulates** For all foreign embassies and consulates in Ecuador, see http://embassy. goabroad.com. **Immigration** Dirección Nacional de Migración, Amazonas 171 y

Language schools in Quito

Quito is one of the most important centres for Spanish language study in Latin America with over 80 schools operating. There is a great variety to choose from. Identify your budget and goals for the course: rigorous grammatical and technical training, fluent conversation skills, getting to know Ecuadoreans or just enough basic Spanish to get you through your trip.

Visit a few places to get a feel for what they charge and offer. Prices vary greatly, from US$5 to US$22 per hour. There is also tremendous variation in teacher qualifications, infrastructure and resource materials. Schools usually offer courses of four or seven hours tuition per day. Many readers suggest that four is enough. Some schools offer packages which combine teaching in the morning and touring in the afternoon, others combine teaching with travel to various attractions throughout the country. A great deal of emphasis has traditionally been placed on one-to-one teaching, but remember that a well-structured small classroom setting is also recommended.

The quality of homestays likewise varies, the cost including half board runs from US$16 to US$20 per day (more for full board). Try to book just one week at first to see how a place suits you. For language courses as well as homestays, deal directly with the people who will provide services to you, avoid intermediaries and always get a detailed receipt.

If you are short on time then it can be a good idea to make your arrangements from home, either directly with one of the schools or through an agency, who can offer you a wide variety of options. If you have more time and less money, then it may be more economical to organize your own studies after you arrive. **South American Explorers** provides a list (free to members) of recommended schools and these may give club members discounts.

We list schools for which we have received positive recommendations each year. This does not imply that schools not mentioned are not recommended.

República, T227 2835, Mon-Fri 0800-1200 and 1500-1800. **Language schools** Many schools offer study-travel programs. The following have received favourable reports: **Academia de Español Quito**, T255 3647. **Amazonas**, www.eduamazonas. com. **Andean Global Studies**, www. andeanglobalstudies.org. **Beraca**, www. beraca.net. **Bipo & Toni's**, www.bipo.net. **Cristóbal Colón**, www.colonspanishschool. com. **Equinox**, www.ecuadorspanish.com. **Instituto Superior**, www.instituto-superior. net. **La Lengua**, www.la-lengua.com. **Mitad del Mundo**, www.mitadmundo. com.ec. **Sintaxis**, www.sintaxis.net. **South American**, www.southamerican.edu.ec. **Universidad Católica**, T299 1700 ext 1388, mejaramillo@puce.edu.ec. **Vida Verde**, www. vidaverde.com. **Medical services** For all emergencies T911. Hospitals: **Metropolitano**, Mariana de Jesús y Occidental, T226 1520, ambulance T226 5020. Very professional and recommended, but expensive. **Clínica Pichincha**, Veintimilla E3-30 y Páez, T256 2296, ambulance T250 1565. Also very good, and expensive. **Voz Andes**, Villalengua Oe 2-37 y Av 10 de Agosto, T226 2142, quick and efficient, fee based on ability to pay, a good place to get vaccines. **Police** T101. Servicio de Seguridad Turística, Reina Victoria y Roca, T254 3983. Report robberies here or at **Fiscalía de Turismo** (Public Prosecutors Office), at **Ministerio de Turismo**, see Tourist information, page 424.

Around Quito

Papallacta → *Phone code: 06. Colour map 1, A4. Population: 950. Altitude: 3200 m.*

At the **Termas de Papallacta** ⓘ *64 km east from Quito, 2 km from the town of Papallacta, 0600-2100, T02-250 4787 (Quito), www.papallacta.com.ec,* the best developed hot springs in the country, are 10 thermal pools, three large enough for swimming, and four cold plunge pools. There are two public complexes of springs: the regular **pools** ⓘ *US$8,* and the **spa centre** ⓘ *US$21 (massage and other special treatments extra).* There are additional pools at the Termas' hotel and cabins (see Where to stay, page 451) for the exclusive use of their guests. The complex is tastefully done and recommended. In addition to the Termas there are nice municipal pools in the village of Papallacta (US$3) and several more economical places to stay (some with pools) on the road to the Termas and in the village. The view, on a clear day, of Antisana while enjoying the thermal waters is superb. Along the highway to Quito, are several additional thermal pools. Note that Quito airport is between Quito and Papallacta.

There are several walking paths in the **Rancho del Cañón private reserve** ⓘ *behind the Termas, US$2 for use of a short trail, to go on longer walks you are required to take a guide for US$8-15 pp.* To the north of this private reserve is **Reserva Cayambe-Coca** ⓘ *T02-211 0370.* A scenic road starts by the Termas information centre, crosses both reserves and leads in 45 km to Oyacachi. A permit from Cayambe-Coca headquartes is required to travel this road even on foot. It is a lovely two-day walk, there is a ranger's station and camping area 1½ hours from Papallacta. Reserva Cayambe-Coca is also accessed from La Virgen, the pass on the road to Quito, where there is a ranger's station. **Ríos Ecuador,** see Tena operators, offer guiding service here.

Refugio de Vida Silvestre Pasochoa

ⓘ *45 mins southeast of Quito by car, very busy at weekends; park office at El Ejido de Amaguaña, T09-9894 5704, Quito office T256 3429, ext 21302.*

This natural park is set in humid Andean forest between 2700 m and 4200 m. The reserve has more than 120 species of birds (unfortunately some of the fauna has been frightened away by the noise of the visitors) and 50 species of trees. There are walks of 30 minutes to eight hours. There are picnic and camping areas. Take a good sleeping bag, food and water.

Western slopes of Pichincha → *Phone code: 02. Altitude: 1200-2800 m.*

Despite their proximity to the capital (two hours from Quito), the western slopes of **Pichincha** and its surroundings are surprisingly wild, with fine opportunities for walking and birdwatching. This scenic area has lovely cloud forests and many nature reserves. The main tourist town in this area is Mindo. To the west of Mindo is a warm subtropical area of clear rivers and waterfalls, with a number of reserves, resorts and lodges.

Paseo del Quinde Two roads go from Quito over the western Cordillera before dropping into the northwestern lowlands. The old route via Nono (the only town of any size along this route) and Tandayapa, is dubbed the Paseo del Quinde (Route of the Hummingbird) or **Ecoruta,** see www.ecorutadelquinde.org. It begins towards the northern end of Avenida Mariscal Sucre (Occidental), Quito's western ring road, at the intersection with Calle Machala. With increased awareness of the need to conserve the cloud forests of the northwest slopes of Pichincha and of their potential for tourism, the number of reserves here is steadily growing. Keen birdwatchers are no longer the only visitors, and the region has much to offer all nature lovers. Infrastructure at reserves varies considerably. Some have comfortable upmarket lodges offering accommodation, meals, guides and transport. Others may require taking your own camping gear, food, and obtaining a permit. There are too many reserves and lodges to mention here; see *Footprint Ecuador* for more details.

At Km 62 on the Paseo del Quinde road is **Bellavista Cloud Forest Reserve**, a 700-ha private reserve with excellent birdwatching and botany in the cloud forest, There are 20 km of trails ranging from wheelchair access to the slippery/suicidal. See Where to stay, page 452.

The new route From the Mitad del Mundo monument the road goes past **Calacalí**, whose plaza has an older monument to the Mitad del Mundo. Beyond Calacalí is a toll (US$0.80 for cars) where a road turns south to Nono and north to Yunguilla. Another road at Km 52 goes to Tandayapa and Bellavista. The main paved road, with heavy traffic at weekends, continues to Nanegalito (Km 56), Miraflores (Km 62), the turn-offs to the old road and to Mindo (Km 79), San Miguel de los Bancos, Pedro Vicente Maldonado and Puerto Quito, before joining the Santo Domingo–Esmeraldas road at La Independencia.

Pululahua ① *park office by the rim lookout, T239 6543, 0800-1700*, is a geobotanical reserve in an inhabited, farmed volcanic caldera. A few kilometres beyond the Mitad del Mundo, off the road to Calacalí, Mirador Ventanillas, a lookout on the rim gives a great view, but go in the morning, as the cloud usually descends around 1300. You can go down to the reserve and experience the rich vegetation and warm microclimate inside. From the mirador: walk down 30 minutes to the agricultural zone then turn left. There are picnic and camping areas. A longer road allows you to drive into the crater via Moraspungo. To walk out this way, starting at the mirador, continue past the village in the crater, turn left and follow the unimproved road up to the rim and back to the main road, a 15-20 km round trip.

In **Nanegalito**, the transport hub for this area, is a **tourist information office** ① *T02-211 6222, Mon-Sun 0900-1700*. Just past the centre is the turn-off to Nanegal and the cloud forest in the 18,500-ha **Maquipucuna Biological Reserve** ① *www.maqui.org, knowledgeable guides: US$25 (Spanish), US$100 (English) per day for a group of 9*, which contains a tremendous diversity of flora and fauna, including spectacled bear, which can be seen when the aguacatillo trees are in fruit (around January) and about 350 species of birds. The reserve has 40 km of trails (US$10 per person) and a lodge (see below).

Next to Maquipucuna is **Santa Lucía** ① *T02-215 7242, www.santaluciaecuador.com*. Access to this reserve is 30 minutes by car from Nanegal and a walk from there. Day tours combining Pululahua, Yunguilla (a community project near Calacalí) and Santa Lucía are available. Bosque Nublado Santa Lucía is a community-based conservation and eco-tourism project protecting a beautiful 650-ha tract of cloud forest. The area is very rich in birds (there is a cock-of-the-rock lek) and other wildlife. There are waterfalls and walking trails and a lodge (see below).

At Armenia (Km 60), a few km beyond Nanegalito, a road heads northwest through Santa Clara, with a handicrafts market on Sunday, to the village and archaeological site of **Tulipe** (14 km; 1450 m). The site consists of several man-made 'pools' linked by water channels. A path leads beside the Río Tulipe in about 15 minutes to a circular pool amid trees. The site **museum** ① *T02-285 0635, www.museodesitiotulipe.com, US$3, Wed-Sun 0900-1600, guided tours (arrange ahead for English)*, has exhibits in Spanish on the Yumbos culture and the colonos (contemporary settlers). There is also an orchid garden. For reserves and tours in the area, see www.tulipecloudforest.org and www.cloudforestecuador.com.

The Yumbos were traders who linked the Quitus with coastal and jungle peoples between AD 800-1600. Their trails are called *culuncos*, 1 m wide and 3 m deep, covered in vegetation for coolness. Several treks in the area follow them. Also to be seen are *tolas*, raised earth platforms; there are some 1500 around Tulipe. **Turismo Comunitario Las Tolas** ① *6 km from Tulipe, T02-286 9488*, offers lodging, food, craft workshops and guides to *tolas* and *culuncos*.

To the northwest of Tulipe are **Gualea** and **Pacto**, beyond which is **$$$$ Mashpi Lodge** and **Reserve**, www.mashpilodge.com. Back along the main road, by Miraflores, is **Tucanopy** (turn north at Km 63.5, closed Wednesday), www.tucanopy.com, a reserve with lodging, trails, canopy ziplines and conservation volunteer opportunities. At Km 79 is the turn-off for Mindo.

Mindo → *Phone code: 02. Colour map 1, A3. Population: 4300. Altitude: 1250 m.*

Mindo, a small town surrounded by dairy farms and lush cloud forest climbing the western slopes of Pichincha, is the main access for the 19,500-ha Bosque Protector Mindo-Nambillo. The town gets very crowded with Quiteños at weekends and holidays. The reserve, which ranges in altitude from 1400 m to 4780 m, features beautiful flora (many orchids and bromeliads), fauna (butterflies, birds including the cock-of-the-rock, golden-headed quetzal and toucan-barbet) and spectacular cloud forest and waterfalls. The region's rich diversity is threatened by proposed mining in the area. **Amigos de la Naturaleza de Mindo** ① *1½ blocks from the Parque Central, T217 0115, US$4 for guided walk along a trail with bird feeders, guides for groups also available*, runs the **Centro de Educación Ambiental** (**CEA**), 4 km from town, within the 17 ha buffer zone, capacity for 25-30 people. Lodging: **$** per person; full board including excursion: **$$** per person; use of kitchen: US$1.50. Arrangements have to be made in advance. During the rainy season, access to the reserve can be rough. Mindo also has orchid gardens and butterfly farms. Activities include visits to waterfalls, with rappelling in the La Isla waterfalls, 'canopy' ziplines, and 'tubing' regattas in the rivers. **Note** There is only one ATM, take cash.

West of Mindo → *Phone code: 02. Colour map 1, A3.*

The road continues west beyond the turn-off to Mindo, descending to the subtropical zone north of Santo Domingo de los Tsáchilas. It goes via San Miguel de los Bancos, Pedro Vicente (PV) Maldonado and Puerto Quito (on the lovely Río Caoni) to La Independencia on the Santo Domingo–Esmeraldas road. From San Miguel de Los Bancos a paved side-road also goes to Santo Domingo. The entire area is good for birdwatching, swimming in rivers and natural pools, walking, kayaking, or simply relaxing in pleasant natural surroundings. There are many reserves, resorts, lodgings and places to visit along the route, of particular interest to birdwatchers. There are tours from Quito. See Where to stay, below, for resorts.

⊙ Around Quito listings

For hotel and restaurant price codes, and other relevant information, see pages 14-17.

🛏 Where to stay

Papallacta *p449*
$$$$-$$$ Hotel Termas Papallacta, at the Termas complex, T289 5060. Comfortable heated rooms and suites, good expensive restaurant, thermal pools set in a lovely garden, nice lounge with fireplace, some rooms with private jacuzzi, also cabins for up to 6, transport from Quito extra. Guests have acces to all areas in the complex and get discounts at the spa. For weekends and holidays book 1 month in advance.

$$ Antizana, on road to the Termas, a short walk from the complex, T289 5016. Simple rooms, private or shared bath, restaurant, pools, a good option.

$$ Coturpa, next to the Municipal baths in Papallacta town, T289 5040. Small fuctional rooms, breakfast available.

$$ La Choza de Don Wilson, at intersection of old unpaved road and road to Termas, T289 5027. Rooms with nice views of the valley, heaters, good popular restaurant, pools, massage, spa, attentive.

East of Papallacta

$$$$ Guango Lodge, near Cuyuja, 9 km east of Papallacta, T02-289 1880 (Quito), www.guangolodge.com. In a 350 ha temperate forest reserve along the Río Papallacta. Includes 3 good meals, nice facilities, excellent birdwatching. Day visits US$5. Reserve ahead.

Western slopes of Pichincha p449
Paseo del Quinde

$$$$ Tandayapa Bird Lodge, T244 7520 (Quito), www.tandayapa.com. Designed and owned by birders. Full board, comfortable rooms, some have a canopy platform for observation, large common area; packages including guide and transport from Quito.

$$$$-$$$ Bellavista Cloud Forest, T211 6232 (Bellavista Lodge), in Quito at Jorge Washington E7-25 y 6 de Diciembre, T290 1536, www.bellavistacloudforest.com. A dramatic lodge perched in beautiful cloud forest, with unique geodesic dome, bamboo house and half-timbered house, suites. Cheaper in dorm with shared bath. Full board, hot showers, birdwatching, the newly discovered olinguito, botany and waterfalls. Camping US$8 pp. Package tours with guide and transport arranged from Quito. Best booked in advance. Recommended.

$$$ San Jorge, T339 0403, www.eco-lodge sanjorge.com. A series of reserves with lodges in bird-rich areas. One is 4 km from Quito (see Hostería San Jorge, page 434), one in Tandayapa at 1500 m and another in Milpe, off the paved road, at 900 m.

The new route

$$$$ Santa Lucía, T02-215 7242, www.santaluciaecuador.com. The lodge with panoramic views is a 1½-hr walk from the access to the reserve. Price includes full board with good food and guiding. There are cabins with private bath, rooms with shared composting toilets and hot showers and dorms (**$** pp including food but not guiding).

$$$$-$$$ Maquipucuna Lodge, T02-250 7200, T09-9237 1945, www.maqui. org. Comfortable rustic lodge, includes full board with good meals using ingredients from own organic garden (vegan available). Shared rooms or private with bath, hot water, electricity. Campsite is 20 mins' walk from main lodge, under US$6 pp (food extra), cooking lessons, chocolate massages.

$$$ Hostería Sumak Pakari, Tulipe, 200 m from the village, T286 4716, www.hosteria sumakpakari.com. Cabins with suites with jacuzzi and rooms set in gardens, includes breakfast and museum fee, terraces with hammocks, pools, restaurant, sports fields.
$ Posada del Yumbo, Tulipe, T286 0121. Up a side street off the main road. Cabins in large property with river view, also simple rooms, electric shower, pool, horse riding. Also run restaurant **La Aldea**, by the archaeological site.

Mindo *p451*
$$$$ Casa Divina, 1.2 km on the road to Cascada de Nambillo, T09-9172 5874, www.mindocasadivina.com. Comfortable 2-storey cabins, lovely location surrounded by 2.7 forested ha, includes breakfast and dinner, bathtubs, guiding extra, US/Ecuadorean-run.
$$$$ El Monte, 2 km from town on road to CEA, then opposite Mariposas de Mindo, cross river on tarabita (rustic cable car), T217 0102, T09-9308 4675, www.ecuadorcloudforest. com. Beautifully constructed lodge in 44-ha property, newer cabins are spacious and very comfortable, includes 3 meals, some (but not all) excursions with a *guía nativo* and tubing, other adventure sports and horse riding are extra, no electricity, reserve in advance. Recommended.
$$$ Séptimo Paraíso, 2 km from Calacalí-La Independencia road along Mindo access road, then 500 m right on a small side road, well signed, T09-9368 4417, www.septimo paraiso.com. All wood lodge in a 420-ha reserve, comfortable, expensive restaurant, pool and jaccuzi, parking, lovely grounds, great birdwatching, walking trails open to non-guests for US$10. Recommended.
$$ Caskaffesu, Sixto Durán Ballén (the street leading to the stadium) y Av Quito, T217 0100, caskaffesu@yahoo.com. Pleasant hostal with nice courtyard, restaurant serves international food, US/Ecuadorean-run.
$$ El Descanso, 300 m from main street, take 1st right after bridge, T217 0213. Nice

house with comfortable rooms, cheaper in loft with shared bath, ample parking. Recommended.
$$ Hacienda San Vicente (Yellow House), 500 m south of the plaza, T217 0124, Quito T02-223 6275. Family-run lodge set in 200 ha of very rich forest, includes excellent breakfast, nice rooms, good walking trails open to non-guests for US$5, reservations required, good value. Highly recommended for nature lovers.
$$-$ Jardín de los Pájaros, 2 blocks from the main street, 1st right after bridge, T217 0159. Family-run hostel, includes good breakfast, small pool, parking, large covered terrace, good value. Recommended.
$ Rubby, by the stadium, T09-9193 1853, rubbyhostal@yahoo.com. Well maintained hostal with homely feel, includes breakfast, other meals on request, private or shared bath, electric shower, nice balcony with hammocks, good value. English spoken, owner Marcelo Arias is a birding guide.
$ Sandy, 1 block from the main street, 1st right after bridge. Family-run hostel in a wooden house, hot water, nice, good value.

West of Mindo *p451*
$$$$ Arashá, 4 km west of PV Maldonado, Km 121, T02-390 0007, Quito T02-244 9881 for reservations, www.arasharesort.com. Well-run resort and spa with pools, waterfalls (artificial and natural) and hiking trails. Comfortable thatched cabins, price includes all meals (world-class chef), use of the facilities (spa extra) and tours, can arrange transport from Quito, attentive staff, popular with families, elegant and very upmarket.
$$ Mirador Río Blanco, San Miguel de los Bancos, main road, at the east end of town, T02-277 0307. Popular hotel/ restaurant serving tropical dishes, small rooms, parking, terrace with bird feeders (many hummingbirds and tanagers) and magnificent views of the river.
$$ Selva Virgen, at Km 132, east of Puerto Quito, T02-390 1317, www.selvavirgen. ec. Nice *hostería* in a 100-ha property owned

by the Universidad Técnica Equinoccial (UTE). Staffed by students. Restaurant, spacious comfortable cabins with a/c, fridge, jacuzzi, and nice porch, cheaper in rooms with ceiling fan, pool, lovely grounds, part of the property is forested and has trails, facilities also open to restaurant patrons.

🍽 Restaurants

Western slopes of Pichincha p449
Pululahua

$$$ El Cráter, on the rim of the crater, access along road to the Mirador, T239 6399, www.elcrater.com. Open 1200-1600. Popular upscale restaurant with excellent views. Fancy hotel.

⚙ What to do

Western slopes of Pichincha p449
Pululahua

Green Horse Ranch, Astrid Muller, T09-8612 5433, www.horseranch.de. 1- to 9-day rides, among the options is a 3-day ride to Bellavista.

Mindo

Mindo Extreme Bird, Sector Saguambi, just out of town on the road to CEA, T217 0188, www.mindobird.com. Birdwatching, regattas, cycling, hiking, waterfalls, English spoken, very helpful.
Vinicio Pérez, T09-947 6867, www.bird watchershouse.corn. Recommended birding guide, he speaks some English.

🚍 Transport

Papallacta p449
Bus From **Quito**, buses bound for Tena or Lago Agrio from Terminal Quitumbe, or buses to Baeza from La Marín (see page 565), 2 hrs, US$2. The bus stop is east of (below) the village, at the junction of the main highway and the old road through town. A taxi to Termas costs US$1pp shared or US$3 private. The access to the Termas

is uphill from the village, off the old road. The complex is a 40-min walk from town. To return to Quito, most buses pass in the afternoon, travelling back at night is not recommended. The Termas also offer van service from Quito, US$110-180.

Refugio de Vida Silvestre Pasochoa
p449
Bus From Quito buses run from El Playón to Amaguaña US$0.50 (ask the driver to let you off at the 'Ejido de Amaguaña'); from there follow the signs. It's about 8-km walk, with not much traffic except at weekends, or book a pick-up from Amaguaña, **Cooperativa Pacheco Jr**, T02-287 7047, about US$6.

Western slopes of Pichincha p449
Pululahua
Bus Take a 'Mitad del Mundo' bus from La Ofelia Metrobus terminal. When boarding, ask if it goes as far as the Pululahua turn-off (some end their route at Mitad del Mundo, others at the Pululahua Mirador turn-off, others continue to Calacalí). It is a 30-min walk from the turn to the rim.

Tulipe
Bus From **Quito**, Estación La Ofelia, from 0615, US$1.50, 1¾ hrs: **Transportes Otavalo**, 6 daily, continue to Pacto (US$2, 2 hrs) and **Transportes Minas** 4 daily, continue to Chontal (US$2.50, 3 hrs). To **Las Tolas**, **Transportes Minas**, daily at 1730, US$2, 2½ hrs or take pickup from Tulipe, US$5.

Mindo p451
Bus From **Quito**, Estación La Ofelia, **Coop Flor del Valle**, T236 4393, Mon-Fri 0800, 0900, 1100, 1300, 1600, Sat and Sun 0740, 0820, 0920, 11, 1300, 1400, 1600 (last one on Sun at 1700 instead of 1600); Mindo-Quito: Mon-Fri 0630, 1100, 1345, 1500, Sat and Sun 0630, 1100 and hourly 1300-1700; US$2.50, 2 hrs; weekend buses fill quickly, buy ahead. You can also take any bus bound for Esmeraldas or San Miguel de los Bancos (see below) and get off at the turn-off for Mindo from where

there are taxis until 1930, US$0.50 pp or US$3 without sharing. **Cooperativa Kennedy** to/from **Santo Domingo** 6 daily, US$4, 3½ hrs, 0400 service from Mindo continues to **Guayaquil**, US$9, 9 hrs.

West of Mindo *p451*
From **Quito**, Terminal Carcelén, departures every 30 mins (**Coop Kennedy** and associates) to Santo Domingo via: **Nanegalito** (US$1.50, 1½ hrs), **San Miguel de los Bancos** (US$2.50, 2½ hrs), **Pedro Vicente Maldonado** (US$3, 3 hrs) and **Puerto Quito** (US$3.75, 3½ hrs). **Trans Esmeraldas** frequent departures from Terminal Carcelén and from their own station in La Mariscal, Santa María 870, also serve these destinations along the Quito–Esmeraldas route.

Northern Highlands

The area north of Quito to the Colombian border is outstandingly beautiful. The landscape is mountainous, with views of the Cotacachi, Imbabura, and Chiles volcanoes, as well as the glacier-covered Cayambe, interspersed with lakes. The region is also renowned for its artesanía.

Quito to Otavalo

On the way from the capital to the main tourist centre in northern Ecuador, the landscape is dominated by the Cayambe volcano.

Quito to Cayambe
At **Calderón**, 32 km north of the centre of Quito, you can see the famous bread figurines being made. Prices are lower than in Quito. On 1-2 November, the graves in the cemetery are decorated with flowers, drinks and food for the dead. The Corpus Christi processions are very colourful. Take a bus at La Ofelia Metrobus terminal.

The Pan-American Highway goes to **Guayllabamba**, home of the Quito zoo (www.quitozoo.org), where it branches, one road going through Cayambe and the second through Tabacundo before rejoining at Cajas. At 10 km past Guayllabamba on the road to Tabacundo, just north of the toll booth, a cobbled road to the left (signed Pirámides de Cochasquí) leads to Tocachi and further on to the **Parque Arqueológico Cochasquí** ① *T09-9822 0686, Quito T399 4405, http://parquecochasqui.blogspot.com, 0900-1600, US$3, entry only with a 1½-hr guided tour.* The protected area contains 15 truncated clay pyramids, nine with long ramps, built between AD 950 and 1550 by the Cara or Cayambi-Caranqui people. Festivals with dancing at the equinoxes and solstices. There is a site museum and views from the pyramids, south to Quito, are marvellous. From Terminal Carcelén, be sure to take a bus that goes on the Tabacundo road and ask to be let off at the turn-off. From there it's a pleasant 8-km walk. A taxi from Tabacundo costs US$12 or US$20 round trip with 1½-hour wait, from Cayambe US$15, US$25 round trip.

On the other road, 8 km before Cayambe, a globe carved out of rock by the Pan-American Highway is at the spot where the French expedition marked the Equator (small shop sells drinks and snacks). A few metres north is **Quitsato** ① *T02-236 3042, www.quitsato.org, US$1,* where studies about the equator and its importance to ancient cultures are carried out. There is a sun dial, 54 m in diameter, and a **solar culture exhibit**, with information about indigenous cultures and archaeological sites along the equator; here too there are special events for the solstices and equinoxes.

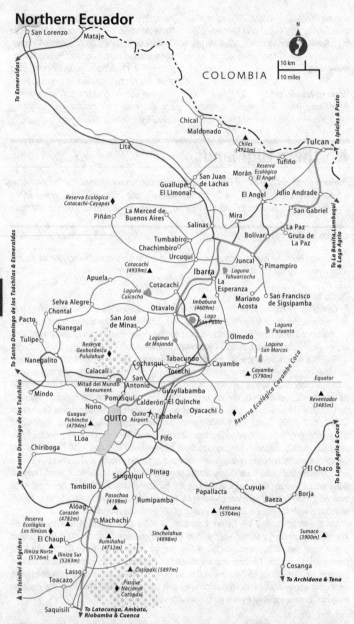

Northern Ecuador

San Lorenzo
Mataje

COLOMBIA

N

10 km
10 miles

To Esmeraldas

Chical
Maldonado
Chiles (4723m)
Tulcán
To Ipiales & Pasto
Tufiño
Lita
Morán
Reserva Ecológica El Angel
Julio Andrade
Guallupe
San Juan de Lachas
El Limonal
El Angel
Reserva Ecológica Cotacachi-Cayapas
San Gabriel
La Merced de Buenos Aires
Salinas
Mira
La Paz
Piñán
Bolívar
Gruta de La Paz
Tumbabiro
Chachimbiro
Urcuquí
Juncal
Pimampiro
To La Bonita, Lumbaquí & Lago Agrio
Cotacachi (4939m)
Ibarra
Laguna Yahuarcocha
Apuela
Cotacachi
La Esperanza
San Francisco de Sigsipamba
Laguna Cuicocha
Imbabura (4609m)
Mariano Acosta
Selva Alegre
Otavalo
Lago San Pablo
Chontal
San José de Minas
Lagunas de Mojanda
Olmedo
Laguna Puruanta
Pacto
Nanegal
Laguna San Marcos
Tulipe
Reserva Geobotánica Pululahua
Cochasquí
Tabacundo
Cayambe
Cayambe (5790m)
Nanegalito
Calacalí
Tocachi
Reserva Ecológica Cayambe Coca
To Santo Domingo de los Tsáchilas & Esmeraldas
Mitad del Mundo Monument
San Antonio
Equator
Mindo
Nono
Pomasqui
Guayllabamba
Reventador (3485m)
Calderón
El Quinche
Guagua Pichincha (4794m)
QUITO
Quito Airport
Oyacachi
Tababela
LLoa
Pifo
To Santo Domingo de los Tsáchilas
Chiriboga
To Lago Agrio & Coca
Sangolquí
Píntag
El Chaco
Tambillo
Pasochoa (4199m)
Rumipamba
Papallacta
Cuyuja
Baeza
Borja
Aláog
Corazón (4782m)
Antisana (5704m)
Machachi
Reserva Ecológica Los Ilinizas
Sincholahua (4898m)
Sumaco (3900m)
El Chaupi
Ruminahui (4712m)
Iliniza Norte (5126m)
Iliniza Sur (5263m)
Lasso
Cotopaxi (5897m)
To Isinliví & Sigchos
Toacazo
Cosanga
Parque Nacional Cotopaxi
To Archidona & Tena
Saquisilí
To Latacunga, Ambato, Riobamba & Cuenca

Cayambe → *Phone code: 02. Colour map 1, A4. Population: 53,700.*

Cayambe, on the eastern (righthand) branch of the highway, 25 km northeast of Guayllabamba, is overshadowed by the snow-capped volcano of the same name. The surrounding countryside consists of a few dairy farms and many flower plantations. The area is noted for its *bizcochos* (biscuits) served with *queso de hoja* (string cheese). At the Centro Cultural Espinoza-Jarrín, is the **Museo de la Ciudad** ① *Rocafuerte y Bolívar, Wed-Sun 0800-1700, free*, with displays about the Cayambi culture and ceramics found at **Puntiachil**, an important but poorly preserved archaeologic site at the edge of town. There is a fiesta in March for the equinox with plenty of local music; also Inti Raymi solstice and San Pedro celebrations in June. Market day is Sunday.

Volcán Cayambe → *Altitude: 5790 m.*

Cayambe, Ecuador's third highest peak, lies within the **Reserva Ecológica Cayambe-Coca** ① *T02-211 0370*. It is the highest point in the world to lie so close to the Equator (3.75 km north). The equator goes over the mountain's flanks. About 1 km south of Cayambe is an unmarked cobbled road heading east via Juan Montalvo, leading in 26 km to the Ruales-Oleas-Berge refuge at 4600 m. The *refugio* was being rebuilt in 2014 and was expected to reopen later that year. The standard climbing route, from the west, uses the refuge as a base. There is a crevasse near the summit which can be very difficult to cross if there isn't enough snow, ask the refuge keeper about conditions. There are nice acclimatization hikes around the refuge. Otavalo and Quito operators offer tours here.

⊙ Quito to Otavalo listings

For hotel and restaurant price codes, and other relevant information, see pages 14-17.

⊜ Where to stay

Cayambe *p457*
$$$ Hacienda Guachalá, south of Cayambe on the road to Cangahua, T236 3042, www.guachala.com. A nicely restored colonial hacienda, the chapel (1580) is built on top of an Inca structure. Simple but comfortable rooms in older section and fancier ones in newer area, fireplaces, delicious meals, covered swimming pool, parking, attentive service, good walking, horses for rent, excursions to nearby pre-Inca ruins, small museum.

$$$-$$ Jatun Huasi, Panamericana Norte Km 1.5, T236 3777. US motel style, cabins and rooms with fireplace and frigo-bar, restaurant, indoor pool, spa, parking.

$$ Shungu Huasi, Camino a Granobles, 1 km northwest of town, T236 1847, www.shunguhuasi.com. Comfortable cabins in a 6.5-ha ranch, excellent Italian restaurant, heaters on request, nice setting, attentive service, offers horse riding and vehicle excursions. Recommended.

$ La Gran Colombia, Panamericana y Calderón, T236 1238. Modern multi-storey building, restaurant, parking, traffic noise in front rooms.

⊘ Restaurants

Cayambe *p457*
$$$ Casa de Fernando, Panamericana Norte Km 1.5. Varied menu, good international food.

$ Aroma, Bolívar 404 y Ascázubi. Large choice of set lunches and à la carte, variety of desserts, very good, closed Wed.

⊖ Transport

Cayambe *p457*
Bus Flor del Valle, from La Ofelia, **Quito**, every 10 mins 0530-2100, US$1.25, 1½ hrs.

Their Cayambe station is at Montalvo y Junín. To **Otavalo**, from traffic circle at Bolívar y Av N Jarrín, every 15 mins, US$0.75, 45 mins.

Volcán Cayambe *p457*
Road Most vehicles can go as far as the **Hacienda Piemonte El Hato** (at about 3500 m) from where it is a 3- to 4-hr walk, longer if heavily laden or if it is windy, but

it is a beautiful walk. Regular pick-ups can often make it to 'la Z', a sharp curve on the road 30-mins' walk to the refugio. 4WDs can often make it to the refugio. Pick-ups can be hired by the market in Cayambe, Junín y Ascázubi, US$35, 1½-2 hrs. Arrange ahead for return transport. A milk truck runs from Cayambe's hospital to the hacienda at 0600, returning between 1700-1900.

Otavalo and around → *Phone code: 06. Colour map 1, A4. Population: 55,000. Altitude: 2530 m.*

Otavalo, only a short distance from the capital, is a must on any tourist itinerary in Ecuador. The Tabacundo and Cayambe roads join at Cajas, then cross the *páramo* and suddenly descend into the land of the *Otavaleños*, a thriving, prosperous group, famous for their prodigious production of woollens. The town itself, consisting of rather functional modern buildings, is one of South America's most important centres of ethno-tourism and its enormous Saturday market, featuring a dazzling array of textiles and crafts, is second to none and not to be missed. Men here wear their hair long and plaited under a broad-brimmed hat; they wear white, calf-length trousers and blue ponchos. The women's colourful costumes consist of embroidered blouses, shoulder wraps and many coloured beads. Indigenous families speak Quichua at home, although it is losing some ground to Spanish with the younger generation. Otavalo is set in beautiful countryside, with mountains, lakes and small villages nearby. The area is worth exploring for three or four days.

Arriving in Otavalo
Tourist offices Contact **iTur** ① *corner of Plaza de Ponchos, Jaramillo y Quiroga, T292 1994, Mon-Fri 0800-1800, Sat 0800-1600,* for local and regional information.

Otavalo
The **Saturday market** comprises four different markets in various parts of the town with the central streets filled with vendors. The *artesanías* market is held 0700-1800, based around the Plaza de Ponchos (Plaza Centenario). The livestock section begins at 0500 until 0900, outside the centre, west of the Panamericana; go west on Calderón from the town centre. The produce market lasts from 0700 till 1400, in Plaza 24 de Mayo; it is scheduled to move to the old stadium, west of the centre in late 2014. The *artesanías* industry is so big that the Plaza de Ponchos is filled with vendors every day of the week. The selection is better on Saturday but prices are a little higher than other days when the atmosphere is more relaxed. Wednesday is also an important market day with more movement than other weekdays. Polite bargaining is appropriate in the market and shops. Otavaleños not only sell goods they weave and sew themselves, but they bring crafts from throughout Ecuador and from Peru and Bolivia. Indigenous people in the market respond better to photography if you buy something first, then ask politely. The **Museo Etnográfico Otavalango** ① *Vía a Selva Alegre Km 1, antigua Fábrica San Pedro, T09-8726 9827, Mon-Sat 0900-1700, call ahead, US$5,* displays on all cultural aspects of Otavaleño life; live presentations of local traditions for groups. The **Museo de Tejidos El Obraje** ① *Sucre 6-08 y Olmedo, T292 0261, US$2, call ahead,* shows the process of traditional Otavalo weaving from shearing to final products. There are good views of town from **Centro de Exposiciones El Colibrí** ① *C Morales past the railway line.*

Around Otavalo

Otavalo weavers come from dozens of communities. Many families weave and visitors should shop around as the less known weavers often have better prices and some of the most famous ones only sell from their homes, especially in Agato and Peguche. The easiest villages to visit are Ilumán (there are also many felt hatmakers in town and *yachacs*, or shamen, mostly north of the plaza – look for signs); Agato; Carabuela (many homes sell crafts including wool sweaters); Peguche. These villages are only 15-30 minutes away and have good bus service; buses leave from the Terminal and stop at Plaza Copacabana (Atahualpa y Montalvo). You can also take a taxi.

To reach the lovely **Cascada de Peguche**, from Peguche's plaza, facing the church, head right and continue straight until the road forks. Take the lower fork to the right, but not

Otavalo

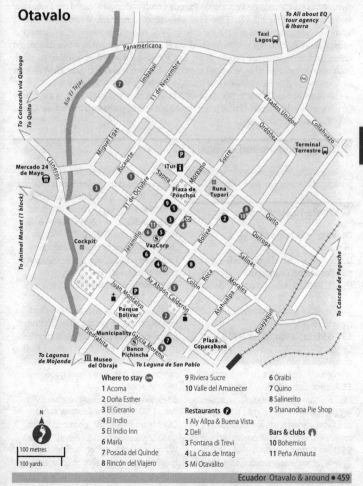

Where to stay		
1 Acoma	9 Riviera Sucre	6 Oraibi
2 Doña Esther	10 Valle del Amanecer	7 Quino
3 El Geranio		8 Salinerito
4 El Indio	**Restaurants**	9 Shanandoa Pie Shop
5 El Indio Inn	1 Aly Allpa & Buena Vista	
6 María	2 Deli	**Bars & clubs**
7 Posada del Quinde	3 Fontana di Trevi	10 Bohemios
8 Rincón del Viajero	4 La Casa de Intag	11 Peña Amauta
	5 Mi Otavalito	

the road that heads downhill. From the top of the falls (left side, excellent views) you can continue the walk to Lago San Pablo. The **Pawkar Raimi** festival is held in Peguche before carnival. At the falls there is a small information centre (contributions are appreciated).

The **Ciclovía** is a bicycle path which runs along the old rail line 21 km between Eugenio Espejo de Cajas and Otavalo. Because of the slope, starting in Cajas is recommended. You can take a tour or hire a bike and take a bus bound for Quito to the bike path.

Lago San Pablo

There is a network of old roads and trails between Otavalo and Lago San Pablo, none of which takes more than two hours to explore. It is worth walking either to or back from the lake for the views. Going in a group is recommended for safety. A nice half-day excursion is via Cascada de Peguche to **Parque Cóndor** ① *on a hill called Curiloma, near the community of Pucará Alto, T304 9399, www.parquecondor.org, Wed-Sun 0930-1700, raptor flight demonstrations at 1130 and 1530, US$4.50, crowded on weekends*, a reserve and birds of prey rehabilitation centre, and back via **El Lechero**, a lookout by a tree considered sacred among indigenous people. From **San Pablo del Lago** it is possible to climb **Imbabura** volcano (4630 m, a serious climb and frequently under cloud), allow at least six hours to reach the summit and four hours for the descent. An alternative access is from La Esperanza or San Clemente (see page 465). Easier, and no less impressive, is the nearby Cerro Huarmi Imbabura, 3845 m, it is not signed but several paths lead there. Take a good map, food and warm clothing.

⊙ Otavalo and around listings

For hotel and restaurant price codes, and other relevant information, see pages 14-17.

⊜ Where to stay

Otavalo *p458, map p459*
In town
Hotels may be full on Fri night before market.
$$$ Posada del Quinde, Quito y Miguel Egas, T292 0750, www.posadaquinde.com. Nicely decorated, all rooms around a lovely garden, also 2 suites, good restaurant, parking, US run.
$$$-$$ El Indio Inn, Bolívar 9-04 y Calderón, T292 2922, www.hotelelindioinn. com. Modern hotel, carpeted rooms and simple suites, restaurant, parking, spa.
$$ Acoma, Salinas 07-57 y 31 de Octubre, T292 6570, www.acomahotel.com. Lovely re-built home in colonial style, parking, nice comfortable rooms, some with balcony, 1 room with bathtub, 2 suites with kitchenette.
$$ Doña Esther, Montalvo 4-44 y Bolívar, T292 0739, www.otavalohotel.com. Nicely

restored colonial house, a hotel for over 100 years, very good restaurant, rooms with nice wooden floors, colourful decor, pleasant atmosphere, transfers to Quito or airport.
$$-$ El Indio, Sucre 12-14 y Salinas, near Plaza de Ponchos, T292 0060, www.hostal elindio.com. In multi-storey building, ask for a room with balcony, simple restaurant, parking, helpful service.
$$-$ Rincón del Viajero, Roca 11-07 y Quiroga, T292 1741, www.hostalrincon delviajero.com. Very pleasant hostel and meeting place. Simple but nicely decorated rooms, includes a choice of good breakfasts, private or shared bath, small parking, rooftop hammocks, sitting room with fireplace, camping, US/Ecuadorean-run, good value. Recommended.
$$-$ Riviera Sucre, García Moreno 380 y Roca, T292 0241, www.rivierasucre.com. Older hotel with ample renovated rooms, good breakfast available, cafeteria, 1 room with shared bath, kitchen facilities, book exchange, bookshop with good selection

of English and German titles, nice common areas, garden and courtyard, good meeting place. Recommended.

$$-$ Valle del Amanecer, Roca y Quiroga, T292 0990. Small rooms, nice courtyard with hammocks, private or shared bath, bike hire, popular.

$ El Geranio, Ricaurte y Morales, T292 0185, hgeranio@hotmail.com. Breakfast available cheaper with electric shower, laundry and cooking facilities, quiet, family-run, popular, runs trips. Good value, recommended.

$ María, Jaramillo y Colón, T292 0672. Bright rooms in multi-storey building, parking for small car. Good value.

$ Santa Fé, Roca 7-34 y García moreno, T292 3640, www.hotelsantafeotavalo.com. Modern, nice pine decoration, restaurant, run by indigenous Otavaleños, good value.

Camping, in Punyaro, Km 2 vía a Mojanda. US$5 pp. Camping area in a rural property, hot shower and Wi-Fi, arrange through Rincón del Viajero, above.

Out of town

$$$$ Ali Shungu Mountaintop Lodge, 5 km west of Otavalo by the village of Yambiro, T09-8950 9945, www.alishungu mountaintoplodge.com. Country inn on a 16 ha private reserve. 4 comfortable nicely decorated guest houses for 6, each with living room, woodstove and kitchenette. Includes breakfast and dinner (vegetarian available), horse riding, US-run.

$$$$ Casa Mojanda, Vía a Mojanda Km 3.5, T09-9972 0890, www.casamojanda.com. Comfortable cabins set in a beautiful hillside. Breakfast and tasty dinner prepared with ingredients from own organic garden and short guided hike to waterfall; each room is decorated with its own elegant touch, outdoor hot tub with great views, quiet, good library, horse riding. Recommended.

$$$ Hacienda Pinsaquí, Panamericana Norte Km 5, 300 m north of the turn-off for Cotacachi, T294 6116, www.hacienda pinsaqui.com. Converted hacienda with 30 suites, one with jacuzzi, restaurant with

lovely dining room, lounge with fireplace, beautiful antiques, colonial ambience, gardens, horse riding, biking.

$$$ Las Palmeras de Quichinche, outside Quichinche, 15 mins by bus from Otavalo, T292 2607, www.laspalmerasinn.com. Cabins with terrace and fireplace in a rural setting, restaurant, parking, nice grounds and views, pool table and ping-pong, British owned.

$$ La Casa de Hacienda, Entrance at Panamericana Norte Km 3, then 300 m east, T269 0245, www.hosteriacasadehacienda. com. Tasteful cabins with fireplace, restaurant, parking, advance reservations required for horse riding.

$$ La Luna de Mojanda, On a side-road going south off the Mojanda road at Km 4, T09-9315 6082, www.lalunaecuador.com. Pleasant hostel in nice surroundings, some rooms with fireplace, heater and private bath, others with shared bath, US$12 pp in dorm, camping US$8 pp, terrace with hammocks, pleasant dining room/lounge, transport information on hostel's website, excursions arranged, popular. Recommended.

$$ Rose Cottage, Vía a Mojanda Km 3, T09-9772 8115, www.rosecottageecuador. com. Various rooms and prices in 7 separate houses, some with private bath, US$10 pp in dorm, camping US$4 pp, restaurant, hammocks, nice views.

Around Otavalo: Peguche p459

$$$ La Casa Sol, near the Cascada de Peguche, T269 0500. Comfortable rustic construction set on a hillside. Rooms and suites with balcony, some with fireplace, lovely attention to detail, restaurant.

$$ Aya Huma, on the railway line in Peguche, T269 0164, www.ayahuma.com. In a country setting between the unused rail tracks and the river. Quiet, pleasant atmosphere, Dutch/Ecuadorean-run, popular. Recommended.

Lago San Pablo p460

$$$ Hacienda Cusín, by the village of San Pablo del Lago to the southeast of the lake, T291 8013, www.haciendacusin.com. A converted 17th-century hacienda with lovely courtyard and garden, fine expensive restaurant, rooms with fireplace, sports facilities (pool, horses, bikes, squash court, games room), library, book in advance, British run. Recommended.

$$$ Puerto Lago, 6 km from Otavalo, just off the Panamericana on the west side of the lake, T292 0920, www.puertolago. com. Modern hostería in a lovely setting on the lakeshore, good expensive restaurant overlooking the lake, rooms and suites with fireplace, very hospitable, a good place to watch the sunset, includes the use of row-boats, pedalos and kayaks, other water sports extra.

$$ Green House, C 24 de Junio, Comunidad Araque, by the east shore of the lake, northwest of San Pablo del Lago, T291 9298, www.araquebyb.hostel.com. Family-run *hostal*, some rooms with bath, others with detached bath, dinner on request, sitting room with fireplace, rooftop terrace with views, transport.

🍴 Restaurants

Otavalo *p458, map p459*
$$ Quino, Roca 7-40 y Juan Montalvo. Tue-Sun 1030-2300, Mon 1730-2300. Traditional coastal cooking and some meat dishes, pleasant seating around patio.
$$-$ Buena Vista, Salinas entre Sucre y Jaramillo, p2, www.buenavistaotavalo.com. 1200-2200, Sat from 0900, closed Tue. Bistro with balcony overlooking Plaza de Ponchos. Good international food, sandwiches, salads, vegetarian options, trout, good coffee, Wi-Fi.
$$-$ Deli, Quiroga 12-18 y Bolívar. Mon-Fri 1000-2100, Sat 0800-2200. Good Mexican and international food, also pizza, nice desserts, pleasant atmosphere, family-run, good value.
$$-$ Fontana di Trevi, Sucre 12-05 y Salinas, 2nd floor. Daily 1300-2100. Overlooking Calle Sucre, good pizza and pasta, nice juices, friendly service.

$$-$ Mi Otavalito, Sucre y Morales. Good for set lunch and international food à la carte.
$$-$ Oraibi, Sucre y Colón. Wed-Sat 0800-2000. Vegetarian food in nice patio setting, pizza, salads, pasta, Mexican, breakfast, Swiss-owned.
$ Aly Allpa, Salinas 509 at Plaza de Ponchos. Daily 0730-2030. Good-value set meals, breakfast and à la carte including trout, vegetarian, meat. Recommended.

Cafés
La Casa de Intag, Colón 465 y Sucre. Mon-Sat 0800-1800. Fair trade cafeteria/shop run by Intag coffee growers and artisans associations. Good organic coffee, breakfast, pancakes, sandwiches, sisal crafts, fruit pulp and more.
Salinerito, Bolívar 10-08 y Morales. Mon-Sat 0800-2200. Café/deli run by the Salinas de Guaranda coop. Good sandwiches, breakfast, coffee and juices. A good place to buy supplies such as cheese, cold cuts and chocolate.
Shanandoa Pie Shop, Salinas y Jaramillo. 1100-2100, Sat from 0900. Good fruit pies, milk shakes and ice cream, popular meeting place, an Otavalo tradition.

🍸 Bars and clubs

Otavalo *p458, map p459*
Otavalo is generally safe but avoid deserted areas at night. Nightlife is concentrated at Morales y Jaramillo and C 31 de Octubre. Peñas are open Fri-Sat from 1930, entrance US$3.
Bohemios, Colón entre Bolívar y Sucre. Live folk music, also Latin music.
Peña Amauta, Morales 5-11 y Jaramillo. Good local bands, welcoming, mainly foreigners.

🎉 Festivals

Otavalo *p458, map p459*
The **end of Jun** combines the Inti Raymi celebrations of the summer solstice (**21 Jun**), with the Fiesta de San Juan

(**24 Jun**) and the **Fiesta de San Pedro y San Pablo** (**29 Jun**). These combined festivities are known as **Los San Juanes** and participants are mostly indigenous. Most of the action takes place in the smaller communities surrounding Otavalo, each one celebrates separately on different dates, some of them for a full week. The celebration begins with a ritual bath, the Peguche waterfall is used by Otavalo residents (a personal spiritual activity, best carried out without visitors and certainly without cameras). In Otavalo, indigenous families have costume parties, which at times spill over onto the streets. In the San Juan neighbourhood, near the Yanayacu baths, there is a week-long celebration with food, drink and music. **Fiesta del Yamor** and **Colla Raimi 1st 2 weeks of Sep**, feature local dishes, amusement parks, bands in the plaza and sporting events. **Oct**, Mes de la cultura, cultural events throughout the month. **Last Oct weekend**, Mojanda Arriba is an annual full day hike from Malchinguí over Mojanda to reach Otavalo for the foundation celebrations.

⏱ What to do

Otavalo *p458, map p459*
Horse riding Several operators offer riding tours. Half-day trips to nearby attractions cost US$25-35. Full-day trips such as Cuicocha or Mojanda cost US$40-50.
Mountain bikes Several tour operators rent bikes and offer cycling tours for US$35-60 a day trip. See also **Ciclovía**, page 460. Rentals cost US$10-12 per day **Hostal Valle del Amanecer** (see Where to stay), good bikes. **La Tierra** craft shop, Salinas 503 y Sucre, Plaza de Ponchos, good equipment. **Taller Ciclo Primaxi**, Ricaurte y Morales and in Peguche.

Tour operators
Most common tours are to indigenous communities, Cuicocha and Mojanda, US$20-30 pp. Independent travel to the Lagunas de Mojanda is not recommended because of public safety problems. Best go with a tour.
All about EQ, Los Corazas 433 y Albarracín, at the north end of town, T292 3633, www.all-about-ecuador.com. Interesting itineraries, trekking and horse riding tours, climbing, cycling, trips to Intag, Piñán, Cayambe, Oyacachi, volunteering on organic farms. English and French spoken. Recommended.
Ecomontes, Sucre y Morales, T292 6244, www.ecomontestour.com. A branch of a Quito operator, trekking, climbing, rafting, also sell tours to Cuyabeno and Galápagos.
Runa Tupari, Sucre y Quito, T292 2320, www.runatupari.com. Arranges indigenous homestays in the Cotacachi area, also the usual tours, trekking, horse riding and cycling trips; also transport.

Train rides
The track from Otavalo to Ibarra is being restored and a tourist ride is expected to operate by late 2014. Train station at Guayaquil y J Montalvo.

🚍 Transport

Otavalo *p458, map p459*
Note Never leave anything in your car or taxi in the street. There are public car parks at Juan Montalvo y Sucre, by Parque Bolívar, and on Quito between 31 de Octubre and Jaramillo.
Bus Terminal at Atahualpa y Ordóñez (no departures after 1830). To **Quito** 2 hrs, US$2, every 10 mins; all depart from the Terminal Carcelén in Quito, **Coop Otavalo** and **Coop Los Lagos** go into Otavalo, buses bound for Ibarra or Tulcán drop you off at the highway, this is inconvenient and not safe at night. From **Quito** or airport by taxi takes 1½ hrs, US$50 one way, US$80 return with 3 hrs wait; shared taxis with **Taxis Lagos** (in Quito, Asunción Oe2-146 y Versalles, T256 5992; in Otavalo, Av Los Sarances y Panamericana, T292 3203), who run a hotel

to hotel service (to/from modern Quito only) and will divert to resorts just off the highway; Mon-Sat hourly, 5 departures on Sun, 1½ hrs, US$9.50 pp, buy ticket at least 1 day before, they also go from Quito to Ibarra. Tour operators also offer tranfers. Bus to **Ibarra**, every 4 mins, US$0.45, 40 mins. To **Peguche**, city bus on Av Atahualpa, every 10 mins, bus stops in front of the terminal and at Plaza Copacabana, US$0.20. To the **Intag region**, 5 daily.

Lago San Pablo *p460*
Bus From **Otavalo** to San Pablo del Lago every 25 mins, more often on Sat, US$0.25, 30 mins; taxi US$4.

⊙ Directory

Otavalo *p458, map p459*
Banks Banco del Austro, Sucre y Quiroga. Banco del Pacífico, Bolívar 614 y García Moreno. **Fax Cambios**, Salinas y Sucre, T292 0501, Mon-Sat 0745-1900, poor rates for cash (7 currencies), 3% commission on TCs. **Vaz Corp**, Sucre 11-13 y Morales, T292 3500, Tue-Sat 0830-1700, exchange 8 currencies, 1.8% comission on TCs (minimum US$2). **Language schools** Instituto Superior de Español, Jaramillo 6-23 y Morales, T292 7354. Mundo Andino Internacional, Salinas 404 y Bolívar, T292 1864, www. mandinospanishschool.com. Salsa and cooking classes included. Otavalo Spanish Institute, 31 de Octubre 47-64 y Salinas, p 3, T292 1404, www.otavalospanish.com, also offers Quichua lessons.

Otavalo to the Colombian border

Northwest of Otavalo is Cotacachi from where a road goes west to the Cotacachi-Cayapas reserve and the subtropical Intag region. The main highway goes north to the city of Ibarra and beyond into the hot Chota Valley from where a branch road goes west to the subtropical valley of the Río Mira and the coastal town of San Lorenzo. The Panamericana reaches the border at the busy town of Tulcán, with its fantastic cemetery topiary.

Cotacachi → *Phone code: 06. Colour map 1, A4. Population: 17,700. Altitude: 2440 m.*
West of the road between Otavalo and Ibarra is Cotacachi, home to a growing expatriate community. Leather goods are made and sold here. There is also access along a secondary road from Otavalo through Quiroga. The **Casa de las Culturas** ⊙ *Bolívar 1334 y 9 de Octubre*, a beautifully refurbished 19th-century building is a monument to peace. It houses a library, café and temporary exhibits. The **Museo de las Culturas** ⊙ *García Moreno 13-41y Bolívar, Mon-Fri 0800-1200, 1400-1700, Sat-Sun 0800-1300, donations appreciated*, renovated in 2013, has good displays of early Ecuadorean history and regional crafts and traditions. For information, **Empresa Pública de Turismo** ⊙ *at Hostería Cuicocha, by the lake (see below), T301 7218*. Additional tourist information and a city map are found in www.cotacachi.gob.ec. Local festivals include **Inti Raymi/San Juan** in June and **Jora** during the September equinox.

Laguna Cuicocha → *Altitude: 3070 m.*
⊙ *15 km from Cotacachi, visitor centre has good natural history and cultural displays, daily 0800-1700.*
This crater lake is part of the **Reserva Ecológica Cotacachi-Cayapas**, which extends from Cotacachi volcano to the tropical lowlands on the Río Cayapas in Esmeraldas. It is a crater lake with two islands, which are closed to the public to protect the native species. There is a well-marked, 8-km path around the lake, which takes four to five hours and provides spectacular

views of the Cotacachi, Imbabura and, occasionally, Cayambe peaks. The best views are in the morning, when condors can sometimes be seen. There is a lookout at 3 km, two hours from the start. Take water and a waterproof jacket. There is a shorter trail which takes 40 minutes. Motor boat rides around the islands, US$3.25 per person for minimum six persons.

Warnings Enquire locally about safety before heading out and don't take valuables. Do not eat the berries which grow near the lake, as some are poisonous. The path around the lake is not for vertigo sufferers.

To the northwest of Otavalo lies the lush subtropical region of **Intag**, reached along a road (being paved in 2014) that follows the southern edge of Cuicocha and continues to the town of **Apuela**. The region's primary cloudforest is threatened by a proposed large-scale copper mine, vigorously opposed by local communities. See **Defensa y Conservación Ecológica de Intag**, www.decoin.org, for local conservation and community development projects. The area's rivers will also be affected by an irrigation and hydroelectric scheme in the Piñan area, see Northwest of Ibarra, below. The **Asociación Agroartesanal de Café Río Intag (AACRI)** ⓘ *on the main street opposite the health centre, T06-264 8489, www.aacri. com*, a fair trade organic coffee grower's association, offers tours of coffee, sisal and sugar cane plantations and processing plants, also lodging and volunteer opportunities. Beyond, are pleasant thermal baths at **Nangulví**. The area is rich in cloud forest and has several nature reserves. On the southwest boundary of the Cotacachi-Cayapas reserve is **Los Cedros Research Station** ⓘ *T09-8460 0274, www.reservaloscedros.org*, 6400 ha of pristine cloud forest, with abundant orchids and bird life. Full board in **$$$** range.

Ibarra and around → *Phone code: 06. Colour map 1, A4. Pop: 137,000. Altitude: 2225 m.*

Ibarra the provincial capital is the main commercial centre and transport hub of the northern highlands. The city has an interesting ethnic mix, with blacks from the Chota valley and Esmeraldas alongside Otavaleños and other highland *indígenas*, mestizos and Colombian immigrants. For information: **Dirección de Turismo de Imbabura** ⓘ *Bolívar y Oviedo, T295 5832, www.imbaburaturismo.gob.ec, Mon-Fri 0800-1300, 1500-1800*, and the municipal tourist office, **i Tur** ⓘ *Sucre y Oviedo, T260 8489, www.touribarra.gob.ec, free Wi-Fi, Mon-Fri 0800-1230, 1400-1730*.

On **Parque Pedro Moncayo** stand the Cathedral, the Municipio and Gobernación. One block away, at Flores y Olmedo, is the smaller Parque 9 de Octubre or **Parque de la Merced** after its church. Beyond the railway station, to the south and west of the centre, is a busy commercial area with several markets beyond which is the bus terminal. The **Museo Regional Sierra Norte** ⓘ *Sucre 7-21 y Oviedo, T260 2093, Mon-Fri, 0830-1700, Sat 1000-1300, 1400-1600*, has interesting displays about cultures from northern Ecuador. **Bosque Protector Guayabillas** ⓘ *Urbanización La Victoria, on the eastern outskirts of town, www. guayabillas.com, daily 0900-1730*, is a 54-ha park on a hill overlooking the city. There are trails, animals, volunteer opportunities, and accommodation. **Virgen del Carmen** festival is on 16 July and **Fiesta de los Lagos** is in the last weekend of September.

Off the main road between Otavalo and Ibarra is **San Antonio de Ibarra**, well known for its wood carvings. It is worth seeing the range of styles and techniques and shopping around in the galleries and workshops. About 8 km from Ibarra on the road to Olmedo is **La Esperanza**, a pretty village in beautiful surroundings. Some 15 km further along, by Angochagua is the community of **Zuleta**. The region is known for its fine embroidery. West of La Esperanza, along a road that starts at Avenida Atahualpa, and also 8 km from Ibarra, is the community of **San Clemente**, which has a very good grassroots tourism project, **Pukyu Pamba**, see Where to stay below. From either La Esperanza or San Clemente you can climb **Cubilche** volcano and **Imbabura**, more easily than from San Pablo del Lago. From the top you can walk down to Lago San Pablo (see page 460). *Guías nativos* are available for these climbs.

Ibarra to the coast The spectacular train ride from Ibarra to San Lorenzo on the Pacific coast no longer operates. A tourist train runs on a small section of this route, see page 472. Some 24 km north of Ibarra is the turn-off west for **Salinas**, a mainly Afro-Ecuadorean village with a Museo de la Sal, and the very scenic road beside the Río Mira down to San Lorenzo. At 41 km from the turn-off are the villages of **Guallupe**, **El Limonal** (see Where to stay, below), and **San Juan de Lachas**, in a lush subtropical area. Ceramic masks and figurines are produced at the latter. In **Lita**, 33 km from Guallupe, there is nice swimming in the river. Beyond is the Río Chuchubi with waterfalls and swimming holes; here is **Las Siete Cascadas resort** ① *entry US$10, guide US$10 per group,* (see Where to stay, below). It is 66 km from Lita to **Calderón**, where this road meets the coastal highway coming from Esmeraldas. Two kilometres before the junction, on the Río Tululbí, is **Hostería Tunda Loma** (see Where to stay, page 556). About 7 km beyond is San Lorenzo (see page 554).

Northwest of Ibarra Along a secondary road to the northwest of Ibarra is the town of **Urcuquí** with Yachay, a university and national research and technology centre, opened in 2014 in a beautiful historic hacienda, and a basic hotel. From just south of Urcuquí, a road leads via Irunguicho towards the **Piñán lakes**, a beautiful, remote, high *páramo* region, part of the Reserva Ecológica Cotacachi-Cayapas. The local community of Piñán (3112 m) has a tourism programme (www.pinantrek.com), with a well-equipped refuge (US$12 per person, meals available), *guías nativos* (US$15 per day) and muleteers (US$12 per day, per horse). Another access to the hamlet of Piñán is via La Merced de Buenos Aires, a village reached form either Tumbabiro (see below) or Guallupe (on the road to the coast). Along the Tumabiro access is the community of Sachapamba, which offers meals and muleteers. The nicest lakes, Donoso and Caricocha, are one-hour walk from the community. They can also be reached walking from either Chachimbiro (see below), Irubí or Cuellaje in the Intag area. Otavalo agencies and hotels in Chachimbiro and Tumababiro also offer trekking tours to Piñán. Note that an irrigation and hydroelectric scheme, proposed in 2014, will affect this beautiful area. Beyond Urcuquí is the friendly town of **Tumbabiro**, with a mild climate, a good base from which to explore this region (several lodgings, see Where to stay page 470); it can also be reached from Salinas on the road to the coast. Some 8 km from Tumbabiro along a side road, set on the slopes of an extinct volcano, is **Chachimbiro**, a good area for walking and horseback riding, with several resorts with thermal baths (see Where to stay, page 470). The largest one, run by the provincial government, is **Santa Agua Chachimbiro** ① *T264 8308, http://imbabura.gob.ec/chachimbiro, 0700-2000, entry to recreational pools US$5, to medicinal pools and spa US$10,* with several hot mineral pools, lodging, restaurants, zipline and horses for riding; weekends can be crowded.

North to Colombia

From Ibarra the Pan-American highway goes past Laguna Yahuarcocha (with a few hotels, a campground, see Where to stay, Ibarra, and many food stalls, busy on weekends) and then descends to the hot dry Chota valley, a centre of Afro-Ecuadorean culture. Beyond the turn-off for Salinas and San Lorenzo, 30 km from Ibarra, the highway divides. One branch follows an older route through Mira and El Angel to Tulcán on the Colombian border. At **Mascarilla**, 1 km along this road, ceramic masks are made (hostal run by the women's craft group, **El Patio de mi Casa**, T09-9449 4029, **$$** full-board). This road is paved and in good condition as far as **El Angel** (3000 m), but deteriorates thereafter. It is passable with 4WD and is a great mountain bike route.

El Angel's main plaza retains a few trees sculpted by José Franco (see Tulcán Cemetery, page 467); market day Monday. The **Reserva Ecológica El Angel** ① *T297 7597, office in El Angel near the Municipio; best time to visit May to Aug,* nearby protects 15,715 ha of *páramo* ranging in altitude from 3400 m to 4768 m. The reserve contains large stands of the velvet-leaved *frailejón* plant, also found in the Andes of Colombia and Venezuela. Also of interest are the spiny *achupallas, bromeliads* with giant compound flowers. The fauna includes *curiquingues* (caracara), deer, foxes, and a few condors. From El Angel follow the poor road north towards Tulcán for 16 km to **El Voladero** ranger station/shelter, where a self-guided trail climbs over a low ridge (30 minutes' walk) to two crystal-clear lakes. Pickups or taxis from the main plaza of El Angel charge US$25 return with one-hour wait for a day trip to El Voladero. A longer route to another area follows an equally poor road to Cerro Socabones, beginning at **La Libertad**, 3.5 km north of El Angel (transport El Angel–Cerro Socabones, US$30 return). It climbs gradually to reach the high *páramo* at the centre of the reserve and, in 40 minutes, the **El Salado** ranger station. From Socabones the road descends to the village of **Morán** (lodging and guides, transport with Sr Calderón, T09-9128 4022), the start of a pleasant three-day walk to Las Juntas, a warm area, off the Ibarra–San Lorenzo road.

Eastern route to the border

The second branch (the modern Pan-American Highway), in good repair but with many heavy lorries, runs east through the warm Chota valley to El Juncal, before turning north to reach Tulcán via Bolívar and San Gabriel. A good paved road runs between Bolívar and El Angel, connecting the two branches.

Bolívar is a neat little town where the houses and the interior of its church are painted in lively pastel colours. At the **Museo Paleontológico** ① by the north entrance to town, US$2, remains of a mammoth, found nearby, can be seen. There is a Friday market.

Some 16 km north of Bolívar is **San Gabriel**, an important commercial centre. The 60-m-high **Paluz** waterfall is 4 km north of town, beyond a smaller waterfall. To the southeast, 11 km from town on the road to Piartal is **Bosque de Arrayanes**, a 16-ha mature forest with a predominance of myrtle trees, some reaching 20 m, taxi US$5.

East of San Gabriel by 20 km is the tiny community of **Mariscal Sucre** also known as Colonia Huaqueña, the gateway to the **Guandera Reserve and Biological Station** ① *the reserve is part of Fundación Jatun Sacha. Reservations should be made at the Quito office, T02-331 7163, www.jatunsacha.org.* You can see bromeliads, orchids, toucans and other wildlife in temperate forest and *frailejón páramo*. From San Gabriel, take a taxi to Mariscal Sucre, one hour, then walk 30 minutes to the reserve, or make arrangements with Jatun Sacha.

Between San Gabriel and Tulcán is the little town of Julio Andrade, with **Hotel Naderic** and a Saturday market (good for horses and other large animals) and, afterwards, paddleball games. This is the beginning of the road to La Bonita, Lumbaqui and Lago Agrio. The road follows the frontier for much of the route. Make enquiries about safety before taking this beautiful route.

Tulcán → *Phone code: 06. Colour map 1, A4. Population: 61,900. Altitude: 2960 m.*

The chilly city of Tulcán is the busy capital of the province of Carchi. There is a great deal of informal trade here with Colombia, a textile and dry goods fair takes place on Thursday and Sunday. The two branches of the Panamericana join at Las Juntas, 2 km south of the city. In the **cemetery** ① *daily 0800-1800,* two blocks from Parque Ayora, the art of topiary is taken to beautiful extremes. Cypress bushes are trimmed into archways, fantastic figures and geometric shapes in *haut* and *bas* relief. To see the stages of this art form, go to the back of the cemetery where young bushes are being pruned. The artistry, started in 1936, is that of the late Sr José Franco, born in El Angel (see above), now buried among the splendour he created. The tradition is carried on by his sons. Around the cemetery is a promenade with fountains, souvenir and flower stalls and the **tourist office**, **Unidad de Turismo** ⓘ *entrance to the cemetery, T298 5760, daily 0800-1800, turismo@gmtulcan.gob.ec, helpful.* Write in advance to request a guided tour of the cemetery. Two blocks south is the **Museo de la Casa de la Cultura** ⓘ *Mon-Fri 0730-1300, 1500-1800,* with a collection of pre-Inca ceramics.

Safety Don't wander about at night. The area around the bus terminal is unsafe. Do not travel outside town (except along the Panamericana) without advance local enquiry.

Border with Colombia: Tulcán-Ipiales

The border is at **Rumichaca** (stone bridge), 5 km from Tulcán. Border posts with immigration, customs and agriculture control are on either side of a concrete bridge over the Río Carchi, opened in 2013, to the east of the natural stone bridge. This well-organized border is open 24 hours. On the Ecuadorean side, next to immigration (T298 6169), is a tourist information office. There are money changers on both sides of the bridge, check all calculations. Ipiales, with all services, is 2 km from the border.

ⓔ Otavalo to the Colombian border listings

For hotel and restaurant price codes, and other relevant information, see pages 14-17.

⬤ Where to stay

Cotacachi *p464*
$$$$ La Mirage, 500 m west of town, T291 5237, www.mirage.com.ec. Luxurious converted hacienda with elegant suites and common areas, includes breakfast and dinner, excellent restaurant, pool, gym and spa (treatments extra), beautiful gardens, tours arranged.
$$ Land of Sun, García Moreno 1376 y Sucre, T291 6009. Refurbished colonial house in the heart of town, restaurant in lovely patio, sauna, parking. Recommended.
$$ Runa Tupari, a system of homestays in nearby villages. Visitors experience life with an indigenous family by taking part in daily activities. The comfortable rooms have space for 3, fireplace, bathroom and hot shower, and cost US$30 pp including breakfast, dinner and transport from Otavalo. Arrange with **Runa Tupari**,

www.runatupari.com, or other Otavalo tour operators.
$$-$ La Cuadra, Peñaherrera 11-46 y González Suárez, T291 6015, www.lacuadra-hostal.com. Modern comfortable rooms, good matresses, private or shared bath, kitchen facilities.
$ Bachita, Sucre 16-82 y Peñaherrera, T291 5063. Simple place, private or shared bath, quiet.
$ Munaylla, 10 de Agosto y Sucre, T291 6169. Centrally located multi-storey building, rooms a bit small, good value.

Laguna Cuicocha *p464*
$$$ Hostería Cuicocha, Laguna Cuicocha, by the pier, T264 8040, www.cuicocha.org. Modern comfortable rooms overlooking the lake, includes breakfast and dinner, restaurant.
$ Cabañas Mirador, on a lookout above the pier, follow the trail or by car follow the road to the left of the park entrance, T09-8682 1699, miradordecuicocha@ yahoo.com. Rustic cabins with fireplace and modern rooms overlooking the lake, good

economical restaurant, trout is the speciality, parking, transport provided to Quiroga (US$4), Cotacachi (US$5), or Otavalo (US$10); owner Ernesto Cevillano is knowledgeable about the area and arranges trips.

Ibarra *p465*

$$$$ Hacienda Pimán, 9 km northeast of town, Quito T02-256 6090, www.hacienda piman.com. Luxuriuosly restored 18th-century hacienda. All inclusive 2- and 3-day packages with a train ride and visit to El Angel Reserve.

$$$ Hacienda Chorlaví, Panamericana Sur Km 4, T293 2222, www.haciendachorlavi. com. In an old hacienda, comfortable rooms, very good expensive restaurant, excellent parrillada, pool and spa, busy on weekends, folk music and crafts on Sat.

$$$ La Estelita, Km 5 Vía a Yuracrucito, T09-9811 6058, www.laestelita.com.ec. Modern hotel 5 km from the city on a hill overlooking town and Laguna Yahuarcocha.

Rooms and suites with lovely views, good restaurant, pool, spa, paragliding.

$$ Montecarlo, Av Jaime Rivadeneira 5-61 y Oviedo, near the obelisk, T295 8266, www. hotelmontecarloibarra.ec. Nice comfortable rooms, buffet breakfast, restaurant, heated pool open on weekends, parking.

$$ Royal Ruiz, Olmedo 9-40 y P Moncayo, T264 4653. Modern, comfortable carpeted rooms, restaurant, solar heated water, parking, long-stay discounts.

$ Fran's Hostal, Gral Julio Andrade 1-58 y Rafael Larrea, near bus terminal, T260 9995. Multi-storey hotel, bright functional rooms.

$ Finca Sommerwind, Autopista Yahuarcocha Km 8, T09-3937 1177, www.finca-sommerwind.com. Campground in a 12-ha ranch by Laguna Yahuarcocha, US$3 pp in tent, US$5 pp for camper vans, electricity, hot shower, laundry facilities.

$ Las Garzas, Flores 3-13 y Salinas, T295 0985. Simple comfortable rooms,

sitting room doubles as café-bar with a pleasant atmosphere.

Around Ibarra
$$$$ Hacienda Zuleta, Imbabura, by Angochahua, along the Ibarra–Cayambe road, T266 2182, Quito T02-603 6874, www.haciendazuleta.com. A 2000-ha working historic hacienda, among the nicest in the country. Superb accommodation and food, 15 rooms with fireplace, price includes all meals (prepared with organic vegetables, trout and dairy produced on the farm) and excursions, advance reservations required.
$$$-$$ Pukyu Pamba, In San Clemente, T266 0045, www.sclemente.com (in French). Part of a community-run program. Nicely built cottages with hot water on family properties, cheaper in more humble family homes, price includes 3 tasty meals and a guided tour, you are expected to participate in the family's activities. Horses and *guías nativos* available for more extended treks and visits to other communities.
$$ Casa Aída, in La Esperanza village, T266 0221. Simple rooms with good beds, includes dinner and breakfast, restaurant, shared bath, hot water, some English spoken, meeting place for climbing Imbabura.

Ibarra to the coast
$$$ Las Siete Cascadas, Km 111, 15 km past Lita, T09-9430 7434, lily_tarupi@hotmail.com. A-frame cabins with balconies in a 204-ha reserve, price includes full board and excursions to waterfalls and the forest, reserve well ahead.
$$-$ Parque Bambú, in El Limonal, about 600 m uphill from the main square, T301 6606, www.bospas.org. Small family-run reserve rich in bird life, private rooms with terrace, cheaper in dorm, splendid views of the valley, good breakfast, tasty meals available, camping, treks and horse-riding trips, can arrange excursions to mangroves, volunteer opportunities, Belgian-run. Knowledgeable and recommended.

Northwest of Ibarra
$$$ Aguasavia, in Chachimbiro,15-min walk from Santa Agua complex, T06-264 8064, www.termasaguasavia.com. Community-run modern hotel in a beautiful setting in the crater of La Viuda Volcano, includes 3 meals, rooms on groud floor with jacuzzi, thermal pools, trips.
$$$ Hacienda San Francisco, in the community of San Francisco, 5 km past Tumbabiro on the road to Chachimbiro, T293 4161, www.hosteriasanfrancisco.com. Intimate family-run inn in tastefully converted hacienda stables, includes breakfast, expensive restaurant, full board packages available, small thermal pool, nice grounds, good walking, horse riding, tennis court, excursions to Piñán, best Thu to Sun when owners are in.
$$$ Santa Agua Chachimbiro, part of the recreational complex, T264 8063, in Ibarra T261 0250. Rooms and cabins (some with jacuzzi), includes 3 meals and access to spa and pools, restaurant, busy on weekends, reserve ahead.
$$$-$$ Hostería Spa Pantaví, 7 km from Salinas, at the entrance to Tumbabiro, T293 4185, Quito reservations T02-234 7476, www.hosteriaspapantavi.com. Stylish inn in a tastefully restored hacienda. Very comfortable rooms, decorated with the owner's original works of art, includes nice breakfast, good restaurant, pool, spa, nice gardens, attentive service, bikes and horses for rent, tours. Recommended.
$ Tío Lauro, 1 block from plaza, Tumbabiro, T293 4148. Nice *residencial*, simple rooms, meals on request, parking, friendly owner.

North to Colombia *p466*
El Angel
$$$ Polylepis Lodge, T09-9403 1467, abutting the reserve, 14 km from El Angel along the road to Socabones. Rustic cabins with fireplace by a lovely 12-ha forest, includes 3 meals (vegetarian on request) and 3 guided walks, jacuzzi.

$$ Las Orquídeas, in the village of Morán, T09-8641 6936, castro503@yahoo.com. Mountain cabin with bunk beds, shared bath, includes 3 meals, horse riding and guide, run by Carlos Castro, a local guide and conservation pioneer.
$ Paisajes Andinos, Riofrío y 2a Transversal, T297 7577. Adequate, private or shared bath.

Eastern Route to the border *p467*
San Gabriel
$ Gabrielita, Mejía y Los Andes, above the agricultural supply shop, T229 1832. Modern hostel, includes breakfast, best in town.

Tulcán *p467*
$$ Grand Hotel Comfort, Colón y Chimborazo, T298 1452, www.grandhotelcomfort.com. Modern highrise hotel with rooms and suites with jacuzzi, fridge, safety box, restaurant with set lunch and à la carte, parking, new in 2013.
$$ Machado, Bolívar 403 y Ayacucho, T298 4221. Includes breakfast, comfy, parking.
$$ Sara Espíndola, Sucre y Ayacucho, on plaza, T298 6209. Comfortable rooms, with breakfast, spa, helpful.
$ Los Alpes, JR Arellano next to bus station, T298 2235. Restaurant, OK, good value.
$ Sáenz Internacional, Sucre y Rocafuerte, T298 1916. Very nice, modern, hot water, good value.
$ Torres de Oro, Sucre y Rocafuerte, T298 0296. Modern, nice, restaurant, parking.

🍴 Restaurants

Cotacachi *p464*
A local speciality is *carne colorada* (spiced pork).
$$ D'Anita, 10 de Agosto, y Moncayo. Daily 0800-2100. Good set meal of the day, local and international dishes à la carte, popular, English spoken, good value.
$$-$ La Marqueza, 10 de Agosto y Bolívar. Daily 0730-2130. Set lunches and à la carte.
Espresso Río Intag, Imbabura y Rocafuerte. Mon-Fri 0800-2000, Sat 1000-2200, Sun 1030-1500. The best coffee, snacks, meeting place.

Ibarra *p465*
$$ El Argentino, Sucre y P Moncayo, at Plazoleta Francisco Calderón. Tue-Sun. Good mixed grill and salads, small, pleasant, outdoor seating.
$$ Flor de Café, Av Teodoro Gómez 6-49 y Atahualpa. Daily. Crêpes, fondue, good breakfasts, bread, yoghurt, cold cuts, coffee.
$$ Pizza El Horno, Rocafuerte 6-38 y Flores. Closed Mon. Italian dishes, live music Sat night.
$$-$ La Cassona, Bolívar 6-47 y Oviedo. Daily. In a nice colonial patio, international, seafood and local dishes, also set lunch.
$ Casa Blanca, Bolívar 7-83. Closed Sun. Family-run, in colonial house with patio, good set lunches and snacks. Recommended.
$ Inti Raymi, Av Pérez Guerrero 6-39 y Bolívar. Good simple vegetarian lunches.

Cafés and heladerías
Café Arte, Salinas 5-43 y Oviedo. Daily from 1700. Café-bar with character, drinks, Mexican snacks, sandwiches, live music Fri-Sat night.
Heladería Rosalía Suárez, Oviedo y Olmedo. Excellent home-made *helados de paila* (fruit sherbets made in large copper basins), an Ibarra tradition since 1896. Highly recommended.
Olor a Café, Flores y Bolívar. Café/bar/cultural centre in an historic home, music, library.

Tulcán *p467*
$ Café Tulcán, Sucre 52-029 y Ayacucho. Café, snacks, desserts, juices, set lunches.
$ Dubai, Chimborazo. Set lunch, à la carte and *comida típica*, popular.
$ Mama Rosita, Sucre entre Boyacá y Atahualpa. Typical Ecuadorean dishes, set lunch.
$ Tequila, Sucre entre Junín y Boyacá. Varied à la carte menu.

🍸 Bars and clubs

Ibarra *p465*
Plazoleta Francisco Calderón on Sucre y Pedro Moncayo, has several café-bars with

outdoor seating and a pleasant atmosphere. **Rincón de Myer**, Olmedo 9-59. A bar with lots of character, attractively restored. **Sambucos** and **Dream Cocktails**, Flores y Sucre. Bars/clubs, the in-places among Ibarreño youth.

◑ What to do

Ibarra *p465*
A unique form of paddle ball, *pelota nacional*, is played in the afternoon at Yacucalle, south of the bus station. Players have huge studded paddles for striking the 1-kg ball.

Cycling
Cycling Zone, Flores y Borja. Well-stocked shop, repairs, rentals, route information.

Paragliding
Fly Ecuador, Oviedo 9-13 y Sánchez Cifuentes, T295 3297, www.flyecuador.com. ec. Tandem flight US$67-90, course US$448, arrange ahead.
Also at **La Estelita**, see Where to stay, above.

Tour operators
EcuaHorizons, Bolívar 4-67 y García Moreno, T295 9904. Bilingual guides for regional tours.
Intipungo, Rocafuerte 6-08 y Flores, T295 7766. Regional tours.

Train rides
A tourist train runs from Ibarra to **Salinas**, 29 km away, Wed-Sun and holidays at 1030, returning 1630, US$15-20 one way, US$20-25 return. When there is high demand, there is also *ferrochiva* (open sided motorized railcar) service at 0800 and 1230, US$15 one way, US$20 return. Purchase tickets in advance at any train station. In Ibarra, at Espejo y Colón, T295 5050, daily 0800-1630 or through T1-800-873637; you need each passenger's passport number and date of birth to purchase tickets. The ride takes 2 hrs with stops. Salinas is a mainly Afro-Ecuadorean town, here are the **Museo**

de la Sal, an ethnographic cultural centre and eateries offering local cuisine. You can continue by bus from Salinas to **San Lorenzo**, see page 554.

◑ Transport

Cotacachi *p464*
Bus Terminal at 10 de Agosto y Salinas by the market. Every 10 mins to/from Otavalo terminal, US$0.25, 25 mins; service alternates between the Panamericana and the Quiroga roads. To **Ibarra**, every 15 mins, US$0.45, 40 mins.

Laguna Cuicocha *p464*
Pick-ups From **Otavalo** US$10. From **Cotacachi**, US$5 one way, US$10 return with short wait. From **Quiroga** US$5. Return service from the lake available from Cabañas El Mirador, same rates.

Los Cedros Research Station
Bus From Estación La Ofelia in Quito, Trans Minas, daily at 0615, 1000, 1530, 1800 to **Chontal**, US$2.50, 3 hrs; then a 5-hr walk; ask in Chontal for mules to carry luggage up. If the road is passable, 1 daily bus from Otavalo to Chontal.

Ibarra *p465*
Bus Terminal is at Av Teodoro Gómez y Av Eugenio Espejo, southwest of the centre, T264 4676. Most inter-city transport runs from here. There are no ticket counters for regional destinations, such as Otavalo, proceed directly to the platforms. City buses go from the terminal to the centre or you can walk in 15 mins. To/from **Quito**, Terminal Carcelén, every 10 mins, US$2.50, 2½ hrs. Shared taxis with **Taxis Lagos** (Quito address under Otavalo Transport, in Ibarra at Flores 924 y Sánchez y Cifuentes, near Parque La Merced, T295 5150), buy ticket at least 1 day ahead, US$9.50 pp, 2½ hrs. To **Tulcán**, with **Expreso Turismo**, 9 daily, US$2.50, 2½ hrs. To **Otavalo**, platform 12, every 4 mins, US$0.45, 40 mins. To **Cotacachi**, platform

15, every 15 mins, US$0.45, 40 mins, some continue to **Quiroga**. To the coast, several companies, some go all the way to **San Lorenzo** US$4, 4 hrs, others only as far as **Lita**, US$3.50, 2 hrs. To **Ambato**, CITA goes via El Quinche and the Quito airport and bypasses Quito, 10 daily, US$5, 5 hrs. To **Baños**, Expreso Baños, also by the airport and bypasses Quito, at 0500 and 1430, US$6, 6 hrs. To **Lago Agrio**, Valle de Chota, at 0915, US$9, via La Bonita. To **Tumbabiro** via Urcuquí, Coop Urcuquí, hourly, US$0.75, 1 hr. To **Chachimbiro**, Coop Urcuquí, at 0700, 0730 and 1200, returning Mon-Fri at 1215 (Sat-Sun at 1300), 1530 and 1630, US$1.25, 1½ hrs, taxi US$40 return. Buses to La Esperanza, Zuleta and San Clemete leave from **Parque Germán Grijalva** (east of the Terminal Terrestre, follow C Sánchez y Cifuentes, south from the centre). To **La Esperanza**, every 20 mins, US$0.25, 30 mins. To **Zuleta**, hourly, US$0.52, 1 hr. To **San Clemente**, frequent, weekdays 0650-1840, Sat-Sun 0720-1500, US$0.25, 30 mins.

North to Colombia p466
El Angel
Bus from **Ibarra** Terminal Terrestre to **Mira**, every 30 mins, US$0.90, 1 hr; to **El Angel**, hourly, US$1.30, 1½ hrs. El Angel to **Mira**, every 30 mins, US$.50, 20 mins. El Angel to **Tulcán**, US$1.30, 1½ hrs. El Angel to **Quito**, US$4, 4 hrs.

Eastern route to the border p467
San Gabriel
Bus From **San Gabriel** to **Tulcán**, vans and jeeps US$0.70, shared taxis US$0.95, 30 mins, all from the main plaza. From San Gabriel to **Ibarra**, buses, US$1.65, 2 hrs. From San Gabriel to **Quito**, buses, US$3.50, 3½ hrs.

Tulcán p467
Air TAME (T224 2101) to **Quito** Tue and Thu.
Bus The bus terminal is 1.5 km uphill from centre; best to take a taxi, US$1. To

Quito, US$4, 5 hrs, every 15 mins, service to Terminal Carcelén, some continue to **Quitumbe**; from Quito, service from both terminals. To **Ibarra**, 2½ hrs, US$2.50. **Otavalo**, US$3, 3 hrs (they don't go in to the Otavalo Terminal, alight at the highway turn-off where taxis are available or transfer in Ibarra). To **Guayaquil**, 20 a day, 13 hrs, US$13. To **Lago Agrio**, 2 a day with **Putumayo**, US$7, 7 hrs, spectacular.

Border with Colombia p467
Bus Minivans and shared taxis (US$1 pp) leave when full from Parque Ayora (near the cemetery); private taxi US$3.50. **Note** These vehicles cross the international bridge and drop you off on the Colombian side, where onward transport waits. Remember to cross back over the bridge for Ecuadorean immigration. Shared taxi border-Tulcán bus terminal, US$1 pp. Colectivo border-Ipiales, US$1.05, taxi US$4.15.

ℹ Directory

Ibarra p465
Banks Banco del Pacífico, Olmedo 715 y Moncayo. Banco Pichincha, Sucre 581 y Flores; Cambio, Sánchez y Cifuentes 10-70 y Velasco, several currencies and TCs. **Medical services** Instituto Médico de Especialidades, Egas 1-83 y Av Teodoro Gómez de La Torre, T295 5612.

Tulcán p467
Banks Banco del Austro, Ayacucho y Bolívar. Banco Pichincha, 10 de Agosto y Sucre. Few places accept credit cards. Nowhere in Tulcán to change TCs. Pesos Colombianos can easily be changed on Parque La Independencia, the bus terminal and the border. **Consulates** Colombia, Bolívar entre Ayacucho y Junín, T298 7302, Mon-Fri 0800-1300, 1430-1530, visas require 3 days.

Cotopaxi, Latacunga and Quilotoa

An impressive roll call of towering peaks lines the route south of Quito, appropriately called the Avenue of the Volcanoes. This area obviously attracts its fair share of trekkers and climbers, while the less active tourist can browse through the many colourful indigenous markets and colonial towns that nestle among the high volcanic cones. The Panamericana heads south from Quito towards the central highlands' hub of Ambato. The perfect cone of Cotopaxi volcano is ever-present and is one of the country's main tourist attractions. Machachi and Latacunga are good bases from which to explore the region and provide access to the beautiful Quilotoa circuit of small villages and vast expanses of open countryside.

Cotopaxi and Latacunga

Machachi → *Phone code: 02. Colour map 1, A3. Population: 29,000. Altitude: 2900 m.*
In a valley between the summits of Pasochoa, Rumiñahui and Corazón, lies the town of **Machachi**, famous for its horsemen (*chagras*), horse riding trips, mineral water springs and crystal clear swimming pools. The water, 'Agua Güitig' or 'Tesalia', is bottled in a plant 4 km from the town, where there is also a sports/recreation complex with one warm and two cold pools, entry US$5. Annual highland 'rodeo', El Chagra, third week in July; tourist information office on the plaza. Just north of Machachi is Alóag, where an important road goes west to Santo Domingo and the coast.

Reserva Ecológica Los Ilinizas → *Phone code: 02. Colour map 1, A/B3.*
Machachi is a good starting point for a visit to the northern section of the **Reserva Ecológica Los Ilinizas**. Below the saddle between the two peaks, at 4740 m, is the **refugio** ① *T8133 3483, office and café in El Chaupi, T367 4125, www.ilinizas-refuge.webs.com, US$15 per night, US$30 with dinner and breakfast, reserve ahead, take sleeping bag,* a shelter with capacity for 25. **Iliniza Norte** (5105 m) although not a technical climb, should not be underestimated, a few exposed, rocky sections require utmost caution. Some climbers suggest using a rope and a helmet is recommended if other parties are there because of falling rock; allow two to four hours for the ascent from the refuge. Take a compass, it's easy to mistake the descent. **Iliniza Sur** (5245 m) involves ice climbing despite the deglaciation: full climbing gear and experience are absolutely necessary. Access to the reserve is through a turn-off west of the Panamericana 6 km south of Machachi, then it's 7 km to the village of El Chaupi, which is a good base for day-walks and climbing **Corazón** (4782 m, not trivial). A dirt road continues from El Chaupi 9 km to 'La Virgen' (statue), pickup US$15. Nearby are woods where you can camp. El Chaupi hotels arrange for horses with muleteer (US$20-25 per animal).

Parque Nacional Cotopaxi → *Phone code: 03. Colour map 1, B4.*
① *Visitors to the park must register at the entrance. Park gates are open 0700-1500, although you can stay until 1800. Visitors arriving with guides not authorized by the park are turned back at the gate. The park administration, a small museum (0800-1200, 1300-1700) and the Paja Blanca restaurant and shelter, are 10 km from the park gates, just before Limpio Pungo. (See also Transport section below.) The museum has a 3D model of the park, information about the volcano and stuffed animals.*
Cotopaxi volcano (5897 m) is at the heart of a much-visited national park. This scenic snow-covered perfect cone is the second highest peak in Ecuador and a very popular climbing

destination. Cotopaxi is an active volcano, one of the highest in the world, and its most recent eruption took place in 1904. Volcanic material from former eruptions can be seen strewn about the *páramo* surrounding Cotopaxi. The northwest flank is most often visited. Here is a high plateau with a small lake (Laguna Limpio Pungo), a lovely area for walking and admiring the delicate flora, and fauna including wild horses and native bird species such as the Andean Lapwing and the Chimborazo Hillstar hummingbird. The lower slopes are clad in planted pine forests, where llamas may be seen. The southwest flank, or Cara Sur, has not received as much impact as the west side. Here too, there is good walking, and you can climb Morurco (4881 m) as an acclimatization hike; condors may sometimes be seen. Just north of Cotopaxi are the peaks of Rumiñahui (4722 m), Sincholagua (4873 m) and Pasochoa (4225 m). To the southeast, beyond the park boundary, are Quilindaña (4890 m) and an area of rugged páramos and mountains dropping down to the jungle. The area has several large haciendas which form the Fundación Páramo (www.fundacionparamo.org), a private reserve with restricted access.

The **main entrance** to Parque Nacional Cotopaxi is approached from Chasqui, 25 km north of Machachi, 6 km north of Lasso. Once through the national park gates, go past Laguna Limpio Pungo to a fork, where the right branch climbs steeply to a parking lot (4600 m). From here it's a 30-minute to one-hour walk to the José Ribas refuge, at 4800 m; beware of altitude sickness. Walking from the highway to the refuge takes an entire day or more. The **El Pedregal entrance**, from the northwest, is accessed from Machachi via Santa Ana del Pedregal (21 km from the Panamericana), or from Sangolquí via Rumipamba and the Río Pita Valley. From Pedregal to the refuge car park is 14 km. There are infrequent buses to Pedregal (two a day) then the hike in is shorter but still a couple of hours. The **Ticatilín access** leads to the southwest flank. Just north of Lasso, a road goes east to the village of San Ramón and on to Ticatilín (a contribution of US\$2 per vehicle may be requested at the barrier here, be sure to close all gates) and Rancho María. From the south, San Ramón is accessed from Mulaló. Beyond Rancho María is the private Albergue Cotopaxi Cara Sur (4000 m, see Where to stay below). Walking four hours from here you reach Campo Alto (4760 m), a climbers' tent camp.

Climbing Cotopaxi The ascent from the Ribas refuge takes five to eight hours, start climbing at 0100 as the snow deteriorates in the sun. A full moon is both practical and a magical experience. Check out snow conditions with the guardian of the refuge before climbing. The route changes from year to year due to deglaciation. Because of the altitude and weather conditions, Cotopaxi is a serious climb, equipment and experience are required. To maximize your chances of reaching the summit, make sure to be well acclimatized beforehand. Glimbing with a guide is compulsory. Agencies in Quito and throughout the Central Highlands offer Cotopaxi climbing trips. Note that some guides encourage tourists to turn back at the first sign of tiredness, don't be pressured, insist on going at your own pace. There is no specific best season to climb Cotopaxi, weather conditions are largely a matter of luck year-round. You can also climb on the southwest flank, where the route is reported easier and safer than on the northwest face, but a little longer. To reach the summit in one day, you have to stay at Campo Alto (see above, and Where to stay below), from where it is six hours to the summit. The last hour goes around the rim of the crater with impressive views.

Lasso → *Phone code: 03. Colour map 1, B3. Altitude: 3000 m.*
Some 30 km south of Machachi is the small town of Lasso, on the railway line and off the Panamericana. In the surrounding countryside are several *hosterías*, converted country estates, offering accommodation and meals. Intercity buses bypass Lasso.

Latacunga → *Phone code: 03. Colour map 1, B3. Population: 103,000. Altitude: 2800 m.*

The capital of Cotopaxi Province is a place where the abundance of light grey pumice has been artfully employed. Volcán Cotopaxi is much in evidence, though it is 29 km away. Provided they are not hidden by clouds, which unfortunately is all too often, as many as nine volcanic cones can be seen from Latacunga; try early in the morning. The colonial character of the town has been well preserved. The central plaza, **Parque Vicente León**, is a beautifully maintained garden (locked at night). There are several other gardens in the town including **Parque San Francisco** and **Lago Flores** (better known as 'La Laguna'). **Casa de los Marqueses de Miraflores** ① *Sánchez de Orellana y Abel Echeverría, T280 1382, Mon-Fri 0800-1200, 1400-1800, Sat 0900-1300, free*, in a restored colonial mansion has a modest museum, with exhibits on **Mama Negra** (see Festivals, page 479), colonial art, archaeology, numismatics, a library and the **Jefatura de Turismo**, see below.

Casa de la Cultura ① *Antonia Vela 3-49 y Padre Salcedo T281 3247, Tue-Fri 0800-1200, 1400-1800, Sat 0800-1500, US$1*, built around the remains of a Jesuit Monastery and the old Monserrat watermill, houses a nice museum with pre-Columbian ceramics, weavings, costumes and models of festival masks; also art gallery, library and theatre. It has week-long festivals with exhibits and concerts for all the local festivities. There is a Saturday **market** on the Plaza de San Sebastián (at Juan Abel Echeverría). Goods for sale include *shigras* (fine stitched, colourful straw bags) and homespun wool and cotton yarn. The produce market, Plaza El Salto has daily trading and larger fairs on Tuesday, Friday and Saturday. A tourist **train** runs from Quito to Latacunga, see page 443.

Tourist offices: Cámara de Turismo de Cotopaxi ① *Quito 14-38 y General Maldonado, T280 1112, www.capturcotopaxi.com/fest.htm, Mon-Fri 0900-1300, 1400-1700*, local and regional information, Spanish only. **Jefatura de Turismo** ① *Casa de los Marqueses, T280 8494, Mon-Fri 0800-1700*, local and regional information and maps.

Latacunga

Where to stay
1 Central
2 Rodelú
3 Rosim
4 Tiana & Tovar Expediciones

Restaurants
1 Café Abuela
2 Chifa China
3 Dragon Rojo
4 El Templario
5 Guadalajara Grill
6 Parilladas La Española
7 Pizzería Buon Giorno

❂ Cotopaxi and Latacunga listings

For hotel and restaurant price codes, and other relevant information, see pages 14-17.

● Where to stay

Machachi *p474*
$$$ Papagayo, in Hacienda Bolívia, west of the Panamericana, take a taxi fom Machachi, T231 0002, www.hosteria-papagayo.com. Nicely refurbished hacienda, pleasant communal areas with fireplace and library, restaurant, jacuzzi, parking, central heating, homely atmosphere, horse riding, biking, tours, popular.
$$ La Estación y Granja, 3 km west of the Panamericana, by railway station outside the village of Aloasí, T230 9246, Quito T02-241 3784. Rooms in a lovely old home and newer section, also cabins, fireplaces, meals available (produce from own garden), parking, family-run, hiking access to Volcán Corazón, reserve ahead.
$$ Sierra Loma, near Aloasí, 700 m south of Machachi train station, T09-9593 8256, www.sierraloma.com. Cabins in the forest for 4, with fireplace, includes breakfast, other meals on request, camping (**$**), package with meals, activities and transport from Quito available.
$ Chiguac, Los Caras y Colón, 4 blocks east of the main park, T231 0396, amsincholagua@gmail.com. Nice family-run hostel, comfortable rooms, good breakfast, other meals available, shared bath. Recommended.

Reserva Ecológica Los Ilinizas *p474*
$$$$ Hacienda Umbria, off the road to El Chaupi, T09-8923 0143, http://hacienda umbria.com. Very exclusive accommodation in a 330-ha working hacienda on the slopes of El Corazón. Rooms with fireplace, gourmet meals with farm produce, open kitchen, outdoor and farm activities.
$$$-$$ Chuquiragua Lodge, 500 m before El Chaupi, then 200 m on a cobbled

road, T367 4046, in Quito: T603 5590, www. ecuadortreasure.com. Inn with lovely views, a variety of rooms and prices, restaurant with roaring fireplace, spa. US$18 pp in dorm, camping US$5 pp with hot shower, horse riding, trekking, climbing, bike tours, and transport from Quito.
$$ La Llovizna, 100 m behind the church, on the way to the mountain, T367 4076. Pleasant hostel, sitting room with fireplace, includes breakfast and dinner, private or shared bath, ping-pong, horse, bike and gear rentals, guiding, book in advance.
$$-$ Nina Rumy, near the bus stop in El Chaupi, T367 4088. Includes breakfast and supper, simple rooms with shared bath, electric shower, family-run and very friendly.

Parque Nacional Cotopaxi *p474*
All these inns are good for acclimatization at altitudes between 3100 m and 3800 m. Just below Limpio Pungo is the **Paja Blanca** shelter (**$** pp with breakfast, hot water) with 2 very basic huts and a couple of campsites (US$2 per tent, no facilities). The **José Ribas refuge** was being rebuilt in 2014 and was expected to reopen later that year. It will have capacity for 100 visitors and a restaurant, no public kitchen, bring a warm sleeping bag.
$$$-$$ Tambopaxi, 3 km south of the El Pedregal access (1 hr drive from Machachi) or 4 km north of the turn-off for the climbing shelter, T02-222 0242 (Quito), www.tambopaxi.com. Comfortable straw-bale mountain shelter at 3750 m. 3 double rooms and several dorms (US$20 pp), duvets, includes breakfast, other meals available, camping US$7.50 pp, horse riding with advance notice.
$$ Albergue Cotopaxi Cara Sur, at the southwestern end of the park, at the end of the Ticatilín road, T09-8461 9264, www. cotopaxicarasur.com (see page 440). Very nice mountain shelter at 4000 m, day use US$1. Includes breakfast and dinner, use of

kitchen, some cabins with private bath, hot shower, transport from Quito and climbing tours available, equipment rental. **Campo Alto** is a very basic tent camp (4780 m, US$8 pp), 4 hrs walk from the shelter, horse to take gear to Campo Alto US$15, muleteer US$15.

Outside the park
$$$$ Hacienda San Agustín de Callo, 2 access roads from the Panamericana, one just north of the main park access (6.2 km); the second, just north of Lasso (4.3 km), T03-271 9160, Quito T02-290 6157, www.incahacienda.com. Exclusive hacienda, the only place in Ecuador where you can sleep and dine in an Inca building, the northernmost imperial-style Inca structure still standing. Rooms and suites with fireplace and bathtub, includes breakfast and dinner, horse rides, treks, bicycles and fishing. Restaurant ($$$) and buildings open to non-guests (US$5-10).
$$$$ Hacienda Santa Ana, 10 mins from north entrance to Cotopaxi National Park, T02-222 4950, www.santaanacotopaxi.com. 17th-century former-Jesuit hacienda in beautiful surroundings. 7 comfortable rooms with fireplaces, central heating, great views, horse riding, hiking, trekking, climbing. Also run **Hotel Sierra Madre** in Quito.
$$$$ Hacienda Yanahurco, on access road to Quilindaña, 2 hrs from Machachi, T09-9612 7759, Quito T02-244 5248, www.haciendayanahurco.com. Large hacienda in wild area, rooms with fireplace or heater, includes meals, 2-4 day programs, all-inclusive.
$$$-$$ Chilcabamba, Loreto del Pedregal, by the northern access to the National Park, T09-9946 0406, T02-237 7098, www.chilcabamba.com. Cabins and rooms, US$30.50 pp in dorm, magnificent views.
$$$-$$ Cuello de Luna, 2 km northwest of the park's main access on a dirt road, T09-9970 0330, www.cuellodeluna.com. Comfortable rooms with fireplace, includes breakfast, other meals available, US$22 pp in dorm (a very low loft). Can arrange tours to Cotopaxi, horse riding and biking.

$$$-$$ Tierra del Volcán, T09-9498 0121, Quito T02-600 9533, www.tierradelvolcan.com. 3 haciendas: **Hacienda El Porvenir**, a working ranch by Rumiñahui, between El Pedregal and the northern access to the park, 3 types of rooms, includes breakfast, set meals available, horses and mountain bikes for hire, camping, zipline; **Hacienda Santa Rita**, by the Río Pita, on the Sangolquí-El Pedregal road, with ziplines, entry US$6, camping US$5 pp; and the more remote, rustic **Hacienda El Tambo** by Quilindaña, southeast of the park. Also offers many adventure activities in the park.
$$ Huagra Corral, 200 m east of Panamericana along the park's main access road, T03-271 9729, Quito T02-380 8427, www.huagracorral.com. Nicely decorated, restaurant, private or shared bath, heaters, convenient location, helpful, reserve ahead.

Lasso p475
$$$$ Hacienda Hato Verde, Panamericana Sur Km 55, by entry to Mulaló, southeast of Lasso, T271 9348, www.haciendahatoverde.com. Lovely old hacienda and working dairy farm near the south flank of Cotopaxi, tastefully restored. 10 rooms with wood-burning stoves, includes breakfast, other meals available; horse riding (for experienced riders), trekking, trip up Cotopaxi Cara Sur, charming hosts.
$$$ Hostería La Ciénega, 2 km south of Lasso, T271 9052. An historic hacienda with nice gardens, rooms with heater or fireplace, good expensive restaurant.
$ Cabañas Los Volcanes, at the south end of Lasso, T271 9524, maexpediciones@yahoo.com. Small hostel, nice rooms, private or shared bath, discounts for HI members. Tours to Cotopaxi.

Latacunga p476, map p476
$$ Rodelú, Quito 16-31, T280 0956, www.rodelu.com.ec. Comfortable popular hotel, restaurant, nice suites and rooms except for a few which are very small, breakfast included starting the 2nd day.

$$-$ Rosim, Quito 16-49 y Padre Salcedo, T280 2172, www.hotelrosim.com. Centrally located, breakfast available, carpeted rooms, quiet and comfortable. Discounts in low season.

$$-$ Tiana, Luis F Vivero N1-31 y Sánchez de Orellana, T281 0147, www.hostaltiana. com. Includes breakfast, drinks and snacks available, private or shared bath, US$10 pp in dorm, nice patio, kitchen facilities, luggage store, popular meeting place, good source of information for Quilotoa Loop.

$ Central, Sánchez de Orellana y Padre Salcedo, T280 2912. A multi-storey hotel in the centre of town, breakfast available, a bit faded but very helpful.

🍴 Restaurants

Machachi *p474*

Not much to choose from in town.

$$$-$$ Café de la Vaca, 4 km south of town on the Panamericana. Daily 0800-1730. Very good meals using produce from their own farm, popular.

$$-$ Pizzeria Di Ragazzo, Av Pablo Guarderas N7-107, north of centre. Is reported good.

Latacunga *p476, map p476*

Few places are open on Sun. Many places along the Panamericana specialize in *chugchucaras*, a traditional pork dish. *Allullas* biscuits and string cheese are sold by the roadside.

$$ Parrilladas La Española, 2 de Mayo 7-175. Mon-Sat 1230-2100. Good grill, popular with locals.

$$-$ Chifa China, Antonia Vela 6-85 y 5 de Junio. Daily 1030-2200. Good Chinese food, large portions.

$$-$ Guadalajara Grill, Quijano y Ordóñez y Vivero. Closed Sun. Good Mexican food.

$$-$ Pizzería Buon Giorno, Maldonado y Sánchez de Orellana. Mon-Sat 1300-2200. Great pizzas and lasagne, large selection. Popular and recommended.

$ Dragon Rojo, Amazonas y Pastaza. Open late. Chinese food, large portions.

Café Abuela, Guayaquil 6-07 y Quito, by Santo Domingo church. Pleasant cosy café/ bar, nicely decorated, drinks, sweets and sandwiches, popular with university students.

El Templario, Luis F Vivero y Sánchez de Orellana. Café/bar, microbrews, tapas, good atmosphere.

✴ Festivals

Latacunga *p476, map p476*

The La Mama Negra is held **23-24 Sep**, in homage to the Virgen de las Mercedes. There are 5 main characters in the parade and hundreds of dancers, some representing the black slaves, others the whites. Mama Negra herself (portrayed by a man) is a slave who dared to ask for freedom in colonial times. The colourful costumes are called the Santísima Trajería. The civic festival of **Mama Negra**, with similar parade, is on the **1st or 2nd Sat in Nov** (but not 2 Nov, Día de los Muertos). It is part of the **Fiestas de Latacunga**, **11 Nov**.

🛍 Shopping

Latacunga *p476, map p476*

Artesanía Otavalo, Guayaquil 5-50 y Quito. A variety of souvenirs from Otavalo.

⚙ What to do

Latacunga *p476, map p476*

All operators offer day trips to **Cotopaxi** and **Quilotoa** (US$40 pp, includes lunch and a visit to a market town if on Thu or Sat, minimum 2 people). Climbing trips to Cotopaxi are around US$170 pp for 2 days (plus *refugio*), minimum 2 people. Trekking trips US$70-80 pp per day. **Note** Many agencies require passport as deposit when renting gear.

Greivag, Guayaquil y Sánchez de Orellana, Plaza Santo Domingo, L5, T281 0510, www.greivagturismo.com. Day trips.

Metropolitan Touring, Calle Guayaquil y Sánchez de Orellana, Plaza Santo

Domingo, L6, T280 2985. See Quito operators. Airline tickets.

Neiges, Guayaquil 6-25, Plaza Santo Domingo, T281 1199, neigestours@hotmail. com. Day trips and climbing.

Tovar Expediciones, at Hostal Tiana, T281 1333. Climbing and trekking.

⊙ Transport

Machachi *p474*
Bus To **Quito**, from El Playón behind the stadium, every 15 mins to Terminal Quitumbe, every 30 mins to Villa Flora and El Trebol, all US$0.75, 1½ hrs. To **Latacunga**, from the monument to El Chagra at the Panamericana, US$0.55, 1 hr.

Reserva Ecológica Los Ilinizas *p474*
Bus From El Playón in Machachi, where buses from Quito arrive (see above), to **El Chaupi** (every 20 mins, US$0.36, ½ hr), from where you can walk to the *refugio* in 7-8 hrs. A pick-up from El Chaupi to 'La Virgen' costs US$10, from Machachi US$25. It takes 3 hrs to walk with a full pack from 'La Virgen' to the *refugio*. Horses can be hired at any of the lodgings in El Chaupi.

Parque Nacional Cotopaxi *p474*
Main park entrance and Refugio Ribas, take a Latacunga bus from Quito and get off at the main access point. Do not take an express bus as you can't get off before Latacunga. At the turn-off to the park there are usually vehicles from a local operator which go to the park. US$40 to the parking lot before the refuge for up to 3 passengers. From **Machachi**, pick-ups go via the cobbled road to El Pedregal on to Limpio Pungo and the refugio parking lot, US$40. From **Lasso**, full day trip to the park, US$70 return, contact **Cabañas los Volcanes**. From **Latacunga**, arrange with tour operators.

To **Cara Sur** from Quito, Cotopaxi Cara Sur offer transport to the **Albergue Cara**

Sur, US$60 per vehicle up to 5 passengers. Alternatively take a Latacunga bound bus and get off at **Pastocalle**, and take a pickup from there, US$15 per vehicle for up to 5 passengers.

Latacunga *p476, map p476*
Air The airport is north of the centre. 1 daily flight to **Guayaquil** and **Coca** with TAME.
Bus Buses leave from the terminal on the Panamericana just south of 5 de Junio, except **Transportes Santa**, which has its own terminal, 2 blocks away at Eloy Alfaro y Vargas Torres, T281 1659, serving **Cuenca** and **Loja** (4 daily), **Machala** and **Guayaquil** (3 daily). To **Quito**, every 15 mins, 2 hrs, US$2. To **Ambato**, 1 hr, US$1. To **Guayaquil**, US$7, 7 hrs. To **Saquisilí**, every 20 mins (see below). Through buses, which are more frequent, do not stop at Latacunga Terminal. During the day (0600-1700), they go along a bypass road 4 blocks west of the Terminal, and have small stations at Puente de San Felipe. At night they stop at the corner of Panamericana and Av 5 de Junio. To **Otavalo**, **Ibarra** and **Tulcán**, bypassing Quito, **Cita Express**, 12 daily from Puente de San Felipe; also with **Expreso Baños**. To **Baños**, every 20 mins from Puente de San Felipe. Buses on the Zumbahua, Quilotoa, Chugchilán, Sigchos circuit are given below.
Note On Thu most buses to nearby communities leave from Saquisilí market instead of Latacunga.

❶ Directory

Latacunga *p476, map p476*
Banks Banco de Guayaquil, Maldonado y Sánchez de Orellana. Banco Pichincha, C Quito, Parque Vicente León. **Medical services** Clínica Latacunga, Sánchez de Orellana 11-79 y Marqués de Maenza, T281 0260. Private, 24 hrs.

Quilotoa Circuit

The popular and recommended 200-km round trip from Latacunga to Pujilí, Zumbahua, Quilotoa crater, Chugchilán, Sigchos, Isinliví, Toacazo, Saquisilí, and back to Latacunga, can be done in two to three days by bus. It is also a great route for biking and only a few sections of the loop are cobbled or rough. Access is from either Pastocalle, north of Lasso or Latacunga. Hiking from one town to another can be challenging, especially when the fog rolls in. For these longer walks hiring a guide might not be unreasonable if you don't have a proper map or enough experience.

Latacunga to Zumbahua

A fine paved road leads west to **Pujilí** ① *15 km, bus US$0.25*, which has a beautiful church. Good market on Sunday, and a smaller one on Wednesday. Colourful Corpus Christi celebrations. Beyond Pujilí, many interesting crafts are practised by the *indígenas* in the **Tigua valley**: paintings on leather, hand-carved wooden masks and baskets. **Chimbacucho**, also known as Tigua, is home to the Toaquiza family, most famous of the Tigua artists. The road goes on to Zumbahua, then over the Western Cordillera to La Maná and Quevedo. This is a great paved downhill bike route. It carries very little traffic and is extremely twisty in parts but is one of the most beautiful routes connecting the highlands with the coast. Beyond Zumbahua are the pretty towns of **Pilaló** (two restaurants, small hostal and petrol pumps), **Esperanza de El Tingo** (two restaurants and lodging at **Carmita's**, T03-281 4657) and **La Maná** (two hotels).

Zumbahua → *Phone code: 03. Colour map 1, B3.*

Zumbahua lies 800 m from the main road, 62 km from Pujilí. It has an interesting Saturday market (starts at 0600) for local produce, and some tourist items. Just below the plaza is a shop selling dairy products and cold drinks. Friday nights involve dancing and drinking. Take a fleece, as it can be windy, cold and dusty. There is a good hospital in town, Italian-funded and run. The Saturday trip to Zumbahua market and the Quilotoa crater is one of the best excursions in Ecuador.

Quilotoa → *Phone code: 03. Colour map 1, B3.*

Zumbahua is the point to turn off for a visit to Quilotoa, a volcanic crater filled by a beautiful emerald lake. From the rim of the crater, 3850 m, several snowcapped volcanoes can be seen in the distance. The crater is reached by a paved road which runs north from Zumbahua (about 12 km, three- to five-hours' walk). There's a 300-m drop down from the crater rim to the water. The hike down takes about 30 minutes (an hour or more to climb back up). The trail starts at the village of Quilotoa, up the slope from the parking area, then, down a steepcanyon-like cut. You can hire a mule to ride up from the bottom of the crater (US$8), best arrange before heading down. There is a basic hostel by the lake and kayaks for rent. Everyone at the crater tries to sell the famous naïve Tigua pictures and carved wooden masks, so expect to be besieged (also by begging children). To the southeast of the crater is the village of Macapungo, which runs the Complejo Turístico Shalalá, see Where to stay, below. The Mirador Shalalá platform on offers great views of the lake. To hike around the crater rim takes 4½ to six hours in clear weather. Be prepared for sudden changes in the weather, it gets very cold at night and can be foggy. Always stay on the trail as trekkers have got lost and hurt themselves. For a shorter loop (three to four hours), start on the regular circuit going left when you reach the rim by Quilotoa village and follow it to Mirador Shalalá, a great place for a picnic; then backtrack for about five minutes and take the path down to the lake. To return, follow a path near the lake until you reach the large trail which takes you back up to Quilotoa village. If you are tired, right there you can hire a horse to take you up.

Chugchilán, Sigchos and Isinliví → Phone code: 03. Colour map 1, B3.

Chugchilán, a village in one of the most scenic areas of Ecuador, is 16 km by paved road from Quilotoa. An alternative to the road is a five- to six-hour walk around part of the Quilotoa crater rim, then down to Guayama, and across the canyon (Río Sigüí) to Chugchilán, 11 km. Outside town is a cheese factory and nearby, at Chinaló, a woodcarving shop. The area has good walking.

Continuing from Chugchilán the road, unpaved, runs to **Sigchos**, the starting point for the Toachi Valley walk, via Asache to San Francisco de las Pampas (0900 bus daily to Latacunga). There is also a highland road to Las Pampas, with two buses from Sigchos. Southeast of Sigchos is **Isinliví**, on the old route to Toacazo and Latacunga. It has a fine woodcarving shop and a pre-Inca *pucará*. Trek to the village of Guantualó, which has a fascinating market on Monday. You can hike to or from Chugchilán (five hours), or from Quilotoa to Isinliví in seven to nine hours.

From Sigchos, a paved road leads to **Toacazo** (**$$ La Quinta Colorada**, T271 6122, www.quintacolorada.com, price includes breakfast and dinner) and on to Saquisilí.

Saquisilí → Phone code: 03. Colour map 1, B3.

Some 16 km southwest of Lasso, and 6 km west of the Panamericana is the small but very important market town of Saquisilí. Its Thursday market (0500-1400) is famous throughout Ecuador for the way in which its seven plazas and some of its streets become jam-packed with people, the great majority of them local *indígenas* with red ponchos and narrow-brimmed felt hats. The best time to visit the market is 0900-1200 (before 0800 for the animal market). Be sure to bargain, as there is a lot of competition. This area has colourful Corpus Christi processions.

⦿ Quilotoa Circuit listings

For hotel and restaurant price codes, and other relevant information, see pages 14-17.

⬤ Where to stay

Latacunga to Zumbahua *p481*
Tigua-Chimbacucho
$$ La Posada de Tigua, 3 km east of Tigua-Chimbacucho, 400 m north of the road, T305 6103, posadadetigua@yahoo.com. Refurbished hacienda, part of a working dairy ranch, 6 rooms, wood-burning stove, includes tasty home-cooked breakfast and dinner, pleasant family atmosphere, horses for riding, trails, nice views.

Zumbahua *p481*
There are only a few phone lines in town, which are shared among several people. Expect delays when calling to book a room.
$ Cóndor Matzi, overlooking the market area, T09-8906 1572 or T03-281 2953 to leave message. Basic but best in town, shared bath, hot water, dinning room with wood stove, kitchen facilities, try to reserve ahead, if closed when you arrive ask at **Restaurante Zumbahua** on the corner of the plaza.
$ Richard, opposite the market on the road in to town, T09-9015 5996. Basic shared rooms and one shower with hot water, cooking facilities, parking.

Quilotoa *p481*

$$ Quilotoa Crater Lake Lodge, on the main road facing the access to Quilotoa, T305 5816. Somewhat faded hacienda-style lodge, includes breakfast and dinner, dining room with fireplace, views.

Humberto Latacunga, a good painter who also organizes treks, runs 3 good hostels, T09-9212 5962, all include breakfast and dinner: **$$ Hostería Alpaca**, www. alpacaquilotoa.com, the most upmarket, rooms with wood stoves; **$$-$ Cabañas Quilotoa**, on the access road to the crater, www.cabanasquilotoa.com, private or shared bath, wood stoves; **$ Hostal Pachamama**, at the top of the hill by the rim of the crater, private bath.
$ Complejo Shalalá, in Macapungo, T09-9312 2983, http://shalala.uphero.com. Community run lodge in a lovely 35-ha cloudforest reserve. Nice cabins, one with wheelchair access, includes breakfast and dinner, restaurant, trails.

Chugchilán *p482*

$$$$-$$$ Black Sheep Inn, below the village on the way to Sigchos, T270-8077, www.blacksheepinn.com. A lovely eco-friendly resort which has received several awards. Includes 3 excellent vegetarian meals, private and shared bath, **$$** pp in dorms, spa, water slide, zipline, arrange excursions. Highly recommended.
$$ Hostal Mama Hilda, on the road in to town, T270 8015. Pleasant family-run hostel, warm atmosphere, large rooms some with wood stoves, includes good dinner and breakfast, private or shared bath, camping, parking, arrange trips. Highly recommended.
$$-$ Hostal Cloud Forest, at the entrance to town, T270 8016, www.cloudforesthostal. com. Simple popular family-run hostel, sitting room with wood stove, includes dinner and great breakfast, restaurant open to public for lunch, private or shared bath, also dorm, parking, very helpful.

Sigchos *p482*

$ Jardín de los Andes, Ilinizas y Tungurahua, T271 2114. Basic but quite clean and friendly.

Isinliví *p482*

$$$-$$ Llullu Llama, T09-9258 0562, www. llullullama.com. Farmhouse with cosy sitting room with wood stove, nicely refurbished in 2013, tastefully decorated rooms, shared ecological bath. Also rustic adobe cabins for four, with bath, stove and small terrace, new in 2014. All include good hearty dinner and breakfast. Warm and relaxing atmosphere, a lovely spot. Recommended.

Saquisilí *p482*

$$ Gilocarmelo, by the cemetery, 800 m from town on the road north to Guaytacama, T09-9966 9734, T02-340 0924. Restored hacienda house in a 4 ha property. Plain rooms with fireplace, restaurant, pool, sauna, jacuzzi, nice garden.
$ San Carlos, Bolívar opposite the Parque Central. A multi-storey building, electric shower, parking, good value, but watch your valuables. Will hold luggage for US$1 while you visit the market.

🚌 Transport

Zumbahua *p481*

Bus Many daily on the Latacunga-Quevedo road (0500-1900, US$1.25, 1½ hrs). Buses on Sat are packed full, get your ticket the day before. A pick-up truck can be hired from Zumbahua to **Quilotoa** for US$5-10 depending on number of passengers; also to **Chugchilán** for around US$30. On Sat mornings there are many trucks leaving the Zumbahua market for Chugchilán which pass Quilotoa. Pick-up Quilotoa–Chugchilán US$25.
Taxi Day-trip by taxi to Zumbahua, Quilotoa, and return to **Latacunga** is about US$60.

Quilotoa *p481*

Bus From the terminal terrestre in Latacunga **Trans Vivero** daily at 1000, 1130, 1230 and 1330, US$2, 2 hrs. Note that this leaves from Latacunga, not Saquisilí market, even on Thu. Return bus direct to Latacunga at 1300. Buses returning at 1400 and 1500 go only as far as Zumbahua, from where you can catch a Latacunga bound bus at the highway. Also, buses going through Zumbahua bound for Chugchilán will drop you at the turn-off, 5 mins from the crater, where you can also pick them up on their way to Zumbahua and Latacunga. Taxi from Latacunga, US$40 one way. For **Shalalá**, Trans Ilinizas from Latacunga to **Macapungo** at 1300, US$1.50, or go to Zumbahua and take a pick-up from there, US$5. From Macapungo it is a 30-min walk to the cabins.

Chugchilán *p482*
Bus From **Latacunga**, daily at 1130 (except Thu) via Sigchos, at 1200 via Zumbahua; on Thu from **Saquisilí market** via Sigchos around 1130, US$2.25, 3 hrs. Buses return to Latacunga daily at 0300 via Sigchos, at 0400 via Zumbahua. On Sun there are 2 extra buses to Latacunga leaving 0900-1000. There are extra buses going as far as Zumbahua Wed 0500, Fri 0600 and Sun between 0900-1000; these continue towards the coast. Milk truck to Sigchos around 0800. On Sat also pick-ups going to/from market in Zumbahua and Latacunga. From **Sigchos**, through buses as indicated above, US$0.60, 1 hr. Pick-up hire to Sigchos US$25, up to 5 people, US$5 additional person. Pickup to **Quilotoa** US$25, up to 5 people, US$5 additional person. Taxi from Latacunga US$60, from Quito US$100.

Sigchos *p482*
Bus From **Latacunga** almost every hour, 0930-1600; returning to Latacunga most buses leave Sigchos before 0700, then at 1430 (more service on weekends); US$1.50, 2 hrs. From **Quito** direct service Mon-Sat at 1400 (more frequent Sun) with **Reina de Sigchos**; also Fri 1700 with **Illinizas**; US$3, 3 hrs. To **La Maná** on the road to Quevedo, via Chugchilán, Quilotoa and Zumbahua, Fri at 0500 and Sun at 0830, US$3.50, 6 hrs (returns Sat at 0730 and Sun at 1530). To **Las Pampas**, at 0330 and 1400, US$2.50, 3 hrs. From Las Pampas to **Santo Domingo**, at 0300 and 0600, US$2.50, 3 hrs.

Isinliví *p482*
From **Latacunga** daily (except Thu), via Sigchos at 1215 (**14 de Octubre**) and direct at 1300 (**Trans Vivero**), on Thu both leave from Saquisilí market around 1100, on Sat the direct bus leaves at 1100 instead of 1300, US$1.80, 2½ hrs. Both buses return to Latacunga 0300-0330, except Wed at 0700 direct, Sun 1245 direct and Mon 1500 via Sigchos. buses fill quickly, be there early. Connections to Chugchilán, Quilotoa and Zumbahua can be made in Sigchos. Bus schedules are posted on www.llullullama.com.

Saquisilí *p482*
Bus Frequent service between **Latacunga** and Saquisilí, US$0.30, 20 mins; many buses daily to/from **Quito** (Quitumbe), 0530-1300, US$2, 2 hrs. Buses and trucks to many outlying villages leave from 1000 onwards. Bus tours from Quito cost US$45 pp, taxis charge US$80, with 2 hrs wait at market.

Ambato → *Phone code: 03. Colour map 1, B3. Population: 182,000. Altitude: 2700 m.*

Almost completely destroyed in the great 1949 earthquake, Ambato lacks the colonial charm of other Andean cities, though its location in the heart of fertile orchard-country has earned it the nickname of 'the city of fruits and flowers' (see Festival, page 486). It is also a transport hub and the principal supply town of the central highlands, with a large Monday market and smaller ones Wednesday and Friday. **Tourist office**: Ministerio de Turismo ① *Guayaquil y Rocafuerte, T282 1800, Mon-Fri 0800-1700*, helpful.

The modern cathedral faces **Parque Montalvo**, where there is a statue of the writer Juan Montalvo (1832-1889), whose **house** ① *Bolívar y Montalvo, T282 4248, US$1*, can be visited. The **Museo de la Provincia** in the Casa del Portal (built 1900), facing Parque Montalvo, has a photo collection.

Northeast of Ambato is the colonial town of **Píllaro**, gateway to **Parque Nacional Los Llanganates**, a beautiful rugged area (for tours see **Sachayacu Explorer**, page 493). The town is known for its colourful festivals: a *diablada* (devils parade) 1-6 January and Corpus Christi.

Ambato to Baños

To the east of Ambato, an important road leads to **Salasaca**, where the *indígenas* sell their weavings; they wear distinctive black ponchos with white trousers and broad white hats. Further east, 5 km, is **Pelileo**, the blue jean manufacturing capital of Ecuador with good views of Tungurahua. There are opportunities for cultural tourism, walking and paragliding in the area (contact **Blue Land Adventures** ① *T03-283 0236, bluelandsalasaca@yahoo.com.ar*). From Pelileo, the road descends to Las Juntas, where the Patate and Chambo rivers meet to form the Río Pastaza. About 1 km east of Las Juntas bridge, the junction with the road to Riobamba is marked by a large sculpture of a macaw and a toucan (locally known as Los Pájaros – the lower bird was destroyed by the volcano). It is a favourite volcano watching site. The road to Baños then continues along the lower slopes of the volcano.

Eight kilometres northeast of Pelileo on a paved side-road is **Patate**, centre of the warm, fruit growing Patate valley. There are excellent views of Volcán Tungurahua from town. The fiesta of **Nuestro Señor del Terremoto** is held on the weekend leading up to 4 February, featuring a parade with floats made with fruit and flowers.

Ambato to Riobamba and Guaranda

After Ambato, the Pan-American Highway runs south to Riobamba (see page 494). About half way is **Mocha**, where guinea pigs (*cuy*) are bred for the table. You can sample roast *cuy* and other typical dishes at stalls and restaurants by the roadside, **Mariadiocelina** is recommended. The highway climbs steeply south of Mocha and at the pass at **Urbina** there are fine views in the dry season of Chimborazo and Carihuayrazo.

To the west of Ambato, a paved road climbs through tilled fields, past the páramos of Carihuayrazo and Chimborazo to the great Arenal (a high desert at the base of the mountain), and down through the Chimbo valley to Guaranda (see page 495). This spectacular journey reaches a height of 4380 m and vicuñas can be seen.

⊙ Ambato listings

For hotel and restaurant price codes, and other relevant information, see pages 14-17.

⊙ Where to stay

Ambato *p484*
$$$ Ambato, Guayaquil 01-08 y Rocafuerte, T242 1791, www.hotelambato.com. A modern hotel near the heart of the city, good restaurant, 1 suite (**$$$$**), squash court, weekend discounts.

$$$ Florida, Av Miraflores 1131, T242 2007, www.hotelflorida.com.ec. Pleasant hotel in a nice setting, restaurant with good set meals, spa, weekend discounts.

$$$ Roka Plaza, Bolívar 20-62 y Guayaquil, T242 3845. Small stylish hotel in a refurbished colonial house in the heart of the city, sushi restaurant.

$$-$ Colony, 12 de Noviembre 124 y Av El Rey, near the bus terminal, T282 5789. A modern hotel with large clean rooms, parking.

$ $-$ **Pirámide Inn**, Cevallos y Mariano Egüez, T242 1920. Comfortable hotel, cafetería, English spoken.

Ambato to Baños *p485*
Salasaca and Pelileo
$ **Hostal Pelileo**, Eloy Alfaro 641, T287 1390. Shared bath, hot water, simple.
$ **Runa Huasi**, in Salasaca, 1 km north off main highway, T09-9984 0125, www. hostalrunahuasi.com. Simple hostel, includes breakfast and fruit, other meals on request, cooking facilities, nice views, guided walks.

Patate
$$$$ **Hacienda Leito**, on the road to El Triunfo, T285 9329, www.haciendaleito. com. Classy hacienda, spacious rooms, includes breakfast and dinner, great views of Tungurahua.
$$$$ **Hacienda Manteles**, in the Leito valley on the road to El Triunfo, T09-9871 5632, Quito T02-223 3484, www. haciendamanteles.com. Nice converted hacienda with wonderful views of Tungurahua and Chimborazo, includes breakfast, dinner, snacks, walk to waterfalls, hiking and horse riding. Reserve ahead.
$$$ **Hostería Viña del Río**, 3 km from town on the old road to Baños, T287 0314, www. hosteriavinadelrio.com. Cabins on a 22 ha ranch, restaurant, pool, spa and mini golf, US$6.72 for day use of facilities.

@ Restaurants

Ambato *p484*
$$ **El Alamo Chalet**, Cevallos 1719 y Montalvo. Open 0800-2300 (2200 Sun). Ecuadorean and international food. Good set meals and à la carte, Swiss-owned.
$$ **La Buena Mesa**, Quito 924 y Bolívar. Mon-Sat 0900-2200. Good French cuisine, also set lunches. Recommended.
$$ **La Fornace**, Cevallos 1728 y Montalvo. Wood oven pizza. Opposite is **Heladería La Fornace**, Cevallos y Castillo. Snacks, sandwiches, ice cream, very popular.

$ **Govinda's**, Cuenca y Quito. Mon-Sat 0800-2030, Sun 0800-1600. Vegetarian set meals and à la carte, also a meditation centre (T282 3182).

Cafés
Crème Brulée, Juan B Vela 08-38 y Montalvo. Daily 0900-2100. Very good coffee and pastries.
Pastelería Quito, JL Mera y Cevallos. Daily 0700-2100. Coffee, pastries, good for breakfast.

@ Festivals

Ambato *p484*
Ambato has a famous festival in **Feb** or **Mar**, the **Fiesta de frutas y flores**, during carnival when there are 4 days of festivities and parades (best Sun morning and Mon night). Must book ahead to get a hotel room.

O Shopping

Ambato *p484*
Leather Ambato is a centre for leather: stores for shoes on Bolívar; jackets, bags, belts on Vela between Lalama and Montalvo. Take a local bus up to the leather town of Quisapincha for the best deals, everyday, but big market on Sat.

O What to do

Ambato *p484*
Train rides An autoferro runs from Ambato to **Urbina** and back via **Cevallos**, Fri-Sun at 0800, US$15. The train station is at Av Gran Colombia y Chile, near the Terminal Terrestre, T252 2623; open Wed-Sun 0800-1630.

O Transport

Ambato *p484*
Bus The main bus station is on Av Colombia y Paraguay, 2 km north of the centre. City buses go there from Plaza Cevallos in the centre, US$0.25. To **Quito**,

3 hrs, US$2.50; also door to door shared taxis with **Servicio Express**, T242 6828 or T09-9924 2795, 9 daily departures (fewer on Sun), US$12. To **Cuenca**, US$8, 6½ hrs. To **Guayaquil**, 6 hrs, US$6. To **Riobamba**, US$1.25, 1 hr. To **Guaranda**, US$2, 3 hrs. To **Ibarra**, via the Quito airport and bypassing Quito, CITA, 8 daily, 5 hrs, US$5. To **Santo Domingo de los Tsáchilas**, 4 hrs, US$4. To **Tena**, US$5, 4½ hrs. To **Puyo**, US$3, 2½ hrs. To **Macas**, US$7, 5½ hrs. To **Esmeraldas**, US$8, 8 hrs. **Note** Buses to **Baños** leave from the Mercado Mayorista and then stop at the edge of town, 1 hr, US$1. Through buses do not go into the terminal, they take the Paso Lateral bypass road.

❻ Directory

Ambato p484
Banks Banco de Guayaquil, JL Mera 514 y Sucre; Banco del Pacífico, Cevallos y Lalama, and Cevallos y Unidad Nacional.

Baños and Riobamba

Baños and Riobamba are both good bases for exploring the Sierra and their close proximity to high peaks gives great opportunities for climbing, cycling and trekking (but check for volcanic activity before you set out). The thermal springs at Baños are an added lure and the road east is one of the best ways to get to the jungle lowlands. On the other hand, anyone with the faintest interest in railways stops in Riobamba to ride the train on the famous section of the line from the Andes to Guayaquil, around the Devil's Nose.

Baños and around → *Phone code: 03. Colour map 1, B4. Population: 15,400. Altitude: 1800 m.*

Baños is nestled between the Río Pastaza and the Tungurahua volcano, only 8 km from its crater. Baños bursts at the seams with hotels, *residenciales*, restaurants and tour agencies. Ecuadoreans flock here on weekends and holidays for the hot springs, to visit the Basílica and enjoy the local *melcochas* (toffees), while escaping the Andean chill in a sub-tropical climate (wettest in July and August). Foreign visitors are also frequent; using Baños as a base for trekking, organizing a visit to the jungle, making local day trips on horseback or by mountain bike, or just plain hanging out.

Arriving in Baños
Tourist offices iTur ① *Oficina Municipal de Turismo, at the Municipio, Halflants y Rocafuerte, opposite Parque Central, Mon-Fri 0800-1230, 1400-1730, Sat-Sun 0800-1600.* Helpful, have colourful maps of the area, some English spoken. There are several private 'tourist information offices' run by travel agencies near the bus station; high-pressure tour sales, maps and pamphlets available. Local artist, J Urquizo, produces an accurate pictorial map of Baños, 12 de Noviembre y Ambato, also sold in many shops. There have been reports of thefts targeting tourists on Quito-Baños buses, take extra care of your hand-luggage.

In 1999, after over 80 years of dormancy, Tungurahua became active again and has remained so until the close of this edition. The level of activity is variable, the volcano can be quiet for weeks or months. Baños continues to be a safe and popular destination and will likely remain so unless the level of volcanic activity greatly increases. **Tungurahua is closed to climbers** and the direct road to Riobamba is often closed, but all else is normal. Since the level of volcanic activity can change, you should enquire locally before visiting Baños. The National Geophysical Institute posts reports on the web at www.igepn.edu.ec.

Places in Baños

The **Manto de la Virgen** waterfall at the southeast end of town is a symbol of Baños. The **Basílica** attracts many pilgrims. The paintings of miracles performed by Nuestra Señora del Agua Santa are worth seeing. There are various thermal baths in town, all charge US$2 unless otherwise noted. The **Baños de la Virgen** ① *0430-1700*, are by the waterfall. They get busy so best visit very early morning. Two small hot pools open evenings only (1800-2200, US$3). The **Piscinas Modernas** ① *Fri-Sun and holidays 0900-1700*, with a water slide, are next door. **El Salado baths** ① *0500-1700, US$3*, several hot pools, plus icy cold river water, repeatedly destroyed by volcanic debris (not safe when activity is high), 1.5 km out of town off the Ambato road. The **Santa Ana baths** ① *Fri-Sun and holidays 0900-1700*, have hot and cold pools in a pleasant setting, just east of town on the road to Puyo. All the baths can be very crowded at weekends and holidays; the brown colour of the water is due to its high mineral content.

Where to stay 🛏
1 Alisamay *B1*
2 Apart-Hotel Napolitano *A4*
3 El Belén *B2*
4 El Oro *B1*
5 Finca Chamanapamba *A4*
6 Isla de Baños *C2*
7 La Casa Verde *A4*
8 La Chimenea *C4*
9 La Floresta *C2*
10 La Petite Auberge *C3*
11 Llanovientos *C1*
12 Los Pinos *B4*
13 Luna Runtún *A3*
14 Plantas y Blanco *C3*
15 Posada del Arte *C4*
16 Princesa María *B1*
17 Puerta del Sol *B4*
18 Samari *A4*
19 Sangay *C4*
20 Santa Cruz *C3*
21 Transilvania *B3*
22 Villa Santa Clara *C4*
23 Volcano *C4*

Restaurants 🍴
1 Ali Cumba *C3*
2 Café Blah Blah *B2*
3 Café Hood *B2*
4 Casa Hood *C3*
5 El Castillo *C3*
6 La Tasca *C3*
7 Mariane *C2*
8 Pancho's *C2*
9 Rico Pan *B2*
10 Swiss Bistro *C3*

Bars & clubs 🍸
11 Buena Vista *B3*
12 Ferchos *B3*
13 Jack Rock *B3*
14 Leprechaun *B3*
15 Peña Ananitay *B3*

As well as the medicinal baths, there is a growing number of spas, in hotels, as independent centres and massage therapists. These offer a combination of sauna, steam bath (Turkish or box), jacuzzi, clay and other types of baths, a variety of massage techniques (Shiatsu, Reiki, Scandinavian) and more.

Around Baños

There are many interesting walks in the Baños area. The **San Martín shrine** is a 45-minute easy walk from town and overlooks a deep rocky canyon with the Río Pastaza thundering below. Beyond the shrine, crossing to the north side of the Pastaza, is the **Ecozoológico San Martín** ① *T274 0552, 0800-1700, US$2.50*, with the **Serpentario San Martín** ① *daily 0900-1800, US$2*, opposite. 50 m beyond is a path to the **Inés María waterfall**, cascading down, but polluted. Further, a *tarabita* (cable-car) and ziplines span the entrance to the canyon. You can also cross the Pastaza by the **Puente San Francisco** road bridge, behind the kiosks across the main road from the bus station. From here a series of trails fans out into the hills, offering excellent views of Tungurahua from the ridge-tops in clear weather. A total of six bridges span the Pastaza near Baños, so you can make a round trip.

On the hillside behind Baños, it is a 45-minute hike to the **statue of the Virgin** (good views). Go to the south end of Calle JL Mera, before the street ends, take the last street to the right, at the end of which are stairs leading to the trail. A steep path continues along the ridge, past the statue. Another trail begins at the south end of JL Mera and leads to the **Hotel Luna Runtún**, continuing on to the village of Runtún (five- to six-hour round-trip). Yet another steep trail starts at the south end of Calle Maldonado and leads in 45 minutes to the **Bellavista cross**, with a lookout and a café (open 0900-2400). You can continue from the cross to Runtún.

The scenic road to Puyo (58 km) has many waterfalls tumbling down into the Pastaza. Many *tarabitas* (cable cars) and ziplines span the Pastaza near Baños offering good views. By the Agoyán dam and bridge, 5 km from town, is **Parque de la Familia** ① *daily 0900-1700, free*, with orchards, gardens, paths and domestic animals. Beyond, the paved road goes through seven tunnels between Agoyán and Río Negro. The older gravel road runs parallel to the new road, directly above the Río Pastaza, and is the preferred route for cyclists who, coming from Baños, should only go through one tunnel at Agoyán and then stay to the right avoiding the other tunnels. Between tunnels there is only the paved road, cyclists must be very careful as there are many buses and lorries. The area has excellent opportunities for walking and nature observation.

At the junction of the Verde and Pastaza rivers, 17 km from Baños is the town of **Río Verde** with snack bars, restaurants and a few places to stay. The Río Verde has crystalline green water and is nice for bathing. The paved highway runs to the north of town, between it and the old road, the river has been dammed forming a small lake where rubber rafts are rented for paddling. Near the paved road is **Orquideario** ① *open 0900-1700, closed Wed, US$1.50*, with nice regional orchids. Before joining the Pastaza the Río Verde tumbles down several falls, the most spectacular of which is **El Pailón del Diablo** (the Devil's Cauldron). Cross the Río Verde on the old road and take the path to the right after the church, then follow the trail down towards the suspension bridge over the Pastaza, for about 20 minutes. Just before the bridge take a side trail to the right (signposted) which leads you to **Paradero del Pailón**, a nice restaurant, and viewing platforms above the falls (US$1.50). The **San Miguel Falls**, smaller but also nice, are some five minutes' walk from the town along a different trail. Cross the old bridge and take the first path to the right, here is **Falls Garden** (US$1.50), with lookout platforms over both sets of falls. Cyclists can leave the bikes at one of the snack bars while visiting the falls and return to Baños by bus.

Baños and around listings

For hotel and restaurant price codes, and other relevant information, see pages 14-17.

Where to stay

Baños *p487, map p488*
Baños has plenty of accommodation but can fill during holiday weekends.

$$$$ Luna Runtún, Caserío Runtún Km 6, T274 0882, www.lunaruntun.com. A classy hotel in a beautiful setting overlooking Baños. Includes dinner, breakfast and use of pools (spa extra), very comfortable rooms with balconies and superb views, lovely gardens. Good service, English, French and German spoken, tours, nanny service.

$$$$ Samari, Vía a Puyo Km 1, T274 1855, www.samarispa.com. Upmarket resort opposite the Santa Ana baths, nice grounds, tastefully decorated hacienda-style rooms and suites, pool and spa, restaurant.

$$$ Finca Chamanapamba, on the east shore of the Río Ulba, a short ride from the road to Puyo, T274 2671, www.chamanapamba.com. 2 nicely finished wooden cabins in a spectacular location overlooking the Río Ulba and just next to the Chamanapamba waterfalls, very good café-restaurant serves German food.

$$$ Posada del Arte, Pasaje Velasco Ibarra y Montalvo, T274 0083, www.posadadelarte.com. Nice cosy inn, restaurant with vegetarian options, pleasant sitting room, some rooms have fireplace, terrace, US run.

$$$ Sangay, Plazoleta Isidro Ayora 100, next to waterfall and thermal baths, T274 0490, www.sangayspahotel.com. A traditional Baños hotel and spa with 3 types of rooms, buffet breakfast, good restaurant specializes in Ecuadorean food, pool and spa open to non-residents 1600-2000 (US$10), parking, tennis and squash courts, games room, car hire, disco, attentive service, mid-week discounts, British/Ecuadorean-run. Recommended.

$$$ Volcano, Rafael Vieira y Montalvo, T274 2140, www.volcano.com.ec. Nice spacious modern hotel, large rooms with fridge, some with views of the waterfall, buffet breakfast, restaurant, heated pool, massage, nice garden.

$$ Alisamay, Espejo y JL Mera, T2741391, www.hotelalisamay.com. Rustic, nice cosy rooms with balconies, includes breakfast and use of spa, gardens with pools.

$$ Apart-Hotel Napolitano, C Oriente 470 y Suárez, T274 2464, napolitano-apart-hotel@hotmail.com. Large comfortable apartments with kitchen, fireplace, pool and spa, garden, parking. A bit pricey, daily rentals or US$600 per month.

$$ Isla de Baños, Halflants 1-31 y Montalvo, T274 0609, www.isladebanios.com. Nicely decorated comfortable hotel, includes European breakfast and steam bath, spa operates when there are enough people, pleasant garden.

$$ La Casa Verde, in Santa Ana, 1.5 km from town on Camino Real, a road parallell and north of the road to Puyo, T09-8659 4189, www.lacasaverde.com.ec. Very nice spacious hotel decorated in pine, the largest rooms in Baños, laundry and cooking facilities, very quiet, New Zealand-run.

$$ La Floresta, Halflants y Montalvo, T274 1824, www.laflorestahotel.com. Nice hotel with large comfortable rooms set around a lovely garden, excellent buffet breakfast, wheelchair accessible, parking, attentive service. Warmly recommended.

$$ La Petite Auberge, 16 de Diciembre y Montalvo, T274 0936, www.lepetit.banios.com. Rooms around a patio, some with fireplace, good upmarket French restaurant, parking, quiet.

$$-$ Los Pinos, Ricardo Zurita y C Ambato, T274 1825. Large hostel with double rooms and dorms (US$8-10 pp), spa, kitchen and laundry facilities, pool table Argentine-run, good value.

$$-$ Puerta del Sol, Ambato y Arrayanes (east end of C Ambato), T274 2265. Modern

hotel, nicer than it looks on the outside, large well-appointed rooms, pleasant dining area, laundry facilities, parking.
$ El Belén, Reyes y Ambato, T274 1024, www.hotelelbelen.com. Nice hostel, cooking facilities, spa, parking, helpful staff.
$ El Oro, Ambato y JL Mera, T274 0736. With bath, US$7 pp in dorm, laundry and cooking facilities, good value, popular. Recommended.
$ La Chimenea, Martínez y Rafael Vieira, T274 2725, www.hostalchimenea.com. Nice hostel with terrace café, breakfast available, private or shared bath, US$7.50 pp in dorm, small pool, jacuzzi extra, parking for small cars, quiet, helpful and good value. Recommended.
$ Llanovientos, Martínez 1126 y Sebastián Baño, T274 0682, www.llanovientos.banios.com. Modern breezy hostel with wonderful views, comfortable rooms, cafeteria, cooking facilities, parking, nice garden. Recommended.
$ Plantas y Blanco, 12 de Noviembre y Martínez, T274 0044, www.plantasyblanco.com. Pleasant popular hostel decorated with plants, private or shared bath, US$6-8 pp in dorm, excellent breakfast available, rooftop cafeteria, steam bath, classic films, bakery, French owned, good value. Repeatedly recommended.
$ Princesa María, Rocafuerte y Mera, T274 1035. Spacious rooms, US$7 pp in dorm, laundry and cooking facilities, parking, popular budget travellers' meeting place, helpful and good value.
$ Santa Cruz, 16 de Diciembre y Martínez, T274 3527, www.santacruzbackpackers.com. Large rooms, US$8 pp in dorm, fireplace in lounge, small garden with hammocks, kitchen facilities, mini pool on roof. New management in 2013.
$ Transilvania, 16 de Diciembre y Oriente, T274 2281, www.hostal-transilvania.com. Multi-storey building with simple rooms, includes breakfast, US$7.90 in dorm, Middle Eastern restaurant, nice views from balconies, large TV and movies in sitting room, pool table, popular meeting place.

$ Villa Santa Clara, 12 de Noviembre y Velasco Ibarra, T274 0349, www.hotelvilla santaclara.com. Nice cabins in a quiet location, laundry facilities, wheelchair accessible, garden, spa, parking.

Around Baños p489
$$$ Miramelindo, Río Verde, just north of the paved road, T249 3004, www.miramelindo.banios.com. Lovely hotel and spa, nicely decorated rooms, good restaurant, pleasant gardens include an orchid collection with over 1000 plants.
$$ Hostería Río Verde, between the paved road and town, T288 4207 (Ambato), www.hosteriarioverde.com. Simple cabins in a rural setting, includes breakfast and use of spa, large pool, restaurant specializes in trout and tilapia.

Restaurants

Baños p487, map p488
$$$ Swiss Bistro, Martínez y Alfaro. Tue-Sat 1200-2300, Sun 1200-1700, Mon 1800-2300. International dishes and Swiss specialities, Swiss-run.
$$$-$$ La Tasca, 12 de Noviembre y Martínez. Wed-Sun 1830-2230, Sat-Sun also 1230-1600. Spanish cuisine, tapas, Spanish-owned.
$$ Mariane, on a small lane by Montalvo y Halflants. Mon-Sat 1300-2200. Excellent authentic Provençal cuisine, large portions, lovely setting, pleasant atmosphere, popular, slow service. Highly recommended. **Hotel Mariane ($$)** at the same location, very clean and pleasant.
$$-$ Café Hood, Maldonado y Ambato, at Parque Central. Open 1000-2200, closed Wed. Mainly vegetarian but also some meat dishes, excellent food, English spoken, always busy. Also rents rooms.
$$-$ Casa Hood, Martínez between Halflants and Alfaro. Open 1200-2200. Largely vegetarian, but also serve some meat dishes, juices, milkshakes, varied menu including Indonesian and Thai dishes,

good set lunch and desserts. Travel books and maps sold, book exchange, repertory cinema, occasional cultural events, nice atmosphere. Popular and recommended.
$ El Castillo, Martínez y Rafael Vieira, in hostel. Open 0800-1000, 1200-1330. Breakfast and good set lunch.

Cafés
Ali Cumba, 12 de Noviembre y Martínez. Daily 0700-1900. Excellent breakfasts, salads, good coffee (filtered, espresso), muffins, cakes, home-made bread, large sandwiches, book exchange. Danish/Ecuadorean-run.
Café Blah Blah, Halflants y Matrínez. Daily 0800-2000. Cosy café serving very good breakfasts, coffee, cakes, snacks and juices, a popular meeting place.
Pancho's, Rocafuerte y Maldonado at Parque Central. Daily 1500-2200. Hamburgers, snacks, sandwiches, coffee,
Rico Pan, Ambato y Maldonado at Parque Central. Mon-Sat 0700-2000, Sun 0700-1300. Good breakfasts, hot bread (including whole wheat), fruit salads and pizzas, also meals.

🍸 Bars and clubs

Baños *p487, map p488*
Eloy Alfaro, between Ambato and Oriente has many bars including:
Buena Vista, Alfaro y Oriente. A good place for salsa and other Latin music.
Ferchos, Alfaro y Oriente. Tue-Sun 1600-2400. Café-bar, modern decor, snacks, cakes, good varied music, German-run.
Jack Rock, Alfaro y Ambato. A favourite traveller hangout.
Leprechaun, Alfaro y Oriente. Popular for dancing, bonfire on weekends, occasional live music.

🎭 Entertainment

Baños *p487, map p488*
Chivas, open-sided buses, cruise town playing music, they take you to different night spots and to a volcano lookout when Tungurahua is active.
Peña Ananitay, 16 de Diciembre y Espejo. Bar, good live music and dancing on weekends, US$2 cover.

🎉 Festivals

Baños *p487, map p488*
During Carnival and Holy Week hotels are full and prices rise.
Oct Nuestra Señora de Agua Santa with daily processions, bands, fireworks, sporting events and partying through the month. Week-long celebrations ending **16 Dec** The town's anniversary, parades, fairs, sports, cultural events. The night of **15 Dec** are the **Verbenas**, when each *barrio* hires a band and parties.

🛍 Shopping

Baños *p487, map p488*
Look out for jaw-aching toffee (*melcocha*) made in ropes in shop doorways, or the less sticky *alfeñique*.
Handicrafts Crafts stalls at Pasaje Ermita de la Vírgen, off C Ambato, by the market. Tagua (vegetable ivory made from palm nuts) crafts on Maldonado y Martínez. Leather shops on Rocafuerte between Halflants and 16 de Diciembre.
Las Orquídeas, Ambato y Maldonado by Parque Central and at **Hostal La Floresta**. Excellent selection of crafts, some guidebooks and coffee-table books.
Latino Shop, Ambato y Alfaro and 4 other locations. For T-shirts.

🎯 What to do

Baños *p487, map p488*
Potentially hazardous activities are popular in Baños, including mountaineering, white water rafting, canyoning, canopying and bridge jumps. Safety standards vary greatly. There is seldom any recourse in the event

of a mishap so these activities are entirely at your own risk.

Bus tours The *chivas* (see entertainment, above) and a **double-decker bus** (C Ambato y Halflants, T274 0596, US$6) visit waterfalls and other attractions. Check about their destination if you have a specific interest such as El Pailón falls.

Canopying or zipline Involves hanging from a harness and sliding on a steel cable. Prices vary according to length, about US$10-20. Cable car, about US$1.50.

Canyoning Many agencies offer this sport, rates US$30 half day, US$50 full day.

Climbing and trekking There are countless possibilities for walking and nature observation near Baños and to the east. Tungurahua has been officially closed to climbers since 1999. There is nobody to stop you from entering the area, but the dangers of being hit by flying volcanic bombs are very real. Operators offer trekking and climbing tours to Cotopaxi and Chimborazo.

Cycling Many places rent bikes, quality varies, US$5-10 per day; check brakes and tyres, find out who has to pay for repairs, and insist on a helmet, puncture repair kit and pump. The following have good equipment: **Carrillo Hermanos**, 16 de Diciembre y Martínez. Rents mountain bikes and motorcycles (reliable machines with helmets, US10 per hr).
Hotel Isla de Baños, cycling tours US$15-20.

Horse riding There are several places, but check their horses as not all are well cared for. Rates around US$6-8 per hr, US$40 per day. The following have been recommended:
Angel Aldaz, Montalvo y JL Mera (on the road to the statue of the Virgin).
Hotel Isla de Baños, see above. Horses for rent; 3½ hrs with a guide and jeep transport costs US$35 pp, English and German spoken.
José & Two Dogs, Maldonado y Martínez, T274 0746. Flexible hours.
Ringo Horses, 12 de Noviembre y Martínez (Apart-hotel El Napolitano). Nice horses, offers rides outside Baños.

Paragliding See www.aeropasion.net; US$60 per day.

Puenting Many operators offer this bungee-jumping-like activity from the bridges around Baños, US$10-15 per jump, heights and styles vary.

Whitewater rafting Fatal accidents have occurred, but not with the agencies listed here. Rates US$30 for half-day, US$60-70 for full-day. The Chambo, Patate and Pastaza rivers are all polluted. **Geotours** and **Wonderful Ecuador** are good (see below).

Tour operators
There are many tour agencies in town, some with several offices, as well as 'independent' guides who seek out tourists on the street (the latter are generally not recommended). Quality varies considerably; to obtain a qualified guide and avoid unscrupulous operators, it is best to seek advice from other travellers who have recently returned from a tour. We have received some critical reports of tours out of Baños, but there are also highly respected and qualified operators here. In all cases, insist on a written contract. Most agencies and guides offer trips to the jungle (US$50-70 per day pp). There are also volcano-watching, trekking and horse tours, in addition to the day trips and sports mentioned above. Several companies run tours aboard a *chiva* (open-sided bus). The following agencies and guides have received positive recommendations but the list is not exhaustive and there are certainly others.
Expediciones Amazónicas, Oriente 11-68 y Halflants, T274 0506.
Explorsierra, Oriente y Halflants, T274 0514. Also rent equipment.
Geotours, Ambato y Halflants, next to Banco Pichincha, T274 1344, www.geotoursbanios. com. Also offer paragliding for US$60.
Imagine Ecuador, 16 de Diciembre y Montalvo, T274 3472, www.imagineecuador.com.
Sachayacu Explorer, Bolívar 229 y Urbina, in Píllaro, T287 5316 or T09-8740 3376, www.parquellanganates.com. Trekking in the Llanganates, jungle tours in

Huaorani territory, Yasuní and as far as Peru, English spoken.
Wonderful Ecuador, Maldonado y Oriente, T274 1580, www.wonderfulecuador.org.

🚌 Transport

Baños *p487, map p488*
Bus City buses run from Alfaro y Martínez east to Agoyán and from Rocafuerte by the market, west to El Salado and the zoo. The long-distance bus station is on the Ambato-Puyo road (Av Amazonas). To **Río Verde** take any Puyo-bound bus, through buses don't go in the station, 20 mins, US$0.50. To **Quito**, US$3.50, 3 hrs, frequent service; going to Quito sit on the right for views of Cotopaxi, buy tickets early for weekends and holidays. For shared taxis from Quito, see **Autovip**, page 447. Note that buses from Quito to Baños are the target of thieves, take a shared taxi or bus to Ambato and transfer there. To **Ambato**, 1 hr, US$0.80. To **Riobamba**, the direct Baños–Riobamba road is sometimes closed due to Tungurahua's volcanic activity (also dangerous after rain), most buses go via Mocha, 1½ hrs, US$2. To **Latacunga**,

2 hrs, US$2. To **Otavalo** and **Ibarra** direct, bypassing Quito, **Expreso Baños**, at 0400 and 1440, US$6, 5½ hrs. To **Guayaquil**, 1 bus per day and one overnight, 6-7 hrs; or change in Riobamba. To **Puyo**, 1½ hrs, US$2. Sit on the right. You can cycle to Puyo and take the bus back (passport check on the way). To **Tena**, 3½ hrs, US$4. To **Misahuallí**, change at Tena. To **Macas**, 4½ hrs, US$6 (sit on the right).

ℹ️ Directory

Baños *p487, map p488*
Banks Banco del Austro, Halflants y Rocafuerte, ATM. Banco del Pacífico, Halflants y Rocafuerte, Parque Central, ATM. **Don Pedro**, Halflants y Martínez, hardware store, open weekends, 3% commission on TCs. Also exchanges Euros and other currencies. **Language schools** Spanish schools charge US$5.50-8 per hr, many also offer homestays. Baños Spanish Center, www.spanishcenter school.com. Home Stay Baños, T274 0453. Mayra's, www.mayraspanishschool.com. Raíces, www.spanishlessons.org.

Riobamba and around

Guaranda and Riobamba are good bases for exploring the Sierra. Riobamba is the bigger of the two and is on the famous railway line from Quito to Guayaquil. Many indigenous people from the surrounding countryside can be seen in both cities on market days. Because of their central location Riobamba and the surrounding province are known as 'Corazón de la Patria' – the heartland of Ecuador – and the city boasts the nickname 'La Sultana de Los Andes' in honour of lofty Mount Chimborazo.

Riobamba → *Phone code: 03. Colour map 1, B3. Population: 162,000. Altitude: 2754 m. See map, page 496.*
The capital of Chimborazo Province has broad streets and many ageing but impressive buildings. **Tourist office**: iTur ① *Av Daniel León Borja y Brasil, T296 3159, Mon-Fri 0800-1230, 1430-1800,* municipal information office. The **Ministerio de Turismo** ① *3 doors from iTur, in the Centro de Arte y Cultura, T294 1213, Mon-Fri 0830-1730,* is very helpful and knowledgeable.
The main square is **Parque Maldonado** around which are the **Cathedral**, the **Municipality** and several colonial buildings with arcades. The Cathedral has a beautiful colonial stone façade and an incongruously modern interior. Four blocks northeast of the railway station is the **Parque 21 de Abril**, named after the Batalla de Tapi, 21 April 1822, the city's independence from Spain. The park, better known as **La Loma de Quito**, affords

an unobstructed view of Riobamba and Chimborazo, Carihuairazo, Tungurahua, El Altar and occasionally Sangay. It also has a colourful tile tableau of the history of Ecuador; ask about safety before visiting. The **Convento de la Concepción** ① *Orozco y España, entrance at Argentinos y J Larrea, T296 5212, Tue-Sat, 0900-1230, 1500-1730, US$3*, has a religious art museum. **Museo del Ministerio de Cultura** ① *Veloz y Montalvo, T296 5501, Mon-Fri 0900-1700, free; temporarily closed in 2014*, has well-displayed exhibits of archaeology and colonial art. **Museo de la Ciudad** ① *Primera Constituyente y Espejo, at Parque Maldonado, T294 4420, Mon-Fri 0800-1230, 1430-1800, free*, in a beautifully restored colonial building, has an interesting historical photograph exhibit and temporary displays.

Riobamba is an important **market** centre where people from many communities congregate. Saturday is the main day when the city fills with colourfully dressed *indígenas* from all over Chimborazo, each wearing their distinctive costume; trading overflows the markets and buying and selling go on all over town. Wednesday is a smaller market day. The 'tourist' market is in the small **Plaza de la Concepción or Plaza Roja** ① *Orozco y Colón, Sat and Wed only, 0800-1500*, is a good place to buy local handicrafts and authentic Indian clothing. The main produce market is **San Alfonso**, Argentinos y 5 de Junio, which on Saturday spills over into the nearby streets and also sells clothing, ceramics, baskets and hats. Other markets in the colonial centre are **La Condamine** ① *Carabobo y Colombia, daily*, largest market on Fridays, **San Francisco** and **La Merced**, near the churches of the same name.

Guano is a carpet-weaving, sisal and leather working town 8 km north of Riobamba. Many shops sell rugs and you can arrange to have these woven to your own design. Buses leave from the Mercado Dávalos, García Moreno y New York, every 15 minutes, US$0.25, last bus back at 1900, taxi US$4.

Guaranda → *Phone code: 03. Colour map 1, B3. Population: 57,500. Altitude: 2650 m.*

This quaint town, capital of Bolívar Province, proudly calls itself 'the Rome of Ecuador' because it is built on seven hills. There are fine views of the mountains all around and a colourful market. Locals traditionally take an evening stroll in the palm-fringed main plaza, **Parque Libertador Simón Bolívar**, around which are the Municipal buildings and a large stone **Cathedral**. Towering over the city, on one of the hills, is an impressive statue of **El Indio Guaranga**; museum (free) and art gallery. Although not on the tourist trail, there are many sights worth visiting in the province, for which Guaranda is the ideal base. Of particular interest is the highland town of **Salinas**, with its community development projects (accommodations and tours available, see Where to stay), as well as the *subtrópico* region, the lowlands stretching west towards the coast.

Market days are Friday (till 1200) and Saturday (larger), when many indigenous people in typical dress trade at the market complex at the east end of Calle Azuay, by Plaza 15 de Mayo (9 de Abril y Maldonado), and at Plaza Roja (Avenida Gen Enríquez). Carnival in Guaranda is among the best known in the country. **Tourist office**: **Oficina Municipal de Turismo** ① *García Moreno entre 7 de Mayo y Convención de 1884, T298 5877, www.guaranda.gob.ec (in Spanish), Mon-Fri 0800-1200, 1400-1800*. Provides Information in Spanish and maps. www. gobiernodebolivar.gob.ec has information in Spanish about regional attractions.

Reserva Faunística Chimborazo → *See also Riobamba Tour operators.*

① *Information from Ministerio del Ambiente, Avenida 9 de Octubre y Duchicela, Quinta Macají, Riobamba, T261 0029, ext107, Mon-Fri 0800-1300, 1400-1700*. Visitors arriving without a guide or with guides not authorized by the ministry are turned back at the gate; exceptions are made for members of alpine clubs, apply for an entry permit at the Ministerio del

Ambiente in Riobamba. The most outstanding features of this reserve, created to protect the camelids (vicuñas, alpacas and llamas) which were re-introduced here, are the beautiful snow-capped volcanos of **Chimborazo** and its neighbour **Carihuayrazo**. Chimborazo, inactive, is the highest peak in Ecuador (6310 m), while Carihuayrazo, 5020 m, is dwarfed by its neighbour. Day visitors can enjoy lovely views, a glimpse of the handsome vicuñas and the rarefied air above 4800 m. There are great opportunities for trekking on the eastern slopes, accessed from **Urbina**, west of the Ambato–Riobamba road, and of course climbing Ecuador's highest peak. Horse riding and trekking tours are offered along the Mocha Valley between the two peaks and downhill cycling from Chimborazo is popular.

To the west of the reserve runs the Vía del Arenal which joins San Juan, along the Riobamba–Guaranda road, with Cruce del Arenal on the Ambato–Guaranda road. A turn-off from this road leads to the main park entrance and beyond to the **Refugio Hermanos Carrel**, a shelter at 4800 m, from where it is a 45-minute walk to **Refugio Whymper** at 5000 m. The shelters were closed for reconstruction in early 2014 and expected to reopen later that year. The access from Riobamba (51 km, paved to the park entrance) is very beautiful. Along the Vía del Arenal past San Juan are a couple of small indigenous communities which grow a few crops and raise llamas and alpacas. They offer lodging and *guías nativos*, the area is good for acclimatization The *arenal* is a large sandy plateau at about 4400 m, to the west of Chimborazo, just below the main park entrance. It can be a harsh, windy place, but it is also very beautiful; take the time to admire the tiny flowers which grow here. This is the best place to see vicuñas, which hang around either in family groups, one male and its harem, or lone males which have been expelled from the group.

Climbing Chimborazo At 6310 m, this is a difficult climb owing to the altitude. Climbers must go with a certified guide working for an operator who has a special permit (*patente*). Rope, ice-axe, helmet and crampons must be used. It is essential to have at least one week's

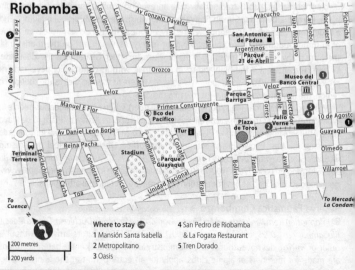

Where to stay 🛏
1 Mansión Santa Isabella
2 Metropolitano
3 Oasis
4 San Pedro de Riobamba
& La Fogata Restaurant
5 Tren Dorado

acclimatization above 3500 m. The best seasons are December and June-September. Deglaciation is making the climb more difficult and ice pinnacles, *penitentes*, sometimes prevent climbers reaching the main, Whymper summit.

The Devil's Nose Train

This spectacular ride is popular with Ecuadorean and foreign tourists alike. In 2014, tourist trains ran from Alausí to Sibambe, the most scenic part of the trip including the **Devil's Nose**, and from Riobamba north to Urbina and south to Colta. The route Riobamba–Alausí–Sibambe is scheduled to operate in 2015. For details see What to do, page 501.

Alausí → *Phone code: 03. Colour map 1, B3. Population: 10,500. Altitude: 2350 m.*

This picturesque town perched on a hillside is where many passengers join the train for the amazing descent over *La Nariz de Diablo* to Sibambe. There is good walking, a Sunday market and a **Fiesta de San Pedro** on 29 June.

Parque Nacional Sangay

Riobamba provides access to the central highland region of **Sangay National Park** ① *information from Ministerio del Ambiente, see Reserva Chimborazo above*, a beautiful wilderness area with excellent opportunities for trekking and climbing. A spectacular but controversial road, good for downhill biking, runs from Riobamba to Macas in the Oriente, cutting through the park. Near Cebadas (with a good cheese factory) a branch road joins from **Guamote**, a quiet, mainly indigenous town on the Pan-American highway, which comes to life during its colourful Thursday market. At **Atillo**, south of Cebadas, an area of lovely páramo dotted with lakes, there is lodging (US$7 per person) and restaurant at **Cabaña Saskines** (T03-230 3290, atillosaskines@hotmail.com). **Sangay** (5230 m) is an active volcano, access to the mountain takes at least three days and is only for those

Restaurants 🍴
1 Bom Café
2 Helados de Paila
3 Jamones La Andaluza & Naranjo's
4 Lulu's
5 Mónaco Pizzería

who can endure long, hard days of walking and severe weather. Climbing Sangay can be dangerous even on a quiet day and a helmet to protect against falling stones is vital, November to January is a good time to climb it. Agencies in Quito and Riobamba offer tours or you can organize an expedition independently. A guide is essential, porters can be hired in the access towns of **Alao** and **Guarguallá**. The latter has a **community tourism project** ① *T03-302 6688, accommodation in Guarguallá Chico US$12 pp, US$21 pp with dinner and breakfast, kitchen facilities. Guías nativos, US$30 per day, porters and horses US$15 per day*. Also in Sangay National Park is the beautiful **El Altar** volcano (5315 m), whose crater is surrounded by nine summits. The most popular climbing and trekking routes begin beyond Candelaria at **Hacienda Releche** (see Where to stay).

For hotel and restaurant price codes, and other relevant information, see pages 14-17.

⊙ Where to stay

Riobamba *p494, map p496*

$$$ Abraspungo, Km 3 on the road to Guano, T236 4275, www.hacienda abraspungo.com. Nice hotel in a country setting, comfortable rooms, includes buffet breakfast, excellent restaurant, parking, attentive service. Recommended.

$$$ La Andaluza, 16 km north of Riobamba along the Panamericana, T294 9371, www. hosteriaandaluza.com. An old hacienda, rooms with heaters and roaring fireplaces, good restaurant, lovely views, good walking.

$$$ Mansión Santa Isabella, Veloz 28-48 y Carabobo, T296 2947, www.mansion santaisabella.com. Lovely restored house with pleasant patio, comfortable rooms most with bathtub, duvets, restaurant serves set lunches and à la carte, bar in stone basement, parking, attentive service, British/Ecuadorean-run. Recommended.

$$$ San Pedro de Riobamba, Daniel L Borja 29-50 y Montalvo, opposite the train station, T294 0586, www. hotelsanpedroderiobamba.com. Elegant hotel in a beautifully restored house in the centre of town, ample comfortable rooms, bathtubs, cafeteria, parking, covered patio, reservations required. Recommended.

$$ Rincón Alemán, Remigio Romero y Alfredo Pareja, Ciudadela Arupos del Norte, T260 3540, www.hostalrinconaleman.com. Family-run hotel in a quiet residential area north of the centre, nice ample rooms, laundry and cooking facilities, parking, fireplace, sauna, gym, garden, terrace, nice views, German spoken.

$$-$ Tren Dorado, Carabobo 22-35 y 10 de Agosto, near the train station, T296 4890, www.hoteltrendorado.com. Modern hotel with nice large rooms, buffet breakfast available (starting 0730, open to non-

guests), restaurant, reliable hot water, good value. Recommended.

$ Metropolitano, Daniel L Borja y Lavalle, near the train station, T296 1714. One of the oldest hotels in Riobamba, built in 1912 and nicely restored. Ample rooms, breakfast available.

$ Oasis, Veloz 15-32 y Almagro, T296 1210, www.oasishostelriobamba.com. Small, pleasant, family-run hostel in a quiet location, laundry facilities, some rooms with kitchen and fridge, shared kitchen for the others, parking, nice garden, Wi-Fi US$1 per day, popular with backpackers. Recommended.

Guaranda *p495*

$$$ La Colina, Av Guayaquil 117, on the road to Ambato, T298 0666, www.complejo lacolina.com. Nicely situated on a quiet hillside overlooking the city. Bright spacious rooms, nice views, small covered swimming pool (not always open) and sauna (weekends only), gardens, parking, tours available.

$$ Bolívar, Sucre 704 y Rocafuerte, T298 0547, http://hotelbolivar.wordpress.com. Pleasant hotel with courtyard, small modern rooms, best quality in the centre of town. Restaurant next door open Mon-Fri for economical breakfasts and lunches.

$$ Mansión del Parque, 10 de Agosto y Sucre, T298 4468. Nicely restored colonial house, spacious rooms, some with balcony, cafeteria, good value.

$ El Marquez, 10 de Agosto y Eloy Alfaro, T298 1053. Pleasant hotel with family atmosphere, newer rooms with private bath are clean and modern, older ones with shared bath are cheaper, parking.

Salinas

$ Hotel Refugio Salinas, 45 min from Guaranda, T221 0044, www.salinerito.com. Pleasant community-run hotel, economical meals on request, private or shared bath, dining/sitting area with fireplace, visits to community projects, walking and horse riding tours, packages available, advance booking advised.

$ La Minga, by the main plaza, T221 0108, www.laminga.ec. Simple rooms with bath and dorms, meals on request, fullboard packages including tour available.

Reserva Faunística Chimborazo *p495*
The following are all good for acclimatization; those in Urbina can be reached by autoferro from either Riobamba or Ambato.

$$ Refugio del Tren, at the Urbina railway station 2 km west of the highway, at 3619 m, T09-981 76400. Converted train station, shared bath, price includes dinner and breakfast, fireplace in common areas and one room, heaters.

$ Casa Cóndor, in Pulinguí San Pablo, Vía del Arenal, T03-235 4034, T09-8650 8152. Basic community-run hostel, dinner and breakfast available, use of cooking facilities extra, tours in the area.

$ Portal Andino, at 4200 m, 4- to 5-hr walk from Urbina, T09-9165 0788. Simple hostel with bunk-beds, shared bath, hot water, use of cooking facilities extra.

$ Posada de la Estación, opposite the Urbina railway station,T09-9969 4867, www.altamontana.net. Comfortable rooms with heaters, shared bath, meals available, wood stoves, magnificent views, trips and equipment arranged, tagua workshop, helpful. Also run **$ Urcu Huasi**, cabins at 4150 m, 10 km (2½ hrs walking) from Urbina, in an area being reforested with polylepis.

Alausí *p497*
$$$$ Posada de las Nubes, on the north side of the Río Chanchán, 7 or 11 km from Alausí depending on the route, best with 4WD, pick-up from Alausí US$7, T293 0535 or T09-9315 0847, www.posadadelasnubes. com. Rustic hacienda house in cloud forest at 2600 m. Rooms are simple to basic for the price, some with bath, full board, hiking and horse riding, advance booking required.
$$$ La Quinta, Eloy Alfaro 121 y M Muñoz, T293 0247, www.hosteria-la-quinta.com.

Nicely restored old house along the rail line to Riobamba. Pleasant atmosphere, some rooms are ample, restaurant, gardens, excellent views, not always open, reserve ahead.
$$ Gampala, 5 de Junio 122 y Loza, T293 0138, www.hotelgampala.com. Nicely refurbished modern rooms and 1 suite with jacuzzi (**$$$**), restaurant and bar with pool table.
$$-$ La Posada del Tren, 5 de Junio y Orozco, T293 1293. Nice, modern, parking.
$$-$ San Pedro, 5 de Junio y 9 de Octubre, T293 0089, hostalsanpedro@hotmail.com. Simple comfortable rooms, a few cheaper rooms in older section, restaurant downstairs, parking, nice owner.

Parque Nacional Sangay *p497*
$ Hostal Capac Urcu, at Hacienda Releche, near the village of Candelaria, T301 4067. Basic rooms in small working hacienda. Use of kitchen (US$6) or meals prepared on request, rents horses for the trek to Collanes, US$11 per horse each way, plus US$12.50 per muleteer each way. Also runs the *refugio* at Collanes (same price), by the crater of El Altar: thatched-roof rustic shelters with solar hot water. The *refugio* is cold, take a warm sleeping bag.

Guamote
$$ Inti Sisa, Vargas Torres y García Moreno, T291 6529, www.intisisa.org. Basic but nice guesthouse, part of a community development project, most rooms with bath, US$18.75 pp in dorm, includes breakfast, other meals available, dining room and communal area with fireplace, horse riding and cycling tours to highland villages, reservations necessary.

🍴 Restaurants

Riobamba *p494, map p496*
Most places closed after 2100 and on Sun.
$$ Lulu's, Veloz 10-41 y Puruha. Tue-Sun 1230-1500, 1800-2200. Bar/restaurant with excellent set lunch and à la carte Ecuadorean and American food, no vegetarian options, nice ambiance.

$$ Mónaco Pizzería, Av de la Prensa y Francisco Aguilar. Mon-Fri 1500-2200, Sat-Sun 1200-2200. Delicious pizza and pasta, nice salads, good food, service and value. Recommended.

$ La Fogata, Av Daniel L Borja y Carabobo, opposite the train station. Daily 0700-2200. Simple but good local food, economical set meals and breakfast.

$ Naranjo's, Daniel L Borja 36-20 y Uruguay. Tue-Sun 1200-1500. Excellent set lunch, friendly service, popular with locals.

Cafés and bakeries

Bom Café, Pichincha 21-37 y 10 de Agosto. Mon-Sat 1000-1300, 1600-2200. Very nice European-style coffee shop, with a good choice of coffee and sandwiches.

Helados de Paila, Espejo y 10 de Agosto. Daily 0900-1900. Excellent home-made ice cream, coffee, sweets, popular.

Jamones La Andaluza, Daniel L Borja y Uruguay. Open 0900–2300. Indoor and outdoor seating, good coffee, sandwiches, salads, variety of cold cuts and cheeses, tapas.

La Abuela Rosa, Brasil y Esmeraldas. Mon-Sat 1600-2100. Cafetería in grandmother's house serving typical Ecuadorean snacks. Nice atmosphere and good service.

Guaranda *p495*

See also Where to stay. Most places close on Sun.

$$ Pizza Buon Giorno, Sucre at Parque Bolívar. Tue-Sun 1200-2200. Pizza and salads.

$$-$ La Bohemia, Convención de 1884 y 10 de Agosto. Mon-Sat 0800-2100. Very good economical set meals and pricier international dishes à la carte, nice decor and ambience, very popular. Recommended.

$$-$ La Estancia, García Moreno y Sucre. Mon 1200-1500, Tue-Sat 1200-2100. Excellent buffet lunch for quality, variety and value, à la carte in the evening, nicely decorated, pleasant atmosphere, popular.

Cafés

Cafetería 7 Santos, Convención de 1884 y Olmedo. Mon-Sat 1000-2200. Pleasant café and bar with open courtyard. Good coffee and snacks, fireplace, live music Fri and Sat, popular.

El Taquito, 10 de Agosto y 9 de Abril. Daily 0700-2200. Small bar with Mexican snacks and meals.

Juad's, Convención de 1884 y Azuay. Mon-Sat 0900-1300, 1500-1900. Very good, popular, cappuccino, hot chocolate, sandwiches, fruit salad, pastries, go early. Recommended.

Salinerito, Plaza Roja. Daily 0800-1300, 1430-1900. Salinas cheese shop also serves coffee, sandwiches and pizza.

Alausí *p497*

$$ El Mesón del Tren, Ricaurte y Eloy Alfaro. Tue-Sun 0700-0930, 1200-1430. Good restaurant, popular with tour groups, breakfast, set lunch and à la carte.

$$ Bukardia, Guatemala 107. Open 1300-2200, closed Wed. Meat specialities, snacks and drinks.

$ Flamingo, Antonio Mora y 9 de Octubre. 0700-2000, closed Sat. Good economical set meals. Also run **$$-$ Ventura Hostal**, simple.

🎵 Bars and clubs

Riobamba *p494, map p496*

Restobar La Rayuela, Daniel L Borja 36-30 y Uruguay. Mon-Sat 1200-2200, Sun 1200-1800. Trendy bar/restaurant, live music on Fri, sandwiches, coffee, salads, pasta.

San Valentín, Daniel L Borja y Vargas Torres. Mon-Sat 1800-0200. Very popular bar, good pizzas and Mexican dishes.

✪ Entertainment

Riobamba *p494, map p496*

Casa de la Cultura, 10 de Agosto y Rocafuerte, T296 0219. Cultural events, cinema on Tue.

Super Cines, at El Paseo Shopping, Vía a Guano, 12 modern cinema halls, some films in 3-D.

Riobamba *p494, map p496*
Fiesta del Niño Rey de Reyes, street parades, music and dancing, starts in **Dec** and culminates on **6 Jan**. Around **21 Apr** there are **independence** celebrations lasting several days, hotel prices rise. **29 Jun** Fiestas Patronales in honour of San Pedro. **11 Nov** is the festival to celebrate the 1st attempt at independence from Spain.

○ Shopping

Riobamba *p494, map p496*
Camping gear Some of the tour operators hire camping and climbing gear. **Marathon Explorer**, at Multiplaza mall, Av Lizarzaburu near the airport. High-end outdoor equipment and clothing. **Protección Industrial**, Rocafuerte 24-51 y Orozco, T296 3017. Outdoor equipment, rope, fishing supplies, rain ponchos. **Handicrafts** Crafts sold at Plaza Roja on Wed and Sat. **Almacén Cacha**, Colón y Orozco, next to the Plaza Roja. A cooperative of indigenous people from the Cacha area, sells woven bags, wool sweaters, and other crafts, good value (closed Sun-Mon).

⊙ What to do

Riobamba and around *p494, map p496*
Mountain biking Guided tours with support vehicle average US$50-60 pp per

day. **Pro Bici**, Primera Constituyente 23-51 y Larrea, T295 1759, www.probici.com. Tours and rentals. **Julio Verne** (see Tour operators), very good tours, equipment and routes.

Tour operators
Most companies offer climbing trips (US$200 pp for 2 days to Chimborazo or Carihuayrazo) and trekking (US$85-100 pp per day).
Andes Trek, Esmeraldas 21-45 y Espejo, T2951275, www.goandestrek.com. Climbing and trekking, transport, equipment rental.
Expediciones Andinas, Vía a Guano, Km 3, across from **Hotel Abraspungo**, T236 4278, www.expediciones-andinas.com. Climbing expeditions run by Marco Cruz, a guide certified by the **German Alpine Club**, operate **$$$** Estrella del Chimborazo lodge on south flank of mountain. Recommended.
Incañán, Brasil 20-28 y Luis A Falconí, T294 0508, www.incanian.com.ec. Trekking, cycling and cultural tours.
Julio Verne, El Espectador 22-25 y Daniel L Borja, 2 blocks from the train station, T296 3436, www.julioverne-travel.com. Climbing, trekking, cycling, jungle and Galápagos trips, transport, equipment rental, English spoken, Ecuadorean/ Dutch-run, very conscientious and reliable. Uses official guides. Highly recommended.
Veloz Coronado, Chile 33-21 y Francia, T296 0916 (after 1900). Climbing and trekking.

The Devil's Nose Train *p497*
In early 2014 the Devil's Nose Train departed from and returned to Alausí, Tue-Sun at

0800, 1100 and 1500 (the latter only if there are enough passengers), 2½ hrs return, US$25-35, includes a snack and folklore dance performance. From Riobamba, an autoferro (motorized rail car) ran from Riobamba to Urbina (Thu–Sun at 0800, US$11) and from Riobamba to Colta (Thu–Sun at 1200, US$15), dress warmly. Purchase tickets well in advance for weekends and holidays at any train station (Riobamba, T296 1038, Mon-Fri 0800-1630, Sat-Sun 0700-1500; Alausí, T293 0126, Tue-Sun 0700-1530), through the call centre (T1800-873637) or by email (reservasriobamba@ferrocarrilesdelecuador.gob.ec, then you have to make a bank deposit). Procedures change frequently, so enquire locally and check www.trenecuador.com.

⊖ Transport

Riobamba p494, map p496
Bus Terminal Terrestre on Epiclachima y Av Daniel L Borja for most long distance buses including to Quito, Guayaquil and Cuenca. **Terminal Oriental**, Espejo y Cordovez, for Baños and the Oriente. **Terminal Intercantonal**, Av Canónigo Ramos about 2.5 km northwest of the Terminal Terrestre, for Guamote, SanJuan and Cajabamba (Colta). Taxi from Terminal Terrestre to Oriental, US$1.50, from Terminal Intercantonal to the other terminals US$2. To **Quito**, US$3.85, 4 hrs, about every 30 mins; also door to door shared taxis with: Montecarlo Trans Vip, T301 5946 or T09-8411 4114, 6 daily, US$18 (US$5 extra for large luggage). To **Guaranda**, US$2, 2 hrs (sit on the right). To **Ambato**, US$1.25, 1 hr. To **Alausí**, see below. To **Cuenca**, 8 a day via Alausí, 5½ hrs, US$6. To **Guayaquil** via Pallatanga, frequent service, US$4.75, 5 hrs, spectacular for the first 2 hrs. The following from Terminal Oriental: to **Baños**, 2 hrs, US$2; to **Puyo** US$4, 4 hrs, to **Macas** via Sangay, 8 daily, 4 hrs, US$5 (sit on the left), also **Unidos** from the Terminal Terrestre at 0900.

Guaranda p495
Bus Terminal at Eliza Mariño Carvajal, on road to Riobamba and Babahoyo; if you are staying in town get off closer to the centre. Many daily buses to: **Ambato**, US$2, 2 hrs. **Riobamba**, see above. **Babahoyo**, US$3, 3 hrs, beautiful ride. **Guayaquil**, US$4, 5 hrs. **Quito**, US$5, 5 hrs.

Reserva Faunística Chimborazo p495
There are no buses that will take you to the shelters. You can take a tour or arrange transport with a tour operator from Riobamba (US$35 one way, US$45 return with wait). You can also take a Riobamba-Guaranda bus, alight at the turn-off for the refuges and walk the remaining steep 8 km (5 km taking short-cuts) to the first shelter. For the eastern slopes, take a trekking tour, arrange transport from an agency or take a bus between Riobamba and Ambato, get off at the turn-off for **Posada La Estación** and Urbina and walk from there.

Alausí p497
Bus To **Riobamba**, 1½ hrs, US$1.90, 84 km. To **Quito**, from 0600 onwards, 8 a day, 6 hrs, US$6; often have to change in Riobamba. To **Cuenca**, 4 hrs, US$5. To **Ambato** hourly, 3 hrs, US$3. To **Guayaquil**, 4 a day, 4 hrs, US$5. **Coop Patria**. Colombia y Orozco, 3 blocks up from the main street; **Trans Alausí**, 5 de Junio y Loza. Many through buses don't go into town, but have to be caught on the highway, taxi from town US$1.

Parque Nacional Sangay p497
To **Atillo** from Parque La Dolorosa, Puruhá y Primera Constituyente, at 0545, 1200, 1500, 1800, US$2, 2 hrs Also Riobamba–**Macas** service goes through Atillo, see above. To **Alao**, from Parque La Dolorosa, 0555, 0630, 0730, 0845 and hourly 1145-1800, US$1.25, 1½ hrs. To **Guarguallá Grande** and **Chico** from Parque La Dolorosa daily at 1345 (return to Riobamba at 0545), US$ 1.75 (Grande), US$2 (Chico), 2 hrs. To **Candelaria**, fromTerminal Oriental, Mon-Fri 0630, 1015,

1215, 1515 and 1700, Sat-Sun 0630, 1215 and 1700 US$1.25, 1½ hrs. Alternatively, take a bus from the same terminal to Penipe, every ½ hr, US$0.40, 40 mins, and hire a pickup truck from there to Candelaria, US$15, 40 mins.

Directory

Riobamba p494, map p496
Banks Several banks with ATMs at Primera Costituyente y García Moreno. **Banco del Pacífico**, Daniel L Borja y Zambrano.

Guaranda p495
Banks Banco Pichincha, Azuay y 7 de Mayo, ATM.

Cuenca and around

Founded in 1557 on the site of the Inca settlement of Tomebamba, much of Cuenca's colonial air has been preserved, with many of its old buildings renovated. Its cobblestone streets, flowering plazas and whitewashed buildings with old wooden doors and ironwork balconies make it a pleasure to explore. The climate is spring-like, but the nights are chilly. In 1999 Cuenca was designated a UNESCO World Heritage Site. It is home to a growing expat retiree community. The area is know for its crafts.

Arriving in Cuenca → *Phone code: 07. Colour map 1, C3. Population: 346,000. Altitude: 2530 m.*
Orientation The **Terminal Terrestre** is on Avenida España, 15 minutes' ride northeast of the centre, T284 2811. The **airport** is five minutes' beyond the Terminal Terrestre, T282 4811. Both can be reached by city bus, but best take a taxi at all hours (US$1.50-2.50 to the centre). The **Terminal Sur** for regional buses within the province is by the Feria Libre El Arenal on Avenida Las Américas. Many city buses pass here.

The city is bounded by the Río Machángara to the north and the Ríos Yanuncay and Tarqui to the south. The Río Tomebamba separates the colonial heart from the newer districts to the south. Avenida Las Américas is a ring road around the north and west of the city and the *autopista*, a multi-lane highway bypasses the city to the south. ▸▸ *See Transport, page 513, for details.*

Tourist offices Ministerio de Turismo ① *Sucre y Benigno Malo, on Parque Calderón next to the Municipio, T282 1035, Mon-Fri, 0800-2000, Sat 0830-1730, Sun 0830-1330, helpful.* **Cámara de Turismo** ①*Terminal Terrestre, T284 5657, Mon-Sat 0830-1200, 1230-1800, information about the city, including city and long distance bus routes; also at the airport. General information from www.cuenca.com.ec. To locate an establishment see www.ubicacuenca.com.*

Safety Though safer than Quito or Guayaquil, routine precautions are advised. Outside the busy nightlife area around Calle Larga, the city centre is deserted and unsafe after 2300, taking a taxi is recommended. The river banks, the Cruz del Vado area (south end of Juan Montalvo), the Terminal Terrestre and all market areas, are not safe after dark.

Places in Cuenca
On the main plaza, **Parque Abdón Calderón**, are the Old Cathedral, **El Sagrario** ① *Mon-Fri 0900-1730, Sat-Sun 0900-1300, US$2,* begun in 1557, and the immense 'New' **Catedral de**

la Inmaculada, started in 1885. The latter contains a famous crowned image of the Virgin, a beautiful altar and an exceptional play of light and shade through modern stained glass. Other churches which deserve a visit are **San Blas**, **San Francisco** and **Santo Domingo**. Many churches are open at irregular hours only and for services. The church of **El Carmen**

Cuenca

Where to stay

1 Carvallo *B3*
2 Casa del Barranco *D3*
3 Casa del Río *C2*
4 Casa Ordóñez *B3*
5 Colonial *B3*
6 El Conquistador *B3*
7 El Príncipe *C3*
8 Hogar Cuencano *D3*
9 Inca Real *B2*
10 La Casona *E3*
11 La Cigale *C3*
12 La Orquídea *B3*
13 La Posada Cuencana *B2*
14 Macondo *A2*
15 Mansión Alcázar *B2*
16 Mercure El Dorado *B3*
17 Milán *C2*
18 Posada del Angel & Mangiare Restaurant *B1*
19 Posada Todos Santos *D4*
20 Santa Lucía *C3*
21 Turista del Mundo *D3*
22 Victoria *D3*
23 Yakumama *C3*

Restaurants

1 Balcón Quiteño *B4*
2 Bananas Café *C2*
3 Café Eucalyptus & Grecia *B3*
4 Coffee Tree *D3*
5 Di Bacco *B2*
6 El Carbón *B3*
7 El Maíz *E5*
8 Mixx Gourmet *C5*

de la Asunción, close to the southwest corner of La Inmaculada, has a flower market in the tiny **Plazoleta El Carmen** in front. There is a colourful daily market in **Plaza Rotary** where pottery, clothes, guinea pigs and local produce, especially baskets, are sold. Thursday is the busiest.

9 Moliendo Café *D3*
10 Néctar *B3*
11 Raymipampa *B3*
12 San Sebas *B1*
13 Tiestos *C3*
14 Tutto Freddo *B3*
15 Viejo Rincón *C3*
16 Villa Rosa *B2*

Bars & clubs 🎵
17 La Mesa Salsoteca *B4*
18 MalAmado *C1*
19 Rue *D3*
20 Wunderbar *D3*

Museo del Monasterio de las Conceptas
ⓘ *Hermano Miguel 6-33 entre Pdte Córdova y Juan Jaramillo, T283 0625, www.museo delasconceptas.org.ec. Mon-Fri 0900-1830, Sat and holidays 1000-1300, US$2.50*, in a cloistered convent founded in 1599, houses a well displayed collection of religious and folk art, in addition to an extensive collection of lithographs by Guayasamín.

Pumapungo ⓘ *C Larga y Huayna Capac, T283 1521, Mon-Fri 0900-1700, Sat 0900-1300*, is a mueum complex on the edge of the colonial city, at the actual site of Tomebamba excavations. Part of the area explored is seen at **Parque Arqueológico Pumapungo**. The **Sala Arqueológica** section contains all the Cañari and Inca remains and artifacts found at this site. Other halls in the premises house the **Sala Etnográfica**, with information on different Ecuadorean cultures, including a special collection of *tsantsas* (shrunken heads from Oriente), the **Sala de Arte Religioso**, the **Sala Numismática** and temporary exhibits. There are also book and music libraries, free cultural videos and music events. Three blocks west of Pumapungo, **Museo Manuel Agustín Landívar** ⓘ *C Larga 2-23 y Manuel Vega, T282 1177, Mon-Fri 0800-1700, Sat 0900-1300, US$1*, is at the site of the small Todos los Santos ruins, with Cañari, Inca and colonial remains; ceramics and artifacts found at the site are also displayed.

Museo de las Culturas Aborígenes ⓘ *C Larga 5-24 y Hermano Miguel, T283 9181, Mon-Fri 0830-1800, Sat 0900-1400, US$2; guided tours in English, Spanish and French, craft shop*, the private collection of Dr J Cordero Íñiguez, has a impressive selection of pre-Columbian archaeology. **Museo Remigio Crespo Toral** ⓘ *C Larga 7-25 y Borreo. T282 1177, Mon-Fri 0900-1300, 1500-1800, Sat 0900-1300, free, temporarily closed in 2014*, in a beautiful colonial house refurbished in 2013, has important history, archaeology and art collections. **Museo del Sombrero** ① *C Larga 10-41 y Gral Torres, T283 1569, Mon-Fri 0900-1800, Sat 0900-1700, Sun 0930-1330*, shop with all the old factory machines for hat finishing.

On Plaza San Sebastián is **Museo Municipal de Arte Moderno** ① *Sucre 1527 y Talbot, T282 0838, Mon-Fri 0900-1700, Sat-Sun 0900-1300, free*, has a permanent contemporary art collection and art library. It holds a biennial international painting competition and other cultural activities. Across the river from the Museo Pumapungo, the **Museo de Artes de Fuego** ① *Las Herrerías y 10 de Agosto, T409 6510, Mon-Fri 0800-1330, 1500-1730, free except for special events*, has a display of wrought iron work and pottery. It is housed in the beautifully restored Casa de Chaguarchimbana. Also south of city, accessed via Avenida Fray Vicente Solano, beyond the football stadium, is Turi church, orphanage and mirador; a tiled panorama explains the magnificent views.

There are sulphur baths at **Baños**, with a domed, blue church in a delightful landscape, 5 km southwest of Cuenca. These are the hottest commercial baths in Ecuador. Above **Hostería Durán** (see Where to stay) are four separate complexes of warm baths, **Merchán**, **Rodas** (www.hosteriarodas.com), **Durán** (www.novaqua.com. ec) and **Piedra de Agua** ① *www.piedradeagua.com.ec, entry US$2-10*. The latter two are better maintained, more exclusive and in addition to having several hot pools, offer a variety of treatments in their spas.

Ingapirca → *Phone code: 07. Colour map 1, B3. Altitude: 3160 m.*

① *Daily 0800-1800, closed public holidays, US$6, including museum and tour in Spanish; bags can be stored. Small café.*

Ecuador's most important Inca ruin, at 3160 m, lies 8.5 km east of the colonial town of **Cañar** (hostales in $ range). Access is from Cañar or **El Tambo**. The Inca Huayna Capac took over the site from the conquered Cañaris when his empire expanded north into Ecuador in the third quarter of the 15th century. Ingapirca was strategically placed on the Royal Highway that ran from Cuzco to Quito and soldiers may have been stationed there. The site shows typical imperial Cuzco-style architecture, such as tightly fitting stonework and trapezoidal doorways. The central structure may have been a solar observatory. Nearby is a throne cut into the rock, the **Sillón del Inca** (Inca's Chair) and the **Ingachugana**, a large rock with carved channels. A 10-minute walk away from the site is the **Cara del Inca**, or 'face of the Inca', an immense natural formation in the rock looking over the landscape. On Friday there is an interesting indigenous market at Ingapirca village.

A tourist autoferro runs from El Tambo 7 km to the small Cañari-Inca archaeological site of **Baños del Inca** or **Coyoctor** ① *site open daily 0800-1700, US$1; 2 departures Wed-Fri, US$7, includes entry to El Tambo museum and Coyoctor site, 5 departures Sat-Sun and holidays, US$5*, a massive rock outcrop carved to form baths, showers, water channels and seats overlooking a small amphitheatre. There is an interpretation centre with information about the site, a hall with displays about regional fiestas and an audiovisual room with tourist information about all of Ecuador.

Inca Trail to Ingapirca

The three-day hike to Ingapirca starts at **Achupallas** (lively Saturday market, one hostel), 25 km from Alausí. The walk is covered by three 1:50,000 *IGM* sheets, Alausí, Juncal and Cañar. The Juncal sheet is most important, the name Ingapirca does not appear on the latter, you may have to ask directions near the end. Also take a compass and GPS. Good camping equipment is essential. Take all food and drink with you as there is nothing along the way. A shop in Achupallas sells basic foodstuffs. There are persistent beggars the length of the hike, especially children. Tour operators in Riobamba and Cuenca offer this trek for about US$250-320 per person, three days, everything included.

East of Cuenca

Northeast of Cuenca, on the paved road to Méndez in the Oriente, is **Paute**, with a pleasant park and modern church. South of Paute, **Gualaceo** is a rapidly expanding, modern town set in beautiful landscape, with a charming plaza and Sunday market. The iTur ① *at the Municipio, Gran Colombia y 3 de Noviembre, Parque Central, T225 5131, Mon-Fri 0800-1300, 1400-1700*, is very helpful, Spanish only. **CIDAP** ① *Loja y Sucre, Wed-Sun 0900-1300, free*, is a small crafts museum. A scenic road goes from Gualaceo to Limón in Oriente (closed for paving in 2014). Many of Ecuador's 4000 species of orchids can be seen at **Ecuagénera** ① *Km 2 on the road to Cuenca, T225 5237, www.ecuagenera.com, Mon-Sat 0730-1630, Sun 0930-1630, US$5 (US$3 pp for groups of 3 or more)*.

South of Gualaceo is **Chordeleg**, a touristy village famous for its crafts in wood, silver and gold filigree, pottery and panama hats. At the Municipio is the **Centro de Interpretación** ① *C 23 de Enero, Mon-Fri 0800-1300, 1400-1700*, an exhibition hall with fascinating local textiles, ceramics and straw work, some of which are on sale at reasonable prices. It's a good uphill walk from Gualaceo to Chordeleg, and a pleasant hour downhill in the other direction. South of Gualaceo, 83 km from Cuenca, **Sígsig**, an authentic highland town where women can be seen weaving hats 'on the move'. It has a Sunday market, two *residenciales* and an archaeology museum. A poor but scenic road goes from Sígsig to Gualaquiza in Oriente.

Parque Nacional Cajas

① *The park office is at Presidente Córdova 7-56 y Luis Cordero, Edif Morejón, p 2, T282 9853, www.etapa.net.ec/PNC, Mon-Fri 0800-1300 and 1500-1800. Entry free, overnight stay US$4 per night. Hiking information for Cajas and other areas around Cuenca in www.thefreeair.com.* Northwest of Cuenca, Cajas is a 29,000-ha national park with over 230 lakes. The *páramo* vegetation, such as chuquiragua and lupin, is beautiful and the wildlife interesting. Cajas is very rich in birdlife; 125 species have been identified, including the condor and many varieties of hummingbird (the violet-tailed metaltail is endemic to this area). On the lakes are Andean gulls, speckled teal and yellow-billed pintails. On a clear morning the views are superb, even to Chimborazo, some 300 km away.

There are two access roads. The paved road from Cuenca to Guayaquil via Molleturo goes through the northern section and is the main route for Laguna Toreadora, the visitors' centre and Laguna Llaviuco. Skirting the southern edge of the park is a gravel secondary road, which goes from Cuenca via San Joaquín to the Soldados entrance and the community of Angas beyond. (See Transport, page 513.) There is nowhere to stay after the *refugio* at Laguna Toreadora (see Where to stay, below) until you reach the lowlands between Naranjal and La Troncal.

The park offers ideal but strenuous walking, at 3150-4450 m altitude, and the climate is rough. There have been deaths from exposure. The best time to visit is August-January, when you may expect clear days, strong winds, night-time temperatures to -8°C and occasional mist. From February to July temperatures are higher but there is much more fog, rain and snow. It is best to arrive in the early morning since it can get very cloudy, wet and cool after about 1300. Cuenca tourist office has a good, one-page map of Cajas, but other local maps are not always exact. It is best to get the IGM maps in Quito (Chaucha, Cuenca, San Felipe de Molleturo, and Chiquintad 1:50,000) and take a compass and GPS. It is easy to get lost.

Cuenca and around listings

For hotel and restaurant price codes, and other relevant information, see pages 14-17.

Where to stay

Cuenca and around *p503, map p504*

$$$$ Carvallo, Gran Colombia 9-52, entre Padre Aguirre y Benigno Malo, T283 2063, www.hotelcarvallo.com.ec. Combination of an elegant colonial-style hotel and art/antique gallery. Very nice comfortable rooms all have bath tubs, restaurant, boutique with exclusive crafts and clothing.

$$$$ Mansión Alcázar, Bolívar 12-55 y Tarqui, T282 3918, www.mansionalcazar. com. Beautifully restored house, a mansion indeed, central, very nice rooms, restaurant serves gourmet international food, lovely gardens, quiet relaxed atmosphere.

$$$$ Oro Verde, Av Ordóñez Lazo, northwest of the centre towards Cajas, T409 0000, www.oroverdehotels.com. Elegant hotel, buffet breakfast, excellent international cuisine offers buffet lunch and à la carte dinner, small pool, parking.

$$$$ Santa Lucía, Borrero 8-44 y Sucre, T282 8000, www.santaluciahotel.com. An elegantly renovated colonial house, very nice comfortable rooms, buffet breakfast, excellent Italian restaurant, safe deposit box.

$$$ Casa Ordóñez, Lamar 8-59 y Benigno Malo, T282 3297, www.casa-ordonez.com. Nicely renovated colonial house with wood floors and 3 inner patios, nicely decorated rooms and common areas, down comforters, no smoking.

$$$ Inca Real, Gral Torres 8-40 entre Sucre y Bolívar, T282 3636, www.hotelincareal. com.ec. Refurbished colonial house with comfortable rooms around patios, good Spanish restaurant, parking.

$$$ La Casona, Miguel Cordero 2-124, near the stadium, T410 3501, www.lacasonahotel. com.ec. Very nice refurbished family home in a residential area, comfortable carpeted rooms, buffet breakfast, restaurant, parking.

$$$ La Posada Cuencana, Tarqui 9-46 y Bolívar, T282 6831. Small family-run hotel, beautiful colonial-style rooms, personalized service by owners.

$$$ Mercure El Dorado, Gran Colombia 787 y Luis Cordero, T283 1390, www. eldoradohotel.com.ec. Elegant modern hotel, rooms have safe and minibar, buffet breakfast, cafeteria, spa, gym, business centre, parking.

$$$ Posada del Angel, Bolívar 14-11 y Estévez de Toral, T284 0695, www. hostalposadadelangel.com. A nicely restored colonial house, comfortable rooms, good Italian restaurant, parking, patio with plants, some noise from restaurant, English spoken, helpful staff. Recommended.

$$$-$$ Victoria, C Larga 6-93 y Borrero, T283 1120, www.grupo-santaana.net. Elegant refurbished hotel overlooking the river, comfortable modern rooms, excellent expensive restaurant, nice views.

$$ Casa del Barranco, Calle Larga 8-41 y Luis Cordero, T283 9763, www.casadel barranco.com. Nicely restored colonial house, some rooms with lovely views over the river, cafeteria overlooking the river.

$$ Colonial, Gran Colombia 10-13 y Padre Aguirre, T284 1644, www.hostalcolonial. com. Refurbished colonial house with beautiful patio, carpeted rooms.

$$ El Príncipe, J Jaramillo 7-82 y Luis Cordero, T284 7287, www.hotelprincipe. com.ec. A refurbished 3-storey colonial house, comfortable rooms around a nice patio with plants, restaurant, parking.

$$ La Orquídea, Borrero 9-31 y Bolívar, T282 4511. Nicely refurbished colonial house, bright rooms, fridge, low season and long term discounts, good value.

$$ Macondo, Tarqui 11-64 y Lamar, T284 0697, www.hostalmacondo.com. Nice restored colonial house, large rooms, buffet breakfast, cooking facilities, pleasant patio with plants, garden, very popular, US-run. Highly recommended.

\$\$ Milán, Pres Córdova 989 y Padre Aguirre, T283 1104, www.hotelmilan.com.ec. Multi-storey hotel with views over market, restaurant, popular.

\$\$ Posada Todos Santos, C Larga 3-42 y Tomás Ordóñez, near the Todos Santos Church, T282 4247, posadatodossantoscue@latinmail.com. Nice tranquil hostel decorated with murals, very good, attentive service, English spoken, group discounts.

\$\$-\$ Casa del Río, Bajada del Padrón 4-07 y C Larga, T282 9659, hostalcasadelrio@hotmail.com. Pleasant quiet hostal on El Barranco overlooking the river, private or shared bath, breakfast available, nice views, attentive service.

\$\$-\$ Turista del Mundo, C Larga 5-79 y Hermano Miguel, T282 9125, esperanzab65@gmail.com. Popular hostel with comfortable rooms, private or shared bath, cooking facilities, nice terrace, very helpful.

\$ Hogar Cuencano, Hermano Miguel 436 y C Larga, T283 4941, celso3515@yahoo.com. Nicely furnished family-run hostal in the heart of the action, private or shared bath, 10 pp in dorm, cafeteria, cooking facilities (0700-1900), clean.

\$ La Cigale, Honorato Vasquez 7-80 y Cordero, T283 5308, lacigalecuencana@yahoo.fr. Very popular hostel with private rooms and dorms for 4 (US\$10 pp) to 6 (US\$7 pp), excellent restaurant (**\$**), can be very noisy.

\$ Yakumama, Cordero 5-66 y Honorato Vásquez, T283 4353, www.hostalyakumama.com. Popular hostel, 2 private rooms and dorms with 2-6 beds US\$7-9 pp, restaurant with Ecuadorean and Swiss dishes, bar, patio with plants and lounging area, terrace with hammocks, can get noisy.

Baños

\$\$\$ Caballo Campana, Vía Misicata-Baños Km 4, on an alternative road from Cuenca to Baños (2 km from Baños, no public transport, taxi US\$5 from the centre of Cuenca), T289 2360, www.caballocampana.com. Nicely rebuilt colonial hacienda house in 28 has with gardens and forest, heated rooms,

suites and cabins, includes buffet breakfast, Ecuadorean and international cuisine, horse riding and lessons, sports fields, discounts for longer stays.

\$\$\$ Hostería Durán, Km 8 Vía Baños, T289 2485, www.hosteriaduran.com. Includes buffet breakfast, restaurant, parking, has well-maintained, very clean pools (US\$6.20 for non-residents), gym, steam bath, transport from Cuenca, camping. There are also a couple of cheap *residenciales*.

Ingapirca *p506*

\$\$\$ Posada Ingapirca, 500 m uphill from ruins, T221 7116, for reservations T283 0064 (Cuenca), www.grupo-santaana.net. Converted hacienda, comfortable rooms, heating, includes typical breakfast, excellent pricey restaurant, good service, great views.

\$ El Castillo, opposite the ruins, T09-9998 3650, cab.castillo@hotmail.com. 3 simple cabins, restaurant with fireplace.

There are a couple of simple places in the village. Also good economical meals at **Intimikuna**, at the entrance to the archaeological site.

El Tambo

This is the nearest town to Ingapirca.

\$ Chasky Wasy, Montenegro next to Banco del Austro, 1 block from the park, T09-9883 0013, tenezaca@hotmail.com. Nice hostel with ample rooms, parking nearby.

\$ Sunshine, Panamericana y Ramón Borrero, at north end of town, T223 3394. Simple, family-run, not always staffed, private or shared bath, restaurant nearby, traffic noise.

Inca Trail to Ingapirca *p506*

\$ Ingañán, Achupallas, T293 0663. Basic, with bath, hot water, meals on request, camping.

East of Cuenca *p507*
Paute

\$\$\$ Hostería Uzhupud, Km 32 Vía a Paute, T225 0329, www.uzhupud.com. Set in the beautiful Paute valley 10 km from town, deluxe, relaxing, rooms at the back have best

views, swimming pools and sauna (US$15 for non-residents), sports fields, horse riding, gardens, lots of orchids. Recommended.
$ Cutilcay, Abdón Calderón, by the river, T225 0133. Older basic hostel, private or shared bath.

Gualaceo
$$-$ Peñón de Cuzay, Sector Bullcay El Carmen on the main road to Cuenca, T217 1515. In one of the weaving communities, spa and pool. Fills on weekends, book ahead.
$ Residencial Gualaceo, Gran Colombia 302 y FA Piedra, T225 5006. Older hotel, clean basic rooms, private or shared bath, parking.

Parque Nacional Cajas p507
There is a *refugio* at **Laguna Toreadora**, cold, cooking facilities, and camping at **Laguna Llaviuco**. Other shelters in the park are primitive.
$$ Hostería Dos Chorreras, Km 21 Vía al Cajas, sector Sayausí, T245 4301, www.hosteriadoschorreras.com. Hacienda-style inn outside the park. Heating, restaurant serves excellent fresh trout, reservations recommended, horse rentals with advanced notice.

🍴 Restaurants

Cuenca *p503, map p504*
There is a wide selection and fast turnover of restaurants. Most places are closed on Sun evening. There are cheap *comedores* at the Mercados 9 de Octubre and 10 de Agosto.
$$$ El Carbón, Borrero 10-69 y Lamar, T283 3711. Mon-Wed 0700-1600, 1800-2200, Thu-Sat until 2400. Excellent charcoal-grilled meat served with a choice of fresh salads, seafood, wide choice of dishes and breakfasts, large portions enough for 2.
$$$ Villa Rosa, Gran Colombia 12-22 y Tarqui, T283 7944. Mon-Fri 1200-1430, 1900-2230. Very elegant restaurant in the centre of town, excellent international and Ecuadorean food and service. A meeting place for business people.

$$$-$$ Balcón Quiteño, Sangurima 6-49 y Borrero, and Av Ordóñez Lazo 311 y los Pinos, T283 1928. Daily 0900-0100. Good Ecuadorean and international food and service, 1960s decor. Popular with locals after a night's partying.
$$$-$$ Tiestos, J Jaramillo 4-89 y M Cueva, T283 5310. Tue-Sat 1230-1500, 1830-2200, Sun 1230-1500. Superb international cuisine prepared on *tiestos*, shallow clay pans, comfortable feel-at-home atmosphere, very popular, reserve ahead.
$$ Café Eucalyptus, Gran Colombia 9-41 y Benigno Malo. Mon-Fri 1700-2300 or later, Sat 1900-0200. A pleasant restaurant, café and bar in an elegantly decorated house. Large menu with dishes from all over the world. British-run, popular. Recommended.
$$ Di Bacco, Tarqui 9-61 y Bolívar, T283 2301, www.cuencadibaccorestaurant.com. Tue-Sun 1200-1500, 1700-2200. Excellent lasagna and other Italian dishes, very good set lunch, live music, theatre and other events (see web page), popular with expats.
$$ El Maíz, C Larga 1-279 y C de los Molinos, T284 0224. Mon-Sat 1200-2100 (variable, call ahead). Good traditional Ecuadorean dishes with some innovations, salads.
$$ Mangiare, Estévez de Toral 8-91 y Bolívar, at Posada del Angel, T282 1360. Mon-Sat 1200-1500, 1730-2230, Sun 1200-1500. Excellent Italian food, home-made pasta, good value, very popular with locals.
$$ Raymipampa, Benigno Malo 8-59, at Parque Calderón. Mon-Fri 0830-2300, Sat-Sun 0930-2230. Good typical and international food in a nice central location, economical set lunch on weekdays, fast service, very popular, at times it is hard to get a table.
$$-$ Néctar, Benigno Malo 10-42 y Gran Colombia, p2, T284 4118. Mon-Sat 1200-1500, Fri 1800-2100. Good economical vegetarian set lunch and à la carte, vegan and raw options.
$$-$ Viejo Rincón, Pres Córdova 7-46 y Borrero. Mon-Fri 0900-2100, Sat 0900-1500. Tasty Ecuadorean food, very good set lunch and à la carte, popular.

$ Good Affinity, Capulíes 1-89 y Gran Colombia. Mon-Sat 0930-1530. Very good vegetarian food, vegan options, economical set lunch, nice garden seating.

$ Grecia, Gran Colombia y Padre Aguirre. Mon-Sat 1200-1500. Good quality and value set lunch.

$ Moliendo Café, Honorato Vásquez y Hermano Miguel. Mon-Sat 1100-2100. Tasty Colombian food including set lunch, friendly service.

Cafés

Bananas Café, C Larga 9-40 y Benigno Malo. Thu-Sun 0800-1600. Breakfast, snacks, light lunches, fruit juices, hot drinks, desserts, attentive service.

Coffee Tree, C Larga y Borrero, Plaza de la Merced. Mon-Thu 0800-2200, Fri-Sat 0800-2400, Sun 0800-2200. Very popular café/restaurant with a varied menu; one of the few places in Cuenca with outdoor seating and open Sun evening. Note that there are plans to remodel and change the name in mid 2014.

Mixx Gourmet, Parque San Blas 2-73 y Tomás Ordóñez. A variety of fruit and liquor flavoured ice cream, popular. Several others nearby.

Monte Bianco, Bolívar 2-80 y Ordóñez and a couple of other locations. Good ice cream and cream cakes, good value.

San Sebas, San Sebastián 1-94 y Sucre, Parque San Sebastián. Tue-Sun 0830-1500. Outdoor café, popular for breakfast, good selection of giant sandwiches and salads.

Tutto Freddo, Bolívar 8-09 y Benigno Malo and several other locations. Daily 0900-2200. Good ice cream, crêpes, pizza, sandwiches and sweets, reasonable prices, popular.

🍸 Bars and clubs

Cuenca *p503, map p504*

Calle Larga is a major destination for night life, with lots of bars with snacks and some restaurants. Av 12 de Abril, along the river near Parque de la Madre, and to the west of the centre, Plaza del Arte, Gaspar de Sangurima y Abraham Sarmiento, opposite Plazoleta El Otorongo, are also popular. Most bars open Wed-Thu until 2300, Fri-Sat until 0200.

La Mesa Salsoteca, Gran Colombia 3-36 entre Vargas Machuca y Tomás Ordóñez (no sign). Latin music, salsa, popular among travellers and locals, young crowd.

MalAmado, C San Roque y Av 12 de Abril. Pleasant atmosphere, good music, food, a good place for dancing, US$10-15.

Rue, at Parque de la Madre, Av 12 de Abril. Nice bar/restaurant with outdoor seating, no cover charge.

Wunderbar, entrance from stairs on Hermano Miguel y C Larga. Mon-Fri 1100-0200, Sat 1500-0200. A café-bar-restaurant, drinks, good coffee and food including some vegetarian. Nice atmosphere, book exchange, German-run.

🎭 Entertainment

Cuenca *p503, map p504*

Cinemas Multicines, Av José Peralta, complex of 5 theatres and food court, also at Mall del Río.

Dance classes Cachumbambe, Remigio Crespo 7-79 y Guayas, p2, T288 2023. Salsa, merengue and a variety of other rhythms, group and individual classes.

🎉 Festivals

Cuenca *p503, map p504*

On **24 Dec** there is an outstanding parade: **Pase del Niño Viajero**, probably the largest and finest Christmas parade in all Ecuador. Children and adults from all the *barrios* and surrounding villages decorate donkeys, horses, cars and trucks with symbols of abundance. Little children in colourful indigenous costumes or dressed up as Biblical figures ride through the streets accompanied by musicians. The parade starts at about 1000 at San Sebastián, proceeds along C Bolívar and ends at San Blas about 5 hrs later. In the days up to, and just after Christmas, there are many smaller parades. **12 Apr** is the **Foundation of Cuenca**. On **Good Friday** there is a fine procession through the town to the Mirador Turi. **May-Jun** Septenario, the religious festival of Corpus Christi, lasts a week. On **3 Nov** is Independence of Cuenca, with street theatre, art exhibitions and night-time dances all over the city. Cuenca hosts the **Bienal de Cuenca**, an internationally famous art competition The next one is due in 2015. Information from Bolívar 13-89, T283 1778, www.bienaldecuenca.org.

O Shopping

Cuenca *p503, map p504*
Camping equipment Bermeo Hnos, Borrero 8-35 y Sucre, T283 1522. **Explorador Andino**, Borrero 7-39 y Sucre. Tatoo/Cikla, Av Remigio Tamariz 2-52 y Federico Proaño, T288 4809, www.ec.tatoo.ws. Good camping, hiking, climbing and biking gear. Also rent bikes. Several other shops near the university, on or near Av Remigio Crespo. Equipment rental from **Apullacta**, see Tour operators.
Handicrafts There are many craftware shops along Gran Colombia, Benigno Malo and Juan Jaramillo alongside Las Conceptas. There are several good leather shops in the arcade off Bolívar between Benigno Malo and Luis Cordero. *Polleras*, traditional skirts worn by indigenous women are found along Gral Torres, between Sucre and Pres Córdova, and on Tarqui, between Pres Córdova and C Larga. For basketwork, take a 15-min bus ride from the Feria Libre (see Markets below) to the village of **San Joaquín**.
Arte, Artesanías y Antigüedades, Borrero y Córdova. Textiles, jewellery and antiques. **Artesa**, L Cordero 10-31 y Gran Colombia, several branches. Modern ceramic tableware. **Centro Artesanal Municipal 'Casa de la Mujer'**, Gral Torres 7-33. Crafts market with a great variety of handicrafts. **Colecciones Jorge Moscoso**, J Jaramillo 6-80 y Borrero. Weaving exhibitions, ethnographic museum, antiques and crafts. **El Barranco**,

Hermano Miguel 3-23 y Av 3 de Noviembre. Artisans' cooperative selling a wide variety of crafts. **El Otorongo**, 3 de Noviembre by Plaza Otorongo, exclusive designs sold at this art gallery/café. **El Tucán**, Borrero 7-35. Good selection. Recommended. **Galápagos**, Borrero 6-75. Excellent selection. **La Esquina de las Artes**, 12 de Abril y Agustín Cueva, shops with exclusive crafts including textiles; also cultural events.
Jewellery Galería Claudio Maldonado, Bolívar 7-75, has unique pre-Columbian designs in silver and precious stones. **Unicornio**, Gran Colombia y Luis Cordero. Good jewellery, ceramics and candelabras.
Panama hats Manufacturers have displays showing the complete hat making process, see also Museo del Sombrero, page 506. K Dorfzaun, Gil Ramírez Dávalos 4-34, near bus station, T286 1707, www.kdorfzaun. com. Good quality and selection of hats and straw crafts, nice styles, good prices. English-speaking guides. **Homero Ortega P e Hijos**, Av Gil Ramírez Dávalos 3-86, T280 1288, www.homeroortega.com. Good quality.
Markets Feria Libre, Av Las Américas y Av Remigio Crespo, west of the centre. The largest market, also has dry goods and clothing, busiest Wed and Sat. **Mercado 9 de Octubre**, Sangurima y Mariano Cueva, busiest on Thu. Nearby at Plaza Rotary, Sangurima y Vargas Machuca, crafts are sold, best selection on Thu. Note this area is not safe. **Mercado 10 de Agosto**, C Larga y Gral Torres. Daily market with a prepared foods and drinks section on the 2nd floor.

O What to do

Cuenca *p503, map p504*
Day tours to Ingapirca or Cajas run about US$45-50 pp. Trekking in Cajas about US$60-100 pp per day, depending on group size.
Apullacta, Gran Colombia 11-02 y Gral Torres, p 2, T283 7815, www.apullacta.com. Run city and regional tours (Cajas, Ingapirca, Saraguro), also adventure tours (cycling, horse riding, canopy, canyoning), sell jungle,

highland and Galápagos trips; also hire camping equipment.

Expediciones Apullacta, Gran Colombia 11-02 y Gral Torres, p2, T283 7815, www.apullacta.com. Run city and regional tours (Cajas, Ingapirca, Saraguro), adventure tours (cycling, horse riding, canopy, canyoning), also sell jungle, highland and Galápagos tours. Camping equipment for hire.

Metropolitan Touring, Sucre 6-62 y Borreo, T284 3223, www.metropolitan-touring.com. A branch of the Quito operator, also sells airline tickets.

Pazhuca Tours, T282 3231, info@pazhucatours.com.ec. Run regional tours and offer transport through **Van Service**, T281 6409, www.vanservice.com.ec, which also run city tours on a double-decker bus. The 1¾-hrs tour includes the main attractions in the colonial city and El Turi lookout. US$5, hourly departures 0900-1900 from the Old Cathedral.

Terra Diversa, C Larga 8-41 y Luis Cordero, T282 3782, www.terradiversa.com. Lots of useful information, helpful staff. Ingapirca, Cajas, community tourism in Saraguro, jungle trips, horse riding, mountain biking and other options. Also sell Galápagos tours and flights. Recommended.

⊖ Transport

Cuenca *p503, map p504*
Air Airport is about a 20-min ride northeast of the centre. To **Quito** and **Guayaquil** with

Aerogal (Aguilar 159 y Solano and Av España, T286 1041), **LAN** (Bolívar 9-18, T283 8078) and TAME (Florencia Astudillo 2-22, T288 9581).
Bus Terminal Sur for local services is at the Feria Libre on Av Las Américas. Many city buses pass here, not a safe area. City buses US$0.25. For the local **Baños**, city buses every 5-10 mins, 0600-2230, buses pass the front of the Terminal Terrestre, cross the city on Vega Muñoz and Cueva, then down Todos los Santos to the river, along 12 de Abril and onto Av Loja.

The long distance **Terminal Terrestre** is on Av España, 15 mins by taxi northeast of centre. Take daytime buses to enjoy scenic routes. To **Riobamba**, 5½ hrs, US$6. To **Baños** (Tungurahua), take a bus to Riobamba and a taxi to the Terminal Oriental. To **Ambato**, 6½ hrs, US$8. To **Quito**, US$10-12, 9 hrs, all buses arrive at Terminal Quitumbe in Quito; **Flota Imbabura** has several nighttime departures which continue to their own terminal in central Quito; van service with **Río Arriba/Atenas** (see To Guayaquil, below), daily at 2300, US$25, 6 hrs. To **Alausí**, 4 hrs, US$5; all Riobamba and Quito-bound buses pass by, but few enter town. To **Loja**, 4 hrs, US$7.50, see www.viajerosinternacional.com; hourly van service with **Elite Tours**, Remigio Crespo 14-08 y Santa Cruz, T420 3088, also **Faisatur**, Remigio Crespo y Brazil, T404 4771, US$12, 3 hrs; taxi US$60. To **Vilcabamba**, van service daily at 1430 from Hostal La Cigale, Honorato Vásquez y Luis Cordero, US$15, 4½ hrs. To **Saraguro**, US$5,

2½ hrs. To **Machala**, 4 hrs, US$5.50, sit on the left, wonderful scenery. To **Huaquillas**, 5 hrs, US$7. To **Guayaquil**, via Cajas and Molleturo, 4 hrs, or via Zhud, 5 hrs, both US$8; also hourly van service, 0500-2100, with Río Arriba/Atenas, Av Remigio Crespo 13-26 y Santa Cruz, near the Feria Libre, T420 3064, US$12, 3 hrs, reserve ahead; several others nearby. To **Macas** via Guarumales or Limón (closed in 2014), 7 hrs, US$8; spectacular scenery but prone to landslides, check in advance if roads are open. To **Gualaquiza**, in the southern Oriente, there are 2 routes, via Gualaceo and Plan de Milagro, US$5 (closed for paving in 2014) and via Sígsig, 6 hrs, US$6.25. To **Chiclayo** (Peru) via Tumbes, **Máncora** and **Piura**, with **Super Semería**, at 2200, US$18, 11 hrs (US$14 as far as Piura or Máncora).To Piura, also **Pullman Sucre**, connecting with CIFA in Huaquillas; direct service to Piura via Macará is available from Loja, 8 hrs.

Taxi US$1.50 for short journey; US$1.50 to the bus station; US$2 to airport; US$5 to Baños.

Ingapirca *p506*

Bus Direct buses **Cuenca** to Ingapirca with Transportes Cañar Mon-Fri at 0900 and 1220, Sat-Sun at 0900, returning 1300 and 1545, US$2.50, 2 hrs. Buses run from Cuenca to Cañar (US$1.50) and El Tambo (US$2) every 15 mins. From **Cañar**, corner of 24 de Mayo and Borrero, local buses leave every 15 mins for Ingapirca, 0600-1800, US$0.50, 30 mins; last bus returns at 1700. The same buses from Cañar go through **El Tambo**, US$0.50, 20 mins. If coming from the north, transfer in El Tambo. Pickup taxi from Cañar US$8, from El Tambo US$5.

Inca Trail to Ingapirca

From **Alausí to Achupallas**, small buses and pickups leave as they fill between 1100 and 1600, US$1, 1 hr. Alternatively, take any bus along the Panamericana south of Alausí, at the turn-off for Achupallas, and a shared pickup from there (best on Thu and Sun), US$0.50. To hire a pick-up from Alausí costs US$12-15, from La Moya US$10.

East of Cuenca *p507*

Bus From Terminal Terrestre in Cuenca: to **Paute**, every 15 mins, US$0.75, 1 hr; to **Gualaceo**, every 15 mins, US$0.60, 50 mins; to **Chordeleg**: every 15 mins from Gualaceo, US$0.25; 15 mins or direct bus from Cuenca, US$0.70, 1 hr; to **Sigsig**, every 30 mins via Gualaceo, US$1.25, 1½ hrs.

Parque Nacional Cajas *p507*

Bus From Cuenca's Terminal Terrestre take any **Guayaquil** bus that goes via Molleturo (not Zhud), US$2, 30 mins to turn-off for

Llaviuco, 45 mins to Toreadora. **Coop Occidental** to Molleturo, 8 a day from the Terminal Sur/Feria Libre, this is a slower bus and may wait to fill up. For the Soldados entrance, catch a bus from Puente del Vado in Cuenca, daily at 0600, US$1.25, 1½ hrs; the return bus passes the Soldados gate at about 1600.

ⓘ Directory

Cuenca *p503, map p504*
Banks Banco del Pacífico, Gran Colombia 23-120 y Av Las Américas and Pres Córdova y Benigno Malo, ATM and TCs. Many banks with ATMs around Sucre y Borrero. **Vazcorp**, Gran Colombia 7-98 y Cordero, T283 3434, Mon-Fri 0830-1730, Sat 0900-1245, change 11 currencies, good rates, 1.8% comission for US$ AMEX TCs. **Car rental** Bombuscaro, España y Elia Liut, opposite the airport, T286 6541. **Also international companies.** **Immigration** E Muñoz 1-42 y Gran

Colombia, T282 1112. **Language courses** Rates US$6-10 per hr. Centro de Estudios Interamericanos (CEDEI), Gran Colombia 11-02 y General Torres, Casilla 597, T283 9003, www.cedei.org. Spanish and Quichua lessons, immersion/volunteering programmes, also run the attached Hostal Macondo. Recommended. **Estudio Internacional Sampere**, Hermano Miguel 3-43 y C Larga, T284 2659, www.sampere.es. At the high end of the price range. **Sí Centro de Español e Inglés**, Bolívar 12-54 y Tarqui, T282 0429, www.sicentrospanishschool. com. Good teachers, competitive prices, homestays, volunteer opportunities, helpful and enthusiastic, tourist information available. Recommended. **Medical services** Emergencies T911. **Hospital Monte Sinaí**, Miguel Cordero 6-111 y Av Solano, near the stadium, T288 5595, several English-speaking physicians. **Hospital Santa Inés**, Av Toral 2-113, T281 7888; Dr Jaime Moreno Aguilar speaks English.

Cuenca to the Peruvian border

From Cuenca various routes go to the Peruvian border, fanning out from the pleasant city of Loja, due south of which is Vilcabamba, famous for its invigorating climate and lovely countryside.

South to Loja
The Pan-American Highway divides about 20 km south of Cuenca. One branch runs south to Loja, the other heads southwest through Girón, the Yunguilla valley (with a small bird reserve, see www.fjocotoco.org) and Santa Isabel (several hotels with pools and spas; cloud forest and waterfalls). The last stretch through sugar cane fields leads to Pasaje and Machala. The scenic road between Cuenca and Loja undulates between high, cold páramo passes and deep desert-like canyons.

Saraguro → *Phone code: 07. Colour map 1, C3. Population: 9500. Altitude: 2500 m.*
On the road to Loja is this old town, where the local people, the most southerly indigenous Andean group in Ecuador, dress all in black. The men are notable for their black shorts and the women for their pleated black skirts, necklaces of coloured beads and silver *topos*, ornate pins fastening their shawls. The town has a picturesque Sunday market and interesting Mass and Easter celebrations. Traditional festivities are held during solstices and equinoxes in surrounding communities. Necklaces and other crafts are sold around the plaza. Saraguro has a community tourism programme with tours and home-stay opportunities with indigenous families. Contact **Fundación Kawsay** ⓘ *18 de Noviembre y Av Loja, T220 0331*, or the **Oficina Municipal de Turismo** ⓘ *C José María Vivar on the main*

plaza, T220 0100 ext 18, Mon-Fri 0800-1200, 1400-1800. See also www.saraguro.org. **Bosque Washapampa**, 6 km south has good birdwatching.

Loja → *Phone code: 07. Colour map 1, C3. Population: 191,000. Altitude: 2060 m.*
This friendly, pleasant highland city, encircled by hills, is a traditional gateway between the highlands and southern Amazonia. Loja has won international awards for its parks and its recycling programme. **Tourist offices**: iTur ① *José Antonio Eguiguren y Bolívar, Parque Central, T258 1251, Mon-Fri 0800-1300, 1500-1800, Sat 0900-1300.* Local and regional information and map, helpful, some English spoken. **Ministerio de Turismo** ① *Bolívar 12-39 y Lourdes, p 3, Parque San Sebastián, T257 2964, Mon-Fri 0830-1330, 1430-1700.* Regional information.

Housed in a beautifully restored house on the main park is the **Centro Cultural Loja** home of the **Museo de la Cultura Lojana** ① *10 de Agosto 13-30 y Bolívar, T257 3004, Mon-Fri 0830-1700, Sat-Sun 1000-1600, free,* with well-displayed archaeology, ethnography, art, and history halls. **Parque San Sebastián** at Bolívar y Mercadillo and the adjoining Calle Lourdes preserve the flavour of old Loja and are worth visiting. Loja is famed for its musicians and has two symphony orchestras. Musical evenings and concerts are often held around the town. The **Museo de Música** ① *Valdivieso 09-42 y Rocafuerte, T256 1342. Mon-Fri 0900-1300, 1500-1900, free,* honours 10 Lojano composers.

Parque Universitario Francisco Vivar Castro (Parque La Argelia) ① *on the road south to Vilcabamba, Tue-Sun 0800-1700, US$1, city bus marked 'Capulí-Dos Puentes' to the park or 'Argelia' to the Universidad Nacional and walk from there,* has trails through the forest to the *páramo.* Across the road is the **Jardín Botánico Reynaldo Espinosa** ① *Mon-Fri 0800-1600, Sat-Sun 0900-1730, US$1,* which is nicely laid out.

Parque Nacional Podocarpus
① *Headquarters at Cajanuma entrance, T302 4862. Limited information from Ministerio del Ambiente in Loja, Sucre 04-55 y Quito, T257 9595, parquepodocarpus@gmail.com, Mon-Fri 0800-1700. In Zamora at Sevilla de Oro y Orellana, T260 6606. Their general map of the park is not adequate for navigation, buy topographic maps in Quito.*
Podocarpus (950 m to 3700 m) is one of the most diverse protected areas in the world. It is particularly rich in birdlife, including many rarities, and includes one of the last major habitats for the Spectacled Bear. The park protects stands of *romerillo* or podocarpus, a native, slow-growing conifer. UNESCO has declared Podocarpus-El Cóndor (Cordillera del Cóndor) as a biosphere reserve. It includes a large area (1.14 million has) in the provinces of Loja and Zamora Chinchipe. The park itself is divided into two areas, an upper premontane section with spectacular walking country, lush cloud forest and excellent birdwatching; and a lower subtropical section, with remote areas of virgin rainforest and unmatched quantities of flora and fauna. Both zones are wet (rubber boots recommended) but there may be periods of dry weather October to January. The upper section is also cold, so warm clothing and waterproofs are indispensable year-round.

Entrances to the upper section: at Cajanuma, 8 km south of Loja on the Vilcabamba road, from the turn-off it is a further 8 km uphill to the guard station; and at San Francisco, 24 km from Loja along the road to Zamora. Entrances to the lower section: Bombuscaro is 6 km from Zamora, the visitor's centre is a 30-minute walk from the car park. **Cajanuma** is the trailhead for the demanding eight-hour hike to **Lagunas del Compadre**, a series of beautiful lakes set amid rock cliffs, camping is possible there (no services). Another trail from Cajanuma leads in one hour to a lookout with views over Loja. At **San Francisco**, the *guardianía* (ranger's station) operated by Fundación Arcoiris, offers nice accommodation (see below). This section of the park is a transition cloud forest at around 2200 m, very rich in birdlife. This is the best place to see podocarpus trees: a trail (four hours return) goes from the shelter to the trees. The **Bombuscaro** lowland section, also very rich in birdlife, has several trails leading to lovely swimming holes on the Bombuscaro River and waterfalls; Cascada La Poderosa is particularly nice.

Conservation groups working in and around the park include: **Arcoiris** ① *Ciprés 12-202 y Acacias, La Pradera, T257 2926, www.arcoiris.org.ec;* **Naturaleza y Cultura Internacional** ① *Av Pío Jaramillo y Venezuela, T257 3691, www.natureandculture.org.*

Loja to the Peruvian border

Of all the crossings from Ecuador to Peru, by far the most efficient and relaxed is the scenic route from Loja to Piura via Macará (see below). Other routes are from Vilcabamba to La Balsa (see page 521), Huaquillas (page 535) and along the Río Napo in the Oriente (page 561). There are smaller border crossings without immigration facilities (passports cannot be stamped) at Jimbura, southeast of Macará; and Lalamor, west of Macará.

Leaving Loja on the main paved highway going west, the airport at **La Toma** (1200 m) is reached after 35 km. La Toma is also called **Catamayo**, where there is lodging. At Catamayo, where you can catch the Loja–Macará–Piura bus, the Pan-American Highway divides: one branch runs west, the other south.

On the western road, at San Pedro de La Bendita, a road climbs to the much-venerated pilgrimage site of **El Cisne**, dominated by its large incongruous French-style Gothic church. Vendors and beggars fill the town and await visitors (see Festivals, page 519). Continuing on the western route, **Catacocha** is spectacularly placed on a hilltop. Visit the Shiriculapo rock for the views. There are pre-Inca ruins around the town; small archaeological **Museo Hermano Joaquín Liebana** ① *T268 3201, 0800-1200, 1400-1800.* From Catacocha, the road runs south to the border at Macará.

Another route south from Catamayo to Macará is via **Gonzanamá**, a sleepy little town (basic *hostales*), famed for the weaving of beautiful *alforjas* (multi-purpose saddlebags), and **Cariamanga**, a regional centre (various hotels, banks). From here the road twists along a ridge westwards to **Colaisaca**, before descending steeply through forests to **Utuana** with a nature reserve (www.fjocotoco.org) and **Sozoranga** (one hotel), then down to the rice paddies of **Macará**, on the border. There is a choice of accommodation here and good road connections to Sullana and Piura in Peru.

Border with Peru: Macará–La Tina The border is at the Río Macará, 2.5 km from Macará, where a new international bridge was opened in 2013. There are plans to build a border complex, in the meantime, immigration, customs and other services are housed in temporary quarters nearby. The border is open 24 hours. Formalities are straightforward, it is a much easier crossing than at Huaquillas. In Macará, at the park where taxis leave for the border, there are money changers dealing in soles. Shared taxi Macará-border, US$0.30, private US$1. On the Peruvian side, minivans and cars run to Sullana; avoid arriving in Sullana after dark.

For hotel and restaurant price codes, and other relevant information, see pages 14-17.

● Where to stay

Saraguro *p515*

$ Achik Huasi, on a hillside above town, T220 0058, or through **Fundación Kawsay**, T220 0331. Community-run *hostería* in a nice setting, private bath, hot water, parking, views, tours, taxi to centre US$1.
$ Saraguro, Loja 03-2 y A Castro, T220 0286. Private or shared bath, nice courtyard, electric shower, family-run, basic, good value.

Loja *p516*

$$$$-$$$ Grand Victoria, B Valdivieso 06-50 y Eguiguren, ½ a block from the Parque Central, T258 3500, www.grandvictoriabh. com. Rebuilt early 20th-century home with 2 patios, comfortable modern rooms and suites, includes buffet breakfast, restaurant, small pool, spa, gym, business centre, frigobar, safety box, parking, weekend discounts.
$$$-$$ Libertador, Colón 14-30 y Bolívar, T256 0779, www.hotellibertador.com.ec. A very good hotel in the centre of town, comfortable rooms and suites, includes buffet breakfast, good restaurant, indoor pool (US$6 for non-guests), spa, parking.
$$ Bombuscaro, 10 de Agosto y Av Universitaria, T257 7021, www.bombuscaro.com.ec. Comfortable rooms and suites, includes buffet breakfast and airport transfers, restaurant, car rental, good service. Recommended.
$ Londres, Sucre 07-51 y 10 de Agosto, T256 1936. Economical hostel in a well-maintained old house, shared bath, hot water, basic, clean, good value.
$ Vinarós, Sucre 11-30 y Azuay, T258 4015, hostalvinaros@hotmail.com. Pleasant hostel with simple rooms, eletric shower, parking, good value.

Parque Nacional Podocarpus *p516*

At **Cajanuma**, there are cabins with beds, bring warm sleeping bag, stove and food. At San Francisco, the *guardianía* (ranger's station), operated by **Fundación Arcoiris** offers rooms with shared bath, hot water and kitchen facilities, US$8 pp if you bring a sleeping bag, US$10 if they provide sheets. Ask to be let off at Arcoiris or you will be taken to Estación San Francisco, 8 km further east. At **Bombuscaro** there are cabins with beds and an area for camping.

Loja to the Peruvian border *p517*
Catamayo

$$ MarcJohn's, Isidro Ayora y 24 de Mayo, at the main park, T267 7631, granhotel marcjohns@hotmail.com. Modern multi-storey hotel, suites with jacuzzi and fridge, fan, restaurant, includes airport transfers.
$$ Rosal del Sol, a short walk from the city on the main road west of town, T267 6517. Ranch-style building, comfortable rooms with fan, restaurant not always open, small pool, parking, includes airport transfer, welcoming owner.
$ Reina del Cisne, Isidro Ayora at the park, T267 7414. Simple adequate rooms, hot water, cheaper with cold water, fan, small pool, gym, parking, good value.

Macará

$ Bekalus, Valdivieso y 10 de Agosto, T269 4043. Simple adequate hostel, a/c, cheaper with fan, cold water.
$ El Conquistador, Bolívar y Abdón Calderón, T269 4057. Comfortable hotel, some rooms are dark, request one with balcony, includes simple breakfast, electric shower, a/c or fan, parking.

⑦ Restaurants

Saraguro *p515*
Several restaurants around the main plaza serve economical meals.

$$-$ **Turu Manka**, 100 m uphill from **Hostal Achik Huasi**. Wide selection. The food is average, but it is still one of the better choices in town.

Loja *p516*
$$ **Lecka**, 24 de Mayo 10-51 y Riofío, T256 3878. Tue-Fri 1630-2200, Sat 1800-2200. Small quaint restaurant serving German specialities, very good food, friendly owners.
$$-$ **Casa Sol**, 24 de Mayo 07-04 y José Antonio Eguiguren. Daily 0830-2330. Small place serving breakfast, economical set lunches and regional dishes in the evening. Pleasant seating on balcony.
$$-$ **Pizzería Forno di Fango**, 24 de Mayo y Azuay, T258 2905. Tue-Sun 1200-2230. Excellent wood-oven pizza, salads and lasagne. Large portions, home delivery, good service and value.
$ **Alivinatu**, 10 de Agosto 12-53 y Bernardo Valdivieso, in the health food shop. Mon-Sat 0830-1400, 1500-1900. Very good fresh fruit or vegetable juices prepared on the spot. Also snacks and set lunches with vegetarian options.
$ **Angelo's**, José Félix de Valdivieso 16-36 y Av Universitaria. Mon-Sat 0800-1600. A choice of good quality set lunches, friendly service.

Cafés
Café Ruskina, Sucre 07-48 y 10 de Agosto. Mon-Sat 0900-1300, 1500-2000. Coffee, cream cakes, other sweets and regional snacks such as *humitas*.
El Sendero, Bolívar 13-13 y Mercadillo, upstairs. Tue-Sat 1530-2200. Fruit juices, coffee and snacks, nice balcony overlooking Parque San Sebastián, ping-pong and other games, library.
Molino Café, José A Eguiguren y Sucre. Mon-Sat 0800-2000. Small place, breakfast, choice of coffees, snacks, sandwiches, economical set lunches.

⊛ Festivals

Loja *p516*
Aug-Sep Fiesta de la Virgen del Cisne, hundreds of faithful accompany the statue of the Virgin in a 3-day 74 km pilgrimage from El Cisne to Loja cathedral, beginning **16 Aug**. The image remains in Loja until **1 Nov** when the return pilgrimage starts. Town is crowded Aug-Sep.

⊘ What to do

Loja *p516*
Aratinga Aventuras, Lourdes 14-80 y Sucre, T258 2434, T08-521 2239, www.exploraves. com. Specializes in birdwatching tours, overnight trips to different types of forest. Pablo Andrade is a knowledgeable guide.

⊖ Transport

Saraguro *p515*
Bus To **Cuenca** US$5, 2½ hrs. To **Loja**, US$1.75, 1½ hrs. Check if your bus leaves from the plaza or the Panamericana.

Loja *p516*
Air The airport is at La Toma (Catamayo), 35 km west (see Loja to the Peruvian border, p517): taxi from airport to Catamayo town US$2, to Loja shared taxi US$5 pp, to hire US$20 (cheaper from Loja) eg with Jaime González, T256 3714 or Paul Izquierdo, T256 3973; to Vilcabamba, US$40. There are 1-2 daily flights to Quito and 1 daily to **Guayaquil** with **TAME** (24 de Mayo y E Ortega, T257 0248).
Bus All buses leave from the Terminal Terrestre at Av Gran Colombia e Isidro Ayora, at the north of town, 10 mins by city bus from the centre; left luggage; US$0.10 terminal tax. Taxi from centre, US$1. To **Cuenca**, almost every hour (www.viajerosinternacional.com), 4 hrs, US$7.50. Van service with **Elite Tours**, 18 de Noviembre 01-13, near Puerta de la Ciudad, T256 0731 and **Faisatur**, 18 de

Noviembre y Av Universitaria, T258 5299, US$12, 3 hrs; taxi US$60. **Machala**, 10 a day, 5-6 hrs, US$6 (3 routes, all scenic: via Piñas, for **Zaruma**, partly unpaved and rough; via Balsas, paved; and via Alamor, for **Puyango petrified forest**). **Quito**, regular US$12-14; Transportes Loja *semi-cama* US$17 to Quitumbe, US$20 to La Mariscal, cama US$40 to La Mariscal, 12 hrs. **Guayaquil**, US$10 regular, US$12 *semi-cama*, 8 hrs. To **Huaquillas**, US$6, 6 hrs direct. To **Zumba** (for Peru), 10 daily including Sur Oriente at 0500 to make connections to Peru the same dayand **Cariamanga** at 0900, US$7.50, 7 hrs but delays possible, road construction in 2014; **Nambija** at 2400 direct to the border at La Balsa (only in the dry season), U$10, 8 hrs. To **Catamayo** (for airport) every 15 mins 0630-1900, US$1, 1hr. To **Macará**, see below. To **Piura (Peru)**, Loja Internacional, via Macará, at 0700, 1300 and 2300 daily, US$12, 8-9 hrs including border formalities . Also Unión Cariamanga at 0600 and 2400.

Parque Nacional Podocarpus *p516*
For **Cajanuma**, take a Vilcabamba bound bus, get off at the turn-off, US$1, it is a pretty 8-km walk from there. Direct transport by taxi to Cajanuma, about US$10 (may not be feasible in the rainy season) or with a tour from Loja. You can arrange a pick up later from the guard station. Pickup from Vilcabamba, US$20. To the **San Francisco section**, take any bus between Loja and Zamora, make sure you alight by the Arcoiris *guardianía* and not at Estación Científica San Francisco which is 8 km east. To the **lower section**: Bombuscaro is 6 km from Zamora, take a taxi US$6 to the entrance, then walk 1 km to the visitor's centre.

Loja to the Peruvian border *p517*
Macará
Bus Transportes Loja and **Cariamanga** have frequent buses, daily from Macará to **Loja**; 6 hrs, US$6. Direct Loja–**Piura** buses can also be boarded in Macará, US$4 to Piura, 3 hrs. Transportes Loja also has service to **Quito**, US$15, 15 hrs, and **Guayaquil**, US$11, 8 hrs.

ⓘ Directory

Loja *p516*
Banks Several banks with ATMs around the Parque Central. **Vazcorp**, B Valdivieso y 10 de Agosto, change euros, Peruvian soles and other South American currencies, also TCs, 1.8% commission. A couple of shops along José Antonio Eguiguren change cash euros and soles. **Embassies and consulates** Peru, Zoilo Rodríguez 03-05, T258 7330, Mon-Fri 0900-1300, 1500-1700. **Medical services** Clínica San Agustín, 18 de Noviembre 10-72 y Azuay, T257 3002.

Vilcabamba to Peru

Vilcabamba → *Phone code: 07. Colour map 1, C3. Population: 4900. Altitude: 1520 m.*
Once an isolated village, Vilcabamba is today home to a thriving and colourful expatriate community. It is popular with travellers and a good place to stop on route between Ecuador and Peru. The whole area is beautiful and tranquil, with an agreeable climate. There are many places to stay and good restaurants. The area offers many great day walks and longer treks, as well as ample opportunities for horse riding and cycling. A number of lovely private nature reserves are situated east of Vilcabamba, towards Parque Nacional Podocarpus. Trekkers can continue on foot through orchid-clad cloud forests to the high *páramos* of Podocarpus. Artisans sell their crafts in front of the school on weekends. Tourist office: iTur ⓘ *Diego Vaca de Vega y Bolívar, on the corner of the main plaza, T264 0090, daily 0800-1300, 1500-1800,* has various pamphlets, helpful.

Rumi Wilco ⓘ *10-min walk northeast of town, take C Agua de Hierro towards C La Paz and turn left, follow signs, US$2 valid for the duration of your stay in Vilcabamba.* This 40-ha private nature reserve has several signed trails. Many of the trees and shrubs are labelled with their scientific and common names. There are great views of town from the higher trails, and it is a very good place to go for a walk. Over 100 species of birds have been identified here. Volunteers are welcome. Climbing **Mandango**, 'the sleeping woman' mountain is a scenic half-day walk. The signed access is along the highway, 250 m south of the bus terminal. Be careful on the higher sections when it is windy and always enquire beforehand about public safety, armed robberies have taken place and tourists have been hurt. South of Vilcabamba, 45 km on the road to Zumba is the 3500-ha bird and orchid rich **Reserva Tapichalaca** ① *T250 5212, www.fjocotoco.org, entry US$15, lodge* **($$$)**.

Border with Peru: La Balsa

Many daily buses run on the scenic road from Loja via Vilcabamba to **Zumba** (see Loja, Transport, page 519), 112 km south of Vilcabamba. It is a 1½-hour rough ride by *ranchera* (open-sided bus) from Zumba to the border at La Balsa, there is a control on the way, keep your passport to hand. La Balsa is just a few houses on either side of the international bridge over the Río Canchis; there are simple eateries, shops, money changers (no banks

Vilcabamba

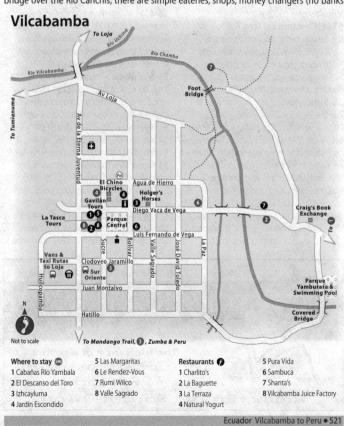

Where to stay
1 Cabañas Río Yambala
2 El Descanso del Toro
3 Izhcayluma
4 Jardín Escondido
5 Las Margaritas
6 Le Rendez-Vous
7 Rumi Wilco
8 Valle Sagrado

Restaurants
1 Charlito's
2 La Baguette
3 La Terraza
4 Natural Yogurt
5 Pura Vida
6 Sambuca
7 Shanta's
8 Vilcabamba Juice Factory

here or in Zumba), and one very basic hotel on the Peruvian side. It is a relaxed border, Ecuadorean customs and immigration are supposedly open 24 hours. The Peruvian border post is open 0800-1300, 1500-2000; entering Peru, visit immigration and the PNP office. On the Peruvian side mototaxis run to **Namballe**, 15 minutes away, and cars run to Namballe and **San Ignacio** when full, two hours, from where there is transport to **Jaén**. This is a faster, more direct route between Vilcabamba and **Chachapoyas** (see the Chacapoyas to Ecuador and the coast section in the Peru chapter) than going via the coast. Parts are rough but it can be done in two days; best take the bus passing Vilcabamba around 0600.

◉ Vilcabamba to Peru listings

For hotel and restaurant price codes, and other relevant information, see pages 14-17.

🛏 Where to stay

Vilcabamba *p520, map p521*
$$$ El Descanso del Toro, 800 m from the centre on the road to Yamburara, T264 0007, www.descansodeltoro.com. Tastefully decorated comfortable rooms, all with jacuzzi, pool, nice grounds, ample parking, attentive staff.
$$-$ Izhcayluma, 2 km south on road to Zumba, T302 5162, www.izhcayluma.com. Popular inn with comfortable rooms and cabins with terrace and hammocks. Very good buffet breakfast included, excellent restaurant with wonderful views, private or shared bath, also dorm US$8.50 pp, very nice grounds, pool, massage centre, yoga centre and lessons, lively bar, billiards, ping-pong, parking, bird-observation platform, walking map and route descriptions, English and German spoken, helpful. Highly recommended.

$$-$ Jardín Escondido, Sucre y Diego Vaca de Vega, T264 0281. Nicely refurbished old house around a lovely patio, bright comfortable rooms, restaurant, cheaper in dorm, small pool, English spoken.
$$-$ Las Margaritas, Sucre y Clodoveo Jaramillo, T264 0051. Small family-run hotel with comfortable nicely furnished rooms, includes good breakfast, intermittent solar-heated water, parking, garden.
$$-$ Le Rendez-Vous, Diego Vaca de Vega 06-43 y La Paz, T09-9219 1180, www.rendezvousecuador.com. Very comfortable rooms with terrace and hammocks around a lovely garden. Private or shared bath, pleasant atmosphere, attentive service, French and English spoken. Recommended.
$ Cabañas Río Yambala, Yamburara Alto, 4 km east of town (taxi US$3), T09-9106 2762, www.vilcabamba-hotel.com. Cabins with cooking facilities in a beautiful tranquil setting on the shores of the Río Yambala, hot water, sauna, monthly rates available. No shops or restaurants nearby, bring food.

Tours to Las Palmas private nature reserve. English spoken.

$ Rumi Wilco, 10-min walk northeast of town, take C Agua de Hierro towards C La Paz and turn left, follow the signs from there, www.rumiwilco.com. Cabins in the Rumi Wilco reserve. Lovely setting on the shores of the river, very tranquil, private or shared bath, laundry facilities, fully furnished kitchens, discounts for long stays and volunteers, camping US$3.50 pp, friendly Argentine owners, English spoken. Recommended.

$ Valle Sagrado, Av de la Eterna Juventud y Luis Fernando de Vega, T09-9936 1699. Basic rooms around nice ample grounds, cheaper in dorm, electric shower, laundry and cooking facilities, parking, trekking tours.

Vilcabamba to Peru: Zumba *p521*
$$-$ Emperador, Colón y Orellana, T230 8063. Adequate rooms, private bath.
$ San Luis, 12 de Febrero y Brasil, T230 8017. Rooms on top floor are nice, private or shared bath, attentive service, refurbished in 2013.

🍴 Restaurants

Vilcabamba *p520, map p521*
Around the Parque Central are many café/bar/restaurants with pleasant sidewalk seating; too many to list, see map, page 521.
$$ Shanta's, 800 m from the centre on the road to Yamburara. Tue-Sun 1300-2100. Specialities are pizza (excellent), trout, frogs legs, filet mignon and *cuy* (with advance notice). Also vegetarian options, good fruit juices and drinks. Nicely decorated rustic setting, pleasant atmosphere and attentive service. Recommended.
$$-$ Natural Yogurt, Bolívar y Diego Vaca de Vega. Daily 0800-2200. Breakfast, home-made yoghurt, a variety of savoury and sweet crêpes, some pasta dishes.
$ Charlito's, Diego Vaca de Vega y Sucre. Tue-Sun 1000-2200. Salads, pasta, pizza, soup, sandwiches with tasty home-made wholemeal bread.

$ Vilcabamba Juice Factory, Sucre y Luis Fernando de Vega, on the Parque Central. Healthy juices, vegan food available, run by a naturopath, popular with expats.
La Baguette, Luis Fernando de Vega y Sucre, small French bakery, great bread and pastries.

⏾ What to do

Vilcabamba *p520, map p521*
See Where to stay, above, for more options.
Cycling El Chino, Sucre y Diego Vaca de Vega, T09-8187 6347, chinobike@gmail.com. Mountain bike tours (US$25-35), rentals (US$2 per hr, US$10 per day) and repairs. Also see **La Tasca Tours**, below.
Horse riding half day US$30, full day with lunch US$40, overnight trips US$60 per day full board.
Gavilán Tours, Sucre y Diego Vaca de Vega, T264 0209, gavilanhorse@yahoo.com. Run by a group of experienced horsemen.
Holger's Horses, Diego Vaca de Vega y Valle Sagrado, T09-8296 1238. Holger Granda, good horses and saddles, German spoken.
La Tasca Tours, Sucre at the plaza, T09-8556 1188. Horse and bike tours with experienced guides, René and Jaime León.
Massage Beauty Care, Diego Vaca de Vega y Valle Sagrado, T09-8122 3456, daily 1000-1800, Karina Zumba, facials, waxing, Reiki, 1 hr US$15; **Shanta's** (see Restaurants, above), T09-8538 5710, Lola Encalada, very good 1½-hr therapeutic massage US$30, also does waxing. Recommended.

⏾ Transport

Vilcabamba *p520, map p521*
Loja to Vilcabamba, a nice 1-hr bus ride; from Loja's Terminal Terrestre, **Vilcabambaturis** minibuses, every 15-30 mins, 0545-2115, US$1.30, 1 hr; or *taxirutas* (shared taxis) from José María Peña y Venezuela, 0600-2000, US$1.75, 45 mins; taxi, US$15. To **Loja**, vans and shared taxis leave from the small terminal behind the market. For **Parque Nacional Podocarpus**, taxis charge

US$20 each way, taking you right to the trailhead at Cajanuma. To **Cuenca** vans at 0800 from Hostería Izhcayluma, then pick up passengers at Hostal Jardín Escondido, US$15, 4-4½ hrs, Cuenca stop at Hostal La Cigale. To **Zumba** buses originating in Loja pass Vilcabamba about 1 hr after departure and stop along the highway in front of the market (1st around 0600, next 1000), US$6.50, 5-6 hrs, expect delays due to road construction in 2014. To **Quito** (Quitumbe) Transportes Loja (tickets sold for this and other routes at Movistar office, Av de la Eterna Juventud y Clodoveo Jaramillo) at 1900, with a stop in Loja, US$18, 13-14 hrs.

Vilcabamba to Peru: Zumba *p521*
Terminal Terrestre in Zumba, 1 km south of the centre. From Zumba to **La Balsa**, *rancheras*

at 0800, 1430 and 1730, US$1.75, 1-1½ hrs. From La Balsa to Zumba at 1200, 1730 and 1930. Taxi Zumba–La Balsa, US$30. To **Loja**, see above. In Zumba, petrol is sold 0700-1700.

ℹ Directory

Vilcabamba *p520, map p521*
Airline offices TAME agent, Bolívar y Montalvo, T264 0437. **Banks** No banks, several standalone ATMs, next to iTur and by the church, but not all cards accepted. **Book exchange** Craig's, in Yamburara, 1 km east of town, follow Diego Vaca de Vega, 2500 books in 12 languages, and art gallery. **Language courses** Spanish classes with Catalina Carrasco, T09-8267 8960, catycarrasco@yahoo.com; Marta Villacrés, T09-9751 3311.

Guayaquil and south to Peru

Guayaquil is hotter, faster and louder than the capital. It is Ecuador's largest city, the country's chief seaport and main commercial centre, some 56 km from the Río Guayas' outflow into the Gulf of Guayaquil. Industrial expansion continually fuels the city's growth. Founded in 1535 by Sebastián de Benalcázar, then again in 1537 by Francisco Orellana, the city has always been an intense political rival to Quito. Guayaquileños are certainly more lively, colourful and open than their Quito counterparts. Since 2000, Guayaquil has cleaned-up and 'renewed' some of its most frequented downtown areas, it boasts modern airport and bus terminals, and the Metrovía transit system.

Thriving banana plantations and other agro-industry are the economic mainstay of the coastal area bordering the east flank of the Gulf of Guayaquil. The Guayas lowlands are subject to flooding, humidity is high and biting insects are fierce. Mangroves characterize the coast leading south to Huaquillas, the main coastal border crossing to Peru.

Arriving in Guayaquil → *Phone code: 04. Colour map 1, B2. Population: 2,370,000. Altitude: 4 m.*
Orientation **José Joaquín de Olmedo** international airport is 15 minutes north of the city centre by car. Not far from the airport is the **Terminal Terrestre** long-distance bus station. Opposite this terminal is the northern terminus of the **Metrovía** rapid transit system. ▶ *See also Transport, page 532.*

A number of hotels are centrally located in the downtown core, along the west bank of the Río Guayas, where you can get around on foot. The city's suburbs sprawl to the north and south of the centre, with middle-class neighbourhoods and some very upscale areas in the north, where some elegant hotels and restaurants are located, and poorer working-class neighbourhoods and slums to the south. Road tunnels under Cerro Santa Ana link the northern suburbs to downtown. Outside downtown, addresses are hard to find; ask for a nearby landmark to help orient your driver. From May-December the climate is dry with often overcast days but pleasantly cool nights, whereas the hot rainy season from January-April can be oppressively humid.

Tourist offices Centro de Información Turística del Municipio ① *Clemente Ballén y Pichincha, at Museo Nahim Isaías, T232 4182, Tue-Fri 0830-1600*, has pamphlets and city maps. There are also information booths at the Malecón 2000 by the clock tower, and at the Terminal Terrestre. **Ministerio de Turismo, Subsecretaría del Litoral** ① *Av Francisco de Orellana, Edif Gobierno del Litoral, p 8 and counter on the ground floor, Ciudadela Kennedy, T268 4274, www.ecuador.travel, Mon-Fri 0900-1700*. Information about the coastal provinces of Ecuador and whale-watching regulations.

Safety The Malecón 2000, parts of Avenida 9 de Octubre, Las Peñas and Malecón del Estero Salado are heavily patrolled and reported safe. The rest of the city requires precautions. Do not go anywhere with valuables. Parque Centenario is also patrolled, but the area around it requires caution. 'Express kidnappings' are of particular concern in Guayaquil; do not take a taxi outside the north end of the Malecón 2000 near the MAAC museum, walk south along the Malecón as far as the **Hotel Ramada**, where there is a taxi stand; whenever possible, call for a radio taxi.

Guayaquil orientation

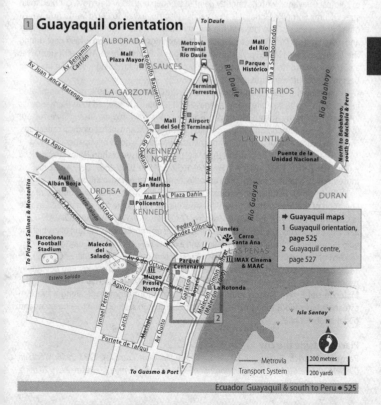

→ **Guayaquil maps**
1 Guayaquil orientation, page 525
2 Guayaquil centre, page 527

Metrovía Transport System

200 metres
200 yards

Places in Guayaquil

A wide, tree-lined waterfront avenue, the Malecón Simón Bolívar runs alongside the Río Guayas from the **Palacio de Cristal**, past **Plaza Olmedo**, the Moorish clock tower, by the imposing **Palacio Municipal** and **Gobernación** and the old Yacht Club to Las Peñas. The riverfront along this avenue is an attractive promenade, known as **Malecón 2000** ① *daily 0700-2400*, where visitors and locals can enjoy the fresh river breeze and take in the views. There are gardens, fountains, childrens' playgrounds, monuments, walkways and an electric vehicle for the handicapped (daily 1000-2000, US$2). You can dine at upmarket restaurants, cafés and food courts. Towards the south end are souvenir shops, a shopping mall and the **Palacio de Cristal** (prefabricated by Eiffel 1905-1907), used as a gallery housing temporary exhibits.

At the north end of the Malecón is an **IMAX** large-screen cinema, and downstairs the **Museo Miniatura** ① *Tue-Sun 0900-2000, US$1.50*, with miniature historical exhibits. Beyond is the Centro Cultural Simón Bolívar, better known as **MAAC, Museo Antropológico y de Arte Contemporaneo** ① *T230 9400, daily 0900-1630, free*, with excellent collections of ceramics and gold objects from coastal cultures and an extensive modern art collection.

North of the Malecón 2000 is the old district of **Las Peñas**, the last picturesque vestige of colonial Guayaquil with its brightly painted wooden houses and narrow, cobbled main street (Numa Pompilio Llona). It is an attractive place for a walk to **Cerro Santa Ana**, which offers great views of the city and the mighty Guayas. It has a bohemian feel, with bars and restaurants. A large open-air exhibition of paintings and sculpture is held here during the *fiestas julianas* (24-25 July). North of La Peñas is **Puerto Santa Ana**, with upmarket apartments, a promenade and three museums: to the romantic singer Julio Jaramillo, to beer in the old brewery, and to football.

By the pleasant, shady **Parque Bolívar** stands the **Cathedral**, in Gothic style, inaugurated in the 1950s. In the park are many iguanas and it is popularly referred to as Parque de las Iguanas. The nearby **Museo Municipal** ① *in the Biblioteca Municipal, Sucre y Chile, Tue-Sat 0900-1700, free, city tours on Sat, also free* has paintings, gold and archaeological collections, shrunken heads, a section on the history of Guayaquil and a good newspaper library.

Between the Parque Bolívar and the Malecón is the **Museo Nahim Isaías** ① *Pichincha y Clemente Ballén, T232 4283, Tue-Fri 0830-1630, Sat-Sun 0900-1600, free*, a colonial art museum with a permanent religious art collection and temporary exhibits.

Halfway up 9 Octubre is **Parque Centenario** with a towering monument to the liberation of the city erected in 1920. Overlooking the park is the museum of the **Casa de la Cultura** ① *9 de Octubre 1200 y P Moncayo, T230 0500, Mon-Fri 0900-1800, Sat 0900-1500, free, English-speaking guides available*, which houses an impressive collection of prehistoric gold items in its archaeological museum; and a photo collection of old Guayaquil.

West of Parque Centenario, the **Museo Presley Norton** ① *Av 9 de Octubre y Carchi, T229 3423, Tue-Sat 0900-1700, free*, has a nice collection of coastal archeology in a beautifully restored house. At the west end of 9 de Octubre are **Plaza Baquerizo Moreno** and the **Malecón del Estero Salado**, another pleasant waterfront promenade along a brackish estuary. It has various monuments, eateries specializing in seafood, and rowing boats and pedal-boats for hire.

Places outside the city

Parque Histórico Guayaquil ① *Vía Samborondón, near Entreríos, T283 2958, Wed-Sun 0900-1630, free; CISA buses to Samborondón leave from the Terminal Terrestre every 20 mins,*

US$0.25. The park recreates Guayaquil and its rural surroundings at the end of the 19th century. There is a natural area with native flora and fauna, a traditions section where you can learn about rural life, an urban section with old wooden architecture, and eateries. A pleasant place for a family outing. The **Botanical Gardens** ① *Av Francisco de Orellana, in Ciudadela Las Orquídeas (bus line 63), T289 9689, daily 0800-1600, US$3, guiding service for*

② Guayaquil centre

N

100 metres
100 yards

Ⓜ Metrovía

➡ Guayaquil maps
1 Guayaquil orientation, page 525
2 Guayaquil centre, page 527

Where to stay 🛏
1 Continental
2 Elite Internacional
3 Grand Hotel Guayaquil
4 Hampton Inn
5 Las Peñas & California Café
6 La Torre

7 Manso
8 Nueve de Octubre
9 Oro Verde
10 Palace
11 Ramada
12 Savoy II
13 Unipark

Restaurants 🍴
1 Asia
2 Fruta Bar
3 La Parrilla del Ñato
4 Las Tres Canastas
5 La Tasca Vasca
6 Ollantay
7 Resaca

up to 5 visitors US$7 (Spanish), US$10 (English), are northwest. There are over 3000 plants, including 150 species of Ecuadorean and foreign orchids (most flower August to December). One area emulates the Amazon rainforest and has monkeys and other animals.

Bosque Protector Cerro Blanco ① *Vía a la Costa, Km 16, T09-8622 5077 (Spanish), fundacionprobosque@ymail.com, US$4, additional guiding fee US$10-15 depending on trails visited, camping US$20 for group of 8, lodge available.* The reserve, run by **Fundación Pro-Bosque**, is set in tropical dry forest with an impressive variety of birds (over 200 species), many reptiles and with sightings of monkeys and other mammals. Unfortunately it is getting harder to see the animals due to human encroachment in the area. Reservations required during weekdays, for groups larger than eight at weekends, and for birders wishing to arrive before or stay after normal opening hours (0800-1600). Take a **CLP** bus from the Terminal Terrestre, a **Cooperativa Chongón** bus from Antepara y 10 de Agosto (hourly) or a taxi (US$8-10). On the other side of the road, at Km 18 is **Puerto Hondo**, where **rowboat trips** ① *through the mangroves are offered, T09-9140 0186, US$15 for a group of 7, 1 hr, reserve ahead.*

Heading east then south from Guayaquil, 22 km beyond the main crossroads at Km 50 on the road to Machala, lies the **Reserva Ecológica Manglares Churute** ① *free entry, camping and use of basic cabins; boat tour US$20-40, depending on group size (2-4 hrs recommended to appreciate the area), arrange several days ahead through the Dirección Regional, Ministerio del Ambiente in Guayaquil, 9 de Octubre y Panamá, Edif Banco Pichincha, p 9, T232 0383, ext 102. Buses (CIFA, Ecuatoriano Pullman, 16 de Junio) leave the Terminal Terrestre every 30 mins, going to Naranjal or Machala; ask to be let off at the Churute information centre. The reserve can also be reached by river.* It is a rich natural area with five different ecosystems created to preserve mangroves in the Gulf of Guayaquil and forests of the Cordillera Churute. Many waterbirds, monkeys, dolphins and other wildlife can be seen. There is a trail through the dry tropical forest (1½ hours' walk) and you can also walk (one hour) to Laguna Canclón or Churute, a large lake where ducks nest. Near the park is **Monoloco Lodge ($)**, www.monoloco.ec, tours available.

⊛ Guayaquil listings

For hotel and restaurant price codes, and other relevant information, see pages 14-17.

⊜ Where to stay

Guayaquil *p526, maps p525 and p527*
Guayaquil has some of the best top-class accommodation in Ecuador. For major chain hotels see: www.hilton.com (**Hilton Colón** and **Hampton Inn**, both excellent), www.ororverdehotels.com (**Oro Verde** and **Unipark**), www.hotelcontinental.com.ec, www.hojo.com (**Howard Johnson**), www.hdoral.com (**Best Western**), www.sheraton.com and www.sonesta.com/guayaquil. There are several refurbished mid-range (**$$**) hotels on Junín between Gen Córdova and Escobedo but decent economy places are few and far between; the latter are concentrated around Parque Centenario, not a safe area.

$$$$ Mansión del Río, Numa Pompilio Llona 120, Las Peñas, T256 6044, www.mansiondelrio-ec.com. Elegant boutique hotel in a 1926 mansion, period European style, river view, buffet breakfast, airport transfers, 10 mins from city centre.

$$$ Castell, Av Miguel H Alcivar y Ulloa, by the Parque Japonés, Kennedy Norte, T268 0190, www.hotelcastell.com. Modern comfortable hotel in a quiet location in the north of the city, includes buffet breakfast, restaurant, a/c, convenient for the airport.

$$$ Grand Hotel Guayaquil, Boyacá 1600
y 10 de Agosto, T232 9690, www.grandhotel
guayaquil.com. A traditional Guayaquil hotel,
central, includes buffet breakfast, good
restaurants, pool, gym and sauna.

$$$ Nazú B&B, Ciudadela La Cogra,
Manzana 1, Villa 2, off Av Carlos Julio
Arosemena Km 3.5 (taxi from bus terminal
or airport US$6-8, Metrovía '28 de Mayo'
stop, best without luggage), T220 1143.
Lovely suburban guesthouse with a variety
of rooms and suites with a/c, includes
dinner and breakfast, pool, parking, terrace
with views of the city, English and German
spoken, refurbished and under new
management in 2014.

$$$ Palace, Chile 214 y Luque, T232 1080,
www.hotelpalaceguayaquil.com.ec. Modern
hotel, includes buffet breakfast, restaurant,
24-hr cafetería, traffic noise on Av Chile side,
good value for business travellers.

$$$ Ramada, Malecón 606 e Imbabura,
T256 5555, www.hotelramada.com. Excellent
location right on the Malecón, rooms facing
the river are more expensive, includes buffet
breakfast, restaurant, a/c, pool, spa.

$$$-$$ Casa Alianza, Av Segunda 318 y
Calle 12, Los Ceibos (taxi from bus terminal
US$6-7, 15-min walk from 'Fe de Guayas'
Metrovía stop, only without luggage), T200
3041. Good hostel, far from the centre, a
variety of rooms and prices, cafetería, a/c,
private or shared bath, group rooms, run by
a Norwegian NGO, Spanish classes available.

$$ La Torre, Chile 303 y Luque, p 13-15,
T253 1316. Popular hotel in a downtown
office tower, long flight of stairs to get into
the building, comfortable rooms, cafetería,
a/c, nice views, reasonably quiet for where
it is, popular, advance booking advised,
good value.

$$ Las Peñas, Escobedo 1215 y Vélez, T232
3355. Nice hotel in a refurbished part of
downtown, ample modern rooms, cafetería,
a/c, quiet despite being in the centre of
town, good value. Recommended.

$$ Manso, Malecón 1406 y Aguirre,
upstairs, T252 6644, www.manso.ec. Nicely

refurbished hostel in a great location
opposite the Malecón. Rooms vary from
fancy with a/c, private bath and river view,
to simpler with shared bath and fan, and a
4-bed dorm (US$15 pp), English spoken.

$$ Savoy II, Junín 627 y Boyacá, T231 0206.
Central location, simple rooms with private
bath, hot water, a/c.

$$ Tangara Guest House, Manuela Sáenz
y O'Leary, Manzana F, Villa 1, Ciudadela
Bolivariana, T228 4445, www.tangara-
ecuador.com. Comfortable hotel in a nice
area by the university and near the Estero
Salado, a/c, fridge, convenient for airport and
bus terminal but also along the flight path,
so it is noisy.

$$-$ Elite Internacional, Baquerizo
Moreno 902 y Junín, T256 5385. Completely
refurbished old downtown hotel, better
rooms have a/c, private bath, hot water;
$ with fan, shared bath and cold water.

$ Nueve de Octubre, 9 de Octubre 736
y García Avilés, T256 4222. Busy 8-storey
hotel in a central location. Simple functional
rooms, those facing the street are larger
but noisy, restaurant, private bath, cold
water, a/c, cheaper with fan, parking extra.
Fills early and does not accept reservations.
Good value.

⑦ Restaurants

Guayaquil *p526, maps p525 and p527*
Main areas for restaurants are the centre
with many in the larger hotels, around
Urdesa and the residential and commercial
neighbourhoods to the north.

$$$ Lo Nuestro, VE Estrada 903 e Higueras,
Urdesa, T238 6398. Daily 1200-2300.
Luxury restaurant with typical coastal
cooking, good seafood platters and stuffed
crabs, colonial décor.

$$$ Manny's, Av Miraflores 112 y C Primera,
Miraflores, T220 2754; also in Urdesa and
Kennedy. Daily 1000-2400. Well-known crab
house with specialities such as *cangrejo al
ajillo* (crab in garlic butter), good quality
and value.

$$$-$$ Cangrejo Criollo, Av Rolando Pareja, Villa 9, La Garzota, T262 6708. Mon-Sat 0900-0100, Sun 0900-2300. Excellent, varied seafood menu.
$$$-$$ La Parrilla del Ñato, VE Estrada 1219 y Laureles in Urdesa; Av Francisco de Orellana opposite the Hilton Colón; Luque y Pichincha downtown; and several other locations, T268 2338. Daily 1200-2300. Large variety of dishes, salad bar, also pizza by the metre, good quality, generous portions. Try the *parrillada de mariscos*, available only at the Urdesa and Kennedy locations. Recommended.
$$$-$$ La Trattoria da Enrico, Bálsamos 504 y las Monjas, Urdesa, T238 7079. Mon-Sat 1230-2330, Sun 1230-2200. Very exclusive Italian restaurant since 1980, the best in food and surroundings, good antipasto.
$$$-$$ Riviera, VE Estrada 707 y Ficus, Urdesa, and Mall del Sol, T288 3790. Daily 1230-2330. Extensive Italian menu, good pasta, antipasto, salads, bright surroundings, good service.
$$$-$$ Sion Lung, VE Estrada 621 y Ficus, Urdesa, also Av Principal, Entre Ríos, T288 8213. Daily 1200-2230. Chinese food, a variety of rice (*chaulafán*) and noodle (*tallarín*) dishes.
$$ La Canoa, at Hotel Continental. Open 24 hrs. Regional dishes rarely found these days, with different specials during the week, a Guayaquil tradition.
$$ La Tasca Vasca, Clemente Ballén 422 y Chimborazo, downtown. Mon-Sat 1200-1600, 1900-2300. Spanish cuisine, specialities include *paella* and *pulpo a la gallega* (octopus).
$$-$ Asia, Sucre 321 y Chile, downtown, also VE Estrada 508 y Las Monjas, Urdesa and in shopping centres in the north. Daily 1100-2130. Chinese food, large portions, popular.
$ Manso, Malecón 1406 y Aguirre, downtown at the hotel. Small dining area serving innovative set lunches and snacks. Tables overlooking the river are nice.
$ Ollantay, Tungurahua 508 y 9 de Octubre, west of downtown. Good vegetarian food.

Cafés and snacks
Aroma Café, Malecón 2000 by Tomás Martínez. Daily 1200-2300. Café, also serves regional food, nice garden setting.
California, Escobedo 1215 y Vélez, below Hotel Las Peñas. Mon-Sat 0700-2000, Sun 0800-1500. Good and popular for breakfast, snacks, drinks, sweets and à la carte meals.
Fruta Bar, Malecón e Imbabura, VE Estrada 608 y Monjas, Urdesa. Excellent fruit juices and snacks, unusual African decor, good music.
Las Tres Canastas, Vélez y García Avilés and several other locations. Breakfast, snacks, safe fruit juices and smoothies.

⊙ Bars and clubs

Guayaquil *p526, maps p525 and p527*
Guayaquil nightlife is not cheap. Most discos charge a cover of around US$5-10 on weekdays, US$10-15 at weekends, and drinks are expensive. There are clubs and bars in most of the major hotels, as well as in the northern suburbs, especially at the Kennedy Mall. Also in vogue are the Las Peñas area, and the Zona Rosa, bounded by the Malecón Simón Bolívar and Rocafuerte, C Loja and C Roca. Both these areas are considered reasonably safe but take a radio taxi back to your hotel. Yellow street cabs have been involved in holdups here.
La Paleta, Escalón 176, Las Peñas. Tue-Sat from 2000. Good music, great drinks and snacks. US$10-15 cover Fri and Sat, popular, reserve.
Praga, Rocafuerte 636 y Mendiburo. Tue-Sat from 1830. US$10-16 cover, live music Fri-Sat. Pleasant atmosphere, several halls, varied music.
Resaca, Malecón 2000, at the level of Junín. Daily 1130-2400. Lovely setting, live tropical music Fri-Sat night. Also serves set lunches on weekdays, regional dishes and pricey drinks.
Vulcano, Rocafuerte 419 y Padre Aguirre. Fri-Sat from 2230. Cover US$7-8. Popular gay bar which attracts a mixed crowd, varied modern music.

⊕ Entertainment

Guayaquil *p526, maps p525 and p527*
Party boats See What to do, below.
Cinemas are at the main shopping
centres and cost US$3-4. The IMAX Cinema,
Malecón 2000, projects impressive films on
its oversize screen.
Theatre Centro Cívico, Quito y Venezuela,
excellent theatre/concert facility, home
to the Guayaquil Symphony which gives
free concerts.

⊕ Festivals

Guayaquil *p526, maps p525 and p527*
The foundation of Guayaquil is celebrated
on **24-25 Jul**, and the city's independence
on **9-12 Oct**. Both holidays are lively and
there are many public events; cultural
happenings are prolonged throughout Oct.

◐ Shopping

Guayaquil *p526, maps p525 and p527*
There are many shopping malls, noisy but air
conditioned for cooling off on hot days.
Camping equipment Casa Maspons,
Ballén 517 y Boyacá. For camping gas.
**Handicrafts Mercado Artesanal del
Malecón 2000**, at the south end of the
Malecón, has many kiosks selling varied
crafts. **Mercado Artesanal**, Baquerizo
Moreno between Loja and J Montalvo.
Greatest variety, almost a whole block of
stalls with good prices. In Albán Borja Mall
are: **El Telar** with a good variety of *artesanías*
and **Ramayana**, with nice ceramics.
Malls Centro Comercial Malecón 2000
is at the south end of the Malecón. **Centro
Comercial San Marino**, Av Francisco de
Orellana y L Plaza Dañín. Huge, one of the
largest in South America. **Mall del Sol** is near
the airport on Av Constitución y Juan Tanca
Marengo. It has craft shops.

◑ What to do

Guayaquil *p526, maps p525 and p527*
Boat tours The gulf islands and
mangroves can be visited on tours from
Guayaquil, Puerto Hondo or Puerto El Morro.
Isla Santay, a Ramsar site wetland with
walking trails has a community tourism
programme, as does **Puná**, the largest of the
islands. **Capitan Morgan**, Muelle Malecón y
Sucre, 1-hr tours on the river with nice city
views, Tue-Fri at 1600, 1800 and 1930, Sat
and Sun at 1230, 1400, 1600, 1800 and 1930,
Fri and Sat also at 2130; US$7. Also 2-hr
party cruises, Thu 2130-2330, Fri-Sat from
2330-0200, US$15, with live music, open bar
and dancing. **Cruceros Discovery**, Muelle
Malecón y Tomás Martínez, 1-hr river cruises,
US$7, Tue-Fri from 1600, Sat-Sun from 1300,
and party trips.
Tour operators A 3-hr city tour costs
about US$14 pp in a group. See Guayaquil
Vision for bus tours of the city. Tours to
coastal haciendas, offer a glimpse of rural life.
Centro Viajero, Baquerizo Moreno 1119 y
9 de Octubre, of 805, T230 1283, T09-9235
7745 24-hr service, www.centroviajero.com.
Custom-designed tours to all regions, travel
information and bookings, flight tickets,
car and driver service, well informed about
options for Galápagos, helpful, English,
French and Italian spoken. Recommended.
Galasam, Edif Gran Pasaje, 9 Octubre 424,
ground floor, T230 4488, www.galapagos-
islands.com. Galápagos cruises, city tours,
tours to reserves near Guayaquil, diving trips,
also run highland and jungle tours and sell
flight tickets.
Guayaquil Visión, ticket booth at Olmedo y
Malecón, T292 5332, www.guayaquilvision.
com. City tours on a double-decker bus,
US$6-17 depending on route, departs from
Plaza Olmedo and the Rotonda, Malecón at
the bottom of 9 de Octubre. Also tours to
attractions outside the city and night-time
party tours.
La Moneda, Av de las Américas 406, Centro de
Convenciones Simón Bolívar, of 2, T269 0900,

ecuador@lamoneda.com.ec. City and coastal tours, whale watching, also other regions. **Metropolitan Touring**, Francisco De Orellana, Edif. World Trade Center, CC Millenium Galery, PB, T263 0900, www.metropolitan-touring.com. High-end land tours and Galápagos cruises.

Train rides The train station is in Durán, across the river from Guayaquil, T215 4254, reservations T1800-873637, www.trenecuador.com, Mon-Fri 0800-1630, Sat-Sun 0730-1530. For information on the luxury *Tren Crucero* from Durán to Quito, see page 444. An *autoferro* runs through rice paddies from Durán to Yaguachi and back Thu-Sun and holidays at 0900 and 1315, US$12, 4 hrs return. A second route is from Durán to Bucay, Sat-Sun and holidays at 0800 returning by bus at 1800, US$20. Tickets are also sold at the railcar in Malecón 2000, Malecón y Aguirre, Wed-Fri 1000-1600, Sat-Sun 1000-1530.

⊖ Transport

Guayaquil *p526, maps p525 and p527*
Air
José Joaquín de Olmedo is a modern airport with all services including banks (change only cash euros at poor rates) and luggage storage. The information booth outside international arrivals (T216 9000, open 24 hrs) has flight, hotel and transport information. It is 15 mins to the city centre by taxi, US$5, and 5-10 mins to the bus terminal, US$3. Fares from the airport to other areas are posted at exit doors and on www.taxiecuadorairport.com. Official airport taxis are more expensive but safer than those out on the street. It is along line 2 of the Metrovía, but neither the Metrovía nor buses to the centre (eg Línea 130 'Full 2') are safe or practical with luggage. For groups, there are van services such as M&M, T216 9294, US$15 to centre.

Many flights daily to **Quito** (sit on the right for the best views) and **Galápagos**, see page 577, with **Aerogal** (Junín 440 y

Córdova, T231 1028, T1-800-237642), **LAN** (Gen Córdova 1042 y 9 de Octubre, and in Mall del Sol, T1-800-101075) and **TAME** (9 de Octubre 424 y Chile, T268 9127 and Galerías Hilton Colón, T268 9135 or T1-700-500800). TAME also flies to **Esmeraldas, Latacunga, Loja** and **Coca**.

Bus Metrovía (T213 0402, www.metrovia-gye.com.ec, US$0.25) is an integrated transport system of articulated buses running on exclusive lanes and *alimentadores* (feeder buses) serving suburbs from the terminuses. One line runs from the Terminal Río Daule, opposite the Terminal Terrestre, in the north, to the Terminal El Guasmo in the south. In the city centre it runs along Boyacá southbound and Pedro Carbo northbound. A second line goes from the Terminal Río Daule along Avenida de las Américas then past the centre to Terminal 25 de Julio in the southern suburbs. A third line goes from the centre (transfer points at Biblioteca Municipal and IESS) along C Sucre to the northwest as far as Bastión Popular and provides access to neighbourhoods such as Urdesa, Miraflores, and Los Ceibos. The Metrovía is a good way of getting around without luggage or valuables. It is very crowded at peak hours.

City buses (US$0.25) are only permitted on a few streets in the centre; northbound buses go along Rumichaca or the *Malecón*, southbound along Lorenzo de Garaicoa or García Avilés. They get very crowded at rush hour.

Taxis Using a radio taxi, such as **Samboroncar**, T284 3883, or **Vipcar**, T239 3000, is recommended. Short trips costs US$2.50, fares from the centre to Urdesa, Policentro or Alborada are around US$4-5. Taxis are supposed to use a meter, but in mid-2014, not all drivers where using them.

Long distance The **Terminal Terrestre**, just north of the airport, is off the road to the Guayas bridge. The Metrovía, opposite the bus station, and many city buses (eg Línea 84 to Parque Centenario) go from to the city centre but these are not safe with luggage; take a taxi (US$3-4). The bus station doubles as a shopping centre with supermarket, shops, banks, post office, calling centres, internet, food courts, etc. Incoming buses arrive on the ground floor, where the ticket offices are also located. Regional buses depart from the second level and long distance (interprovincial) buses depart from the 3rd level. The terminal is very large, so you need to allow extra time to get to your bus. Check the board at the entrance for the location of the ticket counters for your destination, they are colour-coded by region.

Several companies to **Quito**, 8 hrs, US$10, US$12 for express buses which go at night; also non-stop, a/c services, eg **Transportes Ecuador**, Av de las Américas y Hermano Miguel, opposite the airport terminal, T228 9509. To **Cuenca**, 4 hrs via Molleturo/Cajas, 5 hrs via Zhud, both US$8, both scenic; also hourly van service, 0500-2100, with **Río Arriba/Atenas**, Centro de Negocios El Terminal, Bloque C, of 38, Av de las Américas y entrada a Bahía Norte, T09 8488 9269, US$12, 3 hrs, reserve ahead; several others at the same address, departures every 30-40 mins. **Riobamba**, 5 hrs, US$5. To **Santo Domingo de los Tsáchilas**, 5 hrs, US$5. **Manta**, 4 hrs, US$4. **Esmeraldas**, 8 hrs, US$8. To **Bahía de Caráquez**, 6 hrs, US$5. To **Ambato**, 6 hrs, US$6. Frequent buses to **Playas**, 2 hrs, US$2.60; and to **Salinas**, 2½ hrs, US$3.70. To **Santa Elena**, 2hrs, US$2.50, change here for **Puerto López**. To **Montañita** and **Olón**, CLP, at 0520, 0620, 0900, 1300, 1500 and 1640, 3¼hrs, US$5.70. For the **Peruvian border**, to **Huaquillas** direct, 4½-5 hrs, US$6-7; van service with **Transfrosur**, Chile 616 y Sucre, T232 6387, hourly 0500-2000, Sun 0700-2000, 4-4½ hrs, US$13.50; to **Machala**, 3 hrs, US$4-5, also hourly vans with **Oro Guayas**, Clemente Ballén y Chile, T232 0934, US$12, 3 hrs. To **Zaruma**, 8 buses daily, US$6.50, 6 hrs; also

vans, **Rutas Zarumeñas**, T213 0389, US$12, 5 hrs. To **Loja**, with Trans Loja, 8 daily, US$10, 9-10 hrs. Direct bus to **Tumbes** (Peru) 10 daily, 5½ hrs, US$6; to **Piura** (Peru) via **Máncora**, with CIFA, T213 0379, www.cifainternacional.com, regular service at 0720, 1820 and 2100, 10-11 hrs, US$13; and double-decker *bus-cama* at 1950 and 2330, US$17; also with **Ecuatoriano Pullman**, and CIVA, daily at 2130, *semi-cama* US$17, *cama* US$20. To **Chiclayo** (Peru) with **Super Semería**, at 2200 daily, US$25, 12 hrs. To **Lima** with Cruz del Sur, T213 0179, www.cruzdelsur.com.pe, Tue, Fri, Sun at 1400, US$75 (including meals), 27 hrs. With Ormeño, Centro Comercial El Terminal (near Terminal Terrestre), Of C34, T213 0847, 4 weekly to **Lima**, US$80; Sat to **Bogotá**, US$100; Tue and Sun to **Caracas**, US$150.

❶ Directory

Guayaquil *p526, maps p525 and p527*
Banks Most banks have their main branches (with many ATMs) downtown and others in the shopping malls. The airport and Terminal Terrestre both have ATMs. Banco del Pacífico, P Ycaza 200 y Panamá for TCs and cash advances. No *casas de cambio* in centre, only a few street changers along 9 de Octubre dealing in cash euros; be careful. **Car hire** All the main car rental agents are at the airport. **Immigration** Av Río Daule, near the bus terminal, T214 0002. **Medical services** Emergencies T911. Hospitals: a reliable hospital is **Clínica Kennedy**, Av San Jorge y la 9na, T228 9666. Also has branches in Ciudadela La Alborada XIII, Mz-1227 and Entre Ríos. It has many specialists (Dr Roberto Morla speaks German) and a very competent emergency department. Also reliable are: **Clínica Alcívar**, Coronel 2301 y Azuay, T258 0030; **Clínica Guayaquil**, Padre Aguirre 401 y General Córdova, T256 3555 (Dr Roberto Gilbert speaks English and German).

South to Peru

Machala → *Phone code: 07. Colour map 1, C2. Population: 249,000. Altitude: 4 m.*

The capital of the province of El Oro is a booming agricultural town in a major banana producing and exporting region. It is unsafe, somewhat dirty and oppressively hot. For the tourist, the only reasons for stopping here are to go to the beautiful tranquil uplands of El Oro, and to catch a through **CIFA** bus to Peru (also runs from Guayaquil) for the beaches around Máncora. **Tourist office** ① *25 de Junio y 9 de Mayo, Municipio, iturmachala@ hotmail.com, Mon-Fri 0800-1230, 1500-1800, Spanish only.* Some 30 km south along the road to Peru is **Santa Rosa** with the regional airport.

Puerto Bolívar, on the Estero Jambelí among mangroves, is a major export outlet for over two million tonnes of bananas annually. From the old pier canoes cross to the beaches of **Jambelí** (hourly 0730-1500, US$2.40 return) on the far side of the mangrove islands which shelter Puerto Bolívar from the Pacific. The beaches are crowded at weekends, deserted during the week and not very clean. Boats can be rented for excursions to the **Archipiélago de Jambelí**, a maze of islands and channels just offshore, stretching south between Puerto Bolívar and the Peruvian border. These mangrove islands are rich in birdlife (and insects for them to feed on, take repellent), the water is very clear and you may also see fish and reefs.

Zaruma → *Phone code: 07. Colour map 1, C3. Population: 10,800. Altitude: 1300 m.*

Southeast from Machala is the lovely old gold-mining town of Zaruma (118 km). It is reached from Machala by paved road via Piñas, by a scenic dirt road off the main Loja-Machala road, or via Pasaje and Paccha on another scenic dirt road off the Machala-Cuenca road.

Founded in 1549, Zaruma is a delightful town perched on a hilltop, with steep, twisting streets and painted wooden buildings. The **tourist office** ① *in the Municipio, at the plaza, T297 3533, Mon-Fri 0800-1200, 1400-1800, Sat 0900-1600, Sun 0900-1300,* is very friendly and helpful. They can arrange for guides and accommodation with local families. Next door is the small **Museo Municipal** ① *free, ask for the key at the tourist office if closed.* It has a collection of local historical artefacts. The Zaruma area has a number of prehispanic archaeological sites and petroglyphs are also found in the region. Tours with **Oroadventure** ① *at the Parque Central, T297 2761,* or with English speaking guide **Ramiro Rodríguez** ① *T297 2523.* Zaruma is also known for its excellent Arabica coffee freshly roasted in the agricultural store basement, the proud owner will show you around if the store isn´t busy. On top of the small hill beyond the market is a public swimming pool (US$1), from where there are amazing views over the hot, dry valleys. For even grander views, walk up **Cerro del Calvario** (follow Calle San Francisco); go early in the morning as it gets very hot. At **Portovelo**, south of Zaruma, is the largest mine in the area. Its history is told inside a mine shaft at the **Museo Magner Turner** ① *T294 9345, daily 0900-1100, 1400-1700, US$1.* The area has virtually no tourists and is well worth a visit.

Piñas, 19 km west of Zaruma, along the road to Machala is a pleasant town which conserves just a few of its older wooden buildings. Northwest of Piñas, 20 minutes along the road to Saracay and Machala, is **Buenaventura**, to the north of which lies an important area for bird conservation, with over 310 bird species recorded, including many rare ones. The **Jocotoco Foundation** (www.fjocotoco.org) protects a 1500-ha forest in this region, with 13 km of trails, entry US$15, **$$$$** category lodge, advance booking required.

Bosque Petrificado Puyango → *Altitude: 360 m.*

ⓘ *110 km south of Machala, west of the Arenillas–Alamor road, T293 2106 (Machala), bosquepuyango@hotmail.com, 0800-1530, free.* At Puyango, a dry-forest reserve, a great number of petrified trees, ferns, fruits and molluscs, 65 to 120 million years old, have been found. Over 120 species of birds can be seen. There is a camping area, no accommodation in the village, but ask around for floor space or try at the on-site information centre. If not, basic accommodation is available in **Las Lajas**, 20 minutes north (one residencial) and **Alamor**, 20 km south (several hotels, eg **$ Rey Plaza**, T07-268 0256).

Huaquillas → *Phone code: 07. Colour map 1, C2. Population: 50,400. Altitude: 12 m.*

The stiflingly hot Ecuadorean border town of Huaquillas is something of a shopping arcade for Peruvians. The border runs along the Canal de Zarumilla and is crossed by two international bridges, one at the western end of Avenida La República in Huaquillas and a second newer one further south.

Border with Peru: Huaquillas–Tumbes

The best way to cross this border is on one of the international buses that run between Ecuador and Peru. Border formalities are only carried out at the new bridge, far outside the towns of Huaquillas (Ecuador) and Aguas Verdes (Peru). There are two border complexes called CEBAF *(Centro Binacional de Atención Fronteriza)*, open 24 hours, on either side of the bridge; they are about 4 km apart. Both complexes have Ecuadorean and Peruvian customs and immigration officers so you get your exit and entry stamps in the same place. If crossing with your own vehicle however, you have to stop at both border complexes for customs and, on the Ecuadorean side, you also have to stop at the customs *(aduana)* post at Chacras, 7 km from the Ecuadorean CEBAF, on the road to Machala. If you do not take one of the international buses, the crossing is inconvenient. See details in the Peru chapter. A taxi from Huaquillas to the Ecuadorean CEBAF costs US$2.50, to the Peruvian CEBAF US$5. See Peru chapter for transport to Tumbes and beyond. Those seeking a more relaxed crossing to or from Peru should consider Macará (see page 517) or La Balsa (see page 521).

◉ South to Peru listings

For hotel and restaurant price codes, and other relevant information, see pages 14-17.

● Where to stay

Machala *p534*

$$$$ Oro Verde, Circunvalación Norte in Urbanización Unioro, T298 5444, www.oroverde hotels.com. Includes buffet breakfast, 2 restaurants, nice pool (US$6 for non-guests), beautiful gardens, tennis courts, full luxury. Best in town.
$$ Oro Hotel, Sucre y Juan Montalvo, T293 0032, www.orohotel.com. Includes breakfast, pricey restaurant and cheaper café downstairs, a/c, fridge, parking, nice

comfortable rooms but those to the street are noisy, helpful staff. Recommended.
$ San Miguel, 9 de Mayo y Sucre, T292 0474. Good quality and value, some rooms without windows, hot water, a/c, cheaper with fan, fridge, helpful staff.

Zaruma *p534*

$$ Hostería El Jardín, Barrio Limoncito, 10-min walk from centre (taxi US$1.50), T297 2706. Lovely palm garden and terrace with views, internet, parking, comfortable rooms, small zoo, family-run. Recommended.
$$-$ Roland, at entrance to town on road from Portovelo, T297 2800. Comfortable rooms (some are dark) and nicer more

expensive cabins, restaurant with lovely views, pool, parking.
$ Blacio, C Sucre, T297 2045. Hot water, modern, ask for rooms with balcony.
$ Romería, on the plaza facing the church, T297 2173. Old wooden house with balcony, a treat.

Huaquillas p535
$$-$ Hernancor, 1 de Mayo y 10 de Agostso, T299 5467, grandhotelhernancor@gmail.com. Cafeteria, nice rooms with a/c.
$$-$ Sol del Sur, Av La República y Chiriboga, T251 0898, www.soldelsur hotel.amawebs.com. Nice rooms, a/c, small bathrooms, parking.
$ Vanessa, 1 de Mayo y Hualtaco, T299 6263, www.hotelvanessa-ec.com. A/c, internet, fridge, parking, pleasant.

⦿ Restaurants

Machala p534
The best food is found in the better hotels.
$$ Mesón Hispano, Av Las Palmeras y Sucre. Very good grill, attentive service, outstanding for Machala.
$ Chifa Gran Oriental, 25 de Junio entre Guayas y Ayacucho. Good food and service, clean place. Recommended.

Zaruma p534
$$ Giuseppe, C Pichincha s/n. Mon-Sat 1100-2100. Good pizzas.
$$-$ 200 Millas, Av Honorato Márquez, uphill from bus station. Good seafood.
$ Cafetería Uno, C Sucre. Good for breakfast and Zaruma specialities, best *tigrillo* in town.

⦿ Transport

There may be military checkpoints on the roads in this border area, keep your passport to hand.

Machala p534
Air The regional airport is at Santa Rosa, 32 km from Machala; taxi US$12. To **Quito**,

TAME (J Montalvo y Pichincha, T293 0139); 4 daily flights Mon-Fri, 2 on Sat-Sun.
Bus There is no Terminal Terrestre. Do not take night buses into or out of Machala as they are prone to hold-ups. To **Quito**, with **Occidental** (Buenavista entre Sucre y Olmedo), 10 hrs, US$10, 8 daily, with **Panamericana** (Colón y Bolívar), 7 daily. To **Guayaquil**, 3 hrs, US$5, hourly with **Ecuatoriano Pullman** (Colón y Rocafuerte), **CIFA** (Bolívar y Guayas) and **Rutas Orenses** (Tarqui y Rocafuerte), half-hourly, US$5, 3 hrs; also hourly vans with **Oro Guayas**, Guayas y Pichincha, T293 4382, US$12, 3 hrs. There are 3 different scenic routes to **Loja**, each with bus service. They are, from north to south: via **Piñas** and **Zaruma**, partly paved and rough, via **Balsas**, fully paved; and via **Arenillas** and **Alamor**, for **Puyango** petrified forest. Fare to **Loja**, 6 hrs, US$6, several daily with **Trans Loja** (Tarqui y Bolívar). To **Zaruma**, for bus service see below; also vans, **Oro y Plata**, Rocafuerte y Tarqui, US$5, 2 hrs. To **Cuenca,** half-hourly with **Trans Azuay** (Sucre y Junín), 4 hrs, US$5. To **Huaquillas, with** CIFA and Ecuatoriano Pullman, direct, 1½ hr, US$2.30, every 20 mins. To **Piura**, in Peru, with CIFA, 4 a day, US$8-10, 6 hrs; also to **Máncora**, 5 daily, US$6, 5hrs and **Tumbes**, 7 daily, US$3, 3 hrs.

Zaruma p534
Bus To/from Machala with Trans Piñas or TAC, half-hourly, US$3.50, 3 hrs; also vans, Oro y Plata, 10 de Agosto by market, US$5, 2 hrs; and shared taxis (near the terminal), US$7. To **Piñas**, take a Machala bound bus, US$1, 1 hr. To **Guayaquil**, 8 buses daily US$6.50, 6 hrs; also vans, Rutas Zarumeñas, T297 3098, US$12, 5 hrs. To **Quito**, 5 daily, US$11, 12 hrs, note that TAC has a terminal in Quito at Almagro y La Niña; to **Cuenca**, 3 daily (**Trans Azuay** at 0730, US$7, 6 hrs and **Loja**, 4 daily, US$5, 5 hrs (may have to change at Portovelo).

Puyango p535
Puyango is west of the highway: alight from bus at turn-off at the bridge over the Río

Puyango. Bus from **Machala**, Trans Loja 0930, 1300 and 2200, **CIFA** at 0600 and 1500, US$3.50, 2½ hrs. From **Loja**, Trans Loja 0900, 1430 and 1930, US$5, 5 hrs. From **Huaquillas**, Trans Loja at 0730 and **Unión Cariamanga** at 1130, US$2, 1½ hrs. You might be able to hire a pick-up from the main road to the park, US$3. Pick-up from Alamor to Puyango US$25 return, including wait.

Huaquillas p535

Bus There is no Terminal Terrestre, each bus company has its own office, many on Teniente Cordovez. If you are in a hurry, it can be quicker to change buses in Machala or Guayaquil. To **Machala**, with CIFA (Santa Rosa y Machala) and **Ecuatoriano Pullman**, direct, 1½ hrs, US$2.30, every hour between 0800 and 2000; via Arenillas and Santa Rosa, 2 hrs, every 20 mins. To **Quito**, with Occidental, every 2 hrs, 12 hrs, US$10; with **Panamericana**, 11½ hrs, 3 daily via Santo Domingo; 2 daily via **Riobamba** and **Ambato**, 12 hrs. To **Guayaquil**, frequent service with CIFA and Ecuatoriano Pullman, 4½-5 hrs, US$6-7, take a direct bus; van

service to downtown Guayaquil with Transfrosur, C Santa Rosa y Av La República, T299 5288, hourly 0500-2000, Sun 0700-2000, 4-4½ hrs, US$13.50. To **Cuenca**, 8 daily, 5 hrs, US$6. To **Loja**, 6 daily, 6 hrs, US$6.

Directory

Machala p534

Banks Banco del Pacifico, Rocafuerte y Junín, ATM and TCs. For ATM: **Banco de Guayaquil** and **Banco Pichincha**, both at Rocafuerte y Guayas. **Embassies and consulates** Peruvian Consulate, Urb Unioro, Mz 14, V 11, near Hotel Oro Verde, T293 0680, Mon-Fri 0900-1800.

Huaquillas p535

Banks Banks do not change money here. Many street changers deal in soles and US$ cash. Do not change more US$ than you need to get to Tumbes, where there are reliable cambios, but get rid of all your soles here as they are difficult to exchange further inside Ecuador. Only clean, crisp US$ bills are accepted in Peru.

Pacific lowlands

This vast tract of Ecuador covers everything west of the Andes and north of the Guayas delta. Though popular with Quiteños and Guayaquileños, who come here for weekends and holidays, the Pacific Lowlands receive relatively few foreign visitors, which is surprising given the natural beauty, diversity and rich cultural heritage of the coast. Here you can surf, watch whales, visit archaeological sites, or just relax and enjoy some of the best food this country has to offer. Parque Nacional Machalilla protects an important area of primary tropical dry forest, pre-Columbian ruins, coral reef and a wide variety of wildlife. Further north, in the province of Esmeraldas, there are not only well-known party beaches, but also opportunities to visit the remaining mangroves and experience two unique lifestyles: Afro-Ecuadorean on the coast and indigenous Cayapa further inland. Coastal resorts are busy and more expensive from December to April, the temporada de playa.

Guayaquil to Puerto López

Southwest of Guayaquil is the beach resort of Playas and, west of it, the Santa Elena Peninsula, with Salinas at its tip. From the town of Santa Elena, capital of the province of the same name, the coastal road stretches north for 737 km to Mataje on the Colombian border; along the way are countless beaches and fishing villages, and a few cities. Puerto

López is the perfect base for whale watching and from which to explore the beautiful Parque Nacional Machalilla.

Playas and Salinas → *Phone code: 04. Colour map 1, B1. Population: 45,600 and 36,300 respectively.*

The beach resorts of Playas and Salinas remain as popular as ever with vacationing Guayaquileños. The paved toll highway from Guayaquil divides after 63 km at El Progreso (Gómez Rendón). One branch leads to **Playas** (General Villamil), the nearest seaside resort to Guayaquil. Bottle-shaped ceibo (kapok) trees characterise the landscape as it turns into dry, tropical thorn scrub. In Playas a few single-sailed balsa rafts, very simple but highly ingenious, can still be seen among the motor launches returning laden with fish. In high season (*temporada* – December to April), and at weekends, Playas is prone to severe crowding, although the authorities are trying to keep the packed beaches clean and safe (thieving is rampant during busy times). Out of season or midweek, the beaches are almost empty especially north towards Punta Pelado (5 km). Playas has six good surf breaks. There are showers, toilets and changing rooms along the beach, with fresh water, for a fee. Many hotels in our **$$-$** ranges. Excellent seafood and typical dishes from over 50 beach cafés (all numbered and named). Many close out of season. **Tourist office** ① *on the Malecón, Tue-Fri 0800-1200, 1400-1800, Sat-Sun 0900-1600.*

Salinas, surrounded by miles of salt flats, is Ecuador's answer to Miami Beach. **Turismo Municipal** ① *Eloy Alfaro y Mercedes de Jesús Molina, Chipipe, T277 3931, Tue-Fri 0800-1700, Sat 0800-1400.* There is safe swimming in the bay and high-rise blocks of holiday flats and hotels line the seafront. More appealing is the (still urban) beach of Chipipe, west of the exclusive Salinas Yacht Club. In December-April it is overcrowded, its services stretched to the limit. Even in the off season it is not that quiet. On the south shore of the Santa Elena peninsula, 8 km south of La Libertad, built on high cliffs **Punta Carnero**, with hotels in the **$$$-$$** range. To the south is a magnificent 15-km beach with wild surf and heavy undertow, there is whale watching in season.

North to Puerto López
The 'Ruta del Spondylus' north to Puerto López in the province of Manabí parallels the coastline and crosses the Chongón-Colonche coastal range. Most of the numerous small fishing villages along the way have good beaches and are slowly being developed for tourism. Beware of rip currents and undertow.

Valdivia → *Phone code: 04. Colour map 1, B2.*
San Pedro and Valdivia are two unattractive villages which merge together. There are many fish stalls. This is the site of the 5000-year-old Valdivia culture. Many houses offer 'genuine' artefacts (it is illegal to export pre-Columbian artefacts from Ecuador). Juan Orrala, who makes excellent copies, lives up the hill from the **Ecomuseo Valdivia** ① *T08-9011 9856, daily, US$1.50,* which has displays of original artefacts from Valdivia and other coastal cultures. There is also a handicraft section, where artisans may be seen at work, and lots of local information. At the museum is a restaurant and five rooms with bath to let. Most of the genuine artefacts discovered at the site are in museums in Quito and Guayaquil.

Manglaralto → *Phone code: 04. Colour map 1, B2. Population: 30,800*
Located 180 km northwest of Guayaquil, this is the main centre of the region north of Santa Elena. There is a tagua nursery; ask to see examples of worked 'vegetable ivory' nuts. It is a nice place, with a quiet beach, good surf but little shade. **Pro-pueblo** is an

organization working with local communities to foster family-run orchards and cottage craft industry, using tagua nuts, *paja toquilla* (the fibre Panama hats are made from), and other local products. They have a craft shop in town (opposite the park), an office in San Antonio south of Manglaralto, T278 0230, and headquarters in Guayaquil, T268 3569, www.propueblo.com. **Proyecto de Desarrollo Ecoturístico Comunitario** ① *contact Paquita Jara, T09-9174 0143*, has a network of simple lodgings with local families (US\$9 per person), many interesting routes into the Cordillera Chongón Colonche and whale watching and island tours.

Montañita and Olón → *Phone code: 04. Colour map 1, B2.*
About 3 km north of Manglaralto, **Montañita** has mushroomed into a major surf resort, packed with hotels, restaurants, surf-board rentals, tattoo parlours and craft/jewellery vendors. There are periodic police drug raids in Montañita and several foreigners are serving long sentences in jail. At the north end of the bay, 1 km away, is another hotel area with more elbow-room, Baja Montañita (or Montañita Punta, Surf Point). Between the two is a lovely beach where you'll find some of the best surfing in Ecuador. Various competitions are held during the year. At weekends in season, the town is full of Guayaquileños. Beyond an impressive headland and a few minutes north of Montañita is **Olón**, with a spectacular long beach, still tranquil but starting to get some of the overflow from Montañita. Nearby is **El Cangrejal**, a 7-ha dry tropical forest with mangroves.

Ayampe to Salango → *Phone code: 04. Colour map 1, B2.*
North of Montañita, by **La Entrada**, the road winds up and inland through lush forest before continuing to the small, tranquil village of **Ayampe** (tourism is growing here, with many popular places to stay at south end of the beach). North of Ayampe are the villages of **Las Tunas**, **Puerto Rico** and **Río Chico**. There are places to stay all along this stretch of coast. Just north of Río Chico is **Salango**, with an ill-smelling fish-processing plant, but worth visiting for the excellent **Salango archaeological museum** ① *at the north end of town, daily 0900-1200, 1300-1700, US\$1*, housing artefacts from excavations right in town. It also has a craft shop and, at the back, nice rooms with bath in the **\$** range. There is a place for snorkelling offshore, by Isla Salango.

Puerto López → *Phone code: 05. Colour map 1, B2. Population: 11,600.*
This pleasant fishing town is beautifully set in a horseshoe bay. The beach is best for swimming at the far north and south ends, away from the fleet of small fishing boats moored offshore. The town is popular with tourists for watching Humpback Whales from approximately mid-June to September, and for visiting Parque Nacional Machalilla and Isla de la Plata.

Parque Nacional Machalilla
① *Park office in Puerto Lópe, C Eloy Alfaro y García Moreno, daily 0800-1200, 1400-1600.*
The Park extends over 55,000 ha, including Isla de la Plata, Isla Salango, and the magnificent beach of **Los Frailes** and preserves marine ecosystems as well as the dry tropical forest and archaeological sites on shore. At the north end of Los Frailes beach is a trail through the forest leading to a lookout with great views and on to the town of Machalilla (don't take valuables). The land-based part of the park is divided into three sections which are separated by private land, including the town of Machalilla. The park is recommended for birdwatching, especially in the cloud forest of Cerro San Sebastián (see below); there are also howler monkeys, several other species of mammals and reptiles.

About 5 km north of Puerto López, at Buena Vista, a dirt road to the east leads to **Agua Blanca** (park kiosk at entry). Here, 5 km from the main road, in the national park, amid hot, arid scrub, is a small village and a fine, small **archaeological museum** ① 0800-1800, US$5 for a 2-hr guided tour of the museum, ruins (a 45-min walk), funerary urns and sulphur lake, horses can be hired for the visit, camping is possible and there's a cabin and 1 very basic room for rent above the museum for US$5 per person; pick-up from Puerto López US$8, containing some fascinating ceramics from the Manteño civilization. **San Sebastián**, 9 km from Agua Blanca, is in tropical moist forest at 800 m; orchids and birds can be seen and possibly Howler Monkeys. Although part of the national park, this area is administered by the Comuna of Agua Blanca, which charges an entry fee; you cannot go independently. It's five hours on foot or by horse. A tour to the forest costs US$40 per day including guide, horses and camping (minimum two people), otherwise lodging is with a family at extra cost.

Puerto López

N

Not to scale

Where to stay
1 Itapoa
2 La Terraza
3 Mandála
4 Máxima
5 Ruta del Sol
6 Sol Inn
7 Victor Hugo
8 Villa Colombia

Restaurants
1 Bellitalia
2 Carmita
3 Patacón Pisao
4 Whale Café

About 24 km offshore is **Isla de la Plata**. Trips are popular because of the similarities with the Galápagos. Wildlife includes nesting colonies of Waved Albatross (April to November), frigates and three different booby species. Whales can be seen from June to September, as well as sea lions. It is also a pre-Columbian site with substantial pottery finds, and there is good diving and snorkelling, as well as walks. Take a change of clothes, water, precautions against sun and seasickness (most agencies provide snorkelling equipment). You can only visit with a tour and staying overnight is not permitted.

Puerto López to Manta

North of Machalilla, the road forks at **Puerto Cayo**, where whale-watching tours may be organized July-August. One road follows the coast, partly through forested hills, passing Cabo San Lorenzo with its lighthouse. The other route heads inland through the trading centre of **Jipijapa** to **Montecristi**, below an imposing hill, 16 km before Manta. The town is renowned as the centre of the panama hat industry. Also produced are varied straw- and basketware, and wooden barrels which are strapped to donkeys for carrying water. Ask for José Chávez Franco, Rocafuerte 203, where you can see panama hats being made. Some 23 km east of Montecristi is **Portoviejo**, capital of Manabí province, a sweltering unsafe commercial city.

For hotel and restaurant price codes, and other relevant information, see pages 14-17.

● Where to stay

Salinas *p538*

$$$-$$ El Carruaje, Malecón 517, T277 4282. Comfortable rooms, some with ocean view, all facilities, good restaurant, electric shower, a/c, fridge, parking.

$$ Francisco I and II, Enríquez Gallo y Rumiñahui, T277 4106; Malecón y Las Palmeras, T277 3751. Both are very nice, comfortable rooms, restaurant, a/c, fridge pool.

$$ Travel Suites, Av 5 Y C 13, T277 2856, maguerra@telconet.net. Modern, a/c, kitchenette with fridge, very good value in low season.

$ Las Olas, C 17 y Av Quinta, T277 2526, pachecobolivar@hotmail.com. Hot water, a/c, spotless, good value.

$ Porto Rapallo, Av Edmundo Azpiazu y 24 de Mayo, T277 1822. Modern place in a quiet area, hot water, a/c, cheaper with fan, good value.

Valdivia *p538*

$$ Valdivia Ecolodge, at Km 40, just south of San Pedro, T291 6128. Screened cabins without walls in a nice location above the ocean, fresh and interesting. Restaurant, pool and access to nice bathing beach.

Manglaralto *p538*

See also **Proyecto de Desarollo Ecoturístico Comunitario**, page 539.

$$-$ Manglaralto Sunset, 1 block from the Plaza, T09-9440 9687, manglaralto_beach@yahoo.com. Nice modern place, comfortable rooms with a/c, hammocks, cafeteria bar, electric shower, parking.

Montañita *p539*

There are many places to stay in town; the quieter ones are at Montañita Punta. Prices are negotiable in low season.

$$$-$$ Balsa Surf Camp, 50 m from the beach in Montanita Punta, T206 0075, www.balsasurfcamp.com. Very nice spacious cabins with terrace, hammocks in garden, fan, parking, surf classes and rentals, French/Ecuadorean-run. Recommended.

$$ La Casa del Sol, in Montañita Punta, T09-6863 4956, www.casadelsolmontanita.com. A/c, some rooms are dark, fan, restaurant/bar, surf classes and rentals, yoga drop-in (US$8).

$$ Pakaloro, in town at the end of C Guido Chiriboga, T206 0092. Modern 4-storey building with lots of wood, ample rooms with balcony and hammock, fan, shared kitchen, nice setting by the river, good value.

$$ Rosa Mística, Montañita Punta, T09-9798 8383, www.hostalrosamistica.net. Tranquil place, small rooms, cheaper ones away from beach, a/c, garden.

$$-$ La Casa Blanca, C Guido Chiriboga, T09-9918 2501. Wooden house, rooms with bath, mosquito nets, hammocks, good restaurant and bar.

$$-$ Las Palmeras, Malecón at south end of town, T09-8541 9938. Quiet, fan, laundry, English spoken.

$$-$ Sole Mare, on the beach at the north end of Montañita Punta, T206 0119. In a lovely setting on the beach, fan, garden, parking, English spoken, good value. Recommended.

Olón *p539*

$$$ Samai, 10 mins from town by taxi (US$5), T09-462 1316, www.samailodge.com. Rustic cabins in a natural setting, great views, restaurant/bar, pool, jacuzzi, advance booking required.

$$ Isramar, Av Sta. Lucia, ½ block from the beach, T278 8096. Rooms with bath and fan, small garden, restaurant/bar, friendly owner Doris Cevallos.

$$-$ La Mariposa, a block from the beach, near church, T09 8017 8357, www.la mariposahostal.com. 3-storey building, nice ocean views from top floor, Italian-run, English and French also spoken, good value, opened in 2013.

Ayampe to Salango p539
Ayampe
$$ Finca Punta Ayampe, south of other Ayampe hotels, Quito T09-9189 0982, www.fincapuntaayampe.com. Bamboo structure high on a hill with great ocean views, restaurant, hot water, mosquito nets, helpful staff.

$$-$ Cabañas de la Iguana, Ayampe, T08-9016 3825, www.hotelayampe.com. Cabins for 4, mosquito nets, cooking facilities, quiet, relaxed family atmosphere, knowledgeable and helpful, organizes excursions, good choice.

Las Tunas-Puerto Rico
$$$-$$ La Barquita, by Las Tunas, 4 km north of Ayampe, T05-234 7051, www.hosterialabarquita.com. Restaurant and bar are in a boat on the beach with good ocean views, rooms with fan and mosquito nets, pool, nice garden, games, tours, Swiss-run.

Salango p539
$$ Islamar, on a hilltop south of Salango, T09-9385 7580, Guayaquil T04-228 7001, www.hosteria-islamar.com.ec. Ample comfortable cabins, restaurant, lovely views of Isla Salango, camping in your own tent **$** pp, parking for motor-homes. Offers paragliding and diving, Swiss/Ecuadorean-run, advance booking advised.

Puerto López p539, map p540
$$$ Victor Hugo, north along the beach, T230 0054, www.victorhugohotel.com.ec. Ample rooms with bamboo decor, balconies, pool.

$$ La Terraza, on hill overlooking town (moto-taxi US$0.50), T09-8855 4887, www.laterraza.de. Spacious cabins, great views over the bay, gardens, restaurant (only for guests), crystal-clear pool and jacuzzi, parking, German-run.

$$ Mandála, Malecón at north end of the beach, T230 0181, www.hosteriamandala.info. Nice cabins decorated with art, fully wheelchair accessible, gorgeous tropical garden, good restaurant only for guests, fan, mosquito nets, games, music room, Swiss/Italian-run, English spoken, knowledgeable owners. Highly recommended.

$$ Ruta del Sol, Malecón y Mariscal Sucre, T230 0236. Nice modern hotel near the pier, a/c, hot water, restaurant.

$$-$ Itapoa, on a lane off Abdón Calderón, between the Malecón and Montalvo, T09-9314 5894. Thatched cabins around large garden, hot water, cheaper in dorm, family-run, English spoken.

$ Máxima, González Suárez y Machalilla, T230 0310, www.hotelmaxima.org. Cheaper with shared bath, mosquito nets, laundry and cooking facilities, parking, modern, English spoken, good value.

$ Sol Inn, Montalvo entre Eloy Alfaro y Lascano, T230 0248, hostal_solinn@hotmail.com. Bamboo and wood construction, private or shared bath, hot water, fan, laundry and cooking facilities, garden, pool table, popular, relaxed atmosphere.

$ Villa Colombia, García Moreno behind market, T230 0189, www.hostalvillacolombia.com. Rooms with hot water, fan, cooking facilities, mosquito nets, garden with hammocks, small parking area.

Puerto López to Manta p540
There are other places to stay but many close out of season.

$ Luz de Luna, 5 km north of Puerto Cayo on the coastal road, T261 6031, Quito T02-240 0562, www.hosterialuzdeluna.com. On a clean beach, comfortable spacious rooms with balcony, full board **$$**, restaurant, cold water in cabins, shared hot showers available, fan and mosquito net, pool, disco, quieter in low season when discounts are available.

$ Puerto Cayo, south end of beach, Puerto Cayo, T261 6019, T09-9752 1538. Good restaurant, fan, comfortable rooms with hammocks and terrace overlooking the sea.

🍴 Restaurants

Salinas p538

A couple of blocks inland from the Malecón are food stalls serving good *ceviches* and freshly cooked seafood.

$$$ La Bella Italia, Malecón y C 17, near Hotel El Carruaje. Good pizza and international food.

$$$-$$ Amazon, Malecón near Banco de Guayaquil, T277 3671. Elegant upmarket eatery, grill and seafood specialities, good wine list.

$$ Oyster Catcher, Enríquez Gallo entre C 47 y C 50. Oct-May. Restaurant and bar, friendly place, safe oysters, enquire here about birdwatching tours with local expert Ben Haase.

$ El Mayquito, Av 2 y C 12. Simple place with very good food and friendly service.

Montañita p539

$$$-$$ Tikilimbo, opposite Hotel Casa Blanca. Good-quality, vegetarian dishes available.

$$ Hola Ola, in the center of town. Good international food and bar with some live music and dancing, popular.

$$ Marea Pizzeria Bar, 10 de Agosto y Av 2. Open evenings only. Real wood-oven pizza, very tasty. Recommended.

$$ Rocío, 10 de Agosto y Av 2, inside eponymous hotel. Good Mediterranean food.

Salango p539

$$ El Delfín Mágico. Excellent, order meal before visiting museum because all food is cooked from scratch, very fresh and safe.

Puerto López p539, map p540

$$$ Bellitalia, north toward the river, T09- 9617 5183. Mon-Sat 1800-2100. Excellent authentic Italian food, home-made pasta, attentive owners Vittorio and Elena. Reservations required. Highly recommended.

$$ Carmita, Malecón y General Córdova. Tasty fish and seafood, a Puerto López tradition. Try the *camarones en salsa de maní* (prawns in peanut sauce).

$$ Patacón Pisao, Gen Córdova, half a block from the malecón. Colombian food, giant *patacones* and *arepas*.

$$ Whale Café, towards the south end of the Malecón. Good pizza, stir-fried Asian dishes, Thai specialities, sandwiches, vegetarian salads, cakes and pies. Nice breakfast, famous for pancakes. US-run, open irregular hours, evenings only.

⚓ What to do

Salinas p538

Ben Haase, at Museo de Ballenas, Av Enríquez Gallo 1109 entre C47 y C50, T277 7335, T09-9961 9257. Expert English speaking naturalist guide runs birdwatching tours to the Ecuasal salt ponds, US$50 for a small group. Also whale watching and trips to a sea lion colony.

Fernando Félix, T238 4560, T09-9827 4475. English-speaking marine biologist, can guide for whale watching and other nature trips, arrange in advance.

Montañita p539

Surfboard rentals all over town from US$4 per hr, US$15 per day.

Ayampe to Salango p539
Ayampe

Otra Ola, beside Cabañas de la Iguana, www.otraola.com. Surf lessons and board rental, yoga and Spanish classes. Very nice enthusiastic owners, Vanessa and Ryan from Canada.

Puerto López p539, map p540

Whale watching Puerto López is a major centre for trips from Jun to Sep, with many more agencies than we can list; avoid touts on the street. Whales can also be seen elsewhere, but most reliably in Puerto López. There is a good fleet of small boats (16- 20 passengers) running excursions, all have life jackets and a toilet, those with 2 engines are safer. All agencies offer the same tours for the same price. Beware touts offering cheap tours to "La Isla", they take you to Isla Salango not Isla de la Plata. In high season: US$40 pp for whale watching, Isla de la Plata and snorkelling, with a snack and drinks, US$25 for whale watching only (available Jun and Sep). Outside whale season, tours to Isla de la Plata and snorkelling cost US$35. Trips depart from the pier around 0800 and return around 1700. Agencies also offer tours to the mainland sites of the national park. A day tour combining Agua Blanca and Los Frailes costs US$25 pp plus US$5 entry fee. There are also hiking, birdwatching, kayaking, diving (be sure to use a reputable agency, there have been accidents) and other trips. **Aventuras La Plata**, on malecón, T230 0189, www.aventuraslaplata.com. Whale watching tours.

Cercapez, at the Centro Comercial on the highway, T230 0173. All-inclusive trips to San Sebastián, with camping, local guide and food run US$40 pp per day.

Exploramar Diving, Malecón y Gral Córdova, T230 0123, www.exploradiving.com. Quito based, T02-256 3905. Have 2 boats for 8-16 people and their own compressor to fill dive tanks. PADI Dive Master accompanies qualified divers to various sites, but advance notice is required, US$120 pp for all-inclusive diving day tour (2 tanks). Also offer diving lessons. Recommended.

Palo Santo, Malecón y Abdón Calderón, T230 0312, palosanto22@gmail.com. Whale watching tours.

⊖ Transport

Playas p538
Bus Trans Posorja and Trans Villamil to **Guayaquil**, frequent, 2 hrs, US$2.60; taxi US$25.

Salinas p538
Bus To **Guayaquil**, Coop Libertad Peninsular (CLP), María González y León Avilés, every 5 mins, US$3.70, 2½ hrs. For **Montañita, Puerto López** and points north, transfer at La Libertad (not safe, take a taxi between terminals) or Santa Elena. From La Libertad,

every 30 mins to Puerto López, US$4, 2½ hrs; or catch a Guayaquil–Olón bus in Santa Elena.

Manglaralto p538
Bus To **Santa Elena** and **La Libertad**, US$1.25, 1 hr. Transfer in Santa Elena for Guayaquil. To **Guayaquil** direct, see Olón schedule below. To **Puerto López**, 1 hr, US$1.50.

Montañita and Olón p539
Bus Montañita is just a few mins south of Olón, from where **CLP** has direct buses to **Guayaquil** at 0445, 0545, 1000, 1300, 1500, 1700 (same schedule from Guayaquil), US$5.50, 3 hrs; or transfer in Santa Elena, US$1.50, 1½ hrs. To **Puerto López**, every 30 mins, US$2, 45 mins.

Puerto López p539, map p540
Mototaxis all over town, US$0.50.
Bus To **Santa Elena** or **La Libertad**, every 30 mins, US$4, 2½ hrs. To **Montañita** and **Manglaralto**, US$2.50, 1 hr. To **Guayaquil**, direct with **Cooperativa Jipijapa** via Jipijapa, 10 daily, US$4.50, 4 hrs; or transfer in Olón or Santa Elena. Pick-ups for hire to nearby sites are by the market, east of the highway. To/ from **Manta**, direct, hourly, US$3, 2½ hrs; or transfer in Jipijapa. To **Quito** with **Reina del Camino**, office in front of market, daily 0800 and 2000; and **CA Aray**, 5 daily, 9 hrs, US$13; some buses go to Quitumbe others to their private stations.

Parque Nacional Machalilla p539
Bus To **Los Frailes**: take a bus towards Jipijapa (US$0.50), mototaxi (US$5), or a pick-up (US$8), and alight at the turn-off just south of the town of Machalilla, then walk for 30 mins. No transport back to Puerto López after 2000 (but check in advance). **To Agua Blanca**: take tour, a pick-up (US$7), mototaxi (US$10 return with 2 hrs wait) or a bus bound for Jipijapa (US$0.50); it is a hot walk of more than 1 hr from the turning to the village. **To Isla de la Plata**: the island can only be visited on a day trip. Many agencies offer tours, see Puerto López above.

Puerto López to Manta *p540*
Bus From Jipijapa (terminal on the outskirts) to **Manglaralto** (2 hrs, US$2), to **Puerto López** (1 hr, US, 1, these go by Puerto Cayo), to **Manta** (1 hr, US$1), to **Quito** (10 hrs, US$9).

❶ Directory

Montañita *p539*
Banks Banco Bolivariano, and one other ATM (not always working, bring some cash). **Language courses** Montañita

Spanish School, on the main road 50 m uphill outside the village, T206 0116, www.montanitaspanishschool.com.

Puerto López *p539, map p5403*
Banks Banco Pichincha, large building at south end of Malecón, for ATM; only one in town, best bring some cash.
Language courses La Lengua, Abdón Calderón y García Moreno, east of the highway, T09-233 9316 or Quito T02-250 1271, www.la-lengua.com.

Manta and Bahía de Caráquez

Two quite different seaside places: Manta a rapidly growing port city, prospering on fishing and trade; Bahía de Caráquez a relaxed resort town and a pleasant place to spend a few days. It is proud of its 'eco' credentials. Just beyond Bahía, on the other side of the Río Chone estuary, is the village of Canoa, boasting some of the finest beaches in Ecuador.

Manta and around → *Phone code: 05. Colour map 1, B2. Population: 230,000.*
Ecuador's second port after Guayaquil is a busy town that sweeps round a bay filled with all sorts of boats. A constant sea breeze tempers the intense sun and makes the city's *malecones* pleasant places to stroll. At the gentrified west end of town is Playa Murciélago, a popular beach with wild surf (flags indicate whether it is safe to bathe), with good surfing from December to April. Here, the Malecón Escénico has a cluster of bars and seafood restaurants. It is a lively place especially at weekends, when there is good music, free beach aerobics and lots of action. Beyond El Murciélago, along the coastal road are San Mateo, Santa Marianita, San Lorenzo and Puerto Cayo, before reaching Machalilla and Puerto López. The **Museo Centro Cultural Manta** ① *Malecón y C 19, T262 6998, Mon-Fri 0900-1630, Sat-Sun 1000-1500, free*, has a small but excellent collection of archaeological pieces from seven different civilizations which flourished on the coast of Manabí between 3500 BC and AD 1530. Three bridges join the main town with its seedy neighbour, **Tarqui. Tourist offices**: Ministerio de Turismo ① *Paseo José María Egas 1034 (Av 3) y C 11, T262 2944, Mon-Fri 0900-1230, 1400-1700*; Dirección Municipal de Turismo ① *C9 y Av 4, T261 0171, Mon-Fri 0800-1700*; and Oficina de Información ULEAM ① *Malecón Escénico, T262 4099, daily 0900-1700*; all helpful and speak some English. Manta has public safety problems, enquire locally about the current situation.

Crucita → *Phone code: 05. Colour map 1, B2. Population: 14,900.*
A rapidly growing resort, 45 minutes by road from either Manta or Portoviejo, Crucita is busy at weekends and holidays when people flock here to enjoy ideal conditions for paragliding, hang-gliding and kite-surfing. The best season for flights is July to December. There is also an abundance of sea birds in the area. There are many restaurants serving fish and seafood along the seafront. A good one is **Motumbo**, try their *viche*, they also offer interesting tours and rent bikes.

North to Bahía

About 60 km northeast of Manta (30 km south of Bahía de Caráquez) are **San Clemente** and, 3 km south, **San Jacinto**. The ocean is magnificent but be wary of the strong undertow. Both get crowded during the holiday season and have a selection of *cabañas* and hotels. Some 3 km north of San Clemente is **Punta Charapotó**, a high promontory clad in dry tropical forest, above a lovely beach. Here are some nice out-of-the-way accommodations and an out-of-place upmarket property development.

Bahía de Caráquez and around → *Phone code: 05. Colour map 1, B2. Population: 26,400.*

Set on the southern shore at the seaward end of the Chone estuary, Bahía has an attractive riverfront laid out with parks along the Malecón which goes right around the point to the ocean side. The beaches in town are nothing special, but there are excellent beaches nearby between San Vicente and Canoa and at Punta Bellaca (the town is busiest July-August). Bahía has declared itself an 'eco-city', with recycling projects, organic gardens and ecoclubs. Tricycle rickshaws called 'eco-taxis' are a popular form of local transport. Information about the eco-city concept can be obtained from **Río Muchacho Organic Farm** in Canoa (page 550) or the **Planet Drum Foundation**, www.planetdrum.org. **Tourist offices**: Ministerio de Turismo ① *T269 1124, Bolívar y Padre Laennen, Mon-Fri 0830-1300, 1430-1730, Sat 0800-1300, www.bahiadecaraquez.com*; also at the same address **Dirección Municipal** ① *T269 1044*. The **Museo Bahía de Caráquez** ① *Malecón Alberto Santos y Aguilera, T269 2285, Tue-Sat 0830-1630, free,* has an interesting collection of archaeological artefacts from prehispanic coastal cultures, a life-size balsa raft and modern sculpture. Bahía is a port for international yachts, with good service at **Puerto Amistad** ① *T269 3112*.

The Río Chone estuary has several islands with mangrove forest. The area is rich in birdlife, and dolphins may also be seen. **Isla Corazón** has a boardwalk through an area of protected mangrove forest and there are bird colonies at the end of the island which can only be accessed by boat. The village of **Puerto Portovelo** is involved in mangrove reforestation and runs an eco-tourism project (tour with *guía nativo* US$6 per person). You can visit independently, taking a Chone-bound bus from San Vicente or with an agency. Visits here are tide-sensitive, so even if you go independently, it is best to check with the agencies about the best time to visit. Inland near Chone is **La Segua** wetland, very rich in birds; Bahía agencies offer tours here. **Saiananda** ① *5 km from Bahía along the bay, T239 8331, owner Alfredo Harmsen, biologist, reached by taxi or any bus heading out of town, US$2,* is a private park with extensive areas of reforestation and a large collection of animals, a cactus garden and spiritual centre. Also offer first-class accommodation (**$$** including breakfast) and vegetarian meals served in an exquisite dining area over the water.

San Vicente and Canoa → *Phone code: 05. Colour map 1, B2.*

On the north side of the Río Chone, **San Vicente** is reached from Bahía de Caráquez by the longest bridge in Ecuador. Some 17 km beyond, **Canoa**, once a quiet fishing village with a splendid 200-m-wide beach, has grown rapidly and is increasingly popular with Ecuadorean and foreign tourists. It has lost some of its charm along the way, but it is still pleasant on weekdays, crowded, noisy and dirty on weekends and especially holidays. The choice of accommodation and restaurants is very good. The beautiful beach between San Vicente and Canoa is a good walk, horse or bike ride. Horses and bicycles can be hired through several hotels. Surfing is good, particularly during the wet season, December to April. In the dry season there is good wind for windsurfing. Canoa is also a good place for hang-gliding and paragliding. Tents for shade and chairs are rented at the beach for US$3 a day. About 10 km north of Canoa, the **Río Muchacho Organic Farm** (www.riomuchacho. com, see What to do, page 550) accepts visitors and volunteers, it's an eye-opener to rural coastal (*montubio*) culture and to organic farming.

North to Pedernales → *Phone code: 05. Colour map 1, A2. Population: 35,600.*

The coastal road cuts across Cabo Pasado to **Jama** (1½ hours; cabins and several *hostales*), then runs parallel to the beach past coconut groves and shrimp hatcheries, inland across some low hills and across the Equator to **Pedernales**, a market town and crossroads with nice undeveloped beaches to the north. In town, where beaches are less attractive, they cater to the *quiteño* holiday market. A poor unpaved road goes north along the shore to Cojimíes. The main coastal road, fully paved, goes north to Chamanga, El Salto and Esmeraldas. Another important road goes inland to El Carmen, where it divides: one branch to Santo Domingo de los Tsáchilas, another to La Concordia. The latter is the most direct route to Quito.

Santo Domingo de los Tsáchilas → *Phone code: 02. Colour map 1, A3. Population: 319,000.*

In the hills above the western lowlands, Santo Domingo, 129 km from Quito, is an important commercial centre and transport hub. It is capital of the eponymous province. The city is noisy and dangerous, caution is recommended at all times in the market areas, including the pedestrian walkway along 3 de Julio and in peripheral neighbourhoods. Sunday is market day, shops and banks close Monday instead. It was known as 'Santo Domingo de los Colorados', a reference to the traditional red hair dye, made with *achiote* (annatto), worn by the indigenous Tsáchila men. Today the Tsáchila only wear their indigenous dress on special occasions. There are less than 2000 Tsáchilas left, living in eight communities off the roads leading from Santo Domingo towards the coast. Their lands make up a reserve of some 8000 ha. Visitors interested in their culture are welcome at the **Complejo Turístico Huapilú**, in the Comunidad Chigüilpe, where there is a small but interesting museum (contributions expected). Access is via the turn-off east at Km 7 on the road to Quevedo, from where it is 4 km. Tours are run by travel agencies in town. The Santo Domingo area also offers opportunities for nature trips and sports activities, such as rafting. **Cámara de Turismo** ① *Río Mulaute y Av Quito, T275 2146, Mon-Fri 0830-1300, 1430-1800, English spoken.*

⊕ Manta and Bahía de Caráquez listings

For hotel and restaurant price codes, and other relevant information, see pages 14-17.

⊜ Where to stay

Manta and around *p545*

All streets have numbers; those above 100 are in Tarqui (those above C110 are not safe).
$$$$ Oro Verde, Malecón y C 23, T262 9200, www.oroverdehotels.com. Includes buffet breakfast, restaurant, pool, all luxuries.
$$$ Vistalmar, C M1 y Av 24B, at Playa Murciélago, T262 1671. Exclusive hotel overlooking the ocean. Ample cabins and

suites tastefully decorated with art, a/c, pool, cabins have kitchenettes, gardens by the sea. A place for a honeymoon.
$$ Manakin, C 20 y Av 12, T262 0413. A/c, comfortable rooms, small patio, nice common areas.
$$ YorMar, Av 14 entre C 19 y C 20, T262 4375. Nice rooms with small kitchenette and patio, electric shower, a/c, parking.
$$-$ Donkey Den, in Santa Marianita, 20 mins south of Manta, T09-9723 2026, www.donkeydenguesthouse.com. Nice rooms right on the beach where kitesurfing is popular, private or shared bath, dorm

for 5 US$15 pp, cooking facilities, breakfast available, popular with US expats, taxi from Manta US$10.

$ Centenario, C 11 No 602 y Av 5, enquire at nearby Lavamatic Laundry, T262 9245, josesan martin@hotmail.com. Pleasant hostel in a nicely refurbished old home in the centre of town. Shared bath, hot water, fan, cooking facilities, nice views, quiet location, good value.

Tarqui
$$-$ Chávez Inn, Av 106 y C 106, T262 1019. Modern hotel, a/c, fridge, small bright rooms.

Crucita *p545*
$ Cruzita, towards the south end of beach, T234 0068. Very nice hostel right on the beach with great views, meals on request, cold water, fan, small pool, use of kitchen in the evening, parking, good value. Owner Raul Tobar offers paragliding flights and lessons. Recommended.
$ Hostal Voladores, at south end of beach, T234 0200, www.parapentecrucita.com. Simple but nice, restaurant, private or shared bath, hot water, small pool, sea kayaks available. Owner Luis Tobar offers paragliding flights and lessons.
$ Italia, C 9 y 25 de Mayo, at the south end of town, T234 0291. Pleasant place, restaurant serves pizza, electric shower, small pool, parking, nice patio.

North to Bahía *p546*
$$ Peñón del Sol, on the hillside near Punta Charapotó, T09-9941 4149, penondelsol@hotmail.com. Located on a 250-ha dry tropical forest reserve, meals on request, shared bath, cold water, great views, camping possible.
$$-$ Hotel San Jacinto, on the beach between San Jacinto and San Clemente, T261 5516, www.hotelsanjacinto.com. Pleasant location right by the ocean, restaurant, hot water, fan, older place gradually being refurbished and looking good.
$ Sabor de Bamboo, on the ocean side of the road to Punta Charapotó, T09-8024 3562.

Nice simple wooden cabins with sea breeze, cold water, restaurant and bar, music on weekends, wonderfully relaxed place, friendly owner Meier, German and English spoken.

Bahía de Caráquez *p546*
$$$ La Piedra, Circunvalación near Bolívar, T269 0154, www.hotellapiedra.com. Modern hotel with access to the beach and lovely views, good expensive restaurant, a/c, pool (US$2 for non-guests, only in low season), good service, bicycle rentals for guests.
$$-$ La Herradura, Bolívar e Hidalgo, T269 0446, www.laherradurahotel.com. Older well-maintained hotel, restaurant, a/c, cheaper with fan and cold water, nice common areas, cheaper rooms are good value.
$ Bahía Hotel, Malecón y Vinueza. A variety of different rooms, those at the back are nicer, fan, parking.
$ Coco Bongo, Cecilio Intriago y Arenas, T09-8544 0978. Nice hostel with a pleasant atmosphere, private bath, cheaper in dorm, breakfast available, electric shower, ceiling fan, mosquito nets, cooking facilities, popular.

Canoa *p546*
There are over 60 hotels in Canoa.
$$$ Hostería Canoa, 1 km south of town, T261 6380, www.hosteriacanoa.com. Comfortable cabins and rooms, good restaurant and bar, a/c, pool, sauna, whirlpool.
$$ La Vista, on the beach towards the south end of town, T09-9228 8995. All rooms have balconies to the sea, palm garden with hammocks, good value. Recommended.
$ Baloo, on the beach at south end of the village, T261 6355, www.baloo-canoa.com. Wood and bamboo cabins, restaurant, private or shared bath, hot water, British-run.
$ Bambú, on the beach just north of C Principal, T09-8926 5225, www.hotel bambuecuador.com. Pleasant location and atmosphere. A variety of rooms and prices, good restaurant including vegetarian options, private or shared bath, also dorm, camping possible (US$3.50 pp with your own tent), hot water, fan, surfing classes and

board rentals. Dutch/Ecuadorean-owned, very popular and recommended.
$ Coco Loco, on the beach toward the south end of town, T09-8764 6459, www. hostalcoco loco.weebly.com. Pleasant breezy hotel with nice views, café serves breakfast and snacks, bar, private or shared bath, also dorm, hot showers, cooking facilities, surfboard rentals, excellent horse riding, English spoken, popular.

North to Pedernales *p547*
Jama
$$$ Samvara, 300 m from the highway, turn-off 13 km north of Jama, T09-9128 2278, www.samvara-ecolodge.com. Thatched cabins on 6 ha of land, includes breakfast and dinner, beach and pool, lovely secluded setting, camping possible (US$15 pp in on-site tents, US$8 pp in your own tent), Swiss/Ecuadorean-run.
$$$-$$ Punta Prieta Guest House, by Punta Prieta, T09-9225 9146, Quito T02-286 2986, www.puntaprieta.com. Gorgeous setting on a headland high above the ocean with access to pristine beaches. Meals available, comfortable cabins with fridge, suites and rooms with shared bath, balcony with hammocks, nice grounds.
$ Palo Santo, C Melchor Cevallos, by the river in Jama town, T241 0441, luchincevallos@hotmail.com. Thatched cabins on pleasant grounds, cold water, ceiling fan.

Pedernales
There are many other hotels in all price ranges.
$$ Agua Marina, Jaime Roldós 413 y Velasco Ibarra, T268 0491. Modern hotel, cafeteria, a/c, pool, parking.
$$ Cocosolo, on a secluded beach 20 km north of Pedernales (pickups from main park US$1, 30 mins), T09-9921 5078. A lovely hideaway set among palms. Cabins and rooms, camping possible, restaurant, horses for hire, French and English spoken.
$ Mr John, Plaza Acosta y Malecón, 1 block from the beach, T268 0235. Modern hotel,

cold water, fan, parking, rooms facing the beach can be noisy at weekends. Good value.

Santo Domingo de los Tsáchilas *p547*
$$$ Tinalandia, 16 km from Santo Domingo, on the road to Quito, poorly signposted, look for a large rock painted white; T09-9946 7741, in Quito T244 9028, www.tinalandia.com. Includes full board, nice chalets in cloud forest reserve, great food, spring-fed pool, good birdwatching, entry US$10 for non-guests.
$$$ Zaracay, Av Quito 1639, 1.5 km from the centre, T275 0316, www.hotelzaracay.com. Restaurant, gardens and swimming pool, parking, good rooms and service. Advance booking advised, especially on weekends.
$$-$ Royal Class, Cadmo Zambrano y César López, near the bus station, T274 3348. Multi-storey modern hotel, a/c, cheaper with fan, parking, the best choice near the bus station, reasonably quiet location, good value.
$ Safiro Internacional, 29 de Mayo 800 y Loja, T276 0706. Comfortable modern hotel, cafeteria, hot water, a/c, good value.

❼ Restaurants

Manta and around *p545*
Restaurants on Malecón Escénico serve local seafood.
$$ Club Ejecutivo, Av 2 y C 12, top of Banco Pichincha building. First class food and service, great view.
$$ El Marino, Malecón y C 110, Tarqui. Open for lunch only. Classic fish and seafood restaurant, for *ceviches*, *sopa marinera* and other delicacies.
$ Café Trovador, Av 3 y C 11, Paseo José María Egas. Closes 2100. Very good coffee, snacks, sandwiches and economical set lunches.
$ Peberes, Av 1 entre C 13 y C 14. Good quality and set lunch, popular with locals.

Bahía de Caráquez *p546*
$$ Puerto Amistad, on the pier at Malecón y Vinueza. Mon-Sat 1200-2400. Nice setting

over the water, international food and atmosphere, popular with yachties.

$$-$ Arena-Bar Pizzería, Riofrío entre Bolívar y Montúfar, T269 2024. Daily 1700-2400. Restaurant/bar serving good pizza, salads and other dishes, nice atmosphere, also take-away and delivery service. Recommended.

$$-$ Muelle Uno, by the pier where canoes leave for San Vicente. Daily 1000-2400. Good grill and seafood, lovely setting over the water.

$ Doña Luca, Cecilio Intriago y Sergio Plaza, towards the tip of the peninsula. Daily 0800-1800. Simple little place serving excellent local fare, *ceviches*, *desayuno manabita* (a wholesome breakfast), and set lunches. Friendly service, recommended.

Canoa *p546*
$$ Amalur, behind the soccer field. Daily 1200-2100. Fresh seafood and authentic Basque specialities, try the *lomo de chancho adobado*, attentive service, modest portions.
$$-$ Surf Shak, at the beach. Daily 0800-2400. Good for pizza, burgers and breakfast, best coffee in town, Wi-Fi US$1 per hr, popular hangout for surfers, English spoken.
$ Oasis, C Principal, 2 blocks from the beach. Good set meals, tasty and abundant.

Santo Domingo de los Tsáchilas *p547*
$$$ Parrilladas Che Luis, on the road to Quito. Tue-Sun 1200-2300. One of the best grills in town.
$$-$ La Cocina de Consuelo, Av Quito y Chimbo. 0700-2230, Sun and Mon to 1700. Very good à la carte dishes and 4-course set meals.

⏱ What to do

Manta and around *p545*
Delgado Travel, Av 6 y C 13, T262 2813, vtdelgad@hotmail.com. City and regional tours, whale watching trips, Parque Nacional Machalilla, run Hostería San Antonio at El Aromo, 15 km south of Manta.

Canoa *p546*
Canoa Thrills, at the beach next to Surf Shak. Surfing tours and lessons, sea kayaking. Also rent boards and bikes. English spoken.
Río Muchacho Organic Farm, J Santos y Av 3 de Noviembre, T258 8184, www. riomuchacho.com. Bookings for the organic farm and eco-city tours. Hikes from Canoa to Río Muchacho and around Río Muchacho. Knowledgeable and helpful with local information. Recommended.
Wings and Waves, T09-8519 8507 or ask around for Greg. Paragliding flights and lessons.

Santo Domingo de los Tsáchilas *p547*
Turismo Zaracay, 29 de Mayo y Cocaniguas, T275 0546, zaratur@andinanet.net. Tours to Tsáchila commune, minimum 5 persons; rafting, fishing trips, bird- and butterfly-watching tours, English spoken.

⊖ Transport

Manta and around *p545*
Air Eloy Alfaro airport. TAME (T390 5052), Aerogal (T262 8899) and LAN to **Quito** several daily.
Bus Most buses leave from the terminal on C 7 y Av 8 in the centre. A couple of companies have their own private terminals nearby. To **Quito**, 9 hrs, US$7-8, some go to Quitumbe, others continue to private terminals further north. **Guayaquil**, 4 hrs, US$4, hourly. **Esmeraldas**, 3 daily, 10 hrs, US$8. **Santo Domingo**, 7 hrs, US$6. **Portoviejo**, 45 mins, US$0.75, every 10 mins. **Jipijapa**, 1 hr, US$1, every 20 mins. **Bahía de Caráquez**, 3 hrs, US$3, hourly.

Crucita *p545*
Bus Run along the Malecón. There is frequent service to **Portoviejo**, US$1, 1 hr and **Manta**, US$1.20, 1½ hrs.

North to Bahía *p546*
Bus From San Clemente to **Portoviejo**, every 15 mins, US$1.25, 1¼ hrs. To **Bahía**

de Caráquez, US$0.50, 30 mins, a few start in San Clemente in the morning or wait for a through bus at the highway. Mototaxis from San Clemente to Punta Charapotó, US$0.50.

Bahía de Caráquez p546
Boat Motorized canoes (*lanchas* or *pangas*) cross the estuary to **San Vicente**, from the dock opposite C Ante, US$0.30.

Bus The Terminal Terrestre is at the entrance to town. To **Quito**, Reina del Camino, regular service to Quitumbe at 0620 and 2145 (from Quitumbe 1030, 2300), 8 hrs, US$7.50, Ejecutivo to their own station (18 de Septiembre y Larrea) at 0800 and 2215 (from Quito 1200, 2330), US$10. To **Santo Domingo**, 5 hrs, US$5-7.50. To **Guayaquil**, every 30 mins, 6 hrs, US$6-7. To **Portoviejo**, 2 hrs, US$2. To **Manta**, 3 hrs. US$3. To **Puerto López**, change in Manta, Portoviejo or Jipijapa.

San Vicente and Canoa p546
San Vicente
Bus The terminal is by the market on the San Isidro road, take an eco-taxi tricycle to get there. To **Portoviejo**, US$2.50, 2½ hrs. To **Guayaquil**, US$6, 6½ hrs. To **Quito** (Quitumbe), with Reina del Camino at 1000 and 2100 (from Quitumbe 0830 and 2100), US$7.50, 7½ hrs, more services from Bahía, or take a bus to **Pedernales** US$3, 2½ hrs and change. For **Esmeraldas** and northern beaches, take a bus to **Chamanga**, at 0810, 1430 or 1700, US$4.50, 3¼ hrs, and transfer there.

Canoa
Bus To/from **San Vicente**, every 30 mins, 0600-1900, 30 mins, US$0.50; taxi US$5. Taxi to/from Bahía de Caráquez, US$7. To **Pedernales**, hourly 0600-1800, 2 hrs, US$2.50. To **Quevedo**, 4 daily, where you can get a bus to **Quilotoa** and **Latacunga**. To **Quito**, direct bus nightly or transfer in Pedernales or San Vicente.

Pedernales p547
Bus To **Santo Domingo**, every 15 mins, 3½ hrs, US$4, transfer to Quito. To **Quito**

(Quitumbe) direct **Trans Vencedores**, 7 daily via Santo Domingo, US$6.25, 5 hrs; also starting in Jama at 0815 and 2300. To **Chamanga**, hourly 0600-1700, 1½ hrs, US$2, change there for **Esmeraldas**, 3½ hrs, US$3.50. To **Bahía de Caráquez**, shared vans from Plaza Acosta 121 y Robles, T268 1019, 7 daily, US$4.50.

Santo Domingo de los Tsáchilas p547
Bus The bus terminal is on Av Abraham Calazacón, at the north end of town, along the city's bypass. Long distance buses do not enter the city. Taxi downtown, US$1, bus US$0.25. As it is a very important transportation centre, you can get buses going everywhere in the country. To **Quito** via Alóag US$3, 3 hrs; via San Miguel de los Bancos, 5 hrs; also **Sudamericana Taxis**, Cocaniguas y 29 de Mayo, p 2, T275 2567, door to door shared taxi service, 6 daily 0500-1700, US$13, 3 hrs. To **Ambato** US$4, 4 hrs. To **Loja** US$13, 11 hrs. To **Guayaquil** US$5, 5 hrs. To **Huaquillas** US$10, 10 hrs, via Guayaquil. To **Esmeraldas** US$3, 3 hrs. To **Atacames**, US$4, 4hrs. To **Manta** US$6, 7 hrs. To **Bahía de Caráquez** US$5, 6 hrs. To **Pedernales** US$4, 3½ hrs.

ⓘ Directory

Manta and around p545
Banks Many banks with ATMs in the centre. **Language courses** Academia Sur Pacífico, Av 24 y C 15, Edif Barre, p3, T261 0838, www.surpacifico.k12.ec.

Bahía de Caráquez p546
Banks Banco de Guayaquil, Av Bolívar y Riofrío. ATM.

San Vicente and Canoa p546
Banks Banco Pichincha in San Vicente for ATM. No ATMs in Canoa. **Language courses** Sundown, at Sundown Inn, in Canoa, on the beach, 3 km toward San Vicente, contact Juan Carlos, T09-9143 6343, www.ecuadorbeach.com, US$7 per hr.

Northern lowlands

A mixture of palm lined beaches, mangroves (where not destroyed for shrimp production), tropical rainforests, Afro-Ecuadorean and Cayapa Indian communities characterize this part of Ecuador's Pacific lowlands as they stretch north to the Colombian border.

North to Atacames

North of Pedernales the coastal highway veers northeast, going slightly inland, then crosses into the province of Esmeraldas near **Chamanga** (*San José de Chamanga, Population: 4400*), a village with houses built on stilts on the freshwater estuary. This is a good spot from which to explore the nearby mangroves, there is one basic *residencial* and frequent buses north and south. Town is 1 km from the highway. Inland, and spanning the provincial border is the **Reserva Ecológica Mache-Chindul**, a dry forest reserve. North of Chamanga by 31 km and 7 km from the main road along a poor side road is **Mompiche** with a lovely beach and one of Ecuador's best surfing spots. The town and surroundings have been affected by the opening of an international resort complex and holiday real-estate development 2 km south at Punta Portete. The main road continues through El Salto (reported unsafe), the crossroads for **Muisne**, a town on an island with a beach (strong underow), a selection of hostels and a mangrove protection group which offers tours.

The fishing village of **Tonchigüe** is 25 km north of El Salto. South of it, a paved road goes west and follows the shore to **Punta Galera**, along the way is the secluded beach of **Playa Escondida** (see Where to stay, below). Northeast of Tonchigüe by 3 km is Playa de **Same**, with a beautiful, long, clean, grey sandy beach, safe for swimming. The accommodation here is mostly upmarket, intended for wealthy Quiteños, but it is wonderfully quiet in the low season. There is good birdwatching in the lagoon behind the beach and some of the hotels offer whale watching tours in season. Ten kilometres east of Same and 4 km west of Atacames, is **Súa**, a friendly little beach resort, set in a beautiful bay. It gets noisy on weekends and the July to September high season, but is otherwise tranquil.

Atacames → *Phone code: 06. Colour map 1, A2. Population: 18,700.*

One of the main resorts on the Ecuadorean coast, Atacames, 30 km southwest of Esmeraldas, is a real 24-hour party town during the high season (July-September), at weekends and national holidays. Head instead for Súa or Playa Escondida (see above) if you want peace and quiet. Most hotels are on a peninsula between the Río Atacames and the ocean. The main park, most services and the bus stops are south of the river. Information from **Oficina Municipal de Turismo** ① *on the road into town from Esmeraldas, T273 1912, Mon-Fri 0800-1230, 1330-1600.*

Camping on the beach is unsafe. Do not walk along the beach from Atacames to Súa, as there is a risk of mugging. Also the sea can be very dangerous, there is a powerful undertow and people have drowned.

Esmeraldas → *Phone code: 06. Colour map 1, A2. Population: 186,000.*

Capital of the eponymous province, Esmeraldas is a place to learn about Afro-Ecuadorean culture and some visitors enjoy its very relaxed swinging atmosphere. Marimba groups can be seen practising in town, enquire about schedules at the tourist office. Ceramics from La Tolita culture (see below) are found at the **Museo y Centro Cultural Esmeraldas** ① *Bolívar y Piedrahita, US$1, English explanations.* At the **Centro Cultural Afro** ① *Malecón* y J Montalvo, T272 7076, Tue-Sun 0900-1630, free, English explanations, you can see 'La Ruta del Esclavo', an exhibit showing the harsh history of Afro-Ecuadoreans brought as slaves to Ecuador (some English explanations). Despite its wealth in natural resources, Esmeraldas is among the poorest provinces in the country. Shrimp farming has destroyed much mangrove, and timber exports are decimating Ecuador's last Pacific rainforest. **Tourist office**: Ministerio de Turismo ① Bolívar y Ricaurte, Edif Cámara de Turismo, p3, T271 1370, Mon-Fri 0900-1200, 1500-1700. Mosquitoes and malaria are a serious problem throughout Esmeraldas province, especially in the rainy season (January to May). Most residenciales provide mosquito nets (toldos or mosquiteros), or buy one in the market near the bus station. Town suffers from water shortages and is not safe.

North of Esmeraldas

From Esmeraldas, the coastal road goes northeast to Camarones and Río Verde, with a nice beach, from where it goes east to **Las Peñas**, once a sleepy seaside village with a nice wide beach, now a holiday resort. With a paved highway from Ibarra, Las Peñas is the closest beach to any highland capital, only four hours by bus. Ibarreños pack the place on weekends and holidays. From Las Peñas, a secondary road follows the shore north to **La Tola** (122 km from Esmeraldas) where you can catch a launch to Limones. Here the shoreline changes from sandy beaches to mangrove swamp; the wildlife is varied and spectacular, especially the birds. The tallest mangrove trees in the world (63.7 m) are found by **Majagual** to the south. In the village of **Olmedo**, just northwest of La Tola, the Unión de Mujeres runs an ecotourism project; they have accommodation, cheap meals and tours in the area. La Tola itself is not a pleasant place to stay, women especially may be harassed; Olmedo is a better option, see Where to stay below. To the northeast of La Tola and on an island on the northern shore of the Río Cayapas is **La Tolita**, a small, poor village, where the culture of the same name thrived between 300 BC and AD 700. Many remains have been found here, several burial mounds remain to be explored and looters continue to take out artefacts to sell.

Limones (also known as Valdez) is the focus of traffic downriver from much of northern Esmeraldas Province, where bananas from the Río Santiago are sent to Esmeraldas for export. The Cayapa Indians live up the Río Cayapas and can sometimes be seen in Limones, especially during the crowded weekend market, but they are more frequently seen at Borbón (see below). Two shops in Limones sell the very attractive Cayapa basketry. There has been a great deal of migration from neighbouring Colombia to the Limones, Borbón and San Lorenzo areas. Smuggling, including drugs, is big business and there are occasional searches by the authorities. Mosquito-borne diseases are another hazard, always take a net. Accommodation is basic.

Borbón → Phone code: 06. Colour map 1, A3. Population: 8100.

From Las Peñas, the coastal highway runs inland to **Borbón**, upriver from La Tola, at the confluence of the Cayapas and Santiago rivers, a lively, dirty, busy and somewhat dangerous place, with a high rate of malaria. It is a centre of the timber industry that is destroying the last rainforests of the Ecuadorean coast. Ask for Papá Roncón, the King of Marimba, who, for a beer or two, will put on a one-man show. Cayapa handicrafts are sold in town and at the road junction outside town, Afro musical instruments are found at **Artesanía** on 5 de Agosto y Valdez. The local fiestas with marimba music and other Afro-Ecuadorean traditions are held the first week of September. The bakery across from the church is good for breakfast. Sra Marcia, one block from the Malecón serves good regional food.

Upriver from Borbón are Cayapa or Chachi Indian villages and Afro-Ecuadorean communities, you will see the Chachis passing in their canoes and in their open long-houses on the shore. To visit these villages, arrangements can be made through **Hostal Brisas del Río**. Alternatively, around 0700, canoes arrive at the malecón in Borbón and return to their homes around 1000. You can arrange to go with them. For any independent travel in this area take a mosquito net, food and a means of water purification. Upriver along the Río Cayapas, above its confluence with the Río Onzole, are the villages of **Pichiyacu** and **Santa María** (two hours). Beyond is **Zapallo Grande**, a friendly place with many gardens (3½ hours) and **San Miguel**, beautifully situated on a hill at the confluence of the San Miguel and Cayapas rivers (four hours). Along this river are a couple of lodges, the ride is not comfortable but it is an interesting trip. San Miguel is the access to the lowland section of **Reserva Ecológica Cotacachi-Cayapas**, about 30 minutes upriver. The community also runs its own 1200 ha forest reserve, abutting on the national reserve, and has an ecotourism project with accommodation and guiding service.

From Borbón, the costal road goes northeast towards **Calderón** where it meets the Ibarra-San Lorenzo road. Along the way, by the Río Santiago, are the nature reserves of **Humedales de Yalare**, accessed from **Maldonado**, and **Playa de Oro** (see below). From Calderón, the two roads run together for a few kilometres before the coastal road turns north and ends at **Mataje** on the border with Colombia. The road from Ibarra continues to San Lorenzo.

San Lorenzo → *Phone code: 06. Colour map 1, A3. Population: 28,500.*

The hot, humid town of San Lorenzo stands on the Bahía del Pailón, which is characterized by a maze of canals. It is a good place to experience the Afro-Ecuadorean culture including marimba music and dances. There is a local festival 6-10 August and groups practise throughout the year; ask around. At the seaward end of the bay are several beaches without facilities, including San Pedro (one hour away) and Palma Real (1¾ hours). On weekends canoes go to the beaches around 0700-0800 and 1400-1500, US$3. Note that this area is close to the Colombian border and it may not be safe, enquire with the Navy (Marina). From San Lorenzo you can visit several natural areas; launches can be hired for excursions (see Transport, page 558) and trips can be organized. There are mangroves at **Reserva Ecológica Cayapas-Mataje**, which protects islands in the estuary northwest of town. **Reserva Playa de Oro** ① *www.touchthejungle.org, see Where to stay, page 556,* has 10,406 ha of Chocó rainforest, rich in wildlife, along the Río Santiago. Access is from **Selva Alegre** (a couple of basic *residenciales*), off the road to Borbón.

Border with Colombia: San Lorenzo–Tumaco

The Río Mataje is the border with Colombia. From San Lorenzo, the port of Tumaco in Colombia can be reached by a combination of boat and land transport. Because this is a most unsafe region, travellers are advised not to enter Colombia at this border. Go to Tulcán and Ipiales instead.

For hotel and restaurant price codes, and other relevant information, see pages 14-17.

⊛ Where to stay

North to Atacames *p552*
Mompiche
There are several economical places in the town. Camping on the beach is not safe.
$$-$ Iruña, east along the beach, vehicle access only at low tide, T09-9497 5846, teremompiche@yahoo.com. A lovely secluded hideaway with cabins of different sizes and prices. Large terraces and hammocks, meals on request, fan, nice gardens.
$ Gabeal, 300 m east of town, T09-9969 6543. Lovely quiet place with ample grounds and beachfront. Bamboo construction with ocean views, balconies, small rooms and cabins, restaurant serves breakfast and lunch in season, discounts in low season.

Tonchigüe to Punta Galera
$$ Playa Escondida, 10 km west of Tonchigüe and 6 km east of Punta Galera, T273 3106, www.playaescondida.com.ec. A charming beach hideaway set in 100 ha with 500 m beachfront stretching back to dry tropical forest. Run by Canadian Judith Barett on an ecologically sound basis. Nice rustic cabins overlooking a lovely little bay, excellent restaurant (**$$$** with full board), private showers, shared composting toilets, camping US$5 pp, good birdwatching, swimming and walking along the beach at low tide. Also offers volunteer opportunities.

Same
$$$-$$ Cabañas Isla del Sol, at south end of beach, T273 3470, www.cabanasisladelsol.com. Comfortable cabins, meals available in high season, electric shower, a/c, cheaper with fan, pool, boat tours and whale watching in season.
$$ Casa de Amigos, by the entrance to the beach, T247 0102. Restaurant, electric

shower, a/c, nice rooms with balconies, use of kayaks and surfboards included, English and German spoken.
$ La Terraza, on the beach, T247 0320, pepo@hotmail.es. Nice rooms and cabins for 3-4 with balconies, hammocks and large terrace, spacious, hot water, a/c, fan, mosquito net, some rooms have fridge, good restaurant open in season, Spanish-run.

Súa
$ Buganvillas, on the beach, T273 1008. Nice, room 10 has the best views, pool, helpful owners.
$ Chagra Ramos, on the beach, T273 1006. Ageing hotel with balconies overlooking the beach, restaurant, cold water, fan, parking, good service.
$ Sol de Súa, across from beach toward west end of town, T273 1021. Cold water, ceiling fan, mosquito net, simple cabins on ample grounds with palm trees, camping possible.

Atacames *p552*
Prices rise on holiday weekends, discounts may be available in low season. There are many more hotels than we can list.
$$$ Juan Sebastián, towards the east end of the beach, T273 1049. Large upmarket hotel with cabins and suites, restaurant, a/c, 3 pools and small spa (US$10 for non-guests), fridge, parking, popular with Quiteños.
$$ Carluz, behind the stadium, T273 1456. Nice hotel in a good, quiet location. Comfortable suites for 4 and apartments for 6, good restaurant, a/c, fan, pool, fridge, parking.
$$ Cielo Azul, towards the west end of the beach, near the stadium, T273 1813, www.hotelcieloazul.com. Restaurant, fan, pool, fridge, rooms with balconies and hammocks, comfortable and very good.
$$-$ Tahiti, toward east end of beach, T276 0085, lucybritogarcia@yahoo.com.ar. Good restaurant, cheaper with cold water, pool, parking, ample grounds.

$ Chill Inn, Los Ostiones y Malecón, T276 0477, www.chillinnecuador.com. Small backpackers' hostel with bar, good beds, fan, parking, balcony with hammocks, good breakfast available, Swiss-run, helpful.
$ Jarfi, Los Ostiones, 1 block from the beach by the footbridge, T273 1089. Hot water, pool, simple bungalows, good value.

Esmeraldas *p552*

Hotels in the centre are poor; better to stay in the outskirts.
$$ Apart Hotel Esmeraldas, Libertad 407 y Ramón Tello, T272 8700. Good restaurant, a/c, fridge, parking, excellent quality.
$ Andrés, Sucre 812 y Piedrahita, T272 5883. Simple hostel in a multi-storey building, cold water, fan.
$ Galeón, Piedrahita 330 y Olmedo, T272 3820. Cold water, a/c, cheaper with fan, good.
$ Zulema 2, Malecón y Rocafuerte. Modern concrete hostel with large rooms, cold water, fan, parking.

North of Esmeraldas *p553*
Las Peñas

$ Mikey, by the beach, T278 6031. Cabins with kitchenettes, private bath, hot water, pool.

Olmedo

$ Casa del Manglar, a 20-min walk or short boat ride from La Tola, T278 6126 (Catalina Montes or her son Edwin). A wood cabin with porch by the shore. Dormitory for 15 people, meals available, shared bath, mosquito nets, quiet and pleasant. Take drinking water or means of purification. Organizes tours to mangroves, La Tolita and other sights.

Limones

$ Colón, next to the church at the main park, T278 9311. A good hostel for where it is, with bath, cold water, fan.

Borbón *p553*

$ Brisas del Río Santiago, Malecón y 23 de Noviembre, T278 6211. Basic concrete hostel with good air circulation, private bath, cold

water, fan, mosquito net, meeting point for travellers going upriver. Owner Sr Betancourt can arrange canoes for excursions.

San Miguel

In villages like **Pichiyacu** (ethnic Chachi) and Santa María (Afro-Ecuadorean), local families can provide accommodation.
$$$ Eco-Lodge San Miguel, above the village of San Miguel, contact Fundación Verde Milenio, Quito, T02-290 6192, www. verde milenio.org. Community-run lodge with lovely views, 7 bedrooms, shared bath. Price includes transport from Borbón, 3 meals and excursion to the forest. Advance booking advised.

San Lorenzo *p554*

Expect to be mobbed by children wanting a tip to show you to a hotel or restaurant. Also take insect repellent.
$$$ Playa de Oro, on the Río Santiago, upriver from Borbón, contact Ramiro Buitrón at Hotel Valle del Amanecer in Otavalo, T06-292 0990, www.touchthejungle.org. Basic cabins with shared bath, includes 3 meals and guided excursion.
$$ Tunda Loma, Km 17 on the road to Ibarra (taxi from San Lorenzo US$5), T278 0367. Beautifully located on a hill overlooking the Río Tululbí. Wood cabins, includes breakfast, restaurant, warm water, fan, organizes tubing trips on the river and hikes in the forest.
$ Pampa de Oro, C 26 de Agosto y Tácito Ortiz, T278 0214. Adequate family-run hotel, with bath, cold water, fan, mosquito net.
$ San Carlos, C Imbabura near the train station, T278 0284. Simple concrete hotel, private or shared bath, cold water, fan, mosquito nets.

🍴 Restaurants

North to Atacames *p552*
Mompiche

$$-$ Pizza Luz, on the beach between town and Hotel Gabeal. Opens around 1830. Excellent pizza, bar-stool seating, popular.

$ Comedor Margarita, on main street, 2 blocks from the beach. Daily from 0730. Basic *comedor* serving tasty local fare, mostly fish and seafood.

Same

$$$ Seaflower, by the beach at the entrance road. Excellent international food.

Súa

$ Churuco's, diagonally across from the park, 100 m from the beach. Wed-Sun 0900-2100. Simple *comedor* serving good set meals and local snacks, generous portions, good value.

Atacames *p552*

The beach is packed with bars and restaurants offering seafood, too many to list.
$$ Da Giulio, Malecón y Cedros. Weekdays 1700-2300, weekends from 1100. Spanish and Italian cuisine, good pasta.
$$-$ El Tiburón, Malecón y Súa. Good seafood.
$$-$ Le Cocotier, Malecón y Camarones. Very good pizza.

Esmeraldas *p552*

There are restaurants and bars by Las Palmas beach offering regional specialities.
$$ Chifa Asiático, Cañizares y Bolívar. Chinese and seafood, a/c, excellent.
$$-$ El Manglar, Quito y Olmedo. Good *comida esmeraldeña*.
$ Tapao.con, 6 de Diciembre 1717 y Piedrahita. A popular place for typical dishes such as *tapado*, *encocado* and *ceviche*.

San Lorenzo *p554*

$ El Chocó, C Imbabura. Good fish and local specialities. Also economical set lunches and the best *batido de borojó* (milkshake) in town.

⊖ Transport

North to Atacames *p552*

Bus Hourly from **Chamanga** to **Esmeraldas**, US$3.50, 3½ hrs, and to **Pedernales**, US$2, 1½ hrs. **Mompiche** to/from **Esmeraldas**,

5 a day, US$3, 3½ hrs, the last one from Esmeraldas about 1630. To **Playa Escondida**: take a ranchera or bus from Esmeraldas or Atacames for Punta Galera or Cabo San Francisco, 5 a day, US$2, 2 hrs. A taxi from Atacames costs US$12 and a pick-up from Tonchigüe US$5. To **Súa** and **Same**: Buses every 30 mins to and from **Atacames**, 15 mins, US$0.35. Make sure it drops you at Same and not at Club Casablanca.

Atacames *p552*

Bus To **Esmeraldas**, every 15 mins, US$0.80, 1 hr. To **Guayaquil**, US$9, 8 hrs, Trans Esmeraldas at 0830 and 2245. To **Quito**, various companies, about 10 daily, US$8, 7 hrs, Trans Esmeraldas has service from its own terminal in La Mariscal. To **Pedernales**, Coop G Zambrano, 4 daily, US$4, 4 hrs or change in Chamanga.

Esmeraldas *p552*

Air Gen Rivadeneira Airport is along the coastal road heading north. A taxi to the city centre (30 km) costs US$6, buses to the Terminal Terrestre from the road outside the airport pass about every 30 mins. If headed north towards San Lorenzo, you can catch a bus outside the airport. TAME (Bolívar y 9 de Octubre, T272 6863), 1-2 daily flights to **Quito**, continuing to **Cali** (Colombia) Mon, Wed, Fri; to **Guayaquil**, 1 daily Mon, Wed, Fri.
Bus Trans-Esmeraldas (10 de Agosto at Parque Central, recommended) and Panamericana (Colón y Salinas) have *servicio directo* or *ejecutivo* to Quito and Guayaquil, a better choice as they are faster buses and don't stop for passengers; they also run to their own terminals in La Mariscal in Quito. Frequent service to **Quito** via Santo Domingo or via Calacalí, US$7, 6 hrs; ask which terminal they go to before purchasing ticket. To **Ibarra**, 9 hrs, US$10, via Borbón. To **Santo Domingo**, US$3, 3 hrs. To **Ambato**, 6 a day, US$8, 8 hrs. To **Guayaquil**, hourly, US$8, *directo*, 8 hrs. To **Bahía de Caráquez**, via Santo Domingo, US$8, 9 hrs. To **Manta**, US$8, 10 hrs. La Costeñita and El Pacífico, both on

Malecón, to/ from **La Tola**, 8 daily, US$3.75, 3 hrs. To **Borbón**, frequent service, US$3.50, 3 hrs. To **San Lorenzo**, 8 daily, US$4.50, 4 hrs. To **Súa**, **Same** and **Atacames**, every 15 mins from 0630-2030, to Atacames US$0.80, 1 hr. To **Chamanga**, hourly 0500-1900, US$3.50, 3½ hrs, change here for points south.

North of Esmeraldas *p553*
Ferry There are launches between **La Tola** and **Limones** which connect with the buses arriving from Esmeraldas, US$3, 1 hr, and 3 daily Limones–**San Lorenzo**, 2 hrs, US$3. You can also hire a launch to **Borbón**, a fascinating trip through mangrove islands, passing hunting pelicans, approximately US$10 per hr.

Borbón *p553*
Bus To **Esmeraldas**, US$3.50, 3 hrs. To **San Lorenzo**, US$1.60, 1 hr.
Ferry 4 launches a day run to communities upriver, 1030-1100. Check how far each one is going as only one goes as far as **San Miguel**, US$8, 4 hrs.

San Lorenzo *p554*
Bus Buses leave from the train station or environs. To **Ibarra**, 10 daily, 4 hrs, US$4. To **Esmeraldas**, via Borbón, 8 daily, US$4.50, 4 hrs.
Ferry Launch service with **Coopseturi**, T278 0161; and **Costeñita**, both near the pier. All services are subject to change and cancellation. To **Limones**, 4 daily, US$3, 2 hrs. To **La Tola**, US$6, 4 hrs. To **Palma Real**, for beaches, 2 daily, US$3, 2 hrs. To hire a boat for 5 passengers costs US$20 per hr.

Directory

Atacames *p552*
Banks Banco Pichincha, Espejo y Calderón by the plaza, for ATM. There are a few other stand-alone ATMs in town and along the beach.

Esmeraldas *p552*
Banks For ATMs, several banks on C Bolívar in the centre.

San Lorenzo *p554*
Banks Banco Pichincha, C Ponce y Garcés, has the only ATM in town; bring some cash.

The Oriente

East of the Andes the hills fall away to tropical lowlands. Some of this beautiful wilderness remains unspoiled and sparsely populated, with indigenous settlements along the tributaries of the Amazon. Large tracts of jungle are under threat, however: colonists are clearing many areas for agriculture, while others are laid waste by petroleum development. The Ecuadorean jungle, especially the Northern Oriente, has the advantage of being relatively accessible and tourist infrastructure here is well developed. The eastern foothills of the Andes, where the jungle begins, offer the easiest access and a good introduction to the rainforest for those with limited time or money. Further east lie the few remaining large tracts of primary rainforest, teeming with life, which can be visited from several excellent (and generally expensive) jungle lodges. Southern Oriente is as yet less developed for tourism, it offers good opportunities off the beaten path but is threatened by large mining projects.

Arriving in the Oriente
Getting there There are commercial flights from Quito to Lago Agrio, Coca and Macas; and from Guayaquil to Coca via Latucunga. From Quito, Macas and Shell, light aircraft can be chartered to any jungle village with a landing strip. Western Oriente is also accessible by scenic roads which wind their way down from the highlands. Quito, via Baeza, to Lago

Agrio and Coca, Baños to Puyo, and Loja to Zamora are fully paved, as is almost all of the lowland road from Lago Agrio south to Zamora. Other access roads to Oriente are: Tulcán to Lago Agrio via Lumbaqui, Riobamba to Macas, and three diffrent roads from Cuenca. These go to Méndez via Guarumales, Plan de Milagro via Paute (closed for paving in 2014), and Gualaquiza via Sígsig. Some roads are narrow and tortuous and subject to landslides in the rainy season, but all have regular bus service and all can be attempted in a jeep or in an ordinary car with good ground clearance. Deeper into the rainforest, motorized canoes provide the only alternative to air travel.

Jungle tours These fall into four basic types: lodges, guided tours, indigenous ecotourism and river cruises. When staying at a jungle lodge, you will need to take a torch (flashlight), insect repellent, protection against the sun and a rain poncho that will keep you dry when walking and when sitting in a canoe. See also Lodges on the Lower Napo (page 563) and the Upper Napo (page 571). All jungle lodges must be booked in advance. **Guided tours** of varying length are offered by tour operators and independent guides. These should, in principle, be licensed by the Ecuadorean **Ministerio de Turismo**. Tour operators and guides are mainly concentrated in Quito, Baños, Puyo, Tena, Misahuallí, Coca, and, to a lesser extent, Macas and Zamora.

A number of indigenous communities and families offer **ecotourism** programmes in their territories. These are either community-controlled and operated, or organized as joint ventures between the indigenous community or family and a non-indigenous partner. These programmes usually involve guides who are licensed as *guías nativos* with the right to guide within their communities. You should be prepared to be more self-sufficient on such a trip than on a visit to a jungle lodge or a tour with a high-end operator. Take a light sleeping bag, rain jacket, trousers (not only shorts), long-sleeve shirt for mosquitoes, binoculars, torch, insect repellent, sunscreen and hat, water-purifying tablets, and a first aid kit. Wrap everything in several plastic bags to keep it dry. Most lodges provide rubber boots, indepedent guides may not.

River cruises offer a better appreciation of the grandeur of Amazonia, but less intimate contact with life in the rainforest. Passengers sleep and take their meals onboard comfortable river boats, stopping on route to visit local communities and make excursions into the jungle.

Jungle travel without a guide is not recommended. Some indigenous groups prohibit the entry of outsiders to their territory, navigation in the jungle is difficult, and there is a variety of dangerous animals. For your own safety as well as to be a responsible tourist, the jungle is not a place to wander off on your own.

Health and safety A yellow fever vaccination is required. Anti-malarial tablets are recommended, as is an effective insect repellent. There may be police and military checkpoints in the Oriente, so always have your passport handy. Caution is advised in the province of Sucumbíos, enquire about public safety before visiting sites near the Colombian border.

Northern Oriente

Much of the Northern Oriente is taken up by the Parque Nacional Yasuní, the Cuyabeno Wildlife Reserve and most of the Cayambe-Coca Ecological Reserve. The main towns for access are Baeza, Lago Agrio and Coca.

Quito to the Oriente

From Quito to Baeza, a paved road goes via the **Guamaní pass** (4064 m). It crosses the Eastern Cordillera just north of **Volcán Antisana** (5705 m), and then descends via the small village of **Papallacta** (hot springs, see page 449) to the old mission settlement of Baeza. The trip between the pass and Baeza has beautiful views of Antisana (clouds permitting), high waterfalls, *páramo*, cloud forest and a lake contained by an old lava flow.

Baeza → *Phone code: 06. Colour map 1, A4. Population: 2000. Altitude 1900 m.*

The mountainous landscape and high rainfall have created spectacular waterfalls and dense vegetation. Orchids and bromeliads abound. Baeza, in the beautiful Quijos valley, is about 1 km from the main junction of roads from Lago Agrio and Tena. The town itself is divided in two parts: a faded but pleasant **Baeza Colonial** (Old Baeza) and **Baeza Nueva** (New Baeza), where most shops and services are located. There are hiking trails and rafting possibilities in the area.

Beyond Baeza

From Baeza a road heads south to Tena, with a branch going east via Loreto to Coca, all paved. Another paved road goes northeast from Baeza to Lago Agrio, following the Río Quijos past the villages of **Borja** (8 km from Baeza, very good *comedor* **Doña Cleo** along the highway, closed Sun) and **El Chaco** (12 km further, simple accommodation and kayaking at **$ La Guarida del Coyote**) to the slopes of the active volcano **Reventador**, 3560 m. Check www.igepn.edu.ec and enquire locally about volcanic activity before trekking here; simple **$ Hostería El Reventador** at the bridge over the Río Reventador; **Ecuador Journeys** offers tours, see page 442. Half a kilometre south of the bridge is signed access to the impressive 145-m **San Rafael Falls** (part of **Reserva Ecológica Cayambe-Coca**), believed to be the highest in Ecuador. It is a pleasant 45-minute hike through cloud forest to a *mirador* with stunning views of the thundering cascade. Many birds can be spotted along the trail, including cock-of-the-rock, also monkeys and coatimundis. In 2014 the falls could still be visited but the former ranger station had been converted to headquarters of a hydro-electric project (www.ccs.gob.ec) which will use up to 70% of the water in the Río Quijos, leaving only 30% to go over the falls – the death knell for Ecuador's most beautiful cascade.

Lago Agrio → *Phone code: 06. Colour map 1, A5. Population: 63,500. Altitude 300 m.*

The capital of Sucumbíos province is an old oil town with close ties to neighbouring Colombia, and among the places in Ecuador which has been most affected by conflict there. The name comes from Sour Lake, the US headquarters of Texaco, the first oil company to exploit the Ecuadorean Amazon in the 1970s. It is also called Nueva Loja or just 'Lago'. If taking a Cuyabeno tour from Lago Agrio, it is worth leaving Quito a day or two early, stopping en route at Papallacta, Baeza or San Rafael falls. Lago Agrio is not a safe place, return to your hotel by 2000. Alternatively you can overnight at more tranquil **Cascales** (**$ Paraíso Dorado**, small, pleasant), 35 minutes before Lago Agrio, and still meet your tour party in Lago the following morning. There is a border crossing to Colombia north of Lago Agrio but it is also unsafe. Seek local advice from the **Ministerio de Turismo** ① *Narváez y Añazco, upstairs, T283 2488, Mon-Fri 0830-1300, 1400-1800.*

Cuyabeno Wildlife Reserve

This large tract of rainforest, covering 602,000 ha, is located about 100 km east of Lago Agrio along the Río Cuyabeno, which eventually drains into the Aguarico. In the reserve are many lagoons and a great variety of wildlife, including river dolphins, tapirs, capybaras, five species of caiman, ocelots, 15 species of monkey and over 500 species of bird. This is among the best places in Ecuador to see jungle animals. The reserve is very popular with visitors but there have been occasional armed hold-ups of tour groups here, best enquire before booking a tour. Access is either by road from Lago Agrio, or by river along the Río Aguarico. Within the reserve, transport is mainly by canoe. In order to see as many animals as possible and minimally impact their habitat, seek out a small tour group which scrupulously adheres to responsible tourism practices. Most Cuyabeno tours are booked through agencies in Quito.

Coca → *Phone code: 06. Colour map1, A5. Population: 52,400. Altitude 250 m.*

Officially named **Puerto Francisco de Orellana**, Coca is a hot, noisy, bustling oil town at the junction of the Ríos Payamino and Napo. It is the capital of the province of Orellana and is a launch pad from where to visit more remote jungle parts. The view over the water is nice, and the riverfront **Malecón** can be a pleasant place to spend time around sunset; various indigenous groups have craft shops here. Hotel and restaurant provision is adequate, but electricity, water and, ironically for an oil-producing centre, petrol supplies are erratic. Information from **iTur** ① *Chimborazo y Amazonas, by the Malecón, T288 0532, Mon-Sat 0800-1200, 1400-1800, www.orellanaturistica.gob.ec* and the **Ministerio de Turismo** ① *Cuenca y Quito, upstairs, T288 1583, Mon-Fri 0830-1700.*

Jungle tours from Coca Coca provides access to **Parque Nacional Yasuní** and the **Reserva Huaorani**. Tours into the park and reserve really need a minimum of five days but shorter visits of three to four days are worthwhile along the Río Napo, where the lodges are concentrated. Wildlife in this area is under threat: insist that guides and fellow tourists take all litter back and ban all hunting and shooting; it really makes a difference. The majority of tours out of Coca are booked through agencies in Quito but there are a few local operators. Quality varies so try to get a personal recommendation, prices are around US$70-80 per person per day. **Note** If a guide offers a tour to visit the Huaorani, ask to see his/her permission to do so, which should be issued by the Huaorani organization **NAWE**.

The paved road to Coca via Loreto passes through **Wawa Sumaco**, where a rough road heads north to **Sumaco National Park**; 7 km along it is **$$$$-$$$ Wildsumaco** ① *T06-301 8343, www.wildsumaco.com,* a comfortable birdwatching lodge with full board, excellent trails and many rare species. Just beyond is the village of Pacto Sumaco from where a trail runs through the park to the *páramo*-clad summit of **Volcan Sumaco** (3732 m), six to seven days round-trip. Local guides may be hired, there are three nice shelters along the route and a basic community-run hostel in the village (www.sumacobirdwatching.com, try T06-301 8324 but not always staffed).

Coca to Nuevo Rocafuerte and Iquitos (Peru)

Pañacocha is halfway between Coca and Nuevo Rocafuerte, near a magnificent lagoon. Here are a couple of **lodges** (see Lodges on the Lower Napo) and Coca agencies and guides also run tours to the area (see Tour operators). Entry to Pañacocha reserve US$10. There are basic places to stay and eat in Pañacocha village.

Following the Río Napo to Peru is rough, adventurous and requires plenty of time and patience. There are two options: by far the least expensive is to take a motorized canoe from Coca to **Nuevo Rocafuerte** on the border. This tranquil riverside town has simple hotels, eateries, a phone office and basic shops. It can be a base for exploring the endangered southeastern section of **Parque Nacional Yasuní** (see www.yasuni-itt. gob.ec); local guides are available. Ecuadorean immigration for exit stamps is next to the navy dock; if the officer is not in, enquire in town. Peruvian entry stamps are given in **Pantoja**, where there is a decent municipal *hospedaje*, **$ Napuruna**. Shopkeepers in Nuevo Rocafuerte and Pantoja change money at poor rates. In addition to immigration, you may have to register with the navy on either side of the border so have your passport at hand. See Transport, page 566, for boat services Coca–Nuevo Rocafuerte and onward to Pantoja and Iquitos. See also the Peru chapter, under Iquitos Transport.

The second option for river travel to Iquitos is to take a tour with a Coca agency, taking in various attractions on route, and continuing to Iquitos or closer Peruvian ports from which you can catch onward public river transport. Ask carefully about these tours as they may involve many hours sitting in small, cramped craft; confirm all details in advance.

⊚ Northern Oriente listings

For hotel and restaurant price codes, and other relevant information, see pages 14-17.

⊚ Where to stay

Baeza *p560*

$ Gina, Jumandy y Batallón Chimborazo, just off the highway in the old town, T232 0471. Hot water, parking, pleasant, good value.
$ La Casa de Rodrigo, in the old town, T232 0467, rodrigobaeza@andinanet.net. Modern and comfortable, hot water, friendly owner offers rafting trips, kayak rentals and birdwatching.
$ Samay, Av de los Quijos, in the new town, T232 0170. Private or shared bath, electric shower, older place but friendly and adequate, simple rooms, good value.

Around Baeza

$$$$ Cabañas San Isidro, near Cosanga, 19 km south of Baeza, T02-289 1880 (Quito), www.cabanasanisidro.com. A 1200-ha private nature reserve with rich bird life, comfortable accommodation and warm hospitality. Includes 3 excellent meals, reservations required.
$ Hostería El Reventador, on main highway next to bridge over the Río Reventador, turismovolcanreventador@yahoo.com. Meals on request, hot water, pool, simple rooms, busy at weekends, mediocre service but well located for San Rafael Falls and Volcán Reventador.

Lago Agrio *p560*

Virtually everything can be found on the main street, Av Quito.
$$$ Gran Hotel de Lago, Km 1.5 Vía Quito, T283 2415, granhoteldelago@grupodelago. com. Restaurant, a/c, pool, parking, cabins with nice gardens, quiet. Recommended.
$$ Arazá, Quito 536 y Narváez, T283 1287, www.hotel-araza.com. Quiet location away from centre, buffet breakfast, restaurant, a/c, pool (US$5 for non-residents), fridge, parking, comfortable, nice. Recommended.
$$ El Cofán, 12 de Febrero 3915 y Quito, T283 0526, elcofanhotel@yahoo.es. Restaurant, a/c, fridge, parking, older place but well maintained.
$$-$ Lago Imperial, Colombia y Quito, T283 0453, hotellagoimperial@hotmail.com. A/c, cheaper with fan and cold water, central location, good value.
$ Casa Blanca, Quito 228 y Colombia, T283 0181. Electric shower, fan, nice bright rooms.
$ Gran Colombia, Quito y Pasaje Gonzanamá, T283 1032. Good restaurant, hot water, a/c, cheaper with fan and cold water, more expensive rooms also have fridge, parking, centrally located, modern and good value.

Cascales

$ Paraíso Dorado, on the highway at the east end of town, T280 0421. A small place, meals on request, cold water, mosquito nets, very helpful.

Coca *p561*

$$ El Auca, Napo y García Moreno, T288 0600, www.hotelelauca.com. Restaurant, disco on weekends, a/c, cheaper with fan, parking, a variety of different rooms and mini-suites. Comfortable, nice garden with hammocks, English spoken. Popular and centrally located but can get noisy.

$$ Heliconias, Cuenca y Amazonas, T288 2010, heliconiaslady@yahoo.com. Upmarket restaurant, pool (US$5 for non-guests), spotless. Recommended.

$$ La Misión, by riverfront 100 m downriver from the bridge, T288 0260, www.hotela mision.com. A larger hotel, restaurant and disco, a/c and fridge, pool (US$2 for non-guests), parking, a bit faded but still adequate.

$$-$ Amazonas, 12 de Febrero y Espejo, T288 0444, hosteriacoca@hotmail.com. Nice quiet setting by the river, away from centre, restaurant, electric shower, a/c, parking.

$$-$ Río Napo, Bolívar entre Napo y Quito, T288 0872. A/c, cheaper with fan, small modern rooms.

$ Omaguas, Cuenca y Quito, T288 2436, h_omaguas@hotmail.com. Restaurant, hot water, a/c, parking, small modern rooms.

$ San Fermín, Bolívar y Quito, T288 0802. Hot water, a/c (cheaper with fan, shared bath and cold water), ample parking, variety of different rooms, nicely furnished, popular and busy, good value, owner organizes tours. Recommended.

Jungle tours from Coca *p561*
Lodges on the Lower Napo

All Napo lodges count travel days as part of their package, which means that a '3-day tour' spends only 1 day actually in the forest. Most lodges have fixed departure days from Coca (eg Mon and Fri) and it is very expensive to get a special departure on another day. For lodges in Cuyabeno, see page 565; for lodges on the Upper Napo, see page 571, for southern Oriente lodges see page 572.

Amazon Dolphin Lodge, Quito office: Amazonas N24-236 y Colón, T02-250 4037, www.amazondolphinlodge.com. On Laguna de Pañacocha, 4½ hrs downriver from Coca. Special wildlife here includes Amazon river dolphins and giant river otters as well as over 500 species of birds. Cabins with private bath, US$600-700 for 4 days.

Napo Wildlife Center, Quito office: Pje Yaupi N31-90 y Mariana de Jesús, T02-600-5893, USA T1-866-750-0830, UK T0-800-032-5771, www.ecoecuador.org. Operated by and for the local Añangu community, 2½ hrs downstream from Coca. This area of hilly forest is rather different from the low flat forest of some other lodges, and the diversity is slightly higher. There are big caimans and good mammals, including giant otters, and the birdwatching is excellent with 2 parrot clay-licks and a 35-m canopy tower. US$820 for 4 days. Recommended.

La Selva, Quito office: Mariana de Jesús E7-211 y La Pradera, T02-255 0995, www.laselva junglelodge.com. An upmarket lodge, 2½ hrs downstream from Coca on a picturesque lake. Surrounded by excellent forest, especially on the far side of Mandicocha. Bird and animal life is exceptionally diverse. Many species of monkey are seen regularly. A total of 580 bird species have been found, one of the highest totals in the world for a single elevation. Comfortable cabins and excellent meals. High standards, most guides are biologists. 45-m canopy tower. US$765-1100 for 4 days.

Pañacocha Emerald Forest Lodge, Quito office: Ecuador Journeys (see Quito operators), T02-603 5548, www. ecuadorianjourney.com. Located 5 hrs from Coca, on the Río Pañayacu and surrounded by primary forest. Run by the Quito operator and Luis García, a legendary jungle guide. 6 comfortable cabins with solar power, private bath, shower, large deck, common areas, canopy tower, US$440 for 4 days.

Sacha, Quito office: Julio Zaldumbide y Valladolid, T02-256 6090, www.sacha lodge.com. An upmarket lodge 2½ hrs downstream from Coca. Very comfortable cabins, excellent meals. The bird list is outstanding; the local bird expert, Oscar

Tapuy (Coca T06-2881486), can be requested in advance. Canopy tower and 275-m canopy walkway. Several species of monkey are commonly seen. Nearby river islands provide access to a distinct habitat. US$790 for 4 days.

Sani, Quito office: Washington E4-71 y Amazonas, T02-222 8802, www.sanilodge. com. All proceeds go to the Sani Isla community, who run the lodge with the help of outside experts. It is located on a remote lagoon which has 4- to 5-m-long black caiman. This area is rich in wildlife and birds, including many species such as the scarlet macaw which have disappeared from most other Napo area lodges. There is good accommodation and a 35-m canopy tower. An effort has been made to make the lodge accessible to people who have difficulty walking; the lodge can be reached by canoe (total 3½ hrs from Coca) without a walk. US$715 for 4 days. Good value, recommended.

Lodges in the Reserva Huaorani
Huaorani Ecolodge, operated by Tropic Journeys in Nature in Quito (see page 443), a joint venture with several Huaorani communities who staff the lodge; winner of sustainable tourism awards. Small (10 guests), wooden cabins, solar lighting, upgraded in 2013, a spontaneous, rewarding and at times challenging experience. Includes much community involvement, rainforest hikes, conservation area, kayaking (US$40 per day), dug out canoe trips. Tours arrive by small plane from Shell and leave on the Vía Auca to Coca. River journeys are non-motorized except the last stretch from Nenquepare Camp (cabins, refurbished kitchen and bathrooms) where the last night is spent, to the road. From US$730 for 4 days. Prices do not include land and air transport from Quito to the Lodge, or return from Coca to Quito.

Otobo's Amazon Safari, www.rainforest camping.com. 8 day/7 night camping expeditions in Huaorani territory, access by flight from Shell to Bameno (US$1540 pp), or by road from Coca then 2-day motorized canoe journey on the Ríos Shiripuno and Cononaco (US$1050 pp) All meals and guiding included.

Shiripuno, Quito T02-227 1094, www. shiripunolodge.com. A lodge with capacity for 20 people, very good location on the Río Shiripuno, a 4-hr canoe ride downriver from the Vía Auca. Cabins have private bath. The surrounding area has seen relatively little human impact to date. US$360 for 4 days, plus US$20 entry to Huaorani territory.

Coca to Nuevo Rocafuerte and Iquitos *p561*
$ Casa Blanca, Malecón y Nicolás Torres, T238 2184. Rooms with a/c or fan, nice, simple, welcoming. There are a couple of other basic places to stay in town.

🍴 Restaurants

Baeza *p560*
$ El Viejo, east end of Av de los Quijos, the road to Tena in the new town. Daily 0700-2100. Good set meals and à la carte.
$ Gina, Batallón Chimborazo, just off the highway in the old town. Daily 0730-2200. Trout is the speciality, good and popular.

Lago Agrio *p560*
There are good restaurants at the larger hotels (see above); also many cheap *comedores*.

Coca *p561*
$$ Denny's, Alejandro Labaka by the airport. Mon-Sat 0800-2000, Sun 1200-1400. Steaks, ribs and other US-style meals and drinks, friendly.
$$-$ Pizza Choza, Rocafuerte entre Napo y Quito. Daily 1800-2200. Good pizza, friendly owner, English spoken.
$ La Casa del Maito, Espejo entre Quito y Napo. Daily 0700-1700. *Maitos* and other local specialities.
$ Ocaso, Eloy Alfaro entre Napo y Amazonas. Mon-Sat 0600-2100, Sun 0600-1400. Set meals and à la carte, popular with locals.

☼ What to do

Cuyabeno Wildlife Reserve p560
Prices do not include transport to Lago Agrio.
Magic River Tours, Lago Agrio (no storefront), T09-9736 0670, www.magic rivertours.com. Good-quality and value 5- to 8-day canoe tours, half-day paddling, half-day motorized, camping and accommodation in rustic cabins, US$330-800, book well in advance.

The following agencies are all in Quito:
Dracaena, page 441. US$260 for 4 days.
Ecuador Verde País, Calama E6-19 y Reina Victoria, T02-222 0614, www.cabanasjamu. com. Run **Jamu Lodge**, good service, US$230-265 for 4 days.
Galasam, page 531. Operates **Siona Lodge**, www.sionalodge.com, US$360 for 4 days.
Neotropic Turis, Pinto E4-360, Quito, T02-252 1212, www.neotropicturis.com. Operate the **Cuyabeno Lodge** by the Laguna Grande, English speaking guides, US$220-350 for 4 nights.

Coca p561
Jungle tours from Coca
See also page 561.
Ecu-Astonishing, near Hotel La Missión, T288 0251, jjarrin1@msn.com. Julio Jarrín offers tours to his own cabins near Pañacocha.
Luis Duarte, at Casa del Maito (see Restaurants above), T288 2285, cocaselva@ hotmail.com. Regional and trips to Iquitos.
Sachayacu Explorer, in Píllaro near Baños (see page 485), T03-287 5316, info@parquel langanates.com. Although not based in Coca, experienced jungle guide Juan Medina offers recommended jungle tours and trips to Iquitos. Advance arrangements required.
Wildlife Amazon, Robert Vaca at Hotel San Fermín (see Where to stay, above), T288 0802. Jungle tours and trips to Iquitos.

River cruises on the lower Río Napo
Manatee, Quito office: Advantage Travel, Gaspar de Villarroel N 40-143 y 6 de Diciembre, T02-336 0887, www.manatee amazonexplorer.com. This 30-passenger vessel sails between Coca and Pañacocha. US$795 for 4 days. First-class guides, excellent food, en suite cabins. They also operate the new *Anakonda*, www. anakondaamazoncruises.com, a luxury cruise vessel on the Napo.

Coca to Nuevo Rocafuerte and Iquitos p561
Juan Carlos Cuenca, Nuevo Rocafuerte, T06-238 2257, is a *guía nativo* who offers tours to Parque Nacional Yasuní, about US$60 per day.

⊜ Transport

Baeza p560
Bus Buses to and from **Tena** pass right through town. If arriving on a **Lago Agrio** bus, get off at the crossroads (La "Y") and walk or take a pickup for US$0.25. From **Quito**, 5 daily (3 on Sun), with **Trans Quijos**, T02-295 0842, from Don Bosco E1-136 y Av Pichincha (beside the overpass at La Marín, an unsafe area), US$3, 2½ hrs. These continue to Borja and El Chaco.

Lago Agrio p560
Air Airport is 5 km southeast of the centre. TAME (Orellana y 9 de Octubre, T283 0113) and **Aerogal** (at the airport, T283 0333) daily to **Quito**. Book several days in advance. If there is no space available to **Lago Agrio** then you can fly to **Coca** instead, from where it is only 2 hrs by bus on a good road.
Bus Terminal terrestre is north of town, but buses for Coca leave from the market area on Orellana, 3 blocks south of Av Quito. To **Quito** (2 routes: through Cascales, and, slightly longer via Coca and Loreto), US$8, 7-8 hrs. **Baeza** 5 hrs. **Coca**, US$3, 2 hrs. **Tena**, US$7, 7 hrs.

Coca p561
Air Flights to **Quito**, **Latacunga** and **Guayaquil** with TAME (C Quito y Enrique

Castillo, T288 0768) and **Aerogal** (at the airport T288 1742), several daily (fewer on weekends), reserve as far in advance as possible.

Bus Long-distance buses depart from company offices in town; local destinations, including **Lago Agrio**, are served from the terminal on 9 de Octubre north of the centre. To **Quito**, 10 hrs, US$10, several daily 1030-2200. To **Tena**, 5 hrs, US$7. To **Baeza**, US$7.50, 8 hrs. To **Baños**, US$11, 8½ hrs.

River Down the Río Napo to **Nuevo Rocafuerte** on the Peruvian border, 50-passenger motorized canoes leave Coca daily except Sat, 0730, 10-12 hrs; returning at 0500, 12-14 hrs; US$15. Details change often, enquire locally, buy tickets at the dock a day in advance and arrive early for boarding.

From Nuevo Rocafuerte boats can be hired for the 30-km trip down river to the Peruvian border town of **Pantoja**, US$60 per boat, try to share the ride. Departure dates of riverboats from **Pantoja to Iquitos** are irregular, about once a month, be prepared for a long wait. Try to call Iquitos or Pantoja from Coca to enquire about the next sailing; full details are given in the Peru chapter under Iquitos, Transport. For the journey, take a hammock, cup, bowl, cutlery, extra food and snacks, drinking water or purification, insect repellent, toilet paper, soap, towel, cash dollars and soles in small notes; soles cannot be purchased in Coca.

❶ Directory

Lago Agrio *p560*
Banks For ATMs: Banco de Guayquil, Quito y 12 de Febrero; Banco Pichincha, 12 de Febrero y Añasco. Several **Casas de Cambio** on Quito between Colombia and Pasaje Gonzanamá, change euros and Colombian pesos.

Coca *p561*
Banks For ATMs: Banco Pichincha, Quito y Bolívar; Banco Internacional, 9 de Octubre y Cuenca.

Central and southern Oriente

Quito, Baños, Puyo, Tena and Puerto Misahuallí are all starting points for cental Oriente. Further south, Macas, Gualaquiza and Zamora are the main gateways. All have good road connections.

Archidona → *Phone code: 06. Colour map 1, B4. Population: 12,700. Altitude: 550 m.*
Archidona, 65 km south of Baeza and 10 km north of Tena, has a striking, small painted church and not much else but there are some interesting reserves in the surrounding area. The road leaving Archidona's plaza to the east goes to the village of **San Pablo**, and beyond to the Río Hollín. Along this road, 15 km from Archidona, is **Reserva El Para** ⓘ *owned by Orchid Paradise (see Where to stay, page 570); guided tours US$5 per person plus US$20 for transport.* This 500-ha forest reserve has many rare birds and a nice waterfall. Tours can also be arranged to the **Izu Mangallpa Urcu (IMU) Foundation** ⓘ *contact Elias Mamallacta in Archidona, T288 9383 or T08-9045 6942, US$50 per day for accommodation (private rooms, mosquito nets) and guiding, minimum 2 people.* This reserve was set up by the Mamallacta family to protect territory on Galeras mountain. There is easy walking as well as a tougher trek, the forest is wonderful.

Tena and around → *Phone code: 06. Colour map 1, B4. Population: 37,500. Altitude: 500 m.*
Relaxed and friendly, Tena is the capital of Napo Province. It occupies a hill above the confluence of the Ríos Tena and Pano, there are nice views of the Andean foothills often shrouded in mist. Tena is Ecuador's most important centre for whitewater rafting and

also offers ethno-tourism. It makes a good stop en route from Quito to points deeper in Oriente. The road from the north passes the old airstrip and market and heads through the town centre as Avenida 15 de Noviembre on its way to the bus station, nearly 1 km south of the river. Tena is quite spread out. A pedestrian bridge and a vehicle bridge link the two halves of town. **iTur and Ministerio de Turismo** ① *Malecón, sector El Balnerio, Mon-Fri 0730-1230, 1400-1700*, several information offices under one roof. See also map, below.

Misahuallí → *Phone code: 06. Colour map 1, B4. Population: 5300. Altitude: 400 m.*

This small port, at the junction of the Napo and Misahuallí rivers, is perhaps the best place in Ecuador from which to visit the 'near Oriente', but your expectations should be realistic. The area has been colonized for many years and there is no extensive virgin forest nearby (except at **Jatun Sacha** and **Liana Lodge**, see Lodges on the Upper Río Napo, page 571). Access is very easy however, prices are reasonable, and while you will not encounter large animals in the wild, you can still see birds, butterflies and exuberant vegetation – enough to get a taste for the jungle. Beware the troop of urban monkeys by the plaza, who snatch

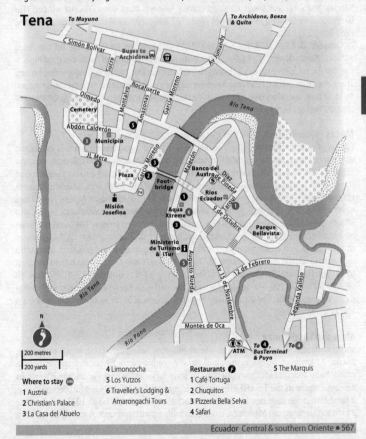

Tena

Where to stay 😑
1 Austria
2 Christian's Palace
3 La Casa del Abuelo
4 Limoncocha
5 Los Yutzos
6 Traveller's Lodging & Amarongachi Tours

Restaurants 🍴
1 Café Tortuga
2 Chuquitos
3 Pizzería Bella Selva
4 Safari
5 The Marquis

food, sunglasses, cameras, etc. There is a fine, sandy beach on the Río Misahuallí, but don't camp on it as the river can rise unexpectedly. A narrow suspension bridge crosses the Río Napo at Misahuallí and joins the road along the south shore. There is an interesting **Mariposario** (butterfly farm) ① *US$2.50*, where several colourful species can be observed and photographed close up, also an orchid garden and an entomologic display. Make arrangements through **Ecoselva** (See What to do, page 574). At Chichicorumi, outside Misahuallí, is **Kamak Maki** ① *US$2.50, T09-9982 7618, www.museokamakmaki.com*, an ethno-cultural museum run by the local Kichwa community.

Puyo → *Phone code: 03. Colour map 1, B4. Population: 40,000. Altitude: 950 m.*

The capital of the province of Pastaza feels more like a lowland city anywhere in Ecuador rather than a typical jungle town. Visits can nonetheless be made to nearby forest reserves and tours deeper into the jungle can also be arranged from Puyo. It is the junction for road travel into the northern and southern Oriente (80 km south of Tena, 130 km north of Macas), and for traffic heading to or from Ambato via Baños; all on paved roads. The Sangay and Altar volcanoes can occasionally be seen from town. **Tourist offices**: iTur ① *Francisco de Orellana y 9 de Octubre, T288 5122, daily 0800-1600; also at Treminal Terrestre, Wed-Sun 0900-1600.*

Omaere ① *T288 3174, Tue-Sun 0900-1700, US$3, access by footbridge off the Paseo Turístico, Barrio Obrero*, is a 15.6-ha ethnobotanical reserve located in the north of Puyo. It has three trails with a variety of plants, an orchidarium and traditional indigenous homes. There are other private reserves of varying quality in the Puyo area and visits are arranged by local tour operators (see page 574). You cannot however expect to see large tracts of undisturbed primary jungle here.

Macas → *Phone code: 07. Colour map 1, B4. Population: 20,700. Altitude: 1050 m.*

Capital of Morona-Santiago province, Macas is situated high above the broad Río Upano valley. It is a pleasant tranquil place, established by missionaries in 1563. **Sangay volcano** (5230 m) can be seen on clear mornings from the plaza, creating an amazing backdrop to the tropical jungle surrounding the town. The modern cathedral, with beautiful stained-glass windows, houses the much-venerated image of La Purísima de Macas. Five blocks north of the cathedral, at Don Bosco y Riobamba, the **Parque Recreacional**, which also affords great views of the Upano Valley, has a small orchid collection. The Sunday market on 27 de Febrero is worth a visit. **Fundación Chankuap** ① *Soasti y Bolívar, T270 1176, www.chankuap.org*, sells a nice variety of locally produced crafts and food products. **Ministerio de Turismo** ① *Bolívar y 24 de Mayo, T270 1480, Mon-Fri 0800-1700.* Macas provides access to **Parque Nacional Sangay** ① *Macas office, Juan de la Cruz y Guamote, T270 2368, Mon-Fri 0800-1300, 1400-1700.* The lowland area of the park has interesting walking with many rivers and waterfalls. See also Sangay Transport (page 502) for notes on the road from Macas to Riobamba.

Macas to Gualaquiza

South of Macas lies one of Ecuador's least touristed areas, promising much to explore. **Sucúa**, 23 km from Macas, is the administrative centre of the Shuar indigenous people who inhabit much of southern Oriente. The town has most services and some attractions nearby; enquire at the **Tourist office** in the Municipio. **Logroño**, 24 km further south, has a large limestone cave nearby; to visit contact Mario Crespo, T07-391 1013. It is another 31 km to (Santiago de) **Méndez**, a crossroads with a modern church. A mostly paved road descends from Cuenca via Paute and Guarumales to Méndez, and another road heads east from Méndez via Patuca to Santiago and San José de Morona, near the Peruvian border. Some 26 km south of Méndez is **Limón** (official name General Leónidas Plaza Gutiérrez), a busy, friendly place, surrounded by impressive hills. From Limón the road climbs steeply 10 km to **Plan de Milagro**, another crossroads, where a great road for birdwatching (closed for paving in 2014), descends from Cuenca via Gualaceo. Next are **Indanza**, 5 km south, then **San Juan Bosco**, 16 km further, with striking views of Cerro Pan de Azucar (2958 m) rising abruptly out of the jungle, before the road reaches Gualaquiza, 55 km ahead.

Gualaquiza → *Phone code 07. Colour map 1, C3. Population 9500. Altitude 850 m.*

A pleasant town with an imposing church on a hilltop, Gualaquiza's pioneer-settlement charm is threatened by large mining projects in the area. Fortunately, tourism offers an alternative as there are also lovely waterfalls, good rivers for tubing, caves and undeveloped archaeological sites nearby. Information and tours from the **Oficina Municipal de Turismo** ① *García Moreno y Gonzalo Pesántez, T278 0783, Mon-Fri 0730-1230, 1330-1630*, and from Leonardo Matoche at **Canela y Café**.

At Gualaquiza a very rough and narrow road forks northwest to climb steeply to Cuenca via **Sígsig**. The paved road south from Gualaquiza passes El Pangui and Yantzaza (55 km), 8 km south of which is **Zumbi**, with basic hotels on the plaza. At Zumbi, a bridge crosses the Río Zamora and a side road goes southeast to Guayzimi and the beautiful **Alto Nangaritza** region, with **Reserva El Zarza**. The upper Río Nangaritza flows through Shuar territory and a magnificent jungle-covered gorge with 200-m-high walls. There are also oilbird caves and other natural attractions. There is bus service to the area from Zamora, and tours are available form **Cabañas Yankuam** (see Where to stay, page 572) and Zamora tour operators. South of Zumbi, the broad valley of the Río Zamora becomes progressively narrower, with forested mountains and lovely views. It is 35 km to Zamora.

Zamora → *Phone code 07. Colour map 1, C3. Population: 14,000. Altitude: 950 m.*

The colonial mission settlement of Zamora, at the confluence of the Ríos Zamora and Bombuscaro, has an increasingly boom-town feeling due to large mining projects in the area. It is reached by road from Gualaquiza (see above) or Loja, 64 km away. The road from Loja is beautiful as it wanders from *páramo* down to high jungle, crossing mountain ranges of cloud forest, weaving high above narrow gorges as it runs alongside the Río Zamora. The town itself is hilly, with a pleasant climate. It gives access to the **Alto Nangaritza** (see above) and is the gateway to the lowland portion of **Parque Nacional Podocarpus** (see page 516). Between town and the park is **Copalinga**, a bird-rich private reserve (see Where to stay, page 572). There are two *orquidearios*, **Tzanka** ① *José Luis Tamayo y Jorge Mosquera, T260 5692, US$2* and **Pafinia** ① *Av del Ejército Km 2, T260 5911*. For information about the town: **Unidad de Turismo** ① *Municipio, Diego de Vaca y 24 de Mayo, by the plaza, T260 5316, ext 110, Mon-Fri 0800-1230, 1400-1730.*

For hotel and restaurant price codes, and other relevant information, see pages 14-17.

ⓦ Where to stay

Archidona p566

$$$$-$$$ Hakuna Matata, Vía Shungu Km 3.9, off the road between Tena and Archidona, T288 9617, www.hakunamat. com. Comfortable cabins in a lovely setting by the Río Inchillaqui. Includes 3 meals, walks, river bathing and horse riding. Excellent food, Belgian hosts, pleasant atmosphere. Warmly recommended.

$$$ Huasquila, Vía Huasquila, Km 3.5, Cotundo, T237 6158, www.huasquila.com. Wheel chair accessible bungalows and Kichwa-style cabins, includes breakfast and dinner, jungle walks, caving, rock art.

$$$ Orchid Paradise, 2 km north of town, T288 9232. Cabins in nice secondary forest with lots of birds. Full board or cheaper with only breakfast, owner organizes tours in the area.

$ Regina, Rocafuerte 446, 1 block north of the plaza, T288 9144. Private or shared bath, cold water, ample parking, pleasant, family-run.

Tena p566, map p567

$$ Christian's Palace, JL Mera y Sucre, T288 6047. Restaurant, a/c, cheaper with fan, pool, modern and comfortable.

$$ La Casa del Abuelo, JL Mera 628, T09-9900 0914, www.tomas-lodge.com. Nice quiet place, comfortable rooms, small garden, hot water, ceiling fan, parking, tours. Recommended.

$$ Los Yutzos, Augusto Rueda 190 y 15 de Noviembre, T09-9567 0160, www.uchutican. com/yutzos. Comfortable rooms and beautiful grounds overlooking the Río Pano, quiet and family-run. A/c, cheaper with fan, parking.

$ Austria, Tarqui y Díaz de Pineda, T288 7205. Spacious rooms, with a/c, cheaper with fan, ample parking, quiet, good value.

$ Limoncocha, Sangay 533, Sector Corazón de Jesús, on a hillside 4 blocks from the bus station, ask for directions, T284 6303, http://limoncocha.tripod.com. Concrete house with terrace and hammocks, some rooms with a/c, private or shared bath, hot water, fan, laundry and cooking facilities, breakfast available, parking, German/Ecuadorean-run, enthusiastic owners organize tours. Out of the way in a humble neighbourhood, good views, pleasant atmosphere, good value.

$ Traveler's Lodging, 15 de Noviembre 438 y 9 de Octubre, T288 6372, www. amarongachi.com. Many different rooms and prices, front ones noisy, best to look around and choose for yourself, some rooms with a/c, cheaper with fan, **Amarongachi Tours** on the premises.

Misahuallí p567

$$$$ El Jardin Aleman, jungle lodge on shores of Río Mishualli, 3 km from town, T289 0122, www.eljardinaleman.com. Comfortable rooms with bath, hot water. Price includes 3 meals and river tour, set in protected rainforest.

$$$$ Hamadryade, behind the Mariposario, 4 km from town, T09-8590 9992, www.hamadryade-lodge.com. Luxury lodge in a 64-ha forest reserve, 5 designer wood cabins, packages include breakfast, dinner and excursions, French chef, pool, lovely views down to the river.

$$$ Hostería Misahuallí, across the river from town, T289 0063, www.hosteria misahualli.com. Cabins for up to 6 in a lovely setting, includes breakfast, other meals on request, electric shower, fan, pool and tennis courts, lovely sunsets.

$$-$ Banana Lodge, 500 m from town on road to Pununo, T289 0190, www.banana lodge.com. Nicely decorated hostel, ample rooms, cheaper in dorm, huge garden with hammocks, breakfast available, cooking facilities, parking, US$4 pp for campervans, opened in 2013, Russian/Ecuadorean-run.

$$-$ Cabañas Río Napo, cross the suspension bridge, then 100 m on the left-hand side, T09-9990 4352. Nice rustic cabins with thatch roof, private bath, hot water, ample grounds along the river, run by a local Kichwa family, enthusiastic and friendly.

$$-$ El Paisano, Rivadeneyra y Tandalia, T289 0027, www.hostalelpaisano.com. Restaurant, hot water, mosquito nets, small pool, helpful.

$ Shaw, Santander on the Plaza, T289 0163, hostalshaw@hotmail.com. Good restaurant, hot water, fan, simple rooms, annexe with kitchen facilities and small pool, operate their own tours, English spoken, very knowledgeable. Good value. Recommended.

Lodges on the Upper Río Napo

Casa del Suizo, Quito office: Julio Zaldumbide y Valladolid, T02-256 6090, www.casadel suizo.com. On north shore at Ahuano, resort with capacity for 200, comfortable rooms, well-tended grounds, pool, gift shop, great river views. Swiss/Ecuadorean-owned. US$99 per night.

Cotococha, Quito office: Muros N27-94 y González Suárez, T512 3358, www.cotococha.com, along the road east of Puerto Napo. Comfortable well-screened cabins. Jungle walks, tubing, waterfalls and community visits. US$320 for 4 days.

Jatun Sacha Biological Station, east of Ahuano and easily accessible by bus, Quito T02-331 7163, www.jatunsacha.org. A 2500-ha reserve for education, research and tourism. 507 birds, 2500 plants and 765 butterfly species have been identified. Basic cabins with shared bath, cold water, good self-guided trails, canopy tower. US$30 per night, day visit US$6, guiding US$20 per group. Good value.

Liana Lodge, on Río Arajuno near its confluence with the Napo, Tena T06 301 7702, www.amazoonico.org. Comfortable cabins with terraces and river views on a 1700-ha reserve. *Centro de rescate* has animals on site. US$250 for 4 days. Recommended. Also arranges stays at **Runa**

Wasi, next door; basic cabins run by the local Kichwa community, US$25 per night with 3 meals, guiding extra.

Yachana, Quito office: Reina Victoria N24-217 y Roca, T02-252 3777, www.yachana.com. Located in the village of Mondaña, 2 hrs downstream from Misahuallí or 2½ hrs upstream from Coca. Proceeds go toward supporting community development projects. For 4 days: US$510-760. Recommended.

Puyo *p568*

$$$$ Altos del Pastaza Lodge, access from Km 16 of Puyo–Macas road, Quito office: Leonardo Murialdo E11-04 y los Nardos, T09-9767 4686, www.altosdelpastazalodge.com. Attractive lodge in 65-ha reserve overlooking the Río Pastaza, pool. Don't expect much wildlife, but a good place to relax, 1- to 4-day packages include meals and walking tours.

$$$$ Las Cascadas Lodge, Quito office: Amazonas N23-87 y Wilson, T02-250 0530, www.surtrek.com. First-class lodge 40 km east of Puyo, 8 rooms with terraces, includes full board, activities and transport from/to Quito, waterfalls; 3- and 4-day packages available.

$$$ El Jardín, Paseo Turístico, Barrio Obrero, T288 6101, www.eljardinrelax.com.ec. Nice rooms and garden, good upmarket restaurant.

$$ Delfín Rosado, Ceslao Marín y Atahualpa, T288 8757. Pool, modern rooms with a/c.

$$ Las Palmas, 20 de Julio y 4 de Enero, 5 blocks from centre, T288 4832, hostal_laspalmas_puyo@yahoo.com. Comfortable new rooms with a/c and fridge, older ones with fan are cheaper (best upstairs), private bath, hot water.

$$ San Luís-Memon's, one block from bus terminal, T288 4064. Nice modern rooms, rooftop terrace with restaurant, good choice for late arrivals or early departures.

$ Colibrí, Av Manabí entre Bolívar y Galápagos, T288 3054. Hot water, private bath, parking, away from centre, simple but nice, good value, offers tours. Recommended.

Southern Oriente jungle lodges

Kapawi, Quito office: Foch E7-38 y Reina Victoria, T02-600 9333, www.kapawi.com. A top-of-the-line lodge located on the Río Capahuari near its confluence with the Pastaza, not far from the Peruvian border. Run by the local Achuar community and accessible only by small aircraft and motor canoe. The biodiversity is good, but more emphasis is placed on ethno-tourism here than at other upmarket jungle lodges. US$1265 for 4 days includes land and air transport from Quito.

Macas *p568*

$$$$ Arrayán y Piedra, Km 7 Vía a Puno, T304 6448. Large resort-style lodging, nice rooms, pool, ample grounds, restaurant with very good food, but variable service.

$$$ Casa Upano, Av La Ciudad, Barrio La Barranca, 1 km from centre, T270 2674, www.realnaturetravel.com. A family-run B&B in a private home, other meals available with advance notice, excellent food, parking, ample comfortable rooms, huge garden with many birds, day visit US$5 with advance notice. Very helpful, English spoken, organize birdwatching tours. Warmly recommended.

$ Casa Blanca, Soasti 14-29 y Sucre, T270 0195. Hot water, small pool, modern and comfortable, very helpful, good value, often full, book in advance.

$ Nivel 5, Juan de la Cruz y Amazonas, T270 1240. Nice modern multi-storey hotel, hot water, fan, pool, parking.

Macas to Gualaquiza *p568*
Sucúa

$$$ Lucelinda, 1 km vía a Cuenca, T274 2118. Comfortable rooms with fans, large clean pool, good restaurant.

$$ Arutam, Vía a Macas Km 1, north of town, T274 0851. Restaurant, pool and sauna, parking, modern comfortable rooms, nice grounds, sports fields, well suited to families.

Several other hotels (**$**) in town.

Méndez

$ Interoceánico, C Quito on the plaza, T276 0245. Hot water, parking, smart and modern, good value.

Limón

$ Dream House, Quito y Bolívar, T277 0166. With restaurant, shared bath, hot water, adequate.

San Juan Bosco

$ Antares, on the plaza, T304 2128. Restaurant, hot water, indoor pool, simple functional rooms, helpful owner.

Gualaquiza *p569*

$ Gran Hotel, Orellana y Gran Pasaje, T278 0722. Modern concrete building, hot water, fan, parking, small rooms, some without windows.

$ Wakis, Orellana 08-52 y Domingo Comín, T278 0138. Older simple place with small rooms, private or shared bath, cold water, enthusiastic owner speaks English.

Alto Nangaritza

$$ Cabañas Yankuam, 3 km south of Las Orquídeas, T260 5739 (Zamora), www.lindoecuadortours.com. Rustic cabins, includes breakfast, other tasty meals on request, private or shared bath, good walking in surrounding jungle-clad hills, organizes trips up the Río Nangaritza. Family-run. Reservations required, 1 week advance notice preferred.

Zamora *p569*

With the ongoing mining boom, many new hotels have opened since 2012.

$$$-$$ Copalinga, Km 3 on the road to the Bombuscaro entrance of Parque Nacional Podocarpus, T09-9347 7013, www.copalinga.com. Comfortable cabins with balcony in a lovely setting, includes very good breakfast, other delicious meals available if arranged in advance, more rustic cabins with shared bath are cheaper, excellent birdwatching, walking trails.

Belgian-run, English, French and Dutch
spoken, attentive, reserve ahead.
Highly recommended.
$$ Samuria, 24 de Mayo y Diego de Vaca,
T260 7801, hotelsamuria@hotmail.com.
Modern bright hotel, comfortable well
furnished rooms, restaurant, parking.
$ Betania, Francisco de Orellana entre
Diego de Vaca y Amazonas, T260 7030,
hotel-betania@hotmail.com. Modern,
functional, breakfast available, hot water.
$ Wampushkar, Diego de Vaca y Pasaje
Vicente Aldeán, T260 7800. Nice modern
hotel, ample rooms, hot water, parking,
good value.

🍴 Restaurants

Tena *p566, map p567*
$$$ The Marquis, Amazonas entre Calderón
y Olmedo, daily 1200-1600, 1800-2200.
Upmarket restaurant serving good steaks.
$$ Chuquitos, García Moreno by the plaza.
Mon-Sat 0800-2100, Sun 1100-2100. Good
food, à la carte only, seating on a balcony
overlooking the river. Pleasant atmosphere,
attentive service and nice views. Popular
and recommended. **Araña Bar** downstairs.
$$ Pizzería Bella Selva, Malecón south of
the footbridge; second location on east side.
Daily 1100-2300. Pizza and pasta.
$ Safari, Av 15 de Noviembre y F Monteros,
Mon-Sat 0700-2300, Sun 0700-1600. Set
meals, good quality and value.
Café Tortuga, Malecón south of the
footbridge, Mon-Sat 0700-1930, Sun
0700-1300. Juices, snacks and sweets,
nice location, spotless, friendly Swiss
owner. Recommended.

Misahuallí *p567*
$$$ El Jardín, 300 m past bridge to
Ahuano. Daily 1200-1600, 1800-2200.
Variety of dishes, beautiful garden setting.
$$-$ Doña Gloria, Arteaga y Rivadeneyra
by corner of plaza. Daily 0730-2030. Good
set meals.

Puyo *p568*
$$$-$$ Tapas y Topes, opposite Parque
Acuático near bus terminal. Daily 1100-1500,
1700-2400. Wide variety of tasty dishes.
$$ Pizzería Buon Giorno, Orellana entre
Villamil y 27 de Febrero. Mon-Sat 1200-2300,
Sun 1400-2300. Good pizza, lasagne and
salads, pleasant atmosphere, very popular.
Recommended.
El Fariseo Café, Atahualpa entre 27 de
Febrero y General Villamil. Open 0700-2200.
Good cakes and the best coffee in town.
Escobar Café, Atahualpa y Orellana.
Daily 0630-2400. Good for early breakfast,
sandwiches, bar at night, attractive
bamboo decor.

Macas *p568*
$$ Junglab, Bolívar entre Guamote y
Amazonas, T270 2448. Tue-Sun 1200-2230.
Delicious creative meals using local produce.
$$-$ La Italiana, Soasti y Sucre. Mon-Sat
1200-2300. Great pizzas, pasta and salads.
$ La Choza de Mama Sara, 10 de Agosto
y 9 de Octubre. Mon-Sat 0830-2100.
Traditional Macabeo cuisine such as
ayampacos and yuca and palm tamales,
served for breakfast. Also a choice of set
lunches, good value.
$ Rincón Manabita, Amazonas y 29 de
Mayo. Mon-Fri 0700-2200, Sat-Sun 0700-
1600. Good breakfasts and a choice of set
meals which are delicious and filling. Also
à la carte.

Zamora *p569*
$ Agate, near main plaza. Mon-Fri midday
only. Good set lunch and à la carte.
$ King Ice, Diego de Vaca y José Luis
Tamayo, by the plaza. Daily 0900-2400.
Snacks and a few à la carte dishes.
Spiga Pan, 24 de Mayo, ½ block downhill
from the plaza. Great bakery with a variety
of hot bread, cream cakes and fresh
fruit yoghurt. A very good option in
this otherwise un-gastronomic town.

● What to do

Tena *p566, map p567*

Rafting tours cost US$50-70 per day, safety standards vary between operators. Avoid touts selling tours on the street.

Amarongachi Tours at Hostal Traveler's Lodging (see Where to stay, above), jungle tours.

AquaXtreme, Malecón Francisco de Orellana 248, T288 8746, www.axtours.com. Offers rafting, kayaking, canyoning and horse riding.

Limoncocha, at Hostal Limoncocha (see Where to stay, above), rafting, kayaking and jungle, English and German spoken.

Ríos Ecuador, Tarqui 230 y Díaz de Pineda, T288 6727, www.riosecuador.com. Highly recommended whitewater rafting and kayak trips, and a 4-day kayaking school (US$320).

Misahuallí *p567*

Jungle tours (US$45-80 pp per day) can be arranged by most hotels as well as the following:

Ecoselva, Santander on the plaza, T289 0019, ecoselva@yahoo.es. Recommended guide Pepe Tapia speaks English and has a biology background. Well organized and reliable.

Runawa Tours, in La Posada hotel, on the plaza, T09-9818 1961, www. misahualliamazon.com. Owner Carlos Santander, tubing, kayak and jungle tours.

Teorumi, on the plaza, T289 0203, www.teorumi.com. Offers tours to the Shiripuno Kichwa community.

Puyo *p568*

All of the following offer jungle tours of varying lengths, US$25-50 pp per day.

Coka Tours, 27 de Febrero y Ceslao Marín, T288 6108, denisecoka@gmail.com.

Naveda Santos, at the Terminal Terrestre, upstairs, T288 3974. Owner, Marco Naveda.

Selvavida Travel, Ceslao Marín y Atahualpa, T288 9729, www.selvavidatravel.com. Specializes in rafting and Parque Nacional Yasuní.

Macas *p568*

Tours to indigenous communities and lowland portions of Parque Nacional Sangay, cost about US$50 per day.

Insondu, Bolívar y Soasti, T270 2533.

Planeta Tours, Domingo Comín 7-35 y Soasti, T270 1328.

Real Nature Travel Company, at Casa Upano, see Where to stay, above. Run by RhoAnn Wallace and professional birdwatching guide Galo Real, English spoken.

Zamora *p569*

BioAventura, at Orquideario Tzanka (see page 569), T09-9381 4472. Fernado Ortega offers downhill bike rides along the old road Loja–Zamora.

Cabañas Yankuam, see page 572. Offer tours to the Alto Nangaritza.

Wellington Valdiviezo, T09-9380 2211, lindozamoraturistico@yahoo.es. Tours to the Alto Nangaritza, Shuar communities, adventure sports, visits to shamans. Contact in advance.

● Transport

Tena *p566, map p567*

Air Airport at Ahuano. TAME to **Quito** on Mon, Wed and Fri.

Bus Run-down Terminal Terrestre on 15 de Noviembre, 1 km from the centre (taxi US$1). To **Quito**, US$6, 5 hrs. To **Ambato**, via Baños, US$5, 4½ hrs. To **Baños**, US$4, 3½ hrs. To **Riobamba**, via Ambato, US$6, 5½ hrs. To **Puyo**, US$3, 2 hrs. To **Coca and Lago Agrio**, fares given above. To **Misahuallí**, see below. To **Archidona**, from Amazonas y Bolívar by market, every 20 mins, US$0.25, 15 mins.

Misahuallí *p567*

Bus Local buses run from the plaza. To **Tena**, hourly 0600-1900, US$1, 45 mins. Make long-distance connections in Tena. To **Quito**, 1 direct bus a day at 0830, US$7, 5 hrs.

River No scheduled passenger service, but motorized canoes for 8-10 passengers can be chartered for touring.

Puyo *p568*

Air The nearest airport to Puyo is at Shell, 13 km. Military flights to jungle villages are not open to foreigners, but light aircraft can be chartered starting around US$300 per hr.
Bus Terminal Terrestre on the outskirts of town, a 10- to 15-min walk from the centre; taxi US$1. To **Baños**, US$2, 1½ hrs. To **Ambato**, US$3, 2½ hrs. To **Quito**, US$5, 5 hrs via Ambato. To **Riobamba**, US$4, 3½ hrs. To **Tena**, see above. To **Macas**, US$5, 2½ hrs.

Macas *p568*

Air Small modern airport within walking distance at Cuenca y Amazonas. To **Quito**, Thu and Sun with TAME (office at airport T270 4940) Sit on left for best views of Volcán Sangay. Air taxis available to jungle villages, US$600 per hr for 9 passengers.
Bus Terminal Terrestre by the market. To **Puyo**, see above. To **Baños**, US$6, 4½ hrs. To **Quito**, via Puyo, Baños and Ambato, US$8, 8 hrs. To **Riobamba** through Parque Nacional Sangay, a beautiful ride, 6 daily, US$5, 4 hrs. To **Cuenca**, US$8, 8 hrs, via Méndez and Guarumales (mostly paved) or via Plan de Milagro and Gualaceo (closed 2014). To **Gualaquiza**, US$8, 8 hrs, where you can get a bus to Zamora and Loja (see below). To **Sucúa**, hourly, US$0.90, 30 min. To **9 de Octubre**, for PN Sangay, US$1.50, 45 mins.

Gualaquiza *p569*

Bus To **Macas**, see above. To **Cuenca**; via Sígsig, 4 daily, US$6.25, 6 hrs; or via Plan de Milagro and Gualaceo (closed 2014). To **Zamora**, US$3.50, 3½ hrs. To **Loja**, US$6, 5½ hrs.

Alto Nangaritza

To **Las Orquídeas**, with Trans Zamora, from Zamora at 0400, 0645, 1115 and 1230, US$3.80, 3½ hrs; from Yantzaza at 0440, 0740, 1150 and 1310, US$2.50, 3½ hrs; with **Unión Yantzaza**, from Yantzaza at 0430, 0930, 1130, 1430 and 1630; from Loja at 1415, 1510, US$6.20, 5½ hrs.

Zamora *p569*

Bus Leave from Terminal Terrestre. To **Loja**, frequent, 1½-2 hrs, US$2.40; to **Gualaquiza**, US$3.50, 3½ hrs, where you transfer for Macas.

⊙ Directory

Tena *p566, map p567*
Banks For ATMs: Banco del Austro, 15 de Noviembre y Díaz de Pineda; Banco Pichincha, 15 de Noviembre y Tena, on the way to bus terminal.

Puyo *p568*
Banks For ATM: Banco del Austro, Atahualpa entre 27 de Febrero y 9 de Octubre; Banco de Guayaquil, Ceslao Marín y 20 de Julio; Banco Pichincha, 10 de Agosto y Orellana.

Macas *p568*
Banks For ATMs: Banco del Austro, Soasti y Domingo Comín; Banco Pichincha, Soasti y 10 de Agosto.

Zamora *p569*
Banks For ATMs: Banco del Austro, Jorge Mosquera by the Plaza; also Banco Pichincha.

Galápagos Islands

A trip to the Galápagos Islands is an unforgettable experience. The islands are world-renowned for their fearless wildlife but no amount of hype can prepare the visitor for such a close encounter with nature. Here you can snorkel with penguins, sea lions and the odd hammerhead shark, watch giant 200-kg tortoises lumbering through cactus forest and enjoy the courtship display of the blue-footed booby and magnificent frigatebird, all in startling close-up.

Lying on the Equator, 970 km west of the Ecuadorean coast, the Galápagos consist of six main islands, 12 smaller islands and over 40 islets. The islands have an estimated population of 27,000, but this does not include many temporary inhabitants. Santa Cruz has 16,600 inhabitants, with Puerto Ayora the main city and tourist centre. San Cristóbal has a population of 7900 with the capital of the archipelago, Puerto Baquerizo Moreno. The largest island, Isabela, is 120 km long and forms over half the total land area of the archipelago, some 2500 people live there, mostly in and around Puerto Villamil on the south coast. Floreana, the first island to be settled, has about 160 residents.

Background

The Galápagos have never been connected with the continent. Gradually, over many hundreds of thousands of years, animals and plants from over the sea somehow migrated there and as time went by they adapted themselves to Galápagos conditions and came to differ more and more from their continental ancestors. Unique marine and terrestrial environments, due to the continuing volcanic formation of the islands in the west of the archipelago and its location at the nexus of several major marine currents, have created laboratory-type conditions where only certain species have been allowed access. The formidable barriers which prevent many species from travelling between the islands, has led to a very high level of endemism. A quarter of the species of shore fish, half of the plants and almost all the reptiles are found nowhere else. In many cases different forms have evolved on the different islands. Charles Darwin recognized this speciation within the archipelago when he visited the Galápagos on the *Beagle* in 1835 and his observations played a substantial part in his formulation of the theory of evolution.

This natural experiment has been under threat ever since the arrival of the first whaling ships and even more so since the first permanent human settlement. New species were introduced and spread very rapidly, placing the endemic species at risk. Quarantine programmes have since been implemented in an attempt to prevent the introduction and spread of even more species, but the rules are not easy to enforce. There have also been campaigns to eradicate some of the introduced species on some islands, but this is inevitably a very slow, expensive and difficult process.

One striking feature of the islands is the tameness of the animals. The islands were uninhabited when they were discovered in 1535 and the animals still have little instinctive fear of man.

Plant and animal species are grouped into three categories. **Endemic species** are those which occur only in the Galápagos and nowhere else on the planet. Examples of Galápagos endemics are the Galápagos marine and Galápagos land iguana, Galápagos fur sea lion, flightless cormorant and the 'daisy tree' (*Scalesia pedunculata*). **Native species** make their homes in the Galápagos as well as other parts of the world. Examples include all three species of boobies, frigate birds and the various types of mangroves. Although not unique to the islands, these native species have been an integral part of the Galápagos ecosystems for a very long time. **Introduced species** on the other hand are very recent arrivals, brought by man, and inevitably the cause of much damage. They include cattle, goats, donkeys, pigs, dogs, cats, rats and over 500 species of plants such as elephant grass (for grazing cattle), and fruit trees. The unchecked expansion of these introduced species has upset the natural balance of the archipelago. The number of tourists also has grown steadily: from 11,800 in 1979, to 68,900 in 2000, to 204,400 in 2013. From 2007 to 2010, Galápagos was on the UNESCO list of endangered World Heritage Sites. Although it is now off the list, promoting environmental conservation and sustainable development in the face of growing tourism and population remains a substantial challenge.

Arriving in the Galápagos Islands → *Phone code: 05. Colour map 5.*

Getting there

Airports at **Baltra**, across a narrow strait from Santa Cruz, and **Puerto Baquerizo Moreno**, on San Cristóbal, receive flights from mainland Ecuador. The two islands are 96 km apart and on most days there are local flights in light aircraft between them, as well as to **Puerto Villamil** on Isabela. There is also speedboat service between Puerto Ayora (Santa Cruz) and the other populated islands. There are no international flights to Galápagos.

AeroGal, LAN and TAME all fly from Quito and Guayaquil to Baltra or San Cristóbal. Baltra receives more flights but there is at least one daily to each destination. You can arrive at one and return from the other. You can also depart from Quito and return to Guayaquil or vice versa, but you may not buy a one-way ticket. The return airfare varies considerably, starting at about US$500 from Quito, US$400 from Guayaquil (2014 prices). See also Fees and inspections, below.

Airport transfers Two buses meet flights from the mainland at Baltra: one runs to the port or *muelle* (10 minutes, no charge) where the cruise boats wait; the other goes to Canal de Itabaca, the narrow channel which separates Baltra from Santa Cruz. It is 15 minutes to the Canal, free, then you cross on a small ferry, US$0.80. On the other side, buses (US$1.80, may involve a long wait while they fill) and pickup truck taxis (US$18 for up to four passengers) run to Puerto Ayora, 45 minutes. For the return trip to the airport, buses leave the *Terminal Terrestre* on Avenida Baltra in Puerto Ayora (2 km from the pier, taxi US$1) at 0700, 0730 and 0830 daily.▶ *See also Transport, page 591.*

Getting around

Emetebe Avionetas ① *Guayaquil at Hotel City Plaza, T04-230 9209, see Directory for local offices*, offers inter-island flights in light aircraft. Two daily flights except Sun between **Puerto Baquerizo Moreno** (San Cristóbal), **Baltra** and **Puerto Villamil** (Isabela). Fares US$155-170 one way; baggage allowance 25 lbs.

Fibras (fibreglass speedboats for about 20 passengers) operate daily between Puerto Ayora and each of Puerto Baquerizo Moreno, Puerto Villamil, and Puerto Velasco Ibarra (Floreana); US$30-35 one way, two hours or more depending on the weather and sea. Tickets are sold by several agencies in Puerto Baquerizo Moreno, Puerto Ayora, and Puerto Villamil. This can be a wild ride in rough seas, life vests should be provided, take drinking water.

Information and advice

A recommended bilingual website is www.galapagospark.org. It describes each visitor site and gives details of guides and tourist vessels operating in the islands.

Tourist offices Puerto Ayora: iTur ① *Av Charles Darwin y 12 de Febrero, T252 6614 ext 22, www.santacruz.gob.ec, Mon-Fri 0730-1230, 1400-1930, Sat-Sun 1600-1930,* has information about Puerto Ayora and Santa Cruz Island; **Ministerio de Turismo** ① *Charles Binford y 12 de Febrero, T252 6174, Mon-Fri 0830-1300, 1430-1700,* is mostly an administrative office but also receives complaints about agencies and vessels. **Puerto Baquerizo Moreno**: **Municipal tourist office** ① *Malecón Charles Darwin y 12 de Febrero, T252 0119 ext 120, Mon-Fri 0730-1230, 1400-1800,* is downstairs at the Municipio. **Ministerio de Turismo** ① *12 de Febrero e Ignacio Hernández, T252 0704, Mon-Fri 0830-1230, 1400-1730,* operates as in Santa Cruz, above. **Puerto Villamil**: **Municipal tourist office** ① *by the park, T252 9002, ext 113, Mon-Fri 0730-1230, 1400-1700,* has local information.

Fees and inspections A US$10 fee is collected at Quito or Guayaquil airport, where a registration form must be completed. You can also pre-register on line at www.gobiernogalapagos.gob.ec, or ask your tour operator to do so for you. Bags are checked prior to flights to Galápagos, no live animals, meat, dairy products, fresh fruit or vegetables may be taken to the islands. On arrival, every foreign visitor must pay a US$100 National Park fee. All fees are cash only. Be sure to have your passport to hand at the airport and keep all fee receipts throughout your stay in the islands. Bags are checked again on departure, as nothing may be taken off the islands. Puerto Villamil charges a US$5 port fee on arrival in Isabela.

Basic rules Do not touch any of the animals, birds or plants. Do not transfer sand, seeds or soil from one island to another. Do not leave litter anywhere; nor take food on to the uninhabited islands, which are also no-smoking zones. There is increasingly close contact between people and sea lions throughout Galápagos. Never touch them however, and keep your distance from the male 'beach-masters', they have been known to bite. Always take food, plenty of water and a compass or GPS if hiking on your own. There are many crisscrossing animal trails and it is easy to get lost. Also watch out for the large-spined opuntia cactus; and the poisonwood tree (*manzanillo*) found near beaches, contact with its leaves or bark can cause severe skin reactions.

What to take A remedy for seasickness is recommended. A good supply of sun block and skin cream to prevent windburn and chapped lips is essential, as are a hat and sunglasses. You should be prepared for dry and wet landings, the latter involving wading ashore; keep photo equipment and other delicate items in plastic bags. The animals are so tame that you will take far more photos than you expected; if you run out of memory cards they can be bought in Puerto Ayora, but best to take your own. Snorkelling equipment is particularly useful as much of the sea-life is only visible under water. The cheaper boats may not provide equipment or it may be of poor quality. If in doubt, bring your own. Good sturdy footwear is important, boots and shoes soon wear out on the abrasive lava terrain. Always bring some US$ cash to Galápagos, there are only a few ATMs and they may be out of order.

Tipping A ship's crew and guides are usually tipped separately. Amounts are often suggested onboard or in agencies' brochures, but these should be considered in light of the quality of service received and your own resources.

Overseas agencies

Galápagos Classic Cruises, 6 Keyes Rd, London NW2 3XA, T020-8933 0613, www. galapagoscruises.co.uk. Specialists in cruises and diving holidays to the islands including tailor-made land tours in Ecuador and additions to Peru and Bolivia on request.
Galápagos Holidays, 14 Prince Arthur Av, Suite 311, Toronto, Ontario M5R 1A9, T416-413 9090, T1-800-661 2512 (toll free), www.galapagosholidays.com.
Galápagos Network, 5805 Blue Lagoon Dr, Suite 160, Miami, FL 33126, T305-2626264, www.ecoventura.com.
INCA, 1311 63rd St, Emeryville, CA 94608, T510-420 1550, www.inca1.com.

International Expeditions, 1 Environs Park, Helena, Alabama, 35080, T205-428 1700, T1-855-232 7134, www.ietravel.com.
Select Latin America, 3.51 Canterbury Court, 1-3 Brixton Road, Kennington Park Business Centre, London SW9 6DE, T020-7407 1478, www.selectlatinamerica. com. Tailor-made holidays and small group tours.
Sol International, PO Box 1738, Kodak, TN 37764, T931-536 4893, T1-800-765 5657, www.solintl.com.
Wilderness Travel, 1102 Ninth St, Berkeley, CA 94710, T510-558 2488, T1-800-368 2794, www.wildernesstravel.com.

If you have problems Raise any issues first with your guide or ship's captain. Serious complaints are rare but may filed with **iTur** or **Ministerio de Turismo** offices in Puerto Ayora or Puerto Baquerizo Moreno, see Tourist offices above.

Best time to visit The Galápagos climate can be divided into a hot season (December-May), when there is a possibility of heavy showers, and the cool or *garúa* (mist) season (June-November), when the days generally are more cloudy and there is often rain or drizzle. July and August can be windy, force four or five. Daytime clothing should be lightweight. (Clothing generally, even on 'luxury cruises', should be casual and comfortable.) At night, however, particularly at sea and at higher altitudes, temperatures fall below 15°C and warm clothing is required. The sea is cold July-October; underwater visibility is best January-March. Ocean temperatures are usually higher to the east and lower at the western end of the archipelago. Despite all these climatic variations, conditions are generally favourable for visiting Galápagos throughout the year.

High season for tourism is June-August and December-January, when last-minute arrangements are generally not possible. Some boats may be heavily booked throughout the year and you should plan well in advance if you want to travel on a specific vessel at a specific time.

Choosing a tour

There are a growing number of options for visiting Galápagos but the best remains the traditional **live-aboard cruise** (*tour navegable*), where you travel and sleep on a yacht, tour boat or cruise ship. These vessels travel at night, arriving at a new landing site each day. Cruises range from three to 14 nights, seven is recommended. Itineraries are controlled by the National Park to distribute cruise boats evenly throughout the islands. All cruises begin with a morning flight from the mainland on the first day and end on the last day with a midday flight back to the mainland. The less expensive boats are normally smaller and less powerful so you see less and spend more time travelling; also the guiding may be mostly in Spanish. The more expensive boats have air conditioning, hot water and private baths.

Galápagos tourist vessels

Name	Description	Capacity	Website
Silversea	cruise ship	100	silversea.com
Galápagos Legend	cruise ship	100	kleintours.com
Xpedition	cruise ship	100	galapagosxpedition.co.uk
Santa Cruz	cruise ship	90	galapagosvoyage.com
Nat Geo Edeavour	cruise ship	80	expeditions.com
Eclipse	cruise ship	48	galapagos-eclipse.com
Nat Geo Islander	cruise ship	48	expeditions.com
Isabela II	cruise ship	40	galapagosvoyage.com
Millenium	cruise ship	40	galasam.net
Coral I	motor yacht	36	kleintours.com
Evolution	cruise ship	32	galapagosexpeditions.com
La Pinta	cruise ship	32	lapintagalapagoscruise.com
Coral II	motor yacht	20	kleintours.com
Eric	motor yacht	20	ecoventura.com
Flamingo I	motor yacht	20	ecoventura.com
Galápagos Adventure	motor yacht	20	various
Letty	motor yacht	20	ecoventura.com
Aída María	motor yacht	16	various
Amigo I	motor vessel	16	various
Anahi	motor catamaran	16	andandotours.com
Angelito I	motor yacht	16	angelitogalapagos.com
Archipel II	motor yacht	16	various
Athala II	motor catamaran	16	various
Beluga	motor yacht	16	enchantedexpeditions.com
Cachalote	2-mast schooner	16	enchantedexpeditions.com
Carina	motor yacht	16	various
Cormorant Evolution	motor catamaran	16	cormorantgalapagos.com
Darwin	motor vessel	16	various
Edén	motor yacht	16	various
Estrella del Mar I	motor yacht	16	galasam.net
Floreana	motor yacht	16	yatefloreana.com
Fragata	motor yacht	16	various
Galap Adventure II	motor yacht	16	various
Galap Journey I	motor catamarans	16	galapagosjourneycruises.com
Galapagos Odyssey	motor yatch	16	galapagosodyssey.com

Name	Description	Capacity	Website
Galapagos Vision I	1-mast catamaran	16	various
Galapagos Voyager	motor yatch	16	galapagos-voyager.com
Galaxy	motor yacht	16	various
Golondrina I	motor vessel	16	various
Grace	motor yatch	16	galapagosexpeditions.com
Gran Monserrat	motor yacht	16	various
Guantanamera	motor yacht	16	various
Integrity	motor yacht	16	various
Liberty	motor yacht	16	various
Majestic	motor vessel	16	www.galasam.com.ec
Mary Anne	3-mast barquentine	16	andandotours.com
Monserrat	motor vessel	16	various
Monserrat II	motor vessel	16	various
Ocean Spray	motor catamaran	16	galapagosoceanspray.com
Pelíkano	motor vessel	16	various
Queen Beatriz	motor catamaran	16	various
Queen of Galap	motor catamaran	16	galasam.net
Reina Silvia	motor yacht	16	reinasilvia.com
Samba	motor yacht	16	various
San José	motor yacht	16	various
San Juan II	motor vessel	16	various
Sea Man II	motor catamaran	16	various
Tip Top II	motor vessel	16	rwittmer.com
Tip Top III	motor yacht	16	rwittmer.com
Tip Top IV	motor yacht	16	rwittmer.com
Treasure of Galap	motor catamaran	16	treasureofgalapagos.com
Xavier III	motor vessel	16	various
Yolita II	motor yacht	16	various
Albatros	motor yacht	14	various
Beagle	2-mast schooner	13	angermeyercruises.com
Amazonía	1-mast catamaran	12	various
Encantada	2-mast schooner	12	scubagalapagos.com
New Flamingo	motor vessel	12	various
Merak	1-mast sailer	8	various

All boats have to conform to certain minimum safety standards; more expensive boats are better equipped. Boats with over 20 passengers take quite a time to disembark and re-embark people, while the smaller boats have a more lively motion, which is important if you are prone to seasickness. Note also that there may be limitations for vegetarians on the cheaper boats. The least expensive boats (economy class) cost about US$200 per person per day and a few of these vessels are dodgy. For around US$250-350 per day (tourist and tourist superior class) you will be on a better, faster boat which can travel more quickly between visitor sites, leaving more time to spend ashore. Over US$400 per day are the first-class and luxury brackets, with far more comfortable and spacious cabins, as well as a superior level of service and cuisine. No boat may sail without a park-trained guide.

The table on page 580 lists live-aboard tour vessels; for dive boats see page 589. The sailing vessels listed also have motors, and many frequently operate under engine power. All details are subject to change. Captains, crews and guides regularly change on all boats. These factors, as well as the sea, weather and your fellow passengers will all influence the quality of your experience.

Island-hopping is another option for visiting Galápagos, whereby you spend a night or two at hotels on some of the four populated islands, travelling between them in speedboats. You cover less ground than on a cruise, see fewer wildlife sites, and cannot visit the more distant islands. Island-hopping is sold in organized packages but visitors in no rush can also travel between and explore the populated islands independently and at their leisure. **Day tours** (*tour diario*) are yet another alternative, based mostly out of Puerto Ayora. Some take you for day-visits to National Park landing sites on nearby unpopulated islands, such as Bartolomé, Seymour, Plazas and Santa Fe (US$140-240), and can be quite good. Others go for the day to the populated islands of Isabela or Floreana, with no stops permitted along the way. The latter require at least four hours of speedboat travel and generally leave insufficient time to enjoy visitor sites; they are not recommended.

None of the above options is cheap, with the flight from the mainland and entry fees alone amounting to about US$600. Galápagos is such a special destination for nature-lovers however, that most agree it is worth saving for and spending on a quality tour. If nature is not your great passion and you are looking mainly for an exotic cruise or beach holiday, then your money will go further and you will likely have a better experience elsewhere.

Booking a tour in advance You can book a Galápagos cruise in several different ways: **1)** over the internet; **2)** from either a travel agency or directly though a Galápagos wholesaler in your home country; **3)** from one of the very many agencies found throughout Ecuador, especially in Quito (see page 441) but also in other tourist centres and Guayaquil (page 531); or **4)** from local agencies, mostly in Puerto Ayora but also in Puerto Baquerizo Moreno. The trade-off is always between time and money: booking from home is most efficient and expensive, last-minute arrangements in Galápagos are cheapest and most time-consuming, while Quito and Guayaquil are intermediate. It is not possible to obtain discounts or make last-minute arrangements in high season (see Best time to visit, above). Surcharges may apply when using a credit card to purchase tours on the islands, there are limits to ATM withdrawals and no cash advances on weekends, so bring cash if looking for a last-minute cruise. Also, if looking for a last-minute sailing, it is best to pay your hotel one night at a time since hoteliers may not refund advance payments. Especially on cheaper boats, check carefully about what is and is not included (eg drinking water, snorkelling equipment, etc).

Puerto Ayora

The islands

Santa Cruz: Puerto Ayora → *Phone code: 05.*
Population: 12,600.

Santa Cruz is the most central of the Galápagos islands and the main town is Puerto Ayora. About 1.5 km from the pier is the **Charles Darwin Research Station** ① *at Academy Bay, www.darwinfoundation. org, office Mon-Fri 0700-1600, visitor areas 0600-1800 daily, free.* A visit to the station is a good introduction to the islands. Collections of several of the rare sub-species of giant tortoise are maintained on the station as breeding nuclei, together with tortoise-rearing pens for the young. The **Centro Comunitario de Educación Ambiental** ① *east end of Charles Binford, Mon-Fri 0730-1200, 1400-1700, Sat morning only, free,* has an aquarium and exhibits about the Galápagos Marine Reserve.

There is a beautiful beach at **Tortuga Bay**, 45 minutes' easy walk (2.5 km each way) west from Puerto Ayora on an excellent cobbled path through cactus forest. Start at the west end of Calle Charles Binford; further on there is a gate where you must register, open 0600-1800 daily, free. Make sure you take sunscreen, drinking water, and beware of the very strong undertow. Do not walk on the dunes above the beach, which are a marine tortoise nesting area. At the west end of Tortuga Bay is a trail to a lovely mangrove-fringed lagoon, with calmer warmer water, shade, and sometimes a kayak for rent.

Las Grietas is a lovely gorge with a natural pool at the bottom which is popular and splendid for bathing. Take a water taxi from the port to the dock at Punta Estrada (five minutes, US$0.50). It is a five-minute walk from here to the **Finch Bay** hotel and 15 minutes further over rough lava boulders to Las Grietas – well worth the trip.

The Puerto Ayora–Baltra road goes through the agricultural zone in the highlands. The community of **Bellavista** is 7 km from the port, and **Santa Rosa** is

15 km beyond. The area has National Park visitor sites, walking possibilities and upmarket lodgings. **Los Gemelos** are a pair of large sinkholes, formed by collapse of the ground above empty magma chambers. They straddle the road to Baltra, beyond Santa Rosa. You can take a taxi or airport bus all the way; otherwise take a bus to Santa Rosa, then walk one hour uphill. There are several **lava tubes** (natural tunnels) on the island. Some are at **El Mirador**, 3 km from Puerto Ayora on the road to Bellavista. Two more lava tubes are 1 km from Bellavista. They are on private land, it costs US$1.50 to enter the tunnels (bring a torch) and it takes about 30 minutes to walk through them. Tours to the lava tubes can be arranged in Puerto Ayora.

The highest point on Santa Cruz Island is **Cerro Crocker** at 864 m. You can hike here and to two other nearby 'peaks' called **Media Luna** and **Puntudo**. The trail starts at Bellavista where a rough trail map is painted as a mural on the wall of the school. The round trip from Bellavista takes six to eight hours. A permit and guide are not required, but a guide may be helpful. Always take food, water and a compass or GPS.

Another worthwhile trip is to the **El Chato Tortoise Reserve**, where giant tortoises can be seen in the wild during the dry season (June to February). In the wet season the tortoises are breeding down in the arid zone. Follow the road that goes past the Santa Rosa school to 'La Reserva'. At the end of the road (about 3 km) you reach a faded wooden memorial to an Israeli tourist who got lost here. Take the trail to the right (west) for about 45 minutes. There are many confusing trails in the reserve itself; take food, water and a compass or GPS. If you have no hiking experience, horses can sometimes be hired at Santa Rosa or arrange a tour from Puerto Ayora.

Tortoises can also be seen at **Cerro Mesa** and at several private ranches, some of which have camping facilities; eg **Butterfly Ranch** ① *Hacienda Mariposa, entry US$3, camping US$25 pp including breakfast, access at Km 16, just before Santa Rosa, walk 1 km from here, make previous arrangements at Moonrise Travel.*

San Cristóbal: Puerto Baquerizo Moreno → *Phone code: 05. Population: 7200.*

Puerto Baquerizo Moreno, on San Cristóbal island, is the capital of the archipelago. Electrical energy here is provided by wind generators in the highlands, see www.eolicsa.com.ec. The town's attractive *malecón* has many shaded seats shared by tourists, residents and sea lions. The **cathedral** ① *on Av Northía y Cobos, 0900-1200, 1600-1800*, has interesting artwork combining religious and Galápagos motifs.

To the north of town, opposite **Playa Mann** (suitable for swimming), is the Galápagos National Park visitor centre or **Centro de Interpretación** ① *T252 0138, ext 123, daily 0700-1700, free.* It has excellent displays of the natural and human history of the islands including contemporary issues, recommended. A good trail goes from the Centro de Interpretación to the northeast through scrub forest to **Cerro Tijeretas**, a hill overlooking town and the ocean, 30 minutes away. From here a rougher trail continues 45 minutes to **Playa Baquerizo**. Frigatebirds nest in this area and can be observed gliding overhead; there are sea lions on the beaches below. To go back from Cerro Tijeretas, if you take the trail which follows the coast, you will end up at **Playa Punta Carola**, a popular surfing beach, too rough for swimming. To the south of Puerto Baquerizo Moreno, 30 minutes' walk past the stadium and high school (ask for directions), is **La Lobería**, a rocky shore with sea lions, Marine Iguanas, and a rough trail leading to beautiful cliffs with many birds, overlooking the sea.

Five buses a day run the 6 km inland from Puerto Baquerizo Moreno to **El Progreso**, US$0.20, 15 minutes, then it's a 2½-hour walk to **El Junco lake**, the largest body of fresh water in Galápagos. Pick-up trucks to El Progreso charge US$2, or you can hire them for touring: US$20 to El Junco (return with wait), US$40 continuing to the beaches at **Puerto Chino** on the other side of the island, past a man-made tortoise reserve. Camping is possible at Puerto Chino with a permit from the National Park, take food and drinking water. At El Junco there is a path to walk around the lake in 20 minutes. The views are lovely in clear weather but it is cool and wet in the *garúa* season, so take adequate clothing. Various small roads fan out from El Progreso and make for pleasant walking. **Jatun Sacha** (www.jatunsacha.org) has a volunteer centre on an old hacienda in the highlands beyond El Progreso, working on eradication of invasive species and a native plant nursery; US$15 taxi ride from town, take repellent.

Boats go to **Punta Pitt** in the far north of San Cristóbal where you can see all three species of booby (US$65 for a tour). Off the northwest coast is **Kicker Rock** (León Dormido), the basalt remains of a crater; many seabirds, including nazca and blue-footed boobies, can be seen around its cliffs (five-hour trip, including snorkelling, recommended, US$40).

Isabela: Puerto Villamil → *Phone code: 05. Population 2300.*

This is the largest island in the archipelago, formed by the coalesced lava flows of six volcanoes. Five are active and each has (or had) its own separate sub-species of giant tortoise. Isabela is also the island which is changing most rapidly, driven by growing land-based tourism. It remains a charming place but is at risk from uncontrolled development. Most residents live in Puerto Villamil. In the highlands, there is a cluster of farms at Santo Tomás. There are several lovely beaches right by town, but mind the strong undertow and ask locally about the best spots for swimming.

It is 8 km west to **Muro de las Lágrimas**, built by convict labour under hideous conditions. It makes a great day-hike or hire a bicycle (always take water). Short side-trails branch off the road to various attractions along the way, and a trail continues from the Muro to nearby hills with lovely views. Along the same road, 30 minutes from town, is the **Centro de Crianza**, a breeding centre for giant tortoises surrounded by lagoons with flamingos and other birds. In the opposite direction, 30 minutes east toward the *embarcadero* (pier) is **Concha de Perla Lagoon**, with a nice access trail through mangroves and a small dock from which you can go swimming with sea lions and other creatures. Tours go to **Las Tintoreras**, a set of small islets in the harbour where white-tipped reef sharks and penguins may be seen in the still crystalline water (US$25 per person). There are also boat tours to **Los Túneles** at Cabo Rosa (US$65 per person, a tricky entrance from the open sea), where fish, rays and turtles can be seen in submerged lava tunnels.

Sierra Negra Volcano has the second-largest basaltic caldera in the world, 9 km by 10 km. It is 19 km (30 minutes) by pickup truck to the park entrance (take passport and National Park entry receipt), where you start the 1½ hour hike to the crater rim at 1000 m. It is a further 1½ hours walk along bare brittle lava rock to **Volcán Chico**, with several fumaroles and more stunning views. You can camp on the crater rim but must take all supplies, including water, and obtain a permit the day before from the National Park office in Puerto Villamil. A tour including transport and lunch costs about US$50 per person. Highland tours are also available to **La Cueva de Sucre**, a large lava tube with many chambers; be sure to take a torch if visiting on your own. A bus to the highlands leaves the market in Puerto Villamil at 0700 daily, US$0.50, ask the driver for directions to the cave and return times.

Floreana: Puerto Velasco Ibarra → *Phone code: 05. Population: 160.*

Floreana is the island with the richest human history and the fewest inhabitants, most living in Puerto Velasco Ibarra. You can easily reach the island with a day-tour boat from

Puerto Ayora, but these do not leave enough time to enjoy the visit. A couple of days stay is recommended, however note that there may not always be space on boats returning to Puerto Ayora, so you must be flexible. Services are limited, one shop has basic supplies and there are a handful of places to eat and sleep, none is cheap (see Where to stay, page 588). Margaret Wittmer, one of the first settlers on Floreana, died in 2000, but you can meet her daughter and granddaughter.

La Lobería is a beautiful little peninsula (which becomes an island at high tide), 15 minutes walk from town, where sea lions, sea turtles, marine iguanas and various birds can be seen. The climate in the highlands is fresh and comfortable, good for walking and birdwatching. A *ranchera* runs up to **Asilo de La Paz**, with a natural spring and tortoise area, Monday to Saturday 0600 and 1500, returning 0700 and 1600; Sun 0700 returning 1000. Or you can walk down in three to four hours, detouring to climb **Cerro Allieri** along the way.

Post Office Bay, on the north side of Floreana, is visited by tour boats. There is a custom (since 1792) for visitors here to place unstamped letters and cards in a barrel, and deliver, free of charge, any addressed to their own destinations.

◉ Galápagos Islands listings

For hotel and restaurant price codes, and other relevant information, see pages 14-17.

● Where to stay

Santa Cruz *p583, map p583*
Puerto Ayora
Reservations are advised in high season.
$$$$ Angemeyer Waterfront Inn, by the dock at Punta Estrada, T252 6561, www. angermeyer-waterfront-inn.com. Gorgeous location overlooking the bay. Includes buffet breakfast, restaurant, very comfortable modern rooms and apartments, some with kitchenettes, a/c, attentive service.
$$$$ Silberstein, Darwin y Piqueros, T252 6277, Quito T02-225 0553, www.hotel silberstein.com. Modern and comfortable with lovely grounds, pool in tropical garden, a/c, buffet breakfast, restaurant, bar, spacious rooms and common areas, very nice.
$$$$ Sol y Mar, Darwin y Binford, T252 6281, www.hotelsolymar.com.ec. Right in town but with a priviledged location overlooking the bay. Inculdes buffet breakfast, restaurant, bar, pool, jacuzzi.
$$$ Estrella de Mar, by the water on a lane off 12 de Febrero, T252 6427. Nice quiet location with views over the bay. A/c, fan, fridge, spacious rooms, sitting area.

$$$ Jean's Home, Punta Estrada, T252 6446. Comfortably refurbished home in a lovely out-of-the-way location, a/c, family-run, English and German spoken.
$$$ Lobo de Mar, 12 de Febrero y Darwin, T252 6188, Quito T02-250 2089, www. lobodemar.com.ec. Modern building with balconies and rooftop terrace, great views over the harbour. A/c, small pool, fridge, modern and comfortable, attentive service.
$$$ Santa Fe Suites, Charles Binford entre Juan Montalvo y Las Ninfas, T252 6419, www.santafegalapagos.com.ec. Spacious modern rooms with kitchenettes (older rooms are smaller and cheaper), a/c, pool.
$$ España, Berlanga y 12 de Febrero, T252 6108, www.hotelespanagalapagos. com. Pleasant and quiet, spacious rooms, a/c (**$** with fan), small courtyard with hammocks, good value.
$$ Peregrina, Darwin e Indefatigable, T252 6323, peregrinagalapagos@yahoo.com. Away from the centre of town, a/c, nice rooms and common areas, small garden, family-run, homely atmosphere.
$ Los Amigos, Darwin y 12 de Febrero, T252 6265. Small place, basic rooms with shared bath, cold water, laundry facilities, use of kitchen for breakfast only, good value.

Highlands of Santa Cruz
$$$$ Galápagos Safari Camp, T09-9179 4259, www.galapagossafaricamp.com. Luxury resort with a central lodge and accommodation in comfortable, en suite tents. Includes breakfast and dinner, swimming pool, organizes tours and activities.
$$$$ Semilla Verde, T301-3079, www.gps.ec. Located on a 5 ha property being reforested with native plants, comfortable rooms and common areas, includes breakfast, other meals available or use of kitchen facilities, British/Ecuadorean-run, family atmosphere.

San Cristóbal *p584*
Puerto Baquerizo Moreno
$$$$ Miconia, Darwin e Isabela, T252 0608.Restaurant, a/c, small pool, large well-equipped gym, modern if somewhat small rooms, some with fridge.
$$$ Blue Marlin, Española y Northia, T252 0253, info@bluemarlingalapagos.ec. Ample modern rooms are mostly wheelchair accessible, bathtubs, a/c, pool, fridge.
$$$ Casablanca, Mellville y Darwin, T252 0392, www.casablancagalapagos.com. Large white house with lovely terrace and views of harbour. Each room is individually decorated by the owner who has an art gallery on the premises.
$$ Bellavista, Darwin y Melville, T252 0352, agat74@yahoo.com. Ample modern rooms with a/c and fridge.
$$ Casa de Nelly, Northía y Roldós, T252 0112. 3-storey building in a quiet location, bright comfortable rooms, a/c, kitchen facilities, family-run.
$$ Mar Azul, Northía y Esmeraldas, T252 0139. Nice comfortable lodgings, electric shower, a/c (cheaper with fan), fridge, kitchen facilities, pleasant. Same family runs 2 more expensive hotels nearby.
$ San Francisco, Darwin y Villamil, T252 0304. Simple rooms with private bath, cold water, fan, kitchen facilities, good value.

El Progreso
$$ Casa del Ceibo, T301 0160, Pto Baquerizo Moreno T252 0248. 2 unique rooms, one up in the branches of a huge kapok tree, the other under its roots. Private bath, hot water, ingenious design, US$1 to visit, advance booking required.

Isabela *p585*
Puerto Villamil
Many hotels have opened in recent years, more than we can list below.
$$$$ La Casa de Marita, at east end of beach, T252 9238, www.galapagosisabela.com. Tastefully chic, includes breakfast, other meals on request, a/c and fridge, very comfortable, each room is slightly different, some have balconies; **$$$** across the road away from the sea. A little gem and recommended.
$$$$-$$$ Albemarle, on the beachfront in town, T252 9489, www.hotelalbemarle.com. Attractive Mediterranean-style construction, restaurant, bright comfortable rooms with wonderful ocean views, a/c, small pool, British/Ecuadorean-run, attentive owner.
$$$ La Laguna, Los Flamencos y Los Petreles, T349 7940. Pleasant rooms with a/c, attractive balconies and common areas, jacuzzi.
$$$-$$ Caleta Iguana, Antonio Gil at west end of the beach, T301 6612, www.caletaiguana.com. Comfortable rooms with fridge and fan, terrace overlooking the ocean, nice views, popular with upmarket surfers.
$$ Casa Isabela on the Beach, on the beachfront in town, T252 9103, casitadelaplaya@hotmail.com, Quito office: Galacruises, www.islasgalapagos.travel. Pleasant house on the beach, rooms with a/c, some have balconies, nice ocean views.
$$ The Jungle, off Antonio Gil at the west edge of town, T301 6690. Nice rooms with a/c, beach views, meals on request, secluded location away from the centre.
$$ San Vicente, Cormoranes y Pinzón Artesano, T252 9140. Very popular and well organized hotel which also offers tours and kayak rentals, includes breakfast, other meals

on request or use of cooking facilities, a/c, jacuzzi, rooms a bit small but nice, family-run.
$ Hostal Villamil, 10 de Marzo y Antonio Gil, T252 9180. A/c, kitchen and laundry facilities, small patio with hammocks, family-run and very friendly, good value. Recommended.

Highlands of Isabela
$$ Campo Duro, T09-8545 3045, refugiodetortugasgigantes@hotmail.com. Camping (tents provided), includes breakfast and dinner, nice ample grounds, giant tortoises may be seen (US$2 to visit), friendly owner.

Floreana: Puerto Velasco Ibarra p585
$$$$ Lava Lodge, book through Tropic Journeys in Nature, www.destination ecuador.com. Wooden cabins on the beach a short distance outside town, family-owned, full board, kayak, snorkel and SUP equipment, guided tours to wildlife and historic sites, popular with groups.
$$$ Hostal Santa María, opposite the school, T252 4904. Nice modern rooms with private bath, hot water, fan, fridge, screened windows, friendly owner Sr Claudio Cruz.
$$$ Hotel Wittmer, right on Black Beach, T252 4873. Lovely location with beautiful sunsets, simple comfortable rooms, electric shower, fan, very good meals available, family-run, German spoken, reservations required.
$$ Sra Lelia Cruz, opposite the school, T252 4901. 2 rooms for rent in a private home, shared bath, hot water, kitchen, meals also available, good value (for Floreana).

❶ Restaurants

Puerto Ayora p583, map p583
$$$ Angermeyer Point, at Punta Estrada across the bay, take a water-taxi, T252 7007. Daily 1800-2230. Former home of Galápagos pioneer and artist Carl Angermeyer, with his works on display. Gorgeous setting over the water (take insect repellent). Excellent, innovative and varied menu, attentive service. Reservations advised. Highly recommended.

$$$ Il Giardino, Charles Darwin y Charles Binford, T252 6627. Open 0800-2230, closed Tue. Very good international food, service and atmosphere, excellent ice cream, very popular.
$$$ Isla Grill, Charles Darwin y Tomás de Berlanga, T252 4461. Tue-Sun 1200-2200. Upmarket grill, seafood and pizza.
$$$ La Dolce Italia, Charles Darwin y 12 de Febrero. Daily 1100-1500, 1800-2200. Italian and seafood, wine list, a/c, pleasant atmosphere, attentive owner.
$$$-$$ La Garrapata, Charles Darwin between 12 de Febrero and Tomás de Berlanga. Mon-Sat 0900-2200. Good food, attractive setting and nice music.
$$ Kiosks, along Charles Binford between Padre Herrera and Rodríguez Lara. Many kiosks serving local fare, including a variety of seafood, outdoor seating, lively informal atmosphere, busy at night.
$$ Rincón del Alma, Charles Darwin e Islas Plaza, across from navy base. Mon-Sat 0830-2100. Traditional old place serving *ceviche* and seafood, also economical set lunch.
$ El Descanso del Guía, Charles Darwin y Los Colonos. Daily 0645-1945. Good set meals, very popular with locals.

Puerto Baquerizo Moreno p584
$$$ Miramar, upstairs at Malecón y Cobos. Daily 1800-2300. Seafood and international dishes, cocktails, lovely ocean views, great sunsets, slow service.
$$$-$$ La Playa, Av de la Armada Nacional, by the navy base. Daily 0930-2330. Varied menu, fish and seafood.
$$$-$$ Rosita, Ignacio de Hernández y General Villamil. Daily 0930-1430, 1700-2230. Old-time yachtie hangout, good food, large portions, nice atmosphere, à la carte and economical set meals. Recommended.
$$$-$$ Sheanovi, Ignacio de Hernández y General Villamil. Daily 1700-2300. Small place with varied menu, nice views from 2nd floor terrace.

$$ Descanso del Marinero, Northia y
Española. Open 0800-2100, closed Tue.
Ceviches and seafood, pleasant outdoor seating.
$ Several simple places serving economical
set meals on Northia between Española and
12 de Febrero.
Mockingbird Café, Española y Hernández.
Mon-Sat 0730-2330, Sun from 0930. Fruit
juices, brownies, snacks, internet.

Isabela *p585*
Puerto Villamil
$$$-$$ There are various outdoor
restaurants around the plaza, all with similar
menus featuring seafood, **Cesar's** and **Los
Delfines** are reported good.
$ Tropical, Las Fragatas ½ block from Plaza.
Daily 1200-1400, 1800-1930. Simple set
lunch, grill at night, popular with locals.

Floreana: Puerto Velasco Ibarra *p585*
Meals available at hotels or from a couple of
restaurants catering to tour groups, **$$$-$$**,
all require advance notice.
$ The Devil's Crown, 100 m from the dock
on the road to the highlands. Set lunch and
dinner on most days, ask in advance.

O Shopping

Most items can be purchased on the islands
but cost more than in mainland Ecuador.
Do not buy anything made of black coral
as it is an endangered species.

Puerto Ayora *p583, map p583*
There is an attractive little **Mercado Artesanal**
(craft market) at Charles Darwin y Tomás de
Berlanga. **Proinsular**, opposite the pier, is the
largest and best stocked supermarket.

Puerto Baquerizo Moreno *p584*
Galamarket, Isabela y Juan José Flores,
is a modern well-stocked supermarket.

O What to do

Puerto Ayora *p583, map p583*
Cycling Mountain bikes can be hired
from travel agencies in town. Prices and
quality vary.
Diving Only specialized diving boats
are allowed to do diving tours. It is not
possible to dive as part of a standard live-
aboard cruise nor are dive boats allowed
to call at the usual land visitor sites. The
following vessels offer live-aboard diving
tours: *Darwin Buddy* and *Wolf Buddy*, www.
buddydive-galapagos.com; *Deep Blue*,
www.deepbluegalapagosdiving.com;
Galápagos Agressor I and II, www.aggressor.
com; *Galápagos Sky*, www.ecoventura.
com; *Humboldt Explorer*, www.galasam.
com. Cruises cost US$4000-5000 for 7 days.
National Park rules prohibit collecting
samples or souvenirs, spear-fishing, touching
animals, or other environmental disruptions.
Experienced dive guides can help visitors
have the most spectacular opportunities
to enjoy the wildlife. There are several
diving agencies in Puerto Ayora, Baquerizo
Moreno and Villamil (see Tour operators,
below) offering courses, equipment rental,
and dives; prices and quality vary. On
offer in Puerto Ayora are diving day trips
(2 dives, US$175-250) and daily tours for
up to 1 week in the central islands. There
is a hyperbaric chamber in Puerto Ayora at
Centro Médico Integral, Marchena y Hanny,
T252 4576, www.sssnetwork.com. Check
if your dive operator is affiliated with this
facility or arrange your own insurance from
home. To avoid the risk of decompression
sickness, divers are advised to stay an extra
day on the islands after their last dive before
flying to the mainland, especially to Quito at
2840 m above sea level.
Dive Center Silberstein, opposite Hotel
Silberstein, T252 6028, www.divingalapagos.
com. Nice comfortable boat for up to
8 guests, English-speaking guides, good
service, dive courses and trips for all levels
of experience.

Galápagos Sub-Aqua, Av Charles Darwin e Isla Floreana, T252 6350, Guayaquil T04-230 5514, www.galapagos-sub-aqua.com. Instructor Fernando Zambrano offers full certificate courses up to PADI divemaster level. Repeatedly recommended.

Nautidiving, Av Charles Darwin, T252 7004, www.nautidiving.com. Offers day trips to central islands as well as longer trips.

Scuba Iguana, Charles Darwin near the research station, T252 6497, www.scuba iguana.com. Matías Espinoza runs this long-time reliable and recommended dive operator. Courses up to PADI divemaster.

Horse riding For riding at ranches in the highlands, enquire at Moonrise Travel.

Snorkelling Masks, snorkels and fins can be rented from travel agencies and dive shops, US$5 a day, deposit required. Closest place to snorkel is by the beach near the Darwin Station.

Surfing There is surfing at Tortuga Bay and at other more distant beaches accessed by boat. There is better surfing near Puerto Baquerizo Moreno on San Cristóbal. The Lonesome George agency rents surfboards, see below.

Tour operators
Avoid touts offering cheap tours at the airport or in the street. Also be wary of agencies who specialize in cut-rate cruises.
Galacruises Expeditions, see page 442.
Galasam, see pages 442, 531 and 565.
Happy Gringo, see page 442.
Lonesome George, Av Baltra y Enrique Fuentes, T252 6245, lonesomegrg@yahoo.com. Run by Victor Vaca. Sells tours and rents: bicycles (US$3 per hr), surf-boards (US$30 per day) snorkelling equipment and motorcycles.
Moonrise Travel, Av Charles Darwin y Charles Binford, T252 6348, www.galapagos moonrise.com. Last-minute cruise bookings, day-tours to different islands, bay tours, airline reservations, run guesthouse in Punta Estrada. Owner Jenny Devine is knowledgeable.

Zenith Travel, JL Mera N24-234 y Cordero, Quito, T252 9993, www.zenithecuador.com. Economical Galápagos cruises, various land tours in Ecuador and Peru. All-gay Galápagos cruises available. Multilingual service, knowledgeable helpful staff, good value.

Puerto Baquerizo Moreno *p584*
Cycling Hire bikes from travel agencies, US$20 per day.
Diving There are several dive sites around San Cristóbal, most popular being Kicker Rock, Roca Ballena and Punta Pitt, full day about US$200, see Tour operators, below.
Kayaking Rentals US$10 per hr; from Islander's Store, Av J Roldós, above cargo pier, T252 0348; and **Galápagos Eco Expedition**, Av de la Armada, next to La Playa restaurant.
Surfing There is good surfing in San Cristóbal, the best season is Dec-Mar. Punta Carola near town is the closest surfing beach; other spots are Canon and Tongo Reef, past the navy base. There is a championship during the local fiesta, the 2nd week of Feb.

Tour operators
Chalo Tours, Darwin y Villamil, T252 0953, chalotours@hotmail.com. Specializes in diving and snorkelling.
Sharksky, Darwin y Española, T252 1188, www.sharksky.com. Highlands, snorkelling, island-hopping, last-minute cruise bookings and gear rental. Also has an office on Isabela. Swiss/Ecuadorean-run, English, German and French spoken, helpful.
Wreck Bay Dive Center, Darwin y Wolf, T252 1663, www.wreckbay.com. Reported friendly and respectful of the environment.

Puerto Villamil *p585*
Hotels also arrange tours. Kayak rentals at **Hotel San Vicente**.
Carapachudo Tours, Escalecias y Tero Real, T252 9451. Mountain biking downhill from Sierra Negra, full day including lunch, US$42. Also rentals: good bikes US$3 per hr, US$20

per day; snorkelling gear US$5 per day; surf boards US$4 per hr.
Galápagos Dive Center, 16 de Marzo y Tero Real, T301 6570. Dive trips, diving gear sale and rental.
Isabela Dive Center, Escalecias y Alberto Gil, T252 9418, www.isabeladivecenter.com.ec. Diving, land and boat tours.

⊖ Transport

Puerto Ayora *p583, map p583*
Sea *Fibras* (fibreglass speedboats) depart daily from the pier near the Proinsular supermarket for the following islands: **San Cristóbal** at 1400; **Isabela** at 0730 and 1400; **Floreana** at 0700; all fares US$30-35.
Pickup truck taxis These may be hired for transport throughout town, US$1. A *ranchera* runs up to the highlands from the **Tropidurus** store, Av Baltra y Jaime Roldóss, 2 blocks past the market: to **Bellavista** US$0.25, 10 mins; **Santa Rosa** US$1, 20 mins. For airport transfers, see page 577.
Water taxis (*taxis acuáticos*) From the pier to Punta Estrada or anchored boats, US$0.60 during the day, US$1 at night.

❶ Directory

Puerto Ayora *p583, map p583*
Airline offices Aerogal, Rodríguez Lara y San Cristóbal, T252 6798. **Emetebe**, at the airport, T252 4755. **LAN**, Av Charles Darwin e Islas Plaza, T1-800-101075. **TAME**, Av Charles Darwin y 12 de Febrero, T252 6527.
Banks Banco del Pacífico, Av Charles Darwin y Charles Binford, T252 6282; also Av Baltra y 10 de Marzo; Mon-Fri 0800-1530, Sat 0930-1230. ATM, cash advances (Mon-Fri) and TCs (US$5 commission per transaction, up to US$200 a day). Also ATMs next to **Proinsular** supermarket; at **Banco Pichincha**, Av Baltra on the way to Highlands and several others. **Medical services** Hospitals: there is a hospital on Av Baltra for first aid and basic care. For anything serious, locals usually fly to the mainland.

Yacht agents Galápagos Ocean Services (Peter Schiess), Charles Darwin next to Garrapata restaurant, T09-9477 0804, www.gos.ec. **Naugala Yacht Services** (Jhonny Romero), T252 7403, www.naugala.com.

Puerto Baquerizo Moreno *p584*
Airline offices Aerogal, at the airport, T252 1118. **Emetebe**, at the airport, T252 0615. **TAME**, Charles Darwin y Manuel J Cobos, T252 1351. **Banks** Banco del Pacífico, Melville y Hernández, same hours and services as in Puerto Ayora. C̶____ ̶___ Wolf y Charles Darwin, for ATM. ̶___ **services** There is a hospital providing ̶___ basic medical care.

Puerto Villamil *p585*
Airline offices Emetebe, Antonio Gil y Las Fragatas, T252 9155. **Banks** There are no banks or ATMs, bring US$ cash. **MoneyGram**, in La Isla supermarket, Tero Real y Escalecias, for international funds transfer.

Contents

Background

Pre-independence history

Earliest settlement

It used to be generally accepted that the earliest settlers in South America were related to people who had crossed the Bering Straits from Asia and drifted through the Americas from about 13,000 years ago (the Clovis model). In recent years, however, a growing number of discoveries from earlier dates in North and South America have raised doubts about this. In South America these include a coastal site in southern Chile called Monte Verde from 14,800 years ago, stone tools from the Serra da Capivara in northeastern Brazil from some 22,000 years ago and paleontological evidence from Uruguay from earlier still. If nothing else, these finds question the theory of a single migration into South America from the north. Other early evidence of human presence has been found at various sites: in the Central Andes (with a radiocarbon date between 12,000 and 9000 BC), northern Venezuela (11,000 BC), southeast Brazil, south-central Chile and Argentine Patagonia (from at least 10,000 BC). After the Pleistocene Ice Age, 8000-7000 BC, rising sea levels and climatic changes introduced new conditions as many mammal species became extinct and coastlands were drowned. A wide range of crops was brought into cultivation and camelids and guinea pigs were domesticated. It seems that people lived nomadically in small groups, mainly hunting and gathering but also cultivating some plants seasonally, until villages with effective agriculture began to appear, it was originally thought, between 2500-1500 BC. The earliest ceramic-making in the western hemisphere was thought to have come from what is now Colombia and Ecuador, around 4000 BC, but fragments of painted pottery were found near Santarém, Brazil, in 1991 with dates of 6000-5000 BC.

On the coast of central Peru settled life developed rapidly. The abundant wealth of marine life produced by the Humboldt Current, especially north of today's Lima, boosted population growth and a shift from nomadic to settled farming in this area. The introduction of sophisticated irrigation systems encouraged higher productivity and population growth, leading to organized group labour which could be devoted to building and making textiles from cotton. Evidence from Caral, Aspero and other sites in the Huaura, Supe, Pativilca and Fortaleza river valleys prove that this process happened much earlier than previously imagined. Caral dates from 2627 BC (other sites have older dates) and is a monumental construction. It flourished for some 500 years and appears to have been a city with primarily a religious, rather than a warlike purpose. The archaeological finds point to Caral and neighbouring sites predating the development of pottery in this region, but artefacts show cultural links with other communities, even as far as the Amazon. Almost contemporaneous with Caral was Ventarrón, a city in Lambayeque, northern Peru, with a temple containing the oldest murals discovered in the Americas. In the central Andes near Huánuco, also in what is now Peru, more advanced architecture was being built at Kotosh. There is evidence of a pre-ceramic culture here, too, but some of the earliest pottery from the site's later phases was found, showing signs of influence from southern Ecuador and the tropical lowlands. Radiocarbon dates of some Kotosh remains are from 1850 BC and Japanese archaeological excavations there in the 1960s revealed a temple with ornamental niches and friezes.

Andean and Pacific coastal civilizations

Chavín and Sechín For the next 1000 years or so up to c900 BC, communities grew and spread inland from the north coast and south along the north highlands. Farmers still lived in simple adobe or rough stone houses but built increasingly large and complex ceremonial centres. As farming became more productive and pottery more advanced, commerce grew and states began to develop throughout central and north-central Peru, with the associated signs of social structure and hierarchies.

Around 900 BC a new era was marked by the rise of two important centres; Chavín de Huántar in the central Andes and Sechín Alto, inland from Casma on the north coast, both now in Peru. The chief importance of Chavín de Huántar was not so much in its highly advanced architecture as in the influence of its cult, coupled with the artistic style of its ceramics and other artefacts. The founders of Chavín may have originated in the tropical lowlands, as some of its carved monoliths show representations of monkeys and felines.

The Chavín cult This was paralleled by the great advances made in this period in textile production and in some of the earliest examples of metallurgy. The origins of metallurgy have been attributed to some gold, silver and copper ornaments found in graves in Chongoyape, near Chiclayo, which show Chavín-style features. But earlier evidence has been discovered at Kuntur Wasi (some 120 km east of the coast at Pacasmayo) where 4000-year old gold has been found, and in the Andahuaylas region, dating from 1800-900 BC. The religious symbolism of gold and other precious metals and stones is thought to have been an inspiration behind some of the beautiful artefacts found in the central Andean area.

The cultural brilliance of Chavín de Huántar was complemented by its contemporary, Sechín, with which it may have combined forces, Sechín being the military power that spread the cultural word of Chavín. The Chavín hegemony broke up around 500 BC, soon after which the Nazca culture began to bloom in southern Peru. This period, up to about AD 500, was a time of great social and cultural development. Sizable towns of 5000-10,000 inhabitants grew on the south coast, populated by artisans, merchants and government and religious officials.

Paracas-Nazca Nazca origins are traced back to about the second century BC, to the Paracas Cavernas and Necropolis, on the coast in the national park near Pisco in Peru. The extreme dryness of the desert here has preserved remarkably the textiles and ceramics in the mummies' tombs excavated. The technical quality and stylistic variety in weaving and pottery rank them among the world's best, and many of the finest examples can be seen in the museums of Lima. The famous Nazca Lines are a feature of the region. Straight lines, abstract designs and outlines of animals are scratched in the dark desert surface forming a lighter contrast that can be seen clearly from the air. There are many theories of how and why the lines were made but no definitive explanation has yet been able to establish their place in South American history. There are similarities between the style of some of the line patterns and that of the pottery and textiles of the same period. Alpaca hair found in Nazca textiles, however, indicates that there must have been strong trade links with highland people.

Moche culture Nazca's contemporaries on the north coast were the militaristic Moche who, from about AD 100-800, built up an empire whose traces stretch from Piura in the north to Huarmey, in the south. The Moche built their capital outside present day Trujillo. The huge pyramid temples of the Huaca del Sol and Huaca de la Luna mark the remains of this city. Moche roads and system of way stations are thought to have been an early inspiration for the Inca network. The Moche increased the coastal population with intensive irrigation projects. Skilful engineering works were carried out, such as the La Cumbre canal, still in use today, and the Ascope aqueduct, both on the Chicama River. The Moche's greatest achievement, however, was its artistic genius. Exquisite ornaments in gold, silver and precious stones were made by its craftsmen. Moche pottery progressed through five stylistic periods, most notable for the stunningly lifelike portrait vases. A wide variety of everyday scenes were created in naturalistic ceramics, telling us more about Moche life than is known about other earlier cultures. Spectacular Moche tombs, discovered at Sipán since 1987, have included semi-precious stones brought from Chile and Argentina, and seashells from Ecuador. The Moche were great navigators.

The cause of the collapse of the Moche Empire around AD 600-700 is unknown, but it may have been started by a 30-year drought at the end of the sixth century, followed by one of the periodic El Niño flash floods (identified by meteorologists from ice thickness in the Andes) and finished by the encroaching forces of the Huari Empire. The decline of the Moche signalled a general tipping of the balance of power in Peru from the north coast to the south sierra.

Huari-Tiwanaku The ascendant Huari-Tiwanaku movement, from AD 600-1000, combined the religious cult of the Tiwanaku site in the Titicaca basin, with the military dynamism of the Huari, based in the central highlands. The two cultures developed independently but they are generally thought to have merged compatibly. Up until their own demise around AD 1440, the Huari-Tiwanaku had spread their empire and influence across much of south Peru, north Bolivia and Argentina. They made considerable gains in art and technology, building roads, terraces and irrigation canals across the country. The Huari-Tiwanaku ran their empire with efficient labour and administrative systems that were later adopted by the Incas. Labour tribute for state projects practised by the Moche were further developed. But the empire could not contain regional kingdoms who began to fight for land and power. As control broke down, rivalry and coalitions emerged, the system collapsed and the scene was set for the rise of the Incas.

Chachapoyas and Chimú cultures After the decline of the Huari Empire, the unity that had been imposed on the Andes was broken. A new stage of autonomous regional or local political organizations began. Among the cultures corresponding to this period were the Chachapoyas in northern highlands and the Chimú. The Chachapoyas people were not so much an empire as a loose-knit 'confederation of ethnic groups with no recognized capital' (Morgan Davis 'Chachapoyas: The Cloud People', Ontario, 1988). But the culture did develop into an advanced society with great skill in road and monument building. Their fortress at Kuélap was known as the most impregnable in the Peruvian Andes. The Chimú culture had two centres. To the north was Lambayeque, near Chiclayo, while to the south, in the Moche Valley near present-day Trujillo, was the great adobe walled city of Chan Chán. Covering 20 sq km, this was the largest pre-Hispanic Peruvian city. Chimú has been classified as a despotic state that based its power on wars of conquest. Rigid social stratification existed and power rested in the hands of the great lord *Siquic* and the lord *Alaec*. These lords were followed in social scale by a group of urban couriers who enjoyed a certain degree of economic power. At the bottom were the peasants and slaves. In 1450, the Chimú kingdom was conquered by the Inca Túpac Yupanqui, the son and heir of the Inca ruler Pachacútec.

Cultures of the northern Andes What is today Ecuador was a densely populated region with a variety of peoples. One of the most important of these was the **Valdivia culture** (3500-1500 BC) on the coast, from which remains of buildings and earthenware figures have been found. A rich mosaic of cultures developed in the period 500 BC to AD 500, after which integration of groups occurred. In the mid-15th century, the relentless expansion of the Inca Empire reached Ecuador. The **Cañaris** resisted until 1470 and the Quitu/Caras were defeated in 1492. Further north, most of the peoples who occupied Colombia were primitive hunters or nomad agriculturists, but one part of the country, the high basins of the Eastern Cordillera, was densely occupied by **Chibcha Indians** who had become sedentary farmers. Their staple foods were maize and the potato, and they had no domestic animal save the dog; the use they could make of the land was therefore limited. Other cultures present in Colombia in the pre-Columbian era were the **Tayrona, Quimbaya, Sinú** and **Calima**. Exhibits of theirs and the Chibcha (Muisca) Indians' goldwork can be seen at the Gold Museum in Bogotá and other cities.

Southern Andes Although there was some influence in southern Bolivia, northern Chile and northern Argentina from cultures such as Tiwanaku, most of the southern Andes was an area of autonomous peoples, probably living in fortified settlements by the time the Incas arrived in the mid-15th century. The conquerors from Peru moved south to the Río Maule in Chile where they encountered the fierce **Mapuches** (Araucanians) who halted their advance.

Amazon Basin Archaeological evidence from the Amazon Basin and Brazil is more scanty than from the Andes or Pacific because the materials used for house building, clothing and decoration were perishable and did not survive the warm, humid conditions of the jungle. Ceramics have been found on Marajó island at the mouth of the Amazon while on the coast much evidence comes from huge shell mounds, called *sambaquis*. Theories about structured societies and their large populations are being revised as aerial photography and forest clearance in the Upper Amazon and Xingu regions of Brazil reveal huge interconnected earthworks, canals, roads and other indicators of city-building. Moreover, falling river levels have uncovered rock carvings estimated between 3000 and 7000 years old near Manaus. The Incas made few inroads into the Amazon so it was the arrival of the Portuguese in 1500 which initiated the greatest change on the Atlantic side of the continent.

The Inca Dynasty
The origins of the Inca Dynasty are shrouded in mythology and shaky evidence. The best known story reported by the Spanish chroniclers talks about Manco Cápac and his sister rising out of Lake Titicaca, created by the sun as divine founders of a chosen race. This was in AD c1200. Over the next 300 years the small tribe grew to supremacy as leaders of the largest empire ever known in the Americas, divided into the four quarters of Tawantinsuyo, all radiating out from Cuzco: Chinchaysuyo, north and northwest; Cuntisuyo, south and west; Collasuyo, south and east; Antisuyo, east.

At its peak, just before the Spanish Conquest, the Inca Empire stretched from the Río Maule in central Chile, north to the present Ecuador-Colombia border, contained most of Ecuador, Peru, west Bolivia, north Chile and northwest Argentina. The area was roughly equivalent to France, Belgium, Holland, Luxembourg, Italy and Switzerland combined, 980,000 sq km. For a brief description of **Inca Society**, see box, page 204. The first Inca ruler, Manco Cápac, moved to the fertile Cuzco region, and established Cuzco as his capital. Successive generations of rulers were fully occupied with local conquests of rivals, such as the Colla and Lupaca to the south, and the Chanca to the northwest. At the end of Inca Viracocha's reign the hated Chanca were finally defeated, largely thanks to the heroism of one of his sons, Pachacútec (Pachacuti Inca Yupanqui), who was subsequently crowned as the new ruler.

From the start of Pachacútec's own reign in 1438, imperial expansion grew in earnest. With the help of his son and heir, Topa Inca, territory was conquered from the Titicaca basin south into Chile, and all the north and central coast down to the Lurín Valley. In 1460-71, the Incas also laid siege to the Chimú. Typical of the Inca method of government, some of the Chimú skills were assimilated into their own political and administrative system, and some Chimú nobles were even given positions in Cuzco.

Perhaps the pivotal event in Inca history came in 1527 with the death of the ruler, Huayna Cápac. Civil war broke out in the confusion over his rightful successor. One of his legitimate sons, Huáscar, ruled the southern part of the empire from Cuzco. Atahualpa, Huáscar's half-brother, governed Quito, the capital of Chinchaysuyo. In 1532, soon after Atahualpa had won the civil war, Francisco Pizarro arrived in Tumbes with 167 *conquistadores*, a third of them on horseback. Atahualpa's army was marching south, probably for the first time, when he clashed with Pizarro at Cajamarca. **Francisco Pizarro**'s only chance against the formidable imperial army he encountered at Cajamarca was a bold stroke. He drew Atahualpa into an ambush, slaughtered his guards and many of his troops, promised him liberty if a certain room were filled with treasure, and finally killed him on the pretext that an Inca army was on its way to free him. Pushing on to Cuzco, he was at first hailed as the executioner of a traitor: Atahualpa had ordered the death of Huáscar in 1533, while himself captive of Pizarro, and his victorious generals were bringing the defeated Huáscar to see his half-brother. Panic followed when the *conquistadores* set about sacking the city, and they fought off with difficulty an attempt by Manco Inca to recapture Cuzco in 1536.

The Spanish conquest

Pizarro's arrival in Peru had been preceded by Columbus' landfall on the Paria Peninsula (Venezuela) on 5 August 1498 and Spanish reconnaissance of the Pacific coast in 1522. Permanent Spanish settlement was established at Santa Marta (Colombia) in 1525 and Cartagena was founded in 1533. Gonzalo Jiménez de Quesada conquered the Chibcha kingdom and founded Bogotá in 1538. Pizarro's lieutenant, Sebastián de Belalcázar, was sent north through Ecuador; he captured Quito with Diego de Almagro in 1534. Gonzalo Pizarro, Francisco's brother, took over control of Quito in 1538 and, during his exploration of the Amazon lowlands, he sent Francisco de Orellana to prospect downriver. Orellana did not return, but drifted down the Amazon, finally reaching the river's mouth in 1542, the first European to cross the continent in this way. Belalcázar pushed north, founding Pasto, Cali and Popayán (Colombia) in 1536, arriving in Bogotá in 1538. Meanwhile, wishing to secure his communications with Spain, Pizarro founded Lima, near the ocean, as his capital in 1535. The same year Diego de Almagro set out to conquer Chile. Unsuccessful, he returned to Peru, quarrelled with Pizarro, and in 1538 fought a pitched battle with Pizarro's men at the Salt Pits, near Cuzco. He was defeated and put to death. Pizarro, who had not been at the battle, was assassinated in his palace in Lima by Almagro's son three years later. In 1541, Pedro de Valdivia founded Santiago de Chile after a renewed attempt to conquer Chile. Like the Incas before them, the Spaniards were unable to master the Mapuches; Valdivia was killed in 1553 and a defensive barrier along the Río Biobío had to be built in order to protect the colony.

Since 1516 European seafarers had visited the Río de la Plata, first Juan de Solís, then Sebastian Cabot and his rival Diego García in 1527. An expedition led by Pedro de Mendoza founded Buenos Aires in 1536, but it was abandoned in 1541. Mendoza sent Juan de Ayolas up the Río Paraná to reach Peru from the east. It is not known for certain what happened to Ayolas, but his lieutenant Domingo Martínez de Irala founded Asunción on the Paraguay in 1537. This was the base from which the Spaniards relaunched their conquest of the Río de la Plata and Buenos Aires was refounded in 1580.

Treasure hunt As Spanish colonization built itself around new cities, the *conquistadores* set about finding the wealth which had lured them to South America in the first place. The great prize came in 1545 when the hill of silver at Potosí (Bolivia) was discovered. Other mining centres grew up and the trade routes to supply them and carry out the riches were established. The Spanish crown soon imposed political and administrative jurisdiction over its new empire, replacing the power of the *conquistadores* with that of governors and bureaucrats. The Viceroyalty of Peru became the major outlet for the wealth of the Americas, but each succeeding representative of the Kingdom of Spain was faced with the twofold threat of subduing the Inca successor state of Vilcabamba, north of Cuzco, and unifying the fierce Spanish factions. Francisco de Toledo (appointed 1568) solved both problems during his 14 years in office: Vilcabamba was crushed in 1572 and the last reigning Inca, Túpac Amaru, put to death. For the next 200 years the Viceroys closely followed Toledo's system, if not his methods. The Major Government – the Viceroy, the *Audiencia* (High Court), and *corregidores* (administrators) – ruled through the Minor Government – Indian chiefs put in charge of large groups of natives: a rough approximation to the original Inca system.

Towards independence
The Indians of Peru rose in 1780, under the leadership of an Inca noble who called himself Túpac Amaru II. He and many of his lieutenants were captured and put to death under torture at Cuzco. Another Indian leader in revolt suffered the same fate in 1814, but this last flare-up had the sympathy of many of the locally born Spanish, who resented their status: inferior to the Spaniards born in Spain, the refusal to give them any but the lowest offices, the high taxation imposed by the home government, and the severe restrictions upon trade with any country but Spain. This was a complaint common to all parts of the Spanish empire and it fostered a twin-pronged independence movement. Given impetus by Napoleon's invasion of Spain in 1808, Simón Bolívar, El Libertador, led a revolution in the north and José de San Martín, with his Army of the Andes, led an uprising through Argentina and Chile. Both converged on Peru.

Bolívar, born in Venezuela in 1783, was involved in the early struggle to free the region from Spanish rule. In 1811 Venezuela declared itself an independent republic, only to be defeated by Spain in 1812. Bolívar led a new revolt in 1813, which was crushed in 1815. He went into exile in Jamaica and Haiti, to return in 1816 with a new army which, in a bold move, he led over the Andes from Venezuela to liberate Nueva Granada (as Colombia was called) at the Battle of Boyacá in 1819. He proclaimed a new republic, Gran Colombia, taking in Colombia, Venezuela and Ecuador. Venezuela was freed at the Battle of Carabobo in 1821.

San Martín's Argentine troops, convoyed from Chile under the protection of the English admiral, Lord Cochrane, landed in southern Peru on 7 September 1820. San Martín proclaimed Peruvian independence at Lima on 28 July 1821, though most of the country was still in the hands of the Viceroy, José de La Serna. Bolívar sent Antonio José de Sucre to

Ecuador where, on 24 May 1822, he gained a victory over La Serna at Pichincha. San Martín, after a meeting with Bolívar at Guayaquil, left for Argentina and a self-imposed exile in France, while Bolívar and Sucre completed the conquest of Peru by defeating La Serna at the battle of Junín (6 August 1824) and the decisive battle of Ayacucho (9 December 1824). For over a year there was a last stand in the Real Felipe fortress at Callao by the Spanish troops under General Rodil before they capitulated on 22 January 1826. Bolívar was invited to stay in Peru, but in 1826 he left for Colombia where he tried to hold Gran Colombia together as a single state. He failed as internal divisions and political ambitions pulled the three new republics apart. While heading for exile, Bolívar died in 1830.

Post-independence history

Peru

After independence
Important events following the ejection of the Spaniards were a temporary confederation between Peru and Bolivia in the 1830s; the Peruvian-Spanish War (1866); and the War of the Pacific (1879-1883), in which Peru and Bolivia were defeated by Chile and Peru lost its southern territory. The 19th and early 20th centuries were dominated by the traditional elites, with landowners holding great power over their workers. Political parties were slow to develop until the 1920s, when socialist thinkers Juan Carlos Mariátegui and Víctor Raúl Haya de la Torre began to call for change. Haya de la Torre formed the Alianza Popular Revolucionaria Americana (APRA), but in the 1930s and 40s he and his party were under threat from the military and the elite.

To the Shining Path
A reformist military Junta took over control of the country in October 1968. Under its first leader, Gen Juan Velasco Alvarado, the Junta instituted a series of measures to raise the personal status and standard of living of the workers and the rural Indians, by land reform, worker participation in industrial management and ownership, and nationalization of basic industries, exhibiting an ideology perhaps best described as 'military socialism'. In view of his failing health Gen Velasco was replaced in 1975 by Gen Francisco Morales Bermúdez and policy (because of a mounting economic crisis and the consequent need to seek financial aid from abroad) swung to the Right. Presidential and congressional elections were held on 18 May 1980, and Fernando Belaúnde Terry was elected President for the second time. His term was marked by growing economic problems and the appearance of the Maoist terrorist movement Sendero Luminoso (Shining Path).

Initially conceived in the University of Ayacucho, the movement gained most support for its goal of overthrowing the whole system of Lima-based government from highland Indians and migrants to urban shanty towns. The activities of Sendero Luminoso and another terrorist group, Túpac Amaru (MRTA), frequently disrupted transport and electricity supplies, although their strategies had to be reconsidered after the arrest of both their leaders in 1992. Víctor Polay of MRTA was arrested in June and Abimael Guzmán of Sendero Luminoso was captured in September; he was sentenced to life imprisonment (although the sentence had to be reviewed in 2003 under legal reforms). Although Sendero did not capitulate, many of its members in 1994-1995 took advantage of the Law of Repentance, which guaranteed lighter sentences in return for surrender, and freedom in exchange for valuable information. Meanwhile, Túpac Amaru was thought to have ceased operations (see below).

The Fujimori years

The April 1985 elections were won by the APRA party leader Alán García Pérez. During his populist, left-wing presidency disastrous economic policies caused increasing poverty and civil instability. In presidential elections held over two rounds in 1990, Alberto Fujimori of the Cambio 90 movement defeated the novelist Mario Vargas Llosa, who belonged to the Fredemo (Democratic Front) coalition. Fujimori, without an established political network behind him, failed to win a majority in either the senate or the lower house. Undeterred, and with massive popular support, President Fujimori dissolved congress and suspended the constitution on 5 April 1992, declaring that he needed a freer hand to introduce free-market reforms, combat terrorism and drug trafficking, and root out corruption.

Elections to a new, 80-member Democratic Constituent Congress (CCD) in November 1992 and municipal elections in February 1993 showed that voters still had scant regard for mainstream political groups. A new constitution drawn up by the CCD was approved by a narrow majority of the electorate in October 1993. Among the new articles were the immediate re-election of the president and, as expected, Fujimori stood for re-election on 9 April 1995. He beat his independent opponent, the former UN General Secretary, Javier Pérez de Cuéllar, by a resounding margin. The coalition that supported him also won a majority in Congress.

The government's success in most economic areas did not accelerate the distribution of foreign funds for social projects. Furthermore, rising unemployment and the austerity imposed by economic policy continued to cause hardship for many. Dramatic events on 17 December 1996 thrust several of these issues into sharper focus. 14 Túpac Amaru terrorist infiltrated a reception at the Japanese Embassy in Lima, taking 490 hostages and demanding the release of their imprisoned colleagues and new measures to raise living standards. Most of the hostages were released and negotiations were pursued during a stalemate that lasted until 22 April 1997. The president took sole responsibility for the successful, but risky assault which freed all the hostages (one died of heart failure) and killed all the terrorists. By not yielding to Túpac Amaru, Fujimori regained much popularity. But this masked the fact that no concrete steps had been taken to ease poverty. It also deflected attention from Fujimori's plans to stand for a third term following his unpopular manipulation of the law to persuade Congress that the new constitution did not apply to his first period in office. As his opponents insisted that Fujimori should not stand, the popularity of Alejandro Toledo, a centrist and former World Bank official of humble origins, surged to such an extent that he and Fujimori were neck-and-neck in the first poll. Toledo and his supporters claimed that Fujimori's slim majority was the result of fraud, a view echoed in the pressure put on the president, by the US government among others, to allow a second ballot. A run-off election was set for 28 May 2000, but all but the authorities pressed for a delay, saying that the electoral system was unprepared and flawed. Toledo boycotted the election and Fujimori was returned unopposed, but with minimal approval. Having won, he proposed to "strengthen democracy".

This pledge proved to be worthless following the airing of a secretly shot video on 14 September 2000 of Fujimori's close aide and head of the National Intelligence Service (SIN), Vladimiro Montesinos, handing US$15,000 to a congressman, Alberto Kouri, to persuade him to switch allegiances to Fujimori's coalition. Fujimori's demise was swift.

His initial reaction was to close down SIN and announce new elections, eventually set for 8 April 2001, at which he would not stand. Montesinos, denied asylum in Panama, was hunted down in Peru, Fujimori personally taking charge of the search. While Montesinos evaded capture, investigators discovered that hundreds of senior figures were under his sway and that he held millions of dollars in overseas bank accounts. As the search continued, Fujimori, on an official visit to Japan, sent congress an email announcing his resignation. Congress rejected this, firing him on charges of being "morally unfit" to govern. An interim president, Valentín Paniagua, was sworn in, with ex-UN Secretary General Javier Pérez de Cuéllar as Prime Minister, and the government set about uncovering the depth of corruption associated with Montesinos and Fujimori. From 2002 onwards, Montesinos was involved in a series of trials and was convicted of a number of crimes. In 2004, prosecutors also sought to charge exiled Fujimori with authorizing deaths squads at Barrios Altos (1991) and La Cantuta (1992) in which 25 people died. This followed the Truth and Reconciliation Committee's report (2003) into the civil war of the 1980s-1990s, which stated that over 69,000 Peruvians had been killed. Declaring from exile in Japan that he would be exonerated and stand for the presidency in 2006, Fujimori flew to Chile in November 2005, but the Chilean authorities jailed him for seven months and then held him on parole until an extradition request was finally approved in September 2007. In December that year the first of several trials began, Fujimori being charged with, but strenuously denying, the Barrios Altos and La Cantuta murders, kidnapping and corruption. He was found guilty of human rights abuses in 2009 and sentenced to 25 years in prison (further convictions followed).

After Fujimori

In the run-up to the 2001 presidential ballot, the front-runner was Alejandro Toledo, with ex-President Alan García as his main opponent. After winning a run-off vote, Toledo pledged to heal the wounds that had opened in Peru since his first electoral battle with the disgraced Fujimori, but his presidency was marked by slow progress on both the political and economic fronts. With the poverty levels still high, few jobs created and a variety of scandals, Toledo's popularity plummeted. Major confrontations and damaging strikes ensued, and charges of corruption were laid at his own door.

The April 2006 elections were contested by Alán García, the conservative Lourdes Flores and Ollanta Humala, a former military officer and unsuccessful coup leader who claimed support from Venezuela's Hugo Chávez and Evo Morales of Bolivia. García and Humala won through to the second round, which García won, in part because many were suspicious of Chávez's interference in Peruvian affairs. García was anxious to overcome his past record as president and pledged to rein in public spending and not squander the benefits of an economy growing consistently since 2005. Throughout his term of office, controversy surrounded García's free-market and mineral exploration policies, with major demonstrations being held over both. Clashes in mid-2009 between indigenous protestors from near Bagua Grande (Amazonas) and police over oil-drilling rights led to over 50 deaths and claims of human rights abuse. The first round of voting to find a successor to García was held on 11 April 2011. The three main candidates were Humala (Gana Perú), former prime minister Pedro Pablo Kuczynski (Alianza por el Gran Cambio) and Keiko Fujimori, daughter of Alberto (Fuerza 2011). No candidate won an outright majority and Humala defeated Fujimori in a second round on 5 June 2011. Humala aimed to tackle poverty and inequality in concert with other moderate left-wing governments such as those of Brazil. He also sought close ties with the US. He inherited a strong economy, which continued to grow at over 5% a year up to end-

2013 (with similar predictions for 2014), largely as a result of investment in mining. Despite being the main motor of the boom, mining was also the chief cause of many conflicts. Violent protests that halted the development of the Conga gold mine in Cajamarca, for example, were the most prominent of up to 200 social and environmental disputes around the country. The government's claim that large-scale projects would benefit the whole country was not matched by improvements in living standards, nor did it alleviate the fears of pollution.

In late 2013 a United Nations Development Programme report reinforced Peru's dilemma of how to translate strong GDP growth into improvements in areas such as health and education. Humala was already hard pressed to achieve his target of reducing the poverty rate from over 25% in 2013 to 15% in 2016. The UNDP paper, like other internationally sponsored reports, also backed up warnings that the reliance on extractive industries posed a serious threat of vulnerability to climate change, to which Peru is especially susceptible. Government and foreign investors in the sector were challenged to show that mines and other works would neither harm the environment nor prevent communities from developing sustainably at their side. The damage from illegal mining, mainly in the Amazon region, was shown to be far worse than previously thought. Deforestation and the dumping of mercury in river systems were the main factors. In its effort to reduce uncontrolled mining, the government faced applications for formalization from almost 73,000 miners in April 2014, despite several protests against the process. Giving greater focus to these problems was the fact that Peru was due to host the UN Climate Change Conference in December 2014.

Bolivia

Coups, mines and wars

Bolivian politics have been the most turbulent in Latin America. Although in the 19th century the army was very small, officers were key figures in power-struggles, often backing different factions of the landowning elite. Between 1840 and 1849 there were 65 attempted *coups d'état*. The longest lasting government of the 19th century was that of Andrés Santa Cruz (1829-1839), but when he tried to unite Bolivia with Peru in 1836, Chile and Argentina intervened to overthrow him. After the War of the Pacific (1879-1883) there was greater stability, but opposition to the political dominance of the city of Sucre culminated in a revolt in 1899 led by business groups from La Paz and the tin-mining areas, as a result of which La Paz became the centre of government.

The Bolivian economy depended on tin exports during the 20th century. Railway construction and the demand for tin in Europe and the USA (particularly in wartime) led to a mining boom after 1900. By the 1920s the industry was dominated by three entrepreneurs, Simón Patiño, Mauricio Hochschild and the Aramayo family, who greatly influenced national politics. The importance of mining and the harsh conditions in the isolated mining camps of the Altiplano led to the rise of a militant miners movement.

Since independence Bolivia has suffered continual losses of territory, partly because of communications difficulties and the central government's inability to control distant provinces. The dispute between Chile and Peru over the nitrate-rich Atacama desert in 1879 soon dragged in Bolivia, which had signed a secret alliance with Peru in 1873. Following its rapid defeat in the War of the Pacific Bolivia lost her coastal provinces. As compensation Chile later agreed to build the railway between Arica and La Paz. When Brazil annexed the rich Acre Territory in 1903, Bolivia was compensated by another railway, but this Madeira-Mamoré line never reached its destination, Riberalta, and proved of little use; it was closed in 1972. There was not even an unbuilt railway to compensate Bolivia for its next loss.

A long-running dispute with Paraguay over the Chaco erupted into war in 1932. Defeat in the so-called Chaco War (1932-1935) resulted in the loss of three quarters of the Chaco.

Modern Bolivia

The Chaco War was a turning point in Bolivian history, increasing the political influence of the army which in 1936 seized power for the first time since the War of the Pacific. Defeat bred nationalist resentment among junior army officers who had served in the Chaco and also led to the creation of a nationalist party, the Movimiento Nacionalista Revolucionario (MNR) led by Víctor Paz Estenssoro. Their anger was directed against the mine owners and the leaders who had controlled Bolivian politics. Between 1936 and 1946 a series of unstable military governments followed. This decade witnessed the apparent suicide in 1939 of one president (Germán Busch) and the public hanging in 1946 of another (Gualberto Villarroel). After a period of civilian government, the 1951 elections were won by the MNR but a coup prevented the party from taking office.

The 1952 revolution In April 1952 the military government was overthrown by a popular revolution in which armed miners and peasants played a major role. Paz Estenssoro became president and his MNR government nationalized the mines, introduced universal suffrage and began the break-up and redistribution of large estates. The economy, however, deteriorated, partly because of the hostility of the US government. Paz's successor, Hernán Siles Zuazo (president from 1956 to 1964), a hero of the 1952 revolution, was forced to take unpopular measures to stabilize the economy. Paz was re-elected president in 1960 and 1964, but shortly afterwards in November 1964 he was overthrown by his vice president, Gral René Barrientos, who relied on the support of the army and the peasants to defeat the miners.

Military rule in the 1970s The death of Barrientos in an air crash in 1969 was followed by three brief military governments. The third, led by Gral Torres, pursued left-wing policies which alarmed many army officers and business leaders. In August 1971 Torres was overthrown by Hugo Banzer, a right-wing colonel who outlawed political parties and trade unions. After Banzer was forced to call elections in 1978, a series of short-lived military governments overruled elections in 1978 and 1979 giving victories to Siles Zuazo. One of these, led by Gral García Meza (1980-1981) was notable for its brutal treatment of opponents and its links to the cocaine trade, which led to its isolation by the international community.

Return to democracy In August 1982 the military returned to barracks and Dr Siles Zuazo assumed the Presidency in a leftist coalition government with support from the communists and trade unions. Under this regime inflation spiralled out of control. The elections of 1985 were won again by Víctor Paz Estenssoro, who imposed a rigorous programme to stabilize the economy. In the elections of 1989, Gonzalo Sánchez de Lozada of the MNR (chief architect of the stabilization programme) failed to win enough votes to prevent Congress choosing Jaime Paz Zamora of the Movimiento de la Izquierda Revolucionaria (MIR), who came third in the elections, as president in August 1989. Paz had made an unlikely alliance with the former military dictator, Hugo Banzer (Acción Democrática Nacionalista).

Although Gonzalo Sánchez de Lozada just failed to gain the required 51% majority to win the presidency in the 1993 elections, the other candidates recognized his victory. The main element in his policies was the capitalization of state assets, in which investors agreed to inject fresh capital into a chosen state-owned company in return for a 50% controlling stake. The other 50% of the shares were distributed to all Bolivians over 18 via a private pension fund scheme. As the programme gained pace, so did opposition to it. In the elections of 1 June 1997, Banzer and the ADN secured 22% of the vote and ADN became the dominant party in a new coalition. After two years of economic austerity, hardship in rural areas, together with unemployment and anger at a US-backed coca eradication programme and a plan to raise water rates led to violent protests and road blocks in many parts of the country. President Banzer was forced to resign in August 2001 because of cancer and his replacement, Vice-President Jorge Quiroga, served the final year of Banzer's term before new elections were held, in which a coalition led by Sánchez de Lozada won an extremely narrow victory. The runner-up was Evo Morales, leader of the coca growers, who campaigned for a restoration of traditional coca production and an end to free market reforms.

Turbulence and the rise of Evo Morales From the outset, Sánchez de Lozada faced economic crisis. Mass demonstrations turned into riots over tax increases and the president was forced to flee the presidential palace in an ambulance. A week later, the cabinet resigned, tax hikes were cancelled, police were awarded a pay rise and Sánchez de Lozada vowed to forego his salary. Subsequent protests over the sale of Bolivian gas to the US became a national uprising and weeks of violent street demonstrations led to Sánchez de Lozada's resignation on 17 October 2003. Vice president Carlos Mesa became president, but survived only until June 2005, when new elections were called. Evo Morales of Movimiento al Socialismo (MAS), self-styled "United States' worst nightmare", beat ex-president Quiroga by a clear majority on 18 December 2005.

Morales' rise to power was precipitated by the continued opposition to gas exports, mass protests by the inhabitants of El Alto calling for a more equal society and his support for coca growers. Morales soon announced elections to a new constituent assembly and, in May 2006, sent troops into the gas fields, provoking foreign hydrocarbon companies to renegotiate their contracts with Bolivia. The Constituent Assembly eventually approved a new socially oriented constitution in November 2007, but the process was marred by procedural irregularities and violence. In 2008, opponents of the Morales government in northern and eastern lowland departments (Santa Cruz, Beni, Pando and Tarija) pressed their case for autonomy, in response to which the Senate called another referendum. The mandate of the president was ratified by a 67% majority and the most important opposition departmental governors were also ratified. A subsequent referendum approved the new constitution by a 61% majority, but predictably voters in the eastern states rejected it. Despite these profound divisions, presidential and congressional elections in December 2009, revealed greater unity as Morales became the first Bolivian president to be democratically reelected (with a 63% majority) and his MAS party won outright majorities in both houses of the legislature.

For most Bolivians, day-to-day concerns revolved around sudden increases in the cost of basic foods, blamed by the government on business leaders seeking to destabilize the administration, and blamed by the opposition on government economic mismanagement. Whatever the cause, high prices and food shortages led to violent demonstrations in 2011, followed by the introduction in June of a new law to ensure food security. Other examples of popular ire were transport strikes which led to the reversal of an increase in fuel prices by 73-83% in December 2010 and month-long mass demonstrations in early 2012 over the government's refusal to raise wages after increasing working hours. Later in the year strikes over low levels of pay for police and army officers led to violence. The government also climbed down over a proposed road through the Isiboro Sécure national park following protests by indigenous people in late 2011, only to change its mind, reopen the project and stimulate more protests in 2012.

In July 2013 the case of the US whistleblower, Edward Snowden, briefly enveloped Bolivia as the plane that was carrying President Morales home from Moscow was forced to land in Vienna after France, Italy, Spain and Portugal were reported to have refused to let it enter their airspace. Rumours that Snowden was on board were unfounded; likewise, accusations that Washington had pressurized the European countries were denied. Many Latin American governments supported Bolivia's assertion that the action was unjustified.

In the first months of 2014 an emergency was declared in the north of the country as persistent rain caused severe flooding. Also at this time there were transport strikes as companies disputed bus fare structures with the government. Overall, though, the economy was registering positive growth (6.5% estimated for GDP for 2013, with slightly less predicted for 2014) and prudent use of the income from sales of natural gas and other commodities gave the country healthy foreign reserves equivalent to about half of GDP. Acute poverty was being reduced, inflation limited to less than 10% and the foreign debt was also cut drastically. In this upbeat climate, opinion polls through 2013 and into 2014 showed that President Morales was receiving support from over 40% of voters, way more than that for any of his rivals in the divided opposition. This gave a boost to the president as his bid to run for a third term in office in October 2014 was approved by the Constitutional Court. The court stated that his first term started before the new constitution of 2009 came into force, so elections in 2014 would mark his second consecutive term, not third. In April 2014, Bolivia lodged a claim at the International Court of Justice in The Hague to regain access to the Pacific Ocean through territory which is currently part of Chile. Bolivia lost the route in the War of the Pacific with Chile in 1879-1883.

Ecuador

After independence
Ecuador decided on complete independence from the Gran Colombia confederation in August 1830, under the presidency of Juan Flores. The country's 19th century history was a continuous struggle between pro-Church conservatives and anti-Church (but nonetheless devoutly Catholic) liberals. There were also long periods of military rule from 1895, when the liberal Gen Eloy Alfaro took power. During the late 1940s and the 1950s there was a prolonged period of prosperity (through bananas, largely) and constitutional rule, but the more typical pattern of alternating civilian and military governments was resumed in the 1960s and 1970s. Apart from the liberal-conservative struggles, there has been long-lasting rivalry between Quito and the Sierra on one hand and Guayaquil and the Costa on the other.

Return to democracy
Following seven years of military rule, the first presidential elections under a new constitution were held in 1979. The ensuing decades of democracy saw an oscillation of power between parties of the centre-right and centre-left. Governments of both political tendencies towed the international economic line and attempted to introduce neoliberal reforms. These measures were opposed by the country's labour organizations and by the indigenous movement, which gained considerable political power. Against a backdrop of this tug-of-war, disenchantment with the political process grew apace with bureaucratic corruption and the nation's economic woes. In 1996 the frustrated electorate swept a flamboyant populist named Abdalá Bucaram to power. His erratic administration lasted less than six months.

A succession of presidents Following an interim government and the drafting of the country's 18th constitution, Ecuador elected Jamil Mahuad, a former mayor of Quito, to the presidency in 1998. Mahuad began his term by signing a peace treaty to end the decades-old and very emotional border dispute with Peru. This early success was his last, as a series of fraudulent bank failures sent the country into an economic and political tailspin. A freeze on bank accounts failed to stop landslide devaluation of the Sucre (Ecuador's currency since 1883) and Mahuad decreed the adoption of the US Dollar in a desperate bid for stability. Less than a month later, on 21 January 2000, he was forced out of office by Ecuador's indigenous people and disgruntled members of the armed forces. The first overt military coup in South America in over two decades, it lasted barely three hours before power was handed to vice-president Gustavo Noboa. Significantly, all of the foregoing years of social unrest were never accompanied by serious bloodshed.

Noboa, a political outsider and academic, stepped into Mahuad's shoes with remarkable aplomb. With assistance from the USA and the International Monetary Fund, his government managed to flesh out and implement the dollarization scheme, thus achieving a measure of economic stability at the cost of deepening poverty. Social unrest diminished, and Ecuadoreans instead attempted to bring about change through the ballot box. In November 2002, Colonel Lucio Gutiérrez, leader of the January 2000 *coup*, was elected president by a comfortable majority. He had run on a populist platform in alliance with the indigenous movement and labour unions, but he soon squandered his support. His administration was lacklustre and only constantly shifting allegiances and high petroleum revenues managed to keep him in power. In late 2004, the dismissal of all the supreme court judges by unconstitutional means – and tear gas – drew local and international criticism. Popular opposition in Quito grew, with peaceful, well-attended protests. The president's response, using heavy-handed police repression, led to mass demonstrations which swept him from office in April 2005. Vice-president Alfredo Palacio replaced him, but had to face persistent strikes. General elections, brought forward to November 2006, were won by Rafael Correa, leader of the Alianza País (AP) movement. He immediately called a national referendum to convene a constituent assembly to redraw the constitution and, the new president hoped, shift the nation's foundations toward the political left. The Constituent Assembly was elected in September 2007 and a referendum gave the new constitution popular approval in September 2008. With re-election of the president now permitted, new elections were held in April 2009 and Correa won comfortably.

By 2010 social tension was increasing, fuelled by Correa's confrontational tone and stalemate over various legal changes under the new constitution. Events came to a head in October when junior police and soldiers, protesting at austerity measures, briefly held Correa captive in a hospital after he had been teargassed. The president was soon released. Meanwhile, government and media maintained a running battle, with a major skirmish in February 2012 when critics of changes to electoral law accused the government of limiting press freedom. Correa maintained that the media had no role to play in political activity. Widespread concern over rising crime led Correa to call a referendum in May 2011 about toughening law enforcement and re-organizing the judiciary, among various unrelated questions, but this rapidly degenerated into a popularity contest, with campaigning and voting focused on whether or not one liked the President, rather than addressing the issues. Correa 'won' by a narrow margin, but a truer test of his popularity came in early 2013 when he stood for reelection as president and defeated all rival candidates in the first round. His Alianza País party also won a majority in Congress. With further four years in power Correa aimed to continue improvements in healthcare, education and roads and further reduce poverty. The high levels of investment in the public sector were largely funded by revenue from oil and borrowing abroad, mostly from China but also with a return to international bond markets in 2014 (the first time in six years). By coincidence or design, Correa announced in August 2013 the cancellation of the YasuníITT conservation initiative, which asked the international community to raise US$3.6 billion to prevent drilling for oil in the Parque Nacional Yasuní. Only US$13 million had been deposited with the UN-based trust fund administering the scheme and Correa claimed that the world had "failed" Ecuador. The liquidation of the fund effectively opened the door to oil companies to extract oil from the Ishpingo-Tambococha-Tiputini region of the park. There was an immediate outcry from indigenous groups and environmentalists and a huge majority of Ecuadoreans were opposed to drilling in what is one of the most diverse regions of the planet.

In June 2012 Julian Assange, founder of WikiLeaks, was granted asylum in the Ecuadorean embassy in London. Assange feared that if he was extradited to Sweden to answer charges of sexual misconduct, as Britain was bound to do, he would be sent to the US to face charges over the leak of secret documents. A year later, with Assange still holed up in the embassy, the Edward Snowden case arose and, unsurprisingly, Ecuador was listed among the countries who might give him sanctuary. It was reported that the Ecuadorean Embassy in London had given Snowden a safe-conduct pass. This was soon revoked, with denials that the government had ever intended to assist Snowden. At the same time, however, Correa included pressure from the US among the reasons for Ecuador renouncing unilaterally its trade preferences under the Andean Trade Promotion and Drug Eradication Pact (ATPDEA). In a further move against the US, the office of military cooperation, with some 20 defence personnel, was closed down in April 2014 after Correa declared that the US had too much influence in the region.

Government

Peru (República del Perú)
Under the constitution of December 1993, there is a single chamber, 120-seat congress. Men and women over 18 are eligible to vote; registration and voting is compulsory until the age of 70. The President, to whom is entrusted the Executive Power, is elected for five years. The country is divided into 25 regions, plus the province of Lima.

Bolivia (Estado Plurinacional de Bolivia)
The Constitution of 2008 vests executive power in the President, who can stand for immediate re-election. The presidential term is five years. The rights of 36 indigenous groups are enshrined in the constitution, including the recognition of indigenous systems of justice. Congress (Asamblea Legislativa Plurinacional) consists of two chambers: the Senate, with 36 seats, and the Chamber of Deputies, with 130 seats. There are nine departments; each is controlled by a Prefecto appointed by the President. **Note** Sucre is the legal capital, La Paz is the seat of government.

Ecuador (República del Ecuador)
The Constitution dates from 2008. There are 24 provinces, including the Galápagos Islands. The president and vice-president are elected for a four-year term and can be re-elected for a second term (once only). The parliament, Asamblea Nacional, is also elected for four years; it currently has 124 seats. The number of *asamblistas* will vary according to the size of the population.

Culture

People

Peru → *Population in 2014 was 30.2 million. Population growth was 1.0%; infant mortality rate 20.21 per 1000 live births; literacy rate 89.6%; GDP per capita US$11,100 (2013).*

Peruvian society is a mixture of native Andean peoples, Afro-Peruvians, Spanish, immigrant Chinese, Japanese, Italians, Germans and, to a lesser extent, indigenous Amazon tribes. The first immigrants were the Spaniards who followed Pizarro's expeditionary force. Their effect, demographically, politically and culturally, has been enormous. Peru's black community is based on the coast, mainly in Chincha, south of Lima, and also in some working-class districts of the capital. Their forefathers were originally imported into Peru in the 16th century as slaves to work on the sugar and cotton plantations on the coast. Large numbers of poor Chinese labourers were brought to Peru in the mid-19th century to work in virtual slavery on the guano reserves on the Pacific coast and to build the railroads in the central Andes. The Japanese community, now numbering some 100,000, established itself in the first half of the 20th century. Like most of Latin America, Peru received many emigrés from Europe seeking land and opportunities in the late 19th century. The country's wealth and political power remains concentrated in the hands of this small and exclusive class of whites, which also consists of the descendants of the first Spanish families.

The **indigenous population** is put at about three million Quechua and Aymara Indians in the Andean region and 200,000-250,000 Amazonian Indians from 40-50 ethnic groups. In the Andes, there are 5000 Indian communities but few densely populated settlements. Their literacy rate is the lowest of any comparable group in South America and their diet is 50% below acceptable levels. About two million Indians speak no Spanish, their main tongue being Quechua; they are largely outside the money economy. Many Indian groups are under threat from colonization, development and road-building projects.

Bolivia → *Population in 2014 was 10.6 million. Population growth was 1.6%; infant mortality rate 38.6 per 1000 live births; literacy rate 91.2%; GDP per capita US$5,5 (2013).*

Of the total population, some two thirds are Indians, the remainder being *mestizos*, Europeans and others. The racial composition varies from place to place: Indian around Lake Titicaca; more than half Indian in La Paz; three-quarters *mestizo* or European in the Yungas, Cochabamba, Santa Cruz and Tarija, the most European of all. There are also about 17,000 blacks, descendants of slaves brought from Peru and Buenos Aires in 16th century, who now live in the Yungas. Since the 1980s, regional tensions between the 'collas' (*altiplano* dwellers) and the 'cambas' (lowlanders) have become more marked. Under 40% of children of school age attend school even though it is theoretically compulsory between 7 and 14.

The most obdurate of Bolivian problems has always been that the main mass of population is, from a strictly economic viewpoint, in the wrong place, the poor Altiplano and not the potentially rich Oriente; and that the Indians live largely outside the monetary system on a self-sufficient basis. Since the land reform of 1952 isolated communities continue the old life but in the agricultural area around Lake Titicaca, the valleys of Cochabamba, the Yungas and the irrigated areas of the south, most peasants now own their land, however small the plot may be. Migration to the warmer and more fertile lands of the east region has been officially encouraged. At the same time roads are now integrating the food-producing eastern zones with the bulk of the population living in the towns of the Altiplano or the west-facing slopes of the Eastern Cordillera.

The **highland Indians** are composed of two groups: those in La Paz and in the north of the Altiplano who speak the guttural Aymara and those elsewhere, who speak Quechua (this includes the Indians in the northern Apolobamba region). Outside the big cities many of them speak no Spanish. In the lowlands are some 150,000 people in 30 groups, including the Ayoreo, Chiquitano, Chiriguano, Garavo, Chimane and Mojo. The **lowland Indians** are, in the main, Guaraní. About 70% of Bolivians are Aymara, Quechua or Tupi-Guaraní speakers. The first two are regarded as national languages, but were not, until very recently, taught in schools.

Ecuador → *Population in the 2010 census was 14.5 million (estimates for 2014 are 15.7 million). Population growth was 1.4%; infant mortality rate 17.9 per 1000 live births; literacy rate 91.6%; GDP per capita US$10,6 (2013).*

Roughly 50% of Ecuador's people live in the coastal region west of the Andes, 45% in the Andean Sierra and 5% in Oriente. Migration is occurring from the rural zones of both the coast and the highlands to the towns and cities, particularly Guayaquil and Quito, and agricultural colonization from other parts of the country is taking place in the Oriente. There has also been an important flux of mostly illegal migrants out of Ecuador, seeking opportunities in the USA and Spain (officially put at 300,000 – probably an underestimate). Meanwhile, Colombian refugees and migrants are becoming an important segment of Ecuador's population. The national average population density is the highest in South America.

There are 900,000 Quichua-speaking **highland Indians** and about 120,000 **lowland Indians**. The following indigenous groups maintain their distinct cultural identity: in the Oriente, Siona, Secoya, Cofán, Huaorani, Zápara, Kichwa del Oriente, Shiwiar, Achuar and Shuar; in the Sierra, Otavalo, Salasaca, Puruhá, Cañari and Saraguro; on the coast, Chachi (Cayapa), Tsáchila (Colorado), Awa (Cuaiquer) and Epera. Many Amazonian Indian communities are fighting for land rights in the face of oil exploration and colonization.

Note Statistics, unless indicated otherwise, are taken from *The CIA World Factbook*, 2012 estimates. GDP per capita is measured at purchasing power parity (PPP).

Music and dance

The pipes of the Andes: Peru, Bolivia and Ecuador

For many, the sprightly pan-pipe and *charango* mandolin music of the Andes, played by a troupe dressed in woven ponchos is synonymous with pre-Columbian South America. Yet while bamboo pipes or *siku*, and split-reed *quena* flutes have been used to make music in the Andes (together with conches and various percussion instruments) for thousands of years, contemporary Andean music is in reality a recent invention, born of a meeting between the indigenous past and the *nueva canción* movement in the late 1950s and early 1960s.

Marching bands of pan pipes swapping notes and melodic lines, accompanied by drum troupes and singers delighted the *conquistadores*. And the music of the Incas and their contemporaries thrives today in remote communities from southern Colombia to Bolivia, where it is played, as it probably always was, at rituals and key community events.

Singing styles, melodies and modes vary from village to village, as do the instruments used, with the more traditional villages only playing percussion and woodwind. Were it not for the rise of left-wing politics in the 1950s Andean music would probably only have trickled out onto the world stage. But as discontent with dictatorship and the ruling élite grew after the Second World War and the Cuban revolution, so South American intellectuals looked to solidarity with the people. And with this came a rediscovery of their artistic and musical traditions (see *nueva canción* above). After the quiet Bolivian revolution of 1952, which saw a left-wing government sweep to power, indigenous Bolivians were afforded the greatest respect they had had since the Spanish conquest. They were granted suffrage, land was re-distributed and the new administration created a governmental department of folklore, one of whose functions was the organization of traditional music festivals. This climate and the influence of Argentine and Chilean groups like **Urubamba** (who formed in 1956 and introduced *El Cóndor Pasa* to Paul Simon) and **Quilapayún** (formed by a group of intellectuals at the Universidad de Chile), inspired a contemporaneous renaissance in Andean music in La Paz. In 1965 a singer and percussionist called Edgar 'Yayo' Joffré formed **Los Jairas**, a quartet who would provide the model for Andean music for the next 50 years.

Los Jairas were arguably the first world-music band, made up of enthusiastic middle-class intellectuals, traditional Andean musicians, a virtuoso classical guitarist called **Alfredo Domínguez** and Domínguez's musical sparring partner, the French-Swiss flute player **Gilbert Favre** (simply called 'El Gringo' by the Bolivian public). Favre was the former lover of the Chilean *nueva canciónera* Violeta Parra and one of the great unsung heroes of international musical co-operation. Los Jairas found a regular haunt in the **Peña Naira** in La Paz, where they re-invented Andean music and became a national sensation. Joffré's melodies and lyrics were imbued with wistful almost operatic melancholy and were accompanied by Ernesto Cavour's flamenco-tinged *charango* and Favre's lilting *quena* flute. All that was missing were the pan-pipes.

These were added by numerous Los Jairas imitators from La Paz to Quito. The most successful were **Los K'jarkas**, a Cochabamba-based trio of brothers with their own music school who penned what has since become the perennial *peña* encore, *Llorando se fue*. K'jarkas both consolidated and built-upon Los Jairas' Andean musical model. They retained the melancholic melodies and musical evocations of glorious pastoral landscapes, adding traditional costume, a stylised logo borrowing motifs from the carvings at Tiwanaku and a few up-tempo numbers drawing on Andean dance rhythms like the *huayno* and the *saya*. Los K'jarkas' fame spread throughout the Andean world, spawning a mini-musical revolution among the Quichua people of Ecuador whose *cachullapi* and *yumbo* dances are an interesting fusion of marching band, modern Andean and traditional Inca music.

In a *peña* in La Paz and Cuzco today what you'll hear is little more than a footnote to Los Jairas and Los K'jarkas, but music in Peru, Ecuador and Bolivia has diversified. Singers like **Emma Junaro** have taken the Andean sound and the *nueva canción* to produce a new, politically sensitive singer-songwriter genre known as **canto nuevo**. Singers like **Susana Baca** have brought the music of **Nicomedes Santa Cruz** and the musicians of African Peru to the attention of the world, through a series of stunning albums and mesmerising shows, and in the shanty towns of Lima and the lowlands of eastern Peru and Ecuador Amazonian **chicha** music has established itself as the new vernacular sound of the poor urban majority.

Land and environment

Peru → *Land area: 1,285,216 sq km.*

The whole of Peru's west seaboard with the Pacific is desert on which rain seldom falls. From this coastal shelf the Andes rise to a high Sierra which is studded with groups of soaring mountains and gouged with deep canyons. The highland slopes more gradually east and is deeply forested and ravined. Eastward from these mountains lie the vast jungle lands of the Amazon Basin.

The **Highlands** (or Sierra), at an average altitude of 3000 m, cover 26% of the country and contain about 50% of the people, mostly Indian, an excessive density on such poor land. Here, high-level land of gentle slopes is surrounded by towering ranges of high peaks including the most spectacular range of the continent, the Cordillera Blanca. This has several ice peaks over 6000 m; the highest, Huascarán, is 6768 m and is a mecca for mountaineers. There are many volcanoes in the south. The north and east highlands are heavily forested up to a limit of 3350 m: the grasslands are between the forest line and the snowline, which rises from 5000 m in the latitude of Lima to 5800 m in the south. Most of the Sierra is covered with grasses and shrubs, with Puna vegetation (bunch grass mixed with low, hairy-leaved plants) from north of Huaraz to the south. Here the indigenous graze llamas, alpacas and sheep providing meat, clothing, transport and even fuel from the animals' dung. Some potatoes and cereals (*quinua, kiwicha* and *kañiwa*) are grown at altitude, but the valley basins contain the best land for arable farming. Most of the rivers which rise in these mountains flow east to the Amazon and cut through the plateau in canyons, sometimes 1500 m deep, in which the climate is tropical. A few go west to the Pacific including the Colca and Cotahuasi in the south, which have created canyons over 3000 m deep.

The **coast**, a narrow ribbon of desert 2250 km long, takes up 11% of the country and holds about 45% of the population. It is the economic heart of Peru, consuming most of the imports and supplying half of the exports. When irrigated, the river valleys are extremely fertile, creating oases which grow cotton throughout the country, sugar cane, rice and export crops such as asparagus in the north, grapes, fruit and olives in the south. At the same time, the coastal current teems with fish and Peru has in the past had the largest catch in the world. The **jungle** covers the forested eastern half of the Andes and the tropical forest beyond, altogether 62% of the country's area, but with only about 5% of the population who are crowded on the river banks in the cultivable land – a tiny part of the area. The few roads have to cope with dense forest, deep valleys, and sharp eastern slopes ranging from 2150 m in the north to 5800 m east of Lake Titicaca. Rivers are the main highways, though navigation is hazardous. The economic potential of the area includes reserves of timber, excellent land for rubber, jute, rice, tropical fruits and coffee and the breeding of cattle. The vast majority of Peru's oil and gas reserves are also east of the Andes.

Bolivia → *Land area: 1,098,581 sq km.*

A harsh, strange land, with a dreary grey solitude except for the bursts of green after rain, Bolivia is the only South American country with no coastline or navigable river to the sea. It is dominated by the Andes and has five distinct geographical areas. The **Andes** are at their widest in Bolivia, a maximum of 650 km. The Western Cordillera, which separates Bolivia from Chile, has high peaks of 5800 m-6500 m and a number of active volcanoes along its crest. The Eastern Cordillera also rises to giant massifs, with several peaks over 6000 m in the Cordillera Real section to the north. The far sides of the Cordillera Real fall away very sharply to the northeast, towards the Amazon Basin. The air is unbelievably clear – the whole landscape is a bowl of luminous light.

The **Altiplano** lies between the Cordilleras, a bleak, treeless, windswept plateau, much of it 4000 m above sea-level. Its surface is by no means flat, and the Western Cordillera sends spurs dividing it into basins. The more fertile northern part has more inhabitants; the southern part is parched desert and almost unoccupied, save for a mining town here and there. Nearly 70% of the population lives on it; over half of the people in towns. **Lake Titicaca**, at the northern end of the Altiplano, is an inland sea of 8965 sq km at 3810 m, the highest navigable water in the world. Its depth, up to 280 m in some places, keeps the lake at an even all-year-round temperature of 10° C. This modifies the extremes of winter and night temperatures on the surrounding land, which supports a large Aymara indigenous population, tilling the fields and the hill terraces, growing potatoes and cereals, tending their sheep, alpaca and llamas, and using the resources of the lake. The **Yungas** and the **Puna** are to the east of the Altiplano. The heavily forested northeastern slopes of the Cordillera Real are deeply indented by the fertile valleys of the Yungas, drained into the Amazon lowlands by the Río Beni and its tributaries, where cacao, coffee, sugar, coca and tropical fruits are grown. Further south, from a point just north of Cochabamba, the Eastern Cordillera rises abruptly in sharp escarpments from the Altiplano and then flattens out to an easy slope east to the plains: an area known as the Puna. The streams which flow across the Puna cut increasingly deep incisions as they gather volume until the Puna is eroded to little more than a high remnant between the river valleys. In these valleys a variety of grain crops and fruits is grown.

The **tropical lowlands** stretch from the foothills of the Eastern Cordillera to the borders with Brazil, Paraguay and Argentina. They take up 70% of the total area of Bolivia, but contain only about 20% of its population. In the north and east the Oriente has dense tropical forest. Open plains covered with rough pasture, swamp and scrub occupy the centre. Before the expulsion of the Jesuits in 1767 this was a populous land of plenty; for 150 years Jesuit missionaries had controlled the area and guided it into a prosperous security. Decline followed but in recent years better times have returned. Meat is now shipped from Trinidad, capital of Beni Department, and from airstrips in the area, to the urban centres of La Paz, Oruro, and Cochabamba. Further south, the forests and plains beyond the Eastern Cordillera sweep down towards the Río Pilcomayo, which drains into the Río de la Plata, getting progressively less rain and merging into a comparatively dry land of scrub forest and arid savannah. The main city of this area is Santa Cruz de la Sierra, founded in the 16th century, now the second city of Bolivia and a large agricultural centre.

Ecuador → *Land area: 272, 045 sq km.*

The Andes, running from north to south, form a mountainous backbone to the country. There are two main ranges, the Central Cordillera and the Western Cordillera, separated by a 400-km long Central Valley, whose rims are about 50 km apart. The rims are joined together, like the two sides of a ladder, by hilly rungs, and between each pair of rungs lies an intermountain basin with a dense cluster of population. These basins are drained by rivers which cut through the rims to run either west to the Pacific or east to join the Amazon. Both rims of the Central Valley are lined with the cones of more than 50 volcanoes. Several of them have long been extinct, for example, Chimborazo, the highest (6310 m). At least eight, however, are still active including Cotopaxi (5897 m), which had several violent eruptions in the 19th century; Pichincha (4794 m), which re-entered activity in 1998 and expelled a spectacular mushroom cloud in October 1999; Sangay (5230 m), one of the world's most active volcanoes, continuously emitting fumes and ash; Tungurahua (5016 m), active since 1999; and Reventador (3562 m), which has erupted several times since 2002. Earthquakes too are common.

The **sierra**, as the central trough of the Andes in known, is home to about 47% of the people of Ecuador, the majority of whom are indigenous. Some of the land is still held in large private estates worked by the Indians, but a growing proportion is now made up of small family farms or is held by native communities, run as cooperatives. Some communities live at subsistence level, others have developed good markets for products using traditional skills in embroidery, pottery, jewellery, knitting, weaving, and carving. The **costa** is mostly lowland at an altitude of less than 300 m, apart from a belt of hilly land which runs northwest from Guayaquil to the coast, where it turns north and runs parallel to the shore to Esmeraldas. In the extreme north there is a typical tropical rain forest, severely endangered by uncontrolled logging. The forests thin out in the more southern lowlands and give way to tropical dry forest. The main agricultural exports come from the lowlands to the southeast and north of Guayaquil. The heavy rains, high temperature and humidity suit the growth of tropical crops. Bananas and mango are grown here while rice is farmed on the natural levees of this flood plain. The main crop comes from the alluvial fans at the foot of the mountains rising out of the plain. Coffee is grown on the higher ground. Shrimp farming was typical of the coast until this was damaged by disease in 1999. The Guayas lowland is also a great cattle-fattening area in the dry season. South of Guayaquil the rainfall is progressively less, mangroves disappear and by the border with Peru, it is semi-arid.

The **Oriente** is east of the Central Cordillera where the forest-clad mountains fall sharply to a chain of foothills (the Eastern Cordillera) and then the jungle through which meander the tributaries of the Amazon. This east lowland region makes up 36% of Ecuador's total territory, but is only sparsely populated by indigenous and agricultural colonists from the highlands. In total, the region has only 5% of the national population, but colonization is now proceeding rapidly owing to population pressure and in the wake of an oil boom in the northern Oriente. There is gold and other minerals in the south. The **Galápagos** are about 1000 km west of Ecuador, on the Equator, and are not structurally connected to the mainland. They mark the junction between two tectonic plates on the Pacific floor where basalt has escaped to form massive volcanoes, only the tips of which are above sea level. Several of the islands have volcanic activity today. Their isolation from any other land has led to the evolution of their unique flora and fauna.

Books

Peru

Culture and history

Bingham, Hiram *Lost City of the Incas*, (new illustrated edition, with introduction by Hugh Thomson, Weidenfeld & Nicolson, London, 2002).

Bowen, Sally *The Fujimori File. Peru and its President 1990-2000* (2000). A very readable account of the last decade of the 20th century; it ends at the election of that year so the final momentous events of Fujimori's term happened after publication. Bowen has also written, with **Jane Holligan**, *The Imperfect Spy: the Many Lives of Vladimiro Montesinos* (2003), Peisa.

Hemming, John *The Conquest of the Incas* (1970). The one, invaluable book on the period of the conquest.

MacQuarrie, Kim *The Last Days of the Incas*, a thrilling account of the events that led to the Incas' final resistance and of the explorers who have tried to uncover the secrets of their civilization (2007) Piatkus.

Mosely, Michael E *The Incas and their Ancestors: The Archaeology of Peru* (2001) Thames and Hudson.

Muscutt, Keith *Warriors of the Clouds: A Lost Civilization in the Upper Amazon of Peru* (1998) New Mexico Press. Excellent coffee table book and Chachapoyas memoir; also refer to its website (www.chachapoyas.com).

Fiction

Alarcón, Daniel *War by Candlelight* (2005), an excellent collection of short stories, written in English, dealing with contemporary life within and outside Peru.

Arguedas, José María (1911-1969) *Los ríos profundos/Deep Rivers* (1958).

Vargas Llosa, Mario (1936-) Peru's best known novelist has written many internationally acclaimed books, eg *La ciudad y los perros/The Time of the Hero* (1962), *La casa verde/The Green House* (1965), *La guerra del fin del mundo/The War of the End of World* (1981), *La fiesta del chivo/The Feast of the Goat* (2000) and *El paraíso en la otra esquina/The Way to Paradise* (2002).

Wilder, Thornton *The Bridge of San Luis Rey* (1941) Penguin.

Travel

Murphy, Dervla *Eight Feet in the Andes* (1983).

Parris, Matthew *Inca-Kola* (1990).

Shah, Tahir *Trail of Feathers* (2001).

Thomson, Hugh *The White Rock* (Phoenix, 2002), describes Thomson's own travels in the Inca heartland, as well as the journeys of earlier explorers. *Cochineal Red: Travels through Ancient Peru* (Weidenfeld & Nicolson, 2006), explores pre-Inca civilizations.

Wright, Ronald *Cut Stones and Crossroads: a Journey in Peru* (1984).

Trekking and climbing

Biggar, John *The Andes. A Guide for Climbers* (1999) Andes Publishing.

Box, Ben and **Steve Frankham** *Footprint Cuzco and the Inca Heartland* (Footprint).

Gómez, Antonio, and **Tomé, Juan José** *La Cordillera Blanca de Los Andes* (1998) Desnivel, Spanish only, climbing guide with some trekking and general information, available locally. Also *Escaladas en los Andes. Guía de la Cordillera Blanca* (1999) Desnivel (Spanish only), a climbing guide.

Ricker, John F *Yuraq Janka, Cordilleras Blanca and Rosko* (1977), The Alpine Club of Canada, The American Alpine Club.

Sharman, David *Climbs of the Cordillera Blanca of Peru* (1995) Whizzo. A climbing guide, available locally, from South American Explorers, as well as from Cordee in the UK and Alpenbooks in the USA.

Simpson, Joe *Touching the Void* (1997) Vintage. A nail-biting account of Simpson's accident in the Cordillera Huayhuasah.

Wildlife

Clements, James F and Shany, Noam *A Field Guide to the Birds of Peru* (2001) Ibis.

Schulenberg, Thomas S, Stotz, Douglas F, et al *Birds of Peru* (2007), Helm. A comprehensive field guide.

TReeS (see under Jungle tours from Puerto Maldonado: Tambopata, for address) publish *Tambopata – A Bird Checklist*, *Tambopata – Mammal, Amphibian & Reptile Checklist* and *Reporte Tambopata*; they also produce tapes and CDs of *Jungle Sounds* and *Birds of Southeast Peru* and distribute other books and merchandise.

Valqui, Thomas *Where toWatch Birds in Peru* (2004), www.granperu.com/bird watchingbook/. Describes 151 sites, how to get there and what to expect once there.

Walker, Barry, and Jon Fjeldsa *Birds of Machu Picchu*.

Bolivia
Birdwatching

Flores, E, and Capriles, C *Aves de la Amazonía Boliviana* (Sagitario, La Paz, 2007). Jungle bird guide withmany photos.

Herzog, Sebastian *Birds of Bolivia*, work in progress, see www.birdsofbolivia.org.

Remsen, J V and Traylor, MA *An Annotated List to the Birds of Bolivia* (Harrell Books, 1989).

Fiction

Cleary, J *Mask of the Andes* (Collins, London, 1982). An entertaining novel set amidst the backdrop of post-1952 revolutionary politics.

Hutchison, R C *Rising* (Penguin, 1982). A gripping tale of conflict between rich creole landowners and the indigenous peasantry.

Santos, R (ed) *The Fat Man from La Paz: Contemporary Fiction from Bolivia* (2000). An extensive collection of short stories by some of Bolivia's finest writers.

History, politics and culture

Anderson, J L *Che Guevara: a Revolutionary Life* (Bantam Press, 1997). A must for any one interested in the life of Guevara and his time in Bolivia.

Escobar, F *De la revolución al Pachakuti* (Garza Azul, La Paz, 2008, in Spanish). A critical look at the Evo Morales government by one of its former insiders.

Ferry, S *I am Rich Potosí* (Monacelli Press, 1999). A fascinating read on the subject of mining.

Kolata, A *Valley of the Spirits* (Wiley & Sons, 1996). By far the most comprehensive book on Tiahuanaco.

Meadows, A *Digging Up Butch and Sundance* (New York: St Martin's Press, 1994). An account of the last days of Butch Cassidy and The Sundance Kid and the attempts to find their graves.

Sivak, M *Jefaso* (Sudamericana, Buenos Aires, 2008, in Spanish). A sympathetic but sincere biography of Bolivia's controversial president, Evo Morales.

Spitzer, L *Hotel Bolivia* (Hill & Wang Pub, 1999). Tells the fascinating story of émigré Jews who fled to Bolivia to escape Hitler's persecution.

Travelogues

Duguid, J *Green Hell: A Chronicle of Travel in the Forests of Eastern Bolivia* (Jonathan Cape, London, 1931). Entertaining account of a journey across the Bolivian Chaco in 1931. By the same author are 2 novels set in the Bolivian jungle: *A Cloak of Monkey Fur* (1936), and *Father Coldstream* (1938).

Fawcett, P *Exploration Fawcett* (Century, 1988). Tells of the famous British explorer's quest to discover El Dorado.

Ghinsberg, Y *Back from Tuichi* (Random House, 1993). The true early-1980s account of an Israeli traveller lost in the jungles of what is now Madidi National Park. His story made Rurrenabaque what it is today. The original is out of print, a more recent version by the same author is *Jungle: A Harrowing True Story of Survival* (Boomerang New Media, 2005).

Jones, T *The Incredible Voyage* (Futura Publications, 1980). The author describes his experiences after spending over 8 months of cruising Lake Titicaca in his sailing cutter Sea Dart.

Meyer, G *Summer at High Altitude* (Alan Ross, London, 1968). A fascinating account of a journey through Bolivia in the mid-1960s with detailed insights into various aspects of Bolivian culture and history.

Young, R *Marching Powder* (Sidgwick & Jackson, 2003). The true story of Thomas McFadden, a small-time English drug dealer jailed in La Paz's San Pedro prison. He gets by giving tours of the prison to gringos.

Trekking and climbing

Biggar, J *The Andes: A Trekking guide*, (Andes, 2001). Features some popular Bolivian treks and some lesser-known ones.

Brain, Y *Bolivia – a climbing guide* (The Mountaineers, Seattle, 1999). Gives comprehensive coverage of Bolivia's mountains.

Brain, Y *Trekking in Bolivia* (The Mountaineers, 1998). A collection of treks in both highland and lowland areas.

Mesili, A *The Andes of Bolivia* (Cima, La Paz, 2004).

Montaño, F, et al *Caminos Precolombinos Departamento de La Paz* (Trópico, La Paz, 2008). Descriptions of ancient trails in the department of La Paz.

Ecuador
Birdwatching

Canaday, C and Jost, L *Common Birds of Amazonian Ecuador* (Ediciones Libri Mundi, Quito, 1997).

Cooper, M and Gellis, R *Plumas* (Latin Web, 2006).

Moore, J *CDs of Ecuadorean birdsongs*. Available at Libri Mundi in Quito.

Ridgely, R and Greenfield, P *Birds of Ecuador* (Cornell University Press, Ithaca, NY, USA, 2001).

Galápagos Islands (general)

Angermeyer, J *My Father's Island* (Anthony Nelson, 1998).

Darwin, C *Voyage of the Beagle* (1839; Penguin, London, 1989).

Treherne, J *The Galápagos Affair* (Jonathan Cape, 1983).

Wittmer, M *Floreana* (Michael Joseph, 1961).

Galápagos field guides

Castro, I and Phillips, A *A Guide to the Birds of the Galápagos Islands* (Christopher Helm, 1996).

Constant, P *Galápagos: A Natural History Guide* (Odyssey, 7th ed, 2007), and *Marine Life of the Galapagos* (Calao Life Experience, 2003).

Horwell, D *Galápagos: the Enchanted Isles* (Dryad Press, 1988).

Hickman, P and Zimmerman, T *Galapagos Marine Life Series* (Sugar Spring Press, 2000).

Humann, P *Reef Fish Identification* (Libri Mundi, 1993).

Jackson, M H *Galápagos: A Natural History Guide* (University of Calgary Press, 1985).

Merlen, G *A Field Guide to the Fishes of Galápagos* (Libri Mundi, 1988).

Schofield, E *Plants of the Galápagos Islands* (Universe Books, New York, 1984).

Trekking and climbing

Brain, Y *Ecuador: A Climbing Guide* (The Mountaineers, Seattle, 2000).

Kunstaetter, R and D *Trekking in Ecuador* (The Mountaineers, Seattle, 2002, www.trekkinginecuador.com).

Rachoweicki, R and Thurber, M *Ecuador: Climbing and Hiking Guide* (Viva Travel Guides, 2009).

Schmudlach, G *Bergfürer Ecuador* (Panico Alpinverlag, 3rd ed, 2009).

Oriente jungle

Kane, J *Savages* (Vintage Books, New York, 1996).

Kimerling, J *Amazon Crude* (Natural Resource Defense Council, 1991; Spanish translation, Abya-Yala, 2006).

Smith, A *The Lost Lady of the Amazon* (Constable, UK, 2003).

Smith, R *Crisis Under the Canopy* (Abya-Yala, Quito).

Whitaker, R *The Mapmaker's Wife* (Basic Books, New York, 2004).

Travelogues

Honigsbaum, M *Valverde's Gold* (Macmillan, London, 2004).

Lourie, P *Sweat of the Sun, Tears of the Moon* (Antheneum, New York, 1991).

Michaux, H *Ecuador* (1929; OUP, 1952).

Miller, T *The Panama Hat Trail* (Abacus, 1986).

Thomsen, M *Living Poor* (University of Washington Press, Seattle, 1969); and *Farm on the River of Emeralds* (Houghton Mifflin, Boston, 1978).

Whymper, E *Travels Amongst the Great Andes of the Equator* (1891; Gibbs M Smith, Salt Lake City, UT, USA, 1987; *Viajes a través de los majestuosos Andes del Ecuador*, Abya-Yala, Quito, 1994)

Contents

Footnotes

Index → *Entries in bold refer to maps*

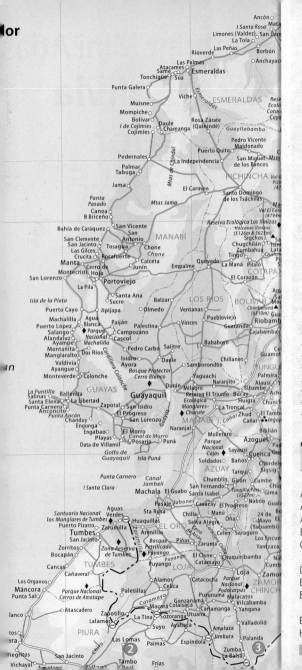

Advertisers' index

Credits

Footprint credits

Editor: Nicola Gibbs
Production and layout: Emma Bryers
Maps: Kevin Feeney
Colour section: Leonie Drake

Publisher: Patrick Dawson
Managing Editor: Felicity Laughton
Advertising: Elizabeth Taylor
Sales and marketing: Kirsty Holmes

Photography credits

Front cover: Biosphoto/Superstock
Back cover: Cem Canbay/Superstock

Colour section

Page i: Superstock: Mint Images/Mint Images
Page ii: Superstock: age fotostock/
age fotostock
Page v: Dreamstime: Jonathan R. Green/
dreamstime.com
Page vi: Shutterstock: Ksenia Ragozina
Page vii: Superstock: age fotostock/
age fotostock
Page viii: Superstock: Visual & Written/
Visual & Written; Hemis.fr/Hemis.fr
Page ix: Superstock: José Enrique Molina/
age fotostock; age fotostock/age fotostock
Page x: Shutterstock: Gleb Aitov
Page xi: Shutterstock: Rafal Cichawa

Printed in India by Thomson Press Ltd,
Faridabad, Haryana

Publishing information

Footprint Peru, Boliva & Ecuador
4th edition
© Footprint Handbooks Ltd
October 2014

ISBN: 978 1 9101200 40
CIP DATA: A catalogue record for this book
is available from the British Library

® Footprint Handbooks and the Footprint
mark are a registered trademark of
Footprint Handbooks Ltd

Published by Footprint
6 Riverside Court
Lower Bristol Road
Bath BA2 3DZ, UK
T +44 (0)1225 469141
F +44 (0)1225 469461
footprinttravelguides.com

Distributed in the USA by
National Book Network, Inc.

Every effort has been made to ensure that
the facts in this guidebook are accurate.
However, travellers should still obtain advice
from consulates, airlines, etc about travel
and visa requirements before travelling.
The authors and publishers cannot
accept responsibility for any loss, injury
or inconvenience however caused.

Map 2 Peru

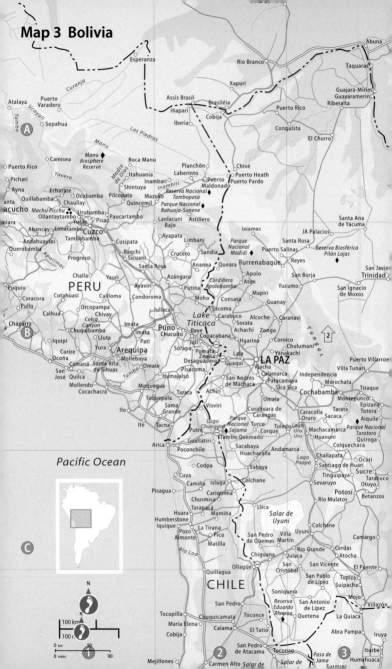

Map 4 Urubamba Valley

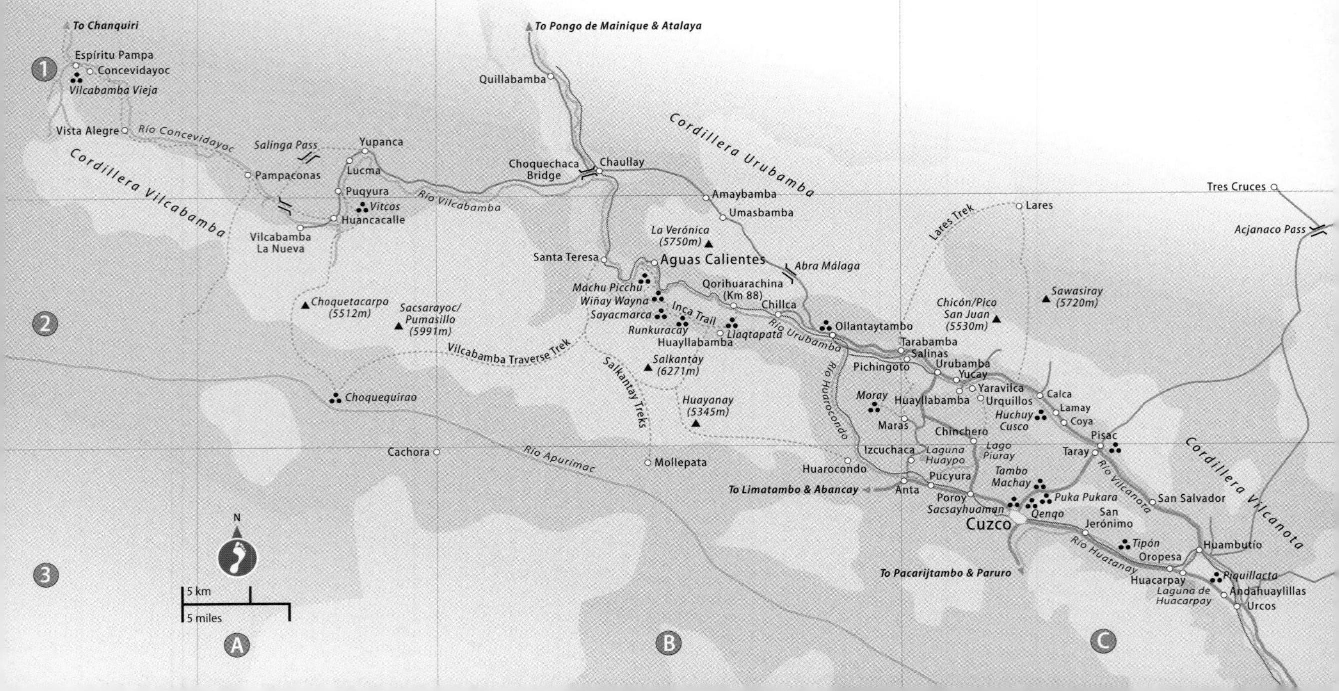

N

5 km
5 miles

A   **B**   **C**

1   **2**   **3**

To Changuiri
Espíritu Pampa
Concevidayoc
Vilcabamba Vieja
Vista Alegre
Río Concevidayoc

Yupanca
Lucma
Puquyura
Vitcos
Huancacalle
Salinga Pass
Pampaconas
Vilcabamba La Nueva
Río Vilcabamba
Cordillera Vilcabamba

Quillabamba
To Pongo de Mainique & Atalaya

Choquechaca Bridge
Chaullay
Santa Teresa

Amaybamba
Umasbamba
Cordillera Urubamba

La Verónica (5750m)
Aguas Calientes
Machu Picchu
Wiñay Wayna
Sayacmarca
Runkuraqay
Inca Trail
Qoriwarachina (Km 88)
Chilca
Abra Málaga

Choquetacarpo (5512m)
Sacsarayoc/ Pumasillo (5991m)

Choquequirao

Cachora

Río Apurímac

Vilcabamba Traverse Trek
Salkantay Treks
Huayllabamba
Salkantay (6271m)
Huaynay (5345m)
Mollepata

Río Urubamba

Ollantaytambo
Pichingoto
Tarabamba
Salinas
Moray
Maras
Pumamarca
Izcuchaca
Huarocondo
Río Huarocondo

Anta
To Limatambo & Abancay

Tres Cruces
Ajíanaco Pass
Lares
Lares Trek

Sawsiray (5720m)
Chicón/Pico San Juan (5530m)

Yanahuara
Yucay
Urubamba
Chinchero
Laguna Huaypo
Lago Piuray
Poroy
Pucyura

Calca
Coya
Lamay
Pisac
Taray

Cordillera Vilcanota
Río Vilcanota
San Salvador
Huambutio
Oropesa
San Jerónimo
Tipón
Huacarpay
Laguna de Huacarpay
Río Huatanay
Piquillacta
Andahuaylillas
Urcos

CUZCO
Saccsayhuamán
Qengo
Puka Pukara
Tambo Machay

Yaravilca
Urquillos
Huchuy Cusco

Map 5 Galápagos Islands

Pacific Ocean

Pinta
Cabo Chalmers
Cabo Ibbetson
Punta Montalvo
Canal de Pinta

Marchena
Punta Mejía
Playa Negra
Punta Calle
Bahía Darwin

Genovesa
Bahía Darwin

Canal de Marchena

° Rocas Nerus

To Isla Marchena 50km

Santiago
Punta Córdova
Buccaneer Cove
Cabo Cowan
Espumilla Beach
James Bay
Puerto Egas
Punta Baquerizo
Cabo Nepean
Punta Albany
Sullivan Bay
Punta Martínez
Rocas Bainbridge
Cabo Sombrero Chino
Cabo Trenton

Bartolomé

Rábida

To Isla Wolf & Isla Darwin
To Isla Wolf & Isla Darwin
Cabo Berkeley
Cabo Flores
Punta Albemarle
Cabo Marshall
Punta Vicente Roca
Bahía Banks
Caleta Black
Punta Tortuga
Punta Flores
Wolf
Darwin

Equator

Fernandina
La Cumbre
Cabo Douglas
Cabo Hammond
Punta Espinosa
Bahía Urbina
Punta Mangle
Canal Bolívar

Isabela
Punta García
Caleta Shipton
Cowley
Punta Alfaro
Mariela
Elizabeth Bay
Perry Isthmus
Volcán Chico
Alcedo
Darwin
Sierra Negra
Mina del Azufre
Santo Tomás
Cerro Azul
Puerto Villamil
Muro de las Lágrimas
Villamil
Roca Unión
Cabo Rosa
Punta Moreno
Caleta Webb
Punta San Juán
Caleta Iguana
Punta Cristóbal
Punta Essex

Canal Isabela
Roca Blanca

Pinzón
Ensenada Flores
Cabo Barrington
Bahía Bowditch
Bahía Conway
Eden
Guy Fawkes
Canal de Pinzón

Los Hermanos
Punta Ballena
Punta Davis
Punta Ballena
Punta Veintimilla
Cabo Napera de Vado (Woodford)
Tortuga

Santa Cruz
Cerro Crocker
Caleta Tortuga Negra
Daphne
El Rosa
Santa Rosa
El Chato Tortoise Reserve
Bellavista
Canal del Norte
Mosquera
Punta Núñez
Punta Rocafuerte
Playa Garrapatero
Puerto Ayora
Charles Darwin Research Station
Academy Bay
Punta Estrada
Tortuga Bay
Punta Nuñez
Canal de Itabaca

North Seymour
Baltra (South Seymour)
Punta del Norte
Gordon Rocks

Plazas

Santa Fé
Canal de Santa Fé

Banco Hancock

Floreana
Post Office Bay
Devil's Crown
Enderby
Punta Cormorant
Punta Crown
Champion
Punta Daylight
Puerto Velasco Ibarra
Black Beach
Punta Ayora
Punta Ensillada (Saddle)
Asilo de la Paz

San Cristóbal
Bahía Hobbs
Punta Pitt
Cabo Norte
Caleta Tortuga
Cerro Brujo
Punta Deda
Bahía Rosa Blanca
Roca Este
Kicker Rock (León Dormido)
Bahía Stephens
Cerro San Joaquín
Punta Bassa
El Junco
El Progreso
Isla Lobos
Puerto Chino
Puerto Baquerizo Moreno
Bahía Wreck
Bahía Agua Dulce (Freshwater)
Roca Ballena (Whale)
Punta Alturas

Arrecife Macgowen

Española
Punta Suárez Blowhole
Gardner
Gardner Bay
Punta Cevallos
Caldwell
Watson

N

10 km
10 miles

Index

Map symbols

□	Capital city	- - - -	Cable car	Ⓢ	Bank
○	Other city, town	┿┿┿┿	Funicular	@	Internet
	International border	🚢	Ferry	♪	Telephone
	Regional border		Pedestrianized street	🏬	Market
⊖	Customs	⊃⊂	Tunnel	🏥	Medical services
⊖	Contours (approx)	→	One way-street	P	Parking
▲	Mountain, volcano	‖‖‖	Steps		Petrol
⇆	Mountain pass	⇌	Bridge	⛳	Golf
	Escarpment	▲▲▲	Fortified wall	⋰	Archaeological site
	Glacier		Park, garden, stadium	♦	National park, wildlife reserve
	Salt flat	●	Sleeping		
	Rocks	❶	Eating	❖	Viewing point
	Seasonal marshland	❶	Bars & clubs	Λ	Campsite
	Beach, sandbank		Building	⌂	Refuge, lodge
⑊	Waterfall	■	Sight		Castle, fort
~	Reef	🏛	Cathedral, church		Diving
	Motorway	🏯	Chinese temple		Deciduous, coniferous, palm trees
	Main road	🏛	Hindu temple		
	Minor road	᛬	Meru		Mangrove
┈┈	Track	◙	Mosque		Hide
┈┈	Footpath	△	Stupa		Vineyard, winery
	Railway	✡	Synagogue		Distillery
⊢■	Railway with station	ⓘ	Tourist office		Shipwreck
✈	Airport	🏛	Museum	✕	Historic battlefield
🚌	Bus station	✉	Post office	⬜	Related map
Ⓜ	Metro station	Ⓟ	Police		

Join us online...

Follow us on **Twitter** and **Facebook** – ask us questions, speak to our authors, swap your stories, and be kept up to date with travel news and exclusive discounts and competitions.

Upload your travel pics to our **Flickr** site – inspire others on where to go next, and have your photos considered for inclusion in Footprint guides.

And don't forget to visit us at **footprint**travelguides.com

Footprint story

It was 1921

Ireland had just been partitioned, the British miners were striking for more pay and the federation of British industry had an idea. Exports were booming in South America – how about a handbook for businessmen trading in that far away continent? The Anglo-South American Handbook was born that year, written by W Koebel, the most prolific writer on Latin America of his day.

1924

Two editions later the book was 'privatized' and in 1924, in the hands of Royal Mail, the steamship company for South America, it became The South American Handbook, subtitled 'South America in a nutshell'. This annual publication became the 'bible' for generations of travellers to South America and remains so to this day. In the early days travel was by sea and the Handbook gave all the details needed for the long voyage from Europe. What to wear for dinner; how to arrange a cricket match with the Cable & Wireless staff on the Cape Verde Islands and a full account of the journey from Liverpool up the Amazon to Manaus: 5898 miles without changing cabin!

1939

As the continent opened up, the South American Handbook reported the new Pan Am flying boat services, and the fortnightly airship service from Rio to Europe on the Graf Zeppelin. For reasons still unclear but with extraordinary determination, the annual editions continued through the Second World War.

1970s

Many more people discovered South America and the backpacking trail started to develop. All the while the Handbook was gathering fans, including literary vagabonds such as Paul Theroux and Graham Greene (who once sent some updates addressed to "The publishers of the best travel guide in the world, Bath, England").

1990s

During the 1990s the company set about developing a new travel guide series using this legendary title as the flagship. By 1997 there were over a dozen guides in the series and the Footprint imprint was launched.

2000s

The series grew quickly and there were soon Footprint travel guides covering more than 150 countries. In 2004, Footprint launched its first thematic guide: *Surfing Europe*, packed with colour photographs, maps and charts. This was followed by further thematic guides such as *Diving the World*, *Snowboarding the World*, *Body and Soul escapes*, *Travel with Kids* and *European City Breaks*.

2014

Today we continue the traditions of the last 91 years that have served legions of travellers so well. We believe that these help to make Footprint guides different. Our policy is to use authors who are genuine experts who write for independent travellers; people possessing a spirit of adventure, looking to get off the beaten track.

Acknowledgements

Peru

Peru was updated jointly by Ben Box and Robert and Daisy Kunstaetter. Ben would like to thank: Claudia Miranda (of *GHL Hoteles* and *Sonesta Collection, Peru*), Verónica Dupuy (*GHL*) and Ricardo Villanueva Wu (*Sonesta*); Miles Buesst (*Rainforest Cruises* and *Cricket Peru*); Mónica Moreno and staff at *Posada del Parque*; Carlos Jiménez of *The Andean Experience Co* and the staff at *Hotel B*; Cecilia Kamiche; Maestro Máximo Laura and Sasha McInnes of *Puchka Perú*; Eduardo Arambarú (*Lima 27*); Joaquín de la Piedra (*Saqra*); Lic Arql Ignacio Alva Meneses of the *Proyecto arqueológico Ventarrón*; and Kieron Heath of *Proyectos Inca*. Robert and Daisy wish to thank: Chris Benway, Alberto and Ayde Cafferata, Rob Dover and Ricardo Espinosa. We should also like to thank Fiona Cameron and Armando Polanco, who updated the Cuzco section this year. Christian Martínez provided much useful information for the Lima gastronomy section and other details on Peru. In addition, we are most grateful to John and Julia Forrest (UK), Michael White (UK), Jaime García Heras (USA), and Heather MacBrayne and Aaron Zarate of *Discover South America*.

Bolivia

Robert and Daisy Kunstaetter, authors of *Footprint Bolivia*, updated the section and would like to thank: Saúl Arias, Jill Benton, Carlos Fiorillo, Petra Huber, Alistair Matthew, Beatriz Michel, Fabiola Mitru, Bastian Müller, Derren Paterson, Tandil Rivera, Mariana Sánchez, Martin Stratker and Remy van den Berg.

Ecuador

Robert and Daisy Kunstaetter, authors of *Footprint Ecuador and the Galápagos*, updated the chapter and would like to thank: Jeaneth Barrionuevo, Jean Brown, Harry Jonitz, Patrick and Baiba Morrow, Popkje van der Ploeg, Michael Resch, Peter Schramm, Iván Suárez and RhoAnn Wallace.

Ben Box

One of the first assignments Ben Box took as a freelance writer in 1980 was subediting work on the *South American Handbook*. The plan then was to write about contemporary Iberian and Latin American affairs, but in no time at all the lands south of the Rio Grande took over, inspiring journeys to all corners of the subcontinent. Ben has contributed to newspapers, magazines and learned tomes, usually on the subject of travel, and became editor of the *South American Handbook* in 1989. He has also been involved in Footprint's Handbooks on *Central America & Mexico*, *Caribbean Islands*, *Brazil*, *Peru*, *Peru, Bolivia & Ecuador* and *Cuzco & the Inca Heartland*. Having a doctorate in Spanish and Portuguese studies from London University, Ben maintains a strong interest in Latin American literature. In the British summer he plays cricket for his local village side and year round he attempts to achieve some level of self-sufficiency in fruit and veg in a rather unruly country garden in Suffolk.

Robert and Daisy Kunstaetter

It was destiny, perhaps, that Daisy Isacovici's childhood dreams of travelling throughout her native Ecuador were not fulfilled until after she met Robert. He hails from Canada, where they met, and shortly thereafter he suggested they wander around South America for a 'year or so'. That was in 1986 and the year proved to be elastic; they have since lived or travelled in every country on the continent. Over the years and miles, Robert and Daisy became regular correspondents for Footprint, helping to update annual editions of the *South American Handbook*. Based back in Ecuador since 1993, they have been closely involved with tourism here as well as in Peru and Bolivia. They are authors, co-authors, contributors or cartographers of over 20 guidebooks and are currently working on a new trekking guide to Peru.